ADVENTURES OF BHARAT MOOSA

Nadakkavu, Kozhikode, Kerala, 673011
www.insightpublica.com
e-mail: insightpublica@gmail.com
Title: **Adventures of Bharat Moosa**
Author: **Jose Prasad**
Translated by: **Muraly TV**
Illustration: Sacheendran Karadka
First Edition: August 2023

Printed and Published by
InsightinPublica Printers & Publishers Pvt. Ltd.
ISBN 978-93-5517-412-3

ADVENTURES OF BHARAT MOOSA

JOSE PRASAD

Translation: Muraly TV

INSIGHT PUBLICA

Jose Prasad is a popular writer in Malayalam Children's Literature with 1000s of published poems, more than 400 published stories and, nearly 30 published articles to his credit. He is a well-known writer in the contemporary children's periodicals in Malayalam.

Jose Prasad is a postgraduate in Malayalam Literature from Calicut University. He did teacher training from SHTTI (Mailapra, Pathanamthitta) and Teachers Education Centre (Kannur University). He studied in St Johns School, Palavayal and Nehru College, Kanjangad.

Jose Prasad was honoured by Kochi International Book Festival Samithi with Mali Smaraka Kavitha Puraskaram in 2023.

Jose Prasad's FIKRU, the superhero, published in Manicheppu Magazine has earned laurels from readers. Jose Prasad has been successfully presenting popular children's stories from foreign languages in Kuttikalude Deepika, a popular fortnightly.

Details of Published Works:

Collection of Poems: Peppare Peppare Peeppi, Kottappurathunni and Kattile Sadhya

Collection of Stories: Minminiyum Kunjaniyanum, Hoppy Muyalinte Christmas Rathri, Aninjorungivanna Poochakal, Lokothara Balakathakal

Novels:

Dr. Chio, published in Chandrika Weekly, Bharat Moosayude Sahasangal and Mayayum Mayavikalum in Balabhumi

Father: Malankadavil Thannikkal Joseph.

Mother: Philomina.

Wife: Soosamma NS (School Teacher).

Daughters: Kavya and Megha (Students)

Address:

Thannikkal House, Bela PO

Kumbala, Kasargod District, Kerala – 671321

Mobile: 9633619174

Email: joseprasadt@gmail.com

Muraly TV is credited with nearly 500 published works in the contemporary periodicals and various online portals in Children's Literature. He writes English stories, poems, rhymes and comics for children of all age groups. The 55-year-old Indian Air Force Veteran has been on a new venture of entertaining and educating children with his numerous literary works based on moral, humour, science, life-lessons and value of social service enriched with his vast experience as a former Air Warrior, a former Administration Manager and also a Solo Adventure Cyclist who transformed the concept of cycling into Social Welfare Missions. His vast travel experience often reflects in his writings.

Muraly has earned numerous honours and awards such as Commendation from the Chief of IAF and Vice Chief of IAF, Appreciations from Air Officer Commanding, Secretariat of Chief of Army Staff, Director IAF Adventure, Southern Naval Command, Directorate of Army Central Welfare Fund, Eye Bank Association Kerala, Air Force Association Karnataka, Star India, Navoujjal Foundation Mathura, Certificate of Kindness from World Records Biennale Foundation, International Achievers Award 2020 by Maitri Peace Foundation India (UP) and Life Time Achievement Award Shourya Kala Ratna Puraskar from Chan Ki Martial Arts Trust Bengaluru. Muraly is Master in Library Information Science, Master in Business Administration, Master in Computer Science and also holds PG diplomas in software, web designing and safety & security management. Muraly did his studies in Kerala, Uttar Pradesh, Rajasthan, New Delhi and Karnataka.

Published Works

Cham Cham Magic (Collection of Stories), Yummy Yellow (Collection of Rhymes)

Father: TC Viswanathan Nair

Mother: Raji Viswanathan

Wife: Indumathy P

Daughter: Chandni M

Address:

Muraly TV, Paradise, 214, 2nd Main Road

Dwaraka Nagar, Chikkabanavara (PO), Bengaluru 560 090

email: muraly2013@gmail.com

Table of Contents

PREFACE

This novel elaborates on the emotions in depth hidden in the hearts of the old generation with a comparison to the new generation in terms of the changed lifestyle in our society. Children stay away from their parents for improving the quality of life of their children but mostly they end up not justifying their acts to both their parents and their children.

Children nowadays go through a tedious and stressful childhood and youth with the heavy loads of their studies, sometimes as per their choice or sometimes for the sake of others' choice to fulfil their dreams. Mostly, children nowadays are forced to follow a life like a robot. They lead a mechanical life, listening to the same words like studies, grade, rank, success, discipline, obedience, fame,·etc.

Parents think they do a lot of sacrifices to shower love on their children by providing the best facilities but children remain unaware of all such feelings of their parents. Grandparents keep waiting for their children and grandchildren with lots of hope. They think one day their dearest ones will return to them.

Everyone is in a mad race of accumulating wealth. People even forget about their SELF and family. They focus on their profession, business, education, and financial growth. Finally, they tend to forget the value of relationships.

I have well-narrated this particular attitude of our society in this novel. Through fun, joy, sorrow, and adventure, different characters in the novel represent the pictures of present-day life in our society. The centre-character of the novel, Bharat Moosa plays a vital role in bridging the gap between the old generation and the new generation with his sincere efforts. The Magical Tree represents the innermost desires of many of us who struggle to fulfil lots of requirements and needs in day-to-day life. I am sure my effort to project the power and beauty of love and friendship in all kinds of relationships will find some positive reflection in the minds of the readers.

Though it is written for children, I am sure that the novel will turn out to be interesting for mature readers too. If my efforts can assure some positive results in the minds of the readers apart from the usual reading for fun and time-pass, I will be happy and grateful.

Jose Prasad

Chapter 1

Mutton Grandpa and Chicken Grandma

Grandpa and Grandma lived in a small house at Pavakka Hills. They had five sons and five daughters. Their daughters after marriage lived at their in-laws' house. Their sons were well-settled in the town. Nobody preferred to keep their old-aged parents and thus Grandpa and Grandma had been living alone for a long time.

One day, Grandma expressed her big wish to Grandpa:

"Hey, our favourite actor Dilip's new film has been released. I came to know from a newspaper. Why don't we watch the film tomorrow?"

"Ah, what's the film's name?"

"C I D Moosa."

"What? C I D Moosa?!"

"Yes, I heard it's a very funny film that would make us laugh like hell for two hours!"

"Wow, then let's watch the film tomorrow itself."

The next morning, after having black coffee and roti, Grandpa and Grandma left Pavakka Hills to watch the film. They boarded a bus from Asan Junction.

There was a heavy rush in the theatre. Grandma stood

in the ladies-queue and cleverly managed two tickets by breaking the line. Other ladies, though annoyed, didn't bother much considering Grandma's old age.

Grandma couldn't control her laugh during the film. Seeing Grandma's laugh, Grandpa also burst into laughter. Watching them laughing to their heart's content, everybody in the theatre laughed uncontrollably.

Grandma and Grandpa liked Moosa's pranks and adventures very much. As the film ended with the scene where a crazy man was flying a helicopter, Grandma angrily said:

"How could they end the film so soon? It's not worth spending two hundred rupees for such a short film! It seems they cheated us!"

"Oh, leave it, I feel hungry after laughing like hell. Come fast, let's go to a hotel and have mutton biriyani."

"You eat mutton biriyani. But I will have chicken biriyani."

"Ah, That's fine. You eat chicken biriyani. Let's walk quickly now."

Grandma and Grandpa walked on the crowded road in search of a good hotel. "Hey, there's a good hotel, Ruchi Rani. It seems good. Let's have stomach-full biriyani now." Grandpa said.

Grandma and Grandpa ate tasty biriyani till their stomachs were about to burst. As they finished eating, Grandpa wanted to urinate. "Where is the toilet?" Grandpa asked the waiter.

"There's no toilet inside the hotel. But there's one outside, go out, take a left, and walk towards the backyard of the hotel, there you'll see one." Replied the waiter.

"You be here, I will be back in a few minutes," Grandpa said to Grandma and walked away. Grandma ordered one lemon tea and enjoyed sipping it slowly.

Grandpa came back and walked to the cash counter to pay the bill. "Oh God, where's my purse?" Grandpa was shocked as he couldn't find his purse in his pocket. Grandpa stood sweating and embarrassed. Grandma felt ashamed.

That's when a boy in a shabby dress came limping. "Grandpa, are you searching for this?" He showed the purse to Grandpa.

Grandpa and Grandma felt relaxed. Grandpa paid the bill and then offered one hundred rupees to the boy.

"No… Grandpa, I don't need money. Instead, can you please buy a meal for me?" asked the boy.

Grandpa ordered a meal for the boy. Both Grandpa and Grandma eagerly watched the boy eating greedily. He stopped eating and started drinking water. That's when Grandpa asked:

"What's your name?"

"I don't have a name, Grandpa."

"What do others call you?"

"Everyone calls me Mottan."

Grandma suddenly got annoyed and said:

"Let him finish his meal peacefully. Why can't you talk to him later?"

Grandpa nodded.

After he finished eating, Grandpa and Grandma comfortably spoke to him and came to know everything about his life. He lost his parents. He is alone in this world. He doesn't even have a name for his identity. And, he can't walk properly like others. As he limped while walking, people started calling him 'Mottan'.

Grandma was deeply touched by his story. Grandma asked:

"Would you like to live with us just like our son? We will be happy to have you in our life!"

His eyes burst into tears.

That evening, the people of Pavakka Hills watched the newcomer, a 16-year-old boy limping alongside Grandpa and Grandma, walking slowly towards their small house!

Chapter 2

The Gold Tree

"Oh, I can't walk anymore. My legs are in pain!" complained Grandma. Grandma got exhausted by walking uphill. Grandma sat on a milestone at Pavakka Hills.

"You were the one who wanted to watch the film! Now, what happened?" Grandpa screamed.

The boy interfered before the quarrel could go out of control. "Don't worry Grandma, I will carry you home."

"Ah, you are unable to walk properly yourself! And, you think of carrying me!" Grandma asked.

Before Grandma could finish her sentence, he had put her on his shoulder. He walked sternly with utmost care.

Grandma enjoyed the journey on his shoulder. Grandma could watch many new scenes which she had never seen before though she had been living at Pavakka Hills for a long time.

He walked fast with his limp leg. Grandpa found it difficult to walk along with him.

Finally, they reached home. Grandpa asked Grandma:

"Don't we need to name him?"

"I already found a name for him!"

"What's that name? Tell me!"

"Moosa"

"Moosa! What type of name is it!"

"Hey, did you forget so soon? Dilip's name in the film is Moosa."

"I don't agree with you. I have found another name for him."

"Oh, then tell me what's that? Let me know!"

"Let's give him our country's name 'Bharatham'."

Grandma didn't approve. Grandma sat angrily, keeping her fingers on her nose.

"OK, then let's modify the name. Hmm... Let's name him 'Bharat'." Grandpa said.

"I don't agree with you. Remember, I only invited him here. So, I myself will decide his name." Grandma was adamant.

The boy got fed up. "Hey, stop quarrelling now. Let my name be 'Bharat Moosa'."

Luckily, that was approved by both Grandpa and Grandma. Thus, the boy finally got a name!

"Freshen yourself first," Grandma said. Grandma gave him a new dress, soap, and a towel. He went to the Shiriya River to take a bath.

Bharat Moosa came back after his bath. Grandpa trimmed his hair.

After dinner, Grandma showed him a bench in the courtyard to sleep.

Grandpa couldn't sleep at all as his mind was highly disturbed. Grandma had slept already. Grandpa thought about his ten children who didn't bother about their old age parents. Grandpa got up from his bed and walked towards the courtyard where Bharat Moosa was sleeping.

"Bharat Moosa, my son...!" Grandpa called the boy.

"Tell me, what do you want Grandpa?"

Grandpa offered him a gold coin and said, "It's for you, my son. My father gave me this gold coin. My sons proved

5

to be useless. You are my son from now on and it's for you!"

"I don't need this gold coin. You offered me a place in your house and that itself is a big thing!"

"You don't think much about it. Tomorrow if I die, there won't be an heir for this!"

Grandpa forcibly gave him the gold coin and warned:

"Let this matter be with us. Even Grandma shouldn't know about it."

The gold coin disturbed Bharat's mind. 'Why should I possess assets that spoil my sleep?' Bharat thought. He dug a pit under the jackfruit tree in the moonlight and hid the gold coin.

The next morning, Bharat Moosa was stunned to see a tree at the same spot where he had dug the coin. And, there was a gold coin lying under the tree. Bharat Moosa picked up the coin and hid it in his pocket!

Chapter 3

New Jeep At Pavakka Hills

Soon, Moosa became a part and parcel of the life of Grandpa and Grandma. Moosa would do any sort of job without any hesitance and thus, he became a great help for the elderly couple. Moosa by himself would understand the requirements and do them voluntarily. He would go to shops. He also would bring wood for cooking.

The next day also, Moosa got a gold coin from the Gold Tree. 'Ah, I have two gold coins now! What should I do with them?' thought Moosa for a while. He got an idea.

Grandma had a piggy bank that she had kept safely in the kitchen. Moosa put the gold coins in the piggy bank.

Later, it became a practice for Moosa that every day, he would pick up the gold coin, and put it in Grandma's piggy bank.

'What will I do once it is full?' thought Moosa as the piggy bank was almost full!

One day, Moosa was massaging Grandma's legs on the veranda. He saw Grandpa with a big kitchen knife walking towards the Gold Tree.

"Oh God, please don't cut that tree, Grandpa!" screamed Moosa.

"What's the need for another tree under the jackfruit tree? I am going to cut it." Grandpa was adamant.

Having left with no other way, finally, Moosa revealed the secret. Both Grandpa and Grandma remained shocked, surprised, and astonished with unbelievable eyes.

Later, as slightly relieved, Grandma asked:

"Where are those coins? Where have you kept them?"

"I have kept them in your piggy bank."

Immediately, Grandma broke her piggy bank and found twenty-two gold coins. One by one, she arranged the coins and asked Moosa:

"What did you understand from these twenty-two coins?"

"Hmm... I understood that I had spent twenty-two days here with you!"

Upon his reply, Grandma and Grandpa laughed wholeheartedly. Grandma repeated the question and asked Grandpa to reply.

"I understand that we are very rich now!" Grandpa replied.

The next day, Grandpa, Grandma, and Moosa went to a jewellery shop in the town with the gold coins. The jeweller weighed all the coins.

"Each coin weighs eight grams. Today's gold rate is five thousand rupees per gram," said the jeweller.

Grandpa received 4 lakh rupees from the jeweller for the gold coins. He kept the amount in his bag. As they reached outside the shop, Grandpa asked:

"What will we do with this money?"

Grandma asked Moosa the same question as she didn't find any way to spend the money.

"Let's buy a jeep, Grandma. I know how much you suffer walking up Pavakka Hills."

"Yes, you are right, my son Moosa." Grandma nodded in agreement.

"Yes, you are right, my son Bharat." Grandpa emphatically said.

They walked in search of a Jeep showroom. Finally, they found a good showroom and bought a new jeep for 4 lakh rupees.

"Who will drive the jeep to our house on Pavakka Hills?"

"Don't worry; our driver will take care of that. He will drop you home." The shop owner said and asked his staff to do the needful.

Grandma and Grandpa were surprised to see a few men loading a bike in their newly purchased jeep.

'I had got a comb free when I bought soap earlier. Is it something like that?' Grandma thought.

"Is it an offer – buy a jeep and get a bike free!" Grandma asked. Laughingly, the shopkeeper replied:

"Nothing like that, Grandma. Who will drop our driver back to this office after he drops you home? He will return on that bike!"

Hiding her embarrassment, Grandma said:

"Moosa, you sit beside the driver and watch how he drives. You are going to be my driver from tomorrow onwards."

"OK, Grandma," Moosa replied as an obedient person.

Thus, for the first time, a jeep appeared at Pavakka Hills. It stopped in front of the house!

Chapter 4

Grandma's Lie

Moosa now got relieved from one of his duties. Grandma herself started collecting the gold coins early in the morning. Since childhood, Grandma has been crazy for money and gold. But, her luck to enjoy all such comforts came too late in her old age only.

Moosa now has a new job, and that is driving. He practiced driving the jeep in the courtyard. Slowly, he became confident in driving the jeep to Asan Junction and returning home safely.

But he was often surrounded by the boys from the adjacent colony. The boys would follow the jeep to Grandpa's house. As the jeep was the first such vehicle at Pavakka Hills, even grownup people followed the jeep in merriment.

'How could Grandma and Grandpa buy a jeep? From where did they get such a huge amount?' Everybody had the same question in their mind.

An unshaken Grandma said:

"Look, he is our dearest son Moosa. He is a millionaire. And, he is now going to live with us forever. He helped us buy this jeep. Next, we are going to construct a big house with his money!"

"Then, what about his parents?" asked the crowd suspiciously.

"Unfortunately, he lost his parents in an air crash. As he doesn't have relatives, he decided to live the rest of his life with us!"

Not only the villagers but Grandpa and Moosa also were stunned at Grandma's lie. Everybody believed Grandma's lie blindly and talked about it at length everywhere!

After the crowd left, Grandpa said:

"Ah, nobody can beat Grandma in lying. Even she begins her day thinking what lies to be made for the day! But I like to hear her lies. I could have written a big book with her limitless lies!". Moosa couldn't resist laughing.

Moosa now started dreaming of building a big house!

Chapter 5

Moosa Becomes Smart

Grandpa, Grandma, and Moosa left for the town with the money that they had made out of twenty gold coins. They started enjoying the Jeep rides too much. They met an engineer in the town to make a building plan for their new house. As the engineer asked for details of facilities, Grandpa said:

"A big living room, a dining room, a kitchen, one bedroom for my wife and I, and one bedroom for my son Bharat. We need a small house without any upstairs."

Suddenly, Grandma said:

"No, that's not enough. We need ten bedrooms with attached bathrooms as we have ten children. Let the house be a duplex."

Moosa at once intervened on seeing Grandpa's angry face. "Most of the people nowadays have a two-story building. Hence, let's plan for a three-story building!" opined Moosa.

The engineer replied, "That's fine, I will make a plan according to your requirements. But it might cost you approximately one crore."

"Ah, that's not at all a problem, Sir," Grandma replied confidently.

They placed an order for construction materials and also

arranged for a supervisor. They bought new dresses. Also, the three of them enjoyed eating their choices of food in a good restaurant. Grandpa ate his favourite mutton biriyani while Grandma enjoyed chicken biriyani. Moosa satisfied himself with a plate of gruel.

Construction works progressed well. Moosa sold gold coins and made the fund available at all times. He made frequent trips on his jeep to the town to procure materials while Grandpa and Grandma kept checking on the ongoing work at home.

Grandma was the one who initiated making a list of invitees for the housewarming ceremony. "Don't we need to invite our children?" asked Grandma.

Grandpa declared:

"We don't need any ungrateful people here. I am not interested in conducting any kind of traditional rituals or celebrations, let's boil milk and inaugurate our house by having milk. That's it!"

"Moosa, where are you? Did you hear this crook man's words?" Grandma screamed. Having got no response, Grandma searched for Moosa and found him laughing alone on the veranda.

Grandma got angry. "Why are you laughing like this? What's the matter? What are you holding in your hand?" asked Grandma.

Moosa showed the item to Grandma and said:

"Grandma, this is a smartphone. It's 4G. Today only I bought it when I went to the town. We can talk to anybody regardless of the distance. There are lots of jokes in TikTok. I couldn't control my laugh!"

Grandma kept blinking as she couldn't understand anything. Grandpa then asked:

"Can you call Kalan? I like to talk to him!"

"Do you know Kalan's number?"

"I don't know!"

Grandma got annoyed. “What do you have to do with Kalan?” asked Grandma.

“Hey, I just want to know how long I am going to live in this world!”

“Ah, leave it. He might have forgotten about you and me! Why do you want to remind him about us unnecessarily?” said Grandma.

‘It seems, this Kalan is a big shot, let me just try to get him online. Anyway, a smartphone is in my hand so it’s not a big deal!’ Moosa thought.

Moosa typed ‘KALAN’ in Google and searched for details. He was surprised to see lots of photos of a curry called ‘KALAN’ along with South Indian Meals in Saravana Bhavan Hotel!

Chapter 6

The Rumour

Moosa decided to put a stop to the ongoing arguments between Grandpa and Grandma regarding the housewarming ceremony. Moosa said:

"Inviting your relatives to the function is all your decision. But don't you feel like inviting the poor residents of Pavakka Hills for a feast?"

Grandpa agreed. Grandma too nodded in agreement. They entrusted the task of inviting the villagers to Moosa. Moosa not only invited the people but also handed over two thousand rupees to those who were found extremely poor and helpless.

Some other works were also progressing side-by-side along with the house construction works. A compound wall was built with laterite stones for Grandpa's half-acre land and a big gate was fixed. Appropriate flooring works were done around the Gold Tree. Grandma started worshipping the Gold Tree at dusk as it had brought prosperity to their life.

Downstairs works had almost come to an end. So, Grandpa and Grandma shifted to their new room. The old house was demolished. Moosa didn't forget to take a photo of the old house before its demolition.

Grandpa asked the painters to write 'Bharat Moosa' in big letters on the jeep's front side and his mobile number in

BHARAT
MOOSA

small letters underneath his name.

The house construction work came to the final stage. Moosa brought furniture and other household items from the town. Ten big cots, three small cots, beds, bed sheets, pillows, two refrigerators, a mixer grinder, a dining table, chairs, tables, teapoys, cupboards, and two sofa sets for the living room…! Moosa didn't forget to fit CCTVs at the gate, sit-out, living room, staircase, and around the house. One CCTV was fitted at the top of the house. All the cameras were connected to Moosa's mobile phone.

In the evening, after paying the workers, Moosa realized that he was running short of money. He had to sell some more gold coins to finish the work.

The next morning at 6 o'clock itself, Moosa had a bath in the Shiriya River as he had planned to leave for the town very early. He expected Grandma with black coffee for him whereas Grandma was found in the sit-out, completely desperate.

"Grandma, get me the gold coins, I need to rush to the town. Money is almost over!"

"Zha Zha Zha Zha…….."

Moosa couldn't make out what Grandma said.

"What happened, Grandma?"

"Zha Zha Zha… ……………………" Grandma stammered.

Moosa felt something had gone wrong with Grandma. Grandma was unable to even get up when Moosa tried to lift her.

"Grandpa… Grandpa…" screamed Moosa.

"Why are you screaming? Is anyone dead? I am in the bathroom." Grandpa replied angrily.

Moosa somehow lifted Grandma and rushed to the jeep. Moosa drove away very fast.

Grandpa found Moosa driving away fast with Grandma as he came out of the bathroom. Grandpa couldn't understand anything.

A few onlookers came running to Grandpa and enquired what happened to Grandma.

"I have no idea," Grandpa said.

"Where is Grandma?" asked one person.

"Moosa took her away."

"Oh, he only got this old lady to kidnap!?"

"Ah, he turned out to be a crook!"

Grandpa closed his ears as he couldn't bear the comments by the villagers.

The rumour spread like wildfire in the village that a 20-year-old boy kidnapped 70-year-old Grandma!

Chapter 7

Pictures Inside The Head

Moosa drove very fast. He pressed the accelerator even while riding downhill roads, taking all the risk. Grandma kept murmuring something or the other but Moosa couldn't understand anything.

As they crossed Asan Junction and entered the good tar road, Grandma got up. Now, Moosa was able to understand a bit of Grandma's talk.

"Moosa, where are you taking me?" asked Grandma.

"Grandma, I am taking you to the hospital."

"I am fine now. There is no need to go to any hospital!" Grandma said.

"Actually, what happened to you?" Moosa asked eagerly.

"My one side got totally numb, even my tongue too!" replied Grandma, "I was unable to stand or walk. Now, I am fine, let's return home. My husband might be worried a lot!"

"Anyway, we came all the way till here, let's meet a doctor. What's the guarantee that the same won't happen again?"

Moosa proceeded to the nearby Government Hospital as he was not carrying much money with him. He took a token for Rs. 2 and visited the doctor. Moosa explained the matter.

The doctor examined Grandma thoroughly and checked her Blood Pressure and Sugar. 'Everything seems to be quite fine.' The doctor thought for a while and then said:

"Grandma's head needs to be scanned."

A nurse took Grandma to the scanning room. Moosa was about to follow them but the doctor stopped him.

"You be here, I need to tell you certain things." The doctor said.

An upset Moosa listened to the doctor.

"Actually, Grandma had suffered from a minor stroke today but luckily escaped. If it happens again, there are chances that Grandma might get paralyzed!"

Moosa sat heartbroken. Doctor continued:

"It usually happens when any small tube in the brain starts leaking. That's the reason I asked for scanning. Anyway, you wait; let me examine the scanning report after it comes. I will advise you based on the report."

Moosa sat on a chair, completely worried and frustrated. Moosa had never prayed to God even when he had starved for many days in the Past but today for the first time he prayed for Grandma.

Grandma came back after a while. "You don't worry Moosa, I am fine!"

Moosa smiled staring at Grandma.

They waited for half an hour more for the scanning report. The doctor examined the report and the film. He said:

"Everything seems to be fine and normal. Still, it's better to visit a neurologist. I am prescribing a few medicines for the time being and ensuring Grandma takes them without fail."

While returning home, Grandma asked Moosa:

"Hey, what's there in that black paper?"

"Hmm... Grandma... That shows the pictures inside your head!"

Grandma excitedly opened the cover and looked at the

film. She smiled staring at the twenty different types of items inside her head.

"Ah, amazing. My husband is in the habit of teasing me saying nothing is there in my head. Let me show him this and stop his pranks hereafter." Grandma smiled.

They reached front of the Metro Hotel. Grandma said:

"I am hungry, let's eat something."

Grandma ate a stomach full of pathiri and chicken curry. Moosa had puttu and black chickpeas curry. They parcelled four pathari and mutton curry for Grandpa.

Grandpa had been eagerly waiting for Moosa and Grandma on the veranda since they left. Grandpa took a sigh of relief upon hearing the sound of the jeep. As Grandma got out of the jeep, Grandpa screamed:

"Where have you been? Where did you go with him without telling me?"

Moosa narrated everything and consoled Grandpa. Grandpa cursed the villagers, "Moosa, you know, the villagers announced you had kidnapped Grandma. Let's not invite any of them to our housewarming!"

"Oh! Grandpa, yesterday itself I invited everybody. What to do now?"

Grandma also was boiling out of anger. "Let me know who the hell he was who spread all such rumours. I will not spare him at all!"

Moosa suddenly burst into laughter and said:

"Grandma, you have been cheating others with your lies! So, this time, they got a chance. Just leave it!"

Chapter 8

The Magical Tree

Finally, the day came – the housewarming of the new house of Grandpa and Grandma.

Actually, three weeks ago, they had shifted to their new house after boiling milk in their new kitchen, one of the customs prevalent in the village. Today, it was a formal function.

As Grandpa and Grandma were fond of biriyani, Moosa had placed an order for biriyani for the function. Moosa had placed an order with caterers for 500 chicken biryani, 300 mutton biriyani, and 200 vegetable biryani.

The invited guests started arriving by 11 o'clock. Grandpa and Grandma wore new dresses. They greeted their guests with a warm welcome. Everybody enjoyed the delicious biriyani and payasam. The guests returned happily with loads of praise for Grandpa and Grandma.

There was one guest who came without an invitation, the ward member Mr. Prakasan. Though he was the ward-member Pavakka Hills, he resided at Asan Junction. He came with his associates in his own car. Mr. Prakasan had brought a big LED TV as a gift for Grandpa and Grandma.

As he entered home, he grinned funnily and hugged Grandpa. He asked his associates to take his photo with Grandpa and Grandma.

‘Ah, luckily I had forgotten to buy a TV!’ whispered Moosa looking at the LED TV brought by Mr. Prakasan.

By 3 o’clock, all the guests left. Lots of food was left over. Moosa carried the food to an orphanage located at Uppala.

Moosa took a bath in the Shiriya River peacefully after a whole day’s tedious work. After dinner, he walked into the courtyard enjoying the shining moonlight. Moosa knew it was ‘Gurupoornima’ day as he had checked the calendar on his mobile. He saw the Gold Tree’s branches swaying in the wind. He felt much affectionate to the tree.

Moosa lit the earthen oil lamp kept under the tree and prayed for a while. Moosa hugged the tree gratefully as it had bestowed unbelievable luck on him.

Moosa felt inexplicable excitement running through his nerves – like a non-dangerous electric current torrent. Suddenly, his handicapped left leg became all right.

Moosa lifted his lungi and stared at his legs. Both legs looked healthy and strong. ‘Oh, I am no more handicapped. I can even participate in the Olympics and win a medal for India!’ Moosa thought. Moosa was a hard-core fan of Usain Bolt!

Moosa jumped in merriment. He ran towards home excitedly. Moosa awoke Grandpa and Grandma from their sleep and narrated the miracle.

“How did it happen?” wondered Grandpa.

“That tree is a Magical Tree, Grandpa. It has supernatural powers!” said Moosa delightedly. Moosa asked Grandma:

“Are you suffering from anything?”

“I have pain in my knees and heels. Also, I find it difficult to get up.”

“If so, let’s go and hug our Magical Tree. I am sure the tree will cure you!”

Grandma came out of the house though it was dark and rushed to the Gold Tree. She hugged the tree but nothing happened.

Grandma said:

"No problem, you became a perfect man. At this old age, we are supposed to live with all sorts of pain and suffering as destined by God. So, there is nothing much to worry about!"

Moosa was in a sweet dream the next morning. He was on the track representing India in the running race. Next to his track, there was Usain Bolt!

Moosa said to Bolt:

"This time, you will be happy with the silver medal!"

The gunshot was heard. Moosa was running with all his might. Suddenly, sprinkles of water fell on his face. Shockingly Moosa opened his eyes and looked around. He found Grandma with a worried and faded face.

"Hey Moosa, today, our Gold Tree didn't give any gold coins!"

Chapter 9

Fragrance Of Jackfruit

"Ah, I just can't believe it!" Moosa rushed to the Gold Tree and checked thoroughly. But there was not a single gold coin underneath!

"Have you revealed the secret to anyone?" asked Grandma.

"No, never! How can I do such a blunder, Grandma?"

Grandma felt someone might have come to know about the Gold Tree and stole the gold coin very early in the morning. But, Moosa's thoughts were in a different direction. Moosa said to Grandma:

"Grandma, just give a hug to the tree, let's see. After all, it blessed us with lots of prosperity!"

Grandma closed her eyes and hugged the Gold Tree. Even though she didn't hear Moosa's voice. After a while, she raised her hands, kissed the tree, and jumped down exactly as the way Moosa had done on the previous day. Grandma jumped like children and screamed in merriment:

"Hey, my knees and heels are cured! Even my spine is fine now. I feel I am thirty years younger now! Let me call Grandpa. Let him also cure his diseases."

"Not today, Grandma. Let him try tomorrow. This tree is capable of curing only one person per day. Didn't we notice it yesterday? Not only that, it lost the power of giving gold

coins as and when it started curing the people. Who knows what more powers this tree possesses?" Moosa said.

"Hey, let's not worry at all! We have got more than enough. Still, we have thirty-two unsold gold coins. More money might cause danger sometimes. Health is more important, right?" Grandma justified.

"Yes, you are right Grandma. Let me have a bath first. I will be back soon." Moosa left for the river with his toothbrush, paste, soap, and towel.

Grandpa's second son Badhran incidentally happened to see his father and mother standing with the Member, Mr. Prakasan on Facebook. Badhran somehow managed to get Prakasan's mobile number and contacted him. Prakasan said:

"Hey, your parents are enjoying the best time in their life now! They have an adopted son, a limper. The reason behind their prosperity is that limper. They have made a three-story bungalow worth 2 crores at Pavakka Hills! Even, they invited people to the housewarming with a 2000 rupees note! I am a witness!"

Badhran couldn't believe his ears. Immediately he called his elder brother Bharathan and explained the matter. Bharathan conveyed the matter to his sisters who then passed the message to all the other brothers. Within a few hours, all ten children came to know about the unexpected luck of Grandpa and Grandma. They decided to visit their parents and find out the facts the very next day. Schools were closed for holidays and thus they had nothing to worry about their children's classes. All of them decided to avail one week's leave and stay with Grandpa and Grandma.

Grandma was relaxing in the front yard after lunch. "Ah, I can smell the fragrance of a fully ripened jackfruit. Moosa, can you climb the jackfruit tree and bring down the ripened fruits?" asked Grandma.

"I am not getting any smell at all!" replied Moosa wonderingly.

"I don't think the jackfruits are fully ripened. If you can pluck a comparatively ready-to-eat jackfruit, we can prepare jackfruit chips and puzhukku." Grandpa expressed his desire.

"From tomorrow, we can start cooking thoran with jackfruit seeds," Grandma added.

Anyway, Moosa decided to climb the jackfruit tree. He changed over his dress, kept a Malappuram Knife on his hip, hung plastic coir on his shoulder, and like a monkey climbed the jackfruit tree. Moosa checked the big-size jackfruits by pressing and knocking on them.

"Not even a single one is ripened, Grandma!" Moosa screamed from the top.

"It's okay, better you bring down two big ready-to-cook jackfruits," Grandma ordered.

But, Moosa was not an expert in deciding about the readiness of the jackfruits. So, he simply selected two big jackfruits and brought them down using the rope. Moosa was astonished to see nine cars coming towards his house one by one as he was about to descend.

It was easy for Moosa to climb the tree but he found it difficult while descending. So, he jumped from ten feet high to reach the ground fast.

Grandma had already left the spot with the jackfruits. Moosa said to Grandpa:

"Grandpa, lots of visitors are coming. I feel, today all our rooms will be full of people!"

"Hey, you are brainless so you feel so. Who is interested in visiting us?"

"Grandpa, you are now a rich man! You are a big shot at Pavakka Hills. Relatives will rush to you once they know about your wealth. Wait and see!"

Moosa had not even completed his sentence when they heard the honks of vehicles at the gate. Moosa rushed to open the gate!

Chapter 10

The Spring Comes

Nine cars reached the courtyard one by one. Four sons and five daughters of Grandpa and Grandma with their family members got off the cars. The youngest son, Kunjiraman had not reached. As he didn't own a car, he was coming by bus.

To the visitors, Moosa looked like a servant in his working attire. Staring at him, Bharathan's wife ordered:

"Carry the entire luggage inside the house."

Moosa counted the children while carrying the luggage. There were 22 children! Moosa felt as if the children had come out of school after the bell rang! Moosa felt happy.

Sons and daughters of Grandpa and Grandma were found exaggerating their love for their parents. Grandpa and Grandma were delighted to see their children. Their face shined as they forgot all their complaints about their children. Even, Moosa's eyes burst into tears on seeing the happiness of Grandpa and Grandma.

Moosa changed over his working dress and wore his dhoti and shirt. By then, the youngest son Kunjiraman reached with his wife. They had no children. Moosa rushed to greet them.

"Please come, all others have arrived already."

Moosa carried their two bags on his shoulder. Kunjiraman asked Moosa on the way:

"Who are you?"

"I am a helper here," Moosa replied humbly.

"Oh, are you the one whom my father has adopted? I heard so!"

"Nothing like that, I just live with them. It's all their mercy!"

Moosa got worried about his future. He sat under the Gold Tree.

A 5-year-old fat boy came to Moosa and asked:

"Brother, what's your name?"

"Bharat Moosa," Moosa replied sternly and seriously.

"Are you CID Moosa?" The boy shot his next question.

'Ah, he is really very funny!' Moosa thought. Moosa instantly sang a song to cheer up the boy:

"Not CID Moosa but I am Bharat Moosa
Not an alcoholic but I often look like a drunkard
I won't spare the cheaters
I will punish the criminals
I will help the helpless
I am friendly and kind-hearted!"

But the boy didn't like Moosa's song. He grinned at Moosa and asked annoyingly:

"Why are you boasting about yourself? The great warrior Tacholi Othenan never praised himself! The songs, vadakkan pattukal about his valour were sung by Pakkanar and not by Othenan himself!"

"Othenan! Who is he? And, what is this vadakkan pattukal?" Moosa wondered. The boy was not ready to leave the topic just like that.

"I want to know what made you boast about yourself. What heroic acts you did!"

"Ah, I have done many daring acts. I defeated a tiger in the forest and made him a domestic animal. I caught a crocodile from the river, removed its tooth, and made it a locket in my garland; I fought with notorious thief Dadi Girija whom even police feared …"

The boy couldn't resist laughing to his heart's content. He said:

"Lie… Lie… Even Munjasan won't lie like this!"

"Hey little boy, I didn't lie at all. Anyway, I made you laugh, right? What's your name dear?" Moosa asked smilingly.

"My name is Samosa." Pranking so, the boy ran away.

Moosa searched Google for details about Tacholi Othenan. Moosa's heart was touched deeply by the heroic acts of the great warrior, Tacholi Othenan. Moosa was interestingly listening to a vadakkan pattu when Grandma came to him with a big list.

"Hey, take your jeep and rush to the market. Bring the items as shown in this list. You know, I am seeing my grandchildren for the first time. It's my duty to treat them well."

While driving the jeep downhill, Moosa thought, 'By any means, I must become Tacholi Othenan! Stories about my heroic acts must be sung like vadakkan pattukal by people around the world.'

Moosa had forgotten about his desire to beat Usain Bolt!

Chapter 11

The Accomplished Liar

Grandpa's third son's youngest son Vikru was the one who had questioned Moosa. Vikru found others also talking about Moosa.

The children had seen Moosa going to the market. As Moosa was away from home, everybody dared to speak about him. The eldest daughter of Grandpa and Grandma, Subhadra asked:

"Father, what's wrong with you? You have 10 children already! What's the need for adopting the 11th one?"

"Ah, what's the use of having 10 children? At this old age, we can't find anybody to help us!" retorted Grandpa.

The eldest son's complaint was something else.

"Why did you give him my name?"

"Your name is Bharathan. His name is Bharat. There's a difference, you know!"

"What special quality did you find in him for adoption?" Badhran, the second son asked.

Grandma replied instantly:

"He does all sorts of work without any hesitation. He is of great help to us in this old age."

"He said he had removed a tooth from a crocodile's mouth and made it a locket in his garland!" Vikru interfered. The children laughed loudly.

"Hey, did you speak to Bharat? And, what else does he say?" The elder sister, Sweta questioned Vikru.

"He defeated a tiger in the forest and made him a domestic animal. He fought with notorious thief Dadi Girija whom even police feared."

Grandpa, Grandma, and everybody stood shocked and surprised.

"Ah, what an accomplished liar he is! How could he master lying like this!" Dinesh, the eldest son of Bharathan wondered.

"It seems we have got a good task. Let him come, we will take him to task!" Subhadra's eldest daughter Viji said.

"Yes, we must show him what we are!" Her younger brother Shaji seconded Viji.

Children waited for Moosa in the front yard anxiously. Vikru stood on the balcony on the third floor looking for Moosa. As the jeep was seen, he ran downstairs and informed others.

Moosa's jeep reached the courtyard. As he came out, the children surrounded him and sang:

"Bharat Moosa is coming

Better let us run away

He might bring a tiger, Ah

There can be a crocodile

He is strong and daring, Ah

Dadi Girija runs away

Bharat Moosa is coming

The biggest liar in the world!"

Moosa angrily blew the horn. The children stopped singing.

"You have enough time to sing. First, you pick up the items and keep them in the kitchen."

Children obeyed Moosa. Finally, there was just one luggage of 70 kilograms of rice. Moosa alone carried it on his shoulder to the store room.

By the time Moosa reached the front yard from the store room, children had reached the spot.

"Brother Moosa, let's go to the forest and catch a tiger." Ganesh, the second son of Bharathan said.

"Brother Moosa, let's go to Shiriya River and pluck a crocodile's tooth." Liji, the second daughter of Subhadra ridiculed him.

'Oh, these children are crossing their limits. I must do something to save my prestige!' thought Moosa.

"Look, the forest is too far, my dear children. We may get stuck there if we go now. Better, let's go to the river which is nearby and catch one crocodile. We can also enjoy bathing in the river. So, get ready with your dress, towel, and soap."

Children screamed in merriment and ran inside the house to pick up their items for bathing. Soon, the children were ready to bathe in the river. Upon hearing the chaos, mothers came out. Vilasini, Grandma's third daughter asked:

"Where are you going?"

"Mom, we are going to the river with Brother Bharat to catch a crocodile." Seven year old Hari replied.

"How dare you take these little kids to the river to catch a crocodile?" Suseela, Grandma's youngest daughter, scolded Moosa.

Grandma intervened:

"Hey, don't worry; there are no crocodiles in the Shiriya River. How could you forget your childhood days? You used to bathe in the river fearlessly. Let these children enjoy the river. After all, our Moosa is there with them!"

Chapter 12

Crocodile's Attack

The children excitedly proceeded to the Shiriya River. 2-year-old Soumya sat on Moosa's shoulder. The elder children, Dinesh and Viji carried the little ones, Sridhanya and Rose.

The vast and deep Shiriya River's crystal-clear water was flowing beautifully, shining in the sunlight. Moosa asked Sridhanya, Rose, and Soumya to sit at the river bank and not to enter the river.

"Your elder sisters will bathe you after we all finish bathing in the river. Till then, you can enjoy watching us playing in the river."

Sridhanya and Rose nodded in agreement but Soumya remained adamant to enter the river. So, Moosa took her to the river.

After a while, Vikru asked:

"Brother Bharat, will you please teach me how to swim?"

Moosa brought Soumya back to the river bank and made her sit beside her elder sisters. Moosa then started Vikru's swimming lessons.

Sanoj, Manoj, Sreerag, Vinod, and Harish were in ecstasy playing in the water. Suddenly, they heard the cries of Rose. Moosa, holding Vikru tightly, rushed to Rose.

Moosa was seeing a live crocodile for the first time in

his life! The crocodile had caught little Rose. It was pulling her leg to carry her off down into the depths of the river. Without thinking much, Moosa challenged the crocodile and tried to open up its mouth by pulling with all his might.

The crocodile thrashed its mighty tail, to and fro in great smacking flails, as it tried to drag little Rose. The crocodile with its tail beat Moosa's head strongly. Though he was hurt, Moosa kept on pulling the crocodile's mouth. By then, Dinesh and Ganesh came running and started beating the crocodile with a big stick. Unable to bear the attack, finally, the crocodile left Rose's legs. Vinod immediately lifted Rose.

The crocodile jumped into the river and swam swiftly to escape from the children's attack with sticks and stones.

Rose's leg was bleeding due to the crocodile's bite. Moosa plucked some medicinal leaves at once. Moosa asked Viji to grind the leaves quickly and make a paste out of them for smearing at Rose's wounds. Moosa was unable to grind as his hands had suffered injuries. Viji kept the leaves on a big stone, collected a pebble, cleaned and washed it, and then ground the leaves. Viji applied the medicinal paste to Rose's wounds.

"Don't be scared, the crocodile won't return," Moosa said to all.

But everybody had lost their mood and enthusiasm.

"Aren't you applying medicine on your wounds?" Jyothi asked Moosa.

"No, it might cure by itself!" replied Moosa.

All of them returned home silently. Moosa handed over Rose to her mother Suseela. Moosa touched Rose's father, Sugunan's feet, and apologized.

"Sugunan, let's rush to the hospital, Rose needs medical care." Sadasivan, Grandma's fourth son told his brother-in-law in a hurry.

Moosa said:

"There is no need to go to any hospital. Just wait, by

tomorrow morning, she will be fine."

Grandma stared at Moosa's face. Moosa winked his eyes. Grandma said at once:

"If Moosa said she would be fine by tomorrow morning, then you can take it for granted. It's my promise."

Everyone looked wondering at Grandma. Nobody said anything thereafter.

That night, Moosa couldn't sleep. 'I never wanted a crocodile to come in real, it was just a lie.' Moosa thought desperately.

'Unknowingly I made a mistake, that too with a 3-year-old kid.' Moosa's thoughts beat around the bush. Moosa remembered the words of Paulo Coelho in his book, The Alchemist – "When you want something, the whole universe conspires in order for you to achieve it"

Two years ago, when Moosa was wandering about the roads in Ernakulam, a poet had given him that book. "It's a useless book. Everything in it is just a lie and nothing else," said the poet!

Chapter 13

Threatening By The 'Little Police'

The next day, early morning at 5 o'clock, Moosa knocked at the door of Sugunan's room. Sugunan's wife, Suseela opened the door.

"Ah, YOU? Why are you disturbing us at this time?" Suseela angrily asked.

"Sister, I just came to see little Rose."

"She is asleep."

Moosa didn't wait for her permission. He entered the room, lifted Rose from the bed, and ran swiftly to the Magical Tree.

"Where are you taking my daughter?" screamed Suseela. But Moosa preferred not to reply.

Rose awoke from sleep and started crying. But as she saw herself in the hands of Moosa, she stopped crying.

Moosa made her stand under the Magical Tree and asked her to touch the tree with her hands. Again, the miracle happened. Rose's wounds got cured leaving behind no scars and marks! Rose's face shined like that of an angel.

Moosa thanked the Magical Tree from the bottom of his heart and returned with Rose.

By then, Sugunan and Suseela had reached the courtyard in search of Rose. Moosa handed over Rose to Suseela and said:

"Look, I have returned your kid without any scars or wounds."

Sugunan and Suseela stood stunned as they couldn't understand anything.

Moosa heard the bell of the paper boy at the gate. Moosa collected the newspaper and started reading it at the sit-out.

After reading the newspaper, Moosa was about to leave for the river with his brush, toothpaste, soap, and towel. Suddenly, the children surrounded him with numerous questions.

"Where are you going, Bharat Brother?" Dinesh asked.

"Just to take a bath."

"Are you again going to face off with that crocodile?" Vinod asked.

"Do you own that crocodile? Is it your pet?" asked Viji.

"Did you deliberately take us to the crocodile's river yesterday?" Ganesan asked sternly.

Moosa replied humbly:

"Oh, my children, please don't mistake me. I even saw a crocodile for the first time in my life yesterday."

"Hey, you only made the crocodile bite little Rose yesterday," Manoj argued.

"When?" Moosa pretended to be innocent as if he knew nothing. Moosa showed his hands to the children and said, "Look, the crocodile had bitten my hands!"

"No, the crocodile bit Rose's leg first," Greeshma screamed.

"Hey, why are you lying unnecessarily? Don't suspect me." Moosa expressed his concern.

"Oh, is it so? Tell me, how did the wounds appear on Rose's leg then? We saw four teeth-marks of the crocodile on her leg!" said Liji.

"What kind of wounds are you talking about? Don't lie and make stories now. Show me her wounds; I am ready to accept any sort of punishment from you if you prove your words." Moosa said.

"We will make you squat 1000 times," Vikru said.

"OK, agreed."

The children rushed to meet Rose. Moosa smilingly went to the river bank.

Moosa found the children waiting for him as he reached home after his bath. The children didn't let him go inside the house.

"Hey, you can't just escape like that. We have some more questions." Harish said.

"Are you a goblin?" asked Viji.

"Are you Mayavi or Luttappi?" Hari asked.

Moosa sadly sang a song as a reply to all:

"Not Luttappi, not Mayavi
Not a goblin, not a magician
But I am a poor orphan
Living with your Grandpa Grandma
Leave me alone if you don't love me
Let me help your Grandpa Grandma"

Moosa's words deeply touched the hearts of the children. They let Moosa go inside the house!

Chapter 14

Kunjulakshmi's Grief

Moosa found the children evading him with suspicious eyes. He found them whispering something as and when they found Moosa on their way. Moosa became suspicious.

Moosa was digging pits for planting banana trees at a few places on the areca nut farm. Vikru approached Moosa while the others stood a little away.

"What happened? Are you not happy with me?" Moosa asked the children.

"Hmm... if you do help, we are ready to be your friend again."

"Ah, is it so? Tell me, what's your demand?"

"We need a swing to play."

"That's all! I will do it. But where will we tie the swing?"

Moosa searched for the right tree for the swing but couldn't find any in the areca nut farm or nearby. Finally, Moosa found a solution.

"In between two areca nut trees, we can tie a strong bamboo stem across and then tie a swing. But we need to go to the river bank and bring bamboo. We also need to collect strong and suitable vines."

"We are also coming with you." The children said in chorus.

"Hey, none of you will come with me. Let me go alone. The crocodile might be waiting." Moosa tried to discourage the children.

Then, Dinesh, the eldest one in the children's gang suggested:

"Children won't go, let the matured people only go today."

Moosa couldn't resist laughing. He asked:

"Who are those mature people here? Raise your hands if you are above 15 years."

Not even a single hand was raised.

"It's OK. Who is there for the above 10 years?"

Dinesh, Ganesh, Harish, Vinod, Jyothi, Viji, Liji, Shaji, and Manoj raised their hands. There were 9 members.

That's when Shaji said: "Girls need not come, let them take care of the kids at home."

Viji got annoyed and said sternly:

"Hey, why is it so? Do you think the vines won't get cut if girls try? Parents are there to take care of the kids, you don't worry about girls!"

Shaji kept quiet. But little ones started crying. Vikru ran inside the home with a faded face. Moosa consoled them and said:

"Don't worry my dear little ones; you will be the first to play when the new swing is ready."

The ten-member gang was about to leave for the river bank when Vikru came and said:

"Aunt Kunjulakshmi is calling Bharat Brother."

"I will just come." Saying so, Moosa went inside the house.

Kunjulakshmi was sitting in Kunjiraman's room with tearful eyes. Moosa anxiously stared at her.

"I know you possess some magical power. I have an issue. Can you sort it out, please?"

"What's your problem?"

"Even after 11 years of marriage life, we have no children."

"Ah, it's a silly matter. Let's sort it out tomorrow itself. You get ready tomorrow morning as if you have to get ready for a temple visit. Rest, you leave to me. I assure you will find your own child playing here after ten months!"

Kunjulakshmi felt relaxed and happy. Moosa, accompanied by the elder children, went to the river bank with a sharp knife.

Lots of bamboo was available at the river bank. Moosa cut a strong one but it didn't fall as it got stuck among other bamboo.

"Hey, all of you sing a sweet song in chorus and pull the stem down using your power." Moosa said to the children. The children quite excitedly did the task and finally, the bamboo fell down.

Moosa cut a piece from the bottom of the stem about 15 feet. Then, he searched for vines suitable for the swing.

Moosa could find a long vine on a big tree. Moosa climbed the tree. Something shocked him! From the top of the tree, he found the crocodile on the other side of the river. It was basking in the muddy land!

Chapter 15

The Crocodile-hunt

Moosa carefully cut the vine. By the time Moosa came down, the children had made the vine just like a rope used in a tug of war. Moosa said to the children:

"I will give you a task now. Keep this vine on a rock and crush it nicely with a big pebble to make it rope."

"Brother Bharat, is it enough to crush both the ends of the vine about one meter?" Dinesh asked.

"No, I want you to crush the entire vine. That's not for tying the swing. I have some other plans."

Moosa went to the bush with his knife. Children couldn't understand anything about Moosa's plan. They started their job and the sound echoed at the river bank as if some stone-workers were working together.

Moosa was busy collecting strong branches with a 'V' shape at the edge. Within ten minutes, he collected four such V-shaped branches and reached the children. By then, the children had made a good rope out of the vine.

"You form two groups and do a tug of war, let me see whether the rope is strong enough or not," Moosa suggested.

"Let boys and girls be different teams and compete," Manoj said.

"Hey, we girls are just three! How is it possible?" Jyothi

asked.

"Never mind, I will join your team. Let the six boys make the other team." Moosa said.

The tug of war started. Moosa's team lost the game.

"Hello, the game is 'best of three'. Wait, we are going to win the next round." Liji said, reminding others about the rules of the game.

Moosa said:

"It was not a competition at all, my children. I was just checking the strength of this rope. Don't worry, the next item is going to be funnier!"

"What's that, brother?" The children asked in chorus.

"We are going for a crocodile-hunt. Let's teach a lesson to that crocodile who bit Rose yesterday. We won't kill him but catch him alive."

"But, where is the crocodile?" asked Viji.

"The crocodile is on the other side of the river bank. Who dares to come with me?"

Everybody raised their hands.

Moosa handed over the rope to Manoj. Moosa then handed over three V-shaped branches to Dinesh, Ganesh, and Shaji. Moosa kept one with him.

Moosa showed them the crocodile basking in a relaxed mood on the other side of the river bank.

"Two members must attack the crocodile from two different directions. Thrust the V-shaped branches at the crocodile making it immovable. Ganesh must attack the crocodile at its tail while Dinesh and Ganesh must focus on attacking at its centre. I will thrust the V-shaped branch at its head." Moosa explained his crocodile-hunt plan.

The children executed the plan like experienced professionals. The crocodile tried once to evade their clutches but to no avail. Moosa handed over his V-shaped branch to Vinod and warned him to be highly vigilant.

Moosa then took the rope from Manoj and tied the crocodile from head to tail.

"Ah, now it can't open its mouth," Moosa assured.

"Now, we must make the crocodile have a nice bath." Moosa pushed the crocodile from the muddy surface to the river. The children enthusiastically pushed the crocodile with the branches into the water.

Meanwhile, Moosa searched Google and found the contact number of the Forest Officer in their area.

"Sir, we have caught a crocodile from the Shiriya River, nearby Pavakka Hills," Moosa informed the matter to the officer.

"How dare you catch a crocodile from the river? Crocodiles are supposed to live in the river and not anywhere else. Who did permit you?" The Forest Officer questioned Moosa.

"Sir, this crocodile is a threat to human life. And, this river is used by many people for bathing and washing clothes. Yesterday, I was attacked by this crocodile. It attacked a 3-year-old child too. If you can't take appropriate action, then I shall contact the Forest Minister."

"Oh, that's not required, we will do the needful. Let me know the exact location."

"Please reach Asan Junction first and then on top of Pavakka Hills, there's Grandpa Kesavan's bungalow." Moosa updated the officer.

Four big children carried the crocodile on their shoulders. The others followed cheerfully, singing and dancing!

Chapter 16

The Magical Fruit

Everybody reached Grandpa's bungalow with the crocodile. As the children were about to offload the crocodile, Moosa said:

"Wait for a minute; let me do a pose with the crocodile."

The children also did different poses for different styles of photos with the crocodile. Moosa then gave his mobile to Dinesh and said:

"I need a different pose."

Moosa took over the crocodile from the children and put it on his shoulder, and stood like a 'farmer with plough'.

The Forest Department Official's vehicle reached Grandpa's bungalow followed by the media personnel and the villagers in a group. There was chaos in Grandpa's courtyard. Member, Prakasan also came with his supporters.

The Forest Officer checked the crocodile and said:

"Ah, this is a gharial usually found in the rivers of Northern India. I am surprised how this is here in our Shiriya River!"

Member Prakasan stubbornly intervened and screamed:

"It's a deliberate act by some miscreants, I am sure about it. I suspect the involvement of the Mine Mafia to scare away the poor residents of Pavakka Hills."

Soon, the TV channels broadcast the news about captur-

ing the deadly crocodile by a few children.

The Forest Officer warned Moosa:

"Beware; we will file a case against you in case this crocodile dies."

Suddenly, Grandpa retorted:

"Don't think so, Moosa is just 16 years old. How can you arrest a child like him?"

"In that case, we can even arrest his parents." The Forest Officer retorted.

Moosa smiled and said:

"Oh, that's really very good. At least, I will know who my parents are!"

The officer instructed his subordinates to take custody of the crocodile. As the Forest Official's vehicle disappeared with the crocodile, Jyothi lamented:

"Oh, they carried our rope too!"

Media personnel had a gala time with the children who were quite interested in giving interviews. They exaggerated their fight with the crocodile and gave much stuff to each reporter.

Member Prakasan approached Moosa and said:

"We should not simply leave this matter. We must find out who the culprits are behind this crocodile-attack."

Moosa stood smiling simply without any reply.

Later in the evening, children spent most of the time in front of the TV watching their faces and speeches curiously and joyously.

But, Moosa was lost in deep thought about Prakasan's suspicion about the Mine Mafia.

The next day, Kunjulakshmi was ready early in the morning. Grandpa told Kunjiraman:

"Hey, you also accompany her. Once, this boy Moosa kidnapped your mother. Don't take risks."

"I don't suspect Bharat at all," Kunjiraman replied to his father confidently.

Moosa guided Kunjulakshmi to the Magical Tree. Moosa helped her get onto the base.

"This is a Magical Tree. Have faith in the tree. Hug and whisper your wish to the tree." Moosa said.

Kunjulakshmi tightly hugged the tree and prayed with her eyes closed. Suddenly, a red coloured fruit, bigger the size of a grape, fell on her head from the tree.

Before it fell on the ground, Moosa caught the fruit in his hands and gave it to Kunjulakshmi.

"Have this fruit with prayers in your heart. I am sure your wish will come true. But don't disclose this matter to anyone now." Moosa said.

Kunjulakshmi's face shined like a Goddess as she ate the fruit and felt its sweetness!

Chapter 17

Playing On The Swing

Moosa kept a knife with him when he went to bathe in the river. He climbed on a tree and cut down a strong vine. He removed its leaves and crushed the vine about one meter at both ends. Thereafter, Moosa bathed in the river.

Moosa scrutinized the areca nut trees and selected two suitable ones that stood one and a half meters away from each other. Moosa tied the bamboo branch across the areca nut trees. He had already tied the ropes at the edges of the bamboo keeping half meter distance between the ropes.

Moosa fixed the seat with a coconut tree stem. "Your swing is ready," Moosa announced. In no time, children surrounded Moosa screaming, 'First ME... First ME!'

Moosa said:

"Let me first swing on this swing and assure safety. In case the rope gets broken, you will fall 'thud' breaking your nose!"

Moosa played on the swing in full swing to assure its strength and stability. Children screamed in merriment. Dinesh and Ganesh pushed the swing with all their might so Moosa could swing swiftly.

Moosa, quite satisfied, got down the swing and made little Soumya sit on the swing at first. Slowly he pushed the

swing by singing delightedly. Children clapped in rhythm.

"Soumya Soumya, swing like wind
Sing a song, swing swing swing
Up and down, down and up
Soumya Soumya, swing like wind
Yonder hills and valleys, Ah
Soumya Soumya, watch them all
It's time to stop your swing
We too want to swing like wind!"

Soumya expressed her unwillingness to get down from the swing. Rose and Sridhanya shouted. Moosa said to Soumya:

"I will let you swing ten more times. After that, you must get down. Look, all are eagerly waiting to play on the swing. Won't you let them swing?"

Soumya nodded. Moosa again pushed the swing for Soumya. Others started counting – "One, Two, Three, Four ...."

It became a habit for the children to spend their days mostly on the swing. Moosa intervened only when they used to quarrel or fight.

Nobody realized how the days had passed by so swiftly in the presence of the merry-making children.

Saturday evening, Grandpa's son Bharat said to Dinesh, Ganesh, and Harish:

"Tomorrow after lunch, we must return. Leave is finished and we need to report to the office from Monday. Start packing your luggage."

Other parents also gave the same instructions to their children. The faces of children faded.

The next morning, children assembled at the areca nut farm. Nobody wanted to leave Grandpa's house.

"Look, we have two weeks' time for the school to reopen. If our parents have no leave then let them return. We will enjoy our holidays here. After two weeks, let them come back. Then, we will go with them without any grievance." Viji opined and the others nodded. The children's strike finally brought them victory as parents were forced to change their decision.

Parents decided to leave all the children at Grandpa's house except the three younger ones. The children became happy.

Thus, Grandpa's children started preparing for the return journey after their holidays. But, Kunjiraman and Kunjulakshmi remained cool as if they had no plan to leave. Moosa asked:

"Aren't you going back?"

Kunjiraman said:

"No, we decided not to leave our parents alone here. We are going to stay here forever!"

"Wow, that's a good decision!" Moosa replied.

Suddenly, Kunjulakshmi asked Kunjiraman:

"We have a good bungalow here with all the facilities. Then, what's the need for you to work like a security guard in the town?"

Moosa smilingly replied:

"Ah, Grandpa has been seriously looking for a security guard for this bungalow!"

"Oh, for that you are here already." Kunjulakshmi laughed at Moosa.

After lunch, everybody got ready to leave. Suddenly, Rose, Sridhanya, and Soumya started crying.

"We don't want to go... we won't come with you..." They screamed. Their mothers tried their best to convince them. The children refused to accept their offers and remained adamant to stay back at Grandpa's house.

Finally, parents had to agree with their stubborn kids. They asked Kunjiraman and Kunjulakshmi to keep a special watch on all the children.

Without children, nine cars, one by one, left Grandpa's house and disappeared from Pavakka Hills!

Chapter 18

Children's Republic

The next morning, Moosa was surprised to see a funny scene on his way back from the river. Grandpa was swinging alone on the children's swing. Grandpa, humming his favourite songs, was in full ecstasy.

Moosa understood the secret behind Grandpa's joy.

"Oh, without my knowledge, you tested the 'hugging magic'. Am I right, Grandpa?"

"Hey Moosa, Grandma only dragged me to the Magical Tree. Don't you see, now I look like a youngster like you?"

As the parents left, the children declared their own freedom in all respects. They often quarrelled and fought for silly reasons.

Grandma handed over a list of items to Moosa after tea. Moosa had certain calculations in his mind as he didn't want the children to engage in unnecessary fights. Moosa decided to buy toys and books for the children.

The children gathered around the jeep as Moosa was about to leave for the market.

"We also wish to accompany you to the market." They demanded.

"Hey, all of you can't be accommodated in this jeep, there's not much place. Look, I will carry two children each day. Is it fine?"

"Look, little ones were given preference for swinging first. Hence, preference for the jeep ride must be given to the older ones." Viji suggested.

Moosa agreed and thus Dinesh and Viji got in the jeep. The jeep left.

Moosa purchased the items as per Grandma's list and then drove the Jeep to a toy shop. Moosa bought one football, one volleyball, four bats for playing badminton with shuttle cocks, two cricket bats, balls, and nets. As desired by Viji, Moosa bought a big carom board and for Dinesh, a chess board too.

"Do you love reading books?" asked Moosa.

"If the stories are interesting, then of course!" replied Viji.

Moosa then took the children to a big bookstall. Dinesh and Viji selected books of their choice.

"Hey, don't forget to select books for the kids." Moosa reminded them.

Moosa casually went through the bookshelves. He saw a known face on the outer cover of a book. He suddenly remembered the poet who had gifted him the book 'The Alchemist', two years ago. The title of the book was 'Poetry of Louis Peter'. Moosa purchased that book too.

Dinesh and Viji selected lots of books. Moosa selected a few children's-periodicals like Balarama and Kalikkudukka. He also purchased colouring books, watercolours, and crayon packets.

Moosa was about to start the jeep when Dinesh asked:

"Can we have some gulab jamuns, please?"

"Oh, we are too late. Grandma might scold us. Better, let's parcel gulab jamuns and have them peacefully at home."

Dinesh and Viji agreed. Moosa bought five packets of gulab jamuns from a nearby bakery.

On the way, Viji said:

"Brother Bharat, you are really great. You don't have any job still you buy whatever we say. You know, our parents don't buy things like that. They only complain about the shortage of money always!"

"Hey, nothing like that, it's all God's blessings!" replied Moosa.

"But, how does God give money to you? How is it possible?" Dinesh asked.

'Ah, I am trapped!' Moosa thought. Moosa suddenly remembered Grandma's lie story and narrated it to the children. Luckily, Dinesh and Viji believed the story!

Moosa distributed the items to all the children. Children soon got engaged, a few reading while a few others played football in the courtyard. The children rejoiced at the zenith of happiness. Moosa handed over the gulab jamun packets to Kunjulakshmi and said:

"Please distribute equally among the children or they will cause chaos here."

Moosa then made an announcement in front of the children:

"Dear children, we have a big task ahead which needs to be completed in three days. Have your lunch and relax for a while. Sharp at 02.30 hours we are going to start making the playgrounds. One court is enough for football and cricket. For volleyball and badminton, we will have a separate court. All of you must work together and make our plan successful."

"Hurray… Hurray…" The children screamed joyously. Moosa searched Google for details for the measurements of various courts!

Chapter 19

The Guests Return

The children enjoyed the task of making the courts. Everyone did their best.

Moosa, with a long plastic thread, made boundaries. The children cut grass and levelled the ground. Moosa cut four headless areca nut trees and made goalposts.

On the fourth day, the courts were ready. Though Moosa had not played any games earlier, he was aware of the rules and regulations of most of the games. Moosa, in the Past, while wandering about aimlessly in the streets had watched elders playing various games.

The children played football, cricket, and volleyball during the day and caroms at night. They learned everything about team play.

They didn't realize how swiftly the days had gone. Finally, the day came – parents reached to pick up their children!

Though they were unwilling to return, they had no other option as the schools were reopening the very next day.

Moosa gifted the books to the children. Grandma gave a gold coin to each child. Grandpa's gift to the children was his loving kiss. Children with tearful eyes said bye to Moosa.

Grandma said:

"Oh, I had never enjoyed my life like this before. Unforgettable days!"

Grandpa said:

"I never thought of earning huge money or assets in my life. I just wanted to live without much trouble. Still, I ensured giving proper education to my children. They all got good jobs and settled well in their life. Then, they neglected us. But now I realize that money is everything, even for happiness!"

Kunjiraman's complaint was something else. He said:

"Mother gave a gold coin to all but not to me!"

Grandma replied:

"I didn't give gold coins to my children but to my grandchildren only. Let your wife give birth to a child. Not just one, but I will give two gold coins to you!"

Kunjulakshmi, with a shy face, smiled innocently. Moosa, pointing towards Grandma and Grandpa, said to Kunjiraman:

"Hey, these two gold treasures are for you, right?"

Kunjiraman nodded. Grandma and Grandpa smiled silently.

Moosa couldn't sleep that night. He remembered the past joyous days with the children. Suddenly, he heard a sound from upstairs!

Moosa silently went upstairs without switching on the lights. The sound was coming from the room where Badhran and Bhanumati had stayed. There was a cupboard in the room and someone was trying to break it. Moosa knew the cupboard key was with Grandma.

Moosa immediately locked the door from outside to prevent the thieves from escaping.

Moosa checked for the presence of Grandma, Grandpa, Kunjiraman, and Kunjulakshmi in their rooms and then informed the police about it.

Moosa tried to know what was going on inside the room,

standing on an iron ladder. As the window was closed, Moosa couldn't see anything inside the room. But Moosa could hear the arguments between the two thieves. Moosa immediately turned on the voice recorder on his mobile and started recording their conversation.

The thieves realized they were trapped inside the room. Hence, they were blaming each other for their bad destiny. Moosa hung the mobile on the ladder to continue the recording and got down the ladder. Moosa called Kunjiraman and conveyed the matter, and then informed Grandpa.

Kunjiraman informed Moosa:

"So much of the sound is coming from the top. It seems they are trying to break open the door with some weapons!"

"No worries, it is a teakwood door. They can't easily break it." Moosa said.

Meanwhile, Grandma reached with a big sickle in her hand. Kunjulakshmi came running with a pestle used for pounding rice. The four of them went upstairs. Moosa rushed outside to keep the gate open for the Police.

While opening the gate, Moosa saw the light of the Police jeep!

Chapter 20

Khader and Poker

Moosa opened the door in the presence of the policemen and switched on the light. Nobody was found! The iron cupboard was kept open!

A policeman pointed his torch under the cot and found two men lying like dead bodies!

"Hey, come out quick or we will push you out with iron rods."

A policeman shouted.

The thieves didn't want to invite unnecessary trouble. They came out one by one and stood with folded hands, pleading for mercy. They were wearing lungi and T-shirt. One was a clean-shaved bald man while the other one bore partial baldness and a big moustache.

A policeman asked the bald man:

"What's your name?"

"Khader"

"What about you?"

"Poker"

"Why did you enter here?"

"No doubt, we came to loot but didn't find anything here, Sir!"

Policeman handcuffed Khader and Poker. The Sub In-

spector told Grandpa:

"Don't worry; we will take care of these culprits. You can go to sleep peacefully."

The SI appreciated Moosa too.

"You made our job very easy. All of you showed a very good presence of mind and reacted well. Usually, people panic and fail to respond properly at crucial times. Very Well Done!"

The SI handed over his visiting card to Moosa and said:

"Don't hesitate to call me for any help, my contact number is here."

The Police left with the thieves. The light of the police jeep slowly disappeared from Pavakka Hills. Moosa closed the gate and went upstairs. Moosa scrutinized the area and realized one entry/exit door was in an open state which made the thieves' entry to the upstairs room very easy.

'The children might have forgotten to close this door!'

Moosa thought while locking that door. Suddenly, he remembered about his mobile phone. Moosa climbed the ladder and checked his mobile phone. Moosa listened to the voice recording. It was not clear but Moosa could understand that the confused thieves were arguing and blaming each other. They even dig out incidents from their unsuccessful past robberies and quarrels. Moosa could make out that they had tried looting banks and jewellery in the past.

Moosa checked the visiting card and found SI's name as Murugesan. Moosa immediately called the SI and informed him about the voice record.

"Oh, that's wonderful! Please forward the voice record through WhatsApp, let me see whether I can make use of it." The Sub Inspector suggested and Moosa forwarded the voice clip immediately. The police jeep was speeding up to the Police Station with the thieves. Khader said:

"Please release us; we didn't loot anything at all!"

"Shut up, tomorrow Magistrate will decide in the court whether to release you or throw you behind bars."

The SI shouted.

Then, Poker said:

"Sir, we are ready to give you one lakh rupees for our immediate release!"

"Ah, one lakh is not a big amount nowadays. You know, there are twenty policemen in the Station."

"Sir, we are ready to give one lakh to each policeman,"

Khader confirmed.

The SI thought for a while and said:

"OK, I will release you if you can pay ten lakh rupees to each policeman."

"Sir, we are not that rich," said Poker, "Anyway, we want to get rid of this trap. Today, we will give you one crore rupees. We need two days to sell some gold and arrange the money. We will handover you the left-over amount without fail."

SI Murugesan realized the thieves were not small-scale snatchers. They first went to Khader's house and stopped the jeep a few distance away from the gate. The policeman opened the handcuff and asked Khader to bring money. Khader went to his house and brought fifty lakh rupees in cloth. SI Murugesan handcuffed Khader again and then the team went to Poker's house.

Poker also promised his words. But SI Murugesan didn't release them after getting the money. The police jeep rushed to the police station.

SI Murugesan ordered the policemen:

"Take out all the money. Let's check."

Policemen arranged the 2000 rupees notes on the SI's table.

"Ah, you have lots of looted money and still you continue looting others!"

SI Murugesan screamed and kicked both Khader and Poker into the lock-up room.

"Oh, you cheated on us!" lamented Khader and Poker.

"Cool your heels in the lock-up for the time being. Have masala dosa breakfast and biriyani lunch tomorrow, then I will release you."

SI Murugesan started examining the voice record message forwarded by Moosa!

Chapter 21

Good News

The next morning, Grandma said to Moosa:

"Hey, you need to take Kunjulakshmi to a doctor. We feel there's good news but needs to be confirmed by a doctor. Finish your breakfast first. It's all the blessings of our Magical Tree!"

"That's really great! Let Kunjiraman and Kunjulakshmi be happy. They waited too long for a child!" Moosa said.

By 9 o'clock, Kunjiraman and Kunjulakshmi got ready and sat on the jeep. Moosa happily drove to the Town Hospital.

As they crossed Asan Junction, Moosa's mobile rang. Moosa parked the jeep at the roadside and attended the call. It was from SI Murugesan.

"Bharat Moosa, can you please come down to the Station right now?"

"Sir, I am already on the way to the town for some urgent work. I will meet you in a few minutes."

"That's fine, come fast." SI Murugesan disconnected the call.

Moosa dropped Kunjiraman and Kunjulakshmi at the hospital and rushed to the Police Station. There was a huge crowd. Newspapers and TV reporters were also seen.

'The reporters might be waiting to take photos of the

thieves.' Moosa thought while walking into the Police Station.

The Circle Inspector was discussing with SI Murugesan.

"Well done, Mr. Bharat Moosa. The voice record helped us crack down on many previous cases like City Bank Robbery and 'Chain Factory Robbery' – the infamous jewellery loot. Their conversation and arguments last night at your home turned out to be vital evidence. Look at these currency notes, it's one crore – their offer to us for their release!" SI Murugesan explained.

The CI shook hands with Moosa and said:

"I am CI Askar Ali. Look, media personnel are eagerly waiting for you!"

Moosa came out of the Police Station with the policemen. SI Murugesan introduced Moosa to the media. CI Askar Ali explained to Moosa about the robberies carried out by Khader and Poker.

"If I am not wrong, you are the person who caught a crocodile from Shiriya River three weeks ago!" a reporter said.

"Yes, I only did that with the help of nine children."

Moosa was narrated about last night's incident. The reporters asked many questions and Moosa replied calmly. Finally, Moosa said:

"Pardon me, I need to go urgently. I actually came to the Town Hospital for an emergency."

Moosa with permission from the CI and the SI rushed to the hospital.

Kunjiraman and Kunjulakshmi were eagerly waiting for the test report.

After some time, they got the test report. They met the doctor. It was good news – Kunjulakshmi is pregnant!

While returning, Kunjulakshmi said to Moosa:

"Bharat, we are speechless! We really don't know how to thank you!"

Moosa decided to celebrate. “We must have sweet payasam today!” Moosa stopped the jeep in front of a provisional store to buy some items.

Grandpa and Grandma were busy watching TV when Moosa reached with Kunjiraman and Kunjulakshmi. Moosa shared the good news with Grandma and Grandpa.

“Wow, a baby is coming to our new house!” Grandma and Grandpa rejoiced.

“And, you know there is yet another good news?” Grandpa asked Moosa.

Moosa stared at Grandpa and the others.

“Hey, the Chief Minister announced a reward of one lakh rupees to Bharat Moosa!” Grandpa screamed!

Chapter 22

Gardner Moosa

'Bank Robbers in Custody'

The next day, all newspapers' front pages covered the adventures of Bharat Moosa. A photo of Moosa with the Police, Khader, and Poker became the talk of the day among the villagers. There was also highlighted news about the Chief Minister's reward of one lakh rupees to Moosa.

While everyone was busy talking about Moosa's adventures, surprisingly Moosa was busy making a kitchen garden at home. He rested only after lunch. At that time, Moosa kept him busy playing chess with Grandpa and Kunjiraman. He always lost the game but Moosa never worried about it. At night, except Kunjulakshmi, everybody played caroms. Kunjulakshmi was busy watching her favourite TV serials.

The days passed by peacefully. But everybody missed the children. All of them eagerly waited for Kunjulakshmi's baby. That had become everybody's most precious wish!

One day, while playing caroms, Moosa said:

"Cow dung is required for the kitchen garden. One load costs about seven thousand rupees. I feel it's better to buy a cow so that we get not only cow dung but also sufficient milk."

"How much does it cost for a cow?" asked Grandpa.

"Approximately, thirty thousand rupees," Moosa replied.

"But, where is the money?" Grandma intervened.

"Grandma, if you can spare one gold coin, I can buy a cow."

"Oh, don't ever think so, my son! I am left with just ten coins only. I will have more grandchildren in the future and then I need to give them one coin each. After a few years, a few of my grandchildren will be getting married. Then, I need to offer them something!" Grandma explained her future plans.

"Do you expect seven thousand rupees worth of vegetables from your kitchen garden if you put seven thousand rupees of cow dung?" Kunjiraman questioned Moosa.

Moosa replied confidently:

"No, we won't get it. But we can eat pure and organic vegetables. Hey, Kunjulakshmi needs more care at this stage. A cow at home will assure pure milk!"

Though Moosa explained the matter elaborately, nothing could be finalized. Everybody left for their usual business.

At night, Moosa got a call from Viji. Viji was calling from her mother's mobile.

"We are very proud of you, Brother Bharat. We read about your adventures in newspapers. What would have happened to Grandpa and Grandma had you not been there with them? And, there's a piece of great news. I got selected for the School Badminton Team. All credit goes to you, brother. You only trained us well. Shaji also got selected for the School Football Team."

Moosa became emotional. With tearful eyes, he said:

"Well done, I am proud of you. But, don't forget to focus on your studies."

"Sure, I will. OK, Good Night brother." Viji disconnected the call.

Moosa felt happy. 'It was really a very good idea to train them.' Moosa thought. Moosa expected calls from the other children too. 'They don't have their own phones; they need to make calls from their parents'phones only. Let me wait.' Moosa murmured.

Moosa slept so soon that day. The next day, he got up late as he heard loud knocks at the door from Grandma.

Grandma gave him a gold coin and said:

"Go, buy a cow and a calf. The cow must give us enough milk, so check thoroughly."

Moosa became happy and went to the town with Kunjiraman.

Initially, they brought materials for making a cowshed. They turned the volleyball court into a cowshed using areca nut tree stems for pillars and aluminium sheets for the roof!

Chapter 23

Santiago

Moosa now has a new friend, a calf. Grandma had named the cow Gowri. This calf is the son of Gowri. Moosa named the calf, Santiago. The name of the shepherd boy in the book, The Alchemist, was Santiago.

Gowri's pure milk, organic vegetables from the kitchen garden, and different kinds of fruits made Kunjulakshmi healthier day by day. Her stomach started bulging more and more. Moosa volunteered to take her to the Town Hospital for the monthly check-up.

Moosa's job has increased a lot nowadays! Moosa would start with cleaning the cowshed and then milking Gowri. Then, he would go to the river bank to bring green grasses for the cow and calf. Afternoon Gowri and Santiago need to be bathed. In the evening, once again, Moosa had to milk the cow. Amidst all these, he had to take care of the kitchen garden.

But Moosa had no complaints. He remained happy always as he knew he could sleep peacefully only after joining Grandpa and Grandma!

In the morning, Moosa used to get six litres of milk from Gowri. Two litres of milk were enough for all at home. Four litres were distributed to the poor people in the neighbourhood freely. In the evening, Moosa would not milk Gowri much as he wanted only two liters of milk. The rest of the

milk was left for little Santiago.

When exhausted, Moosa would sit in the swing and relax. Santiago would stand beside him and nod his head whenever Moosa chatted.

One afternoon, suddenly, the pain started for Kunjulakshmi. Moosa took her to the Town Hospital along with the others. Kunjulakshmi got admitted to the hospital. Moosa and Grandpa returned home while Kunjiraman stayed back at the hospital. Moosa had to take care of Gowri and Santiago!

At night, Moosa received a message from Kunjiraman – 'Kunjulakshmi delivered a baby boy. Both mother and child are fine.'

Moosa immediately informed the good news to Grandpa. Grandpa's face bloomed with joy and peace!

Moosa forwarded Kunjiraman's message to Grandpa's children. 'The Annual exam is starting. Or else, children would have reached here,' Moosa thought.

Grandpa checked the calendar and laughingly said:

"Ha Ha, February 29th is the birthday of the baby. He needs to wait for four years to celebrate his birthdays!"

After dinner, Moosa asked Grandpa:

"Grandpa, should I be with you tonight in your room?"

Grandpa felt Moosa was cutting jokes out of him. Hence, he asked angrily:

"Do you think you are my wife? What do you think about me? Without anybody's help, I took care of ten children. I am seventy-five years old and still, I am not afraid of anything or anybody. If you are scared, then let me know. You can sleep in my room!"

"Ah, don't underestimate me, Grandpa. For 16 years, I used to sleep in the streets. I don't know what fear is!" Moosa also replied sternly.

Pin-drop-silence prevailed for a while. Both of them became very emotional. Grandpa hugged Moosa and said:

"Hey, you are my eleventh son, my dear. I know you love me more than anybody."

Moosa wiped off his tears and said:

"My life is indebted to you, Grandpa. Whatever I am today is just because of Grandpa and Grandma!"

Grandpa advised Moosa:

"Better die but never do anything that's against your consciousness. Don't beg in front of anyone even if you are starving. Keep helping others but never expect anything in return. Be grateful to God. Don't keep enmity in your mind forever against someone. Learn the art of forgiving. Never underestimate others. Don't hurt others. Don't be greedy for wealth and fame; they will automatically come to you if you work hard."

That night, before sleeping, Moosa noted down Grandpa's advice in his mobile notepad!

Chapter 24

The Lost Necklace

As Grandma was not at home, Grandpa and Moosa were having only gruel at all times – breakfast, lunch, and dinner. Curry was nothing but a mixture of chilli, onion, and salt. Moosa had planted sixty tapioca but nothing was ready to eat.

Anyway, their 'gruel days' got over as soon as Grandma came back home from the hospital with the baby. Moosa looked at the baby. 'Wow, he is so handsome!' Moosa murmured. Grandpa kissed the baby on his forehead.

The baby became the centre of attraction at home. Everybody fought for their turn to play with the baby. But, Moosa only had limited time to be with the baby. Moosa called him 'Kunju'. Once, Moosa brought Santiago inside the house for Kunju. Everybody laughed at Moosa that day!

One month passed by so soon after the baby's birth. It was April 1st. Moosa had been waiting for this day eagerly for quite some time as the annual vacation was starting for the children. The last working day for the school was yesterday. Grandpa's sons and daughters had promised that they would bring their children to Grandpa's bungalow during vacation.

In the morning itself, Moosa kept the gate open. His eyes anxiously waited for the cars to come with his dearest children. Instead, the police jeep came!

CI Askar Ali and SI Murugesan informed Moosa about a piece of shocking news - Khader and Poker escaped from the jail last night. Also, a robbery took place at Nellikkunne Devi Temple, three kilometers away from the town. The gold necklace of the Goddess was stolen!

The police doubted the involvement of both Khader and Poker.

CI Askar Ali explained the case:

"The priest and the Temple Committee President Mr. Gopalan were the first who came to know about the robbery when they opened the temple this morning. The gold necklace was made of three kilograms of gold, donated by the devotees three years ago. We couldn't make out how the thieves made entry inside the temple. The lock is intact and even the roof is not broken!"

SI Murugesan added up:

"We couldn't get any evidence from the spot. It's a matter of prestige for the Police now. We can't show our faces to anyone if the culprits are not caught today. We need your help."

Moosa couldn't resist laughing. He asked:

"Sir, what can I do? The entire Police Department couldn't get a lead. And, what can this silly boy do alone in this complicated case?"

"Don't think you are alone. The entire Police Department is with you. We need your support." CI Askar Ali compelled Moosa.

Moosa thought for a while and said:

"OK, let me inform Grandpa and Grandma."

Moosa explained the matter to Grandpa and Grandma. Both of them encouraged Moosa to do his best. Finally, Moosa got ready for his next mission.

Moosa, for the first time, wore pants. He looked smart in his newly stitched pants and shirt. Moosa took his Jeep's key. He went to the Magical Tree and bowed his head for its blessing. Surprisingly, a leaf from the tree fell on Moosa's head. Moosa, with prayers, kept the leaf inside his pants pocket.

Moosa said to the Police:

"Let's first visit the priest. You start; I will follow you on my jeep."

Within half an hour, the three jeeps reached the priest's house. The priest and his wife gave them a warm welcome.

The priest looked in his forties. He had a tuft at the centre of his bald head. His beautiful wife looked ten years younger than her husband. Only the husband and wife were residing in that house. They had no children.

By then, Mr. Gopalan reached with a few members of the Temple Committee.

Moosa told the priest:

"I like to hear everything about the gold necklace from your face. Come on, be quick."

The priest started explaining everything that happened last night after he closed the temple. Moosa didn't utter a word but observed his facial expressions. Moosa also noticed the priest's wife. Once the priest concluded, Moosa said:

"I need to talk to you privately."

Moosa went to the bedroom with the priest and bolted the door!

Chapter 25

Temple Thief

The priest started shivering. Moosa shouted, "Where's the necklace?"

With folded hands, the priest begged, "Sir, I don't know anything."

Moosa pulled him by his tuft. The priest screamed in pain.

"I know you are the culprit. You only stole the necklace. Did you forget about the CCTVs installed in the temple? Hey, speak out the truth or I will kill you."

"Oh, leave me, Sir. I admit I only stole the necklace. I know the Goddess will curse me for my sin. But it all happened because of my darling!"

"Who is your darling?" Moosa shouted.

"She is my wife only, Sir. She forced me to do this sin. Repeatedly I refused to commit this crime but…"

"But what?" screamed Moosa.

"She threatened me that she would leave me forever."

"Oh… Tell me, where did you keep the necklace?" Moosa came to the point.

"She has hidden it in the kitchen, Sir. It's kept inside the ash heap!"

Moosa opened the door and approached the lady with a

stern and serious look. "Go and bring the necklace… Make it fast; your husband has revealed the truth." Moosa shouted.

The lady's face became pale. She was about to fall down. Someone suddenly carried her to the room.

Moosa rushed to the kitchen. He took a stick and searched for the necklace in the ash heap. Everybody looked shocked and speechless as Moosa took out the necklace from the ash heap.

Moosa handed over the necklace to Mr. Gopalan, and told CI Askar Ali:

"Sir, please don't file a case. The poor priest was threatened by his greedy wife. If you file a case, then the media will come to know and people will make many hues and cries. Who knows whether this couple will end up in suicide? Let's not carry that sin on our head, just leave it, Sir."

SI Murugesan asked the priest and his wife:

"You don't even have a child. Then, why are you so greedy?"

The priest and the lady remained silent. Moosa smilingly replied:

"Who said they have no children? They have already fostered a child!"

Nobody could understand what Moosa was saying. Everybody looked confused. Moosa then looked at SI Murugesan and said:

"Murugesan Sir already said the name of their child; 'Greediness'!"

Everybody laughed loudly. CI Askar Ali asked the Temple Committee Members:

"Should we forgive them?"

The members nodded in agreement.

"That's fine. Please report to the Station and withdraw your case."

The policemen thanked Moosa. Then, Mr. Gopalan came

with an envelope for Moosa.

"Sir, it's a small compliment for you. Please accept."

"What's this?" Moosa asked.

"Fifty thousand rupees, Sir. We had made an offering to the Goddess that we would hand over fifty thousand rupees to the person who would recover the necklace. We know you don't need this amount; you may use it for some charity purpose."

The CI and the SI gestured to Moosa to accept it. Moosa politely received the amount.

"Then, what about our Khader and Poker?" SI Murugesan asked Moosa.

"Sir, they are thieves, they will commit some crime today or tomorrow. Let's wait and catch them." Moosa replied confidently.

Moosa started his jeep and drove fast. 'Children might have reached home!' Moosa thought. At the same time, some other thoughts were also wavering in his mind. 'What should I do with this money? Whom should I give?'

That's when Moosa happened to see an orphanage at the roadside. He parked the jeep outside the gate and walked in. Children were having their lunch - gruel with green gram. Moosa watched those unlucky children who had no home to go to during vacation.

Moosa walked into the Admin Office. He saw an old man. Moosa asked:

"How many children are here, Sir?"

"Sixty-five."

"Are they only fed with gruel and green gram daily?"

"No... No... We provide them rice and sambar three times a week."

"Why can't you give them biriyani once a week?"

"Hey, who are you to ask me all these?"

"Please don't mind, I am just a philanthropist. My name is Bharat Moosa."

"Okey. But, Mr. Moosa, please understand that I have been running this orphanage with lots of difficulties. Somehow, I manage donations from some well-wishers and take care of these orphans!"

"What will be the cost in case we wish to provide them with biriyani once a week?"

The old man thought for a while and said, "Approximately, seven thousand rupees."

"OK, from today onwards, I take the responsibility of giving them biriyani once a week."

Moosa took out the envelope from his pocket and counted the money. "Please accept twenty-eight thousand rupees. It is enough for four weeks this month. Every month, I will come and hand over you the required amount."

The old man gratefully received the money and handed over the payment receipt to Moosa.

"I am Moidu Haji. I take care of this orphanage. Kindly give me your contact number, Sir." The old man requested.

"With pleasure, Sir" Moosa gave his phone number to Moidu Haji and smilingly walked out.

Chapter 26

Fight With The Robbers

Moosa is now left with twenty-two thousand rupees. Moosa decided to buy something for the children and went to a bookstall. He bought story books, novels, and poems for the children. For the kids, Moosa bought some toys.

Moosa crossed Asan Junction and entered Pavakka Hills Road. As he reached a sharp curve, he found another Jeep in the middle of the road blocking his way. Moosa felt something fishy and immediately reversed his jeep about fifty meters. Moosa soon called SI Murugesan and informed him about the situation:

"Sir, I am stuck on the road. I just crossed Asan Junction and entered Pavakka Hills Road. My life is in danger, please come fast."

Without waiting for the SI's reply, Moosa immediately cut the call and made another call to Kunjiraman.

"Some miscreants have blocked my way; I am on the Pavakka Hills road. Please come fast with some people."

Moosa found five people approaching him aggressively. Moosa recognized Khader and Poker among them. 'The other three might be professional goondas,' Moosa thought. Moosa looked at their knives and swords.

Moosa had purchased a small black gun along with other

toys for the children. Moosa hid the gun in his pocket and faced the miscreants boldly.

"Ah, you dared to apprehend us!" Khader shouted.

"You silly fool, how did you think we would never come out of jail?" Poker screamed.

"Today, we are going to cut you into pieces. We don't care even if we have to return to jail." Khader threatened Moosa.

Moosa suddenly took out his gun and aimed at the miscreants boldly. They stood shocked for a while but Poker shouted at the next moment:

"Hey fool, by the time you shoot one person, the other four people will cut you into pieces."

"Oh, then, let the first bullet be for you," Moosa shouted, aiming at Poker.

"Ah, I have three children. Don't shoot me, please." Poker cried.

"Then, let me shoot this culprit." Moosa aimed his gun at Khader.

"Oh NO, I have four children," Khader screamed.

Moosa wanted to do some time-pass till his rescue team came. Moosa aimed his gun at the fat man:

"What about you?"

"Sir, please don't kill us. We don't want to hurt you. We are doing this job for our livelihood. These thieves offered us money to kill you."

"Oh, how much do you charge?"

"Five thousand rupees, Sir."

"I offer ten thousand rupees to each one of you. Just eliminate Khader and Poker forever."

"Sir, we won't kill them but we are ready to cut their legs. But you must give us some money in advance."

"Hey, the Police are here!" looking at the police jeep, one of the miscreants screamed. They tried to escape from the spot. But before they could start their jeep, Kunjiraman

with many villagers had surrounded them with long sticks.

Kunjiraman's team smashed the Jeep. Kunjiraman poured two litters of kerosene on the jeep and screamed:

"We are going to burn the jeep. Jump out and save your life."

The five culprits jumped out of the jeep. The villagers thrashed them black and blue.

"Let's break their legs so that they don't walk hereafter," Kunjiraman shouted.

The miscreants lay on the floor helplessly, bleeding and screaming in pain. Villagers handed over the culprits to the police. Later, they pushed the miscreant's jeep into the deep valley. SI Murugesan asked Moosa:

"How did you challenge them? Any weapons with you!"

Moosa handed over his gun to SI Murugesan and said:

"Sir, it's a toy. I just bought it for Grandpa's grandchildren!"

Everybody burst into laughter. SI Murugesan said:

"Thank you, Bharat. You sorted out two big issues in a day and saved our skin. You kept up the prestige of the Police Department. And, it's good that everyone can now lead a peaceful life."

Children were anxiously waiting for Moosa. As the jeep entered Grandpa's bungalow, children cheered up and surrounded Moosa. Moosa hugged little Soumya and shook hands with the other children. Children sang loudly in chorus:

"Not CID Moosa but he is Bharat Moosa

Not an alcoholic but often looks like a drunkard

He won't spare the cheaters

He will punish the criminals

He will help the helpless

He is friendly and kind-hearted!"

Moosa smiled innocently. It was the beginning of yet another vacation with lots of joy and adventures!

The Most Successful Way of JEE Preparation

DPP

Daily Practice Problems

JEE Main & Advanced

Graph & Derivatives

MATHEMATICS Vol-7

The Most Successful Way of JEE Preparation

DPP

Daily Practice Problems

JEE Main & Advanced

Graph & Derivatives

MATHEMATICS Vol-7

Amit M Agarwal

arihant
ARIHANT PRAKASHAN (SERIES), MEERUT

DPP
Daily Practice Problems

arihant

ARIHANT PRAKASHAN (SERIES), MEERUT

卐 Administrative & Production Offices

Corporate Office 'Ramchhaya' 4577/15, Agarwal Road, Darya Ganj, New Delhi -110002
Tele: 011- 47630600, 43518550; Fax: 011- 23280316

Head Office Kalindi, TP Nagar, Meerut (UP) - 250002
Tel: 0121-2401479, 2512970, 4004199; Fax: 0121-2401648

卐 Sales & Support Offices

Agra, Ahmedabad, Bengaluru, Bareilly, Chennai, Delhi, Guwahati, Hyderabad, Jaipur, Jhansi, Kolkata, Lucknow, Meerut, Nagpur & Pune

卐 ISBN : 978-93-13193-55-5

Published by Arihant Publications (I) Ltd.

Production Team

Publishing Managers	Mahendra Singh Rawat & Keshav Mohan	*Inner Designer*	Mazher Chaudhary
Project Head	Sorabh Chaudhary	*Page Layouting*	Sunil Sharma, Hemant
Cover Designer	Shanu Mahad	*Proof Reading*	Himanshu

For further information about the products from Arihant, log on to www.arihantbooks.com or email to info@arihantbooks.com

/arihantpub /@arihantpub Arihant Publications /arihantpub

ABOUT DPP

Daily Practice Problems

Indian Institutes of Technology better known as IITs have always been the dream destination of each science group students who want to pursue their career as Engineers. These are the institutes which have got very high value not even in India but in the whole world. To get the admission in such institutes one need to face entrance Examinations; JEE Main & JEE Advanced, out of which JEE Main is considered as the preliminary exam & JEE Advanced is the final exam to get into the IITs. Approximately per year 12 lakh students enroll themselves for JEE Main and only the top 2.25 lakh in JEE Main merit can attempt for JEE Advanced, the fact clearly express the degree of toughness of JEE Main & JEE Advanced.

To have success in such an exam one needs to be very planned & systematic in its preparation. A very popular wise saying 'Rome was not built in a day' suggests that to achieve a big target like IITs we need to work continuously. For continuous work, one need to have proper planning that how much work he/she has to do on regular basis, i.e., on daily basis. Each student preparing for JEE has many books but unfortunately none of them gives the students a plan for daily studies, which is the most effective success key for JEE.

Keeping the daily practice needs of the students in mind we have come up with DPP Series (Daily Practice Problems) having approximately 26 books. The primary focus of this series is on achieving success through practice & proper planning. For that we have divided the whole syllabus of JEE Main & JEE Advanced; Physics, Chemistry & Mathematics, into different volumes (around 8 volumes of Mathematics & 9 volumes each of Physics & Chemistry), each volume has Daily Practice Problems Sheets having specific questions on various Topics of the individual chapter of the volume ensuring the complete Practice & Assessment of the topic.

In this way we have tried to give you an effective daily planning for JEE keeping in mind the daily hours that a student can devote to his practice, you are just required to practice one sheet of each subject on daily basis. This habit of daily practice will keep you away from exam stress and thoughts like; how much I have prepared/am I preparing properly or not/ do I need to study more on daily basis or what I am doing is ok, etc., which regularly tease your mind and can give you panic at any stage of your preparation.

Some special features that we have tried to incorporate in our Daily Practice Problems (DPP) series are discussed below

1. Micro Level coverage of all the topics of a Chapter/ Unit given in JEE Main & Advanced Syllabus.
2. Each DPP has various types of questions; Subjective Questions, Single/ Multiple Correct Options, Statements type, Comprehension based, Integer Value Answer type, Matching, etc., making you practice & ready for all the question formats of JEE.
3. New & innovative questions in each DPP challenging & improving your problem solving skills.
4. Along with Topical Coverage, Revisal DPPs for JEE Main & JEE Advanced with each Chapter, covering multidisciplinary questions proving comprehensive practice.
5. JEE Main & JEE Advanced Archive (collection of last 13 years' exams questions) with each chapter.
6. Complete Solutions for each DPP.

We hope that DPP series will prove to be very beneficial for the students preparing for JEE, by giving them daily practice in a systematic & planned manner. The suggestions/criticism from the students, teachers & parents about DPP series will be welcomed whole heartedly and we promise to update this series accordingly from time to time.

DPP
Daily Practice Problems

DAILY TASKS...

1 METHODS OF DIFFERENTIATION

2 LIMITS

DPP

Daily Practice Problems

3 CONTINUITY AND DIFFERENTIABILITY

4 APPLICATIONS OF DERIVATIVES

1. Methods of Differentiation

DPP
DAILY PRACTICE PROBLEMS

DPP-1 First Principle and Fundamental Theorems

Subjective Questions

Working Space

Direction (Q. Nos. 1-4) *These questions are subjective in nature, need to be solved completely on notebook.*

1 Differentiate each of the following by first principle.

i. $f(x) = \tan x$
ii. $f(x) = \cot(2x+1)$
iii. $f(x) = \sqrt{\sin x}$
iv. $f(x) = \tan\sqrt{x}$
v. $f(x) = \dfrac{\sin x}{x}$
vi. $f(x) = \sin x + \cos x$

2 Differentiate the following w.r.t. x.

i. $(x^2 - 4x + 5)(x^3 - 2)$
ii. $(3x+8)^{7/3} \cdot (x+7)^{-3}$
iii. $\dfrac{1-\sqrt{x}}{1+\sqrt{x}}$
iv. $\dfrac{(x^2+1)(x+3)}{x}$

3 Differentiate the following functions w.r.t. x.

i. $\sqrt{a+\sqrt{a+x}}$
ii. $\sqrt{4+\sqrt{4+\sqrt{4+x^2}}}$
iii. $\dfrac{\sqrt{a+x}-\sqrt{a-x}}{\sqrt{a+x}+\sqrt{a-x}}$
iv. $\log(x+\sqrt{x^2+a^2})$
v. 10^{10^x}
vi. $\log\left[\tan\left(\dfrac{\pi}{4}+\dfrac{x}{2}\right)\right]$

4 Differentiate the following w.r.t. x.

i. $e^{ax} \cdot \cot(bx+c)$
ii. $\sqrt{\log\left\{\sin\left(\dfrac{x^2}{3}-1\right)\right\}}$
iii. $\log_{\sin x} \cos x$
iv. $\log_e(\sec x + \tan x)$
v. $\log_e(\sin\sqrt{x^2+1})$
vi. $\log_e\left(\dfrac{x+\sqrt{x^2-a^2}}{x-\sqrt{x^2-a^2}}\right)$

Only One Option Correct Type

Direction (Q. Nos. 5-17) *This section contains 13 multiple choice questions. Each question has four choices (a), (b), (c) and (d), out of which ONLY ONE is correct.*

5 If $y = \dfrac{\sec x - \tan x}{\sec x + \tan x}$, then $\dfrac{dy}{dx}$ is

a. $2\sec x(\sec x - \tan x)$
b. $-2\sec x(\sec x - \tan x)^2$
c. $2\sec x(\sec x + \tan x)^2$
d. $-2\sec x(\sec x + \tan x)^2$

6 If $y = \dfrac{1+x^2+x^4}{1+x+x^2}$ and $\dfrac{dy}{dx} = ax + b$, then the values of a and b are

a. $a = 2, b = 1$ b. $a = -2, b = 1$ c. $a = 2, b = -1$ d. $a = -2, b = -1$

7 Which of the following could be the sketch graph of $y = \dfrac{d}{dx}(x \log_e x)$?

a. 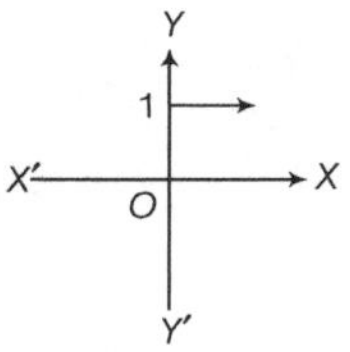

b. 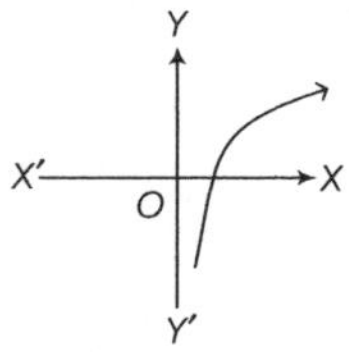

c. 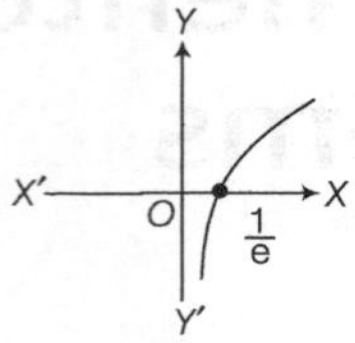

d. 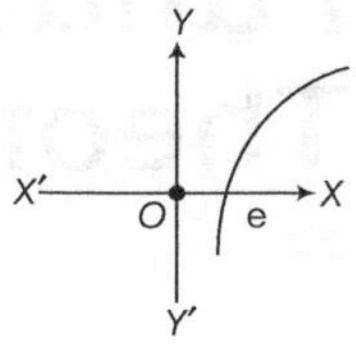

8 Differential coefficient of

$\left(x^{\frac{l+m}{m-n}}\right)^{\frac{1}{n-l}} \cdot \left(x^{\frac{m+n}{n-l}}\right)^{\frac{1}{l-m}} \cdot \left(x^{\frac{n+l}{l-m}}\right)^{\frac{1}{m-n}}$ w.r.t. x is

a. 1 b. 0 c. −1 d. x^{lmn}

9 If $y = \dfrac{1}{1+x^{n-m}+x^{p-m}} + \dfrac{1}{1+x^{m-n}+x^{p-n}} + \dfrac{1}{1+x^{m-p}+x^{n-p}}$, then $\dfrac{dy}{dx}$ at $x = e^{m^{n^p}}$ is equal to

a. e^{mnp} b. $e^{mn/p}$ c. $e^{np/m}$ d. None of these

10 If $f(x) = \log_x(\log x)$, then $f'(x)$ at $x = e$ is

a. $\dfrac{1}{e}$ b. 1 c. e d. None of these

11 Let $f(x)$ be a polynomial in x, then the second derivative of $f(e^x)$ is

a. $f''(e^x)\cdot e^x + f'(e^x)$ b. $f''(e^x)\cdot e^{2x} + f'(e^x)\cdot e^{2x}$
c. $f''(e^x)\cdot e^{2x}$ d. $f''(e^x)\cdot e^{2x} + f'(e^x)\cdot e^x$

12 If $f'(x) = \sqrt{2x^2 - 1}$ and $y = f(x^2)$, then $\dfrac{dy}{dx}$ at $x = 1$ is

a. 2 b. 1
c. −2 d. −1

13 If $y = f\left(\dfrac{2x-1}{x^2+1}\right)$ and $f'(x) = \sin x$, then $\dfrac{dy}{dx}$ is equal to

a. $\dfrac{1+x-x^2}{(1+x^2)^2}\sin\left(\dfrac{2x-1}{x^2+1}\right)$ b. $\dfrac{2(1+x-x^2)}{(1+x^2)^2}\cdot\sin\left(\dfrac{2x-1}{x^2+1}\right)$
c. $\dfrac{1-x+x^2}{(1+x^2)^2}\cdot\sin\left(\dfrac{2x-1}{x^2+1}\right)$ d. None of these

14 If $8f(x) + 6f\left(\dfrac{1}{x}\right) = x + 5$ and $y = x^2 f(x)$, then $\dfrac{dy}{dx}$ at $x = -1$ is

a. 0 b. $\dfrac{1}{14}$ c. $-\dfrac{1}{14}$ d. None of these

15 If $f(x) = x^n$, then the values of $f(1) - \dfrac{f^1(1)}{1!} + \dfrac{f^2(1)}{2!} - \dfrac{f^3(1)}{3!} + \dots + \dfrac{(-1)^n \cdot f^n(1)}{n!}$ is (where, $f^n(x)$ denotes nth order derivative) **[AIEEE 2002]**

a. n b. 1 c. 2^n d. 0

Working Space

16 Let $f(x)$ be a polynomial function of second degree. If $f(1) = f(-1)$ and a, b, c are in an AP. Then, $f'(a), f'(b), f'(c)$ are in **[AIEEE 2003]**

a. AP
b. GP
c. HP
d. None of these

17 Let $f : (-1, 1) \to R$ be a differentiable function, $f(0) = -1$ and $f'(0) = 1$. If $g(x) = [f\{2f(x) + 2\}]^2$, then $g'(0)$ is **[AIEEE 2010]**

a. 4
b. –4
c. 0
d. –2

One or More than One Options Correct Type

Direction (Q. Nos. 18-20) *This section contains 3 multiple choice questions. Each question has four choices (a), (b), (c) and (d), out of which ONE or MORE THAN ONE are correct.*

18 If $y = \tan x \cdot \tan 2x \cdot \tan 3x$, then $\frac{dy}{dx}$ is

a. $3\sec^2 3x \cdot \tan 2x \cdot \tan x + \sec^2 x \cdot \tan 2x \cdot \tan 3x + 2\sec^2 2x \cdot \tan 3x \cdot \tan x$
b. $2y(\operatorname{cosec} 2x + 2\operatorname{cosec} 4x + 3\operatorname{cosec} 6x)$
c. $3\sec^2 3x - 2\sec^2 2x - \sec^2 x$
d. $\sec^2 x + 2\sec^2 2x + 3\sec^2 3x$

19 If $y = e^{\sqrt{x}} + e^{-\sqrt{x}}$, then $\frac{dy}{dx}$ is

a. $\frac{e^{\sqrt{x}} - e^{-\sqrt{x}}}{2\sqrt{x}}$
b. $\frac{e^{\sqrt{x}} - e^{-\sqrt{x}}}{2x}$
c. $\frac{1}{2\sqrt{x}}\sqrt{y^2 - 4}$
d. $\frac{1}{2\sqrt{x}}\sqrt{y^2 + 4}$

20 Two functions f and g have first and second derivatives at $x = 0$ and satisfy the relations, $f(0) = \frac{2}{g(0)}$, $f'(0) = 2g'(0) = 4g(0)$, $g''(0) = 5f''(0) = 6f(0) = 3$. Then,

a. if $h(x) = \frac{f(x)}{g(x)}$, then $h'(0) = \frac{15}{4}$
b. if $k(x) = f(x) \cdot g(x) \cdot \sin x$, then $k'(0) = 2$
c. $\lim_{x \to 0} \frac{g'(x)}{f'(x)} = \frac{1}{2}$
d. None of these

One Integer Value Correct Type

Direction (Q. Nos. 21-25) *This section contains 5 questions. When worked out will result in an integer from 0 to 9 (both inclusive).*

21 If $f(x) = \lambda x^2 + \mu x + 12$, $f'(4) = 15$ and $f'(2) = 11$, then $\lambda + \mu$ is

22 If $f(x) = 2\log_e(x - 2) - x^2 + 4x + 1$, where the solution set of $f'(x) \geq 0$ is $[a, b]$, then $(a + b)$ is

23 If $f(x) = (ax + b)\sin x + (cx + d)\cos x$, then the values of a, b, c and d such that $f'(x) = x\cos x$ for all x, then $(a + b + c + d)$ is

24 If $f(x) = x^n$, then the value of $f(1) + \frac{f^1(1)}{1!} + \frac{f^2(1)}{2!} + \frac{f^3(1)}{3!} + \dots + \frac{f^n(1)}{n!} = \lambda^n$ (where, $f^r(x)$ denotes the rth order derivative of $f(x)$ w.r.t. x), then λ is

25 If $f'(x) = \sqrt{3x^2 + 6}$ and $y = f(x^3)$, then at $x = 1$, $\left(\frac{dy}{dx}\right)$ is equal to

DPP-2 Differentiation of Inverse Trigonometric and Implicit Functions

Subjective Questions

Working Space

Direction *(Q. Nos. 1 and 2) These questions are subjective in nature, need to be solved completely on notebook.*

1 Differentiate the following w.r.t. x.

i. $\tan^{-1}(\sqrt{1+x^2}+x)$

ii. $\tan^{-1}\left(\dfrac{\cos x}{1+\sin x}\right)$

iii. $\sin^{-1}\left(\sqrt{\dfrac{1+x^2}{2}}\right)$

iv. $\sin^{-1}(x^2\sqrt{1-x^2}+x\sqrt{1-x^4})$

v. $\tan^{-1}\left(\dfrac{\sqrt{1+x^2}+\sqrt{1-x^2}}{\sqrt{1+x^2}-\sqrt{1-x^2}}\right)$

vi. $\tan^{-1}\left(\dfrac{\sqrt{1+x^2}-1}{x}\right)$

vii. $\cot^{-1}\left(\dfrac{\sqrt{1+\sin x}+\sqrt{1-\sin x}}{\sqrt{1+\sin x}-\sqrt{1-\sin x}}\right)$

viii. $\tan^{-1}\left(\dfrac{1-x}{1+x}\right)+\tan^{-1}\left(\dfrac{x+2}{1-2x}\right)$

2 Find $\dfrac{dy}{dx}$, if

i. $xy^3 - yx^3 = x$

ii. $x^3 + y^3 = 3axy$

iii. $x\log_e y + y\log_e x = 5$

Only One Option Correct Type

Direction *(Q. Nos. 3-14) This section contains 12 multiple choice questions. Each question has four choices (a), (b), (c) and (d), out of which ONLY ONE is correct.*

3 If $y = \cos^{-1}(\cos x)$, then $\dfrac{dy}{dx}$ at $x = \dfrac{5\pi}{4}$ is

a. 1

b. -1

c. $\dfrac{1}{\sqrt{2}}$

d. $-\dfrac{1}{\sqrt{2}}$

4 If $\sin(xy) + \cos(xy) = 0$, then $\dfrac{dy}{dx}$ is

a. $\dfrac{y}{x}$

b. $-\dfrac{y}{x}$

c. $-\dfrac{x}{y}$

d. $\dfrac{x}{y}$

Working Space

5 If $y = \sin^{-1}\left(\frac{x^2-1}{x^2+1}\right) + \sec^{-1}\left(\frac{x^2+1}{x^2-1}\right)$, $|x| > 1$, then $\frac{dy}{dx}$ is equal to

a. $\frac{x}{x^4-1}$ b. $\frac{x^2}{x^4-1}$

c. 0 d. 1

6 If $y = x - x^2$, then the derivative of y^2 w.r.t. x^2 is

a. $2x^2 + 3x - 1$ b. $2x^2 - 3x + 1$

c. $2x^2 + 3x + 1$ d. None of these

7 If $x\sqrt{1+y} + y\sqrt{1+x} = 0$, then $\frac{dy}{dx}$ is

a. $\frac{1}{(1+x)^2}$ b. $-\frac{1}{(1+x)^2}$

c. $\frac{1}{(1+x^2)}$ d. $\frac{1}{(1+x)}$

8 If $y = \sin^{-1}(x\sqrt{1-x} + \sqrt{x}\sqrt{1-x^2})$ and $\frac{dy}{dx} = \frac{1}{2\sqrt{x(1-x)}} + p$, then p is equal to

a. 0 b. $\frac{1}{\sqrt{1-x}}$

c. $\sin^{-1}\sqrt{x}$ d. $\frac{1}{\sqrt{1-x^2}}$

9 If $ax^2 + 2hxy + by^2 = 0$, then $\frac{dy}{dx}$ is

a. $\frac{y}{x}$ b. $\frac{x}{y}$

c. $-\frac{x}{y}$ d. None of these

10 If $\cos^{-1}\left(\frac{x^2-y^2}{x^2+y^2}\right) = \log a$, then $\frac{dy}{dx}$ is

a. $-\frac{x}{y}$ b. $-\frac{y}{x}$

c. $\frac{y}{x}$ d. $\frac{x}{y}$

11 If $x^2 \cdot e^y + 2xye^x + 13 = 0$, then $\frac{dy}{dx}$ is

a. $\frac{-2xe^{y-x} - 2y(x+1)}{x(xe^{y-x}+2)}$ b. $\frac{2x \cdot e^{x-y} + 2y(x+1)}{x(xe^{y-x}+2)}$

c. $\frac{-2xe^{x-y} + 2y(x+1)}{x(xe^{y-x}+2)}$ d. None of these

12 If $y = \log_y x$, then $\frac{dy}{dx}$ is **[AIEEE 2002]**

a. $\frac{1}{x + \log_e y}$ b. $\frac{1}{\log_e x \cdot (1+y)}$

c. $\frac{1}{x(1+\log_e y)}$ d. $\frac{1}{y + \log_e x}$

Working Space

13 If $y = \sec(\tan^{-1} x)$, then $\frac{dy}{dx}$ at $x = 1$ is **[AIEEE 2013]**

a. $\frac{1}{\sqrt{2}}$
b. $\frac{1}{2}$
c. 1
d. $\sqrt{2}$

14 If $\log_e(x + y) = 2xy$, then $y'(0)$ is **[IIT JEE 2004]**

a. 1
b. −1
c. 2
d. 0

One or More than One Options Correct Type

Direction (Q. Nos. 15-17) This section contains 3 multiple choice questions. Each question has four choices (a), (b), (c) and (d), out of which ONE or MORE THAN ONE are correct.

15 If $y + \log_e(1 + x) = 0$, then which of the following is true?

a. $e^y = xy' + 1$
b. $y' = -\frac{1}{(x+1)}$
c. $y' + e^y = 0$
d. $y' = e^y$

16 If $y^2 + b^2 = 2xy$, then $\frac{dy}{dx}$ equals

a. $\frac{1}{xy - b^2}$
b. $\frac{y}{y - x}$
c. $\frac{xy - b^2}{(y - x)^2}$
d. $\frac{xy - b^2}{y}$

17 If $\sqrt{y + x} + \sqrt{y - x} = c$, then $\frac{dy}{dx}$ is

a. $\frac{2x}{c^2}$
b. $\frac{x}{y + \sqrt{y^2 - x^2}}$
c. $\frac{y - \sqrt{y^2 - x^2}}{x}$
d. $\frac{c^2}{2y}$

Comprehension Type

Direction (Q. Nos. 18-23) This section contains 2 paragraphs, each describing theory, experiments, data, etc. Six questions related to the paragraphs have been given. Each question has only one correct answer among the four given options (a), (b), (c) and (d).

Passage I

Let $f(x) = \sin^{-1}\left(\frac{2x}{1 + x^2}\right)$.

18 The value of $f'(2)$ is

a. 2/5
b. −2/5
c. 1/5
d. −1/5

19 The value of $f'(1/2)$ is

a. 8/5
b. 4/5
c. 2/5
d. −2/5

20 The value of $f'(1)$ is

a. −1
b. 1
c. 1/5
d. Does not exist

Passage II

Working Space

Let $f(x) = \cos^{-1}\left(\frac{1-x^2}{1+x^2}\right)$.

21 The value of $f'(1)$ is

a. 1
b. −1
c. 2
d. −2

22 The value of $f'(-1)$ is

a. 1
b. −1
c. 2
d. −2

23 The value of $f'(0)$ is

a. 1
b. −1
c. 2
d. Does not exist

One Integer Value Correct Type

Direction *(Q. Nos. 24 and 25) This section contains 2 questions. When worked out will result in an integer from 0 to 9 (both inclusive).*

24 If $f(x) = \tan^{-1}\left(\frac{1}{x^2+x+1}\right) + \tan^{-1}\left(\frac{1}{x^2+3x+3}\right) + \tan^{-1}\left(\frac{1}{x^2+5x+7}\right) + \cdots \infty$ terms. Then, the value of $|f'(0)|$ is

25 If $xe^{xy} = y + \sin^2 x$, then at $x = 0$, $\frac{dy}{dx}$ is

DPP-3 Logarithmic Series, Infinite Series and Differentiation of One With Respect to Other

Subjective Questions

Working Space

Direction (Q. Nos. 1- 6) *These questions are subjective in nature, need to be solved completely on notebook.*

1 Differentiate the following w.r.t. x.

i. x^x

ii. x^{x^x}

iii. $(\sin x)^{\cos^{-1} x}$

iv. $\dfrac{\sqrt{x}\,(x+4)^{3/2}}{(4x-3)^{4/3}}$

v. $x^{\sin x - \cos x} + \left(\dfrac{x^2-1}{x^2+1}\right)$

2 Find $\dfrac{dy}{dx}$ for the following.

i. $y = \sqrt{x + \sqrt{x + \sqrt{x + \cdots \infty}}}$

ii. $y = \sqrt{\sin x + \sqrt{\sin x + \sqrt{\sin x + \cdots \infty}}}$

iii. $y = \sqrt{\cos x + \sqrt{\cos x + \sqrt{\cos x + \cdots \infty}}}$

iv. $y = \sqrt{\log_e x + \sqrt{\log_e x + \sqrt{\log_e x + \cdots \infty}}}$

3 If $x = \dfrac{1-t^2}{1+t^2}$, $y = \dfrac{2t}{1+t^2}$, then prove that $\dfrac{dy}{dx} = -\dfrac{x}{y}$.

4 If $x = \sec\theta - \cos\theta$, $y = \sec^n \theta - \cos^n \theta$, then show that

$$(x^2+4)\left(\frac{dy}{dx}\right)^2 = n^2(y^2+4).$$

5 Differentiate the following.

i. $\tan^{-1}\left(\dfrac{1+2x}{1-2x}\right)$ w.r.t. $\sqrt{1+4x^2}$

ii. $\tan^{-1}\left(\dfrac{\sqrt{1+x^2}-1}{x}\right)$ w.r.t. $\tan^{-1} x$

6 Find $\dfrac{dy}{dx}$, if

i. $x = a\left(\cos t + \dfrac{1}{2}\log_e \tan^2 \dfrac{t}{2}\right)$ and $y = a\sin t$

ii. $x = \sin t\sqrt{\cos 2t}$ and $y = \cos t\sqrt{\cos 2t}$

Only One Option Correct Type

Working Space

Direction (Q. Nos. 7-14) *This section contains 8 multiple choice questions. Each question has four choices (a), (b), (c) and (d), out of which ONLY ONE is correct.*

7 If $x = \frac{1+t}{t^3}$, $y = \frac{3}{2t^2} + \frac{2}{t}$, then $x \cdot \left(\frac{dy}{dx}\right)^3 - \left(\frac{dy}{dx}\right)$ is

a. 0
b. −1
c. 1
d. 2

8 If $y = x^{x^{x^2}}$, then $\frac{dy}{dx}$ is

a. $2\log_e x \cdot x^{x^2}$
b. $(2\log_e x + 1) \cdot x^{x^2}$
c. $(2\log_e x + 1) \cdot x^{x^2+1}$
d. None of these

9 If $x = 3\cos\theta - 2\cos^3\theta$ and $y = 3\sin\theta - 2\sin^3\theta$, then $\frac{dy}{dx}$ is **[AIEEE 2002]**

a. $\sin\theta$
b. $\cos\theta$
c. $\tan\theta$
d. $\cot\theta$

10 If $x = e^{y + e^{y + \dots \infty}}$, $x > 0$, then $\frac{dy}{dx}$ is **[AIEEE 2004]**

a. $\frac{x}{1+x}$
b. $\frac{1}{x}$
c. $\frac{1-x}{x}$
d. $\frac{1+x}{x}$

11 If $x^m \cdot y^n = (x+y)^{m+n}$, then $\frac{dy}{dx}$ is **[AIEEE 2006]**

a. $\frac{x+y}{xy}$
b. xy
c. $\frac{x}{y}$
d. $\frac{y}{x}$

12 Let y be an implicit function of x defined by $x^{2x} - 2x^x \cot y - 1 = 0$. Then, $y'(1)$ equals **[AIEEE 2009]**

a. $\log_e 2$
b. $-\log_e 2$
c. −1
d. 1

13 If $f(x) = \prod_{n=1}^{100} (x-n)^{n(101-n)}$, then $\frac{f(101)}{f'(101)}$ is equal to

a. 5050
b. $\frac{1}{5050}$
c. 10010
d. $\frac{1}{10010}$

14 The derivative of $\sin^{-1}\left(\frac{x}{\sqrt{1+x^2}}\right)$ w.r.t. $\cos^{-1}\left(\frac{1-x^2}{1+x^2}\right)$, $(x > 0)$ is

a. 1
b. 2
c. $\frac{1}{2}$
d. $\frac{-1}{2}$

Working Space

One or More than One Options Correct Type

Direction (Q. Nos. 15-19) *This section contains 5 multiple choice questions. Each question has four choices (a), (b), (c) and (d), out of which ONE or MORE THAN ONE are correct.*

15 The differential coefficient of $\sin^{-1}\left(\frac{t}{\sqrt{1+t^2}}\right)$ w.r.t. $\cos^{-1}\left(\frac{1}{\sqrt{1+t^2}}\right)$ is

a. $1, \forall t > 0$
b. $-1, \forall t < 0$
c. $1, \forall t \in R$
d. None of these

16 If $x = \cos t$, $y = \log_e t$, then

a. $\frac{dy}{dx} = \frac{-2}{\pi}$ at $t = \frac{\pi}{2}$
b. $\frac{dy}{dx} = \frac{4}{\pi^2}$ at $t = \frac{\pi}{2}$
c. $\frac{dy}{dx} = \frac{144}{\pi^2}$ at $t = \frac{\pi}{6}$
d. $\frac{dy}{dx} = \frac{-12}{\pi}$ at $t = \frac{\pi}{6}$

17 If $2^x + 2^y = 2^{x+y}$, then $\frac{dy}{dx}$ is equal to

a. $\frac{-2^y}{2^x}$
b. $\frac{1}{1-2^x}$
c. $1-2^y$
d. $\frac{2^x(1-2^y)}{2^y(2^x-1)}$

18 If $x^p \cdot y^q = (x+y)^{p+q}$, then $\frac{dy}{dx}$ is

a. independent of p
b. independent of q
c. dependent on both p and q
d. $\frac{y}{x}$

19 The functions $u = e^x \cdot \sin x$ and $v = e^x \cdot \cos x$ satisfy the equation

a. $v\frac{du}{dx} - u\frac{dv}{dx} = u^2 + v^2$
b. $v\frac{du}{dx} + u\frac{dv}{dx} = u^2 + v^2$
c. $\frac{du}{dx} + \frac{dv}{dx} = 2v$
d. $\frac{du}{dx} + \frac{dv}{dx} = 2u$

Matching List Type

Direction (Q. No. 20) *Choices for the correct combination of elements from Column I and Column II are given as options (a), (b), (c) and (d), out of which one is correct.*

20 Match the Column I with Column II and mark the correct option from the codes given below.

	Column I		Column II
i.	If $y = \cos^{-1}(\cos x)$, then y' at $x = 5$ is equal to	p.	-1
ii.	For the function $f(x) = \log_e \tan\left(\frac{\pi}{4} + \frac{x}{2}\right)$, if $\frac{dy}{dx} = \sec x + p$, then p is equal to	q.	0
iii.	The derivative of $\tan^{-1}\left(\frac{1+x}{1-x}\right)$ at $x = -1$ is	r.	1/2
iv.	The derivative of $\frac{\log\lvert x\rvert}{x}$ at $x = -1$ is	s.	1

Codes

	i	ii	iii	iv
a.	p	q	r	s
b.	q	p	r	s
c.	s	r	q	p
d.	r	s	p	q

One Integer Value Correct Type

Working Space

Direction (Q. Nos. 21-25) This section contains 5 questions. When worked out will result in an integer from 0 to 9 (both inclusive).

21 Let $f(x) = x + \cfrac{1}{2x + \cfrac{1}{2x + \cfrac{1}{2x + \cfrac{1}{2x + \cdots \infty}}}}$, then the value of $\frac{f(100) \cdot f'(100)}{100}$ is

22 If $y = \tan^{-1}\left(\frac{u}{\sqrt{1-u^2}}\right)$ and $x = \sec^{-1}\left(\frac{1}{2u^2 - 1}\right)$, $u \in \left(0, \frac{1}{\sqrt{2}}\right) \cup \left(\frac{1}{\sqrt{2}}, 1\right)$, then $\left|2\frac{dy}{dx}\right|$ is

23 If $y = \tan^{-1}\left(\frac{x}{1+\sqrt{1-x^2}}\right) + \sin\left(2\tan^{-1}\sqrt{\frac{1-x}{1+x}}\right)$, then $\left|2\frac{dy}{dx}\right|$ at $x = 0$ is

24 On differentiating $y = \cos^{-1}\left(\frac{1-x^2}{1+x^2}\right)$ w.r.t. $\tan^{-1} x$, state where function is not differentiable at x.

25 Suppose $f(x)$ and $g(x)$ are two functions such that $f, g : R \to R$, $f(x) = \log_e(1+\sqrt{1+x^2})$ and $g(x) = \log_e(x + \sqrt{1+x^2})$. Then, the value of $x \cdot e^{g(x)} \cdot \left[f\left(\frac{1}{x}\right)\right]' + g'(x)$ at $x = 1$ is

DPP-4 Higher Order Derivatives and Differentiation of Inverse Functions

Subjective Questions

Working Space

Direction *(Q. Nos. 1-17) These questions are subjective in nature, need to be solved completely on notebook.*

1 If $y = A\sin mx + B\cos mx$, then show that $\frac{d^2y}{dx^2} + m^2y = 0$.

2 If $y = A\cos(\log x) + B\sin(\log x)$, then show that $x^2y_2 + xy_1 + y = 0$.

3 If $\log_e y = \tan^{-1} x$, then show that $(1 + x^2)y_2 + (2x - 1)y_1 = 0$.

4 If $y = \tan x$, then show that $y_2 = 2yy_1$.

5 If $y = \tan x + \sec x$, then show that $y_2 = \frac{\cos x}{(1 - \sin x)^2}$.

6 If $y = \tan^{-1} x$, then show that $(1 + x^2)y_2 + 2x\, y_1 = 0$.

7 If $x = a(1 - \cos\theta)$, $y = a(\theta + \sin\theta)$, then show that $\frac{d^2y}{dx^2} = -\frac{1}{2}\operatorname{cosec}^2\left(\frac{\theta}{2}\right)\cdot\left(\frac{1}{a\sin\theta}\right)$.

8 If $x = a\cos^3\theta$, $y = a\sin^3\theta$, then show that $\frac{d^2y}{dx^2} = \frac{1}{3a}\cdot\sec^4\theta\cdot\operatorname{cosec}\theta$.

9 If $y = \frac{ax + b}{x^2 + c}$, then show that $(2xy_1 + y)y_3 = 3(xy_2 + y_1)y_2$.

10 If $(a + bx)e^{y/x} = x$, then show that $x^3 \cdot y_2 = (xy_1 - y)^2$.

11 If $y = \left[\left(\log(x + \sqrt{x^2 + 1}\right)\right]^2$, then show that $(1 + x^2)y_2 + xy_1 = 2$.

12 If $y = \frac{\sin^{-1} x}{\sqrt{1 - x^2}}$, then show that $(1 - x^2)y_2 - 3xy_1 - y = 0$.

13 If $y = (x + \sqrt{x^2 + 1})^m$, then show that $(x^2 + 1)y_2 + xy_1 - m^2y = 0$.

14 If $y = e^{ax}\cdot\sin bx$, then show that $y_2 - 2ay_1 + (a^2 + b^2)y = 0$.

15 If $y = e^x\tan^{-1} x$, then show that $(1 + x^2)\,y_2 - 2(1 - x + x^2)\,y_1 + (1 - x)^2 y = 0$.

Working Space

16 If $y = \log\left(\frac{x^2}{e^x}\right)$, then show that $y_2 = -\frac{2}{x^2}$.

17 If $y = (\tan^{-1} x)^2$, then show that $(x^2 + 1)^2 \cdot y_2 + 2x \cdot (x^2 + 1) \cdot y_1 = 2$.

Only One Option Correct Type

Direction (Q. Nos. 18-26) *This section contains 9 multiple choice questions. Each question has four choices (a), (b), (c) and (d), out of which ONLY ONE is correct.*

18 Let $e^{f(x)} = \log_e x$. If $g(x)$ is the inverse function of $f(x)$, then $g'(x)$ equals

a. e^x b. $e^x + x$ c. $e^{x + e^x}$ d. $e^{x + \log_e x}$

19 Let g be the inverse function of f and $f'(x) = \frac{x^{10}}{1 + x^2}$. If $g(2) = a$, then $[g'(2)]$ is

a. $\frac{a}{2^{10}}$ b. $\frac{1 + a^2}{a^{10}}$ c. $\frac{a^{10}}{1 + a^2}$ d. $\frac{1 + a^{10}}{a^2}$

20 If $u = ax + b$, then $\frac{d^n}{dx^n}[f(ax + b)]$ is equal to

a. $\frac{d^n}{dx^n}[f(u)]$ b. $a \cdot \frac{d^n}{dx^n}[f(u)]$

c. $a^n \cdot \frac{d^n}{dx^n}[f(u)]$ d. $a^{-n} \cdot \frac{d^n}{dx^n}[f(u)]$

21 If $y = x + e^x$, then $\frac{d^2x}{dy^2}$ is

a. e^x b. $-\frac{e^x}{(1 + e^x)^3}$ c. $-\frac{e^x}{(1 + e^x)^2}$ d. $\frac{1}{(1 + e^x)^2}$

22 If $y^2 = P(x)$ is a polynomial of degree 3, then $2 \cdot \frac{d}{dx}\left(y^3 \cdot \frac{d^2y}{dx^2}\right)$ is

a. $P'''(x) \cdot P(x)$ b. $P'''(x) + P(x)$

c. $P'''(x) \cdot P''(x)$ d. a constant

23 If $x^2 + y^2 = 1$, then **[IIT JEE 2000]**

a. $y \cdot y'' - 2(y')^2 + 1 = 0$ b. $y \cdot y'' + (y')^2 + 1 = 0$

c. $y \cdot y'' - (y')^2 - 1 = 0$ d. $y \cdot y'' + 2(y')^2 + 1 = 0$

24 If $f''(x) = -f(x)$ and $g(x) = f'(x)$ and $F(x) = \left[f\left(\frac{x}{2}\right)\right]^2 + \left[g\left(\frac{x}{2}\right)\right]^2$ and given that $F(5) = 5$, then $F(10)$ is **[IIT JEE 2006]**

a. 5 b. 10

c. 0 d. 15

25 The value of $\frac{d^2x}{dy^2}$ equals **[IIT JEE 2007]**

a. $\left(\frac{d^2y}{dx^2}\right)^{-1}$ b. $-\left(\frac{d^2y}{dx^2}\right)^{-1} \cdot \left(\frac{dy}{dx}\right)^{-3}$

c. $\left(\frac{d^2y}{dx^2}\right) \cdot \left(\frac{dy}{dx}\right)^{-2}$ d. $-\left(\frac{d^2y}{dx^2}\right) \cdot \left(\frac{dy}{dx}\right)^{-3}$

Working Space

26 Let $g(x) = \log_e f(x)$, where $f(x)$ is a twice differentiable positive function on $(0, \infty)$ such that $f(x+1) = x\,f(x)$. Then, for $N = 1, 2, 3, \cdots, g''\left(N+\frac{1}{2}\right) - g''\left(\frac{1}{2}\right)$, is

a. $-4\left\{1+\frac{1}{9}+\frac{1}{25}+\cdots+\frac{1}{(2N-1)^2}\right\}$

b. $4\left\{1+\frac{1}{9}+\frac{1}{25}+\cdots+\frac{1}{(2N-1)^2}\right\}$

c. $-4\left\{1+\frac{1}{9}+\frac{1}{25}+\cdots+\frac{1}{(2N+1)^2}\right\}$

d. $4\left\{1+\frac{1}{9}+\frac{1}{25}+\cdots+\frac{1}{(2N+1)^2}\right\}$

Comprehension Type

Direction *(Q. Nos. 27-29) This section contains a paragraph, describing theory, experiments, data, etc. Three questions related to the paragraph have been given. Each question has only one correct answer among the four given options (a), (b), (c) and (d).*

Passage

An operator Δ is defined to operate on differentiable functions defined as follows:

If $f(x)$ is a differentiable function, then $\Delta[f(x)] = \lim_{h\to 0}\frac{f^3(x+h)-f^3(x)}{h}$, $g(x)$ is differentiable function such that the slope of tangent to the curve $y = g(x)$ at any point $[a, g(a)]$ is equal to $2e^a(a+1)$, also $g(0) = 0$.

27 The value of $\Delta[g(x)]$ at $x = \log_e 2$ is

a. $24\log_e 2\{2\log_e 2+2\}$

b. $\log_e(4e^3)\log_e^2 2$

c. $96\log_e(4e^2)\cdot\log_e^2 2$

d. $192\log_e(4e)\cdot\log_e^2 2$

28 The value of $\Delta[\Delta(x+2)]$ at $x = 0$ is

a. $2^5\cdot 3^9$

b. $2^9\cdot 3^5$

c. $2^4\cdot 3^5$

d. $2^6\cdot 3^4$

29 The value of $\lim_{x\to 0}\frac{\Delta g(x)}{\log_e(\cos 2x)}$ is

a. -12

b. 12

c. 24

d. -24

One Integer Value Correct Type

Direction *(Q. Nos. 30-35) This section contains 6 questions. When worked out will result in an integer from 0 to 9 (both inclusive).*

30 If the function $f(x) = x^3 + e^{x/2}$ and $g(x) = f^{-1}(x)$, then the value of $g'(1)$ is **[IIT JEE 2009]**

31 If $x^2 + y^2 = 2$ and $2y_2 + a\cdot y^{-3} = 0$, then a is

32 If $y = \frac{a}{2}(e^{x/a} + e^{-x/a})$ and $\frac{d^2y}{dx^2} = 4y$, then $|2a|$ is

33 If $f(x)$ is twice differentiable such that $f''(x) = -f(x)$ and $f'(x) = g(x)$. If $h(x)$ is a twice differentiable function such that $h'(x) = [f(x)]^2 + [g(x)]^2$. If $h(0) = 2$, $h(1) = 4$. Then, the equation $y = h(x)$ represents a straight line with slope

34 If $y = (\sin^{-1}x)^2 + (\cos^{-1}x)^2$, then $(1-x^2)\cdot y_2 - xy_1$ is

35 If $f(x) = x^2 - 4x - 3$, $x > 2$ and let $g(x)$ be the inverse of f. Then, the value of $8[g'(x)]$ at $f(x) = 9$ is

SET - 1

Revisal Problems for JEE Main

Only One Option Correct Type

Direction *(Q. Nos. 1-17) This section contains 17 multiple choice questions. Each question has four choices (a), (b), (c) and (d), out of which ONLY ONE is correct.*

Working Space

1 Let $y = \dfrac{x^8 + x^4 + 1}{x^4 + x^2 + 1}$. If $\dfrac{dy}{dx} = ax^3 + bx$, then

a. $a = 4, b = 2$ b. $a = 4, b = -2$
c. $a = -2, b = 4$ d. None of these

2 Let $f(x)$ be a polynomial of degree 3 such that $f(3) = 1$, $f'(3) = -1$, $f''(3) = 0$ and $f'''(3) = 12$. Then, the value of $f'(1)$ is

a. 12 b. 23
c. −13 d. None of these

3 If $f(x) = 2\tan^{-1} x + \cos^{-1}\left(\dfrac{1 - x^2}{1 + x^2}\right)$, then

a. $f'(-2) = \dfrac{4}{5}$ b. $f'(-1) = -1$
c. $f'(x) = 0$, for all $x < 0$ d. None of these

4 Let $f(x) = \sqrt{x - 1} + \sqrt{x + 24 - 10\sqrt{x - 1}}$, $1 < x < 26$ be real valued function, then $f'(x)$ for $1 < x < 26$ is

a. 0 b. $\dfrac{1}{\sqrt{x - 1}}$
c. $2\sqrt{x - 1}$ d. None of these

5 If $y = f(x)$ is an odd differentiable function defined on $(-\infty, \infty)$ such that $f'(3) = -2$, then $f'(-3)$ equals

a. 4 b. 2 c. −2 d. 0

6 If $f(x) = \cos x \cdot \cos 2x \cdot \cos 2^2 x \dots \cdot \cos 2^{n-1} x$ and $n > 1$, then $f'\left(\dfrac{\pi}{2}\right)$ is

a. 1 b. 0 c. −1 d. None of these

7 If $f'(x) = \sqrt{2x^2 - 1}$ and $y = f(x^2)$, then $\dfrac{dy}{dx}$ at $x = 1$ is

a. 2 b. 1 c. −2 d. None of these

8 Let f and g be differentiable function satisfying $g'(a) = 2$, $g(a) = b$ and $fog = I$ (identity function), then $f'(b)$ is

a. 2 b. 2/3 c. 1/2 d. None of these

9 Let f be a differentiable function defined for all $x \in R$ such that $f(x^3) = x^5$ for all $x \in R$, $x \neq 0$, then the value of $f'(8)$ is

a. 20 b. $\dfrac{20}{3}$ c. $\dfrac{50}{3}$ d. None of these

10 If $y = \sin^{-1}(\sin x)$, then $\dfrac{dy}{dx}$ at $x = \dfrac{\pi}{2}$ is

a. 1 b. −1 c. non-existent d. None of these

11 Let $y = x^3 - 8x + 7$ and $x = f(t)$. If $\dfrac{dy}{dt} = 2$ and $x = 3$ at $t = 0$, then $\dfrac{dx}{dt}$ at $t = 0$ is given by

a. 1 b. 14/2 c. 2/19 d. None of these

Working Space

12 If $f(x) = |x|^{|\sin x|}$, then $f'(\pi/4)$ equals

a. $\left(\frac{\pi}{4}\right)^{1/\sqrt{2}} \cdot \left(\frac{\sqrt{2}}{2} \cdot \log\frac{4}{\pi} - \frac{2\sqrt{2}}{\pi}\right)$ b. $\left(\frac{\pi}{4}\right)^{1/\sqrt{2}} \cdot \left(\frac{\sqrt{2}}{2} \cdot \log\frac{4}{\pi} + \frac{2\sqrt{2}}{\pi}\right)$

c. $\left(\frac{\pi}{4}\right)^{1/\sqrt{2}} \cdot \left(\frac{\sqrt{2}}{2} \cdot \log\frac{\pi}{4} - \frac{2\sqrt{2}}{\pi}\right)$ d. $\left(\frac{\pi}{4}\right)^{1/\sqrt{2}} \cdot \left(\frac{\sqrt{2}}{2} \log\frac{\pi}{4} + \frac{2\sqrt{2}}{\pi}\right)$

13 If $x = at^2$ and $y = 2at$, then $\frac{d^2y}{dx^2}$ is

a. $\frac{-1}{t^2}$ b. $\frac{1}{2at}$ c. $\frac{-1}{t^3}$ d. $\frac{-1}{2at^3}$

14 If $y = (\sin x)^{\tan x}$, then $\frac{dy}{dx}$ is

a. $(\sin x)^{\tan x} \cdot (1 + \sec^2 x \cdot \log \sin x)$ b. $\tan x \cdot (\sin x)^{\tan x - 1} \cdot \cos x$

c. $(\sin x)^{\tan x} \cdot \sec^2 x \cdot \log(\sin x)$ d. $\tan x \cdot (\sin x)^{\tan x - 1}$

15 If $y = \cfrac{x}{a + \cfrac{x}{b + \cfrac{x}{a + \cfrac{x}{b + \cfrac{x}{a + \cdots \infty}}}}}$, then $\frac{dy}{dx}$ is

a. $\frac{a}{ab + 2ay}$ b. $\frac{b}{ab + 2by}$ c. $\frac{a}{ab + 2by}$ d. $\frac{b}{ab + 2ay}$

16 If $f(x) = x^n$, then the value of $f(1) - \frac{f^1(1)}{1!} + \frac{f^2(1)}{2!} - \frac{f^3(1)}{3!} + \cdots + \frac{(-1)^n \cdot f^n(1)}{n!}$ is

a. 2^{n-1} b. 0 c. 1 d. 2^n

17 If $f(x) = x + \frac{x^2}{2!} + \frac{x^3}{3!} + \cdots + \frac{x^n}{(n-1)!}$, then $f(0) + f^1(0) + f^2(0) + \cdots + f^n(0)$ is equal to

a. $\frac{n(n+1)}{2}$ b. $\frac{n^2+1}{2}$ c. $\left[\frac{n(n+1)}{2}\right]^2$ d. $\frac{n(n+1)(2n+1)}{6}$

Statement Type

Direction *(Q. Nos. 18-20)* ***This section is based on Statement I and Statement II. Select the correct answer from the codes given below.***

a. Both Statement I and Statement II are correct and Statement II is the correct explanation of Statement I
b. Both Statement I and Statement II are correct but Statement II is not the correct explanation of Statement I
c. Statement I is correct but Statement II is incorrect
d. Statement II is correct but Statement I is incorrect

18 **Statement I** If $f(x)$ is a continuous function defined from R to Q and $f(5) = 3$, then differential coefficient of $f(x)$ w.r.t. x will be 0.

Statement II Differentiation of constant function is always zero.

19 **Statement I** Derivative of $\sin^{-1}\left(\frac{2x}{1+x^2}\right)$ w.r.t. $\cos^{-1}\left(\frac{1-x^2}{1+x^2}\right)$ is 1 for $0 < x < 1$.

Statement II $\sin^{-1}\left(\frac{2x}{1+x^2}\right) = \cos^{-1}\left(\frac{1-x^2}{1+x^2}\right)$ for $-1 \le x \le 1$.

20 Consider $f(x) = \frac{x}{x^2 - 1}$ and $g(x) = f''(x)$.

Statement I Graph of $g(x)$ is concave up for $x > 1$.

Statement II $\frac{d^n[f(x)]}{dx^n} = \frac{(-1)^n \cdot n!}{2}\left\{\frac{1}{(x+1)^{n+1}} + \frac{1}{(x-1)^{n+1}}\right\}, n \in N$.

SET - 2

Revisal Problems for JEE Advanced

Only One Option Correct Type

Working Space

Direction *(Q. Nos. 1-7) This section contains 7 multiple choice questions. Each question has four choices (a), (b), (c) and (d), out of which ONLY ONE is correct.*

1 If $y = f(x)$ and $x = g(y)$ are inverse of each other. Then, $g'(y)$ and $g''(y)$ in terms of derivative of $f(x)$ is

a. $-\frac{f''(x)}{[f'(x)]^3}$ b. $\frac{f''(x)}{[f'(x)]^3}$ c. $-\frac{f''(x)}{[f'(x)]^2}$ d. None of these

2 If $x = \frac{1+t}{t^3}$ and $y = \frac{3}{2t^2} + \frac{2}{t}$, then $x(y')^3 - y'$ is

a. 1 b. 2 c. 3 d. -1

3 If $f(x) = x^3 + x^2 f'(1) + xf''(2) + f'''(3)$ for all $x \in R$, then $f(x)$ is

a. $x^3 - 5x^2 + 2x - 6$ b. $x^3 - 5x^2 - 2x - 6$ c. $x^3 - 5x^2 + 2x + 6$ d. $x^3 + 5x^2 - 2x + 6$

4 If $f(x) = |x - 2|$, then $f'[f(x)]$ is equal to

a. 1, when $x \ge 2$ b. -1, when $x \ge 2$
c. 2, when $x < 0$ d. 1, when $0 < x < 2$ or $x \ge 4$

5 If $f(x) = \frac{x}{1+|x|}$, then $f'(-1)$ is

a. 1/4 b. 0 c. $-1/2$ d. not exist

6 If $f(0) = a$, $f'(0) = b$, $g(0) = 0$, and $(fog)'(0) = c$, then $g'(0)$ is

a. a b. b c. c d. c/b

7 If $f(1) = 3$, $f'(1) = 2$ and $f''(1) = 4$ and let $f^{-1}(x) = g(x)$, then $g''(3)$ is equal to

a. 1 b. $-1/2$ c. -2 d. None of these

Comprehension Type

Direction *(Q. Nos. 8-15) This section contains 3 paragraphs, each describing theory, experiments, data, etc. Eight questions related to the paragraphs have been given. Each question has only one correct answer among the four given options (a), (b), (c) and (d).*

Passage I

A non-zero polynomial with real coefficients has the property that $f''(x) \cdot f'(x) = f(x)$.

8 The leading coefficient of $f(x)$ is

a. 1/6 b. 1/9 c. 1/12 d. 1/18

9 The degree of $f(x)$ is

a. 2 b. 3 c. 4 d. 5

10 The value of $f'''(x)$ is

a. 1/18 b. 1/3 c. 1/9 d. 1/6

Passage II

The ends A and B of a rod of length $\sqrt{5}$ units are sliding along the curve $y = 2x^2$. Let x_A and x_B be the x-coordinates of both the ends.

11 The moment when A is at (0, 0) and B is at (1, 2). The derivative $\frac{dx_B}{dx_A}$ is

a. 1/9 b. 1/7 c. 1/5 d. None of these

Working Space

12 The moment when A is at (1, 2) and B is at (0, 0). The derivative $\frac{dx_B}{dx_A}$ is

a. 16 b. 8 c. 9 d. 2

Passage III

Equation $x^n - 1 = 0$, $n > 1$, $n \in N$ has roots $1, a_1, a_2, \ldots, a_{n-1}$.

13 The value of $(1 - a_1)(1 - a_2) \cdots (1 - a_{n-1})$ is

a. $\frac{n^2}{2}$ b. n c. $(-1)^n \cdot n$ d. None of these

14 The value of $\sum_{r=1}^{n-1} \frac{1}{2 - a_r}$ is

a. $\frac{2^{n-1} \cdot (n-2) + 1}{2^n - 1}$ b. $\frac{2^n (n-2) + 1}{2^n - 1}$ c. $\frac{2^{n-1}(n-1) - 1}{2^n - 1}$ d. None of these

15 The value of $\sum_{r=1}^{n-1} \frac{1}{1 - a_r}$ is

a. $\frac{n}{4}$ b. $\frac{n(n-1)}{2}$ c. $\frac{n-1}{2}$ d. None of these

Matching List Type

Direction (*Q. No. 16*) *Choices for the correct combination of elements from Column I and Column II are given as options (a), (b), (c) and (d), out of which one is correct.*

16 Match the Column I with Column II and mark the correct option from the codes given below.

	Column I		Column II
i.	If $f'(x) = \sqrt{3x^2 + 6}$ and $y = f(x^3)$, then at $x = 1$, $\frac{dy}{dx}$ is	p.	-2
ii.	If f is a differentiable function such that $f(xy) = f(x) + f(y)$; $x, y \in R$, then $f(e) + f(1/e)$ is	q.	-1
iii.	If f is a twice differentiable function such that $f''(x) = -f(x)$ and $f'(x) = g(x)$. If $h(x) = [f(x)]^2 + [g(x)]^2$ and $h(5) = 9$, then $h(10)$ is	r.	0
iv.	$y = \tan^{-1}(\cot x) + \cot^{-1}(\tan x)$, $\frac{\pi}{2} < x < \pi$, then $\frac{dy}{dx}$ is	s.	9

Codes

	i	ii	iii	iv		i	ii	iii	iv
a.	s	r	s	p	b.	p	q	r	s
c.	q	p	r	r	d.	s	p	q	q

One Integer Value Correct Type

Direction (*Q. Nos. 17-21*) *This section contains 5 questions. When worked out will result in an integer from 0 to 9 (both inclusive).*

17 If f and g are differentiable functions such that $g'(a) = 2$ and $g(a) = b$ and if fog is an identity function, then $4f'(b)$ is

18 If $f(x) = \sqrt{x + 2\sqrt{2x - 4}} + \sqrt{x - 2\sqrt{2x - 4}}$, then the value of $10 f'(102^+)$ is

19 Suppose the function $f(x) - f(2x)$ has the derivative 5 at $x = 1$ and derivative 7 at $x = 2$. The derivative of the function $f(x) - f(4x)$ at $x = 1$ has the value $10 + \lambda$, then the value of λ is

20 If $x + y = 3e^2$, then $D(x^y)$ vanishes when x equals λe^2, then the value of λ is

21 Let $h(x)$ be differentiable for all x and let $f(x) = (kx + e^x) h(x)$, where k is some constant. If $h(0) = 5$, $h'(0) = -2$ and $f'(0) = 18$, then the value of k is

JEE Main & AIEEE Archive

(Compilation of Last 13 Years' Questions)

1 If $x = -1$ and $x = 2$ are extreme points of $f(x) = \alpha \log|x| + \beta x^2 + x$, then **(JEE Main 2014)**

a. $\alpha = -6, \beta = \frac{1}{2}$ b. $\alpha = -6, \beta = -\frac{1}{2}$

c. $\alpha = 2, \beta = -\frac{1}{2}$ d. $\alpha = 2, \beta = \frac{1}{2}$

2 If $y = \sec(\tan^{-1} x)$, then $\frac{dy}{dx}$ at $x = 1$ is equal to **(JEE Main 2013)**

a. $\frac{1}{\sqrt{2}}$ b. $\frac{1}{2}$

c. 1 d. $\sqrt{2}$

3 $\frac{d^2x}{dy^2}$ is equal to **(AIEEE 2011)**

a. $-\left(\frac{d^2y}{dx^2}\right)^{-1}\left(\frac{dy}{dx}\right)^{-3}$ b. $\left(\frac{d^2y}{dx^2}\right)\left(\frac{dy}{dx}\right)^{-2}$

c. $-\left(\frac{d^2y}{dx^2}\right)\left(\frac{dy}{dx}\right)^{-3}$ d. $\left(\frac{d^2y}{dx^2}\right)^{-1}$

4 Let y be an implicit function of x defined by $x^{2x} - 2x^x \cot y - 1 = 0$. Then, $y'(1)$ is equal to **(AIEEE 2009)**

a. -1 b. 1

c. $\log 2$ d. $-\log 2$

5 If $x^m y^n = (x+y)^{m+n}$, then $\frac{dy}{dx}$ is equal to **(AIEEE 2006)**

a. $\frac{x+y}{xy}$ b. xy c. $\frac{x}{y}$ d. $\frac{y}{x}$

6 If $x = e^{y + e^{y + \dots \infty}}$, $x > 0$, then $\frac{dy}{dx}$ is equal to **(AIEEE 2004)**

a. $\frac{x}{1+x}$ b. $\frac{1}{x}$

c. $\frac{1-x}{x}$ d. $\frac{1+x}{x}$

7 Let $f(x)$ be a polynomial function of second degree. If $f(1) = f(-1)$ and a, b, c are in an AP, then $f'(a), f'(b), f'(c)$ are in **(AIEEE 2003)**

a. AP

b. GP

c. HP

d. Arithmetic-Geometric progression

8 If $f(x) = x^n$, then the value of

$$f(1) - \frac{f'(1)}{1!} + \frac{f''(1)}{2!} - \frac{f'''(1)}{3!} + \dots + \frac{(-1)^n f^n(1)}{n!}$$ is **(AIEEE 2003)**

a. 2^n b. 2^{n-1}

c. 0 d. 1

9 If $y = (x + \sqrt{1+x^2})^n$, then $(1+x^2)\frac{d^2y}{dx^2} + x\frac{dy}{dx}$ is equal to **(AIEEE 2002)**

a. $n^2 y$ b. $-n^2 y$

c. $-y$ d. $2x^2 y$

10 If $\sin y = x \sin(a+y)$, then $\frac{dy}{dx}$ is equal to **(AIEEE 2002)**

a. $\frac{\sin a}{\sin^2(a+y)}$ b. $\frac{\sin^2(a+y)}{\sin a}$

c. $\sin a \sin^2(a+y)$ d. $\frac{\sin^2(a-y)}{\sin a}$

11 If $x^y = e^{x-y}$, then $\frac{dy}{dx}$ is equal to **(AIEEE 2002)**

a. $\frac{1+x}{1+\log x}$ b. $\frac{1-\log x}{1+\log x}$

c. $\frac{\log x}{(1+\log x)^2}$ d. Not defined

JEE Advanced & IIT JEE Archive

(Compilation of Last 10 Years' Questions)

1 Let $f(x) = x \sin \pi x$, $x > 0$. Then, for all natural numbers n, $f'(x)$ vanishes at

(2013 Adv., One or More than One Options Correct Type)

a. a unique point in the interval $\left(n, n + \frac{1}{2}\right)$

b. a unique point in the interval $\left(n + \frac{1}{2}, n + 1\right)$

c. a unique point in the interval $(n, n + 1)$

d. two points in the interval $(n, n + 1)$

2 $\frac{d^2x}{dy^2}$ equals **(2007, Only One Option Correct Type)**

a. $\left(\frac{d^2y}{dx^2}\right)^{-1}$

b. $-\left(\frac{d^2y}{dx^2}\right)^{-1}\left(\frac{dy}{dx}\right)^{-3}$

c. $\left(\frac{d^2y}{dx^2}\right)\left(\frac{dy}{dx}\right)^{-2}$

d. $-\left(\frac{d^2y}{dx^2}\right)\left(\frac{dy}{dx}\right)^{-3}$

2. Limits

DPP
DAILY PRACTICE PROBLEMS

DPP-1 Definition of Limits and $\left(\frac{0}{0}\right)$ Form on Algebraic

Subjective Questions

Working Space

Direction *(Q. Nos. 1 and 2) These questions are subjective in nature, need to be solved completely on notebook.*

1 For the function g whose graph is given, state the value of each quantity, if it exists.

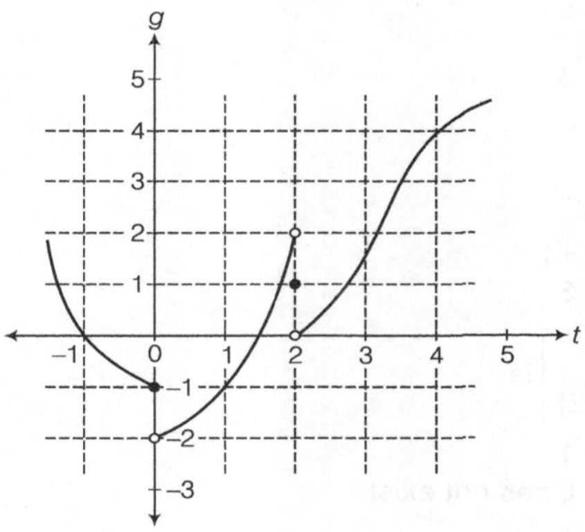

i. $\lim_{t \to 0^-} g(t)$ ii. $\lim_{t \to 0^+} g(t)$ iii. $\lim_{t \to 0} g(t)$

iv. $\lim_{t \to 2^-} g(t)$ v. $\lim_{t \to 2^+} g(t)$ vi. $\lim_{t \to 2} g(t)$

vii. $g(2)$ viii. $\lim_{t \to 4} g(t)$

2 For the function f whose graph is given, state the value of each quantity, if it exists.

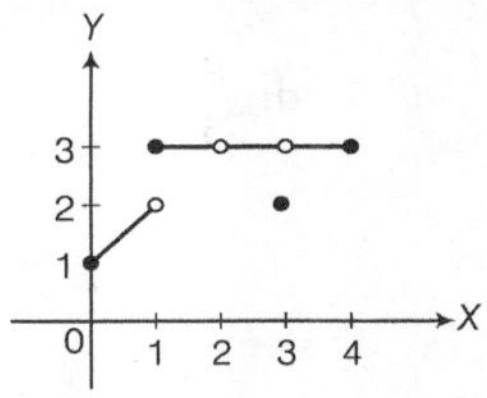

i. $\lim_{x \to 1} f(x)$ ii. $\lim_{x \to 2} f(x)$ iii. $\lim_{x \to 3} f(x)$

iv. $\lim_{x \to 1.99} f(x)$ v. $\lim_{x \to 3^-} f(x)$

Only One Option Correct Type

Working Space

Direction (Q. Nos. 3-20) *This section contains 18 multiple choice questions. Each question has four choices (a), (b), (c) and (d), out of which ONLY ONE is correct.*

3 The value of $\lim_{x \to a} \frac{x^m - a^m}{x^n - a^n}$ is

a. $\frac{m}{n}$

b. $\frac{m-n}{m+n}$

c. a^{m-n}

d. $\frac{m}{n} \cdot a^{m-n}$

4 The value of $\lim_{x \to 1} \frac{(x + x^2 + x^3 + \cdots + x^n) - n}{x - 1}$ is

a. $\frac{n+1}{2}$

b. $\frac{n(n+1)}{2}$

c. $\frac{n(n-1)}{2}$

d. 0

5 If $\lim_{x \to 1} \frac{x^4 - 1}{x - 1} = \lim_{x \to k} \frac{x^3 - k^3}{x^2 - k^2}$, then the value of k is

a. 8

b. $\frac{4}{3}$

c. $\frac{8}{3}$

d. 4

6 If $\lim_{x \to -a} \frac{x^9 + a^9}{x + a} = 9$, then the value of a is

a. 0

b. ± 1

c. 2

d. 3

7 The value of $\lim_{x \to 2} \left[\frac{1}{x(x-2)^2} - \frac{1}{(x^2 - 3x + 2)} \right]$ is

a. 2

b. 1

c. 0

d. Does not exist

8 The value of $\lim_{x \to 1} \left(\frac{1}{1-x} - \frac{3}{1-x^3} \right)$ is

a. 0

b. −1

c. 1

d. 2

9 The value of $\lim_{x \to \sqrt{2}} \left(\frac{x^4 - 4}{x^2 + 3x\sqrt{2} - 8} \right)$ is

a. $\frac{6}{5}$ b. $\frac{7}{5}$ c. $\frac{8}{5}$ d. $\frac{9}{5}$

10 The value of $\lim_{x \to 2} \frac{\sqrt{1 + \sqrt{2 + x}} - \sqrt{3}}{x - 2}$ is

a. $8\sqrt{3}$

b. $4\sqrt{3}$

c. $\sqrt{3}$

d. $\frac{1}{8\sqrt{3}}$

11 The value of $\lim_{x \to 1} \frac{x^m - 1}{x^n - 1}$, where m and n are integers, is

a. mn b. 0 c. $\frac{m}{n}$ d. Does not exist

Working Space

12 The value of $\lim_{x \to 0} \frac{\sqrt{1+x^2}-1}{x^2}$ is

a. $\frac{1}{2}$ b. 1
c. 2 d. –1

13 The value of $\lim_{x \to 0} \frac{\sqrt{1+x}-\sqrt{1-x}}{2x}$ is

a. 1 b. 2
c. 3 d. $\frac{1}{2}$

14 The value of $\lim_{x \to 0} \frac{\sqrt{1+x^2}-1}{\sqrt{16+x^2}-4}$ is

a. 4 b. 3
c. 2 d. 1

15 The value of $\lim_{x \to 1} \frac{\sqrt[n]{x}-1}{\sqrt[m]{x}-1}$, where m and n are integers, is

a. $\frac{m}{n}$ b. $\frac{n}{m}$
c. mn d. Does not exist

16 The value of $\lim_{x \to 1} \frac{\sqrt[3]{1+x^2}-\sqrt[3]{1-2x}}{x+x^2}$ is

a. $\frac{1}{2}$ b. $\frac{3}{2}$
c. $\frac{3}{4}$ d. $\frac{4}{3}$

17 The value of $\lim_{x \to 1} \frac{\sqrt[3]{7+x^2}-\sqrt{3+x^2}}{x-1}$ is

a. $-\frac{1}{3}$ b. $\frac{3}{2}$
c. $-\frac{1}{4}$ d. $\frac{1}{4}$

18 The value of $\lim_{x \to 2} \frac{\sqrt{x-2}+\sqrt{x}-\sqrt{2}}{\sqrt{x^2-4}}$ is

a. 1 b. 2
c. $\frac{1}{2}$ d. $\frac{1}{4}$

19 The value of $\lim_{x \to 1} \frac{4x^3-x^2+2x-5}{x^6+5x^3-2x-4}$ is

a. $\frac{1}{19}$ b. $\frac{5}{19}$
c. $\frac{7}{19}$ d. $\frac{12}{19}$

20 The value of $\lim_{x \to a} \frac{\sqrt{a+2x}-\sqrt{3x}}{\sqrt{3a+x}-2\sqrt{x}}$, $a \neq 0$ is

a. $\frac{2}{\sqrt{3}}$ b. $\frac{2}{3\sqrt{3}}$ c. $\frac{1}{\sqrt{3}}$ d. $\frac{1}{2\sqrt{3}}$

DPP-2 Questions Based on $\left(\frac{\infty}{\infty}\right)$ Form

Subjective Question

Working Space

Direction *(Q. No. 1) This question is subjective in nature, need to be solved completely on notebook.*

1 The value of $\lim_{x \to \infty} \frac{a_0 x^m + a_1 x^{m-1} + a_2 x^{m-2} + \cdots + a_m}{b_0 x^n + b_1 x^{n-1} + b_2 x^{n-2} + \cdots + b_n}$, where $a_0, b_0 \neq 0$ and m, n are positive integers, when

i. $m > n$

ii. $m = n$

iii. $m < n$

Only One Option Correct Type

Direction *(Q. Nos. 2-17) This section contains 16 multiple choice questions. Each question has four choices (a), (b), (c) and (d), out of which ONLY ONE is correct.*

2 The value of $\lim_{x \to \infty} \left(\frac{x^2 + 1}{x + 1} - ax - b\right) = 0$, then

a. $a = 1, b = -1$ b. $a = -1, b = 1$
c. $a = 1, b = 1$ d. $a = b = 0$

3 The value of $\lim_{x \to \infty} \left(\frac{x^2 - 1}{x + 1} - ax - b\right) = 2$, then

a. $a = 1, b = 1$ b. $a = 1, b = -3$
c. $a = -1, b = -1$ d. $a = -1, b = 3$

4 The value of $\lim_{x \to \infty} \left(\frac{x^2 + 1}{x + 1} - ax - b\right) = \infty$, then

a. $a = 1, b = 1$ b. $a = 1, b \neq 1$
c. $a \neq 1, b \in R$ d. $a < 1, b \in R$

5 The value of $\lim_{n \to \infty} \frac{(n + 1)^4 - (n - 1)^4}{(n + 1)^4 + (n - 1)^4}$ is

a. 1 b. 0
c. ∞ d. None of these

6 The value of $\lim_{n \to \infty} \frac{(2n + 1)^4 - (n - 1)^4}{(2n + 1)^4 + (n - 1)^4}$ is

a. 1 b. $\frac{15}{17}$
c. $\frac{13}{17}$ d. $\frac{11}{17}$

Working Space

7 The value of $\lim_{n\to\infty} \frac{\sqrt[3]{n^3+2n-1}}{n+2}$ is

a. 0
b. −1
c. 1
d. Does not exist

8 The value of $\lim_{n\to\infty} \frac{n!}{(n+1)!-n!}$ is

a. −1
b. 1
c. 0
d. $\frac{3}{2}$

9 The value of $\lim_{n\to\infty} \frac{\sqrt{n^3+2n^2+1}+\sqrt[5]{n^4+1}}{\sqrt[4]{n^6+2n^5+2}+\sqrt[5]{n^7+3n^3+1}}$ is

a. 1
b. $\frac{3}{2}$
c. 2
d. 0

10 The value of $\lim_{n\to\infty} \frac{\sqrt[4]{n^5+2}-\sqrt[3]{n^2+1}}{\sqrt[5]{n^4+2}-\sqrt{n^3+1}}$ is

a. 0
b. 1
c. $\frac{4}{5}$
d. $\frac{3}{2}$

11 The value of $\lim_{n\to\infty} \frac{(n+2)!+(n+1)!}{(n+3)!}$ is

a. 1
b. $\frac{1}{2}$
c. $\frac{3}{2}$
d. 0

12 The value of $\lim_{n\to\infty} \left\{\frac{1}{1\cdot 2}+\frac{1}{2\cdot 3}+\frac{1}{3\cdot 4}+\cdots+\frac{1}{(n-1)\cdot n}\right\}$ is

a. $\frac{1}{4}$
b. $\frac{1}{6}$
c. $\frac{1}{3}$
d. 1

13 The value of $\lim_{x\to\infty} \left(\frac{x^3}{2x^2-1}-\frac{x^2}{2x+1}\right)$ is

a. $\frac{1}{4}$
b. $\frac{1}{6}$
c. $\frac{1}{3}$
d. 1

14 The value of $\lim_{x\to\infty} \frac{(x+1)^{10}+(x+2)^{10}+\cdots+(x+100)^{10}}{x^{10}+10^{10}}$ is

a. 1
b. 0
c. 100
d. 50

15 The value of $\lim_{x\to\infty} x^{3/2}\{\sqrt{x^3+1}-\sqrt{x^3-1}\}$ is

a. $\frac{3}{2}$
b. $\frac{1}{2}$
c. 1
d. 0

Working Space

16 The value of $\lim_{x \to \infty} \left[\sqrt{x^2 - x + 1} - (ax + b)\right] = 0$, then

a. $a = 1, b = \frac{1}{2}$
b. $a = -1, b = \frac{1}{2}$
c. $a = 1, b = -\frac{1}{2}$
d. $a \in R, b = \frac{1}{2}$

17 The value of $\lim_{n \to \infty} \frac{1 \cdot n + 2 \cdot (n-1) + 3 \cdot (n-2) + \cdots + (n-1) \cdot 2 + n \cdot 1}{1^2 + 2^2 + \cdots + n^2}$ is

a. $\frac{1}{2}$
b. $\frac{1}{4}$
c. 0
d. Does not exist

One or More than One Options Correct Type

Direction (Q. Nos. 18 and 19) *This section contains 2 multiple choice questions. Each question has four choices (a), (b), (c) and (d), out of which ONE or MORE THAN ONE are correct.*

18 If $f(x) = \frac{\sqrt{x^2 + 2}}{3x - 6}$, then

a. $\lim_{x \to -\infty} f(x) = -\frac{1}{3}$
b. $\lim_{x \to \infty} f(x) = \frac{1}{3}$
c. $\lim_{x \to -\infty} f(x) = \frac{1}{3}$
d. $\lim_{x \to \infty} f(x) = -\frac{1}{3}$

19 If $L = \lim_{x \to \infty} \frac{(ax + 1)^n}{x^n + A}$, then L is equal to

a. a^n, if $n \in N$
b. ∞, if $n \in Z^-$ and $a = A = 0$
c. $\frac{1}{1 + A}$, if $n = 0$
d. a^n, if $n \in Z^-$, $A = 0$ and $a \neq 0$

Matching List Type

Direction (Q. No. 20) *Choices for the correct combination of elements from Column I and Column II are given as options (a), (b), (c) and (d), out of which one is correct.*

20 Let $\phi(x) = \frac{a_0 x^m + a_1 x^{m+1} + \cdots + a_k \cdot x^{m+k}}{b_0 x^n + b_1 x^{n+1} + \cdots + b_l \cdot x^{n+l}}$, where $a_0 \neq 0, b_0 \neq 0$, then find $\lim_{x \to 0} \phi(x)$.

Match the Column I with Column II and mark the correct option from the codes given below.

	Column I		Column II
i.	$m > n$	p.	∞
ii.	$m = n$	q.	$-\infty$
iii.	$m < n$ and $(n - m)$ is even, $\frac{a_0}{b_0} > 0$	r.	$\frac{a_0}{b_0}$
iv.	$m < n$ and $(n - m)$ is even, $\frac{a_0}{b_0} < 0$	s.	0

Codes

	i	ii	iii	iv		i	ii	iii	iv
a.	s	r	p	q	b.	p	s	r	q
c.	p	q	s	r	d.	r	p	s	q

Working Space

One Integer Value Correct Type

Direction *(Q. Nos. 21-25) This section contains 5 questions. When worked out will result in an integer from 0 to 9 (both inclusive).*

21 If $f(x)=\sum_{\lambda=1}^{n}\left(x-\frac{1}{\lambda}\right)\cdot\left(x-\frac{1}{\lambda+1}\right)$, then the value of $\lim_{n\to\infty} f(0)$ is

22 If $\lim_{x\to\infty} f(x)$ exists, is finite, non-zero and $\lim_{x\to\infty}\left[f(x)+\frac{3f(x)-1}{f^2(x)}\right]=3$, then the value of $\lim_{x\to\infty} f(x)$ is

23 If limit of $f(x)=\begin{cases} x^3+a, & x<-1 \\ bx+x, & -1\le x<1 \\ cx^2, & x\ge 1\end{cases}$ exits at $x=1$, $x=-1$ and both are equal, then the value of $a+b+c$ is

24 Let $P_n=\prod_{r=2}^{n}\left(\frac{r^3-1}{r^3+1}\right)$, then the value of $3\left(\lim_{n\to\infty} P_n\right)$ is

25 Let $P_n=\frac{1}{n^4}\left[1\cdot\left(\sum_{k=1}^{n} k\right)+3\cdot\left(\sum_{k=1}^{n-1} k\right)+5\cdot\left(\sum_{k=1}^{n-2} k\right)+\cdots+(2n-1)\cdot 1\right]$, then the value of $12\cdot\left(\lim_{n\to\infty} P_n\right)$ is

DPP-3 Exponential, Logarithmic and Trigonometric Forms

Subjective Questions

Working Space

Direction (Q. Nos. 1-5) *These questions are subjective in nature, need to be solved completely on notebook.*

1 Solve the following:

i. $\lim_{x \to 0} \frac{\sin \alpha x}{\tan \beta x}$

ii. $\lim_{x \to 0} \frac{x^3 \cdot \cot x}{1 - \cos x}$

iii. $\lim_{n \to \infty} \frac{\sin \frac{a}{n}}{\tan\left(\frac{b}{n+1}\right)}$

iv. $\lim_{h \to 0} \frac{(a+h)^2 \cdot \sin(a+h) - a^2 \cdot \sin a}{h}$

2 Solve the following:

i. $\lim_{x \to a} \frac{e^x - e^a}{x - a}$

ii. $\lim_{x \to 0} \frac{2^x - 1}{\sqrt{1+x} - 1}$

iii. $\lim_{x \to 0} \frac{e^{\tan x} - e^x}{\tan x - x}$

3 Solve the following:

i. $\lim_{x \to e} \frac{\log_e x - 1}{x - 1}$

ii. $\lim_{x \to 0} \frac{\log_e(5+x) - \log_e(5-x)}{x}$

iii. $\lim_{x \to 0} \frac{a^{\tan x} - a^{\sin x}}{x^3}$

iv. $\lim_{x \to 2} \frac{(x-2)}{\log_a(x-1)}$

v. $\lim_{x \to \frac{\pi}{2}} \frac{2^{-\cos x} - 1}{x\left(x - \frac{\pi}{2}\right)}$

vi. $\lim_{x \to 0} \frac{27^x - 9^x - 3^x + 1}{\sqrt{2} - \sqrt{1+\cos x}}$

4 Solve the following:

i. $\lim_{x \to 0} \frac{1 - \cos^3 x}{x \sin 2x}$

ii. $\lim_{x \to 0} \frac{1 + \sin x - \cos x}{1 - \sin x - \cos x}$

iii. $\lim_{x \to 0} \left(\frac{1}{\sin x} - \frac{1}{\tan x}\right)$

iv. $\lim_{x \to 0} \frac{\cos \alpha x - \cos \beta x}{x^2}$

v. $\lim_{x \to 0} \frac{2x - \sin^{-1} x}{2x + \tan^{-1} x}$

vi. $\lim_{x \to 0} \frac{\tan 3x - 2x}{3x - \sin^2 x}$

vii. $\lim_{\alpha \to 0} \left(\frac{\tan \alpha - \sin \alpha}{\alpha^3}\right)$

viii. $\lim_{y \to 0} \frac{(x+y)\sec(x+y) - x \sec x}{y}$

Working Space

5 Solve the following:

i. $\lim_{x \to \frac{\pi}{2}} \dfrac{\cos 3x + 3\cos x}{\left(\dfrac{\pi}{2} - x\right)^3}$

ii. $\lim_{x \to \frac{\pi}{6}} \dfrac{\sin\left(x - \dfrac{\pi}{6}\right)}{\left(\sqrt{\dfrac{3}{2}} - \cos x\right)}$

iii. $\lim_{x \to \pi} \dfrac{\sin x}{1 - \dfrac{x^2}{\pi^2}}$

iv. $\lim_{x \to \frac{\pi}{4}} \dfrac{\sqrt{2} - \cos x - \sin x}{(4x - \pi)^2}$

Only One Option Correct Type

Direction *(Q. Nos. 6-16) This section contains 11 multiple choice questions. Each question has four choices (a), (b), (c) and (d), out of which ONLY ONE is correct.*

6 The value of $\lim_{x \to 0} \dfrac{\cos^{-1}(1 - x)}{\sqrt{x}}$ is

a. $\dfrac{1}{\sqrt{2}}$

b. $\sqrt{2}$

c. 1

d. 0

7 The value of $\lim_{x \to 0} \dfrac{\sin [\log_e(1 + x)]}{\log(1 + \sin x)}$ is

a. 0

b. $\dfrac{1}{2}$

c. $\dfrac{1}{4}$

d. 1

8 The value of $\lim_{x \to 0} \dfrac{(4^x - 1)^3}{\sin\left(\dfrac{x}{p}\right) \cdot \log\left(1 + \dfrac{x^2}{3}\right)}$ is

a. $9p(\log_e 4)$

b. $3p(\log_e 4)^3$

c. $12p(\log_e 4)^3$

d. None of these

9 The value of $\lim_{x \to 0} \dfrac{\sin(6x^2)}{\log_e[\cos(2x^2 - x)]}$ is

a. 12

b. −12

c. 6

d. −6

10 The value of $\lim_{x \to \infty} \dfrac{x^3 \cdot \sin\left(\dfrac{1}{x}\right) + x + 1}{x^2 + x + 1}$ is

a. 0

b. $\dfrac{1}{2}$

c. 1

d. None of these

11 The value of $\lim_{n \to \infty} n \cos\left(\dfrac{\pi}{4n}\right) \cdot \sin\left(\dfrac{\pi}{4n}\right)$ is

a. $\dfrac{\pi}{3}$

b. $\dfrac{\pi}{4}$

c. $\dfrac{\pi}{6}$

d. None of these

Working Space

12 Let α and β be the distinct roots of $ax^2 + bx + c = 0$, then the value of $\lim_{x \to \alpha} \frac{1 - \cos(ax^2 + bx + c)}{(x - \alpha)^2}$ is **[AIEEE 2005]**

a. $\frac{a^2}{2}(\alpha - \beta)^2$
b. 0
c. $\frac{a^2}{2}(\alpha + \beta)^2$
d. $\frac{1}{2}(\alpha - \beta)^2$

13 The value of $\lim_{x \to 0} \frac{(1 - \cos 2x)(3 + \cos x)}{x \tan 4x}$ is **[JEE Advanced 2013]**

a. $-\frac{1}{4}$
b. $\frac{1}{2}$
c. 1
d. 2

14 If $\lim_{x \to 0} \frac{[(a - n) \cdot nx - \tan x] \cdot \sin nx}{x^2} = 0$, where n is non-zero real number, then a is equal to **[IIT JEE 2003]**

a. 0
b. $\frac{n+1}{n}$
c. n
d. $n + \frac{1}{n}$

15 The value of $\lim_{x \to 0} \frac{\sin(\pi \cos^2 x)}{x^2}$ is **[IIT JEE 2001]**

a. $-\pi$
b. π
c. $\frac{\pi}{2}$
d. 1

16 The value of $\lim_{x \to 0} \frac{x \tan 2x - 2x \tan x}{(1 - \cos 2x)^2}$ is **[IIT JEE 1999]**

a. 2
b. -2
c. $\frac{1}{2}$
d. $-\frac{1}{2}$

One or More than One Options Correct Type

***Direction** (Q. Nos. 17 and 18) This section contains 2 multiple choice questions. Each question has four choices (a), (b), (c) and (d), out of which ONE or MORE THAN ONE are correct.*

17 If $I = \lim_{x \to 0} \frac{x(1 + a\cos x) - b\sin x}{x^3} = \lim_{x \to 0} \frac{1 + a\cos x}{x^2} - \lim_{x \to 0} \frac{b \sin x}{x^3}$, where $I \in R$, then

a. $(a, b) = (-1, 0)$
b. a and b are any real numbers
c. $I = 0$
d. $I = \frac{1}{2}$

18 If $\lim_{x \to 0} \frac{\sin 2x + a \sin x}{x^3} = p$ (finite), then

a. $a = -2$
b. $a = -1$
c. $p = -2$
d. $p = -1$

Working Space

Comprehension Type

Direction *(Q. Nos. 19-21) This section contains a paragraph, describing theory, experiments, data, etc. Three questions related to the paragraph have been given. Each question has only one correct answer among the four given options (a), (b), (c) and (d).*

Passage

Consider $f(x)=\dfrac{\sin x+ae^{x}+be^{-x}+c\log(1+x)}{x^{3}}$, where a, b and c are real numbers.

19 If $\lim\limits_{x\to 0^+} f(x)$ is finite, then the value of $(a+b+c)$ is

a. 0
b. 1
c. 2
d. −2

20 If $\lim\limits_{x\to 0^+} f(x)=l$ (finite), then the value of l is

a. −2
b. $-\dfrac{1}{2}$
c. −1
d. $-\dfrac{1}{3}$

21 Using the values of a, b, c as found above, the value of $\lim\limits_{x\to 0^+} x f(x)$ is

a. 0
b. $\dfrac{1}{2}$
c. $-\dfrac{1}{2}$
d. 2

One Integer Value Correct Type

Direction *(Q. Nos. 22-24) This section contains 3 questions. When worked out will result in an integer from 0 to 9 (both inclusive).*

22 If $f(x)=\dfrac{2\sqrt{2}-(\cos x+\sin x)^{3}}{1-\sin 2x}$, then the value of $\sqrt{2}\left[\lim\limits_{x\to\pi/4} f(x)\right]$ is

23 If $\lim\limits_{x\to 0}(x^{-3}\sin 3x+ax^{-2}+b)$ exists and is equal to zero, then the value of $|2(a+b)|$ is

24 If $f(x)=\sqrt{(1-\cos x)+\sqrt{(1-\cos x)+\sqrt{(1-\cos x)+\sqrt{(1-\cos x)+\cdots\infty}}}}-1$, then the value of $2\cdot\left[\lim\limits_{x\to 0}\dfrac{f(x)}{x^{2}}\right]$ is

DPP-4 Problems Based on $(1)^{\infty}$ and $(\infty)^0$ Forms

Subjective Question

Direction (Q. No. 1) *This question is subjective in nature, need to be solved completely on notebook.*

Working Space

1 Solve the following:

i. $\lim_{x \to \infty} \left(1+\frac{2}{x}\right)^x$

ii. $\lim_{x \to 0} (1+\sin x)^{2\cot x}$

iii. $\lim_{x \to 1} (\log_3 3x)^{\log_x 3}$

iv. $\lim_{x \to 0} (\cos x)^{\cot x}$

Only One Option Correct Type

Direction (Q. Nos. 2-18) *This section contains 17 multiple choice questions. Each question has four choices (a), (b), (c) and (d), out of which ONLY ONE is correct.*

2 The value of $\lim_{x \to \infty} \left(\frac{x^2 - 2x + 1}{x^2 - 4x + 2}\right)^x$ is

a. e^2 b. e c. $1/e$ d. $1/e^2$

3 The value of $\lim_{x \to 0} (\cos x + a\sin bx)^{\frac{1}{x}}$ is

a. $e^{\frac{a}{b}}$ b. $e^{\frac{b}{a}}$ c. e^{ab} d. e

4 The value of $\lim_{x \to 0} \left[\tan\left(\frac{\pi}{4} + x\right)\right]^{\frac{1}{x}}$ is

[IIT JEE 1993]

a. e b. $1/e$

c. $1/e^2$ d. e^2

5 The value of $\lim_{x \to \infty} \left(\frac{3x - 4}{3x + 2}\right)^{\frac{x+1}{3}}$ is

a. $e^{\frac{2}{3}}$ b. $e^{-\frac{2}{3}}$

c. $e^{\frac{1}{3}}$ d. e^2

6 The value of $\lim_{x \to \infty} \left(1+\frac{1}{a + bx}\right)^{c+dx}$ is

a. $e^{\frac{d}{b}}$ b. $e^{\frac{b}{d}}$

c. $e^{\frac{a}{c}}$ d. $e^{\frac{c}{a}}$

Working Space

7 The value of $\lim_{x \to 0} \left\{\frac{2}{x^3}(\tan x - \sin x)\right\}^{\frac{2}{x^2}}$ is

a. e^2
b. $\sqrt{e}$
c. $\frac{1}{e}$
d. -1

8 If $\lim_{x \to \lambda} \left(2 - \frac{\lambda}{x}\right)^{\lambda \tan\left(\frac{\pi x}{2\lambda}\right)} = \frac{1}{e}$, then λ is equal to

a. $-\pi$
b. π
c. $\frac{\pi}{2}$
d. $-\frac{2}{\pi}$

9 The value of $\lim_{x \to 1} \left[\operatorname{cosec} \frac{\pi x}{2}\right]^{\frac{1}{1-x}}$ (where, $[\cdot]$ denotes greatest integer function) is

a. 0
b. 1
c. ∞
d. Does not exist

10 The value of $\lim_{x \to 0} \{(1+x)^{\frac{2}{x}}\}$ (where, $\{\cdot\}$ denotes fractional part of x) is

a. $e^2 - 7$
b. $e^2 - 8$
c. $e^2 - 6$
d. None of these

11 The value of $\lim_{n \to \infty} (4^n + 5^n)^{\frac{1}{n}}$ is

a. 4
b. $\frac{5}{4}$
c. e^4
d. 5

12 The value of $\lim_{x \to \infty} \left(\frac{1^{1/x} + 2^{1/x} + \cdots + n^{1/x}}{n}\right)^{nx}$ is

a. e^n
b. $n!$
c. $e^{1/n}$
d. None of these

13 The value of $\lim_{x \to 0} \left(\frac{1+\tan x}{1+\sin x}\right)^{\operatorname{cosec} x}$ is

a. e
b. $\frac{1}{e}$
c. 1
d. None of these

14 Let $f : R \to R$ be such that $f(1) = 3$ and $f'(1) = 6$, then $\lim_{x \to 0} \left\{\frac{f(1+x)}{f(1)}\right\}^{\frac{1}{x}}$ equals **[IIT JEE 2002]**

a. 1
b. $e^{\frac{1}{2}}$
c. e^2
d. e^3

15 If $\lim_{x \to \infty} \left(1 + \frac{a}{x} + \frac{b}{x^2}\right)^{2x} = e^2$, then the values of a and b are **[AIEEE 2004]**

a. $a \in R$ and $b = 2$
b. $a = 1$ and $b \in R$
c. $a \in R$ and $b \in R$
d. $a = 1$ and $b = 2$

Working Space

16 For $x > 0$, $\lim_{x \to 0} \left[(\sin x)^{\frac{1}{x}} + \left(\frac{1}{x}\right)^{\sin x} \right]$ is equal to **[IIT JEE 2006]**

a. 0
b. −1
c. 1
d. 2

17 For $x \in R$, $\lim_{x \to \infty} \left(\frac{x-3}{x+2}\right)^x$ is equal to **[IIT JEE 2000]**

a. e
b. e^{-1}
c. e^{-5}
d. e^5

18 The value of $\lim_{x \to 0} \left(\frac{1+5x^2}{1+3x^2}\right)^{\frac{1}{x^2}}$ is **[IIT JEE 1996]**

a. e
b. e^{-1}
c. e^2
d. e^{-2}

One or More than One Options Correct Type

Direction (Q. Nos. 19 and 20) *This section contains 2 multiple choice questions. Each question has four choices (a), (b), (c) and (d), out of which ONE or MORE THAN ONE are correct.*

19 If $\lim_{x \to 0} (\cos x + a \sin bx)^{\frac{1}{x}} = e^2$, then the possible values of a and b are

a. $a = 1$ and $b = 2$
b. $a = 2$ and $b = 1$
c. $a = 3$ and $b = \frac{2}{3}$
d. $a = \frac{2}{3}$ and $b = 3$

20 Let $\lim_{x \to \infty} (2^x + a^x + e^x)^{\frac{1}{x}} = L$, then which of the following is/are correct?

a. If $L = a\ (a > 0)$, then the range of a is (e, ∞)
b. If $L = 2e\ (a > 0)$, then the range of a is $\{2e\}$
c. If $L = e\ (a > 0)$, then the range of a is $(0, e)$
d. If $L = 2a\ (a > 1)$, then the range of a is $\left(\frac{e}{2}, \infty\right)$

Comprehension Type

Direction (Q. Nos. 21-26) *This section contains 2 paragraphs, each describing theory, experiments, data, etc. Six questions related to the paragraphs have been given. Each question has only one correct answer among the four given options (a), (b), (c) and (d).*

Passage I

Consider two functions $f(x) = \lim_{n \to \infty} \left(\cos \frac{x}{\sqrt{n}}\right)^n$ and $g(x) = -x^{4b}$

where, $b = \lim_{x \to \infty} (\sqrt{x^2 + x + 1} - \sqrt{x^2 + 1})$.

21 The value of $f(x)$ is

a. e^{-x^2}
b. $e^{\frac{-x^2}{2}}$
c. e^{x^2}
d. $e^{\frac{x^2}{2}}$

Working Space

22 The value of $g(x)$ is

a. $-x^2$ b. x^2
c. x^4 d. $-x^4$

23 The number of solutions of $f(x) + g(x) = 0$ is

a. 2 b. 4
c. 0 d. 1

Passage II

Given, $g(x) = \sin\left(\frac{1}{x}\right)$, $h(x) = x^2 + 2x + (\lambda + 1)$ and $u(x) = \frac{1}{x} + \cos\left(\frac{1}{x^2}\right)$.

Let $f(x) = \lim_{n \to \infty} \frac{x^{2n+1}g(x) + h(x)}{x^{2n} + 3x \cdot u(x)}$

24 If $\lim_{x \to 0} f(x) = 2$, then the value of λ is

a. 10 b. 5
c. 2 d. Does not exist

25 The value of $\lim_{x \to \infty} f(x)$ is

a. 0 b. 2
c. 5 d. 1

26 If $\lim_{x \to -2} f(x) = l$, then $[l]$ (where, $[\cdot]$ denotes greatest integer function), is equal to

a. 0 b. 1
c. -1 d. 2

One Integer Value Correct Type

***Direction** (Q. Nos. 27-30) This section contains 4 questions. When worked out will result in an integer from 0 to 9 (both inclusive).*

27 If $\lim_{x \to 1} (1 + ax + bx^2)^{\frac{c}{x-1}} = e^3$, then $\frac{1}{17}\left(\left|\frac{5b}{a}\right| + 4bc\right)$ is equal to

28 If $\lim_{x \to 0} (1 + ax + bx^2)^{\frac{2}{x}} = e^3$, then $2a$ is equal to

29 If $\lim_{x \to \infty} \left(1 + \frac{1}{x^n}\right)^x = L$ (when $n > 1$), then L is equal to

30 If $\lim_{x \to 0} [\cos x + a^3 \sin(b^6 x)]^{\frac{1}{x}} = e^{512}$, then the value of ab^2 is

DPP-5 Applications of RHL and LHL

Subjective Questions

Working Space

Direction *(Q. Nos. 1-3) These questions are subjective in nature, need to be solved completely on notebook.*

1 Which of the following statements are true for the function f defined for $-1 \le x \le 3$ in the figure shown?

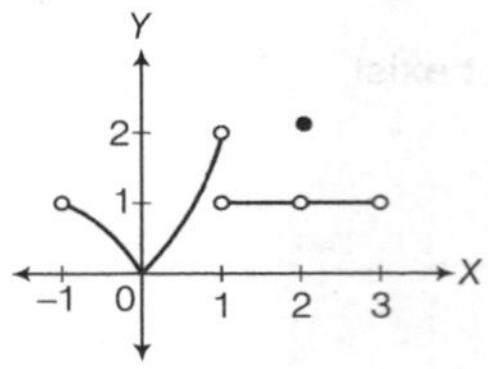

i. $\lim\limits_{x \to -1^+} f(x) = 1$

ii. $\lim\limits_{x \to 2} f(x)$ does not exist

iii. $\lim\limits_{x \to 1^-} f(x) = 2$

iv. $\lim\limits_{x \to 0^+} f(x) = \lim\limits_{x \to 0^-} f(x)$

2 Evaluate the limit of

i. $f(x) = \begin{cases} \dfrac{|x-4|}{x-4}, & x \neq 4 \\ 0, & x = 4 \end{cases}$ at $x = 4$.

ii. $f(x) = \begin{cases} 1 + x^2, & \text{if } 0 \le x \le 1 \\ 2 - x, & \text{if } x > 1 \end{cases}$ at $x = 1$.

iii. $f(x) = \begin{cases} 5x - 4, & \text{if } 0 < x \le 1 \\ 4x^3 - 3x, & \text{if } 1 < x < 2 \end{cases}$ at $x = 1$.

3 If f is an even function, then prove that $\lim\limits_{x \to 0^-} f(x) = \lim\limits_{x \to 0^+} f(x)$.

Only One Option Correct Type

Direction *(Q. Nos. 4-22) This section contains 19 multiple choice questions. Each question has four choices (a), (b), (c) and (d), out of which ONLY ONE is correct.*

4 The value of $\lim\limits_{x \to 0^-} \dfrac{\cos^{-1}(1-x)}{\sqrt{x}}$ is

a. $\dfrac{1}{\sqrt{2}}$

b. $\sqrt{2}$

c. 1

d. Does not exist

5 The value of $\lim\limits_{x \to 0} \sin^{-1}(\sec x)$ is

a. $\pi/2$

b. 1

c. 0

d. None of these

Working Space

6 The value of $\lim\limits_{x \to 1} (1 - x + [x - 1] + [1 - x])$ (where, $[x]$ denotes greatest integer function of x), is

a. 0 b. 1
c. −1 d. Does not exist

7 The value of $\lim\limits_{x \to \pi/2} \left[\dfrac{x - \dfrac{\pi}{2}}{\cos x}\right]$ (where, $[x]$ denotes greatest integer function) is

a. −1 b. 0
c. −2 d. Does not exist

8 The value of $\lim\limits_{x \to \pi/4} (1 + [x])^{\frac{1}{\log(\tan x)}}$ (where, [·] denotes greatest integer function) is

a. 0 b. 1
c. e d. $\dfrac{1}{e}$

9 The value of $\lim\limits_{x \to \pi/2} [\sin x]$ (where, [·] denotes greatest integer function) is

a. 0 b. −1
c. 1 d. Does not exist

10 The value of $\lim\limits_{x \to 2} \left\{\dfrac{x}{2}\right\}$ (where, {·} denotes the fractional part of x) is

a. 0 b. −1
c. 1 d. Does not exist

11 The value of $\lim\limits_{x \to \pi} \text{Sgn}\, [\tan x]$ (where, [·] denotes the greatest integer function) is

a. 0 b. −1
c. 1 d. Does not exist

12 The value of $\lim\limits_{x \to 1} \sin^{-1} (\log_e x)$ is

a. 0 b. −1
c. 1 d. Does not exist

13 If $f(x) = \begin{cases} x^2 + 2, & x \geq 2 \\ 1 - x, & x < 2 \end{cases}$ and $g(x) = \begin{cases} 2x, & x > 1 \\ 3 - x, & x \leq 1 \end{cases}$, then $\lim\limits_{x \to 1} f[g(x)]$ is equal to

a. 4 b. 6
c. 0 d. Does not exist

14 The value of $\lim\limits_{x \to 1^-} ([x])^{1-x}$ (where, [·] denotes the greatest integer function) is

a. 0 b. 1
c. −1 d. Does not exist

15 The value of $\lim\limits_{x \to a^-} \left(\dfrac{|x|^3}{a} - \left[\dfrac{x}{a}\right]^3\right)$ $(a > 0)$ (where, [·] denotes greatest integer function) is

a. $a^2 + 1$ b. a^2
c. $a^2 - 1$ d. $-a^2$

16 The value of $\lim_{x \to \infty} \sec^{-1}\left(\frac{x}{x+1}\right)$ is

a. 0 b. $\frac{\pi}{2}$ c. π d. Does not exist

17 If $f(x) = \begin{cases} \frac{\tan^2\{x\}}{x^2 - [x]^2}, & x > 0 \\ 1, & x = 0 \\ \sqrt{\{x\}\cot\{x\}}, & x < 0 \end{cases}$

where, $[x]$ is the integral part of x and $\{x\}$ is the fractional part of x, then

a. $\lim_{x \to 0} f(x) = 1$
b. $\lim_{x \to 0^-} f(x) = \cot 1$
c. $\cot^{-1}[\lim_{x \to 0^-} f(x)]^2 = 1$
d. None of these

18 The value of $\lim_{\theta \to 0}\left(\left[\frac{n\sin\theta}{\theta}\right] + \left[\frac{n\tan\theta}{\theta}\right]\right)$, where $[\cdot]$ is greatest integer function and $n \in N$, is

a. $2n$
b. $2n+1$
c. $2n-1$
d. Does not exist

19 The value of $\lim_{x \to 1} \frac{\sqrt{1 - \cos 2(x-1)}}{(x-1)}$ is **[AIEEE 2011]**

a. $\sqrt{2}$
b. $-\sqrt{2}$
c. Does not exist
d. None of these

20 The value of $\lim_{x \to \infty} \frac{\log_e x^x - [x]}{[x]}$, where $[x]$ denotes greatest integer function, is **[AIEEE 2002]**

a. -1 b. 0 c. 1 d. Does not exist

21 Let $f : R \to [0, \infty)$ be such that $\lim_{x \to 5} f(x)$ exists and $\lim_{x \to 5} \frac{[f(x)]^2 - 9}{|x - 5|} = 0$, then $\lim_{x \to 5} f(x)$ equals **[AIEEE 2011]**

a. 3 b. 0 c. 1 d. 2

22 Let $\alpha(a)$ and $\beta(a)$ be the roots of the equation

$$(\sqrt[3]{1+a} - 1)x^2 + (\sqrt{1+a} - 1)x + (\sqrt[6]{1+a} - 1) = 0,$$

where $a > -1$. Then, $\lim_{a \to 0^+} \alpha(a)$ and $\lim_{a \to 0^+} \beta(a)$ are **[IIT JEE 2012]**

a. $-\frac{5}{2}$ and 1
b. $-\frac{1}{2}$ and -1
c. $-\frac{7}{2}$ and 2
d. $-\frac{9}{2}$ and 3

One or More than One Options Correct Type

Direction *(Q. Nos. 23-26) This section contains 4 multiple choice questions. Each question has four choices (a), (b), (c) and (d), out of which ONE or MORE THAN ONE are correct.*

23 Let $f(x) = \frac{x^2 - 9x + 20}{x - [x]}$, where $[x]$ denotes greatest integer function, then

a. $\lim_{x \to 5^-} f(x) = 0$
b. $\lim_{x \to 5^+} f(x) = 1$
c. $\lim_{x \to 5} f(x)$ does not exist
d. None of these

Working Space

24 Let $f(x) = \dfrac{\cos 2 - \cos 2x}{x^2 - |x|}$, then

a. $\lim\limits_{x \to -1} f(x) = 2\sin 2$

b. $\lim\limits_{x \to 1} f(x) = 2\sin 2$

c. $\lim\limits_{x \to -1} f(x) = 2\cos 2$

d. $\lim\limits_{x \to 1} f(x) = 2\cos 2$

25 Let $f(x) = |x|^{\sin x}$, then

a. $\lim\limits_{x \to 0^-} f(x) = 1$ b. $\lim\limits_{x \to 0^+} f(x) = 1$ c. $\lim\limits_{x \to 0} f(x) = 1$ d. limit does not exist

26 Let $f(x) = \dfrac{|x + \pi|}{\sin x}$, then

a. $f(-\pi^+) = -1$

b. $f(-\pi^+) = 1$

c. $\lim\limits_{x \to -\pi} f(x)$ does not exist

d. $\lim\limits_{x \to \pi} f(x)$ does not exist

Comprehension Type

Direction (Q. Nos. 27-29) This section contains a paragraph, describing theory, experiments, data, etc. Three questions related to the paragraph have been given. Each question has only one correct answer among the four given options (a), (b), (c) and (d).

Passage

Let $f(x) = \begin{cases} x^2 + 1, & x < 1 \\ x^3, & x \geq 1 \end{cases}$, $g(x) = 2^x$ and $h(x) = \dfrac{\sin x}{x}$.

27 $|f[h(0^+)] - f[h(0^-)]|$ is equal to

a. 3 b. 0 c. 1 d. 2

28 $|f[g(0^+)] - f[g(0^-)]|$ is equal to

a. 3 b. 0 c. 1 d. 2

29 $|f[g\{h(0^+)\}] - f[g\{h(0^-)\}]|$ is equal to

a. 3 b. 0 c. 1 d. 2

One Integer Value Correct Type

Direction (Q. Nos. 30-35) This section contains 6 questions. When worked out will result in an integer from 0 to 9 (both inclusive).

30 The value of $\lim\limits_{x \to 0} |x|^{[\cos x]}$ (where, [·] denotes greatest integer function) is

31 If $L = \lim\limits_{x \to 1^-} 2^{-2(1-x)^{-1}}$ and $M = \lim\limits_{x \to 1^+} 2^{-2(1-x)^{-1}}$, then $(L + M)$ is equal to

32 The value of $\lim\limits_{x \to 0} \left[\log(1 + x) \cdot \dfrac{\tan x}{|x|}\right]$ (where, [·] denotes the greatest integer function) is

33 The value of $\lim\limits_{x \to 0^+} \dfrac{\log(-\cos 3x + \cos x)}{\log(\sin x)}$ is

34 The value of $\left|\lim\limits_{x \to 0} \left[(1 - e^x) \cdot \dfrac{\sin x}{|x|}\right]\right|$ (where, [·] denotes greatest function) is

35 The value of $\lim\limits_{x \to 0} \left[\dfrac{3\sin 3x}{x}\right] - \left[\dfrac{2\sin 2x}{x}\right]$ (where, [·] denotes greatest integer function) is

DPP-6 Limit of Expansions, Dual Behaviour, Newton- Leibnitz Rule and Conversion into Definite Integral

Only One Option Correct Type

Direction (Q. Nos. 1-11) *This section contains 11 multiple choice questions. Each questions has four choices (a), (b), (c) and (d), out of which ONLY ONE is correct.*

Working Space

1 The value of a and b such that $\lim_{x \to 0} \frac{x(1 + a\cos x) - b\sin x}{x^3} = 1$, are **[IIT JEE 1996]**

a. $\frac{5}{2}$ and $\frac{3}{2}$
b. $\frac{5}{2}$ and $-\frac{3}{2}$
c. $-\frac{5}{2}$ and $\frac{-3}{2}$
d. None of these

2 The integer n for which $\lim_{x \to 0} \frac{(\cos x - 1)(\cos x - e^x)}{x^n}$ is a finite non-zero number, is **[IIT JEE 2002]**

a. 1
b. 2
c. 3
d. 4

3 The value of $\lim_{x \to 0} \frac{(1 + x)^{1/x} - e}{x}$ is

a. 1
b. $\frac{e}{2}$
c. $-\frac{e}{2}$
d. $\frac{2}{e}$

4 The value of $\lim_{x \to 0^+} \frac{e^{1/x} + 1}{e^{1/x} - 1}$ is equal to

a. 0
b. 1
c. −1
d. 2

5 The value of $\lim_{x \to 0^-} \frac{e^{1/x} + 1}{e^{1/x} - 1}$ is equal to

a. 0
b. 1
c. −1
d. 2

6 The value of $\lim_{n \to \infty} \frac{[x] + [2x] + \cdots + [nx]}{n^2}$ is

a. x
b. $\frac{x}{2}$
c. $2x$
d. $\frac{x}{4}$

Working Space

7 The value of $\lim_{n\to\infty}\frac{[1^2x]+[2^2x]+\cdots+[n^2x]}{n^3}$ is

a. x b. $\frac{x}{2}$
c. $\frac{x}{3}$ d. $\frac{x}{6}$

8 The value of $\lim_{x\to 0}\frac{\int_0^{x^2}\sec^2 t\,dt}{x\sin x}$ is equal to **[AIEEE 2003]**

a. 2 b. 1
c. 0 d. 3

9 Let $f: R\to R$ be a differentiable function having $f(2)=6$, $f'(2)=\frac{1}{48}$. Then,

$\lim_{x\to 2}\int_6^{f(x)}\frac{4t^3dt}{x-2}$ equals **[AIEEE 2005]**

a. 18 b. 12
c. 36 d. 24

10 The value of $\lim_{n\to\infty}\left(\frac{1}{\sqrt{n^2}}+\frac{1}{\sqrt{n^2+1^2}}+\frac{1}{\sqrt{n^2+2^2}}+\cdots+\frac{1}{\sqrt{n^2+n^2}}\right)$ is

a. 1 b. $\log(\sqrt{2})$ c. 0 d. $\log(1+\sqrt{2})$

11 If $f(x)$ is defined as $f:(-1,1)\to R$ and is differentiable on $(-1,1)$. It is given that $f'(0)=\lim_{n\to\infty}n\left[f\left(\frac{1}{n}\right)\right]$ also $f(0)=0$. Then, the value of $\lim_{n\to\infty}\left[\frac{2}{\pi}(1+n)\cos^{-1}\left(\frac{1}{n}\right)-n\right]$ given that $\left|\cos^{-1}\left(\frac{1}{n}\right)\right|\le\frac{\pi}{2}$ is **[IIT JEE 2004]**

a. $\frac{1}{\pi}$ b. $\frac{1}{\pi-2}$
c. $\frac{\pi-2}{\pi}$ d. π

Comprehension Type

Direction *(Q. Nos. 12-14) This section contains a paragraph, which describing theory, experiments, data, etc. Three questions related to the paragraph have been given. Each question has only one correct answer among the four given options (a), (b), (c) and (d).*

Passage

Suppose $\lim_{x\to 0}\frac{\int_0^x\frac{t^2}{(a+t^r)^{1/p}}dt}{bx-\sin x}=c$, where $p\in N$, $p\ge 2$, $a>0$, $r>0$ and $b\ne 0$.

12 If c exists and is non-zero, then

a. $b>1$ b. $0<b<1$ c. $b<0$ d. $b=1$

13 If $p=3$ and $c=1$, then the value of a is

a. 3 b. $\frac{3}{2}$ c. 8 d. 6

14 If $p=2$ and $a=9$ and c exists, then the value of c is

a. $\frac{1}{3}$ b. $\frac{3}{2}$ c. $\frac{2}{3}$ d. $\frac{3}{4}$

One Integer Value Correct Type

Working Space

Direction *(Q. Nos. 15- 20) This section contains 6 questions. When worked out will result in an integer from 0 to 9 (both inclusive).*

15 The value of $\lim_{n \to \infty} \frac{\{1^4 + 2^4 + 3^4 + \cdots + n^4\}}{n^5} = \lambda$, then 10λ is equal to

16 The value of $\lim_{n \to \infty} \left\{\frac{1}{n} + \frac{1}{n+1} + \frac{1}{n+2} + \cdots + \frac{1}{2n}\right\} = \log \lambda$, then λ is equal to

17 The value of $\lim_{n \to \infty} \left\{\frac{n}{n^2 + 1^2} + \frac{n}{n^2 + 2^2} + \cdots + \frac{n}{n^2 + n^2}\right\} = \lambda$, then the value of $\sin 2\lambda$ is

18 The value of $\left[\lim_{n \to \infty} \frac{(n!)^{\frac{1}{n}}}{n}\right]$ (where, [·] denotes greatest integer function), is

19 Let $f(x)$ be a function such that $\lim_{x \to 0} \frac{f(x)}{x} = 1$. If $\lim_{x \to 0} \frac{x(1 + a\sin x) - b\sin x}{\{f(x)\}^3}$ is finite, then the value of $|a + b|$ is

20 If $\lim_{n \to \infty} \{(1+x)(1+x^2)(1+x^4)\cdots(1+x^{2^n})\} = f(x)$ for $|x| < 1$, then $f\left(\frac{1}{2}\right)$ is equal to

SET - 1

Revisal Problems for JEE Main

Only One Option Correct Type

Working Space

Direction (Q. Nos. 1-45) *This section contains 45 multiple choice questions. Each question has four choices (a), (b), (c) and (d), out of which ONLY ONE is correct.*

1 The value of $\lim_{x \to 2} \dfrac{\sin(e^{x-2}-1)}{\log_e(x-1)}$ is

a. 0
b. -1
c. 2
d. 1

2 The value of $\lim_{n \to \infty} \dfrac{-3n+(-1)^n}{4n-(-1)^n}$ is

a. $-\dfrac{3}{4}$
b. $-\dfrac{3}{4}$, if n is even; $\dfrac{3}{4}$, if n is odd
c. 1, if n is even; does not exist, if n is odd
d. Does not exist

3 The value of $\lim_{x \to \infty} \left[x - x^2 \cdot \log\left(1+\dfrac{1}{x}\right)\right]$ is

a. $\dfrac{1}{2}$
b. $\dfrac{3}{2}$
c. $\dfrac{1}{3}$
d. 1

4 The value of $\lim_{x \to \infty} \left(\dfrac{x+2}{x-2}\right)^{x+1}$ is

a. e^4
b. e^{-4}
c. e^2
d. None of these

5 The value of $\lim_{x \to 0^+} (1+\tan^2\sqrt{x})^{\frac{5}{x}}$ is

a. e^5
b. e^2
c. e
d. None of these

6 The value of $\lim_{x \to \infty} \left(\dfrac{x^2-2x+1}{x^2-4x+2}\right)^x$ is

a. 1
b. 2
c. e^2
d. e

7 The limiting value of $(\cos x)^{\frac{1}{\sin x}}$ as $x \to 0$ is

a. 1
b. e
c. 0
d. None of these

8 The $\lim_{x \to a} \left(2-\dfrac{a}{x}\right)^{\tan\left(\frac{\pi x}{2a}\right)}$ is

a. $e^{-a/\pi}$
b. $e^{-2a/\pi}$
c. $e^{-2/\pi}$
d. 1

Working Space

9 The value of $\lim_{n \to \infty} \frac{5^{n+1} + 3^n - 2^{2n}}{5^n + 2^n + 3^{2n+3}}$ is

a. 5 b. 3
c. 1 d. 0

10 The value of $\lim_{x \to \infty} \frac{x^n}{e^x} = 0$ (where, n is an integer) for

a. no value of n
b. all values of n
c. only negative values of n
d. only positive values of n

11 The value of $\lim_{x \to 0} \frac{\sin^{-1} x - \tan^{-1} x}{x^3}$ is

a. 0 b. $\frac{1}{2}$
c. 1 d. None of these

12 The value of $\lim_{x \to \frac{\pi}{2}} \frac{\left(1 - \tan\frac{x}{2}\right) \cdot (1 - \sin x)}{\left(1 + \tan\frac{x}{2}\right) \cdot (\pi - 2x)^3}$ is

a. $\frac{1}{16}$ b. $-\frac{1}{16}$
c. $\frac{1}{32}$ d. $-\frac{1}{32}$

13 The value of $\lim_{x \to -\infty} \frac{x^2 \cdot \sin\left(\frac{1}{x}\right)}{\sqrt{9x^2 + x + 1}}$ is

a. 1/3 b. −1/3
c. 0 d. Does not exist

14 If α and β are the roots of $ax^2 + bx + c = 0$. Then, $\lim_{x \to \alpha} (1 + ax^2 + bx + c)^{\frac{1}{x-\alpha}}$ is equal to

a. $a(\alpha - \beta)$ b. $\log_e |a(\alpha - \beta)|$
c. $e^{a(\alpha - \beta)}$ d. $e^{a|\alpha - \beta|}$

15 Let α and β be the roots of $ax^2 + bx + c = 0$, where $1 < \alpha < \beta$, then $\lim_{x \to x_0} \frac{|ax^2 + bx + c|}{ax^2 + bx + c} = 1$.

State which of the following statements is incorrect?

a. $a > 0$ and $x_0 < 1$
b. $a > 0$ and $x_0 > \beta$
c. $a < 0$ and $\alpha < x_0 < \beta$
d. $a < 10$ and $x_0 < 1$

16 The value of $\lim_{x \to 0^+} \log_{\sin\left(\frac{x}{2}\right)} \sin x$ is equal to

a. 1 b. 0
c. 4 d. $\frac{1}{4}$

17 The value of $\lim_{x \to 0} \frac{1 - \cos x \cdot \sqrt{\cos 2x}}{x^2}$ is

a. $\frac{1}{2}$ b. $-\frac{1}{2}$
c. $\frac{3}{2}$ d. 1

Working Space

18 If $f(x)=\begin{cases}\sin x, & x \neq n\pi, n=0, \pm 1, \pm 2, \ldots \\ 2, & \text{otherwise}\end{cases}$ and $g(x)=\begin{cases}x^2+1, & x \neq 0, 2 \\ 4, & x=0 \\ 5, & x=2\end{cases}$, then the value of $\lim_{x \to 0} g[f(x)]$ is

a. 1
b. 0
c. 4
d. Does not exist

19 The graph of function $f(x)=\lim_{t \to 0}\left(\frac{2x}{\pi} \cdot \cot^{-1}\frac{x}{t^2}\right)$ is

a. 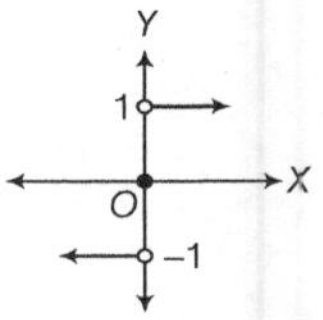

b. 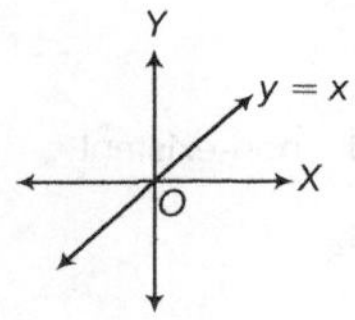

c. 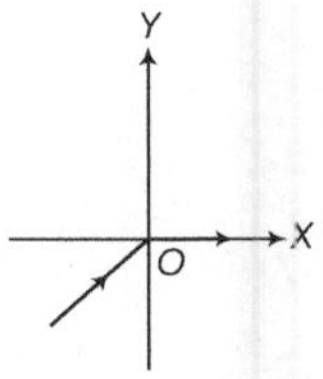

d. 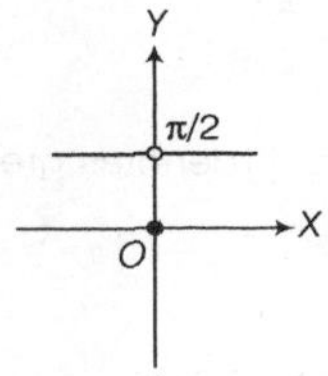

20 The value of $\lim_{y \to 0}\left(\frac{\lim_{x \to \infty} \exp\left[x \log\left(1+\frac{ay}{x}\right)\right]-\exp\left[x \log\left(1+\frac{by}{x}\right)\right]}{y}\right)$ is

a. $a+b$
b. $a-b$
c. $b-a$
d. $-(a+b)$

21 The value of $\lim_{x \to 0}\frac{\sin(\pi \cos^2 x)}{x^2}$ is

a. $-\pi$
b. π
c. $\frac{\pi}{2}$
d. 1

22 The value of $\lim_{x \to 0}\frac{x \tan 2x-2x \tan x}{(1-\cos 2x)^2}$ is

a. 2
b. -2
c. $\frac{1}{2}$
d. $-\frac{1}{2}$

23 If $\lim_{x \to 0}\frac{axe^x-b\log_e(1+x)+cxe^{-x}}{x^2 \sin x}=2$, then $(a-b+c)$ is equal to

a. 0
b. 3
c. 24
d. 12

24 The value of $\lim_{n \to \infty}(\sqrt[3]{8n^2-n^3}+n)$ is

a. $\frac{1}{3}$
b. $\frac{8}{3}$
c. $-\frac{1}{3}$
d. $-\frac{8}{3}$

25 The value of $\lim_{x \to 0}(x^{16}+4x^{12}-3x^4)\left[\frac{1}{x^4}\right]$ (where, $[\cdot]$ denotes greatest integer function) is

a. 0
b. -3
c. 4
d. non-existent

Working Space

26 If $\lim_{n \to \infty} (\sqrt{2n^2 + n} - \lambda\sqrt{2n^2 - n}) = \frac{1}{\sqrt{2}}$ (where, λ is a real number), then

a. $\lambda = 1$ b. $\lambda = -1$
c. $\lambda = \pm 1$ d. $\lambda \in (-\infty, 1)$

27 The value of $\lim_{x \to -1} \frac{1}{\sqrt{|x| - \{x\}}}$ (where, $\{\cdot\}$ denotes the fractional part of x) is

a. $\frac{1}{2}$ b. 1
c. ∞ d. Does not exist

28 The value of $\lim_{x \to 0} \frac{\log(\sin 3x)}{\log(\sin x)}$ is

a. 0 b. 1
c. 2 d. non-existent

29 The value of $\lim_{x \to 0} \frac{x^8}{1 - \cos x\,[1 - \cos(1 - \cos x)]}$ is

a. 32 b. 64
c. 128 d. 256

30 The value of $\lim_{x \to 0} \left(\left[\frac{-5\sin x}{x}\right] + \left[\frac{6\sin x}{x}\right]\right)$ (where, $[\cdot]$ denotes greatest integer function) is

a. 0 b. 1
c. 2 d. -12

31 The minimum value of k, if $\lim_{x \to 0} \frac{[(k - \alpha)\alpha x - \tan x] \cdot \sin \alpha x}{x^2} = 0$ (α being a positive integer) is

a. $\alpha + \frac{1}{\alpha}$ b. 1
c. 2 d. α^2

32 The value of $\lim_{x \to \frac{1}{\sqrt{2}}} \frac{2\sin^{-1} x - \frac{\pi}{2}}{1 - 2x^2}$ is

a. -1 b. 0
c. 1 d. Does not exist

33 The value of $\lim_{x \to 0} \frac{(\cos x)\log(1 + x) - x\cos x - \log(1 + x) + x}{x^4}$ is

a. 0 b. $\frac{1}{2}$
c. $\frac{1}{4}$ d. $\frac{1}{8}$

34 The value of $\lim_{x \to 0} \left[\frac{\sin(\text{Sgn}\, x)}{\text{Sgn}\, x}\right]$ (where, $[\cdot]$ denotes greatest integer function and $\text{Sgn}(x)$ denotes signum function) is

a. 0 b. 1
c. -1 d. Does not exist

35 Let $a = \min\{x^2 + 2x + 3, x \in R\}$ and $b = \lim_{\theta \to 0} \frac{1 - \cos\theta}{\theta^2}$, then the value of $\sum_{r=0}^{n} a^r b^{n-r}$ is

a. $\frac{2^{n+1} - 1}{3 \cdot 2^n}$

b. $\frac{2^{n+1} + 1}{3 \cdot 2^n}$

c. $\frac{4^{n+1} - 1}{3 \cdot 2^n}$

d. None of the above

Working Space

36 If $\lim_{x \to 0} \frac{x(1+a\cos x) - b\sin x}{x^3} = 1$, then

a. $a = -\frac{5}{2}$ and $b \in R$
b. $a = -\frac{3}{2}$ and $b = \frac{1}{2}$
c. $a = -\frac{3}{2}$ and $b = -\frac{5}{2}$
d. $a = -\frac{5}{2}$ and $b = -\frac{3}{2}$

37 If x is a real number in [0, 1], then the value of $f(x) = \lim_{m \to \infty} \lim_{n \to \infty} \{1 + \cos^{2m}(n!\pi x)\}$, is

a. 1, for all x
b. 2 or 1, according as x is rational or irrational
c. 1 or 2, according as x is rational or irrational
d. 2, for all x

38 The value of $\lim_{x \to 0} \frac{\sin x^{2012} - x^{2012} \cdot \cos x^{2012} + (x^3)^{2012}}{x^{2012}(e^{5x^{2012}} - 1 - 5x^{2012})}$ is

a. $\frac{8}{75}$
b. $\frac{1}{3}$
c. $\frac{4}{3}$
d. $-\frac{1}{3}$

39 If $\alpha_n \in \left[0, \frac{\pi}{4}\right)$ is a root of equation $\tan\alpha + \cot\alpha = n$, $n \ge 2$, then $\lim_{n \to \infty} (\sin\alpha_n + \cos\alpha_n)^n$ is

a. 0
b. 1
c. 2
d. e

40 The value of $\lim_{n \to \infty} \left[\frac{n^{n+1}e}{(n+1)^n} - n\right]$ is

a. 0
b. 1/2
c. 1
d. 0

41 Let $f(x) = \lim_{n \to \infty} \frac{1}{\left(\frac{3}{\pi}\tan^{-1}2x\right)^{2n} + 5}$. Then, the set of values of x for which $f(x) = 0$ is

a. $|2x| > \sqrt{3}$
b. $|2x| < \sqrt{3}$
c. $|2x| \ge \sqrt{3}$
d. None of these

42 The value of $\lim_{x \to 0} \frac{|\cos(\sin 3x)| - 1}{x^2}$ is

a. $-\frac{9}{2}$
b. $-\frac{3}{2}$
c. $\frac{3}{2}$
d. $\frac{9}{2}$

43 The value of $\lim_{x \to 0} \left(2^{x-1} + \frac{1}{2}\right)^{\frac{1}{x}}$ is

a. $\sqrt{2}$
b. $\frac{1}{2}\log_e 2$
c. $\log_e 2$
d. 2

44 $\lim_{x \to 0^-} (-\log(\{x\} + |[x]|))^{\{x\}}$ (where, $[\cdot]$ and $\{\cdot\}$ denote greatest integer and fractional part of x) is equal to

a. 0
b. 1
c. 2
d. $\log\left(\frac{1}{2}\right)$

45 The value of $\lim_{x \to \infty} \left[\frac{(1+x)^x}{x^x \cdot e}\right]^x$ is

a. $\sqrt{e}$
b. $\frac{1}{\sqrt{e}}$
c. e
d. $\frac{1}{e}$

Statement Type

Working Space

Direction *(Q. Nos. 46-50) This section is based on Statement I and Statement II. Select the correct answer from the codes given below.*

a. Both Statement I and Statement II are correct and Statement II is the correct explanation of Statement I
b. Both Statement I and Statement II are correct but Statement II is not the correct explanation of Statement I
c. Statement I is correct but Statement II is incorrect
d. Statement II is correct but Statement I is incorrect

46 **Statement I** $\lim_{x\to 0}\left[\frac{\sin x}{x}\right] \neq \left[\lim_{x\to 0}\frac{\sin x}{x}\right]$ (where, [·] represents greatest integer function).

Statement II $\lim_{x\to a} h[g(x)] = h[\lim_{x\to a} g(x)]$, if $y = h(x)$ is continuous at $x = \lim_{x\to a} g(x)$.

47 **Statement I** $\lim_{x\to 0}\frac{\sqrt{\frac{1-\cos 2x}{2}}}{x}$ does not exist.

Statement II $\lim_{x\to 0}\frac{\sin x}{x} = 1$.

48 **Statement I** $\lim_{x\to 0}\left[\tan\left(\frac{\pi}{4}+x\right)\right]^{\frac{1}{x}} = e$.

Statement II $\lim_{x\to a}[1+f(x)]^{g(x)} = e^{\lim_{x\to a} f(x)g(x)}$, if $\lim_{x\to a} f(x) = 0$ and $\lim_{x\to a} g(x) = \infty$.

49 **Statement I** $\lim_{x\to\infty}\left(\frac{2x^4+3x^3+7x}{3x^4+2x^2+3x}\right) = \frac{2}{3}$.

Statement II If $P(x)$ and $Q(x)$ are two polynomials with rational coefficients, then $\lim_{x\to\infty}\frac{P(x)}{Q(x)} = \frac{\text{Leading coefficient of } P(x)}{\text{Leading coefficient of } Q(x)}$.

50 **Statement I** $\lim_{n\to\infty}\left(\sqrt{n^2+n+1} - \left[\sqrt{n^2+n+1}\right]\right)$, where $n \in I$ and [·] denotes greatest integer function is 1/2.

Statement II $\lim_{n\to\infty}\frac{a_0x^n + a_1x^{n-1}+\cdots+a_n}{b_0x^n+b_1x^{n-1}+\cdots+b_n} = \frac{a_0}{b_0}$ and $(n < \sqrt{n^2+n+1} < n+1)$.

SET - 2

Revisal Problems
for JEE Advanced

Only One Option Correct Type

Working Space

Direction *(Q. Nos. 1-23) This section contains 23 multiple choice questions. Each question has four choices (a), (b), (c) and (d), out of which ONLY ONE is correct.*

1 Let $l = \lim_{x \to \infty} \left(\frac{x+1}{x-1}\right)^x$, then $\{l\}$ (where, $\{x\}$ denotes the fractional part of x), is

a. $8 - e^2$
b. $7 - e^2$
c. $e^2 - 6$
d. $e^2 - 7$

2 For a certain value of c, $\lim_{x \to -\infty} [(x^5 + 7x^4 + 2)^c - x]$ is finite and non-zero. The value of c and the value of limit are

a. $\frac{1}{5}$ and $\frac{7}{5}$
b. 0 and 1
c. 1 and $\frac{7}{5}$
d. None of these

3 The value of $\lim_{x \to \infty} [\sqrt[3]{(x+a)(x+b)(x+c)} - x]$ is

a. $\sqrt{abc}$
b. $\frac{a+b+c}{3}$
c. abc
d. $(abc)^{1/3}$

4 The value of $\lim_{n \to \infty} \left[\left(\frac{n}{n+1}\right)^{\alpha} + \sin\frac{1}{n}\right]^n$, when $\alpha \in Q$, is

a. $e^{-\alpha}$
b. $-\alpha$
c. $e^{1-\alpha}$
d. $e^{1+\alpha}$

5 The value of $\lim_{n \to \infty} \sum_{r=1}^{n} \frac{r}{n^2 + n + r}$ is

a. 0
b. $\frac{1}{3}$
c. $\frac{1}{2}$
d. 1

6 The function $f(x) = \lim_{n \to \infty} \frac{x^{2n} - 1}{x^{2n} + 1}$ is identical with the function

a. $g(x) = \text{Sgn}(x - 1)$
b. $h(x) = \text{Sgn}(\tan^{-1} x)$
c. $u(x) = \text{Sgn}(|x| - 1)$
d. None of these

7 Which one of the following statement is true?

a. If $\lim_{x \to c} f(x) \cdot g(x)$ and $\lim_{x \to c} f(x)$ exist, then $\lim_{x \to c} g(x)$ exists
b. If $\lim_{x \to c} [f(x) + g(x)]$ and $\lim_{x \to c} f(x)$ exist, then $\lim_{x \to c} g(x)$ exists
c. If $\lim_{x \to c} f(x) \cdot g(x)$ exists, then $\lim_{x \to c} f(x)$ and $\lim_{x \to c} g(x)$ exist
d. If $\lim_{x \to c} [f(x) + g(x)]$ exists, then $\lim_{x \to c} f(x)$ and $\lim_{x \to c} g(x)$ exist

8 The value of $\lim_{x \to 1} \frac{\sin^2(x^3 + x^2 + x - 3)}{1 - \cos(x^2 - 4x + 3)}$ is

a. 18
b. $\frac{9}{2}$
c. 9
d. None of these

Working Space

9 The graph of function f contains the point $P(1, 2)$ and $Q(s, r)$. The equation of secant line through P and Q is $y = \left(\frac{s^2 + 2s - 3}{s - 1}\right) x - 1 - s$. The value of $f'(1)$ is

a. 2 b. 3
c. 4 d. non-existent

10 The value of $\lim_{n \to \infty} \frac{1^2 \cdot n + 2^2 \cdot (n-1) + 3^2 \cdot (n-2) + \cdots + n^2 \cdot 1}{1^3 + 2^3 + 3^3 + \cdots + n^3}$ is

a. $\frac{1}{3}$ b. $\frac{2}{3}$
c. $\frac{1}{2}$ d. $\frac{1}{6}$

11 The value of $\lim_{x \to \infty} \frac{\cot^{-1}(x^{-a} \log_a x)}{\sec^{-1}(a^x \log_x a)}$, $(a > 1)$ is

a. 1 b. 0
c. $\frac{\pi}{2}$ d. Does not exist

12 Given, $l_1 = \lim_{x \to \frac{\pi}{4}} \cos^{-1}\left[\sec\left(x - \frac{\pi}{4}\right)\right]$; $l_2 = \lim_{x \to \frac{\pi}{4}} \sin^{-1}\left[\operatorname{cosec}\left(x + \frac{\pi}{4}\right)\right]$;

$l_3 = \lim_{x \to \frac{\pi}{4}} \tan^{-1}\left[\cot\left(x + \frac{\pi}{4}\right)\right]$; $l_4 = \lim_{x \to \frac{\pi}{4}} \cot^{-1}\left[\tan\left(x - \frac{\pi}{4}\right)\right]$, where [·] denotes greatest integer function, then which of the following limits exist?

a. l_1 and l_2 b. l_1 and l_3
c. l_1 and l_4 d. All of these

13 The value of $\lim_{x \to \infty} \frac{\cot^{-1}(\sqrt{x+1} - \sqrt{x})}{\sec^{-1}\left[\left(\frac{2x-1}{x-1}\right)^x\right]}$ is

a. 1 b. 0
c. $\frac{\pi}{2}$ d. non-existent

14 The value of $\lim_{n \to \infty} \cos(\pi\sqrt{n^2 + n})$, when n is an integer, is

a. 1 b. −1
c. 0 d. does not exist

15 The value of $\lim_{x \to 0} (1 + \log^2_{\cos \frac{x}{2}} \cos x)^2$ is

a. 4 b. 9
c. 289 d. non-existent

16 The value of $\lim_{x \to 0} \frac{(\tan\{x\} - 1)\sin\{x\}}{\{x\}(\{x\} - 1)}$ (where, $\{x\}$ denotes the fractional part of x), is

a. 1 b. tan1
c. sin1 d. non-existent

17 The value of $\lim_{x \to 0^-} (\log\{x\} + |[x]|)^{\{x\}}$ is

a. 0 b. 1
c. $\log_e 2$ d. $\log_e\left(\frac{1}{2}\right)$

18 If $P_n = \prod_{k=1}^{n}\left(1 + \frac{2}{k^2 + 3k}\right)$, then $\lim_{n \to \infty} P_n$ is equal to

a. 1 b. 3
c. 5 d. 7

Working Space

19 For $n \in N$, let $a_n = \sum_{k=1}^{n} 2k$ and $b_n = \sum_{k=1}^{n} (2k-1)$. Then, $\lim_{n \to \infty} (\sqrt{a_n} - \sqrt{b_n})$ is equal to

a. 1 b. $\frac{1}{2}$

c. 0 d. 2

20 The value of $\lim_{x \to 0} (\sin^{-1}[\sin x] + \cos^{-1}[\cos x] - 2\tan^{-1}[\tan x])$ (where, [·] denotes greatest integer function), is

a. π b. $\frac{\pi}{2}$

c. $\frac{3\pi}{2}$ d. Does not exist

21 Let $l = \lim_{x \to 2} \frac{[x]}{\{x\}}$ and $m = \lim_{x \to 2} \frac{\{x\}}{[x]}$, where [·] and {·} denotes greatest integer function and fractional part of x, then

a. l exists but m does not
b. m exists but l does not
c. both l and m exist
d. neither l nor m exists

22 The value of $\lim_{n \to \infty} \sum_{r=1}^{n} \frac{r^2}{n^3 + n^2 + r}$ is

a. $\frac{1}{3}$ b. $\frac{1}{2}$

c. $\frac{2}{3}$ d. 1

23 Let $\lim_{x \to 0} \frac{[x]^2}{x} = l$ and $\lim_{x \to 0} \frac{[x^2]}{x^2} = m$ (where, [·] denotes greatest Integer function), then

a. l exists but m does not exist
b. m exists but l does not exist
c. l and m both exist
d. neither l nor m exists

One or More than One Options Correct Type

***Direction** (Q. Nos. 24-28) This section contains 5 multiple choice questions. Each question has four choices (a), (b), (c) and (d), out of which ONE or MORE THAN ONE are correct.*

24 Let $f(x) = x + \sqrt{x^2 + 2x}$ and $g(x) = \sqrt{x^2 + 2x} - x$, then

a. $\lim_{x \to \infty} g(x) = 1$ b. $\lim_{x \to \infty} f(x) = 1$

c. $\lim_{x \to -\infty} f(x) = -1$ d. $\lim_{x \to -\infty} g(x) = -1$

25 If $A = \lim_{x \to 0} \frac{\sin^{-1}(\sin x)}{\cos^{-1}(\cos x)}$ and $B = \lim_{x \to 0} \frac{[|x|]}{x}$ (where, [·] denotes greatest integer function), then

a. $A = 1$ b. A does not exist

c. $B = 0$ d. $B = 1$

26 Let $f(x) = \begin{cases} |x|, & -2 \le x \le 0 \\ e^x - 1, & 0 < x \le 5 \end{cases}$, $g(x) = \begin{cases} -x-1, & -1 \le x \le 0 \\ \frac{4x-3}{5}, & 0 < x \le 3 \end{cases}$, then

a. $\lim_{x \to 0^-} f[g(x)] = 1$

b. $\lim_{x \to 0^-} f[g(2^x)] = 1$

c. $\lim_{x \to 0^+} f[g(2^x)] = e^{1/5} - 1$

d. $\lim_{x \to 0^+} f[g(2^x)] = \lim_{x \to 0^-} f[g(2^x)]$

Working Space

27 The value(s) of n for which $\lim_{x \to 1} \frac{e^{x-1} - x}{(x-1)^n}$ exists is/are

a. 1 b. 2
c. 3 d. 4

28 Let $f : \left(-\frac{\pi}{2}, \frac{\pi}{2}\right) \to R$, $f(x) = \begin{cases} \lim_{n \to \infty} \left[\frac{(\tan x)^{2n} + x^2}{\sin^2 x + (\tan x)^{2n}}\right]; & x \neq 0 \\ 1; & x = 0 \end{cases}$

which of the following holds good?

a. $f\left(-\frac{\pi^-}{4}\right) = f\left(\frac{\pi^+}{4}\right)$ b. $f\left(-\frac{\pi^-}{4}\right) = f\left(-\frac{\pi^+}{4}\right)$
c. $f\left(\frac{\pi^-}{4}\right) = f\left(\frac{\pi^+}{4}\right)$ d. $f(0^+) = f(0) = f(0^-)$

Matching List Type

***Direction** (Q. Nos. 29 and 30) Choices for the correct combinations of elements from Column I and Column II are given as options (a), (b), (c) and (d), out of which one is correct.*

29 Match the Column I with Column II and mark the correct option from the codes given below.

	Column I		Column II
i.	$\lim_{x \to \infty} (\sqrt{x + \sqrt{x}} - \sqrt{x - \sqrt{x}})$ equals	p.	-2
ii.	$\lim_{x \to 0} \frac{\sin 2x - 2\tan x}{\log(1 + x^3)}$ equals	q.	-1
iii.	$\lim_{x \to 0^+} [\log \sin^3 x - \log(x^4 + ex^3)]$ equals	r.	0
iv.	Let $\tan(2\pi \lvert\sin\theta\rvert) = \cot(2\pi \lvert\cos\theta\rvert)$, where $\theta \in R$ and $f(x) = (\lvert\sin\theta\rvert + \lvert\cos\theta\rvert)^x$. The value of $\lim_{x \to \infty} \left[\frac{2}{f(x)}\right]$ (where, $[\cdot]$ denotes greatest integer function) equals	s.	1

Codes

	i	ii	iii	iv
a.	p	s	r	q
b.	s	p	q	r
c.	r	q	p	s
d.	q	r	s	p

30 Match the Column I with Column II and mark the correct option from the codes given below.

	Column I		Column II
i.	$\lim_{n \to \infty} \cos^2 [\pi \sqrt[3]{n^3 + n^2 + 2n})]$, ($n \in$ integer) is	p.	$\frac{1}{2}$
ii.	$\lim_{n \to \infty} n \sin(2\pi \sqrt{1 + n^2})$, ($n \in N$) is	q.	$\frac{1}{4}$
iii.	$\lim_{n \to \infty} (-1)^n \sin(\pi \sqrt{n^2 + 0.5n + 1}) \sin\left(\frac{(n+1)\pi}{4n}\right)$, ($n \in N$) is	r.	π
iv.	If $\lim_{x \to \infty} \left(\frac{x + a}{x - a}\right)^x = e$, where a is real constant, then value of a is	s.	non-existent

Codes

	i	ii	iii	iv
a.	q	r	p	p
b.	r	p	q	q
c.	s	r	q	p
d.	p	q	s	r

Comprehension Type

Working Space

***Direction** (Q. Nos. 31-33) This section contains a paragraph, which describing theory, experiments, data, etc. Three questions related to the paragraph have been given. Each question has only one correct answer among the four given options (a), (b), (c) and (d).*

Passage

Let $f(x)$ be a function continuous, $\forall x \in R$ except at $x = 0$. Such that $f'(x) < 0, \forall x \in (-\infty, 0)$ and $f'(x) > 0, \forall x \in (0, \infty)$. Let $\lim_{x \to 0^+} f(x) = 2$, $\lim_{x \to 0^-} f(x) = 3$ and $f(0) = 4$.

31 The value of λ for which $2\left[\lim_{x \to 0} f(x^3 - x^2)\right] = \lambda\left[\lim_{x \to 0} f(2x^4 - x^5)\right]$ is

a. $\frac{4}{3}$ b. 2
c. 3 d. 5

32 The value of $\lim_{x \to 0^+} \frac{f(-x) \cdot x^2}{\left\{\frac{1 - \cos x}{[x]}\right\}}$, where $[\cdot]$ denotes greatest integer function and $\{\cdot\}$ denotes fractional part function, is

a. 6 b. 12
c. 18 d. 24

33 The value of $\lim_{x \to 0^-} \left(\left[3f\left(\frac{x^3 - \sin^3 x}{x^4}\right)\right] - f\left[\frac{\sin x^3}{x}\right]\right)$, where $[\cdot]$ denotes greatest integer function, is

a. 3 b. 5
c. 7 d. 9

One Integer Value Correct Type

***Direction** (Q. Nos. 34-40) This section contains 7 questions. When worked out will result in an integer from 0 to 9 (both inclusive).*

34 Let $f(x)$ be a twice differentiable function and $f''(0) = 2$, then $\lim_{x \to 0} \frac{2f(x) - 3f(2x) + f(4x)}{x^2}$ is

35 The value of $\lim_{x \to 0} \frac{ex}{e - (1 + x)^{\frac{1}{x}}}$ is

36 Let $a_1, a_2, a_3, \ldots, a_n$ be sequence of real numbers with $a_{n+1} = a_n + \sqrt{1 + a_n^2}$ and $a_0 = 0$, if $\lim_{n \to \infty} \frac{a_n}{2^{n-1}}$ is $\frac{k}{\pi}$, then k is

37 Suppose $x_1 = \tan^{-1} 2 > x_2 > x_3 > \ldots$ are positive real numbers satisfying $\sin(x_{n+1} - x_n) + 2^{-(n+1)} \cdot \sin x_n \cdot \sin x_{n+1} = 0$ for $n > 1$ and $l = \lim_{n \to \infty} x_n$. Then, the value of $[4l]$ (where, $[\cdot]$ denotes the greatest integer function), is

38 If $\lim_{n \to \infty} \sum_{r=1}^{n} \frac{kr}{1 \times 3 \times 5 \times 7 \times \cdots \times (2r + 1)} = 1$, then k^2 is equal to

39 If $a_1 = 1$ and $a_n = n(1 + a_{n-1}), \forall n \geq 2$, then $\lim_{n \to \infty} \left[\left(1 + \frac{1}{a_1}\right)\left(1 + \frac{1}{a_2}\right) \cdots \left(1 + \frac{1}{a_n}\right)\right] \cdot \frac{1}{e}$ is

40 The value of $\lim_{n \to \infty} \{(\sqrt{3} + 1)^{2n}\}$ (where, $[\cdot]$ denotes greatest integer function), is

JEE Main & AIEEE Archive

(Compilation of Last 13 Years' Questions)

1 $\lim_{x \to 0} \frac{(1-\cos 2x)(3+\cos x)}{x \tan 4x}$ is equal to **(JEE Main 2015)**

a. 4 b. 3
c. 2 d. $\frac{1}{2}$

2 Let $f(x)$ be a polynomial of degree four having extreme value at $x = 1$ and $x = 2$. If $\lim_{x \to 0}\left[1+\frac{f(x)}{x^2}\right] = 3$, then $f(2)$ is equal to **(JEE Main 2015)**

a. -8 b. -4
c. 0 d. 4

3 $\lim_{x \to 0} \frac{\sin(\pi \cos^2 x)}{x^2}$ is equal to **(JEE Main 2014)**

a. $\frac{\pi}{2}$ b. 1
c. $-\pi$ d. π

4 $\lim_{x \to 0} \frac{(1-\cos 2x)(3+\cos x)}{x \tan 4x}$ is equal to **(JEE Main 2013)**

a. $-\frac{1}{4}$ b. $\frac{1}{2}$
c. 1 d. 2

5 $\lim_{x \to 2}\left(\frac{\sqrt{1-\{\cos 2(x-2)\}}}{x-2}\right)$ is equal to

a. $\sqrt{2}$ b. $-\sqrt{2}$ **(AIEEE 2011)**
c. $\frac{1}{\sqrt{2}}$ d. Does not exist

6 Let $f : R \to [0, \infty)$ be such that $\lim_{x \to 5} f(x)$ exists and $\lim_{x \to 5} \frac{[f(x)]^2 - 9}{\sqrt{|x-5|}} = 0$. Then, $\lim_{x \to 5} f(x)$ is equal to **(AIEEE 2011)**

a. 3 b. 0
c. 1 d. 2

7 If function $f(x)$ is differentiable at $x = a$, then $\lim_{x \to a} \frac{x^2 f(a) - a^2 f(x)}{x-a}$ is equal to **(AIEEE 2011)**

a. $2af(a) + a^2 f'(a)$
b. $-a^2 f'(a)$
c. $af(a) - a^2 f'(a)$
d. $2af(a) - a^2 f'(a)$

8 Let $f : R \to R$ be a positive increasing function with $\lim_{x \to \infty} \frac{f(3x)}{f(x)} = 1$. Then, $\lim_{x \to \infty} \frac{f(2x)}{f(x)}$ is equal to **(AIEEE 2010)**

a. 1 b. $\frac{2}{3}$
c. $\frac{3}{2}$ d. 3

9 If α and β are the distinct roots of $ax^2 + bx + c = 0$, then $\lim_{x \to \alpha} \frac{1-\cos(ax^2+bx+c)}{(x-\alpha)^2}$ is equal to **(AIEEE 2005)**

a. $\frac{1}{2}(\alpha-\beta)^2$ b. $-\frac{a^2}{2}(\alpha-\beta)^2$
c. 0 d. $\frac{a^2}{2}(\alpha-\beta)^2$

10 If $\lim_{x \to \infty}\left(1+\frac{a}{x}+\frac{b}{x^2}\right)^{2x} = e^2$, then the values of a and b are **(AIEEE 2004)**

a. $a \in R, b \in R$
b. $a = 1, b \in R$
c. $a \in R, b = 2$
d. $a = 1, b = 2$

11 $\lim_{x \to \frac{\pi}{2}} \frac{\left[1-\tan\left(\frac{x}{2}\right)\right](1-\sin x)}{\left[1+\tan\left(\frac{x}{2}\right)\right](\pi-2x)^3}$ is equal to **(AIEEE 2003)**

a. $\frac{1}{8}$ b. 0
c. $\frac{1}{32}$ d. ∞

12 If $\lim_{x \to 0} \frac{\log(3+x)-\log(3-x)}{x} = k$, then the value of k is **(AIEEE 2003)**

a. 0 b. $-1/3$
c. $2/3$ d. $-2/3$

13 $\lim_{x \to 0} \frac{\sqrt{1-\cos 2x}}{\sqrt{2}x}$ is equal to **(AIEEE 2002)**

a. λ b. -1
c. zero d. Does not exist

14 $\lim_{x \to \infty}\left(\frac{x^2+5x+3}{x^2+x+2}\right)^x$ is equal to **(AIEEE 2002)**

a. e^4 b. e^2
c. e^3 d. e

15 For $x \in R$, $\lim_{x \to \infty}\left(\frac{x-3}{x+2}\right)^x$ is equal to **(AIEEE 2002)**

a. e b. e^{-1}
c. e^{-5} d. e^5

16 Let $f(2) = 4$ and $f'(2) = 4$. Then, $\lim_{x \to 2} \frac{xf(2)-2f(x)}{x-2}$ is given by **(AIEEE 2002)**

a. 2 b. -2
c. -4 d. 3

JEE Advanced & IIT JEE Archive

(Compilation of Last 10 Years' Questions)

1 Let $f(x) = \sin\left[\frac{\pi}{6}\sin\left(\frac{\pi}{2}\sin x\right)\right]$ for all $x \in R$ and $g(x) = \frac{\pi}{2}\sin x$ for all $x \in R$. Let $(fog)(x)$ denotes $f[g(x)]$ and $(gof)(x)$ denotes $g[f(x)]$. Then, which of the following is (are) true? **(2015 Adv., One or More than One Options Correct Type)**

a. Range of f is $\left[-\frac{1}{2}, \frac{1}{2}\right]$

b. Range of fog is $\left[-\frac{1}{2}, \frac{1}{2}\right]$

c. $\lim_{x\to 0}\frac{f(x)}{g(x)} = \frac{\pi}{6}$

d. There is an $x \in R$ such that $(gof)(x) = 1$

2 Let m and n be two positive integers greater than 1. If $\lim_{\alpha\to 0}\left(\frac{e^{\cos(\alpha^n)} - e}{\alpha^m}\right) = -\left(\frac{e}{2}\right)$, then the value of $\frac{m}{n}$ is **(2015 Adv., Integer Type)**

3 The largest value of the non-negative integer a for which $\lim_{x\to 1}\left\{\frac{-ax + \sin(x-1) + a}{x + \sin(x-1) - 1}\right\}^{\frac{1-x}{1-\sqrt{x}}} = \frac{1}{4}$ is **(2014 Adv., Integer Type)**

4 Let $\alpha(a)$ and $\beta(a)$ be the roots of the equation $(\sqrt[3]{1+a} - 1)x^2 - (\sqrt{1+a} - 1)x + (\sqrt[6]{1+a} - 1) = 0$, where $a > -1$. Then, $\lim_{a\to 0^+}\alpha(a)$ and $\lim_{a\to 0^+}\beta(a)$ are **(2012, Only One Option Correct Type)**

a. $-\frac{5}{2}$ and 1 b. $-\frac{1}{2}$ and -1

c. $-\frac{7}{2}$ and 2 d. $-\frac{9}{2}$ and 3

5 If $\lim_{x\to\infty}\left(\frac{x^2 + x + 1}{x + 1} - ax - b\right) = 4$, then **(2012, Only One Option Correct Type)**

a. $a = 1, b = 4$ b. $a = 1, b = -4$

c. $a = 2, b = -3$ d. $a = 2, b = 3$

6 If $\lim_{x\to 0}[1 + x\log(1 + b^2)]^{\frac{1}{x}} = 2b\sin^2\theta$, $b > 0$ and $\theta \in (-\pi, \pi]$, then the value of θ is **(2011, Only One Option Correct Type)**

a. $\pm\frac{\pi}{4}$ b. $\pm\frac{\pi}{3}$

c. $\pm\frac{\pi}{6}$ d. $\pm\frac{\pi}{2}$

7 Let $p(x)$ be a polynomial of degree 4 having extremum at $x = 1, 2$ and $\lim_{x\to 0}\left(1 + \frac{p(x)}{x^2}\right) = 2$. Then, the value of $p(2)$ is **(2010, Integer Type)**

8 Let $L = \lim_{x\to 0}\frac{a - \sqrt{a^2 - x^2} - \frac{x^2}{4}}{x^4}$, $a > 0$. If L is finite, then **(2009, One or More than One Options Correct Type)**

a. $a = 2$ b. $a = 1$

c. $L = \frac{1}{64}$ d. $L = \frac{1}{32}$

JEE Archive

9 Let $g(x)=\dfrac{(x-1)^n}{\log\cos^m(x-1)}$; $0<x<2$, m and n are integers, $m\neq 0$, $n>0$ and let p be the left hand derivative of $|x-1|$ at $x=1$. If $\lim_{x\to 1^+} g(x)=p$, then

(2008, Only One Option Correct Type)

a. $n=1, m=1$
b. $n=1, m=-1$
c. $n=2, m=2$
d. $n>2, m=n$

10 $\lim_{x\to\frac{\pi}{4}} \dfrac{\int_2^{\sec^2 x} f(t)\,dt}{x^2-\frac{\pi^2}{16}}$ equals

(2007, Only One Option Correct Type)

a. $\frac{8}{\pi}f(2)$
b. $\frac{2}{\pi}f(2)$
c. $\frac{2}{\pi}f\left(\frac{1}{2}\right)$
d. $4f(2)$

11 For $x>0$, $\lim_{x\to 0}\left[(\sin x)^{1/x}+\left(\frac{1}{x}\right)^{\sin x}\right]$ is equal to

(2006, Only One Option Correct Type)

a. 0
b. -1
c. 1
d. 2

3. Continuity and Differentiability

DPP-1 Graphical Transformaton

Only One Option Correct Type

Working Space

Direction (*Q. Nos.* 1-15) *This section contains 15 multiple choice questions. Each question has four choices (a), (b), (c) and (d), out of which ONLY ONE is correct.*

1 The graph for $y = \log_{0.5}|x|$ is

a. 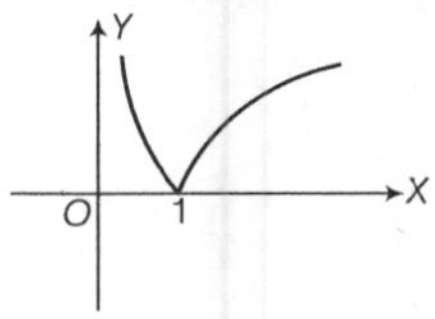

b. 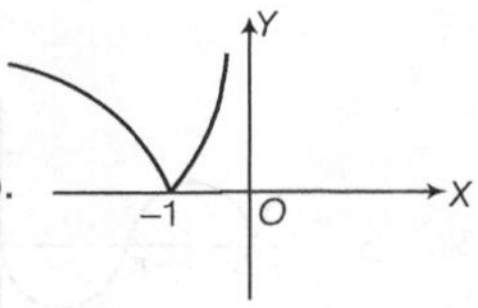

c. 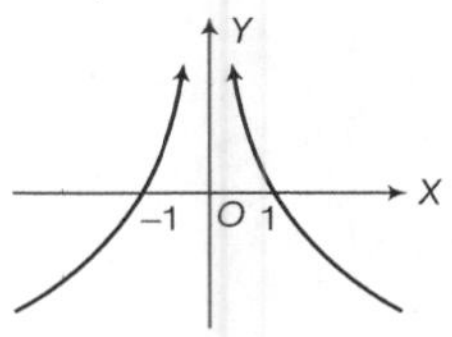

d. 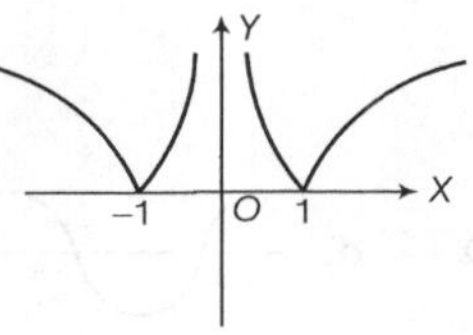

2 The graph for $y = |x - 2|$ is

a. 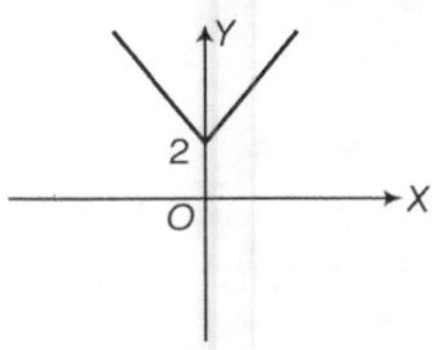

b. 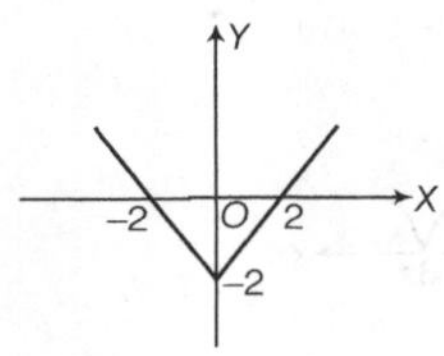

c. 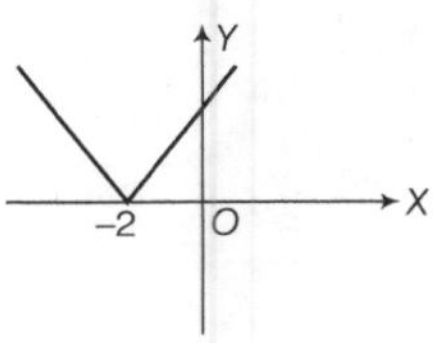

d. 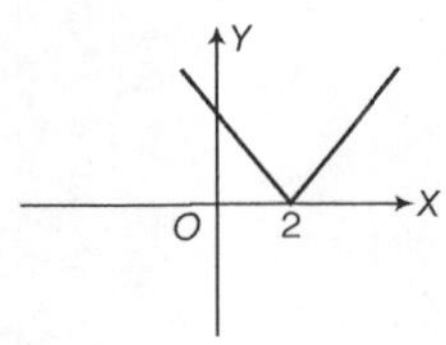

3 The graph for $y = |x + 2|$ is

a. 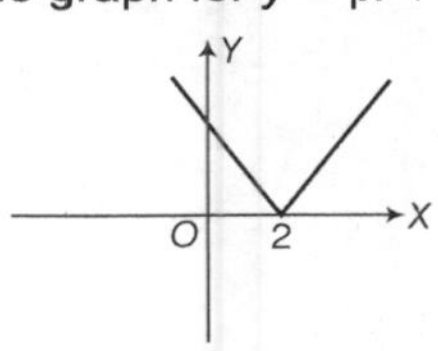

b. 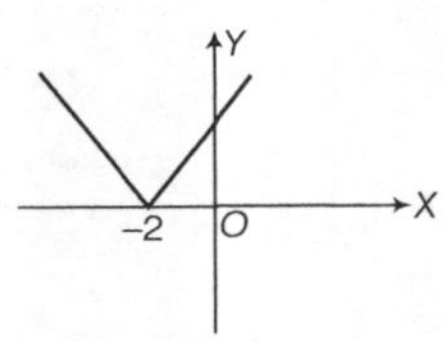

c. 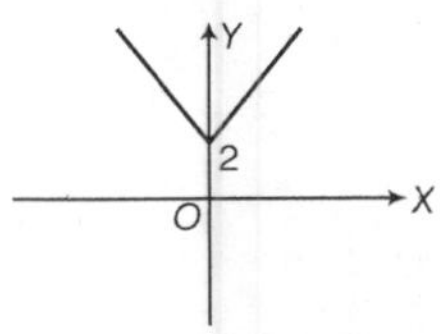

d. 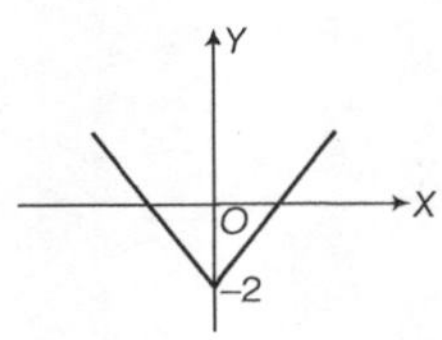

Working Space

4 The graph for $y = \left|\left|\frac{1}{x}\right| - 3\right|$ is

a. 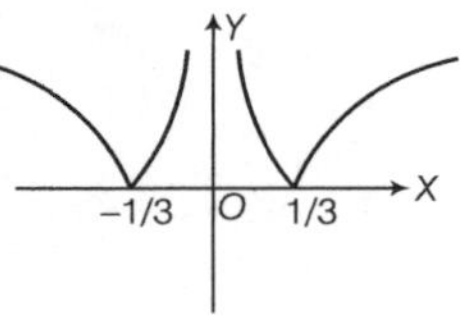

b. 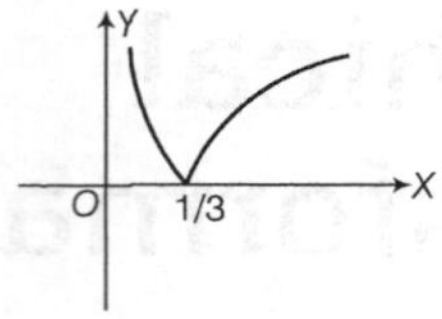

c. 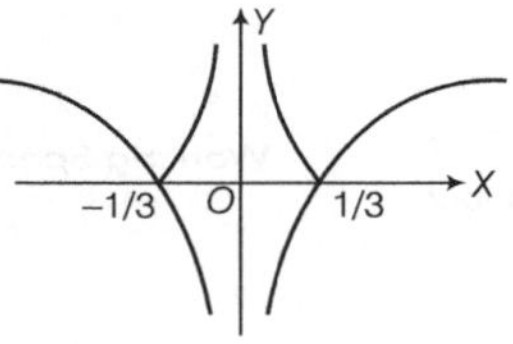

d. 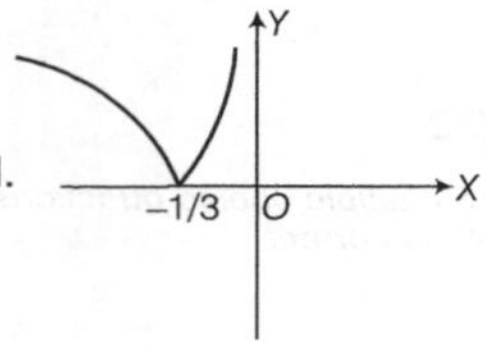

5 The graph for $y = \sin(|x|)$ is

a. 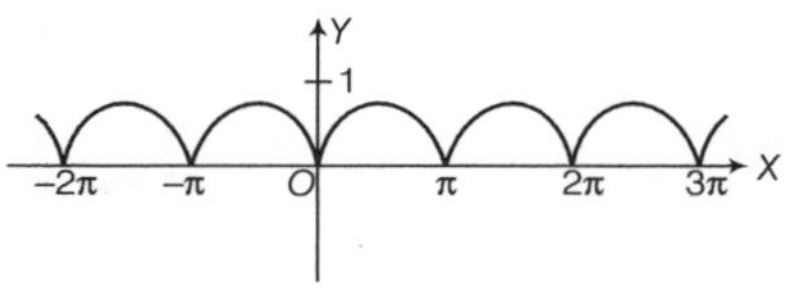

b. 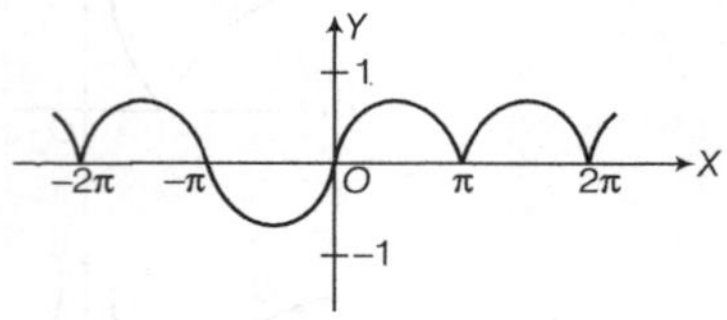

c. 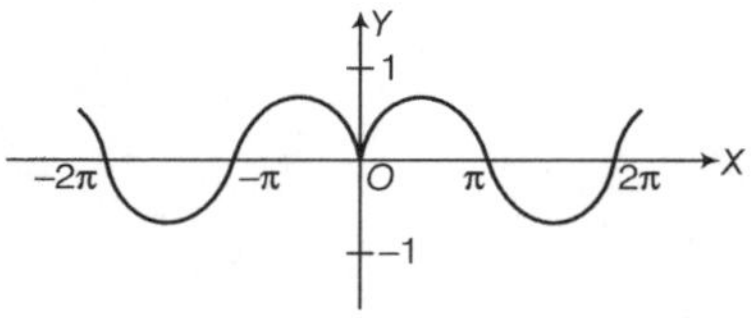

d. 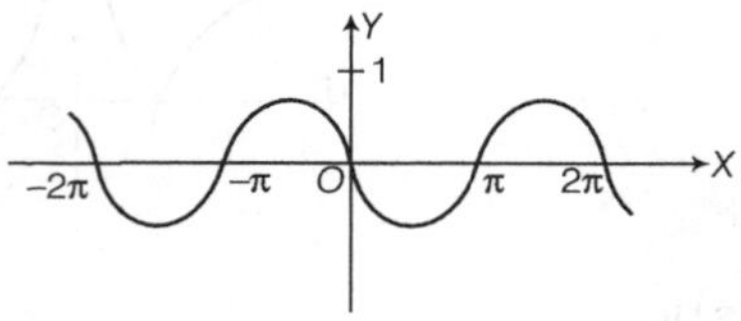

6 The graph for $y = |\sin x|$ is

a. 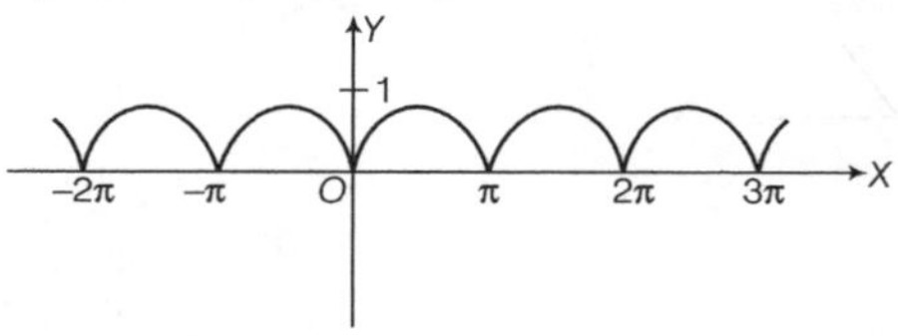

b. 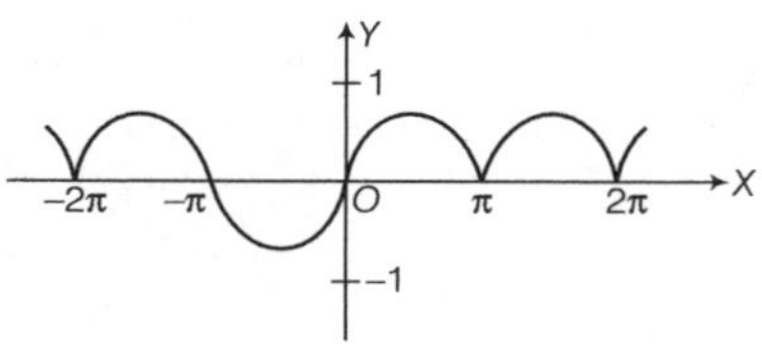

c. 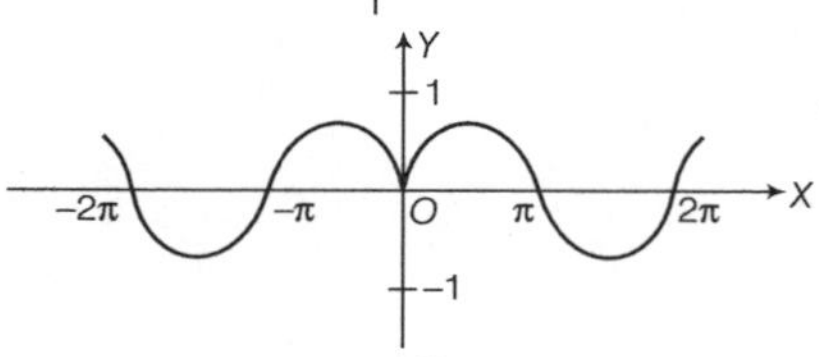

d. 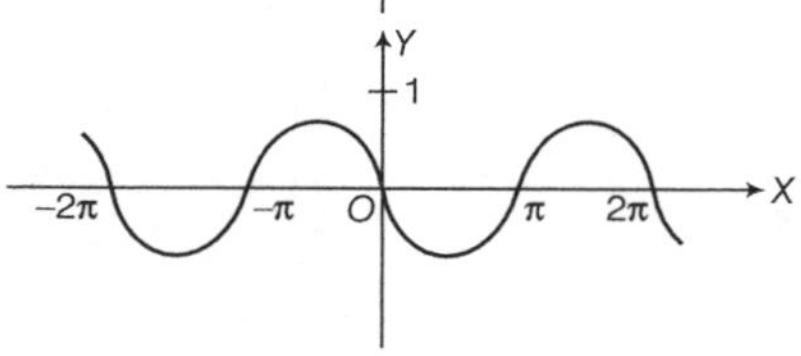

Working Space

7 The graph for $y = \left|\sin x + \frac{1}{2}\right|$ is

a. 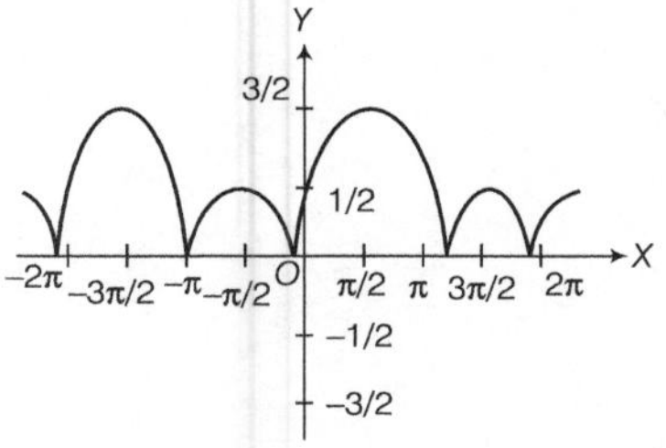

b. 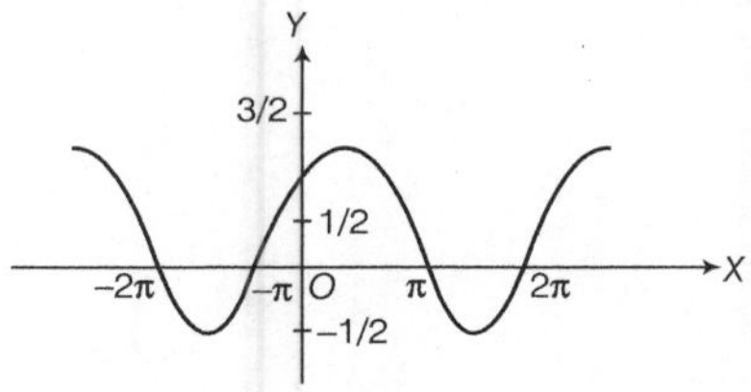

c. 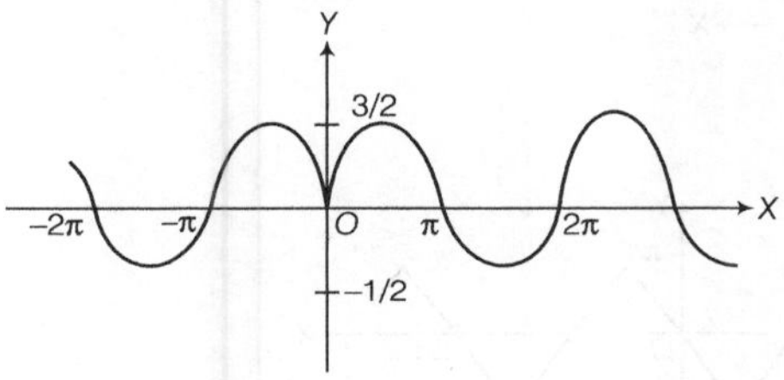

d. 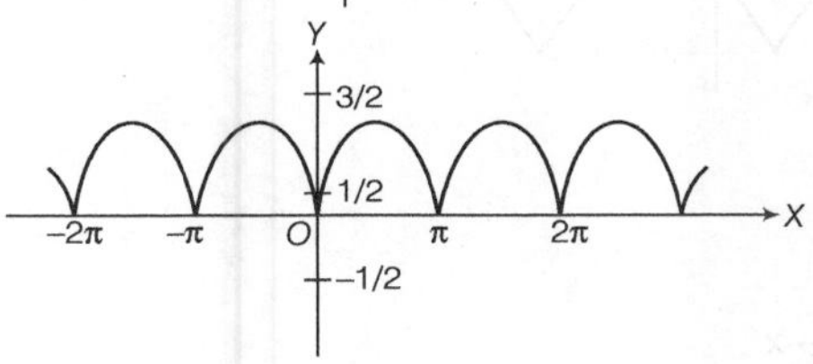

8 The graph for $y = 2^{\{x\}}$ is

a. 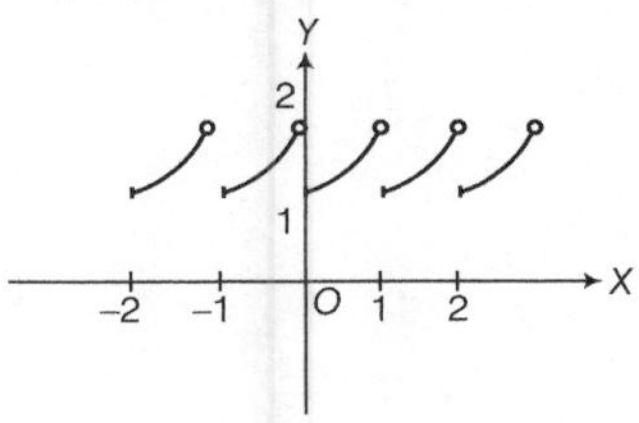

b. 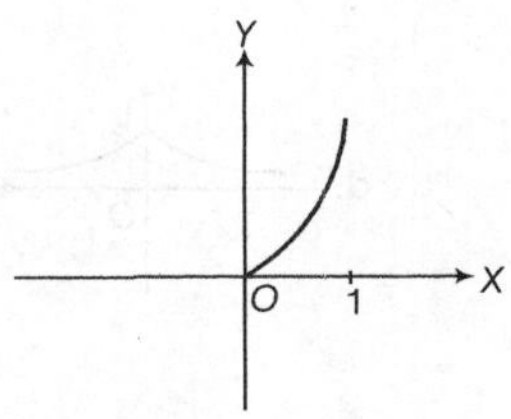

c. 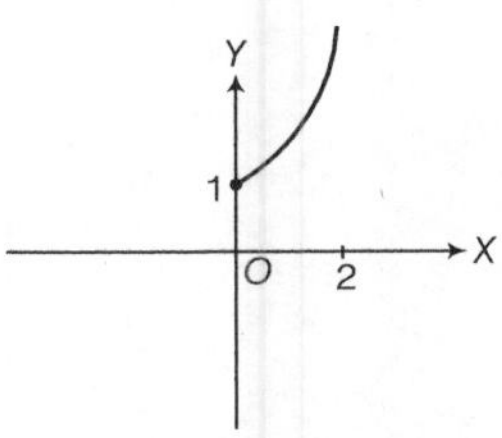

d. 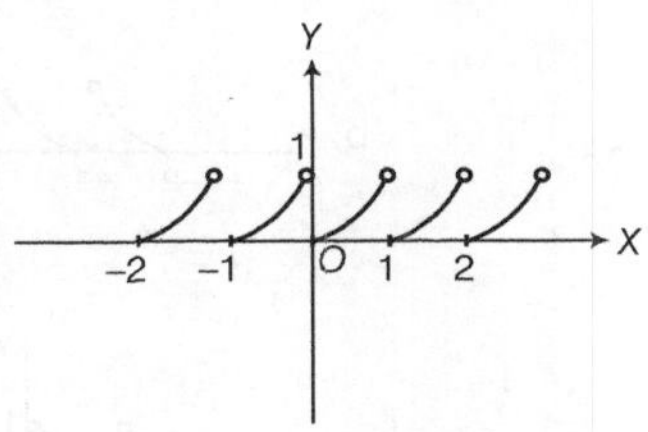

Working Space

9 The graph for $y = \sin^{-1} x$, where $-1 \le x \le 1$, is

a. 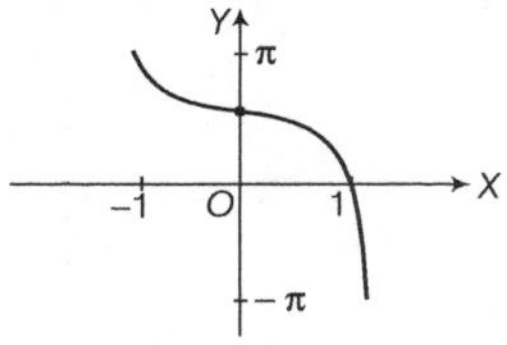

b. 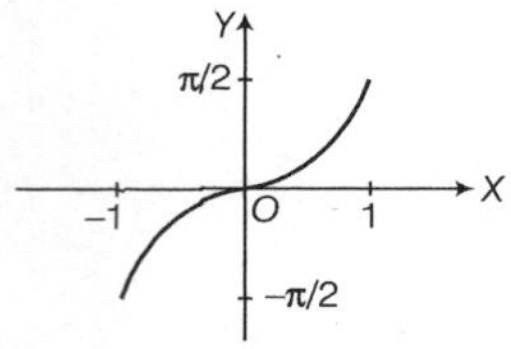

c. 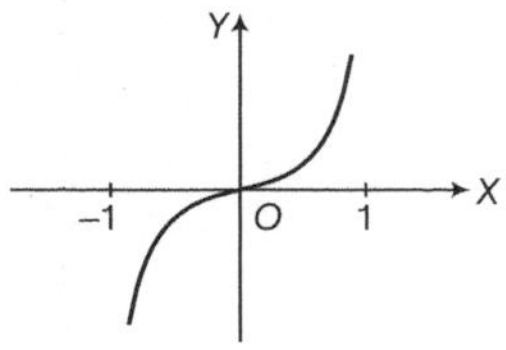

d. 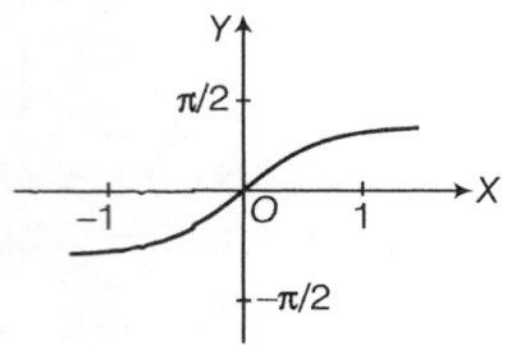

10 The graph for $y = \sin^{-1}(\sin x)$ is

a. 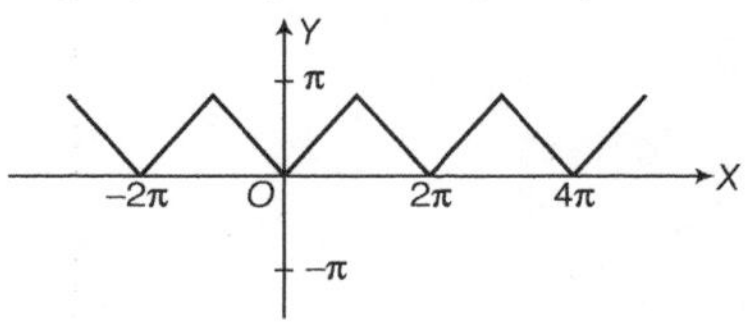

b. 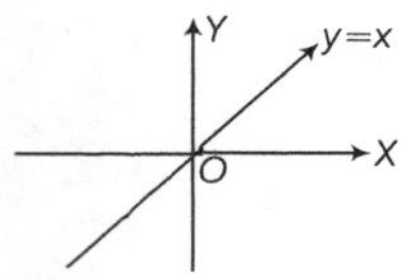

c. 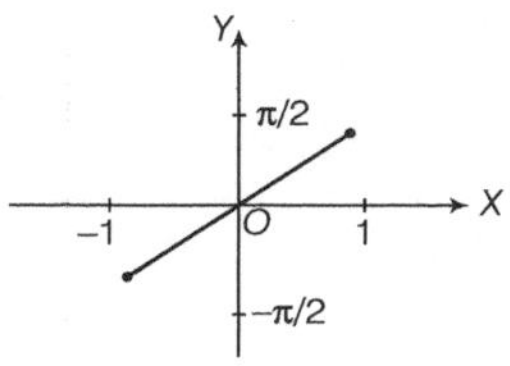

d. 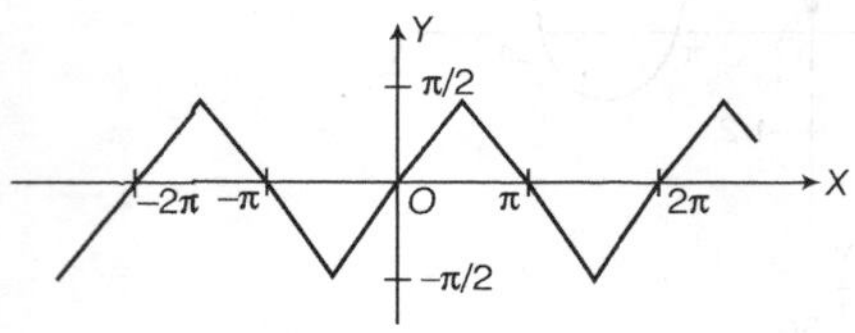

11 The graph for $y = 3^{-|x|}$ is

a. 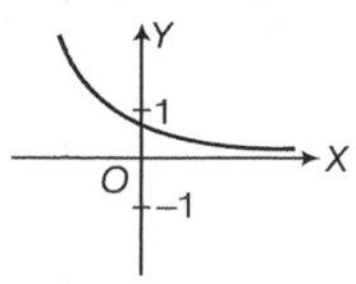

b. 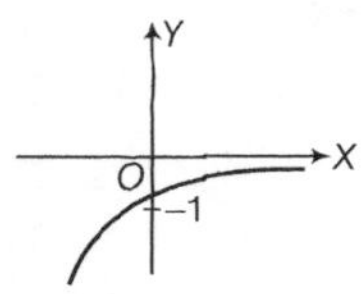

c. 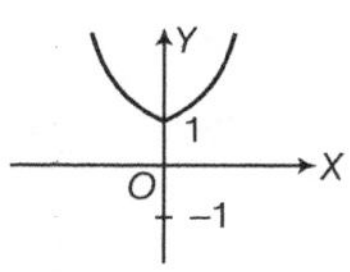

d. 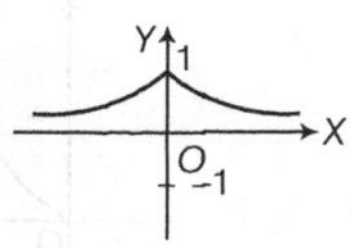

12 The graph for $y = \sqrt{x - [x]}$ is

a. 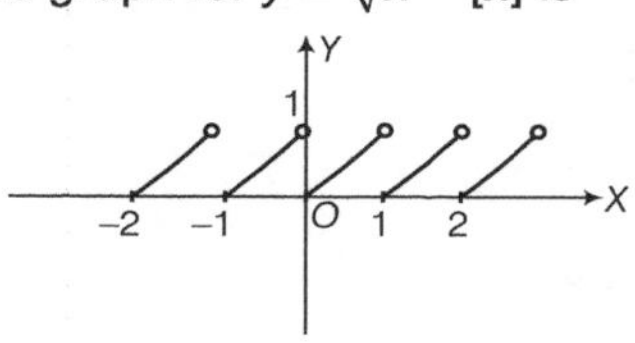

b. 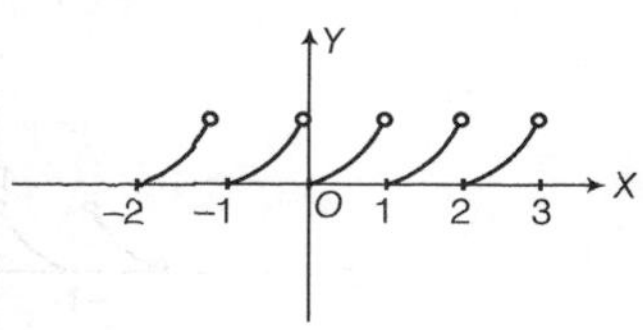

c. 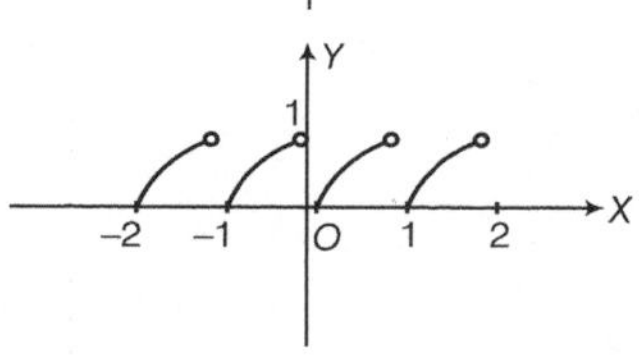

d. 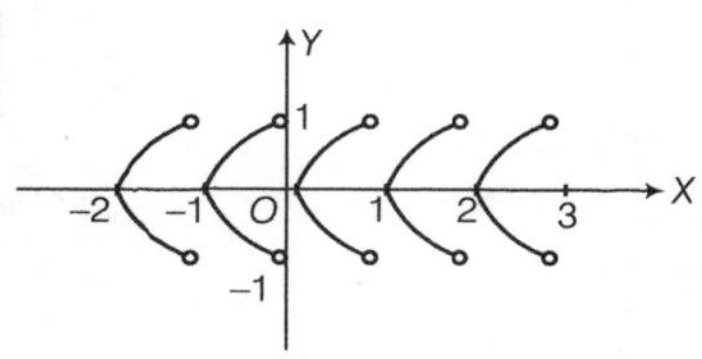

Working Space

13 The graph for $y = |[x] + \sqrt{x - [x]}|$ is

a. 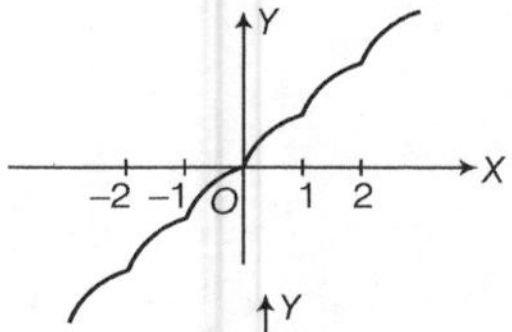

b. 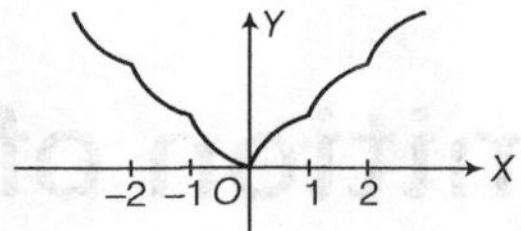

c. 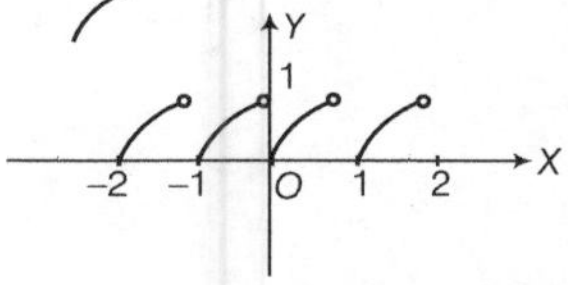

d. 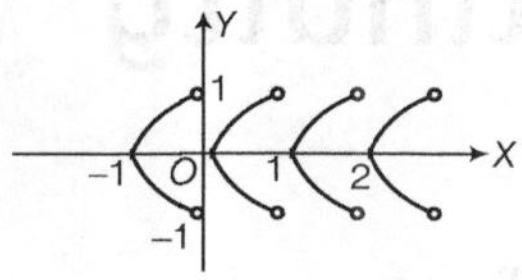

14 The graph for $y = |[x] + \sqrt{x - [x]}|$ is

a. 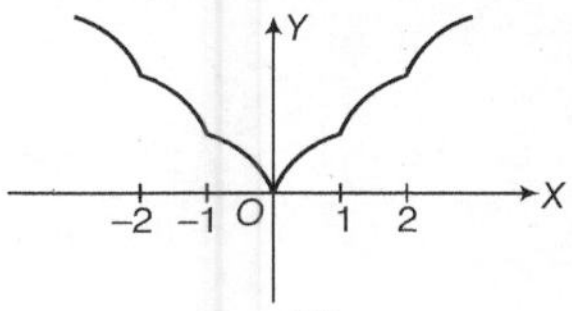

b. 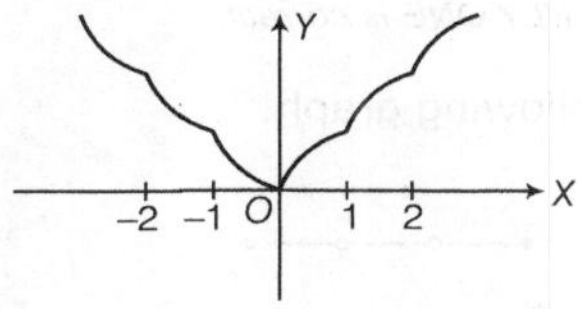

c. 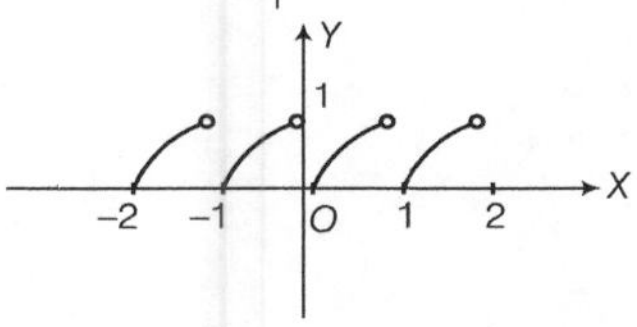

d. 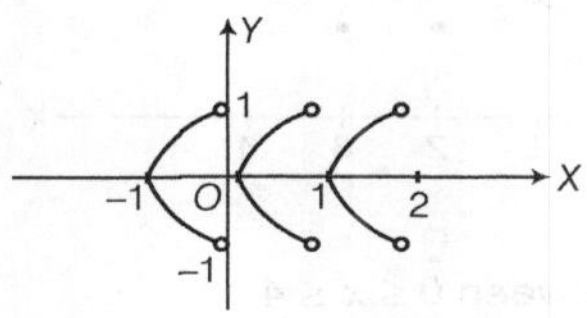

15 The graph for $y = [|x|]$ is

a. 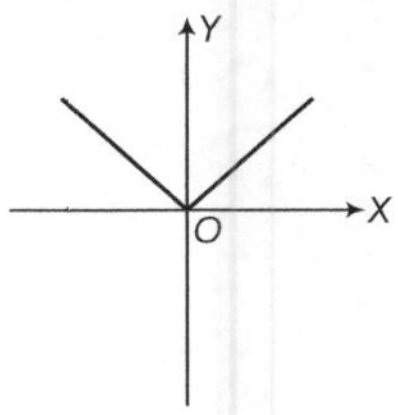

b. 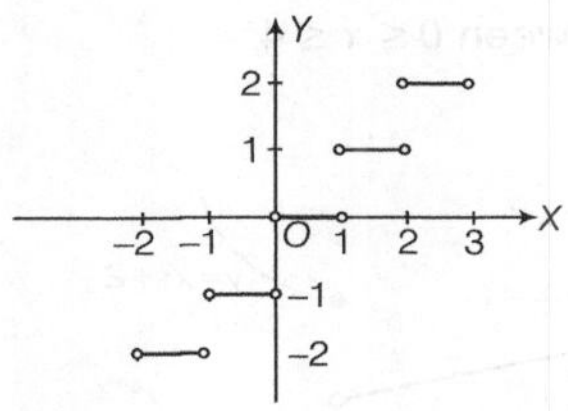

c. 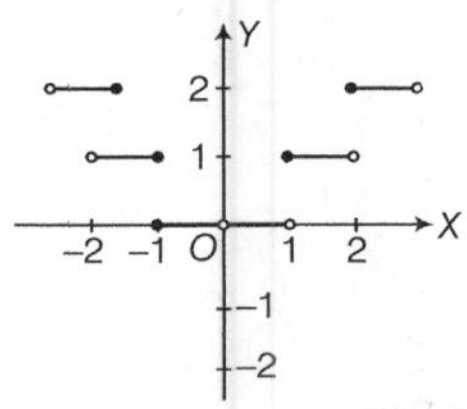

d. 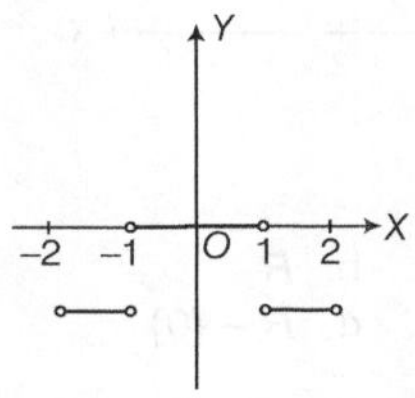

DPP-2 Definition of Continuity

Only One Option Correct Type

Working Space

Direction *(Q. Nos. 1-10) This section contains 10 multiple choice questions. Each question has four choices (a), (b), (c) and (d), out of which ONLY ONE is correct.*

1 Discuss the continuity of the following graph.

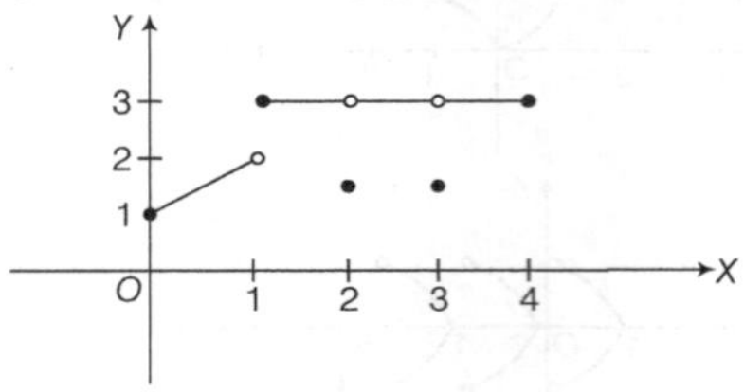

a. Discontinuous at 2 points between $0 \le x \le 4$
b. Discontinuous at 3 points between $0 \le x \le 4$
c. Discontinuous at 4 points between $0 \le x \le 4$
d. Discontinuous at 5 points between $0 \le x \le 4$

2 The function $f(x)$ is shown as

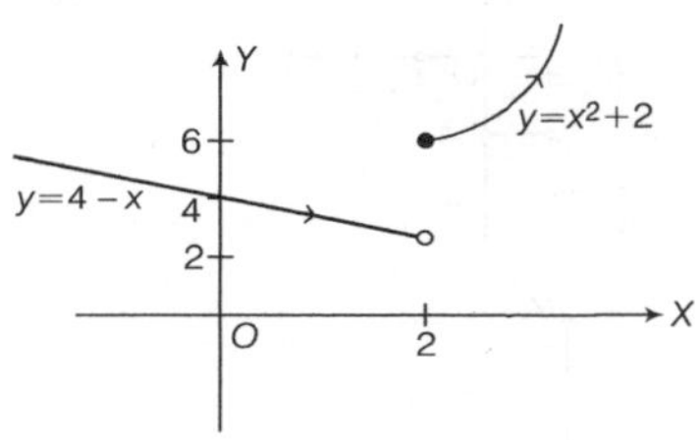

is continuous for x belongs to

a. $R - \{2\}$
b. R
c. $R - \{0, 2\}$
d. $R - \{0\}$

3 Which of the following statements is true for the function f defined for $-1 \le x \le 3$ in the figure shown below?

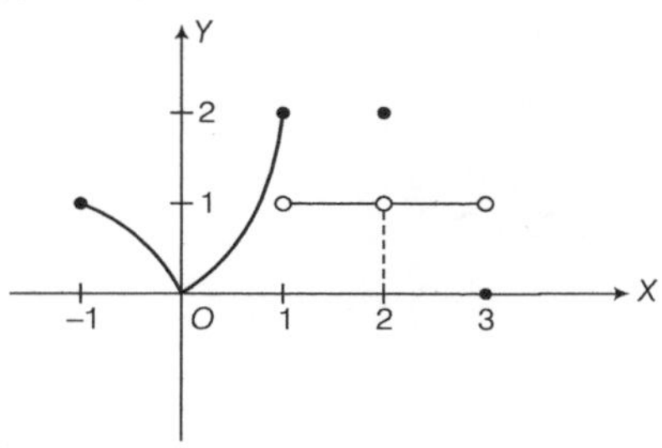

a. Discontinuous at $x = 0$
b. Continuous at $x = 1$
c. Discontinuous at $x = 2$
d. Continuous at $x = 3$

Working Space

4 The function $f(x) = [x] + [-x]$ is continuous for

a. $x \in R$
b. $x \in R - \{0\}$
c. $x \in R -$ Integer
d. $x \in [0, \infty)$

5 The function $y = \sqrt{x - [x]}$ is continuous for

a. $x \in R$
b. $x \in R - \{0\}$
c. $x \in R -$ Integer
d. $x \in [0, \infty)$

6 The function $y = [x] + \sqrt{x - [x]}$ is continuous for

a. $x \in R$
b. $x \in R - \{0\}$
c. $x \in R -$ Integer
d. $x \in [0, \infty)$

7 If $f(x) = \begin{cases} |x-1|, & x \geq 0 \\ -|x|, & x < 0 \end{cases}$, then $f(x)$ is continuous for

a. $x \in R$
b. $x \in R - \{1\}$
c. $x \in R - \{0\}$
d. None of these

8 If $f(x) = |[x] - 1|$, then $f(x)$ is continuous for

a. $x \in R$
b. $x \in R -$ Integer
c. $[0, \infty)$
d. $(-\infty, 0]$

9 If $f(x) = [\sin x]$, where $x \in [0, 2\pi]$, then $f(x)$ is discontinuous at x equals

a. $\{\pi/2, 3\pi/2\}$
b. $\{\pi/2, \pi, 2\pi\}$
c. $\{\pi, 2\pi\}$
d. $\{0, \pi/2, \pi, 2\pi\}$

10 If $f(x) = \min\{\tan x, \cot x\}$, then $f(x)$ is discontinuous at

a. $x \in n\pi$
b. $x \in \frac{n\pi}{2}$
c. $x \in (2n+1)\frac{\pi}{2}$
d. None of these

DPP-3 Continuity at a Point

Subjective Questions

Working Space

Direction (Q. Nos. 1-10) *These questions are subjective in nature, need to be solved completely on notebook.*

1 Find the value of k, so that the function $f(x) = \begin{cases} kx + 1, \text{if } x \le \pi \\ \cos x, \text{ if } x > \pi \end{cases}$ is continuous at $x = \pi$.

2 Show that the function $f(x) = \begin{cases} \dfrac{\sin x}{x} + \cos x, & x \ne 0 \\ 2, & x = 0 \end{cases}$ is continuous at $x = 0$.

3 Show that $f(x) = 2x - |x|$ is continuous at $x = 0$.

4 For what value of k, is the following function continuous at $x = 0$?

$$f(x) = \begin{cases} \dfrac{1 - \cos 4x}{8x^2}, & x \ne 0 \\ k, & x = 0 \end{cases}$$

5 Discuss the continuity of the function $f(x) = \begin{cases} x, & \text{if } 0 \le x < 1/2 \\ 1/2, & \text{if } x = 1/2 \\ 1 - x, & \text{if } x > 1/2 \end{cases}$ at $x = \dfrac{1}{2}$.

6 Examine the continuity of the function

$$f(x) = \begin{cases} \dfrac{|\sin x|}{x}, & x \ne 0 \\ 1, & x = 0 \end{cases} \text{ at } x = 0.$$

7 If the function $f(x) = \begin{cases} 3ax + b, & \text{if } x > 1 \\ 11, & \text{if } x = 1 \\ 5ax - 2b, & \text{if } x < 1 \end{cases}$ is continuous at $x = 1$, find the values of a and b.

8 Examine the continuity of the function

$$f(x) = \begin{cases} x \sin \dfrac{1}{x}, & x \ne 0 \\ 0, & x = 0 \end{cases} \text{ at } x = 0.$$

9 If $f(x)$ is continuous at $x = 0$, find the values of a, b and c, where

$$f(x) = \begin{cases} \dfrac{\sin(a + 1)x + \sin x}{x}, & \text{if } x < 0 \\ c, & \text{if } x = 0. \\ \dfrac{\sqrt{x + bx^2} - \sqrt{x}}{bx^{3/2}}, & \text{if } x > 0 \end{cases}$$

Working Space

10 If $f(x) = \{x\}$ and $g(x) = [x]$, (where, {} and [·] denote the fractional part and greatest integer function respectively), then discuss the continuity of

i. $h(x) = f(x) \cdot g(x)$ at $x = 1$
ii. $h(x) = f(x) + g(x)$ at $x = 1$
iii. $h(x) = f(x) - g(x)$ at $x = 1$

Only One Option Correct Type

Direction *(Q. Nos. 11-24) This section contains 14 multiple choice questions. Each question has four choices (a), (b), (c) and (d), out of which ONLY ONE is correct.*

11 If $f(x) \begin{cases} x + 2, & \text{when } x < 1 \\ 4x - 1, & \text{when } 1 \le x \le 3 \\ x^2 + 5, & \text{when } x > 3 \end{cases}$, then the correct statement is

a. $\lim_{x \to 1} f(x) = \lim_{x \to 3} f(x)$
b. $f(x)$ is continuous at $x = 3$
c. $f(x)$ is continuous at $x = 1$
d. $f(x)$ is continuous at $x = 1$ and 3

12 If $f(x) = \begin{cases} \dfrac{1}{e^{4x} + 1}, & x \neq 0 \\ 0, & x = 0 \end{cases}$, then

a. $\lim_{x \to 0^+} f(x) = 1$
b. $\lim_{x \to 0^-} f(x) = 0$
c. $f(x)$ is discontinuous at $x = 0$
d. $f(x)$ is continuous at $x = 0$

13 If $f(x) = \begin{cases} \dfrac{x^2 - (a + 2)x + 2a}{x - 2}, & x \neq 2 \\ 2, & x = 2 \end{cases}$ is continuous at $x = 2$, then a is equal to

a. 0
b. 1
c. −1
d. 2

14 If $f(x) = \begin{cases} \dfrac{\log(1 + 2ax) - \log(1 - bx)}{x}, & x \neq 0 \\ k, & x = 0 \end{cases}$ is continuous at $x = 0$, then k is equal to

a. $2a + b$
b. $2a - b$
c. $b - 2a$
d. $a + b$

15 If $f(x) = \begin{cases} [x] + [-x], & x \neq 2 \\ \lambda \quad , & x = 2 \end{cases}$ (where, [·] denotes greatest integer function), f is continuous at $x = 2$, then λ is equal to

a. −1
b. 0
c. 1
d. 2

16 If $f(x) = \begin{cases} \dfrac{1 - \cos 4x}{x^2}, & x < 0 \\ a, & x = 0 \\ \dfrac{\sqrt{x}}{\sqrt{16 + \sqrt{x}} - 4}, & x > 0 \end{cases}$, then the correct statement is

a. $f(x)$ is continuous at $x = 0$ and the value of $a = 8$
b. $f(x)$ is continuous at $x = 0$ and the value of $a = 6$
c. $f(x)$ is discontinuous at $x = 0$ and the value of $a = 4$
d. $f(x)$ is continuous at $x = 0$ and the value of $a = 2$

Working Space

17 The function $f(x)=\dfrac{1}{\log|x|}$ is discontinuous at

a. one point
b. two points
c. three points
d. infinite number of points

18 Which of the following functions has finite number of points of discontinuity in R (where, [·] denotes greatest integer)?

a. $\tan x$
b. $\dfrac{|x|}{x}$
c. $x+[x]$
d. $\sin[\pi x]$

19 If $f(x)=\dfrac{1-\tan x}{4x-\pi}$, $x\neq\dfrac{\pi}{4}$, $x\in\left[0,\dfrac{\pi}{2}\right)$ is a continuous function, then $f\left(\dfrac{\pi}{4}\right)$ is equal to **[AIEEE 2004]**

a. $-\dfrac{1}{2}$
b. $\dfrac{1}{2}$
c. 1
d. -1

20 The value of $f(0)$, so that $f(x)=\dfrac{\sqrt{a^2-ax+x^2}-\sqrt{a^2+ax+x^2}}{\sqrt{a+x}-\sqrt{a-x}}$ becomes continuous for all x, is given by

a. $a\sqrt{a}$
b. $-\sqrt{a}$
c. $\sqrt{a}$
d. $-a\sqrt{a}$

21 If $f(x)=\dfrac{x-e^x+\cos 2x}{x^2}$, where $x\neq 0$, is continuous at $x=0$, then (where, {} and $[x]$ denote the fractional part and greatest integer)

a. $f(0)=\dfrac{5}{2}$
b. $[f(0)]=-2$
c. $\{f(0)\}=-0.5$
d. $[f(0)]\cdot\{f(x)\}=-1.5$

22 Let $f(x)=\dfrac{x(1+a\cos x)-b\sin x}{x^3}$, $x\neq 0$ and $f(0)=1$. The values of a and b, so that f is continuous function, are

a. 5/2, 3/2
b. 5/2, – 3/2
c. –5/2, – 3/2
d. None of these

23 The function $f:R-\{0\}\to R$ given by $f(x)=\dfrac{1}{x}-\dfrac{2}{e^{2x}-1}$ can be made continuous at $x=0$ defining $f(0)$ as **[AIEEE 2007]**

a. 2
b. -1
c. 0
d. 1

24 The value of p and q for which the function **[AIEEE 2011]**

$$f(x)=\begin{cases}\dfrac{\sin(p+1)x+\sin x}{x}, & x<0\\ q, & x=0\\ \dfrac{\sqrt{x+x^2}-\sqrt{x}}{x^{3/2}}, & x>0\end{cases}$$

is continuous for all x in R, are

a. $p=-3/2, q=1/2$
b. $p=1/2, q=3/2$
c. $p=1/2, q=-3/2$
d. $p=5/2, q=1/2$

Working Space

One or More than One Options Correct Type

Direction (Q. Nos. 25-27) This section contains 3 multiple choice questions. Each question has four choices (a), (b), (c) and (d), out of which ONE or MORE THAN ONE are correct.

25 The value(s) of x for which $f(x) = \dfrac{e^{\sin x}}{4 - \sqrt{x^2 - 9}}$ is continuous, is (are)

a. 3
b. –3
c. 5
d. all $x \in (-\infty, -3] \cup [3, \infty)$

26 Which of the following functions not defined at $x = 0$ has/have removable discontinuity at the origin?

a. $f(x) = \dfrac{1}{1 + 2^{\cot x}}$

b. $f(x) = \cos\left(\dfrac{|\sin x|}{x}\right)$

c. $f(x) = x \sin \dfrac{\pi}{x}$

d. $f(x) = \dfrac{1}{\log|x|}$

27 Let $f(x) = [x]$ and $g(x) = \begin{cases} 0, & x \in Z \\ x^2, & x \in R - Z \end{cases}$, then (where, [·] denotes greatest integer function)

a. $\lim_{x \to 1} g(x)$ exists but $g(x)$ is not continuous at $x = 1$
b. $\lim_{x \to 1} f(x)$ does not exist and $f(x)$ is not continuous at $x = 1$
c. $g(x)$ is continuous at $x = 0$
d. $g(x)$ is discontinuous at $x = 0$

Statement Type

Direction (Q. Nos. 28-31) This section is based on Statement I and Statement II. Select the correct answer from the codes given below.

a. Both Statement I and Statement II are correct and Statement II is the correct explanation of Statement I
b. Both Statement I and Statement II are correct and Statement II is not the correct explanation of Statement I
c. Statement I is correct but Statement II is incorrect
d. Statement II is correct but Statement I is incorrect

28 **Statement I** $f(x) = \sin x + [x]$ is discontinuous at $x = 0$.

Statement II If $g(x)$ is continuous and $h(x)$ is discontinuous at $x = a$, then $g(x) + h(x)$ will necessarily be discontinuous at $x = a$.

29 Consider $f(x) = \begin{cases} 2\sin(a\cos^{-1} x), & \text{if } x \in (0, 1) \\ \sqrt{3}, & \text{if } x = 0 \\ ax + b, & \text{if } x < 0 \end{cases}$

Statement I If $b = \sqrt{3}$ and $a = 2/3$, then $f(x)$ is continuous in $(-\infty, 1)$.

Statement II If a function is defined on an interval I and limit exists at every point of interval I, then function is continuous in I.

Working Space

30 Let $f(x) = \begin{cases} \dfrac{\cos x - e^{-x^2/2}}{x^3}, & x \neq 0 \\ 0, & x = 0 \end{cases}$, then

Statement I $f(x)$ is continuous at $x = 0$.

Statement II $\lim_{x \to 0} \dfrac{\cos x - e^{-x^2/2}}{x^3} = -1/12$

31 Let $f(x) = \begin{cases} Ax - B, & x \leq -1 \\ 2x^2 + 3xA + B, & x \in (-1, 1] \\ 4, & x > 1 \end{cases}$

Statement I $f(x)$ is continuous at all x, if $A = 3/4$, $B = -1/4$.

Statement II Polynomial function is always continuous.

Comprehension Type

Direction *(Q. Nos. 32-34) This section contains a paragraph, describing theory, experiments, data, etc. Three questions related to the paragraph have been given. Each question has only one correct answer among the four given options (a), (b), (c) and (d).*

Passage

If $S_n = \dfrac{x}{x+1} + \dfrac{x^2}{(x+1)(x^2+1)} + \cdots + \dfrac{x^{2^n}}{(x+1)(x^2+1)\cdots(x^{2^n}+1)}$, $x > 1$ and $\lim_{n \to \infty} S_n = L$.

$$g(x) = \begin{cases} \dfrac{\sqrt{ax+b} - 1}{x}, & x \neq 0 \\ 1, & x = 0 \end{cases}$$

$h: R \to R$, $h(x) = x^9 - 6x^8 - 2x^7 + 12x^6 + x^4 - 7x^3 + 6x^2 + x - 7$.

32 If $g(x)$ is continuous at $x = 0$, then $(a + b)$ is equal to

a. 0
b. 1
c. 2
d. 3

33 If $g(x)$ is continuous at $x = 0$, then the value of $g'(0)$ is

a. L
b. $\dfrac{h(6)}{2}$
c. $a - 2b$
d. Does not exist

34 Identify the incorrect option.

a. $h(x)$ is surjective
b. Domain of $g(x) \in [-1/2, \infty)$
c. $h(x)$ is bounded
d. $L = 1$

DPP-4 Continuity for Composition of Functions

Subjective Questions

Working Space

Direction (Q. Nos. 1-5) *These questions are subjective in nature, need to be solved completely on notebook.*

1 Find the interval for which the function given by the following expressions are continuous.

i. $f(x)=\dfrac{3x+7}{x^2-5x+6}$ ii. $f(x)=\dfrac{1}{|x|-1}-\dfrac{x^2}{2}$

iii. $f(x)=\dfrac{\sqrt{x^2+1}}{1+\sin^2 x}$ iv. $f(x)=\tan\left(\dfrac{\pi x}{2}\right)$

2 If $f(x) = x + \{-x\} + [x]$, where [·] and {} denote the fractional part and greatest integer function. Discuss the continuity of f in $[-2, 2]$.

3 If $f(x)=\dfrac{x^2+1}{x^2-1}$ and $g(x) = \tan x$, then discuss the continuity of $(fog)(x)$.

4 Let $f(x)=\begin{cases}1+x, & 0\le x\le 2\\ 3-x, & 2<x\le 3\end{cases}$. Determine the composite function $g(x) = f[f(x)]$ and hence the point of discontinuity of g, if any.

5 Find the point of discontinuity of $y = f(u)$, where $f(u)=\dfrac{3}{2u^2+5u-3}$ and $u=\dfrac{1}{x+2}$.

Only One Option Correct Type

Direction (Q. Nos. 6-14) *This section contains 9 multiple choice questions. Each question has four choices (a), (b), (c) and (d), out of which ONLY ONE is correct.*

6 The function $f(x)=\dfrac{4-x^2}{4x-x^3}$ is

a. discontinuous at only one point in its domain
b. discontinuous at two points in its domain
c. discontinuous at three points in its domain
d. continuous everywhere in its domain

7 If $f(x)=\begin{cases}-4\sin x+\cos x, & \text{for } x\le -\pi/2\\ a\sin x+b, & \text{for } -\pi/2<x<\pi/2\\ \cos x+2, & \text{for } \pi/2\le x\end{cases}$ is continuous for all x, then the values of a and b are

a. −1, 3 b. 1, − 3
c. 1, 3 d. −1, − 3

Working Space

8 In [1, 3], the function $[x^2 + 1]$, [·] denote the greatest integer function, is continuous

a. for all x
b. for all x except at nine points
c. for all x except at seven points
d. for all x except at eight points

9 The number of points of discontinuity of $f(x) = [2x^3 - 5]$ in [1, 2) is equal to (where, [·] denotes greatest integer function)

a. 14
b. 13
c. 10
d. 8

10 Given, $f(x) = \begin{cases} |x+1|, & \text{if } x < -2 \\ 2x + 3, & \text{if } -2 \le x < 0 \\ x^2 + 3, & \text{if } 0 \le x < 3 \\ x^3 - 15, & \text{if } 3 \le x \end{cases}$, then the number of points of discontinuity of $f(x)$ is

a. 0
b. 1
c. 2
d. 3

11 Let $f : R \to R$ be a continuos function, $\forall\, x \in R$ and $f(x) = 5$, $\forall x \in$ irrational. Then, the value of $f(3)$ is

a. 1
b. 2
c. 5
d. Cannot be determined

12 Let $f(x)$ be a continuous function which satisfies $f(x^2 + 1) = \dfrac{x^2}{f(2^x) - 1}$ and $f(x) > 0$ for all $x \in R$, then $\lim\limits_{x \to 1} f(x)$ is equal to

a. 2
b. 4
c. 1
d. Does not exist

13 If $f(x) = \dfrac{1}{(x+1)(x-2)}$ and $g(x) = \dfrac{1}{x^2}$, then the points of discontinuity of $f[g(x)]$ are

a. $\left\{-1, 0, 1, \dfrac{1}{\sqrt{2}}\right\}$
b. $\left\{-\dfrac{1}{2}, -1, 0, 1, \dfrac{1}{\sqrt{2}}\right\}$
c. $\{0, 1\}$
d. $\left\{0, 1, \dfrac{1}{\sqrt{2}}\right\}$

14 Let function f be defined as $f : R^+ \to R^+$ and function g is defined as $g : R^+ \to R^+$. Functions f and g are continuous in their domain. Suppose, the function $h(x) = \lim\limits_{n \to \infty} \dfrac{x^n f(x) + x^2}{x^n + g(x)}$, $x > 0$. If $h(x)$ is continuous in its domain, then $f(1) \cdot g(1)$ is equal to

a. 2
b. 1
c. 1/2
d. 0

One or More than One Options Correct Type

Direction (Q. Nos. 15-19) *This section contains 5 multiple choice questions. Each question has four choices (a), (b), (c) and (d), out of which ONE or MORE THAN ONE are correct.*

15 $f(x)$ is continuous at $x = 0$, then which of the following are always true?

a. $\lim\limits_{x \to 0} f(x) = 0$
b. $f(x)$ is continuous at $x = 1$
c. $g(x) = x^2 f(x)$ is continuous at $x = 0$
d. $\lim\limits_{x \to 0^+} [f(x) - f(0)] = 0$

Working Space

16 Indicate all correct alternatives, if $f(x) = \frac{x}{2} - 1$, then on the interval $[0, \pi]$.

a. $\tan[f(x)]$ and $\frac{1}{f(x)}$ are both continuous

b. $\tan[f(x)]$ and $\frac{1}{f(x)}$ are both discontinuous

c. $\tan[f(x)]$ and $f^{-1}(x)$ are both continuous

d. $\tan[f(x)]$ is continuous but $\frac{1}{f(x)}$ is not continuous

17 If $f(x) = \frac{2\cos x - \sin 2x}{(\pi - 2x)^2}$, $g(x) = \frac{e^{-\cos x} - 1}{8x - 4\pi}$ and $h(x) = \begin{cases} f(x), & x < \pi/2 \\ g(x), & x \geq \pi/2 \end{cases}$. Then, which of the following does not hold?

a. h is continuous at $x = \pi/2$

b. h has an irremovable discontinuity at $x = \pi/2$

c. h has a removable discontinuity at $x = \pi/2$

d. $f\left(\frac{\pi^+}{2}\right) = g\left(\frac{\pi^-}{2}\right)$

18 If $f(x) = \cos\left[\frac{\pi}{x}\right] \cdot \cos\left(\frac{\pi}{2}(x-1)\right)$, where [·] denotes greatest integer function. Then, $f(x)$ is continuous at

a. $x = 0$ b. $x = 1$ c. $x = 2$ d. None of these

19 Given, $f(x) = \begin{cases} b([x]^2 + [x]) + 1, & \text{for } x \geq -1 \\ \sin[\pi(x + a)], & \text{for } x < -1 \end{cases}$ (where, [·] denotes greatest integer function), then for what values of a and b, the function is continuous at $x = -1$?

a. $a = 2n + 3/2, b \in R; n \in I$ b. $a = 4n + 2, b \in R; n \in I$

c. $a = 4n + 3/2, b \in R^+; n \in I$ d. $a = 4n + 1, b \in R^+; n \in I$

Matching List Type

Direction (Q. No. 20) *Choices for the correct combination of elements from Column I and Column II are given as options (a), (b), (c) and (d), out of which one is correct.*

20 Match the Column I with Column II and mark the correct option from the codes given below.

	Column I		Column II
i.	If $f(x) = \begin{cases} \sin\{x\}, & x < 1 \\ \cos x + a, & x \geq 1 \end{cases}$ (where, {·} denotes fractional part) such that $f(x)$ is continuous at $x = 1$. If $\lvert k \rvert = \frac{a}{\sqrt{2}\sin\frac{(4-\pi)}{4}}$, then k is equal to	p.	1
ii.	If the function $f(x) = \frac{1 - \cos(\sin x)}{x^2}$ is continuous at $x = 0$, then $f(0)$ is equal to	q.	0
iii.	If $f(x) = \begin{cases} x, & x \in Q \\ 1 - x, & x \notin Q \end{cases}$, then the values of x at which $f(x)$ is continuous, is	r.	−1
		s.	1/2

Codes

	i	ii	iii		i	ii	iii
a.	p,r	s	s	b.	p	r,s	q
c.	r	p	q	d.	p	q	r

Comprehension Type

Direction (Q. Nos. 21-23) This section contains a paragraph, describing theory, experiments, data, etc. Three questions related to the paragraph have been given. Each question has only one correct answer among the four given options (a), (b), (c) and (d).

Passage

A man leaves his home early in the morning to have a walk. He arrives at a junction of road *A* and road *B* as shown in figure given below. He takes the following steps in later journey.

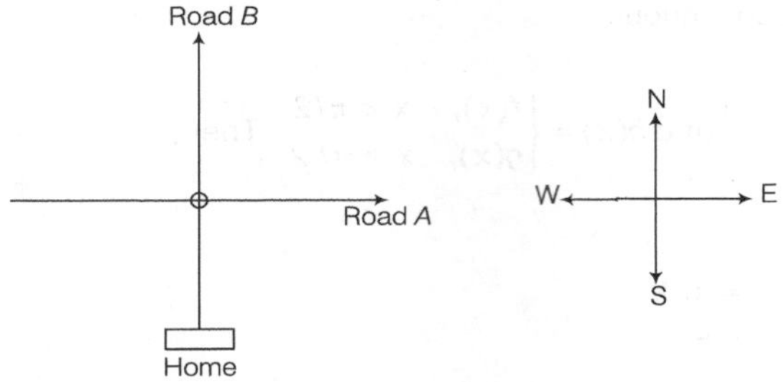

i. 1 km in North direction.
ii. Changes direction and moves in North-East direction for $2\sqrt{2}$ km.
iii. Changes direction and moves Southwards for distance of 2 km.
iv. Finally he changes the direction and moves in South-East direction and moves in South-East direction to reach road *A* again.

Visible/Invisible path The path traced by the man in the direction parallel to road *A* and road *B* is called invisible path, the remaining path traced is visible.

Visible points The points about which the man changes direction are called visible points except the point from where he changes direction last time. Now, if road *A* and road *B* are taken as *X*-axis and *Y*-axis, then visible path and visible points represent the graph of $y = f(x)$.

21 The value of x at which the function is discontinuous, is

a. 2 b. 0
c. 1 d. 3

22 The value of x at which $fof(x)$ is discontinuous, is

a. 0 b. 1
c. 2 d. 3

23 If $f(x)$ is periodic with period 3, then $f(19)$ is equal to

a. 2 b. 3
c. 19 d. None of these

One Integer Value Correct Type

Direction (Q. Nos. 24 and 25) This section contains 2 questions. When worked out will result in an integer from 0 to 9 (both inclusive).

24 The number of points, where $f(x) = [\sin x + \cos x]$ (where, [·] denotes greatest integer), $x \in (0, 2\pi)$ is not continuous, is

25 For the function $f(x) = \dfrac{1}{x + 2^{\frac{1}{x-2}}}$, $x \neq 2$, then the number of values of x at which $f(x)$ is discontinuous, is

DPP-5 Differentiability at a Point

Subjective Questions

Working Space

Direction *(Q. Nos. 1-5) These questions are subjective in nature, need to be solved completely on notebook.*

1 Test the continuity and differentiability of the function defined as under at $x = 1$ and $x = 2$, $f(x) = \begin{cases} x, & x \le 1 \\ 2 - x, & 1 < x \le 2. \\ -2 + 3x - x^2, & x > 2 \end{cases}$

2 Examine the differentiability of $f(x) = \sqrt{1 - e^{-x^2}}$ at $x = 0$.

3 If $f(x) = \begin{cases} ax^2 - b, & \text{if } |x| < 1 \\ -\dfrac{1}{|x|}, & \text{if } |x| \ge 1 \end{cases}$ is derivable at $x = 1$. Find the values of a and b.

4 A function f is defined as follows

$$f(x) = \begin{cases} 1, & \text{for } -\infty < x < 0 \\ 1 + \sin x, & \text{for } 0 \le x < \pi/2 \\ 2 + (x - \pi/2)^2, & \text{for } \pi/2 \le x < \infty \end{cases}$$

Discuss the continuity and differentiability at $x = 0$ and $x = \pi/2$.

5 Show that the function $f(x) = \begin{cases} x^m \cdot \sin(1/x), & x > 0 \\ 0, & x = 0 \end{cases}$ is

i. differentiable at $x = 0$, if $m > 1$.

ii. continuous but not differentiable at $x = 0$, if $0 < m \le 1$.

iii. neither continuous nor differentiable, if $m \le 0$.

Only One Option Correct Type

Direction *(Q. Nos. 6-19) This section contains 14 multiple choice questions. Each question has four choices (a), (b), (c) and (d), out of which ONLY ONE is correct.*

6 If a function $f(x)$ is defined as $f(x) = \begin{cases} -x, & x \le 0 \\ x^2, & 0 < x \le 1, \\ x^2 - x + 1, & x > 1 \end{cases}$ then

a. $f(x)$ is differentiable at $x = 0$ and $x = 1$

b. $f(x)$ is differentiable at $x = 0$ but not at $x = 1$

c. $f(x)$ is differentiable at $x = 1$ but not at $x = 0$

d. $f(x)$ is not differentiable at $x = 0$ and $x = 1$

Working Space

7 If $f(x)\begin{cases} x\left(\dfrac{e^{1/x}-e^{-1/x}}{e^{1/x}+e^{-1/x}}\right), & x \neq 0 \\ 0, & x=0 \end{cases}$, then at $x = 0$, $f(x)$ is

a. differentiable
b. not differentiable
c. $f'(0^+) = -1$
d. $f'(0^-) = 1$

8 If $f(x) = x^3\,\text{Sgn}(x)$, then

a. f is differentiable at $x = 0$
b. f is continuous but not differentiable at $x = 0$
c. $f'(0^-) = 1$
d. None of the above

9 The function $f(x) = (x^2 - 1)\,|x^2 - 3x + 2| + \cos(|x|)$ is not differentiable at $x =$

a. -1
b. 0
c. 1
d. 2

10 Let $f(x) = \begin{cases} g(x)\cos(1/x), & \text{if } x \neq 0 \\ 0, & \text{if } x = 0 \end{cases}$, where $g(x)$ is an even function, differentiable at $x = 0$, passing through the origin. Then, $f'(0)$ is equal to

a. 1
b. 0
c. 2
d. Does not exist

11 If $f(x) = \begin{cases} xe^{-\left(\frac{1}{|x|}+\frac{1}{x}\right)}, & x \neq 0 \\ 0, & x = 0 \end{cases}$, then $f(x)$ is **[AIEEE 2003]**

a. discontinuous everywhere
b. continuous as well as differentiable at all x
c. continuous for all x but not differentiable at $x = 0$
d. neither differentiable nor continuous at $x = 0$

12 Let $f: R \to R$ be a function defined by $f(x) = \max\{x, x^3\}$, the set of all points, where $f(x)$ is not differentiable, is **[IIT JEE 2001]**

a. $\{-1, 1\}$
b. $\{-1, 0\}$
c. $\{0, 1\}$
d. $\{-1, 0, 1\}$

13 The left hand derivative of $f(x) = [x]\sin(\pi x)$ at $x = k$, k is an integer is (where, [·] denotes greatest integer function) **[IIT JEE 2001]**

a. $(-1)^k \cdot (k-1)\pi$
b. $(-1)^{k-1} \cdot (k-1)\pi$
c. $(-1)^k \cdot k\pi$
d. $(-1)^{k-1} \cdot k\pi$

14 Which of the following function is differentiable at $x = 0$? **[IIT JEE 2001]**

a. $\cos(|x|) + |x|$
b. $\cos(|x|) - |x|$
c. $\sin(|x|) + |x|$
d. $\sin(|x|) - |x|$

15 The function given by $y = ||x| - 1|$ is differentiable for all real numbers except the points **[IIT JEE 2003]**

a. $\{0, 1, -1\}$
b. ± 1
c. 1
d. -1

16 Let $g(x) = \dfrac{(x-1)^n}{\log_e \cos^m (x-1)}$, $0 < x < 2$, m and n are integers, $m \neq 0$, $n > 0$ and let p be the left hand derivative of $|x - 1|$ at $x = 1$. If $\lim\limits_{x \to 1^+} g(x) = p$, then **[IIT JEE 2008]**

a. $n = 1, m = 1$
b. $n = 1, m = -1$
c. $n = 2, m = 2$
d. $n > 2, m = n$

Working Space

17 Let $f(x)=\begin{cases} x^2\left|\cos\left(\frac{\pi}{x}\right)\right|, & x\neq 0 \\ 0, & x=0 \end{cases}, x\in R$, then f is **[IIT JEE 2012]**

a. differentiable both at $x=0$ and at $x=2$
b. differentiable at $x=0$ but not differentiable at $x=2$
c. not differentiable at $x=0$ but differentiable at $x=2$
d. differentiable neither at $x=0$ nor at $x=2$

18 The set of points, where $f(x)=\dfrac{x}{1+|x|}$ is differentiable, is **[AIEEE 2009]**

a. $(-\infty,-1)\cup(-1,\infty)$
b. $(-\infty,\infty)$
c. $(0,\infty)$
d. $(-\infty,0)\cup(0,\infty)$

19 If the function $f(x)$ is differentiable at $x=a$, then $\lim\limits_{x\to a}\dfrac{x^2f(a)-a^2f(x)}{x-a}$ is **[AIEEE 2011]**

a. $2af(a)+a^2f'(a)$
b. $-a^2f'(a)$
c. $af(a)-a^2f'(a)$
d. $2af(a)-a^2f'(a)$

One or More than One Options Correct Type

Direction *(Q. Nos. 20-26) This section contains 7 multiple choice questions. Each question has four choices (a), (b), (c) and (d), out of which ONE or MORE THAN ONE are correct.*

20 If $f(x)=\begin{cases} \dfrac{x\log(\cos x)}{\log(1+x^2)}, & \text{if } x\neq 0 \\ 0, & \text{if } x=0 \end{cases}$, then

a. f is continuous at $x=0$
b. f is continuous at $x=0$ but not differentiable at $x=0$
c. f is differentiable at $x=0$
d. f is not continuous at $x=0$

21 Let $f(x)=\begin{cases} (x-e)2^{-2^{\frac{1}{e-x}}}, & x\neq e \\ 0, & x=e \end{cases}$, then

a. f is continuous and differentiable at $x=e$
b. f is continuous but not differentiable at $x=e$
c. f is neither continuous nor differentiable at $x=e$
d. geometrically f has sharp corner at $x=e$

22 Let [·] be greatest integer function, then $f(x)=\dfrac{\sin\frac{1}{4}\pi[x]}{[x]}$ is

a. not continuous at any point
b. continuous at $x=3/2$
c. discontinuous at $x=2$
d. differentiable at $x=1/3$

23 If $f(x)=3(2x+3)^{2/3}+2x+3$, then

a. $f(x)$ is continuous but not differentiable at $x=-3/2$
b. $f(x)$ is differentiable at $x=0$
c. $f(x)$ is continuous at $x=0$
d. $f(x)$ is differentiable but not continuous at $x=-3/2$

Working Space

24 Given that the derivative $f'(a)$ exists, indicate which of the following statement(s) is/are always?

a. $f'(a) = \lim_{h \to a} \frac{f(h) - f(a)}{h - a}$

b. $f'(a) = \lim_{h \to 0} \frac{f(a) - f(a-h)}{h}$

c. $f'(a) = \lim_{h \to 0} \frac{f(a+2t) - f(a)}{t}$

d. $f'(a) = \lim_{t \to 0} \frac{f(a+2t) - f(a+t)}{2t}$

25 If $f(x) = \min\{1, x^2, x^3\}$, then **[IIT JEE 2006]**

a. $f(x)$ is continuous, $\forall x \in R$

b. $f'(x) > 0, \forall x > 1$

c. $f(x)$ is not differentiable but continuous, $\forall x \in R$

d. $f(x)$ is not differentiable for two values of x

26 If $f(x) = \begin{cases} -x - \pi/2, & x \le -\pi/2 \\ -\cos x, & -\pi/2 < x \le 0 \\ x - 1, & 0 < x \le 1 \\ \log_e x, & x > 1 \end{cases}$, then **[IIT JEE 2011]**

a. $f(x)$ is continuous at $x = -\pi/2$

b. $f(x)$ is not differentiable at $x = 0$

c. $f(x)$ is differentiable at $x = 1$

d. $f(x)$ is differentiable at $x = -3/2$

Statement Type

Direction *(Q. Nos. 27-30) This section is based on Statement I and Statement II. Select the correct answer from the codes given below.*

a. Both Statement I and Statement II are correct and Statement II is the correct explanation of Statement I

b. Both Statement I and Statement II are correct and Statement II is not the correct explanation of Statement I

c. Statement I is correct but Statement II is incorrect

d. Statement II is correct but Statement I is incorrect

27 Consider $f(x) = ax^2 + bx + c$, $a, b, c \in R$ and $a \ne 0$.

Statement I If $f(x) = 0$ has two distinct positive real roots, then number of non-differentiable points of $y = |f(-|x|)|$ is 1.

Statement II Graph of $y = f(|x|)$ is symmetrical about Y-axis.

28 **Statement I** $|x^3|$ is differentiable at $x = 0$.

Statement II If $f(x)$ is differentiable at $x = a$, then $|f(x)|$ is also differentiable at $x = a$.

29 **Statement I** $f(x) = |x| \cdot \sin x$ is differentiable at $x = 0$.

Statement II If $f(x)$ is not differentiable and $g(x)$ is differentiable at $x = a$, then $f(x) \cdot g(x)$ will be differentiable at $x = a$.

30 Consider the function $f(x) = \cos(\sin^{-1} x)$, differentiable in $(-1, 1)$.

Statement I $f(x)$ is bounded in $(-1, 1)$.

Statement II If a function is differentiable in (a, b), then it is bounded in $[a, b]$.

Working Space

Comprehension Type

Direction (*Q. Nos.* 31-33) *This section contains a paragraph, each describing theory, experiments, data, etc. Three questions related to the paragraph have been given. Each question has only one correct answer among the four given options (a), (b), (c) and (d).*

Passage

$$f(x)=\begin{cases}2+(x-1)^2, & x<1\\ 2, & 1\le x\le 3,\\ 2-(x-3)^2, & x>3\end{cases} \qquad g(x)=\begin{cases}2+\sqrt{-x}, & x<0\\ x+2, & 0\le x\le 4,\\ 3x-6, & x>4\end{cases}$$

$$h(x)=\begin{cases}4+ae^x, & x<0\\ x+2, & 0\le x\le 3\\ b^2-7b+18-\dfrac{3}{x}, & x>3\end{cases}$$

and $\quad k(x)=\sqrt{1+x\sqrt{1+(x+1)\sqrt{1+(x+2)(x+4)}}},\ x>0.$

31 Which of the following is continuous at each point of its domain?

a. $f(x)$ b. $g(x)$
c. $k(x)$ d. All of these

32 The value of (a, b) for which $h(x)$ is continuous, $\forall\, x \in R$, is

a. (4, 3) b. (−2, 3)
c. (3, 4) d. None of these

33 Which of the following function is not differentiable at exactly two points of its domain?

a. $f(x)$ b. $g(x)$
c. $k(x)$ d. None of these

One Integer Value Correct Type

Direction (*Q. Nos.* 34 *and* 35) *This section contains* 2 *questions. When worked out will result in an integer from* 0 *to* 9 (*both inclusive*).

34 Let f be differentiable at $x=0$ and $f'(0)=1$. Then, $\lim\limits_{h\to 0}\dfrac{f(h)-f(-2h)}{h}$ equals

35 If the right hand derivative of $f(x)=[x]\tan(\pi x)$ (where, [·] denotes greatest integer function) at $x=7$ is $k\pi$, then k is equal to

DPP-6 Differentiability in the Interval

Subjective Questions

Working Space

***Direction** (Q. Nos. 1-5) These questions are subjective in nature, need to be solved completely on notebook.*

1 Draw a graph of the function, $y = [x] + |1 - x|, -1 \le x \le 3$. Determine the points, if any, where this function is not differentiable (where, [·] denotes the greatest integer function).

2 Discuss the continuity and derivability of $f(x) = \begin{cases} \left|x - \frac{1}{2}\right|, & 0 \le x < 1 \\ x \cdot [x], & 1 \le x < 2 \end{cases}$ (where, [·] denotes the greatest integer function).

3 If $f'(2) = 4$, then evaluate $\lim\limits_{x \to 0} \dfrac{f(1 + \cos x) - f(2)}{\tan^2 x}$.

4 Let the function $f : R \to R$ be given by $f(x + y) = f(x) \cdot f(y)$ for all $x, y \in R$ and $f(x) \ne 0$ for any $x \in R$. If the function $f(x)$ is differentiable at $x = 0$, show that $f'(x) = f'(0) f(x)$ for all $x \in R$. Also, determine $f(x)$.

5 Let R be the set of real numbers and $f : R \to R$ be such that for all x and y in R $|f(x) - f(y)| \le |x - y|^3$. Prove that $f(x)$ is constant.

Only One Option Correct Type

***Direction** (Q. Nos. 6-17) This section contains 12 multiple choice questions. Each question has four choices (a), (b), (c) and (d), out of which ONLY ONE is correct.*

6 Which of the following functions is continuous everywhere in its domain but at least one point where it is not differentiable?

a. $f(x) = x^{1/3}$
b. $f(x) = \dfrac{|x|}{x}$
c. $f(x) = e^{-x}$
d. $f(x) = \tan x$

7 If $f(x) = \begin{cases} x + \{x\} + x \sin\{x\}, & \text{for } x \ne 0 \\ 0, & \text{for } x = 0 \end{cases}$,

where {} denotes fractional part of x, then

a. f is continuous and differentiable at $x = 0$
b. f is continuous but not differentiable at $x = 0$
c. f is neither continuous nor differentiable at $x = 0$
d. None of the above

8 Let $f(x) = x^3$ and $g(x) = |x|$, then at $x = 0$, the composite function

a. *gof* is derivable but *fog* is not
b. *fog* is derivable but *gof* is not
c. *gof* and *fog* both are derivable
d. neither *gof* nor *fog* is derivable

Working Space

9 Let the function f, g and h be defined as follows:

$$f(x)=\begin{cases} x\sin\left(\frac{1}{x}\right), & \text{for} -1\le x\le 1 \text{ and } x\ne 0 \\ 0, & \text{for } x=0 \end{cases},$$

$$g(x)=\begin{cases} x^2\cdot\sin\left(\frac{1}{x}\right), & \text{for} -1\le x\le 1 \text{ and } x\ne 0 \\ 0, & \text{for } x=0 \end{cases} \text{ and}$$

$$h(x)=|x|^3, \text{ for } -1\le x\le 1$$

Which of these functions are differentiable at $x = 0$?

a. f and g b. f and h c. g and h d. None of these

10 Identify the correct statement.

a. If $f(x)$ is derivable at $x=a$, $|f(x)|$ will also derivable at $x=a$
b. If $f(x)$ is continuous at $x=a$, $|f(x)|$ too will be continuous at $x=a$
c. If $f(x)$ is discontinuous at $x=a$, $|f(x)|$ will also be discontinuous at $x=a$
d. If $|f(x)|$ is continuous at $x=a$, $f(x)$ too will be continuous at $x=a$

11 A function f defined as $f(x)=x[x]$ for $-1\le x\le 3$ (where, [·] denotes greatest integer function) is

a. continuous at all points in the domain of f but non-derivable at a finite number of points
b. discontinuous at all points and hence non-derivable at all points in the domain of f
c. discontinuous at a finite number of points but not derivable at all points in the domain of f
d. discontinuous and also non-derivable at a finite number of point of f

12 If for all values of x and y, $f(x+y)=f(x)\cdot f(y)$ and $f(5)=2$, $f'(0)=3$, then $f'(5)$ is **[AIEEE 2002]**

a. 3 b. 4 c. 5 d. 6

13 Suppose $f(x)$ is differentiable at $x=1$, $\lim\limits_{h\to 0}\frac{f(1+h)}{h}=5$, then $f'(1)$ equals **[AIEEE 2005]**

a. 3 b. 4 c. 5 d. 6

14 If f is a real-valued differentiable function satisfying $|f(x)-f(y)|\le(x-y)^2$, $x, y\in R$ and $f(0)=0$, then $f(1)$ equals **[AIEEE 2005]**

a. -1 b. 0 c. 2 d. 1

15 The set of points, where $f(x)=\frac{x}{1+|x|}$ is differentiable, is **[AIEEE 2006]**

a. $(-\infty,-1)\cup(-1,\infty)$
b. $(-\infty,\infty)$
c. $(0,\infty)$
d. $(-\infty,0)\cup(0,\infty)$

16 The domain of derivative of the function $f(x)=\begin{cases}\tan^{-1}x, & \text{if } |x|\le 1 \\ \frac{1}{2}(|x|-1), & \text{if } |x|>1\end{cases}$, is **[IIT JEE 2002]**

a. $R-\{0\}$
b. $R-\{1\}$
c. $R-\{-1\}$
d. $R-\{-1, 1\}$

17 Let $f: R\to R$ be such that $f(1)=3$, $f'(1)=6$, then $\lim\limits_{x\to 0}\left[\frac{f(1+x)}{f(1)}\right]^{1/x}$ equals

a. 1
b. $e^{1/2}$
c. e^2
d. e^3

Working Space

One or More than One Options Correct Type

Direction *(Q. Nos. 18-26) This section contains 9 multiple choice questions. Each question has four choices (a), (b), (c) and (d), out of which ONE or MORE THAN ONE are correct.*

18 Let $f(x)=\begin{cases} 2x+3, & -3 \le x < -2 \\ x+1, & -2 \le x < 0 \\ x+2, & 0 \le x \le 1 \end{cases}$. At what points the function is/are not differentiable in the point $[-3, 1]$?

a. -2 b. 0
c. 1 d. $1/2$

19 If $f(x)=\cos\pi(|x|+[x])$, then $f(x)$ is/are (where, [·] denotes greatest integer function)

a. continuous at $x=1/2$ b. continuous at $x=0$
c. differentiable in $(2, 4)$ d. differentiable in $(0, 1)$

20 If $f(x)=|x+1|(|x|+|x-1|)$, then at what points the function is/are not differentiable at in the interval $[-2, 2]$?

a. -1 b. 0
c. 1 d. $1/2$

21 Let $h(x)=\min\{x, x^2\}$, for every real number x, then

a. h is continuous for all x b. h is differentiable for all x
c. $h'(x)=1$ for all $x>1$ d. h is not differentiable at two values of x

22 If $f(x)=1+[\cos x]x$, in $0 < x \le \pi/2$ (where, [·] denotes greatest integer function), then

a. it is continuous in $0 < x < \pi/2$ b. it is differentiable in $0 < x < \pi/2$
c. its maximum value is 2 d. it is not differentiable in $0 < x < \pi/2$

23 If $f(x)=[x\sin\pi x]$, then f is (where, [·] denotes greatest integer function)

a. continuous at $x=0$ b. continuous in $(-1, 0)$
c. differentiable in $(-1, 1)$ d. All of these

24 Let f be a differentiable function on the open interval (a, b). Which of the following statements must be true?

I. f is continuous on the closed interval $[a, b]$.
II. f is bounded on the open interval (a, b).
III. If $a < a_1 < b_1 < b$ and $f(a_1) < 0 < f(b_1)$, then there is a number c such that $a_1 < c < b_1$ and $f(c)=0$.

a. I and II b. I and III
c. II and III d. Only III

25 Let $f(x)=\cos x$ and $H(x)=\begin{cases} \min[f(t): 0 \le t \le x], & \text{for } 0 \le x \le \pi/2 \\ \pi/2 - x, & \text{for } \pi/2 < x \le 3 \end{cases}$, then

a. $H(x)$ is continuous and derivable in $[0, 3]$
b. $H(x)$ is continuous but not derivable at $x=\pi/2$
c. $H(x)$ is neither continuous nor derivable at $x=\pi/2$
d. maximum value of $H(x)$ in $[0, 3]$ is 1

26 Let $f: R \to R$ be a function such that $f(x+y)=f(x)+f(y), \forall x, y \in R$.
If $f(x)$ is differentiable at $x=0$, then **[IIT JEE 2011]**

a. $f(x)$ is differentiable only in a finite interval containing zero
b. $f(x)$ is continuous, $\forall x \in R$
c. $f'(x)$ is constant, $\forall x \in R$
d. $f(x)$ is differentiable except at finitely many points

Working Space

Matching List Type

Direction (Q. No. 27) Choices for the correct combination of elements from Column I and Column II are given as options (a), (b), (c) and (d), out of which one is correct.

27 Match the Column I with Column II and mark the correct option from the given codes.

	Column I		Column II
i.	The number of the values of x in $(0, 2\pi)$, where the function $f(x) = \frac{\tan x + \cot x}{2} - \left\lvert \frac{\tan x - \cot x}{2} \right\rvert$ is continuous but not differentiable, is	p.	2
ii.	The number of points, where the function $f(x) = \min\{1, 1 + x^3, x^2 - 3x + 3\}$ is non-derivable, is	q.	0
iii.	The number of points, where $f(x) = (x + 4)^{1/3}$ is non-differentiable, is	r.	4
iv.	Consider $f(x) = \begin{cases} -\frac{\pi}{2}\log\left(\frac{2x}{\pi}\right) + \frac{\pi}{2}, & 0 < x \le \pi/2 \\ \sin^{-1}(\sin x), & \pi/2 < x < 3\pi/2 \end{cases}$. The number of points in $(0, 3\pi/2)$, where $f(x)$ is non-differentiable, is	s.	1

Codes

	i	ii	iii	iv			i	ii	iii	iv
a.	p	q	r	s		b.	r	s	p	q
c.	r	p	s	q		d.	q	p	r	s

Comprehension Type

Direction (Q. Nos. 28-30) This section contains a paragraph, each describing theory, experiments, data, etc. Three questions related to the paragraph have been given. Each question has only one correct answer among the four given options (a), (b), (c) and (d).

Passage

Let f be a function that is differentiable everywhere and that has the following properties:

i. $f(x) > 0$

ii. $f'(0) = -1$

iii. $f(-x) = \frac{1}{f(x)}$ and $f(x + h) = f(x) \cdot f(h)$

A standard result: $\int \frac{f'(x)}{f(x)} dx = \log|f(x)| + C$.

28 The range of $f(x)$ is

a. R b. $R - \{0\}$
c. R^+ d. $(0, e)$

29 The range of the function $\Delta = |f(x)|$ is

a. $[0, 1]$ b. $[0, 1)$
c. $(0, 1]$ d. None of these

30 The function $y = f(x)$ is

a. odd b. even
c. increasing d. decreasing

SET - 1

Revisal Problems for JEE Main

Only One Option Correct Type

Direction (Q. Nos. 1-36) This section contains 36 multiple choice questions. Each question has four choices (a), (b), (c) and (d), out of which ONLY ONE is correct.

Working Space

1 If $f(x)=\begin{cases} x, & x\le 1 \\ x^2+bx+c, & x>1 \end{cases}$ and $f'(x)$ exists finitely for all $x \in R$, then

a. $b=-1, c\in R$
b. $c=1, b\in R$
c. $b=1, c=-1$
d. $b=-1, c=1$

2 The number of points in (1, 3), where $f(x)=a^{[x^2]}$, $a>1$ is not differentiable, is

a. 0
b. 3
c. 5
d. 7

3 Let $f(x)=[x^2-3]$ (where, $[\cdot]$ denotes greatest integer function). Then, the number of points in the interval (1, 2), where the function is discontinuous, is

a. 4
b. 2
c. 6
d. None of these

4 Let $f(x)=$ degree $(u^{x^2}+u^2+2u+3)$, then at $x=\sqrt{2}$, $f(x)$ is

a. continuous but not differentiable
b. differentiable
c. discontinuous
d. None of these

5 Let $f: R\to R$ be a function given by $f(x+y)=f(x)\cdot f(y)$ for all $x, y\in R$. If $f(x)\ne 0$ all $x\in R$ and $f'(0)=\log 2$, then $f(x)$ is equal to

a. x^2
b. 2^x
c. $x(\log 2)$
d. e^{2x}

6 Let $f: R\to R$ be a function given by $f(x+y)=f(x)\cdot f(y)$ for all $x, y, \in R$. If $f'(0)=2$, then $f(x)$ is equal to

a. Ae^x
b. Ae^{2x}
c. $2x$
d. None of these

7 Let $f(x)=|x|$ and $g(x)=[x]$, where $[\cdot]$ denotes greatest integer function. Then, $(fog)'(-2)$ is

a. 0
b. 1
c. −1
d. non-existent

8 Let $f(x)=\cos x$ and $g(x)=[x+1]$, where $[\cdot]$ denotes greatest integer function. Then, $(gof)'(\pi/2)$ is

a. 0
b. 1
c. −1
d. non-existent

9 If $f(x)=x^5\cdot \text{Sgn}(x)$, then at $x=0$, $f(x)$ is

a. everywhere continuous and differentiable
b. everywhere continuous but not differentiable
c. everywhere differentiable but not continuous
d. neither continuous nor differentiable

10 If f is periodic function, then

a. f' and f'' are also periodic
b. f' is periodic but f'' is not periodic
c. f'' is periodic but f' is not periodic
d. None of these

11 If $f(x)=\begin{cases} x[x], & 0\le x<2 \\ (x-1)[x], & 2\le x<3 \end{cases}$, where $[\cdot]$ denotes greatest integer function, then

a. both $f'(1)$ and $f'(2)$ do not exist
b. $f'(1)$ exists but $f'(2)$ does not exist
c. $f'(2)$ exists but $f'(1)$ does not exist
d. both $f'(1)$ and $f'(2)$ exist

Working Space

12 If $f(x)=\begin{cases} 4, & -3<x<-1 \\ 5+x, & -1\le x<0 \\ 5-x, & 0\le x<2 \\ x^2+x-3, & 2\le x<3 \end{cases}$, then $f(|x|)$ is

a. differentiable but not continuous in (–3, 3)
b. continuous but not differentiable in (–3, 3)
c. continuous as well as differentiable in (–3, 3)
d. neither continuous nor differentiable in (–3, 3)

13 If $f(x)=[\sin^2 x]$, where [·] denotes greatest integer function, then

a. f is everywhere continuous
b. f is everywhere differentiable
c. f is a constant function
d. None of these

14 If $f'(2)=6$ and $f'(1)=4$, then $\lim_{h\to 0}\frac{f(2h+2+h^2)-f(2)}{f(h-h^2+1)-f(1)}$ is equal to

a. 3
b. –3/2
c. 3/2
d. Does not exist

15 Let a function $f(x)$ defined on [3, 6] be given by $f(x)=\begin{cases}\log_e[x], & 3\le x<5\\ |\log_e x|, & 5\le x<6\end{cases}$, then $f(x)$ is

a. continuous and differentiable on [3, 6]
b. continuous on [3, 6) but not differentiable at $x = 4, 5$
c. differentiable on [3, 6) but not continuous at $x = 4, 5$
d. None of the above

16 If $f(x)=\text{Sgn}(x)=\begin{cases}\frac{|x|}{x}, & x\ne 0\\ 0, & x=0\end{cases}$ and $g(x)=f[f(x)]$, then at $x = 0$, $g(x)$ is

a. continuous and differentiable
b. continuous but not differentiable
c. differentiable but not continuous
d. neither continuous nor differentiable

17 Let $f(x)=\sin x$, $g(x)=[x+1]$ and $h(x)=gof(x)$, where [·] is greatest integer function, then $h'(\pi/2)$ is

a. 1
b. –1
c. non-existent
d. None of these

18 If function $f(x)$ is given by $f(x)=\begin{cases}(\sin x)^{1/(\pi-2x)}, & x\ne\pi/2\\ \lambda, & x=\pi/2\end{cases}$ is continuous at $x=\pi/2$, then λ is

a. e
b. 1
c. 0
d. None of these

19 If $f(x)=|x-2|$ and $g(x)=f[f(x)]$, then $g'(x)$ for $x>4$ is

a. 1
b. 2
c. –1
d. None of these

20 Let $f:[0,1]\to[0,1]$ be a continuous function, then

a. $f(x)=x$ for atleast one $x\in(0,1)$
b. $f(x)$ will be differentiable in [0, 1]
c. $f(x)+x=0$ for atleast one x such that $0\le x\le 1$
d. None of the above

21 Let $f(x)$ be a continuous function defined for $1\le x\le 3$. If $f(x)$ takes rational values for all x and $f(2)=10$, then the value of $f(4)$ is

a. 20
b. 5
c. 10
d. None of these

22 Let $f(x)=(-1)^{[x^3]}$, where [·] denotes greatest integer function, then

a. $f(x)$ is discontinuous at $x=n^{1/3}, n\in Z$
b. $f(3/2)=1$
c. $f'(x)=0$ for all $x\in(-1,1)$
d. None of these

Working Space

23 Let $f(x) = [n + p\sin x]$, $x \in (0, \pi)$, $n \in Z$, p is a prime number and $[\cdot]$ denotes the greatest integer function. The number of points at which $f(x)$ is not differentiable is

a. p
b. $p - 1$
c. $2p + 1$
d. $2p - 1$

24 If $f(x) = x + \tan x$ and $g(x)$ is the inverse of $f(x)$, then $g'(x)$ is equal to

a. $\dfrac{1}{1 + [g(x) - x]^2}$
b. $\dfrac{1}{2 + [g(x) + x]^2}$
c. $\dfrac{1}{2 + [g(x) - x]^2}$
d. None of these

25 The number of points of non-differentiable of $f(x) = \sin\{\pi(x - [x])\}$ in $(-\pi/2, \pi/2)$, where $[\cdot]$ denotes the greatest integer function, is

a. 4
b. 5
c. 3
d. 2

26 Let $f : R \to R$ be a function satisfying $f(x + y) = f(x) + 2y^2 + kxy$ for all $x, y \in R$. If $f(1) = 2$ and $f(2) = 8$, then $f(x)$ is equal to

a. $2x^2$
b. $6x - 4$
c. $x^2 + 3x - 2$
d. $-x^2 + 9x - 6$

27 Let $f : R \to R$ be a function given by $f(x + y) = f(x) \cdot f(y)$ for all $x, y \in R$. If $f(x) = 1 + x \cdot g(x) + x^2 g(x) \cdot \phi(x)$ such that $\lim\limits_{x \to 0} g(x) = a$ and $\lim\limits_{x \to 0} \phi(x) = b$, then $f'(x)$ is equal to

a. $(a + b)\, f(x)$
b. $af(x)$
c. $b\, f(x)$
d. $ab\, f(x)$

28 Let $f : R \to R$ be a function satisfying $f(x + y) = f(x) \cdot f(y)$ for all $x, y \in R$. If $f(x) = x^3 \cdot g(x)$ for all $x, y \in R$, where $g(x)$ is continuous, then $f'(x)$ is

a. $g(0)$
b. $g'(x)$
c. 0
d. None of these

29 Let $f : R \to R$ be a function satisfying $f(x + y) = f(x) + \lambda xy + 3x^2y^2$ for all $x, y \in R$. If $f(3) = 4$ and $f(5) = 52$, then $f'(x)$ is equal to

a. $10x$
b. $-10x$
c. $20x$
d. $128x$

30 Let f be a differentiable function satisfying the condition:
$f\left(\dfrac{x}{y}\right) = \dfrac{f(x)}{f(y)}$ for all $x, y (\neq 0) \in R$ and $f(y) \neq 0$. If $f'(1) = 2$, then $f'(x)$ is equal to

a. $2f(x)$
b. $\dfrac{f(x)}{x}$
c. $2xf(x)$
d. $\dfrac{2f(x)}{x}$

31 Let f and g be differentiable function satisfying $g'(a) = 2$, $g(a) = b$ and $fog = I$ (identity function). Then, $f'(b)$ is equal to

a. 2
b. 2/3
c. 1/2
d. None of these

32 If g is the inverse of a function f and $f'(x) = \dfrac{1}{1 + x^n}$, then $g'(x)$ is eqal to

a. $\dfrac{1}{1 + \{g(x)\}^n}$
b. $1 + \{g(x)\}^n$
c. $\{g(x)\}^n - 1$
d. None of these

33 If $f(x + y) = 2f(x) \cdot f(y)$ for all x, y, where $f'(0) = 3$ and $f(4) = 2$, then $f'(4)$ is equal to

a. 6
b. 12
c. 4
d. None of these

34 Let $f\left(\dfrac{x + y}{2}\right) = \dfrac{f(x) + f(y)}{2}$ for real values of x and y. If $f'(0)$ exists and equals to -1 and $f(0) = 1$, then $f'(2)$ is equal to

a. -1
b. 1
c. 0
d. None of these

35 Let $f(x)=p[x]+qe^{-|x|}+r|x|^2$, where p, q and r are real constants. If $f(x)$ is differentiable at $x=0$, then

a. $q=0, r=0, p\in R$
b. $p=0, r=0, q\in R$
c. $p=0, q=0, r\in R$
d. None of these

Working Space

36 Let $f: R \to R$ be a function given by $f(x+y)=f(x)\cdot f(y)$ for all $x, y\in R$. If $f(x)=1+x\,g(x)\cdot \log_e 2$, where $\lim_{x\to 0} g(x)=1$, then $f'(x)$ is equal to

a. $\log_e 2^{f(x)}$
b. $\log_e [f(x)]^2$
c. $\log_e 2$
d. None of these

Statement Type

Direction ***(Q. Nos. 37-40) This section is based on Statement I and Statement II. Select the correct answer from the codes given below.***

a. Both Statement I and Statement II are correct and Statement II is the correct explanation of Statement I
b. Both Statement I and Statement II are correct and Statement II is not the correct explanation of Statement I
c. Statement I is correct but Statement II is incorrect
d. Statement II is correct but Statement I is incorrect

37 Define $f(x)$ as the product of two real functions $f_1(x)=x, x\in R$ and $f_2(x)=\begin{cases}\sin\frac{1}{x}, & x\neq 0\\ 0, & x=0\end{cases}$ as

$$F(x)=\begin{cases} f_1(x)\,f_2(x), & x\neq 0\\ 0, & x=0\end{cases}$$

Statement I $F(x)$ is continuous on R.
Statement II $f_1(x)$ and $f_2(x)$ are continuous on R.

38 Let $f(x)=x-x^2$ and $g(x)=\{x\}$ for $x\in R$, where $\{\cdot\}$ denotes the fractional part of x.

Statement I $f[g(x)]$ will be continuous, $\forall\, x\in R$.
Statement II $f(0)=f(1)$ and $g(x)$ is periodic with period 1.

39 Let $h(x)=f_1(x)+f_2(x)+\ldots+f_n(x)$, where $f_1(x), f_2(x), \ldots, f_n(x)$ are real valued functions of x.

Statement I $f(x)=|\cos|x||+\cos^{-1}(\text{Sgn}\,x)+|\log_e x|$ is not differentiable at 3 points in $(0, 2\pi)$.

Statement II Exactly one function $f_i(x), i=1,2,\ldots,n$ not differentiable and the rest of the function differentiable at $x=a$ makes $h(x)$ not differentiable at $x=a$.

40 **Statement I** $f(x)=|x|\sin x$ is differentiable at $x=0$.

Statement II If $g(x)$ is not differentiable at $x=a$ and $h(x)$ is differentiable at $x=a$. Then, $g(x)\,h(x)$ cannot be differentiable at $x=a$.

SET - 2

Revisal Problems
for JEE Advanced

Only One Option Correct Type

Working Space

Direction *(Q. Nos. 1-11) This section contains 11 multiple choice questions. Each question has four choices (a), (b), (c) and (d), out of which ONLY ONE is correct.*

1 If $f(x)$ and $g(x)$ are two differentiable functions at $x = x_0$, then the function defined as, $h(x) = \max\{f(x), g(x)\}$

a. is always differentiable at $x = x_0$
b. is never differentiable at $x = x_0$
c. is differentiable at $x = x_0$, when $f(x_0) \neq g(x_0)$
d. cannot be differentiable at $x = x_0$, if $f(x_0) = g(x_0)$

2 For $x > 0$, let $h(x) = \begin{cases} 1/q, & \text{if } x = p/q \\ 0, & \text{if } x \text{ is irrational} \end{cases}$, where p and $q > 0$ are relatively prime integers, then which one does not hold good?

a. $h(x)$ is discontinuous for all x in $(0, \infty)$
b. $h(x)$ is continuous for each irrational in $(0, \infty)$
c. $h(x)$ is discontinuous for each rational in $(0, \infty)$
d. $h(x)$ is not derivable for all x in $(0, \infty)$

3 Given, $f(x) = \dfrac{e^x - \cos 2x - x}{x^2}$ for $x \in R - \{0\}$ and $g(x) = \begin{cases} f(\{x\}), & \text{for } n < x < n + \frac{1}{2} \\ f(1 - \{x\}), & \text{for } n + \frac{1}{2} \leq x < n + 1, n \in I, \\ 5/2, & \text{otherwise} \end{cases}$

where $\{x\}$ denotes fractional part of x, then $g(x)$ is

a. discontinuous at all integral values of x only
b. continuous everywhere except for $x = 0$
c. discontinuous at $x = n + 1/2$; $n \in I$ and at some $x \in I$
d. continuous everywhere

4 Let $f(x) = \dfrac{2\cos x - \sin 2x}{(\pi - 2x)^2}$, $g(x) = \dfrac{e^{-\cos x} - 1}{8x - 4\pi}$ and $h(x) = \begin{cases} f(x), & \text{for } x < \pi/2 \\ g(x), & \text{for } x > \pi/2 \end{cases}$, then which of the following holds?

a. h is continuous at $x = \pi/2$
b. h has an irremovable discontinuity at $x = \pi/2$
c. h has a removable discontinuity at $x = \pi/2$
d. $f\left(\dfrac{\pi^+}{2}\right) = g\left(\dfrac{\pi^-}{2}\right)$

5 Consider the function $f(x) = \begin{cases} x\{x\} + 1, & 0 \leq x < 1 \\ 2 - \{x\}, & 1 \leq x < 2 \end{cases}$, where $\{x\}$ denotes the fractional part of x. Which one of the following statement is incorrect?

a. $\lim_{x \to 1} f(x)$ exists
b. $f(0) \neq f(2)$
c. $f(x)$ is continuous in $[0, 2]$
d. None of these

6 Consider $f(x) = \left[\dfrac{2(\sin x - \sin^3 x) + |\sin x - \sin^2 x|}{2(\sin x - \sin^3 x) - |\sin x - \sin^2 x|}\right]$, $x \neq \dfrac{\pi}{2}$ for $x \in (0, \pi)$ and $f\left(\dfrac{\pi}{2}\right) = 3$, where $[\cdot]$ denotes greatest integer function, then

a. f is continuous and differentiable at $x = \pi/2$
b. f is continuous but not differentiable at $x = \pi/2$
c. f is neither continuous nor differentiable at $x = \pi/2$
d. None of the above

Working Space

7 Let $[x]$ denotes the integral part of $x \in R, g(x) = x - [x]$. Let $f(x)$ be any continuous function with $f(0) = f(1)$, then the function $h(x) = f[g(x)]$

a. has finitely many discontinuity
b. is discontinuous at some $x = c$
c. is continuous on R
d. is a constant function

8 If $f(x + y) = f(x) + f(y) + |x| y + xy^2, \forall x, y \in R$ and $f'(0) = 0$, then

a. f need not be differentiable at every non-zero x
b. f is differentiable for all x
c. f is twice differentiable at $x = 0$
d. None of the above

9 Let f be a differentiable function on the open internal (a, b). Which of the following statements must be true?

I. f is continuous on the closed interval $[a, b]$
II. f is bounded on the open interval (a, b)
III. If $a < a_1 < b_1 < b$ and $f(a_1) < 0 < f(b_1)$, then there is a number c such that $a_1 < c < b_1$ and $f(c) = 0$.

a. I and II
b. I and III
c. II and III
d. Only III

10 Let $f(x) = \max\{|x^2 - 2|x||, |x|\}$ and $g(x) = \min\{|x^2 - 2|x||, |x|\}$, then

a. both $f(x)$ and $g(x)$ are non-differentiable at 5 points
b. $f(x)$ is not differentiable at 5 points and $g(x)$ is not differentiable at 7 points
c. number of points of non-differentiability for $f(x)$ and $g(x)$ are 7 and 5 respectively
d. both $f(x)$ and $g(x)$ are non-differentiable at 3 and 5 points respectively

11 Given $f(x) = \begin{cases} b([x]^2 + [x]) + 1, & \text{for } x \geq 1 \\ \sin(\pi(x + a)), & \text{for } x < -1 \end{cases}$,

where $[x]$ denotes greatest integer function of x, then for what values of a and b, the function is continuous at $x = -1$?

a. $a = 2n + 3/2, b \in R; n \in I$
b. $a = 4n + 2, b \in R; n \in I$
c. $a = 4n + 3/2; b \in R^+; n \in I$
d. $a = 4n + 1, b \in R^+; n \in I$

One or More than One Options Correct Type

Direction (Q. Nos. 12-16) *This section contains 5 multiple choice questions. Each question has four choices (a), (b), (c) and (d), out of which ONE or MORE THAN ONE are correct.*

12 Let $f(x) = \min(x^3, x^2)$ and $g(x) = [x]^2 + \sqrt{\{x\}^2}$, where $[\cdot]$ and $\{\cdot\}$ denote greatest integer and fractional part of x. Then, which of the following holds?

a. f is continuous for all x
b. g is discontinuous for all $x \in I$
c. f is differentiable for all $x \in (1, \infty)$
d. g is not differentiable for all $x \in I$

13 The function, $f(x) = [|x|] - |[x]|$, where $[x]$ denotes greatest integer function

a. is continuous for all positive integers
b. is discontinuous for all non-positive integers
c. has finite number of elements in its range
d. is such that its graph does not lie above the X-axis

14 Which of the following statement(s) is (are) correct?

a. If $f(x)$ is differentiable, $\forall x \in [0, 1]$, then $f'(x)$ must be bounded in $[0, 1]$
b. There exists a bijective function $f : [0, 1] \to [0, 1]$ which is not continuous
c. Let $f : [-1, 2] \to R$ be defined as $f(x) = x^2 - \cos \pi x + 4$, then $f(c) = 2\pi$ for some $c \in (-1, 2)$
d. If $f(x) = 3 + x + e^x$, then $(f^{-1})'(4)$ is equal to $(1/2)$

Working Space

15 Let $f(x)$ be twice differentiable function such that $f''(x) < 0$ in [0, 2], then

a. $f(0) + f(2) = 2f(c)$, $0 < c < 2$
b. $f(0) + f(2) = 2f(1)$
c. $f(0) + f(2) > 2f(1)$
d. $f(0) + f(2) < 2f(1)$

16 Let $f(x) = \begin{cases} |x|^p \sin\frac{1}{x} + x|\tan x|^q, & \text{if } x \neq 0, p,q \in N \\ 0, & \text{if } x = 0 \end{cases}$.

If $f(x)$ is derivable at $x = 0$, then the ordered pair (p, q) is

a. (1, 2)
b. (2, 1)
c. (3, 2)
d. (2, 2)

Matching List Type

Direction *(Q. No. 17) Choices for the correct combination of elements from Column I and Column II are given as options (a), (b), (c) and (d), out of which one is correct.*

17 Match the Column I with Column II and mark the correct option from the given codes.

	Column I		Column II
i.	$f(x) = \begin{cases} x + 1, \text{ if } x < 0 \\ \cos x, \text{ if } x \geq 0 \end{cases}$, at $x = 0$ is	p.	continuous
ii.	For every $x \in R$, the function $g(x) = \frac{\sin(\pi[x - \pi])}{1 + [x]^2}$ (where, [x] denotes fractional part of x) is	q.	differentiable
iii.	$h(x) = \sqrt{\{x\}^2}$ (where, $\{x\}$ denotes fractional part of x), then for all $x \in I$, is	r.	discontinuous
iv.	$k(x) = \begin{cases} x^{1/\log x}, \text{ if } x \neq 1 \\ e, \quad \text{ if } x = 1 \end{cases}$, at $x = 1$ is	s.	non-derivable

Codes

	i	ii	iii	iv
a.	p,q	r,s	s,p	p,r
b.	p,s	p,q	r,s	p,q
c.	s,r	p,r	r,s	q,r
d.	r,p	p,q	p,r	q,s

Comprehension Type

Direction *(Q. Nos. 18-37) This section contains 7 paragraphs, each describing theory, experiments, data, etc. Twenty questions related to the paragraphs have been given. Each question has only one correct answer among the four given options (a), (b), (c) and (d).*

Passage I

Consider the function $f(x)$ twice differentiable of degree four symmetrical to line $x = 1$ defined as $f: R \to R$ and $f''(2) = 0$.

18 The sum of roots of the cubic $f'(x) = 0$ is

a. 0
b. 1
c. 2
d. 3

19 If $f(1) = 0$ and $f(2) = 1$, then the value of $f(3)$ is

a. 6/5
b. 7/5
c. 8/5
d. 9/5

20 The distance between two horizontal tangents of the curve $f(x)$ is

a. 6/5
b. 7/5
c. 8/5
d. 9/5

Passage II

Let $f: R \to R$ be a function defined as $f(x) = \begin{cases} 1 - |x|, & |x| \leq 1 \\ 0, & |x| > 1 \end{cases}$ and

$g(x) = f(x - 1) + f(x + 1), \forall x \in R$.

21 The number of solutions of $f(x) = g(x)$, $|x| < 2$, is/are

a. 1
b. 2
c. 3
d. 4

Working Space

22 The number of points at which $g(x)$ is discontinuous, is/are

a. 0 b. 1
c. 2 d. 4

23 The number of points at which $g(x)$ is non-differentiable, is/are

a. 3 b. 4
c. 5 d. 6

Passage III

f be a polynomial function such that $f(x)f(y)+2=f(x)+f(y)+f(xy)$ for all $x, y \in [0, \infty)$ and $f(x)$ is one-one function on $[0, \infty)$ with $f(0)=1$ and $f'(1)=2$.

24 $f(x)$ is given by

a. $1+\frac{2x^3}{3}$ b. x^2+1
c. $1+\frac{3}{2}x^2$ d. $1+\frac{3x^4}{4}$

25 The number of discontinuity of $g(x)=\left[\frac{1}{f(x)}\right]$ on [0, 10] is (where, [·] denotes greatest integer function)

a. 1 b. 0
c. 10 d. 11

26 If $h(x)=\min\left\{\frac{2}{f(x)}, x^2, |1-|x||\right\}$, then the number of points of non-differentiability of $h(x)$ is

a. 3 b. 4
c. 5 d. 6

Passage IV

Let $f(x)=f_1(x)-2f_2(x)$, $f_1(x)=\begin{cases}\max\{x^2,|x|\} & \text{for } x\in[-1,1]\\ \min\{x^2,|x|\} & \text{for } |x|>1\end{cases}$

and $f_2(x)=\begin{cases}\max\{x^2,|x|\} & \text{for } x\in[-1,1]\\ \min\{x^2,|x|\} & \text{for } |x|>1\end{cases}$

27 The number of points, where $f'(x)$ vanishes or does not exist, is

a. 1 b. 2 c. 3 d. 4

28 If $g(x)=|f(x)|$, then the number of points, where the function is non-differentiable, is

a. 0 b. 1 c. 3 d. 4

Passage V

Let $f(x)=\max\{|x^2-1|, |x-1|\}$ and $g(x)=\int_a^x f(t)dt$, $x\in R$.

29 The value of $f(x)$ is

a. $f(x)=\begin{cases}x^2-1, & x\le -2\\ 1-x, & -2<x\le 0\\ 1-x^2, & 0<x\le 1\\ x-1, & x>1\end{cases}$ b. $f(x)=\begin{cases}x^2-1, & x\le -2\\ 1-x^2, & -2<x\le 0\\ 1-x, & 0<x\le 1\\ x-1, & x>1\end{cases}$

c. $f(x)=\begin{cases}x^2-1, & x\le 1\\ x-1, & x>1\end{cases}$ d. $f(x)=\begin{cases}x-1, & x\le 1\\ x^2-1, & x>1\end{cases}$

30 The function $f(x)$ is continuous for x belongs to

a. $R-\{0,1\}$ b. $R-\{-2,0,1\}$
c. R d. None of these

31 The function $g(x)$ is differentiable for

a. $R-\{0,1\}$ b. $R-\{-2,0,1\}$
c. R d. None of these

Working Space

Passage VI

Let $f(x) = \begin{cases} [x], & -2 \le x \le -1/2 \\ 2x^2 - 1, & -1/2 < x \le 2 \end{cases}$ and $g(x) = f(|x|) + |f(x)|$, where [·] represents greatest integer function.

32 The number of points, where $|f(x)|$ is non-differentiable, is

a. 3 b. 4 c. 2 d. 5

33 The number of points, where $g(x)$ is non-differentiable, is

a. 4 b. 5 c. 2 d. 3

34 The number of points, where $g(x)$ is discontinuous, is

a. 1 b. 2
c. 3 d. None of these

Passage VII

If $f(x) = \text{mid}\{g(x), h(x), p(x)\}$ means the function which will be second in order when values of the three function at a particular value of x are arranged, then for

$$f(x) = \text{mid}\left\{(x-1), (x-3)^2, 3 - \frac{(x-3)^2}{2}\right\}, x \in [1, 4]$$

35 The numerical value of difference between the LHD and RHD at the point $x = 2$ for $f(x)$ in $x \in [1, 4]$ will be

a. 0 b. 2 c. 3 d. 4

36 The greatest value of $f(x)$ in [1, 4] will be

a. $1 + \sqrt{3}$ b. $2 + \sqrt{3}$ c. $3 + \sqrt{3}$ d. None of these

37 The rate of change of x w.r.t. $f(x)$ at $x = 3$ will be

a. 1 b. 3/2 c. 2 d. $-3/2$

One Integer Value Correct Type

***Direction** (Q. Nos. 38-44) This section contains 7 questions. When worked out will result in an integer from 0 to 9 (both inclusive).*

38 Let $f(x) = [x] + [x + 1/4] + [x + 2/4] + [x + 3/4]$. Then, the number of points of discontinuity of $f(x)$ in [0, 1] is (where, [·] denotes greatest integer function)

39 If $f(x)$ is a continuous function, $\forall x \in R$ and the range of $f(x)$ is $(2, \sqrt{21})$ and $g(x) = \left[\frac{f(x)}{c}\right]$ is continuous, $\forall x \in R$, then the least positive integral value of c is (where, [·] denotes greatest integer function)

40 The only integer lying in the interval (0, 4), where the function $f(x) = \lim_{n \to \infty} \left(\cos \frac{\pi x}{2}\right)^{2n}$ is discontinuous, is

41 Let $f(x) = x^3 - x^2 + x + 1$, $g(x) = \begin{cases} \max[f(t)], 0 \le t \le x, & \text{if } 0 \le x \le 1 \\ 3 - x, & \text{if } 1 < x \le 2 \end{cases}$, then the number of points in (0, 2), where $g(x)$ is not differentiable is

42 The number of continuous functions $f(x)$ satisfying $[f(x)]^2 = x$, $\forall x \in R$ and continuous on R, is

43 The number of points of discontinuity of $f(x) = [2x]^2 - \{2x\}^2$ (where, [·] and {·} denote greatest integer and fractional part respectively) in the interval (−2, 2), are

44 Let $f(x)$ be a function which is differentiable any number of times $f(2x^2 - 1) = 2x^3 f(x), \forall x \in R$, then $f^{2016}(0)$ is equal to (where, $f^n(x) = n$th order derivative of f at x)

JEE Main & AIEEE Archive

(Compilation of Last 13 Years' Questions)

1 If the function, $g(x)=\begin{cases} k\sqrt{x+1}, 0 \le x \le 3 \\ mx+12, 3 < x \le 5 \end{cases}$ is differentiable, then the value of $k+m$ is : **(JEE Main 2015)**

a. 2 b. $\frac{16}{5}$

c. $\frac{10}{3}$ c. 4

2 If f and g are differentiable functions in $(0, 1)$ satisfying $f(0)=2=g(1), g(0)=0$ and $f(1)=6$, then for some $c \in]0,1[$, **(JEE Main 2014)**

a. $2f'(c)=g'(c)$
b. $2f'(c)=3g'(c)$
c. $f'(c)=g'(c)$
d. $f'(c)=2g'(c)$

3 If $f: R \to R$ is a function defined by $f(x)=[x]\cos\left(\frac{2x-1}{2}\right)\pi$, where $[x]$ denotes the greatest integer function, then f is **(AIEEE 2012)**

a. continuous for every real x
b. discontinuous only at $x=0$
c. discontinuous only at non-zero integral values of x
d. continuous only at $x=0$

4 Consider the function $f(x)=|x-2|+|x-5|, x \in R$.

Statement I $f'(4)=0$

Statement II f is continuous in $[2, 5]$, differentiable in $(2, 5)$ and $f(2)=f(5)$. **(AIEEE 2012)**

a. Both Statement I and Statement II are correct and Statement II is the correct explanation of Statement I
b. Both Statement I and Statement II are correct and Statement II is not the correct explanation of Statement I
c. Statement I is correct but Statement II is incorrect
d. Statement II is correct but Statement I is incorrect

5 The values of p and q for which the function

$$f(x)=\begin{cases} \frac{\sin(p+1)x+\sin x}{x}, & x<0 \\ q, & x=0 \\ \frac{\sqrt{x+x^2}-\sqrt{x}}{x^{3/2}}, & x>0 \end{cases}$$

is continuous for all x in R, are **(AIEEE 2011)**

a. $p=\frac{5}{2}, q=\frac{1}{2}$

b. $p=-\frac{3}{2}, q=\frac{1}{2}$

c. $p=\frac{1}{2}, q=\frac{3}{2}$

d. $p=\frac{1}{2}, q=-\frac{3}{2}$

6 Define $f(x)$ as the product of two real functions $f_1(x)=x, x \in IR$ and $f_2(x)=\begin{cases} \sin\frac{1}{x}, \text{if } x \ne 0 \\ 0 \quad, \text{if } x=0 \end{cases}$ as follows

$$f(x)=\begin{cases} f_1(x)\cdot f_2(x), & \text{if } x \ne 0 \\ 0, & \text{if } x=0. \end{cases}$$

Statement I $f(x)$ is continuous on IR.

Statement II $f_1(x)$ and $f_2(x)$ are continuous on IR. **(AIEEE 2011)**

a. Both Statement I and Statement II are correct and Statement II is the correct explanation of Statement I
b. Both Statement I and Statement II are correct and Statement II is not the correct explanation of Statement I
c. Statement I is correct but Statement II is incorrect
d. Statement II is correct but Statement I is incorrect

7 If $f: (-1, 1) \to R$ be a differentiable function with $f(0)=-1$ and $f'(0)=1$. Let $g(x)=[f(2f(x)+2)]^2$. Then, $g'(0)$ is equal to **(AIEEE 2010)**

a. 4 b. -4
c. 0 d. -2

8 Let $f(x)=x|x|$ and $g(x)=\sin x$.

Statement I gof is differentiable at $x=0$ and its derivative is continuous at that point.

Statement II gof is twice differentiable at $x=0$. **(AIEEE 2009)**

a. Both Statement I and Statement II are correct and Statement II is the correct explanation of Statement I
b. Both Statement I and Statement II are correct and Statement II is not the correct explanation of Statement I
c. Statement I is correct but Statement II is incorrect
d. Statement II is correct but Statement I is incorrect

9 Let $f(x)=\begin{cases} (x-1)\sin\frac{1}{(x-1)}, & \text{if } x \ne 1 \\ 0, & \text{if } x=1 \end{cases}$.

Then, which one of the following is true? **(AIEEE 2008)**

a. f is differentiable at $x=1$ but not at $x=0$
b. f is neither differentiable at $x=0$ nor at $x=1$
c. f is differentiable at $x=0$ and at $x=1$
d. f is differentiable at $x=0$ but not at $x=1$

10 The function $f : R/\{0\} \to R$ given by
$$f(x) = \frac{1}{x} - \frac{2}{e^{2x}-1}$$
can be made continuous at $x = 0$ by defining $f(0)$ as **(AIEEE 2007)**

a. 2 b. −1 c. 0 d. 1

11 The set of points where $f(x) = \frac{x}{1+|x|}$ is differentiable is **(AIEEE 2006)**

a. $(-\infty, -1) \cup (-1, \infty)$
b. $(-\infty, \infty)$
c. $(0, \infty)$
d. $(-\infty, 0) \cup (0, \infty)$

12 If $f(x)$ is differentiable at $x = 1$ and $\lim_{h \to 0} \frac{1}{h} f(1+h) = 5$, then $f'(1)$ is equal to **(AIEEE 2005)**

a. 6 b. 5 c. 4 d. 3

13 Let f be differentiable for all x. If $f(1) = -2$ and $f'(x) \geq 2$ for $x \in [1, 6]$, then **(AIEEE 2005)**

a. $f(6) = 5$
b. $f(6) < 5$
c. $f(6) < 8$
d. $f(6) \geq 8$

14 If f is a real-valued differentiable function satisfying $|f(x) - f(y)| \leq (x-y)^2$; $x, y \in R$ and $f(0) = 0$, then $f(1)$ is equal to **(AIEEE 2005)**

a. 1 b. 2 c. 0 d. −1

15 Let $f(x) = \frac{1-\tan x}{4x - \pi}$, $x \neq \frac{\pi}{4}$, $x \in \left[0, \frac{\pi}{2}\right]$. If $f(x)$ is continuous in $\left[0, \frac{\pi}{2}\right]$, then $f\left(\frac{\pi}{4}\right)$ is equal to **(AIEEE 2004)**

a. 1 b. 1/2
c. −1/2 d. −1

16 Let $f(a) = g(a) = k$ and their nth derivatives $f^n(a), g^n(a)$ exist and are not equal for some n. Further, if
$$\lim_{x \to a} \frac{f(a)g(x) - f(a) - g(a)f(x) + g(a)}{g(x) - f(x)} = 4,$$
then the value of k is **(AIEEE 2003)**

a. 4 b. 2
c. 1 d. 0

17 If $f(x) = \begin{cases} xe^{-\left(\frac{1}{|x|} + \frac{1}{x}\right)}, & x \neq 0 \\ 0, & x = 0 \end{cases}$, then $f(x)$ is **(AIEEE 2003)**

a. continuous as well as differentiable for all x
b. continuous for all x but not differentiable at $x = 0$
c. neither differentiable nor continuous at $x = 0$
d. discontinuous everywhere

JEE Advanced & IIT JEE Archive

(Compilation of Last 10 Years' Questions)

1 Let $f : R \to R$ be a continuous odd function, which vanishes exactly at one point and $f(1) = \frac{1}{2}$. Suppose that $F(x) = \int_{-1}^{x} f(t)\,dt$ for all $x \in [-1, 2]$ and $G(x) = \int t\,|f\{f(t)\}|\,dt$ for all $x \in [-1, 2]$. If $\lim_{x \to a} \frac{F(x)}{G(x)} = \frac{1}{4}$, then the value of $f\left(\frac{1}{2}\right)$ is **(2015 Adv., Integer Type)**

2 Let $g : R \to R$ be a differentiable function with $g(0) = 0, g'(1) \neq 0$. Let $f(x) = \begin{cases} \frac{x}{|x|} g(x), & x \neq 0 \\ 0, & x = 0 \end{cases}$ and $h(x) = e^{|x|}$ for all $x \in R$. Let $(fo\,h)(x)$ denot $f\{h(x)\}$ and $(hof)(x)$ denote $h\{f(x)\}$. Then which of the following is (are) true?

(2015 Adv., One or More than One Options Corect Type)

a. f is differentiable at $x = 0$
b. h is differentiable at $x = 0$
c. $fo\,h$ is differentiable at $x = 0$
d. $ho\,f$ is differentiable at $x = 0$

3 Let $f : R \to R$ and $g : R \to R$ be respectively given by $f(x) = |x| + 1$ and $g(x) = x^2 + 1$. Define $h : R \to R$ by $h(x) = \begin{cases} \max\{f(x), g(x)\}, & \text{if } x \leq 0 \\ \min\{f(x), g(x)\}, & \text{if } x > 0. \end{cases}$

The number of points at which $h(x)$ is not differentiable, is **(2014 Adv., Integer Type)**

4 Let $f : [a, b] \to [1, \infty)$ be a continuous function and $g : R \to R$ be defined as

$$g(x) = \begin{cases} 0, & \text{if } x < a \\ \int_a^x f(t)dt, & \text{if } a \leq x \leq b \\ \int_a^b f(t)dt, & \text{if } x > b \end{cases}$$ Then,

(2014 Adv., One or More than One Options Correct Type)

a. $g(x)$ is continuous but not differentiable at a
b. $g(x)$ is differentiable on R
c. $g(x)$ is continuous but not differentiable at b
d. $g(x)$ is continuous and differentiable at either a or b but not both

5 Let $f(x) = \begin{cases} x^2 \left|\cos \frac{\pi}{x}\right|, & x \neq 0, x \in R, \\ 0, & x = 0 \end{cases}$ then f is

(2012, Only One Option Correct Type)

a. differentiable both at $x = 0$ and at $x = 2$
b. differentiable at $x = 0$ but not differentiable at $x = 2$
c. not differentiable at $x = 0$ but differentiable at $x = 2$
d. differentiable neither at $x = 0$ nor at $x = 2$

6 Let $f : [1, \infty) \to [2, \infty)$ be differentiable function such that $f(1) = 2$. If $6\int_1^x f(t)dt = 3x\,f(x) - x^3$ for all $x \geq 1$, then the value of $f(2)$ is **(2011, Integer Type)**

7 Let $f : R \to R$ be a function such that $f(x + y) = f(x) + f(y), \forall x, y \in R$. If $f(x)$ is differentiable at $x = 0$, then

(2011, One or More than One Options Correct Type)

a. $f(x)$ is differentiable only in a finite interval containing zero
b. $f(x)$ is continuous, $\forall x \in R$
c. $f'(x)$ is constant, $\forall x \in R$
d. $f(x)$ is differentiable except at finitely many points

8 If $f(x) = \begin{cases} -x - \pi/2, & x \leq -\pi/2 \\ -\cos x, & -\pi/2 < x \leq 0 \\ x - 1, & 0 < x \leq 1 \\ \ln x, & x > 1 \end{cases}$, then

(2011, One or More than One Options Correct Type)

a. $f(x)$ is continuous at $x = -\pi/2$
b. $f(x)$ is not differentiable at $x = 0$
c. $f(x)$ is differentiable at $x = 1$
d. $f(x)$ is differentiable at $x = -3/2$

9 Let f and g be real valued functions defined on interval $(-1, 1)$ such that $g''(x)$ is continuous, $g(0) \neq 0$, $g'(0) = 0$, $g''(0) \neq 0$, and $f(x) = g(x)\sin x$.

Statement I $\lim_{x \to 0} [g(x)\cos x - g(0)\text{cosec}\, x] = f''(0)$.

Statement II $f'(0) = g(0)$. **(2008, Statement Type)**

a. Both Statement I and Statement II are correct and Statement II is the correct explanation of Statement I
b. Both Statement I and Statement II are correct and Statement II is not the correct explanation of Statement I
c. Statement I is correct but Statement II is incorrect
d. Statement II is correct but Statement I is incorrect

10 In the following, $[x]$ denotes the greatest integer less than or equal to x. **(2007, Matching Type)**

	Column I		Column II
i.	$x\|x\|$	p.	continuous in $(-1, 1)$
ii.	$\sqrt{\|x\|}$	q.	differentiable in $(-1, 1)$
iii.	$x + [x]$	r.	strictly increasing $(-1, 1)$
iv.	$\|x-1\| + \|x+1\|$	s.	not differentiable atleast at one point in $(-1, 1)$

Codes

	i	ii	iii	iv
a.	p,q,r	p,s	r,s	p,q
b.	p,r,s	q,s	p,s	q,r
c.	q,r	p,q,s	q,s	p,q
d.	p,q	q,r,s	p,s	q,r,s

11 If $f''(x) = -f(x)$, where $f(x)$ is a continuous double differentiable function and $g(x) = f'(x)$. If $F(x) = \left[f\left(\frac{x}{2}\right)\right]^2 + \left[g\left(\frac{x}{2}\right)\right]^2$ and $F(5) = 5$, then $F(10)$ is

(2006, Only One Option Correct Type)

a. 0 b. 5
c. 10 d. 25

Passage for Q. Nos. (12 and13)

Given that for each $a \in (0, 1)$,
$\lim_{h \to 0^+} \int_h^{1-h} t^{-a}(1-t)^{a-1} dt$ exists. Let this limit be $g(a)$. In addition, it is given that the function $g(a)$ is differentiable on $(0, 1)$.

(2007, Comprehension Type)

12 The value of $g(1/2)$ is

a. π
b. 2π
c. $\pi/2$
d. $\pi/4$

13 The value of $g'(1/2)$ is

a. $\pi/2$ b. π
c. $-\pi/2$ d. 0

14 If $f(x) = \min\{1, x^2, x^3\}$, then

(2006, One or More than One Options Correct Type)

a. $f(x)$ is continuous everywhere
b. $f(x)$ is continuous and differentiable everywhere
c. $f(x)$ is not differentiable at two points
d. $f(x)$ is not differentiable at one point

15 Let f be twice differentiable function satisfying $f(1) = 1, f(2) = 4, f(3) = 9$, then

(2005, Only One Option Correct Type)

a. $f''(x) = 2, \forall\ x \in (R)$
b. $f'(x) = 5 = f''(x)$, for some $x \in (1, 3)$
c. there exists atleast one $x \in (1, 3)$ such that $f''(x) = 2$
d. None of the above

16 If f is a differentiable function satisfying $f\left(\frac{1}{n}\right) = 0$ for all $n \geq 1, n \in I$, then **(2005, Only One Option Correct Type)**

a. $f(x) = 0, x \in (0, 1]$
b. $f'(0) = 0 = f(0)$
c. $f(0) = 0$ but $f'(0)$ not necessarily zero
d. $|f(x)| \leq 1, x \in (0, 1]$

17 Let $f(x) = ||x| - 1|$, then points, where $f(x)$ is not differentiable, is/are **(2005, Only One Option Correct Type)**

a. $0, \pm 1$ b. ± 1 c. 0 d. 1

4. Applications of Derivatives

DPP

DAILY PRACTICE PROBLEMS

DPP-1 Derivative as Rate Measure

Subjective Questions

Working Space

Direction *(Q. Nos. 1-8) These questions are subjective in nature, need to be solved completely on notebook.*

1 The area of expanding rectangle is increasing at the rate 48 cm^2/s. The length of rectangle is always equal to square of the breadth. At what rate the length is increasing at the instant when the breadth is 4.5 cm?

2 The radius of balloon is increasing at the rate 10 cm/s. At what rate is the surface of the balloon increasing when the radius is 15 cm?

3 The volume of cube is increasing at a constant rate. Prove that the increase in surface area varies inversely as the length of edge of the cube.

4 An airforce plane is ascending vertically at the rate of 100 km/h. If radius of the Earth is r km. Then, how fast is the area of the Earth visible from the plane, increasing at 3 min after it started ascending?

5 A ladder 5 m long is leaning against a wall. The bottom of the ladder is pulled along the ground, away from the wall, at the rate 2 m/s. How fast is the height on the wall decreasing when the foot of the ladder is 4 m away from the wall?

6 Sand is pouring from a pipe at the rate 12 cm^3/s. The falling sand forms a cone on the ground in such a way that the height of the cone is always one-sixth of the radius of the base. How fast is the height of the sand-cone increasing when the height is 4 cm?

7 A kite is 120 m high and 130 m of string is out. If the kite is moving away horizontally at the rate of 52 m/s, then find the rate at which the string is being paid out.

8 At what points of the ellipse $16x^2 + 9y^2 = 400$ does the ordinates decreases at the same rate at which the abscissa increases?

Only One Option Correct Type

Direction *(Q. Nos. 9-13) This section contains 5 multiple choice questions. Each question has four choices (a), (b), (c) and (d), out of which ONLY ONE is correct.*

9 A 13 ft ladder is leaning against a wall when its base starts to slide away. At the instant when the base is 12 ft away from the wall, the base is moving away from the wall at the rate of 5 ft/s. The rate at which the angle θ between the ladder and the ground is changing, is

a. $-\frac{12}{13}$ rad/s
b. -1 rad/s
c. $-\frac{13}{12}$ rad/s
d. $\frac{10}{13}$ rad/s

Working Space

10 Water is poured into an inverted conical vessel of which the radius of the base is 2 m and height 4 m at the rate of 77 L/min. The rate at which the water level is rising at the instant when the depth is 70 cm, is

a. 10 cm/min
b. 20 cm/min
c. 40 cm/min
d. None of these

11 A point is moving along the curve $y^3 = 27x$. The interval in which the abscissa changes at slower rate, then the ordinate is

a. $(-3, 3)$
b. $(-\infty, \infty)$
c. $(-1, 1)$
d. $(-\infty, -3) \cup (3, \infty)$

12 A particle moves along the curve $y = x^{3/2}$ in the first quadrant in such a way that its distance from the origin increases at the rate of 11 units/s. The value of dx/dt when $x = 3$, is

a. 4
b. 9/ 2
c. $3\sqrt{3}/2$
d. None of these

13 If x and y are the sides of two squares such that $y = x - x^2$. Then, the rate of change, if the area of second square with respect to the first square, when $x = 2$, is

a. 1
b. 4
c. 3
d. 6

Matching List Type

***Direction** (Q. No. 14) Choices for the correct combination of elements from Column I and Column II are given as options (a), (b), (c) and (d), out of which one is correct.*

14 Match the Column I with Column II and mark the correct option from the codes given below.

	Column I		Column II
i.	Circular plate is expanded by heat from radius 5 cm to 5.06 cm, then approximate increase in area is	p.	4
ii.	If an edge of cube is increased by 1%, then percentage increase in volume is	q.	0.6π
iii.	If rate of decrease of $\frac{x^2}{2} - 2x + 5$ is twice the rate of decrease of x, then x is equal to (rate of decrease is non-zero)	r.	3
iv.	The rate of increase in area of an equilateral triangle of side 15 cm, when each side is increasing at the rate 0.1 cm/s, is	s.	$3\sqrt{3}/4$
		t.	0.8π

Codes

	i	ii	iii	iv
a.	p	q	t	s
b.	q	r	p	s
c.	r	s	p	q
d.	s	r	t	p

Working Space

Comprehension Type

Direction *(Q. Nos. 15-18) This section contains 2 paragraphs, each describing theory, experiments, data, etc. Four questions related to the paragraphs have been given. Each question has only one correct answer among the four given options (a), (b), (c) and (d).*

Passage I

A spherical balloon is being inflated, so that its volume increases uniformly at the rate of 40 cm^3/min.

15 At $r = 8$, its surface area increases at the rate of

a. 8 cm^2/min
b. 10 cm^2/min
c. 20 cm^2/min
d. None of these

16 When $r = 8$, then the increase in radius in the next $\frac{1}{2}$ min is

a. 0.025 cm
b. 0.050 cm
c. 0.075 cm
d. 0.01 cm

Passage II

Water is poured at a constant rate of π m^3/s into an inverted right circular conical container of semi-vertical angle 45°.

17 The rate at which the depth of water is rising, when the depth is 2 m (assume that the container has a height exceeding 2 m), is

a. 0.5
b. 0.25
c. 1
d. 0.75

18 The rate at which the top surface area of water is increasing m/s, when the depth is 1 m, is

a. 2π
b. π
c. 0.5π
d. 1.5π

One Integer Value Correct Type

Direction *(Q. Nos. 19 and 20) This section contains 2 questions. When worked out will result in an integer from 0 to 9 (both inclusive).*

19 If the rate of change in the volume of sphere is equals to the rate of change in its radius, then the radius is $\frac{1}{k\sqrt{\pi}}$. The value of k is

20 A man 1.6 m high walks at the rate of 30 m/min away from a lamp which is 4 m above ground. If k is the rate at which the man's shadow is lengthening, then the value of $\frac{k}{4}$ is

DPP-2 Tangents and Normals

Subjective Questions

Working Space

Direction (Q. Nos. 1-6) *These questions are subjective in nature, need to be solved completely on notebook.*

1 Find the equation of normal to the curve $3x^2 - y^2 = 8$, which is parallel to the line $x + 3y = 4$.

2 Show $\frac{x}{a} + \frac{y}{b} = 1$ touches the curve $y = be^{-x/a}$ at the point, where the curve crosses the axis of y.

3 If the straight line $x\cos\alpha + y\sin\alpha = p$ touches $\frac{x^2}{a^2} + \frac{y^2}{b^2} = 1$, then prove that $p^2 = a^2\cos^2\alpha + b^2\sin^2\alpha$.

4 If $x\cos\alpha + y\sin\alpha = p$ touches $x^m y^n = a^{m+n}$, then prove that $p^{m+n} \cdot m^m \cdot n^n = (m+n)^{m+n} \cdot \cos^m\alpha \cdot \sin^n\alpha \cdot a^{m+n}$.

5 Show that the curves $x = y^2$ and $xy = k$ cut at right angled, if $8k^2 = 1$.

6 Tangents are drawn from the origin to the curve $y = \sin x$. Prove that their points of contact lie on $x^2y^2 = (x^2 - y^2)$.

Only One Option Correct Type

Direction (Q. Nos. 7-30) *This section contains 24 multiple choice questions. Each question has four choices (a), (b), (c) and (d), out of which ONLY ONE is correct.*

7 The equation of tangent to the curve $x = a\cos^3 t$, $y = a\sin^3 t$ at t point is

a. $x\sec t - y\operatorname{cosec} t = a$
b. $x\sec t + y\operatorname{cosec} t = a$
c. $x\operatorname{cosec} t - y\sec t = a$
d. $x\operatorname{cosec} t + y\sec t = a$

8 The equation of normal to the curve $y = x + \sin x\cos x$ at $x = \pi/2$ is

a. $x = 2$
b. $x = \pi$
c. $x + \pi = 0$
d. $2x = \pi$

9 The equation of normal to the curve $x + y = x^y$, where it cuts X-axis, is

a. $y = x + 1$
b. $y = -x + 1$
c. $y = x - 1$
d. $y = -x - 1$

10 If a variable tangent to the curve $x^2y = c^3$ makes intercepts a, b on X and Y-axes respectively, then the value of a^2b is

a. $27c^3$
b. $\frac{4}{27}c^3$
c. $\frac{27}{4}c^3$
d. $\frac{4}{9}c^3$

Working Space

11 The number of values of c such that the straight line $3x + 4y = c$ touches the curve $\frac{x^4}{2} = x + y$, is

a. 0 b. 1 c. 2 d. 4

12 Let $f(x) = x^3 + ax + b$ with $a \neq b$ and suppose that tangent lines to the graph of f at $x = a$ and $x = b$ have the same gradient. Then, the value of $f(1)$ is

a. 0
b. 1
c. $\frac{-1}{3}$
d. $\frac{2}{3}$

13 The tangent to the curve $3xy^2 - 2x^2y = 1$ at $(1, 1)$ meets the curve again the point

a. $(16/5, 1/20)$
b. $(-16/5, -1/20)$
c. $(1/20, 16/5)$
d. None of these

14 The curve $y - e^{xy} + x = 0$ has a vertical tangent at

a. $(1, 1)$
b. $(0, 1)$
c. $(1, 0)$
d. no point

15 A curve with equation of the form $y = ax^4 + bx^3 + cx + d$ has zero gradient at the point $(0, 1)$ and also touches the X-axis at the point $(-1, 0)$, then the values of x for which the curve has a negative gradient, are

a. $x > -1$
b. $x < 1$
c. $x < -1$
d. $-1 \le x \le 1$

16 The coordinates of point(s) at each of which the tangents to the curve $y = x^3 - 3x^2 - 7x + 6$ cut off on the positive semi-axis OX a line segment half that on the negative semi-axis OY is given by

a. $(-1, 9)$
b. $(3, -15)$
c. $(1, -3)$
d. None of these

17 The cubic polynomial $f(x) = ax^3 + bx^2 + cx + d$ has a graph which is tangent to the X-axis at 2, has an other x-intercept at -1, and has y-intercept at -2 as shown. The value of $a + b + c + d$ is

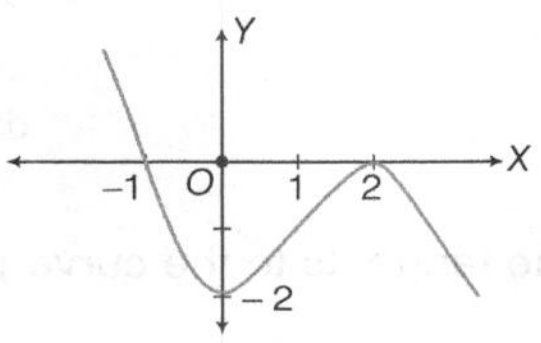

a. -2
b. -1
c. 0
d. 1

18 Consider the curve represented parametrically by the equation $x = t^3 - 4t^2 - 3t$ and $y = 2t^2 + 3t - 5$, where $x \in R$. If H denotes the number of point on the curve where the tangent is horizontal and V the number of point where the tangent is vertical, then

a. $H = 2$ and $V = 1$
b. $H = 1$ and $V = 2$
c. $H = 2$ and $V = 2$
d. $H = 1$ and $V = 1$

19 At the point $P(a, a^n)$ on the graph of $y = x^n$ $(n \in N)$ in the first quadrant a normal is drawn. The normal intersects the Y-axis at the point $(0, b)$, if $\lim_{a \to 0} b = 1/2$, then n equals

a. 1
b. 3
c. 2
d. 4

20 The equation of a line through the point $\left(\frac{1}{2}, 2\right)$ and tangent to the parabola $y = -\frac{x^2}{2} + 2$ and secant to the curve $y = \sqrt{4 - x^2}$, is

a. $2x + 2y - 5 = 0$
b. $2x + 2y - 9 = 0$
c. $y = 2$
d. None of these

Working Space

21 If the tangent at P of the curve $y^2 = x^3$ intersects the curve again at Q and the straight lines OP, OQ make angles α, β with the X-axis, where O is the origin. Then, $\frac{\tan\alpha}{\tan\beta}$ has the value equal to

a. -1
b. -2
c. 2
d. $\sqrt{2}$

22 The normal to the curve $x = a(1+\cos\theta)$, $y = a\sin\theta$ at θ always passes through the fixed point

a. $(a, 0)$
b. $(0, a)$
c. $(0, 0)$
d. (a, a)

23 The equation of tangent to the curve $y = x + \frac{4}{x^2}$, which is parallel to the X-axis, is **[AIEEE 2010]**

a. $y = 0$
b. $y = 1$
c. $y = 2$
d. $y = 3$

24 The intercept on X-axis made by tangents to the curve, $y = \int_0^x |t|\, dt$, $x \in R$, which are parallel to the line $y = 2x$, are equal to **[IIT JEE 2013]**

a. ± 1
b. ± 2
c. ± 3
d. ± 4

25 The normal to the curve, $y = f(x)$ at the point (3, 4) makes an angle $3\pi/4$ with the positive X-axis, then $f'(3)$ is equal to

a. -1
b. $-3/4$
c. $4/3$
d. 1

26 The points on the curve $y^3 + 3x^2 = 12y$, where the tangents is vertical, is

a. $\left(\pm\frac{4}{\sqrt{3}}, -2\right)$
b. $\left(\pm\sqrt{\frac{11}{3}}, 1\right)$
c. $(0, 0)$
d. $\left(\pm\frac{4}{\sqrt{3}}, 2\right)$

27 Angle between the tangents to the curve $y = x^2 - 5x + 6$ at the points (2, 0) and (3, 0), is **[AIEEE 2006]**

a. $\pi/2$
b. $\pi/6$
c. $\pi/4$
d. $\pi/3$

28 The tangent to the curve $y = e^x$ drawn at the point (c, e^c) intersects the line joining the points $(c-1, e^{c-1})$ and $(c+1, e^{c+1})$ **[IIT JEE 2007]**

a. on the left of $x = c$
b. on the right of $x = c$
c. at no point
d. at all points

29 At any point of a curve $\sqrt{\frac{\text{subnormal}}{\text{subtangent}}}$ is

a. the abscissa of that point
b. the ordinate of that point
c. slope of the tangent at that point
d. slope of the normal at that point

30 The length of subnormal of the curve $y^2 = 8ax$ $(a > 0)$ is

a. $2a$
b. $4a$
c. $6a$
d. $8a$

One or More than One Options Correct Type

Working Space

Direction (Q. Nos. 31-38) *This section contains 8 multiple choice questions. Each question has four choices (a), (b), (c) and (d), out of which ONE or MORE THAN ONE are correct.*

31 Which of the following pair(s) of curves is/are orthogonal?

a. $y^2 = 4ax; y = e^{-x/2a}$ b. $y^2 = 4ax; x^2 = 4ay$
c. $xy = a^2; x^2 - y^2 = b^2$ d. $y = ax; x^2 + y^2 = c^2$

32 If $\frac{x}{a} + \frac{y}{b} = 1$ is a tangent to the curve $x = kt$, and $y = k/t$, where $k > 0$, then

a. $a > 0, b > 0$ b. $a > 0, b < 0$ c. $a < 0, b > 0$ d. $a < 0, b < 0$

33 The coordinates of the point(s) on the graph of the function $f(x) = \frac{x^3}{3} - \frac{5x^2}{2} + 7x - 4$, where the tangent drawn cut-off intercepts from the coordinate axes which are equal in magnitude but opposite in sign, is

a. (2, 8/3) b. (3, 7/2) c. (1, 5/6) d. None of these

34 If the line $ax + by + c = 0$ is a normal to the curve $xy = 1$, then **[IIT JEE 1996]**

a. $a > 0, b > 0$ b. $a > 0, b < 0$
c. $a < 0, b > 0$ d. $a < 0, b < 0$

35 The angle at which the curve $y = ke^{kx}$ intersects the Y-axis, is

a. $\tan^{-1} k^2$ b. $\cot^{-1}(k^2)$
c. $\sin^{-1}\left(\frac{1}{\sqrt{1+k^4}}\right)$ d. $\sec^{-1}(\sqrt{1+k^4})$

36 The abscissa of the point on the curve $\sqrt{xy} = a + x$, $(a > 0)$ the tangent at which cuts off equal intercepts from the coordinates axes is

a. $a/\sqrt{2}$ b. $-a/\sqrt{2}$ c. $a\sqrt{2}$ d. $-a\sqrt{2}$

37 The equation of a tangent to the curve $y \cot x = y^3 \tan x$ at the point, where the abscissa is $\pi/4$, is

a. $4x + 2y = \pi + 2$ b. $4x - 2y = \pi + 2$
c. $x = 0$ d. $y = 0$

38 The normal to the curve $x = a(\cos\theta + \theta\sin\theta)$, $y = a(\sin\theta - \theta\cos\theta)$ at any point θ is such that

a. it passes through the origin b. it makes angle $\left(\frac{\pi}{2} + \theta\right)$ with the X-axis
c. it passes through $\left(\frac{a\pi}{2}, -a\right)$ d. it is a constant distance from the origin

Comprehension Type

Direction (Q. Nos. 39-44) *This section contains 2 paragraphs, each describing theory, experiments, data, etc. Six questions related to the paragraphs have been given. Each question has only one correct answer among the four given options (a), (b), (c) and (d).*

Passage I

Consider the function $f(x) = x^2 f(1) - xf'(2) + f''(3)$, such that $f(0) = 2$.

39 The value of $f'(1)$ is

a. 0 b. 1
c. 2 d. 3

Working Space

40 The equation of tangent to $y = f(x)$ at $x = 3$ is

a. $y = x - 7$
b. $y = \frac{x}{4} - 7$
c. $y = 4x - 7$
d. None of these

41 The angle of intersection of $y = f(x)$ and $y = 2e^{2x}$ is

a. $\tan^{-1}(3/4)$
b. $\tan^{-1}(4/3)$
c. 0
d. $\tan^{-1}(6/7)$

Passage II

If a continuous function f defined on the real line R, assumes positive and negative values in R, then the equation $f(x) = 0$ has a root in R. e.g. If it is known that a continuous function f on R is positive at some point and its minimum value is negative, then the equation $f(x) = 0$ has a root in R. Consider $f(x) = ke^x - x$ for all real x, where k is a real constant. **[IIT JEE 2007]**

42 The line $y = x$ meets $y = ke^x$ for $k \le 0$ at

a. no point
b. one point
c. two points
d. more than two points

43 The positive value of k for which $ke^x - x = 0$ has only one root is

a. $1/e$
b. 1
c. e
d. $\log_e 2$

44 For $k > 0$, the set of all values of k for which $ke^x - x = 0$ has two distinct roots, is

a. $(0, 1/e)$
b. $(1/e, 1)$
c. $(1/e, \infty)$
d. $(0, 1)$

One Integer Value Correct Type

Direction *(Q. Nos. 45-50) This section contains 6 questions. When worked out will result in an integer from 0 to 9 (both inclusive).*

45 The least positive integer value of a, so that the line $(3 - a)x + ay + (a^2 - 1) = 0$ is normal to the curve $xy = 1$, is

46 If $x + 4y = 14$ is normal to the curve $y^2 = \alpha x^3 - \beta$ at (2, 3), then the value of $(\alpha + \beta)$ is

47 The angle of intersection of the curves $y = [|\sin x| + |\cos x|]$ and $x^2 + y^2 = 5$, where [·] denotes the greatest integer function is $\tan^{-1}(k)$. Then, k is equal to

48 Let A be the area bounded by the axes of reference and the normal to $y = \log_e x$ at a point (1, 0), then $2A$ is equal to

49 Let α be the angle in radians between $\frac{x^2}{36} + \frac{y^2}{4} = 1$ and the circle $x^2 + y^2 = 12$ at their points of intersection. If $\alpha = \tan^{-1}\left(\frac{k}{2\sqrt{3}}\right)$, then the value of k is

50 The chord of parabola $y = -p^2x^2 + 5px - 4$ touches the curve $y = \frac{1}{1-x}$ at the point $x = 2$ and is bisected by that point, then the number of values of p are

DPP-3 Mean Value Theorem

Subjective Questions

Working Space

Direction *(Q. Nos. 1-9) These questions are subjective in nature, need to be solved completely on notebook.*

1 Verify Rolle's theorem for $f(x) = (x - a)^m \cdot (x - b)^n$ on $[a, b]$; where m, n being positive integer.

2 Check the validity of Rolle's theorem for the function $y = x^3 + 4x^2 - 7x - 10$ in the interval $[-1, 2]$.

3 Verify Lagrange's mean value theorem for $f(x) = x^3 - 2x^2 - x + 3$ in $[0, 1]$.

4 If the equation $a_0x^n + a_1x^{n-1} + a_2x^{n-2} + \cdots + a_{n-1}x = 0$ has a positive root α, then prove that the equation $na_0x^{n-1} + (n-1)a_1x^{n-2} + \cdots + a_{n-1} = 0$ also have a positive root smaller than α.

5 If $f(x)$ and $g(x)$ are differentiable for $0 \le x \le 2$ such that $f(0) = 5$, $g(0) = 0$, $f(2) = 8$, $g(2) = 1$. Show that there exists a number c satisfying $0 < c < 2$ and $f'(c) = 3g'(c)$.

6 If f, ϕ and ψ are continuous in $[a, b]$ and derivable in $]a, b[$, then show that there is a value 'c' lying between a and b such that

$$\begin{vmatrix} f(a) & f(b) & f'(c) \\ \phi(a) & \phi(b) & \phi'(c) \\ \psi(a) & \psi(b) & \psi'(c) \end{vmatrix} = 0.$$

7 The function $y = \dfrac{2 - x^2}{x^4}$ takes on equal value at the end-points of the interval $[-1, 1]$. Make sure the derivative of this function does not vanish at any of the interval $[-1, 1]$ and explain this deviation from Rolle's theorem.

8 With the aid of Lagrange's formula, prove that $\dfrac{a-b}{a} \le \log\left(\dfrac{a}{b}\right) \le \dfrac{a-b}{b}$, for the condition $0 < b \le a$.

9 Let $f : [0, 4] \to R$ be a differentiable function. **[IIT JEE 2003]**

i. Show that there exists $a, b \in [0, 4]$, $[f(4)]^2 - [f(0)]^2 = 8f'(a) \cdot f(b)$.

ii. Show that there exists α, β with $0 < \alpha < \beta < 2$ such that $\int_0^4 f(t)\,dt = 2\{[\alpha f(\alpha^2)] + \beta f[(\beta^2)]\}$.

Only One Option Correct Type

Working Space

Direction (Q. Nos. 10-18) *This section contains 9 multiple choice questions. Each question has four choices (a), (b), (c) and (d), out of which ONLY ONE is correct.*

10 Rolle's theorem in the indicated intervals will not be valid for which of the following function?

a. $f(x)=\begin{cases}\dfrac{\sin x}{x}, & x\neq 0\\ 1, & x=0\end{cases};x\in[-1,1]$

b. $g(x)=\begin{cases}\dfrac{1-\cos x}{x}, & x\neq 0\\ 0, & x=0\end{cases};x\in[-2\pi,2\pi]$

c. $h(x)=\begin{cases}\dfrac{1-\cos x}{x^2}, & x\neq 0\\ \dfrac{1}{2}, & x=0\end{cases};x\in[-2\pi,2\pi]$

d. $k(x)=\begin{cases}x\sin\left(\dfrac{1}{x}\right), & x\neq 0\\ 0, & x=0\end{cases};x\in\left[-\dfrac{1}{\pi},\dfrac{1}{2\pi}\right]$

11 Consider the function for $x\in[-2,3]$,

$$f(x)=\begin{cases}\dfrac{x^3-2x^2-5x+6}{x-1}, & x\neq 1\\ -6, & x=1\end{cases}, \text{ then}$$

a. f is discontinuous at $x=1 \Rightarrow$ Rolle's is not applicable in $[-2, 3]$
b. $f(-2)\neq f(3) \Rightarrow$ Rolle's theorem is not applicable in $[-2, 3]$
c. f is not derivable in $(-2, 3) \Rightarrow$ Rolle's theorem is not applicable
d. Rolle's theorem is applicable as f satisfies all the conditions and c of Rolle's theorem is $1/2$

12 If the function $f(x)=2x^2+3x+5$ satisfies LMVT at $x=2$ on the closed interval $[1, a]$, then the value of a is

a. 3
b. 4
c. 6
d. 8

13 Consider the function $f(x)=8x^2-7x+5$ on the interval $[-6, 6]$. The value of c that satisfies the conclusion of the mean value theorem, is

a. $-7/8$
b. -4
c. $7/8$
d. 0

14 Let f be a function which is continuous and differentiable for all real x. If $f(2)=-4$ and $f'(x)\geq 6$ for all $x\in[2,4]$, then

a. $f(4)\leq 8$
b. $f(4)\geq 8$
c. $f(4)\geq 12$
d. None of these

15 If $f(x)=x^3+7x-1$, then $f(x)$ has a zero between $x=0$ and $x=1$. The theorem which best describes this, is

a. Rolle's theorem
b. Mean Value theorem
c. Maximum-minimum value theorem
d. Intermediate value theorem

Working Space

16 Consider $f(x) = |1 - x|$, $1 \le x \le 2$ and $g(x) = f(x) + b\sin\left(\frac{\pi}{2}x\right)$, $1 \le x \le 2$, then which of the following is correct?

a. Rolle's theorem is applicable to both f, g and $b = 3/2$
b. LMVT is not applicable to f and Rolle's theorem, if applicable to g with $b = 1/2$
c. LMVT is applicable to f and Rolle's theorem is applicable to g with $b = 1$
d. Rolle's theorem is not applicable to both f, g for any real b

17 Let $f(x) = \begin{cases} x^{\alpha} \log_e x, & x > 0 \\ 0, & x = 0 \end{cases}$. Rolle's theorem is applicable to f for $x \in [0, 1]$, if α is equal to **[IIT JEE 2004]**

a. -2
b. -1
c. 0
d. $1/2$

18 If $P(x) = 51x^{101} - 2323\,x^{100} - 45x + 1035$, then Rolle's is applicable for **[IIT JEE 2004]**

a. $(45, 46)$
b. $(45, 46^{1/3})$
c. $(45^{1/100}, 46)$
d. $(45, 46^{1/100})$

One or More than One Options Correct Type

Direction (Q. Nos. 19 and 20) This section contains 2 multiple choice questions. Each question has four choices (a), (b), (c) and (d), out of which ONE or MORE THAN ONE are correct.

19 Let $f(x) = 8x^3 - 6x^2 - 2x + 1$, then

a. $f(x) = 0$ has no root in $(0, 1)$
b. $f(x) = 0$ has atleast one root $\in (0, 1)$
c. $f'(c) = 0$ vanishes for some $c \in (0, 1)$
d. None of the above

20 If $f(0) = f(1) = f(2) = 0$ and function $f(x)$ is twice differentiable in $(0, 2)$ and continuous in $[0, 2]$. Then, which of the following is/are true?

a. $f''(c) = 0, \forall c \in (0, 2)$
b. $f'(c) = 0$, for atleast two $c \in (0, 2)$
c. $f'(c) = 0$, for exactly one $c \in (0, 2)$
d. $f''(c) = 0$, for atleast one $c \in (0, 2)$

Statement Type

Direction (Q. Nos. 21 and 22) This section is based on Statement I and Statement II. Select the correct answer from the codes given below.

a. Both Statement I and Statement II are correct and Statement II is the correct explanation of Statement I
b. Both Statement I and Statement II are correct but Statement II is not the correct explanation of Statement I
c. Statement I is correct but Statement II is incorrect
d. Statement II is correct but Statement I is incorrect

21 **Statement I** The quadratic equation $10x^2 - 28x + 17 = 0$ has atleast one root $\in [1, 2]$.

Statement II $f(x) = e^{10x}(x - 1)(x - 2)$ satisfy all the condition of Rolle's theorem in $[1, 2]$.

22 Let $f(x) = 2 + \cos x$ for all x. **[IIT JEE 2007]**

Statement I For each real t, there exists a point c in $[t, t + \pi]$ such that $f'(c) = 0$.

Statement II $f(t) = f(t + 2\pi)$ for each real t.

Matching List Type

Direction *(Q. No. 23) Choices for the correct combination of elements from Column I and Column II are given as options (a), (b), (c) and (d), out of which one is correct.*

23 Match the Column I with Column II and mark the correct option from the codes given below.

	Column I		Column II
i.	The equation $x\log x = 3 - x$ has atleast one root in	p.	[0, 1]
ii.	If $27a + 9b + 3c + d = 0$, then the equation $4ax^3 + 3bx^2 + 2cx + d = 0$ has atleast one root in	q.	[1, 3]
iii.	If $c = \sqrt{3}$ and $f(x) = x + 1/x$, then interval in which LMVT is applicable is	r.	[0, 3]
iv.	If $c = 1/2$ and $f(x) = 2x - x^2$, then interval in which LMVT is applicable for $f(x)$	s.	[−1, 1]

Codes

	i	ii	iii	iv		i	ii	iii	iv
a.	p	q	r	s	b.	p,q	r	s	p
c.	q,r	r	q	p	d.	s	r	q	p

One Integer Value Correct Type

Direction *(Q. Nos. 24 and 25) This section contains 2 questions. When worked out will result in an integer from 0 to 9 (both inclusive).*

24 Suppose that f is differentiable for all x, such that $f'(x) \le 2$ for all x. If $f(1) = 2$ and $f(4) = 8$, then $f(2)$ has the value equal to

25 If $f(x)$ and $g(x)$ are two differentiable functions in [0, 2] such that $f''(x) - g''(x) = 0$, $f'(1) = 2$, $g'(1) = 4$, $f(2) = 3$, $g(2) = 9$, then $|f(x) - g(x)|$ at 3/2 is equal to

DPP-4 Monotonic Functions

Only One Option Correct Type

Direction (Q. Nos. 1-22) This section contains 22 multiple choice questions. Each question has four choices (a), (b), (c) and (d), out of which ONLY ONE is correct.

Working Space

1 The function $f(x) = x^2 (x-2)^2$ is

a. increasing in $(0, 1) \cup (2, \infty)$
b. decreasing in $(0, 1) \cup (2, \infty)$
c. decreasing function
d. increasing function

2 The function $f(x) = \tan x - x, \forall x \in R - \{(2n+1)\pi/2\}$ is

a. always increases
b. always decreases
c. never decreases
d. sometimes increases and sometimes decreases

3 The function $f(x) = x^3 + 6x^2 + (9+2k)x + 1$ is an increasing function, if

a. $k \geq 3/2$ b. $k > 3/2$
c. $k < 3/2$ d. $k \leq 3/2$

4 The value of a for which the function $f(x) = \sin x - \cos x - ax + b$ decreases for all real values of x, is

a. $a \geq -\sqrt{2}$ b. $a \leq -\sqrt{2}$
c. $a \leq \sqrt{2}$ d. $a \geq \sqrt{2}$

5 If $f(x) = \int \left(2 - \frac{1}{1+x^2} - \frac{1}{\sqrt{1+x^2}}\right) dx$, then f is

a. increasing in $(0, \infty)$ and decreasing in $(-\infty, 0)$
b. increasing in $(-\infty, 0)$ and decreasing in $(0, \infty)$
c. increasing in $(-\infty, \infty)$
d. decreasing in $(-\infty, \infty)$

6 The length of largest interval in which function $f(x) = 4x - \tan 2x$ is monotonic, is

a. $\pi/2$ b. $\pi/4$
c. $\pi/8$ d. $\pi/16$

7 The function $f(x) = \tan^{-1}(\sin x + \cos x)$ is an increasing function in **[AIEEE 2007]**

a. $(\pi/4, \pi/2)$ b. $(-\pi/2, \pi/4)$
c. $(0, \pi/2)$ d. $(-\pi/2, \pi/2)$

8 For all $x \in (0, 1)$, **[IIT JEE 2000]**

a. $e^x < 1 + x$ b. $\log_e(1+x) < x$
c. $\sin x > x$ d. $\log_e x > x$

Working Space

9 Let $f(x) = \int e^x (x-1)(x-2)dx$, then f decreases in the interval **[IIT JEE 2000]**

a. $(-\infty, 2)$
b. $(-2, -1)$
c. $(1, 2)$
d. $(2, \infty)$

10 If $f(x) = xe^{x(1-x)}$, then $f(x)$ is **[IIT JEE 2001]**

a. increasing on $[-1/2, 1]$
b. decreases on R
c. increasing on R
d. decreasing on $[-1/2, 1]$

11 The length of a longest interval in which the function $3\sin x - 4\sin^3 x$ is increasing, is **[IIT JEE 2002]**

a. $\pi/3$
b. $\pi/2$
c. $3\pi/2$
d. π

12 If $f(x) = \dfrac{x}{\sin x}$ and $g(x) = \dfrac{x}{\tan x}$, where $0 < x \le 1$, then in this interval

a. both $f(x)$ and $g(x)$ are increasing functions
b. both $f(x)$ and $g(x)$ are decreasing functions
c. $f(x)$ is an increasing function
d. $g(x)$ is an increasing function

13 If $f(x) > x$, $\forall \in R$, then the equation $f[f(x)] - x = 0$ has

a. atleast one real root
b. more than one real root
c. no real root, if $f(x)$ is polynomial and one real root, if $f(x)$ is not a polynomial
d. no real root at all

14 A function $y = f(x)$ is given by $x = \dfrac{1}{1+t^2}$ and $y = \dfrac{1}{t(1+t^2)}$ for all $t > 0$, then f is

a. increasing in $(0, 3/2)$ and decreasing in $(3/2, \infty)$
b. increasing in $(0, 1)$
c. increasing in $(0, \infty)$
d. None of the above

15 The function $f(x) = \dfrac{\log(\pi + x)}{\log(e + x)}$, is

a. increasing on $(0, \infty)$
b. decreasing on $(0, \infty)$
c. increasing on $(0, \pi/e)$, decreasing on $(\pi/e, \infty)$
d. None of the above

16 Number of solution(s) satisfying the equation $3x^2 - 2x^3 = \log_2(x^2+1) - \log_2 x$, is

a. 1
b. 2
c. 3
d. None of these

17 If $f(x) = a^{\{|x| \text{Sgn} x\}}$, $g(x) = a^{[a^{|x|} \text{Sgn} x]}$ for $a > 0$, $a \ne 1$ and $x \in R$, where $\{\}$ and $[\cdot]$ denote the fractional part and greatest integer function respectively, then which of the following statements holds good for the function $h(x)$, where $(\log a)\, h(x) = \log(f(x)) + \log[g(x)]$?

a. h is even and increasing for $a > 1$
b. h is odd and decreasing for $a < 1$
c. h is even and decreasing for $a < 1$
d. h is odd and increasing for $a > 1$

Working Space

18 The value of p for which the function $f(x) = \left(\frac{\sqrt{p+4}}{1-p}\right) x^5 - 3x + \log 5$ decreases for all real x, is

a. $(-\infty, \infty)$
b. $\left[-4, \frac{3-\sqrt{21}}{2}\right] \cup (1, \infty)$
c. $\left[-3, \frac{5-\sqrt{27}}{2}\right] \cup (2, \infty)$
d. $(1, \infty)$

19 If $f(x) = x^3 + bx^2 + cx + d$, $0 < b^2 < c$, then $f(x)$ **[IIT JEE 2004]**

a. is strictly increasing
b. has a local maxima
c. has a local minima
d. has bounded area

20 Let the function $g : (-\infty, \infty) \to (-\pi/2, \pi/2)$ be given by $g(u) = 2\tan^{-1}(e^u) - \pi/2$. Then, g is **[IIT JEE 2008]**

a. even and is strictly increasing in $(0, \infty)$
b. odd and is strictly decreasing in $(-\infty, \infty)$
c. odd and is strictly increasing in $(-\infty, \infty)$
d. neither even nor odd but is strictly increasing in $(-\infty, \infty)$

21 If $f(x) = \frac{a\sin x + b\cos x}{c\sin x + d\cos x}$ is monotonically increasing, then

a. $ad \geq bc$
b. $ad < bc$
c. $ad \leq bc$
d. $ad > bc$

22 Let $f(x) = x^3 + ax^2 + bx + 5\sin^2 x$ be an increasing function in the set of real numbers R. Then, a and b satisfy the condition

a. $a^2 - 3b - 15 \geq 0$
b. $a^2 - 3b + 15 \leq 0$
c. $a^2 - 3b - 15 < 0$
d. $a > 0$ and $b > 0$

One or More than One Options Correct Type

Direction (Q. Nos. 23-30) *This section contains 8 multiple choice questions. Each question has four choices (a), (b), (c) and (d), out of which ONE or MORE THAN ONE are correct.*

23 Let $h(x) = f(x) - [f(x)]^2 + [f(x)]^3$ for every real number x, then

a. h is increasing, whenever f is increasing
b. h is increasing, whenever f is decreasing
c. h is decreasing, whenever f is decreasing
d. nothing can be said in general

Working Space

24 If $f(x)=\begin{cases}3x^2+12x-1, & -1\le x\le 2\\ 37-x, & 2<x\le 3\end{cases}$, then

a. $f(x)$ is increasing on $(-1, 2)$
b. $f(x)$ is continuous on $[-1, 3]$
c. $f'(2)$ does not exist
d. $f(x)$ has the maximum value at $x = 2$

25 Let f and g be two functions defined on an interval I such that $f(x) \ge 0$ and $g(x) \le 0$, for all $x \in I$ and f is strictly decreasing on I while g is strictly increasing on I, then

a. the product function fg is strictly increasing on I
b. the product function fg is strictly decreasing on I
c. $fog(x)$ is monotonically increasing on I
d. $fog(x)$ is monotonically decreasing on I

26 Let $f(x)$ be a non-constant twice differentiable function defined on $(-\infty, \infty)$ such that $f(x) = f(1-x)$ and $f'(1/4) = 0$, then **[IIT JEE 2008]**

a. $f''(x)$ vanishes atleast twice on $[0, 1]$
b. $f'(1/2) = 0$
c. $\int_{-1/2}^{1/2} f(x)dx = 0$
d. $\int_0^{1/2} f(t)e^{\sin \pi t} = \int_{1/2}^{1} f(1-t)e^{\sin \pi t}dt$

27 For the function $f(x) = x\cos(1/x)$, $x \ge 1$ **[IIT JEE 2009]**

a. for atleast one x in the interval $[1, \infty)$, $f(x+2) - f(x) < 2$
b. $\lim_{x\to\infty} f'(x) = 1$
c. for all x in the interval $[1, \infty)$, $f(x+2) - f(x) > 2$
d. $f'(x)$ is strictly decreasing in the interval $[1, \infty)$

28 Let f be a real valued function defined on the interval $[0, \infty)$ by

$f(x) = \log_e x + \int_0^x \sqrt{1+\sin t}\, dt$, then which of the following statement(s) is/are true? **[IIT JEE 2010]**

a. $f''(x)$ exists for all $x \in (0, \infty)$
b. $f'(x)$ exists for all $x \in (0, \infty)$ and $f'(x)$ is continuous on $(0, \infty)$ but not differentiable on $(0, \infty)$
c. There exists $\alpha > 1$ such that $|f'(x)| < |f(x)|$ for all $x \in (0, \infty)$
d. There exists $\beta > 0$ such that $|f(x)| + |f'(x)| \le \beta$ for all $x \in (0, \infty)$

29 If $f(x) = \int_0^x e^t (t-2)(t-3)\, dt$, $\forall x \in (0, \infty)$, then **[IIT JEE 2012]**

a. f is increasing on $(2, 3)$
b. f is decreasing on $(2, 3)$
c. there exists some $c \in (0, \infty)$ such that $f''(c) = 0$
d. f has a local minimum at $x = 3$

30 Let $f(x) = x\sin(\pi x)$, $x > 0$. Then, for all natural numbers n, $f'(x)$ vanishes at **[IIT JEE 2013]**

a. an unique point in the interval $(n, n+1/2)$
b. an unique point in the interval $(n+1/2, n+1)$
c. an unique point in the interval $(n, n+1)$
d. two points in the interval $(n, n+1)$

Working Space

Statement Type

Direction *(Q. Nos. 31 and 32) This section is based on Statement I and Statement II. Select the correct answer from the codes given below.*

a. Both Statement I and Statement II are correct and Statement II is the correct explanation of Statement I
b. Both Statement I and Statement II are correct but Statement II is not the correct explanation of Statement I
c. Statement I is correct but Statement II is incorrect
d. Statement II is correct but Statement I is incorrect

31 Let $f : R \to R$, $f(x) = x^3 + x^2 + 3x + \sin x$.

Statement I $f(x)$ is one-one, because

Statement II $f(x)$ is decreasing function.

32 **Statement I** The greatest of the numbers 1, $2^{1/2}, 3^{1/3}, 4^{1/4}, 5^{1/5}, 6^{1/6}, 7^{1/7}$ is $3^{1/3}$.

Statement II $x^{1/x}$ is increasing for $0 < x < e$ and decreasing for $x > e$.

Comprehension Type

Direction *(Q. Nos. 33-40) This section contains 3 paragraphs, each describing theory, experiments, data, etc. Eight questions related to the paragraphs have been given. Each question has only one correct answer among the four given options (a), (b), (c) and (d).*

Passage I

$f : (0, \infty) \to (-\pi/2, \pi/2)$ be defined as, $f(x) = \arctan(\log_e x)$.

33 The above function can be classified as

a. injective but not surjective
b. surjective but not injective
c. neither injective nor surjective
d. both injective as well as surjective

34 The graph of $y = f(x)$ is best represented by

a.
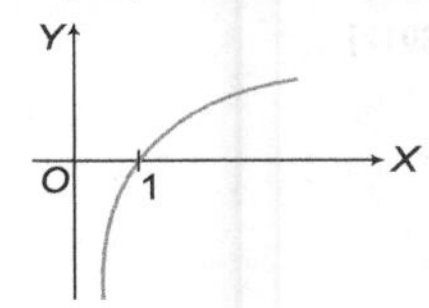

b.
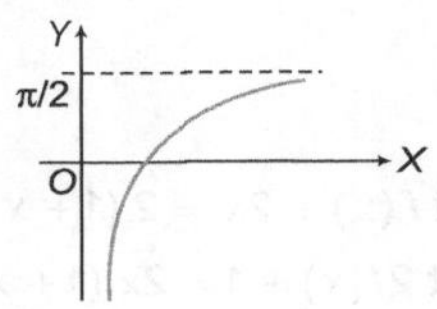

c.
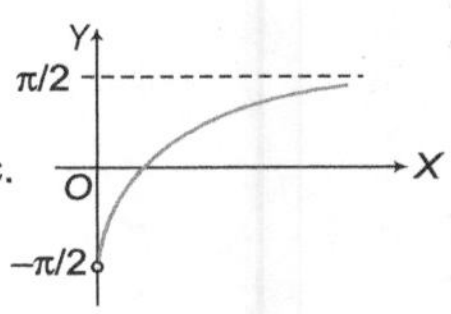

d.
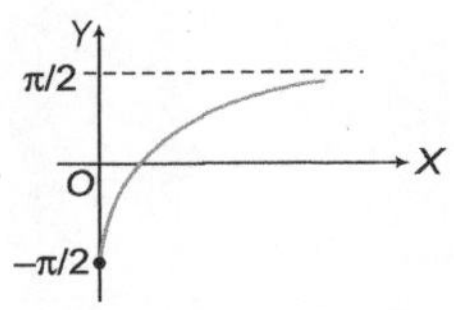

35 If x_1, x_2 and x_3 are the points at which $g(x) = [f(x)]$ is discontinuous (where, [·] denotes the greatest integer function), then $(x_1 + x_2 + x_3)$ is

a. 2
b. 3
c. greater than 3
d. belong to (2, 3)

Passage II

Consider the polynomial function $f(x) = 3x^4 - 4x^3 - 12x^2 + 5$, this function has monotonicity as given below:

Interval	Function $f(x)$
$(-\infty, -a_1)$	decreasing
(a_1, a_2)	increasing
(a_2, a_3)	decreasing
(a_3, ∞)	increasing

A rectangle *ABCD* is formed such that
$l(AB) =$ Portion of the tangent to the curve
$y = f(x)$ at $x = a_1$, intercepted between the lines $x = a_1$ and $x = a_3$.
$l(BC) =$ Portion of the line $x = a_3$ intercepted between the curve and *X*-axis.

36 Triplet (a_1, a_2, a_3) is given by

a. $(-1, 0, 2)$
b. $(0, -1, 2)$
c. $(2, -1, 0)$
d. $(2, 0, -1)$

37 The area of rectangle *ABCD* is

a. 51 sq units
b. 57 sq units
c. 87 sq units
d. 81 sq units

38 The equation $f(x) = 0$ has

a. 2 real and 2 imaginary roots
b. 2 complex and 2 irrational roots
c. 4 real and distinct roots
d. 2 real coincident and 2 irrational roots

Passage III

Let $f(x) = (1 - x)^2 \sin^2 x + x^2$ for all $x \in R$, and let $g(x) = \int_1^x \left[\frac{2(t-1)}{t+1} - \log t\right] f(t)dt$ for all $x \in (1, \infty)$. **[IIT JEE 2012]**

39 Consider the statements :

P : There exists some $x \in R$ such that $f(x) + 2x = 2(1 + x^2)$

Q : There exists some $x \in R$ such that $2f(x) + 1 = 2x(1 + x)$. Then,

a. both *P* and *Q* are true
b. *P* is true and *Q* is false
c. *P* is false and *Q* is true
d. both *P* and *Q* are false

40 Which of the following is true?

a. *g* is increasing on $(1, \infty)$
b. *g* is decreasing on $(1, \infty)$
c. *g* is increasing on (1, 2) and decreasing on $(2, \infty)$
d. *g* is decreasing on (1, 2) and increasing on $(2, \infty)$

DPP-5 Maxima and Minima

Subjective Questions

Direction (Q. Nos. 1-12) *These questions are subjective in nature, need to be solved completely on notebook.*

Working Space

1 Find the points of local maxima/minima of following functions.

i. $f(x) = 2x^3 - 21x^2 + 36x - 20$

ii. $f(x) = -(x-1)^3 (x+1)^2$

iii. $f(x) = x \log_e x$

iv. $y = \dfrac{3x^2 + 4x + 4}{x^2 + x + 1}$

2 Find the absolute maxima/minima value of following functions.

i. $f(x) = 4x - \dfrac{x^2}{2}; x \in \left[-2, \dfrac{9}{2}\right]$

ii. $f(x) = 3x^4 - 8x^3 + 12x^2 - 48x + 25; x \in [0, 3]$

iii. $f(x) = \sin x + \dfrac{1}{2}\cos 2x; x \in \left[0, \dfrac{\pi}{2}\right]$

3 Prove that the perimeter of a right angled triangle of given hypotenuse, say k is maximum when the triangle is isosceles.

4 A wire of length 28 m is to be cut into two pieces. One of the pieces is to be made into square and the other into a circle. What should be length of the two pieces, so that the combined area of the square and circle is minimum?

5 Prove that the semi-vertical angle of a cone of maximum volume and of given slant height l is $\tan^{-1}\sqrt{2}$.

6 Show that a conical tent of given capacity will require least amount of canvas, if its height is $\sqrt{2}$ times the radius of the base.

7 Show that the semi-vertical angle of the right cone of given total surface (including area of base) and maximum volume is $\sin^{-1}(1/3)$.

8 A window is in the form of a rectangle above which there is a semi-circle. If perimeter of window is p cm, then show that the window will allow maximum possible light only when the radius of the semi-circle is $\left(\dfrac{p}{\pi + 4}\right)$ cm.

9 A window of perimeter P (including the base of the arch) is in the form of a rectangle surrounded by a semi-circle. The semi-circular portion is fitted with a coloured glass while the rectangular part is fitted with a clear glass. The clear glass transmits three times as much light per square metre as the coloured glass does. What is the ratio for the sides of the rectangle, so that the window transmits the maximum light?

10 Find the points on the curve $ax^2 + 2hxy + ay^2 = c, c > h > a > 0$, whose distance from the origin is minimum.

Working Space

11 Find the point on the curve $4x^2 + a^2y^2 = 4a^2, 4 < a^2 < 8$ that is farthest from the point $(0, -2)$.

12 Let S be a square of unit area. Consider any quadrilateral which has one vertex on each side of S. If a, b, c and d denote the length of the sides of the quadrilateral, then prove that $2 \le a^2 + b^2 + c^2 + d^2 \le 4$.

Only One Option Correct Type

Direction (Q. Nos. 13-30) *This section contains 18 multiple choice questions. Each question has four choices (a), (b), (c) and (d), out of which ONLY ONE is correct.*

13 If the function $f(x) = 2x^3 - 9ax^2 + 12a^2x + 1$, where $a > 0$, attains its maximum and minimum at p and q respectively such that $p^2 = q$, then a is

a. 1/2 b. 3
c. 1 d. 2

14 The function $f(x) = \frac{x}{2} + \frac{2}{x}$ has a local minimum at

a. $x = -2$ b. $x = 0$
c. $x = 1$ d. $x = 2$

15 A triangular park is enclosed on two sides by a fence and on the third side by a straight river bank. The two sides having fence are of same length x. The maximum area enclosed by the park is

a. $\sqrt{\frac{x^3}{8}}$ b. $\frac{1}{2}x^2$
c. πx^2 d. $\frac{3}{2}x^2$

16 Given $P(x) = x^4 + ax^3 + bx^2 + cx + d$ such that $x = 0$ is the only real root of $P'(x) = 0$. If $P(-1) < P(1)$, then in the interval $[-1, 1]$

a. $P(-1)$ is the minimum but $P(1)$ is not the maximum at P
b. neither $P(-1)$ is the minimum nor $P(1)$ is the maximum at P
c. $P(-1)$ is the minimum and $P(1)$ is the maximum at P
d. $P(-1)$ is not the minimum but $P(1)$ is the maximum at P

17 Let $f : R \to R$ be defined by $f(x) = \begin{cases} k - 2x, & \text{if } x \le -1 \\ 2x + 3, & \text{if } x > -1 \end{cases}$. If f has a local minimum at $x = -1$, then least possible value of k is

a. 1 b. 0
c. $-1/2$ d. -1

18 For $x \in \left(0, \frac{5\pi}{2}\right)$, define $f(x) = \int_0^x \sqrt{t} \sin t \, dt$, then f has **[AIEEE 2011]**

a. local minimum at π and local maximum at 2π
b. local minimum at 2π and local maximum at π
c. local maximum at π and 2π
d. local minimum at π and 2π

19 The real number k for which the equation $2x^3 + 3x + k = 0$ has two distinct real roots in $[0, 1]$ **[JEE Advanced 2013]**

a. lies between 1 and 2
b. lies between 2 and 3
c. lies between -1 and 0
d. does not exist

Working Space

20 Let $f(x) = \begin{cases} |x|, & \text{for } 0 < |x| \le 2 \\ 1, & \text{for } x = 0 \end{cases}$. Then, at $x = 0$, f has

a. a local maximum
b. no local maximum
c. a local minimum
d. no extremum

21 Let $f(x) = (1 + b^2)x^2 + 2bx + 1$ and $m(b)$ is the minimum value of $f(x)$. As b varies, the range of $m(b)$ is

a. $[0, 1]$
b. $\left(0, \frac{1}{2}\right]$
c. $\left[\frac{1}{2}, 1\right]$
d. $(0,1]$

22 A straight line L with negative slope passes through the point (8, 2) and cuts the positive coordinates axes at points P and Q. Then, the absolute minimum of $OP + OQ$, as L varies (where O is origin), is

a. 15
b. 16
c. 17
d. 18

23 If $f(x) = \begin{cases} x, & 0 \le x \le 1 \\ 2 - e^{x-1}, & 1 < x \le 2 \\ x - e, & 2 < x \le 3 \end{cases}$ and $g(x) = \int_0^x f(t)\,dt$, $x \in [0, 3]$, then $g(x)$ has

a. local maxima at $x = 1 + \log 2$ and local minima at $x = e$
b. local maxima at $x = 1$ and local minima at $x = 2$
c. no local maxima
d. no local minima

24 The total number of local maxima and local minima of the function $f(x) = \begin{cases} (2 + x)^3, & -3 < x \le -1 \\ x^{2/3}, & -1 < x < 2 \end{cases}$, is

a. 0
b. 1
c. 2
d. 3

25 Let f, g and h be real valued functions defined on the interval [0, 1] by $f(x) = e^{x^2} + e^{-x^2}$, $g(x) = xe^{x^2} + e^{-x^2}$ and $h(x) = x^2e^{x^2} + e^{-x^2}$. If a, b and c denote respectively, the absolute maximum of f, g and h on [0, 1], then **[IIT JEE 2010]**

a. $a = b$ and $c \ne b$
b. $a = c$ and $a \ne b$
c. $a \ne b$ and $c \ne b$
d. $a = b = c$

26 For all $a, b \in R$, the function $f(x) = 3x^4 - 4x^3 + 6x^2 + ax + b$ has

a. no extremum
b. exactly one extremum
c. exactly two extremum
d. three extremum

27 A rectangle has one side on the positive Y-axis and one side on the positive X-axis. The upper right hand vertex on the curve $y = \frac{\log x}{x^2}$. The maximum area of the rectangle is

a. $\frac{1}{e}$ sq unit
b. $\frac{1}{2\sqrt{e}}$ sq unit
c. 1 sq unit
d. $\sqrt{e}$ sq unit

Working Space

28 The set of values of a for which the function $f(x) = \frac{ax^3}{3} + (a + 2)x^2 + (a - 1)x + 2$ possess a negative point of inflection, is

a. $(-\infty, -2) \cup (0, \infty)$
b. $\left\{\frac{-4}{5}\right\}$
c. $(-2, 0)$
d. empty set

29 The coordinates of the point P on the graph of the function $y = e^{-|x|}$, where area of triangle made by tangent and the coordinate axes has the greatest area, is

a. $\left(\pm 1, \frac{1}{e}\right)$
b. $\left(e, \frac{1}{e}\right)$
c. $\left(\pm\frac{1}{2}, \frac{1}{e^2}\right)$
d. None of these

30 The least value of a for which the equation $\frac{4}{\sin x} + \frac{1}{1 - \sin x} = a$ has atleast one solution m in the interval $(0, \pi/2)$, is

a. 3
b. 5
c. 7
d. 9

One or More than One Options Correct Type

Direction (Q. Nos. 31-35) *This section contains 5 multiple choice questions. Each question has four choices (a), (b), (c) and (d), out of which ONE or MORE THAN ONE are correct.*

31 A rectangular sheet of fixed perimeter with sides having their lengths in the ratio 8 : 15 is converted into an open rectangular box by folding after removing squares of equal area from all four corners. If the total area of removed squares is 100, the resulting box has maximum volume. Then, the lengths of sides of the rectangular sheet are **[JEE Advanced 2013]**

a. 24
b. 32
c. 45
d. 60

32 The function $f(x) = 2|x| + |x - 2| - ||x + 2| - 2|x||$ has a local minimum or a local maximum at x is equal to **[JEE Advanced 2013]**

a. -2
b. $-2/3$
c. 2
d. $2/3$

33 The function $f(x) = \int_0^x \sqrt{1 - t^4}\, dt$ is such that

a. it is defined on the interval $[-1, 1]$
b. it is an increasing function
c. it is an odd function
d. the point $(0, 0)$ is the point of inflection

34 The function $f(x) = \frac{\sin(x + a)}{\sin(x + b)}$ has no maxima or minima, if

a. $b - a = n\pi, n \in I$
b. $b - a = (2n + 1)\pi, n \in I$
c. $b - a = 2n\pi, n \in I$
d. None of these

35 $f(x)$ is cubic polynomial which has local maximum at $x = -1$. If $f(2) = 18$, $f(1) = -1$ and $f'(x)$ has local minima at $x = 0$, then

a. the distance between $(-1, 2)$ and $(a, f(a))$, where $x = a$, the point of local minima is $2\sqrt{5}$
b. $f(x)$ is increasing for $x \in [1, 2\sqrt{5}]$
c. $f(x)$ has local minima at $x = 1$
d. has value of $f(0) = 5$

Matching List Type

Working Space

***Direction** (Q. No. 36) Choices for the correct combination of elements from Column I and Column II are given as options (a), (b), (c) and (d), out of which one is correct.*

36 For the function $f(x) = x^4 (12\log_e x - 7)$. Match the Column I with Column II and mark the correct option from the codes given below.

	Column I		Column II
i.	If $x = a$ is the point of inflection, then $8a$ is equal to	p.	3
ii.	If e^t is a point of minima, then $12t$ is equal to	q.	1
iii.	If graph is concave downward in (d, e), then $d + 3e$ is equal to	r.	4
iv.	If graph is concave upward in (p, ∞), then the least value of p is	s.	8

Codes

	i	ii	iii	iv
a.	r	p	q	s
b.	s	r	p	q
c.	p	q	r	s
d.	r	q	s	p

Comprehension Type

***Direction** (Q. Nos. 37-42) This section contains 2 paragraphs, each describing theory, experiments, data, etc. Six questions related to the paragraphs have been given. Each question has only one correct answer among the four given options (a), (b), (c) and (d).*

Passage I

Suppose $f(x)$ is a real valued polynomial function of degree 6 satisfying the following conditions.

i. f has minimum value at $x = 0$ and 2.

ii. f has maximum value at $x = 1$.

iii. For all x, $\lim_{x \to 0} \frac{1}{x} \log \begin{vmatrix} \frac{f(x)}{x} & 1 & 0 \\ 0 & \frac{1}{x} & 1 \\ 1 & 0 & \frac{1}{x} \end{vmatrix} = 2.$

37 The number of solution of the equation $8f(x) - 1 = 0$ is

a. 1 b. 2
c. 3 d. 4

38 The range of $f(x)$ is

a. $\left[-\frac{32}{15}, \infty\right)$ b. $\left[-\frac{4}{15}, \infty\right)$
c. $\left(-\infty, \frac{2}{15}\right]$ d. None of these

39 If the area bounded by $y = f(x)$, X-axis, $x = \pm 1$, is a/b, where a, b are relatively prime, then the value of $\tan^{-1}(a - b)$ is

a. $\pi/4$ b. $-\pi/4$
c. $\pi/3$ d. $\pi/6$

Working Space

Passage II

Consider the function $f : (-\infty, \infty) \to (-\infty, \infty)$ defined by $f(x) = \dfrac{x^2 - ax + 1}{x^2 + ax + 1}$, $0 < a < 2$.

40 Which of the following is true? **[IIT JEE 2008]**

a. $(2+a)^2 f''(1) + (2-a)^2 f''(-1) = 0$
b. $(2-a)^2 f''(1) - (2+a)^2 \cdot f''(-1) = 0$
c. $f'(1) f'(-1) = (2-a)^2$
d. $f'(1) \cdot f'(-1) = -(2+a)^2$

41 Which of the following is true?

a. $f(x)$ is decreasing on $(-1, 1)$ and has a local minimum at $x = 1$
b. $f(x)$ is increasing on $(-1, 1)$ and has a local maximum at $x = 1$
c. $f(x)$ is increasing on $(-1, 1)$ but has neither a local maximum nor a local minimum at $x = 1$
d. $f(x)$ is decreasing on $(-1, 1)$ but has neither a local maximum nor a local minimum at $x = 1$

42 Let $g(x) = \int_0^{e^x} \dfrac{f'(t)dt}{1+t^2}$, then which of the following is true?

a. $g'(x)$ is positive on $(-\infty, 0)$ and negative on $(0, \infty)$
b. $g'(x)$ is negative on $(-\infty, 0)$ and positive on $(0, \infty)$
c. $g'(x)$ changes sign on both $(-\infty, 0)$ and $(0, \infty)$
d. $g'(x)$ does not change sign on $(-\infty, \infty)$

One Integer Value Correct Type

Direction (Q. Nos. 43-50) This section contains 8 questions. When worked out will result in an integer from 0 to 9 (both inclusive).

43 The maximum value of the function $f(x) = 2x^3 - 15x^2 + 36x - 48$ on the set $A = \{x : x^2 + 20 \le 9x\}$ is

44 Let $p(x)$ be a polynomial of degree 4 having extremum at $x = 1, 2$ and $\lim_{x \to 0}\left[1 + \dfrac{p(x)}{x^2}\right] = 2$, then the value of $p(2)$ is

45 Let f be a function defined on R (the set of all real numbers) such that $f'(x) = 2010(x - 2009)(x - 2010)^2(x - 2011)^3(x - 2012)^4$, for all $x \in R$. If g is a function defined on R with values in the interval $(0, \infty)$ such that $f(x) = \log[g(x)]$ for all $x \in R$. Then, the number of points in R at which g has a local maximum is **[IIT JEE 2010]**

46 Let $f : R \to R$ be defined as $f(x) = |x| + |x^2 - 1|$. The total number of points at which f attains either a local maximum or a local minimum, is **[IIT JEE 2012]**

47 Let $P(x)$ be a real polynomial of least degree which has a local maximum at $x = 1$ and a minimum at $x = 3$. If $P(1) = 6$ and $P(3) = 2$, then $P'(0)$ is **[IIT JEE 2012]**

48 For a circle $x^2 + y^2 = r^2$, find the value of r for which the area enclosed by the tangents drawn from the point $P(6, 8)$ to the circle and the chord of contact is maximum.

49 If the function $f(x) = x^4 + bx^2 + 8x + 1$ has a horizontal tangent at a point of inflection for the same value of x, then the value of $|b|$ is equal to

50 For constant number a, consider the function $f(x) = ax + \cos 2x + \sin x + \cos x$ on R such that $f(u) < f(v)$ for $u < v$. If the range of a for any real number u, v is $\left[\dfrac{m}{n}, \infty\right)$, then the value of $(m - n)$, is

SET - 1

Revisal Problems for JEE Main

Only One Option Correct Type

Working Space

Direction (Q. Nos. 1-30) *This section contains 30 multiple choice questions. Each question has four choices (a), (b), (c) and (d), out of which ONLY ONE option is correct.*

1 Let $f(x)$ be a non-zero function whose all successive derivative exist and are non-zero. If $f(x)$, $f'(x)$ and $f''(x)$ are in GP and $f(0)=1$, $f'(0)=1$, Then

a. $f'(x)<0, \forall x \in R$ b. $f''(x)<1, \forall x \in R$
c. $f''(0) \neq f'''(0)$ d. $f''(x)>0, \forall x \in R$

2 Tangent of acute angle between the curves $y=|x^2-1|$ and $y=|x^2-3|$ at their points of intersection, is

a. 0 b. $4\sqrt{2}/3$
c. $4\sqrt{2}/7$ d. $2\sqrt{2}$

3 A particle moving on a curve has the position at time t given by $x=f'(t)\sin t+f''(t)\cos t$ and $y=f'(t)\cos t-f''(t)\sin t$, where f is thrice differentiable function. Then, the velocity of particle at time t is

a. $f'(t)+f''(t)$ b. $f'(t)-f'''(t)$
c. $f'(t)+f'''(t)$ d. None of these

4 If $f:[0, 4] \to R$ is a differentiable function. Then, for some $a, b \in (0, 4)$, $f^2(4)-f^2(0)$ is

a. $8f'(a) \cdot f(b)$ b. $4f'(b) \cdot f(a)$
c. $2f'(b) \cdot f(a)$ d. $f'(b) \cdot f(a)$

5 The set of values of a for which the function $f(x)=8ax-a\sin 6x-7x-\sin 5x$ increases and has no critical points for all $x \in R$, is

a. $[-1, 1]$ b. $(-\infty, -6)$
c. $(6, \infty)$ d. $[6, \infty)$

6 Let $f(x)=\{x\}$ (where, $\{\cdot\}$ denotes fractional part of x) for $f(x)$, $x=5$ is

a. a point of local maxima
b. a point of local minima
c. neither a point of local minima nor local maximum
d. None of the above

7 The equation $x^3-3x+[a]=0$ (where, $[\cdot]$ denotes the greatest integer function) will have three real and distinct roots, if

a. $a \in (-\infty, 2)$ b. $a \in (0, 2)$
c. $a \in (-\infty, -2) \cup (0, \infty)$ d. $a \in [-1, 2)$

8 A function is defined as $f(x)=ax^2-b|x|$, where a and b are constants, $x=0$ will be a point of maxima of $f(x)$ is

a. $a>0, b>0$ b. $a>0, b<0$
c. $a<0, b<0$ d. $a<0, b>0$

9 If $f(x)=2x^3-3(a+1)x^2+6ax-12$ has local maximum at x_1 and local minimum at x_2 and if $2x_1=x_2$, then the value of a is

a. 1 b. 1/2
c. -1 d. 2

10 Let $f(x)$ be defined as $f(x)=\begin{cases} \tan^{-1}\alpha-5x^2, & 0<x<1 \\ -6x, & x \geq 1 \end{cases}$, $f(x)$ can have a local maximum at $x=1$, if value of α is

a. 0 b. -1 c. $-\tan 1$ d. -2

Working Space

11 A truck is to be driven 300 km on a highway at a constant speed of x km/h. Speed rules of highway required that $30 \le x \le 60$. The fuel cost ₹10 per litre and is consumed at the rate of $2 + \frac{x^2}{100}$ L/h. The wages of the driver are ₹200 per hour. The most economical speed to drive the truck (in km/h) is

a. 30   b. 60

c. $30\sqrt{3}$ d. $20\sqrt{3}$

12 Slope of tangent to the curve $y = 2e^x \sin\left(\frac{\pi}{4} - \frac{x}{2}\right)\cos\left(\frac{\pi}{4} - \frac{x}{2}\right)$, where $0 \le x \le 2\pi$, is minimum at x is equal to

a. 0   b. π

c. 2π d. None of these

13 The lateral edge of a regular hexagonal pyramid is 1 cm. If the volume is maximum, then its height must be equal to

a. 1/3   b. 2/3

c. $1/\sqrt{3}$ d. 1

14 Let $f(x) = \begin{cases} \frac{4-x}{2-\sqrt{x}}, & \text{for } 0 < x < 4 \\ 4, & \text{for } x = 4 \\ 16 - 3x, & \text{for } 4 < x < 6 \end{cases}$, then which of the following does f have on the interval (0, 6)?

I. $\log [f(x)]$ exists.   II. f is continuous.

III. f is monotonic.

a. Only I   b. Only II

c. Only III   d. I and II

15 Consider, the function $f(x) = \begin{cases} x \sin(\pi/x), & \text{for } x > 0 \\ 0, & \text{for } x = 0 \end{cases}$. Then, the number of points in (0, 1), where the derivative $f'(x)$ vanishes, is

a. 0   b. 1

c. 2   d. infinite

16 The number of roots of $x^2 \cdot e^{|x|} = 1$ is

a. 2   b. 4

c. 6   d. infinite

17 A function $y = f(x)$ has a second order derivative $f''(x) = 6(x-1)$. If its graph passes through the point (2, 1) and at that point the tangent to the graph is $y = 3x - 5$, then the function is

a. $(x-1)^2$ b. $(x-1)^3$

c. $(x+1)^3$ d. $(x+1)^2$

18 If $f(x)$ is a twice differentiable function such that $f(a) = 0$, $f(b) = 2$, $f(c) = -1$, $f(d) = 2$, $f(e) = 0$, where $a < b < c < e$. Then, the minimum number of zeros of $g(x) = [f'(x)]^2 + f''(x) \cdot f(x)$ in the interval $[a, e]$ is

a. 4   b. 5   c. 6   d. 7

19 Let $f(x) = \begin{cases} \sin \frac{\pi x}{2}, & 0 \le x < 1 \\ 3 - 2x, & x \ge 1 \end{cases}$, then

a. $f(x)$ has local maxima at $x = 1$

b. $f(x)$ has local minima at $x = 1$

c. $f(x)$ does not have any local extrema at $x = 1$

d. $f(x)$ has a global minima at $x = 1$

20 Two sides of triangle have lengths a cm and b cm. If the triangle is to have the maximum area, then the length of the median from the vertex containing the sides a and b is

a. $\frac{1}{2}\sqrt{a^2 + b^2}$ b. $\frac{2a + b}{3}$

c. $\sqrt{\frac{a^2 + b^2}{3}}$ d. $\frac{a + 2b}{3}$

Working Space

21 The equation of a straight line passing through (1, 4). If the sum of its positive intercepts on the coordinate axes is the smallest, is

a. $2x + y - 6 = 0$ b. $x + 2y - 9 = 0$
c. $y + 2x + 6 = 0$ d. None of these

22 A solid rectangular brick is to be made from 1 cu ft of clay. The brick must be 3 times as long as it is wide. The width of brick for which it will have minimum surface area is a, then a^3 is

a. $(2/9)^{1/3}$ b. 2/9
c. 8/729 d. 3/2

23 Let h be a twice continuously differentiable positive function on an open interval J, let $g(x) = \log_e [h(x)]$ for each $x \in J$. Suppose $[h'(x)]^2 > h''(x)\, h(x)$ for each $x \in J$, then

a. g is increasing on J
b. g is decreasing on J
c. g is concave up on J
d. g is concave down on J

24 Function $f(x), g(x)$ are defined on $[-1, 3]$ and $f''(x) > 0,\ g''(x) > 0,\ \forall\, x \in [-1, 3]$. Then, which of the following is always true?

a. $f(x) - g(x)$ is concave upwards on $(-1, 3)$
b. $f(x)g(x)$ is concave upwards on $(-1, 3)$
c. $f(x)g(x)$ does not have a critical point on $(-1, 3)$
d. $f(x) + g(x)$ is concave upwards on $(-1, 3)$

25 The number of solution(s) satisfying the equation $3x^2 - 2x^3 = \log_2(x^2 + 1) - \log_2 x$ is

a. 1 b. 2
c. 3 d. None of these

26 Let $P(x) = a_0 + a_1x^2 + a_2x^4 + \cdots + a_nx^{2n}$ be a polynomial in a real variable x with $0 < a_0 < a_1 < a_2 < \cdots < a_n$. The function $P(x)$ has

a. neither a maximum nor a minimum
b. only one maximum
c. only one minimum
d. only one maximum and only one minimum

27 A spherical balloon is filled with $4500\pi\ m^3$ of helium gas. If a leak in the balloon causes the gas to escape at the rate of $72\pi\ m^3$/min, then the rate (in m/min) at which the radius of the balloon decreases 49 min after the leakage began is

a. 9/2 b. 9/7
c. 7/9 d. 2/9

28 Let $f : R \to R$ be defined by $f(x) = \begin{cases} b - 2x, & \text{if } x \le -1 \\ 2x + 3, & \text{if } x > -1 \end{cases}$. If f has a local minimum at $x = -1$, then a possible value of b is equal to

a. 0 b. −1/2
c. −1 d. 1

29 If $a < b < c < d$ and $x \in R$, then the least value of the function $f(x) = |x - a| + |x - b| + |x - c| + |x - d|$ is

a. $c - d + b - a$
b. $c + d - b - a$
c. $c + d - b + a$
d. $c + b - d + a$

30 The intervals of increase of $f(x)$ defined by $f(x) = \int_{-1}^{x} (t^2 + 2t)(t^2 - 1)\,dt$ is

a. $(-\infty, -3/2) \cup (0, 3) \cup (10, \infty)$
b. $(-\infty, -2) \cup (-1/2, 1/2) \cup (4, \infty)$
c. $(-\infty, -2) \cup (-1, 0) \cup (1, \infty)$
d. $(-\infty, -2) \cup (-3/4\ 1/4) \cup (1, \infty)$

Working Space

Statement Type

***Direction** (Q. Nos. 31-40) This section is based on Statement I and Statement II. Select the correct answer from the codes given below.*

a. Both Statement I and Statement II are correct and Statement II is the correct explanation of Statement I
b. Both Statement I and Statement II are correct but Statement II is not the correct explanation of Statement I
c. Statement I is correct but Statement II is incorrect
d. Statement II is correct but Statement I is incorrect

31 **Statement I** The ratio of length of tangent to length of normal is inversely proportional to numerical value of the ordinate of point of tangency at the curve $y^2 = 4ax$.

Statement II The length of normal and tangent to a curve $y = f(x)$ is $|y\sqrt{1+m^2}|$ and $\left|y\dfrac{\sqrt{1+m^2}}{m}\right|$, where $m = \dfrac{dy}{dx}$.

32 **Statement I** The curves $y^2 = 16x$ and $x^2 = 16y$ are orthogonal curves.

Statement II Two curves are said to be orthogonal,if they intersect each other at right angle at each point of intersection.

33 **Statement I** Shortest distance between $|x| + |y| = 2$ and $x^2 + y^2 = 16$ is $4 - \sqrt{2}$.

Statement II Shortest distance between the two differentiable curves lies along the common normal.

34 **Statement I** $\dfrac{2e^{x_1} + e^{x_2}}{3} > e^{\left(\frac{2x_1 + x_2}{3}\right)}$, where e is a Napier's constant.

Statement II If $f'(x)$ and $f''(x)$ are positive for all $x \in R$, then $f(x)$ increases with concavity up $\forall x \in R$ and any chord lies above the curve.

35 Consider, $f(x)$ is a function such that $f(1) = 1$, $f(2) = 4$ and $f(3) = 9$.

Statement I $f''(x) = 2$ for some $x \in (1, 3)$.
Statement II $g(x) = x^2 \Rightarrow g''(x) = 2, \forall x \in R$.

36 **Statement I** If $f(x)$ is increasing function with concavity upwards, then concavity of $f^{-1}(x)$ is also upwards.
Statement II If $f(x)$ is decreasing function with concavity upwards, then concavity of $f^{-1}(x)$ is also upwards.

37 **Statement I** Let $f(x) = 5 - 4(x-2)^{2/3}$, then at $x = 2$, the function $f(x)$ attains neither least value nor greatest value.
Statement II $x = 2$ is the only critical point of $f(x)$.

38 **Statement I** The function $f(x) = x$ is increasing for all x.

Statement II If $f(x)$ and $g(x)$ both are increasing (a, b). Then, $f(x) \cdot g(x)$ must be increasing in (a, b).

39 Consider the polynomial function $f(x) = \dfrac{x^7}{7} - \dfrac{x^6}{6} + \dfrac{x^5}{5} - \dfrac{x^4}{4} + \dfrac{x^3}{3} - \dfrac{x^2}{2} + x$.

Statement I The equation $f(x) = 0$ cannot have two or more roots.
Statement II Rolle's theorem is not applicable for $y = f(x)$ on any interval $[a, b]$, where $a, b \in R$.

40 **Statement I** $f(x) = \log_{e+x}(\pi + x)$ is strictly increasing for all $x > 0$.

Statement II $\pi + x > e + x, \forall x > 0$.

SET - 2

Revisal Problems
for JEE Advanced

Only One Option Correct Type

Working Space

Direction *(Q. Nos. 1-27) This section contains 27 multiple choice questions. Each question has four choices (a), (b), (c) and (d), out of which ONLY ONE option is correct.*

1 Difference between the greatest and the least values of the function $f(x) = x(\log x - 2)$ on $[1, e^2]$ is

a. 2 b. e c. e^2 d. 1

2 The number of positive integral values of a for which the curve $y = a^x$ intersects the line $y = x$, is

a. 0 b. 1 c. 2 d. more than 2

3 The bottom of legs of a three legged table are the vertices of an isosceles triangle with sides 5, 5 and 6. The legs are to be braced at the bottom by three wires in the shape of a Y. The minimum length of the wire needed for this purpose is

a. $4 + 3\sqrt{3}$ b. 10 c. $3 + 4\sqrt{3}$ d. $1 + 6\sqrt{2}$

4 Let $g : [1, 6] \to [0, \infty)$ be a real values differentiable function satisfying $g'(x) = \dfrac{2}{x + g(x)}$ and $g(1) = 0$, then the maximum value of g cannot exceed

a. $\log_e 2$ b. $\log_2 6$ c. $6\log_e 2$ d. $2\log_e 6$

5 A horse runs along a circle with a speed of 20 km/h. A lantern is at the centre of the circle. A fence is along the tangent to the circle at the point at which the horse starts. The speed with which the shadow of the horse moves along the fence at the moment when it covers 1/8 of the circle in km/h, is

a. 20 b. 40 c. 30 d. 60

6 The lateral edge of a regular hexagonal pyramid is 1 cm. If the volume is maximum, then its height must be equal to

a. 1/3 b. 2/3
c. $1/\sqrt{3}$ d. 1

7 Let $f(x)$ and $g(x)$ be two continuous functions defined from $R \to R$, such that $f(x_1) > f(x_2)$ and $g(x_1) < g(x_2)$, $\forall\, x_1, x_2$, then solution set of $f[g(\alpha^2 - 2\alpha)] > f[g(3\alpha - 4)]$ is

a. R b. ϕ
c. (1, 4) d. $R - [1, 4]$

8 If the function $f(x) = \dfrac{t + 3x - x^2}{x - 4}$, where t is a parameter has a maximum, then the range of values of t is

a. (0, 4) b. $(0, \infty)$
c. $(-\infty, 4)$ d. $(4, \infty)$

9 The graph of $y = f(x)$ is shown. Let $F(x)$ be an anti-derivative of $f(x)$. Then, $F(x)$ has

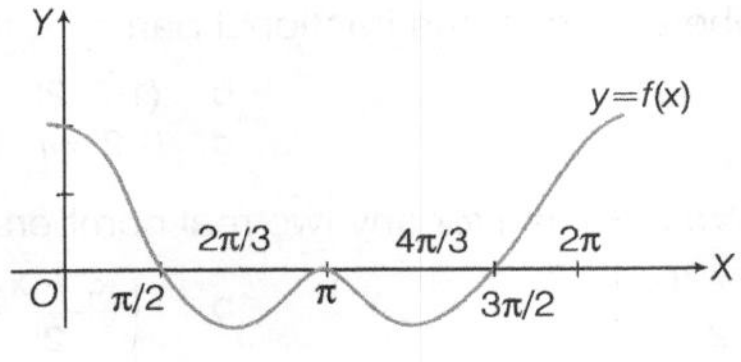

a. points of inflexion at $x = 0, \dfrac{2\pi}{3}, \pi, \dfrac{4\pi}{3}$ and 2π, a local maximum at $x = \pi/2$ and a local minimum at $x = 3\pi/2$

b. points of inflexion at $x = 0, \dfrac{2\pi}{3}, \pi, \dfrac{4\pi}{3}$ and 2π, a local minimum at $x = \pi/2$ and a local maximum at $x = \dfrac{3\pi}{2}$

c. point of inflexion at $x = \pi$, a local maximum at $x = \pi/2$ and a local minimum at $x = 3\pi/2$

d. points of inflexion at $x = \pi$, a local minimum at $x = \pi/2$ and a local maximum at $x = 3\pi/2$

Working Space

10 The number of critical points of the function, $f(x)=\frac{2}{3}\sqrt{x^3}-\frac{x}{2}+\int_1^x\left(\frac{1}{2}+\frac{1}{2}\cos 2t-\sqrt{t}\right)dt$ which lie in the interval $[-2\pi, 2\pi]$, is

a. 2
b. 4
c. 6
d. 8

11 For a steamer the consumption of petrol (per hour) varies as the cube of its speed (in km). If the speed of the current is steady at c km/h. Then, the most economical speed of the steamer going against the current will be

a. $1.25c$
b. $1.5c$
c. $1.75c$
d. $2c$

12 If the point of minima of the function $f(x)=1+a^2x-x^3$ satisfy the inequality $\frac{x^2+x+2}{x^2+5x+6}<0$, then a must lie in the interval

a. $(-3\sqrt{3}, 3\sqrt{3})$
b. $(-2\sqrt{3}, -3\sqrt{3})$
c. $(2\sqrt{3}, 3\sqrt{3})$
d. $(-3\sqrt{3}, -2\sqrt{3})\cup(2\sqrt{3}, 3\sqrt{3})$

13 The number of solutions of equation $3\tan x + x^3 = 2$ in $(0, \pi/4)$ is

a. 0
b. 1
c. 2
d. 3

14 If f be a continuous function in $[0, 1]$, differentiable in $(0, 1)$ such that $f(1)=0$, then their exists some $c \in (0, 1)$ such that

a. $cf'(c)-f(c)=0$
b. $f'(c)+cf(c)=0$
c. $f'(c)-cf(c)=0$
d. $cf'(c)+f(c)=0$

15 There are 50 apple trees in an orchard. Each tree produces 800 apples. For each additional tree planted in the orchard, the output per additional tree drops by 10 apples. Number of trees that should be added to the existing orchard for maximising the output of trees, is

a. 5
b. 10
c. 15
d. 20

16 If $M(x_0, y_0)$ is the point on the curve $3x^2-4y^2=72$, which is nearest to the line $3x+2y+1=0$, then the value of (x_0+y_0) is equal to

a. 3
b. -3
c. 9
d. -9

17 In which one of the following intervals Rolle's theorem holds good for $y=x^2\sin\left(\frac{1}{x}\right)+x^3\cos\left(\frac{1}{2x}\right)$?

a. $\left[\frac{1}{\pi}, \frac{2}{\pi}\right]$
b. $\left[\frac{1}{3\pi}, \frac{1}{\pi}\right]$
c. $\left[\frac{1}{2\pi}, \frac{1}{\pi}\right]$
d. $\left[\frac{1}{\pi}, \frac{3}{\pi}\right]$

18 If $f'(x)>0, \forall x \in R$, $f'(3)=0$ and $g(x)=f(\tan^2 x-2\tan x+4)$, $0<x<\pi/2$, then $g(x)$ increases in

a. $(0, \pi/4)$
b. $(\pi/4, \pi/2)$
c. $(\pi/4, \pi/3)$
d. $(0, \pi/3)$

19 If $f'(x)=|x|-\{x\}$, where $\{\cdot\}$ denotes fractional part of x, then $f(x)$ is decreasing in

a. $(-1/2, 0)$
b. $(1/2, 2)$
c. $(-1/2, 2)$
d. $(1/2, \infty)$

20 If $f'(x)>0$, $f''(x)>0, \forall x \in R$, then for any two real numbers x_1 and x_2 $(x_1 \neq x_2)$

a. $f\left(\frac{x_1+x_2}{2}\right)>\frac{f(x_1)+f(x_2)}{2}$
b. $f\left(\frac{x_1+x_2}{2}\right)=\frac{f(x_1)+f(x_2)}{2}$
c. $f\left(\frac{x_1+x_2}{2}\right)<\frac{f(x_1)+f(x_2)}{2}$
d. None of these

Working Space

21 Let $f'(\sin x) < 0$, $f''(\sin x) > 0$, $\forall x \in \left(0, \frac{\pi}{2}\right)$ and $g(x) = f(\sin x) + f(\cos x)$, then the interval in which $g(x)$ is increasing, is

a. $(\pi/4, \pi)$
b. $(\pi, 3\pi/2)$
c. $(\pi/4, \pi/2)$
d. $(0, \pi/4)$

22 If $f(x) = \begin{cases} x - 1, & x \geq 1 \\ [a+1] - x^3 + 1, & x < 1 \end{cases}$ has minimum at $x = 1$, then (where $[\cdot]$ denotes the greatest integer function)

a. $a \geq -1$
b. $a \leq -1$
c. $-1 \leq a \leq 1$
d. $a \neq 0$

23 $f(x)$ is twice differentiable function such that $f(x) + f''(x) = -x|\sin x|f'(x)$, where $x \geq 0$. Given that $f(0) = -3$, $f'(0) = 4$ the maximum value of $f(x)$ is

a. 4
b. 3
c. 5
d. Does not exist

24 If $a, b \in R$ distinct numbers satisfying $|a-1| + |b-1| = |a| + |b| = |a+1| + |b+1|$, then the minimum value of $|a - b|$ is

a. 3
b. 0
c. 1
d. 2

25 If $f(x) = f(x-1)|x^2 - 2007x + 2010| + \sin[(x-1)]\log_e x$ has

a. local minimum at $x = 1$
b. local maximum at $x = 1$
c. no local extremum at $x = 1$
d. None of these

26 The function $f(x) = |px - q| + r|x|$, $x \in (-\infty, \infty)$, where $p > 0, q > 0, r > 0$ assumes its minimum value only on one point of

a. $p \neq q$
b. $r \neq q$
c. $r \neq p$
d. $p = q = r$

27 If $f: R \to R$ and $g: R \to R$ are two functions such that $f(x) + f''(x) = -xg(x) \cdot f'(x)$ and $g(x) > 0$, $\forall x \in R$, then the functions $f^2(x) + [f'(x)]^2$ has

a. a maximum at $x = 0$
b. a minimum at $x = 0$
c. a point of inflexion at $x = 0$
d. None of these

One or More than One Options Correct Type

Direction (Q. Nos. 28-35) *This section contains 8 multiple choice questions. Each question has four choices (a), (b), (c) and (d), out of which ONE or MORE THAN ONE are correct.*

28 Let $f(x) = (x^2 - 1)^n \cdot (x^2 + x + 1)$, then $f(x)$ has local extremum at $x = 1$, when

a. $n = 2$
b. $n = 3$
c. $n = 4$
d. $n = 6$

29 The function $f(x) = \begin{cases} x + 2, & \text{if } x < -1 \\ x^2, & \text{if } -1 \leq x < 1 \\ (x-2)^2, & \text{if } x \geq 1 \end{cases}$

a. is continuous for all $x \in R$
b. is continuous but not differentiable for all $x \in R$
c. is such that $f'(x)$ change its sign exactly twice
d. has two local maxima and two local minima

30 Which of the following inequalities always hold good in (0, 1)?

a. $x > \tan^{-1} x$
b. $\cos x < 1 - \frac{x^2}{2}$
c. $1 + x\log(x + \sqrt{1 + x^2}) > \sqrt{1 + x^2}$
d. $x^2 - \frac{x^2}{2} < \log(1 - x)$

Working Space

31 If $f(x)$ is continuous and differentiable, $\forall x \in R$ and $f'(c) = 0$ for exactly two real values of c, then the number of real and distinct values of d for which $f(d) = 0$ can be

a. 1 b. 2
c. 3 d. 4

32 If $\lim_{x \to a} f(x) = \lim_{x \to a} [f(x)]$ (a is a finite quantity), (where [·] denotes the greatest integer function), then

a. $\lim_{x \to a} f(x)$ is an integer
b. $\lim_{x \to a} f(x)$ needed not be an integer
c. $f(x)$ has a local minima at $x = a$
d. $f(x)$ has a local maxima at $x = a$

33 Which of the following functions fail to satisfy the condition of Rolle's theorem on the interval $[-1, 1]$?

a. $f(x) = |x| [x]$
b. $f(x) = \begin{cases} \frac{\tan x}{x}, & x \neq 0 \\ 0, & x = 0 \end{cases}$
c. $f(x) = \{x\} + \{-x\}$
d. $f(x) = |x| - \sin|x|$

34 Let $f(x) = 1 + x \log(x + \sqrt{x^2 + 1}) - \sqrt{1 + x^2}$ and $h(x) = f(x) - f^2(x) + f^3(x)$. Then

a. $h(x)$ is increasing in $(0, \infty)$
b. $h(x)$ is decreasing in $(-\infty, 0)$
c. $h(x)$ is increasing on R
d. $h(x)$ is decreasing on R

35 Let $f(x) = a(x - x_1)(x - x_2)$, where a, x_1 and x_2 are real numbers such that $a \neq 0$ and $x_1 + x_2 = 0$. Then, which of the following statements is/are always correct?

a. $f(x)$ is increasing in $(-\infty, 0)$ and decreasing in $(0, \infty)$
b. $f(x)$ is decreasing in $(-\infty, 0)$ and increasing in $(0, \infty)$
c. $f(x)$ is non-monotonic on R
d. $f(x)$ has an extremum point

Comprehension Type

Direction (Q. Nos. 36-44) ***This section contains 3 paragraphs, each describing theory, experiments, data, etc. Nine questions related to the paragraphs have been given. Each question has only one correct answer among the four given options (a), (b), (c) and (d).***

Passage I

Consider, the function $f(x) = \dfrac{x^2}{x - 1}$.

36 The interval in which f is increasing is

a. $(-1, 1)$ b. $(-\infty, -1) \cup (-1, 0)$
c. $(-\infty, \infty) - \{-1, 1\}$ d. $(0, 1) \cup (1, \infty)$

37 If f is defined from $R - \{-1, 1\} \to R$, then f is

a. injective but not surjective
b. surjective but not injective
c. injective as well as surjective
d. neither injective nor surjective

38 f has

a. local maxima but no local minima
b. local minima but no local maxima
c. both local maxima and local minima
d. neither local minima nor local maxima

Passage II

Let $f(x)$ be a real valued continuous function on R defined as $f(x) = x^2 e^{-|x|}$.

39 The value of k for which the curve $y = kx^2$ $(k > 0)$ intersect the curve $y = e^{|x|}$ at exactly two points, is

a. e^2 b. $e^2/2$ c. $e^2/4$ d. $e^2/8$

40 The area bounded by ordinates at points of local maximum, the curve $y = f(x)$ and X-axis, is

a. $\frac{4(e^2 - 5)}{e^2}$ b. $\frac{e^2 + 5}{e}$ c. $\frac{2(e^2 + 5)}{e^2}$ d. 4

41 The range of function $f(x)$ is

a. $\left[0, \frac{2}{e^2}\right]$ b. $\left[0, \frac{4}{e^2}\right]$

c. $\left[0, \frac{4}{e}\right]$ d. $(0, e^2)$

Passage III

Consider the functions $f(x) = \frac{x}{2^x}$ and $g(x) = \max\{f(t) : x \le t \le x + 1\}$.

42 Which of the following statement is incorrect?

a. $f(x)$ is increasing in $\left(-\infty, \frac{1}{\log_e 2}\right)$ and decreasing in $\left(\frac{1}{\log_e 2}, \infty\right)$

b. Local maximum value of $f(x)$ exists

c. Local minimum value of $f(x)$ does not exist

d. $f(x)$ changes its concavity at 2 points

43 If $f(x) = k$ has 2 distinct real roots, then the range of k is

a. $(0, 1/e)$ b. $\left(0, \frac{1}{e\log_e 2}\right)$

c. $\left(\frac{1}{e\log_e 2}, \infty\right)$ d. $(-\infty, 0)$

44 The value of function $g(x)$ is

a. $(x + 1)2^{-x+1}$ b. $(x - 1)2^{-x-1}$ c. $x \cdot 2^{-x}$ d. $(x + 1)2^{-(x+1)}$

One Integer Value Correct Type

***Direction** (Q. Nos. 45-50) This section contains 6 questions. When worked out will result in an integer from 0 to 9 (both inclusive).*

45 Let P be the point on the curve $4x^2 + \alpha^2 y^2 = 4\alpha^2$, $0 < \alpha^2 < 8$, whose distance from $Q(0, -2)$ is greatest. If R is the reflection of P in the X-axis, then the least distance of R form the line $3x - 4y + 7 = 0$ is

46 The minimum value of the function $f(x) = \frac{\tan(x + \pi/6)}{\tan x}$ is

47 The minimum distance between the curves $f(x) = e^x$ and $g(x) = \log_e x$ is $\sqrt{k}$, then k is

48 The lower corner of a leaf in a book is folded over, so as to just reach the inner edge of the page. The fraction of width folded over, if the area of the folded part is minimum is p/q, where $p, q \in N$, then the least value of $(p + q)$ is

49 A parabola of the form $y = ax^2 + bx + c$ with $a > 0$ intersects the graph of $f(x) = \frac{1}{x^2 - 4}$. Then, the minimum number of points of intersection is

50 If the largest positive value of the function $f(x) = \sqrt{8x - x^2} - \sqrt{14x - x^2 - 48}$ is $\sqrt{k}$, where $k \in N$, then the number of positive divisors of k is

JEE Main & AIEEE Archive

(Compilation of Last 13 Years' Questions)

1 The normal to curve $x^2 + 2xy - 3y^2 = 0$ at (1, 1) **(JEE Main 2015)**

a. does not meet the curve again
b. meets the curve again in second quadrant
c. meets the curve again in third quadrant
d. meets the curve again in fourth quadrant

2 The intercepts on X-axis made by tangents to the curve, $y = \int_0^x |t|\, dt,\ x \in R$, which are parallel to the line $y = 2x$, are equal to **(JEE Main 2013)**

a. ± 1 b. ± 2
c. ± 3 d. ± 4

3 A spherical balloon is filled with 4500π cu m of helium gas. If a leak in the balloon causes the gas to escape at the rate of 72π cu m/min, then the rate (in m/min) at which the radius of the balloon decreases 49 min after the leakage began is **(AIEEE 2012)**

a. $\frac{9}{7}$ b. $\frac{7}{9}$ c. $\frac{2}{9}$ d. $\frac{9}{2}$

4 Let $a, b \in R$ be such that the function f given by $f(x) = \log|x| + bx^2 + ax, x \neq 0$ has extreme values at $x = -1$ and $x = 2$.

Statement I f has local maximum at $x = -1$ and at $x = 2$.

Statement II $a = \frac{1}{2}$ and $b = \frac{-1}{4}$. **(AIEEE 2012)**

a. Both Statement I and Statement II are correct and Statement II is the correct explanation of Statement I
b. Both Statement I and Statement II are correct but Statement II is not the correct explanation of Statement I
c. Statement I is correct but Statement II is incorrect
d. Statement II is correct but Statement I is incorrect

5 For $x \in \left(0, \frac{5\pi}{2}\right)$, define $f(x) = \int_0^x \sqrt{t}\, \sin t\, dt$.

Then, f has **(AIEEE 2011)**

a. local minimum at π and 2π
b. local minimum at π and local maximum at 2π
c. local maximum at π and local minimum at 2π
d. local maximum at π and 2π

6 Let f be a function defined by

$$f(x) = \begin{cases} \frac{\tan x}{x}, & x \neq 0 \\ 1, & x = 0 \end{cases}$$

Statement I $x = 0$ is point of minima of f.

Statement II $f'(0) = 0$ **(AIEEE 2011)**

a. Both Statement I and Statement II are correct and Statement II is the correct explanation of Statement I
b. Both Statement I and Statement II are correct but Statement II is not the correct explanation of Statement I
c. Statement I is correct but Statement II is incorrect
d. Statement II is correct but Statement I is incorrect

7 The equation of the tangent to the curve $y = x + \frac{4}{x^2}$, i.e. parallel to the X-axis, is **(AIEEE 2010)**

a. $y = 0$ b. $y = 1$
c. $y = 2$ d. $y = 3$

8 Let $f: R \to R$ be defined by

$$f(x) = \begin{cases} k - 2x, & \text{if } x \le -1 \\ 2x + 3, & \text{if } x > -1 \end{cases}.$$

If f has a local minimum at $x = -1$, then a possible value of k is **(AIEEE 2010)**

a. 1 b. 0
c. $-\frac{1}{2}$ d. -1

9 Given, $P(x) = x^4 + ax^3 + bx^2 + cx + d$ such that $x = 0$ is the only real root of $P'(x) = 0$. If $P(-1) < P(1)$, then in the interval $[-1, 1]$ **(AIEEE 2009)**

a. $P(-1)$ is the minimum and $P(1)$ is the maximum of P
b. $P(-1)$ is not minimum but $P(1)$ is the maximum of P
c. $P(-1)$ is the minimum and $P(1)$ is not the maximum of P
d. neither $P(-1)$ is the minimum nor $P(1)$ is the maximum of P

10 How many real solutions does the equation $x^7 + 14x^5 + 16x^3 + 30x - 560 = 0$ have? **(AIEEE 2008)**

a. 5 b. 7
c. 1 d. 3

11 If the cubic $x^3 - px + q$ has three distinct real roots, where $p > 0$ and $q > 0$. Then, which one of the following holds? **(AIEEE 2008)**

a. The cubic has maxima at both $\sqrt{\frac{p}{3}}$ and $-\sqrt{\frac{p}{3}}$
b. The cubic has minima at $\sqrt{\frac{p}{3}}$ and maxima at $-\sqrt{\frac{p}{3}}$
c. The cubic has minima at $-\sqrt{\frac{p}{3}}$ and maxima at $\sqrt{\frac{p}{3}}$
d. The cubic has minima at both $\sqrt{\frac{p}{3}}$ and $-\sqrt{\frac{p}{3}}$

12 A value of c for which the conclusion of mean value theorem holds for the function $f(x) = \log_e x$ on the interval (1, 3) is **(AIEEE 2007)**

a. $2\log_3 e$ b. $\frac{1}{2}\log_e 3$
c. $\log_3 e$ d. $\log_e 3$

13 The normal to a curve at $P(x, y)$ meets the X-axis at G. If the distance of G from the origin is twice the abscissa of P, then the curve is a/an **(AIEEE 2007)**

a. ellipse b. parabola
c. circle d. hyperbola

14 Let $f: R \to R$ be a function defined by $f(x) = \min\{x+1, |x|+1\}$. Then, which one of the following is true? **(AIEEE 2007)**

a. $f(x) \geq 1, \forall x \in R$
b. $f(x)$ is not differentiable at $x = 1$
c. $f(x)$ is differentiable everywhere
d. $f(x)$ is not differentiable at $x = 0$

15 The function $f(x) = \tan^{-1}(\sin x + \cos x)$ is an increasing function in **(AIEEE 2006)**

a. $\left(\frac{\pi}{4}, \frac{\pi}{2}\right)$ b. $\left(\frac{-\pi}{2}, \frac{\pi}{4}\right)$ c. $\left(0, \frac{\pi}{2}\right)$ d. $\left(\frac{-\pi}{2}, \frac{\pi}{2}\right)$

16 Angle between the tangents to the curve $y = x^2 - 5x + 6$ at the points (2, 0) and (3, 0) is **(AIEEE 2006)**

a. $\frac{\pi}{2}$ b. $\frac{\pi}{6}$ c. $\frac{\pi}{4}$ d. $\frac{\pi}{3}$

17 The function $f(x) = \frac{x}{2} + \frac{2}{x}$ has a local minimum at **(AIEEE 2006)**

a. $x = -2$ b. $x = 0$ c. $x = 1$ d. $x = 2$

18 If x is real, then the maximum value of $\frac{3x^2 + 9x + 17}{3x^2 + 9x + 7}$ is **(AIEEE 2006)**

a. 41 b. 1 c. $\frac{17}{7}$ d. $\frac{1}{4}$

19 A function is matched below against an interval, where it is supposed to be increasing. Which of the following pair is incorrectly matched? **(AIEEE 2005)**

	Interval	Function
a.	$(-\infty, -4)$	$x^3 + 6x^2 + 6$
b.	$\left(-\infty, \frac{1}{3}\right]$	$3x^2 - 2x + 1$
c.	$[2, \infty)$	$2x^3 - 3x^2 - 12x + 6$
d.	$(-\infty, \infty)$	$x^3 - 3x^2 + 3x + 3$

20 The normal to the curve, $x = a(\cos\theta + \theta\sin\theta)$, $y = a(\sin\theta - \theta\cos\theta)$ at any point θ is such that **(AIEEE 2005)**

a. it is at a constant distance from the origin
b. it passes through $\left(\frac{a\pi}{2}, -a\right)$
c. it makes angle $\frac{\pi}{2} - \theta$ with the X-axis
d. it passes through the origin

21 A spherical iron ball 10 cm in radius is coated with a layer of ice of uniform thickness that melts at a rate of 50 cm^3/min. When the thickness of ice is 15 cm, then the rate at which the thickness of ice decreases, is **(AIEEE 2005)**

a. $\frac{5}{6\pi}$ cm/min b. $\frac{1}{54\pi}$ cm/min
c. $\frac{1}{18\pi}$ cm/min d. $\frac{1}{36\pi}$ cm/min

22 A lizard, at an initial distance of 21 cm behind an insect, moves from rest with an acceleration of 2 cm/s^2 and pursues the insect which is crawling uniformly along a straight line at a speed of 20 cm/s. Then, the lizard will catch the insect after **(AIEEE 2005)**

a. 24 s b. 21 s
c. 1 s d. 20 s

23 If $u = \sqrt{a^2\cos^2\theta + b^2\sin^2\theta} + \sqrt{a^2\sin^2\theta + b^2\cos^2\theta}$, then the difference between the maximum and minimum values of u^2 is given by **(AIEEE 2004)**

a. $2(a^2 + b^2)$ b. $2\sqrt{a^2 + b^2}$
c. $(a + b)^2$ d. $(a - b)^2$

24 A point on the parabola $y^2 = 18x$ at which the ordinate increases at twice the rate of the abscissa, is **(AIEEE 2004)**

a. (2, 4) b. (2, – 4)
c. $\left(-\frac{9}{8}, \frac{9}{2}\right)$ d. $\left(\frac{9}{8}, \frac{9}{2}\right)$

25 A function $y = f(x)$ has a second order derivative $f''(x) = 6(x - 1)$. If its graph passes through the point (2, 1) and at that point, the tangent to the graph is $y = 3x - 5$, then the function is **(AIEEE 2004)**

a. $(x - 1)^2$ b. $(x - 1)^3$
c. $(x + 1)^3$ d. $(x + 1)^2$

26 The normal to curve $x = a(1 + \cos\theta)$, $y = a\sin\theta$ at θ always passes through the fixed point **(AIEEE 2004)**

a. $(a, 0)$ b. $(0, a)$
c. $(0, 0)$ d. (a, a)

27 The real number x when added to its inverse gives the minimum value of the sum at x equal to **(AIEEE 2003)**

a. 2 b. 1 c. –1 d. –2

28 If the function $f(x) = 2x^3 - 9ax^2 + 12a^2x + 1$, where $a > 0$, attains its maximum and minimum at p and q respectively, such that $p^2 = q$, then a is equal to **(AIEEE 2003)**

a. 3 b. 1
c. 2 d. 1/2

29 The function $f(x) = \cot^{-1} x + x$ increases in the interval **(AIEEE 2002)**

a. $(1, \infty)$ b. $(-1, \infty)$
c. $(-\infty, \infty)$ d. $(0, \infty)$

30 The greatest value of $f(x) = (x + 1)^{1/3} - (x - 1)^{1/3}$ on (0, 1) is **(AIEEE 2002)**

a. 1 b. 2
c. 3 d. 1/3

31 The two curves $x^3 - 3xy^2 + 2 = 0$ and $3x^2y - y^3 - 2 = 0$ **(AIEEE 2002)**

a. cut at right angle b. touch each other
c. cut at an angle $\frac{\pi}{3}$ d. cut at an angle $\frac{\pi}{6}$

JEE Advanced & IIT JEE Archive

(Compilation of Last 10 Years' Questions)

1 A cylindrical container is to be made from certain solid material with the following constraints. It has a fixed inner volume of $V\ \text{mm}^3$, has a 2 mm thick solid wall and is open at the top. The bottom of the container is a solid circular disc of thickness 2 mm and is of radius equal to the outer radius of the container.

If the volume of the material used to make the container is minimum when the inner radius of the container is 10 mm, then the value of $\frac{V}{250\pi}$ is **(2015 Adv., Integer Type)**

2 Consider the hyperbola $H: x^2 - y^2 = 1$ and a circle S with centre N. Suppose that H and S touch each other at a point $P(x_1, y_1)$ with $x_1 > 1$ and $y_1 > 0$. The common tangent to H and S at P intersects the X-axis at point M. If (l, m) is the centroid of the triangle ΔPMN, then the correct expression(s) is(are) **(2015 Adv., One or More than One Options Correct Type)**

a. $\frac{dl}{dx_1} = 1 - \frac{1}{3x_1^2}$ for $x_1 > 1$

b. $\frac{dm}{dx_1} = \frac{x_1}{3\left[\sqrt{x_1^2 - 1}\right]}$ for $x_1 > 1$

c. $\frac{dl}{dx_1} = 1 + \frac{1}{3x_1^2}$ for $x_1 > 1$

d. $\frac{dm}{dy_1} = \frac{1}{3}$ for $y_1 > 1$

3 Let $f, g : [-1, 2] \to R$ be continuous functions which are twice differentiable on the interval $(-1, 2)$. Let the values of f and g at the points -1, 0 and 2 be as given in the following table: **(2015 Adv., One or More than One Options Correct Type)**

	$x = -1$	$x = 0$	$x = 2$
$f(x)$	3	6	0
$g(x)$	0	1	-1

In each of the intervals $(-1, 0)$ and $(0, 2)$, the function $(f - 3g)''$ never vanishes. Then, the correct statement(s) is(are)

a. $f'(x) - 3g'(x) = 0$ has exactly three solutions in $(-1, 0) \cup (0, 2)$

b. $f'(x) - 3g'(x) = 0$ has exactly one solution in $(-1, 0)$

c. $f'(x) - 3g'(x) = 0$ has exactly one solution in $(0, 2)$

d. $f'(x) - 3g'(x) = 0$ has exactly two solutions in $(-1, 0)$ and exactly two solutions in $(0, 2)$

4 Let $f : (0, \infty) \to R$ be given by

$f(x) = \int_{1/x}^{x} e^{-\left(t + \frac{1}{t}\right)} \frac{dt}{t}$.

Then, **(2014 Adv., One or More than One Options Correct Type)**

a. $f(x)$ is monotonically increasing on $[1, \infty)$

b. $f(x)$ is monotonically decreasing on $[0, 1)$

c. $f(x) + f\left(\frac{1}{x}\right) = 0$, for all $x \in (0, \infty)$

d. $f(2^x)$ is an odd function of x on R

5 The slope of tangent to the curve $(y - x^5)^2 = x(1 + x^2)^2$ at the point $(1, 3)$ is **(2014 Adv., Integer Type)**

6 A rectangular sheet of fixed perimeter with sides having their lengths in the ratio $8:15$ is converted into an open rectangular box by folding after removing squares of equal area from all four corners. If the total area of removed squares is 100, then resulting box has maximum volume. The lengths of the sides of the rectangular sheet are **(2013 Adv., One or More than One Options Correct Type)**

a. 24 b. 32

c. 45 d. 60

7 The function $f(x) = 2|x| + |x + 2| - ||x + 2| - 2|x||$ has a local minimum or a local maximum at x is equal to **(2013 Adv., One or More than One Options Correct Type)**

a. -2 b. $\frac{-2}{3}$

c. 2 d. $\frac{2}{3}$

8 The number of points in $(-\infty, \infty)$ for which $x^2 - x\sin x - \cos x = 0$ is **(2013 Adv., Only One Option Correct Type)**

a. 6 b. 4

c. 2 d. 0

9 A vertical line passing through the point $(h, 0)$ intersects the ellipse $\frac{x^2}{4} + \frac{y^2}{3} = 1$ at the points P and Q. Let the tangents to the ellipse at P and Q meet at the point R. If $\Delta(h) =$ area of the ΔPQR, $\Delta_1 = \max_{1/2 \le h \le 1} \Delta(h)$ and $\Delta_2 = \min_{1/2 \le h \le 1} \Delta(h)$, then $\frac{8}{\sqrt{5}}\Delta_1 - 8\Delta_2$ is equal to **(2013 Adv., Integer Type)**

10 Let $f : R \to R$ be defined as $f(x) = |x| + |x^2 - 1|$. The total number of points at which f attains either a local maximum or a local minimum is **(2012, Integer Type)**

11 Let $p(x)$ be a real polynomial of least degree which has a local maximum at $x = 1$ and a local minimum at $x = 3$. If $p(1) = 6$ and $p(3) = 2$, then $p'(0)$ is equal to **(2012, Integer Type)**

JEE Archive

12 If $f(x)=\int_0^x e^{t^2}(t-2)(t-3)\,dt,\ \forall\ x\in(0,\infty)$, then

(2012, One or More than One Options Correct Type)

a. f has a local maximum at $x=2$
b. f is decreasing on $(2, 3)$
c. there exists some $c\in(0,\infty)$ such that $f''(c)=0$
d. f has a local minimum at $x=3$

13 The number of distinct real roots of $x^4-4x^3+12x^2+x-1=0$ is **(2011, Integer Type)**

14 The maximum value of the expression $\dfrac{1}{\sin^2\theta+3\sin\theta\cos\theta+5\cos^2\theta}$ is **(2010, Integer Type)**

15 Let f be a real valued differentiable function on R (the set of all real numbers) such that $f(1)=1$. If the y-intercept of the tangent at any point $P(x, y)$ on the curve $y=f(x)$ is equal to the cube of the abscissa of P, then the value of $f(-3)$ is

(2010, Integer Type)

16 Let f be a function defined on R (the set of all real numbers) such that $f'(x)=2010(x-2009)(x-2010)^2(x-2011)^3(x-2012)^4,\ \forall\ x\in R$.
If g is a function defined on R with values in the interval $(0,\infty)$ such that $f(x)=\ln\{g(x)\},\ \forall\ x\in R$, then the number of points in R at which g has a local maximum is **(2010, Integer Type)**

17 Let f be a real valued function defined on the interval $(0,\infty)$, by $f(x)=\ln x+\int_0^x\sqrt{1+\sin t}\,dt$. Then, which of the following statement(s) is (are) true ?

(2010, One or More than One Options Correct Type)

a. $f''(x)$ exists for all $x\in(0,\infty)$
b. $f'(x)$ exists for all $x\in(0,\infty)$ and f' is continuous on $(0,\infty)$ but not differentiable on $(0,\infty)$
c. there exists $\alpha>1$ such that $|f'(x)|<|f(x)|$ for all $x\in(\alpha,\infty)$
d. there exists $\beta>0$ such that $|f(x)|+|f'(x)|\le\beta$ from all $x\in(0,\infty)$

18 Let f, g and h be real valued functions defined on the interval $[0, 1]$ by $f(x)=e^{x^2}+e^{-x^2}$, $g(x)=xe^{x^2}+e^{-x^2}$ and $h(x)=x^2e^{x^2}+e^{-x^2}$. If a, b and c denote respectively, the absolute maximum of f, g and h on $[0, 1]$, then

(2010, Only One Option Correct Type)

a. $a=b$ and $c\ne b$
b. $a=c$ and $a\ne b$
c. $a\ne b$ and $c\ne b$
d. $a=b=c$

19 Let f be a real valued function defined on the interval $(-1, 1)$ such that $e^{-x}f(x)=2+\int_0^x\sqrt{t^4+1}\,dt$, for all $x\in(-1,1)$ and let f^{-1} be the inverse function of f. Then, $(f^{-1})'(2)$ is equal to **(2010, Only One Option Correct Type)**

a. 1 b. 1/3
c. 1/2 d. 1/e

20 The maximum value of the function $f(x)=2x^3-15x^2+36x-48$ on the set $A=\{x\mid x^2+20\le 9x\}$ is **(2009, Integer Type)**

21 For the function $f(x)=x\cos\dfrac{1}{x},\ x\ge 1$,

(2009, One or More than One Options Correct Type)

a. for atleast one x in the interval $[1,\infty)$, $f(x+2)-f(x)<2$
b. $\lim\limits_{x\to\infty}f'(x)=1$
c. for all x in the interval $[1,\infty)$, $f(x+2)-f(x)>2$
d. $f'(x)$ is strictly decreasing in the interval $[1,\infty)$

22 Let the function $g:(-\infty,\infty)\to\left(-\dfrac{\pi}{2},\dfrac{\pi}{2}\right)$ be given by $g(u)=2\tan^{-1}(e^u)-\dfrac{\pi}{2}$. Then, g is

(2008, Only One Option Correct Type)

a. even and is strictly increasing in $(0,\infty)$
b. odd and is strictly decreasing in $(-\infty,\infty)$
c. odd and is strictly increasing in $(-\infty,\infty)$
d. neither even nor odd but is strictly increasing in $(-\infty,\infty)$

23 The total number of local maxima and local minima of the function $f(x)=\begin{cases}(2+x)^3, & -3<x\le -1\\ x^{2/3}, & -1<x<2\end{cases}$ is

(2008, Only One Option Correct Type)

a. 0 b. 1
c. 2 d. 3

24 Let the functions defined in Column I have domain $(-\pi/2, \pi/2)$. Match the following columns and select the correct option given below. **(2008, Matching Type)**

	Column I		Column II
i.	$x+\sin x$	p.	Increasing
ii.	$\sec x$	q.	Decreasing
		r.	Neither increasing nor decreasing

Codes

	i	ii
a.	p	r
b.	p,q	r
c.	q	r
d.	r	p

Passage for Q. Nos. (25-27)

Consider the function $f:(-\infty,\infty)\to(-\infty,\infty)$ defined by $f(x)=\dfrac{x^2-ax+1}{x^2+ax+1};\ 0<a<2$.

(2008, Comprehension Type)

25 Which of the following is true?

a. $(2+a)^2f''(1)+(2-a)^2f''(-1)=0$
b. $(2-a)^2f''(1)-(2+a)^2f''(-1)=0$
c. $f'(1)f'(-1)=(2-a)^2$
d. $f'(1)f'(-1)=-(2+a)^2$

26 Which of the following is true?

a. $f(x)$ is decreasing on $(-1, 1)$ and has a local minimum at $x = 1$

b. $f(x)$ is increasing on $(-1, 1)$ and has a local maximum at $x = 1$

c. $f(x)$ is increasing on $(-1, 1)$ but has neither a local maximum nor a local minimum at $x = 1$

d. $f(x)$ is decreasing on $(-1, 1)$ but has neither a local maximum nor a local minimum at $x = 1$

27 Let $g(x) = \int_0^{e^x} \frac{f'(t)}{1+t^0} dt$. Which of the following is true?

a. $g'(x)$ is positive on $(-\infty, 0)$ and negative on $(0, \infty)$

b. $g'(x)$ is negative on $(-\infty, 0)$ and positive on $(0, \infty)$

c. $g'(x)$ changes sign on both $(-\infty, 0)$ and $(0, \infty)$

d. $g'(x)$ does not change sign $(-\infty, \infty)$

28 The tangent to the curve $y = e^x$ drawn at the point (c, e^c) intersects the line joining the points $(c-1, e^{c-1})$ and $(c+1, e^{c+1})$

(2007, Only One Option Correct Type)

a. on the left of $x = c$

b. on the right of $x = c$

c. at no point

d. at all points

29 If $f(x)$ is cubic polynomial which has local maximum at $x = -1$. If $f(2) = 18$, $f(1) = -1$ and $f'(x)$ has local minimum at $x = 0$, then

(2006, One or More than One Options Correct Type)

a. the distance between $(-1, 2)$ and $\{a, f(a)\}$, where $x = a$ is the point of local minima is $2\sqrt{5}$

b. $f(x)$ is increasing for $x \in [1, 2\sqrt{5}]$

c. $f(x)$ has local minima at $x = 1$

d. the value of $f(0) = 5$

30 If $f(x) = \begin{cases} e^x & , 0 \le x \le 1 \\ 2 - e^{x-1} & , 1 < x \le 2 \\ x - e & , 2 < x \le 3 \end{cases}$ and $g(x) = \int_0^x f(t)\,dt$, $x \in [1, 3]$, then **(2006, One or More than One Options Correct Type)**

a. $g(x)$ has local maxima at $x = 1 + \log_e 2$ and local minima at $x = e$

b. $f(x)$ has local maxima at $x = 1$ and local minima at $x = 2$

c. $g(x)$ has no local minima

d. $f(x)$ has no local maxima

31 The second degree polynomial $f(x)$, satisfying $f(0) = 0$, $f(1) = 1$, $f'(x) > 0$ for all $x \in (0, 1)$

(2005, Only One Option Correct Type)

a. $f(x) = \phi$

b. $f(x) = ax + (1-a)x^2; \forall a \in (0, \infty)$

c. $f(x) = ax + (1-a)x^2, a \in (0, 2)$

d. No such polynomial

32 The tangent at $(1, 7)$ to the curve $x^2 - y - 6$ touches the circle $x^2 + y^2 + 16x + 12y + c = 0$ at

(2005, Only One Option Correct Type)

a. $(6, 7)$ b. $(-6, 7)$ c. $(6, -7)$ d. $(-6, -7)$

33 A line $L: y = mx + 3$ meets Y-axis at $E(0, 3)$ and the arc of the parabola $y^2 = 16x, 0 \le y \le 6$ at the point $F(x_0, y_0)$. The tangent to the parabola at $F(x_0, y_0)$ intersects the Y-axis at $G(0, y_1)$. The slope m of the line L is chosen such that the area of the ΔEFG has a local maximum.

Match the Column I with Column II and mark the correct option from the codes given below. **(2005, Matching Type)**

	Column I		Column II
i.	m is equal to	p.	1/2
ii.	Maximum area of ΔEFG is	q.	4
iii.	y_0 is equal to	r.	2
iv.	y_1 is equal to	s.	1

Codes

	i	ii	iii	iv
a.	s	p	q	r
b.	r	s	p	q
c.	p	r	q	s
d.	p	r	s	q

JEE Archive

Answers *with* Explanations

Answers

1. Methods of Differentiation

DPP-1 First Principle and Fundamental Theorems

1. (i) $\sec^2 x$ (ii) $\frac{-2}{\sin^2(2x+1)}$ (iii) $\frac{\cos x}{2\sqrt{\sin x}}$ (iv) $\frac{\sec^2\sqrt{x}}{2\sqrt{x}}$ (v) $\frac{x\cos x - \sin x}{x^2}$ (vi) $\cos x - \sin x$

2. (i) $5x^4 - 16x^3 + 15x^2 - 4x + 8$ (ii) $(25-2x)(3x+8)^{4/3}(x+7)^{-4}$ (iii) $\frac{-1}{\sqrt{x}(1+\sqrt{x})^2}$ (iv) $\frac{2x^3+3x^2-3}{x^2}$

3. (i) $\frac{1}{4(\sqrt{a+\sqrt{a+x}})(\sqrt{a+x})}$ (ii) $\frac{x}{4\sqrt{4+\sqrt{4+\sqrt{4+x^2}}}\sqrt{4+\sqrt{4+x^2}}\sqrt{4+x^2}}$

(iii) $\frac{2a}{(\sqrt{a+x}+\sqrt{a-x})^2\sqrt{a^2-x^2}}$ (iv) $\frac{1}{\sqrt{x^2+a^2}}$ (v) $10^{10^x}\cdot 10^x(\log 10)^2$ (vi) $\sec x$

4. (i) $e^{ax}[a\cot(bx+c) - b\operatorname{cosec}^2(bx+c)]$ (ii) $\frac{x\cot\left(\frac{x^2}{3}-1\right)}{3\log\left\{\sin\left(\frac{x^2}{3}-1\right)\right\}}$

(iii) $-(\tan x + \log_{\sin x}\cos x\cot x)\log_{\sin x} e$ (iv) $\sec x$ (v) $\frac{x\cot\sqrt{x^2+1}}{\sqrt{x^2+1}}$ (vi) $\frac{1}{2\sqrt{x^2-a^2}}$

5. *b*	**6.** *c*	**7.** *c*	**8.** *b*	**9.** *d*	**10.** *a*	**11.** *d*	**12.** *a*	**13.** *b*	**14.** *c*
15. *d*	**16.** *a*	**17.** *b*	**18.** *a,b,c*	**19.** *a,c*	**20.** *a,b,c*	**21.** 8	**22.** 5	**23.** 2	**24.** 2
25. 9									

DPP-2 Differentiation of Inverse Trigonometric and Implicit Functions

1. (i) $\frac{1}{2(1+x^2)}$ (ii) $\frac{-1}{2}$ (iii) $\frac{x}{\sqrt{1-x^4}}$ (iv) $\frac{2x+\sqrt{1+x^2}}{\sqrt{1-x^4}}$ (v) $\frac{-x}{\sqrt{1-x^4}}$ (vi) $\frac{1}{2(1+x^2)}$ (vii) $\frac{1}{2}$ (viii) 0

2. (i) $\frac{1+3x^2y-y^3}{3xy^2-x^3}$ (ii) $\frac{ay-x^2}{y^2-ax}$ (iii) $\frac{-y}{x}\left(\frac{x\log y+y}{x+y\log x}\right)$

3. *b*	**4.** *b*	**5.** *c*	**6.** *b*	**7.** *b*	**8.** *d*	**9.** *a*	**10.** *b*	**11.** *a*	**12.** *c*
13. *a*	**14.** *a*	**15.** *a,b,c*	**16.** *b,c*	**17.** *a,b*	**18.** *b*	**19.** *a*	**20.** *d*	**21.** *a*	**22.** *b*
23. *d*	**24.** 1	**25.** 1							

DPP-3 Logarithmic Series, Infinite Series and Differentiation of One With Respect to Other

1. (i) $x^x(1+\log x)$ (ii) $x^{x^x}x^{x-1}[x-\log x + x(\log x)^2+1]$ (iii) $(\sin x)^{\cos^{-1}x}\left(\cot x\cos^{-1}x - \frac{\log\sin x}{\sqrt{1-x^2}}\right)$

(iv) $\frac{\sqrt{x}(x+4)^{3/2}}{(4x-3)^{4/3}}\left[\frac{1}{2x}+\frac{3}{2x+8}-\frac{16}{12x-9}\right]$ (v) $x^{\sin x-\cos x}\left[\frac{\sin x-\cos x}{x}+(\cos x+\sin x)\log x\right]+\frac{4x}{(x^2+1)^2}$

2. (i) $\frac{1}{2y-1}$ (ii) $\frac{\cos x}{2y-1}$ (iii) $\frac{\sin x}{1-2y}$ (iv) $\frac{1}{x(2y-1)}$

5. (i) $\frac{1}{2x\sqrt{1+4x^2}}$ (ii) $\frac{1}{2}$

6. (i) $\tan t$ (ii) $-\tan 3t$

7. *c*	**8.** *c*	**9.** *d*	**10.** *c*	**11.** *d*	**12.** *c*	**13.** *b*	**14.** *c*	**15.** *a,b*	**16.** *a,d*
17. *a,b,c,d*		**18.** *a,b,d*	**19.** *a,c*	**20.** *a*	**21.** 1	**22.** 1	**23.** 1	**24.** 0	**25.** 0

DPP-4 Higher Order Derivatives and Differentiation of Inverse Functions

18. *c*	**19.** *b*	**20.** *c*	**21.** *b*	**22.** *a*	**23.** *b*	**24.** *b*	**25.** *d*	**26.** *a*	**27.** *c*
28. *d*	**29.** *a*	**30.** 2	**31.** 4	**32.** 1	**33.** 2	**34.** 4	**35.** 1		

Revisal Problems (JEE Main)

1. *b* 2. *b* 3. *c* 4. *a* 5. *c* 6. *a* 7. *a* 8. *c* 9. *b* 10. *c*
11. *c* 12. *d* 13. *d* 14. *a* 15. *d* 16. *b* 17. *a* 18. *a* 19. *c* 20. *b*

Revisal Problems (JEE Advanced)

1. *a* 2. *a* 3. *c* 4. *d* 5. *a* 6. *d* 7. *b* 8. *d* 9. *b* 10. *b*
11. *a* 12. *c* 13. *b* 14. *a* 15. *c* 16. *a* 17. 2 18. 1 19. 9 20. 1
21. 3

JEE Main & AIEEE Archive

1. *c* 2. *a* 3. *c* 4. *a* 5. *d* 6. *c* 7. *a* 8. *c* 9. *a* 10. *b*
11. *c*

JEE Advanced & IIT JEE Archive

1. *b,c* 2. *d*

2. Limits

DPP-1 Definition of Limits and $\left(\frac{0}{0}\right)$ Form on Algebraic

1. (i) −1 (ii) −2 (iii) Does not exist (iv) 2 (v) 0 (vi) Does not exist (vii) 1 (viii) 4
2. (i) Does not exist (ii) 3 (iii) 3 (iv) 3 (v) 3
3. *d* 4. *b* 5. *c* 6. *b* 7. *d* 8. *b* 9. *c* 10. *d* 11. *c* 12. *a*
13. *d* 14. *a* 15. *a* 16. *a* 17. *a* 18. *c* 19. *d* 20. *b*

DPP-2 Questions Based on $\left(\frac{\infty}{\infty}\right)$ Form

1. (i) $\begin{cases} \infty, & \frac{a_0}{b_0}>0 \\ -\infty, & \frac{a_0}{b_0}<0 \end{cases}$ (ii) a_0/b_0 (iii) 0

2. *a* 3. *b* 4. *d* 5. *b* 6. *b* 7. *c* 8. *c* 9. *a* 10. *a* 11. *d*
12. *d* 13. *a* 14. *c* 15. *c* 16. *c* 17. *a* 18. *a,b* 19. *a,b,c,d* 20. *a*
21. 1 22. 1 23. 0 24. 2 25. 1

DPP-3 Exponential, Logarithmic and Trigonometric Forms

1. (i) $\frac{\alpha}{\beta}$ (ii) 2 (iii) $\frac{a}{b}$ (iv) $2a\sin a + a^2\cos a$ 2. (i) e^a (ii) $2\log 2$ (iii) 1
3. (i) $\frac{1}{e}-1$ (ii) $\frac{2}{5}$ (iii) $\frac{1}{2}\log_e a$ (iv) $\log_e a$ (v) $\frac{2}{\pi}\log_e 2$ (vi) $8\sqrt{2}(\log 3)^2$
4. (i) $\frac{3}{4}$ (ii) −1 (iii) 0 (iv) $\frac{\beta^2-\alpha^2}{2}$ (v) $\frac{1}{3}$ (vi) $\frac{1}{3}$ (vii) $\frac{1}{2}$ (viii) $\sec x(1+x\tan x)$
5. (i) −4 (ii) −2 (iii) $\frac{\pi}{2}$ (iv) $\frac{1}{16\sqrt{2}}$
6. *b* 7. *d* 8. *b* 9. *a* 10. *c* 11. *b* 12. *a* 13. *d* 14. *d* 15. *b*
16. *c* 17. *a,d* 18. *a,d* 19. *a* 20. *d* 21. *a* 22. 3 23. 3 24. 1

DPP-4 Problems Based on $(1)^\infty$ and $(\infty)^0$ Forms

1. (i) e^2 (ii) e^2 (iii) e (iv) 1
2. *a* 3. *c* 4. *d* 5. *b* 6. *a* 7. *b* 8. *c* 9. *b* 10. *a* 11. *d*
12. *b* 13. *c* 14. *c* 15. *b* 16. *c* 17. *c* 18. *c* 19. *a,b,c,d* 20. *a,b,c* 21. *b*
22. *a* 23. *a* 24. *b* 25. *d* 26. *a* 27. 1 28. 3 29. 1 30. 8

DPP-5 Applications of RHL and LHL

1. (i), (iii) and (iv) are true **2.** (i) Does not exist (ii) Does not exist (iii) 1

4. *d* **5.** *d* **6.** *c* **7.** *c* **8.** *b* **9.** *a* **10.** *d* **11.** *d* **12.** *a* **13.** *b*
14. *a* **15.** *b* **16.** *d* **17.** *c* **18.** *c* **19.** *c* **20.** *a* **21.** *a* **22.** *b*
23. *a,b,c* **24.** *a,b* **25.** *a,b,c* **26.** *a,b,c,d* **27.** *b* **28.** *c* **29.** *b* **30.** 1 **31.** 1
32. 0 **33.** 2 **34.** 1 **35.** 5

DPP-6 Limit of Expansions, Behaviour, Newton-Leibnitz Rule and Conversion into Definite Integral

1. *c* **2.** *c* **3.** *c* **4.** *b* **5.** *c* **6.** *b* **7.** *c* **8.** *b* **9.** *a* **10.** *d*
11. *c* **12.** *d* **13.** *c* **14.** *c* **15.** 2 **16.** 2 **17.** 1 **18.** 0 **19.** 1 **20.** 2

Revisal Problems (JEE Main)

1. *d* **2.** *a* **3.** *a* **4.** *a* **5.** *a* **6.** *c* **7.** *a* **8.** *c* **9.** *d* **10.** *b*
11. *b* **12.** *c* **13.** *b* **14.** *c* **15.** *d* **16.** *a* **17.** *c* **18.** *a* **19.** *c* **20.** *b*
21. *b* **22.** *c* **23.** *a* **24.** *b* **25.** *b* **26.** *a* **27.** *b* **28.** *b* **29.** *c* **30.** *a*
31. *c* **32.** *a* **33.** *c* **34.** *a* **35.** *c* **36.** *d* **37.** *b* **38.** *a* **39.** *d* **40.** *b*
41. *a* **42.** *a* **43.** *a* **44.** *d* **45.** *b* **46.** *a* **47.** *b* **48.** *d* **49.** *c* **50.** *a*

Revisal Problems (JEE Advanced)

1. *d* **2.** *a* **3.** *b* **4.** *c* **5.** *c* **6.** *c* **7.** *b* **8.** *a* **9.** *c* **10.** *a*
11. *a* **12.** *a* **13.** *a* **14.** *c* **15.** *c* **16.** *d* **17.** *c* **18.** *b* **19.** *b* **20.** *b*
21. *d* **22.** *a* **23.** *b* **24.** *a,c* **25.** *b,c* **26.** *a,c,d* **27.** *a,b* **28.** *a,d* **29.** *b* **30.** *a*
31. *c* **32.** *b* **33.** *b* **34.** 6 **35.** 2 **36.** 4 **37.** 3 **38.** 4 **39.** 1 **40.** 1

JEE Main & AIEEE Archive

1. *c* **2.** *c* **3.** *d* **4.** *d* **5.** *d* **6.** *a* **7.** *d* **8.** *a* **9.** *d* **10.** *b*
11. *c* **12.** *c* **13.** *d* **14.** *a* **15.** *c* **16.** *c*

JEE Advanced & IIT JEE Archive

1. *a,b,c* **2.** 2 **3.** 2 **4.** *b* **5.** *b* **6.** *d* **7.** 0 **8.** *a,c* **9.** *c* **10.** *a*
11. *c*

3. Continuity and Differentiability

DPP-1 Graphical Transformation

1. *c* **2.** *d* **3.** *b* **4.** *a* **5.** *c* **6.** *a* **7.** *a* **8.** *a* **9.** *b* **10.** *d*
11. *d* **12.** *c* **13.** *a* **14.** *b* **15.** *c*

DPP-2 Definition of Continuity

1. *b* **2.** *a* **3.** *c* **4.** *c* **5.** *c* **6.** *a* **7.** *c* **8.** *b* **9.** *b* **10.** *b*

DPP-3 Continuity at a Point

1. $\frac{-2}{\pi}$ **4.** 1 **7.** $a=3, b=2$ **9.** $a=-3/2, b \in R$ and $c=1/2$ **11.** *c* **12.** *c* **13.** *a*
14. *a* **15.** *a* **16.** *a* **17.** *c* **18.** *b* **19.** *a* **20.** *b* **21.** *d* **22.** *c* **23.** *d*
24. *a* **25.** *a,b* **26.** *b,c,d* **27.** *a,b,c* **28.** *a* **29.** *c* **30.** *c* **31.** *b* **32.** *d* **33.** *b*
34. *c*

DPP-4 Continuity for Composition of Functions

1. (i) $x \in R-\{2,3\}$ (ii) $x \in R-\{-1,1\}$ (iii) $x \in \{-\infty, \infty\}$ (iv) $x \in R-(2n+1), n \in I$

4. $x=1, 2$ 5. $x=0,-2,-7/3$ 6. *d* 7. *a* 8. *d* 9. *b* 10. *b* 11. *c* 12. *a*
13. *b* 14. *b* 15. *c,d* 16. *c,d* 17. *a,c,d* 18. *b,c* 19. *a,c* 20. *a* 21. *a* 22. *b,c*
23. *a* 24. 5 25. 1

DPP-5 Differentiability at a Point

3. $a=1/2, b=3/2$ 6. *d* 7. *b* 8. *a* 9. *d* 10. *b* 11. *c* 12. *d* 13. *a*
14. *d* 15. *a* 16. *c* 17. *b* 18. *b* 19. *d* 20. *a,c* 21. *b,d* 22. *b,c* 23. *a,c*
24. *a,b* 25. *a,c* 26. *b,c,d* 27. *b* 28. *c* 29. *c* 30. *d* 31. *a* 32. *c* 33. *b*
34. 3 35. 7

DPP-6 Differentiability in the Interval

1. At all integral in $-1 < x \le 3$ 3. −2 4. $e^{xf'(0)}$ 6. *a* 7. *c* 8. *c* 9. *c* 10. *b*
11. *d* 12. *d* 13. *c* 14. *b* 15. *b* 16. *d* 17. *c* 18. *a,b* 19. *a,d*
20. *a,b,c* 21. *a,c,d* 22. *a,b* 23. *d* 24. *d* 25. *a,d* 26. *b,c* 27. *c* 28. *c* 29. *c*
30. *d*

Revisal Problems for (JEE Main)

1. *d* 2. *d* 3. *b* 4. *a* 5. *b* 6. *b* 7. *d* 8. *d* 9. *a* 10. *a*
11. *a* 12. *b* 13. *d* 14. *a* 15. *d* 16. *d* 17. *c* 18. *b* 19. *a* 20. *a*
21. *c* 22. *a* 23. *d* 24. *d* 25. *c* 26. *a* 27. *b* 28. *c* 29. *b* 30. *d*
31. *c* 32. *b* 33. *b* 34. *a* 35. *c* 36. *a* 37. *c* 38. *b* 39. *a* 40. *c*

Revisal Problems for (JEE Advanced)

1. *c* 2. *a* 3. *d* 4. *b* 5. *c* 6. *a* 7. *c* 8. *b* 9. *d* 10. *b*
11. *a* 12. *a,c* 13. *a,b,c,d* 14. *b,c,d* 15. *a,d* 16. *b,c,d* 17. *b* 18. *d* 19. *c* 20. *d*
21. *b* 22. *a* 23. *c* 24. *b* 25. *a* 26. *d* 27. *c* 28. *c* 29. *a* 30. *c*
31. *b* 32. *a* 33. *c* 34. *b* 35. *c* 36. *b* 37. *a* 38. 4 39. 5
40. 2 41. 1 42. 4 43. 6 44. 0

JEE Main & AIEEE Archive

1. *a* 2. *d* 3. *a* 4. *b* 5. *b* 6. *c* 7. *b* 8. *c* 9. *d* 10. *d*
11. *b* 12. *b* 13. *d* 14. *c* 15. *c* 16. *a* 17. *b*

JEE Advanced & IIT JEE Archive

1. 7 2. *a,d* 3. 3 4. *a,c* 5. *b* 6. 8/3 7. *b,c* 8. *a,b,c,d* 9. *b* 10. *a*
11. *b* 12. *a* 13. *d* 14. *a,d* 15. *c* 16. *b* 17. *a*

4. Applications of Derivatives

DPP-1 Derivative as Rate Measure

1. 7.11cm/s 2. $1200\,\pi\,\text{cm}^2/\text{s}$ 4. $\frac{200\,\pi r^3}{(r+5)^2}$ 5. $\frac{8}{3}$ m/s 6. $\frac{1}{48\pi}$ cm/s
7. 20 m/s 8. $\left(3, \frac{16}{3}\right)$ and $\left(-3, \frac{-16}{3}\right)$
9. *b* 10. *b* 11. *c* 12. *a* 13. *c* 14. *b* 15. *b* 16. *a* 17. *b* 18. *a*
19. 2 20. 5

Answers

DPP-2 Tangents and Normals

1. $x+3y+8=0$ and $x+3y-8=0$ 7. *b* 8. *d* 9. *c* 10. *c* 11. *b* 12. *b*
13. *b* 14. *c* 15. *c* 16. *b* 17. *b* 18. *b* 19. *c* 20. *a* 21. *b* 22. *a*
23. *d* 24. *a* 25. *d* 26. *d* 27. *a* 28. *a* 29. *c* 30. *b* 31. *a,b,c,d* 32. *a,d*
33. *a,b* 34. *b,c* 35. *b,c* 36. *a,b* 37. *a,b,d* 38. *b,d* 39. *a* 40. *c* 41. *d* 42. *b*
43. *a* 44. *a* 45. 4 46. 9 47. 2 48. 1 49. 4 50. 2

DPP-3 Mean Value Theorem

10. *d* 11. *d* 12. *a* 13. *d* 14. *b* 15. *b* 16. *c* 17. *d* 18. *c* 19. *b,c*
20. *b,d* 21. *a* 22. *b* 23. *c* 24. 4 25. 5

DPP-4 Monotonic Functions

1. *a* 2. *a* 3. *a* 4. *d* 5. *c* 6. *b* 7. *b* 8. *b* 9. *c* 10. *a*
11. *a* 12. *c* 13. *d* 14. *b* 15. *b* 16. *a* 17. *d* 18. *b* 19. *a* 20. *c*
21. *a* 22. *b* 23. *a,c* 24. *a,b,c,d* 25. *a,d* 26. *a,b,c,d* 27. *b,c,d* 28. *b,c* 29. *b,c,d* 30. *b,c*
31. *c* 32. *a* 33. *d* 34. *c* 35. *c* 36. *a* 37. *d* 38. *d* 39. *c* 40. *b*

DPP-5 Maxima and Minima

4. $\frac{112}{\pi+4}$ (square), $\frac{28\pi}{\pi+4}$ (circle) 9. $6+\pi:6$ 11. (0, 2) 13. *d* 14. *d* 15. *b* 16. *d*
17. *d* 18. *b* 19. *d* 20. *a* 21. *d* 22. *d* 23. *a* 24. *c* 25. *d* 26. *b*
27. *b* 28. *a* 29. *a* 30. *d* 31. *a,c* 32. *a,b* 33. *a,b,c,d* 34. *a,b,c* 35. *b,c* 36. *b*
37. *d* 38. *a* 39. *b* 40. *a* 41. *a* 42. *b* 43. 7 44. 0 45. 1 46. 5
47. 9 48. 5 49. 6 50. 9

Revision Problems (JEE Main)

1. *d* 2. *c* 3. *c* 4. *a* 5. *d* 6. *b* 7. *d* 8. *a* 9. *b* 10. *d*
11. *b* 12. *b* 13. *c* 14. *b* 15. *d* 16. *a* 17. *b* 18. *c* 19. *a* 20. *a*
21. *a* 22. *b* 23. *d* 24. *d* 25. *a* 26. *c* 27. *d* 28. *c* 29. *b* 30. *c*
31. *a* 32. *d* 33. *d* 34. *a* 35. *b* 36. *d* 37. *d* 38. *c* 39. *a* 40. *d*

Revisal Problems (JEE Advanced)

1. *b* 2. *b* 3. *a* 4. *d* 5. *b* 6. *c* 7. *c* 8. *c* 9. *c* 10. *b*
11. *b* 12. *d* 13. *b* 14. *d* 15. *c* 16. *b* 17. *b* 18. *b* 19. *a* 20. *c*
21. *c* 22. *a* 23. *c* 24. *d* 25. *c* 26. *c* 27. *a* 28. *a,c,d* 29. *a,b,d*
30. *a,c,d* 31. *a,b,c* 32. *a,c* 33. *a,b,c* 34. *a,b* 35. *c,d* 36. *b* 37. *d* 38. *a* 39. *c*
40. *a* 41. *b* 42. *d* 43. *b* 44. *d* 45. 3 46. 3 47. 2 48. 5 49. 2
50. 6

JEE Main & AIEEE Archive

1. *d* 2. *a* 3. *c* 4. *b* 5. *c* 6. *b* 7. *d* 8. *d* 9. *b* 10. *c*
11. *b* 12. *a* 13. *d* 14. *c* 15. *b* 16. *a* 17. *d* 18. *a* 19. *b* 20. *a*
21. *c* 22. *b* 23. *d* 24. *d* 25. *b* 26. *a*` 27. *b* 28. *c* 29. *c* 30. *b*
31. *a*

JEE Advanced & IIT JEE Archive

1. 4 2. *a,b,d* 3. *b,c* 4. *a,c,d* 5. 8 6. *a,c* 7. *a,b* 8. *c* 9. 9 10. 5
11. 9 12. *a,b,c,d* 13. 2 14. 2 15. 9 16. 1 17. *b,c* 18. *d* 19. *b* 20. 7
21. *b,c,d* 22. *c* 23. *c* 24. *a* 25. *a* 26. *a* 27. *b* 28. *a* 29. *b,c* 30. *a,b*
31. *c* 32. *d* 33. *a*

1. Methods of Differentiation

DPP-1 First Principle and Fundamental Theorems

1. (i) We have,

$$f(x) = \tan x$$

$$\Rightarrow f'(x) = \lim_{h \to 0} \frac{f(x+h) - f(x)}{h}$$

$$= \lim_{h \to 0} \frac{\tan(x+h) - \tan x}{h}$$

$$= \lim_{h \to 0} \frac{\sin(x+h-x)}{h\cos(x+h)\cos x}$$

$$\left[\because \tan x - \tan y = \frac{\sin(x-y)}{\cos x \cos y}\right]$$

$$= \lim_{h \to 0} \frac{\sin h}{h} \times \lim_{h \to 0} \frac{1}{\cos(x+h)\cos x}$$

$$\therefore \quad f'(x) = 1 \times \frac{1}{\cos^2 x} = \sec^2 x$$

(ii) We have,

$$f(x) = \cot(2x+1)$$

$$\Rightarrow f'(x) = \lim_{h \to 0} \frac{f(x+h) - f(x)}{h}$$

$$= \lim_{h \to 0} \frac{\cot[2(x+h)+1] - \cot(2x+1)}{h}$$

$$= \lim_{h \to 0} \frac{-\sin(2x+2h+1-2x-1)}{h\sin(2x+2h+1)\sin(2x+1)}$$

$$\left[\because \cot x - \cot y = \frac{-\sin(x-y)}{\sin x \sin y}\right]$$

$$= \lim_{h \to 0} \frac{-2\sin 2h}{2h} \times \lim_{h \to 0} \frac{1}{\sin(2x+2h+1)\sin(2x+1)}$$

$$\therefore \quad f'(x) = \frac{-2}{\sin^2(2x+1)}$$

(iii) We have,

$$f(x) = \sqrt{\sin x}$$

$$\Rightarrow f'(x) = \lim_{h \to 0} \frac{f(x+h) - f(x)}{h}$$

$$= \lim_{h \to 0} \frac{\sqrt{\sin(x+h)} - \sqrt{\sin x}}{h}$$

$$= \lim_{h \to 0} \frac{\sin(x+h) - \sin x}{h(\sqrt{\sin(x+h)} + \sqrt{\sin x})}$$

$$= \lim_{h \to 0} \frac{2\sin\frac{h}{2}\cos\left(x + \frac{h}{2}\right)}{h(\sqrt{\sin(x+h)} + \sqrt{\sin x})}$$

$$\left[\because \sin x - \sin y = 2\sin\frac{(x-y)}{2}\cos\frac{(x+y)}{2}\right]$$

$$= \lim_{h \to 0} \frac{\sin\frac{h}{2}}{\frac{h}{2}} \times \lim_{h \to 0} \frac{\cos\left(x+\frac{h}{2}\right)}{\sqrt{\sin(x+h)} + \sqrt{\sin x}}$$

$$\therefore \quad f'(x) = 1 \times \frac{\cos x}{2\sqrt{\sin x}} = \frac{\cos x}{2\sqrt{\sin x}}$$

(iv) We have,

$$f(x) = \tan\sqrt{x}$$

$$\Rightarrow f'(x) = \lim_{h \to 0} \frac{f(x+h) - f(x)}{h}$$

$$= \lim_{h \to 0} \frac{\tan\sqrt{x+h} - \tan\sqrt{x}}{h}$$

$$= \lim_{h \to 0} \frac{\sin(\sqrt{x+h} - \sqrt{x})}{h\cos\sqrt{(x+h)}\cdot\cos\sqrt{x}}$$

$$= \lim_{h \to 0} \frac{\sin(\sqrt{x+h} - \sqrt{x})(\sqrt{x+h} - \sqrt{x})}{h\sqrt{(x+h)} - \sqrt{x}}$$

$$\times \lim_{h \to 0} \frac{1}{\cos\sqrt{x+h}\cos\sqrt{x}}$$

$$= \lim_{h \to 0} \frac{\sin(\sqrt{x+h} - \sqrt{x})}{(\sqrt{x+h} - \sqrt{x})} \times \lim_{h \to 0} \frac{\sqrt{x+h} - \sqrt{x}}{h}$$

$$\times \frac{1}{\cos^2\sqrt{x}}$$

$$= \frac{1}{\cos^2\sqrt{x}} \times \lim_{h \to 0} \frac{x+h-x}{h\sqrt{x+h} + \sqrt{x}}$$

$$\therefore \quad f'(x) = \frac{1}{\cos^2\sqrt{x}} \times \frac{1}{2\sqrt{x}} = \frac{\sec^2\sqrt{x}}{2\sqrt{x}}$$

(v) We have,

$$f(x) = \frac{\sin x}{x}$$

$$\Rightarrow f'(x) = \lim_{h \to 0} \frac{f(x+h) - f(x)}{h}$$

$$= \lim_{h \to 0} \frac{\frac{\sin(x+h)}{x+h} - \frac{\sin x}{x}}{h}$$

$$= \lim_{h \to 0} \frac{x\sin(x+h) - x\sin x - h\sin x}{h(x+h)\,x}$$

$$= \lim_{h \to 0} \frac{x[\sin(x+h) - \sin x]}{h(x+h)\,x} - \frac{h(\sin x)}{h(x+h)x}$$

$$= \lim_{h \to 0} \frac{2x\sin\frac{h}{2}\cos\left(x+\frac{h}{2}\right)}{h(x+h)x} - \lim_{h \to 0} \frac{h\sin x}{h(x+h)x}$$

$$= \lim_{h \to 0} \frac{\sin\frac{h}{2}}{\frac{h}{2}} \times \lim_{h \to 0} \frac{x\cos\left(x+\frac{h}{2}\right)}{(x+h)x} - \frac{\sin x}{x^2}$$

$$\therefore \quad f'(x) = \frac{1 \times x\cos x}{x^2} - \frac{\sin x}{x^2} = \frac{x\cos x - \sin x}{x^2}$$

(vi) We have,

$$f(x) = \sin x + \cos x$$

$$\Rightarrow f'(x) = \lim_{h \to 0} \frac{f(x+h) - f(x)}{h}$$

$$= \lim_{h \to 0} \frac{\sin(x+h) + \cos(x+h) - \sin x - \cos x}{h}$$

$$= \lim_{h \to 0} \frac{\sin(x+h) - \sin x}{h} + \lim_{h \to 0} \frac{\cos(x+h) - \cos x}{h}$$

$$= \lim_{h \to 0} \frac{2\sin\frac{h}{2}\cos\left(x+\frac{h}{2}\right)}{h} + \lim_{h \to 0} \frac{-2\sin\left(x+\frac{h}{2}\right)\sin\frac{h}{2}}{h}$$

$$= \lim_{h \to 0} \frac{\sin\frac{h}{2}}{\frac{h}{2}} \times \lim_{h \to 0} \cos\left(x+\frac{h}{2}\right) + \lim_{h \to 0} -\sin\left(x+\frac{h}{2}\right)$$

$$\times \lim_{h \to 0} \frac{\sin\frac{h}{2}}{\frac{h}{2}}$$

$$\Rightarrow \quad f'(x) = \cos x - \sin x$$

2. (i) We have,

$$f(x) = (x^2 - 4x + 5)(x^3 - 2)$$

$$\Rightarrow f'(x) = (x^2 - 4x + 5)(x^3 - 2)' + (x^3 - 2)(x^2 - 4x + 5)'$$

$$\left[\because \frac{d(uv)}{dx} = v\frac{du}{dx} + u\frac{dv}{dx}\right]$$

$$= (x^2 - 4x + 5)(3x^2) + (x^3 - 2)(2x - 4)$$

$$= 3x^4 - 12x^3 + 15x^2 + 2x^4 - 4x^3 - 4x + 8$$

$$\therefore \quad f'(x) = 5x^4 - 16x^3 + 15x^2 - 4x + 8$$

(ii) We have,

$$f(x) = (3x + 8)^{7/3} \cdot (x + 7)^{-3}$$

$$= (3x + 8)^{7/3}[(x + 7)^{-3}]' + (x + 7)^{-3}[(3x + 8)^{7/3}]'$$

$$= (3x + 8)^{7/3}[-3(x + 7)^{-4}] + (x + 7)^{-3} \times \frac{7}{3}(3x + 8)^{4/3} \cdot 3$$

$$= -3(3x + 8)^{7/3}(x + 7)^{-4} + 7(x + 7)^{-3} \cdot (3x + 8)^{4/3}$$

$$= (3x + 8)^{4/3}(x + 7)^{-4}[-3(3x + 8) + 7(x + 7)]$$

$$= (3x + 8)^{4/3}(x + 7)^{-4}[-9x - 24 + 7x + 49]$$

$$\therefore f(x) = (25 - 2x)(3x + 8)^{4/3}(x + 7)^{-4}$$

(iii) We have,

$$f(x) = \frac{1 - \sqrt{x}}{1 + \sqrt{x}}$$

$$\Rightarrow f'(x) = \frac{(1 + \sqrt{x})(1 - \sqrt{x})' - (1 - \sqrt{x})(1 + \sqrt{x})'}{(1 + \sqrt{x})^2}$$

$$\left[\because \left(\frac{u}{v}\right)' = \frac{vu' - uv'}{v^2}\right]$$

$$= \frac{(1 + \sqrt{x})\left(\frac{-1}{2\sqrt{x}}\right) - (1 - \sqrt{x})\left(\frac{1}{2\sqrt{x}}\right)}{(1 + \sqrt{x})^2}$$

$$= \frac{1}{2\sqrt{x}} \frac{(-1 - \sqrt{x} - 1 + \sqrt{x})}{(1 + \sqrt{x})^2}$$

$$\therefore \quad f'(x) = \frac{-1}{\sqrt{x}(1 + \sqrt{x})^2}$$

(iv) We have,

$$f(x) = \frac{(x^2 + 1)(x + 3)}{x}$$

$$= \frac{x^3 + 3x^2 + x + 3}{x}$$

$$= x^2 + 3x + 1 + \frac{3}{x}$$

$$\therefore \quad f'(x) = 2x + 3 + 0 - \frac{3}{x^2}$$

$$= \frac{2x^3 + 3x^2 - 3}{x^2}$$

3. (i) We have,

$$f(x) = \sqrt{a + \sqrt{a + x}}$$

$$\therefore \quad f'(x) = \frac{d\sqrt{a + \sqrt{a + x}}}{d(a + \sqrt{a + x})} \times \frac{d(a + \sqrt{a + x})}{dx}$$

$$= \frac{1}{2\sqrt{a + \sqrt{a + x}}} \times \left(0 + \frac{1}{2\sqrt{a + x}}\right)$$

$$= \frac{1}{4(\sqrt{a + \sqrt{a + x}})(\sqrt{a + x})}$$

(ii) We have,

$$f(x) = \sqrt{4 + \sqrt{4 + \sqrt{4 + x^2}}}$$

$$\therefore f'(x) = \frac{d\left(\sqrt{4 + \sqrt{4 + \sqrt{4 + x^2}}}\right)}{d(4 + \sqrt{4 + \sqrt{4 + x^2}})} \times \frac{d(4 + \sqrt{4 + \sqrt{4 + x^2}})}{d(4 + \sqrt{4 + x^2})} \times \frac{d(4 + \sqrt{4 + x^2})}{dx}$$

$$= \frac{1}{2\sqrt{4 + \sqrt{4 + \sqrt{4 + x^2}}}} \times \left(0 + \frac{1}{2\sqrt{4 + \sqrt{4 + x^2}}}\right) \times \left(0 + \frac{1}{2\sqrt{4 + x^2}}\right) \times 2x$$

$$= \frac{x}{4\sqrt{4 + \sqrt{4 + \sqrt{4 + x^2}}}\sqrt{4 + \sqrt{4 + x^2}}\sqrt{4 + x^2}}$$

(iii) We have,

$$f(x) = \frac{\sqrt{a + x} - \sqrt{a - x}}{\sqrt{a + x} + \sqrt{a - x}}$$

$$\therefore \quad f'(x) = \frac{\left[\begin{array}{l}(\sqrt{a + x} + \sqrt{a - x})(\sqrt{a + x} - \sqrt{a - x})' \\ -(\sqrt{a + x} - \sqrt{a - x})(\sqrt{a + x} + \sqrt{a - x})'\end{array}\right]}{(\sqrt{a + x} + \sqrt{a - x})^2}$$

$$= \frac{\left[\begin{array}{l}(\sqrt{a + x} + \sqrt{a - x})\left(\frac{1}{2\sqrt{a + x}} + \frac{1}{2\sqrt{a - x}}\right) \\ -(\sqrt{a + x} - \sqrt{a - x})\left(\frac{1}{2\sqrt{a + x}} - \frac{1}{2\sqrt{a - x}}\right)\end{array}\right]}{(\sqrt{a + x} + \sqrt{a - x})^2}$$

$$= \frac{1}{2\sqrt{a + x}\sqrt{a - x}} \frac{\left[\begin{array}{l}(\sqrt{a + x} + \sqrt{a - x})^2 \\ + (\sqrt{a + x} - \sqrt{a - x})^2\end{array}\right]}{(\sqrt{a + x} + \sqrt{a - x})^2}$$

$$= \frac{2(a + x + a - x)}{2\sqrt{a + x}\sqrt{a - x}(\sqrt{a + x} + \sqrt{a - x})^2}$$

$$= \frac{2a}{(\sqrt{a + x} + \sqrt{a - x})^2\sqrt{a^2 - x^2}}$$

(iv) We have,

$$f(x) = \log(x + \sqrt{x^2 + a^2})$$

$$\therefore f'(x) = \frac{d\log(x + \sqrt{x^2 + a^2})}{d(x + \sqrt{x^2 + a^2})} \times \frac{d(x + \sqrt{x^2 + a^2})}{dx}$$

$$= \frac{1}{x + \sqrt{x^2 + a^2}} \times \left(1 + \frac{1}{2\sqrt{x^2 + a^2}} \times 2x\right)$$

$$= \frac{1}{x + \sqrt{x^2 + a^2}}\left(1 + \frac{x}{\sqrt{x^2 + a^2}}\right)$$

$$= \frac{1}{x + \sqrt{x^2 + a^2}}\left(\frac{\sqrt{x^2 + a^2} + x}{\sqrt{x^2 + a^2}}\right)$$

$$= \frac{1}{\sqrt{x^2 + a^2}}$$

(v) We have,

$$f(x) = 10^{10^x}$$

$$\therefore \quad f'(x) = \frac{d10^{10^x}}{d10^x} \times \frac{d10^x}{dx}$$

$$= 10^{10^x}\log 10 \cdot 10^x \log 10$$

$$= 10^{10^x} \cdot 10^x (\log 10)^2$$

(vi) We have,

$$f(x) = \log\left[\tan\left(\frac{\pi}{4} + \frac{x}{2}\right)\right]$$

$$\therefore \quad f'(x) = \frac{d\log\left[\tan\left(\frac{\pi}{4}+\frac{x}{2}\right)\right]}{d\tan\left(\frac{\pi}{4}+\frac{x}{2}\right)} \times \frac{d\tan\left(\frac{\pi}{4}+\frac{x}{2}\right)}{dx}$$

$$= \frac{1}{\tan\left(\frac{\pi}{4}+\frac{x}{2}\right)} \times \sec^2\left(\frac{\pi}{4}+\frac{x}{2}\right) \times \frac{1}{2}$$

$$= \frac{1}{2\sin\left(\frac{\pi}{4}+\frac{x}{2}\right)\cos\left(\frac{\pi}{4}+\frac{x}{2}\right)}$$

$$= \frac{1}{\sin\left(\frac{\pi}{2}+x\right)} = \frac{1}{\cos x} = \sec x$$

4. (i) We have,

$$f(x) = e^{ax} \cdot \cot(bx + c)$$

$$\therefore \quad f'(x) = e^{ax} \cdot [\cot(bx+c)]' + \cot(bx+c)\,(e^{ax})'$$

$$= e^{ax}[-\operatorname{cosec}^2(bx+c)\cdot b] + \cot(bx+c)\,(e^{ax}\cdot a)$$

$$= e^{ax}[a\cot(bx+c) - b\operatorname{cosec}^2(bx+c)]$$

(ii) We have,

$$f(x) = \sqrt{\log\left\{\sin\left(\frac{x^2}{3}-1\right)\right\}}$$

$$\therefore \quad f'(x) = \frac{d\sqrt{\log\left\{\sin\left(\frac{x^2}{3}-1\right)\right\}}}{d\log\left\{\sin\left(\frac{x^2}{3}-1\right)\right\}} \times \frac{d\log\left\{\sin\left(\frac{x^2}{3}-1\right)\right\}}{d\sin\left(\frac{x^2}{3}-1\right)} \times \frac{d\sin\left(\frac{x^2}{3}-1\right)}{dx}$$

$$= \frac{1}{2\sqrt{\log\left\{\sin\left(\frac{x^2}{3}-1\right)\right\}}} \times \frac{1}{\sin\left(\frac{x^2}{3}-1\right)} \times \cos\left(\frac{x^2}{3}-1\right) \times \frac{2x}{3}$$

$$= \frac{x\cot\left(\frac{x^2}{3}-1\right)}{3\log\left\{\sin\left(\frac{x^2}{3}-1\right)\right\}}$$

(iii) We have,

$$f(x) = \log_{\sin x}\cos x$$

$$\Rightarrow \quad f(x) = \frac{\log\cos x}{\log\sin x} \qquad \left[\because \log_a b = \frac{\log b}{\log a}\right]$$

$$\therefore \quad f'(x) = \frac{(\log\sin x)(\log\cos x)' - (\log\cos x)(\log\sin x)'}{(\log\sin x)^2}$$

$$= \frac{(\log\sin x)(-\tan x) - \log\cos x(\cot x)}{(\log\sin x)^2}$$

$$= -(\tan x + \log_{\sin x}\cos x\cot x)\log_{\sin x} e$$

(iv) We have,

$$f(x) = \log_e(\sec x + \tan x)$$

$$\therefore \quad f'(x) = \frac{d\log_e(\sec x + \tan x)}{d(\sec x + \tan x)} \times \frac{d(\sec x + \tan x)}{dx}$$

$$= \frac{1}{\sec x + \tan x} \times (\sec x\tan x + \sec^2 x)$$

$$= \sec x$$

(v) We have,

$$f(x) = \log_e \sin\sqrt{x^2+1}$$

$$\therefore \quad f'(x) = \frac{d\log_e\sin\sqrt{x^2+1}}{d\sin\sqrt{x^2+1}} \times \frac{d\sin\sqrt{x^2+1}}{d\sqrt{x^2+1}} \times \frac{d\sqrt{x^2+1}}{d(x^2+1)} \times \frac{d(x^2+1)}{dx}$$

$$= \frac{1}{\sin\sqrt{x^2+1}} \times \cos\sqrt{x^2+1} \times \frac{1}{2\sqrt{x^2+1}} \times 2x$$

$$= \frac{x\cot\sqrt{x^2+1}}{\sqrt{x^2+1}}$$

(vi) We have,

$$f(x) = \log_e\left(\frac{x+\sqrt{x^2-a^2}}{x-\sqrt{x^2-a^2}}\right)$$

$$\Rightarrow \quad f(x) = \log_e(x+\sqrt{x^2-a^2}) - \log(x-\sqrt{x^2-a^2})$$

$$\left[\because \log\frac{a}{b} = \log a - \log b\right]$$

$$\therefore \quad f'(x) = \left(\frac{1}{x+\sqrt{x^2-a^2}}\right)\left(1+\frac{2x}{2\sqrt{x^2-a^2}}\right) - \left[\left(\frac{1}{x-\sqrt{x^2-a^2}}\right)\left(1-\frac{2x}{2\sqrt{x^2-a^2}}\right)\right]$$

$$= \frac{1}{\sqrt{x^2-a^2}} + \frac{1}{\sqrt{x^2-a^2}}$$

$$= \frac{1}{2\sqrt{x^2-a^2}}$$

5. (b) We have,

$$y = \frac{\sec x - \tan x}{\sec x + \tan x}$$

$$\Rightarrow \quad y = (\sec x - \tan x)^2$$

$$\therefore \quad \frac{dy}{dx} = 2(\sec x - \tan x)(\sec x\tan x - \sec^2 x)$$

$$= -2\sec x(\sec x - \tan x)^2$$

6. (c) We have,

$$y = \frac{1+x^2+x^4}{1+x+x^2} = \frac{(1-x+x^2)(1+x+x^2)}{(1+x+x^2)}$$

$$y = 1 - x + x^2$$

$$\frac{dy}{dx} = 2x - 1 \qquad \text{...(i)}$$

Also, we have

$$\frac{dy}{dx} = ax + b \qquad \text{...(ii)}$$

From Eqs. (i) and (ii), we get $a = 2$, $b = -1$

7. (c) We have, $y = \frac{d}{dx}(x\log_e x)$

$$\Rightarrow \quad y = x(\log_e x)' + (\log_e x)(x)'$$

$$= \frac{x}{x} + \log_e x = 1 + \log_e x$$

$$\Rightarrow \quad y = 1 + \log_e x$$

Graph of $y = 1 + \log_e x$ is

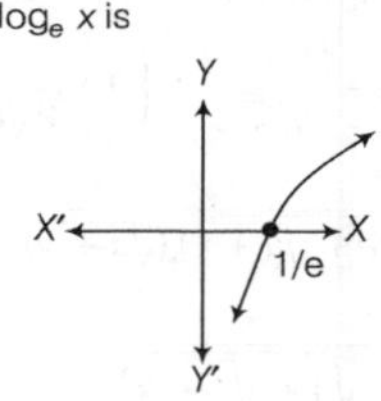

8. (b) Let $y = \left(x^{\frac{l+m}{m-n}}\right)^{\frac{1}{n-l}} \cdot \left(x^{\frac{m+n}{n-l}}\right)^{\frac{1}{l-m}} \cdot \left(x^{\frac{n+l}{l-m}}\right)^{\frac{1}{m-n}}$

$$= x^{\frac{l+m}{(m-n)(n-l)} + \frac{m+n}{(n-l)(l-m)} + \frac{n+l}{(l-m)(m+n)}}$$

$$= x^{\frac{l^2 - m^2 + m^2 - n^2 + n^2 - l^2}{(m-n)(n-l)(l-m)}} = x^0 = 1$$

$\therefore \quad \frac{dy}{dx} = 0$

9. (d) We have,

$$y = \frac{1}{1 + x^{n-m} + x^{p-m}} + \frac{1}{1 + x^{m-n} + x^{p-n}} + \frac{1}{1 + x^{m-p} + x^{n-p}}$$

$$= \frac{x^m}{x^m + x^n + x^p} + \frac{x^n}{x^n + x^m + x^p} + \frac{x^p}{x^p + x^m + x^n}$$

$\Rightarrow \quad y = \frac{x^m + x^n + x^p}{x^m + x^n + x^p} = 1$

$\Rightarrow \quad \frac{dy}{dx} = 0$

$\therefore \quad \left(\frac{dy}{dx}\right)_{x = e^{m^{n^p}}} = 0$

10. (a) We have, $f(x) = \log_x(\log x)$

$\Rightarrow \quad f(x) = \frac{\log(\log x)}{\log x}$

or $\quad f'(x) = \frac{\log x \frac{1}{x \log x} - \frac{\log \log x}{x}}{(\log x)^2}$

$\therefore \quad f'(e) = \frac{\frac{\log e}{e \log e} - \frac{\log(\log e)}{e}}{(\log e)^2}$

$$= \frac{1}{e}$$

11. (d) Let $y = f(e^x) \quad \Rightarrow \quad \frac{dy}{dx} = f'(e^x) \cdot e^x$

$\therefore \quad \frac{d^2y}{dx^2} = e^x [f'(e^x)]' + [f'(e^x)](e^x)'$

$$= e^x f''(e^x) \cdot e^x + f'(e^x) \cdot e^x$$

$$= f''(e^x) \cdot e^{2x} + f'(e^x) \cdot e^x$$

12. (a) We have, $y = f(x^2)$ and $f'(x) = \sqrt{2x^2 - 1}$

$\because \quad y = f(x^2) \quad \Rightarrow \quad \frac{dy}{dx} = f'(x^2) \cdot 2x$

$\Rightarrow \quad = \sqrt{2x^4 - 1} \cdot 2x \qquad [\because f'(x) = \sqrt{2x^2 - 1}]$

$\therefore \quad \left(\frac{dy}{dx}\right)_{x=1} = 2$

13. (b) We have, $y = f\left(\frac{2x - 1}{x^2 + 1}\right)$ and $f'(x) = \sin x$

$\because \quad y = f\left(\frac{2x-1}{x^2+1}\right)$

$\Rightarrow \quad \frac{dy}{dx} = f'\left(\frac{2x-1}{x^2+1}\right) \cdot \frac{(x^2+1)(2) - (2x-1)(2x)}{(x^2+1)}$

$$= f'\left(\frac{2x-1}{x^2+1}\right)\left[\frac{2(1 + x - x^2)}{x^2+1}\right]$$

$$= \sin\left(\frac{2x-1}{x^2+1}\right) \cdot \frac{2(1 + x - x^2)}{(x^2+1)^2} \qquad [\because f'(x) = \sin x]$$

14. (c) We have,

$$8f(x) + 6f\left(\frac{1}{x}\right) = x + 5 \qquad \text{...(i)}$$

Replace x by $\frac{1}{x}$ in Eq. (i), we get

$$8f\left(\frac{1}{x}\right) + 6f(x) = \frac{1}{x} + 5 \qquad \text{...(ii)}$$

On solving Eqs. (i) and (ii), we get

$$f(x) = \frac{1}{28}\left(8x - \frac{6}{x} + 10\right)$$

Now, $\quad y = x^2 f(x)$

$\Rightarrow \quad y = \frac{x^2}{28}\left(8x - \frac{6}{x} + 10\right) = \frac{1}{28}(8x^3 - 6x + 10x^2)$

$\Rightarrow \quad \frac{dy}{dx} = \frac{1}{28}(24x^2 - 6 + 20x)$

$\therefore \quad \left(\frac{dy}{dx}\right)_{x=-1} = \frac{1}{28}(24 - 6 - 20) = \frac{-2}{28} = \frac{-1}{14}$

15. (d) We have, $\quad f(x) = x^n$

$$f^1(x) = nx^{n-1}$$

$$f^2(x) = n(n-1)x^{n-2}$$

$$f^3(x) = n(n-1)(n-2)x^{n-3}$$

Similarly, $f^n(x) = n(n-1)(n-2)\cdots[n-(n-1)]x^{n-n}$

Now, $\quad f(x) - \frac{f'(x)}{1!} - \frac{f^2(x)}{2!} + \frac{f^3(x)}{3!} + \cdots + \frac{(-1)^n \cdot f^n(x)}{n!}$

$$= x^n - {}^nC_1 x^{n-1} + {}^nC_2 x^{n-2} + \cdots + (-1)^{n-1} \cdot 1$$

$$= (x-1)^n$$

$$[\because (x-1)^n = x^n - {}^nC_1 x^{n-1} \cdots (-1)^n \cdot 1]$$

$\Rightarrow \quad f(1) - \frac{f'(1)}{1!} + \frac{f^2(1)}{2!} + \cdots + \frac{(-1)^n \cdot f^n(1)}{n!} = (1-1)^n = 0$

16. (a) Gvien, $f(x)$ is a polynomial function of second degree.

Let $\quad f(x) = \alpha x^2 + \beta x + \gamma$

We have, $\quad f(1) = f(-1)$

$\therefore \quad \alpha + \beta + \gamma = \alpha - \beta + \gamma$

$\Rightarrow \quad \beta = 0$

$\therefore \quad f(x) = \alpha x^2 + \gamma$

Now, $\quad f'(x) = 2\alpha x$

$f'(a) = 2\alpha a$, $f'(b) = 2\alpha b$ and $f'(c) = 2\alpha c$

Here, a, b, c are in an AP.

$\therefore f'(a)$, $f'(b)$ and $f'(c)$ are also in an AP.

17. (b) We have, $g(x) = [f\{2f(x) + 2\}]^2$, $f(0) = -1$ and $f'(0) = 1$

$$g'(x) = 2[f\{2f(x) + 2\}] \cdot f'[2f(x) + 2] \cdot 2f'(x)$$

$$g'(0) = 2[f\{2f(0) + 2\} \cdot f'[2f(0) + 2] \cdot 2f'(0)$$

$$= 2[f(-2+2) f'(-2+2) \cdot 2f'(0)]$$

$$= 2[f(0) \cdot f'(0) \cdot 2f'(0)]$$

$$= 2[-1 \cdot 1 \cdot 2 \cdot 1] = -4 \quad [\because f(0) = -1 \text{ and } f'(0) = 1]$$

18. (a,b,c) We have, $y = \tan x \cdot \tan 2x \cdot \tan 3x$

On applying product rule, we get

$$\frac{dy}{dx} = \tan x \cdot \tan 2x \cdot 3\sec^2 3x + \tan x \cdot \tan 3x \cdot 2\sec^2 x + \tan 2x \cdot \tan 3x \cdot \sec^2 x$$

$$= 3\sec^2 3x \cdot \tan 2x \cdot \tan x + \sec^2 x \cdot \tan 2x \cdot \tan 3x + 2\sec^2 2x \cdot \tan x \cdot \tan 3x$$

Now, $y = \tan x \tan 2x \tan 3x$

On taking log both sides, we get

$$\log y = \log \tan x + \log \tan 2x + \log \tan 3x$$

On differentiating w.r.t. x, we get

$$\frac{1}{y}\frac{dy}{dx}=\frac{\sec^2 x}{\tan x}+\frac{2\sec^2 2x}{\tan 2x}+\frac{3\sec^3 3x}{\tan 3x}$$

$$\frac{1}{y}\frac{dy}{dx}=\frac{2}{2\sin x\cos x}+\frac{4}{2\sin 2x\cos 2x}+\frac{6}{2\sin 3x\cos 3x}$$

$$\frac{dy}{dx}=2y\,(\text{cosec}\,2x+2\text{cosec}\;4x+3\text{cosec}\;6x)$$

We know that,

$$\tan x\tan 2x\tan 3x=\tan 3x-\tan 2x-\tan x$$

$$\therefore \quad \frac{dy}{dx}=3\sec^2 3x-2\sec^2 2x-\sec^2 x$$

19. (a,c) We have,

$$y=e^{\sqrt{x}}+e^{-\sqrt{x}}$$

$$\therefore \quad \frac{dy}{dx}=e^{\sqrt{x}}\times\frac{1}{2\sqrt{x}}-\frac{e^{-\sqrt{x}}}{2\sqrt{x}}$$

$$=\frac{e^{\sqrt{x}}-e^{-\sqrt{x}}}{2\sqrt{x}}=\frac{[(e^{\sqrt{x}}-e^{-\sqrt{x}})^2]^{1/2}}{2\sqrt{x}}$$

$$=\frac{\sqrt{(e^{\sqrt{x}})^2+(e^{-\sqrt{x}})^2-2}}{2\sqrt{x}}$$

$$=\frac{\sqrt{(e^{\sqrt{x}})^2+(e^{-\sqrt{x}})^2+2-4}}{2\sqrt{x}}$$

$$=\frac{\sqrt{(e^{\sqrt{x}}+e^{-\sqrt{x}})^2-4}}{2\sqrt{x}}=\frac{\sqrt{y^2-4}}{2\sqrt{x}}$$

20. (a,b,c) We have,

$$f(0)=\frac{2}{g(0)},\ f'(0)=2g'(0)=4g(0)$$

$$g''(0)=5f''(0)=6f(0)=3$$

Now, on solving these equations, we get

$$f(0)=\frac{1}{2}, g(0)=4,\ f'(0)=16,\ g'(0)=8$$

$$f''(0)=\frac{3}{5},\ g''(0)=3$$

(a) We have, $h(x)=\dfrac{f(x)}{g(x)}$

$$h'(x)=\frac{g(x)f'(x)-g'(x)f'(x)}{[g(x)]^2}$$

$$\therefore \quad h'(0)=\frac{g(0)f'(0)-g'(0)f(0)}{g(0)^2}$$

$$=\frac{4\times 16-8\times\frac{1}{2}}{(4)^2}=\frac{15}{4}$$

(b) $k(x)=f(x)\cdot g(x)\cdot\sin x$

$k'(x)=f(x)\,g(x)\cos x+f(x)\sin x\,g'(x)+g(x)\sin x\,f'(x)$

$k'(0)=f(0)g(0)\cos 0+f(0)\sin 0\,g'(0)+g(0)\sin 0\,f'(0)$

$k'(0)=\frac{1}{2}\times 4\times 1+0+0=2$

(c) $\lim\limits_{x\to 0}\dfrac{g'(x)}{f'(x)}$

$$\Rightarrow \quad \frac{g'(0)}{f'(0)}=\frac{1}{2}$$

21. (8) We have,

$$f(x)=\lambda x^2+\mu x+12$$

$$f'(x)=2\lambda x+\mu$$

$$f'(4)=8\lambda+\mu=15 \qquad \ldots\text{(i)}$$

and $\quad f'(2)=4\lambda+\mu=11 \qquad \ldots\text{(ii)}$

On solving Eqs. (i) and (ii), we get

$$\lambda=1 \quad\text{and}\quad \mu=7$$

$$\therefore \quad \lambda+\mu=1+7=8$$

22. (5) We have, $f(x)=2\log_e(x-2)-x^2+4x+1 \qquad [x\neq 2,\ x>2]$

$$\Rightarrow \quad f'(x)=\frac{2}{x-2}-2x+4$$

$$=\frac{2}{x-2}-2\,(x-2)$$

$$=2\left[\frac{1}{x-2}-x-2\right]$$

$$=2\left[\frac{1-(x^2-4x+4)}{x-2}\right]$$

$$f'(x)=2\,\frac{(-x^2+4x-3)}{x-2}$$

$$f'(x)=\frac{-2(x-3)(x-1)}{x-2}$$

$$\because \quad f'(x)\geq 0$$

$$\therefore \quad \frac{-2\,(x-3)(x-1)}{x-2}\geq 0$$

$$\frac{2\,(x-3)(x-1)}{x-2}\leq 0$$

+ − + − on $-\infty$ … 1 … 2 … 3 … ∞

$x\in[2,3] \qquad [\because x>2]$

$$\Rightarrow \quad a=2,\ b=3$$

$$\therefore \quad a+b=2+3=5$$

23. (2) We have,

$$f(x)=(ax+b)\sin x+(cx+d)\cos x$$

$$\Rightarrow \quad f'(x)=(ax+b)\cos x+a\sin x+c\cos x-(cx+d)\sin x$$

$$=a\,x\cos x+b\cos x+a\sin x+c\cos x-c\,x\sin x-d\sin x$$

$$=a\,x\cos x+(b+c)\cos x+(a-d)\sin x-c\,x\sin x$$

But we have, $f'(x)=x\cos x$

$$\therefore \quad b+c=0,\quad a-d=0,\quad c=0 \quad\text{and}\quad a=1$$

$$\Rightarrow \quad a+b+c+d=(1+0+0+1)=2$$

24. (2) We have,

$$f(x)=x^n$$

$$f^1(x)=nx^{n-1}$$

$$f^2(x)=n(n-1)\,x^{n-2}$$

$$\vdots \qquad \vdots$$

$$f^n(x)=n!$$

Now, $\quad f(x)+\dfrac{f^1(x)}{1!}+\dfrac{f^2(x)}{2!}+\cdots+\dfrac{f^n(x)}{n!}$

$$=x^n+\frac{nx^{n-1}}{1!}+\frac{n(n-2)x^{n-2}}{2!}+\cdots+\frac{n!}{n!}$$

$$=x^n+{}^nC_1x^{n-1}+{}^nC_2x^{n-2}+\cdots+{}^nC_n$$

Hence, $\quad (x+1)^n=f(x)+\dfrac{f^1(x)}{1!}+\dfrac{f^2(x)}{2!}+\cdots+\dfrac{f^n(x)}{n!}$

On putting $x=1$ both sides, we get

$$2^n=f(1)+\frac{f^1(1)}{1!}+\frac{f^2(1)}{2!}+\cdots+\frac{f^n(1)}{n!}$$

$$\therefore \quad \lambda=2$$

25. (9) We have, $y=f(x^3)$ and $f'(x)=\sqrt{3x^2+6}$

Now, $\quad \dfrac{dy}{dx}=f'(x^3)\cdot 3x^2$

$$=\sqrt{3x^6+6}\cdot 3x^2 \qquad \left[\because f'(x)=\sqrt{3x^2+6}\right]$$

$$\therefore \quad \left(\frac{dy}{dx}\right)_{x=1}=\sqrt{3+6}\cdot 3$$

$$=3\times 3=9$$

DPP-2 Differentiation of Inverse Trigonometric and Implicit Functions

1. (i) Let $y = \tan^{-1}(\sqrt{1+x^2} + x)$

Put $x = \tan\theta \Rightarrow \theta = \tan^{-1} x$

$$y = \tan^{-1}(\sqrt{1+\tan^2\theta} + \tan\theta)$$
$$= \tan^{-1}(\sec\theta + \tan\theta)$$
$$= \tan^{-1}\left(\frac{1+\sin\theta}{\cos\theta}\right)$$
$$= \tan^{-1}\left[\frac{(\cos\theta/2 + \sin\theta/2)^2}{\cos^2\theta/2 - \sin^2\theta/2}\right]$$
$$= \tan^{-1}\left[\frac{\cos\theta/2 + \sin\theta/2}{\cos\theta/2 - \sin\theta/2}\right]$$
$$= \tan^{-1}\tan(\pi/4 + \theta/2)$$
$$= \pi/4 + \theta/2$$
$$\Rightarrow \quad y = \pi/4 + \frac{1}{2}\tan^{-1} x$$

On differentiating w.r.t. x, we get

$$\Rightarrow \quad \frac{dy}{dx} = \frac{1}{2(1+x^2)}$$

(ii) Let $y = \tan^{-1}\left(\frac{\cos x}{1+\sin x}\right)$

$$= \tan^{-1}\frac{(\cos^2 x/2 - \sin^2 x/2)}{(\cos x/2 + \sin x/2)^2}$$
$$= \tan^{-1}\left(\frac{\cos x/2 - \sin x/2}{\cos x/2 + \sin x/2}\right)$$
$$= \tan^{-1}\tan(\pi/4 - x/2)$$
$$y = \pi/4 - x/2$$
$$\therefore \quad \frac{dy}{dx} = -\frac{1}{2}$$

(iii) Let $y = \sin^{-1}\sqrt{\frac{1+x^2}{2}}$

Put $x^2 = \cos\theta \Rightarrow \theta = \cos^{-1} x^2$

$$\Rightarrow \quad y = \sin^{-1}\sqrt{\frac{1+\cos\theta}{2}}$$
$$= \sin^{-1}\sqrt{\frac{2\cos^2\frac{\theta}{2}}{2}}$$
$$= \sin^{-1}\cos\frac{\theta}{2}$$
$$= \sin^{-1}\sin\left(\frac{\pi}{2} - \frac{\theta}{2}\right)$$
$$= \frac{\pi}{2} - \frac{\theta}{2}$$
$$\Rightarrow \quad y = \frac{\pi}{2} - \frac{1}{2}\cos^{-1} x^2$$
$$\therefore \quad \frac{dy}{dx} = -\frac{1}{2}\left[\frac{-1}{\sqrt{1-x^4}} \times (2x)\right]$$
$$= \frac{x}{\sqrt{1-x^4}}$$

(iv) Let $y = \sin^{-1}(x^2\sqrt{1-x^2} + x\sqrt{1-x^4})$

$$y = \sin^{-1} x^2 + \sin^{-1} x$$

$[\because \sin^{-1} x + \sin^{-1} y = \sin^{-1}(x\sqrt{1-y^2} + y\sqrt{1-x^2})]$

$$\therefore \quad \frac{dy}{dx} = \frac{2x}{\sqrt{1-x^4}} + \frac{1}{\sqrt{1-x^2}} = \frac{2x + \sqrt{1+x^2}}{\sqrt{1-x^4}}$$

(v) Let $y = \tan^{-1}\left(\frac{\sqrt{1+x^2} + \sqrt{1-x^2}}{\sqrt{1+x^2} - \sqrt{1-x^2}}\right)$

Put $x^2 = \cos\theta \Rightarrow \theta = \cos^{-1} x^2$

$$y = \tan^{-1}\left(\frac{\sqrt{1+\cos\theta} + \sqrt{1-\cos\theta}}{\sqrt{1+\cos\theta} - \sqrt{1-\cos\theta}}\right)$$
$$= \tan^{-1}\left[\frac{\sqrt{2}\cos\theta/2 + \sqrt{2}\sin\theta/2}{\sqrt{2}\cos\theta/2 - \sqrt{2}\sin\theta/2}\right]$$
$$= \tan^{-1}\left(\frac{\cos\theta/2 + \sin\theta/2}{\cos\theta/2 - \sin\theta/2}\right)$$
$$= \tan^{-1}\tan(\pi/4 + \theta/2)$$
$$= \frac{\pi}{4} + \theta/2$$
$$\Rightarrow \quad y = \frac{\pi}{4} + \frac{1}{2}\cos^{-1} x^2$$
$$\therefore \quad \frac{dy}{dx} = \frac{1}{2}\left(\frac{-1}{\sqrt{1-x^4}}\right)\cdot(2x) = \frac{-x}{\sqrt{1-x^4}}$$

(vi) Let $y = \tan^{-1}\left(\frac{\sqrt{1+x^2} - 1}{x}\right)$

Put $x = \tan\theta \Rightarrow \theta = \tan^{-1} x$

$$\Rightarrow \quad y = \tan^{-1}\frac{(\sqrt{1+\tan^2\theta} - 1}{\tan\theta}$$
$$= \tan^{-1}\left(\frac{\sec\theta - 1}{\tan\theta}\right)$$
$$= \tan^{-1}\left(\frac{1-\cos\theta}{\sin\theta}\right)$$
$$= \tan^{-1}\tan\theta/2$$
$$= \theta/2$$
$$\Rightarrow \quad y = \frac{1}{2}\tan^{-1} x$$
$$\therefore \quad \frac{dy}{dx} = \frac{1}{2(1+x^2)}$$

(vii) Let $y = \cot^{-1}\left(\frac{\sqrt{1+\sin x} + \sqrt{1-\sin x}}{\sqrt{1+\sin x} - \sqrt{1-\sin x}}\right)$

$$y = \cot^{-1}\left(\frac{\cos x/2 + \sin x/2 + \cos x/2 - \sin x/2}{\cos x/2 + \sin x/2 - \cos x/2 + \sin x/2}\right)$$

$$\left[\begin{aligned}\because 1 + \sin x &= (\cos x/2 + \sin x/2)^2,\\ 1 - \sin x &= (\cos x/2 - \sin x/2)^2\end{aligned}\right]$$

$$= \cot^{-1}\left(\frac{\cos x/2}{\sin x/2}\right)$$
$$= \cot^{-1}\cot x/2 = x/2$$
$$\therefore \quad \frac{dy}{dx} = \frac{1}{2}$$

(viii) Let $y = \tan^{-1}\left(\frac{1-x}{1+x}\right) + \tan^{-1}\left(\frac{x+2}{1-2x}\right)$

$$\Rightarrow \quad y = \tan^{-1}1 - \tan^{-1}x + \tan^{-1}x + \tan^{-1}2$$

$$\left[\because \tan^{-1}x - \tan^{-1}y = \tan^{-1}\left(\frac{x-y}{1+xy}\right)\right]$$

$$\Rightarrow \quad y = \tan^{-1}1 + \tan^{-1}2$$
$$\therefore \quad \frac{dy}{dx} = 0$$

2. (i) We have, $xy^3 - yx^3 = x$

On differentiating w.r.t. x, we get

$$\left[x\left(3y^2\frac{dy}{dx}\right) + y^3\right] - \left[y(3x^2) + x^3\frac{dy}{dx}\right] = 1$$

$$\Rightarrow \quad 3xy^2\frac{dy}{dx} + y^3 - 3x^2y - x^3\frac{dy}{dx} = 1$$

$$\Rightarrow \quad \frac{dy}{dx}(3xy^2 - x^3) = 1 + 3x^2y - y^3$$

$$\Rightarrow \quad \frac{dy}{dx} = \frac{1 + 3x^2y - y^3}{3xy^2 - x^3}$$

(ii) We have, $x^3 + y^3 = 3axy$

On differentiating w.r.t. x, we get

$$3x^2 + 3y^2\frac{dy}{dx} = 3a\left(x\frac{dy}{dx} + y\right)$$

$$\Rightarrow \quad \frac{dy}{dx}(3y^2 - 3ax) = 3ay - 3x^2$$

$$\therefore \quad \frac{dy}{dx} = \frac{3(ay - x^2)}{3(y^2 - ax)} = \frac{ay - x^2}{y^2 - ax}$$

(iii) We have,

$$x\log y + y\log x = 5$$

On differentiating w.r.t. x, we get

$$\frac{x}{y}\frac{dy}{dx} + \log y + \frac{y}{x} + \log x\frac{dy}{dx} = 0$$

$$\Rightarrow \quad \frac{dy}{dx}\left(\frac{x}{y} + \log x\right) = -\left(\log y + \frac{y}{x}\right)$$

$$\therefore \quad \frac{dy}{dx} = \frac{-y}{x}\left(\frac{x\log y + y}{x + y\log x}\right)$$

3. (b) We have, $y = \cos^{-1}\cos x$ at $x = 5\pi/4$

$$y = \begin{cases} x, & x \in (0, \pi) \\ \pi - \cos^{-1}\cos x, & x \in \left(\pi, \frac{3\pi}{2}\right) \end{cases}$$

$$\Rightarrow \quad y = \pi - \cos^{-1}\cos x$$

$$\Rightarrow \quad y = \pi - x$$

$$\therefore \quad \frac{dy}{dx} = -1$$

4. (b) We have,

$$\sin(xy) + \cos(xy) = 0$$

$$\Rightarrow \quad \sin(xy) = -\cos(xy)$$

$$\Rightarrow \quad \tan(xy) = -1$$

$$\Rightarrow \quad xy = \tan^{-1}(-1)$$

$$\Rightarrow \quad xy = 3\pi/4$$

On differentiating w.r.t. x, we get

$$x\frac{dy}{dx} + y = 0$$

$$\therefore \quad \frac{dy}{dx} = \frac{-y}{x}$$

5. (c) We have,

$$y = \sin^{-1}\left(\frac{x^2 - 1}{x^2 + 1}\right) + \sec^{-1}\left(\frac{x^2 + 1}{x^2 - 1}\right)$$

$$y = \operatorname{cosec}^{-1}\left(\frac{x^2 + 1}{x^2 - 1}\right) + \sec^{-1}\left(\frac{x^2 + 1}{x^2 - 1}\right)$$

$$y = \frac{\pi}{2} \qquad [\because \operatorname{cosec}^{-1}x + \sec^{-1}x = \pi/2]$$

$$\therefore \quad \frac{dy}{dx} = 0$$

6. (b) We have,

$$y = x - x^2 \quad \ldots(i)$$

$$\Rightarrow \quad \frac{dy}{dx} = 1 - 2x \quad \ldots(ii)$$

Let $u = y^2$ and $v = x^2$

$$\frac{du}{dx} = 2y\frac{dy}{dx}$$

and $$\frac{dv}{dx} = 2x$$

$$\therefore \quad \frac{du}{dv} = \frac{2y\,dy/dx}{2x} = \frac{(x - x^2)(1 - 2x)}{x}$$

[from Eqs. (i) and (ii)]

$$= (1 - x)(1 - 2x) = 2x^2 - 3x + 1$$

7. (b) We have,

$$x\sqrt{1 + y} + y\sqrt{1 + x} = 0$$

$$\Rightarrow \quad x\sqrt{1 + y} = -y\sqrt{1 + x}$$

$$\Rightarrow \quad x^2(1 + y) = y^2(1 + x)$$

$$\Rightarrow \quad x^2 - y^2 + x^2y - y^2x = 0$$

$$\Rightarrow \quad (x - y)(x + y + xy) = 0$$

$$\Rightarrow \quad x + y + xy = 0 \qquad [x - y \neq 0]$$

$$\Rightarrow \quad y = \frac{-x}{1 + x}$$

$$\therefore \quad \frac{dy}{dx} = -\left[\frac{(1 + x)(1) - x}{(1 + x)^2}\right] = \frac{-1}{(1 + x)^2}$$

8. (d) We have,

$$y = \sin^{-1}(x\sqrt{1 - x^2} + \sqrt{x}\sqrt{1 - x^2})$$

$$y = \sin^{-1}x + \sin^{-1}\sqrt{x}$$

$$[\because \sin^{-1}x + \sin^{-1}y = \sin^{-1}(x\sqrt{1 - y^2} + y\sqrt{1 - x^2})]$$

$$\frac{dy}{dx} = \frac{1}{\sqrt{1 - x^2}} + \frac{1}{\sqrt{1 - x}} \times \frac{1}{2\sqrt{x}}$$

$$\frac{dy}{dx} = \frac{1}{\sqrt{1 - x^2}} + \frac{1}{2\sqrt{x(1 - x)}} \quad \ldots(i)$$

But we have given,

$$\frac{dy}{dx} = \frac{1}{2\sqrt{x(1 - x)}} + p$$

From Eq. (i),

$$p = \frac{1}{\sqrt{1 - x^2}}$$

9. (a) We have,

$$ax^2 + 2hxy + by^2 = 0$$

On differentiating w.r.t. x, we get

$$2ax + 2h\left(x\frac{dy}{dx} + y\right) + 2by\frac{dy}{dx} = 0$$

$$\Rightarrow \quad \frac{dy}{dx} = \frac{-(ax + hy)}{(hx + by)}$$

$$\Rightarrow \quad \frac{dy}{dx} = \frac{y}{x}$$

$$\left[\begin{array}{l} \because ax^2 + 2hxy + by^2 = 0 \\ ax^2 + hxy = -(by^2 + hxy) \\ \Rightarrow -\left(\frac{ax + hy}{by + hx}\right) = \frac{y}{x} \end{array}\right]$$

10. (b) We have, $\cos^{-1}\left(\frac{x^2-y^2}{x^2+y^2}\right)=\log a$

$$\Rightarrow \frac{x^2-y^2}{x^2+y^2}=\cos(\log a)$$

On differentiating w.r.t. x, we get

$$\frac{(x^2+y^2)\left(2x-2y\frac{dy}{dx}\right)-(x^2-y^2)\left(2x+2y\frac{dy}{dx}\right)}{(x^2+y^2)^2}=0$$

$$\Rightarrow (x^2+y^2)\left(2x-2y\frac{dy}{dx}\right)-(x^2-y^2)\left(2x+2y\frac{dy}{dx}\right)=0$$

$$\Rightarrow 2x(x^2+y^2)-2y\frac{dy}{dx}(x^2+y^2)-2x(x^2-y^2)-2y\frac{dy}{dx}(x^2-y^2)=0$$

$$\Rightarrow 2y\frac{dy}{dx}(x^2+y^2+x^2-y^2)=2x(x^2-y^2-x^2-y^2)$$

$$\therefore \frac{dy}{dx}=-\frac{y}{x}$$

11. (a) We have, $x^2\cdot e^y+2xye^x+13=0$

On differentiating w.r.t. x, we get

$$x^2e^y\frac{dy}{dx}+2xe^y+2xye^x+2xe^x\frac{dy}{dx}+2ye^x=0$$

$$\Rightarrow \frac{dy}{dx}(x^2e^y+2xe^x)=-(2xe^y+2xye^x+2ye^x)$$

$$\Rightarrow \frac{dy}{dx}=\frac{-2xe^y-2ye^x(x+1)}{x(xe^y+2e^x)}$$

$$\Rightarrow \frac{dy}{dx}=\frac{-2xe^{y-x}-2y(x+1)}{x(xe^{y-x}+2)}$$

12. (c) We have, $y=\log_y x$

$$\Rightarrow y=\frac{\log_e x}{\log_e y} \quad \left[\because \log_a b=\frac{\log b}{\log a}\right]$$

$$\Rightarrow y\log_e y=\log_e x$$

On differentiating w.r.t. x, we get

$$(1+\log_e y)\frac{dy}{dx}=\frac{1}{x}$$

$$\Rightarrow \frac{dy}{dx}=\frac{1}{x(1+\log_e y)}$$

13. (a) We have,

$$y=\sec(\tan^{-1}x)$$

On differentiating w.r.t. x, we get

$$\frac{dy}{dx}=\sec(\tan^{-1}x)\tan(\tan^{-1}x)\times\frac{1}{1+x^2}$$

$$\left(\frac{dy}{dx}\right)_{x=1}=\sec(\tan^{-1}1)\times\tan(\tan^{-1}1)\times\frac{1}{1+1}$$

$$=\sec\frac{\pi}{4}\times\tan\frac{\pi}{4}\times\frac{1}{2}=\frac{\sqrt{2}}{2}=\frac{1}{\sqrt{2}}$$

14. (a) We have, $\log_e(x+y)=2xy$

Put $x=0$, then $y=1$

On differentiating w.r.t. x, we get

$$\frac{1}{x+y}\left(1+\frac{dy}{dx}\right)=2x\frac{dy}{dx}+2y$$

$$\frac{dy}{dx}\left(\frac{1}{x+y}-2x\right)=2y-\frac{1}{x+y}$$

$$\frac{dy}{dx}=\frac{2y(x+y)-1}{1-2x(x+y)}$$

$$\therefore \left(\frac{dy}{dx}\right)_{\substack{x=0\\y=1}}=\frac{2-1}{1-0}=1$$

15. (a,b,c) We have, $y+\log_e(1+x)=0$

$$\Rightarrow y=-\log_e(1+x) \Rightarrow y=\log_e(1+x)^{-1}$$

$$\Rightarrow e^y=\frac{1}{1+x} \quad \ldots(i)$$

$$\Rightarrow xe^y+e^y=1$$

On differentiating w.r.t. x, we get

$$xe^yy'+e^y+e^yy'=0$$

$$xy'+y'+1=0 \quad \ldots(ii)$$

$$\Rightarrow y'=-\frac{1}{x+1} \Rightarrow y'=-e^y \quad \left[\because e^y=\frac{1}{1+x}\right]$$

$$\Rightarrow y'+e^y=0$$

From Eq. (ii), $xy'+y'+1=0 \Rightarrow xy'+1=-y'$

$$\Rightarrow xy'+1=e^y$$

16. (b,c) We have, $y^2+b^2=2xy$

$$\Rightarrow 2xy-y^2=b^2$$

On differentiating w.r.t. x, we get

$$2x\frac{dy}{dx}+2y-2y\frac{dy}{dx}=0 \Rightarrow \frac{dy}{dx}(x-y)=-y$$

$$\Rightarrow \frac{dy}{dx}=\frac{y}{y-x}$$

On multipling by $(y-x)$ both numerator and denominator, we get

$$\Rightarrow \frac{dy}{dx}=\frac{y(y-x)}{(y-x)^2}=\frac{y^2-xy}{(y-x)^2}=\frac{2xy-b^2-xy}{(y-x)^2}=\frac{xy-b^2}{(y-x)^2}$$

17. (a,b) We have, $\sqrt{y+x}+\sqrt{y-x}=c$

On differentiating w.r.t. x, we get

$$\frac{1}{2\sqrt{y+x}}\left(\frac{dy}{dx}+1\right)+\frac{\left(\frac{dy}{dx}-1\right)}{2\sqrt{y-x}}=0$$

$$\Rightarrow \frac{dy}{dx}\left(\frac{1}{\sqrt{y+x}}+\frac{1}{\sqrt{y-x}}\right)=\frac{1}{\sqrt{y-x}}-\frac{1}{\sqrt{y+x}}$$

$$\Rightarrow \frac{dy}{dx}(\sqrt{y-x}+\sqrt{y+x})=\sqrt{y+x}-\sqrt{y-x}$$

$$\Rightarrow \frac{dy}{dx}=\frac{\sqrt{y+x}-\sqrt{y-x}}{\sqrt{y+x}+\sqrt{y-x}}$$

$$\Rightarrow \frac{dy}{dx}=\frac{y+x-y+x}{(\sqrt{y+x}+\sqrt{y-x})^2}=\frac{2x}{c^2}$$

$$[\because \sqrt{y+x}+\sqrt{y-x}=c]$$

$$\therefore \frac{dy}{dx}=\frac{2x}{y+x+y-x+2\sqrt{y^2-x^2}}=\frac{x}{y+\sqrt{y^2-x^2}}$$

Explanations for Q. Nos. (18-20)

We have, $f(x)=\sin^{-1}\frac{2x}{1+x^2}$

$$f(x)=\begin{cases}2\tan^{-1}x, & -1\le x\le 1\\ \pi-2\tan^{-1}x, & x>1\end{cases}; \quad f'(x)=\begin{cases}\frac{2}{1+x^2}, & -1\le x\le 1\\ \frac{-2}{1+x^2}, & x>1\end{cases}$$

$$\Rightarrow f'(2)=\frac{-2}{1+2^2}=\frac{-2}{5}$$

$$\Rightarrow f'\left(\frac{1}{2}\right)=\frac{2}{1+\left(\frac{1}{2}\right)^2}=\frac{8}{5} \Rightarrow f'(1^-)=\frac{2}{1+1}=1$$

$$f'(1^+)=\frac{-2}{1+1}=-1$$

$$f'(1^-)\ne f'(1^+)$$

$\therefore f'(1)$ does not exist.

18. (b) 19. (a) 20. (d)

Explanations for Q. Nos. (21-23)

We have,

$$f(x) = \cos^{-1}\left(\frac{1 - x^2}{1 + x^2}\right)$$

$$f(x) = \begin{cases} 2\tan^{-1}x, & x \ge 0 \\ -2\tan^{-1}x, & x < 0 \end{cases}$$

$$f'(x) = \begin{cases} \dfrac{2}{1 + x^2}, & x \ge 0 \\ \dfrac{-2}{1 + x^2}, & x < 0 \end{cases}$$

$$f'(x) = \begin{cases} \dfrac{2}{1 + x^2}, & x > 0 \\ \text{does not exist}, & x = 0 \\ \dfrac{-2}{1 + x^2}, & x < 0 \end{cases}$$

$\Rightarrow \quad f'(1) = \dfrac{2}{1 + 1} = \dfrac{2}{2} = 1$

$\Rightarrow \quad f'(-1) = \dfrac{-2}{1 + 1} = \dfrac{-2}{2} = -1$

$\Rightarrow \quad f'(0) =$ does not exist

21. (a)

22. (b)

23. (d)

24. (1) We have,

$$f(x) = \tan^{-1}\frac{1}{x^2 + x + 1} + \tan^{-1}\frac{1}{x^2 + 3x + 3} + \tan^{-1}\frac{1}{x^2 + 5x + 7} + \cdots \infty$$

$$\Rightarrow \quad f(x) = \tan^{-1}\left[\frac{(x + 1) - x}{1 + (x + 1)(x)}\right] + \tan^{-1}\left[\frac{(x + 2) - (x + 1)}{1 + (x + 2)(x + 1)}\right] + \tan^{-1}\left[\frac{(x + 3) - (x + 2)}{1 + (x + 3)(x + 2)}\right] + \cdots$$

$$\Rightarrow \quad f(x) = \tan^{-1}(x + 1) - \tan^{-1}x + \tan^{-1}(x + 2) - \tan^{-1}(x + 1) + \tan^{-1}(x + 3) - \tan^{-1}(x + 2) + \cdots$$

$$\Rightarrow \quad f(x) = \frac{\pi}{2} - \tan^{-1}x \qquad \left[\because \tan^{-1}\infty = \frac{\pi}{2}\right]$$

$$\Rightarrow \quad f'(x) = \frac{-1}{1 + x^2} \Rightarrow f'(0) = -1 \Rightarrow |f'(0)| = |-1| = 1$$

25. (1) We have, $xe^{xy} = y + \sin^2 x$

When $x = 0$, then $y = 0$

Now, on differentiating w.r.t. x, we get

$$xe^{xy}\left(x\frac{dy}{dx} + y\right) + e^{xy} = \frac{dy}{dx} + 2\sin x\cos x$$

$$\Rightarrow \quad \frac{dy}{dx}(x^2e^{xy} - 1) = 2\sin x\cos x - e^{xy} - xye^{xy}$$

$$\Rightarrow \quad \frac{dy}{dx} = \frac{\sin 2x - e^{xy}(1 + xy)}{x^2e^{xy} - 1}$$

$$\therefore \quad \left(\frac{dy}{dx}\right)_{x=0} = \frac{0 - e^0}{0 - 1} = e^0 = 1 \qquad [\because x = 0 \text{ and } y = 0]$$

DPP-3 Logarithmic Series, Infinite Series and Differentiation of One With Respect to Other

1. (i) Let $y = x^x$

On taking log both sides, we get

$$\log y = x\log x$$

On differentiating w.r.t. x, we get

$$\frac{1}{y}\frac{dy}{dx} = \frac{x}{x} + \log x$$

$$\Rightarrow \quad \frac{dy}{dx} = y(1 + \log x) = x^x(1 + \log x)$$

(ii) Let $y = x^{x^x}$

On taking log both sides, we get

$$\log y = x^x \log x$$

Again, on taking log both sides, we get

$$\log(\log y) = \log x^x + \log(\log x)$$

$$\Rightarrow \quad \log(\log y) = x\log x + \log(\log x)$$

On differentiating w.r.t. x, we get

$$\frac{1}{y\log y}\frac{dy}{dx} = 1 + \log x + \frac{1}{x\log_x}$$

$$\frac{dy}{dx} = y\log y\left(1 + \log x + \frac{1}{x\log x}\right)$$

$$= x^{x^x}x^x\log x\,\frac{(x\log x + x(\log x)^2 + 1)}{x\log x}$$

$$= x^{x^x}x^{x-1}[x\log x + x(\log x)^2 + 1]$$

(iii) Let $y = (\sin x)^{\cos^{-1}x}$

On taking log both sides, we get

$$\log y = \cos^{-1}x\log\sin x$$

On differentiating w.r.t. x, we get

$$\frac{1}{y}\frac{dy}{dx} = \cos^{-1}x\left(\frac{1}{\sin x} \times \cos x\right) - \frac{1}{\sqrt{1 - x^2}}\log\sin x$$

$$\Rightarrow \quad \frac{dy}{dx} = y\left(\cot x\cos^{-1}x - \frac{\log\sin x}{\sqrt{1 - x^2}}\right)$$

$$\therefore \quad \frac{dy}{dx} = (\sin x)^{\cos^{-1}x}\left(\cot x\cos^{-1}x - \frac{\log\sin x}{\sqrt{1 - x^2}}\right)$$

(iv) Let $y = \dfrac{\sqrt{x}(x + 4)^{3/2}}{(4x - 3)^{4/3}}$

On taking log both sides, we get

$$\log y = \frac{1}{2}\log x + \frac{3}{2}\log(x + 4) - \frac{4}{3}\log(4x - 3)$$

On differentiating w.r.t. x, we get

$$\frac{1}{y}\frac{dy}{dx} = \frac{1}{2x} + \frac{3}{2(x + 4)} - \frac{4 \times 4}{3(4x - 3)}$$

$$\frac{1}{y}\frac{dy}{dx} = \frac{1}{2x} + \frac{3}{2(x + 4)} - \frac{16}{3(4x - 3)}$$

$$\frac{dy}{dx} = y\left[\frac{1}{2x} + \frac{3}{2(x + 4)} - \frac{16}{3(4x - 3)}\right]$$

$$\Rightarrow \quad \frac{dy}{dx} = \frac{\sqrt{x}(x + 4)^{3/2}}{(4x - 3)^{4/3}}\left[\frac{1}{2x} + \frac{3}{2x + 8} - \frac{16}{12x - 9}\right]$$

(v) Let $y = x^{\sin x - \cos x} + \dfrac{x^2 - 1}{x^2 + 1}$

$$\Rightarrow \quad y = e^{(\sin x - \cos x)\log x} + \frac{x^2 - 1}{x^2 + 1} \qquad [\because u^v = e^{v\log u}]$$

On differentiating w.r.t. x, we get

$$\frac{dy}{dx} = e^{(\sin x - \cos x)\log x}\left[\frac{\sin x - \cos x}{x} + (\cos x + \sin x)\log x\right] + \frac{(x^2+1)(2x) - (x^2-1)(2x)}{(x^2+1)^2}$$

$$\therefore \quad \frac{dy}{dx} = x^{\sin x - \cos x}\left[\frac{\sin x - \cos x}{x} + (\cos x + \sin x)\log x\right] + \frac{4x}{(x^2+1)^2}$$

2. (i) We have, $y = \sqrt{x + \sqrt{x + \sqrt{x + \cdots \infty}}}$

$$y = \sqrt{x + y} \quad \Rightarrow \quad y^2 = x + y$$

$$\Rightarrow \quad y^2 - y = x$$

On differentiating w.r.t. x, we get

$$(2y-1)\frac{dy}{dx} = 1$$

$$\therefore \quad \frac{dy}{dx} = \frac{1}{2y-1}$$

(ii) We have, $y = \sqrt{\sin x + \sqrt{\sin x + \sqrt{\sin x + \cdots \infty}}}$

$$y = \sqrt{\sin x + y}$$

$$\Rightarrow \quad y^2 = \sin x + y$$

$$\Rightarrow \quad y^2 - y = \sin x$$

On differentiating w.r.t. x, we get

$$(2y-1)\frac{dy}{dx} = \cos x$$

$$\frac{dy}{dx} = \frac{\cos x}{2y-1}$$

(iii) We have, $y = \sqrt{\cos x + \sqrt{\cos x + \cdots \infty}}$

$$\Rightarrow \quad y = \sqrt{\cos x + y} \quad \Rightarrow \quad y^2 = \cos x + y$$

$$\Rightarrow \quad y^2 - y = \cos x$$

On differentiating w.r.t. x, we get

$$(2y-1)\frac{dy}{dx} = -\sin x$$

$$\Rightarrow \quad \frac{dy}{dx} = \frac{\sin x}{1-2y}$$

(iv) We have, $y = \sqrt{\log_e x + \sqrt{\log_e x + \cdots \infty}}$

$$\Rightarrow \quad y = \sqrt{\log_e x + y} \quad \Rightarrow \quad y^2 = \log_e x + y$$

$$\Rightarrow \quad y^2 - y = \log_e x.$$

On differentiating w.r.t. x, we get

$$(2y-1)\frac{dy}{dx} = \frac{1}{x}$$

$$\Rightarrow \quad \frac{dy}{dx} = \frac{1}{x(2y-1)}$$

3. We have, $x = \dfrac{1-t^2}{1+t^2}$ and $y = \dfrac{2t}{1+t^2}$

$$\frac{dx}{dt} = \frac{(1+t^2)(-2t) - (1-t^2)2t}{(1+t^2)^2}$$

$$\Rightarrow \quad \frac{dx}{dt} = \frac{-2t(1+t^2+1-t^2)}{(1+t^2)^2} = \frac{-4t}{(1+t^2)^2}$$

and

$$\frac{dy}{dt} = \frac{(1+t^2)(2) - (2t)(2t)}{(1+t^2)^2}$$

$$\Rightarrow \quad \frac{dy}{dt} = \frac{2(1+t^2-2t^2)}{(1+t^2)^2} = \frac{2(1-t^2)}{(1+t^2)^2}$$

$$\therefore \quad \frac{dy}{dx} = \frac{dy}{dt} \times \frac{dt}{dx} = \frac{2(1-t^2)}{-4t} = -\frac{x}{y}$$

Hence proved.

4. We have,

$$x = \sec\theta - \cos\theta$$

and

$$y = \sec^n\theta - \cos^n\theta$$

$$\frac{dx}{d\theta} = \sec\theta\tan\theta + \sin\theta$$

$$= \tan\theta(\sec\theta + \cos\theta)$$

$$= \tan\theta\sqrt{(\sec\theta - \cos\theta)^2 + 4}$$

$$= \tan\theta\sqrt{(x^2+4)}$$

and

$$\frac{dy}{d\theta} = n\sec^{n-1}\theta\sec\theta\tan\theta + n\cos^{n-1}\theta\sin\theta$$

$$= n\sec^n\theta\tan\theta + n\cos^{n-1}\theta\sin\theta$$

$$= n\tan\theta(\sec^n\theta + \cos^n\theta)$$

$$= n\tan\theta\sqrt{(\sec^n\theta - \cos^n\theta)^2 + 4}$$

$$= n\tan\theta\sqrt{y^2+4}$$

$$\frac{dy}{dx} = \frac{n\tan\theta\sqrt{y^2+4}}{\tan\theta\sqrt{x^2+4}}$$

$$\therefore \quad \left(\frac{dy}{dx}\right)^2 = \frac{n^2(y^2+4)}{x^2+4}$$

$$\Rightarrow \quad (x^2+4)\left(\frac{dy}{dx}\right)^2 = n^2(y^2+4)$$

5. (i) Let $u = \tan^{-1}\left(\dfrac{1+2x}{1-2x}\right)$ and $v = \sqrt{1+4x^2}$

$$u = \tan^{-1}\left(\frac{1+\tan\theta}{1-\tan\theta}\right) \quad [\because \text{put } 2x = \tan\theta]$$

$$u = \tan^{-1}\tan\left(\frac{\pi}{4} + \theta\right)$$

$$u = \frac{\pi}{4} + \theta$$

$$u = \frac{\pi}{4} + \tan^{-1}2x$$

$$\Rightarrow \quad \frac{du}{dx} = \frac{2}{1+4x^2}$$

and

$$\frac{dv}{dx} = \frac{8x}{2\sqrt{1+4x^2}}$$

$$\therefore \quad \frac{du}{dv} = \frac{\dfrac{2}{1+4x^2}}{\dfrac{4x}{\sqrt{1+4x^2}}} = \frac{1}{2x\sqrt{1+4x^2}}$$

(ii) Let $u = \tan^{-1}\left(\dfrac{\sqrt{1+x^2}-1}{x}\right)$, $v = \tan^{-1}x$

$$u = \tan^{-1}\left(\frac{\sqrt{1+\tan^2\theta}-1}{\tan\theta}\right) \quad [\because \text{put } x = \tan\theta]$$

$$u = \tan^{-1}\left(\frac{\sec\theta - 1}{\tan\theta}\right)$$

$$u = \tan^{-1}\left(\frac{1-\cos\theta}{\sin\theta}\right) = \tan^{-1}\tan\frac{\theta}{2}$$

$$u = \theta/2 = \frac{1}{2}\tan^{-1}x$$

$$\Rightarrow \quad \frac{du}{dx} = \frac{1}{2(1+x^2)}$$

and

$$\frac{dv}{dx} = \frac{1}{1+x^2}$$

$$\therefore \quad \frac{du}{dv} = \frac{1}{2}$$

6. (i) We have,

$$x = a\left(\cos t + \frac{1}{2}\log_e \tan^2 t/2\right),\ y = a\sin t$$

$\Rightarrow$ $x = a(\cos t + \log_e \tan t/2)$

$$\frac{dx}{dt} = a\left(-\sin t + \frac{1}{\tan t/2}\times\sec^2 t/2\times\frac{1}{2}\right)$$

$$\frac{dx}{dt} = a\left(-\sin t + \frac{1}{2\sin t/2\cos t/2}\right)$$

$$\frac{dx}{dt} = a\left(-\sin t + \frac{1}{\sin t}\right) = \frac{a\cos^2 t}{\sin t}$$

and $\dfrac{dy}{dt} = a\cos t$

$\therefore$ $\dfrac{dy}{dx} = \dfrac{a\cos t}{a\dfrac{\cos^2 t}{\sin t}} = \tan t$

(ii) We have,

$$x = \sin t\sqrt{\cos 2t},\ y = \cos t\sqrt{\cos 2t}$$

$$\frac{dx}{dt} = \cos t\sqrt{\cos 2t} - \frac{\sin t\sin 2t}{\sqrt{\cos 2t}}$$

$$\frac{dx}{dt} = \frac{\cos t\cos 2t - \sin t\sin 2t}{\sqrt{\cos 2t}} = \frac{\cos 3t}{\sqrt{\cos 2t}}$$

and $\dfrac{dy}{dt} = -\sin t\sqrt{\cos 2t} - \dfrac{\cos t\sin 2t}{\sqrt{\cos 2t}}$

$$\frac{dy}{dt} = -\frac{\sin t\cos 2t - \cos t\sin 2t}{\sqrt{\cos 2t}} = -\frac{\sin 3t}{\sqrt{\cos 2t}}$$

$\therefore$ $\dfrac{dy}{dx} = \dfrac{-\sin 3t}{\sqrt{\cos 2t}} \div \dfrac{\cos 3t}{\sqrt{\cos 2t}} = \dfrac{-\sin 3t}{\cos 3t}$

$= -\tan 3t$

7. (c) We have, $x = \dfrac{1+t}{t^3},\ y = \dfrac{3}{2t^2} + \dfrac{2}{t}$

$$x = \frac{1}{t^3} + \frac{1}{t^2}$$

and $\dfrac{dx}{dt} = \dfrac{-3}{t^4} - \dfrac{2}{t^3}$

$$\frac{dy}{dx} = \frac{-\dfrac{1}{t^2}\left(\dfrac{3}{t}+2\right)}{\dfrac{-1}{t^3}\left(\dfrac{3}{t}+2\right)} = t$$

$\therefore$ $x\left(\dfrac{dy}{dx}\right)^3 - \dfrac{dy}{dx} = xt^3 - t = 1$

8. (c) We have, $y = x^{x^2}$

On taking log both sides, we get

$$\log y = x^2\log_e x$$

On differentiating w.r.t. x, we get

$$\frac{1}{y}\frac{dy}{dx} = \frac{x^2}{x} + 2x\log_e x$$

$$\frac{dy}{dx} = y(x + 2x\log_e x)$$

$\Rightarrow$ $\dfrac{dy}{dx} = x^{x^2}\cdot x(1 + 2\log_e x)$

$\Rightarrow$ $\dfrac{dy}{dx} = x^{x^2+1}(2\log_e x + 1)$

9. (d) We have,

$$x = 3\cos\theta - 2\cos^3\theta$$

$$y = 3\sin\theta - 2\sin^3\theta$$

$$\frac{dx}{d\theta} = -3\sin\theta + 6\cos^2\theta\sin\theta$$

$$\frac{dx}{d\theta} = 3\sin\theta(-1 + 2\cos^2\theta)$$

and $\dfrac{dy}{d\theta} = 3\cos\theta - 6\sin^2\theta\cos\theta$

$$\frac{dy}{d\theta} = 3\cos\theta(1 - 2\sin^2\theta)$$

$\therefore$ $\dfrac{dy}{dx} = \dfrac{3\cos\theta(1-2\sin^2\theta)}{3\sin\theta(-1+2\cos^2\theta)}$

$[\because 1 - 2\sin^2\theta = 2\cos^2\theta - 1 = \cos 2\theta]$

$= \cot\theta$

10. (c) We have, $x = e^{y + e^{y+\cdots\infty}}$

$$x = e^{y+x}$$

On taking log both sides, we get

$$\log x = (x + y)\log_e e$$

$\Rightarrow$ $\log x = x + y$

On differentiating w.r.t. x, we get

$$\frac{1}{x} = 1 + \frac{dy}{dx}$$

$\Rightarrow$ $\dfrac{dy}{dx} = \dfrac{1-x}{x}$

11. (d) We have,

$$x^m\cdot y^n = (x+y)^{m+n}$$

On taking log both sides, we get

$$\log x^m y^n = \log(x+y)^{m+n}$$

$\Rightarrow$ $m\log x + n\log y = (m+n)\log(x+y)$

On differentiating w.r.t. x, we get

$$\frac{m}{x} + \frac{n}{y}\frac{dy}{dx} = \frac{(m+n)}{x+y}\left(1 + \frac{dy}{dx}\right)$$

$\Rightarrow$ $\dfrac{dy}{dx}\left(\dfrac{n}{y} - \dfrac{m+n}{x+y}\right) = \left(\dfrac{m+n}{x+y} - \dfrac{m}{x}\right)$

$\Rightarrow$ $\dfrac{dy}{dx}\left(\dfrac{xn + ny - my - ny}{y(x+y)}\right) = \left(\dfrac{mx + nx - mx - my}{x(x+y)}\right)$

$\therefore$ $\dfrac{dy}{dx} = \dfrac{y}{x}$

12. (c) We have, $x^{2x} - 2x^x\cot y - 1 = 0$

On putting $x = 1$, we get

$$y = \pi/2$$

$$x^{2x} - 2x^x\cot y + \cot^2 y = 1 + \cot^2 y$$

$\Rightarrow$ $(x^x - \cot y)^2 = \operatorname{cosec}^2 y$

$\Rightarrow$ $x^x = \cot y \pm \operatorname{cosec} y$

On differentiating w.r.t. x, we get

$$x^x(1 + \log x) = -(\operatorname{cosec}^2 y \pm \operatorname{cosec} y\cot y)\frac{dy}{dx}$$

$$x^x(1 + \log x) = -\operatorname{cosec} y x^x\frac{dy}{dx}$$

$\Rightarrow$ $\dfrac{dy}{dx} = \dfrac{1 + \log x}{-\operatorname{cosec} y}$

$\therefore$ $\left(\dfrac{dy}{dx}\right)_{x=1,\ y=\pi/2} = \dfrac{1+0}{-1} = -1$

13. (b) We have,

$$f(x) = \prod_{n=1}^{100}(x-n)^{n(101-n)}$$

$\Rightarrow$ $f(x) = (x-1)^{100}\times(x-2)^{2\times 99}\times(x-3)^{3\times 98}\times\cdots(x-100)^{100}$

On taking log both sides, we get

$$\log f(x) = 100\log(x-1) + 2\times 99\log(x-2) + 3\times 98\log(x-3) + \cdots + 100\log(x-100)$$

On differentiating w.r.t. x, we get

$$\frac{1}{f(x)}f'(x) = \frac{100}{x-1} + \frac{2\times 99}{x-2} + \frac{3\times 98}{x-3} + \cdots + \frac{100}{x-100}$$

$$\frac{f'(101)}{f(101)} = \frac{100}{100} + \frac{2\times 99}{99} + \frac{3\times 98}{98} + \cdots + \frac{100}{1}$$

$$\frac{f'(101)}{f(101)} = 1+2+3+4+\cdots+100$$

$$\frac{f'(101)}{f(101)} = 5050 \Rightarrow \frac{f(101)}{f'(101)} = \frac{1}{5050}$$

14. (c) Let $u = \sin^{-1}\frac{x}{\sqrt{1+x^2}}$ and $v = \cos^{-1}\left(\frac{1-x^2}{1+x^2}\right)$

$$u = \tan^{-1}x, x>0 \qquad \left[\because \sin^{-1}\frac{x}{\sqrt{1+x^2}} = \tan^{-1}x\right]$$

and $v = 2\tan^{-1}x, x>0 \qquad \left[\because \cos^{-1}\left(\frac{1-x^2}{1+x^2}\right) = 2\tan^{-1}x\right]$

$\therefore \quad \frac{du}{dx} = \frac{1}{1+x^2}$

and $\quad \frac{dv}{dx} = \frac{1}{2(1+x^2)}$

$\Rightarrow \quad \frac{du}{dv} = \frac{1}{2}$

15. (a,b) Let $u = \sin^{-1}\frac{t}{\sqrt{1+t^2}}$

and $v = \cos^{-1}\frac{1}{\sqrt{1+t^2}}$

$$\Rightarrow \quad u = \begin{cases} \tan^{-1}t, & t\ge 0 \\ -\tan^{-1}t, & t<0 \end{cases}$$

$$\text{and} \quad v = \begin{cases} \tan^{-1}t, & t\ge 0 \\ \tan^{-1}t, & t<0 \end{cases}$$

$$\Rightarrow \quad \frac{du}{dt} = \begin{cases} \frac{1}{1+t^2}, & t\ge 0 \\ -\frac{1}{1+t^2}, & t<0 \end{cases}$$

$$\text{and} \quad \frac{dv}{dt} = \begin{cases} \frac{1}{1+t^2}, & t\ge 0 \\ \frac{1}{1+t^2}, & t<0 \end{cases}$$

$$\therefore \quad \frac{du}{dv} = \begin{cases} 1, & t\ge 0 \\ -1, & t<0 \end{cases}$$

16. (a,d) We have, $x = \cos t$, $y = \log_e t$

$$\frac{dx}{dt} = -\sin t, \frac{dy}{dt} = \frac{1}{t}$$

$$\frac{dy}{dx} = \frac{-1}{t\sin t}$$

$$\therefore \quad \left(\frac{dy}{dx}\right)_{t=\pi/2} = \frac{-2}{\pi}$$

$$\text{and} \quad \left(\frac{dy}{dx}\right)_{t=\pi/6} = \frac{-12}{\pi}$$

17. (a,b,c,d) We have, $2^x + 2^y = 2^{x+y}$

On differentiating w.r.t. x, we get

$$2^x\log 2 + 2^y\log 2\frac{dy}{dx} = 2^{x+y}\left(1+\frac{dy}{dx}\right)\log 2$$

$$\Rightarrow \quad 2^x + 2^y\frac{dy}{dx} = 2^{x+y}\left(1+\frac{dy}{dx}\right)$$

$$\Rightarrow \quad \frac{dy}{dx}(2^y - 2^{x+y}) = 2^{x+y} - 2^x$$

$$\Rightarrow \quad \frac{dy}{dx} = \frac{2^{x+y}-2^x}{2^y-2^{x+y}}$$

$$\Rightarrow \quad \frac{dy}{dx} = \frac{2^x(2^y-1)}{2^y(1-2^x)} = \frac{2^x(1-2^y)}{2^y(2^x-1)}$$

$$\text{or} \quad \frac{dy}{dx} = \frac{2^x+2^y-2^x}{2^y-2^x-2^y} \qquad [\because 2^{x+y} = 2^x+2^y]$$

$$\frac{dy}{dx} = \frac{-2^y}{2^x} \quad \Rightarrow \quad \frac{dy}{dx} = \frac{2^{x+y}-2^x}{2^y(1-2^x)}$$

$$\frac{dy}{dx} = \frac{2^y}{2^y(1-2^x)} = \frac{1}{1-2^x} \quad [\because 2^y = 2^{x+y}-2^x]$$

$$\Rightarrow \quad \frac{dy}{dx} = \frac{2^x(2^y-1)}{2^y-2^{x+y}}$$

$$\Rightarrow \quad \frac{dy}{dx} = \frac{2^x(2^y-1)}{-2^x} \qquad [\because 2^x = 2^{x+y}-2^y]$$

$$\therefore \quad \frac{dy}{dx} = 1-2^y$$

18. (a,b,d) We have, $x^p\cdot x^q = (x+y)^{p+q}$

On taking log both sides, we get

$$p\log x + q\log y = (p+q)\log(x+y)$$

On differentiating w.r.t. x, we get

$$\frac{p}{x} + \frac{q}{y}\frac{dy}{dx} = \frac{p+q}{x+y}\left(1+\frac{dy}{dx}\right)$$

$$\Rightarrow \quad \frac{dy}{dx}\left(\frac{q}{y} - \frac{p+q}{x+y}\right) = \frac{p+q}{x+y} - \frac{p}{x}$$

$$\therefore \quad \frac{dy}{dx} = \frac{y}{x}$$

19. (a,c) We have, $u = e^x\cdot\sin x$, $v = e^x\cdot\cos x$

$$\frac{du}{dx} = e^x\sin x + e^x\cos x$$

$$\text{and} \quad \frac{dv}{dx} = e^x\cos x - e^x\sin x$$

$$\frac{du}{dx} + \frac{dv}{dx} = 2e^x\cos x$$

$$\Rightarrow \quad \frac{du}{dx} + \frac{dv}{dx} = 2v$$

$$\Rightarrow \quad \frac{du}{dx} = u+v \text{ and } \frac{dv}{dx} = v-u$$

$$\therefore \quad v\frac{du}{dx} = uv+v^2 \text{ and } u\frac{dv}{dx} = uv-u^2$$

$$\Rightarrow \quad v\frac{du}{dx} - u\frac{dv}{dx} = v^2+u^2$$

20. (a) (i) We have,

$$y = \cos^{-1}(\cos x)$$

$$y = \begin{cases} x, & 0\le x\le\pi \\ 2\pi - x, & \pi\le x\le 2\pi \end{cases}$$

$$\frac{dy}{dx} = \begin{cases} 1, & 0\le x\le\pi \\ -1, & \pi\le x\le 2\pi \end{cases}$$

$$\because \quad 5\in[\pi, 2\pi]$$

$$\therefore \quad \left(\frac{dy}{dx}\right)_{x=5} = -1$$

(ii) We have, $f(x) = \log_e\tan\left(\frac{\pi}{4}+\frac{x}{2}\right)$

$$f'(x) = \frac{1}{\tan\left(\frac{\pi}{4}+\frac{x}{2}\right)}\times\sec^2\left(\frac{\pi}{4}+\frac{x}{2}\right)\times\frac{1}{2}$$

$$f'(x) = \frac{1}{2\sin\left(\frac{\pi}{4}+\frac{x}{2}\right)\cos\left(\frac{\pi}{4}+\frac{x}{2}\right)}$$

$$f'(x) = \frac{1}{\sin\left(\frac{\pi}{2}+x\right)} = \frac{1}{\cos x} = \sec x$$

$\therefore \quad p = 0$

(iii) Let $\quad y = \tan^{-1}\left(\frac{1+x}{1-x}\right)$

$$y = \tan^{-1} 1 + \tan^{-1} x$$

$$\therefore \quad \frac{dy}{dx} = \frac{1}{1+x^2}$$

$$\Rightarrow \quad \left(\frac{dy}{dx}\right)_{x=-1} = \frac{1}{2}$$

(iv) Let $\quad y = \frac{\log|x|}{x}$

$$\frac{dy}{dx} = \frac{-\log|x|}{x^2} + \frac{1}{x^2}$$

$$\left(\frac{dy}{dx}\right)_{x=-1} = \frac{-\log 1}{1} + \frac{1}{1} = 1$$

Hence, (i) $\rightarrow$ (p), (ii) $\rightarrow$ (q), (iii) $\rightarrow$ (r), (iv) $\rightarrow$ (s)

21. (1) We have,

$$f(x) = x + \cfrac{1}{2x + \cfrac{1}{2x + \cfrac{1}{2x + \cfrac{1}{2x + \cdots \infty}}}}$$

$$\Rightarrow \quad f(x) = x + \frac{1}{x + f(x)}$$

$$\Rightarrow \quad f(x) - x = \frac{1}{x + f(x)}$$

$\Rightarrow \quad [f(x)]^2 - x^2 = 1$

On differentiating w.r.t. x, we get

$$2f(x)\cdot f'(x) - 2x = 0$$

$$f(x)\, f'(x) = x \Rightarrow \frac{f(x)\cdot f'(x)}{x} = 1$$

$$\therefore \quad \frac{f(100)\cdot f'(100)}{100} = 1$$

22. (1) We have, $y = \tan^{-1}\frac{u}{\sqrt{1-u^2}}$, $x = \sec^{-1}\frac{1}{2u^2-1}$

$$y = \sin^{-1} u$$

and $\quad x = 2\cos^{-1} u$

$$\Rightarrow \quad \frac{dy}{du} = \frac{1}{\sqrt{1-u^2}}$$

and $\quad \frac{dx}{du} = \frac{-2}{\sqrt{1-u^2}}$

$$\Rightarrow \quad \frac{dy}{dx} = -\frac{1}{2}$$

$$\therefore \quad \left|2\frac{dy}{dx}\right| = \left|2 \times \frac{-1}{2}\right| = 1$$

23. (1) We have,

$$y = \tan^{-1}\frac{x}{1+\sqrt{1-x^2}} + \sin\left(2\tan^{-1}\sqrt{\frac{1-x}{1+x}}\right) \quad \ldots\text{(i)}$$

On puting $x = \cos\theta$ in Eq. (i), we get

$$y = \tan^{-1}\frac{\cos\theta}{1+\sin\theta} + \sin\left[2\tan^{-1}\sqrt{\frac{1-\cos\theta}{1+\cos\theta}}\right]$$

$$y = \tan^{-1}\left(\frac{\cos\theta/2 - \sin\theta/2}{\cos\theta/2 + \sin\theta/2}\right) + \sin\left(2\tan^{-1}\tan\frac{\theta}{2}\right)$$

$$y = \tan^{-1}\tan\left(\frac{\pi}{4} - \frac{\theta}{2}\right) + \sin\theta$$

$$y = \frac{\pi}{4} - \frac{\theta}{2} + \sin\theta$$

$$y = \frac{\pi}{4} - \frac{1}{2}\cos^{-1} x + \sin(\cos^{-1} x)$$

$$\Rightarrow \quad \frac{dy}{dx} = \frac{1}{2\sqrt{1-x^2}} - \frac{\cos(\cos^{-1} x)}{\sqrt{1-x^2}}$$

$$\therefore \quad \left(\frac{dy}{dx}\right)_{x=0} = \frac{1}{2} - 1 = -\frac{1}{2}$$

$$\Rightarrow \quad \left|2\frac{dy}{dx}\right| = \left|2 \times \frac{-1}{2}\right| = 1$$

24. (0) We have,

$$y = \cos^{-1}\left(\frac{1-x^2}{1+x^2}\right)$$

$$y = \begin{cases} 2\tan^{-1} x, & x \ge 0 \\ -2\tan^{-1} x, & x < 0 \end{cases}$$

$$\frac{dy}{dx} = \begin{cases} \frac{2}{1+x^2}, & x \ge 0 \\ \frac{-2}{1+x^2}, & x < 0 \end{cases}$$

$$\therefore \quad \frac{d(\tan^{-1} x)}{dx} = \frac{1}{1+x^2},\ x \in (-\infty, \infty)$$

$$\Rightarrow \quad \left[\frac{dy}{d(\tan^{-1} x)}\right]_{x=0} = \text{does not exist}$$

$$\left[\because \left(\frac{dy}{dx}\right)_{x=0} = \text{does not exist}\right]$$

25. (0) $\quad f\left(\frac{1}{x}\right) = \log\left(\frac{x+\sqrt{x^2+1}}{x}\right)$

$$f\left(\frac{1}{x}\right) = \log\left(x + \sqrt{1+x^2}\right) - \log x$$

On differentiating w.r.t. x, we get

$$f'\left(\frac{1}{x}\right) = \left(\frac{1}{x+\sqrt{1+x^2}}\right)\left(1 + \frac{2x}{2\sqrt{1+x^2}}\right) - \frac{1}{x}$$

$$= \frac{1}{\sqrt{1+x^2}} - \frac{1}{x}$$

Now, $\quad \left[f'\left(\frac{1}{x}\right)\right]_{x=1} = \frac{1}{\sqrt{2}} - 1 = \frac{(1-\sqrt{2})}{\sqrt{2}} \quad \ldots\text{(i)}$

Also, $\quad g(x) = \log\left(x + \sqrt{1+x^2}\right)$

$$\therefore \quad g'(x) = \frac{1}{\sqrt{1+x^2}}$$

$$\Rightarrow \quad [g'(x)]_{x=1} = \frac{1}{\sqrt{2}} \quad \ldots\text{(ii)}$$

Thus, $\quad \left[x\cdot e^{g(x)}\cdot\left\{f\left(\frac{1}{x}\right)\right\}' + g'(x)\right]_{\text{at } x=1}$

$$= \left[1\cdot(1+\sqrt{2})\cdot\frac{(1-\sqrt{2})}{\sqrt{2}} + \frac{1}{\sqrt{2}}\right]$$

$$= \frac{-(2-1)}{\sqrt{2}} + \frac{1}{\sqrt{2}}$$

$$= \frac{-1}{\sqrt{2}} + \frac{1}{\sqrt{2}} = 0$$

DPP-4 Higher Order Derivatives and Differentiation of Inverse Functions

1. We have, $y = A\sin mx + B\cos mx$

$$\frac{dy}{dx} = A\cos mx \cdot m + B(-\sin mx)\cdot m$$
$$= m(A\cos mx - B\sin mx)$$
$$\frac{d^2y}{dx^2} = m\{-A\sin mx \cdot m - B\cos mx \cdot m\}$$
$$= -m^2\{A\sin mx + B\cos mx)$$
$$\frac{d^2y}{dx^2} = -m^2y$$
$$\therefore \quad \frac{d^2y}{dx^2} + m^2y = 0$$

2. We have, $y = A\cos(\log x) + B\sin(\log x)$

Then, $y_1 = -A\sin(\log x)\cdot\frac{1}{x} + B\cos(\log x)\cdot\frac{1}{x}$

or $xy_1 = -A\sin(\log x) + B\cos(\log x)$

Again on differentiating w.r.t. x, we get

$$xy_2 + y_1 = -A\cos(\log x)\cdot\frac{1}{x} - B\sin(\log x)\cdot\frac{1}{x}$$
$$\Rightarrow \quad x^2y_2 + xy_1 = -[A\cos(\log x) + B\sin(\log x)]$$
$$\Rightarrow \quad x^2y_2 + xy_1 = -y$$
$$\therefore \quad x^2y_2 + xy_1 + y = 0$$

3. We have, $\log_e y = \tan^{-1} x$

$$\Rightarrow \quad y = e^{\tan^{-1} x}$$

On differentiating w.r.t. x, we get

$$y_1 = e^{\tan^{-1} x}\cdot\frac{1}{1+x^2}$$

or $(1+x^2)\, y_1 = y$

Again on differentiating w.r.t. x, we get

$$(1+x^2)\, y_2 + y_1 2x = y_1$$
$$\Rightarrow (1+x^2)y_2 + (2x-1)y_1 = 0$$

4. We have, $y = \tan x$

On differentiating w.r.t. x, we get

$$y_1 = \sec^2 x = 1 + \tan^2 x = 1 + y^2$$

Again on differentiating w.r.t. x, we get

$$y_2 = 2y\,y_1$$

5. We have, $y = \tan x + \sec x$

On differentiating w.r.t. x, we get

$$y_1 = \sec^2 x + \sec x \tan x$$

or $y_1 = \sec x\,(\sec x + \tan x)$

$$= \frac{1+\sin x}{\cos^2 x} = \frac{1+\sin x}{1-\sin^2 x}$$
$$\therefore \quad y_1 = \frac{1}{1-\sin x}$$

Again on differentiating w.r.t. x, we get

$$y_2 = -\frac{1}{(1-\sin x)^2}\times(-\cos x)$$
$$\therefore \quad y_2 = \frac{\cos x}{(1-\sin x)^2}$$

6. We have, $y = \tan^{-1} x$

$$y_1 = \frac{1}{1+x^2}$$
$$\Rightarrow \quad (1+x^2)y_1 = 1$$

On differentiating w.r.t. x, we get

$$(1+x^2)y_2 + y_1 2x = 0$$
$$\therefore \quad (1+x^2)y_2 + 2xy_1 = 0$$

7. We have, $x = a(1-\cos\theta)$ and $y = a(\theta + \sin\theta)$

$$\Rightarrow \quad \frac{dx}{d\theta} = a\sin\theta \quad\text{and}\quad \frac{dy}{d\theta} = a(1+\cos\theta)$$
$$\Rightarrow \quad \frac{dy}{dx} = \frac{\frac{dy}{d\theta}}{\frac{dx}{d\theta}} = \frac{a(1+\cos\theta)}{a\sin\theta} = \frac{1+2\cos^2\frac{\theta}{2}-1}{2\sin\frac{\theta}{2}\cos\frac{\theta}{2}}$$
$$\therefore \quad \frac{dy}{dx} = \cot\frac{\theta}{2}$$

Now, on differentiating w.r.t. x, we get

$$\frac{d}{dx}\left(\frac{dy}{dx}\right) = \frac{d^2y}{dx^2} = -\text{cosec}^2\frac{\theta}{2}\cdot\frac{1}{2}\cdot\frac{d\theta}{dx}$$
$$\therefore \quad \frac{d^2y}{dx^2} = -\frac{1}{2}\cdot\text{cosec}^2\frac{\theta}{2}\cdot\frac{1}{a\sin\theta}$$

8. We have, $x = a\cos^3\theta$ and $y = \sin^3\theta$

Now, $\frac{dx}{d\theta} = 3a\cos^2\theta\,(-\sin\theta)$

and $\frac{dy}{d\theta} = 3a\sin^2\theta\cdot\cos\theta$

$$\therefore \quad \frac{dy}{dx} = \frac{3a\sin^2\theta\cdot\cos\theta}{-3a\cos^2\theta\cdot\sin\theta} = -\tan\theta$$
$$\frac{d^2y}{dx^2} = -\sec^2\theta\cdot\frac{d\theta}{dx}$$
$$= -\sec^2\theta\cdot\frac{1}{-3a\cos^2\theta\cdot\sin\theta}$$
$$\therefore \quad \frac{d^2y}{dx^2} = \frac{1}{3a}\sec^4\theta\cdot\text{cosec}\theta$$

9. We have, $y = \frac{ax+b}{x^2+c}$

or $y\,(x^2+c) = ax + b$

Now, on differentiating w.r.t. x, we get

$$y\cdot 2x + (x^2+c)y_1 = a$$

Again on differentiating w.r.t. x, we get

$$y\cdot 2 + 2x\,y_1 + (x^2+c)y_2 + y_1\cdot 2x = 0$$

or $\frac{4xy_1 + 2y}{y_2} = -x^2 - c$

Now, on differentiating w.r.t. x, we get

$$\frac{y_2[4xy_2 + y_1 4 + 2y_1] - (4xy_1 + 2y)y_3}{(y_2)^2} = -2x$$
$$\Rightarrow \quad y_2(4xy_2 + 6y_1) - 2(2xy_1 + y)y_3 = -2x(y_2)^2$$
$$\Rightarrow \quad y_2(4xy_2 + 2xy_2 + 6y_1) = 2(2xy_1 + y)y_3$$
$$\Rightarrow \quad 6(xy_2 + y_1)y_2 = 2\,(2xy_1 + y)y_3$$
$$\therefore \quad (2xy_1 + y)y_3 = 3(xy_2 + y_1)y_2$$

10. We have, $(a+bx)e^{\frac{y}{x}} = x$

or $e^{\frac{y}{x}} = \frac{x}{a+bx}$

On taking log both sides, we get

$$\frac{y}{x} = \log\frac{x}{a+bx}$$

or $y = x\cdot[\log x - \log(a+bx)]$

Now, on differentiating w.r.t. x, we get

$$y_1 = x\left[\frac{1}{x} - \frac{1}{a+bx}\cdot b\right] + \log x - \log(a+bx)$$

or $$y_1 = 1 - \frac{bx}{a+bx} + \log x - \log(a+bx)$$

$$y_1 = \frac{a}{a+bx} + \log\frac{x}{a+bx}$$

or $$xy_1 = \frac{ax}{a+bx} + y$$

or $$\frac{ax}{a+bx} = xy_1 - y \quad \ldots\text{(i)}$$

Now, on differentiating again w.r.t. x, we get

$$\frac{(a+bx)\,a - ax\cdot b}{(a+bx)^2} = xy_2 + y_1 - y_1$$

$\therefore$ $$\frac{a^2}{(a+bx)^2} = xy_2$$

On multiplying both sides by x^2 and then using Eq. (i), we get

or $$x^3\cdot y_2 = \left(\frac{ax}{a+bx}\right)^2 = (xy_1 - y)^2$$

11. We have,

$$y = [\log(x + \sqrt{1+x^2})]^2$$

On differentiating w.r.t. x, we get

$$y_1 = \frac{2\log(x+\sqrt{1+x^2})}{x+\sqrt{1+x^2}}\left[1 + \frac{1}{2\sqrt{1+x^2}}\cdot 2x\right]$$

$$y_1 = \frac{2\log(x+\sqrt{1+x^2})}{x+\sqrt{1+x^2}} \times \frac{x+\sqrt{1+x^2}}{\sqrt{1+x^2}}$$

Now, on cross-multiplying and then squaring on both sides, we get

$$(1+x^2)y_1^2 = 4\,[\log(x+\sqrt{1+x^2})]^2$$

$$(1+x^2)y_1^2 = 4y$$

Again on differentiating w.r.t. x, we get

$$(1+x^2)2y_1y_2 + y_1^2\cdot 2x = 4y_1$$

$\therefore$ $$(1+x^2)y_2 + xy_1 = 2$$

12. We have, $$y = \frac{\sin^{-1}x}{\sqrt{1-x^2}}$$

or $$\sqrt{1-x^2}\cdot y = \sin^{-1}x$$

On differentiating w.r.t. x, we get

$$\sqrt{1-x^2}\;y_1 + y\cdot\frac{1}{2\sqrt{1-x^2}}\cdot(-2x) = \frac{1}{\sqrt{1-x^2}}$$

$\Rightarrow$ $$(1-x^2)y_1 - xy = 1$$

$\Rightarrow$ $$(1-x^2)y_2 + y_1(-2x) - xy_1 - y = 0$$

$\therefore$ $$(1-x^2)y_2 - 3xy_1 - y = 0$$

13. We have, $y = (x + \sqrt{1+x^2})^m$

Then, $$y_1 = m(x+\sqrt{1+x^2})^{m-1}\cdot\left(1 + \frac{1}{2\sqrt{1+x^2}}2x\right)$$

$\Rightarrow$ $$y_1 = \frac{m(x+\sqrt{1+x^2})^m}{\sqrt{1+x^2}} \Rightarrow (1+x^2)\,y_1^2 = m^2y^2$$

Again on differentiating w.r.t. x, we get

$$(1+x^2)2y_1y_2 + y_1^2 2x = 2m^2yy_1$$

$\therefore$ $$(1+x^2)y_2 + xy_1 - m^2y = 0$$

14. We have, $y = e^{ax}\cdot\sin bx$

$$y_1 = e^{ax}\cdot\cos bx\cdot b + \sin bx\cdot e^{ax}\cdot a$$

$\therefore$ $$y_1 = b\cdot e^{ax}\cdot\cos bx + ay$$

or $$y_2 = b\cdot e^{ax}(-\sin bx)\cdot b + \cos bx\cdot b\cdot e^{ax}\cdot a + ay_1$$

$\because$ $$y_2 = -b^2y + a(y_1 - ay) + ay_1$$

$$= -b^2y + ay_1 - a^2y + ay_1$$

$\therefore$ $$y_2 = 2ay_1 - (a^2+b^2)y \text{ or } y_2 - 2ay_1 + (a^2+b^2)y = 0$$

15. We have, $y = e^x\cdot\tan^{-1}x$, $\quad y_1 = e^x\cdot\dfrac{1}{1+x^2} + \tan^{-1}x\cdot e^x$

$$(1+x^2)y_1 = e^x + y(1+x^2)$$

$$(1+x^2)y_2 + y_1 2x = e^x + y\cdot 2x + (1+x^2)y_1$$

$\Rightarrow$ $$(1+x^2)y_2 + y_1(2x - 1 - x^2) = 2xy + e^x$$

$\Rightarrow$ $$(1+x^2)y_2 + y_1(2x-1-x^2) = 2xy + (1+x^2)y_1 - y(1+x^2)$$

$\Rightarrow$ $$(1+x^2)y_2 + y_1(2x - 2 - 2x^2) + y(1-x)^2 = 0$$

$\therefore$ $$(1+x^2)y_2 - 2(1 - x + x^2)y_1 + (1-x)^2y = 0$$

16. We have, $y = \log\left(\dfrac{x^2}{e^x}\right) \Rightarrow y = 2\log x - x$

$\Rightarrow$ $$y_1 = \frac{2}{x} - 1$$

$\therefore$ $$y_2 = -\frac{2}{x^2}$$

17. We have, $y = (\tan^{-1}x)^2$

$\therefore$ $$y_1 = 2\tan^{-1}x\cdot\frac{1}{1+x^2}$$

or $$(1+x^2)y_1 = 2\sqrt{y}$$

or $$(1+x^2)^2(y_1)^2 = 4y$$

Now, on differentiating w.r.t. x, we get

$$(1+x^2)^2\,2y_1y_2 + (y_1)^2\,2\,(1+x^2)\cdot 2x = 4y_1$$

$$(1+x^2)^2\,y_2 + (1+x^2)2y_1\cdot x = 2$$

$\therefore$ $$(1+x^2)^2y_2 + 2x(1+x^2)y_1 = 2$$

18. (c) We have, $g(x) = f^{-1}(x)$

$\therefore$ $$gof(x) = x$$

$\Rightarrow$ $$g'of(x)\cdot f'(x) = 1$$

or $$g'of(x) = \frac{1}{f'(x)}$$

and we have $$f(x) = \log_e\log_e x$$

$$f'(x) = \frac{1}{\log_e x}\cdot\frac{1}{x}$$

$\therefore$ $$g'of(x) = x\log_e x$$

Now, put $f(x) = t$ i.e. $\log_e\log_e x = x$

which gives $x = e^{e^t}$

$\Rightarrow$ $$g'(t) = e^{e^t}\cdot e^t = e^{t+e^t}$$

$\therefore$ $$g'(x) = e^{x+e^x}$$

19. (b) We have, $g(x) = f^{-1}(x)$

$\therefore$ $$fog(x) = x$$

On differentiating w.r.t. x, we get

$$f'og(x)\cdot g'(x) = 1$$

Now, on putting $x = 2$, we get

$$f'og(2)\cdot g'(2) = 1 \qquad [\because g(2) = a]$$

$$f'(a)\cdot g'(2) = 1$$

$\therefore$ $$g'(2) = \frac{1}{f(a)} = \frac{1+a^2}{a^{10}}$$

20. (c) We have, $u = ax + b$

$$\frac{d}{dx} f(ax+b) = f'(ax+b)\cdot a = f'(u)\cdot a$$

$$\frac{d^2}{dx^2} f'(ax+b) = f''(u)\cdot a\cdot a = a^2 f''(u)$$

Similarly, $\frac{d^n}{dx^n}[f(ax+b)] = a^n \cdot \frac{d^n}{dx^n}[f(u)]$

21. (b) We have, $y = x + e^x$

$$\frac{dy}{dx} = 1 + e^x$$

$$\because \quad \frac{dx}{dy} = \frac{1}{1+e^x}$$

Now, on differentiating w.r.t. y, we get

$$\frac{d^2x}{dy^2} = -\frac{1}{(1+e^x)^2} \times e^x \cdot \frac{dx}{dy}$$

$$\therefore \quad \frac{d^2x}{dy^2} = -\frac{e^x}{(1+e^x)^3}$$

22. (a) We have, $y^2 = P(x)$

$$\therefore \quad 2y\frac{dy}{dx} = P'(x)$$

or

$$2\cdot\frac{dy}{dx} = \frac{P'(x)}{y}$$

Now, on differentiating w.r.t. x, we get

$$2\frac{d^2y}{dx^2} = \frac{y\cdot P''(x) - P'(x)\cdot\frac{dy}{dx}}{y^2}$$

$$\Rightarrow \quad 2y^2\frac{d^2y}{dx} = y\cdot P''(x) - P'(x)\cdot\frac{P'(x)}{2y}$$

$$\Rightarrow \quad 2y^3\frac{d^2y}{dx^2} = y^2\cdot P''(x) - \frac{[P'(x)]^2}{2}$$

$$\therefore \quad 2y^3\frac{d^2y}{dx^2} = P(x)\cdot P''(x) - \frac{[P'(x)]^2}{2}$$

Now, on differentiating w.r.t. x, we get

$$\frac{d}{dx}\left(2y^3\frac{d^2y}{dx^2}\right) = P(x)\cdot P'''(x) + P''(x)\,P'(x) - \frac{2P'(x)\,P''(x)}{2}$$

$$\therefore \quad 2\frac{d}{dx}\left(y^3\frac{d^2y}{dx^2}\right) = P(x)\cdot P'''(x)$$

23. (b) We have, $x^2 + y^2 = 1$

$$\Rightarrow \quad 2x + 2yy' = 0$$

$$\Rightarrow \quad x + yy' = 0$$

Now, on again differentiating w.r.t. x, we get

$$1 + yy'' + y'\cdot y' = 0$$

$$\therefore \quad yy'' + (y')^2 + 1 = 0$$

24. (b) We have,

$$F(x) = \left[f\left(\frac{x}{2}\right)\right]^2 + \left[g\left(\frac{x}{2}\right)\right]^2$$

$$F'(x) = 2f\left(\frac{x}{2}\right)\cdot f'\left(\frac{x}{2}\right)\cdot\frac{1}{2} + 2g\left(\frac{x}{2}\right)\cdot g'\left(\frac{x}{2}\right)\cdot\frac{1}{2}$$

$$= f\left(\frac{x}{2}\right)g\left(\frac{x}{2}\right) + g\left(\frac{x}{2}\right)\left[-f\left(\frac{x}{2}\right)\right] = 0$$

$[\because f''(x) = -f(x)$ and $g(x) = f'(x)]$

$\because \quad F'(x) = 0$

This shows, $F(x)$ is a constant function.

$\because \quad F(x) = C$

We have, $F(5) = 5$

$\therefore \quad F(10) = 10$

25. (d) Since, $\frac{dx}{dy} = \frac{1}{\frac{dy}{dx}} = \left(\frac{dy}{dx}\right)^{-1}$

$$\frac{d}{dy}\left(\frac{dx}{dy}\right) = \frac{d}{dx}\left(\frac{dy}{dx}\right)^{-1}\cdot\frac{dx}{dy}$$

$$\therefore \quad \frac{d^2x}{dy^2} = -\left(\frac{d^2y}{dx^2}\right)\left(\frac{dy}{dx}\right)^{-2}\cdot\frac{dx}{dy}$$

$$= -\left(\frac{d^2y}{dx^2}\right)\left(\frac{dy}{dx}\right)^{-3}$$

26. (a) We have, $g(x) = \log_e f(x)$

$$f(x) = e^{g(x)}$$

$$e^{g(x+1)} = f(x+1) = xf(x) = xe^{g(x)}$$

$$\therefore \quad g(x+1) = \log x + g(x)$$

$$g(x+1) - g(x) = \log x \quad \dots\text{(i)}$$

Now, on replacing x by $x - \frac{1}{2}$, we get

$$g\left(x+\frac{1}{2}\right) - g\left(x-\frac{1}{2}\right) = \log\left(x-\frac{1}{2}\right) = \log(2x-1) - \log 2$$

$$g'\left(x+\frac{1}{2}\right) - g'\left(x-\frac{1}{2}\right) = \frac{1}{2x-1}\times 2$$

or

$$g''\left(x+\frac{1}{2}\right) - g''\left(x-\frac{1}{2}\right) = \frac{-4}{(2x-1)^2} \quad \dots\text{(ii)}$$

On putting $x = 1, 2, 3 \cdots N$ in Eq. (ii) and then adding, we get

$$g''\left(N+\frac{1}{2}\right) - g''\left(\frac{1}{2}\right) = -4\left\{1 + \frac{1}{9} + \frac{1}{25} + \cdots + \frac{1}{(2N-1)^2}\right\}$$

27. (c) We have, $\left(\frac{dy}{dx}\right)_{\text{at }[a,\ g(a)]} = g'(a) = 2e^a(a+1)$

$$\because \quad g'(x) = 2e^x(x+1)$$

$$g(x) = 2xe^x + k$$

Put $x = 0$, we get $k = 0$

$$g(x) = 2xe^x \quad \dots\text{(i)}$$

We have, $\Delta[f(x)] = \lim_{h\to 0}\frac{f^3(x+h) - f^3(x)}{h}$

$$= \lim_{h\to 0}\frac{f(x+h) - f(x)}{h} \times f^2(x+h) + f^2(x) + f(x+h)\,f(x)$$

$$\because \quad \Delta[f(x)] = f'(x)\lim_{h\to 0} f^2(x+h) + f^2(x) + f(x+a)\,f(x)$$

$$= 3f'(x)\,f^2(x)$$

Now, $\Delta[g(x)] = 3g'(x)\cdot g^2(x)$

$$= 3\cdot(2xe^x + e^x\cdot 2)4x^2e^{2x}$$

$$= 24x^2e^{2x}(x+1)e^x$$

$$= 24x^2e^{3x}(x+1)$$

Now, $\Delta[g(\log_e 2)] = 24(\log_e 2)^2\cdot e^{3\log_e 2}(\log_e 2 + 1)$

$$= 24(\log 2)^2\cdot 8(1 + \log_e 2)$$

$$= 24 \times 4(\log 2)^2(2 + 2\log_e 2)$$

$$= 96(\log_e 2)^2(2\log_e e + 2\log_e 2)$$

$$= 96(\log_e 2)^2\log_e(4e^2)$$

28. (d) $\Delta(x+2) = 3(x+2)'(x+2)^2 = 3(x+2)^2$

Now, $\Delta[\Delta(x+2)] = 3\cdot\frac{d}{dx}[3(x+2)^2]\cdot 9(x+2)^4$

$$= 3\cdot 6(x+2)\cdot 9(x+2)^4$$

$$= 162(x+2)^5$$

$$\therefore \quad \Delta[\Delta(x+2)]_{\text{at } x=0} = 162\cdot 2^5 = 2^6\cdot 3^4$$

29. (a) We have, $\lim_{x \to 0} \frac{\Delta[g(x)]}{\log\cos 2x}$

$$= \lim_{x \to 0} \frac{24x^2e^{3x}(x+1)}{\log_e \cos 2x}$$

$$= 24 \cdot \lim_{x \to 0} \frac{x^2(x+1)}{\log_e \cos 2x} \quad \left[\frac{0}{0} \text{ form}\right]$$

$$= 24 \cdot \lim_{x \to 0} \frac{3x^2 + 2x}{-\frac{\tan 2x}{2x} \times 2x \times 2} \quad \left[\because \lim_{x \to 0} \frac{\tan x}{x} = 1\right]$$

$$= 24 \lim_{x \to 0} \frac{x(3x+2)}{-2x \times 2}$$

$$= -12 \lim_{x \to 0} \frac{3x+2}{2}$$

$$= \frac{-12(2)}{2}$$

$$= -12$$

30. (2) We have, $g(x) = f^{-1}(x)$

$\therefore \quad gof(x) = x$

$g'of(x) \cdot f'(x) = 1$

$\Rightarrow \quad g'of(x) = \dfrac{1}{3x^2 + e^{\frac{x}{2}} \cdot \frac{1}{2}}$

Put $x = 0$, we get

$g'of(0) = \dfrac{2}{0+1}$ and $f(0) = 1$

$\therefore \quad g'(1) = 2$

31. (4) We have, $x^2 + y^2 = 2$

$x^2 = 2 - y^2$

$2x \cdot \dfrac{dx}{dy} = -2y$

$\therefore \quad \dfrac{dy}{dx} = -\dfrac{x}{y}$

$y_2 = -\left[\dfrac{y \cdot 1 - x \cdot y_1}{y^2}\right]$

$y^2y_2 = -y + xy_1 = -y + x\left(\dfrac{-x}{y}\right)$

$y^2 y_2 = \dfrac{-y^2 - x^2}{y}$

$y^3y_2 = -2$

$\because \quad y_2 + 2y^{-3} = 0$

or $\quad 2y_2 + 4y^{-3} = 0$

Hence, on comparing, we get $a = 4$.

32. (1) We have, $y = \dfrac{a}{2}(e^{\frac{x}{a}} + e^{\frac{-x}{a}})$

$\dfrac{dy}{dx} = \dfrac{a}{2}\left(e^{\frac{x}{a}} \cdot \dfrac{1}{a} - e^{\frac{-x}{a}} \cdot \dfrac{1}{a}\right)$

$\dfrac{dy}{dx} = \dfrac{1}{2}(e^{\frac{x}{a}} - e^{-\frac{x}{a}})$

$\dfrac{d^2y}{dx^2} = \dfrac{1}{2}\left(e^{\frac{x}{a}} \cdot \dfrac{1}{a} + e^{\frac{-x}{a}} \cdot \dfrac{1}{a}\right)$

$= \dfrac{1}{2a}(e^{\frac{x}{a}} + e^{-\frac{x}{a}}) = \dfrac{1}{2a} \times \dfrac{2y}{a}$

$\therefore \quad \dfrac{d^2y}{dx^2} = \dfrac{y}{a^2}$

On comparing, we get

$\dfrac{1}{a^2} = 4$

$a = \pm \dfrac{1}{2}$

$2a = \pm 1$

$\therefore \quad |2a| = 1$

33. (2) We have,

$h'(x) = [f(x)]^2 + [g(x)]^2$

$h''(x) = 2f(x) \cdot f'(x) + 2g(x) \cdot g'(x)$

$= 2f(x) \cdot g(x) + 2g(x)[-f(x)]$

$h''(x) = 0$

$\because \quad h'(x) =$ Constant function

$\therefore \quad h(x)$ is a linear function.

Let $\quad h(x) = lx + m$

$h(0) = m = 2$

and $\quad h(1) = l + m = 4$

$l = 2$

$h(x) = 2x + 2$

$\therefore$ Slope of the line = 2

34. (4) We have,

$y = (\sin^{-1} x)^2 + (\cos^{-1} x)^2$

$\Rightarrow \quad y_1 = 2\sin^{-1} x \cdot \dfrac{1}{\sqrt{1-x^2}} + 2\cos^{-1} x\left(-\dfrac{1}{\sqrt{1-x^2}}\right)$

$\Rightarrow \quad \sqrt{1-x^2}\, y_1 = 2(\sin^{-1} x - \cos^{-1} x)$

$\Rightarrow \quad \sqrt{1-x^2}\, y_2 + y_1 \dfrac{1}{2\sqrt{1-x^2}}(-2x) = 2 \cdot \left(\dfrac{1}{\sqrt{1-x^2}} + \dfrac{1}{\sqrt{1-x^2}}\right)$

$\therefore \quad (1-x^2)\, y_2 - xy_1 = 4$

35. (1) We have, $g(x) = f^{-1}(x)$

and $\quad f(x) = x^2 - 4x - 3$

$f'(x) = 2x - 4$

Now, $\quad gof(x) = x$

$g'of(x) \cdot f'(x) = 1$

$g'of(x) = \dfrac{1}{2x-4}$

Put $x = 6$,

$g'of(6) = g'(9) = \dfrac{1}{8}$

$\therefore \quad 8g'(x)$ at $f(x) = 9$ is 1.

Revisal Problems (JEE Main)

1. (b) We have, $y = \frac{x^8 + x^4 + 1}{x^4 + x^2 + 1}$

$\Rightarrow \quad y = \frac{(x^4 + x^2 + 1)(x^4 - x^2 + 1)}{x^4 + x^2 + 1} = x^4 - x^2 + 1$

$\Rightarrow \quad \frac{dy}{dx} = 4x^3 - 2x$

$\therefore \quad a = 4$ and $b = -2$

2. (b) Let $f(x) = ax^3 + bx^2 + cx + d$

$f'(x) = 3ax^2 + 2bx + c$

$f''(x) = 6ax + 2b$

$f'''(x) = 6a$

$f'''(3) = 12 = 6a \Rightarrow a = 2$

$f''(3) = 0 = 36 + 2b \Rightarrow b = -18$

$f'(3) = -1 = 54 - 108 + c \Rightarrow c = 53$

$\therefore \quad f'(x) = 6x^2 - 36x + 53$

$\Rightarrow \quad f'(1) = 6 - 36 + 53 = 23$

3. (c) We have, $f(x) = 2\tan^{-1}(x) + \cos^{-1}\left(\frac{1-x^2}{1+x^2}\right)$

$$\Rightarrow \quad f(x) = \begin{cases} 2\tan^{-1}x + 2\tan^{-1}x, & x \ge 0 \\ 2\tan^{-1}x - 2\tan^{-1}x, & x < 0 \end{cases}$$

$$\Rightarrow \quad f(x) = \begin{cases} 4\tan^{-1}x, & x \ge 0 \\ 0, & x < 0 \end{cases}$$

$$\Rightarrow \quad f'(x) = \begin{cases} \frac{4}{1+x^2}, & x \ge 0 \\ 0, & x < 0 \end{cases}$$

4. (a) We have,

$f(x) = \sqrt{x-1} + \sqrt{x + 24 - 10\sqrt{x-1}} \quad [\because 1 < x < 26]$

$\Rightarrow \quad f(x) = \sqrt{x-1} + \sqrt{[(\sqrt{x-1}) - 5]^2}$

$\Rightarrow \quad f(x) = \sqrt{x-1} + |\sqrt{x-1} - 5|$

$\Rightarrow \quad f(x) = \sqrt{x-1} - \sqrt{x+1} + 5 \quad [\because 1 < x < 26]$

$\Rightarrow \quad f(x) = 5$

$\therefore \quad f'(x) = 0$

5. (c) We have, $f(x)$ is an odd differentiable function.

$\therefore f'(x)$ is an even function.

$\Rightarrow \quad f^{-1}(-x) = f'(x)$

$\Rightarrow \quad f^{-1}(-3) - f'(3) = -2$

6. (a) Here, $f(x) = \cos x \cdot \cos 2x \cdot \cos 2^2 x \ldots \cos 2^{n-1} x$

$$f(x) = \frac{\sin 2^n x}{2^n \sin x}$$

On differentiating both sides, we get

$$f'(x) = \frac{1}{2^n}\left[\frac{\sin x \cdot 2^n \cdot \cos 2^n x - \sin 2^n x \cdot \cos x}{\sin^2 x}\right]$$

$$\therefore \quad f'\left(\frac{\pi}{2}\right) = \frac{1}{2^n}\left[\frac{1 \times 2^n \times 1 - 0}{(1)^2}\right]$$

$$\Rightarrow \quad f'\left(\frac{\pi}{2}\right) = 1$$

7. (a) We have, $f'(x) = \sqrt{2x^2 - 1}$ and $y = f(x^2)$

$\frac{dy}{dx} = f'(x^2)\, 2x$

$\frac{dy}{dx} = \sqrt{2x^4 - 1} \cdot 2x \quad [\because f'(x) = \sqrt{2x^2 - 1}]$

$\left(\frac{dy}{dx}\right)_{x=1} = \sqrt{2 - 1} \cdot 2 = 2$

8. (c) We have, $g'(a) = 2, g(a) = b$ and $fog = I$

$\therefore \quad fog = x \Rightarrow f(gx) = x$

On differentiating w.r.t. x, we get

$f'(gx) \cdot g'(x) = 1$

$f'[g(x)] = \frac{1}{g'(x)}$

$f'[g(a)] = \frac{1}{g'(a)}$

$f'(b) = \frac{1}{2} \quad [\because g'(a) = 2, g(a) = b]$

9. (b) We have, $f(x^3) = x^5$

On differentiating w.r.t. x, we get

$f'(x^3) \cdot 3x^2 = 5x^4$

$f'(x^3) = \frac{5}{3}x^2 \Rightarrow f'(2^3) = \frac{5}{3}2^2$

$f'(8) = \frac{20}{3}$

10. (c) We have, $y = \sin^{-1}(\sin x)$

$$y = \begin{cases} x, & \frac{-\pi}{2} \le x \le \frac{\pi}{2} \\ \pi - x, & \frac{\pi}{2} \le x \le \pi \end{cases}$$

$$\Rightarrow \quad \frac{dy}{dx} = \begin{cases} 1, & \frac{\pi}{2} \le x \le \frac{\pi}{2} \\ \text{does not exist}, & x = \frac{\pi}{2} \\ -1, & x > \frac{\pi}{2} \end{cases}$$

11. (c) We have, $y = x^3 - 8x + 7$ and $x = f(t)$

Put $x = f(t)$

$y = [f(t)]^3 - 8f(t) + 7$

$\frac{dy}{dt} = 3[f(t)]^2 \cdot f'(t) - 8f'(t)$

$\left[\frac{dy}{dt}\right]_{t=0} = 3[f(0)]^2 \cdot f'(0) - 8f'(0)$

$2 = 3 \times 9 \cdot f'(0) - 8f'(0) \quad [\because f(0) = 3]$

$\therefore \quad f'(0) = \frac{2}{19}$

12. (d) We have, $f(x) = |x|^{|\sin x|}$

On taking log both sides, we get

$\log f(x) = |\sin x| \log |x|$

On differentiating w.r.t. x, we get

$\frac{f'(x)}{f(x)} = \frac{|\sin x|}{|x|} + |\cos x| \log |x|$

$$\Rightarrow \quad f'(x) = f(x)\left[\frac{|\sin x|}{|x|} + |\cos x| \log |x|\right]$$

$$\Rightarrow \quad f'(x) = (x)^{|\sin x|}\left[\frac{|\sin x|}{|x|} + |\cos x| \log |x|\right]$$

$$\Rightarrow \quad f'\left(\frac{\pi}{4}\right) = \left(\frac{\pi}{4}\right)^{\sin\frac{\pi}{4}}\left[\frac{\sin\frac{\pi}{4}}{\left|\frac{\pi}{4}\right|} + \cos\frac{\pi}{4}\log\frac{\pi}{4}\right]$$

$$\Rightarrow \quad f'\left(\frac{\pi}{4}\right) = \left(\frac{\pi}{4}\right)^{\frac{1}{\sqrt{2}}}\left[\frac{2\sqrt{2}}{\pi} + \frac{1}{\sqrt{2}}\log\frac{\pi}{4}\right]$$

$$\therefore \quad f'\left(\frac{\pi}{4}\right) = \left(\frac{\pi}{4}\right)^{\frac{1}{\sqrt{2}}}\left[\frac{\sqrt{2}}{2}\log\left(\frac{\pi}{4}\right) + \frac{2\sqrt{2}}{\pi}\right]$$

13. (d) We have, $x = at^2$ and $y = 2at$

$$\frac{dx}{dt} = 2at \quad \text{and} \quad \frac{dy}{dt} = 2a$$

$$\frac{dy}{dx} = \frac{2a}{2at} = \frac{1}{t}$$

$$\Rightarrow \frac{d^2y}{dx^2} = \frac{-1}{t^2}\left(\frac{dt}{dx}\right) \Rightarrow \frac{d^2y}{dx^2} = \frac{-1}{t^2}\left(\frac{1}{2at}\right)$$

$$\therefore \frac{d^2y}{dx^2} = \frac{-1}{2at^3}$$

14. (a) We have, $y = (\sin x)^{\tan x}$

On taking log both sides, we get

$$\log y = \tan \log \sin x$$

On differentiating w.r.t. x, we get

$$\frac{1}{y}\frac{dy}{dx} = \frac{\tan x \cdot \cos x}{\sin x} + \sec^2 x \log \sin x$$

$$\frac{dy}{dx} = y(1 + \sec^2 x \log \sin x)$$

$$\frac{dy}{dx} = (\sin x)^{\tan x} \cdot (1 + \sec^2 x \cdot \log \sin x)$$

15. (d) We have, $y = \cfrac{x}{a + \cfrac{x}{b + \cfrac{x}{a + \cfrac{x}{b + \cfrac{x}{a + \cdots \infty}}}}}$

$$\Rightarrow y = \frac{x}{a + \frac{x}{b + y}} \Rightarrow y = \frac{x(b + y)}{ab + ay + x}$$

$$\Rightarrow aby + ay^2 + xy = xb + xy \quad \Rightarrow aby + ay^2 = xb$$

On differentiating w.r.t. x, we get

$$(ab + 2ay)\frac{dy}{dx} = b$$

$$\frac{dy}{dx} = \frac{b}{ab + 2ay}$$

16. (b) We have, $f(x) = x^n$

$$f'(x) = nx^{n-1}$$

$$f^2(x) = n(n-1)\,x^{n-2}$$

$$f^3(x) = n(n-1)\,)(n-2)\,x^{n-3}$$

$$\vdots$$

$$f^n(x) = n(n-1)\,(n-2)\cdots 3 \times 2 \times 1$$

$$\Rightarrow f(1) - \frac{f'(1)}{1!} + \frac{f^2(1)}{2!} - \frac{f^3(1)}{3!} + \cdots + \frac{(-1)^n \cdot f^n(1)}{n!}$$

$$= 1 - \frac{n}{1!} + \frac{n(n-1)}{2!} - \frac{n(n-1)\,(n-2)}{3} + \cdots + \frac{(-1)^n n!}{n!}$$

$$= {}^nC_0 - {}^nC_1 + {}^nC_2 - {}^nC_3 + \cdots (-1)^n\, {}^nC_n$$

$$[\because n(n-1)\cdots[r-(r+1)]\,!r! = {}^nC_r]$$

$$= 0$$

17. (a) We have, $f(x) = x + \dfrac{x^2}{1!} + \dfrac{x^3}{2!} + \cdots + \dfrac{x^n}{(n-1)!}$

$$f'(x) = 1 + \frac{2x}{1!} + \frac{3x^2}{2!} + \cdots + \frac{nx^{n-1}}{(n-1)!}$$

$$f^2(x) = 2 + \frac{3 \cdot 2x}{2!} + \cdots + \frac{n(n-1)x^{n-2}}{(n-1)!}$$

$$f^n(x) = \frac{n!}{(n-1)!}$$

$$\Rightarrow f(0) + f'(0) + f^2(0) + \cdots + f^n(0) = 0 + 1 + 2 + 3 + \cdots + x$$

$$= \frac{n(n+1)}{2}$$

18. (a) $f(x)$ is a continuous function $f : R \to Q$.

$f : R \to 0$, iff $f(x)$ is constant function.

$$f(5) = 3$$

$\therefore$ $f(x) = 3$

or $f'(x) = 0$

$$f(0) = 0$$

So, Statement I and Statement II both are correct and Statement II is the correct explanation of Statement I.

19. (c) Let $f(x) = \sin^{-1}\dfrac{2x}{1 + x^2}$

and $g(x) = \cos^{-1}\left(\dfrac{1 - x^2}{1 + x^2}\right)$

$$f(x) = \begin{cases} 2\tan^{-1} x\,, & -1 \le x \le 1 \\ \pi - 2\tan^{-1} x\,, & x > 1 \\ -\pi - 2\tan^{-1} x\,, & x < -1 \end{cases}$$

$$g(x) = \begin{cases} 2\tan^{-1} x & x \ge 0 \\ -2\tan^{-1} x\,, & x < 0 \end{cases}$$

$$f'(x) = \begin{cases} \dfrac{2}{1 + x^2}\,, & -1 \le x \le 1 \\ \dfrac{-2}{1 + x^2}\,, & x > 1 \\ \dfrac{-2}{1 + x^2}\,, & x < -1 \end{cases}$$

$$g'(x) = \begin{cases} \dfrac{2}{1 + x^2}\,, & x \ge 0 \\ \dfrac{-2}{1 + x^2}\,, & x < 0 \end{cases}$$

$$\frac{f'(x)}{g'(x)} = 1, \quad 0 < x \le 1$$

$$\therefore f(x) \ne g(x),\ -1 \le x \le 1$$

So, Statement I is correct and Statement II is incorrect.

20. (b) We have, $f(x) = \dfrac{x}{x^2 - 1}$

$$f(x) = \frac{x}{(x+1)\,(x-1)}$$

$$f(x) = \frac{1}{2}\left[\frac{1}{x+1} + \frac{1}{x-1}\right]$$

$$f'(x) = \frac{1}{2}\left[\frac{-1}{(x+1)^2} - \frac{1}{(x-1)^2}\right]$$

$$f''(x) = \frac{(-1)(-2)}{2}\left[\frac{1}{(x+1)^3} + \frac{1}{(x-1)^3}\right]$$

$$f^n(x) = \frac{(-1)^n \cdot n!}{2}\left[\frac{1}{(x+1)^{n+1}} + \frac{1}{(x-1)^{n+1}}\right]$$

Now, $g(x) = f''(x)$

$$g'(x) = f'''(x)$$

$$g''(x) = f''''(x)$$

$$\Rightarrow g''(x) = \frac{(-1)^4\, 4!}{2}\left[\frac{1}{(x+1)^5} + \frac{1}{(x-1)^5}\right]$$

$$g''(x) = \frac{4!}{2}\left[\frac{1}{(x+1)^5} + \frac{1}{(x-1)^5}\right]$$

$$g''(1) > 0$$

$\therefore$ Graph of $g(x)$ is concave up for $x > 1$.

Hence, Statement I and Statement II both are correct and Statement II is not correct explanation of Statement I.

Revisal Problems (JEE Advanced)

1. (a) Here, $\frac{dy}{dx} = f'(x)$ and $\frac{dx}{dy} = g'(y)$

$$\Rightarrow \quad g'(y) = \frac{1}{f'(x)} \quad \ldots(i)$$

Again on differentiating w.r.t. y, we get

$$g''(y) = \frac{d}{dy}\left[\frac{1}{f'(x)}\right] = -\frac{1}{[f'(x)]^2}\cdot f''(x)\left(\frac{dx}{dy}\right)$$

$$= -\frac{f''(x)}{[f'(x)]^2}\cdot\frac{1}{f'(x)} = -\frac{f''(x)}{[f'(x)]^3}$$

2. (a) Given, $x = \frac{1+t}{t^3}$ and $y = \frac{3}{2t^2} + \frac{2}{t}$

On differentiating w.r.t. t, we get

$$\frac{dx}{dt} = \frac{t^3 - (1+t)(3t^2)}{t^6}$$

$$= \frac{t^3 - 3t^2 - 3t^3}{t^6} = \frac{-(2t^3 + 3t^2)}{t^6}$$

$$= -\frac{(2t+3)}{t^4}$$

and $$\frac{dy}{dt} = \frac{-3}{t^3} - \frac{2}{t^2} = \frac{-(3+2t)}{t^3}$$

$$\therefore \quad \frac{dy}{dx} = \frac{-(2t+3)}{t^3} \div \frac{-(2t+3)}{t^4}$$

$$= \frac{-(2t+3)}{t^3} \times \frac{t^4}{-(2t+3)} = t$$

Now, $$x(y')^3 - y' = \left(\frac{1+t}{t^3}\right)(t)^3 - (t) = 1 + t - t = 1$$

3. (c) Here, $f(x) = x^3 + x^2 f'(1) + xf''(2) + f'''(3)$

Put $f'(1) = a$, $f''(2) = b$, $f'''(3) = c$ $\quad\ldots(i)$

$$\therefore \quad f(x) = x^3 + ax^2 + bx + c$$

$$f'(x) = 3x^2 + 2ax + b$$

or $$f'(1) = 3 + 2a + b \quad \ldots(ii)$$

$$f''(x) = 6x + 2a$$

or $$f''(2) = 12 + 2a \quad \ldots(iii)$$

$$f'''(x) = 6 \quad \text{or} \quad f'''(3) = 6 \quad \ldots(iv)$$

From Eqs. (i) and (iv), $c = 6$

From Eqs. (i), (ii) and (iii), $a = -5, b = 2$

$$\therefore \quad f(x) = x^3 - 5x^2 + 2x + 6$$

4. (d) Here, $$f(x) = \begin{cases} 2 - x, & x < 2 \\ x - 2, & x \ge 2 \end{cases}$$

$$\Rightarrow \quad f[f(x)] = \begin{cases} 2 - f(x), & f(x) < 2 \\ f(x) - 2, & f(x) \ge 2 \end{cases} = \begin{cases} x, & 0 < x < 2 \\ -x, & x \le 0 \\ 4 - x, & 2 \le x < 4 \\ x - 4, & x \ge 4 \end{cases}$$

$$\therefore \quad f'[f(x)] = \begin{cases} 1, & 0 < x < 2 \\ -1, & x \le 0 \\ -1, & 2 \le x < 4 \\ 1, & x \ge 4 \end{cases}$$

5. (a) $\because$ $$f(x) = \frac{x}{1 + |x|}$$

$$\therefore \quad f(x) = \frac{x}{1-x}, \text{ when } x < 0$$

$$\Rightarrow \quad f'(x) = \frac{(1-x)\cdot 1 - x(-1)}{(1-x)^2}, \text{ when } x < 0$$

$$f'(x) = \frac{1}{(1-x)^2}, \text{ when } x < 0$$

$$\therefore \quad f'(-1) = \frac{1}{4}$$

6. (d) Let $g(x) = t$

$$f[g(x)] = f(t)$$

$$f'(t) = \frac{d}{dx}[f(t)]\cdot g'(x)$$

Now, $g(0) = 0$, i.e. $t = 0$

$$[f'\{g(x)\}]_{x=0} = f'(0) = b$$

$$[f\{g(x)\}]_{x=0}' = [f'\{g(x)\}\cdot g'(x)]_{x=0} = f'(0)\cdot g'(0)$$

$$\therefore \quad c = b\cdot g'(0)$$

$$\Rightarrow \quad g'(0) = \frac{c}{b}$$

7. (b) As we know

$$\frac{d^2x}{dy^2} = \frac{-\frac{d^2y}{dx^2}}{\left(\frac{dy}{dx}\right)^3}$$

i.e. $$g''(y) = -\frac{f''(x)}{[f'(x)]^3}$$

$$\therefore \quad g''(3) = -\frac{4}{2^3} = -\frac{1}{2}$$

Explanations for Q. Nos. (8-10)

Let degree of $f(x) = n$

$\therefore$ Degree of $f'(x) = (n-1)$, degree of $f''(x) = (n-2)$

Since, $f''(x)\cdot f'(x) = f(x)$

$\Rightarrow$ $(n-1) + (n-2) = n$

$\therefore$ $n = 3$

So, degree of $f(x) = 3$

Hence, $$f(x) = ax^3 + bx^2 + cx + d$$

$$f'(x) = 3ax^2 + 2bx + c$$

$$f''(x) = 6ax + 2b$$

$$f'''(x) = 6a$$

as $f''(x)\cdot f'(x) = f(x)$

$$(6ax + 2b)(3ax^2 + 2bx + c) = ax^3 + bx^2 + c + d$$

On comparing coefficient of x^3, we get

$$18a^2 = a$$

$$\Rightarrow \quad a = \frac{1}{18} \quad [a \ne 0]$$

$\therefore$ Leading coefficient of $f(x) = \frac{1}{18}$

$$f'''(x) = 6a = \frac{1}{3}$$

8. (d) **9.** (b) **10.** (b)

Explanations for Q. Nos. (11 and 12)

We have, $$y = 2x^2$$

$$(AB)^2 = (x_B - x_A)^2 + (2x_B^2 - 2x_A^2)^2 = 5$$

$$(x_B - x_A)^2 + 4(x_B^2 - x_A^2)^2 = 5$$

On differentiating w.r.t. x_A and denoting $\frac{dx_B}{dx_A} = D$, we get

$$2(x_B - x_A)\cdot(D - 1) + 8(x_B^2 - x_A^2)\cdot(2x_B\cdot D - 2x_A) = 0 \quad \ldots(i)$$

Now, when $A(0, 0)$ and $B(1, 2)$

$$\Rightarrow \quad x_A = 0, x_B = 1$$

Now, Eq. (i) reduces to

$$2(1-0)(D-1) + 8(1-0)\cdot\{2D - 0\} = 0$$

$$\Rightarrow \quad 2D - 2 + 16D = 0$$

$$\therefore \quad D = \frac{1}{9} \quad \text{or} \quad \frac{dx_B}{dx_A} = \frac{1}{9}$$

Again, when $A(1, 2)$ and $B(0, 0)$

$\Rightarrow \quad x_A = 1, x_B = 0$

Now Eq. (i) reduces to

$$2(0-1)(D-1) + 8(0-1)\{0-2\} = 0$$

$\Rightarrow \quad D = 9$

or $\quad \dfrac{dx_B}{dx_A} = 9$

11. (a) **12.** (c)

13. (b) Since, $1, a_1, a_2, \cdots, a_{n-1}$ are roots of $x^n - 1 = 0$, then

$$x^n - 1 = (x-1)(x-a_1)(x-a_2)\cdots(x-a_{n-1})$$

$\Rightarrow \quad \dfrac{x^n - 1}{x-1} = (x-a_1)(x-a_2)\cdots(x-a_{n-1})$

$\therefore \quad \lim\limits_{x\to 1} \dfrac{x^n-1}{x-1} = \lim\limits_{x\to 1}(x-a_1)(x-a_2)\cdots(x-a_{n-1})$

$\Rightarrow \quad n = (1-a_1)(1-a_2)\cdots(1-a_{n-1})$

14. (a) $\log(x^n - 1) = \log(x-1) + \log(x-a_1) + \log(x-a_2) + \cdots + \log(x-a_{n-1})$

On differentiating w.r.t. x, we get

$$\frac{n\cdot x^{n-1}}{x^n-1} = \frac{1}{x-1} + \frac{1}{x-a_1} + \frac{1}{x-a_2} + \cdots + \frac{1}{x-a_{n-1}} \quad \ldots(\text{i})$$

On putting $x = 2$, we get

$$\frac{n\cdot 2^{n-1}}{2^n-1} = 1 + \frac{1}{2-a_1} + \frac{1}{2-a_2} + \cdots + \frac{1}{2-a_{n-1}}$$

$\therefore \quad \sum\limits_{r=1}^{n-1} \dfrac{1}{2-a_r} = \dfrac{2^{n-1}\cdot(n-2)+1}{2^n-1}$

15. (c) From Eq. (i),

$$\frac{nx^{n-1}}{x^n-1} = \frac{1}{x-1} + \frac{1}{x-a_1} + \frac{1}{x-a_2} + \cdots + \frac{1}{x-a_{n-1}}$$

$\therefore \quad \dfrac{1}{x-a_1} + \dfrac{1}{x-a_2} + \cdots + \dfrac{1}{x-a_{n-1}} = \dfrac{nx^{n-1}}{x^n-1} - \dfrac{1}{x-1}$

Taking limit $x \to 1$, we get

$$\sum_{r=1}^{n-1} \frac{1}{1-a_r} = \frac{n-1}{2}$$

16. (a)

(i) $\because y = f(x^3)$

$\therefore \quad \dfrac{dy}{dx} = f'(x^3)\cdot 3x^2$

$\left(\dfrac{dy}{dx}\right)_{x=1} = f'(1)\cdot 3 = 9$

(ii) $\because f(xy) = f(x) + f(y)$

Put $x = y = 1$, $\quad f(1) = f(1) + f(1)$

$\therefore \quad f(1) = 0$

Also, $\quad f(1) = f(e) + f(1/e)$, i.e. $x = e$, $y = 1/e$

$\therefore \quad f(e) + f(1/e) = 0$

(iii) $\because f''(x) = -f(x)$ and $g(x) = f'(x)$

$\therefore \quad g'(x) = f''(x) = -f(x) \quad \ldots(\text{i})$

Also, $\quad h(x) = [f(x)]^2 + [g(x)]^2$

$\therefore \quad h'(x) = 2f(x)\cdot f'(x) + 2g(x)\cdot g'(x)$

$= 2f(x)\cdot g(x) - 2g(x)\cdot f(x) = 0$

$\therefore \quad h(x) = C, \forall x \in R$

Here, $\quad h(5) = 9$

$\therefore \quad h(10) = 9$

(iv) $\because y = \tan^{-1}(\cot x) + \cot^{-1}(\tan x)$, $\dfrac{\pi}{2} < x < \pi$

$\therefore \quad \dfrac{dy}{dx} = \dfrac{-\operatorname{cosec}^2 x}{1+\cot^2 x} + \dfrac{-1\cdot\sec^2 x}{1+\tan^2 x}$

$= -1 - 1 = -2$

Hence, (i) $\to$ (s), (ii) $\to$ (r), (iii) $\to$ (s), (iv) $\to$ (p)

17. (2) Let $\quad f[g(x)] = x$

$\Rightarrow \quad f'[g(x)]\cdot g'(x) = 1$

$\Rightarrow \quad f'[g(a)]\cdot g'(a) = 1$

$\Rightarrow \quad f'(b)\cdot 2 = 1$

$\therefore \quad 4f'(b) = 2$

18. (1) $f(x) = \sqrt{(\sqrt{x-2}+\sqrt{2})^2} + \sqrt{(\sqrt{x-2}-\sqrt{2})^2}$

$= |\sqrt{x-2}+\sqrt{2}| + |\sqrt{x-2}-\sqrt{2}|$

For $\sqrt{x-2}$ to exist, $x \ge 2$.

Also, $\quad \sqrt{x-2}+\sqrt{2} > 0$

$\sqrt{x-2}-\sqrt{2} \ge 0$

$\Rightarrow \quad x \ge 4$

$\therefore \quad f(x) = \begin{cases} \sqrt{x-2}+\sqrt{2}+\sqrt{x-2}-\sqrt{2}, & x \ge 4 \\ \sqrt{x-2}+\sqrt{2}-\sqrt{x-2}+\sqrt{2}, & 2 \le x < 4 \end{cases}$

$= \begin{cases} 2\sqrt{x-2}, & x \ge 4 \\ 2\sqrt{2}, & 2 \le x < 4 \end{cases}$

$\therefore \quad 10f'(102^+) = 10\cdot\dfrac{1}{\sqrt{102-2}} = 1$

19. (9) Let $y = f(x) - f(2x)$

$y' = f'(x) - 2f'(2x)$

$y'(1) = f'(1) - 2f'(2) = 5 \quad \ldots(\text{i})$

and $\quad y'(2) = f'(2) - 2f'(4) = 7 \quad \ldots(\text{ii})$

Now, let $\quad y = f(x) - f(4x)$

$y' = f'(x) - 4f'(4x)$

$y'(1) = f'(1) - 4f'(4) \quad \ldots(\text{iii})$

On substituting $f'(2) = 7 + 2f'(4)$ in Eq. (i), we get

$f'(1) - 2[7 + 2f'(4)] = 5 \quad \Rightarrow \quad f'(1) - 4f'(4) = 19$

$\Rightarrow \quad 19 = 10 + \lambda$

$\therefore \quad \lambda = 9$

20. (1) Here, $\quad y = 3e^2 - x$

$\therefore \quad x^y = x^{3e^2 - x}$

$\Rightarrow \quad f(x) = x^{3e^2 - x}$

Now, on taking log and then differentiating, we get

$\log f(x) = (3e^2 - x)\log x$

$\dfrac{1}{f(x)}\cdot f'(x) = \dfrac{3e^2 - x}{x} - \log x$

$\therefore \quad f'(x) = 0$

$\Rightarrow \quad \dfrac{3e^2 - x}{x} - \log x = 0$

$\Rightarrow \quad 3e^2 = x(1 + \log x)$

$\Rightarrow \quad x = e^2$

$\therefore \quad \lambda = 1$

21. (3) $\quad f'(x) = (kx + e^x)h'(x) + h(x)\cdot(k + e^x)$

$f'(0) = h'(0) + h(0)(k+1)$

$18 = -2 + 5(k+1)$

$\therefore \quad k = 3$

JEE Main & AIEEE Archive

1. (c) Here, $x = -1$ and $x = 2$ are extreme points of $f(x) = \alpha \log|x| + \beta x^2 + x$, then

$$f'(x) = \frac{\alpha}{x} + 2\beta x + 1$$

$$\therefore \quad f'(-1) = -\alpha - 2\beta + 1 = 0 \quad \ldots(i)$$

[at extreme point, $f'(x) = 0$]

and $$f'(-2) = \frac{\alpha}{2} + 4\beta + 1 = 0 \quad \ldots(ii)$$

On solving Eqs. (i) and (ii), we get

$$\alpha = 2, \beta = -\frac{1}{2}$$

2. (a) Given,

$$y = \sec(\tan^{-1} x)$$

Let $$\tan^{-1} x = \theta$$

$$\Rightarrow \quad x = \tan\theta$$

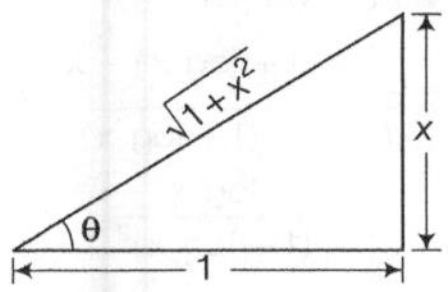

$$\therefore \quad y = \sec\theta = \sqrt{1 + x^2}$$

On differentiating w.r.t. x, we get

$$\frac{dy}{dx} = \frac{1}{2\sqrt{1 + x^2}} \cdot 2x$$

At $x = 1$,

$$\frac{dy}{dx} = \frac{1}{\sqrt{2}}$$

3. (c) Here, $\frac{dx}{dy} = \left(\frac{dy}{dx}\right)^{-1}$

On differentiating both sides w.r.t. y, we get

$$\frac{d^2x}{dy^2} = -\left(\frac{dy}{dx}\right)^{-2} \cdot \frac{d}{dy}\left(\frac{dy}{dx}\right)$$

$$= -\left(\frac{dy}{dx}\right)^{-2} \cdot \frac{d}{dy}\left(\frac{dy}{dx}\right) \cdot \frac{dx}{dx}$$

$$= -\left(\frac{dy}{dx}\right)^{-2} \cdot \frac{d}{dx} \cdot \left(\frac{dy}{dx}\right) \cdot \frac{dx}{dy}$$

$$= -\left(\frac{dy}{dx}\right)^{-2} \cdot \frac{d^2y}{dx^2} \cdot \left(\frac{dy}{dx}\right)^{-1}$$

$$= -\left(\frac{dy}{dx}\right)^{-3} \cdot \left(\frac{d^2y}{dx^2}\right)$$

4. (a) $$x^{2x} - 2x^x \cot y - 1 = 0 \quad \ldots(i)$$

Now, $$x = 1$$

$$\therefore \quad 1 - 2\cot y - 1 = 0$$

$$\Rightarrow \quad \cot y = 0$$

$$\Rightarrow \quad y = \frac{\pi}{2}$$

On differentiating Eq. (i) w.r.t. x, we get

$$2x^{2x}(1 + \log x) - 2[x^x(-\operatorname{cosec}^2 y)\frac{dy}{dx} + \cot y \, x^x (1 + \log x)] = 0$$

At $\left(1, \frac{\pi}{2}\right)$,

$$2(1 + \log 1) - 2\left[1(-1)\left(\frac{dy}{dx}\right)_{\left(1, \frac{\pi}{2}\right)} + 0\right] = 0$$

$$\Rightarrow \quad 2 + 2\left(\frac{dy}{dx}\right)_{\left(1, \frac{\pi}{2}\right)} = 0$$

$$\therefore \quad \left(\frac{dy}{dx}\right)_{\left(1, \frac{\pi}{2}\right)} = -1$$

5. (d) Given that, $x^m y^n = (x + y)^{m+n}$

On taking log both sides, we get

$$m \log x + n \log y = (m + n)\log(x + y)$$

On differentiating w.r.t. x, we get

$$\frac{m}{x} + \frac{n}{y}\frac{dy}{dx} = \frac{(m + n)}{(x + y)}\left(1 + \frac{dy}{dx}\right)$$

$$\Rightarrow \quad \frac{dy}{dx}\left(\frac{m + n}{x + y} - \frac{n}{y}\right) = \frac{m}{x} - \frac{m + n}{x + y}$$

$$\Rightarrow \quad \frac{dy}{dx}\left(\frac{my + ny - nx - ny}{y(x + y)}\right) = \frac{mx + my - mx - nx}{x(x + y)}$$

$$\therefore \quad \frac{dy}{dx} = \frac{y}{x}$$

6. (c) Given that, $$x = e^{y + e^{y + \ldots \infty}}$$

$$\therefore \quad x = e^{y + x}$$

On taking log both sides, we get

$$\log x = (y + x)$$

On differentiating w.r.t. x, we get

$$\frac{1}{x} = \frac{dy}{dx} + 1 \Rightarrow \frac{dy}{dx} = \frac{1 - x}{x}$$

7. (a) Let $$f(x) = Ax^2 + Bx + C$$

$$\therefore \quad f(1) = A + B + C$$

and $$f(-1) = A - B + C$$

$$\because \quad f(1) = f(-1) \quad \text{[given]}$$

$$\Rightarrow \quad A + B + C = A - B + C$$

$$\Rightarrow \quad 2B = 0 \Rightarrow B = 0$$

$$\therefore \quad f(x) = Ax^2 + C$$

$$\Rightarrow \quad f'(x) = 2Ax$$

$$\therefore \quad f'(a) = 2Aa$$

$$f'(b) = 2Ab$$

and $$f'(c) = 2Ac$$

Also, a, b, c are in an AP.

So, $2Aa$, $2Ab$ and $2Ac$ are in AP.

Hence, $f'(a)$, $f'(b)$ and $f'(c)$ are also in an AP.

8. (c) $$f(x) = x^n \quad \Rightarrow \quad f(1) = 1$$

$$f'(x) = nx^{n-1} \quad \Rightarrow \quad f'(1) = n$$

$$f''(x) = n(n-1)x^{n-2} \quad \Rightarrow \quad f''(1) = n(n-1)$$

… … … … … … …

… … … … … … …

$$f^n(x) = n(n-1)(n-2)\ldots 2 \cdot 1$$

$$\Rightarrow \quad f^n(1) = n(n-1)(n-2)\ldots 2 \cdot 1$$

Now, $f(1) - \frac{f'(1)}{1!} + \frac{f''(1)}{2!} - \frac{f'''(1)}{3!} + \ldots + \frac{(-1)^n f^n(1)}{n!}$

$$= 1 - \frac{n}{1!} + \frac{n(n-1)}{2!} - \frac{n(n-1)(n-2)}{3!} + \ldots + \frac{(-1)^n n(n-1)(n-2)\ldots 2\cdot 1}{n!}$$

$[\because (1-x)^n = 1 - {}^nC_1 x + {}^nC_2 x^2 - {}^nC_3 x^3 + \ldots + (-1)^n\, {}^nC_n]$

$$= (1-1)^n = 0$$

9. (a) $\because$ $y = (x + \sqrt{1+x^2})^n$ ...(i)

On differentiating w.r.t. x, we get

$$\frac{dy}{dx} = n(x + \sqrt{1+x^2})^{n-1} \cdot \left(1 + \frac{2x}{2\sqrt{1+x^2}}\right)$$

$$= \frac{n(x+\sqrt{1+x^2})^n}{\sqrt{1+x^2}}$$

$\Rightarrow$ $(1+x^2)\left(\frac{dy}{dx}\right)^2 = n^2y^2$ [from Eq. (i)]

Again on differentiating w.r.t. x, we get

$$(1+x^2)\cdot 2\frac{dy}{dx}\cdot\frac{d^2y}{dx^2} + 2x\left(\frac{dy}{dx}\right)^2 = n^2 2y\frac{dy}{dx}$$

$\therefore$ $(1+x^2)\frac{d^2y}{dx^2} + x\frac{dy}{dx} = n^2y$

10. (b) $\because$ $\sin y = x\sin(a+y)$

$\Rightarrow$ $x = \frac{\sin y}{\sin(a+y)}$

On differentiating w.r.t. y, we get

$$\frac{dx}{dy} = \frac{\sin(a+y)\cos y - \sin y\cos(a+y)}{\sin^2(a+y)}$$

$\Rightarrow$ $\frac{dx}{dy} = \frac{\sin a}{\sin^2(a+y)}$

$\therefore$ $\frac{dy}{dx} = \frac{\sin^2(a+y)}{\sin a}$

11. (c) Since, $x^y = e^{x-y}$

On taking log both sides, we get

$$y\log x = (x-y)\log_e e$$

$\Rightarrow$ $y = \frac{x}{1+\log x}$

On differentiating w.r.t. x, we get

$$\frac{dy}{dx} = \frac{(1+\log x) - x\cdot\frac{1}{x}}{(1+\log x)^2} = \frac{\log x}{(1+\log x)^2}$$

JEE Advanced & IIT JEE Archive

1. (b,c) **Concept Involved** This question is based on the concept of transcendental equation and should be solved with the help of graph.

$$f(x) = x\sin\pi x,\ x > 0$$

$$f'(x) = \sin\pi x + \pi x\cos\pi x = 0$$

$\Rightarrow$ $\tan\pi x = -\pi x$

Let $f(x) = \tan\pi x$ and $g(x) = -\pi x$

which could be plotted as

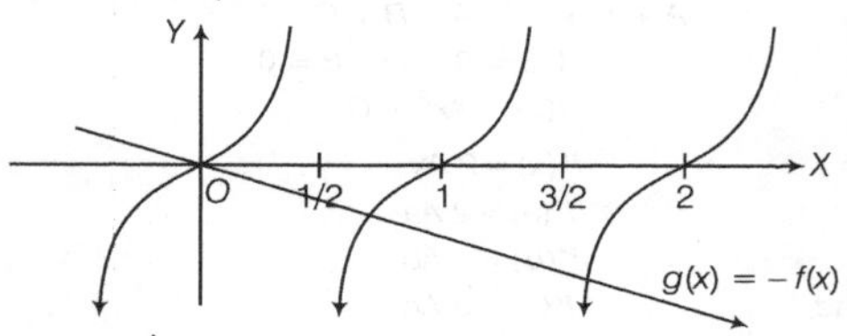

Clearly, $f(x)$ and $g(x)$ intersect, when $\frac{1}{2} < x < 1$ or $\frac{3}{2} < x < 2$

or $\frac{5}{2} < x < 3$

$\therefore$ A unique point in $\left(n + \frac{1}{2}, n+1\right)$ or $(n, n+1)$.

2. (d) Since, $\frac{dx}{dy} = \frac{1}{dy/dx} = \left(\frac{dy}{dx}\right)^{-1}$

$\Rightarrow$ $\frac{d}{dy}\left(\frac{dx}{dy}\right) = \frac{d}{dx}\left(\frac{dy}{dx}\right)^{-1}\frac{dx}{dy}$

$\therefore$ $\frac{d^2x}{dy^2} = -\left(\frac{d^2y}{dx^2}\right)\left(\frac{dy}{dx}\right)^{-2}\left(\frac{dx}{dy}\right)$

$$= -\left(\frac{d^2y}{dx^2}\right)\left(\frac{dy}{dx}\right)^{-3}$$

2. Limits

DPP-1 Definition of Limits and $\left(\frac{0}{0}\right)$ Form on Algebraic

1. According to the figure,

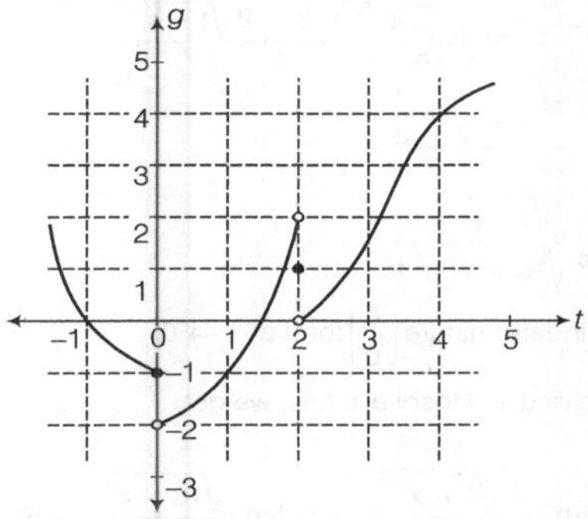

(i) $\lim_{t \to 0^-} g(t) = -1$ (because the value −1 only exists at $t < 0$)

(ii) $\lim_{t \to 0^+} g(t) = -2$

(iii) $\lim_{t \to 0} g(t) =$ does not exist (RHL ≠ LHL)

(iv) $\lim_{t \to 2^-} g(t) = 2$

(v) $\lim_{t \to 2^+} g(t) = 0$

(vi) $\lim_{t \to 2} g(t) =$ does not exist

(vii) $g(2) = 1$

(viii) $\lim_{t \to 4} g(t) = 4$

2. According to the figure,

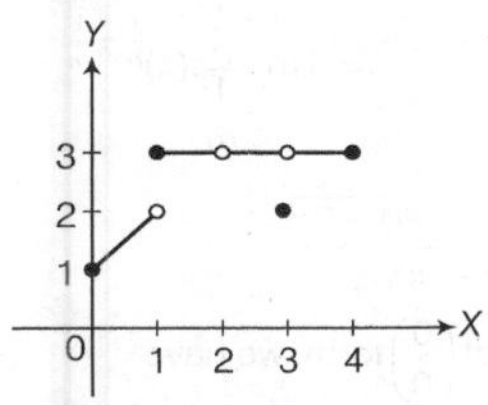

(i) $\lim_{x \to 1} f(x) =$ does not exist (RHL ≠ LHL)

(ii) $\lim_{x \to 2} f(x) = 3$

(iii) $\lim_{x \to 3} f(x) = 3$

(iv) $\lim_{x \to 1.99} f(x) = 3$

(v) $\lim_{x \to 3^-} f(x) = 3$

3. (d) $\lim_{x \to a} \frac{x^m - a^m}{x^n - a^n}$

As, it is $\left(\frac{0}{0}\right)$ form,

On applying L' Hospital's rule i.e. differentiating numerator and denominator, we get

$$\lim_{x \to a} \frac{m x^{m-1} - 0}{n x^{n-1} - 0} = \lim_{x \to a} \frac{m}{n} x^{m-n}$$

On applying limits, we get

$$= \frac{m}{n}(a)^{m-n}$$

4. (b) $\lim_{x \to 1} \frac{(x + x^2 + x^3 + \dots + x^n) - n}{x - 1}$

As, it is $\left(\frac{0}{0}\right)$ form.

On applying L' Hospital's rule, we get

$$\lim_{x \to 1} \frac{(1 + 2x + 3x^2 + \dots + nx^{n-1}) - 0}{1}$$

On applying limits, we get

$$1 + 2 + 3 + 4 + \dots + n = \frac{n(n+1)}{2}$$

5. (c) Given, $\lim_{x \to 1} \frac{x^4 - 1}{x - 1} = \lim_{x \to k} \frac{x^3 - k^3}{x^2 - k^2}$

As, it is $\left(\frac{0}{0}\right)$ form.

On applying L' Hospital's rule, we get

$$\lim_{x \to 1} \frac{4x^3 - 0}{1 - 0} = \lim_{x \to k} \frac{3x^2 - 0}{2x - 0}$$

$$\Rightarrow \quad 4 = \frac{3k}{2}$$

$$\therefore \quad k = \frac{8}{3}$$

6. (b) Given, $\lim_{x \to -a} \frac{x^9 + a^9}{x + a} = 9$

As, it is $\left(\frac{0}{0}\right)$ form.

On differentiating numerator and denominator, we get

$$\lim_{x \to -a} \frac{9x^8 + 0}{1 + 0} = 9$$

$$\Rightarrow \quad 9(-a)^8 = 9$$

$$\Rightarrow \quad (-a)^8 = 1$$

$$\therefore \quad a = \pm 1$$

7. (d) $\lim_{x \to 2} \left[\frac{1}{x(x-2)^2} - \frac{1}{x^2 - 3x + 2}\right]$

$$= \lim_{x \to 2} \left[\frac{1}{x(x-2)^2} - \frac{1}{(x-2)(x-1)}\right]$$

On applying $\lim_{x \to 2}$, we get

$$\frac{1}{0} - \frac{1}{0} = \infty - \infty$$

So, convert it into $\left(\frac{0}{0}\right)$ form.

$$\therefore \quad \lim_{x \to 2} \left(\frac{1}{x-2}\right)\left[\frac{1}{x(x-2)} - \frac{1}{(x-1)}\right]$$

$$= \lim_{x \to 2} \frac{1}{(x-2)} \left[\frac{-x^2 + 3x - 1}{x(x-1)(x-2)}\right]$$

$$= \lim_{x \to 2} \left[\frac{-x^2 + 3x - 1}{x(x-1)(x-2)^2}\right]$$

On applying limits, we get

$$= \frac{-4 + 6 - 1}{2(2-1)(2-2)^2} = \frac{1}{0} = \infty$$

8. (b) $\lim_{x\to 1}\left(\frac{1}{1-x}-\frac{3}{1-x^3}\right)$

It is a $(\infty - \infty)$ form.

We have to convert it into either $\left(\frac{0}{0}\right)$ or $\left(\frac{\infty}{\infty}\right)$ form.

Now, $\lim_{x\to 1}\left[\frac{1-x^3-3(1-x)}{(1-x)(1-x)^3}\right]$

$$= \lim_{x\to 1}\left[\frac{1-x^3-3+3x}{1-x^3-x+x^4}\right]$$

$$= \lim_{x\to 1}\left[\frac{-x^3+3x-2}{x^4-x^3-x+1}\right]$$

At $x = 1$, it is a $\left(\frac{0}{0}\right)$ form.

On applying L' Hospital's rule, we get

$$\lim_{x\to 1}\left[\frac{-3x^2+3}{4x^3-3x^2-1}\right]$$

Still at $x \to 1$, it is a $\left(\frac{0}{0}\right)$ form.

$\therefore$ $\lim_{x\to 1}\left[\frac{-6x}{12x^2-6x}\right] = \lim_{x\to 1}\left[\frac{-6}{12x-6}\right]$

$$= \frac{-6}{12-6} = \frac{-6}{6} = -1$$

9. (c) $\lim_{x\to\sqrt{2}}\left(\frac{x^4-4}{x^2+3x\sqrt{2}-8}\right)$

At $x = \sqrt{2}$, it is an indeterminate $\left(\frac{0}{0}\right)$ form.

On applying L' Hospital's rule, we get

$$\lim_{x\to\sqrt{2}}\left(\frac{4x^3}{2x+3\sqrt{2}}\right) = \frac{4(2\sqrt{2})}{2\sqrt{2}+3\sqrt{2}} = \frac{8}{5}$$

10. (d) $\lim_{x\to 2}\frac{\sqrt{1+\sqrt{2+x}}-\sqrt{3}}{x-2}$

At $x \to 2$, it is an indeterminate $\left(\frac{0}{0}\right)$ form.

On applying L' Hospital's rule

$$\lim_{x\to 2}\frac{1}{2}\cdot\frac{1}{\sqrt{1+\sqrt{2+x}}}\cdot\frac{1}{2\sqrt{2+x}}$$

$$= \frac{1}{2}\cdot\frac{1}{\sqrt{1+2}}\cdot\frac{1}{2\sqrt{4}} = \frac{1}{8\sqrt{3}}$$

11. (c) $\lim_{x\to 1}\frac{x^m-1}{x^n-1}$

It is an indeterminate $\left(\frac{0}{0}\right)$ form.

On applying L'Hospital's rule, we get

$$\lim_{x\to 1}\frac{mx^{m-1}}{nx^{n-1}} = \lim_{x\to 1}\left(\frac{m}{n}\right)x^{m-n} = \frac{m}{n}$$

12. (a) $\lim_{x\to 0}\frac{\sqrt{1+x^2}-1}{x^2}$

It is an indeterminate $\left(\frac{0}{0}\right)$ form.

On applying L' Hospital's rule, we get

$$\lim_{x\to 0}\frac{\frac{1}{2\sqrt{1+x^2}}\cdot 2x}{2x} = \lim_{x\to 0}\frac{1}{2\sqrt{1+x^2}} = \frac{1}{2}$$

13. (d) $\lim_{x\to 0}\frac{\sqrt{1+x}-\sqrt{1-x}}{2x}$ $\left[\frac{0}{0}\text{form}\right]$

On applying L' Hospital's rule, we get

$$\lim_{x\to 0}\frac{\frac{1}{2\sqrt{1+x}}-\frac{1}{2\sqrt{1-x}}(0-1)}{2}$$

$$= \lim_{x\to 0}\frac{\frac{1}{2\sqrt{1+x}}+\frac{1}{2\sqrt{1-x}}}{2}$$

$$= \frac{\frac{1}{2}+\frac{1}{2}}{2} = \frac{1}{2}$$

14. (a) $\lim_{x\to 0}\frac{\sqrt{1+x^2}-1}{\sqrt{16+x^2}-4}$

It is an indeterminate $\left(\frac{0}{0}\right)$ form at $x \to 0$.

On applying, L' Hospital's rule, we get

$$\lim_{x\to 0}\frac{\frac{1}{2\sqrt{1+x^2}}\cdot 2x}{\frac{1}{2\sqrt{16+x^2}}\cdot 2x} = \lim_{x\to 0}\frac{\sqrt{16+x^2}}{\sqrt{1+x^2}} = \sqrt{16} = 4$$

15. (a) $\lim_{x\to 1}\frac{\sqrt[n]{x}-1}{\sqrt[m]{x}-1}$

It is an $\left(\frac{0}{0}\right)$ indeterminate form.

On applying L' Hospital's rule, we get

$$= \lim_{x\to 1}\frac{\frac{1}{n}(x)^{\frac{1}{n}-1}}{\frac{1}{m}(x)^{\frac{1}{m}-1}}$$

$$= \lim_{x\to 1}\frac{\frac{1}{n}}{\frac{1}{m}}(x)^{\frac{1}{n}-\frac{1}{m}} = \frac{m}{n}$$

16. (a) $\lim_{x\to 1}\frac{\sqrt[3]{1+x^2}-\sqrt[3]{1-2x}}{x+x^2}$

At $x \to 1$, it is not $\left(\frac{0}{0}\right)$ form, we have

$$= \frac{(2)^{\frac{1}{3}}-(-1)^{\frac{1}{3}}}{2} = \frac{1}{2}$$

17. (a) $\lim_{x\to 1}\frac{\sqrt[3]{7+x^2}-\sqrt{3+x^2}}{x-1}$

It is an indeterminate $\left(\frac{0}{0}\right)$ form.

On applying L' Hospital's rule, we get

$$\lim_{x\to 1}\frac{\frac{1}{3}(7+x^2)^{\frac{-2}{3}}\cdot 2x-\frac{1}{2}(3+x^2)^{\frac{-1}{2}}\cdot 2x}{1-0}$$

$$= \frac{1}{3}(8)^{\frac{-2}{3}}\cdot 2-\frac{2}{2}(4)^{\frac{-1}{2}}$$

$$= \frac{2}{3}(2)^{-2}-\frac{2}{2}(2)^{-1}$$

$$= \frac{2}{3}\left[\frac{1}{4}\right]-\frac{1}{2} = -\frac{1}{3}$$

18. (c) $\lim_{x \to 2} \frac{\sqrt{x-2} + \sqrt{x} - \sqrt{2}}{\sqrt{x^2 - 4}}$

At $x \to 2$, it is an indeterminate $\left(\frac{0}{0}\right)$ form.

On applying L' Hospital's rule, we get

$$\lim_{x \to 2} \frac{\frac{1}{2\sqrt{x-2}} \cdot 1 + \frac{1}{2\sqrt{x}} - 0}{\frac{1}{2\sqrt{x^2-4}} \cdot 2x}$$

$$= \lim_{x \to 2} \frac{\frac{1}{2}\left[\frac{1}{\sqrt{x-2}} + \frac{1}{\sqrt{x}}\right]}{\frac{x}{\sqrt{x-2}\sqrt{x+2}}} = \lim_{x \to 2} \frac{\frac{1}{2}\left[\frac{\sqrt{x} + \sqrt{x-2}}{\sqrt{x}\sqrt{x-2}}\right]}{\frac{x}{\sqrt{x-2}\sqrt{x+2}}}$$

$$= \lim_{x \to 2} \frac{1}{2}\left[\frac{\sqrt{x} + \sqrt{x-2}}{x\sqrt{x}}\right]\sqrt{x+2}$$

$$= \frac{1}{2}\left[\frac{\sqrt{2}}{2\sqrt{2}}\right]\sqrt{2+2}$$

$$= \frac{1}{2} \cdot \left[\frac{1}{2}\right] \cdot 2 = \frac{1}{2}$$

19. (d) $\lim_{x \to 1} \frac{4x^3 - x^2 + 2x - 5}{x^6 + 5x^3 - 2x - 4}$ $\left[\frac{0}{0} \text{form}\right]$

On applying L' Hospital's rule, we get

$$\lim_{x \to 1} \frac{12x^2 - 2x + 2}{6x^5 + 15x^2 - 2}$$

$$= \frac{12 - 2 + 2}{6 + 15 - 2} = \frac{12}{19}$$

20. (b) $\lim_{x \to a} \frac{\sqrt{a + 2x} - \sqrt{3x}}{\sqrt{3a + x} - 2\sqrt{x}}$

At $x \to a$, it is an indeterminate $\left(\frac{0}{0}\right)$ form.

On applying L' Hospital's rule, we get

$$= \lim_{x \to a} \frac{\frac{1}{2\sqrt{a+2x}} \cdot 2 - \frac{1}{2\sqrt{3x}} \cdot 3}{\frac{1}{2\sqrt{3a+x}} \cdot 1 - 2 \cdot \frac{1}{2\sqrt{x}}}$$

$$= \lim_{x \to a} \frac{\frac{1}{\sqrt{a+2x}} - \frac{3}{2\sqrt{3x}}}{\frac{1}{2\sqrt{3a+x}} - \frac{1}{\sqrt{x}}}$$

$$= \frac{\frac{1}{\sqrt{3a}} - \frac{3}{2\sqrt{3a}}}{\frac{1}{2\sqrt{4a}} - \frac{1}{\sqrt{a}}}$$

$$= \frac{\frac{1}{\sqrt{3a}}\left[1 - \frac{3}{2}\right]}{\frac{1}{4\sqrt{a}} - \frac{1}{\sqrt{a}}}$$

$$= \frac{\frac{1}{\sqrt{3a}}\left[\frac{-1}{2}\right]}{\frac{1}{\sqrt{a}}\left[\frac{1}{4} - 1\right]}$$

$$= \frac{\frac{1}{\sqrt{3}}\left[-\frac{1}{2}\right]}{\left[\frac{-3}{4}\right]} = \frac{4}{3} \cdot \frac{1}{2\sqrt{3}} = \frac{2}{3\sqrt{3}}$$

DPP-2 Questions Based on $\left(\frac{\infty}{\infty}\right)$ Form

1. $\lim_{x \to \infty} \frac{a_0x^m + a_1x^{m-1} + a_2x^{m-2} + \cdots + a_m}{b_0x^n + b_1x^{n-1} + b_2x^{n-2} + \cdots + b_n}$

where $a_0, b_0 \neq 0$ and m, n are positive integers.

(i) When $m > n$, then

$$\lim_{x \to \infty} \frac{a_0x^m + a_1x^{m-1} + a_2x^{m-2} + \cdots + a_m}{b_0x^n + b_1x^{n-1} + b_2x^{n-1} + \cdots + b_n}$$

$$= \lim_{x \to \infty} \frac{a_0 + a_1x^{-1} + a_2x^{-2} + \cdots + a_mx^{-m}}{b_0 + b_1x^{-1} + b_2x^{-2} + \cdots + b_nx^{-n}}$$

The general solution becomes

$$\lim_{x \to \infty} \frac{a_0}{b_0} x^{m-n}$$

$$\lim_{x \to \infty} \frac{a_0}{b_0}(\infty) = \begin{cases} \infty, & \frac{a_0}{b_0} > 0 \\ -\infty, & \frac{a_0}{b_0} < 0 \end{cases}$$

(ii) When $m = n$, then

$$\lim_{x \to \infty} \frac{a_0}{b_0} x^{m-n}$$

$$\lim_{x \to \infty} \frac{a_0}{b_0} x^0 = \left(\frac{a_0}{b_0}\right)$$

(iii) When $m < n$, then

$$\lim_{x \to \infty} \frac{a_0}{b_0} x^{m-n} = \lim_{x \to \infty} \frac{a_0}{b_0} x^{m-n}$$

$$= \frac{a_0}{b_0 \cdot (\infty)} = 0$$

2. (a) $\lim_{x \to \infty} \left(\frac{x^2 + 1}{x + 1} - ax - b\right) = 0$

It is a $(\infty - \infty)$ form, first convert it in to $\left(\frac{\infty}{\infty}\right)$ form.

$$\lim_{x \to \infty} \frac{x^2 + 1 - ax(x+1) - b(x+1)}{x + 1}$$

$$= \lim_{x \to \infty} \frac{(1-a)x^2 - (a+b)x + (1-b)}{x + 1} \quad \left[\frac{\infty}{\infty} \text{ form}\right]$$

On differentiating numerator and denominator, we get

$$\lim_{x \to \infty} \frac{2(1-a)x - (a+b)}{1} = 0$$

On comparing both sides, we get

$1 - a = 0$ and $a + b = 0$

$a = 1$ and $b = -a$

Hence, $a = 1$ and $b = -1$.

3. (b) Given, $\lim_{x \to \infty} \left(\frac{x^2 - 1}{x + 1} - ax - b\right) = 2$

$$\Rightarrow \lim_{x \to \infty} \left[\frac{(x-1)(x+1)}{(x+1)} - ax - b\right] = 2$$

$$\Rightarrow \lim_{x \to \infty} (x - 1 - ax - b) = 2$$

$$\Rightarrow \lim_{x \to \infty} (1-a)x - (1+b) = 2$$

On comparing both the sides, we get

$-(1 + b) = 2$ and $1 - a = 0$

Hence, $b = -3$ and $a = 1$.

4. (d) Given, $\lim_{x \to \infty} \left[\frac{x^2+1}{x+1} - ax - b\right] = \infty$

$$\Rightarrow \lim_{x \to \infty} \frac{x^2 + 1 - ax(x+1) - b(x+1)}{x+1} = \infty \quad \left[\frac{\infty}{\infty} \text{ form}\right]$$

$$\Rightarrow \lim_{x \to \infty} \frac{(1-a)x^2 - (a+b)x + (1-b)}{x+1} = \infty$$

$$\Rightarrow 1 - a > 0$$

$$\Rightarrow a < 1 \text{ and } b \in R$$

5. (b) $\lim_{n \to \infty} \frac{(n+1)^4 - (n-1)^4}{(n+1)^4 + (n-1)^4}$

$$= \lim_{n \to \infty} \left[\frac{\frac{(n+1)^4}{(n-1)^4} - 1}{\frac{(n+1)^4}{(n-1)^4} + 1}\right]$$

$$= \lim_{n \to \infty} \frac{\frac{\left(1+\frac{1}{n}\right)^4}{\left(1-\frac{1}{n}\right)^4} - 1}{\frac{\left(1+\frac{1}{n}\right)^4}{\left(1-\frac{1}{n}\right)^4} + 1} = \frac{1-1}{1+1} = 0$$

6. (b) $\lim_{n \to \infty} \frac{(2n+1)^4 - (n-1)^4}{(2n+1)^4 + (n-1)^4}$

$$= \lim_{n \to \infty} \frac{\left(2+\frac{1}{n}\right)^4 - \left(1-\frac{1}{n}\right)^4}{\left(2+\frac{1}{n}\right)^4 + \left(1-\frac{1}{n}\right)^4}$$

$$= \frac{\left(2+\frac{1}{\infty}\right)^4 - \left(1-\frac{1}{\infty}\right)^4}{\left(2+\frac{1}{\infty}\right)^4 + \left(1-\frac{1}{\infty}\right)^4}$$

$$= \frac{16-1}{16+1} = \frac{15}{17}$$

7. (c) $\lim_{n \to \infty} \frac{\sqrt[3]{n^3 + 2n - 1}}{n+2}$

$$= \lim_{n \to \infty} \frac{(n^3 + 2n - 1)^{1/3}}{n+2}$$

$$= \lim_{n \to \infty} \frac{n\left(1 + \frac{2}{n^2} - \frac{1}{n^3}\right)^{1/3}}{n\left(1+\frac{2}{n}\right)}$$

$$= \lim_{n \to \infty} \frac{\left(1 + \frac{2}{n^2} - \frac{1}{n^3}\right)^{1/3}}{\left(1+\frac{2}{n}\right)}$$

$$= \left(\frac{1+0-0}{1+0}\right) = 1$$

8. (c) $\lim_{n \to \infty} \frac{n!}{(n+1)! - n!}$

$$= \lim_{n \to \infty} \frac{n!}{(n+1)n! - n!} = \lim_{n \to \infty} \frac{1}{(n+1)-1}$$

$$= \lim_{n \to \infty} \frac{1}{n} = 0$$

9. (a) $\lim_{n \to \infty} \frac{\sqrt{n^3 + 2n^2 + 1} - \sqrt[5]{n^4 + 1}}{\sqrt[4]{n^6 + 2n^5 + 2} + \sqrt[5]{n^7 + 3n^3 + 1}}$

$$= \lim_{n \to \infty} \frac{n^{3/2}\left(1 + \frac{2}{n} + \frac{1}{n^3}\right)^{1/2} - n^{4/5}\left(1 + \frac{1}{n^4}\right)^{1/5}}{n^{6/4}\left(1 + \frac{2}{n} + \frac{2}{n^6}\right)^{1/4} + n^{7/5}\left(1 + \frac{3}{n^4} + \frac{1}{n^7}\right)^{1/5}}$$

$$= \lim_{n \to \infty} \frac{\left(1 + \frac{2}{n} + \frac{1}{n^3}\right)^{1/2} - n^{-7/10}\left(1 + \frac{1}{n^4}\right)^{1/5}}{\left(1 + \frac{2}{n} + \frac{2}{n^6}\right)^{1/4} + n^{-1/10}\left(1 + \frac{1}{n^4}\right)^{1/5}}$$

On applying limit $n \to \infty$, we get

$$= \frac{(1+0+0)^{1/2} - 0(1+0)^{1/5}}{(1+0+0)^{1/4} + 0(1+0)^{1/5}} = 1$$

10. (a) $\lim_{n \to \infty} \frac{\sqrt[4]{n^5 + 2} - \sqrt[3]{n^2 + 1}}{\sqrt[5]{n^4 + 2} - \sqrt{n^3 + 1}}$

$$= \lim_{n \to \infty} \frac{n^{5/4}\left(1 + \frac{2}{n^5}\right)^{1/4} - n^{2/3}\left(1 + \frac{1}{n^2}\right)^{1/3}}{n^{4/5}\left(1 + \frac{2}{n^4}\right)^{1/5} - n^{3/2}\left(1 + \frac{1}{n^3}\right)^{1/2}}$$

On dividing numerator and denominator by the highest powers of n i.e. $n^{3/2}$, we get

$$= \lim_{n \to \infty} \left[\frac{\frac{n^{5/4}}{n^{3/2}}\left(1 + \frac{2}{n^5}\right)^{1/4} - \frac{n^{2/3}}{n^{3/2}}\left(1 + \frac{1}{n^2}\right)^{1/3}}{\frac{n^{4/5}}{n^{3/2}}\left(1 + \frac{2}{n^4}\right)^{1/5} - \frac{n^{3/2}}{n^{3/2}}\left(1 + \frac{1}{n^3}\right)^{1/2}}\right]$$

$$= \lim_{n \to \infty} \left[\frac{\frac{1}{n^{1/4}}\left(1 + \frac{2}{n^5}\right)^{1/4} - \frac{1}{n^{5/6}}\left(1 + \frac{1}{n^2}\right)^{1/3}}{\frac{1}{n^{7/10}}\left(1 + \frac{2}{n^4}\right)^{1/5} - \left(1 + \frac{1}{n^3}\right)^{1/2}}\right]$$

$$= \frac{0-0}{0-1} = 0$$

11. (d) $\lim_{n \to \infty} \frac{(n+2)! + (n+1)!}{(n+3)!}$

$$= \lim_{n \to \infty} \frac{(n+2)(n+1)! + (n+1)!}{(n+3)(n+2)(n+1)!}$$

$$= \lim_{n \to \infty} \frac{(n+2+1)}{(n+3)(n+2)}$$

$$= \lim_{n \to \infty} \frac{n+3}{(n+3)(n+2)}$$

$$= \lim_{n \to \infty} \frac{1}{(n+2)}$$

$$= \lim_{n \to \infty} \frac{\frac{1}{n}}{\left(1+\frac{2}{n}\right)} = 0$$

12. (d) $\lim_{n \to \infty} \left\{\frac{1}{1 \cdot 2} + \frac{1}{2 \cdot 3} + \frac{1}{3 \cdot 4} + \cdots + \frac{1}{(n-1) \cdot n}\right\}$

$$= \lim_{n \to \infty} \left[\left(\frac{1}{1} - \frac{1}{2}\right) + \left(\frac{1}{2} - \frac{1}{3}\right) + \left(\frac{1}{3} - \frac{1}{4}\right) + \cdots + \left(\frac{1}{n-1} - \frac{1}{n}\right)\right]$$

$$= \lim_{n \to \infty} \left[1 - \frac{1}{n}\right]$$

$$= 1 - 0 = 1$$

13. (a) $\lim_{x\to\infty}\left(\frac{x^3}{2x^2-1}-\frac{x^2}{2x+1}\right)$

$$= \lim_{x\to\infty}\left[\frac{x^3(2x+1)-x^2(2x^2-1)}{(2x^2-1)(2x+1)}\right]$$

$$= \lim_{x\to\infty}\left[\frac{2x^4+x^3-2x^4+x^2}{(2x^2-1)(2x+1)}\right]$$

$$= \lim_{x\to\infty}\left[\frac{x^3+x^2}{(2x^2-1)(2x+1)}\right]$$

$$= \lim_{x\to\infty}\frac{x^3\left(1+\frac{1}{x}\right)}{x^3\left(2-\frac{1}{x^2}\right)\left(2+\frac{1}{x}\right)}=\frac{1}{4}$$

14. (c) $\lim_{x\to\infty}\frac{(x+1)^{10}+(x+2)^{10}+\cdots+(x+100)^{10}}{x^{10}+10^{10}}$

$$= \lim_{x\to\infty}\frac{x^{10}\left[\left(1+\frac{1}{x}\right)^{10}+\left(1+\frac{2}{x}\right)^{10}+\cdots+\left(1+\frac{100}{x}\right)^{10}\right]}{x^{10}\left[1+\frac{10^{10}}{x^{10}}\right]}$$

$$= 1+1+1+\cdots+1 = 100$$

15. (c) $\lim_{x\to\infty}x^{3/2}\{\sqrt{x^3+1}-\sqrt{x^3-1}\}$

$$= \lim_{x\to\infty}x^{3/2}\left\{\frac{(x^3+1)-(x^3-1)}{(x^3+1)^{1/2}+(x^3-1)^{1/2}}\right\}$$

$$\left[\because a^2-b^2=(a-b)(a+b) \quad \therefore a-b=\frac{a^2-b^2}{a+b}\right]$$

$$= \lim_{x\to\infty}x^{3/2}\left\{\frac{2}{x^{3/2}\left\{\left(1+\frac{1}{x^3}\right)^{1/2}+\left(1-\frac{1}{x^3}\right)^{1/2}\right\}}\right\}$$

$$= \lim_{x\to\infty}\frac{2}{\left(1+\frac{1}{x^3}\right)^{1/2}+\left(1-\frac{1}{x^3}\right)^{1/2}}=\frac{2}{2}=1$$

16. (c) Given, $\lim_{x\to\infty}[\sqrt{x^2-x+1}-(ax+b)]=0$

$$\Rightarrow \lim_{x\to\infty}(\sqrt{x^2-x+1}-ax-b)=0$$

$$\Rightarrow \lim_{x\to\infty}\left[x\left(1-\frac{1}{x}+\frac{1}{x^2}\right)^{1/2}-ax-b\right]=0$$

$$\Rightarrow \lim_{x\to\infty}\left[x\left\{1-\frac{1}{2}\left(\frac{1}{x}+\frac{1}{x^2}\right)+\cdots\right\}-ax-b\right]=0$$

$$\Rightarrow \lim_{x\to\infty}\left[x(1-a)-\left(\frac{1}{2}+b\right)-\frac{1}{2x}-\frac{1}{2x^2}-\cdots\right]=0$$

On comparing, $1-a=0$ and $b+\frac{1}{2}=0$

$\therefore$ $a=1$ and $b=-\frac{1}{2}$

17. (a) $\lim_{n\to\infty}\frac{1\cdot n+2\cdot(n-1)+3\cdot(n-2)+\cdots+(n-1)\cdot 2+n\cdot 1}{1^2+2^2+\cdots+n^2}$

$$= \lim_{n\to\infty}\left[\frac{\Sigma n(n-1)}{\frac{n(n+1)(2n+1)}{6}}\right]=\lim_{n\to\infty}\frac{\Sigma n^2-\Sigma n}{\left[\frac{n(n+1)(2n+1)}{6}\right]}$$

$$= \lim_{n\to\infty}\frac{\left[\frac{n(n+1)(2n+1)}{6}-\frac{n(n+1)}{2}\right]}{\frac{n(n+1)(2n+1)}{6}}=\lim_{n\to\infty}\frac{1}{2}\frac{(2n-5)}{(2n+1)}=\frac{1}{2}$$

18. (a,b) We have,

$$f(x)=\frac{\sqrt{x^2+2}}{3x-6}$$

Now, $\lim_{x\to\infty}f(x)=\lim_{x\to\infty}\frac{\sqrt{x^2+2}}{3x-6}=\lim_{x\to\infty}\frac{x\sqrt{1+\frac{2}{x^2}}}{x\left(3-\frac{6}{x}\right)}=\frac{1}{3}$

and $\lim_{x\to-\infty}f(x)=\lim_{x\to-\infty}\frac{\sqrt{x^2+2}}{3x-6}=\lim_{x\to-\infty}\frac{-x\sqrt{1+\frac{2}{x^2}}}{x\left(3-\frac{6}{x}\right)}=\frac{-1}{3}$

19. (a,b,c,d) We have, $L=\lim_{x\to\infty}\frac{(ax+1)^n}{x^n+A}$

(a) If $n\in N$, then $L=\lim_{x\to\infty}\frac{x^n\left(a+\frac{1}{x}\right)^n}{x^n\left(1+\frac{A}{x^n}\right)}=a^n$

(b) If $n\in Z^-$ and $a=A=0$, then

$$L=\lim_{x\to\infty}\frac{(ax+1)^n}{x^n+A}$$

$$=\lim_{x\to\infty}\frac{1}{x^n}=\infty \qquad [\because n\in(-\infty,0)]$$

(c) If $n=0$, then $L=\lim_{x\to\infty}\frac{(ax+1)^n}{x^n+A}$

$$=\frac{1}{1+A}$$

(d) If $n\in Z^-$, $A=0$ and $a\neq 0$, then

$$L=\lim_{x\to\infty}\frac{(ax+1)^n}{x^n}$$

$$=\lim_{x\to\infty}\left(a+\frac{1}{x}\right)^n=a^n$$

20. (a) $\lim_{x\to 0}\phi(x)=\lim_{x\to 0}\frac{a_0x^m+a_1x^{m+1}+\cdots+a_kx^{m+k}}{b_0x^n+b_1x^{n+1}+\cdots+b_lx^{n+l}}$

$$=\lim_{x\to 0}\frac{x^m(a_0+a_1x+\cdots+a_kx^k)}{x^n(b_0+b_1x+\cdots+b_lx^l)}$$

$$=\lim_{x\to 0}\left(\frac{a_0}{b_0}\right)x^{m-n}$$

$$=\begin{cases}0, & \text{if } m>n\\ \left(\frac{a_0}{b_0}\right), & \text{if } m=n\\ \infty\left(\frac{a_0}{b_0}\right)=\infty, & \text{if } m<n \text{ and } (n-m) \text{ is even, } \frac{a_0}{b_0}>0\\ \infty\left(\frac{a_0}{b_0}\right)=-\infty, & \text{if } m<n \text{ and } (n-m) \text{ is even; } \frac{a_0}{b_0}<0\end{cases}$$

Hence, (i) → (s), (ii) → (r), (iii) → (p), (iv) → (q)

21. (1) We have,

$$f(x)=\sum_{\lambda=1}^{n}\left(x-\frac{1}{\lambda}\right)\left(x-\frac{1}{\lambda+1}\right)$$

$$\therefore f(0)=\sum_{\lambda=1}^{n}\frac{1}{\lambda(\lambda+1)}=\frac{1}{1\times 2}+\frac{1}{2\times 3}+\cdots+\frac{1}{n(n+1)}$$

$$=\left(1-\frac{1}{2}\right)+\left(\frac{1}{2}-\frac{1}{3}\right)+\cdots+\left(\frac{1}{n}-\frac{1}{n+1}\right)$$

$$=1-\frac{1}{n+1}$$

Thus, $\lim_{n\to\infty}f(0)=1$

22. (1) If $\lim_{x\to\infty} f(x) = l$, then

$$\lim_{x\to\infty}\left[f(x) + \frac{3f(x)-1}{f^2(x)}\right] = 3$$

$$\Rightarrow \quad l + \frac{3l-1}{l^2} = 3$$

$$\Rightarrow \quad l^3 + 3l - 1 = 3l^2$$

$$\Rightarrow \quad l^3 - 3l^2 + 3l - 1 = 0$$

$$\Rightarrow \quad (l-1)^3 = 0$$

$$\Rightarrow \quad l = 1$$

$$\therefore \quad \lim_{x\to\infty} f(x) = 1$$

23. (0) Since, $\lim_{x\to 1} f(x) = \lim_{x\to -1} f(x)$

Here, $\lim_{x\to 1} f(x)$ exists.

$$\Rightarrow \quad \lim_{x\to 1^+} f(x) = \lim_{x\to 1^-} f(x)$$

$$\Rightarrow \quad c = b + 1 \qquad \ldots\text{(i)}$$

Also, $\lim_{x\to -1} f(x)$ exists.

$$\Rightarrow \quad \lim_{x\to -1^+} f(x) = \lim_{x\to -1^-} f(x)$$

$$\Rightarrow \quad -b - 1 = a - 1 \qquad \ldots\text{(ii)}$$

From Eqs. (i) and (ii), if both limits are equal, then $b + 1 = 0$

$$\Rightarrow \quad c = 0, 1 - a = 0$$

$$\therefore \quad a = 1, b = -1, c = 0$$

$$\Rightarrow \quad a + b + c = 0$$

24. (2) We have, $P_n = \prod_{r=2}^{n}\left(\frac{r^3-1}{r^3+1}\right)$,

Now, $\lim_{n\to\infty} P_n = \lim_{n\to\infty}\prod_{r=2}^{n}\left(\frac{r^3-1}{r^3+1}\right)$

$$= \lim_{n\to\infty}\left(\frac{2^3-1}{2^3+1}\right)\left(\frac{3^3-1}{3^3+1}\right)\cdots\left(\frac{n^3-1}{n^3+1}\right)$$

$$= \lim_{n\to\infty}\left(\frac{2-1}{2+1}\cdot\frac{2^2+1+2}{2^2+1-2}\right)\left(\frac{3-1}{3+1}\cdot\frac{3^2+1+3}{3^2+1-3}\right)\cdots\left(\frac{n-1}{n+1}\cdot\frac{n^2+1+n}{n^2+1-n}\right)$$

$$= \lim_{n\to\infty}\left(\frac{2-1}{2+1}\cdot\frac{3-1}{3+1}\cdots\frac{n-1}{n+1}\right)\left(\frac{2^2+1+2}{2^2+1-2}\cdot\frac{3^2+1+3}{3^3+1-3}\cdots\frac{n^2+1+n}{n^2+1-n}\right)$$

$$= \lim_{n\to\infty}\left(\frac{1}{3}\cdot\frac{2}{4}\cdot\frac{3}{5}\cdot\frac{4}{6}\cdots\frac{n-2}{n}\cdot\frac{n-1}{n+1}\right)\left(\frac{7}{3}\cdot\frac{13}{7}\cdot\frac{21}{13}\cdots\frac{(n^2+n+1)}{(n^2-n+1)}\right)$$

$$= \lim_{n\to\infty}\left(\frac{1\cdot 2}{n(n+1)}\right)\cdot\left(\frac{n^2+n+1}{3}\right)$$

$$= \lim_{n\to\infty}\frac{2}{3}\cdot\frac{n^2+n+1}{n^2+n} = \frac{2}{3}$$

$$\therefore \quad 3\left(\lim_{n\to\infty} P_n\right) = 2$$

25. (1) $P_n = \frac{1}{n^4}\left[\sum_{r=1}^{n}(2r-1)\cdot\sum_{k=1}^{n-r+1} k\right]$

$$= \frac{1}{n^4}\left[\sum_{r=1}^{n}(2r-1)\cdot\frac{\{(n-r+1)(n-r+2)\}}{2}\right]$$

$$= \frac{1}{2n^4}\left[\sum_{r=1}^{n}(2r-1)\{(n+1)(n+2) - r(2n+3) + r^2\}\right]$$

$$= \frac{1}{2n^4}\left[\sum_{r=1}^{n}(n+1)(n+1)\cdot(2r-1) - \sum_{r=1}^{n}(2n+3)(2r^2-r) + \sum_{r=1}^{n}(2r^3-r^2)\right]$$

$$= \frac{1}{2n^4}\left[(n+1)(n+1)\cdot n^2 - 2(2n+3)\cdot\frac{n(n+1)(2n+1)}{6} - \frac{(2n+3)\cdot n(n+1)}{2} + 2\cdot\frac{n^2(n+1)^2}{4} - \frac{n(n+1)(2n+1)}{6}\right]$$

$$\therefore \quad \lim_{n\to\infty} P_n = \left(\frac{1-\frac{4}{3}+\frac{1}{2}}{2}\right) = \frac{\frac{3}{2}-\frac{4}{3}}{2} = \frac{1}{12}$$

$$\Rightarrow \quad 12\cdot\left(\lim_{n\to\infty} P_n\right) = 1$$

DPP-3 **Exponential, Logarithmic and Trigonometric Forms**

1. (i) $\lim_{x\to\infty}\frac{\sin\alpha x}{\tan\beta x}$

$$= \lim_{x\to 0}\frac{\frac{\sin\alpha x}{\alpha x}\cdot\alpha x}{\frac{\tan\beta x}{\beta x}\cdot\beta x} = \left(\frac{\alpha}{\beta}\right)\frac{\lim_{x\to 0}\frac{\sin\alpha x}{\alpha x}}{\lim_{x\to 0}\frac{\tan\beta x}{\beta x}} = \frac{\alpha}{\beta}$$

(ii) $\lim_{x\to 0}\frac{x^3\cdot\cot x}{1-\cos x} = \lim_{x\to 0}\frac{x^3\cdot\cot x}{2\sin^2 x/2}$

$$= \lim_{x\to 0}\frac{4x\cot x}{2\,\frac{\sin\frac{x}{2}}{\frac{x}{2}}\cdot\frac{\sin\frac{x}{2}}{\frac{x}{2}}}$$

$$= \lim_{x\to 0}\frac{4\cdot\cos x\,\frac{x}{\sin x}}{2\,\frac{\sin\frac{x}{2}}{\frac{x}{2}}\,\frac{\sin\frac{x}{2}}{\frac{x}{2}}}$$

$$= 2\cos 0 = 2$$

(iii) $\lim_{n\to\infty}\frac{\sin\frac{a}{n}}{\tan\left(\frac{b}{n+1}\right)} = \lim_{n\to\infty}\frac{\frac{\sin\frac{a}{n}}{\left(\frac{a}{n}\right)}\cdot\left(\frac{a}{n}\right)}{\frac{\tan\left(\frac{b}{n+1}\right)}{\left(\frac{b}{n+1}\right)}\cdot\left(\frac{b}{n+1}\right)}$

$$= \lim_{n\to\infty}\frac{\frac{a}{n}}{\frac{b}{(n+1)}} = \lim_{n\to 0}\frac{a}{\frac{b}{\left(1+\frac{1}{n}\right)}} = \frac{a}{b}$$

(iv) $\lim_{h\to 0}\frac{(a+h)^2\sin(a+h) - a^2\sin a}{h}$

It is an indeterminate $\left(\frac{0}{0}\right)$ form.

On applying L' Hospital's rule, we get

$$\lim_{h\to 0} 2(a+h)\sin(a+h) + \cos(a+h)(a+h)^2 - 0$$

$$= 2a\sin a + a^2\cos a$$

2. (i) $\lim_{x \to a} \frac{e^x - e^a}{x - a}$

It is an indeterminate $\left(\frac{0}{0}\right)$ form.

$\therefore \quad = \lim_{x \to a} \frac{e^x - 0}{1 - 0} = \lim_{x \to a} e^x = e^a$

(ii) $\lim_{x \to 0} \frac{2^x - 1}{\sqrt{1 + x} - 1}$

It is an indeterminate $\left(\frac{0}{0}\right)$ form.

$\therefore \lim_{x \to 0} \frac{2^x \log 2 - 0}{\frac{1}{2\sqrt{1+x}} - 0} = \frac{2^0 \log 2}{\frac{1}{2}} = 2\log 2$

(iii) $\lim_{x \to 0} \frac{e^{\tan x} - e^x}{\tan x - x}$

It is an indeterminate $\left(\frac{0}{0}\right)$ form.

$\therefore \lim_{x \to 0} \frac{e^x [e^{\tan x - x} - 1]}{\tan x - x}$

$= \lim_{x \to 0} e^x \cdot \lim_{x \to 0} \left[\frac{e^{\tan x - x} - 1}{\tan x - x}\right]$

$= e^0 \cdot 1 = 1$

3. (i) $\lim_{x \to e} \frac{\log_e x - 1}{x - 1}$

It is an indeterminate $\left(\frac{0}{0}\right)$ form.

So, applying L' Hospital's rule, we get

$= \lim_{x \to e} \frac{\frac{1}{x} - 1}{1 - 0} = \frac{1}{e} - 1$

(ii) $\lim_{x \to 0} \frac{\log_e(5 + x) - \log_e(5 - x)}{x}$

It is an indeterminate $\left(\frac{0}{0}\right)$ form.

So, applying L' Hospital's rule, we get

$\lim_{x \to 0} \frac{1}{5 + x}(1) - \frac{1}{(5 - x)}(-1)$

$= \lim_{x \to 0} \cdot \frac{1}{5 + x} + \frac{1}{5 - x}$

$= \frac{1}{5} + \frac{1}{5} = \frac{2}{5}$

(iii) $\lim_{x \to 0} \frac{a^{\tan x} - a^{\sin x}}{x^3}$

$= \lim_{x \to 0} \frac{1}{x^3} a^{\sin x} [a^{\tan x - \sin x} - 1]$

$= \lim_{x \to 0} \frac{1}{x^3} a^{\sin x} \left[\frac{a^{\tan x - \sin x} - 1}{(\tan x - \sin x)}\right] (\tan x - \sin x)$

$= \lim_{x \to 0} \frac{1}{x^3} a^{\sin x} (\tan x - \sin x) \cdot \lim_{x \to 0} \frac{[a^{\tan x - \sin x} - 1]}{(\tan x - \sin x)}$

$= \lim_{x \to 0} \frac{1}{x^3} a^{\sin x} (\tan x - \sin x) \log_e a$

$= \lim_{x \to 0} \frac{\sin x(1 - \cos x)}{x^3} a^{\sin x} \log_e a$

$= \lim_{x \to 0} \left(\frac{\sin x}{x}\right) \lim_{x \to 0} \frac{2\sin^2 x/2}{(x/2)^2 \cdot 4} \lim_{x \to 0} a^{\sin x} (\log_e a)$

$= \frac{1}{2} \log_e a$

(iv) $\lim_{x \to 2} \frac{(x - 2)}{\log_a(x - 1)}$

$= \lim_{x \to 2} \frac{1}{\frac{1}{(x - 1)} \log_e a}$ [using L' Hospital's rule]

$= \log_e a$

(v) $\lim_{x \to \frac{\pi}{2}} \frac{2^{-\cos x} - 1}{x\left(x - \frac{\pi}{2}\right)}$

$= \lim_{x \to \frac{\pi}{2}} \frac{2^{-\cos x} \sin x \log_e 2}{\left(x - \frac{\pi}{2}\right) + x}$ [using L' Hospital's rule]

$= \lim_{x \to \frac{\pi}{2}} \frac{2^{-\cos x} \sin x \log_e 2}{2\pi - \frac{\pi}{2}} = \frac{2}{\pi} \log_e 2$

(vi) $\lim_{x \to 0} \frac{27^x - 9^x - 3^x + 1}{\sqrt{2} - \sqrt{1 + \cos x}}$

$= \lim_{x \to 0} \frac{9^x \cdot 3^x - 9^x - 3^x + 1}{\sqrt{2} - \sqrt{2} \cos \frac{x}{2}}$

$= \lim_{x \to 0} \frac{(9^x - 1)(3^x - 1)}{\sqrt{2}\left[1 - \cos \frac{x}{2}\right]}$

$= \lim_{x \to 0} \left(\frac{9^x - 1}{x}\right)\left(\frac{3^x - 1}{x}\right) \cdot \frac{1}{\sqrt{2}} x^2 \cdot \frac{1}{2\sin^2 \frac{x}{4}}$

$= \lim_{x \to 0} \left(\frac{9^x - 1}{x}\right)\left(\frac{3^x - 1}{x}\right) \cdot \frac{1}{\sqrt{2}} \left(\frac{\frac{x^2}{16}}{\sin^2 \frac{x}{4}}\right) 8$

$\frac{8}{\sqrt{2}} (\log 9)(\log 3) = 8\sqrt{2} (\log 3)^2$

4. (i) $\lim_{x \to 0} \frac{1 - \cos^3 x}{x \sin 2x}$

$= \lim_{x \to 0} \frac{(1 - \cos x)(1 + \cos^2 x + \cos x)}{2x \sin x \cos x}$

$= \lim_{x \to 0} \frac{(1 + \cos^2 x + \cos x)}{2\cos x} \cdot \lim_{x \to 0} \left(\frac{1 - \cos x}{x \sin x}\right)$

$= \frac{3}{2} \lim_{x \to 0} \frac{2\sin^2 \frac{x}{2}}{x \cdot 2\sin \frac{x}{2} \cos \frac{x}{2}} = \frac{3}{2} \lim_{x \to 0} \frac{\tan \frac{x}{2}}{\frac{x}{2} \cdot 2} = \frac{3}{4}$

(ii) $\lim_{x \to 0} \frac{1 + \sin x - \cos x}{1 - \sin x - \cos x}$

It is an indeterminate $\left(\frac{0}{0}\right)$ form.

$\lim_{x \to 0} \frac{0 + \cos x - (-\sin x)}{0 - \cos x - (-\sin x)}$ [using L' Hospital's rule]

$= \lim_{x \to 0} \frac{\cos x + \sin x}{-\cos x + \sin x} = \frac{1 + 0}{-1 + 0} = -1$

(iii) $\lim_{x \to 0} \left(\frac{1}{\sin x} - \frac{1}{\tan x}\right)$

$= \lim_{x \to 0} \left(\frac{1}{\sin x} - \frac{\cos x}{\sin x}\right)$

$= \lim_{x \to 0} \frac{(1 - \cos x)}{\sin x}$

$= \lim_{x \to 0} \frac{0 - (-\sin x)}{\cos x}$ [using L' Hospital's rule]

$= \lim_{x \to 0} \frac{\sin x}{\cos x} = 0$

(iv) $\lim_{x \to 0} \frac{\cos \alpha x - \cos \beta x}{x^2}$

$= \lim_{x \to 0} \frac{-\alpha \sin \alpha x + \beta \sin \beta x}{2x}$ [using L' Hospital's rule]

$= \lim_{x \to 0} \frac{-\alpha^2 \cos \alpha x + \beta^2 \cos \beta x}{2} = \frac{\beta^2 - \alpha^2}{2}$

(v) $\lim_{x \to 0} \frac{2x - \sin^{-1} x}{2x + \tan^{-1} x}$

It is an indeterminate $\left(\frac{0}{0}\right)$ form.

$\therefore \quad \lim_{x \to 0} \frac{2 - \frac{1}{\sqrt{1 - x^2}}}{2 + \frac{1}{1 + x^2}} = \lim_{x \to 0} \frac{2 - \frac{1}{\sqrt{1 - x^2}}}{2 + \frac{1}{1 + x^2}}$

$= \frac{2 - \frac{1}{\sqrt{1}}}{2 + \frac{1}{1}} = \frac{2 - 1}{2 + 1} = \frac{1}{3}$

(vi) $\lim_{x \to 0} \frac{\tan 3x - 2x}{3x - \sin^2 x}$

It is an indeterminate $\left(\frac{0}{0}\right)$ form.

$\lim_{x \to 0} \frac{\sec^2 3x \cdot 3 - 2}{3 - 2 \sin x \cos x}$

$= \lim_{x \to 0} \frac{3 \sec^2 3x - 2}{3 - 2 \sin x \cos x} = \frac{3 - 2}{3 - 2\,(0)} = \frac{1}{3}$

(vii) $\lim_{\alpha \to 0} \frac{\tan \alpha - \sin \alpha}{\alpha^3}$

$= \lim_{\alpha \to 0} \frac{1}{\alpha^3} \left(\frac{\sin \alpha}{\cos \alpha} - \sin \alpha\right) = \lim_{\alpha \to 0} \frac{\sin \alpha}{\alpha^3} \left(\frac{1 - \cos \alpha}{\cos \alpha}\right)$

$= \lim_{\alpha \to 0} \frac{\sin \alpha}{\alpha} \cdot \lim_{\alpha \to 0} \frac{2 \sin^2 \frac{\alpha}{2}}{\left(\frac{\alpha}{2}\right)^2 \cdot 4} \cdot \lim_{\alpha \to 0} \frac{1}{\cos \alpha} = 1 \cdot \frac{2}{4} \cdot \frac{1}{1} = \frac{1}{2}$

(viii) $\lim_{y \to 0} \frac{(x + y) \sec (x + y) - x \sec x}{y}$

It is an indeterminate $\left(\frac{0}{0}\right)$ form.

$\lim_{y \to 0} \frac{(0 + 1) \sec (x + y) + [\sec (x + y) \tan (x + y)]\,(x + y) - 0}{1}$

[using L' Hospital's rule]

$= \lim_{y \to 0} \sec (x + y) + (x + y)\,[\sec (x + y) \tan (x + y)]$

$= \sec x + x \sec x \tan x$

$= \sec x\,(1 + x \tan x)$

5. (i) $\lim_{x \to \frac{\pi}{2}} \frac{\cos 3x + 3 \cos x}{\left(\frac{\pi}{2} - x\right)^3}$

$= \lim_{x \to \frac{\pi}{2}} \frac{4 \cos^3 x - 3 \cos x + 3 \cos x}{\left(\frac{\pi}{2} - x\right)^3} = \lim_{x \to \frac{\pi}{2}} \frac{4 \cos^3 x}{\left(\frac{\pi}{2} - x\right)^3}$

$= \lim_{x \to \frac{\pi}{2}} \frac{12 \cos^2 x (-\sin x)}{3 \left(\frac{\pi}{2} - x\right)^2 (-1)}$

$= \lim_{x \to \frac{\pi}{2}} \frac{12\,[2 \cos x\,(\sin^2 x) + \cos^2 x (-\cos x)]}{6 \left(\frac{\pi}{2} - x\right)(-1)}$

$= \lim_{x \to \frac{\pi}{2}} \frac{12}{6} \left[\frac{2 (-\sin^3 x) + 2 (2 \sin x \cos^2 x) + 3 \cos^2 x \sin x}{(0 - 1)\,(-1)}\right]$

$= 2\,[2 (-1)^3 + 0 + 0] = -4$

(ii) $\lim_{x \to \frac{\pi}{6}} \frac{\sin\left(x - \frac{\pi}{6}\right)}{\left(\frac{\sqrt{3}}{2} - \cos x\right)}$

$= \lim_{x \to \frac{\pi}{6}} \frac{\left(x - \frac{\pi}{6}\right)(1)}{0 - \sin x} = \lim_{x \to \frac{\pi}{6}} - \frac{\cos\left(x - \frac{\pi}{6}\right)}{\sin x}$

$= \frac{-\cos 0}{\sin \frac{\pi}{6}} = \frac{-1}{\frac{1}{2}} = -2$

(iii) $\lim_{x \to \pi} \frac{\sin x}{1 - \frac{x^2}{\pi^2}} = \lim_{x \to \pi} \frac{\cos x}{\frac{-2x}{\pi^2}}$

$= \frac{-1 \times \pi^2}{-2\pi} = \frac{\pi}{2}$

(iv) $\lim_{x \to \frac{\pi}{4}} \frac{\sqrt{2} - \cos x - \sin x}{(4x - \pi)^2}$

$= \lim_{x \to \frac{\pi}{4}} \frac{0 - (-\sin x) - \cos x}{2\,(4x - \pi) \cdot 4}$

$= \lim_{x \to \frac{\pi}{4}} \frac{\cos x + \sin x}{8[4 - 0]} = \frac{1}{32} \left[\frac{1}{\sqrt{2}} + \frac{1}{\sqrt{2}}\right]$

$= \frac{2}{\sqrt{2}} \cdot \frac{2}{32} = \frac{1}{16\sqrt{2}}$

6. (b) $\lim_{x \to 0} \frac{\cos^{-1}(1 - x)}{\sqrt{x}}$

$= \lim_{x \to 0} \frac{-\frac{1}{\sqrt{1 - (1 - x)^2}}(0 - 1)}{\frac{1}{2\sqrt{x}}}$ [using L' Hospital's rule]

$= \lim_{x \to 0} \frac{\frac{1}{\sqrt{1 - 1 - x^2 + 2x}}}{\frac{1}{2\sqrt{x}}}$

$= \lim_{x \to 0} \frac{2\sqrt{x}}{\sqrt{2x - x^2}} = \lim_{x \to 0} \frac{2}{\sqrt{2 - x}} = \frac{2}{\sqrt{2}} = \sqrt{2}$

7. (d) $\lim_{x \to 0} \frac{\sin\,[\log_e (1 + x)]}{\log (1 + \sin x)}$

It is an indeterminate $\left(\frac{0}{0}\right)$ form.

$= \lim_{x \to 0} \frac{\cos [\log_e (1 + x)] \cdot \frac{1}{(1 + x)} \cdot (1)}{\frac{1}{(1 + \sin x)} (0 + \cos x)}$ [using L' Hospital's rule]

$= \frac{\cos (\log_e 1) \cdot (1)}{1 \cdot \cos 0} = \frac{\cos 0}{\cos 0} = \frac{1}{1} = 1$

8. (b) $\lim_{x \to 0} \frac{(4^x - 1)^3}{\sin\left(\frac{x}{p}\right) \cdot \log\left(1 + \frac{x^2}{3}\right)}$

It is an indeterminate $\left(\frac{0}{0}\right)$ form.

$= \frac{\lim_{x \to 0} \left(\frac{4^x - 1}{x}\right)^3 \cdot x^3}{\lim_{x \to 0} \frac{\sin\left(\frac{x}{p}\right)}{\left(\frac{x}{p}\right)} \cdot \left(\frac{x}{p}\right) \cdot \lim_{x \to 0} \frac{\log\left(1 + \frac{x^2}{3}\right)}{\frac{x^2}{3}} \cdot \left(\frac{x^2}{3}\right)}$

$= \lim_{x \to 0} \frac{x^3 (\log_e 4)^3}{\frac{x^3}{3p}} = 3p\,(\log_e 4)^3$

9. (a) $\lim_{x \to 0} \dfrac{\sin(6x^2)}{\log_e[\cos(2x^2 - x)]}$

$$= \lim_{x \to 0} \frac{\cos(6x^2)\cdot 12x}{\dfrac{1}{\cos(2x^2 - x)}[-\sin(2x^2 - x)]\cdot(4x - 1)}$$

$$= \lim_{x \to 0} \frac{12\,[x\cos(6x^2)]}{\dfrac{\sin(2x^2 - x)}{\cos(2x^2 - x)}(1 - 4x)}$$

$$= \lim_{x \to 0} \frac{12x\cos(6x^2)}{\dfrac{\sin(2x^2 - x)}{(2x^2 - x)}\cdot\dfrac{(2x^2 - x)}{\cos(2x^2 - x)}(1 - 4x)}$$

$$= \lim_{x \to 0} \frac{12\cos 6x^2}{\dfrac{(2x - 1)}{\cos(2x^2 - x)}(1 - 4x)} = 12$$

10. (c) We have, $\lim_{y \to \infty} \dfrac{x^3\cdot\sin\left(\dfrac{1}{x}\right) + x + 1}{x^2 + x + 1}$ Put $\dfrac{1}{x} = y$

$$\Rightarrow \lim_{y \to 0} \frac{\dfrac{1}{y^3}\cdot\sin(y) + \dfrac{1}{y} + 1}{\dfrac{1}{y^2} + \dfrac{1}{y} + 1} = \lim_{x \to 0} \frac{\dfrac{1}{y^2}\left[\dfrac{\sin y}{y} + y + y^2\right]}{\dfrac{1}{y^2}\left[1 + y + y^2\right]}$$

$$= \lim_{y \to 0} \frac{\dfrac{\sin y}{y} + y + y^2}{1 + y + y^2} = 1$$

11. (b) $\lim_{n \to \infty} n\cos\left(\dfrac{\pi}{4n}\right)\cdot\sin\left(\dfrac{\pi}{4n}\right)$

$$= \lim_{n \to \infty} n\cos\left(\frac{\pi}{4n}\right)\left[\frac{\sin\left(\dfrac{\pi}{4n}\right)}{\left(\dfrac{\pi}{4n}\right)}\right]\cdot\frac{\pi}{4n}$$

$$= \lim_{n \to \infty} n\cos\left(\frac{\pi}{4\pi}\right)\cdot\left(\frac{\pi}{4n}\right)\lim_{n \to \infty}\frac{\sin\left(\dfrac{\pi}{4n}\right)}{\left(\dfrac{\pi}{4n}\right)}$$

$$= \lim_{n \to \infty} \frac{\pi}{4}\cos\left(\frac{\pi}{4n}\right) = \frac{\pi}{4}$$

12. (a) $\lim_{x \to \alpha} \dfrac{1 - \cos(ax^2 + bx + c)}{(x - \alpha)^2}$

As α and β are two distinct roots.

$\therefore \quad ax^2 + bx + c = a(x - \alpha)(x - \beta)$

i.e. $\quad \alpha, \beta = \dfrac{-b \pm \sqrt{b^2 - 4ac}}{2a}$

$$= \lim_{x \to \alpha} \frac{1 - \cos[(x - \alpha)(x - \beta)a]}{(x - \alpha)^2}$$

$$= \lim_{x \to \alpha} \frac{2\sin^2\dfrac{[(x - \alpha)(x - \beta)a]}{2}}{(x - \alpha)^2}$$

$$= \lim_{x \to \alpha} \frac{2\sin^2\dfrac{[(x - \alpha)(x - \beta)a]}{2}}{\left[\dfrac{(x - \alpha)(x - \beta)a}{2}\right]^2} a^2\left(\frac{x - \beta}{4}\right)^2$$

$$= \lim_{x \to \alpha} \frac{2}{4}a^2(x - \beta)^2$$

$$= \frac{a^2}{2}(\alpha - \beta)^2$$

13. (d) $\lim_{x \to 0} \dfrac{(1 - \cos 2x)(3 + \cos x)}{x\tan 4x}$

$$= \lim_{x \to 0}\left[\frac{[1 - (1 - 2\sin^2 x)](3 + \cos x)}{x\tan 4x}\right]$$

$$= \lim_{x \to 0} \frac{(2\sin^2 x)(3 + \cos x)}{x\left(\dfrac{\tan 4x}{4x}\right)\cdot 4x} = \lim_{x \to 0} \frac{2\left(\dfrac{\sin x}{x}\right)^2(3 + \cos x)}{4\left(\dfrac{\tan 4x}{4x}\right)}$$

$$= \frac{2}{4}\,\frac{\lim_{x \to 0}\left(\dfrac{\sin x}{x}\right)^2\cdot\lim_{x \to 0}(3 + \cos x)}{\lim_{x \to 0}\dfrac{\tan 4x}{4x}} = \frac{2}{4}\cdot 4 = 2$$

14. (d) Given, $\quad \lim_{x \to 0} \dfrac{[(a - n)nx - \tan x]\sin nx}{x^2} = 0$

$$\Rightarrow \quad \lim_{x \to 0} \frac{[(a - n)nx - \tan x]}{x}\cdot\lim_{x \to 0}\left(\frac{\sin nx}{nx}\right)\cdot n = 0$$

$$\Rightarrow \quad \lim_{x \to 0}\left[\frac{(a - n)nx - \tan x}{x}\right]n = 0$$

$$\Rightarrow \quad n\cdot\lim_{x \to 0}\left(\frac{anx - n^2x - \tan x}{x}\right) = 0$$

$$\Rightarrow \quad \lim_{x \to 0} n\cdot(an - n^2 - \sec^2 x) = 0$$

$$\Rightarrow \quad n(an - n^2 - 1) = 0$$

$$\Rightarrow \quad an^2 - n^3 - n = 0$$

$$\Rightarrow \quad n^2a = n^3 + n$$

$$\therefore \quad a = n + \frac{1}{n}$$

15. (b) $\lim_{x \to 0} \dfrac{\sin(\pi\cos^2 x)}{x^2}$

$$= \lim_{x \to 0} \frac{\cos(\pi\cos^2 x)\cdot\pi[2\cos x(-\sin x)]}{2x}$$

$$= \lim_{x \to 0}\cos(\pi\cos^2 x)\cdot(-\pi)\lim_{x \to 0}\left(\frac{\sin x}{x}\right)\lim_{x \to 0}\cos x$$

$$= (\cos\pi)(-\pi)\cdot 1\cdot 1$$

$$= (-1)(-\pi) = \pi$$

16. (c) $\lim_{x \to 0} \dfrac{x\tan 2x - 2x\tan x}{(1 - \cos 2x)^2}$

$$= \lim_{x \to 0} \frac{\left[x\left(\dfrac{2\tan x}{1 - \tan^2 x}\right) - 2x\tan x\right]}{(2\sin^2 x)^2} = \lim_{x \to 0} \frac{2x\tan x\left(\dfrac{\tan^2 x}{1 - \tan^2 x}\right)}{4\sin^4 x}$$

$$= \lim_{x \to 0} \frac{2x\dfrac{\tan^3 x}{1 - \tan^2 x}}{4\left(\dfrac{\sin x}{x}\right)^4\cdot x^4} = \lim_{x \to 0} \frac{2x\tan^3 x}{4x^4\left(\dfrac{\sin x}{x}\right)^4}$$

$$= \lim_{x \to 0} \frac{2\left(\dfrac{\tan x}{x}\right)^3}{4\left(\dfrac{\sin x}{x}\right)^4} = \frac{2}{4}\,\frac{\lim_{x \to 0}\left(\dfrac{\tan x}{x}\right)^3}{\lim_{x \to 0}\left(\dfrac{\sin x}{x}\right)^4} = \frac{2}{4} = \frac{1}{2}$$

17. (a,d) $I = \lim_{x \to 0} \dfrac{x(1 + a\cos x) - b\sin x}{x^3}$

$$= \lim_{x \to 0} \frac{(1 + a\cos x)}{x^3} - \lim_{x \to 0} \frac{b\sin x}{x^3}$$

$$= \underset{\text{I}}{\lim_{x \to 0} \frac{1 + a\cos x}{x^2}} - \underset{\text{II}}{\lim_{x \to 0} \frac{b\sin x}{x^3}}$$

I exists only when $a = -1$ and II exists only when $b = 0$

i.e. $(a, b) = (-1, 0)$.

$$\therefore \quad I = \lim_{x \to 0} \frac{1 - \cos x}{x^2} = \lim_{x \to 0} \frac{2\sin^2\dfrac{x}{2}}{x^2} = \lim_{x \to 0} \frac{2\sin^2\dfrac{x}{2}}{\left(\dfrac{x}{2}\right)^2\cdot 4}$$

$$= \frac{2}{4}\lim_{x \to 0}\left[\frac{\sin\dfrac{x}{2}}{\dfrac{x}{2}}\right]^2 = \frac{1}{2}$$

18. (a,d) $\lim_{x \to 0} \frac{\sin 2x + a\sin x}{x^3} = p$

$$= \lim_{x \to 0} \frac{2\cos 2x + a\cos x}{3x^2} \quad \text{[using L' Hospital's rule]}$$

We require $2\cos 2x + a\cos x = 0, \forall x = 0$ as denominator is zero.

$\therefore \quad a = -2$

Now, $$p = \lim_{x \to 0} \frac{2\cos 2x - 2\cos x}{3x^2}$$

$$= \lim_{x \to 0} \frac{-4\sin 2x + 2\sin x}{6x}$$

$$= \lim_{x \to 0} \frac{-8\cos 2x + 2\cos x}{6}$$

$$= -1$$

Explanations for Q. Nos. (19 -21)

Here, $f(x) = \frac{\sin x + ae^x + be^{-x} + c\log(1+x)}{x^3}$

If $\lim_{x \to 0^+} f(x)$ is finite.

$\Rightarrow \quad \lim_{x \to 0^+} \frac{\sin x + ae^x + be^{-x} + c\log(1+x)}{x^3}$,

For this to be $\left(\frac{0}{0}\right)$ form,

$$a + b = 0 \quad \text{...(i)}$$

By using L' Hospital's rule, we get

$$\Rightarrow \lim_{x \to 0^+} \frac{\cos x + ae^x - be^{-x} + \frac{c}{1+x}}{3x^2}$$

Again, for $\left(\frac{0}{0}\right)$ form $\Rightarrow 1 + a - b + c = 0$ ...(ii)

Again, by using L' Hospital's rule, we get

$$\Rightarrow \lim_{x \to 0^+} \frac{-\sin x + ae^x + be^{-x} - \frac{c}{(1+x)^2}}{6x}$$

Again, for $\left(\frac{0}{0}\right)$ form, $a + b - c = 0$ ...(iii)

Again, using L' Hospital's rule, we get

$$\Rightarrow \lim_{x \to 0^+} \frac{-\cos x + ae^x - be^{-x} + \frac{2c}{(1+x)^3}}{6} = \frac{-1 + a - b + 2c}{6} \quad \text{...(iv)}$$

From Eqs. (i), (ii) and (iii), we get

$$c = 0, a + b = 0 \text{ and } a - b = -1$$

$\Rightarrow \quad c = 0, a = -1/2, b = 1/2$

$\therefore \quad (a + b + c) = 0$

Also, if $\lim_{x \to 0^+} f(x) = l$

$$\Rightarrow l = \frac{-1 + a - b + 2c}{6} = \frac{-1 - \frac{1}{2} - \frac{1}{2} + 0}{6} = \frac{-1}{3}$$

$\therefore \quad l = -\frac{1}{3}$

Also, $$\lim_{x \to 0^+} xf(x) = \lim_{x \to 0^+} \frac{x \cdot [\sin x + ae^x + be^{-x} + c\log(1+x)]}{x^3}$$

$$= \lim_{x \to 0^+} \frac{[\sin x + ae^x + be^{-x} + c\log(1+x)]}{x^2}$$

$$= \lim_{x \to 0^+} \frac{\left(\cos x + ae^x - be^{-x} + \frac{c}{1+x}\right)}{2x},$$

[by L' Hospital's rule]

$$= \lim_{x \to 0^+} \frac{-\sin x + ae^x + be^{-x} - \frac{c}{(1+x^2)}}{2}, \quad \text{[by L' Hospital's rule]}$$

$$= \left(\frac{a + b - c}{2}\right) = 0$$

19. (a)

20. (d)

21. (a)

22. (3) Given, $f(x) = \frac{2\sqrt{2} - (\cos x + \sin x)^3}{1 - \sin 2x}$

Now, $$\lim_{x \to \frac{\pi}{4}} f(x) = \lim_{x \to \frac{\pi}{4}} \frac{2\sqrt{2} - (\cos x + \sin x)^3}{1 - \sin 2x} \quad \left[\frac{0}{0}\text{form}\right]$$

$$= \lim_{x \to \frac{\pi}{4}} \frac{-3(\cos x + \sin x)^2 (-\sin x + \cos x)}{-2\cos 2x}$$

$$= \lim_{x \to \frac{\pi}{4}} \frac{-3(\cos x + \sin x)(\cos^2 x - \sin^2 x)}{-2\cos 2x}$$

$$= \lim_{x \to \frac{\pi}{4}} \frac{-3(\cos x + \sin x)\cos 2x}{-2\cos 2x}$$

$$= \lim_{x \to \frac{\pi}{4}} \frac{3(\cos x + \sin x)}{2}$$

$$= \frac{3}{2} \cdot \left(\frac{1}{\sqrt{2}} + \frac{1}{\sqrt{2}}\right)$$

$$= \frac{3}{\sqrt{2}}$$

Then, $\sqrt{2} \times \lim_{x \to \frac{\pi}{4}} f(x) = \sqrt{2} \cdot \frac{3}{\sqrt{2}} = 3$

23. (3) Given, $\lim_{x \to 0} \frac{\sin 3x + ax + bx^3}{x^3} = 0$

By using L' Hospital's rule, we get

$$\lim_{x \to 0} \frac{3\cos 3x + a + 3bx^2}{3x^2} = 0 \quad \left[\frac{0}{0}\text{ form}\right]$$

$\therefore \quad 3 + a = 0$

Again, using L' Hospital's rule, we get

$$\Rightarrow \lim_{x \to 0} \frac{-9\sin 3x + 6bx}{6x} = 0$$

$$\Rightarrow \lim_{x \to 0} \left(-\frac{9}{2} \cdot \frac{\sin 3x}{3x} + b\right) = 0$$

$$\Rightarrow -\frac{9}{2} + b = 0$$

$\therefore \quad b = \frac{9}{2}$ and $a = -3$

$\Rightarrow \quad |2(a + b)| = 3$

24. (1) Let $y = \sqrt{(1 - \cos x) + \sqrt{(1 - \cos x) + \sqrt{(1 - \cos x) + \cdots \infty}}}$

$\Rightarrow \quad y = \sqrt{(1 - \cos x) + y}$

On solving, we get $y = \frac{1 + \sqrt{1 + 4(1 - \cos x)}}{2}$

$$\therefore \lim_{x \to 0} \frac{f(x)}{x^2} = \lim_{x \to 0} \frac{\frac{1 + \sqrt{1 + 4(1 - \cos x)}}{2} - 1}{x^2}$$

$$= \lim_{x \to 0} \frac{\sqrt{1 + 4(1 - \cos x)} - 1}{2x^2}$$

$$= \lim_{x \to 0} \frac{1 + 4(1 - \cos x) - 1}{2x^2[\sqrt{1 + 4(1 - \cos x)} + 1]}$$

$$= \lim_{x \to 0} \frac{4 \cdot 2\sin^2 x/2}{2 \cdot 4x^2/4 \cdot [\sqrt{1 + 4(1 - \cos x)} + 1]}$$

$$= 1 \cdot 1 \cdot \frac{1}{2} = \frac{1}{2}$$

$$\therefore \quad 2\left[\lim_{x \to 0} \frac{f(x)}{x^2}\right] = 1$$

DPP-4 Problems Based on $(1)^\infty$ and $(\infty)^0$ Forms

1. (i) Let $f(x)=\lim_{x\to\infty}\left(1+\frac{2}{x}\right)^x$ [1^∞ form]

$\Rightarrow f(x)=\lim_{x\to 0}(1+x)^{2/x}$

On taking log both sides, we get

$$\log f(x)=\lim_{x\to 0}\frac{2}{x}\log(1+x)=\lim_{x\to 0}2\left[\frac{\log(1+x)}{x}\right]=2\lim_{x\to 0}\left[\frac{\log(1+x)}{x}\right]$$

$\Rightarrow \log f(x)=2$

$\therefore f(x)=e^2$

(ii) Let $f(x)=\lim_{x\to 0}(1+\sin x)^{2\cot x}$

$\Rightarrow f(x)=\lim_{x\to 0}(1+\sin x)^{\frac{2\cos x}{\sin x}}$

On taking log both sides, we get

$$\log f(x)=\lim_{x\to 0}\frac{2\cos x}{\sin x}\log(1+\sin x)=2\lim_{x\to 0}\cos x\lim_{x\to 0}\log\frac{(1+\sin x)}{\sin x}$$

$\Rightarrow \log f(x)=2$

$\therefore f(x)=e^2$

(iii) Let $f(x)=\lim_{x\to 1}(\log_3 3x)^{\log_x 3}$

$$=\lim_{x\to 1}(\log_3 3+\log_3 x)^{\log_x 3}=\lim_{x\to 1}(1+\log_3 x)^{\log_x 3}=e^{\lim_{x\to 1}\log_x 3\cdot\log_3 x}=e^1=e$$

(iv) $\lim_{x\to 0}(\cos x)^{\cot x}=\lim_{x\to 0}[1+(\cos x-1)]^{\cot x}$

$$=e^{\lim_{x\to 0}(\cos x-1)\cdot\cot x}=e^{\lim_{x\to 0}\frac{-2\sin^2 x/2}{\tan x}}=e^{\lim_{x\to 0}\frac{-2\sin^2 x/2}{x^2/4}\cdot\frac{x^2/4}{x}\cdot\frac{x}{\tan x}}=e^0=1$$

2. (a) $\lim_{x\to\infty}\left(\frac{x^2-2x+1}{x^2-4x+2}\right)^x$

$$=\lim_{x\to\infty}\left(1+\frac{2x-1}{x^2-4x+2}\right)^x=e^{\lim_{x\to\infty}\frac{(2x-1)x}{(x^2-4x+2)}}=e^{\lim_{x\to\infty}\frac{x^2\left[2-\frac{1}{x}\right]}{x^2\left[1-\frac{4}{x}+\frac{2}{x^2}\right]}}=e^2$$

3. (c) $\lim_{x\to 0}(\cos x+a\sin bx)^{1/x}$

$$=e^{\lim_{x\to 0}\frac{1}{x}(\cos x+a\sin bx-1)}$$

$$=e^{\lim_{x\to 0}(-\sin x+ab\cos bx)}\quad\left[\begin{array}{l}\text{using,}\\ \lim_{x\to a}[f(x)]^{\phi(x)}=e^{\lim_{x\to a}\phi(x)[f(x)-1]}\\ \text{as } f(x)\to 1 \text{ and } \phi(x)\to\infty \text{ as } x\to a\end{array}\right]$$

$$=e^{ab}$$

4. (d) $\lim_{x\to 0}\left[\tan\left(\frac{\pi}{4}+x\right)\right]^{1/x}$

$$=\lim_{x\to 0}\left[\frac{1+\tan x}{1-\tan x}\right]^{1/x}=e^{\lim_{x\to 0}\frac{1}{x}\left[\frac{1+\tan x}{1-\tan x}-1\right]}$$

$$=e^{\lim_{x\to 0}\frac{2\tan x}{x(1-\tan x)}}=e^{\lim_{x\to 0}2\left(\frac{\tan x}{x}\right)\left(\frac{1}{1-\tan x}\right)}=e^2$$

5. (b) $\lim_{x\to\infty}\left(\frac{3x-4}{3x+2}\right)^{\frac{x+1}{3}}$

$$=\lim_{x\to\infty}\left[1-\frac{6}{3x+2}\right]^{\frac{x+1}{3}}=e^{\lim_{x\to\infty}\frac{-6(x+1)}{3(3x+2)}}$$

$$=e^{\lim_{x\to\infty}\frac{-2(x+1)}{(3x+2)}}=e^{\lim_{x\to\infty}\frac{-2}{3}\frac{\left(1+\frac{1}{x}\right)}{\left(1+\frac{2}{3x}\right)}}=e^{-\frac{2}{3}}$$

6. (a) $\lim_{x\to\infty}\left(1+\frac{1}{a+bx}\right)^{c+dx}$

$$=e^{\lim_{x\to\infty}\left(\frac{c+dx}{a+bx}\right)}=e^{\lim_{x\to\infty}\frac{d}{b}\left[\frac{1+\frac{c}{dx}}{1+\frac{a}{bx}}\right]}=e^{\frac{d}{b}}$$

7. (b) $\lim_{x\to 0}\left\{1+\frac{2}{x^3}(\tan x-\sin x)-1\right\}^{2/x^2}$

$$=e^{\lim_{x\to 0}\frac{[2(\tan x-\sin x)-x^3]\cdot 2}{x^5}}$$

$$=e^{\lim_{x\to 0}\frac{2\left[2\left\{\left(x-\frac{x^3}{3}+\frac{2x^5}{15}-\cdots\right)-\left(x-\frac{x^3}{3!}+\frac{x^5}{5!}\cdots-x^3\right)\right\}\right]}{x^5}}$$

$$=e^{\lim_{x\to 0}\frac{2\left[2\left(\frac{x^5}{8}+x^7\text{ and higher powers of x}\right)\right]}{x^5}}$$

$$=e^{1/2}=\sqrt{e}$$

8. (c) $\lim_{x\to\lambda}\left(2-\frac{\lambda}{x}\right)^{\lambda\tan\left(\frac{\pi x}{2\lambda}\right)}=\frac{1}{e}$

$$=\lim_{x\to\lambda}\left[2-\frac{\lambda}{x}\right]^{\lambda\tan\left(\frac{\pi x}{2\lambda}\right)}=e^{\lim_{x\to\lambda}\lambda\tan\left[\frac{\pi x}{2\lambda}\right]\left[2-\frac{\lambda}{x}-1\right]}$$

$$=e^{\lim_{x\to\lambda}\lambda\tan\left[\frac{\pi x}{2\lambda}\right]\left[1-\frac{\lambda}{x}\right]}=e^{\lim_{x\to\lambda}\frac{\lambda\left[1-\frac{\lambda}{x}\right]}{\cot\left[\frac{\pi x}{2\lambda}\right]}}$$

$$=e^{\lim_{x\to\lambda}\frac{\lambda^2/x^2}{-\text{cosec}^2\left[\frac{\pi x}{2\lambda}\right]\cdot\frac{\pi}{2\lambda}}}=e^{\lim_{x\to\lambda}\left(\frac{\lambda^2}{x^2}\right)(-1)\frac{\sin^2\left[\frac{\pi x}{2\lambda}\right]}{\left(\frac{\pi}{2\lambda}\right)}}$$

$$=e^{\lim_{x\to\lambda}\frac{-\lambda^2\sin^2\left[\frac{\pi x}{2\lambda}\right]}{\left(\frac{2\lambda}{\pi}\right)\left(\frac{\pi}{2\lambda}\right)^2x^2}}$$

$$=e^{\lim_{x\to\lambda}\left(\frac{-2\lambda}{\pi}\right)\frac{\sin^2\left[\frac{\pi x}{2\lambda}\right]}{\left(\frac{\pi x}{2\lambda}\right)^2}}=e^{\frac{-2\lambda}{\pi}}=e^{-1}$$

$\Rightarrow -\lambda\cdot\left(\frac{2}{\pi}\right)=-1$

$\therefore \lambda=\frac{\pi}{2}$

9. (b) $\lim_{x\to 1}\left[\text{cosec}\,\dfrac{\pi x}{2}\right]^{\frac{1}{1-x}}$

$$= \lim_{x\to 1}\left\{1+\left(\text{cosec}\,\frac{\pi x}{2}-1\right)\right\}^{\frac{1}{1-x}}$$

$$= e^{\lim_{x\to 1}\frac{\text{cosec}\frac{\pi x}{2}-1}{1-x}} = e^{\lim_{x\to 1}\frac{-\text{cosec}\frac{\pi x}{2}\cdot\cot\frac{\pi x}{2}\cdot\frac{\pi}{2}}{-1}}$$

$$= e^0 = 1$$

10. (a) Here, $\lim_{x\to 0}\left\{(1+x)^{2/x}\right\}$

$$= \left\{\lim_{x\to 0}(1+x)^{2/x}\right\} = \left\{e^{\lim_{x\to 0}x\cdot\frac{2}{x}}\right\}$$

$$= \{e^2\} = e^2 - 7 \qquad \left[\because e^2 \sim (2.732)^2 \sim 7.463 \quad \therefore \{e^2\} = e^2 - 7\right]$$

11. (d) $\lim_{n\to\infty}(4^n + 5^n)^{1/n}$

$$= \lim_{n\to\infty} 5\left[\left(\frac{4}{5}\right)^n + 1\right]^{1/n} = 5\,[0+1]^0$$

$$= 5 \qquad \left[\because \frac{4}{5} < 1, \left(\frac{4}{5}\right)^n \to 0 \text{ as } n\to\infty\right]$$

12. (b) $\lim_{x\to\infty}\left[\dfrac{1^{1/x}+2^{1/x}+\cdots+n^{1/x}}{n}\right]^{nx}$

Let $y = \dfrac{1}{x}$, then

$$= \lim_{y\to 0}\left[\frac{1^y+2^y+\cdots+n^y}{n}\right]^{n/y}$$

$$= e^{\lim_{y\to 0}\frac{n}{y}\left[\frac{1^y+2^y+3^y+\cdots+n^y}{n}-1\right]}$$

$$= e^{\lim_{y\to 0}\left[\frac{1^y+2^y+3^y+\cdots+n^y-n}{y}\right]}$$

$$= e^{\lim_{y\to 0}\left[\left(\frac{1^y-1}{y}\right)+\left(\frac{2^y-1}{y}\right)+\left(\frac{3^y-1}{y}\right)+\cdots+\left(\frac{n^y-1}{y}\right)\right]}$$

$$= e^{(\log 1+\log 2+\log 3+\cdots+\log n)} = e^{\log(1\cdot 2\cdot 3\cdots n)} = n!$$

13. (c) $\lim_{x\to 0}\left(\dfrac{1+\tan x}{1+\sin x}\right)^{1/\sin x}$

$$= \lim_{x\to 0}\frac{\left[\left(1+\dfrac{\sin x}{\cos x}\right)^{\frac{\cos x}{\sin x}}\right]^{1/\cos x}}{(1+\sin x)^{1/\sin x}}$$

$$= \frac{e^{\lim_{x\to 0}\left[\frac{\cos x}{\sin x}\cdot\frac{\sin x}{\cos x}\right]^{1/\cos x}}}{e^{\lim_{x\to 0}\sin x\cdot\frac{1}{\sin x}}} = \frac{e^{\lim_{x\to 0}\frac{1}{\cos x}}}{e^{\lim_{x\to 0}1}} = \frac{e^1}{e^1} = 1$$

14. (c) $\lim_{x\to 0}\left\{\dfrac{f(1+x)}{f(1)}\right\}^{1/x}$

$$= e^{\lim_{x\to 0}\frac{1}{x}\left\{\frac{f(1+x)}{f(1)}-1\right\}} = e^{\lim_{x\to 0}\left\{\frac{f(1+x)-f(1)}{x\,f(1)}\right\}}$$

$$= e^{\lim_{x\to 0}\left\{\frac{f(1+x)-f(1)}{x}\cdot\frac{1}{f(1)}\right\}}$$

$$= e^{\lim_{x\to 0}\left\{\frac{f(1+x)-f(1)}{x}\right\}\frac{1}{f(1)}}$$

$$= e^{f'(1)/f(1)} = e^{6/3} = e^2$$

15. (b) $\lim_{x\to\infty}\left(1+\dfrac{a}{x}+\dfrac{b}{x^2}\right)^{2x} = e^2$

$$\Rightarrow \quad e^{\lim_{x\to\infty}2\left(\frac{a}{x}+\frac{b}{x^2}\right)x} = e^2 \quad \Rightarrow \quad e^{\lim_{x\to\infty}\left(2a+\frac{2b}{x}\right)} = e^2$$

$$\Rightarrow \quad e^{\lim_{x\to\infty}2\left(a+\frac{b}{x}\right)} = e^2 \qquad \left[\because \lim_{x\to\infty}(1+x)^{1/x} = e\right]$$

On comparing both sides, we get

$$e^{2a} = e^2$$

$$\Rightarrow \quad e^a = e^1$$

$$\therefore \quad a = 1 \text{ and } b \in R$$

16. (c) $\lim_{x\to 0}\left[(\sin x)^{1/x} + \left(\dfrac{1}{x}\right)^{\sin x}\right]$

$$= \lim_{x\to 0}(\sin x)^{1/x} + \lim_{x\to 0}\left(\frac{1}{x}\right)^{\sin x}$$

$$= 0 + \lim_{x\to 0} e^{\log\left(\frac{1}{x}\right)^{\sin x}} = e^{\lim_{x\to\infty}\frac{\log\left(\frac{1}{x}\right)}{\text{cosec}\,x}}$$

[using L' Hospital's rule]

$$= e^{\lim_{x\to 0}\frac{x\left(-\frac{1}{x^2}\right)}{\text{cosec}\,x\cot x}} = e^{\lim_{x\to 0}\frac{\sin x}{x}\tan x} = e^0 = 1$$

17. (c) $\lim_{x\to\infty}\left(\dfrac{x-3}{x+2}\right)^x = \lim_{x\to\infty}\left(\dfrac{1-\dfrac{3}{x}}{1+\dfrac{2}{x}}\right)^x$

$$= \frac{\lim_{x\to\infty}\left[\left(1-\dfrac{3}{x}\right)^{-x/3}\right]^{-3}}{\lim_{x\to\infty}\left[\left(1+\dfrac{2}{x}\right)^{x/2}\right]^2} = \frac{e^{-3}}{e^2} = e^{-5}$$

18. (c) $\lim_{x\to 0}\left(\dfrac{1+5x^2}{1+3x^2}\right)^{1/x^2} = e^{\lim_{x\to 0}\frac{1}{x^2}\left[\frac{1+5x^2}{1+3x^2}-1\right]}$

$$= e^{\lim_{x\to 0}\frac{1}{x^2}\left[\frac{2x^2}{1+3x^2}\right]} = e^{\lim_{x\to 0}\left[\frac{2}{1+3x^2}\right]}$$

$$= e^2$$

19. (a,b,c,d) Given, $\lim_{x\to 0}(\cos x + a\sin x bx)^{1/x} = e^2$

$$\Rightarrow \quad e^{\lim_{x\to 0}\frac{1}{x}(\cos x + a\sin bx - 1)} = e^2$$

$$\Rightarrow \quad e^{\lim_{x\to 0}\left[\frac{-\sin x + ab\cos bx - 0}{1}\right]} = e^2$$

[using L' Hospital's rule]

$$\Rightarrow \quad e^{ab} = e^2$$

Now, according to the options all are correct because product of all given values of a and b in the options is equal to 2.

20. (a,b,c) Here, $L = \lim_{x\to\infty}(2^x + a^x + e^x)^{1/x}$

Case I When $a > e$, then

$$L = \lim_{x\to\infty} a\cdot\left\{1+\left(\frac{2}{a}\right)^x+\left(\frac{e}{a}\right)^x\right\}^{1/x}$$

Since, $\quad \dfrac{2}{a} < 1 \quad$ and $\quad \dfrac{e}{a} < 1$

$$\Rightarrow \quad \left(\frac{2}{a}\right)^x \to 0, \left(\frac{e}{a}\right)^x \to 0, \text{ as } \quad x\to\infty$$

$$\therefore \quad L = a\cdot\{1+0+0\}^0 = a$$

$$\Rightarrow \quad L = a$$

Case II When $a < e$, then

$$L = \lim_{x \to \infty} (2^x + a^x + e^x)^{1/x}$$

$$= \lim_{x \to \infty} e \left[1 + \left(\frac{a}{e}\right)^x + \left(\frac{2}{e}\right)^x\right]^{1/x}$$

$$= e \left[\text{as} \left(\frac{a}{e}\right)^x \to 0 \text{ and } \left(\frac{2}{e}\right)^x \to 0, \text{ when } x \to \infty\right]$$

Case III When $a = 2e$, then

$$L = \lim_{x \to \infty} [2^x + (2e)^x + e^x]^{1/x} = 2e \lim_{x \to \infty}\left[1 + \frac{1}{e^x} + \frac{1}{2^x}\right]^{1/x}$$

$$= 2e$$

Explanations for Q. Nos. (21-23)

Given, $f(x) = \lim_{n \to \infty} \left(\cos \frac{x}{\sqrt{n}}\right)^n = e^{\lim_{n \to \infty}\left(\cos \frac{x}{\sqrt{n}} - 1\right) \cdot n}$

On substituting $n = 1/t^2$, we get

$$f(x) = e^{\lim_{t \to 0} \frac{\cos tx - 1}{t^2}} = e^{\lim_{t \to 0} \frac{-2\sin^2 \frac{tx}{2}}{t^2}}$$

$$= e^{\lim_{t \to 0} \frac{-2\sin^2 \frac{tx}{2}}{t^2x^2/4} \cdot \frac{x^2}{4}}$$

$\therefore \quad f(x) = e^{-x^2/2}$

Also, $\quad g(x) = -x^{4b}$ [given]

and $\quad b = \lim_{x \to \infty} (\sqrt{x^2 + x + 1} - \sqrt{x^2 + 1})$

$$= \lim_{x \to \infty} \frac{(x^2 + x + 1) - (x^2 + 1)}{\sqrt{x^2 + x + 1} + \sqrt{x^2 + 1}} = \frac{1}{2}$$

$\therefore \quad g(x) = -x^{4 \cdot \frac{1}{2}} = -x^2$

Now, $\quad f(x) = -g(x)$

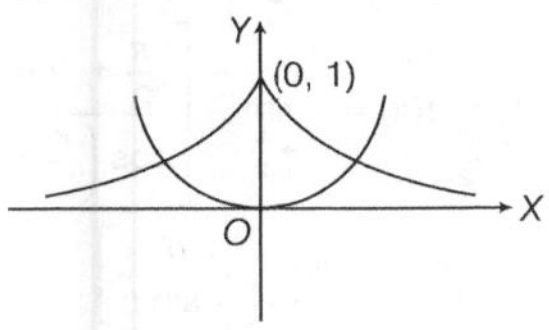

By observation graph of $f(x)$ and $-g(x)$, they intersect each other at two points.

$\therefore$ Number of solutions is 2.

21. (b) **22.** (a) **23.** (a)

24. (b) Given, $\lim_{x \to 0} f(x) = 2$

and $f(x) = \lim_{n \to \infty} \dfrac{x^{2n+1}\, g(x) + h(x)}{x^{2n} + 3x \cdot u(x)}$

$$= \lim_{n \to \infty} \frac{x^{2n+1} \cdot \sin\left(\frac{1}{x}\right) + [x^2 + 2x + (\lambda + 1)]}{x^{2n} + 3x \cdot \left[\frac{1}{x} + \cos\left(\frac{1}{x^2}\right)\right]}$$

$$= \lim_{n \to \infty} \frac{x^{2n} \cdot \left[\frac{\sin\left(\frac{1}{x}\right)}{\frac{1}{x}}\right] + x^2 + 2x + (\lambda + 1)}{x^{2n} + 3\left[1 + x \cdot \cos\left(\frac{1}{x^2}\right)\right]}$$

$$= \frac{x^2 + 2x + (\lambda + 1)}{3\left[1 + x \cdot \cos\left(\frac{1}{x^2}\right)\right]} \quad [\text{as } x \to 0]$$

Now, $\lim_{x \to 0} f(x) = \lim_{x \to 0} \dfrac{x^2 + 2x + \lambda + 1}{3\left[1 + x \cdot \cos\left(\frac{1}{x^2}\right)\right]} = 2$

$\Rightarrow \quad \dfrac{\lambda + 1}{3} = 2 \Rightarrow \lambda = 5$

25. (d) As, $x \to \infty$

$$\lim_{x \to \infty} f(x) = \lim_{x \to \infty} \lim_{n \to \infty} \frac{x^{2n} \cdot \left[\frac{\sin(1/x)}{1/x}\right] + x^2 + 2x + (\lambda + 1)}{x^{2n} + 3\,[1 + x\cos(1/x^2)]}$$

$= 1$

26. (a) As, $x \to -2$

$$\lim_{x \to -2} f(x) = 2\sin\left(\frac{1}{2}\right) = l \Rightarrow [l] = 0$$

27. (1) Given, $\lim_{x \to 1} (1 + ax + bx^2)^{\frac{c}{x-1}} = e^3$

$\Rightarrow \quad e^{\lim_{x \to 1} \frac{(ax + bx^2) \cdot c}{(x - 1)}} = e^3$

$\Rightarrow \quad \lim_{x \to 1} \dfrac{c \cdot (ax + bx^2)}{x - 1} = 3$

For limit to exists, $\quad c\,(a + b) = 0$ ...(i)

$\Rightarrow \quad \lim_{x \to 1} \dfrac{c\,(a + 2bx)}{1} = 3$ [using L' Hospital's rule]

$\Rightarrow \quad c\,(a + 2b) = 3$ ...(ii)

From Eqs. (i) and (ii), we get

$b = -a$ and $bc = 3$

$\therefore \quad \dfrac{1}{17}\left(\left|\dfrac{5b}{a}\right| + 4bc\right) = \dfrac{1}{17}(5 + 12) = 1$

28. (3) Given, $\lim_{x \to 0} (1 + ax + bx^2)^{2/x} = e^3$

$\Rightarrow \quad e^{\lim_{x \to 0} \frac{2}{x}(ax + bx^2)} = e^3$

$\Rightarrow \quad e^{\lim_{x \to 0} (2a + 2bx)} = e^3$

$\Rightarrow \quad e^{\lim_{x \to 0} 2(a + bx)} = e^3 \quad \left[\because \lim_{x \to 0}\left(1 + \frac{1}{x}\right)^x = 1\right]$

On comparing, we get $\quad a = \dfrac{3}{2}$

$\therefore \quad 2a = 2 \cdot \dfrac{3}{2} = 3$

29. (1) Given, $\lim_{x \to \infty} \left(1 + \dfrac{1}{x^n}\right)^x = L$ $(n > 1)$

$\Rightarrow \quad e^{\lim_{x \to \infty} x \cdot \frac{1}{x^n}} = L$

$e^{\lim_{x \to \infty} x^{1-n}} = L \quad [\text{as } n > 1, \therefore x^{1-n} \to 0, \forall\, x \to \infty]$

$\Rightarrow \quad e^0 = L$

$\Rightarrow \quad L = 1$

30. (8) Given, $\lim_{x \to 0} [1 + \cos x + a^3 \cdot \sin(b^6x) - 1]^{1/x} = e^{512}$

$\Rightarrow \quad e^{\lim_{x \to 0} \frac{a^3 \cdot \sin(b^6x) + \cos x - 1}{x}} = e^{512}$

$\Rightarrow \quad \lim_{x \to 0} \dfrac{a^3 \cdot \sin(b^6x) + \cos x - 1}{x} = 512$

$\Rightarrow \quad \lim_{x \to 0} \dfrac{a^3\cos(b^6x) \cdot b^6 - \sin x}{1} = 512$

$\Rightarrow \quad a^3 \cdot b^6 = 512$

$\therefore \quad ab^2 = 8$

DPP-5 **Applications of RHL and LHL**

1. From the given graph,

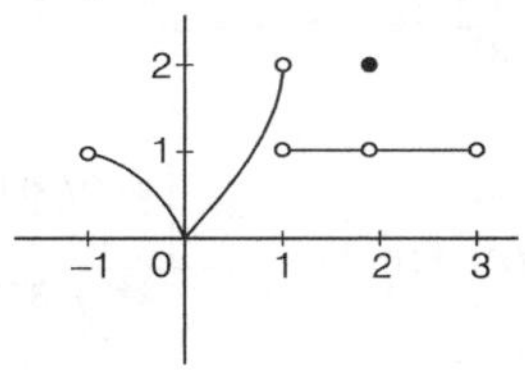

(i) $\lim_{x \to -1^+} f(x) = 1$

(ii) $\lim_{x \to 2} f(x) = 1$

(iii) $\lim_{x \to 1^-} f(x) = 2$

(iv) $\lim_{x \to 0^+} f(x) = 0$ and $\lim_{x \to 0^-} f(x) = 0$

So, (i), (iii) and (iv) are true.

2. (i) We have, $f(x) = \begin{cases} \dfrac{|x-4|}{x-4}, & x \neq 4 \\ 0, & x = 4 \end{cases}$

$$\lim_{x \to 4^-} f(x) = \lim_{x \to 4-h} \frac{|4-h-4|}{4-h-4}$$

$$= \lim_{h \to 0} \frac{h}{-h} = -1$$

and $\lim_{x \to 4^+} f(x) = \lim_{x \to 4+h} \dfrac{|4+h-4|}{4+h-4}$

$$= \lim_{h \to 0} \frac{h}{h} = 1$$

$\because$ $\lim_{x \to 4^-} f(x) \neq \lim_{x \to 4^+} f(x)$

Hence, $\lim_{x \to 4} f(x)$ does not exist.

(ii) We have, $f(x) = \begin{cases} 1 + x^2, & \text{if } 0 \le x \le 1 \\ 2 - x, & \text{if } \quad x > 1 \end{cases}$

$$\lim_{x \to 1^-} f(x) = \lim_{x \to 1^-} 1 + x^2 = 1 + 1 = 2$$

and $\lim_{x \to 1^+} f(x) = \lim_{x \to 1^+} 2 - x = 2 - 1 = 1$

$\therefore$ $\lim_{x \to 1^-} f(x) \neq \lim_{x \to 1^+} f(x)$

Hence, $\lim_{x \to 1} f(x)$ does not exist.

(iii) We have, $f(x) = \begin{cases} 5x - 4, & 0 < x \le 1 \\ 4x^3 - 3x, & 1 < x < 2 \end{cases}$

$$\lim_{x \to 1^-} f(x) = \lim_{x \to 1^-} 5x - 4 = 5 - 4 = 1$$

and $\lim_{x \to 1^+} f(x) = \lim_{x \to 1^+} 4x^3 - 3x = 4 - 3 = 1$

$\because$ $\lim_{x \to 1^-} f(x) = \lim_{x \to 1^+} f(x) = 1$

$\therefore$ $\lim_{x \to 1} f(x) = 1$

3. We have, $f(x)$ is an even function.

$\therefore$ $f(-x) = f(x)$

$$\lim_{x \to 0^-} f(x) = \lim_{x \to 0-h} f(0-h) = \lim_{h \to 0} f(-h)$$

and $\lim_{x \to 0^+} f(x) = \lim_{x \to 0+h} f(0+h) = \lim_{h \to 0} f(h)$

$\therefore$ $f(x)$ is an even function.

$$f(-h) = f(h)$$

$\therefore$ $\lim_{x \to 0^-} f(x) = \lim_{x \to 0^+} f(x)$

Hence proved.

4. (d) We have,

$$\lim_{x \to 0^-} \frac{\cos^{-1}(1-x)}{\sqrt{x}}$$

$$= \lim_{x \to 0-h} \frac{\cos^{-1}[1-(0-h)]}{\sqrt{0-h}}$$

$$= \lim_{h \to 0} \frac{\cos^{-1} h}{\sqrt{-h}} \text{ does not exist.}$$

[$\because \sqrt{-h}$ is not defined]

5. (d) We have, $\lim_{x \to 0} \sin^{-1}(\sec x)$

$$-1 \le \sin^{-1} x \le 1$$

But $\qquad \sec x \in (-\infty, -1) \cup (1, \infty)$

$\therefore$ $\lim_{x \to 0} \sin^{-1}(\sec x)$ is not defined.

6. (c) We have, $\lim_{x \to 1} (1 - x + [x-1] + [1-x])$

$$= \lim_{x \to 1} (1 - x - 1) \qquad [\because [x] + [-x] = -1]$$

$$= -1$$

7. (c) We have, $\lim_{x \to \frac{\pi}{2}} \left[\dfrac{x - \frac{\pi}{2}}{\cos x} \right]$

Now, $\lim_{x \to \frac{\pi^-}{2}} f(x) = \lim_{x \to \frac{\pi}{2} - h} \left[\dfrac{\frac{\pi}{2} - h - \frac{\pi}{2}}{\cos\left(\frac{\pi}{2} - h\right)} \right]$

$$= \lim_{h \to 0} \left[\frac{-h}{\sin h} \right]$$

$$= -2$$

and $\lim_{x \to \frac{\pi^+}{2}} f(x) = \lim_{x \to \frac{\pi}{2} + h} \left[\dfrac{\frac{\pi}{2} + h - \frac{\pi}{2}}{\cos\left(\frac{\pi}{2} + h\right)} \right]$

$$= \lim_{h \to 0} \left[\frac{h}{-\sin h} \right]$$

$$= -2$$

$\therefore$ $\lim_{x \to 0} f(x) = -2$

8. (b) We have, $\lim_{x \to \frac{\pi}{4}} (1 + [x])^{\frac{1}{\log(\tan x)}}$

Now, $\lim_{x \to \frac{\pi^-}{4}} f(x) = \lim_{x \to \frac{\pi}{4} - h} \left(1 + \left[\frac{\pi}{4} - h\right]\right)^{\frac{1}{\log\left[\tan\left(\frac{\pi}{4} - h\right)\right]}}$

$$= \lim_{h \to 0} (1 + 0)^{\frac{1}{0}} \qquad \left[\because \left(\frac{\pi}{4} - h\right) = 0\right]$$

$$= 1^{\infty} = 1$$

and $\lim_{x \to \frac{\pi^+}{4}} f(x) = \lim_{x \to \frac{\pi}{4} + h} \left(1 + \left[\frac{\pi}{4} + h\right]\right)^{\frac{1}{\log \tan\left(\frac{\pi}{4} + h\right)}}$

$$= \lim_{h \to 0} 1^{\infty} = 1 \qquad \left[\because \left(\frac{\pi}{4} + h\right) = 0\right]$$

$\therefore$ $\lim_{x \to \pi/4} f(x) = 1$

9. (a) We have, $\lim_{x \to \frac{\pi}{2}} [\sin x]$

Graph of $[\sin x]$ is

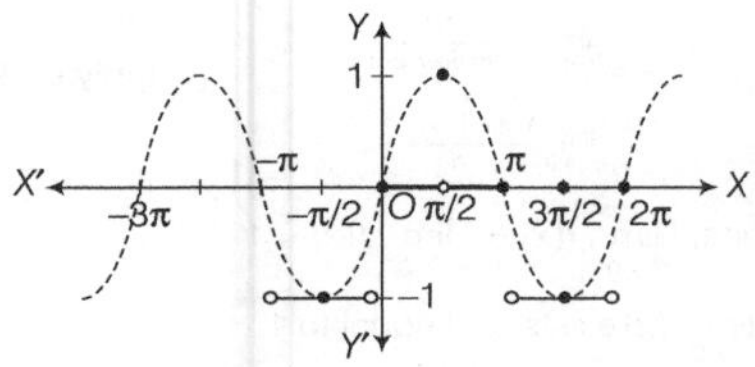

From the above graph,

$$\lim_{x \to \frac{\pi^-}{2}} [\sin x] = 0$$

and $$\lim_{x \to \frac{\pi^+}{2}} [\sin x] = 0$$

$\because$ $$\lim_{x \to \frac{\pi}{2}} [\sin x] = 0$$

10. (d) We have, $\lim_{x \to 2} \left\{\frac{x}{2}\right\}$

Graph of $\left\{\frac{x}{2}\right\}$ is

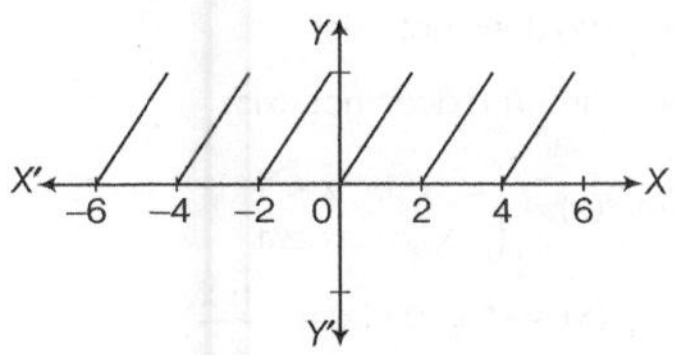

From the above graph,

$$\lim_{x \to 2^-} \left\{\frac{x}{2}\right\} \neq \lim_{x \to 2^+} \left\{\frac{x}{2}\right\}$$

Hence, $\lim_{x \to 2} \left\{\frac{x}{2}\right\}$ does not exist.

11. (d) We have, $\lim_{x \to \pi^-} \text{Sgn}\,[\tan x]$

Now, $\lim_{x \to \pi^-} \text{Sgn}\,[\tan x] = -1$

and $\lim_{x \to \pi^+} \text{Sgn}\,[\tan x] = 0$

$\therefore$ $\lim_{x \to \pi} \text{Sgn}\,[\tan x]$ does not exist.

12. (a) We have, $\lim_{x \to 1} \sin^{-1} (\log_e x)$

$$= \sin^{-1} (\log_e 1) = \sin^{-1} (0) = 0$$

13. (b) We have, $f(x) = \begin{cases} x^2 + 2, & x \geq 2 \\ 1 - x, & x < 2 \end{cases}$

and $g(x) = \begin{cases} 2x, & x > 1 \\ 3 - x, & x \leq 1 \end{cases}$

Now, $f[g(x)] = \begin{cases} [g(x)]^2 + 2, & g(x) \geq 2 \\ 1 - [g(x)], & g(x) < 2 \end{cases}$

$\Rightarrow$ $f[g(x)] = \begin{cases} 4x^2 + 2, & x \geq 1 \\ (3 - x)^2 + 2, & x < 1 \end{cases}$

$\therefore$ $\lim_{x \to 1} f[g(x)] = 6$

14. (a) We have, $\lim_{x \to 1^-} (x)^{1 - x}$

$\Rightarrow$ $\lim_{x \to (1 - h)} (1 - h)^{1 - h - 1} = 0$ $\quad [\because (1 - h) = 0]$

15. (b) We have, $\lim_{x \to a^-} \left(\frac{|x|^3}{a} - \left[\frac{x}{a}\right]^3\right)$

$$= \lim_{x \to a - h} \left(\frac{|a - h|^3}{a} - \left[\frac{a - h}{a}\right]^3\right)$$

$$= \lim_{h \to 0} \left(\frac{|a|^3}{a} - \left[1 - \frac{h}{a}\right]^3\right) \quad \left[\because \left[1 - \frac{h}{a}\right] = 0\right]$$

$$= a^2$$

16. (d) We have, $\lim_{x \to \infty} \sec^{-1} \left(\frac{x}{x + 1}\right)$

For $x > 0$, $\frac{x}{x + 1} < 1$

$\therefore$ $\sec^{-1} \left(\frac{x}{x + 1}\right)$ is not defined.

Hence, $\lim_{x \to \infty} \sec^{-1} \left(\frac{x}{x + 1}\right)$ does not exist.

17. (c) We have, $\lim_{x \to 0^+} f(x) = \lim_{x \to 0^+} \frac{\tan^2 \{x\}}{x^2 - [x]^2}$

$$= \lim_{x \to 0^+} \frac{\tan^2 x}{x^2} = 1$$

$$[\because x \to 0^+ ;\ [x] = 0 \Rightarrow \{x\} = x]$$

Also, $\lim_{x \to 0^-} f(x) = \lim_{x \to 0^-} \sqrt{\{x\} \cot \{x\}}$

$$= \sqrt{\cot 1} \quad \left[\begin{array}{l}\because \{x\} = x - [x] \\ \Rightarrow x \to 0^- \Rightarrow \{x\} = 1 - h = 1\}\end{array}\right]$$

Also, $\cot^{-1} \left[\lim_{x \to 0^-} f(x)\right]^2 = \cot^{-1} (\sqrt{\cot 1})^2 = \cot^{-1} (\cot 1) = 1$

18. (c) We have, $\lim_{\theta \to 0} \left(\left[\frac{n \sin \theta}{\theta}\right] + \left[\frac{n \tan \theta}{\theta}\right]\right)$

We know that, $\lim_{\theta \to 0} \frac{\sin \theta}{\theta} = 1$ $\quad \left[\because \frac{\sin \theta}{\theta} < 1\right]$

$\Rightarrow$ $\lim_{\theta \to 0} \left[\frac{n \sin \theta}{\theta}\right] = n - 1$

Similarly, $\lim_{\theta \to 0} \left(\frac{n \tan \theta}{\theta}\right) = n$ $\quad \left[\because \frac{\tan \theta}{\theta} > 1\right]$

$\therefore$ $\lim_{\theta \to 0} \left(\left[\frac{n \sin \theta}{\theta}\right] + \left[\frac{n \tan \theta}{\theta}\right]\right) = n - 1 + n = 2n - 1$

19. (c) We have, $\lim_{x \to 1} \frac{\sqrt{1 - \cos 2 (x - 1)}}{(x - 1)}$

$$= \lim_{x \to 1} \frac{\sqrt{2}\,|\sin (x - 1)|}{x - 1} \quad [\because \sqrt{1 - \cos 2x} = \sqrt{2}\,|\sin x|]$$

$$= \frac{\sqrt{2}\,|\sin (x - 1)|}{x - 1} = \begin{cases} \dfrac{-\sqrt{2} \sin (x - 1)}{x - 1}, & x \leq 1 \\[2ex] \dfrac{\sqrt{2} \sin (x - 1)}{x - 1}, & x \geq 1 \end{cases}$$

$\because$ $\lim_{x \to 1^-} f(x) = -\sqrt{2}$ and $\lim_{x \to 1^+} f(x) = \sqrt{2}$

$\Rightarrow$ $\lim_{x \to 1^-} f(x) \neq \lim_{x \to 1^+} f(x)$

$\therefore$ $\lim_{x \to 1} f(x)$ does not exist.

20. (a) We have, $\lim_{x \to \infty} \frac{\log_e x^x - [x]}{[x]}$

$$= \lim_{x \to \infty} \frac{x \log_e x - [x]}{[x]}$$

$$= \lim_{x \to \infty} \left(\frac{x \log_e x}{[x]} - 1\right) = 0 - 1 = -1 \left[\because \lim_{x \to \infty} \frac{\log x}{[x]} = 0\right]$$

21. (a) We have, $\lim_{x \to 5} \frac{[f(x)]^2 - 9}{|x - 5|} = 0$

$\Rightarrow \quad \lim_{x \to 5} [f(x)]^2 - 9 = 0 \Rightarrow \lim_{x \to 5} [f(x)]^2 = 9$

$\Rightarrow \quad \lim_{x \to 5} f(x) = \pm 3$

$\because$ Range of $f(x) \geq 0$

$\therefore \quad \lim_{x \to 5} f(x) = 3$

22. (b) We have,

$(\sqrt[3]{1+a} - 1)\, x^2 + (\sqrt{1+a} - 1)\, x + \sqrt[6]{1+a} - 1 = 0$

Let $1 + a = y^6 \Rightarrow a \to 0, y \to 1$

$\therefore \quad (y^2 - 1)\, x^2 + (y^3 - 1)\, x + y - 1 = 0$

$\Rightarrow \quad (y - 1)\{(y + 1)\, x^2 + (y^2 + y + 1)\, x + 1\} = 0$

$\Rightarrow \quad 2x^2 + 3x + 1 = 0 \quad [\because y \to 1]$

$\Rightarrow \quad (2x + 1)(x + 1) = 0$

$\Rightarrow \quad x = -1, -\frac{1}{2}$

$\therefore \quad \lim_{a \to 0^+} \alpha(a) = -1$

and $\quad \lim_{a \to 0^+} \beta(a) = -\frac{1}{2}$

23. (a,b,c) We have, $f(x) = \frac{x^2 - 9x + 20}{x - [x]} = \frac{(x - 5)(x - 4)}{x - [x]}$

(a) $\lim_{x \to 5^-} f(x) = \lim_{x \to (5 - h)} \frac{(5 - h - 5)(5 - h - 4)}{(5 - h) - [5 - h]}$

$= \lim_{h \to 0} \frac{h(1 - h)}{(1 - h)} \quad [\because [5 - h] = 4]$

$= \lim_{h \to 0} h = 0$

(b) $\lim_{x \to 5^+} f(x) = \lim_{x \to (5 + h)} \frac{(5 + h - 5)(5 + h - 4)}{(5 + h) - [5 + h]}$

$= \lim_{h \to 0} \frac{h(1 + h)}{h} \quad [\because [5 + h] = 5]$

$= \lim_{h \to 0} (1 + h) = 1$

$\lim_{x \to 5^-} f(x) \neq \lim_{x \to 5^+} f(x)$

$\therefore \lim_{x \to 5} f(x)$ does not exist.

24. (a,b) We have, $f(x) = \frac{\cos 2 - \cos 2x}{x^2 - |x|}$

$\Rightarrow \quad f(x) = \frac{2 \sin (x + 1) \sin (x - 1)}{x^2 - |x|}$

$\Rightarrow \quad f(x) = \begin{cases} \frac{2 \sin (x + 1) \sin (x - 1)}{x(1 + x)}, & x < 0 \\ \frac{2 \sin (x + 1) \sin (x - 1)}{x(x - 1)}, & x \geq 0 \end{cases}$

$\Rightarrow \lim_{x \to -1} f(x) = \lim_{x \to -1} \frac{2 \sin (x + 1) \sin (x - 1)}{x(x + 1)} = 2 \sin 2$

$\therefore \quad \lim_{x \to 1} f(x) = \lim_{x \to 1} \frac{-2 \sin (x + 1) \sin (x - 1)}{x(x - 1)} = 2 \sin 2$

25. (a,b,c) We have, $f(x) = |x|^{\sin x} \Rightarrow f(x) = \begin{cases} -x^{\sin x}, & x < 0 \\ x^{\sin x}, & x \geq 0 \end{cases}$

(a) $\lim_{x \to 0^-} f(x) = \lim_{x \to 0^-} -x^{\sin x} = e^{\lim_{x \to 0^-} -\sin x \log (x)}$

$= e^{\lim_{h \to 0} -\sin h \log h} = e^{\lim_{h \to 0} -\frac{\log h}{\operatorname{cosec} h}}$

$= e^{\lim_{h \to 0} \frac{-1/h}{-\operatorname{cosec} h \cos h}}$ [apply L' Hospital's rule]

$= e^{\lim_{h \to 0} \frac{\sin h}{h} \tan h} = e^0 = 1$

(b) $\lim_{x \to 0^+} f(x) = \lim_{x \to 0^+} x^{\sin x} = e^{\lim_{x \to 0^+} \sin x \log x}$

$= e^{\lim_{x \to 0^+} \sin h \log h} = e^{\lim_{h \to 0} \frac{\log h}{\operatorname{cosec} h}}$

$= e^{\lim_{h \to 0} \frac{1/h}{-\operatorname{cosec} h \cot h}}$ [$\because$ apply L' Hospital's rule]

$= e^{\lim_{h \to 0} \frac{-\sin h \tan h}{h}} = e^0 = 1$

(c) Hence, $\lim_{x \to 0^-} f(x) = \lim_{x \to 0^+} f(x) = 1$

$\therefore \lim_{x \to 0} f(x)$ exists and equal to 1.

26. (a,b,c,d) We have, $f(x) = \frac{|x + \pi|}{\sin x}$

(a) $\lim_{x \to -\pi^+} f(x) = \lim_{x \to -\pi + h} \frac{|-\pi + h + \pi|}{\sin(-\pi + h)}$

$= \lim_{h \to 0} \frac{|h|}{-\sin h} = -1$

(b) $\lim_{x \to -\pi^-} f(x) = \lim_{x \to -\pi - h} \frac{|-\pi - h + \pi|}{\sin(-\pi - h)}$

$= \lim_{h \to 0} \frac{h}{\sin h} = 1$

(c) $\lim_{x \to -\pi^+} f(x) \neq \lim_{x \to -\pi^-} f(x)$

$\therefore \lim_{x \to -\pi} f(x)$ does not exist.

Similarly, $\lim_{x \to \pi} f(x)$ does not exist.

27. (b) We have, $f(x) = \begin{cases} x^2 + 1, & x < 1 \\ x^3, & x \geq 1 \end{cases}$

$g(x) = 2^x$ and $h(x) = \frac{\sin x}{x}$

Now, $\quad f[h(x)] = \begin{cases} \frac{\sin^2 x}{x^2} + 1, & \frac{\sin x}{x} < 1 \\ \frac{\sin^3 x}{x^3}, & \frac{\sin x}{x} \geq 1 \end{cases}$

$\Rightarrow \quad f[h(x)] = \frac{\sin^2 x}{x^2} + 1$

$f[h(0^+)] = \lim_{x \to 0^+} \frac{\sin^2 x}{x^2} + 1 = 1 + 1 = 2$

and $\quad f[h(0^-)] = \lim_{x \to 0^-} \frac{\sin^2 x}{x^2} + 1 = 1 + 1 = 2$

$\therefore \quad |f[h(0^+)] - f[h(0^-)]| = |2 - 2| = 0$

28. (c) Now, $f[g(x)] = \begin{cases} (2^x)^2 + 1, & 2^x < 1 \\ (2^x)^3, & 2^x \geq 1 \end{cases}$

and $\quad f[g(x)] = \begin{cases} 4^x + 1, & x < 0 \\ 8^x, & x \geq 0 \end{cases}$

Also, $\quad f[g(0^+)] = \lim_{x \to 0^+} 8^x = 8^0 = 1$

and $\quad f[g(0^-)] = \lim_{x \to 0^-} 4^x + 1 = 1 + 1 = 2$

$\therefore |f[g(0^+)] - f[g(0^-)]| = |1 - 2| = 1$

29. (b) $f[g(hx)] = \begin{cases} 4^{\frac{\sin x}{x}} + 1, & 2^{\frac{\sin x}{x}} < 1 \\ 8^{\frac{\sin x}{x}}, & 2^{\frac{\sin x}{x}} \geq 1 \end{cases}$

Now, $\quad fg[h(0^+)] = \lim_{x \to 0^+} 4^{\frac{\sin x}{x}} + 1 = 4^{\lim_{x \to 0^+} \frac{\sin x}{x}} + 1 = 4 + 1 = 5$

and $\quad fg[h(0^-)] = \lim_{x \to 0^-} 4^{\frac{\sin x}{x}} + 1 = 4^{\lim_{x \to 0^-} \frac{\sin x}{x}} + 1 = 4 + 1 = 5$

$\therefore \quad |f[g\{h(0^+)\}] - f[g\{(h(0^-)\}]| = |5 - 5| = 0$

30. (1) We have, $\lim_{x \to 0} |x|^{[\cos x]}$

Now, $\lim_{x \to 0^+} f(x) = \lim_{x \to 0^+} |0 + h|^{[\cos(0+h)]} = h^0 = 1$

and $\lim_{x \to 0^-} f(x) = \lim_{x \to 0^-} |0 - h|^{[\cos(0-h)]} = h^0 = 1$

$\therefore \lim_{x \to 0} |x|^{[\cos x]} = 1$

31. (1) We have, $L = \lim_{x \to 1^-} 2^{-2(1-x)^{-1}}$

and $M = \lim_{x \to 1^+} 2^{-2(1-x)}$

Now, $L = \lim_{x \to 1^-} 2^{-2(1-x)^{-1}} = \lim_{x \to (1-h)} 2^{-2(h)^{-1}}$

$= \lim_{h \to 0} \frac{1}{2^{2/h}} = 0$

and $M = \lim_{x \to 1^+} 2^{-2(1-x)^{-1}} = \lim_{x \to (1+h)} 2^{-2(-h)}$

$= \lim_{h \to 0} 2^{2h} = 1$

$\therefore L + M = (0 + 1) = 1$

32. (0) We have, $\lim_{x \to 0} \left[\log(1+x) \cdot \frac{\tan x}{|x|}\right]$

Let $f(x) = \log(1+x) \cdot \frac{\tan x}{|x|}$

$\lim_{x \to 0^-} f(x) = \lim_{x \to (0-h)} \log(1-h) \cdot \frac{\tan(-h)}{|-h|}$

$= \lim_{h \to 0} \log(1-h) \cdot \frac{(-\tan h)}{h} = 0$

$\Rightarrow \lim_{x \to 0^+} f(x) = \lim_{x \to (0+h)} \log(1+h) \cdot \frac{\tan h}{|h|}$

$= \lim_{n \to 0} \log(1+h) \cdot \frac{\tan h}{h} = 0$

$\because \lim_{x \to 0} \left[\log(1+x) \cdot \frac{\tan x}{|x|}\right] = [0] = 0$

33. (2) We have, $\lim_{x \to 0^+} \frac{\log(-\cos 3x + \cos x)}{\log(\sin x)}$

$= \lim_{x \to 0^+} \frac{\log(-4\cos^3 x + 3\cos x + \cos x)}{\log(\sin x)}$

$= \lim_{x \to 0^+} \frac{\log 4\cos x \sin^2 x}{\log \sin x}$

$= \lim_{h \to 0} \frac{\log 4 + \log \cos h + 2 \log \sin h}{\log \sin h}$

$= \lim_{h \to 0} \frac{0 - \tan h + 2\cot h}{\cot h}$ [apply L' Hospital's rule]

$= \lim_{h \to 0} -\tan^2 h + 2 = 2$

34. (1) We have, $\lim_{x \to 0} \left[(1-e^x)\frac{\sin x}{|x|}\right]$

Let $f(x) = (1-e^x)\frac{\sin x}{|x|}$

$$f(x) = \begin{cases} \frac{(e^x - 1)\sin x}{x}, & x < 0 \\ \frac{(1-e^x)\sin x}{x}, & x > 0 \end{cases}$$

We know that, $\lim_{x \to 0} \frac{\sin x}{x} = 1$

$\therefore \lim_{x \to 0} [e^x - 1] = -1, x < 0$

and $\lim_{x \to 0} [1 - e^x] = -1, x > 0$

$\therefore |\lim_{x \to 0} f(x)| = |-1| = 1$

35. (5) We have, $\lim_{x \to 0} \left[\frac{3\sin 3x}{x}\right] - \left[\frac{2\sin 2x}{x}\right]$

$= \lim_{x \to 0} \left[\frac{9\sin 3x}{3x}\right] - \left[\frac{4\sin 2x}{2x}\right]$

$= 8 - 3 = 5$ $\left[\because \lim_{x \to 0} \left[\frac{x \sin x}{x}\right] = x - 1\right]$

DPP-6 Limit of Expansions, Dual Behaviour, Newton-Leibnitz Rule and Conversion into Definite Integral

1. (c) Given, $\lim_{x \to 0} \frac{x(1 + a\cos x) - b\sin x}{x^3} = 1$

$$\Rightarrow \lim_{x \to 0} \frac{x\left\{1 + a\left(1 - \frac{x^2}{2!} + \frac{x^4}{4!} - \cdots\right)\right\} - b\left\{x - \frac{x^3}{3!} + \frac{x^5}{5!} - \cdots\right\}}{x^3} = 1$$

$$\Rightarrow \lim_{x \to 0} \frac{x(1 + a - b) + x^3\left(-\frac{a}{2} + \frac{b}{6}\right) + x^5 \cdots}{x^3} = 1$$

$\Rightarrow (1 + a - b) = 0$ and $\frac{-a}{2} + \frac{b}{6} = 1$

On solving, we get $a = -5/2$ and $b = -3/2$

2. (c) $\lim_{x \to 0} \frac{(\cos x - 1)(\cos x - e^x)}{x^n}$

We know that, $\cos x = 1 - \frac{x^2}{2!} + \frac{x^4}{4!} - \frac{x^6}{6!} + \cdots \infty$

and $e^x = 1 + \frac{x}{1!} + \frac{x^2}{2!} + \frac{x^3}{3!} + \cdots \infty$

$$\Rightarrow \lim_{x \to 0} \frac{\left[\left\{\left(1 - \frac{x^2}{2!} + \frac{x^4}{4!} - \frac{x^6}{6!} + \cdots \infty\right) - 1\right\} \left\{\left(1 - \frac{x^2}{2!} + \frac{x^4}{4!} - \frac{x^6}{6!} + \cdots \infty\right) - \left(1 + \frac{x}{1!} + \frac{x^2}{2!} + \frac{x^3}{3!} + \cdots \infty\right)\right\}\right]}{x^n}$$

$$\Rightarrow \lim_{x \to 0} \frac{\left[\left(\frac{-x^2}{2!} + \frac{x^4}{4!} - \frac{x^6}{6!} + \cdots \infty\right)\left(\frac{-x}{1!} - \frac{2x^2}{2!} - \frac{x^3}{3!} + \frac{x^4}{4!} - \frac{x^5}{5!} - \frac{x^6}{6!} + \cdots \infty\right)\right]}{x^n}$$

$$\Rightarrow \lim_{x \to 0} \frac{x^3\left(-\frac{1}{2!} + \frac{x^2}{4!} - \frac{x^4}{6!} + \cdots \infty\right)\left(-1 - x - \frac{x^2}{3!} + \frac{x^3}{4!} - \cdots \infty\right)}{x^n}$$

For the above limit to be finite and non-zero i.e. $\frac{1}{2}$.

$\therefore n = 3$

3. (c) $\lim_{x\to 0}\frac{(1+x)^{1/x}-e}{x}$

$$= \lim_{x\to 0}\frac{e\left(1-\frac{x}{2}+\frac{11x^2}{24}+\cdots\right)-e}{x}$$

$$= \lim_{x\to 0}\frac{e\cdot x\left\{-\frac{1}{2}+\frac{11x}{24}+\cdots\right\}}{x} = -\frac{e}{2}$$

4. (b) $\lim_{x\to 0^+}\frac{e^{1/x}+1}{e^{1/x}-1}$

As $x\to 0^+ \Rightarrow \quad x>0 \Rightarrow e^{1/x}<1$

$\therefore \quad \lim_{h\to 0}\frac{e^{1/h}+1}{e^{1/h}-1}$ i.e. $e^{1/h}>1$

$$= \lim_{h\to 0}\frac{1+\frac{1}{e^{1/h}}}{1-\frac{1}{e^{1/h}}} = \lim_{h\to 0}\frac{1+e^{-1/h}}{1-e^{-1/h}} = \frac{1+e^{-\infty}}{1-e^{-\infty}} = 1$$

5. (c) $\lim_{x\to 0^-} = \frac{e^{1/x}+1}{e^{1/x}-1}$

As $x\to 0^- \quad \Rightarrow \quad x<0 \Rightarrow e^{1/x}>1$

$\therefore \quad \lim_{h\to 0}\frac{e^{1/-h}+1}{e^{1/-h}-1} = \frac{e^{-\infty}+1}{e^{-\infty}-1}$

$$= \frac{0+1}{0-1} = -1$$

6. (b) $\lim_{n\to\infty}\frac{[x]+[2x]+\cdots+[nx]}{n^2}$

$nx-1<[nx]\le nx$

Putting $n = 1, 2, 3, \ldots, n$ and adding them

$$x\Sigma n - n < \Sigma[nx] \le x\Sigma n$$

$$x\cdot\frac{\Sigma n}{n^2}-\frac{1}{n} < \frac{\Sigma[nx]}{n^2} \le x\cdot\frac{\Sigma n}{n^2} \qquad \ldots\text{(i)}$$

Now, $\lim_{n\to\infty}\left\{x\cdot\frac{\Sigma n}{n^2}-\frac{1}{n}\right\} = x\cdot\lim_{n\to\infty}\frac{\Sigma n}{n^2}-\lim_{n\to\infty}\frac{1}{n}$

$$= x\lim_{n\to\infty}\frac{n(n+1)}{2n^2}-0 = \frac{x}{2}$$

and $\lim_{n\to\infty} x\cdot\frac{\Sigma n}{n^2} = x\cdot\lim_{n\to 0}\frac{\Sigma n}{n^2} = \frac{x}{2}$

As two limits are equal by Eq. (i) i.e. $x/2$.

7. (c) $\lim_{n\to\infty}\frac{[1^2x]+[2^2x]+\cdots+[n^2x]}{n^3}$

$n^2x-1<[n^2x]\le n^2x$,

Putting $n = 1, 2, 3, \cdots, n$, we get

$$x\,\Sigma n^2 - n < \Sigma[n^2x] \le x\Sigma n^2$$

$$x\frac{\Sigma n^2}{n^3}-\frac{1}{n^2} < \frac{\Sigma[n^2x]}{n^3} \le x\frac{\Sigma n^2}{n^3} \qquad \ldots\text{(i)}$$

$\Rightarrow \quad \lim_{n\to\infty}\left\{x\cdot\frac{\Sigma n^2}{n^3}-\frac{1}{n^2}\right\} = x\cdot\lim_{n\to\infty}\frac{\Sigma n^2}{n^3}-\lim_{n\to\infty}\frac{1}{n^2}$

$$= x\cdot\lim_{n\to\infty}\frac{n(n+1)(2n+1)}{6n^3}-0$$

$$= x\cdot\lim_{n\to\infty}\frac{\left(1+\frac{1}{n}\right)\left(2+\frac{1}{n}\right)}{6}$$

$$= x\cdot\frac{2}{6} = \frac{x}{3}$$

and $\lim_{n\to\infty} x\frac{\Sigma n^2}{n^3} = \frac{x}{3}$

As two limits are equal i.e. $x/3$.

8. (b) $\lim_{x\to 0}\frac{\int_0^{x^2}\sec^2 t\,dt}{x\sin x}$

$$= \lim_{x\to 0}\frac{\frac{d}{dx}\int_0^{x^2}\sec^2 t\,dt}{\frac{d}{dx}(x\sin x)} = \lim_{x\to 0}\frac{\sec^2 x^2\cdot 2x}{\sin x + x\cos x}$$

$$= \lim_{x\to 0}\frac{2x\sec^2 x^2}{x\left(\frac{\sin x}{x}+\cos x\right)} = \frac{2\times 1}{1+1} \qquad \left[\because \lim_{x\to 0}\frac{\sin x}{x} = 1\right]$$

$= 1$

9. (a) We have, $f: R\to R;\ f(2) = 6,\ f'(2) = \frac{1}{48}$

Now, $\lim_{x\to 2}\int_6^{f(x)}\frac{4t^3dt}{x-2} = \lim_{x\to 2}\frac{4\{f(x)\}^3}{1}\cdot f'(x)$

$$= 4\{f(2)\}^3\cdot f'(2)$$

$$= 4\times(6)^3\cdot\frac{1}{48} = 18$$

10. (d) $\lim_{n\to\infty}\sum_{r=0}^{n}\frac{1}{\sqrt{n^2+r^2}}$

$$= \lim_{n\to\infty}\frac{1}{n}\cdot\sum_{r=0}^{n}\frac{1}{\sqrt{1+(r/n)^2}}$$

$$= \int_0^1\frac{dx}{\sqrt{1+x^2}} \Rightarrow [\log|x+\sqrt{1+x^2}|]_0^1$$

$$= \log(1+\sqrt{2})$$

11. (c) Given, $f'(0) = \lim_{n\to\infty} n\left[f\left(\frac{1}{n}\right)\right]$ and $f(0) = 0$

$\therefore \lim_{n\to\infty}\left[\frac{2}{\pi}(n+1)\cos^{-1}\left(\frac{1}{n}\right)-n\right]$

$$= \lim_{n\to\infty} n\left[\frac{2}{\pi}\left(1+\frac{1}{n}\right)\cos^{-1}\frac{1}{n}-1\right]$$

Let $\quad f(x) = \frac{2}{\pi}(1+x)\cos^{-1}x - 1$

Now, $\quad f'(x) = \frac{2}{\pi}\left[(1+x)\frac{-1}{\sqrt{1-x^2}}+\cos^{-1}x\right]$

$$f'(0) = \frac{2}{\pi}\left[-1+\frac{\pi}{2}\right] = \frac{2}{\pi}\left[\frac{\pi-2}{2}\right] = \left(\frac{\pi-2}{\pi}\right)$$

Explanations for Q. Nos. (12–14)

Here, $\quad c = \lim_{x\to 0}\frac{\int_0^x\frac{t^2}{(a+t^r)^{1/p}}dt}{bx-\sin x}$

$$= \lim_{x\to 0}\frac{x^2}{(a+x^r)^{1/p}}\cdot\frac{1}{b-\cos x}$$

If it exists, then $b-1=0 \Rightarrow b=1$

and $\quad c = \lim_{x\to 0}\frac{x^2}{(a+x^r)^{1/p}}\cdot\frac{1}{1-\cos x}$

$$= \lim_{x\to 0}\frac{1}{(a+x^r)^{1/p}}\cdot\frac{x^2}{(1-\cos x)}$$

$$= \frac{2}{a^{1/p}}$$

$\therefore \quad b = 1$

If $p = 3$ and $c = 1$, then $a = 8$

If $p = 2$ and $a = 9$, then $c = 2/3$

12. (d) **13.** (c) **14.** (c)

15. (2) $\lim_{n\to\infty} \frac{1^4+2^4+3^4+\cdots+n^4}{n^5} = \lambda$

$$\Rightarrow \lim_{n\to\infty} \frac{1}{n}\cdot\sum_{r=1}^{n}\left(\frac{r}{n}\right)^4 = \lambda$$

$$\Rightarrow \int_0^1 x^4 dx = \lambda$$

$$\Rightarrow \left(\frac{x^5}{5}\right)_0^1 = \lambda$$

$$\therefore \lambda = 1/5 \Rightarrow 10\lambda = 2$$

16. (2) Given, $\lim_{n\to\infty}\left\{\frac{1}{n}+\frac{1}{n+1}+\frac{1}{n+2}+\cdots+\frac{1}{2n}\right\} = \log\lambda$

$$\Rightarrow \lim_{n\to\infty}\frac{1}{n}\left\{\frac{1}{1+\frac{0}{n}}+\frac{1}{1+\frac{1}{n}}+\frac{1}{1+\frac{2}{n}}+\cdots+\frac{1}{1+\frac{n}{n}}\right\} = \log\lambda$$

$$\Rightarrow \lim_{n\to\infty}\frac{1}{n}\sum_{r=0}^{n}\frac{1}{1+\left(\frac{r}{n}\right)}$$

Put $\frac{r}{n} = x \Rightarrow \frac{1}{n} = dx$

At $r = 0$, $r = n$

$\Rightarrow \quad x = 1$

$$\therefore \int_0^1 \frac{1}{1+x}dx = [\log(1+x)]_0^1$$

$$= \log 2 - \log 1 = \log 2$$

As $\quad \log 2 = \log\lambda$

$\therefore \quad \lambda = 2$

17. (1) Given, $\lim_{n\to\infty}\left\{\frac{n}{n^2+1^2}+\frac{n}{n^2+2^2}+\cdots+\frac{n}{n^2+n^2}\right\} = \lambda$

$$\Rightarrow \lim_{n\to\infty}\frac{1}{n}\left[\frac{1}{1+\left(\frac{1}{n}\right)^2}+\frac{1}{1+\left(\frac{2}{n}\right)^2}+\cdots+\frac{1}{1+\left(\frac{n}{n}\right)^2}\right] = \lambda$$

$$\Rightarrow \lim_{n\to\infty}\frac{1}{n}\sum_{r=1}^{n}\frac{1}{1+\left(\frac{r}{n}\right)^2} = \lambda$$

Let $\frac{r}{n} = x \Rightarrow \frac{1}{n} = dx$

When $r = 1$, then $r = n$

$\Rightarrow \quad x = 1$

$$\Rightarrow \int_0^1 \frac{1}{1+x^2}dx = \lambda$$

$$\Rightarrow \lambda = [\tan^{-1}x]_0^1 = \tan^{-1}(1) - \tan^{-1}(0) = \left(\frac{\pi}{4}\right)$$

Now, $\sin 2\lambda = \sin 2\cdot\frac{\pi}{4} = \sin\frac{\pi}{2} = 1$

18. (0) $\left[\lim_{n\to\infty}\frac{(n!)^{1/n}}{n}\right] = \left[\lim_{n\to\infty}\left(\frac{n!}{n^n}\right)^{1/n}\right]$

$$f(x) = \left[\lim_{n\to\infty}\left(\frac{n!}{n^n}\right)^{1/n}\right] \quad \ldots(i)$$

Now, let $A = \left(\frac{n!}{n^n}\right)^{1/n}$

Then, $A = \lim_{n\to\infty}\left[\frac{1}{n}\cdot\frac{2}{n}\cdot\frac{3}{n}\cdots\frac{n}{n}\right]^{1/n}$

$$\log A = \lim_{n\to\infty}\frac{1}{n}\left[\log\left(\frac{1}{n}\right)+\log\left(\frac{2}{n}\right)+\log\left(\frac{3}{n}\right)+\cdots+\log\left(\frac{n}{n}\right)\right]$$

$$= \lim_{n\to\infty}\frac{1}{n}\sum_{r=1}^{n}\log\left(\frac{r}{n}\right)$$

Put $\frac{r}{n} = x \Rightarrow \frac{1}{n} = dx$ and limits becomes 0 to 1.

$$\therefore \log A = \int_0^1 \log x dx = [x\log x]_0^1 - \int_0^1 x\cdot\frac{1}{x}$$

$$\Rightarrow \log A = [x\log x - x]_0^1$$

$$\Rightarrow \log A = -1$$

$$\Rightarrow A = e^{-1}$$

From Eq. (i), $f(x) = [A] = [e^{-1}]$, where $[\cdot]$ is a greatest integer function.

$$= \left[\frac{1}{e}\right] = [0.3678] \cong 0$$

As, $\left\{0 < \left[\frac{1}{e}\right] \le 1\right\}$

19. (1) Given, $\lim_{x\to 0}\frac{f(x)}{x} = 1$

$$\therefore \lim_{x\to 0}\frac{x(1+a\sin x) - b\sin x}{\left\{\frac{f(x)}{x}\right\}^3\cdot x^3}$$

$$= \lim_{x\to 0}\frac{x(1+a\sin x) - b\sin x}{x^3}$$

$$= \lim_{x\to 0}\frac{(1+a\sin x) + x(a\cos x) - b\cos x}{3x^2}$$

For limit to exists, $1 - b = 0 \Rightarrow b = 1$

$$\therefore \lim_{x\to 0}\frac{a\cos x + a\cos x - ax\sin x + b\sin x}{6x}$$

$$\lim_{x\to 0}\frac{2a\cos x - ax\sin x + b\sin x}{6x},$$

For limit to exists, $a = 0$

$\therefore \quad |a+b| = 1$

20. (2) $\lim_{n\to\infty}\{(1+x)(1+x^2)(1+x^4)\cdots(1+x^{2^n})\} = f(x), \ |x| < 1$

$$= \lim_{n\to\infty}\frac{(1-x)(1+x)(1+x^2)(1+x^4)\cdots(1+x^{2^n})}{(1-x)}$$

$$= \lim_{n\to\infty}\frac{(1-x^2)(1+x^2)(1+x^4)\cdots(1+x^{2^n})}{1-x}$$

$$= \lim_{n\to\infty}\frac{1-x^{2^{n+1}}}{1-x} = \frac{1}{1-x}, \forall |x| < 1$$

$$\therefore f(x) = \frac{1}{1-x}, \forall |x| < 1$$

Now, $f\left(\frac{1}{2}\right) = \frac{1}{1-\frac{1}{2}} = 2$

$$\Rightarrow f\left(\frac{1}{2}\right) = 2$$

Revisal Problems (JEE Main)

1. (d) $\lim_{x \to 2} \frac{\sin(e^{x-2}-1)}{\log_e(x-1)}$

It is a $\frac{0}{0}$ indeterminate form.

$\Rightarrow \lim_{x \to 2} \frac{\cos(e^{x-2}-1)\cdot e^{x-2}\cdot 1}{\frac{1}{(x-1)}\cdot(1-0)}$ [using L' Hospital's rule]

$$= \lim_{x \to 2} \frac{e^{x-2}\cos(e^{x-2}-1)(x-1)}{1}$$

$$= e^0 \cos(e^0-1)(2-1) = 1\cos 0\cdot(1) = 1$$

2. (a) $\lim_{n \to \infty} \frac{-3n+(-1)^n}{4n-(-1)^n}$

$$= \lim_{n \to \infty} \frac{-3n\left[1+\frac{(-1)^n}{3n}\right]}{4n\left[1-\frac{(-1)^n}{4n}\right]} = \frac{-3n}{4n} = \frac{-3}{4}$$

3. (a) $\lim_{x \to \infty} \left[x - x^2\cdot\log\left(1+\frac{1}{x}\right)\right]$

Let $y = \frac{1}{x}$, then

$$= \lim_{y \to 0} \frac{1}{y} - \frac{1}{y^2}\log(1+y)$$

$$= \lim_{y \to 0} \frac{y-\log(1+y)}{y^2} \quad \left[\frac{0}{0}\text{ form}\right]$$

$$= \lim_{y \to 0} \frac{1-\frac{1}{1+y}}{2y} \quad \text{[using L' Hospital's rule]}$$

$$= \lim_{y \to 0} \frac{y}{2y(1+y)} = \frac{1}{2}$$

4. (a) $\lim_{x \to \infty} \left(\frac{x+2}{x-2}\right)^{x+1}$

$$\Rightarrow e^{\lim_{x \to \infty}(x+1)\left(\frac{x+2}{x-2}-1\right)} = e^{\lim_{x \to \infty}\frac{4(x+1)}{(x-2)}}$$

$$= e^{\lim_{x \to \infty}\frac{4\left(1+\frac{1}{x}\right)}{\left(1-\frac{2}{x}\right)}} = e^4$$

5. (a) $\lim_{x \to 0^+} (1+\tan^2\sqrt{x})^{\frac{5}{x}}$

$$\Rightarrow e^{\lim_{x \to 0^+}\frac{5\tan^2\sqrt{x}}{x}} = e^{\lim_{h \to 0}\frac{5\tan^2\sqrt{0+h}}{0+h}}$$

$$= e^{\lim_{h \to 0}\frac{5\tan^2\sqrt{h}}{h}}$$

$$= e^{\lim_{h \to 0} 5\left[2\tan\sqrt{h}\sec^2\sqrt{h}\cdot\frac{1}{2\sqrt{h}}\right]}$$

$$= e^{\lim_{h \to 0} 5\cdot\frac{\tan\sqrt{h}}{\sqrt{h}}\sec^2\sqrt{h}}$$

$$= e^{5\lim_{h \to 0}\frac{\tan\sqrt{h}}{h}\lim_{h \to 0}\sec^2\sqrt{h}} = e^5$$

6. (c) $\lim_{x \to \infty} \left(\frac{x^2-2x+1}{x^2-4x+2}\right)^x$

$$= e^{\lim_{x \to \infty} x\left(\frac{x^2-2x+1}{x^2-4x+2}-1\right)}$$

$$= e^{\lim_{x \to \infty}\frac{x(2x-1)}{x^2-4x+2}} = e^{\lim_{x \to \infty}\frac{\left(2-\frac{1}{x}\right)x^2}{x^2\left(1-\frac{4}{x}+\frac{2}{x^2}\right)}} = e^2$$

7. (a) $\lim_{x \to 0} (\cos x)^{\frac{1}{\sin x}}$

$$= e^{\lim_{x \to 0}\left(\frac{\cos x - 1}{\sin x}\right)}$$

$$= e^{\lim_{x \to 0}\frac{-\sin x}{\cos x}} \Rightarrow e^{-0} = 1$$

8. (c) $\lim_{x \to a} \left(2-\frac{a}{x}\right)^{\tan\left(\frac{\pi x}{2a}\right)}$

$$= e^{\lim_{x \to a}\left(2-\frac{a}{x}-1\right)\tan\left(\frac{\pi x}{2a}\right)}$$

$$= e^{\lim_{x \to a}\left(1-\frac{a}{x}\right)\left(\tan\frac{\pi x}{2a}\right)}$$

$$= e^{\lim_{x \to a}\frac{\left(1-\frac{a}{x}\right)}{\cot\frac{\pi x}{2a}}} = e^{\lim_{x \to a}\frac{0+\frac{a}{x^2}}{-\operatorname{cosec}^2\left(\frac{\pi x}{2a}\right)\frac{\pi}{2a}}}$$

$$= e^{\lim_{x \to a}\left(\frac{-2}{\pi}\right)\sin^2\left(\frac{\pi x}{2a}\right)}$$

$$= e^{-2/\pi}$$

9. (d) $\lim_{n \to \infty} \frac{5^{n+1}+3^n-2^{2n}}{5^n+2^n+3^{2n+3}}$

$$= \lim_{n \to \infty} \frac{5\cdot5^n+3^n-4^n}{5^n+2^n+27\cdot3^{2n}}$$

$$= \lim_{n \to \infty} \frac{5^n\left[5+\left(\frac{3}{5}\right)^n-\left(\frac{4}{5}\right)^n\right]}{5^n\left[1+\left(\frac{2}{5}\right)^n+27\cdot\left(\frac{9}{5}\right)^n\right]}$$

We know that,

$$\lim_{n \to \infty}\left(\frac{a}{b}\right)^n \to 0, \forall\, a < b$$

$$\lim_{n \to \infty}\left(\frac{a}{b}\right)^n \to \infty, \forall\, a > b$$

$$\therefore \lim_{n \to \infty}\left[\frac{5+\left(\frac{3}{5}\right)^n-\left(\frac{4}{5}\right)^n}{1+\left(\frac{2}{5}\right)^n+27\cdot\left(\frac{9}{5}\right)^n}\right] = \frac{5+0-0}{1+0+\infty} = \frac{5}{\infty} = 0$$

10. (b) $\lim_{x \to \infty} \frac{x^n}{e^x} = 0$

Case I n is a positive integer.

$$\lim_{x \to \infty}\frac{x^n}{e^x} = \lim_{x \to \infty}\frac{nx^{n-1}}{e^x}$$

$$= \lim_{x \to \infty}\frac{n(n-1)x^{n-2}}{e^x}$$

$$= \lim_{x \to \infty}\frac{n!}{e^x} = 0$$

Case II n is a negative integer.

$$\lim_{x \to \infty}\frac{x^n}{e^\infty} = \lim_{x \to \infty}\frac{x^{-m}}{e^x}$$

[putting $n = -m$, where m is a + ve integer]

$$= \lim_{x \to \infty}\frac{1}{x^m e^x} = \frac{1}{\infty} = 0$$

Case III When $n = 0$

$$\lim_{x \to \infty}\frac{x^n}{e^x} = \lim_{x \to \infty}\frac{1}{e^x} = \frac{1}{\infty} = 0$$

Hence, $\lim_{x \to \infty}\frac{x^n}{e^x} = 0$, for all values of n.

11. (b) $\lim_{x \to 0} \frac{\sin^{-1} x - \tan^{-1} x}{x^3}$

$$= \lim_{x \to 0} \frac{\frac{1}{\sqrt{1-x^2}} - \frac{1}{1+x^2}}{3x^2}$$

$$= \lim_{x \to 0} \frac{(1+x^2) - \sqrt{1-x^2}}{3x^2 (1+x^2) \sqrt{1-x^2}}$$

$$= \lim_{x \to 0} \frac{(1+x^2)^2 - (1-x^2)}{3x^2 (1+x^2)\sqrt{1-x^2}(1+x^2+\sqrt{1-x^2})}$$

$$= \lim_{x \to 0} \frac{x^4 + 3x^2}{3x^2 (1+x^2)\sqrt{1-x^2}(1+x^2+\sqrt{1-x^2})}$$

$$= \lim_{x \to 0} \frac{x^2 + 3}{3(1+x^2)(\sqrt{1-x^2})(1+x^2+\sqrt{1-x^2})}$$

$$= \frac{3}{6} = \frac{1}{2}$$

12. (c) $\lim_{x \to \frac{\pi}{2}} \frac{(1-\tan x/2)\cdot(1-\sin x)}{(1+\tan x/2)\cdot(\pi - 2x)^3}$

Put $x = \frac{\pi}{2} - h$ as $x \to \frac{\pi}{2}, h \to 0$

$$= \lim_{h \to 0} \frac{1-\tan\left(\frac{\pi}{4}+\frac{h}{2}\right)}{1+\tan\left(\frac{\pi}{4}+\frac{h}{2}\right)} \frac{(1-\cos h)}{(2h)^3}$$

$$= \lim_{h \to 0} \tan h/2 \frac{2\sin^2 h/2}{8h^3}$$

$$= \lim_{h \to 0} \frac{1}{4}\frac{\tan h/2}{h/2 \times 2} \times \left(\frac{\sin h/2}{h/2}\right) \times \frac{1}{4}$$

$$= \lim_{h \to 0} \frac{1}{32}\left(\frac{\tan h/2}{h/2}\right)\left(\frac{\sin h/2}{h/2}\right)^2 = \frac{1}{32}$$

13. (b) $\lim_{x \to -\infty} \frac{x^2 \cdot \sin\left(\frac{1}{x}\right)}{\sqrt{9x^2 + x + 1}}$

Let $x = -\frac{1}{y}$

$$= \lim_{y \to 0} \frac{-\frac{1}{y^2}\sin y}{\left(\frac{9}{y^2} - \frac{1}{y} + 1\right)^{1/2}}$$

$$= \lim_{y \to 0} \frac{-\sin y}{\left(\sqrt{9 - y + y^2}\right) y} = -\frac{1}{3}$$

14. (c) α and β are the roots of $ax^2 + bx + c = 0$

i.e. $\quad ax^2 + bx + c = a(x-\alpha)(x-\beta)$

$\Rightarrow \quad \lim_{x \to \alpha} (1 + ax^2 + bx + c)^{1/x-\alpha}$

$$\Rightarrow e^{\lim_{x \to \alpha}\left[\frac{ax^2+bx+c}{(x-\alpha)}\right]} = e^{\lim_{x \to \alpha}\frac{a(x-\alpha)(x-\beta)}{(x-\alpha)}}$$

$$= e^{\lim_{x \to \alpha} a(x-\beta)} = e^{a(\alpha-\beta)}$$

15. (d) Here, $\frac{|ax^2+bx+c|}{ax^2+bx+c} = \frac{|a|\,|(x-\alpha)(x-\beta)|}{a(x-\alpha)(x-\beta)}$

$$= \begin{cases} \frac{a|(x-\alpha)(x-\beta)|}{a(x-\alpha)(x-\beta)}, & a > 0 \\ \frac{-a|(x-\alpha)(x-\beta)|}{a(x-\alpha)(x-\beta)}, & a < 0 \end{cases}$$

$$= \begin{cases} 1, & a > 0 \text{ and } (x < \alpha \text{ or } x > \beta) \\ -1, & a > 0 \text{ and } (\alpha < x < \beta) \\ -1, & a < 0 \text{ and } (x < \alpha \text{ or } x > \beta) \\ 1, & a < 0 \text{ and } (\alpha < x < \beta) \end{cases}$$

$\therefore \quad \lim_{x \to x_0} \frac{|ax^2+bx+c|}{ax^2+bx+c} = 1$

when, $\begin{cases} a > 0 \text{ and } (x < \alpha \text{ or } x > \beta) \\ a < 0 \text{ and } (\alpha < x < \beta) \end{cases}$

16. (a) $\lim_{x \to 0^+} \log_{\sin\left(\frac{x}{2}\right)}(\sin x)$

$$= \lim_{x \to 0^+} \frac{\log\sin\left(\frac{x}{2}\right)}{\log\sin x}$$

$$= \lim_{h \to 0} \frac{\log\sin\left(\frac{h}{2}\right)}{\log\sin h} = \lim_{h \to 0} \frac{\frac{1}{\sin\left(\frac{h}{2}\right)}\cos\left(\frac{h}{2}\right)\cdot\frac{1}{2}}{\frac{1}{\sin h}\cdot\cos h}$$

$$= \lim_{h \to 0} \frac{\frac{\frac{h}{2}}{\sin\left(\frac{h}{2}\right)}\cos\left(\frac{h}{2}\right)}{\left(\frac{h}{\sin h}\right)\cos h}$$

$$= 1$$

17. (c) $\lim_{x \to 0} \frac{1 - \cos x \cdot \sqrt{\cos 2x}}{x^2}$ $\quad \left[\frac{0}{0}\text{form}\right]$

$$= \lim_{x \to 0} \frac{0 - \left[(-\sin x)\cdot\sqrt{\cos 2x} + \frac{1}{2\sqrt{\cos 2x}}(-2\sin 2x)\cdot\cos x\right]}{2x}$$

$$= \lim_{x \to 0} \frac{\sin x\sqrt{\cos 2x}}{2x} + \frac{1}{2\sqrt{\cos 2x}}\frac{(2\sin 2x)}{2x}\cdot\cos x$$

$$= \frac{1}{2}\lim_{x \to 0}\frac{\sin x}{x}\sqrt{\cos 2x} + \lim_{x \to 0}\frac{\sin 2x}{2x}\cdot\frac{1}{\sqrt{\cos 2x}}\cdot\cos x$$

$$= \frac{1}{2} + 1 = \frac{3}{2}$$

18. (a) $f(x) = \begin{cases} \sin x, & x \neq n\pi\ ;\ n = 0, \pm 1, \pm 2 + \ldots \\ 2, & \text{otherwise} \end{cases}$

and $\quad g(x) = \begin{cases} x^2 + 1, & x \neq 0, 2 \\ 4, & x = 0 \\ 5, & x = 2 \end{cases}$

Now, $\lim_{x \to 0} g[f(x)]$

$$g[f(x)] = \begin{cases} [f(x)]^2 + 1; & f(x) \neq 2 \\ 5; & f(x) = 2 \end{cases}$$

$$g[f(x)] = \begin{cases} \sin^2 x + 1; & x \neq n\pi \\ 5; & x = n\pi \end{cases}$$

$$\text{RHL} = g\lim_{h \to 0}[f(0+h)]$$

$$= \lim_{h \to 0} \sin^2 h + 1 = 1$$

$$\text{LHL} = \lim_{h \to 0} g[f(0-h)]$$

$$= \lim_{h \to 0} (\sin^2 h + 1) = 1$$

$\therefore \lim_{x \to 0} g[f(x)] = 1$

19. (c) $f(x) = \lim_{t \to 0} \left(\frac{2x}{\pi} \cdot \cot^{-1} \frac{x}{t^2} \right)$

$$= \begin{cases} \frac{2x}{\pi} \cdot \cot^{-1}(\infty), & x \geq 0 \\ \frac{2x}{\pi} \cdot \cot^{-1}(-\infty), & x < 0 \end{cases}$$

$$f(x) = \begin{cases} 0, & x \geq 0 \\ 2x, & x < 0 \end{cases}$$

$\therefore$ Graph of $f(x)$ is

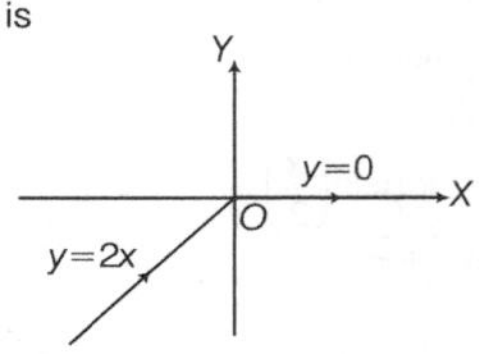

20. (b) $\lim_{y \to 0} \left\{ \lim_{x \to \infty} \frac{\exp\left[x \log\left(1 + \frac{ay}{x}\right)\right] - \exp\left[x \log\left(1 + \frac{by}{x}\right)\right]}{y} \right\}$

Let $x = \frac{1}{z}$, $x \to \infty$, $z \to 0$

$$= \lim_{y \to 0} \left\{ \lim_{z \to 0} \frac{e^{\frac{\log[1 + (ay)z]}{z}} - e^{\frac{\log[1 + (by)z]}{z}}}{y} \right\}$$

$$= \lim_{y \to 0} \left\{ \lim_{z \to 0} \frac{e^{(ay)\frac{\log[1 + (ay)z]}{(ay)z}} - e^{by\frac{\log[1 + (by)z]}{(by)z}}}{y} \right\}$$

$$= \lim_{y \to 0} \left\{ \frac{e^{ay} - e^{by}}{y} \right\}$$

$$= \lim_{y \to 0} \left\{ \frac{e^{(a-b)y} - 1}{y} \right\} e^{by} = \lim_{y \to 0} \left\{ \frac{e^{(a-b)y} - 1}{(a-b)y} \right\} e^{by} (a - b)$$

$= (a - b)$

21. (b) $\lim_{x \to 0} \frac{\sin(\pi \cos^2 x)}{x^2}$

$$= \lim_{x \to 0} \frac{\cos(\pi \cos^2 x) \cdot \pi \cdot 2\cos x(-\sin x)}{2x}$$

$$= \lim_{x \to 0} \pi \cos(\pi \cos^2 x) \cos x \left(-\frac{\sin x}{x} \right)$$

$$= \pi(-1) \cdot 1(-1) = \pi$$

22. (c) $\lim_{x \to 0} \frac{x \tan 2x - 2x \tan x}{(1 - \cos 2x)^2}$

$$= \lim_{x \to 0} \frac{x \frac{2\tan x}{1 - \tan^2 x} - 2x \tan x}{(1 - 1 + 2\sin^2 x)^2} = \lim_{x \to 0} \frac{2x \tan x \left(\frac{1}{1 - \tan^2 x} - 1 \right)}{4\sin^4 x}$$

$$= \lim_{x \to 0} \frac{2x \tan^3 x}{(1 - \tan^2 x)\, 4\sin^4 x} = \lim_{x \to 0} \frac{1}{2} \frac{\frac{\tan^3 x}{x^3}}{(1 - \tan^2 x) \frac{\sin^4 x}{x^4}}$$

$$= \frac{1}{2}$$

23. (a) $\lim_{x \to 0} \frac{axe^x - b\log_e(1 + x) + cxe^{-x}}{x^2 \cdot \sin x} = 2$

$$\Rightarrow \lim_{x \to 0} \frac{axe^x - b\log(1 + x) + cxe^{-x}}{x^3} = 2$$

$$\Rightarrow \lim_{x \to 0} \frac{ae^x + axe^x - \frac{b}{1 + x} + ce^{-x} - cxe^{-x}}{3x^2} = 2$$

For limit to exist, $a - b + c = 0$

24. (b) $\lim_{n \to \infty} (\sqrt[3]{8n^2 - n^3} + n)$

$$= \lim_{n \to \infty} (\sqrt[3]{8n^2 - n^3} + \sqrt[3]{n^3})$$

$$= \lim_{n \to \infty} \frac{8n^2 - n^3 + n^3}{(8n^2 - n^3)^{2/3} + (n^3)^{2/3} - (8n^2 - n^3)^{1/3} n}$$

$$= \lim_{n \to \infty} \frac{8n^2}{n^2\left(\frac{8}{n} - 1\right)^{2/3} + n^2 - n^2\left(\frac{8}{n} - 1\right)^{1/3}}$$

$$= \lim_{n \to \infty} \frac{8}{\left(\frac{8}{n} - 1\right)^{2/3} + 1 - \left(\frac{8}{n} - 1\right)^{1/3}}$$

$$= \frac{8}{3}$$

25. (b) $\lim_{x \to 0} \frac{(x^{16} + 4x^{12} - 3x^4)}{[x^4]}$

$$= \lim_{x \to 0} \frac{x^{16} + 4x^{12} - 3x^4}{x^4}$$

$$= \lim_{x \to 0} x^{12} + 4x^8 - 3 = -3$$

26. (a) $\lim_{n \to \infty} (\sqrt{2n^2 + n} - \lambda\sqrt{2n^2 - n}) = \frac{1}{\sqrt{2}}$

$$\Rightarrow \lim_{n \to \infty} \frac{(2n^2 + n) - \lambda^2(2n^2 - n)}{\sqrt{2n^2 + n} + \lambda\sqrt{2n^2 - n}} = \frac{1}{\sqrt{2}}$$

$$\Rightarrow \lim_{n \to \infty} \frac{(1 - \lambda)^2 \cdot 2n^2 + (1 + \lambda^2)n}{\sqrt{2n^2 + n} + \lambda\sqrt{2n^2 - n}} = \frac{1}{\sqrt{2}}, \text{ for limit to exist}$$

$$1 - \lambda^2 = 0 \Rightarrow \lambda = \pm 1 \quad \ldots\text{(i)}$$

$$\therefore \lim_{n \to \infty} \frac{n(1 + \lambda^2)}{\sqrt{2n^2 + n} + \lambda\sqrt{2n^2 - n}} = \frac{1}{\sqrt{2}}$$

$$\Rightarrow \frac{(1 + \lambda^2)}{\sqrt{2} + \lambda\sqrt{2}} = \frac{1}{\sqrt{2}}$$

$$\Rightarrow 1 + \lambda^2 = 1 + \lambda, \text{ where } \lambda \neq 0 \quad \ldots\text{(ii)}$$

From Eqs. (i) and (ii), we get

$$\lambda = 1$$

27. (b) We have, $\lim_{x \to -1} \frac{1}{\sqrt{|x| - \{x\}}}$

RHL

$$= \lim_{h \to 0} \frac{1}{\sqrt{|-1 + h| - \{-1 + h\}}} = \lim_{h \to 0} \frac{1}{\sqrt{|-1 + h| - [1 - (1 - h)]}} = 1$$

LHL

$$= \lim_{h \to 0} \frac{1}{\sqrt{|-1 - h| - \{-1 - h\}}} = \lim_{h \to 0} \frac{1}{\sqrt{|1 + h| - [1 - (1 + h)]}} = 1$$

28. (b) $\lim_{x \to 0} \frac{\log(\sin 3x)}{\log(\sin x)}$

$$= \lim_{x \to 0} \frac{\frac{1}{\sin 3x} \cos 3x \cdot 3}{\frac{1}{\sin x} \cos x} = \lim_{x \to 0} \frac{\frac{3x}{\sin 3x} \cos 3x}{\frac{x}{\sin x} \cos x} = 1$$

29. (c) $\lim_{x \to 0} \frac{x^8}{[1 - \cos x\{1 - \cos(1 - \cos x)\}]}$

$$= \lim_{x \to 0} \frac{x^8}{1 - \cos[1 - \cos(2\sin^2 x/2)]}$$

$$= \lim_{x \to 0} \frac{x^8}{1 - \cos[2\sin^2(\sin^2 x/2)]}$$

$$= \lim_{x \to 0} \frac{x^8}{[2\sin^2\{\sin^2(\sin^2 x/2)\}]}$$

$$= \lim_{x \to 0} \frac{x^8}{2 \cdot (x/2)^8} = \lim_{x \to 0} \frac{1}{2 \cdot \frac{1}{2^8}} = 2^7 = 128$$

30. (a) $\lim_{x \to 0}\left(\left[\frac{-5\sin x}{x}\right]+\left[\frac{6\sin x}{x}\right]\right)$

$$= \lim_{x \to 0}(-5+5) \quad \left[\begin{array}{l} \because \quad \frac{\sin x}{x} < 1 \\ \Rightarrow \ -4 > \frac{-5\sin x}{x} > -5 \text{ and } 5 < \frac{6\sin x}{x} < 6 \end{array}\right]$$

$= 0$

31. (c) $\lim_{x \to 0}\left[\frac{(k-\alpha)\alpha x}{x} - \frac{\tan x}{x}\right]\cdot\frac{\sin \alpha x}{\alpha x}\cdot\alpha = 0$

$\Rightarrow \quad [(k-\alpha)\alpha - 1]\alpha = 0$

$\Rightarrow \quad k-\alpha = 1/\alpha \quad \text{or} \quad k = \alpha + 1/\alpha \geq 2$

$\therefore$ Minimum value of $k = 2$

32. (a) $\lim_{x \to \frac{1}{\sqrt{2}}} \frac{2\sin^{-1}x - \frac{\pi}{2}}{1-2x^2}$

$$= \lim_{x \to \frac{1}{\sqrt{2}}} \frac{\frac{2}{\sqrt{1-x^2}} - 0}{-4x} = \frac{\frac{2}{\sqrt{1-\frac{1}{2}}}}{-4\cdot\frac{1}{\sqrt{2}}} = \frac{2\sqrt{2}}{-2\sqrt{2}} = -1$$

33. (c) $\lim_{x \to 0} \frac{(\cos x)\log(1+x) - x\cos x - \log(1+x) + x}{x^4}$

$$= \lim_{x \to 0} \frac{\log(1+x)(\cos x - 1) - x\cos x + x}{x^4}$$

$$= \lim_{x \to 0} \frac{(\cos x - 1)[\log(1+x) - x]}{x^4}$$

$$= \lim_{x \to 0} \frac{-2\sin^2\frac{x}{2}}{\left(\frac{x^2}{4}\right)\cdot 4} \lim_{x \to 0} \frac{\log(1+x) - x}{x^2}$$

$$= \left(-\frac{1}{2}\right)\lim_{x \to 0} \frac{\frac{1}{1+x} - 1}{2x}$$

$$= \left(\frac{-1}{2}\right)\lim_{x \to 0} \frac{-x}{2x(1+x)}$$

$$= \left(\frac{-1}{2}\right)\lim_{x \to 0} -\frac{1}{2(1+x)} = \left(\frac{-1}{2}\right)\left(\frac{-1}{2}\right) = \frac{1}{4}$$

34. (a) $\lim_{x \to 0}\left[\frac{\sin(\operatorname{Sgn} x)}{\operatorname{Sgn} x}\right]$

$$\operatorname{Sgn}(x) = \begin{cases} 0, & x = 0 \\ \operatorname{Sgn}(x), & x \neq 0 \end{cases}$$

$$\therefore \quad \lim_{x \to 0}\left[\frac{\sin(\operatorname{Sgn} x)}{\operatorname{Sgn} x}\right]$$

$$= \lim_{t \to 1^-}[t] = 0 \quad \left[\because \frac{\sin(\operatorname{Sgn} x)}{\operatorname{Sgn} x} = t\right]$$

35. (c) $x^2 + 2x + 3 = (x+1)^2 + 2 \geq 1$, so $a = 2$

and $b = \lim_{\theta \to 0} \frac{1-\cos\theta}{\theta^2} = \lim_{\theta \to 0} \frac{2\sin^2\frac{\theta}{2}}{\left(\frac{\theta}{2}\right)^2\cdot 4} = \frac{1}{2}$

$$\therefore \quad \sum_{r=0}^{n} a^r b^{n-r} = b^n + ab^{n-1} + a^2b^{n-2} + \cdots + a^n$$

$$= \frac{b^n\left[1-\left(\frac{a}{b}\right)^{n+1}\right]}{1-\frac{a}{b}} = \frac{\left(\frac{1}{2}\right)^n[1-(4)^{n+1}]}{1-4}$$

$$= \frac{4^{n+1}-1}{3\cdot 2^n}$$

36. (d) $\lim_{x \to 0} \frac{x(1+a\cos x) - b\sin x}{x^3} = 1$ [using L' Hospital's Rule]

$$\Rightarrow \quad \lim_{x \to 0} \frac{(1+a\cos x) + x(-a\sin x) - b\cos x}{3x^2} = 1$$

For limit to exist

$$1 + a - b = 0 \qquad \ldots\text{(i)}$$

Again, on applying L' Hospital's Rule

$$\Rightarrow \quad \lim_{x \to 0} \frac{-a\sin x - a\sin x - ax\cos x + b\sin x}{6x} = 1$$

$$\Rightarrow \quad \lim_{x \to 0} \frac{\sin x(b-2a)}{6x} - \frac{ax\cos x}{6x} = 1$$

$$\Rightarrow \quad \frac{(b-2a)}{6} - \frac{a}{6} = 1$$

$$\Rightarrow \quad b - 3a = 6 \qquad \ldots\text{(ii)}$$

On solving Eqs. (i) and (ii), we get

$$a = -5/2 \quad \text{and} \quad b = -3/2$$

37. (b) $f(x) = \lim_{m \to \infty}\lim_{n \to \infty}\{1 + \cos^{2m}(n!\,\pi x)\}$

We know that, $|\cos\theta| \leq 1, \forall\theta$

So, if $|\cos n!\,px| < 1$, when $x \in$ irrational.

$$\lim_{m \to \infty}\lim_{n \to \infty}(1 + \cos^{2m} n!\,\pi x) = (1+0) = 1$$

and if $|\cos n!\,px| = 1$; $x \in$ rational

$$\lim_{m \to \infty}\lim_{n \to \infty}(1 + \cos^{2m} n!\,\pi x) = \lim_{m \to \infty}\lim_{n \to \infty}(1 + 1^{2m})$$

$$= \lim_{m \to \infty}\lim_{n \to \infty}(1+1) = 2$$

38. (a) $\lim_{x \to 0} \frac{\sin x^{2012} - x^{2012}\cdot\cos x^{2012} + (x^3)^{2012}}{x^{2012}\cdot(e^{5x^{2012}} - 1 - 5x^{2012})}$,

Put $x^{2012} = t$

Then, $\quad \lim_{t \to 0} \frac{\sin t - t\cdot\cos t + t^3}{t(e^{5t} - 1 - 5t)}$

$$= \lim_{t \to 0} \frac{\left(t - \frac{t^3}{3!} + \frac{t^5}{5!} - \cdots\right) - t\left(1 - \frac{t^2}{2!} + \frac{t^4}{4!} - \cdots\right) + t^3}{t\left[\left(1 + 5t + \frac{(5t)^2}{2!} + \cdots\right)\right] - 1 - 5t}$$

$$= \lim_{t \to 0} \frac{t^3\left(\frac{-1}{6} + \frac{1}{2} + 1\right) + t^5\cdots}{t^3\left(\frac{25}{2} + t\cdots\right)}$$

$$= \frac{\frac{-1}{6} + \frac{1}{2} + 1}{\frac{25}{2}} = \frac{\frac{8}{6}}{\frac{25}{2}} = \frac{8}{75}$$

39. (d) Here, $\tan\alpha + \cot\alpha = n$

$$\Rightarrow \quad \frac{1}{\sin\alpha\cos\alpha} = n \ \Rightarrow \ \sin 2\alpha = \frac{2}{n} \qquad \ldots\text{(i)}$$

$\therefore \quad \sin 2\alpha_n = \frac{2}{n}$, as α_n is root

$$\lim_{n \to \infty}(\sin\alpha_n + \cos\alpha_n)^n$$

$$= \lim_{n \to \infty}[(\sin\alpha_n + \cos\alpha_n)^2]^{n/2}$$

$$= \lim_{n \to \infty}[1 + \sin 2\alpha_n]^{n/2}$$

$$= \lim_{n \to \infty}\left[1 + \frac{2}{n}\right]^{n/2}$$

$$= e^{\lim_{n \to \infty}\frac{2}{n}\cdot\frac{n}{2}} = e$$

40. (b) $\lim_{n \to \infty} n\left[\frac{e}{\left(1+\frac{1}{n}\right)^n} - 1\right]$, let $\frac{1}{n} = x$

$$\Rightarrow \quad \lim_{x \to 0} \frac{\frac{e}{(1+x)^{1/x}} - 1}{x} = \lim_{x \to 0} \frac{e - (1+x)^{1/x}}{x \cdot (1+x)^{1/x}}$$

$$= \lim_{x \to 0} \frac{e - e\left(1 - \frac{x}{2} + \frac{11x^2}{24} \cdots\right)}{x} \cdot \lim_{x \to 0} \frac{1}{(1+x)^{1/x}}$$

$$= \lim_{x \to 0} \frac{\frac{x}{2} \cdot e\left(1 - \frac{11}{12}x \cdots\right)}{x} \cdot \lim_{x \to 0} \frac{1}{(1+x)^{1/x}}$$

$$= \frac{e}{2} \cdot \frac{1}{e} = \frac{1}{2}$$

41. (a) $f(x) = \lim_{n \to \infty} \frac{1}{\left(\frac{3}{\pi}\tan^{-1} 2x\right)^{2n} + 5} = 0$

when, $\left|\frac{3}{\pi}\tan^{-1} 2x\right| > 1$

$\Rightarrow \quad |\tan^{-1} 2x| > \pi/3 \Rightarrow |2x| > \sqrt{3}$

42. (a) $\lim_{x \to 0} \frac{|\cos(\sin 3x)| - 1}{x^2}$

We have, $|\cos(\sin 3x)| = \begin{cases} \cos(\sin 3x), & x > 0 \\ \cos(\sin 3x), & x < 0 \end{cases}$

$$\text{RHS} = \lim_{x \to 0^+} \frac{\cos(\sin 3x) - 1}{x^2} = \lim_{h \to 0} \frac{\cos(\sin 3h) - 1}{h^2}$$

$$= \lim_{h \to 0} \frac{-\sin(\sin 3h)\cos 3h \cdot (3)}{2h}$$

$$= \lim_{h \to 0} \frac{-\sin(\sin 3h)}{\sin 3h} \cdot \frac{\sin 3h}{3h}(3)\frac{3}{2}\cos 3h = \frac{-9}{2}$$

$$\text{LHS} = \lim_{x \to 0^-} \frac{\cos(\sin 3x) - 1}{x^2} = \lim_{h \to 0} \frac{\cos(\sin 3h) - 1}{h^2}$$

$$= \lim_{h \to 0} \frac{-\sin(\sin 3h)\cos 3h(3)}{2h}$$

$$= \lim_{h \to 0} \frac{-\sin h(\sin 3h)}{\sin 3h} \frac{\sin 3h}{3h} \cdot (3)\frac{(3)}{2}\cos 3h = \frac{-9}{2}$$

43. (a) $\lim_{x \to 0} \left(2^{x-1} + \frac{1}{2}\right)^{1/x}$

$$= e^{\lim_{x \to 0}\left(\frac{2^x - 1}{2x}\right)} = e^{\frac{1}{2}\lim_{x \to 0} \frac{2^x - 1}{x}}$$

$$= e^{\frac{1}{2}\log 2}$$

$$= e^{\log\sqrt{2}} = \sqrt{2}$$

44. (d) $\lim_{h \to 0} [-\log(\{0-h\} + |[-h]|]^{\{-h\}}$

$$\Rightarrow \quad = \lim_{h \to 0} [-\log(1 - h + 1)]^{1-h}$$

$$= -\log 2 = \log\left(\frac{1}{2}\right)$$

45. (b) $\lim_{x \to 0} \left[\frac{(1+x)^x}{x^x \cdot e}\right]^x$, put $\frac{1}{x} = y$

$$\Rightarrow \quad \lim_{y \to 0} \left[\frac{(1+y)^{1/y}}{e}\right]^{1/y} = e^{\lim_{y \to 0} \frac{(1+y)^{1/y} - e}{ey}}$$

$$\Rightarrow \quad e^{\lim_{y \to 0} \frac{e(1 - y/2 + 11y^2/24) - e}{ey}}$$

$$e^{\lim_{y \to 0}\left(-\frac{1}{2} + \frac{11y}{12} \cdots\right)}$$

$$e^{-1/2} = \frac{1}{\sqrt{e}}$$

46. (a) **Statement I** $\underbrace{\lim_{x \to 0}\left[\frac{\sin x}{x}\right]}_{\text{I}} \neq \underbrace{\left[\lim_{x \to 0} \frac{\sin x}{x}\right]}_{\text{II}}$

Case I $\lim_{x \to 0}\left[\frac{\sin x}{x}\right]$

$$\text{LHL} = \lim_{x \to 0^-}\left[\frac{\sin x}{x}\right] = \lim_{t \to 1^-} [t] = 0$$

i.e. $\lim_{x \to 0}\left[\frac{\sin x}{x}\right] = 0$

$$\text{RHL} = \lim_{x \to 0^+}\left[\frac{\sin x}{x}\right] = \lim_{t \to 1^+} [t] = 0$$

Case II $\left[\lim_{x \to 0} \frac{\sin x}{x}\right]$

$$\text{LHL} = \left[\lim_{x \to 0^-} \frac{\sin x}{x}\right] = \left[\lim_{h \to 0} \frac{\sin(0-h)}{-h}\right] = \left[\lim_{h \to 0} \frac{-\sin h}{-h}\right] = [1] = 1$$

$$\text{RHL} = \left[\lim_{x \to 0^+} \frac{\sin x}{x}\right] = \left[\lim_{h \to 0} \frac{\sin(0+h)}{(0+h)}\right] = \left[\lim_{h \to 0} \frac{\sin h}{h}\right] = [1] = 1$$

$$\left[\lim_{x \to 0} \frac{\sin x}{x}\right] = [1] = 1$$

Case I $\neq$ Case II

Statement II $\lim_{x \to a} h[g(x)] = h[\lim_{x \to a} g(x)]$, if $y = h(x)$ is continuous at $x = \lim_{x \to a} g(x)$.

So, Statement I and Statement II both are correct and Statement II is correct explanation of Statement I.

47. (b) **Statement I** $\frac{\sqrt{\frac{1 - \cos 2x}{2}}}{x} = \lim_{x \to 0} \frac{|\sin x|}{x}$

$$\text{LHL} = \lim_{x \to 0^-} \frac{|\sin x|}{x} = \lim_{h \to 0} \frac{|\sin(-h)|}{h} = \lim_{h \to 0} \frac{\sin h}{-h} = -1$$

$$\text{RHL} = \lim_{x \to 0^+} \frac{|\sin x|}{x} = \lim_{h \to 0} \frac{|\sin(0+h)|}{(0+h)} = \lim_{h \to 0} \frac{\sin h}{h} = 1$$

$\therefore$ LHL $\neq$ RHL

So, $\lim_{x \to 0} \frac{\sqrt{\frac{1 - \cos 2x}{2}}}{x}$ does not exist.

Statement II $\lim_{x \to 0} \frac{\sin x}{x} = 1$

$$\text{LHL} = \lim_{x \to 0^-} \frac{\sin x}{x} = \lim_{h \to 0} \frac{-\sin h}{-h} = \lim_{h \to 0} \frac{\sin h}{h} = 1$$

$$\text{RHL} = \lim_{x \to 0^+} \frac{\sin x}{x} = \lim_{h \to 0} \frac{\sin h}{h} = 1$$

$\therefore$ LHL = RHL

So, Statements I and II both are correct but Statement II is not the correct explanation of Statement I.

48. (d) **Statement I** $\lim_{x \to 0}\left[\tan\left(\frac{\pi}{4} + x\right)\right]^{1/x}$

$$= \lim_{x \to 0}\left(\frac{\tan\frac{\pi}{4} + \tan x}{\tan\frac{\pi}{4} - \tan x}\right)^{1/x}$$

$$= \lim_{x \to 0}\left(\frac{1 + \tan x}{1 - \tan x}\right)^{1/x}$$

$$= e^{\lim_{x \to 0} \frac{1}{x}\left(\frac{1 + \tan x}{1 - \tan x} - 1\right)} = e^{\lim_{x \to 0} \frac{1}{x} \frac{2\tan x}{(1 - \tan x)}} = e^2$$

Statement II $\lim_{x \to a} [1 + f(x)]^{g(x)} = e^{\lim_{x \to a} f(x) g(x)}$,

If $\lim_{x \to a} f(x) = 0$ and $\lim_{x \to a} g(x) = \infty$

So, Statement II is correct but Statement I is incorrect.

49. (c) **Statement I** $\lim_{x \to \infty} \left(\frac{2x^4 + 3x^3 + 7x}{3x^4 + 2x^2 + 3x}\right)$

$$= \lim_{x \to \infty} \left(\frac{2 + \frac{3}{x} + \frac{7}{x^3}}{3 + \frac{2}{x^2} + \frac{3}{x^3}}\right) = \frac{2}{3}$$

n

Statement II $\lim_{x \to \infty} \frac{P(x)}{Q(x)} = \frac{\text{Leading coefficient of } P(x)}{\text{Leading coefficient of } Q(x)}$

$P(x)$ and $Q(x)$ are two unknown polynomials.

So, Statement I is correct but Statement II is incorrect.

50. (a) **Statement I**

$$\lim_{n \to \infty}\left(\sqrt{n^2+n+1} - \left[\sqrt{n^2+n+1}\right]\right)$$

$$\Rightarrow \quad (n) < \left[\sqrt{n^2+n+1}\right] < (n+1)$$

$$= \lim_{n \to \infty} \sqrt{n^2+n+1} - n$$

$$= \lim_{n \to \infty} \frac{n^2+n+1-n^2}{\sqrt{n^2+n+1}+n}$$

$$= \lim_{n \to \infty} \frac{n\left(1+\frac{1}{n}\right)}{n\left(\sqrt{1+\frac{1}{n}+\frac{1}{n^2}}+1\right)}$$

$$= \frac{1}{2}$$

Statement II

$$\lim_{n \to \infty} \frac{a_0x^n + a_1x^{n-1} + \cdots + a_n}{b_0x^n + b_1x^{n-1} + \cdots + b_n} = \frac{a_0}{b_0}$$

As $n < \sqrt{n^2+n+1} < (n+1)$

$\therefore \quad \frac{a_0}{b_0}$ [take x^n common from numerator and denominator]

So, Statement I and Statement II are correct and Statement II is the correct explanation of Statement I.

Revisal Problems (JEE Advanced)

1. (d) We have, $I = \lim_{x \to \infty} \left(\frac{x+1}{x-1}\right)^x$

$$= \lim_{x \to \infty} \left(\frac{x-1+1+1}{x-1}\right)^x = \lim_{x \to \infty} \left[\frac{(x-1)+2}{(x-1)}\right]^x$$

$$= \lim_{x \to \infty} \left[1 + \frac{2}{(x-1)}\right]^x$$

Clearly, it is of the form 1^∞ and we know if $\lim_{x \to a} f(x) = 1$ and $\lim_{x \to a} g(x) = \infty$, then $\lim_{x \to a} [f(x)]^{g(x)} = e^{\lim_{x \to a} \{f(x)-1\} g(x)}$

$\therefore$ We have, $\quad I = e^{\lim_{x \to \infty} \left\{\left(1+\frac{2}{(x-1)}\right)-1\right\}x}$

$$e^{\lim_{x \to \infty} \frac{2x}{x-1}} = e^{\lim_{x \to \infty} 2} = e^2 \quad \text{[using L' Hospital's rule]}$$

Now, $\quad \{I\} = \{e^2\} = \{7.389\} = 0.389 = e^2 - 7$

2. (a) Consider $\lim_{x \to -\infty} [(x^5 + 7x^4 + 2)^c - x]$

$$= \lim_{x \to -\infty} \left[x^{5c}\left(1+\frac{7}{x}+\frac{2}{x^5}\right)^c - x\right]$$

$$= \lim_{x \to -\infty} x\left[x^{5c-1}\left(1+\frac{7}{x}+\frac{2}{x^5}\right)^c - 1\right] \quad \ldots(i)$$

Now, as the limit exists, therefore it should be of the form $\infty \times 0$, which is possible only, if

$$5c - 1 = 0 \Rightarrow c = \frac{1}{5}$$

Now, on substituting $c = \frac{1}{5}$ in Eq. (i), we get

$\lim_{x \to -\infty} [(x^5 + 7x^4 + 2)^{1/5} - x]$

$$= \lim_{x \to -\infty} x\left[\left(1+\frac{7}{x}+\frac{2}{x^5}\right)^{1/5} - 1\right]$$

$$= \lim_{x \to -\infty} x\,((1+t)^{1/5} - 1), \text{ where } t = \frac{7}{x} + \frac{2}{x^5}$$

$$= \lim_{x \to -\infty} x\left[\left(1+\frac{t}{5}-\frac{2}{25}t^2+\cdots\right)-1\right],$$

since, if n is any rational number, then

$\left[(1+x)^n = 1 + nx + \frac{n(n-1)}{1\cdot 2}x^2 + \cdots\right]$

$$= \lim_{x \to -\infty} x\left(\frac{t}{5} - \frac{2}{25}t^2 + \cdots\right), \text{ where } t = \frac{7}{x} + \frac{2}{x^5}$$

$$= \lim_{x \to -\infty} x\left[\frac{1}{5}\left(\frac{7}{x}+\frac{2}{x^5}\right) - \frac{2}{25}\left(\frac{7}{x}+\frac{2}{x^5}\right)^2 + \cdots\right]$$

$$= \lim_{x \to -\infty} \left[\frac{1}{5}\left(7+\frac{2}{x^4}\right) - \frac{2}{25}x\left(\frac{7}{x}+\frac{2}{x^5}\right)^2 + \cdots\right] = \frac{7}{5}$$

3. (b) Consider

$$\lim_{x \to \infty} (\sqrt[3]{(x+a)(x+b)(x+c)} - x) = \lim_{x \to \infty} [(x+a)(x+b)(x+c)^{1/3} - x]$$

$$\lim_{x \to \infty} \{(x^2 + (a+b)x + ab)(x+c)\}^{1/3} - x]$$

$$= \lim_{x \to \infty} [(x^3 + (a+b+c)x^2 + (ab+bc+ca)x + abc)^{1/3} - x]$$

$$= \lim_{x \to \infty} \left[x\left(1 + \frac{(a+b+c)}{x} + \frac{(ab+bc+ca)}{x^2} + \frac{abc}{x^3}\right)^{1/3} - x\right]$$

$$= \lim_{x \to \infty} x\left[\left(1 + \frac{(a+b+c)}{x} + \frac{(ab+bc+ca)}{x^2} + \frac{abc}{x^3}\right)^{1/3} - 1\right]$$

$$= \lim_{x \to \infty} x[(1+t)^{1/3} - 1],$$

where $t = \frac{(a+b+c)}{x} + \frac{(ab+bc+ca)}{x^2} + \frac{abc}{x^3}$

$$= \lim_{x \to \infty} x\left[\left(1+\frac{1}{3}t+\cdots\right)-1\right],$$

$\left[\begin{array}{l}\text{since, if } n \text{ is any rational number, then}\\ (1+x)^n = 1 + nx + \frac{n(n-1)}{1\cdot 2}x^2 + \frac{n(n-1)(n-2)}{1\cdot 2\cdot 3}x^3 + \cdots\end{array}\right]$

$$= \lim_{x \to \infty} x\left[\frac{1}{3}\left(\frac{(a+b+c)}{x} + \frac{(ab+bc+ca)}{x^2} + \frac{abc}{x^3}\right) + \cdots\right]$$

$$= \lim_{x \to \infty} \left[\frac{1}{3}\left((a+b+c) + \frac{(ab+bc+ca)}{x} + \frac{abc}{x^2}\right) + \cdots\right]$$

$$= \frac{a+b+c}{3}$$

4. (c) Consider

$$\lim_{n\to\infty}\left[\left(\frac{n}{n+1}\right)^{\alpha}+\sin\frac{1}{n}\right]^n=\lim_{n\to\infty}\left[\left(\frac{1}{1+\frac{1}{n}}\right)^{\alpha}+\sin\frac{1}{n}\right]^n$$

which is of the form 1^{∞} and we know if $\lim_{x\to a} f(x)=1$ and $\lim_{x\to a} g(x)=\infty$, then $\lim_{x\to a}\{f(x)\}^{g(x)}=e^{\lim_{x\to a}\{f(x)-1\}g(x)}$

∴ We have,

$$\lim_{n\to\infty}\left[\left(\frac{n}{n+1}\right)^{\alpha}+\sin\frac{1}{n}\right]^n=e^{\lim_{n\to\infty}\left\{\left(\frac{n}{n+1}\right)^{\alpha}+\sin\frac{1}{n}-1\right\}n}$$

$$=e^{\lim_{n\to\infty} n\sin\frac{1}{n}+\lim_{n\to\infty} n\left\{\left(\frac{n}{n+1}\right)^{\alpha}-1\right\}}$$

$$=e^{1+\lim_{n\to\infty} n\left\{\left(\frac{n}{n+1}\right)^{\alpha}-1\right\}} \quad \ldots(i)$$

$$\left[\because \lim_{n\to\infty}\frac{\sin(1/n)}{1/n}=1\right]$$

Now, consider $\lim_{n\to\infty} n\left\{\left(\frac{n}{n+1}\right)^{\alpha}-1\right\}=\lim_{n\to\infty} n\left\{\left(\frac{1}{1+\frac{1}{n}}\right)^{\alpha}-1\right\}$

Now, let $\frac{1}{n}=y$, then $n\to\infty \Rightarrow y\to 0$

$$\Rightarrow \lim_{n\to\infty} n\left\{\left(\frac{n}{n+1}\right)^{\alpha}-1\right\}=\lim_{y\to 0}\frac{1}{y}\left\{\left(\frac{1}{1+y}\right)^{\alpha}-1\right\}$$

$$=\lim_{y\to 0}\frac{1}{y}\left\{\frac{1-(1+y)^{\alpha}}{(1+y)^{\alpha}}\right\}$$

$$=\lim_{y\to 0}\frac{1}{y}\{1-(1+y)^{\alpha}\}\times\lim_{y\to 0}\frac{1}{(1+y)^{\alpha}}$$

$$=\lim_{y\to 0}\frac{1-(1+y)^{\alpha}}{y} \quad \left[\because \lim_{y\to 0}\frac{1}{(1+y)^{\alpha}}=1\right]$$

$$=\lim_{y\to 0}\frac{1-\left(1+\alpha y+\frac{\alpha(\alpha-1)}{2}y^2+\cdots\right)}{y}$$

[using binomial theorem for rational index]

$$=\lim_{y\to 0} -\alpha-\frac{\alpha(\alpha-1)}{2}y+\cdots=-\alpha$$

From Eq. (i), we get

$$\lim_{n\to\infty}\left(\left(\frac{n}{n+1}\right)^{\alpha}+\sin\frac{1}{n}\right)^n=e^{1-\alpha}$$

5. (c) Let $f(n)=\sum_{r=1}^{n}\frac{r}{n^2+n+r}$

$$=\frac{1}{n^2+n+1}+\frac{2}{n^2+n+2}+\frac{3}{n^2+n+3}+\cdots+\frac{n}{n^2+n+n}$$

Now, consider

$$g(n)=\frac{1}{n^2+n+n}+\frac{2}{n^2+n+n}+\frac{3}{n^2+n+n}+\cdots+\frac{n}{n^2+n+n}$$

$$=\frac{1}{n^2+2n}+\frac{2}{n^2+2n}+\frac{3}{n^2+2n}+\cdots+\frac{n}{n^2+2n}$$

$$=\frac{1+2+3+\cdots+n}{n^2+2n}=\frac{\frac{n(n+1)}{2}}{n(n+2)}=\frac{n+1}{2(n+2)}$$

and $h(n)=\frac{1}{n^2+n+1}+\frac{2}{n^2+n+1}+\frac{3}{n^2+n+1}+\cdots+\frac{n}{n^2+n+1}$

$$=\frac{1+2+3+\cdots+n}{n^2+n+1}=\frac{n(n+1)}{2(n^2+n+1)}=\frac{n^2+n}{2(n^2+n+1)}$$

Clearly, it can be observed that

$$g(n)<f(n)<h(n) \quad \ldots(i)$$

Also, $\lim_{n\to\infty} g(n)=\frac{1}{2}$

and $\lim_{n\to\infty} h(n)=\frac{1}{2}$

∴ By using Sandwich theorem in Eq. (i), we get

$$\lim_{n\to\infty} f(n)=\frac{1}{2}$$

6. (c) We have,

$$f(x)=\lim_{n\to\infty}\frac{x^{2n}-1}{x^{2n}+1}$$

Case I If $|x|<1$, then $f(x)=\lim_{n\to\infty}\frac{x^{2n}-1}{x^{2n}+1}=\frac{0-1}{0+1}$

$$\left[\because \lim_{n\to\infty} x^{2n}=0, \text{ if } |x|<1\right]$$

$=-1$

Case II If $|x|>1$, then

$$f(x)=\lim_{n\to\infty}\frac{x^{2n}-1}{x^{2n}+1}=\lim_{n\to\infty}\left(\frac{1-\frac{1}{x^{2n}}}{1+\frac{1}{x^{2n}}}\right)$$

$$=\frac{1-0}{1+0} \quad \left[\because \lim_{n\to\infty} x^{2n}=\infty, \text{ if } |x|>1\right]$$

$=1$

Case III If $|x|=1$, then

$$f(x)=\lim_{n\to\infty}\frac{x^{2n}-1}{x^{2n}+1}$$

$$=\lim_{n\to\infty}\frac{1-1}{1+1}=0 \quad [\because |x|=1\Rightarrow x=\pm 1]$$

Thus, $f(x)=\begin{cases}-1, & \text{if } |x|<1\\ 0, & \text{if } |x|=1\\ 1, & \text{if } |x|>1\end{cases}=\text{Sgn}(|x|-1)$

7. (b)

(a) This is false. Consider $f(x)=x$ and $g(x)=\text{cosec}\, x$, then

$$\lim_{x\to 0} f(x)\cdot g(x)=\lim_{x\to 0}\frac{x}{\sin x}=1$$

$$\lim_{x\to 0} f(x)=\lim_{x\to 0} x=0$$

but $\lim_{x\to 0} g(x)=\lim_{x\to 0}\frac{1}{\sin x}$ does not exist

(b) This is true. As we can write $g=(f+g)-f$ and by algebra of limit, we get

$$\lim_{x\to c} g(x)=\lim_{x\to c}\{f(x)+g(x)\}-\lim_{x\to c} f(x),$$

which exist as $\lim_{x\to c}\{f(x)+g(x)\}$ and $\lim_{x\to c} f(x)$ exist.

(c) This is false. Consider $f(x)=\begin{cases}2, & \text{if } x\le 0\\ 3, & \text{if } x>0\end{cases}$

and $g(x)=0$, then $f(x)\cdot g(x)=0$ and so $\lim_{x\to 0} f(x)\cdot g(x)=0$ (exist), while $\lim_{x\to 0} f(x)$ does not exist.

(d) This is false. Consider $f(x)=x-\sin\left(\frac{1}{x}\right)$ and $g(x)=\sin\left(\frac{1}{x}\right)$, then $f(x)+g(x)=x$ and so $\lim_{x\to 0}\{f(x)+g(x)\}=\lim_{x\to c} x=0$, while $\lim_{x\to 0} f(x)$ and $\lim_{x\to 0} g(x)$ does not exist.

8. (a) Consider $\lim\limits_{x\to 1} \dfrac{\sin^2(x^3+x^2+x-3)}{1-\cos(x^2-4x+3)}$

$$= \lim_{x\to 1} \frac{\sin^2(x^3+x^2+x-3)}{(x^3+x^2+x-3)^2} \times \frac{(x^3+x^2+x-3)^2}{1-\cos(x^2-4x+3)}$$

$$= \lim_{x\to 1}\left[\frac{\sin(x^3+x^2+x-3)}{(x^3+x^2+x-3)}\right]^2 \times \lim_{x\to 1}\frac{(x^3+x^2+x-3)^2}{1-\cos(x^2-4x+3)}$$

$$= 1\times \lim_{x\to 1}\frac{(x^2-4x+3)^2}{2\sin^2\left(\dfrac{x^2-4x+3}{2}\right)}\cdot\frac{(x^3+x^2+x-3)^2}{(x^2-4x+3)^2}$$

$$\left[\because \lim_{x\to 1} x^3+x^2+x-3=0\right]$$

$$= \lim_{x\to 1}\frac{4\left(\dfrac{x^2-4x+3}{2}\right)^2}{2\sin^2\left(\dfrac{x^2-4x+3}{2}\right)} \times \lim_{x\to 1}\left(\frac{x^3+x^2+x-3}{x^2-4x+3}\right)^2$$

$$= 2\times \lim_{x\to 1}\left[\frac{\left(\dfrac{x^2-4x+3}{2}\right)}{\sin\left(\dfrac{x^2-4x+3}{2}\right)}\right]^2 \times \lim_{x\to 1}\left(\frac{x^3+x^2+x-3}{x^2-4x+3}\right)^2$$

$$= 2\times\left[\lim_{x\to 1}\left(\frac{x^3+x^2+x-3}{x^2-4x+3}\right)\right]^2$$

$$= 2\left(\lim_{x\to 1}\frac{3x^2+2x+1}{2x-4}\right)^2 \quad \text{[using L' Hospital's rule]}$$

$$= 2\left(\frac{6}{-2}\right)^2 = 2(-3)^2 = 18$$

9. (c) Clearly , by definition $f'(1)$ is the limit of the slope of the secant line, when $s \to 1$.

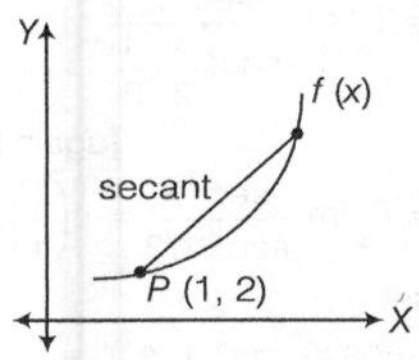

Thus, $f'(1) = \lim\limits_{s\to 1}\dfrac{s^2+2s-3}{s-1}$

Since, equation of secant is of the form $y = mx + c$, therefore,

$$\text{slope} = \frac{s^2+2s-3}{s-1}$$

$$= \lim_{s\to 1}\frac{(s-1)(s+3)}{(s-1)} = \lim_{s\to 1} s+3 = 4$$

Alternate Method

On substituting $x = s$ into the equation of the secant line, we get

$$y = \frac{(s^2+2s-3)}{(s-1)}s - 1 - s$$

$$= \frac{(s-1)(s+3)}{(s-1)}s - 1 - s$$

$$= (s+3)s - 1 - s = s^2 + 3s - 1 - s$$

$$= s^2 + 2s - 1$$

This is $f(s)$, i.e. $f(s) = s^2 + 2s - 1$ and its derivative is $f'(s) = 2s + 2$. So, $f'(1) = 4$.

10. (a) Consider

$$\lim_{n\to\infty}\frac{1^2\cdot n + 2^2\cdot(n-1) + 3^2\cdot(n-2) + \cdots + n^2\cdot 1}{1^3+2^3+3^3+\cdots+n^3}$$

$$= \lim_{n\to\infty}\frac{1^2\cdot n + 2^2\cdot(n-1) + 3^2\cdot(n-2) + \cdots + n^2\{n-(n-1)\}}{\Sigma n^3} \quad \ldots\text{(i)}$$

Now, consider
Numerator

$$= n(1^2+2^2+3^2+\cdots+n^2) - \{1\cdot 2^2 + 2\cdot 3^2 + \cdots + (n-1)\cdot n^2\}$$

$$= n\Sigma n^2 - \sum_{r=2}^{n}(r-1)r^2$$

$$= n\Sigma n^2 - \sum_{r=2}^{n}(r^3-r^2) = n\Sigma n^2 - \sum_{r=1}^{n}(r^3-r^2)$$

$$= n\Sigma n^2 - \sum_{r=1}^{n} r^3 + \sum_{r=1}^{n} r^2 = n\Sigma n^2 - \Sigma n^3 + \Sigma n^2$$

$$= (n+1)\Sigma n^2 + \Sigma n^3$$

Now from Eq. (i), we get

$$\lim_{n\to\infty}\frac{1^2\cdot n + 2^2\cdot(n-1) + 3^2\cdot(n-2) + \cdots + n^2}{1^3+2^3+3^3+\cdots+n^3}$$

$$= \lim_{n\to\infty}\frac{[(n+1)\Sigma n^2 - \Sigma n^3]}{\Sigma n^3} = \lim_{n\to\infty}\frac{(n+1)\Sigma n^2}{\Sigma n^3} - 1$$

$$= \lim_{n\to\infty}\frac{(n+1)n(n+1)(2n+1)}{6n^2(n+1)^2} \times 4 - 1$$

$$\left[\because \Sigma n^2 = \frac{n(n+1)(2x+1)}{6},\ \Sigma n^3 = \frac{n^2(n+1)^2}{4}\right]$$

$$= \lim_{n\to\infty}\frac{(2n+1)}{3n} - 1$$

$$= \frac{2}{3}\left[\lim_{n\to\infty}\left(2+\frac{1}{n}\right)\right] - 1$$

$$= \frac{2}{3}\times 2 - 1 = \frac{4}{3} - 1 = \frac{1}{3}$$

Alternate Method

Let $I = \dfrac{1^2\cdot n + 2^2\cdot(n-1) + 3^2\cdot(n-2) + \cdots + n^2}{1^3+2^3+\cdots+n^3}$

$$= \frac{1^2\cdot n + 2^2\cdot(n-1) + 3^2\cdot(n-2) + \cdots + n^2}{1^3+2^3+3^3+\cdots+n^3} + 1 - 1$$

$$= \frac{[1^2\cdot n + 2^2\cdot(n-1) + 3^2\cdot(n-2) + \cdots + n^2] + (1^3+2^3+\cdots+n^3)}{1^3+2^3+\cdots+n^3} - 1$$

$$= \frac{(1^2n+1^3) + [2^2(n-1)+2^3] + \cdots + (n^2+n^3)}{1^3+2^3+\cdots+n^3} - 1$$

$$= \frac{1^2(n+1) + 2^2(n+1) + \cdots + n^2(n+1)}{\Sigma n^3} - 1$$

$$= \frac{(n+1)(1^2+2^2+\cdots+n^2)}{\Sigma n^3} - 1$$

$$= \frac{(n+1)\Sigma n^2}{\Sigma n^3} - 1$$

$$= \frac{(n+1)n(n+1)(2x+1)}{6\cdot n^2(n+1)^2} \times 4 - 1$$

$$= \frac{2}{3}\frac{(2n+1)}{n} - 1$$

Thus, $\lim\limits_{n\to\infty} I = \lim\limits_{n\to\infty}\dfrac{2}{3}\left(2+\dfrac{1}{n}\right) - 1$

$$= \frac{4}{3} - 1 = \frac{1}{3}$$

11. (a) Consider

$$\lim_{x\to\infty}\frac{\cot^{-1}(x^{-a}\log_a x)}{\sec^{-1}(a^x\log_x a)}=\lim_{x\to\infty}\frac{\cot^{-1}\left(\dfrac{\log_a x}{x^a}\right)}{\sec^{-1}\left(\dfrac{a^x}{\log_a x}\right)}\quad\ldots(i)$$

Note that $\lim_{x\to\infty}\left(\frac{\log_a x}{x^a}\right)=\lim_{x\to\infty}\left(\frac{\frac{1}{x}\times\log_a e}{ax^{a-1}}\right)$

[using L' Hospital's rule]

$$=\lim_{x\to\infty}\left(\frac{\log_a e}{ax^a}\right)=0$$

[$\because a>1$ and $x\to\infty$]

and $\lim_{x\to\infty}\left(\frac{a^x}{\log_a x}\right)=\lim_{x\to\infty}\left(\frac{a^x\log_e a}{\log_a e\cdot\frac{1}{x}}\right)$

[using L' Hospital's rule]

$$=\lim_{x\to\infty}\left(\frac{x\cdot a^x\log_e a}{\log_a e}\right)$$

$$=\infty$$

From Eq. (i), we get

$$\lim_{x\to\infty}\frac{\cot^{-1}(x^{-a}\log_a x)}{\sec^{-1}(a^x\log_x a)}=\frac{\cot^{-1}(0)}{\sec^{-1}(\infty)}=\frac{\frac{\pi}{2}}{\frac{\pi}{2}}=1$$

12. (a) By using graph, we can see that

when $x\to\frac{\pi^+}{4}$, $\sec\left(x-\frac{\pi}{4}\right)\to1^+\Rightarrow\left[\sec\left(x-\frac{\pi}{4}\right)\right]=1$

$$\operatorname{cosec}\left(x+\frac{\pi}{4}\right)\to1^+\Rightarrow\left[\operatorname{cosec}\left(x+\frac{\pi}{4}\right)\right]=1$$

$$\cot\left(x+\frac{\pi}{4}\right)\to0^-\Rightarrow\left[\cot\left(x+\frac{\pi}{4}\right)\right]=-1$$

$$\tan\left(x-\frac{\pi}{4}\right)\to0^+\Rightarrow\left[\tan\left(x-\frac{\pi}{4}\right)\right]=0$$

and when $x\to\frac{\pi^-}{4}$,

$$\sec\left(x-\frac{\pi}{4}\right)\to1^+\Rightarrow\left[\sec\left(x-\frac{\pi}{4}\right)\right]=1$$

$$\operatorname{cosec}\left(x+\frac{\pi}{4}\right)\to1^+\Rightarrow\left[\operatorname{cosec}\left(x+\frac{\pi}{4}\right)\right]=1$$

$$\cot\left(x+\frac{\pi}{4}\right)\to0^+\Rightarrow\left[\cot\left(x+\frac{\pi}{4}\right)\right]=0$$

$$\tan\left(x-\frac{\pi}{4}\right)\to0^-\Rightarrow\left[\tan\left(x-\frac{\pi}{4}\right)\right]=-1$$

Thus, $\lim_{x\to\frac{\pi}{4}}\left[\sec\left(x-\frac{\pi}{4}\right)\right]=1,$

$$\lim_{x\to\frac{\pi}{4}}\left[\operatorname{cosec}\left(x+\frac{\pi}{4}\right)\right]=1$$

but $\lim_{x\to\frac{\pi}{4}}\left[\cot\left(x+\frac{\pi}{4}\right)\right]$

and $\lim_{x\to\frac{\pi}{4}}\left[\tan\left(x-\frac{\pi}{4}\right)\right]$ does not exist.

Hence, l_1, l_2 exist and equal to 0 and $\frac{\pi}{2}$ respectively but l_3 and l_4 does not exist.

[since, if $\lim_{x\to a}g(x)$ does not exist, then $\lim_{x\to a}fog(x)=f[\lim_{x\to a}g(x)]$ does not exist]

13. (a) Consider $\lim_{x\to\infty}\sqrt{x+1}-\sqrt{x}=\lim_{x\to\infty}\frac{1}{\sqrt{x+1}+\sqrt{x}}=0$

and $\lim_{x\to\infty}\left(\frac{2x-1}{x-1}\right)^x=\lim_{x\to\infty}\left(2+\frac{1}{x-1}\right)^x=2^\infty=\infty$

$$\therefore\quad\lim_{x\to\infty}\frac{\cot^{-1}(\sqrt{x+1}-\sqrt{x})}{\sec^{-1}\left(\left(\frac{2x-1}{x-1}\right)^x\right)}=\frac{\cot^{-1}(0)}{\sec^{-1}(\infty)}=\frac{\frac{\pi}{2}}{\frac{\pi}{2}}=1$$

14. (c) Consider

$$\lim_{n\to\infty}\cos(\pi\sqrt{n^2+n})=\lim_{n\to\infty}\cos\left[n\pi\left(1+\frac{1}{n}\right)^{1/2}\right]$$

$$=\lim_{n\to\infty}\cos\left[n\pi\left\{1+\frac{1}{2n}+\frac{1}{2}\left(\frac{1}{2}-1\right)\frac{1}{2!}\frac{1}{n^2}+\cdots\right\}\right]$$

$$=\lim_{n\to\infty}\cos\left[\left\{n+\frac{1}{2}+\frac{1}{2}\left(\frac{1}{2}-1\right)\frac{1}{2!}\cdot\frac{1}{n}+\cdots\right\}\right]$$

$$=\lim_{n\to\infty}\cos\left[\frac{\pi}{2}\left\{2n+1+\left(\frac{1}{2}-1\right)\frac{1}{2!}\right\}\cdot\frac{1}{n}+\cdots\right]$$

$$=\lim_{n\to\infty}\cos((2n+1)\pi/2)$$

$$\left[\text{as } n\to\infty,\text{ therefore }\left(\frac{1}{2}-1\right)\frac{1}{2!}\frac{1}{n}+\cdots\to0\right]$$

$$=\lim_{n\to\infty}0=0$$

15. (c) Consider

$$\lim_{x\to0}(1+\log^2_{\cos x/2}\cos x)^2=\lim_{x\to0}\left[1+\left(\frac{\log_e\cos x}{\log_e\cos x/2}\right)^2\right]^2\quad\ldots(i)$$

Now, consider

$$\lim_{x\to0}\frac{\log_e\cos x}{\log_e\cos x/2}=\lim_{x\to0}\frac{\frac{1}{\cos x}(-\sin x)}{\frac{1}{\cos x/2}(-\sin x/2)\times\frac{1}{2}}$$

[using L' Hospital's rule]

$$=\lim_{x\to0}\frac{2\tan x}{\tan x/2}\quad\left[\frac{0}{0}\text{ form}\right]$$

$$=2\lim_{x\to0}\frac{\sec^2 x}{\sec^2\frac{x}{2}\cdot\frac{1}{2}}$$

[again using L' Hospital's rule]

$$=4\lim_{x\to0}\frac{\sec^2 x}{\sec^2 x/2}=4\left(\frac{1}{1}\right)=4$$

From Eq. (i), we get

$$\lim_{x\to0}(1+\log^2_{\cos x/2}\cos x)^2=(1+4^2)^2=(1+16)^2=17=289$$

16. (d) Consider, $\lim_{x\to0^+}\frac{[\tan(\{x\}-1)]\sin\{x\}}{\{x\}(\{x\}-1)}$

$$=\lim_{h\to0}\frac{[\tan(\{0+h\}-1)]\sin\{0+h\}}{\{0+h\}(\{0+h\}-1)}$$

$$=\lim_{h\to0}\frac{[\tan(h-1)]\sin h}{h(h-1)}=\lim_{h\to0}\frac{\tan(h-1)}{(h-1)}\times\lim_{h\to0}\frac{\sin h}{h}$$

$$=\frac{\tan(-1)}{-1}\times1=\tan1\quad\ldots(i)$$

and $\lim_{x\to0^-}\frac{[\tan(\{x\}-1)]\sin\{x\}}{\{x\}(\{x\}-1)}$

$$=\lim_{h\to0}\frac{[\tan(\{0-h\}-1)]\sin\{0-h\}}{\{0-h\}(\{0-h\}-1)}$$

$$=\lim_{h\to0}\frac{[\tan\{(1-h)-9\}]\sin(1-h)}{(1-h)\{(1-h)-1\}}\quad[\because\{0-h\}=1-h]$$

$$=\lim_{h\to0}\frac{\tan(-h)\sin(1-h)}{(1-h)(-h)}=\lim_{h\to0}\frac{\tan h}{h}\times\lim_{h\to0}\frac{\sin(1-h)}{(1-h)}$$

$$=1\times\frac{\sin1}{1}=\sin1\quad\ldots(ii)$$

From Eqs. (i) and (ii), we get

$\lim_{x\to0}\frac{[\tan(\{x\}-1)]\sin\{x\}}{\{x\}(\{x\}-1)}$ does not exist.

17. (c) Consider $\lim_{x \to 0^-} [\log(\{x\} + |[x]|)]^{\{x\}}$

$$= \lim_{h \to 0} [\log(\{0-h\} + |[0-h]|)]^{\{0-h\}}$$

$$= \lim_{h \to 0} [\log((1-h) + |-1|)]^{(1-h)}$$

$$[\because \{0-h\} = 1-h \text{ and } [0-h] = -1]$$

$$= \lim_{h \to 0} [\log((1-h)+1)]^{(1-h)}$$

$$= \lim_{h \to 0} [\log(2-h)]^{(1-h)} = \log_e 2$$

18. (b) We have,

$$P_n = \prod_{k=1}^{n} \left(1 + \frac{2}{k^2 + 3k}\right)$$

$$= \prod_{k=1}^{n} \left(\frac{k^2 + 3k + 2}{k^2 + 3k}\right)$$

$$= \prod_{k=1}^{n} \left[\frac{(k+1)(k+2)}{k(k+3)}\right]$$

$$= \left(\frac{2 \cdot 3}{1 \cdot 4}\right) \times \left(\frac{3 \cdot 4}{2 \cdot 5}\right) \times \left(\frac{4 \cdot 5}{3 \cdot 6}\right) \cdots \left[\frac{(n+1)(n+2)}{n(n+3)}\right]$$

$$= \frac{3 \cdot [2 \cdot 3 \cdot 4 \cdots (n+1)]}{(1 \cdot 2 \cdot 3 \cdots n) \cdot (n+3)}$$

$$\Rightarrow \quad P_n = \frac{3(n+1)!}{n!\,(n+3)} = \frac{3(n+1)}{(n+3)}$$

Now, $\lim_{n \to \infty} P_n = 3 \lim_{n \to \infty} \frac{(n+1)}{(n+3)} = 3 \lim_{n \to \infty} \frac{\left(1 + \frac{1}{n}\right)}{\left(1 + \frac{3}{n}\right)} = 3$

19. (b) We have, $a_n = \sum_{k=1}^{n} 2k$ and $b_n = \sum_{k=1}^{n} (2k-1)$, where $n \in N$.

Clearly, $a_n = 2 \sum_{k=1}^{n} k = 2 \frac{n(n+1)}{2} = n^2 + n$

and $b_n = \sum_{k=1}^{n} (2k) - \sum_{k=1}^{n} 1 = 2 \frac{(n)(n+1)}{2} - n$

$$= n^2 + n - n = n^2$$

Now, $\lim_{n \to \infty} (\sqrt{a_n} - \sqrt{b_n}) = \lim_{n \to \infty} (\sqrt{n^2 + n} - \sqrt{n^2})$

$$= \lim_{n \to \infty} (\sqrt{n^2 + n} - n)$$

$$= \lim_{n \to \infty} \frac{n}{\sqrt{n^2 + n} + n} = \lim_{n \to \infty} \frac{1}{\sqrt{1 + \frac{1}{n}} + 1}$$

[dividing numerator and denominator by n^2]

$$= \frac{1}{2}$$

20. (b) We can see that

when $x \to 0^+$, $\sin x \to 0^+ \Rightarrow [\sin x] = 0$

$\cos x \to 1^- \Rightarrow [\cos x] = 0$

$\tan x \to 0^+ \Rightarrow [\tan x] = 0$

and when $x \to 0^-$,

$\sin x \to 0^- \Rightarrow [\sin x] = -1$

$\cos x \to 1^- \Rightarrow [\cos x] = 0$

$\tan x \to 0^- \Rightarrow [\tan x] = -1$

Now, $\lim_{x \to 0^+} (\sin^{-1}[\sin x] + \cos^{-1}[\cos x] - 2\tan^{-1}[\tan x])$

$$= \sin^{-1}(0) + \cos^{-1}(0) - 2\tan^{-1}(0)$$

$$= 0 + \frac{\pi}{2} - 2(0) = \frac{\pi}{2}$$

and $\lim_{x \to 0^-} (\sin^{-1}[\sin x] + \cos^{-1}[\cos x] - 2\tan^{-1}[\tan x])$

$$= \sin^{-1}(-1) + \cos^{-1}(0) - 2\tan^{-1}(-1)$$

$$= -\sin^{-1}(1) + \cos^{-1}(0) + 2\tan^{-1}(1)$$

$$= \frac{-\pi}{2} + \frac{\pi}{2} + 2 \cdot \frac{\pi}{4} \qquad \left[\begin{array}{l}\because \sin^{-1}(-x) = -\sin^{-1}(x) \\ \tan^{-1}(-x) = -\tan^{-1}(x)\end{array}\right]$$

$$= \frac{\pi}{2}$$

Hence, $\lim_{x \to 0} (\sin^{-1}[\sin x] + \cos^{-1}[\cos x] - 2\tan^{-1}[\tan x]) = \frac{\pi}{2}$

21. (d) Consider $\lim_{x \to 2^+} \frac{[x]}{\{x\}} = \lim_{h \to 0} \frac{[2+h]}{\{2+h\}}$

$$= \lim_{h \to 0} \frac{2}{h}, \text{ which does not exist.}$$

Thus, $\lim_{x \to 2} \frac{[x]}{\{x\}} = l$, does not exist.

Now, consider

$$\lim_{x \to 2^+} \frac{\{x\}}{[x]} = \lim_{h \to 0} \frac{\{2+h\}}{[2+h]} = \lim_{h \to 0} \frac{h}{2} = 0$$

and $\lim_{x \to 2^-} \frac{\{x\}}{[x]} = \lim_{h \to 0} \frac{\{2-h\}}{[2-h]} = \lim_{h \to 0} \frac{\{1 + (1-h)\}}{1}$

$$= \lim_{h \to 0} (1-h) = 1$$

Thus, $\lim_{x \to 2} \frac{\{x\}}{[x]} = m$, does not exist.

Hence, neither l nor m exists.

22. (a) Let $f(n) = \sum_{r=1}^{n} \frac{r^2}{n^3 + n^2 + r}$

$$= \frac{1^2}{n^3 + n^2 + 1} + \frac{2^2}{n^3 + n^2 + 2} + \cdots + \frac{n^2}{n^3 + n^2 + n} \quad \ldots \text{(i)}$$

Now, consider

$$g(n) = \frac{1^2}{n^3 + n^2 + n} + \frac{2^2}{n^3 + n^2 + n} + \cdots + \frac{n^2}{n^3 + n^2 + n} \quad \ldots \text{(ii)}$$

$$= \frac{(1^2 + 2^2 + \cdots + n^2)}{n^3 + n^2 + n}$$

$$= \frac{\Sigma n^2}{n^3 + n^2 + n} = \frac{n(n+1)(2n+1)}{6(n^3 + n^2 + n)}$$

$$= \frac{(n+1)(2n+1)}{6(n^2 + n + 1)} \quad \ldots \text{(iii)}$$

$$\text{and } h(n) = \frac{1^2}{n^3 + n^2 + 1} + \frac{2^2}{n^3 + n^2 + 1} + \cdots + \frac{n^2}{n^2 + n + 1} \quad \ldots \text{(iv)}$$

$$= \frac{(1^2 + 2^2 + \cdots + n^2)}{n^3 + n^2 + 1}$$

$$= \frac{\Sigma n^2}{n^3 + n^2 + 1} = \frac{n(n+1)(2n+1)}{6(n^3 + n^2 + 1)} \quad \ldots \text{(v)}$$

From Eqs. (i), (ii) and (iv), we get

$$g(n) < f(n) < h(n) \quad \ldots \text{(vi)}$$

Also, from Eqs. (iii) and (v), we have

$$\lim_{n \to \infty} g(n) = \lim_{n \to \infty} \frac{\left(1 + \frac{1}{n}\right)\left(2 + \frac{1}{n}\right)}{6\left(1 + \frac{1}{n} + \frac{1}{n^2}\right)} = \frac{2}{6} = \frac{1}{3}$$

and $\lim_{n \to \infty} h(n) = \lim_{n \to \infty} \frac{\left(1 + \frac{1}{n}\right)\left(2 + \frac{1}{n}\right)}{6\left(1 + \frac{1}{n} + \frac{1}{n^3}\right)} = \frac{2}{6} = \frac{1}{3}$

$\therefore$ By applying Sandwich theorem in Eq. (vi), we get

$$\lim_{n \to \infty} f(n) = \frac{1}{3}$$

23. (b) Clearly, $\frac{[x]^2}{x} = \begin{cases} 0, & 0 < x < 1 \\ \frac{1}{x}, & -1 < x < 0 \end{cases}$

and $\frac{[x^2]}{x^2} = \begin{cases} 0, & 0 < x < 1 \\ 0, & -1 < x < 0 \end{cases}$

Now, consider $\lim_{x \to 0^+} \frac{[x]^2}{x} = 0$ and $\lim_{x \to 0^-} \frac{[x]^2}{x} = \lim_{x \to 0^-} \frac{1}{x}$, which does not exist.

Hence, $\lim_{x \to 0} \frac{[x]^2}{x} = l$ does not exist.

Also, $\lim_{x \to 0^+} \frac{[x^2]}{x^2} = 0$ and $\lim_{x \to 0^-} \frac{[x^2]}{x^2} = 0$

$\Rightarrow \lim_{x \to 0} \frac{[x^2]}{x^2} = m = 0$, exist

Hence, m exists but l does not.

24. (a,c)

(a) Consider

$$\lim_{x \to \infty} g(x) = \lim_{x \to \infty} \sqrt{x^2 + 2x} - x = \lim_{x \to \infty} \frac{2x}{\sqrt{x^2 + 2x} + x}$$

$$= \lim_{x \to \infty} \frac{2}{\sqrt{1 + \frac{2}{x}} + 1} = \frac{2}{2} = 1$$

(b) Consider $\lim_{x \to \infty} f(x) = \lim_{x \to \infty} x + \sqrt{x^2 + 2x} \to \infty$

$\therefore \lim_{x \to \infty} f(x)$ does not exist.

(c) Consider $\lim_{x \to -\infty} f(x) = \lim_{y \to \infty} f(-y)$ [put $x = -y$]

$$= \lim_{y \to \infty} -y + \sqrt{y^2 - 2y} = \lim_{y \to \infty} \sqrt{y^2 - 2y} - y$$

$$= \lim_{y \to \infty} \frac{-2y}{\sqrt{y^2 - 2y} + y} = \lim_{y \to \infty} \frac{-2}{\sqrt{1 - \frac{2}{y}} + 1}$$

$$= \frac{-2}{2} = -1$$

(d) Consider

$$\lim_{x \to -\infty} g(x) = \lim_{y \to \infty} g(-y) \quad \text{[put } x = -y\text{]}$$

$$= \lim_{y \to \infty} \sqrt{y^2 - 2y} + y \to \infty$$

Hence, $\lim_{x \to -\infty} g(x)$ does not exist.

25. (b, c) We know that, $\sin^{-1}(\sin x) = x$, if $-\frac{\pi}{2} \le x \le \frac{\pi}{2}$

and $\cos^{-1}(\cos x) = \begin{cases} x, & 0 \le x \le \pi \\ -x, & -\pi \le x \le 0 \end{cases}$

$\therefore \lim_{x \to 0^+} \frac{\sin^{-1}(\sin x)}{\cos^{-1}(\cos x)} = \lim_{x \to 0^+} \frac{x}{x} = 1$

and $\lim_{x \to 0^-} \frac{\sin^{-1}(\sin x)}{\cos^{-1}(\cos x)} = \lim_{x \to 0^-} \frac{x}{(-x)} = -1$

Hence, $\lim_{x \to 0} \frac{\sin^{-1}(\sin x)}{\cos^{-1}(\cos x)} = A$, does not exist.

Now, consider

$$\lim_{x \to 0^+} \frac{[|x|]}{x} = \lim_{h \to 0} \frac{[|0 + h|]}{0 + h}$$

$$= \lim_{h \to 0} \frac{[|h|]}{h} = \lim_{h \to 0} \frac{[h]}{h}$$

$$= \lim_{h \to 0} \frac{0}{h} = 0$$

and $\lim_{x \to 0^-} \frac{[|x|]}{x} = \lim_{h \to 0} \frac{[|0 - h|]}{0 - h} = \lim_{h \to 0} \frac{[h]}{-h} = 0$

$\Rightarrow \lim_{x \to 0} \frac{[|x|]}{x} = 0 = B$

26. (a,c,d)

(a) $\lim_{x \to 0^-} f[g(x)] = \lim_{h \to 0} f(-1) = |-1| = 1$

(b) $\lim_{x \to 0^-} f[g(2^x)] = f[g(1^-)] = f(1/5) = e^{1/5 - 1}$

(c) $\lim_{x \to 0^+} f[g(2^x)] = f[g(1^+)] = f(1/5) = e^{1/5 - 1}$

27. (a,b) For $n = 1$, we have

$$\lim_{x \to 1} \frac{e^{x-1} - x}{x - 1} = \lim_{x \to 1} \frac{e^{x-1} - 1 - (x - 1)}{(x - 1)}$$

$$= \lim_{x \to 1} \frac{e^{(x-1)} - 1}{(x - 1)} - 1 = 1 - 1 = 0$$

For $n = 2$, we have

$$\lim_{x \to 1} \frac{e^{x-1} - x}{(x - 1)^2} = \lim_{x \to 1} \frac{e^{x-1} - 1}{2(x - 1)} \quad \text{[using L' Hospital's rule]}$$

$$= \lim_{x \to 1} \frac{e^{x-1}}{2} \quad \text{[again, using L' Hospital's rule]}$$

$$= \frac{1}{2}$$

For $n = 3$, we have

$$\lim_{x \to 1} \frac{e^{x-1} - x}{(x - 1)^3} = \lim_{x \to 1} \frac{e^{x-1} - 1}{3(x - 1)^2} \quad \text{[using L' Hospital's rule]}$$

$$= \lim_{x \to 1} \frac{e^{x-1}}{3 \times 2\,(x - 1)}$$

[again, using L' Hospital's rule]

$$= \frac{1}{6} \lim_{x \to 1} \frac{e^{x-1}}{(x - 1)} \to \infty$$

Thus, the value of n cannot be greater than 2.

28. (a,d) $f(x) = \begin{cases} \lim_{n \to \infty} \left[\frac{(\tan x)^{2n} + x^2}{\sin^2 x + (\tan x)^{2n}} \right], & x \ne 0 \\ 1, & x = 0 \end{cases}$

Now, $f\left(\frac{\pi^+}{4}\right) = 1, f\left(-\frac{\pi^-}{4}\right) = 1$

$$f\left(-\frac{\pi^+}{4}\right) = \frac{\pi^2/16}{1/2} = \frac{\pi^2}{8}, \ f\left(\frac{\pi^-}{4}\right) = \frac{\pi^2}{8}$$

$\therefore f(0^+) = 1, f(0^-) = 1 = f(0)$

29. (b)

(i) Consider $\lim_{x \to \infty} (\sqrt{x + \sqrt{x}} - \sqrt{x - \sqrt{x}})$

$$= \lim_{x \to \infty} \frac{(\sqrt{x + \sqrt{x}})^2 - (\sqrt{x - \sqrt{x}})^2}{\sqrt{x + \sqrt{x}} + \sqrt{x - \sqrt{x}}}$$

$$= \lim_{x \to \infty} \frac{2\sqrt{x}}{\sqrt{x + \sqrt{x}} + \sqrt{x - \sqrt{x}}}$$

$$= \lim_{x \to \infty} \frac{2}{\sqrt{1 + \frac{1}{\sqrt{x}}} + \sqrt{1 - \frac{1}{\sqrt{x}}}} = 1$$

(ii) Consider $\lim_{x \to 0} \frac{\sin 2x - 2\tan x}{\log(1 + x^3)}$

$$= \lim_{x \to 0} \frac{\sin 2x - 2\tan x}{x^3} \times \lim_{x \to 0} \frac{x^3}{\log(1 + x^3)}$$

$$= \lim_{x \to 0} \left(\frac{2\sin x \cos x - \frac{2\sin x}{\cos x}}{x^3} \right) \times 1$$

$$= \lim_{x \to 0} \frac{2\sin x(\cos^2 x - 1)}{x^3 \cos x} = \lim_{x \to 0} \frac{-2\sin^3 x}{x^3} \times \lim_{x \to 0} \frac{1}{\cos x}$$

$$= -2 \times 1 = -2$$

(iii) Consider $\lim_{x \to 0^+} [\log \sin^3 x - \log(x^4 + ex^3)]$

$$= \lim_{x \to 0^+} \log\left(\frac{\sin^3 x}{x^4 + ex^3}\right)$$

$$= \lim_{x \to 0^+} \log\left(\frac{\sin^3 x}{x^3(x + e)}\right)$$

$$= \log\left(\lim_{x \to 0^+} \frac{\sin^3 x}{x^3(x + e)}\right)$$

$$\left[\because \lim_{x \to a} \log f(x) = \log\left(\lim_{x \to a} f(x)\right)\right]$$

$$= \log\left(\frac{1}{e}\right) = -\log e = -1$$

(iv) We have, $\tan(2\pi|\sin\theta|) = \cot(2\pi|\cos\theta|)$

$$= \tan\left(\frac{\pi}{2} - 2\pi|\cos\theta|\right)$$

$$\Rightarrow \quad 2\pi|\sin\theta| = n\pi + \frac{\pi}{2} - |\cos\theta|\, 2\pi$$

$$\Rightarrow \quad 2\pi(|\sin\theta| + |\cos\theta|) = n\pi + \frac{\pi}{2}$$

$$\Rightarrow \quad |\sin\theta| + |\cos\theta| = \frac{n}{2} + \frac{1}{4} \qquad \ldots\text{(i)}$$

As we know, $1 \le |\sin\theta| + |\cos\theta| \le \sqrt{2}$

$$\Rightarrow \quad 1 \le \frac{n}{2} + \frac{1}{4} \le \sqrt{2} \qquad \text{[using Eq. (i)]}$$

$$\Rightarrow \quad 4 \le 2n + 1 \le 4\sqrt{2}$$

$$\Rightarrow \quad \frac{3}{2} \le n \le \frac{4\sqrt{2} - 1}{2}$$

Thus, the only possible value of n is 2.

Now, on substituting $n = 2$ in Eq. (i), we get

$$|\sin\theta| + |\cos\theta| = \frac{5}{4} \Rightarrow f(x) = \left(\frac{5}{4}\right)^x$$

Now, consider $\lim_{x \to \infty}\left[\frac{2}{f(x)}\right] = \lim_{x \to \infty}\left[2\left(\frac{4}{5}\right)^x\right]$

$$= 0 \qquad \left[\because \lim_{x \to \infty}\left(\frac{4}{5}\right)^x = 0\right]$$

Hence, (i) → (s), (ii) → (p), (iii) → (q), (iv) → (r)

30. (a)

(i) Let $I = \lim_{n \to \infty} \cos^2[\pi(\sqrt[3]{n^3 + n^2 + 2n})]$

$$= \lim_{n \to \infty} \cos^2\left(\pi\sqrt[3]{n^3 + n^2 + 2n} - n\pi\right)$$

[since, $\cos^2 x$ is periodic with period π]

Now, consider

$$\lim_{n \to \infty} \sqrt[3]{n^3 + n^2 + 2n} - n = \lim_{n \to \infty} n\left[\left(1 + \frac{1}{n} + \frac{2}{n^2}\right)^{1/3} - 1\right]$$

$$= \lim_{n \to \infty} n\left[\left\{1 + \left(\frac{1}{n} + \frac{2}{n^2}\right)\right\}^{1/3} - 1\right]$$

$$= \lim_{n \to \infty} n\left[1 + \frac{1}{3}\cdot\left(\frac{1}{n} + \frac{2}{n^2}\right) + \cdots - 1\right]$$

$$= \lim_{n \to \infty} n\left[\frac{1}{3}\left(\frac{1}{n} + \frac{2}{n^2}\right) + \cdots\right]$$

$$= \lim_{n \to \infty}\left[\frac{1}{3}\left(1 + \frac{2}{n}\right) + \cdots\right] = \frac{1}{3}$$

$$\therefore \quad I = \lim_{n \to \infty} \cos^2[\pi(\sqrt[3]{n^3 + n^2 + 2n} - n)]$$

$$= \lim_{n \to \infty} \cos^2\left(\frac{\pi}{3}\right) = \left(\frac{1}{2}\right)^2 = \frac{1}{4}$$

(ii) Consider

$$\lim_{n \to \infty} n\sin(2\pi\sqrt{1 + n^2})$$

$$= \lim_{n \to \infty} n\sin(2\pi\sqrt{1 + n^2} - 2n\pi)$$

[since, $\sin x$ is periodic with period 2π]

$$= \lim_{n \to \infty} n\sin[2\pi(\sqrt{1 + n^2} - n)]$$

$$= \lim_{n \to \infty} n\sin\left(\frac{2\pi(\sqrt{1 + n^2} - n)}{(\sqrt{1 + n^2} + n)}(\sqrt{1 + n^2} + n)\right)$$

$$= \lim_{n \to \infty} n\sin\left(\frac{2\pi}{\sqrt{1 + n^2} + n}\right)$$

$$= \lim_{n \to \infty} \frac{n\sin\left(\frac{2\pi}{\sqrt{1 + n^2} + n}\right)}{\left(\frac{2\pi}{\sqrt{1 + n^2} + n}\right)} \times \left(\frac{2\pi}{\sqrt{1 + n^2} + n}\right)$$

$$= \lim_{n \to \infty} \frac{2n\pi}{\sqrt{1 + n^2} + n} = \lim_{n \to \infty} \frac{2n\pi}{n\left(\sqrt{\frac{1}{n^2} + 1} + 1\right)}$$

$$= \lim_{n \to \infty} \frac{2\pi}{\sqrt{\frac{1}{n^2} + 1} + 1} = \frac{2\pi}{2} = \pi$$

(iii) Consider

$$\lim_{n \to \infty} (-1)^n \sin(\pi\sqrt{n^2 + 0.5n + 1})\sin\left[\frac{(n + 1)\pi}{4n}\right]$$

$$= \lim_{n \to \infty} (-1)^n \sin\left[\pi\sqrt{n^2 + \frac{n}{2} + 1}\right] \times \lim_{n \to \infty} \sin\left[\frac{\pi}{4}\left(1 + \frac{1}{4}\right)\right]$$

$$\lim_{n \to \infty} (-1)^n (-1)^{n-1} \sin\left(n\pi - \pi\sqrt{n^2 + \frac{n}{2} + 1}\right) \times \frac{1}{\sqrt{2}}$$

$$= \lim_{n \to \infty} (-1)^{2n-1} \sin\left(\pi\,\frac{\left(n - \sqrt{n^2 + \frac{n}{2} + 1}\right)\left(n + \sqrt{n^2 + \frac{n}{2} + 1}\right)}{n + \sqrt{n^2 + \frac{n}{2} + 1}}\right) \times \frac{1}{\sqrt{2}}$$

$$= \frac{1}{\sqrt{2}} \lim_{n \to \infty} (-1)^{2n-1} \sin\left[\frac{\pi\left(n^2 - n^2 - \frac{n}{2} - 1\right)}{n\left(1 + \sqrt{1 + \frac{1}{2n} + \frac{1}{n^2}}\right)}\right]$$

$$= \frac{1}{\sqrt{2}} \lim_{n \to \infty} (-1)^{2n} \sin\left[\frac{\pi\left(\frac{n}{2} + 1\right)}{n\left(1 + \sqrt{1 + \frac{1}{2n} + \frac{1}{n^2}}\right)}\right]$$

$$= \frac{1}{\sqrt{2}} \lim_{n \to \infty} (-1)^{2n} \sin\left[\frac{\pi\left(\frac{1}{2} + \frac{1}{n}\right)}{\left(1 + \sqrt{1 + \frac{1}{2n} + \frac{1}{2n^2}}\right)}\right]$$

$$= \frac{1}{\sqrt{2}} \lim_{n \to \infty} \sin\left[\frac{\pi\left(\frac{1}{2} + \frac{1}{n}\right)}{\left(1 + \sqrt{1 + \frac{1}{2n} + \frac{1}{n^2}}\right)}\right]$$

$$= \frac{1}{\sqrt{2}}\sin\left(\frac{\pi}{4}\right) = \frac{1}{\sqrt{2}} \times \frac{1}{\sqrt{2}}$$

$$= \frac{1}{2}$$

(iv) Consider $\lim_{x \to \infty} \left(\frac{x+a}{x-a}\right)^x = e$ [1^∞ form]

$\Rightarrow \quad e^{\lim_{x \to \infty}\left(\frac{x+a}{x-a}-1\right)x} = e$

$\Rightarrow \quad e^{\lim_{x \to \infty} \frac{2ax}{x-a}} = e$

$\Rightarrow \quad e^{\lim_{x \to \infty}\left(\frac{2a}{1-\frac{a}{x}}\right)} = e$

$\Rightarrow \quad e^{2a} = e$

$\therefore \quad a = \frac{1}{2}$

Hence, (i) $\to$ (q), (ii) $\to$ (r), (iii) $\to$ (p), (iv) $\to$ (p)

Explanations for Q. Nos. (31-33)

We have, $f(x)$ is exist for all $x \in R-\{0\}$, with $f'(x) < 0, \forall x \in (-\infty, 0)$ and $f'(x) > 0, \forall x \in (0, \infty)$.

Also, $\lim_{x \to 0^-} f(x) = 3$; $\lim_{x \to 0^+} f(x) = 2$ and $f(0) = 4$

$\therefore$ Graph of $f(x)$ will be

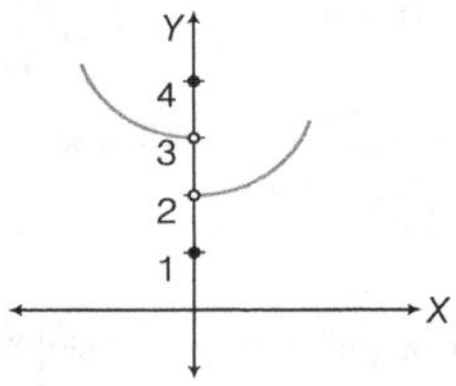

$\Rightarrow$ Clearly, as $x \to 0$, $x^3 - x^2 = x^2(x-1) \to 0^-$

and as $x \to 0, 2x^4 - x^5 = x^4(2 - x^5) \to 0^+$

$\therefore \quad \lim_{x \to 0} f(x^3 - x^2) = f(0^-) = 3$

and $\quad \lim_{x \to 0} f(2x^4 - x^5) = f(0^+) = 2$

Now, consider

$$2\left[\lim_{x \to 0} f(x^3 - x^2)\right] = \lambda\left[\lim_{x \to 0} f(2x^4 - x^5)\right]$$

$\Rightarrow \quad 2 \times 3 = \lambda(2)$

$\therefore$ On comparing, $\lambda = 3$

Now, consider,

$$\lim_{x \to 0^+} \frac{f(-x)\,x^2}{\left\{\frac{1-\cos x}{[f(x)]}\right\}} = \lim_{x \to 0^+} \frac{f(-x)\,x^2}{\left(\frac{1-\cos x}{[f(x)]}\right) - \left[\frac{1-\cos x}{[f(x)]}\right]}$$

[$\because \{x\} = x - [x]$]

$$= \lim_{x \to 0^+} \frac{3x^2}{\left(\frac{1-\cos x}{2}\right) - 0}$$

[$\because \lim_{x \to 0^+} f(-x) = f(0^-) = 3$]

$\lim_{x \to 0^+} [f(x)] = [f(0^+)] = [2] = 2$

and $x \to 0^+ \Rightarrow \cos x \to 1^-$

$\therefore [1 - \cos x] = 0$

$$= 6 \lim_{x \to 0^+} \frac{x^2}{2\sin^2\frac{x}{2}} = 3 \lim_{x \to 0^+} \frac{4 \times \frac{x^2}{4}}{\sin^2\frac{x}{2}}$$

$$= 12 \lim_{x \to 0^+} \frac{\left(\frac{x}{2}\right)^2}{\left[\sin\left(\frac{x}{2}\right)\right]^2} = 12 \times 1 = 12$$

Again, consider

$$\lim_{x \to 0^-}\left(\frac{x^3 - \sin^3 x}{x^4}\right) = \lim_{x \to 0^-} \frac{(x - \sin x)(x^2 + \sin^2 x + x\sin x)}{x^4}$$

$$= \lim_{x \to 0^-}\left(\frac{x - \sin x}{x^3}\right)\left(\frac{x^2 + \sin^2 x + x\sin x}{x^2}\right)\cdot x$$

$$= \lim_{x \to 0^-}\left(\frac{1}{6}\right)(3)\cdot x \to 0^-$$

$$\left[\because \lim_{x \to 0^-} \frac{x - \sin x}{x^3} = \lim_{x \to 0^-} \frac{1 - \cos x}{3x^2} = \lim_{x \to 0^-} \frac{\sin x}{6x} = \frac{1}{6}\right.$$

and $\lim_{x \to 0^-} \frac{x^2 + \sin^2 x + x\sin x}{x^2}$

$$\left. = \lim_{x \to 0^-}\left(1 + \frac{\sin^2 x}{x^2} + \frac{\sin x}{x}\right) = 1 + 1 + 1 = 3\right]$$

$\Rightarrow$ As $x \to 0^- \quad \Rightarrow \quad \frac{x^3 - \sin^3 x}{x^4} \to 0^-$

Now, consider

Then, $\lim_{x \to 0^-} \frac{\sin x^3}{x} = \lim_{x \to 0^-} \frac{\sin x^3}{x^3}\cdot x^2 = \lim_{x \to 0^-} x^2 \to 0^+$

$\therefore \quad \lim_{x \to 0^-} f\left(\frac{x^3 - \sin^3 x}{x^4}\right) = f(0^-) = 3$

and $\quad \lim_{x \to 0^-} f\left(\left[\frac{\sin x^3}{x}\right]\right) = f(0) = 4$

$$\left[\because \left[\frac{\sin x^3}{x}\right] = 0, \text{ as } \frac{\sin x^3}{x} \to 0^+\right]$$

Hence,

$$\lim_{x \to 0^-}\left[3f\left(\frac{x^3 - \sin^3 x}{x^4}\right)\right] - f\left(\left[\frac{\sin^3 x}{x}\right]\right) = [3 \times 3] - 4$$

$$= 9 - 4 = 5$$

31. (c) **32.** (b) **33.** (b)

34. (6) Consider

$$\lim_{x \to 0} \frac{2f(x) - 3f(2x) + f(4x)}{x^2} = \lim_{x \to 0} \frac{2f'(x) - 6f'(2x) + 4f'(4x)}{2x}$$

[using L' Hospital's rule]

$$= \lim_{x \to 0} \frac{2f''(x) - 12f''(2x) + 16f''(4x)}{2}$$

[again, applying L' Hospital's rule]

$= \lim_{x \to 0} f''(x) - 6f''(2x) + 8f''(4x)$

$= f''(0) - 6f''(0) + 8f''(0)$

$= 2 - 12 + 16$ [$\because f''(0) = 2$]

$= 6$

35. (2) Consider

$$\lim_{x \to 0} \frac{ex}{e - (1+x)^{1/x}} = \lim_{x \to 0} \frac{ex}{e - e^{\frac{1}{x}\log(1+x)}}$$

$$= \lim_{x \to 0} \frac{ex}{e - e^{\frac{1}{x}\left(x - \frac{x^2}{2} + \frac{x^3}{3} - \dots\right)}}$$

$$= \lim_{x \to 0} \frac{ex}{e - e^{\left(1 - \frac{x}{2} + \frac{x^2}{3} - \dots\right)}}$$

$$= \lim_{x \to 0} \frac{ex}{e - e\cdot e^{\left(-\frac{x}{2} + \frac{x^2}{3} - \dots\right)}}$$

$$= \lim_{x \to 0} \frac{x}{1 - e^{\left(-\frac{x}{2} + \frac{x^2}{3} - \dots\right)}}$$

$$= \lim_{x \to 0} \frac{x}{1 - \left[1 + \left(-\frac{x}{2} + \frac{x^2}{3} - \cdots\right) + \frac{1}{2!}\left(\frac{-x}{2} + \frac{x^2}{3} - \cdots\right)^2 + \cdots\right]}$$

$$= \lim_{x \to 0} \frac{x}{-\left(-\frac{x}{2} + \frac{x^2}{3} \cdots\right) - \frac{1}{2!}\left(-\frac{x}{2} + \frac{x^2}{3} - \cdots\right)^2 + \cdots}$$

$$= \lim_{x \to 0} \frac{1}{-\left(-\frac{1}{2} + \frac{x}{3} - \cdots\right) - \frac{1}{2!} x\left(-\frac{1}{2} + \frac{x}{3} \cdots\right)^2 + \cdots}$$

$$= \frac{1}{-\left(\frac{-1}{2}\right)} = 2$$

36. (4) We have, $a_{n+1} = a_n + \sqrt{1 + a_n^2}$

Let $a_n = \cot(\alpha_n)$

$\Rightarrow \quad a_{n+1} = \cot(\alpha_n) + \operatorname{cosec}(\alpha_n)$

$$= \frac{\cos(\alpha_n) + 1}{\sin(\alpha_n)} = \frac{2\cos^2(\alpha_n/2)}{2\sin(\alpha_n/2)\cos(\alpha_n/2)} = \cot\left(\frac{\alpha_n}{2}\right) \quad \ldots \text{(i)}$$

Now, on putting $n = 1$, we get

$$a_1 = \cot(\alpha_1) \quad \text{and} \quad a_1 = a_0 + \sqrt{1 + a_0^2} = 1$$

$$\Rightarrow \quad \cot(\alpha_1) = 1 \quad \text{or} \quad \alpha_1 = \frac{\pi}{4}$$

Now, from Eq. (i), we get

$$a_2 = \cot\left(\frac{\alpha_1}{2}\right) = \cot\left(\frac{\pi}{8}\right) = \cot\left(\frac{\pi}{4 \cdot 2}\right)$$

$$a_3 = \cot\left(\frac{\alpha_2}{2}\right) = \cot\left(\frac{\pi}{4 \cdot 2^2}\right)$$

$$a_4 = \cot\left(\frac{\alpha_3}{2}\right) = \cot\left(\frac{\pi}{4 \cdot 2^3}\right)$$

$$\vdots$$

$$a_n = \cot\left(\frac{\pi}{4 \cdot 2^{n-1}}\right)$$

Hence, $\displaystyle \lim_{x \to \infty} \frac{a_n}{2^{n-1}} = \lim_{n \to \infty} \frac{\cot\left(\frac{\pi}{4 \cdot 2^{n-1}}\right)}{2^{n-1}}$

$$= \lim_{n \to \infty} \frac{1}{\tan\left(\frac{\pi}{4 \cdot 2^{n-1}}\right) 2^{n-1}} = \lim_{n \to \infty} \frac{\frac{1}{\tan\left(\frac{\pi}{4} \cdot \frac{1}{2^{n-1}}\right)}}{\frac{1}{2^{n-1}} \times \left(\frac{\pi}{4}\right)} \times \left(\frac{\pi}{4}\right)$$

$$= \frac{1}{1 \times \frac{\pi}{4}} = \frac{4}{\pi}$$

37. (3) $\sin(x_{n+1} - x_n) + 2^{-(n+1)} \cdot \sin x_n \cdot \sin x_{n+1} = 0$

$$\Rightarrow \quad \cot x_{n+1} - \cot x_n = 2^{-(n+1)}$$

$$\Rightarrow \quad \cot x_n - \cot x_{n-1} = 2^{-n}$$

$$\vdots \qquad \vdots$$

$$\Rightarrow \quad \cot x_2 - \cot x_1 = 2^{-2}$$

On adding,

$$\cot x_{n+1} - \cot x_1 = \frac{1}{2^2} + \frac{1}{2^3} + \cdots + \frac{1}{2^{n+1}}$$

$$\Rightarrow \quad \cot x_{n+1} = \frac{1}{2} + \frac{1}{2^2} + \frac{1}{2^3} + \cdots + \frac{1}{2^{n+1}}$$

$$\therefore \quad \lim_{n \to \infty} \cot x_{n+1} = \frac{1/2}{1 - 1/2} = 1$$

$$\therefore \quad \lim_{n \to \infty} x_{n+1} = \pi/4$$

or $\displaystyle \lim_{n \to \infty} x_n = \pi/4 = l$

$$\therefore \quad 4l = \pi \Rightarrow [4l] = 3$$

38. (4) $\displaystyle \lim_{n \to \infty} \sum_{r=1}^{n} \frac{kr}{1 \times 3 \times 5 \times \cdots \times (2r+1)} = 1$

$$\Rightarrow \quad \frac{k}{2} \cdot \lim_{n \to \infty} \sum_{r=1}^{n} \left[\frac{1}{1 \times 3 \times 5 \cdots \times (2r-1)} - \frac{1}{1 \times 3 \times 5 \times \cdots \times (2r+1)}\right] = 1$$

$$\Rightarrow \quad \frac{k}{2} \lim_{n \to \infty} \left[\left(1 - \frac{1}{1 \times 3}\right) + \left(\frac{1}{1 \times 3} - \frac{1}{1 \times 3 \times 5}\right) + \cdots + \left(\frac{1}{1 \times 3 \times \cdots \times (2n-1)} - \frac{1}{1 \times 3 \times \cdots \times (2n+1)}\right)\right] = 1$$

$$\Rightarrow \quad \frac{k}{2} \lim_{n \to \infty} \left[1 - \frac{1}{1 \times 3 \times 5 \times \cdots \times (2n+1)}\right] = 1$$

$$\Rightarrow \quad \frac{k}{2} \times 1 = 1$$

$$\Rightarrow \quad k = 2$$

$$\therefore \quad k^2 = 4$$

39. (1) We have,

$$a_n = n(1 + a_{n-1})$$

$$\Rightarrow \quad a_{n-1} + 1 = \frac{a_n}{n} \quad \ldots \text{(i)}$$

Now, consider

$$\lim_{n \to \infty} \left[\left(1 + \frac{1}{a_1}\right)\left(1 + \frac{1}{a_2}\right) \cdots \left(1 + \frac{1}{a_n}\right)\right] \frac{1}{e}$$

$$= \frac{1}{e} \lim_{n \to \infty} \frac{(a_1 + 1)}{a_1} \times \frac{(a_2 + 1)}{a_2} \times \frac{(a_3 + 1)}{a_3} \cdots \times \frac{(a_n + 1)}{a_n}$$

$$= \frac{1}{e} \lim_{n \to \infty} \left(\frac{a_2}{2}\right)\left(\frac{a_3}{3}\right)\left(\frac{a_4}{4}\right) \cdots \left(\frac{a_{n+1}}{n+1}\right) \times \frac{1}{a_1 a_2 a_3 \cdots a_n}$$

[using Eq. (i)]

$$= \frac{1}{e} \lim_{n \to \infty} \frac{a_{n+1}}{(n+1)!} \quad [\because a_1 = 1]$$

$$= \frac{1}{e} \lim_{n \to \infty} \frac{a_n + 1}{n!} \quad \text{[using Eq. (i)]}$$

$$= \frac{1}{e} \lim_{n \to \infty} \left(\frac{1}{n!} + \frac{a_n}{n!}\right)$$

$$= \frac{1}{e} \lim_{n \to \infty} \left(\frac{1}{n!} + \frac{(1 + a_{n-1})}{(n-1)!}\right) \quad \text{[using Eq. (i)]}$$

$$= \frac{1}{e} \lim_{n \to \infty} \left(\frac{1}{n!} + \frac{1}{(n-1)} + \frac{a_{n-1}}{(n-1)!}\right)$$

$$= \frac{1}{e} \lim_{n \to \infty} \left(\frac{1}{n!} + \frac{1}{(n-1)!} + \frac{1}{(n-2)!} + \cdots + \frac{1}{(2!)} + \frac{1}{1!} + \frac{a_1}{1!}\right)$$

$$= \frac{1}{e} \lim_{n \to \infty} \left(1 + \frac{1}{1!} + \frac{1}{2!} + \cdots + \frac{1}{n!}\right)$$

$$= \frac{1}{e}\left(1 + \frac{1}{1!} + \frac{1}{2!} + \cdots \infty\right)$$

$$= \frac{1}{e} \cdot e = 1 \quad \left[\because e = 1 + \frac{1}{1!} + \frac{1}{2!} + \cdots \infty\right]$$

40. (1) Let $(\sqrt{3} + 1)^{2n} = I + f$, $F = (\sqrt{3} - 1)^{2n}$.

If $I + f + F =$ Even integer, $0 < f, F < 1$

$$\Rightarrow \quad 0 < F + f < 2$$

$$\Rightarrow \quad f + F = 1$$

$$\Rightarrow \quad \{(\sqrt{3} + 1)^{2n}\} = f = 1 - F$$

$$\therefore \quad \lim_{n \to \infty} f = \lim_{n \to \infty} (1 - F)$$

$$= \lim_{n \to \infty} [1 - (\sqrt{3} - 1)^{2n}] = 1$$

JEE Main & AIEEE Archive

1. (c) $\lim_{x \to 0} \frac{(1-\cos 2x)(3+\cos x)}{x \tan 4x}$

$$= \lim_{x \to 0} \frac{2\sin^2 x(3+\cos x)}{x\tan 4x} = \lim_{x\to 0} \frac{2\frac{\sin^2}{x^2}(3+\cos x)}{4\left(\frac{x\tan 4x}{4x^2}\right)} = 2$$

2. (c) $\lim_{x\to 0}\left[1+\frac{f(x)}{x^2}\right] = 3 \Rightarrow \lim_{x\to 0}\frac{f(x)}{x^2} = 2$

$\therefore \quad f(x) = ax^4 + bx^3 + 2x^2 + 0x + 0$

$f'(x) = 4ax^3 + 3bx^2 + 4x$

$f'(1) = 4a + 3b + 4 = 0 \qquad$ (i)

$f'(2) = 32a + 12b + 8 = 0$

$\Rightarrow \quad 8a + 3b + 2 = 0 \qquad$ ...(ii)

On solving Eqs. (i) and (ii), we get

$$a = \frac{1}{2}, b = -2$$

$\therefore \quad f(x) = \frac{x^4}{2} - 2x^3 + 2x^2$

Now, $\quad f(2) = 8 - 16 + 8 = 0$

3. (d) $\lim_{x\to 0}\frac{\sin(\pi\cos^2 x)}{x^2}$

$$= \lim_{x\to 0}\frac{\sin\pi(1-\sin^2 x)}{x^2} = \lim_{x\to 0}\frac{\sin(\pi - \pi\sin^2 x)}{x^2}$$

$$= \lim_{x\to 0}\frac{\sin(\pi\sin^2 x)}{x^2} = \lim_{x\to 0}\frac{\sin(\pi\sin^2 x)}{\pi\sin^2 x}\times(\pi)\left(\frac{\sin^2 x}{x^2}\right)$$

$= \pi \qquad \left[\because \lim_{x\to 0}\frac{\sin x}{x} = 1\right]$

4. (d) Let $I = \lim_{x\to 0}\frac{(1-\cos 2x)}{x^2}\cdot\frac{(3+\cos x)}{1}\cdot\frac{x}{\tan 4x}$

$$= \lim_{x\to 0}\frac{2\sin^2 x}{x^2}\cdot\frac{3+\cos x}{1}\cdot\frac{x}{\tan 4x}$$

$$= 2\lim_{x\to 0}\left(\frac{\sin x}{x}\right)^2\cdot\lim_{x\to 0}(3+\cos x)\cdot\lim_{x\to 0}\frac{4x}{4\tan 4x}$$

$\because \quad \lim_{\theta\to 0}\frac{\sin\theta}{\theta} = 1$ and $\lim_{\theta\to 0}\frac{\theta}{\tan\theta} = 1$

$\therefore \quad I = 2\cdot(1)^2\cdot(3+\cos 0^\circ)\cdot\frac{1}{4}(1)$

$$= 2\cdot 1\cdot(3+1)\cdot\frac{1}{4} = 2\cdot 4\cdot\frac{1}{4} = 2$$

5. (d) $\lim_{x\to 2}\frac{\sqrt{1-\cos 2(x-2)}}{(x-2)} = \lim_{x\to 2}\frac{\sqrt{2\sin^2(x-2)}}{(x-2)}$

$$= \lim_{x\to 2}\frac{\sqrt{2}\,|\sin(x-2)|}{(x-2)}$$

RHL at $x = 2$,

$$\lim_{h\to 0}\frac{\sqrt{2}\,|\sin(2+h-2)|}{(2+h)-2} = \lim_{h\to 0}\frac{\sqrt{2}\,|\sin h|}{h}$$

$$= \lim_{h\to 0}\frac{\sqrt{2}\sin h}{h} = \sqrt{2}$$

LHL at $x = 2$,

$$\lim_{h\to 0}\frac{\sqrt{2}\,|\sin(2-h-2)|}{(2-h)-2} = \lim_{h\to 0}\frac{\sqrt{2}\,|\sin(-h)|}{-h}$$

$$= \lim_{h\to 0}\frac{\sqrt{2}\sin h}{-h} = -\sqrt{2}$$

So, the limit does not exist.

6. (a) Given, $\lim_{x\to 5} f(x)$ exists and $\lim_{x\to 5}\frac{[f(x)]^2 - 9}{\sqrt{|x-5|}} = 0$

$\Rightarrow \quad \lim_{x\to 5}[f(x)]^2 - 9 = 0$

$\Rightarrow \quad \left(\lim_{x\to 5}[f(x)]\right)^2 = 9$

$\therefore \quad \lim_{x\to 5} f(x) = 3, -3$

But $\quad f : R \to [0, \infty)$

$\therefore \quad$ Range of $f(x) \geq 0$

$\Rightarrow \quad \lim_{x\to 5} f(x) = 3$

7. (d) Here, $\lim_{x\to a}\frac{x^2 f(a) - a^2 f(x)}{x - a}$

$$= \lim_{x\to a}\frac{2xf(a) - a^2 f'(x)}{1-0} \qquad \text{[using L' Hospital's rule]}$$

$$= 2af(a) - a^2 f'(a)$$

8. (a) Since, $f(x)$ is a positive increasing function.

$\Rightarrow \quad 0 < f(x) < f(2x) < f(3x)$

$\Rightarrow \quad 0 < 1 < \frac{f(2x)}{f(x)} < \frac{f(3x)}{f(x)}$

$\Rightarrow \quad \lim_{x\to\infty} 1 \leq \lim_{x\to\infty}\frac{f(2x)}{f(x)} \leq \lim_{x\to\infty}\frac{f(3x)}{f(x)}$

By Sandwich theorem, $\lim_{x\to\infty}\frac{f(2x)}{f(x)} = 1$

9. (d) $\lim_{x\to\alpha}\frac{1-\cos(ax^2+bx+c)}{(x-\alpha)^2}$

$$= \lim_{x\to\alpha}\frac{2\sin^2\left(\frac{ax^2+bx+c}{2}\right)}{(x-\alpha)^2}$$

$$= \lim_{x\to\alpha}\frac{2\sin^2\left[\frac{a}{2}(x-\alpha)(x-\beta)\right]}{\left(\frac{a}{2}\right)^2(x-\alpha)^2(x-\beta)^2}\left(\frac{a}{2}\right)^2(x-\beta)^2$$

$$= \lim_{x\to\alpha}\frac{a^2}{2}(x-\beta)^2 \qquad \left[\because \lim_{x\to 0}\frac{\sin x}{x} = 1\right]$$

$$= \frac{a^2}{2}(\alpha-\beta)^2$$

10. (b) Now, $\lim_{x\to\infty}\left(1+\frac{a}{x}+\frac{b}{x^2}\right)^{2x}$

$$= \lim_{x\to\infty}\left(1+\frac{a}{x}+\frac{b}{x^2}\right)^{2x\left(\frac{\frac{a}{x}+\frac{b}{x^2}}{\frac{a}{x}+\frac{b}{x^2}}\right)}$$

$$= e^{\lim_{x\to\infty} 2x\left(\frac{a}{x}+\frac{b}{x^2}\right)} \qquad \left[\because \lim_{x\to\infty}(1+x)^{1/x} = e\right]$$

$$= e^{2a}$$

But $\lim_{x\to\infty}\left(1+\frac{a}{x}+\frac{b}{x^2}\right)^{2x} = e^2 \Rightarrow e^{2a} = e^2$

$\therefore \quad a = 1$

and $\quad b \in R$

11. (c) $\lim_{x\to\frac{\pi}{2}}\frac{\left(1-\tan\frac{x}{2}\right)(1-\sin x)}{\left(1+\tan\frac{x}{2}\right)(\pi-2x)^3}$

Let $x = \frac{\pi}{2} - h$ as $x \to \frac{\pi}{2}, h \to 0$

$$\therefore \lim_{h\to 0}\frac{1-\tan\left(\frac{\pi}{4}-\frac{h}{2}\right)}{1+\tan\left(\frac{\pi}{4}-\frac{h}{2}\right)}\cdot\frac{(1-\cos h)}{(2h)^3}$$

$$= \lim_{h\to 0}\tan\left[\frac{\pi}{4}-\left(\frac{\pi}{4}-\frac{h}{2}\right)\right]\cdot\frac{2\sin^2\frac{h}{2}}{8h^3}\left[\because \tan\left(\frac{\pi}{4}-x\right) = \frac{1-\tan x}{1+\tan x}\right]$$

$$= \lim_{h\to 0} \frac{1}{4} \cdot \frac{\tan\frac{h}{2}}{\frac{h}{2}\times 2} \times \left(\frac{\sin\frac{h}{2}}{\frac{h}{2}}\right)^2 \times \frac{1}{4}$$

$$= \frac{1}{32} \lim_{h\to 0}\left(\frac{\tan\frac{h}{2}}{\frac{h}{2}}\right) \lim_{h\to 0}\left(\frac{\sin\frac{h}{2}}{\frac{h}{2}}\right)^2$$

$$= \frac{1}{32} \qquad \left[\because \lim_{\theta\to 0}\frac{\sin\theta}{\theta} = 1 \text{ and } \lim_{\theta\to 0}\frac{\tan\theta}{\theta} = 1\right]$$

12. (c) $\because \lim_{x\to 0} \frac{\log(3+x) - \log(3-x)}{x} = k$

$$\Rightarrow \lim_{x\to 0} \frac{\left(\frac{1}{3+x} + \frac{1}{3-x}\right)}{1} = k \qquad \text{[using L'Hospital's rule]}$$

$$\Rightarrow \frac{1}{3} + \frac{1}{3} = k$$

$$\therefore k = \frac{2}{3}$$

13. (d) Now, $\lim_{x\to 0} \frac{\sqrt{1-\cos 2x}}{\sqrt{2}x} = \lim_{x\to 0}\frac{\sqrt{2}\,|\sin x|}{\sqrt{2}x} = \lim_{x\to 0}\frac{|\sin x|}{x}$

Let $f(x) = \frac{|\sin x|}{x}$

Now, LHL $= \lim_{h\to 0}\frac{|\sin(0-h)|}{0-h} = \lim_{h\to 0}\frac{\sin h}{-h} = -1$

and RHL $= \lim_{h\to 0}\frac{|\sin(0+h)|}{0+h} = \lim_{h\to 0}\frac{\sin h}{h} = 1$

$\because$ LHL $\neq$ RHL

Hence, $\lim_{x\to 0}\frac{|\sin x|}{x}$ does not exist.

14. (a) $\lim_{x\to\infty}\left(\frac{x^2+5x+3}{x^2+x+2}\right)^x = \lim_{x\to\infty}\left(1 + \frac{4x+1}{x^2+x+2}\right)^x$

$$= \lim_{x\to\infty}\left[\left(1 + \frac{4x+1}{x^2+x+2}\right)^{1/\frac{(4x+1)}{x^2+x+2}}\right]^{\frac{(4x+1)x}{x^2+x+2}}$$

$$= e^{\lim_{x\to\infty}\frac{\left(4+\frac{1}{x}\right)}{1+\frac{1}{x}+\frac{2}{x^2}}} = e^4 \qquad \left[\because \lim_{x\to 0}\left(1+\frac{1}{x}\right)^x = e\right]$$

15. (c) $\lim_{x\to\infty}\left(\frac{x-3}{x+2}\right)^x = \lim_{x\to\infty}\left[1 - \frac{5}{x+2}\right]^x$

$$= \lim_{x\to\infty}\left[\left\{1 + \left(\frac{-5}{x+2}\right)\right\}^{1/\left(\frac{-5}{x+2}\right)}\right]^{\left(\frac{-5x}{x+2}\right)}$$

$$= e^{\lim_{x\to\infty}\left(-\frac{5}{1+2/x}\right)} \qquad \left[\because \lim_{x\to\infty}\left(1+\frac{1}{x}\right)^x = e\right]$$

$$= e^{-5}$$

16. (c) $\lim_{x\to 2}\frac{xf(2) - 2f(x)}{x-2}$

$$= \lim_{x\to 2}\frac{xf(2) - 2f(2) + 2f(2) - 2f(x)}{x-2}$$

$$= \lim_{x\to 2}\frac{f(2)(x-2) - 2\{f(x) - f(2)\}}{x-2}$$

$$= f(2) - 2\lim_{x\to 2}\frac{f(x)-f(2)}{x-2} \qquad \left[\because f'(x) = \lim_{x\to a}\frac{f(x)-f(a)}{x-a}\right]$$

$$= f(2) - 2f'(2) = 4 - 2\times 4 = -4$$

JEE Advanced & IITJEE Archive

1. (a,b,c) Given, $f(x) = \sin\left[\frac{\pi}{6}\sin\left(\frac{\pi}{2}\sin x\right)\right]$ and $g(x) = \frac{\pi}{2}\sin x$

$$f[g(x)] = \sin\left[\frac{\pi}{6}\sin\left\{\frac{\pi}{2}\sin\left(\frac{\pi}{2}\sin x\right)\right\}\right]$$

$$\lim_{x\to 0}\frac{f(x)}{g(x)} = \frac{\sin\frac{\pi}{6}\left[\sin\left(\frac{\pi}{2}\sin x\right)\right]}{\frac{\pi}{6}\sin\left(\frac{\pi}{2}\sin x\right)} \times \frac{\frac{\pi}{6}\sin\left(\frac{\pi}{2}\sin x\right)}{\frac{\pi}{2}\sin x} = \frac{\pi}{6}$$

$$g[f(x)] = \frac{\pi}{2}\sin\left[\sin\left\{\frac{\pi}{6}\sin\left(\frac{\pi}{2}\sin x\right)\right\}\right]$$

$$-\frac{\pi}{2}\sin\left(\frac{1}{2}\right) \le g[f(x)] \le \frac{\pi}{2}\sin\frac{1}{2}$$

$$-0.73 \le g[f(x)] \le 0.73$$

2. (2) Given,

$$\lim_{\alpha\to 0}\left(\frac{\cos(\alpha^n) - e}{\alpha^m}\right) = -\frac{e}{2} \Rightarrow \lim_{\alpha\to 0}\frac{e\{e^{\cos(\alpha^n)-1} - 1\}}{\alpha^m} = -\frac{e}{2}$$

$$\Rightarrow \lim_{\alpha\to 0}\frac{e\{e^{\cos(\alpha^n)-1} - 1\}}{\alpha^m} = -\frac{e}{2}$$

$$\Rightarrow \lim_{\alpha\to 0}\frac{e\{e^{\cos(\alpha^n)-1} - 1\}}{\alpha^m\{\cos(\alpha^n) - 1\}}\{\cos(\alpha^n) - 1\} = -\frac{e}{2}$$

$$\Rightarrow \lim_{\alpha\to 0}\frac{-e\left\{2\sin^2\frac{\alpha^n}{2}\right\}}{\alpha^m\left(\frac{\alpha^n}{2}\right)^2}\cdot\left(\frac{\alpha^n}{2}\right)^2 = \frac{-e}{2}$$

$$\Rightarrow \lim_{\alpha\to 0}\frac{-e\left\{2\sin^2\frac{\alpha^n}{2}\right\}}{\alpha^m\left(\frac{\alpha^n}{2}\right)^2}\cdot\left(\frac{\alpha^n}{2}\right)^2 = \frac{-e}{2}$$

$$\Rightarrow \lim_{\alpha\to 0}\frac{-e}{2}\cdot\alpha^{2n-m} = -\frac{e}{2} \Rightarrow 2n - m = 0 \Rightarrow \frac{m}{n} = 2$$

3. (2) **Plan** $\lim_{x\to 0}\frac{\sin x}{x} = 1$

Given, $\lim_{x\to 1}\left\{\frac{\sin(x-1) + a(1-x)}{(x-1) + \sin(x-1)}\right\}^{\frac{(1+\sqrt{x})(1-\sqrt{x})}{1-\sqrt{x}}} = \frac{1}{4}$

$$\Rightarrow \lim_{x\to 1}\left\{\frac{\frac{\sin(x-1)}{(x-1)} - a}{1 + \frac{\sin(x-1)}{(x-1)}}\right\}^{1+\sqrt{x}} = \frac{1}{4}$$

$$\Rightarrow \left(\frac{1-a}{2}\right)^2 = \frac{1}{4} \Rightarrow (a-1)^2 = 1 \Rightarrow a = 2 \text{ or } 0$$

But for $a = 2$, base of above limit approaches $-1/2$ and exponent approaches to 2 and since base cannot be negative, hence limit does not exist.

4. (b) **Concept Involved** To make the quadratic into simple form we should eliminate radical sign.

Description of Situation As for given equation when $a \to 0$ the equation reduces to identity in x.

i.e. $ax^2 + bx + c = 0$, for all $x \in R$ or $a = b = c \to 0$

Thus, first we should make above equation independent from coefficients as 0.

Let $a + 1 = t^6$. Thus, when $a \to 0, t \to 1$.

$\therefore \quad (t^2 - 1)x^2 + (t^3 - 1)x + (t - 1) = 0$

$\Rightarrow \quad (t - 1)\{(t + 1)x^2 + (t^2 + t + 1)x + 1\} = 0 \quad$ [as $t \to 1$]

$\Rightarrow \quad 2x^2 + 3x + 1 = 0$

$\Rightarrow \quad 2x^2 + 2x + x + 1 = 0$

$\Rightarrow \quad (2x + 1)(x + 1) = 0$

Thus, $\quad x = -1, -1/2$ or $\lim_{a \to 0^+} \alpha(a) = -1$

and $\quad \lim_{a \to 0^+} \beta(a) = -1/2$

5. (b) **Concept Involved** $\left(\frac{\infty}{\infty}\right)$ form

$$\lim_{x \to \infty} \frac{a_0x^n + a_1x^{n-1} + \ldots + a_n}{b_0x^m + b_1x^{m-1} + \ldots + b_m} = \begin{cases} 0, & \text{if } n = m \\ \frac{a_0}{b_0}, & \text{if } n < m \\ +\infty, & \text{if } n > m \text{ and } a_0b_0 > 0 \\ -\infty, & \text{if } n > m \text{ and } a_0b_0 < 0 \end{cases}$$

Description of Situation As to make degree of numerator equal to degree of denominator.

$$\lim_{x \to \infty}\left(\frac{x^2 + x + 1}{x + 1} - ax - b\right) = 4$$

$\Rightarrow \quad \lim_{x \to \infty} \frac{x^2 + x + 1 - ax^2 - ax - bx - b}{x + 1} = 4$

$\Rightarrow \quad \lim_{x \to \infty} \frac{x^2(1 - a) + x(1 - a - b) + (1 - b)}{x + 1} = 4$

Here, we make degree of numerator = degree of denominator

$\therefore \quad 1 - a = 0 \Rightarrow a = 1$

and $\quad \lim_{x \to \infty} \frac{x(1 - a - b) + (1 - b)}{x + 1} = 4$

$\Rightarrow \quad 1 - a - b = 4 \Rightarrow b = -4$

6. (d) Here, $\lim_{x \to 0} \{1 + x\log(1 + b^2)\}^{1/x}$ $\quad (1^\infty$ form)

$\Rightarrow \quad e^{\lim_{x \to 0} \{x \log(1 + b^2)\} \cdot \frac{1}{x}}$

$\Rightarrow \quad e^{\log(1 + b^2)} = (1 + b^2) \quad \ldots$(i)

Given, $\lim_{x \to 0} \{1 + x\log(1 + b^2)\}^{1/x} = 2b \sin^2\theta$

$\Rightarrow \quad (1 + b^2) = 2b\sin^2\theta$

$\therefore \quad \sin^2\theta = \frac{1 + b^2}{2b} \quad \ldots$(ii)

By AM $\geq$ GM, $\frac{b + \frac{1}{b}}{2} \geq \left(b \cdot \frac{1}{b}\right)^{1/2} \Rightarrow \frac{b^2 + 1}{2b} \geq 1 \quad \ldots$(iii)

From Eqs. (ii) and (iii), $\sin^2\theta = 1 \Rightarrow \theta = \pm\frac{\pi}{2}$ as $\theta \in (-\pi, \pi]$

7. (0) Let $\quad p(x) = ax^4 + bx^3 + cx^2 + dx + e$

$\Rightarrow \quad p'(x) = 4ax^3 + 3bx^2 + 2cx + d$

$\therefore \quad p'(1) = 4a + 3b + 2c + d = 0 \quad \ldots$(i)

and $\quad p'(2) = 32a + 12b + 4c + d = 0 \quad \ldots$(ii)

Since, $\quad \lim_{x \to 0}\left(1 + \frac{p(x)}{x^2}\right) = 2 \quad$ (given)

$\therefore \quad \lim_{x \to 0} \frac{ax^4 + bx^3 + (c + 1)x^2 + dx + e}{x^2} = 2$

$\Rightarrow \quad c + 1 = 2, d = 0, e = 0 \Rightarrow c = 1$

From Eqs. (i) and (ii),

$4a + 3b = -2$

and $\quad 32a + 12b = -4$

$\Rightarrow \quad a = \frac{1}{4}$ and $b = -1$

$\therefore \quad p(x) = \frac{x^4}{4} - x^3 + x^2 \Rightarrow p(2) = \frac{16}{4} - 8 + 4$

$\Rightarrow \quad p(2) = 0$

8. (a,c) $\quad L = \lim_{x \to 0} \frac{a - \sqrt{a^2 - x^2} - \frac{x^2}{4}}{x^4}, a > 0$

$$= \lim_{x \to 0} \frac{a - a\cdot\left[1 - \frac{2}{2}\cdot\frac{x^2}{a^2} + \frac{\frac{1}{2}\left(\frac{1}{2} - 1\right)}{2}\cdot\frac{x^4}{a^4} - \ldots\right] - \frac{x^2}{4}}{x^4}$$

$$= \lim_{x \to 0} \frac{\frac{x^2}{2a} + \frac{1}{8}\cdot\frac{x^4}{a^3} + \ldots - \frac{x^2}{4}}{x^4}$$

Since, L is finite, then $2a = 4 \Rightarrow a = 2$

$\therefore \quad L = \lim_{x \to 0} \frac{1}{8 \cdot a^3} = \frac{1}{64}$

9. (c) Given, $g(x) = \frac{(x - 1)^n}{\log\cos^m(x - 1)}$; $0 < x < 2$, $m \neq 0$, n are integers

and $|x - 1| = \begin{cases} x - 1; & x \geq 1 \\ 1 - x; & x < 1 \end{cases}$

The left hand derivative of $|x - 1|$ at $x = 1$ is $p = -1$.

Also, $\lim_{x \to 1^+} g(x) = p = -1$

$\Rightarrow \quad \lim_{h \to 0} \frac{(1 + h - 1)^n}{\log\cos^m(1 + h - 1)} = -1 \Rightarrow \lim_{h \to 0} \frac{h^n}{\log\cos^m h} = -1$

$\Rightarrow \quad \lim_{h \to 0} \frac{h^n}{m\log\cos h} = -1$

$\Rightarrow \quad \lim_{h \to 0} \frac{n \cdot h^{n-1}}{m\frac{1}{\cos h}(-\sin h)} = -1 \quad$ [using L'Hospital's rule]

$\Rightarrow \quad \lim_{h \to 0}\left(-\frac{n}{m}\right)\cdot\frac{h^{n-2}}{\left(\frac{\tan h}{h}\right)} = -1 \Rightarrow \left(\frac{n}{m}\right)\lim_{h \to 0}\frac{h^{n-2}}{\left(\frac{\tan h}{h}\right)} = 1$

$\Rightarrow \quad n = 2$ and $\frac{n}{m} = 1$

$\therefore \quad m = n = 2$

10. (a) $\lim_{x \to \frac{\pi}{4}} \frac{\int_2^{\sec^2 x} f(t)\,dt}{x^2 - \frac{\pi^2}{16}} = \lim_{x \to \pi/4} \frac{f(\sec^2 x)2\sec x\sec x\tan x}{2x} \quad \left[\frac{0}{0} \text{ form}\right]$

[using L' Hospital's rule]

$= \frac{2f(2)}{\pi/4} = \frac{8f(2)}{\pi}$

11. (c) Here, $\lim_{x \to 0} (\sin x)^{1/x} + \lim_{x \to 0}\left(\frac{1}{x}\right)^{\sin x}$

$= 0 + \lim_{x \to 0} e^{\log\left(\frac{1}{x}\right)^{\sin x}}$

$= e^{\lim_{x \to 0} \frac{\log(1/x)}{\operatorname{cosec} x}} \quad \left[\begin{array}{l}\lim_{x \to 0} (\sin x)^{1/x} \to 0, \\ \text{as (decimal)}^\infty \to 0\end{array}\right]$

On applying L'Hospital's rule, we get

$= e^{\lim_{x \to 0} \frac{x\left(-\frac{1}{x^2}\right)}{-\operatorname{cosec} x\cot x}} = e^{\lim_{x \to 0} \frac{\sin x}{x}\tan x}$

$= e^0 = 1$

3. Continuity and Differentiability

DPP-1 Graphical Transformation

1. (c) We know that, if graph of $y = f(x)$ is given, then the graph of $f(|x|)$ can be obtained by the following steps

(i) Leaving the graph of $f(x)$ on the right of Y-axis as it is i.e. consider the graph of $f(x)$ for $x \geq 0$.

(ii) Taking the mirror image of the graph of $f(x)$, lying on right of Y-axis, about Y-axis $f(x)$.

Now, as the graph of $y = f(x) = \log_{0.5} x$ is a decreasing graph given as

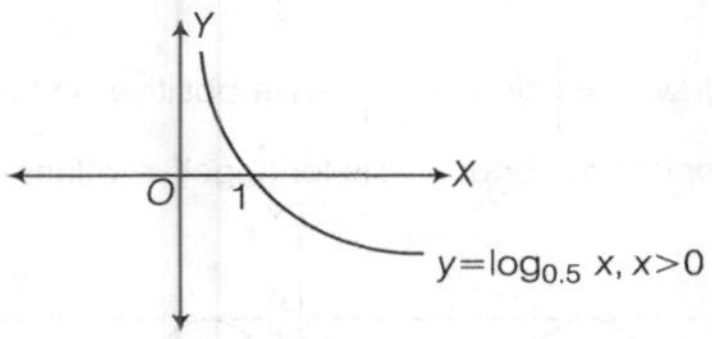

and $(x) \to f(|x|)$

By taking mirror image about Y-axis for $x > 0$, we get the graph of $y = \log_{0.5}|x|$ i.e.

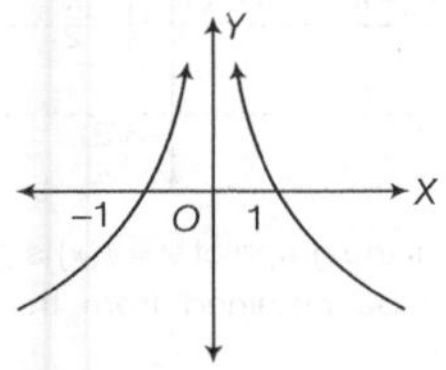

2. (d) We know that, if $f(x)$ changes to $f(x - a)$, where a is positive, then the graph of $f(x - a)$ can be obtained by shifting the graph of $f(x)$ through 'a' units towards right.

Now, as the graph of $y = f(x) = |x|$ is

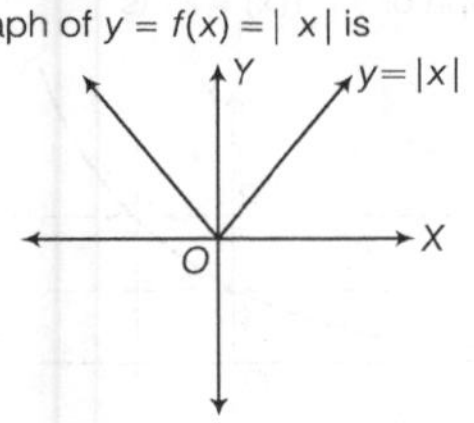

and $f(x) \to f(x - 2)$

$\therefore$ The graph of $y = |x - 2|$ is

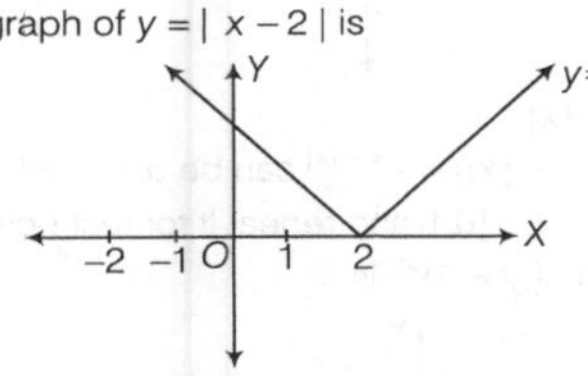

3. (b) We know that, if $f(x)$ changes to $f(x + a)$, where a is positive, then the graph of $f(x + a)$ can be obtained by shifting the graph of $f(x)$ through 'a' units towards left.

Now, as the graph of $y = f(x) = |x|$ is

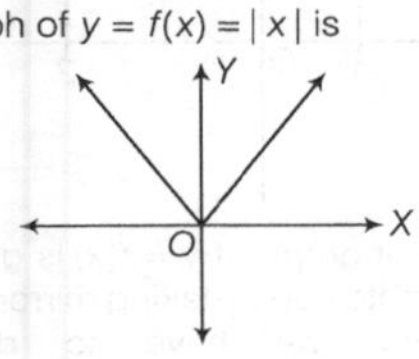

and $f(x) \to f(x + 2)$

$\therefore$ The graph of $y = |x + 2|$ is

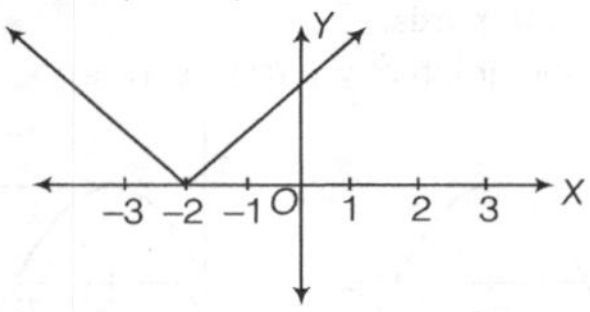

4. (a) We have, $y = \left|\left|\frac{1}{x}\right| - 3\right|$

To draw the graph of $y = \left|\left|\frac{1}{x}\right| - 3\right|$, we follow certain steps. First we plot $\frac{1}{x}$ and then successively $\left|\frac{1}{x}\right|, \left|\frac{1}{x}\right| - 3$ and $\left|\left|\frac{1}{x}\right| - 3\right|$.

(i) Consider, $y = \frac{1}{x}$

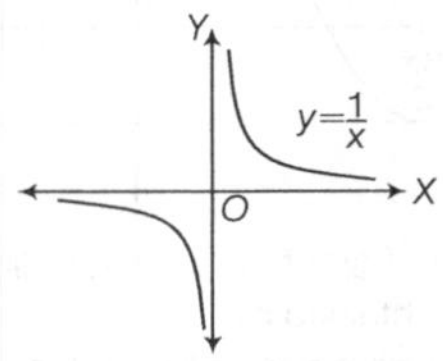

(ii) To draw $y = \left|\frac{1}{x}\right|$, leave positive part as it is and take mirror image about X-axis for negative values of y.

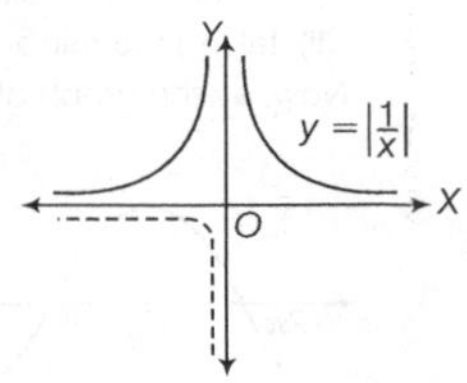

[if $y = f(x)$ is given, then the graph of $y = |f(x)|$ can be obtained by

(a) leaving the positive part of $f(x)$ as it is

(b) taking the image of negative part of $f(x)$ about X-axis.

(iii) To draw $y = \left|\frac{1}{x}\right| - 3$, shift 3 units below the above graph.

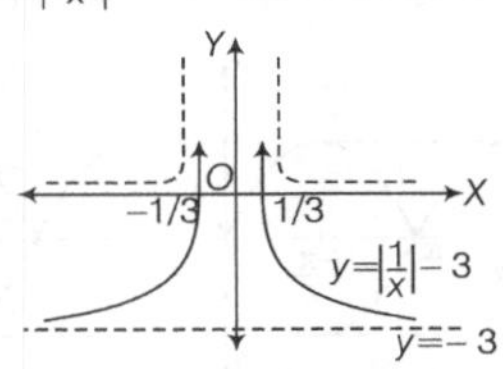

[$\because$ if $y = f(x)$ is given, then the graph of $y = f(x) - a$ can be obtained by shifting the graph of $f(x)$ downward through 'a' units].

(iv) To draw $y = \left|\left|\frac{1}{x}\right| - 3\right|$, leave positive part as it is and take mirror image about X-axis for negative values of y.

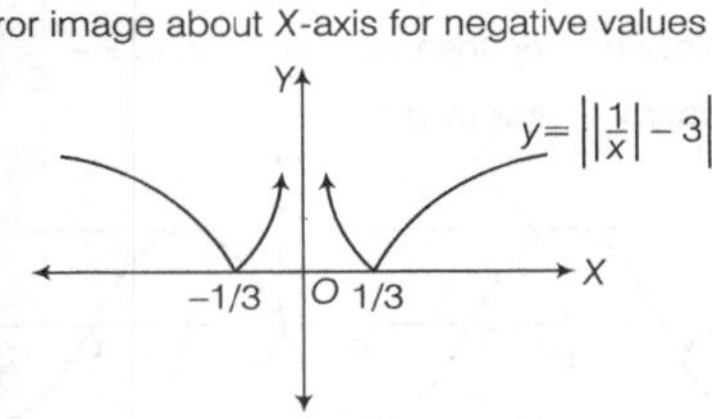

5. (c) We know that, if graph of $y = f(x)$ is given, then the graph of $y = f(|x|)$ can be obtained by the following steps

(i) Leaving the graph of $f(x)$ on the right of Y-axis as it is i.e. consider the graph of $f(x)$ for $x \geq 0$.

(ii) Taking the mirror image of the graph of $f(x)$, lying on the right of Y-axis, about Y-axis.

Now, as the graph of $y = f(x) = \sin x$ is

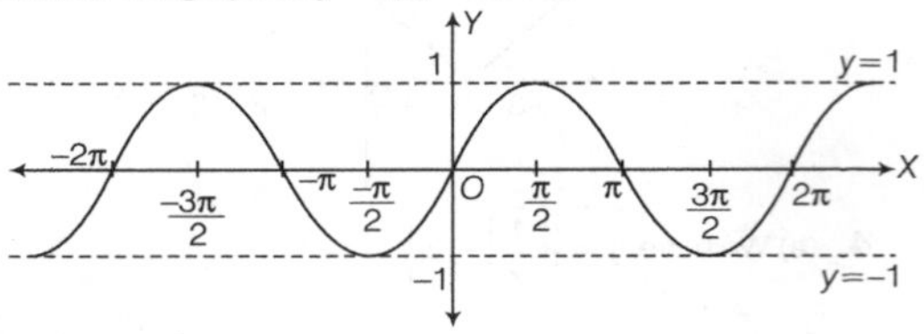

and $\qquad f(x) \to f(|x|)$

$\therefore$ Graph of $y = f(|x|) = \sin(|x|)$ is given by

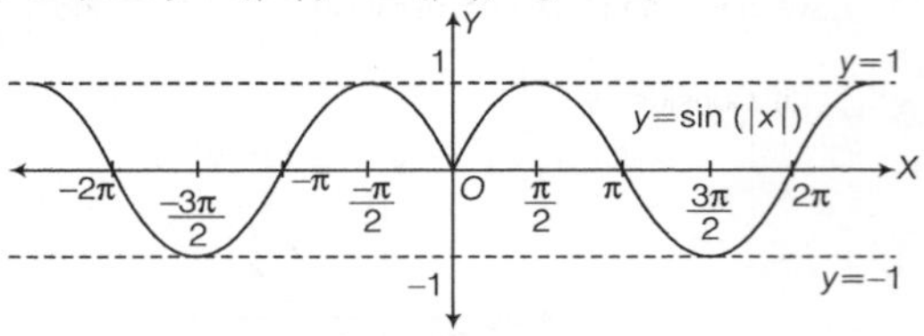

6. (a) We know that, if graph of $y = f(x)$ is given, then the graph of $y = |f(x)|$ can be obtained by

(i) leaving the positive part of $f(x)$ as it is.

(ii) taking the mirror image of negative part of $f(x)$ about X-axis.

Now, as the graph of $y = f(x) = \sin x$ is

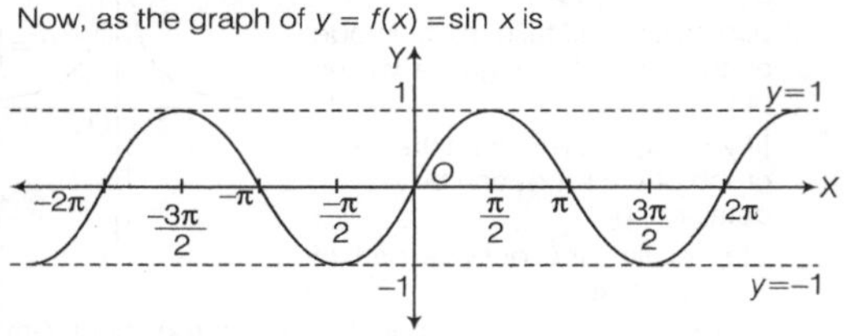

and $f(x) \to |f(x)|$

$\therefore$ Graph of $y = |f(x)| = |\sin x|$ is given by leaving positive part as it is and by taking the image of negative part of $f(x)$ about X-axis.

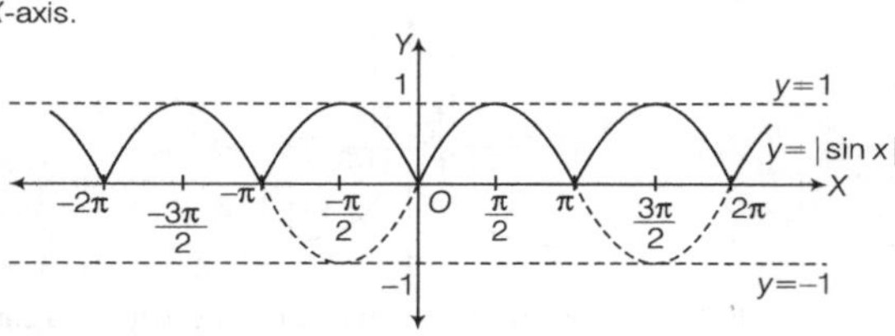

7. (a) We have, $y = \left|\sin x + \frac{1}{2}\right|$

To draw the graph of $y = \left|\sin x + \frac{1}{2}\right|$, we follow the certain steps.

First we plot $\sin x$ and then successively $\sin x + \frac{1}{2}, \left|\sin x + \frac{1}{2}\right|$.

(i) Consider $y = \sin x$, its graph is

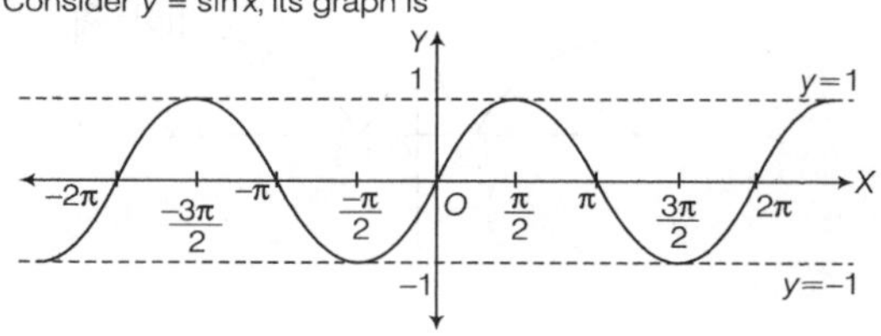

(ii) To draw, $y = \sin x + \frac{1}{2}$, shift the graph of $y = \sin x$ upward through $\frac{1}{2}$ units.

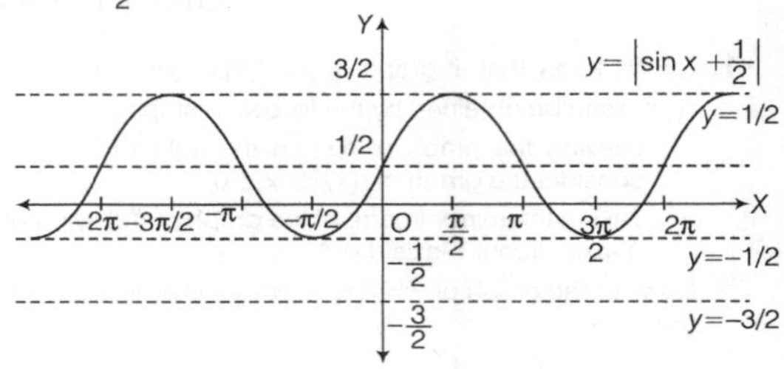

(iii) To draw $y = \left|\sin x + \frac{1}{2}\right|$, leave positive part as it is and take mirror image about X-axis for negative values of y.

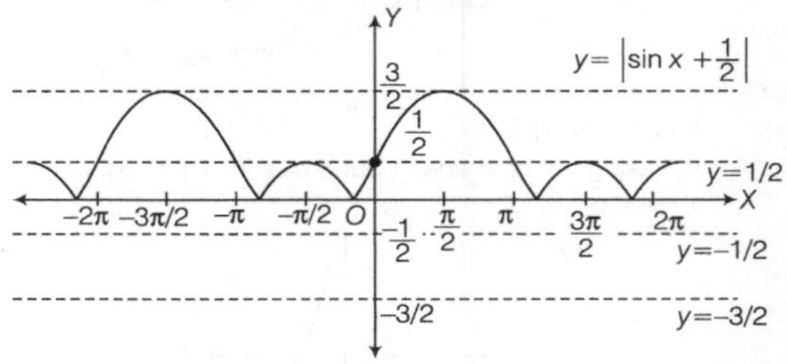

8. (a) We know that, if the graph of $y = f(x)$ is given then, the graph of $y = f(x - [x])$ can be obtained from the graph of $f(x)$ by the following rule

"Retain the graph of $f(x)$ for values of x lying between interval $[0, 1)$ and repeat it for rest of points."

Here, we have to draw the graph of $y = 2^{\{x\}} = 2^{x - [x]}$

Now, as the graph of $y = f(x) = 2^x$ is

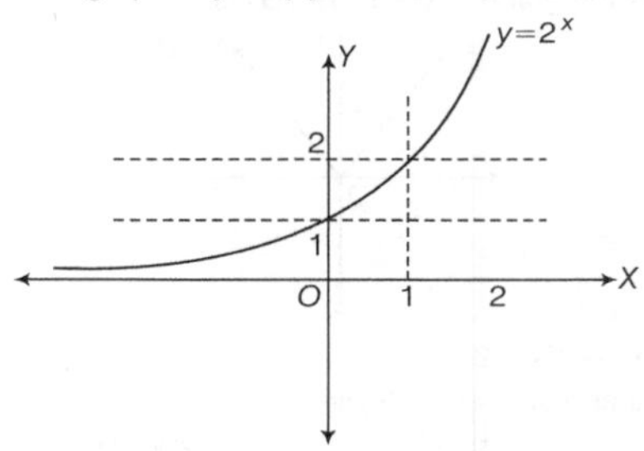

and $f(x) \to f(x - [x])$

$\therefore$ Graph of $y = f(x - [x]) = 2^{x - [x]}$ can be obtained by retaining the graph of 2^x for $x \in [0,1)$ and repeat it for rest points.

Hence, the graph of $y = 2^{\{x\}}$ is

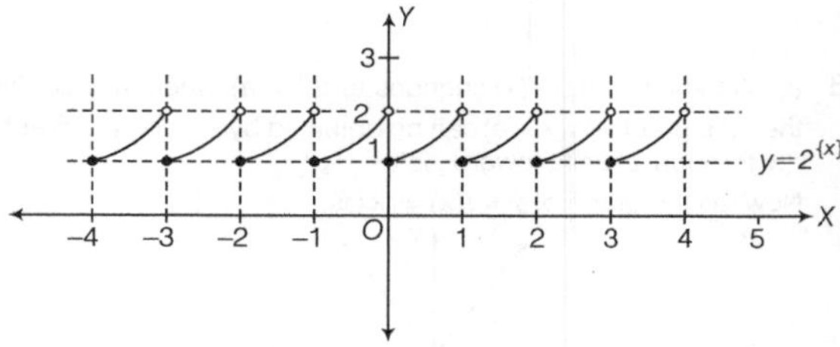

9. (b) We know that, if graph of $y = f(x)$ is given, then the graph of $y = f^{-1}(x)$ can be obtained by taking mirror image of $f(x)$ about the line $y = x$. Here, we have to draw the graph of $y = \sin^{-1} x, -1 \leq x \leq 1$.

Now, as the graph of $y = f(x) = \sin x$ is

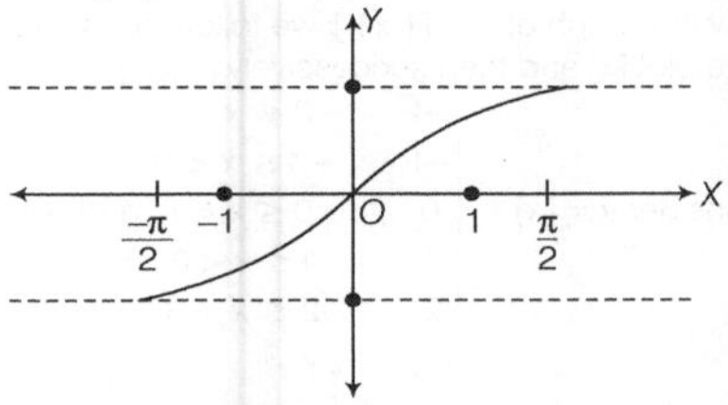

and $\qquad f(x) \to f^{-1}(x)$

$\therefore$ The graph of $y = \sin^{-1} x$ can be obtained by taking mirror image of $f(x)$ about the line $y = x$.

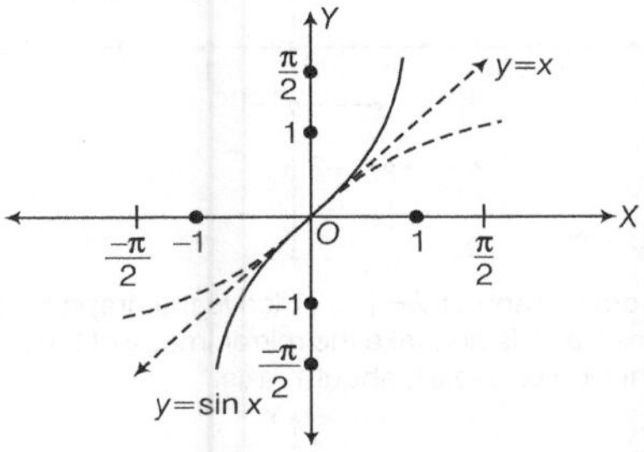

10. (d) We have, $y = \sin^{-1}(\sin x)$.

As, we know $y = \sin^{-1}(\sin x)$ is periodic with period 2π.

$\therefore$ To draw the graph of $y = \sin^{-1}(\sin x)$, we will draw the graph for one interval of length 2π and repeat it for entire values of x.

$$\because \quad \sin^{-1}(\sin x) = \begin{cases} x, & -\frac{\pi}{2} \le x \le \frac{\pi}{2} \\ \pi - x, & -\frac{\pi}{2} \le \pi - x \le \frac{\pi}{2} \end{cases}$$

$$\left(\text{i.e. } \frac{\pi}{2} \le x \le \frac{3\pi}{2}\right)$$

$$\text{or} \quad \sin^{-1}(\sin x) = \begin{cases} x, & -\frac{\pi}{2} \le x \le \frac{\pi}{2} \\ \pi - 2, & \frac{\pi}{2} \le x \le \frac{3\pi}{2} \end{cases}$$

Thus, $y = \sin^{-1}(\sin x)$ has been defined for $-\frac{\pi}{2} \le x \le \frac{3\pi}{2}$ that has length 2π. So, its graph could be plotted as

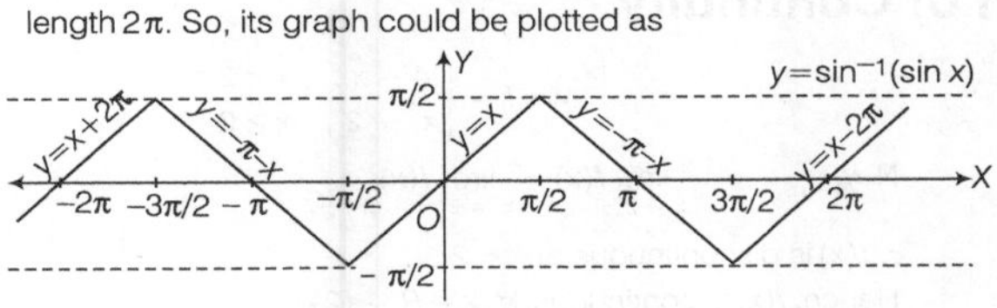

11. (d) We have, $y = 3^{-|x|}$

To draw the graph of $y = 3^{-|x|}$, we follow certain steps

First, we plot 3^x and then successively 3^{-x}, $3^{-|x|}$.

(i) Consider $y = 3^x$, its graph is

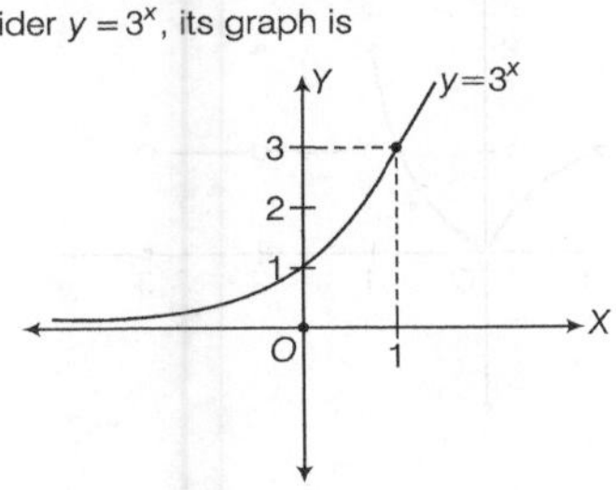

(ii) To draw the graph of $y = 3^{-x}$, take the image of above curve about Y-axis.

[$\because$ if $y = f(x)$ is given, then the graph of $y = f(-x)$ is given by taking the image of $f(x)$ about Y-axis].

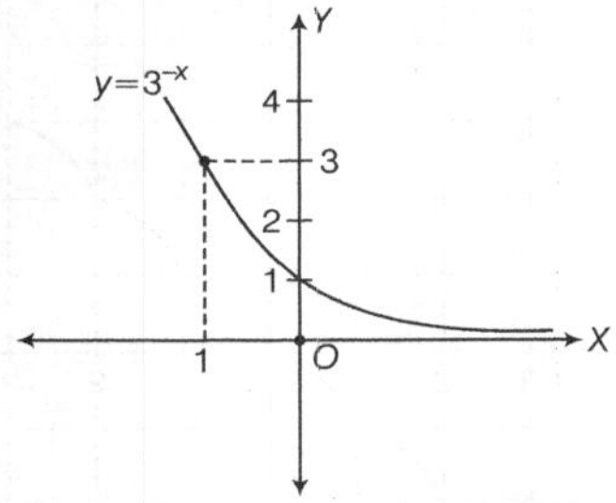

(iii) To draw the graph of $y = 3^{-|x|}$, leave the graph lying right side of Y-axis as it is and take the mirror image of the portion lying on right of Y-axis, about Y-axis.

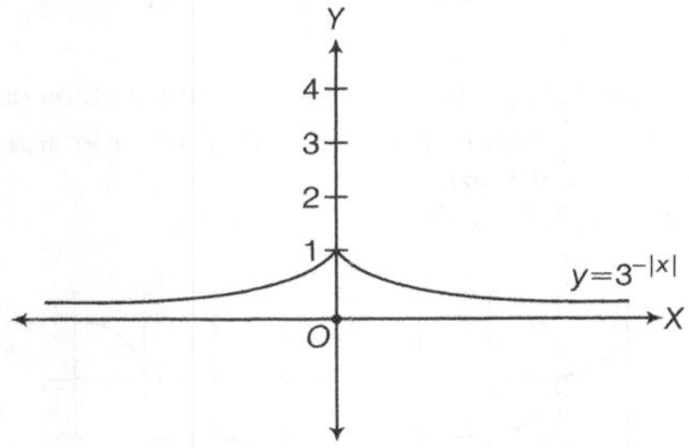

12. (c) We know that, if $y = f(x)$ is given, then the graph of $f(x - [x])$ can be obtained from the graph of $f(x)$ by the following rule "Retain the graph of $f(x)$ for values of x lying between interval $[0, 1]$ and repeat it for rest of points."

Here, we have to draw the graph of $y = \sqrt{x - [x]}$.

Now, as the graph of $y = f(x) = \sqrt{x}$ is

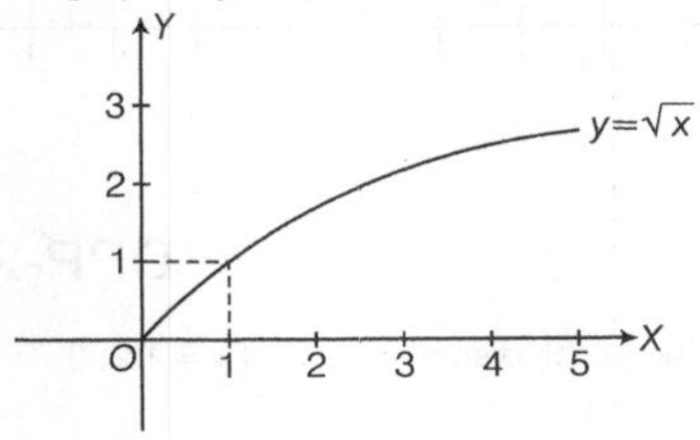

and $\qquad f(x) \to f(x - [x])$

$\therefore$ Graph of $y = f(x - [x]) = \sqrt{x - [x]}$ can be obtained by retaining the graph of $\sqrt{x}$ for $x \in [0,1]$ and repeat it for rest points.

Hence, the graph of $y = \sqrt{x - [x]}$ is

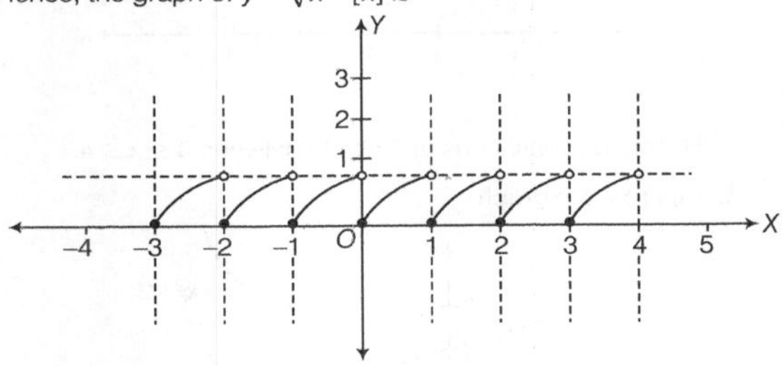

13. (a) The graph of $y = [x] + \sqrt{x - [x]}$ can be obtained by the graph of $y = \sqrt{x - [x]}$ by translating it by $[x]$ units in upward or downward direction according as $[x] > 0$ or $[x] < 0$.

Thus, the graph for $y = [x] + \sqrt{x - [x]}$ is

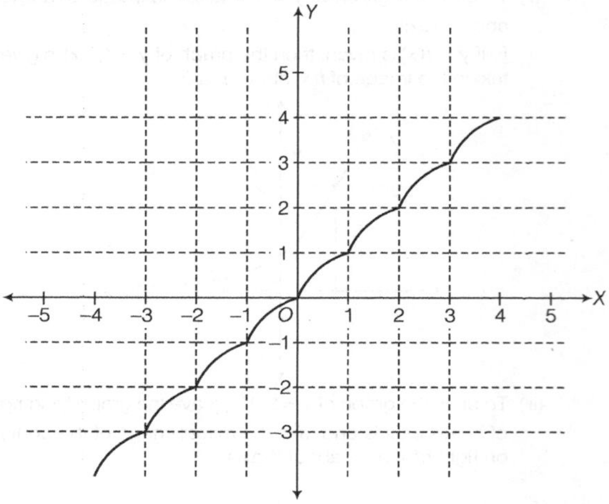

14. (b) The graph of $y = |[x] + \sqrt{x - [x]}|$ can be obtained by leaving the positive part as it is and by taking mirror image of negative part of $f(x)$ about X-axis.

Thus, the graph for $y = |[x] + \sqrt{x - [x]}|$ is

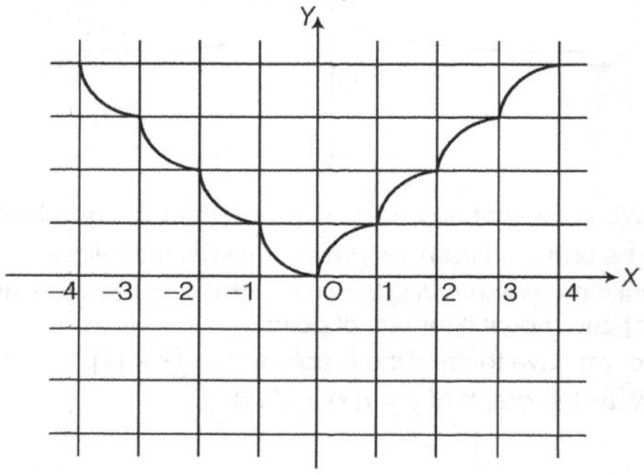

15. (c) We have, $y = [|x|]$

To draw the graph of $y = [|x|]$, we follow certain steps

First, we plot $[x]$ and then successively $[|x|]$.

(i) Consider $y = [x] = \begin{cases} -2, & -2 \le x < -1 \\ -1, & -1 \le x < 0 \\ 0, & 0 \le x < 1 \\ 1, & 1 \le x < 2 \\ 2, & 2 \le x < 3 \end{cases}$ and so on its graph is

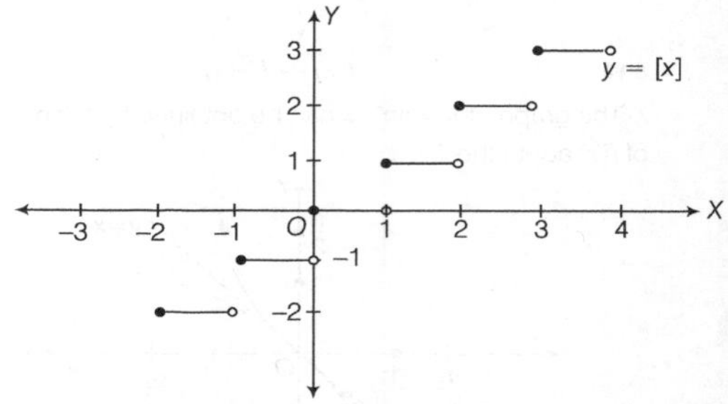

(ii) To draw graph of $y = [|x|]$, leave the graph lying right side of Y-axis, as it is and take the mirror image of the portion lying on right side on Y-axis, about Y-axis.

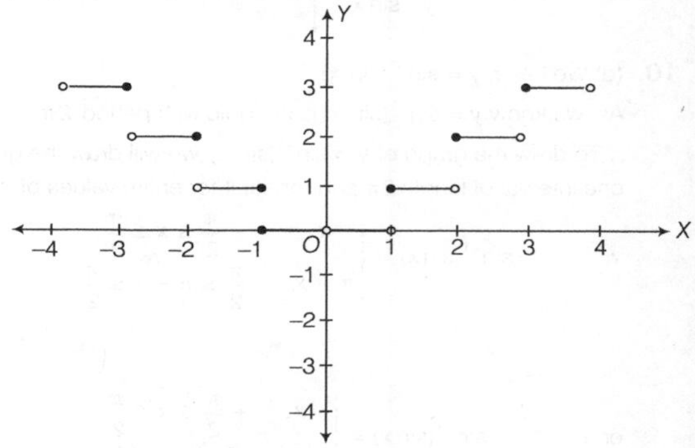

DPP-2 **Definition of Continuity**

1. (b) From the graph discontinuous at $x = 1, 2, 3$.

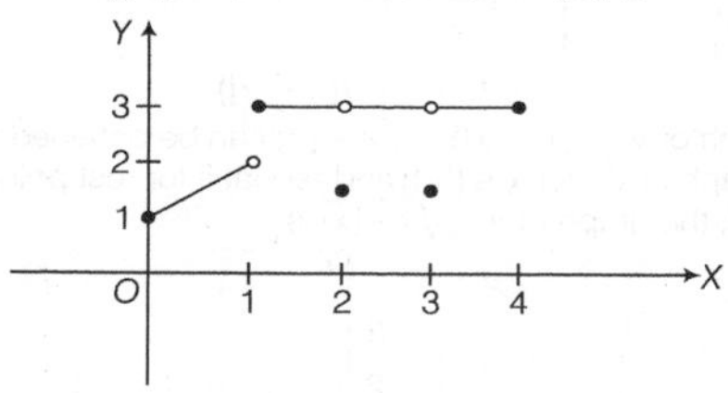

Hence, discontinuous at 3 points between $0 \le x \le 4$.

2. (a) From the graph,

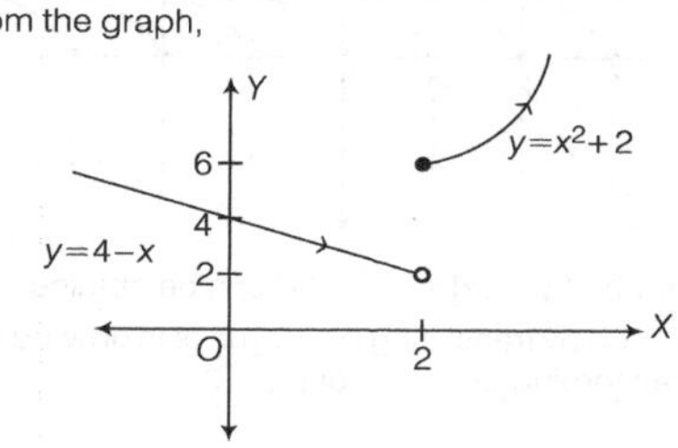

$$y = f = \begin{cases} 4 - x, & x < 2 \\ x^2 + 2, & x \ge 2 \end{cases}$$

Now, $\lim_{x \to 2^-} f(x) \ne \lim_{x \to 2^+} f(x)$

$\therefore f(x)$ is discontinuous at $x = 2$.

Hence, $f(x)$ is continuous, $\forall\ x \in R - \{2\}$.

3. (c) From the graph, $f(x)$ is continuous at $x = 0$ and discontinuous at $x = 1, 2$ and 3.

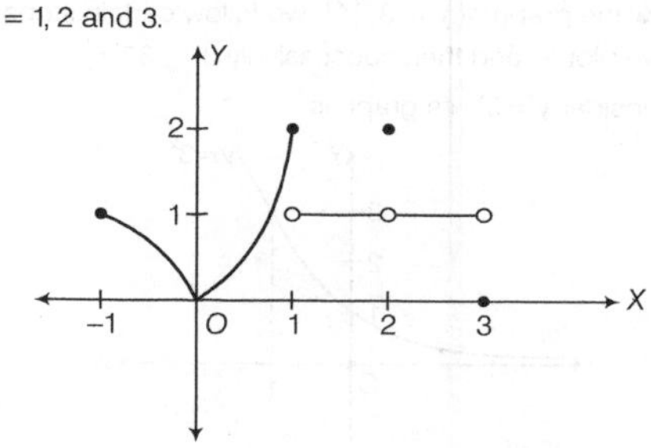

4. (c) We have, $f(x) = [x] + [-x]$

$$f(x) = \begin{cases} 0, & x \in \text{Integer} \\ -1, & x \notin \text{Integer} \end{cases}$$

$\therefore$ $f(x)$ is continuous, $\forall\ x \in R - \text{Integer}$.

5. (c) We have, $y = \sqrt{x - [x]}$

$\Rightarrow$ $y = \sqrt{\{x\}}$ $\quad [\because x - [x] = \{x\}]$

$\therefore$ The graph of $\sqrt{\{x\}}$ is

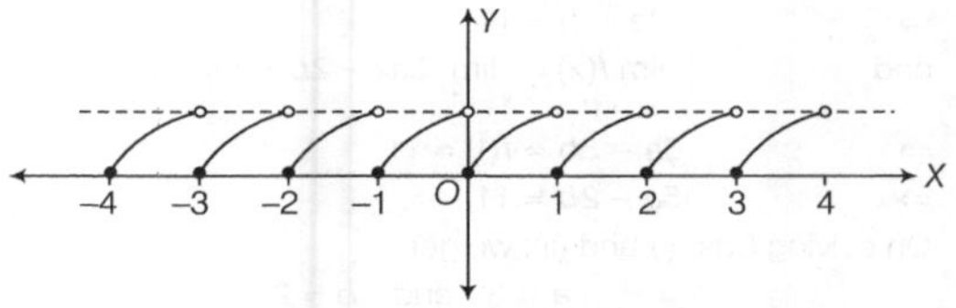

From the graph, $f(x)$ is continuous, $\forall\ x \in R - \text{Integer}$.

6. (a) We have, $y = [x] + \sqrt{x - [x]}$

$$y = \begin{cases} \sqrt{x}, & \text{if } 0 \le x < 1 \\ 1 + \sqrt{x-1}, & \text{if } 1 \le x < 2 \text{ and so on} \\ 2 + \sqrt{x-2}, & \text{if } 2 \le x < 3 \end{cases}$$

$\therefore$ The graph of $y = [x] + \sqrt{x - [x]}$ is

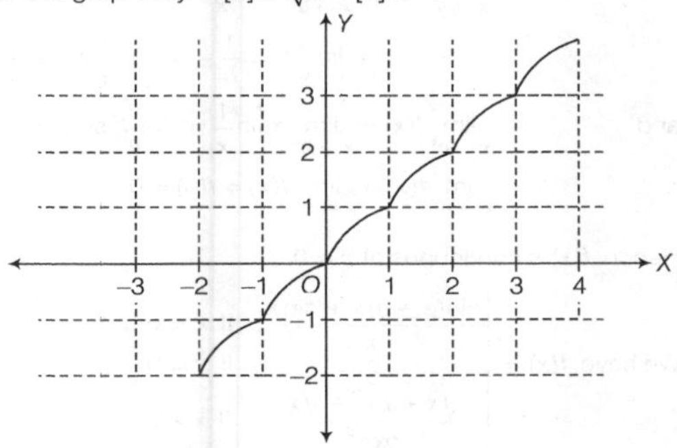

From the graph, $f(x)$ is continuous, $\forall\ x \in R$.

7. (c) We have, $f(x) = \begin{cases} |x-1|, & \text{if } x \ge 0 \\ -|x|, & \text{if } x < 0 \end{cases}$

$\therefore$ $\lim_{x \to 0^-} f(x) = |0 - 1| = 1$

and $\lim_{x \to 0^+} f(x) = -|x| = 0$

$\therefore$ $\lim_{x \to 0^-} f(x) \ne \lim_{x \to 0^+} f(x)$

$\therefore$ $f(x)$ is discontinuous at $x = 0$.

Hence, $f(x)$ is continuous, $\forall\ x \in R - \{0\}$.

8. (b) We have, $f(x) = |[x] - 1|$

Let a be any integer.

$\therefore$ $\lim_{x \to a^+} f(x) = \lim_{x \to a+h} |[a+h] - 1| = |a - 1|$ $\quad [\because [a+h] = a]$

and $\lim_{x \to a^-} f(x) = \lim_{x \to a-h} |[a-h] - 1] = [a-2]$ $\quad [\because [a-h] = a-1]$

$\therefore$ $\lim_{x \to a^+} f(x) \ne \lim_{x \to a^-} f(x)$

So, $f(x)$ is discontinuous at integer point.

$\therefore$ $f(x)$ is continuous, $\forall\ x \in R -$ Integer.

9. (b) Graph of $y = [\sin x]$ is $x \in [0, 2\pi]$.

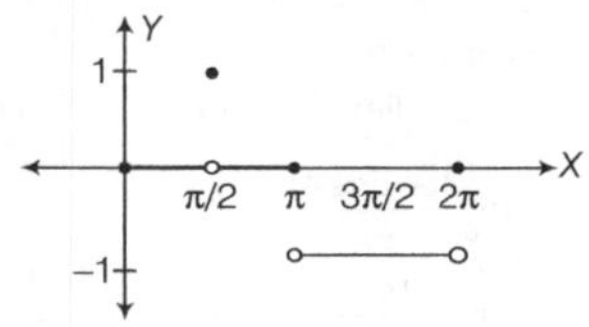

From the graph, $f(x)$ is discontinuous at $x = \frac{\pi}{2}, \pi, 2\pi$.

10. (b) Graph of min $\{\tan x, \cot x\}$ is

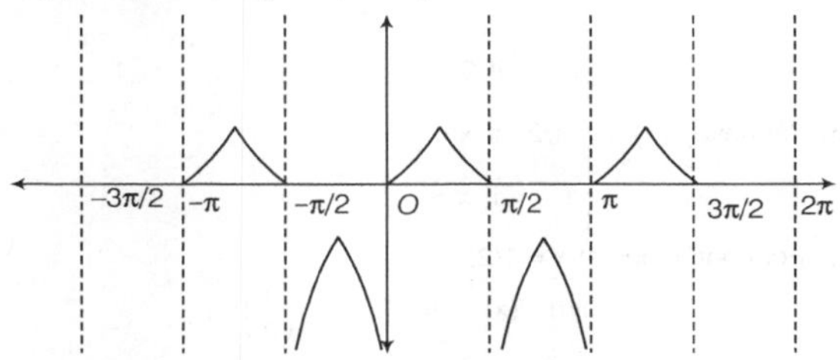

From the graph, $f(x)$ is discontinuous at

$x = \pm\pi, \pm\pi/2, 0, \cdots$

$\therefore$ $x = \frac{n\pi}{2}, xn \in I$

DPP-3 Continuity at a Point

1. We have,

$$f(x) = \begin{cases} kx + 1, & \text{if } x \le \pi \\ \cos x, & \text{if } x > \pi \end{cases}$$

$f(x)$ is continuous at $x = \pi$.

$\therefore$ $\lim_{x \to \pi^-} f(x) = \lim_{x \to \pi^+} f(x) = f(\pi)$

$\Rightarrow$ $\lim_{x \to \pi^-} kx + 1 = \lim_{x \to \pi^+} \cos x$

$\Rightarrow$ $k\pi + 1 = \cos \pi$

$\Rightarrow$ $k\pi + 1 = -1$

$\Rightarrow$ $k = -\frac{2}{\pi}$

2. We have,

$$f(x) = \begin{cases} \frac{\sin x}{x} + \cos x, & x \ne 0 \\ 2, & x = 0 \end{cases}$$

$$\lim_{x \to 0^-} f(x) = \lim_{x \to 0^-} \left(\frac{\sin x}{x} + \cos x\right) = \lim_{h \to 0} \left(\frac{\sin h}{h} + \cos h\right) = 1 + 1 = 2$$

$$\lim_{x \to 0^+} f(x) = \lim_{x \to 0^+} \left(\frac{\sin x}{x} + \cos x\right) = \lim_{h \to 0} \left(\frac{\sin h}{h} + \cos h\right) = 1 + 1 = 2$$

$\therefore$ $\lim_{x \to 0^+} f(x) = \lim_{x \to 0^+} f(x)$

$= f(0) = 2$

Hence, $f(x)$ is continuous at $x = 2$.

3. We have, $f(x) = 2x - |x|$

$$f(x) = \begin{cases} 2x + x, & x < 0 \\ 2x - x, & x \geq 0 \end{cases}$$

$$f(x) = \begin{cases} 3x, & x < 0 \\ x, & x \geq 0 \end{cases}$$

For continuous at $x = 0$,

$$\lim_{x \to 0^-} f(x) = \lim_{x \to 0^+} f(x) = f(0)$$

$$\lim_{x \to 0^-} f(x) = 3x = 0$$

$$\lim_{x \to 0^+} f(x) = x = 0$$

$$\therefore \lim_{x \to 0^-} f(x) = \lim_{x \to 0^+} f(x) = f(0) = 0$$

Hence, $f(x)$ is continuous at $x = 0$.

4. We have, $f(x) = \begin{cases} \dfrac{1 - \cos 4x}{8x^2}, & x \neq 0 \\ k, & x = 0 \end{cases}$

$f(x)$ is continuous at $x = 0$.

$$\therefore \quad \lim_{x \to 0} f(x) = f(0)$$

$$\Rightarrow \quad \lim_{x \to 0} \frac{1 - \cos 4x}{8x^2} = k \quad [\because f(0) = k]$$

$$\Rightarrow \quad \lim_{x \to 0} \frac{2\sin^2 2x}{8x^2} = k$$

$$\Rightarrow \quad \lim_{x \to 0} \left(\frac{\sin 2x}{2x}\right)^2 = k \Rightarrow 1 = k$$

$$\therefore \quad k = 1$$

5. We have, $f(x) = \begin{cases} x, & \text{if } 0 \leq x < \frac{1}{2} \\ 1/2, & \text{if } x = \frac{1}{2} \\ 1 - x, & \text{if } x > \frac{1}{2} \end{cases}$

For continuous at $x = 1/2$,

$$\lim_{x \to \frac{1}{2}^-} f(x) = \lim_{x \to \frac{1}{2}} f(x) = f\left(\frac{1}{2}\right)$$

$$\Rightarrow \quad \lim_{x \to \frac{1}{2}^-} f(x) = \lim_{x \to \frac{1}{2}^-} x = \frac{1}{2}$$

and $$\lim_{x \to \frac{1}{2}^+} f(x) = \lim_{x \to \frac{1}{2}^+} (1 - x) = 1 - \frac{1}{2} = \frac{1}{2}$$

$$\therefore \quad \lim_{x \to \frac{1}{2}^-} f(x) = \lim_{x \to \frac{1}{2}^+} f(x) = f\left(\frac{1}{2}\right) = \frac{1}{2} \quad \left[\because f\left(\frac{1}{2}\right) = \frac{1}{2}\right]$$

Hence, $f(x)$ is continuous at $x = \frac{1}{2}$.

6. We have, $f(x) = \begin{cases} \dfrac{(\sin x)}{x}, & \text{if } x \neq 0 \\ 1, & \text{if } x = 0 \end{cases}$

$$\Rightarrow \quad f(x) = \begin{cases} \dfrac{-\sin x}{x}, & \text{if } x < 0 \\ 1, & \text{if } x = 0 \\ \dfrac{\sin x}{x} & \text{if } x > 0 \end{cases}$$

For continuous at $x = 0$,

$$\lim_{x \to 0^-} f(x) = \lim_{x \to 0^+} f(x) = f(0)$$

$$\Rightarrow \quad \lim_{x \to 0^-} f(x) = \lim_{x \to 0^-} \frac{-\sin x}{x} = -1$$

and $$\lim_{x \to 0^+} f(x) = \lim_{x \to 0^+} \frac{\sin x}{x} = 1$$

$$\therefore \quad \lim_{x \to 0^-} f(x) \neq \lim_{x \to 0^+} f(x)$$

Hence, $f(x)$ is discontinuous at $x = 0$.

7. We have, $f(x) = \begin{cases} 3ax + b, & \text{if } x > 1 \\ 11, & \text{if } x = 1 \\ 5ax - 2b, & \text{if } x < 1 \end{cases}$ is continuous at $x = 1$.

$$\therefore \quad \lim_{x \to 1} f(x) = \lim_{x \to 1^+} f(x) = f(1)$$

$$\Rightarrow \quad \lim_{x \to 1^-} f(x) = \lim_{x \to 1^-} 3ax + b = 3a + b$$

$$\Rightarrow \quad 3a + b = f(1) = 11 \quad [\because f(1) = 11]$$

$$\Rightarrow \quad 3a + b = 11 \quad \ldots(i)$$

and $$\lim_{x \to 1^+} f(x) = \lim_{x \to 1^+} 5ax - 2b = 5a - 2b$$

$$\Rightarrow \quad 5a - 5b = f(1) = 11$$

$$\Rightarrow \quad 5a - 2b = 11 \quad \ldots(ii)$$

On solving Eqs. (i) and (ii), we get

$$a = 3 \text{ and } b = 2$$

8. We have, $f(x) = \begin{cases} x\sin \dfrac{1}{x}, & x \neq 0 \\ 0, & x = 0 \end{cases}$

For continuous at $x = 0$,

$$\lim_{x \to 0^-} f(x) = \lim_{x \to 0^+} f(x) = f(0)$$

$$\Rightarrow \quad \lim_{x \to 0^-} f(x) = \lim_{x \to 0^-} x\sin\frac{1}{x}$$

$$= \lim_{h \to 0} h\sin\frac{1}{h} = 0 \quad \left[\because 1 \leq \sin\frac{1}{h} \leq 1\right]$$

and $$\lim_{x \to 0^+} f(x) = \lim_{x \to 0^+} x\sin\frac{1}{x} = \lim_{h \to 0} h\sin\frac{1}{h} = 0$$

$$\therefore \quad \lim_{x \to 0^-} f(x) = \lim_{x \to 0^+} f(x) = f(0) = 0$$

Hence, $f(x)$ is continuous at $x = 0$.

9. We have, $f(x) = \begin{cases} \dfrac{\sin(a + 1)x + \sin x}{x}, & \text{if } x < 0 \\ c, & \text{if } x = 0 \\ \dfrac{\sqrt{x + bx^2} - \sqrt{x}}{bx^{3/2}}, & \text{if } x > 0 \end{cases}$

$f(x)$ is continuous at $x = 0$.

$$\therefore \quad \lim_{x \to 0^-} f(x) = \lim_{x \to 0^+} f(x) = f(0)$$

$$\Rightarrow \quad \lim_{x \to 0^-} f(x) = \lim_{x \to 0^-} \frac{\sin(a + 1)x + \sin x}{x}$$

$$= \lim_{x \to 0^-} \frac{\sin(a + 1)x}{x} + \lim_{x \to 0^-} \frac{\sin x}{x}$$

$$= \lim_{x \to 0^-} \frac{(a + 1)\sin(a + 1)x}{(a + 1)x} + \lim_{x \to 0^-} \frac{\sin x}{x}$$

$$= a + 1 + 1 = a + 2$$

$$\Rightarrow \quad \lim_{x \to 0^-} f(x) = f(0) = c$$

$$\therefore \quad a + 2 = c \quad \ldots(i)$$

and $$\lim_{x \to 0^+} f(x) = \lim_{x \to 0^+} \frac{\sqrt{x + bx^2} - \sqrt{x}}{bx^{3/2}}$$

$$= \lim_{x \to 0^+} \frac{x + bx^2 - x}{bx^{3/2}(\sqrt{x + bx^2} + \sqrt{x})}$$

$$= \lim_{x \to 0^+} \frac{\sqrt{x}}{\sqrt{x}\left(\sqrt{1 + \frac{b}{x}} + 1\right)} = \frac{1}{2}$$

$$\therefore \quad \lim_{x \to 0^+} f(x) = f(0)$$

$$\Rightarrow \quad \frac{1}{2} = c \quad \ldots(ii)$$

From Eqs. (i) and (ii), $a = -\frac{3}{2}$

$$\therefore \quad a = -\frac{3}{2}, b \in R \text{ and } c = \frac{1}{2}$$

10. We have,

$$f(x) = \{x\} \text{ and } g(x) = [x]$$

(i) $h(x) = f(x) \cdot g(x)$

$\Rightarrow \quad h(x) = \{x\}\,[x]$

For continuos at $x = 1$,

$$\lim_{x \to 1^-} h(x) = \lim_{x \to 1^+} h(x) = h(1)$$

$$\lim_{x \to 1^-} h(x) = \lim_{x \to 1^-} \{x\}\,[x]$$

$$= \lim_{x \to (1-h)} \{1-h\}\,[1-h]$$

$$= \lim_{h \to 0} \{1-h\}\,[1-h]$$

$$= \lim_{h \to 0} h \times 0 = 0$$

$$[\because \{x\} = x,\ 0 \le x < 1,\ [1-h] = 0]$$

and $\quad \lim_{x \to 1^+} h(x) = \lim_{x \to 1^+} \{x\}\,[x]$

$$= \lim_{x \to (1+h)} \{1+h\}\,[1+h]$$

$$= \lim_{h \to b} h(1) \quad \left[\begin{array}{l} \because \{x\} = x - 1,\ 1 \le x < 2 \\ \text{and } [x] = 1,\ 1 \le x < 2 \end{array}\right]$$

$$= 0 \times 1 = 0$$

$\therefore \quad \lim_{x \to 1^-} h(x) = \lim_{x \to 1^+} h(x) = h(1) = 0$

Hence, $h(x)$ is continuous at $x = 1$.

(ii) $h(x) = f(x) + g(x) \Rightarrow h(x) = \{x\} + [x]$

$\Rightarrow \quad h(x) = x - [x] + [x] = x \quad [\because \{x\} = x - [x]]$

Clearly, $h(x)$ is continuous at $x = 1$.

(iii) $h(x) = f(x) - g(x) \Rightarrow h(x) = \{x\} - [x]$

$\Rightarrow \quad h(x) = x - 2[x]$

For continuous at $x = 1$,

$$\lim_{x \to 1^-} h(x) = \lim_{x \to 1^+} h(x) = h(1)$$

$$\lim_{x \to 1^-} h(x) = \lim_{x \to 1^-} x - 2\,[x]$$

$$= \lim_{x \to (1-h)} (1-h) - 2\,[1-h]$$

$$= \lim_{h \to 0} 1 - h - 0 = 1 \quad [\because [1-h] = 0]$$

and $\quad \lim_{x \to 1^+} h(x) = \lim_{x \to 1^+} x - 2[x]$

$$= \lim_{x \to (1+h)} (1+h) - 2\,[1+h]$$

$$= \lim_{h \to 0} 1 + h - 2 \quad [\because [1+h] = 1]$$

$$= -1$$

$\therefore \quad \lim_{x \to 1^-} h(x) \ne \lim_{x \to 1^+} h(x)$

Hence, $f(x)$ is discontinuous at $x = 1$.

11. (c) We have, $f(x) = \begin{cases} x + 2, & x < 1 \\ 4x - 1, & 1 \le x \le 3 \\ x^2 + 5, & x > 3 \end{cases}$

$$\lim_{x \to 1^-} f(x) = \lim_{x \to 1^-} x + 2 = 1 + 2 = 3 \quad \ldots\text{(i)}$$

$$\lim_{x \to 1^+} f(x) = \lim_{x \to 1^+} 4x - 1 = 4 - 1 = 3 \quad \ldots\text{(ii)}$$

$$\lim_{x \to 3^-} f(x) = \lim_{x \to 3^-} 4x - 1 = 12 - 1 = 11 \quad \ldots\text{(iii)}$$

$$\lim_{x \to 3^+} f(x) = \lim_{x \to 3^+} x^2 + 5 = 9 + 5 = 14 \quad \ldots\text{(iv)}$$

From Eqs. (i) and (ii), $\lim_{x \to 1^-} f(x) = \lim_{x \to 1^+} f(x) = f(1) = 3$

$\therefore f(x)$ is continuos at $x = 1$.

From Eqs. (iii) and (iv), $\lim_{x \to 3^-} f(x) \ne \lim_{x \to 3^+} f(x)$

$\therefore f(x)$ is discontinuous at $x = 3$.

12. (c) We have, $f(x) = \begin{cases} \dfrac{1}{e^{4x} + 1}, & \text{if } x \ne 0 \\ 0, & \text{if } x = 0 \end{cases}$

$$\lim_{x \to 0^-} f(x) = \lim_{x \to 0^-} \frac{1}{e^{4x} + 1}$$

$$= \lim_{x \to (0-h)} \frac{1}{e^{-4h} + 1}$$

$$= \lim_{h \to 0} \frac{1}{e^{-4h} + 1} = \frac{1}{e^0 + 1} = \frac{1}{2}$$

$$\lim_{x \to 0^+} f(x) = \lim_{x \to 0^+} \frac{1}{e^{4x} + 1}$$

$$= \lim_{x \to (0+h)} \frac{1}{e^{4h} + 1}$$

$$= \frac{1}{e^0 + 1} = \frac{1}{2}$$

$\therefore \quad \lim_{x \to 0^-} f(x) = \lim_{x \to 0^+} f(x) \ne f(0) = 0$

Hence, $f(x)$ is discontinuous.

13. (a) We have,

$$f(x) = \begin{cases} \dfrac{x^2 - (a+2)x + 2a}{x - 2}, & x \ne 2 \\ 2, & x = 2 \end{cases}$$

$f(x)$ is continuous at $x = 2$.

$\therefore \quad \lim_{x \to 2} f(x) = f(2)$

$$\Rightarrow \quad \lim_{x \to 2} \frac{x^2 - (a+2)x + 2a}{x - 2} = 2 \quad [\because f(2) = 2]$$

$$\Rightarrow \quad \lim_{x \to 2} \frac{(x-a)(x-2)}{x-2} = 2$$

$$\Rightarrow \quad 2 - a = 2$$

$$\therefore \quad a = 0$$

14. (a) We have, $f(x) = \begin{cases} \dfrac{\log(1 + 2ax) - \log(1 - bx)}{x}, & \text{if } x \ne 0 \\ k, & \text{if } x = 0 \end{cases}$

$f(x)$ is continuous at $x = 0$.

$\therefore \quad \lim_{x \to 0} f(x) = f(0)$

$$\Rightarrow \quad \lim_{x \to 0} \frac{\log(1 + 2ax) - \log(1 - bx)}{x} = k \quad [\because f(0) = k]$$

$$\Rightarrow \quad \lim_{x \to 0} \frac{\log(1 + 2ax) \cdot 2a}{2ax} - \lim_{x \to 0} \frac{\log(1 - bx) \cdot (-b)}{-bx} = k$$

$$\Rightarrow \quad 2a + b = k \quad \left[\because \lim_{x \to 0} \frac{\log(1 + x)}{x} = 1\right]$$

15. (a) We have, $\quad f(x) = \begin{cases} [x] + [-x], & x \ne 2 \\ \lambda, & x = 2 \end{cases}$

$f(x)$ is continuous at $x = 2$.

$\therefore \quad \lim_{x \to 0} f(x) = f(2)$

$$\Rightarrow \quad \lim_{x \to 0} [x] + [-x] = \lambda \quad [\because f(2) = \lambda]$$

$$\Rightarrow \quad -1 = \lambda$$

$$\left[\begin{array}{l} \because [x] + [-x] = 0,\ x \in \text{Integer} \\ \text{and } [x] + [-x] = -1,\ x \notin \text{Integer} \end{array}\right]$$

$\therefore \quad \lambda = -1$

16. (a) We have, $f(x) = \begin{cases} \dfrac{1 - \cos 4x}{x^2}, & \text{if } x < 0 \\ a, & \text{if } x = 0 \\ \dfrac{\sqrt{x}}{\sqrt{16 + \sqrt{x}} - 4}, & \text{if } x > 0 \end{cases}$

For $f(x)$ is continuous at $x = 0$,

$$\lim_{x \to 0^-} f(x) = \lim_{x \to 0^+} f(x) = f(0)$$

Now, $\lim_{x \to 0^-} f(x) = \lim_{x \to 0^-} \frac{1 - \cos 4x}{x^2}$

$$= \lim_{h \to 0} \frac{1 - \cos 4h}{h^2}$$

$$= \lim_{h \to 0} \frac{4 \times 2\sin^2 2h}{(2h)^2} = 8$$

and $\lim_{x \to 0^+} f(x) = \lim_{x \to 0^+} \frac{\sqrt{x}}{\sqrt{16 + \sqrt{x}} - 4}$

$$= \lim_{h \to 0} \frac{\sqrt{h}}{\sqrt{16 + \sqrt{h}} - 4}$$

$$= \lim_{h \to 0} \frac{\sqrt{h}\,(\sqrt{16 + \sqrt{h}} + 4)}{16 + \sqrt{h} - 16}$$

$$= \lim_{h \to 0} \sqrt{16 + \sqrt{h}} + 4 = 8$$

$\therefore$ $\lim_{x \to 0^-} f(x) = \lim_{x \to 0^+} f(x) = f(0)$

$\therefore$ $8 = 8 = a$ $\quad [\because f(0) = a]$

Hence, $f(x)$ is continuous at $x = 0$, and the value of a is 8.

17. (c) We have, $f(x) = \frac{1}{\log|x|}$

$f(x)$ is not depend at $x = 0, \pm 1$.

$\therefore$ $f(x)$ is discontinuous at three points.

18. (b) (a) $\tan x$ is discontinuous at $x = \frac{n\pi}{2}, n \in I$.

(b) $\frac{|x|}{x}$ is discontinuous at $x = \{-1, 0, 1\}$.

(c) $x + [x]$ is discontinuous at $x \in$ Integer.

(d) $\sin[\pi x]$ is discontinuous at $x \in n$ or $\left(n + \frac{1}{2}\right)$.

Hence, $\frac{|x|}{x}$ has finite number of points of discontinuity.

19. (a) We have, $f(x) = \frac{1 - \tan x}{4x - \pi}, x \neq \pi/4$

$f(x)$ is continuous at $x = \pi/4$.

$\therefore$ $\lim_{x \to \frac{\pi}{4}} f(x) = f\left(\frac{\pi}{4}\right)$

$$f\left(\frac{\pi}{4}\right) = \lim_{x \to \frac{\pi}{4}} \frac{1 - \tan x}{4x - \pi}$$

$$= \lim_{x \to \frac{\pi}{4} + h} \frac{1 - \tan\left(\frac{\pi}{4} + h\right)}{4\left(\frac{\pi}{4} + h\right) - \pi}$$

$$= \lim_{h \to 0} \frac{1 - \frac{1 + \tan h}{1 - \tan h}}{4h} = \lim_{h \to 0} \frac{-2\tan h}{4h(1 - \tan h)} = \frac{-1}{2}$$

20. (b) We have, $f(x) = \frac{\sqrt{a^2 - ax + x^2} - \sqrt{a^2 + ax + x^2}}{\sqrt{a + x} - \sqrt{a - x}}$

$f(x)$ is continuous at $x = 0$.

$\therefore$ $\lim_{x \to 0} f(x) = f(0)$

$$\Rightarrow f(0) = \lim_{x \to 0} \frac{\sqrt{a^2 - ax + x^2} - \sqrt{a^2 + ax + x^2}}{\sqrt{a + x} - \sqrt{a - x}}$$

$$= \lim_{x \to 0} \frac{[(a^2 - ax + x^2) - (a^2 + ax + x^2)]\,(\sqrt{a + x} + \sqrt{a - x})}{(a + x) - (a - x)\,(\sqrt{a^2 - ax + x^2} + \sqrt{a^2 + ax + x^2})}$$

$$= \lim_{x \to 0} \frac{-2ax\,(\sqrt{a + x} + \sqrt{a - x})}{2x(\sqrt{a^2 - ax + x^2} + \sqrt{a^2 + ax + x^2})}$$

$$= \frac{-2a\sqrt{a}}{2a} = -\sqrt{a}$$

21. (d) We have, $f(x) = \frac{x - e^x + \cos 2x}{x^2}, x \neq 0$

$f(x)$ is continuous at $x = 0$.

$\therefore$ $\lim_{x \to 0} f(x) = f(0)$

$\Rightarrow$ $f(0) = \lim_{x \to 0} \frac{x - e^x + \cos 2x}{x^2}$

$\Rightarrow$ $f(0) = \lim_{x \to 0} \frac{1 - e^x + 2\sin 2x}{2x}$

[applying L' Hospital's rule]

$\Rightarrow$ $f(0) = \lim_{x \to 0} \frac{-e^x - 4\cos 2x}{2}$

$\Rightarrow$ $f(0) = \frac{-5}{2}$

$\therefore$ $[f(0)] = \left[\frac{-5}{2}\right] = -3$

and $\{f(0)\} = \left\{\frac{-5}{2}\right\} = 0.5$

$\therefore$ $[f(0)]\{f(0)\} = -3 \times 0.5 = -1.5$

Alternate Method

$$f(x) = \frac{x - e^x + \cos 2x}{x^2}, x \neq 0$$

$$= \lim_{x \to 0} \frac{x - e^x + 1 - (1 - \cos 2x)}{x^2}$$

$$= \lim_{x \to 0} \left[\frac{x - e^x + 1}{x^2} - \frac{1 - \cos 2x}{x^2}\right]$$

$$= \lim_{x \to 0} \left[\frac{(x + 1) - \left(1 + x + \frac{x^2}{2}\right)}{x^2} - \frac{2\sin^2 x}{x^2}\right]$$

[using expansion of e^x]

$$= \frac{-1}{2} - 2 = \frac{-5}{2}$$

For continuity, $f(0) = \frac{-5}{2}$

Now, $[f(0)] = -3$, $\{f(0)\} = \left\{\frac{-5}{2}\right\} = \frac{1}{2}$

$\therefore$ $[f(0)]\{f(0)\} = \frac{-3}{2} = -1.5$

22. (c) We have, $f(x) = \frac{x(1 + a\cos x) - b\sin x}{x^3}, x \neq 0$ and $f(0) = 1$

$f(x)$ is continuous at $x = 0$.

$\Rightarrow$ $f(0) = \lim_{x \to 0} \frac{x \cdot (1 + a\cos x) - b\sin x}{x^3}$

$$= \lim_{x \to 0} \frac{x(-a\sin x) + (1 + a\cos x) - b\cos x}{3x^2},$$

[using L'Hospital's rule]

$\Rightarrow$ $1 + a - b = 0$ [for limit to exists] ...(i)

Again, using L' Hospital's rule

$$= \lim_{x \to 0} \frac{-a\sin x - a x\cos x - a\sin x + b\sin x}{6x}$$

$$= \lim_{x \to 0} \frac{(b - 2a)\sin x}{6x} - \frac{ax\cos x}{6x}$$

$$f(0) = \frac{b - 2a}{6} - \frac{a}{6}$$

$\Rightarrow$ $1 = \frac{b - 3a}{6}$

$\Rightarrow$ $b - 3a = 6$ ...(ii)

From Eqs. (i) and (ii), we get

$$a = -\frac{5}{2} \text{ and } b = -\frac{3}{2}$$

23. (d) $\lim_{x \to 0} \left(\frac{1}{x} - \frac{2}{e^{2x} - 1}\right) = \lim_{x \to 0} \frac{e^{2x} - 1 - 2x}{x(e^{2x} - 1)}$

$$= \lim_{x \to 0} \frac{2e^{2x} - 2}{(e^{2x} - 1) + 2xe^{2x}}$$

[by L' Hospital's rule]

$$= \lim_{x \to 0} \frac{4e^{2x}}{4e^{2x} + 4xe^{2x}}$$

[by L' Hospital's rule]

$$= 1$$

So, $f(x)$ is continuous at $x = 0$.

$\therefore \quad \lim_{x \to 0} f(x) = f(0)$

$\Rightarrow \quad f(0) = 1$

24. (a) Here, $f(x) = \begin{cases} \frac{\sin(p+1)x + \sin x}{x}, & x < 0 \\ q, & x = 0 \\ \frac{\sqrt{x + x^2} - \sqrt{x}}{x^{3/2}}, & x > 0 \end{cases}$

Since, $f(x)$ is continuous for $x \in R$.

So, $f(x)$ is continuous at $x = 0$.

RHL at $x = 0$,

$$\lim_{h \to 0} \frac{\sqrt{h + h^2} - \sqrt{h}}{h^{3/2}} = \lim_{h \to 0} \frac{\sqrt{h}\{\sqrt{h+1} - 1\}}{h\sqrt{h}}$$

$$= \lim_{h \to 0} \left(\frac{\sqrt{h+1} - 1}{h} \times \frac{\sqrt{h+1} + 1}{\sqrt{h+1} + 1}\right)$$

$$= \lim_{h \to 0} \frac{(h+1) - 1}{h\{\sqrt{h+1} + 1\}}$$

$$= \lim_{h \to 0} \frac{1}{\sqrt{h+1} + 1} = \frac{1}{2} \quad \ldots \text{(i)}$$

LHL at $x = 0$,

$$\lim_{h \to 0} \frac{\sin(p+1)(-h) + \sin(-h)}{-h}$$

$$= \lim_{h \to 0} \frac{\sin(p+1)h}{h} + \frac{\sin h}{h}$$

$\Rightarrow \quad p + 1 + 1 = p + 2 \quad \ldots \text{(ii)}$

$f(0) = q \quad \ldots \text{(iii)}$

From Eqs. (i), (ii) and (iii)

$$q = \frac{1}{2} \text{ and } p = \frac{-3}{2}$$

25. (a,b) Given, $f(x) = \frac{e^{\sin x}}{4 - \sqrt{x^2 - 9}}$

$f(x)$ is continuous, where it is defined

$4 - \sqrt{x^2 - 9} = 0$

$\Rightarrow \quad \sqrt{x^2 - 9} = 4$

$\Rightarrow \quad x^2 - 9 = 16$

$\Rightarrow \quad x^2 = 25$

$x = \pm 5$

$f(x)$ is discontinuous at $x = \pm 5$

and $\quad x^2 - 9 \geq 0$

$\Rightarrow \quad x^2 \geq 9$

$\Rightarrow \quad x \geq \pm 3$

$\therefore f(x)$ is continuous for $x = \pm 3$.

26. (b,c,d)

(a) Given, $f(x) = \frac{1}{1 + 2^{\cot x}}$

Clearly, $f(x)$ is defined for $x = 0$.

(b) Given, $f(x) = \cos\left(\frac{|\sin x|}{x}\right)$

Clearly, it is not defined at $x = 0$.

(c) Given, $f(x) = x \sin\frac{\pi}{x}$

Clearly, it is not defined at $x = 0$.

(d) Given, $f(x) = \frac{1}{\log|x|}$

Clearly, it is not defined at $x = 0$.

Among there four functions, $\cos\left(\frac{|\sin x|}{x}\right)$, $x\sin\frac{\pi}{x}$ and $\frac{1}{\log|x|}$ have removable discontinuity which can be removed by redefining the function.

27. (a,b,c)

Since, $\lim_{x \to 1^-} g(x) = \lim_{x \to 1^+} g(x) = 1$ and $g(1) = 0$

$g(x)$ is not continuous at $x = 1$ but $\lim_{x \to 1} g(x)$ exists, we have

$$\lim_{x \to 1^-} f(x) = \lim_{h \to 0} + (1 - h) = \lim_{h \to 0} [1 - h] = 0$$

and $\quad \lim_{x \to 1^+} f(x) = \lim_{h \to 0} f(1 + h) = \lim_{h \to 0} [1 + h] = 1$

So, $\lim_{x \to 1} f(x)$ does not exist and hence $f(x)$ is not continuous at $x = 1$

Again, we have $gof(x) = g[f(x)] = g([x]) = 0, \forall x \in R$

So, $gof(x)$ is continuous for all x.

We have, $\quad fog(x) = f[g(x)] = \begin{cases} f(0), & \text{if } n \in Z \\ f(x^2), & \text{if } x \in R - Z \end{cases}$

$$= \begin{cases} 0, & \text{if } x \in Z \\ [x^2], & \text{if } x \in R - Z \end{cases}$$

which is clearly not continuous.

28. (a) $\lim_{x \to 0^+} \sin x + [x] = 0$, $\lim_{x \to 0^-} (\sin x + [x]) = -1$

Thus, limit does not exist. So, $f(x)$ is discontinuous at $x = 0$.

Hence, Statement II is fundamental property and is correct explanation of Statement I.

29. (c) $f(x) = \begin{cases} 2\sin(a\cos^{-1} x), & \text{if } x \in (0, 1) \\ \sqrt{3}, & \text{if } x = 0 \\ ax + b, & \text{if } x < 0 \end{cases}$

and $\quad a = \frac{2}{3}, b = \sqrt{3}$

$\therefore \quad f(x) = \begin{cases} 2\sin\left(\frac{2}{3}\cos^{-1} x\right), & \text{if } x \in (0, 1) \\ \sqrt{3}, & \text{if } x = 0 \\ \frac{2}{3}x + \sqrt{3}, & \text{if } x < 0 \end{cases}$

At $x = 0$,

$$\text{LHL} = \lim_{x \to 0^-} f(x) = \lim_{h \to 0} f(0 - h)$$

$$= \frac{2}{3}(0 - h) + \sqrt{3} = \sqrt{3}$$

$$\text{RHL} = \lim_{x \to 0^+} f(x) = \lim_{h \to 0} f(0 + h)$$

$$= 2\sin\left[\frac{2}{3}\cos^{-1}(0 + h)\right]$$

$$= 2 \times \frac{\sqrt{3}}{2} = \sqrt{3}$$

$\therefore \quad \text{LHL} = \text{RHL} = \sqrt{3}$

Now, $f(0) = \sqrt{3}$

So, $f(x)$ is continuous at $x = 0$ only.

Hence, Statement II is incorrect.

30. (c) $\lim_{x \to 0} \frac{\cos x - e^{-x^2/2}}{x^3}$ $\left[\frac{0}{0} \text{ form}\right]$

$= \lim_{x \to 0} \frac{-\sin x - e^{-x^2/2}(-x)}{3x^2}$ [by L' Hospital's rule]

$= \lim_{x \to 0} \frac{-\sin x + xe^{-x^2/2}}{3x^2}$ $\left[\frac{0}{0} \text{ form}\right]$

$= \lim_{x \to 0} \frac{-\cos x + (e^{-x^2/2} + xe^{-x^2/2}(-x)}{6x}$

(by L' Hospital's rule)

$= \lim_{x \to 0} = \frac{-\cos x + e^{-x^2/2}(1 - x^2)}{6x}$ $\left[\frac{0}{0} \text{ form}\right]$

$= \lim_{x \to 0} \frac{\sin x + (-2x) e^{-x^2/2} + (1 - x^2) e^{-x^2/2} (-x)}{6}$

$= \lim_{x \to 0} \frac{\sin x + e^{-x^2/2}(-2x - x + x^3)}{6} = 0$

Also, $f(0) = 0$

So, $f(x)$ is continuous at $x = 0$.

Statement II $\lim_{x \to 0} \frac{\cos x - e^{-x^2/2}}{4} = 0$

Hence, Statement I is correct but Statement II is incorrect.

31. (b) We know that, polynomial function is everywhere continuous.

∴ Statement II is correct.

Statement I Let $A = 3/4, B = -1/4$

∴ $f(x) = \begin{cases} \frac{3}{4}x + 1/4, & \text{if } x \le -1 \\ 2x^2 + \frac{3}{4}x - \frac{1}{4}, & \text{if } x \in (-1, 1) \\ 4, & \text{if } x > 1 \end{cases}$

LHL at $x = -1$,

$\lim_{x \to -1^-} f(x) = \lim_{h \to 0} f(-1 - h) = \frac{3}{4}(-1 - h) + \frac{1}{4} = -\frac{1}{2}$

RHL at $x = -1$, $\lim_{x \to -1^+} f(x) = \lim_{h \to 0} f(-1 + h)$

$= 2(-1 + h)^2 + \frac{9}{4}(-1 + h) - \frac{1}{4}$

$= 2 - \frac{9}{4} - \frac{1}{4} = \frac{8 - 10}{4} = \frac{-1}{2}$

Also, $f(-1) = \frac{-3}{4} + \frac{1}{4} = \frac{-1}{2}$

∴ $f(x)$ is continuous at $x = -1$.

For $x > 1$, $f(x) = 4$ [constant]

∴ $f(x)$ is continuous for all x.

32. (d) Here, $g(x)$ is continuous at $x = 0$.

∴ $g(0) = \lim_{x \to 0} \frac{\sqrt{ax + b} - 1}{x}$

For this to exists, $\sqrt{b} - 1 = 0 \Rightarrow b = 1$

$\Rightarrow \quad 1 = \lim_{x \to 0} \frac{\sqrt{ax + 1} - 1}{x}$

$\Rightarrow \quad 1 = \lim_{x \to 0} \frac{(ax + 1) - 1}{x \cdot [\sqrt{ax + 1} + 1]}$

$\Rightarrow \quad 1 = \lim_{x \to 0} \frac{a}{\sqrt{ax + 1} + 1}$

$\Rightarrow \quad 1 = \frac{a}{2}$

∴ $a = 2$ and $b = 1$

Now, $a + b = 3$

33. (b) We have,

$g(x) = \begin{cases} \frac{\sqrt{2x + 1} - 1}{x}, & x \ne 0 \\ 1, & x = 0 \end{cases}$

∴ $g'(0) = \lim_{h \to 0} \frac{\frac{\sqrt{2h + 1} - 1}{h} - 1}{h}$

$= \lim_{h \to 0} \frac{\sqrt{2h + 1} - (1 + h)}{h^2} \times \frac{[\sqrt{2h + 1} + (1 + h)]}{[\sqrt{2h + 1} + (1 + h)]}$

$= \lim_{h \to 0} \frac{-h^2}{h^2 [\sqrt{2h + 1} + (1 + h)]}$

$= -\frac{1}{2} = \frac{h(6)}{2}$

34. (c) Here, $g(x) = \begin{cases} \frac{\sqrt{1 + 2x} - 1}{x}, & x \ne 0 \\ 1, & x = 0 \end{cases}$

∴ Domain of $g(x) \in \left[-\frac{1}{2}, \infty\right)$,

Range of $h(x) \in R =$ Codomain

So, it is surjective and unbounded.

Now, $I = \lim_{n \to \infty} S_n$

$= \lim_{n \to \infty} \left\{1 - \frac{1}{(x + 1)(x^2 + 1) \dots (x^{2^n} + 1)}\right\}, x > 1$

$= 1 - 0$

$= 1$

DPP-4 **Continuity for Composition of Functions**

1. (i) Given, $f(x) = \frac{3x+7}{x^2 - 5x + 6}$

We know that a rational function is everywhere continuous except at the point, where denominator is zero.

∴ $x^2 - 5x - 6 = 0$

$\Rightarrow \quad (x-2)(x-3) = 0 \Rightarrow \quad x = 2, 3$

Hence, $f(x)$ is continuous everywhere except at $x=2$ and $x=3$.

∴ Required interval is $x \in R - \{2, 3\}$.

(ii) Given,

$f(x) = \frac{1}{|x| - 1} - \frac{x^2}{2} \Rightarrow f(x) = \frac{2 - x^2(|x| - 1)}{2(|x| - 1)}$

Given function in sum of a modulus function and polynomial function, both are continuous. But $f(x)$ is also a rational function, it is continuous everywhere except at the point where denominator is zero.

∴ $2(|x| - 1) = 0 \Rightarrow |x| - 1 = 0$

$\Rightarrow \quad |x| = 1 \Rightarrow x = \ne 1$

Hence, the required interval is $x \in R - \{-1, 1\}$.

(iii) Given, $f(x) = \frac{\sqrt{x^2 + 1}}{1 + \sin^2 x}$

It is a rational function, continuous everywhere because $1 + \sin^2 x$ cannot be zero for any value of x.

Hence, required interval is $x \in R$ i.e $x \in (-\infty, \infty)$.

(iv) Given, $f(x) = \tan\left(\frac{\pi}{2}x\right)$

We know that tangent function is continuous everywhere except at the point, where it does not defined.

We also know that $\tan x$ is not defined at odd multiple of $\frac{\pi}{2}$.

$\therefore \quad x \neq 2n+1, n \in I$

$\Rightarrow \quad x \in R-(2n+1), n \in I$

2. Given, $f(x) = x + \{-x\} + [x]$

We have to check continuity at $x=n, n \in I$ and $n \in [-2, 2]$.

$$\text{LHL} = \lim_{x \to h^-} f(x) = \lim_{x \to 0} f(n-h)$$
$$= \lim_{x \to 0} n-h+\{-n+h\}+[n-h]$$
$$= \lim_{x \to 0} n-h+h+n-1 = 2n-1$$
$$\text{RHL} = \lim_{x \to h^+} f(x) = \lim_{x \to 0} f(n+h)$$
$$= \lim_{x \to 0} n+h+\{-n-h\}+[n+h]$$
$$= \lim_{x \to 0} n+h+1-h+n = 2n+1$$

Since, LHL $\neq$ RHL

$\therefore$ $f(x)$ is discontinuous at integral point.

3. Given, $f(x) = \frac{x^2+1}{x^2-1}$ and $g(x) = \tan x$

$$\therefore \quad fog(x) = f[g(x)] = \frac{[g(x)]^2+1}{[g(x)]^2-1}$$
$$fog(x) = \frac{\tan^2 x+1}{\tan^2 x-1}$$

$fog(x)$ is continuous for all x except, where

$\tan^2 x - 1 = 0 \Rightarrow \tan^2 x = 1$

$\Rightarrow \tan x = \pm 1 \Rightarrow x = n\pi \pm \frac{\pi}{4}$

Also, $fog(x)$ is discontinuous, where $g(x)$ is not defined. We know that $\tan x$ is not defined at $x = (2n+1)\frac{\pi}{4}$.

$\therefore$ $fog(x)$ discontinuous at $x = n\pi \pm \frac{\pi}{4}$ and $x = (2n+1)\pi/2$.

4. $$g(x) = f[f(x)] = \begin{cases} f(1+x), & \text{if } 0 \le x \le 2 \\ f(3-x), & \text{if } 2 < x \le 3 \end{cases} = \begin{cases} f(1+x), \text{ if } 0 \le x \le 1 \\ f(1+x), \text{ if } 1 \le x \le 2 \\ f(1+x), \text{ if } 2 \le x \le 3 \end{cases}$$

$x \in [0, 1] \Rightarrow (1+x) \in [1, 2]$

$x \in [1, 2] \Rightarrow (1+x) \in [2, 3]$

$x \in [2, 3] \Rightarrow (3-x) \in [0, 1]$

$$\text{Hence, } g(x) = \begin{cases} f(1+x), \text{ for } 0 \le x \le 1 \Rightarrow 1 \le x+1 \le 2 \\ f(1+x), \text{ for } 1 \le x \le 2 \Rightarrow 2 \le x+1 \le 3 \\ f(1+x), \text{ for } 2 \le x \le 3 \Rightarrow 0 \le 3-x \le 1 \end{cases}$$

Now, if $(1+x) \in [1, 2]$, then

$f(1+x) = 1+1+x = 2+x$ ...(i)

[from original definition of $f(x)$]

Similarly, if $(1+x) \in (2, 3)$, then

$f(1+x) = 3-(1+x) = 2-x$ ...(ii)

of $\quad 3-x \le (0, 1)$

$f(3-x) = 1+(3-x) = 4-x$ ...(iii)

Using Eqs. (i), (ii) and (iii), we get

$$g(x) = \begin{cases} 2+x, & 0 \le x \le 1 \\ 2-x, & 1 < x \le 2 \\ 4-x, & 2 < x \le 3 \end{cases}$$

Since, $g(x)$ changes the equality sign at $x=1$ and $x=2$.

Thus, to check continuity at $x=1$ and $x=2$.

At $x=1$, $\text{LHL} = \lim_{x \to n^-} g(x) = \lim_{x \to n^-} (2+x) = 3$

$\text{RHL} = \lim_{x \to 0^+} g(x) = \lim_{x \to 1^+} (2-x) = 1$

As LHL $\neq$ RHL, $g(x)$ is not continuous at $x=1$.

At $\quad x=2$,

$\text{LHL} = \lim_{x \to 2^-} g(x) = \lim_{x \to 2^-} (2-x) = 0$

$\text{RHL} = \lim_{x \to 2^+} g(x) = \lim_{x \to 2^+} (4-x) = 2$

LHL $\neq$ RHL, $g(x)$ is discontinuous $x=2$.

Thus, $g(x)$ is discontinuous at $x=1, 2$.

5. Given, $\quad f(u) = \frac{3}{2u^2+5u-3}$ and $u = \frac{1}{x+2}$

Since, $u = \frac{1}{x+2}$ is not defined for $x=-2$.

$\therefore$ u is discontinuous at $x=-2$.

Also, $\quad f(u) = \frac{3}{2u^2+5u-3} = \frac{3}{(2u-1)(u+3)}$

Clearly, $f(u)$ is not defined at $u=-3, \frac{1}{2}$

When $u=-3$, then $\frac{1}{x+2} = -3 \Rightarrow -3x-6=1$

$\Rightarrow \quad x = \frac{-7}{3}$

when, $u = \frac{1}{2}$, then $\frac{1}{x+2} = \frac{1}{2} \Rightarrow x=0$

$\therefore$ $f(u)$ is discontinuous at $x = 0, -2, \frac{-7}{3}$.

6. (d) Given, $f(x) = \frac{4-x^2}{4x-x^3} \Rightarrow f(x) = \frac{4-x^2}{x(4-x^2)}$

Clearly, $f(x)$ is not defined at $x = 0, \pm 2$.

$\therefore$ $f(x)$ is discontinuous at $x = 0, \pm 2$.

Also, domain of f is $R - \{-2, 0, 2\}$.

Hence, $f(x)$ is continuous every where in its domain.

7. (a) Given, $$f(x) = \begin{cases} -4\sin x + \cos x, & \text{if } x \le -\pi/2 \\ a\sin x + b, & \text{if } -\pi/2 < x < \frac{\pi}{2} \\ \cos x + 2, & \text{if } -\pi/2 \le x \end{cases}$$

LHL at $x = \frac{-\pi}{2}$,

$$\lim_{x \to -\frac{\pi}{2}^-} f(x) = \lim_{h \to 0} -4\sin\left(\frac{-\pi}{2}-h\right) + \cos\left(\frac{-\pi}{2}-h\right)$$
$$= \lim_{h \to 0} 4\cos h - \sin h = 4$$

RHL at $x = \frac{-\pi}{2}$,

$$\lim_{x \to -\frac{\pi}{2}^-} f(x) = \lim_{h \to 0} a\sin\left(\frac{-\pi}{2}-h\right) + b$$
$$= \lim_{h \to 0} (-a\cos h + b) - a + b$$

$\because f(x)$ is continuous at $x = \frac{-\pi}{2}$.

$\therefore \quad -a+b=4$ ...(i)

Now, LHL at $x = \frac{\pi}{2}$,

$$\lim_{x \to \frac{\pi}{2}^-} f(x) = \lim_{h \to 0} a\sin\left(\frac{\pi}{2}-h\right) + b = a+b$$

RHL at $x = \frac{\pi}{2}$,

$$\lim_{x \to \frac{\pi}{2}^+} f(x) = \lim_{h \to 0} \cos\left(\frac{\pi}{2}+h\right) + 2 = 2 \Rightarrow a+b=2 \quad \text{...(ii)}$$

On solving Eqs. (i) and (ii), we get

$a=-1, b=3$

8. (d) Given, $f(x) = [x^2+1] = [x^2]+1$

Now, x^2 is monotonic in the range of [1,3].

Hence, $[x^2]$ is discontinuous when x^2 is integer.

$\therefore \quad x^2 = 2, 3, 4, \ldots, 9$

or $\quad x = \sqrt{2}, \sqrt{3}, \sqrt{4}, \sqrt{5}, \sqrt{6}, \sqrt{7}, \sqrt{8}, \sqrt{9}$

Note *It is right continuous at $x=1$ but not left continuous at $x=3$.*

$\therefore \quad \lim_{x\to 1^+} [x^2+1] = 2 = f(1)$

and $\quad \lim_{x\to 3^-} [x^2+1] = 9 \neq 10 = f(3)$

Hence, $f(x)$ is continuous for all x except eight points.

9. (b) Given, $f(x) = [2x^3-5] = [2x^3]-5$

$(2x^3)$ is monotonic in the range [1, 2].

$\therefore (2x^3)$ is discontinuous at integral point in (1,2).

$\therefore 2x^3 = 3, 4, 5, 6, 7, 8, 9, 10, 11, 12, 13, 14, 15.$

Hence, $f(x)$ is discontinuous at 13 points.

10. (b) Given, $f(x) = \begin{cases} |x+1|, \text{ if } x<-2 \\ 2x+3, \text{ if } -2\le x<0 \\ x^2+3, \text{ if } 0\le x<3 \\ x^3-15, \text{ if } 3\le x \end{cases} \Rightarrow f(x) = \begin{cases} -(x+1), \text{ if } x<-2 \\ 2x+3, \text{ if } -2\le x<0 \\ x^2+3, \text{ if } 0\le x<3 \\ x^3-15, \text{ if } 3\le x \end{cases}$

At $x=-2$,

$f(-2^-) = \lim_{h\to 0} -(-2-h+1) = 1$

$f(-2^+) = \lim_{h\to 0} 2(-2+h)+3 = -1$

$f(x)$ is discontinuous at $x=-2$.

Now, at $x=0$,

$f(0^-) = f(0^+) = f(0) = 3$

$\therefore f(x)$ is continuous at $x=0$.

At $x=3$,

$f(3^-) = f(3^+) = f(3) = 12$

$f(x)$ is continuous at $x=3$.

Hence, only point of discontinuity is $x=-2$.

11. (c) As, $f(x)$ is continuous for all $x \in R$ and $f(x) = 5, \forall\ x \in$ irrational number

$\Rightarrow f(x)$ must be constant.

$\therefore \quad f(x) = f(3) = 5$

12. (a) Given, $\quad f(x^2+1) = \dfrac{2}{f(2^x)-1}, f(x)>0 \quad$ ...(i)

Put $t = x^2+1$, then $\quad x = \sqrt{t-1}$

$\therefore \quad f(t) = \dfrac{2}{f(2^{\sqrt{t-1}})-1}$

$\Rightarrow \quad f(x) = \dfrac{2}{f(2^{\sqrt{x-1}})-1} \quad$ ...(ii)

From Eq. (i), $\quad f(1) = \dfrac{2}{f(1)-1} \Rightarrow f(1)^2 - f(1) = 2$

$\Rightarrow \quad f(1)^2 - f(1) - 2 = 0 \Rightarrow f(1) = 2, -1$

$\Rightarrow \quad f(1) = 2 \quad [\because f(x)>0 \text{ for all } x\in R]$

Now, $\quad \lim_{x\to 1} f(x) = \lim_{x\to 1} \dfrac{2}{f(2^{\sqrt{x-1}})-1} \quad$ [using Eq. (ii)]

$= \dfrac{2}{f(1)-1} = \dfrac{2}{2-1} \quad [\because f(1) = 2]$

$= 2$

13. (b) Given, $\quad f(x) = \dfrac{1}{(x-1)(x-2)}$ and $g(x) = \dfrac{1}{x^2}$

Now, $\quad f[g(x)] = \dfrac{1}{[g(x)-1][g(x)-2]}$

Clearly, $g(x)$ is not defined at $x=0$.

$\therefore g(x)$ is discontinuous at $x=0$.

Also $f(x)$ is not defined at $x=1, 2$.

$f[g(x)]$ is also not defined at $x=1, 2$

When $g(x)=1$, the $x=\pm 1$

When $g(x)=2$, the $x = \dfrac{\pm 1}{\sqrt{2}}$

Hence, the point of discontinuity of $f[g(x)]$ are $\dfrac{-1}{\sqrt{2}}, -1, 0, 1, \dfrac{1}{\sqrt{2}}$.

14. (b) We have, $h(x) = \lim_{n\to\infty} \dfrac{x^{n+1}f(x)+x^2}{x^n+g(x)}, x>0$

$\therefore \quad h(x) = \begin{cases} \dfrac{x^2}{g(x)}, & 0<x<1 \\ f(x), & x>1 \\ \dfrac{f(1)+1}{1+g(1)}, & x=1 \end{cases}$

Since, $h(x)$ is continuous for $x>1$.

$\therefore \quad h(1) = h(1^+) = h(1^-)$

$\Rightarrow \quad \dfrac{1}{g(1)} = f(1)$

$\Rightarrow \quad f(1)\cdot g(1) = 1$

15. (c,d)

Given, $f(x)$ is continuous at $x=0$.

(a) $\lim_{x\to 0} f(x) = 0$ [may or may not be true]

(b) $f(x)$ is continuous at $x=0$,

$\therefore$ It may or may not be continuous at $x=1$.

(c) $g(x) = x^2 f(x)$ is continuous at $x=0$, because x^2 and $f(x)$ both are continuous at $x=0$.

(d) Since, $f(x)$ is continuous at $x=0$.

$\therefore \lim_{x\to 0} f(x) = f(0)$

$\Rightarrow \lim_{x\to 0} [f(x) - f(0)] = 0$

16. (c,d) Given, $\quad f(x) = \dfrac{x}{2} - 1$

Since, $f(x)$ is polynomial, if is continuous everywhere.

$f(x)$ is one-one and onto.

$\therefore \quad y = \dfrac{x}{2} - 1 \Rightarrow 2y = x-2$

$\Rightarrow \quad x = 2y+2 \Rightarrow x = 2(y+1)$

$\Rightarrow \quad f^{-1}(x) = 2(x+1)$

$f^{-1}(x)$ is also a polynomial function.

It is also continuous.

$\tan[f(x)] = \tan\left(\dfrac{x}{2} - 1\right)$

It is continuous in $(0, \pi)$.

Now, $\quad \dfrac{1}{f(x)} = \dfrac{2}{x-2}$

it is not continuous at $x=2$.

17. (a,c,d) Given, $h(x) = \begin{cases} \dfrac{2\cos x - \sin 2x}{(\pi - 2x)^2}, & x<\dfrac{\pi}{2} \\ \dfrac{e^{-\cos x} - 1}{8x - 4\pi}, & x>\dfrac{\pi}{2} \end{cases}$

LHL at $x = \dfrac{\pi}{2}$,

$= \lim_{h\to 0} \dfrac{2\sin h - \sin 2h}{4h^2}$

$= \lim_{h\to 0} \dfrac{2\sin h(1-\cos h)}{4h^2} = 0$

RHL at $x = \frac{\pi}{2}$,

$$= \lim_{h\to 0} \frac{e^{\sin h}-1}{8\left(\frac{\pi}{2}+h\right)-4\pi} = \lim_{h\to 0} \frac{e^{\sin h}-1}{8h}\cdot\frac{\sin h}{\sin h}$$

$$= \frac{1}{8}$$

$\Rightarrow h(x)$ is discontinuous at $x = \frac{\pi}{2}$.

Irremovable discontinuity at $x = \frac{\pi}{2}$.

Also, $f\left(\frac{\pi^+}{2}\right) = 0$ and $g\left(\frac{\pi^-}{2}\right) = \frac{1}{8}$

$\Rightarrow \quad f\left(\frac{\pi^+}{2}\right) \neq g\left(\frac{\pi^-}{2}\right)$

18. (b,c) Given, $f(x)=\cos\left[\frac{\pi}{x}\right].\cos\left[\frac{\pi}{2}(x-1)\right]$

Now, $\lim_{x\to 0} f(x)=\cos\left[\frac{\pi}{0}\right]\cos\left(\frac{-\pi}{2}\right)$

$\Rightarrow \lim_{x\to 0} f(x)$ does not define.

$$\lim_{x\to 1} f(x)=\cos[\pi]\cdot\cos 0=\cos[\pi]$$

$\Rightarrow \quad f(1) = \cos[\pi]$

$\therefore f(x)$ is continuous at $x=1$.

$$\lim_{x\to 2} f(x)=\cos\left[\frac{\pi}{2}\right]\cos\frac{\pi}{2}=0$$

$$f(2)=\cos\left[\frac{\pi}{2}\right]\cdot 0=0$$

Hence, $f(x)$ is continuous at $x=1, 2$.

19. (a,c) Given, $f(x)=\begin{cases} b([x]^2+[x])+1, & \text{for } x\geq -1 \\ \sin[\pi(x+a)], & \text{for } x<-1 \end{cases}$

At $x=-1$,

$$\text{LHL} = \lim_{h\to 0} \sin[\pi\{-1-h\}+a] = \sin(a-1)\pi$$

$$\text{RHL} = \lim_{h\to 0} b\{[-1+h]^2[-1+h]\}+1=1$$

$\because f(x)$ is continuous at $x=-1$.

$\therefore \quad \sin(a-1)\pi=1$

$\Rightarrow \quad \sin(a-1)\pi=\sin\frac{\pi}{2}$

$\Rightarrow \quad a=2n+\frac{3}{2}$ or $4n+\frac{3}{2} \Rightarrow b\in R$

20. (a) (i) $f(1^+) = a+\cos 1$, $f(1^-) = \sin 1$.

Since, $f(x)$ is continuous.

$\Rightarrow \quad a = \sin 1 - \cos 1$

$$|k| = \frac{a}{\sqrt{2}\sin\left(1-\frac{\pi}{4}\right)} = \frac{\sin 1-\cos 1}{\sin 1-\cos 1} = 1$$

$\therefore \quad k = 1, -1$

(ii) $f(x)=\frac{1-\cos(\sin x)}{x^2}$

$$\lim_{x\to 0} f(x) = \lim_{x\to 0}\frac{1-\cos(\sin x)}{x^2} \quad \left[\frac{0}{0}\text{ form}\right]$$

$$= \lim_{x\to 0^+}\frac{\sin(\sin x)\cos x}{2x} \quad \text{[by L' Hospital's rule]} \left[\frac{0}{0}\text{ form}\right]$$

$$= \lim_{x\to 0}\frac{\cos(\sin x)\cdot\cos^2 x-\sin(\sin x)\sin x}{2} = \frac{1}{2}$$

$\because f(x)$ is continuous at $x=0$.

$\therefore \quad \lim_{x\to 0} f(x)=f(0)$

$\Rightarrow \quad f(0)=\frac{1}{2}$

(iii) $f(x)$ is continuous at some $x=a$, where $x=1-x$ or $x=\frac{1}{2}$.

Hence, $f(x)$ is continuous at $x=\frac{1}{2}$.

We have, $f\left(\frac{1}{2}\right)=\frac{1}{2}$

If $x\to\frac{1^+}{2}$, then x may be rational or irrational

i.e $f\left(\frac{1^+}{2}\right)=\frac{1}{2}$ or $1-\frac{1}{2}=\frac{1}{2}$

If $x\to\frac{1^-}{2}$, then x may be rational or irrational

i.e $f\left(\frac{1^-}{2}\right)=\frac{1}{2}$ or $1-\frac{1}{2}=\frac{1}{2}$

So, f is continuous at $x=\frac{1}{2}$.

For some other point say $x=1$, $f(1)=1$

if $x\to 1^+$, may be rational or irrational.

$f(1^+)=1$ or $1-1=0$

So, $f(1^+)$ oscillates between 1 and 0 which causes discontinuity at $x=1$.

Similarly, $f(x)$ oscillates between 0 and 1 for all $x\in R-\left\{\frac{1}{2}\right\}$.

Hence, (i) $\to$ (p,r), (ii) $\to$ (s), (iii) $\to$ (s)

Explanations for Q. Nos. (21-23)

From the given statement

Graph for $y = f(x)$ is

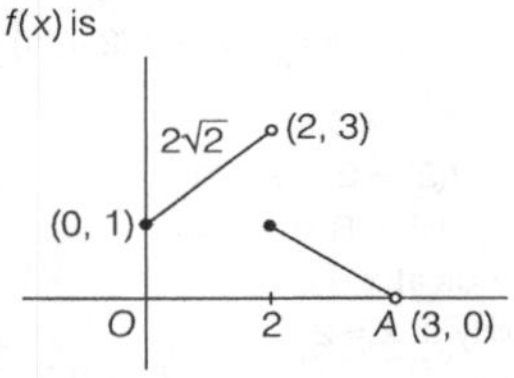

$\therefore \quad f(x) = \begin{cases} x+1, & 0\leq x<2 \\ 6-2x, & 2\leq x\leq 3 \end{cases}$

$f(x)$ is discontinuous at $x = 2$.

$(fof)(x)$ is discontinuous at $x = 1, 2$.

$$f(x+3) = f(x)$$

$\Rightarrow \quad f(19) = f(3\times 6+1) = f(1) = 2$

21. (a) **22.** (b,c) **23.** (a)

24. (5) Given, $f(x)=[\sin x+\cos x]=[g(x)]$, where

$g(x)=\sin x+\cos x$

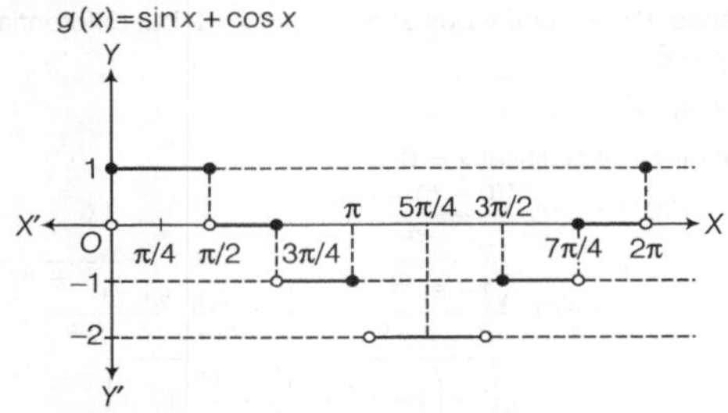

Clearly, from the graph $f(x)$ is discontinuous at

$$x=0, \frac{\pi}{2}, \frac{3\pi}{4}, \pi, \frac{3\pi}{2}, \frac{7\pi}{4}, 2\pi$$

$$\therefore \quad x\in\left\{\frac{\pi}{2}, \frac{3\pi}{4}, \pi, \frac{3\pi}{2}, \frac{7\pi}{4}\right\}$$

25. (1) Clearly, domain of $f(x) \in R - \{1\}$

$\therefore f(x)$ is discontinuous only at one point.

DPP-5 Differentiability at a Point

1. Given, $f(x) = \begin{cases} x, & \text{if } x \le 1 \\ 2 - x, & \text{if } 1 < x \le 2 \\ -2 + 3x - x^2, & \text{if } x > 2 \end{cases}$

For continuity at $x = 1$,

$$\text{LHL} = \lim_{x \to 1^-} f(x) = \lim_{h \to 0} f(1 - h) = \lim_{h \to 0} (1 - h) = 1$$

$$\text{RHL} = \lim_{x \to 1^+} f(x) = \lim_{h \to 0} f(1 + h) = \lim_{h \to 0} 2 - (1 + h) = 1$$

and $f(1) = 2 - 1 = 1$

$\because$ LHL = RHL = $f(1)$

$\therefore$ $f(x)$ is continuous at $x = 1$

For differentiability at $x = 1$,

$$Lf'(1^-) = \lim_{h \to 0} \frac{f(1-h) - f(1)}{-h} = \lim_{h \to 0} \frac{(1-h) - 1}{-h} = 1$$

$$Rf'(1^+) = \frac{f(1+h) - f(1)}{h} = \lim_{h \to 0} \frac{2 - (1+h) - 1}{h} = -1$$

$\because$ $Lf'(1^-) \ne Rf'(1^+)$

$\therefore$ $f(x)$ is not differentiable at $x = 1$.

For continuity at $x = 2$,

$$\text{LHL} = \lim_{x \to 2^-} f(x) = \lim_{h \to 0} f(2 - h)$$

$$= \lim_{h \to 0} 2 - (2 - h) = 0$$

$$\text{RHL} = \lim_{x \to 2+} f(x) = \lim_{h \to 0} f(2 + h)$$

$$= \lim_{h \to 0} -2 + 3(2 + h) - (2 + h)^2$$

$$= 0$$

and $f(2) = 2 - 2 = 0$

$\because$ LHL = RHL = $f(2)$

$\therefore$ $f(x)$ is continuous at $x = 2$.

For differentiability at $x = 2$,

$$Lf'(2^-) = \lim_{h \to 0} \frac{f(2-h) - f(2)}{-h}$$

$$= \lim_{h \to 0} \frac{2 - (2-h) - 0}{-h} = -1$$

$$Rf'(2^+) = \lim_{h \to 0} \frac{f(2+h) - f(2)}{h}$$

$$= \lim_{h \to 0} \frac{-2 + 3(2+h) - 2(2+h)^2}{h} = -1$$

$\because$ $Lf'(2^-) = Rf'(2^+)$

$\therefore$ $f(x)$ is differentiable at $x = 2$.

Hence, $f(x)$ is continuous at $x = 1$ and $x = 2$ but differentiable only at $x = 2$.

2. Given, $f(x) = \sqrt{1 - e^{-x^2}}$

For differentiability at $x = 0$,

$$Lf'(0^-) = \lim_{h \to 0} \frac{f(0-h) - f(0)}{-h}$$

$$= \lim_{h \to 0} \frac{\sqrt{1 - e^{-(0-h)^2}} - 0}{-h} = \lim_{h \to 0} \frac{\sqrt{1 - e^{-h^2}}}{-h}$$

$$= \lim_{h \to 0} \frac{\sqrt{1 - \left(1 - h^2 + \frac{h^4}{2!} + \frac{h^6}{3!} + \cdots\right)}}{-h}$$

$$= \lim_{h \to 0} \frac{\sqrt{h^2 - \frac{h^4}{2!} + \frac{h^6}{3!} + \cdots}}{-h}$$

$$= \lim_{h \to 0} \frac{h^2\sqrt{1 - \frac{h^2}{2!} + \frac{h^4}{3!} + \cdots}}{-h} = -1$$

$$Rf'(0^+) = \lim_{h \to 0} \frac{f(0+h) - f(0)}{h}$$

$$= \lim_{h \to 0} \frac{\sqrt{1 - e^{-(0+h)^2}} - 0}{h}$$

$$= \lim_{h \to 0} \frac{\sqrt{1 - e^{-h^2}}}{h}$$

$$= \lim_{h \to 0} \frac{\sqrt{1 - \left(1 - h^2 + \frac{h^4}{2!} + \frac{h^6}{3!} + \cdots\right)}}{h}$$

$$= \lim_{h \to 0} \frac{\sqrt{h^2 - \frac{h^4}{2!} + \frac{h^6}{3!} - \cdots}}{h}$$

$$= \lim_{h \to 0} \frac{h\sqrt{1 - \frac{h^2}{2!} + \frac{h^4}{3!} - \cdots}}{h}$$

$$= \lim_{h \to 0} \sqrt{1 - \frac{h^2}{2!} + \frac{h^4}{3!} - \cdots}$$

$$= 1$$

$\because$ $Lf'(0^-) \ne Rf'(0^+)$

$\therefore$ $f(x)$ is not differentiable at $x = 0$.

3. Given, $f(x) = \begin{cases} ax^2 - b, & \text{if } |x| < 1 \\ -\frac{1}{|x|}, & \text{if } |x| \ge 1 \end{cases}$

$$\Rightarrow \quad f(x) = \begin{cases} ax^2 - b, & \text{if } -1 < x < 1 \\ \frac{1}{x}, & \text{if } x \le -1 \\ -\frac{1}{x}, & \text{if } x \ge 1 \end{cases}$$

$\because$ $f(x)$ is differentiable function.

$$\therefore \quad f'(x) = \begin{cases} 2ax, & \text{if} -1 < x < 1 \\ -\frac{1}{x^2}, & \text{if } x \le -1 \\ \frac{1}{x^2}, & \text{if} x \ge 1 \end{cases}$$

Now, $Lf'(1^-) = Rf'(1^+)$ [$\because f(x)$ is differentiable at $x = 1$]

$\therefore$ $2a = 1$ ...(i)

$\Rightarrow$ $a = \frac{1}{2}$

Since, $f(x)$ is differentiable at $x = 1$, it must be continuous at $x = 1$.

$\therefore$ LHL at $x = 1$ = RHL at $x = 1$

$\Rightarrow$ $a - b = -1$ ...(ii)

On solving Eqs. (i) and (ii), we get

$$a = \frac{1}{2}, b = \frac{3}{2}$$

4. We have, $f(x) = \begin{cases} 1, & \text{for } -\infty < x < 0 \\ 1 + \sin x, & \text{for } 0 \le x < \frac{\pi}{2} \\ 2 + \left(x - \frac{\pi}{2}\right)^2, & \text{for } \frac{\pi}{2} \le x < \infty \end{cases}$

For continuity at $x = 0$,

$$\text{LHL} = \lim_{x \to 0^-} f(x)$$

$$= \lim_{h \to 0} (0 - h) = 1$$

$$\text{RHL} = \lim_{x \to 0^+} f(x) = \lim_{h \to 0} (0 + h)$$

$$= \lim_{h \to 0} 1 + \sin(0 + h) = 1$$

and $\quad f(0) = 1$

$\because \quad$ LHL = RHL = $f(0)$

$\therefore$ $f(x)$ is continuous at $x = 0$.

For differentiability at $x = 0$,

$$Lf'(0^-) = \lim_{h \to 0} \frac{f(0-h) - f(0)}{-h} = \lim_{h \to 0} \frac{1-1}{-h} = 0$$

$$Rf'(0^+) = \lim_{h \to 0} \frac{f(0+h) - f(0)}{h}$$

$$= \lim_{h \to 0} \frac{1 + \sin(0+h) - 1}{h}$$

$$= \lim_{h \to 0} \frac{\sin h}{h}$$

$$= 1 \qquad \left[\because \lim_{\theta \to 0} \frac{\sin\theta}{\theta} = 1\right]$$

$\because \quad Lf'(0^-) \neq Rf'(0^+)$

$\therefore$ $f(x)$ is not differentiable at $x = 0$.

For continuity at $x = \frac{\pi}{2}$,

$$\text{LHL} = \lim_{x \to \frac{\pi}{2}^-} f(x) = \lim_{h \to 0} f\left(\frac{\pi}{2} - h\right)$$

$$= \lim_{h \to 0} 1 + \sin\left(\frac{\pi}{2} - h\right)$$

$$= \lim_{h \to 0} 1 + \cos h = 2$$

$$\text{RHL} = \lim_{x \to \frac{\pi}{2}^+} f(x) = \lim_{h \to 0} f\left(\frac{\pi}{2} + h\right)$$

$$= \lim_{h \to 0} 2 + \left(\frac{\pi}{2} + h - \frac{\pi}{2}\right)^2 = 2$$

and $\quad f\left(\frac{\pi}{2}\right) = 2 + \left(\frac{\pi}{2} - \frac{\pi}{2}\right)^2 = 2$

$\because \quad \text{LHL} = \text{RHL} = f\left(\frac{\pi}{2}\right)$

$\therefore$ $f(x)$ is continuous at $x = \frac{\pi}{2}$.

For differentiability at $x = \frac{\pi}{2}$,

$$Lf'\left(\frac{\pi^-}{2}\right) = \lim_{h \to 0} \frac{f\left(\frac{\pi}{2} - h\right) - f\left(\frac{\pi}{2}\right)}{-h}$$

$$= \lim_{h \to 0} \frac{1 + \sin\left(\frac{\pi}{2} - h\right) - 2}{-h}$$

$$= \lim_{h \to 0} \frac{\sin\left(\frac{\pi}{2} - h\right) - 1}{-h}$$

$$= \lim_{h \to 0} \frac{\cos h - 1}{-h}$$

$$= 0$$

$$Rf'\left(\frac{\pi^+}{2}\right) = \lim_{h \to 0} \frac{f\left(\frac{\pi}{2} + h\right) - f\left(\frac{\pi}{2}\right)}{h}$$

$$= \lim_{h \to 0} \frac{2 + \left\{\left(\frac{\pi}{2} + h\right) - \frac{\pi}{2}\right\}^2 - 2}{h}$$

$$= 0$$

$\because \quad Lf'\left(\frac{\pi^-}{2}\right) = Rf'\left(\frac{\pi^+}{2}\right)$

$\therefore$ $f(x)$ is differentiable at $x = \frac{\pi}{2}$.

5. We have, $\quad f(x) = \begin{cases} x^m \sin(1/x), & \text{if } x > 0 \\ 0, & \text{if } x = 0 \end{cases}$

Now, $\quad f'(0) = \lim_{h \to 0} \frac{f(h) - 0}{h}$

$$= \lim_{h \to 0} \frac{h^m \sin 1/h}{h} = \lim_{h \to 0} h^{m-1} \sin\left(\frac{1}{h}\right)$$

(i) When $m > 1$,

$$f'(0) = \lim_{h \to 0} h^{m-1} \sin\left(\frac{1}{h}\right) = 0$$

$\therefore$ $f(x)$ is differentiable when $m > 1$.

(ii) This limit will not exist, if $m - 1 \leq 0$.

$\Rightarrow \quad m \leq 1$

Now, $\quad \lim_{x \to 0} f(x) = \lim_{x \to 0} x^m \sin\left(\frac{1}{x}\right) = 0$, if $m > 0$.

Also, $\quad f(0) = 0$

$\therefore$ $f(x)$ is continuous but not differentiable when $0 < m \leq 1$.

(iii) When $\quad m \leq 0$, let $m = -a$

$\therefore \quad \lim_{x \to 0} x^{-a} \sin\left(\frac{1}{x}\right) = \lim_{x \to 0} \frac{\sin(1/x)}{x^a} = \infty$

Hence, limit does not exist.

$f(x)$ is not continuous when $m \leq 0$.

Also, $\quad f'(0) = \lim_{h \to 0} h^{m-1} \sin \cdot (1/h)$

$$= \lim_{h \to 0} h^{-a-1} \sin \cdot (1/h) = \lim_{h \to 0} \frac{\sin(1/h)}{h^{a+1}} = \infty$$

$\therefore$ $f(x)$ is not differentiable when $m \leq 0$.

Hence, $f(x)$ is neither continuous nor differentiable, if $m \leq 0$.

6. (d) $f(x) = \begin{cases} -x, & \text{if } x \leq 0 \\ x^2, & \text{if } 0 < x \leq 1 \\ x^2 - x + 1, & \text{if } x > 1 \end{cases}$

For differentiability at $x = 0$,

$$Lf'(0^-) = \lim_{h \to 0} \frac{f(0-h) - f(0)}{-h}$$

$$= \lim_{h \to 0} \frac{-(0-h) - 0}{-h}$$

$$= -1$$

$$Rf'(0^+) = \lim_{h \to 0} \frac{f(0+h) - f(0)}{h}$$

$$= \lim_{h \to 0} \frac{(0 + h^2) - 0}{h}$$

$$= 0$$

$Lf'(0^-) \neq Rf'(0^+)$

$\therefore$ $f(x)$ is differentiable at $x = 0$.

For differentiability at $x = 1$,

$$Lf'(1^-) = \lim_{h \to 0} \frac{f(1-h) - f(1)}{-h}$$

$$= \lim_{h \to 0} \frac{(1-h)^2 - 1}{-h}$$

$$= \lim_{h \to 0} \frac{1 + h^2 - 2h - 1}{-h} = 2$$

$$Rf'(1^+) = \lim_{h \to 0} \frac{f(1+h) - f(1)}{h}$$

$$= \lim_{h \to 0} \frac{(1+h)^2 - (1+h) + 1 - 1}{h}$$

$$= \lim_{h \to 0} \frac{(1+h)(1+h-1)}{h} = 1$$

$\because \quad Lf'(1^-) \neq Rf'(1^+)$

$\therefore$ $f(x)$ is not differentiable at $x = 1$.

7. (b) We have,

$$f(x) = \begin{cases} x\left(\dfrac{e^{1/x} - e^{-1/x}}{e^{1/x} + e^{-1/x}}\right), & \text{if } x \neq 0 \\ 0, & \text{if } x = 0 \end{cases}$$

Now, $Lf'(0^-) = \lim_{h \to 0} \dfrac{f(0-h) - f(0)}{-h}$

$$= \lim_{h \to 0} \frac{-h\left(\dfrac{e^{-1/h} - e^{1/h}}{e^{-1/h} + e^{1/h}}\right)}{-h}$$

$$= \lim_{h \to 0} \left(\frac{e^{-2/h} - 1}{e^{-2/h} + 1}\right)$$

$$= -1$$

$$Rf'(0^+) = \lim_{h \to 0} \frac{f(0+h) - f(0)}{h}$$

$$= \lim_{h \to 0} \frac{h\left(\dfrac{e^{1/h} - e^{-1/h}}{e^{1/h} + e^{-1/h}}\right)}{h}$$

$$= \lim_{h \to 0} \frac{1 - e^{-2/h}}{1 + e^{-2/h}} = 1$$

$\because$ $Lf'(0^-) \neq Rf'(0^+)$.

$\therefore$ $f(x)$ is not differentiable at $x = 0$.

8. (a) Given $f(x) = x^3 \operatorname{Sgn}(x)$

or $f(x) = \begin{cases} x^3, & \text{if } x > 0 \\ 0, & \text{if } x = 0 \\ -x^3, & \text{if } x < 0 \end{cases}$

To check differentiability at $x = 0$,

$$Lf'(0^-) = \lim_{h \to 0} \frac{f(0-h) - f(0)}{-h}$$

$$= \lim_{h \to 0} \frac{-(0-h)^3 - 0}{-h}$$

$$= \lim_{h - 0} \frac{h^3}{-h}$$

$$= 0$$

$$Rf'(0) = \lim_{h \to 0} \frac{f(0+h) - f(0)}{h}$$

$$= \lim_{h \to 0} \frac{(0+h)^3 - 0}{h}$$

$$= \lim_{h \to 0} \frac{h^3}{h} = 0$$

$\therefore$ $f(x)$ is differentiable at $x = 0$.

9. (d) $f(x) = (x^2 - 1)|x^2 - 3x + 2| + \cos(|x|)$

$$= (x-1)(x+1) \cdot |(x-1)(x-2)| + \cos x$$

$(x-1)|x-1|$ and $\cos x$ are differentiable for all x, but $|x-2|$ is not differentiable at $x = 2$.

Hence, $f(x)$ is non-differentiable at $x = 2$.

10. (b) Given, $f(x) = \begin{cases} g(x)\cos\left(\dfrac{1}{x}\right), & \text{if } x \neq 0 \\ 0, & \text{if } x = 0 \end{cases}$

Since, $g(x)$ is an even function, then

$$g(x) = g(-x) \Rightarrow g'(x) = -g'(-x)$$

$\Rightarrow$ $g'(0) = -g'(0) \Rightarrow g'(0) = 0$

Now, $f'(0) = \lim_{h \to 0} y \dfrac{(0+h)\cos(1/h) - 0}{h}$

$$= \lim_{h \to 0} \frac{g(h)\cos(1/h)}{h}$$

$$= \lim_{h \to 0} g(0)\cos(1/h) = 0$$

11. (c) Given, $f(x) = \begin{cases} x\, e^{-\left(\frac{1}{|x|} + \frac{1}{x}\right)}, & x \neq 0 \\ 0, & x = 0 \end{cases}$

$\Rightarrow$ $f(x) = \begin{cases} x \cdot e^{-\left(-\frac{1}{x} + \frac{1}{x}\right)} = x, & x < 0 \\ x \cdot e^{-2/x}, & x > 0 \\ 0, & x = 0 \end{cases}$

Clearly, $\lim_{x \to 0^-} f(x) = \lim_{x \to 0} x = 0$

$$\lim_{x \to 0^+} f(x) = \lim_{x \to 0} x \cdot e^{-2/x} = 0$$

Also, $f(0) = 0$

$\therefore$ $\lim_{x \to 0^-} f(x) = \lim_{x \to 0^+} f(x) = f(0)$

So, $f(x)$ is continuous at $x = 0$.

Now, $Lf'(0) = \lim_{h \to 0} \dfrac{f(0-h) - f(0)}{-h}$

$$= \lim_{h \to 0} \frac{0 - h - 0}{-h} = 1$$

$$Rf'(0^+) = \lim_{h \to 0} \frac{f(0+h) - f(0)}{h}$$

$$= \frac{(0+h) \cdot e^{-\frac{2}{0+h}} - 0}{h}$$

$$= 0$$

$\because$ $Lf'(0) \neq Rf'(0^-)$

$\therefore$ $f(x)$ is not differentiable at $x = 0$.

12. (d) We have, $f(x) = \max.\{x, x^3\}$

$\Rightarrow$ $f(x) = \begin{cases} x, & \text{if } x \leq -1 \\ x^3, & \text{if } -1 \leq x < 0 \\ x, & \text{if } 0 \leq x \leq 1 \\ x^3, & \text{if } 1 \leq x \end{cases}$

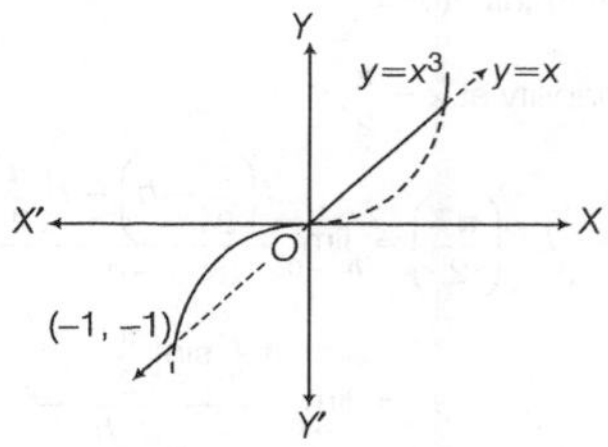

The continuous line shown in the above figure represent the graph of $f(x)$.

Clearly, $f(x)$ is not differentiable at $x = -1, 0, 1$.

13. (a) We have,

$$f(x) = [x] \sin \pi x$$

$\therefore$ $Lf'(k^-) = \lim_{x \to k^-} \dfrac{f(x) - f(k)}{x - k}$

$\lim_{h \to 0} \dfrac{f(k-h) - f(k)}{-h}$

$$= \lim_{h \to 0} \frac{[k-h]\sin(\pi k - \pi h) - [k]\sin \pi k}{-h}$$

$$= \lim_{h \to 0} \frac{(-1)^{k-1}[k-h]\sin \pi h - 0}{-h}$$

$$= \lim_{h \to 0} (-1)^k \frac{[k-h]\sin \pi h}{h}$$

$$= (-1)^k (k-1) \lim_{h \to 0} \frac{\sin \pi h}{h}$$

$$= (-1)^k (k-1)\pi$$

14. (d) We have, $\cos|x| = \begin{cases} \cos x, & \text{if } x \geq 0 \\ \cos(-x), & \text{if } x < 0 \end{cases}$

$\Rightarrow$ $\cos|x| = \cos x$ for all $x \in R$

Similarly, $\sin|x| = \begin{cases} \sin x, & \text{if } x \geq 0 \\ \sin(-x) = -\sin x, & \text{if } x < 0 \end{cases}$

Let $f(x) = \cos|x| + |x|$ and $g(x) = \cos|x| - |x|$

Since, $\cos x$ is everywhere differentiable and $|x|$ is not differentiable at $x = 0$.

Therefore, $f(x)$ and $g(x)$ are not differentiable at $x = 0$.

Let $u(x) = \sin(|x|) + |x|$, then

$$u(x) = \begin{cases} \sin x + x, & x \geq 0 \\ -\sin x - x, & x < 0 \end{cases}$$

Now, $Lf'(0^-) = \left\{\frac{d}{dx}(-\sin x - x)\right\}_{\text{at } x=0}$

$= (-\cos x - 1)_{\text{at } x=0} = -2$

$Rf'(0^+) = \left\{\frac{d}{dx}(\sin x + x)\right\}_{\text{at } x=0}$

$= \{\cos x + 1\}_{\text{at } x=0} = 2$

Clearly, $Lf'(0^-) \neq Rf'(0^+)$

So, $\mu(x)$ is not differentiable at $x = 0$.

Let $v(x) = \sin|x| - |x|$, then

$$v(x) = \begin{cases} -\sin x + x, & \text{if } x < 0 \\ \sin x - x, & \text{if } x \geq 0 \end{cases}$$

$Lf'(0^-) = \left\{\frac{d}{dx}(-\sin x + x)\right\}_{\text{at } x=0}$

$= \{-\cos x + 1\}_{\text{at } x=0} = 0$

$Rf'(0^+) = \left\{\frac{d}{dx}(\sin x - x)\right\}_{\text{at } x=0}$

$= (\cos x - 1)_{\text{at } x=0} = \cos 0 - 1 = 0$

$\therefore$ $Lf'(0^-) = Rf'(0^+)$

So, $v(x)$ is differentiable at $x = 0$.

15. (a) Given, $f(x) = ||x| - 1|$

It is not differentiable, when $|x| = 0$ i.e. $x = 0$.

and when $|x| - 1 = 0$ i.e. $x = \pm 1$

Alternate Method

The graph of $y = ||x| - 1|$ is as follows

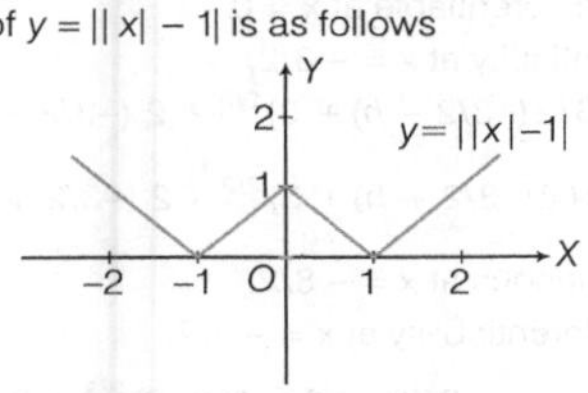

The graph of function has sharp turn at $x = -1, 0, 1$.

Hence, it is not differentiable at $x = -1, 0, 1$.

16. (c) Given, $g(x) = \frac{(x-1)^n}{\log_e \cos^m(x-1)}$, $0 < x < 2, m \neq 0, n$ are integers

and $|x-1| = \begin{cases} x-1, & x \geq 1 \\ 1-x, & x < 1 \end{cases}$

The left hand derivative of $|x-1|$ at $x = 1$ is $p = -1$.

Also, $\lim_{x \to 1^+} g(x) = p = -1$

$$\lim_{h \to 0} \frac{(1+h-1)^n}{\log \cos^m(1+h-1)} = -1$$

$\Rightarrow$ $\lim_{h \to 0} \frac{h^n}{\log \cos^m h} = -1$

$\Rightarrow$ $\lim_{h \to 0} \frac{h^n}{m \log \cos h} = -1$

$\Rightarrow$ $\lim_{h \to 0} \frac{nh^{n-1}}{m \times \frac{1}{\cos h} \times (-\sin h)} = -1$

[using L' Hospital's rule]

$\Rightarrow$ $\lim_{h \to 0} \left(\frac{-n}{m}\right) \frac{h^{n-1}}{\frac{\sin h}{\cos h}} = -1$

$\Rightarrow$ $\frac{n}{m} \lim_{h \to 0} \frac{h^{n-2}}{\frac{\tan h}{h}} = 1$

$\therefore$ $n = 2$ and $\frac{n}{m} = 1 \Rightarrow m = n = 2$

17. (b) Given, $f(x) = \begin{cases} x^2\left|\cos\left(\frac{\pi}{x}\right)\right|, & x \neq 0 \\ 0, & x = 0 \end{cases}, x \in R$

To check differentiability at $x = 0$,

$Rf'(0^+) = \lim_{h \to 0} f\frac{(0+h) - f(0)}{h}$

$= \lim_{h \to 0} \frac{h^2\left|\cos\frac{\pi}{h}\right| - 0}{h} = \lim_{h \to 0} h \cdot \left|\cos\frac{\pi}{h}\right| = 0$

$Lf'(0^-) = \lim_{h \to 0} \frac{f(0-h) - f(0)}{-h}$

$= \lim_{h \to 0} \frac{h^2\left|\cos\left(\frac{-\pi}{h}\right)\right| - 0}{-h} = 0$

So, $f(x)$ is differentiable at $x = 0$.

To check differentiability at $x = 2$,

$Rf'(2^+) = \lim_{h \to 0} \frac{f(2+h) - f(2)}{h}$

$= \lim_{h \to 0} \frac{(2+h)^2\left|\cos\left(\frac{\pi}{2+h}\right)\right| - 0}{h}$

$= \lim_{h \to 0} \frac{(2+h)^2 \cos\left(\frac{\pi}{2+h}\right)}{h}$

$= \lim_{h \to 0} \frac{(2+h)^2 \sin\left(\frac{\pi}{2} - \frac{\pi}{2+h}\right)}{h}$

$= \lim_{h \to 0} \frac{(2+h)^2 \sin\left[\frac{\pi h}{2(2+h)}\right]}{h \frac{\pi}{2(2+h)}} \cdot \frac{\pi}{2(2+h)}$

$= \pi$

$Lf'(2^-) = \lim_{h \to 0} \frac{f(2-h) - f(2)}{-h}$

$= \lim_{h \to 0} (2-h)^2 \left|\cos\left(\frac{\pi}{2-h}\right)\right| - 2^2 \left|\cos\frac{\pi}{2}\right|$

$= \lim_{h \to 0} \frac{(2-h)^2 - \left(\cos\frac{\pi}{2-h}\right) - 0}{-h}$

$= \lim_{h \to 0} \frac{-(2-h)^2 - \sin\left(\frac{\pi}{2} - \frac{\pi}{2-h}\right)}{h}$

$= \lim_{h \to 0} \frac{(2-h)^2 \sin\left[-\frac{\pi h}{2(2-h)}\right]}{h \times \frac{-\pi}{2(2-h)}} \times \frac{-\pi}{2(2-h)}$

$= -\pi$

Thus, $f(x)$ is not differentiable at $x = 2$.

18. (b) Given, $f(x) = \frac{x}{1+|x|}$

Here, $f(x)$ is defined for all real values of x.

$\therefore$ It is differentiable in $(-\infty, \infty)$.

19. (d) $\lim_{x \to a} \frac{x^2 f(a) - a^2 f(x)}{x - a}$ $\left[\frac{0}{0} \text{ form}\right]$

$$= \lim_{x \to a} \frac{2x f(a) - a^2 f'(x)}{1 - 0} \quad \text{[using L' Hospital's rule]}$$

$$= 2a f(a) - a^2 f'(a)$$

20. (a,c) We have, $\lim_{x \to 0} \frac{f(x) - f(0)}{x - 0}$

$$= \lim_{x \to 0} \frac{\log \cos x}{\log(1 + x^2)}$$

$$= \lim_{x \to 0} \frac{\log(1 - 1 + \cos x)}{\log(1 + x^2)} \cdot \left(\frac{1 - \cos x}{1 - \cos x}\right)$$

$$= \lim_{x \to 0} \frac{\log\{1 - (1 - \cos x)\}}{1 - \cos x} \cdot \frac{1 - \cos x}{\log(1 + x^2)}$$

$$= - \lim_{x \to 0} \frac{\log\{1 - (1 - \cos x)\}}{-(1 - \cos x)} \cdot \frac{2\sin^2 x/2}{4(x/2)^2} \cdot \frac{x^2}{\log(1 + x^2)}$$

$$= -1/2$$

Hence, $f(x)$ is differentiable at $x = 0$, and $f(x)$ is continuous at $x = 0$.

21. (b,d) Given, $f(x) = \begin{cases} (x - e)2^{-2^{\frac{1}{e-x}}}, & x \neq e \\ 0, & x = e \end{cases}$

To check continuity at $x = e$,

$$\lim_{x \to e} f(x) = \lim_{x \to e} (x - e)\, 2^{-2^{\frac{1}{e-x}}} = 0$$

Also, $f(e) = 0$

$\because$ $\lim_{x \to e} f(x) = f(e) = 0$

$\therefore$ $f(x)$ is continuous at $x = e$.

To check differentiability at $x = e$,

$$Lf'(e) = \lim_{h \to 0} \frac{f(e - h) - f(e)}{-h}$$

$$= \lim_{h \to 0} \frac{(-h)\, 2^{(-2)^{1/h}} - 0}{-h} = \lim_{h \to 0} 2^{-2^{1/h}} = 0$$

$$Rf'(e) = \lim_{h \to 0} \frac{f(e + h) - f(e)}{h}$$

$$= \lim_{h \to 0} \frac{h \times 2^{-2^{1/h}} - 0}{h} = 1$$

$\therefore$ $f(x)$ is non-differentiable at $x = e$.

Since, $f(x)$ is not differentiable at $x = e$

$\therefore$ It must gave sharp edge at $x = e$.

22. (b,c)We have, $f(x) = \frac{\sin\frac{\pi}{4}[x]}{[x]}$

To check continuity at $x = 3/2$,

$$\text{LHL} = \lim_{h \to 0} \frac{\sin\frac{\pi}{4}[3/2 - h]}{[3/2 - h]}$$

$$= \lim_{h \to 0} \sin\frac{\pi}{4} = \frac{1}{\sqrt{2}}$$

$$\text{RHL} = \lim_{h \to 0} \frac{\sin\frac{\pi}{4}\left[\frac{3}{2} + h\right]}{\left[\frac{3}{2} + h\right]}$$

$$= \lim_{h \to 0} \sin\frac{\pi}{4} = \frac{1}{\sqrt{2}}$$

$\therefore$ $f(x)$ is continuous at $x = 3/2$.

To check continuity at $x = 2$,

$$f(2^+) = \lim_{h \to 0} \frac{\sin\frac{\pi}{4}[2 + h]}{[2 + h]} = \frac{1}{2}$$

$$f(2^-) = \lim_{h \to 0} \frac{\sin\frac{\pi}{4}[2 - h]}{[2 - h]} = \lim_{h \to 0} \frac{\sin\frac{\pi}{4}}{1} = \frac{1}{\sqrt{2}}$$

$\therefore$ $f(x)$ is discontinuous at $x = 2$.

23. (a,c) Given, $f(x) = 3(2x + 3)^{2/3} + 2x + 3$

To check contunity at $x = 0$,

$$\text{LHL} = \lim_{h \to 0} 3\{2(0 - h) + 3\}^{2/3} + 2(0 - h) + 3$$

$$= \lim_{h \to 0} 3\{-2h + 3\}^{2/3} - 2h + 3$$

$$= 3 \cdot (3)^{2/3} + 3 = 3^{5/3} + 3$$

$$\text{RHL} = \lim_{h \to 0} 3\{2(0 + h) + 3\}^{2/3} + 2(0 + h) + 3$$

$$= \lim_{h \to 0} 3\{2h + 3\}^{2/3} + 2h + 3$$

$$= 3 \cdot (3)^{2/3} + 3 = 3^{5/3} + 3$$

$$f(0) = 3^{5/3} + 3$$

$\therefore$ $f(x)$ is continuous at $x = 0$.

To check differentiability at $x = 0$,

$$Lf'(0) = \lim_{h \to 0} \frac{3\{2(0 - h) + 3\}^{2/3} + 2(0 - h) + 3}{-h}$$

$$\lim_{h \to 0} \frac{3(3 - 2h)^{2/3} - 2h + 3}{-h}$$

$$= \lim_{h \to 0} \frac{3^{5/3}\left\{1 - \frac{2}{3}h\right\}^{2/3} - 2h + 3}{-h}$$

$$= \lim_{h \to 0} \frac{3^{5/3}\left(1 - \frac{2}{3} \times \frac{2}{3}h + \frac{\frac{2}{3} \times \left(\frac{-1}{3}\right)\left(\frac{2}{3}h\right)^2 + \cdots}{2!}\right) - 2h + 3}{-h}$$

$$= \text{Does not exist}$$

$\therefore$ $f(x)$ is not differentiable at $x = 0$.

To check continuity at $x = -3/2$,

$$\text{LHL} = \lim_{h \to 0} 3\{2(-3/2 - h) + 3\}^{2/3} + 2(-3/2 - h) + 3 = 0$$

$$\text{RHL} = \lim_{h \to 0} 3\{2(-3/2 + h) + 3\}^{2/3} + 2(-3/2 + h) + 3 = 0$$

$\therefore$ $f(x)$ is continuous at $x = -3/2$.

To check differentiability at $x = -3/2$,

$$Lf'\left(-\frac{3}{2}\right) = \lim_{h \to 0} \frac{3\{2(-3/2 - h) + 3\}^{2/3} + 2(-3/2 - h) + 3}{-h}$$

$$= \lim_{h \to 0} \frac{3\{(-2h)^{2/3} - 3 - 2h + 3}{-h}$$

$$= \lim_{h \to 0} \frac{3\{(-2h)^{2/3} - 2h\}}{-h}$$

$$= \lim_{h \to 0} 3\{(-2)^{2/3} h^{-1/3} - 2\} = -6$$

$$Rf' = \left(-\frac{3}{2}\right) \lim_{h \to 0} \frac{3\left\{2\left(\frac{-3}{2} + h\right) + 3\right\}^{2/3} + 2\left(\frac{-3}{2} + h\right) + 3}{h}$$

$$= \lim_{h \to 0} \frac{3\{(2h)^{2/3}\} + 2h}{h} = \lim_{h \to 0} 3\{(2)^{2/3} h^{1/3} + 2\}$$

$$= 6$$

$$Lf'(-3/2) \neq Rf'(-3/2)$$

$\therefore$ $f(x)$ is not differentiable at $x = -3/2$.

24. (a,b) $f'(a)$ exists if

$$\lim_{h \to 0} \frac{f(a-h) - f(a)}{-h} = \lim_{h \to 0} \frac{f(a+h) - f(a)}{h}$$

or $$\lim_{h \to 0} \frac{-f(a-h) + f(a)}{h} = \lim_{h \to 0} \frac{f(a+h) - f(a)}{h}$$

$\Rightarrow$ $$f'(a) = \frac{f(a) - f(a-h)}{h}$$

Also, $$f'(a) = \lim_{h \to 0} \frac{f(h) - f(a)}{h - a}$$

25. (a,c) Given, $f(x) = \min\{1, x^2, x^3\}$

which could be graphical shown as below.

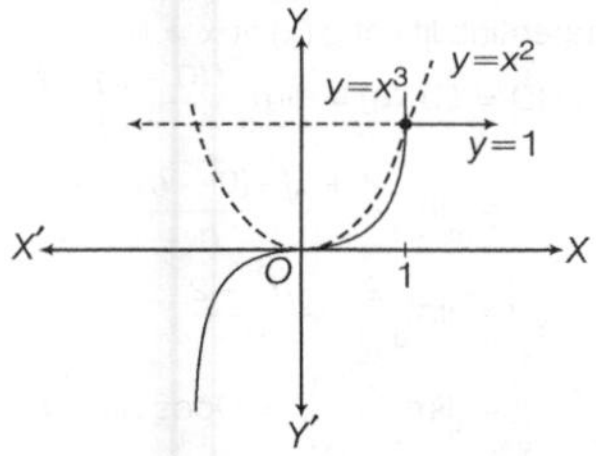

$\Rightarrow f(x)$ is continuous for all $x \in R$ and not differentiable at $x = 1$ due to sharp edge.

26. (b,c,d) We have, $f(x) = \begin{cases} -x - \pi/2, & \text{if } x \le -\pi/2 \\ -\cos x, & \text{if } -\pi/2 < x < 0 \\ x - 1, & \text{if } 0 < x \le 1 \\ \log x, & \text{if } x > 1 \end{cases}$

Continuity at $x = -\frac{\pi}{2}$,

$$f\left(-\frac{\pi}{2}\right) = -\left(-\frac{\pi}{2}\right) - \frac{\pi}{2} = 0$$

$$\text{RHL} = \lim_{h \to 0} -\cos\left(-\frac{\pi}{2} + h\right) = 0$$

$\therefore f(x)$ is continuous at $x = -\frac{\pi}{2}$.

Continuity at $x = 0$, $f(0) = -1$

$$\text{RHL} = \lim_{h \to 0} (0 + h) - 1 = -1$$

$\therefore f(x)$ is continuous at $x = 0$.

Continuity at $x = 1$,

$$f(1) = 0$$

$$\text{RHL} = \lim_{h \to 0} \log(1 + h) = 0$$

$\therefore f(x)$ is continuous at $x = 1$.

Hence, $$f'(x) = \begin{cases} -1, & x \le -\pi/2 \\ \sin x, & -\pi/2 < x \le 0 \\ 1, & 0 < x \le 1 \\ \frac{1}{x}, & x > 1 \end{cases}$$

Differentiability at $x = 0$, LHD $= 0$, RHD $= 1$

$\therefore f(x)$ is not differentiable at $x = 0$.

Differentiability at $x = 1$, LHD $= 1$, RHD $= 1$

$\therefore f(x)$ is differentiable at $x = 1$.

Also, for $x = -3/2$,

$$f(x) = -x - \frac{\pi}{2}$$

$\therefore f(x)$ is differentiable at $x = -3/2$.

27. (b) Graph for $y = f(x)$ is

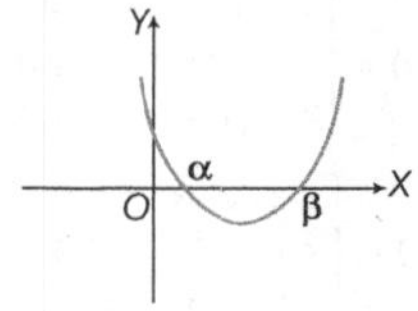

Graph for $y = f(-x)$ is

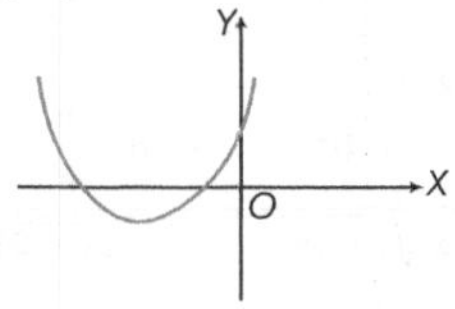

Graph for $y = |f(-x)|$ is

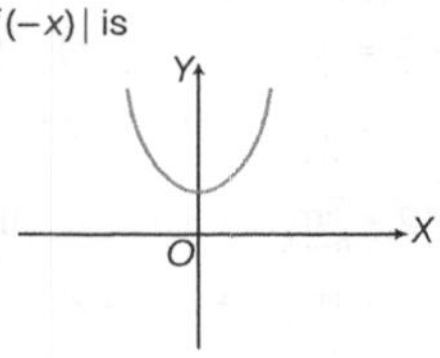

$\therefore$ Not differentiable at 1 point.

$\Rightarrow$ Statement I is correct.

Statement II is correct, as $y = f(|x|)$ is symmetrical about Y-axis.

28. (c) Graph of $|x^3|$ is shown below:

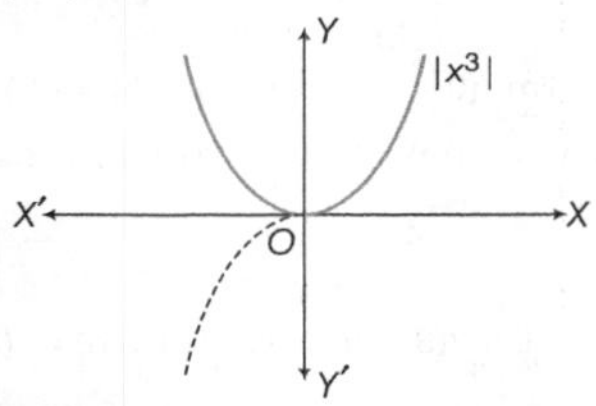

Clearly, it is differentiable at $x = 0$, because there is a unique tangent to the curve at $x = 0$.

Clearly, Statement II is incorrect.

29. (c) We have $f(x) = |x| \cdot \sin x$

$\therefore$ $$Lf'(0) = \lim_{h \to 0} \frac{(0-h)\sin(0-h) - 0}{-h}$$

$$= \lim_{h \to 0} \frac{-h \sin h}{-h} = 0$$

$$Rf'(0) = \lim_{h \to 0} \frac{(0+h)\sin(0+h) - 0}{h}$$

$$= \lim_{h \to 0} \frac{h \sin h}{h} = 0$$

$$Lf'(0) = Rf'(0)$$

$\therefore f(x)$ is differentiable at $x = 0$.

Clearly, Statement II is incorrect.

30. (d) We have $f(x) = \cos(\sin^{-1} x)$

We know that, $$-\frac{\pi}{2} \le \sin^{-1} x \le \frac{\pi}{2}$$

$\therefore$ $$\cos 1 \le \cos(\sin^{-1} x) \le 1$$

Hence, $f(x)$ is bounded in $[\cos 1, 1]$.

31. (a) Given functions are

$$f(x)=\begin{cases}2+(x-1)^2, & x<1\\ 2, & 1\le x\le 3\\ 2-(x-3)^2, & x>3\end{cases}$$

$$g(x)=\begin{cases}2+\sqrt{-x}, & x<0\\ x+2, & 0\le x\le 4\\ 3x-6, & x>4\end{cases}$$

$$h(x)=\begin{cases}4+ae^x, & x<0\\ x+2, & 0\le x\le 3\\ b^2-7b+18-\dfrac{3}{x}, & x>3\end{cases}$$

and $k(x)=\sqrt{1+x\sqrt{1+(x+1)\sqrt{1+(x+2)(x+4)}}},\ x>0$

To check continuity of $f(x)$ at $x=1$,

$$\text{LHD}=\lim_{h\to 0} 2+\{(1-h)-1\}^2$$

$$=\lim_{h\to 0} 2+(-h)^2=2$$

$$\text{RHD}=\lim_{h\to 0} 2+\{(1+h)-1\}^2$$

$$=\lim_{h\to 0} 2+(h)^2=2$$

and $f(1)=2$

$\therefore$ $f(x)$ is continuous at $x=1$.

32. (c) Since $h(x)$ is continuous, $\forall n\in R$.

$\therefore$ $\text{LHL}=\text{RHL}=f(0)$ ...(i)

and $\text{LHL}=\text{RHL}=f(3)$ ...(ii)

From Eq. (i), $\lim_{h\to 0} f(0-h)=\lim_{h\to 0} f(0+h)=f(0)$

$$\Rightarrow \lim_{h\to 0} 4+ae^{(0-h)}=\lim_{h\to 0}(0+h)+2=2$$

$$\Rightarrow 4+a=2$$

$$\Rightarrow a=-2 \quad ...(iii)$$

From Eq. (ii), $\lim_{h\to 0} f(3-h)=\lim_{h\to 0} f(3+h)=f(3)$

$$\Rightarrow \lim_{h\to 0} 3-h+2=\lim_{h\to 0} b^2-7b+18-\frac{3}{(3+h)}=5$$

$$\Rightarrow 5-b^2-7b+17$$

$$\Rightarrow b^2-7b+17=5$$

$$\Rightarrow b^2-7b+12=0$$

$$\Rightarrow b^2-4b-3b+12=0$$

$$\Rightarrow b(b-4)-3(b-4)=0$$

$$\Rightarrow (b-4)(b-3)=0$$

$$\therefore b=3,4$$

33. (b) To check differentiability of $f(x)$ at $x=1$,

$$\text{LHD}=Lf'(1)=\lim_{h\to 0}\frac{f(1-h)-f(1)}{-h}$$

$$=\lim_{h\to 0}\frac{2+\{(1-h)-1\}^2-2}{-h}$$

$$=\lim_{h\to 0}\frac{2+h^2-2}{-h}=0$$

$$\text{RHD}=Rf'(1)=\lim_{h\to 0}\frac{f(1+h)-f(1)}{h}$$

$$=\lim_{h\to 0}\frac{2-2}{h}=0$$

$\therefore$ $f(x)$ is differentiable at $x=1$.

Now, to check differentiability of $f(x)$ at $x=3$,

$$\text{LHD}=Lf'(3)=\lim_{h\to 0}\frac{f(3-h)-f(3)}{-h}$$

$$=\lim_{h\to 0}\frac{2-2}{-h}=0$$

$$\text{RHD}=Rf'(3)=\lim_{h\to 0}\frac{f(3+h)-f(3)}{h}$$

$$=\lim_{h\to 0}\frac{2-\{(3+h)-3\}^2-2}{h}$$

$$=0$$

$\therefore$ $f(x)$ is differentiable at $x=1$ and $x=3$.

To check differentiability at $g(x)$ at $x=0$,

$$\text{LHD}=Lg'(0)=\lim_{h\to 0}\frac{f(0-h)-f(0)}{-h}$$

$$=\lim_{h\to 0}\frac{2+\sqrt{-(0-h)}-2}{-h}$$

$$=\lim_{h\to 0}\frac{2+\sqrt{h}-2}{-h}$$

$$=\lim_{h\to 0}-\frac{1}{\sqrt{h}}=\text{Does not exist}$$

$$\text{RHD}=Rg'(0)=\lim_{h\to 0}\frac{f(0+h)-f(0)}{h}$$

$$=\lim_{h\to 0}\frac{(0+h)+2-2}{h}$$

$$=-1$$

$\therefore$ $g(x)$ is not differentiability at $x=1$.

To check differentiability of $g(x)$ at $x=4$,

$$\text{LHD}=Lg'(4)=\lim_{h\to 0}\frac{f(4-h)-f(4)}{-h}$$

$$=\lim_{h\to 0}\frac{4-h+2-6}{-h}=1$$

$$\text{RHD}=Rg'(4)=\lim_{h\to 0}\frac{3(4+h)-6-6}{h}$$

$$=\lim_{h\to 0}\frac{3(4+h)}{h}=\text{Does not exist}$$

$\therefore$ $g(x)$ is not differentiable at $x=4$.

Hence, $g(x)$ is not differentiable at exactly two points.

34. (3) We have,

$$\lim_{h\to 0}\frac{f(h)-f(-2h)}{h} \qquad \left[\frac{0}{0}\text{ form}\right]$$

$$=\lim_{h\to 0}\frac{f'(h)+2f'(-2h)}{1} \quad \text{[by L' Hospital's rule]}$$

$$=f'(0)+2f'(0)$$

$$=3f'(0)=3$$

35. (7) We have,

$$f(x)=[x]\tan x(\pi x)$$

Now, $$Rf'(7)=\lim_{h\to 0}\frac{[7+h]\tan\pi(7+h)-7\tan 7\pi}{h}$$

$$=\lim_{h\to 0}\frac{7\cdot\tan\pi(7+h)-7\tan 7\pi}{h}$$

$$=7\cdot\lim_{h\to 0}\frac{\tan\pi(7+h)-\tan 7\pi}{h}=7\cdot\pi$$

$\therefore$ $k=7$

DPP-6 Differentiability in the Interval

1. We have,

$$f(x) = [x] + |1 - x|, -1 \le x \le 3$$

$f(x)$ can be written as

$$f(x) = \begin{cases} -1 + 1 - x, & \text{for } -1 \le x < 0 \\ 0 + 1 - x, & \text{for } 0 \le x < 1 \\ 1 - 1 + x, & \text{for } 1 \le x < 2 \\ 2 - 1 + x, & \text{for } 2 \le x < 3 \end{cases}$$

$$\therefore \quad f(x) = \begin{cases} -x, & \text{for } -1 \le x < 0 \\ 1 - x, & \text{for } 0 \le x < 1 \\ x, & \text{for } 1 \le x < 2 \\ 1 + x, & \text{for } 2 \le x < 3 \\ 5, & \text{for } x = 3 \end{cases}$$

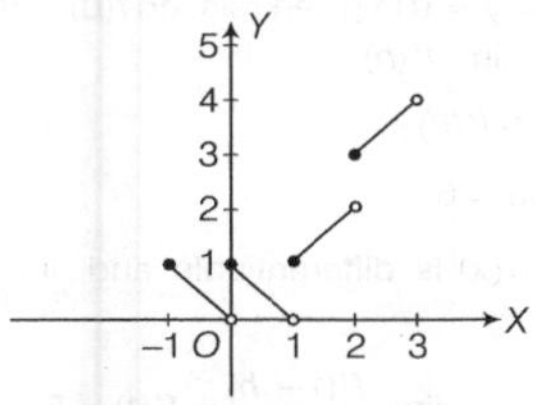

Hence, $f(x)$ is not differentiable at all integral in $-1 < x \le 3$.

2. Check continuity at $x = 1$,

$$\text{LHL} = \lim_{x \to 1^-} f(x)$$

$$= \lim_{x \to 1} \left|x - \frac{1}{2}\right| = \frac{1}{2}$$

$$\text{RHL} = \lim_{x \to 1^+} f(x)$$

$$= \lim_{x \to 1^+} x[x] = 1$$

Clearly, $f(x)$ is discontinuous at $x = 1$.

Now, check differentiability at $x = 1$,

$$\text{LHD} = Lf'(1) = \lim_{x \to 1^-} \frac{f(x) - f(1)}{x - 1}$$

$$= \lim_{x \to 1} \frac{\left|x - \frac{1}{2}\right| - 1}{x - 1}$$

$$= \lim_{x \to 1} \frac{x - \frac{3}{2}}{x - 1} = \infty$$

$$\text{RHD} = Rf'(1) = \lim_{x \to 1^+} \frac{f(x) - f(1)}{x - 1}$$

$$= \lim_{x \to 1} \frac{x[1] - 1}{x - 1}$$

$$= \lim_{x \to 1} \frac{x - 1}{x - 1} = 1$$

$\therefore f(x)$ is not differentiable at $x = 1$.

Hence, $f(x)$ is not continuous at $x = 1$ and $f(x)$ is not differentiable at $x = \frac{1}{2}, 1$.

3. We have,

$$\lim_{x \to 0} \frac{f(1 + \cos x) - f(2)}{\frac{\tan^2 x}{x^2} \times x^2}$$

$$\therefore \quad \lim_{x \to 0} \frac{f(1 + \cos x) - f(2)}{x^2}$$

It is $\frac{0}{0}$ form, hence apply L'Hospital's rule, we get

$$\lim_{x \to 0} \frac{f'(1 + \cos x) \cdot (-\sin x)}{2x}$$

$$= f'(2) \cdot \left(-\frac{1}{2}\right)$$

$$= -\frac{1}{2} \cdot 4 = -2$$

4. Since, $f'(x) = \lim_{h \to 0} \frac{f(x + h) - f(x)}{h}$

$$= \lim_{h \to 0} \frac{f(x) \cdot f(h) - f(x)}{h}$$

$$= f(x) \cdot \lim_{h \to 0} \frac{f(h) - 1}{h}$$

Since, $f(x)$ is differentiable.

$\because f(0) = 1$ must be zero.

$$\Rightarrow \quad f(0) = 1$$

$$f'(x) = f(x) \cdot f'(0)$$

$$\text{or} \quad \int \frac{f'(x)}{f(x)} = \int f'(0)\, dx$$

$$\log f(x) = f'(0) \cdot x + C$$

Put $x = 0$, we get $C = 0$

$$\therefore \quad \log f(x) = x \cdot f'(0)$$

$$\Rightarrow \quad f(x) = e^{x \cdot f'(0)}$$

5. We know that, $\lim_{x \to 0} |f(x)| \to 0.$

If $f(x) \to 0$, we have

$$|f(x) - f(y)| \le |x - y|^3, \forall\ x, y \in R$$

Let x be any real number and let y be chosen in the neighbourhood of x, then

$$\left|\frac{f(x) - f(y)}{x - y}\right| < |x - y|^2$$

$$\lim_{y \to x} \left|\frac{f(x) - f(y)}{x - y}\right| \le \lim_{y \to x} |x - y|^2$$

$$\therefore \quad |f'(x)| \le 0$$

$$\Rightarrow \quad f'(x) = 0$$

So, $f(x)$ is a constant function.

6. (a) (a) We have, $f(x) = x^{1/3}$

Its domain is R and it is continuous everywhere, but $f'(x) = \frac{1}{3} x^{-2/3}$ which is not defined at $x = 0$.

$f(x)$ is not differentiable at $x = 0$.

(b) We have, $f(x) = \frac{|x|}{x} = \begin{cases} 1, & \text{if } x > 0 \\ -1, & \text{if } x < 0 \end{cases}$

It domain is $x \ne 0$,

which is continuous and differentiable at $x = 0$.

(c) We have, $f(x) = e^{-x}$ is continuous and differentiable in its domain.

(d) We have, $f(x) = \tan x$ is continuous and differentiable in its domain.

7. (c) RHL at $x = 0$,

$$= \lim_{h \to 0} h + \{h\} + h \sin\{h\}$$

$$= \lim_{h \to 0} h + h + h \sin h = 0$$

LHL at $x = 0$,

$$= \lim_{h \to 0} (-h) + \{-h\} - h \cdot \sin\{-h\}$$

$$= \lim_{h \to 0} -h + 1 - h - h \cdot \sin(1-h) = 1$$

Since, RHL $\neq$ LHL

$\therefore$ Neither continuous nor differentiable at $x = 0$.

8. (c) We have, $f(x) = x^3$ and $g(x) = |x|$

$\therefore$ $gof(x) = |f(x)| = |x^3|$

and $fog(x) = [g(x)]^3 = |x|^3$

Clearly, at $x = 0$, both are differentiable i.e. derivable.

9. (c) At $x = 0$

$$Lf'(0) = \frac{f(0-h) - f(0)}{-h}$$

$$= \lim_{h \to 0} \frac{-h\sin\left(-\frac{1}{h}\right) - 0}{-h}$$

$$= \lim_{h \to 0} -\sin\left(\frac{1}{h}\right)$$

which is not unique.
Hence, $f(x)$ is not differentiable at $x = 0$.

Now, $$Lg'(0) = \lim_{h \to 0} \frac{f(0-h) - f(0)}{-h}$$

$$= \lim_{h \to 0} \frac{h^2 \sin\left(-\frac{1}{h}\right) - 0}{-h}$$

$$= \lim_{h \to 0} h\sin\left(\frac{1}{h}\right) = 0 \times (\text{Finite}) = 0$$

and $$Rg'(0) = \lim_{h \to 0} \frac{f(0+h) - f(0)}{h}$$

$$= \lim_{h \to 0} \frac{h^2 \sin\left(\frac{1}{h}\right) - 0}{h}$$

$$= \lim_{h \to 0} h\sin\frac{1}{h}$$

$$= 0 \times (\text{Finite}) = 0$$

$\therefore$ $g(x)$ is differentiable at $x = 0$ and $h(x)$ is also differentiable at $x = 0$.

10. (b)

(a) Let take an example.

$f(x) = \sin x$ is differentiable at $x = \pi$, but $|\sin x|$ is not differentiable at $x = \pi$.

Hence, option (a) is incorrect.

(b) True, because $f(x) = \sin x$ is continuous at $x = a$, then $f(x) = |\sin x|$ is also continuous at $x = a$.

11. (d) We have,

$$f(x) = x[x] = \begin{cases} -x & ,\text{for } -1 \le x < 0 \\ 0 & ,\text{for } 0 \le x < 1 \\ x & ,\text{for } 1 \le x < 2 \\ 2x & ,\text{for } 2 \le x < 3 \\ 3x & ,\text{for } x = 3 \end{cases}$$

which is discontinuous at $x = 0, 1, 2$ and 3.

$$f'(x) = \begin{cases} -1 & ,\text{for } -1 \le x < 0 \\ 0 & ,\text{for } 0 \le x < 1 \\ 1 & ,\text{for } 1 \le x < 2 \\ 2 & ,\text{for } 2 \le x < 3 \\ 3 & ,\text{for } x = 3 \end{cases}$$

Clerly, $f(x)$ is not differentiable at $x = 0, 1, 2$ and 3.

12. (d) $$f'(5) = \lim_{h \to 0} \frac{f(5+h) - f(5)}{h}$$

$$= \lim_{h \to 0} \frac{f(5) \cdot f(h) - f(5)}{h}$$

$$= f(5) \cdot \lim_{h \to 0} \frac{f(h) - 1}{h}$$

which is $\frac{0}{0}$ form.

[put $x = y = 0$ in given relation $f(0) = f(0) - f(0) \Rightarrow f(0) = 1$]

$$\therefore \quad f'(5) = f(5) \lim_{h \to 0} f'(h)$$

$$= f(5) \cdot f'(0)$$

$$= 2 \cdot 3 = 6$$

13. (c) We have, $f(x)$ is differentiable and $\lim_{h \to 0} \frac{f(1+h)}{h}$ is 5, when $f(1) = 0$.

$$\therefore \quad \lim_{h \to 0} \frac{f'(1+h)}{1} = f'(1) = 5$$

14. (b) We have, $f(0) = 0$ and $|f(x) - f(y)| \le (x - y)^2$

On taking $\lim x \to y$ on both sides, we get

$$\lim_{x \to y} \frac{|f(x) - f(y)|}{|x - y|} \le \lim_{x \to y} |x - y|$$

or $$\lim_{x \to y} \left|\frac{f(x) - f(y)}{x - y}\right| \le \lim_{x \to y} |x - y|$$

$|f'(x)| \le 0$ which is not negative.

$\therefore |f'(x)| = 0$

$f(x)$ is constant function.

$\therefore f(1) = f(0) = 0$

15. (b) We have, $f(x) = \frac{x}{1 + |x|}$ its domain is R.

or $$f(x) = \begin{cases} \frac{x}{1+x}, & \text{for } x \ge 0 \\ \frac{x}{1-x}, & \text{for } x < 0 \end{cases}$$

$$\Rightarrow \quad f'(x) = \begin{cases} \frac{1}{(x+1)^2}, & x > 0 \\ \frac{1}{(1-x)^2}, & x < 0 \end{cases}$$

Clearly, $f'(x)$ is continuous at $x = 0$.

$\therefore$ $f(x)$ is differentiable everywhere.

16. (d) We have,

$$f(x) = \begin{cases} \frac{1}{2}(-x-1), & \text{if } x < -1 \\ \tan^{-1} x, & \text{if } -1 \le x \le 1 \\ \frac{1}{2}(x-1), & \text{if } x > 1 \end{cases}$$

$f(x)$ is discontinuous at $x = -1$ and $x = 1$

$\therefore$ Domain of $f'(x)$ is $R - \{-1, 1\}$.

17. (c) We have,

$$f(1) = 3 \text{ and } f'(1) = 6$$

Now, $$\lim_{x \to 0} \left(\frac{f(1+x)}{f(1)} \right)^{1/x} \qquad [1^{\infty} \text{ form}]$$

$\therefore$ $$e^{\lim_{x \to 0} \frac{f(1+x) - f(1)}{f(1)} \times \frac{1}{x}}$$

or $$e^{\frac{1}{f(1)} \lim_{x \to 0} \frac{f'(1+x) - 0}{1}} = e^{1/3 \cdot f'(1)} = e^{1/3 \times 6} = e^2$$

18. (a,b) We have,

$$f(x) = \begin{cases} 2x + 3, & \text{for } -3 \le x < -2 \\ x + 1, & \text{for } -2 \le x < 0 \\ x + 2, & \text{for } 0 \le x \le 1 \end{cases}$$

We check differentiability at $x = -2$

LHD = 2 and RHD = + 1

$\therefore$ $f(x)$ is not differentiable not continuous at $x = 0$.

$\therefore$ Also, $f(x)$ is not differentiable at $x = 0$.

19. (a,d) We have, $f(x) = \cos \pi (|x| + [x])$

Check continuity at $x = \frac{1}{2}$,

$$\lim_{x \to 1/2} \cos \pi \left(|x| + \left[\frac{1}{2} \right] \right) = \lim_{x \to 1/2} \cos \pi x$$

$$= \cos \frac{\pi}{2} = 0, \text{ which is finite.}$$

So, it is continuous

$\therefore$ Continuity at $x = 0$,

$$\text{LHL} = \lim_{x \to 0^-} f(x) = \lim_{h \to 0} f(0 - h)$$

$$= \lim_{h \to 0} \cos \pi(|0 - h| + [-h])$$

$$= \lim_{h \to 0} \cos \pi (h - 1)$$

$$= \cos(-\pi) = -1$$

$$\text{RHL} = \lim_{h \to 0} f(0 + h)$$

$$= \lim_{h \to 0} \cos \pi (h + 0)$$

$$= \cos 0 = 1$$

$\therefore$ It is discontinuous at $x = 0$.

We know that $[x]$ is not ciffrentiable at x = Integer

$\therefore$ Option (c) is incorrect.

$\therefore$ $f(x) = \cos \pi (|x| + 0) = \cos \pi |x| = \cos \pi x$

Hence, $f(x)$ is differentiable in (0, 1).

20. (a,b,c) We have,

$$f(x) = |x + 1|(|x| + |x - 1|)$$

$$f(x) = \begin{cases} -(x+1)(-x-x+1); & -2 \le x < -1 \\ (x+1)(-x-x+1); & -1 \le x < 0 \\ (x+1)(x-x+1); & 0 \le x < 1 \\ (x+1)(x+x-1); & 1 \le x < 2 \end{cases}$$

$$= \begin{cases} -(x+1)(1-2x); & -2 \le x < -1 \\ (x+1)(1-2x); & -1 \le x < 0 \\ x+1; & 0 \le x < 1 \\ (x+1)(2x-1); & 1 \le x \le 2 \end{cases}$$

$$= \begin{cases} 2x^2 + x - 1; & -2 \le x < -1 \\ -2x^2 - x + 1; & -1 \le x < 0 \\ x + 1; & 0 \le x < 1 \\ 2x^2 + x - 1; & 1 \le x \le 2 \end{cases}$$

Now, $$f'(x) = \begin{cases} 4x + 1; & -2 \le x < -1 \\ -4x - 1 & -1 \le x < 0 \\ 1; & 0 \le x < 1 \\ 4x + 1; & 1 \le x \le 2 \end{cases}$$

Clearly, $f(x)$ is not differentiable at $x = -1, 0$ and 1.

21. (a,c,d) We have,

$$h(x) = \min\{x, x^2\}$$

$\therefore$ $$h(x) = \begin{cases} x, & \text{if } x < 0 \\ x^2, & \text{if } 0 \le x < 1 \\ x, & \text{if } x \ge 1 \end{cases}$$

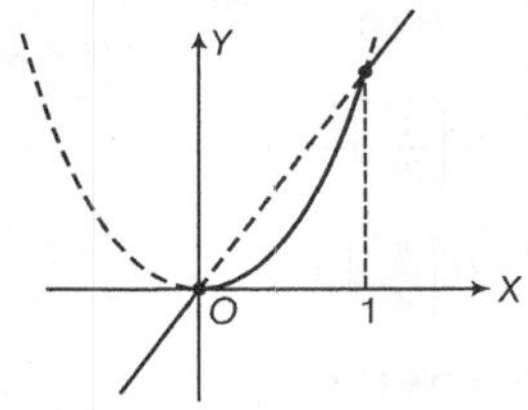

Clearly, $h(x)$ is continuous for all $x \in R$.

$$h'(x) = \begin{cases} 1, & \text{if } x < 0 \\ 2x, & \text{if } 0 \le x < 1 \\ 1, & \text{if } x \ge 1 \end{cases}$$

$\therefore$ $h'(x) = 1$ for all $x > 1$

and $h(x)$ is not differentiable at $x = 0$ and 1.

22. (a,b) We have, $f(x) = 1 + [\cos x]x$

We know that in $0 < x \le \frac{\pi}{2}$, $[\cos x] = 0$

$\therefore$ $f(x) = 1$, which is a constant function.

$\therefore$ $f(x)$ is continuous and differentiable everywhere.

23. (d) We have, for $-1 < x < 1$

$\Rightarrow$ $$0 \le x \sin \pi x \le \frac{1}{2}$$

Also, $x \sin \pi x$ becomes negative and numerically less than 1, when x is slightly greater than 1 and so by definition of $[x]$.

$f(x) = [x \sin \pi x] = -1$, when $1 < x < 1 + h$.

Thus, $f(x)$ is constant and equal to 0 in the closed internal $[-1, 1]$ and so $f(x)$ is continuous and differentiable in the open interval $(-1, 1)$.

At $x = 1$, $f(x)$ is discontinuous, since

$$\lim_{h \to 0} (1 - h) = 0$$

and $$\lim_{h \to 0} (1 + h) = -1$$

$\therefore$ $f(x)$ is not differentiable at $x = 1$.

24. (d)

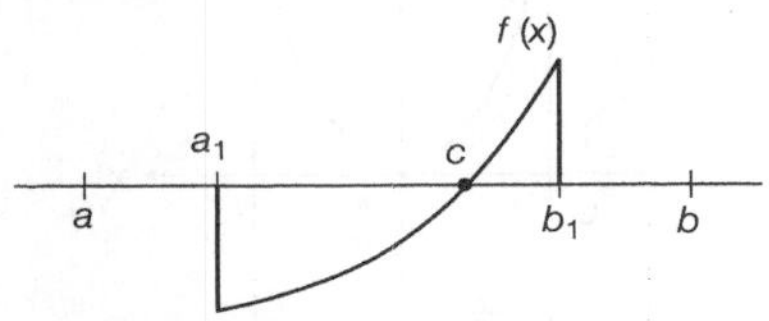

Statement I and Statement II are incorrect.

Let $f(x) = \frac{1}{x}$, $0 < x < 1$

Statement III is correct. Apply mean value theorem to f on the closed interval $[a, b]$.

25. (a,d) $H(x) = \begin{cases} \min\{f(t) : 0 \le t \le x\}, & \text{for } 0 \le x \le \pi/2 \\ \frac{\pi}{2} - x, & \text{for } \pi/2 < x \le 3 \end{cases}$

$$= \begin{cases} \cos x, & \text{for } 0 \le x \le \pi/2 \\ \frac{\pi}{2} - x, & \text{for } \pi/2 < x \le 3 \end{cases}$$

[as, $\min\{f(t) : 0 \le t \le x\}$ for $0 \le x \le \frac{\pi}{2}$

$= \cos x, 0 \le x \le \frac{\pi}{2}$, as $\cos x$ is decreasing]

$\therefore H(x)$ is continuous at $x = \frac{\pi}{2}$.

$$H'(x) = \begin{cases} -\sin x, & 0 \le x \le \pi/2 \\ -1, & \pi/2 < x \le 3 \end{cases}$$

$$H'\left(\frac{\pi}{2}^+\right) = -1$$

$$H'\left(\frac{\pi}{2}^-\right) = -1$$

$\therefore H(x)$ is differentiable at $x = \frac{\pi}{2}$.

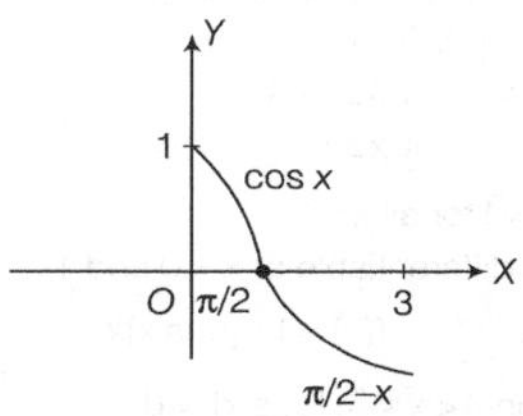

Also, $H(x)$ is maximum at $x = 0$.

$\Rightarrow$ Maximum value of $H(x) = 1$

26. (b,c) We have,

$$f(x+y) = f(x) + f(y)$$

Clearly, $f(x) = Kx$ satisfy the above condition and which is differentiable at $x = 0$.

We see that $f(x)$ continuous everywhere $f'(x) = K$, which is also continuous everywhere.

27. (c) (i) We have,

$$f(x) = \frac{\tan x + \cot x}{2} - \left|\frac{\tan x - \cot x}{2}\right|$$

$$= \begin{cases} \tan x, \text{for } 0 < x < \frac{\pi}{4} \\ \cot x, \text{for } \frac{\pi}{4} < x < \frac{\pi}{2} \end{cases}$$

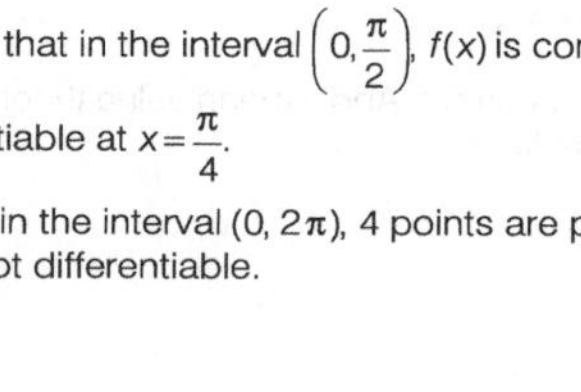

We see that in the interval $\left(0, \frac{\pi}{2}\right)$, $f(x)$ is continuous but not differentiable at $x = \frac{\pi}{4}$.

Hence, in the interval $(0, 2\pi)$, 4 points are present at which $f(x)$ is not differentiable.

(ii)

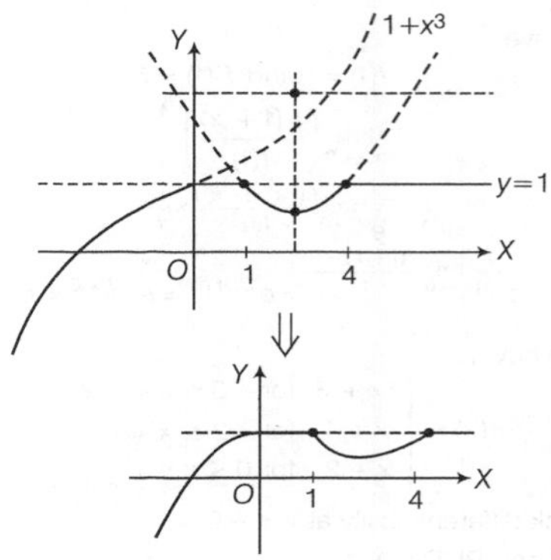

$$f(x) = \begin{cases} 1 + x^3, & \text{if } x < 0 \\ 1, & \text{if } 0 \le x < 1 \\ x^2 - 3x + 3, & \text{if } 1 \le x < 4 \\ 1, & \text{if } x \ge 4 \end{cases}$$

There is two sharp points, hence it is not differentiable at two points.

(iii) We have, $f(x) = (x+4)^{1/3}$

$$f'(x) = -\frac{1}{3}(x+4)^{-2/3} = -\frac{1}{3(x+4)^{2/3}}$$

which in not defined on $x = -4$.

Hence, $f(x)$ is not differentiable at $x = -4$.

(iv) $f(x) = \begin{cases} \frac{-\pi}{2}\log\left(\frac{2x}{\pi}\right) + \frac{\pi}{2}; & \text{if } 0 < x \le \pi/2 \\ \sin^{-1}(\sin x); & \text{if } \frac{\pi}{2} < x < 3\pi/2 \end{cases}$

or $f(x) = \begin{cases} \frac{-\pi}{2}\log\frac{2x}{\pi} + \frac{\pi}{2}, & \text{if } 0 < x \le \pi/2 \\ \pi - x, & \text{if } \frac{\pi}{2} < x < 3\pi/2 \end{cases}$

$$f'(x) = \begin{cases} \frac{-\pi}{2x}, & \text{if } 0 < x \le \frac{\pi}{2} \\ -1, & \text{if } \frac{\pi}{2} < x < \frac{3\pi}{2} \end{cases}$$

Clearly, $f'(x)$ is continuous at $x = \frac{\pi}{2}$.

$\therefore f(x)$ is differentiable everywhere.

Hence, (i) $\to$(r), (ii)$\to$(p), (iii)$\to$(s), (iv)$\to$(q)

Explanations for Q. Nos. (28-30)

We have, $f(x+h) = f(x) \cdot f(h)$

We know that, $f(x) = a^{Kx}$

$$f'(x) = a^{Kx} \cdot K \cdot \log_e a$$

$$f'(0) = K \cdot \log_e a = -1$$

$\therefore$ $K = -1$ and $a = e$

$$f(-x) = a^{Kx} = \frac{1}{a^{Kx}} = \frac{1}{f(x)}$$

We see that $f(x) = e^{-x}$ satisfying the above condition.

$\therefore$ Range of $f(x) = R^+$

Now, the range of $|f(x)|$ is $(0,1)|$ for $x > 0$

We have, $f(x) > 0$

So, the range is (0, 1].

Clearly, $f(x) = e^{-x}$ is strictly decreasing function .

28. (c) **29.** (c) **30.** (d)

Revisal Problems (JEE Main)

1. (d) We know that differentiable function is always continuous, hence first check continuity at $x = 1$.

$$\text{LHL} = 1$$
$$\text{RHL} = 1 + b + c$$
$$\because \quad 1 + b + c = 1$$
$$b + c = 0 \qquad \ldots\text{(i)}$$

Now, $$f'(x) = \begin{cases} 1; & x \le 1 \\ 2x + b; & x > 1 \end{cases}$$

$$\because \quad \text{LHD} = 1$$
and $$\text{RHD} = 2 + b$$
$$\Rightarrow \quad b + 2 = 1$$
$$\Rightarrow \quad b = -1$$
$$\therefore \quad c = 1$$

2. (d) We know that,

$$[x^2] = \begin{cases} 0;\, 0 \le x^2 < 1 \Rightarrow -1 < x < 1 \\ 1;\, 1 \le x^2 < 2 \Rightarrow -\sqrt{2} < x \le -1 \text{ or } 1 \le x < \sqrt{2} \\ 2;\, 2 \le x^2 < 3 \Rightarrow -\sqrt{3} < x \le -\sqrt{2} \text{ or } \sqrt{2} \le x < \sqrt{3} \\ 3;\, 3 \le x^2 < 4 \Rightarrow -2 < x \le -\sqrt{3} \text{ or } \sqrt{3} \le x < 2 \\ 4;\, 4 \le x^2 < 5 \Rightarrow -\sqrt{5} < x \le -2 \text{ or } 2 \le x < \sqrt{5} \\ 5;\, 5 \le x^2 < 6 \Rightarrow -\sqrt{6} < x \le -\sqrt{5} \text{ or } \sqrt{5} \le x < \sqrt{6} \\ 6;\, 6 \le x^2 < 7 \Rightarrow -\sqrt{7} < x \le -\sqrt{6} \text{ or } \sqrt{6} \le x < \sqrt{7} \\ 7;\, 7 \le x^2 < 8 \Rightarrow -\sqrt{8} < x \le -\sqrt{7} \text{ or } \sqrt{7} \le x < \sqrt{8} \\ 8;\, 8 \le x^2 < 9 \Rightarrow -3 < x \le -\sqrt{8} \text{ or } \sqrt{8} \le x < 3 \end{cases}$$

We see that there is 7 points in (1, 3), where $[x^2]$ is not differentiable.

$\because q^{[x^2]}$ is not differentiable at 7 points.

3. (b) We have, $f(x) = [x^2 - 3]$

$$= \begin{cases} 0;\, 0 \le x^2 - 3 < 1 \Rightarrow 3 \le x^2 < 4 \Rightarrow \sqrt{3} \le x < 2 \\ -1;\, -1 \le x^2 - 3 < 0 \Rightarrow 2 \le x^2 < 3 \Rightarrow \sqrt{2} \le x < \sqrt{3} \\ -2;\, -2 \le x^2 - 3 < -1 \Rightarrow 1 \le x^2 < 2 \Rightarrow 1 \le x < \sqrt{2} \end{cases}$$

We see that, in $x \in (1, 2)$ there are two points, where $f(x)$ is not differentiable.

By graph

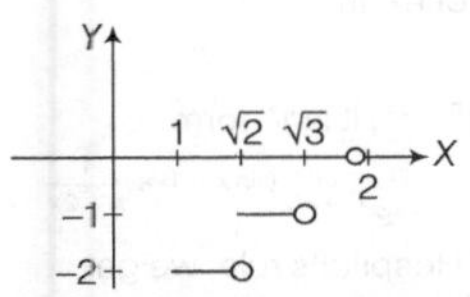

$x = \sqrt{2}$ and $x = \sqrt{3}$, where $f(x)$ is not differentiable.

4. (a) We have, $f(x) = \text{degree of } (u^{x^2} + u^2 + 2u + 3)$

$$\Rightarrow \quad f(x) = \begin{cases} x^2, & x > \sqrt{2} \\ 2, & x \le \sqrt{2} \end{cases}$$

$$\therefore \quad \lim_{x \to \sqrt{2}^-} f(x) = 2 = f(2)$$

and $$\lim_{x \to \sqrt{2}^+} f(x) = \lim_{x \to \sqrt{2}} x^2 = (\sqrt{2})^2 = 2$$

$$\therefore \quad \lim_{x \to \sqrt{2}^-} f(x) = \lim_{x \to \sqrt{2}^+} f(x) = f(\sqrt{2})$$

So, $f(x)$ is continuous at $x = \sqrt{2}$.

Now, $$Lf'(\sqrt{2}) = \left(\frac{d}{dx}(2)\right)_{\text{at } x = \sqrt{2}} = 0$$

$$Rf'(\sqrt{2}) = \left[\frac{d}{dx}(x^2)\right]_{\text{at } x = 2}$$
$$= 2\sqrt{2}$$

Clearly, $$Lf'(\sqrt{2}) \ne Rf'(\sqrt{2})$$

$\therefore f(x)$ is not differentiable at $x = \sqrt{2}$.

5. (b) Here, $$f'(x) = \lim_{h \to 0} \frac{f(x + h) - f(x)}{h}$$
$$= \lim_{h \to 0} \frac{f(x) \cdot f(h) - f(x)}{h} = f(x) \cdot \lim_{h \to 0} \frac{f(h) - 1}{h} = f(x) \cdot f'(0)$$

Now, $$\frac{f'(x)}{f(x)} = \log 2 \qquad [\because f'(0) = \log 2]$$

Integrating both sides, w.r.t. x, we get

$$\log|f(x)| = (\log 2) \cdot x + C \qquad [\because f(0) = 1]$$

Put $$x = 0$$
$$\log|1| = 0 + C$$
$$\Rightarrow \quad C = 0$$
$$\therefore \quad \log|f(x)| = x \cdot \log 2$$
or $$\log|f(x)| = \log(2^x)$$
$$\Rightarrow \quad f(x) = 2^x$$

6. (b) Here, $$f'(x) = \lim_{h \to 0} \frac{f(x + h) - f(x)}{h} = f(x) \cdot f'(0)$$

$$\Rightarrow \quad f'(x) = 2f(x) \text{ or } \int \frac{f'(x)}{f(x)} dx = 2\int dx$$

$$\Rightarrow \quad \log|f(x)| = 2x + c$$
$$\therefore \quad f(x) = e^{2x + c} = e^c \cdot e^{2x} = A \cdot e^{2x}$$

7. (d) We have, $f(x) = |x|$ and $g(x) = [x]$

$$fog(x) = |g(x)| = |[x]|$$

Sketching the graph of $fog(x)$,

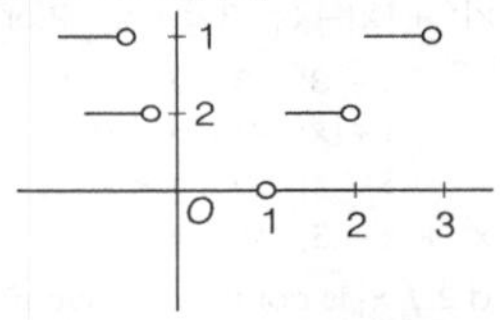

We see that, at $x = 2$ $fog(x)$ is not differentiable.

Hence, $(fog)'(2)$ does not exist.

8. (d) We have, $f(x) = \cos x$ and $g(x) = [x + 1]$

$$gof(x) = [f(x) + 1] = [\cos x + 1]$$
$$= 1 + [\cos x]$$

Sketching the graph

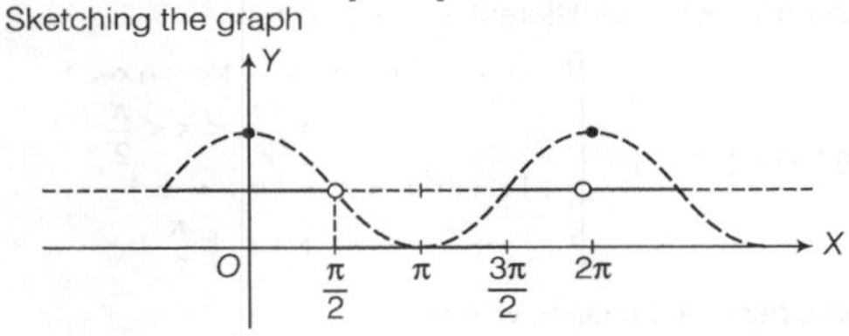

We see that at $x = \frac{\pi}{2}$, $gof(x)$ is not differentiable.

Hence, $(gof)'\left(\frac{\pi}{2}\right)$ does not exist.

9. (a) We have, $$f(x) = x^5 \text{Sgn}(x) = \begin{cases} x^5, & x > 0 \\ 0, & x = 0 \\ -x^5, & x < 0 \end{cases}$$

At $x = 0$, $\quad$ LHL = RHL = 0 = $f(0)$

So, $f(x)$ is continuous everywhere.

$$f'(x) = \begin{cases} 5x^4; & x > 0 \\ 0; & x = 0 \\ -5x^4; & x < 0 \end{cases}$$

$f'(x)$ is also continuous at $x = 0$, since $f(x)$ is differentiable everywhere.

10. (a) Let $f(x)$ be a periodic function with period T.

Then, $f(x+T) = f(x)$ for all n

Now, $f'(x) = \lim_{h \to 0} \frac{f(x+h) - f(x)}{h}$

$\therefore$ $f'(x+T) = \lim_{h \to 0} \frac{f(x+T+h) - f(x+T)}{h}$

$\Rightarrow$ $f'(x+T) = \lim_{h \to 0} \frac{f(x+h) - f(x)}{h} = f'(x)$ for all x

Similarly, $f''(x+T) = f''(x)$ for all x.

Hence, f' and f'' are also periodic with same period.

11. (a) $f(x) = \begin{cases} 0, & 0 \le x < 1 \\ x, & 1 \le x < 2 \\ 2(x-1), & 2 \le x < 3 \end{cases}$

$f(x)$ is not continuous at $x = 1$ but continuous at $x = 2$.

$$f'(x) = \begin{cases} 0, & 0 \le x < 1 \\ 1, & 1 \le x < 2 \\ 2, & 2 \le x < 3 \end{cases}$$

Clearly, $f(x)$ is not differentiable at $x = 1, 2$.

$\therefore$ Both $f'(1)$ and $f'(2)$ do not exist.

12. (b) $f(|x|) = \begin{cases} 4, & -3 < |x| < -1 \\ 5 + |x|, & -1 \le |x| < 0 \\ 5 - |x|, & 0 \le |x| < 2 \\ |x|^2 + |x| - 3, & 2 \le |x| < 3 \end{cases}$

$\Rightarrow f(|x|) = \begin{cases} 5 - |x|; & -2 < x \le 0 \text{ or } 0 \le x < 2 \\ |x|^2 + |x| - 3; & -3 < x \le -2 \text{ or } 2 \le x < 3 \end{cases}$

$\Rightarrow f(|x|) = \begin{cases} x^2 - x - 3; & -3 < x \le -2 \\ 5 + x; & -2 < x \le 0 \\ 5 - x; & 0 \le x < 2 \\ x^2 + x - 3; & 2 \le x < 3 \end{cases}$

At $x = -2$, 0 and 2, $f|x|$ is continuous because LHL = RHL.

Now, $f'(|x|) = \begin{cases} 2x - 1; & -3 < x \le -2 \\ +1; & -2 < x \le 0 \\ -1; & 0 \le x < 2 \\ 2x + 1; & 2 \le x < 3 \end{cases}$

Clearly, $f'(|x|) = 0$ does not continuous at $x = -2$, 0 and 2.

Hence, $f(|x|)$ is not differentiable in $(-3, 3)$.

13. (d) $f(x) = [\sin^2 x] = \begin{cases} 0; 0 \le \sin^2 x < 1 \Rightarrow -1 < \sin x < 1 \\ \qquad \Rightarrow \frac{-\pi}{2} < x < \frac{\pi}{2} \\ 1; 1 \le \sin^2 x < 2 \Rightarrow \sin x = \pm 1 \\ \qquad \Rightarrow x = \pm \frac{\pi}{2} \end{cases}$

$f(x)$ is periodic function, with period π.

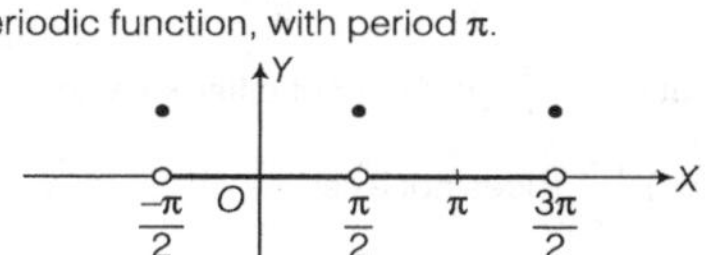

We see that $f(x)$ is discontinuous and not differentiable at

$$x = (2n+1)\frac{\pi}{2}$$

$f(x)$ is not constant function.

14. (a) We have, $\lim_{h \to 0} \frac{f(2h + 2 + h^2) - f(2)}{f(h - h^2 + 1) - f(1)}$

It is $\frac{0}{0}$ form, hence apply L' Hospital's rule,

$$\lim_{h \to 0} \frac{f'(2h + 2 + h^2)(2 + 2h)}{f'(h - h^2 + 1)(1 - 2h)} = \frac{f'(2) \cdot 2}{f'(1)} = \frac{2 \cdot 6}{4} = \frac{12}{4} = 3$$

15. (d) $f(x) = \begin{cases} \log_e 3; & 3 \le x < 4 \\ \log_e 4; & 4 \le x < 5 \\ \log_e x; & 5 \le x < 6 \end{cases}$

Clearly, $f(x)$ is discontinuous at $x = 4$ and 5.

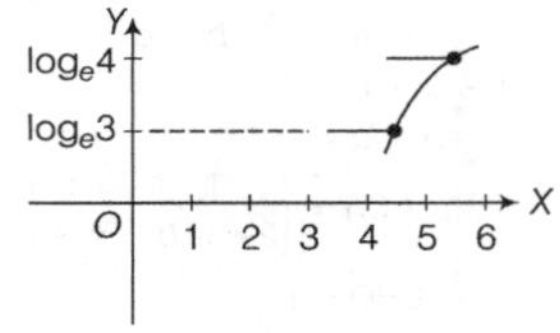

By graph, $f(x)$ is not differentiable at $x = 4$ and 5.

16. (d) We have, $f(x) = \text{Sgn}(x)$

$g(x) = fof(x) = \text{Sgn}(\text{Sgn}(x))$

$\therefore$ $g(x) = \begin{cases} 1, & \text{if Sgn}(x) > 0 \\ -1, & \text{if Sgn}(x) < 0 \\ 0, & \text{if Sgn } x = 0 \end{cases}$

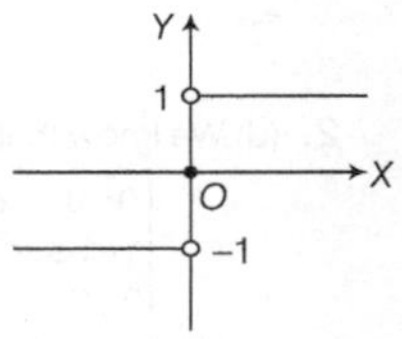

or $g(x) = \begin{cases} 1, & \text{if } x > 0 \\ -1, & \text{if } x < 0 \\ 0, & \text{if } x = 0 \end{cases}$

$\therefore g(x)$ is neither continuous nor differentiable.

17. (c) $h(x) = gof(x) = [f(x) + 1] = [\sin x + 1]$

$\therefore$ $h(x) = 1 + [\sin x]$

or $h(x) = \begin{cases} 1, & \text{if } 0 \le x < \pi/2 \\ 1, & \text{if } \pi/2 < x < \pi \end{cases}$

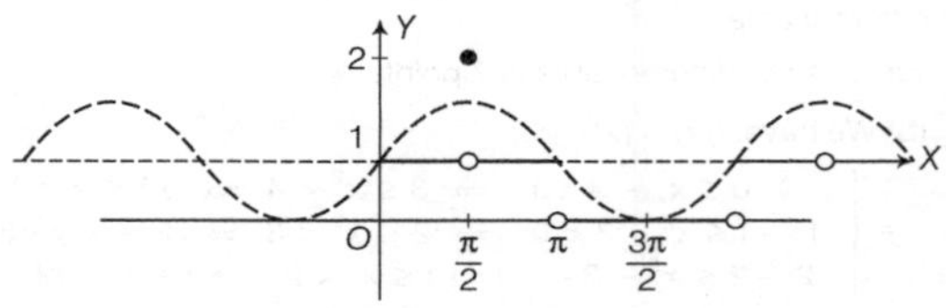

Clearly, $h(x)$ discontinuous at $x = \frac{\pi}{2}$.

$\therefore h'\left(\frac{\pi}{2}\right)$ does not exist.

18. (b) $\lim_{x \to \pi/2} (\sin x)^{\frac{1}{\pi - 2x}}$, it is 1^∞ form.

$\because$ $e^{\lim_{x \to \pi/2} (\sin x - 1) \times \frac{1}{\pi - 2x}}$

On applying L' Hospital's rule, we get

$$e^{\lim_{x \to \pi/2} \frac{\cos x}{-2}} = e^0 = 1$$

$\therefore$ $\lambda = 1$

19. (a) We have, $f(x) = |x - 2| = \begin{cases} x - 2, & \text{if } x \ge 2 \\ -x + 2, & \text{if } x < 2 \end{cases}$

$$g(x) = fof(x) = \begin{cases} f(x) - 2, & \text{if } f(x) \ge 2 \\ 2 - f(x), & \text{if } f(x) < 2 \end{cases}$$

$$g(x) = \begin{cases} x - 2 - 2; & x - 2 \ge 2; & x \ge 2 \\ 2 - x + 2; & x - 2 < 2; & x \ge 2 \\ 2 - x - 2; & 2 - x \ge 2; & x < 2 \\ 2 - 2 + x; & 2 - x < 2; & x < 2 \end{cases}$$

$$g(x) = \begin{cases} x - 4; & x \ge 4; x \ge 2 & \Rightarrow & x \ge 4 \\ 4 - x; & x < 4; x \ge 2 & \Rightarrow & 2 < x < 4 \\ -x; & x < 0; x < 2 & \Rightarrow & x < 0 \\ x; & x > 0; x < 2 & \Rightarrow & 0 < x < 2 \end{cases}$$

or $x > 4$ $g'(x) = x - 4$

$\because$ $g'(x) = 1$

20. (a) We have, $f : [0, 1] \to [0, 1]$

$f(x)$ is continuous and domain and range is same.

$\because f(x)$ is identical function.

$\therefore f(x) = x$ for atleast one $x \in (0, 1)$.

21. (c) As $f(x)$ is continuous in $[1, 3]$.

$\therefore f(x)$ will attain all values between $f(1)$ and $f(3)$.

As $f(x)$ takes rational values for all x and there are innumerable irrational values between $f(1)$ and $f(3)$, which implies that $f(x)$ can take rational values for all x, if $f(x)$ has a constant rational values at all points between $x = 1$ and $x = 3$.

So, $\quad f(2) = f(4) = 10$

22. (a) We have, $f(x) = (-1)^{[x^3]}$

(a) Since, x^3 is integer when $x = n^{1/3}; n \in z$ and at integer $[x]$ is discontinuous.

$\because f(x)$ is discontinuous at $x = n^{1/3}$; $n \in Z$.

(b) $f\left(\frac{3}{2}\right) = (-1)^{\left[\frac{27}{8}\right]} = (-1)^3 = -1$

(c) $f'(x) = 0$ but not differentiable at $x = 0$ in the interval $(-1, 1)$.

23. (d) $f(x) = [n + p\sin x]$

$= n + [p\sin x]$

$f(x)$ is not differentiable at those points, where $p\sin x$ is an integer.

$p\sin x$ is an integer of $\sin x = 1, -1$ and $\frac{x}{p}$

i.e. $x = \frac{\pi}{2}, \frac{-\pi}{2}, \sin^{-1}\frac{r}{p}, \pi - \sin^{-1}\frac{r}{p}$

where, $\quad 0 \le r \le p - 1$

But $\quad x = \frac{-\pi}{2}, 0$

$\therefore$ Function is not differentiable at $x = \frac{\pi}{2}$,

$\sin^{-1}\frac{r}{p}, \pi - \sin^{-1}\frac{r}{p}$, where $0 < r < p - 1$

So, the required number of points are

$$1 + 2(p - 1) = 2p - 1$$

24. (d) We have, $f(x) = x + \tan x$

$$fog(x) = g(x) + \tan[g(x)]$$

$$\Rightarrow \quad x = g(x) + \tan[g(x)]$$

$$1 = g'(x) + \frac{1}{1 + [g(x)]^2} \cdot g'(x)$$

$$g'(x) = \frac{1}{1 + \sec^2[g(x)]}$$

or $\quad g'(x) = \frac{1}{2 + \tan^2[g(x)]}$

$$g'(x) = \frac{1}{2 + [x - g(x)]^2}$$

25. (c) We have, $f(x) = \sin\{\pi(x - [x]\}$ in $\left(-\frac{\pi}{2}, \frac{\pi}{2}\right)$.

Since, $f(x)$ is not differentiable at those point, where $x - [x]$ is not differentiable.

i.e. x is an integer in the interval $\left(-\frac{\pi}{2}, \frac{\pi}{2}\right)$.

$x = -1, 0, 1$ are integers in the interval $\left(-\frac{\pi}{2}, \frac{\pi}{2}\right)$.

26. (a) We have, $f(x + y) = f(x) + 2y^2 + kxy \quad \ldots$(i)

Putting $x = 1$ and $y = 1$ in Eq. (i), we get

$$f(2) = f(1) + 2 + k$$

$$8 = 2 + 2 + k \Rightarrow k = 4$$

Now, differentiating Eq. (i) w.r.t. x, treating y constant, we get

$$f'(x + y) = f'(x) + ky \quad \ldots\text{(ii)}$$

Again differentiating Eq. (i) w.r.t. y, treating x constant, we get

$$f'(x + y) = 4y + kx \quad \ldots\text{(iii)}$$

Now, dividing Eqs. (ii) by (iii), we get

$$1 = \frac{f'(x) + ky}{4y + kx}$$

$$4y + 4x = f'(x) + 4y \quad \text{[putting } k = 4]$$

$$\therefore \quad f'(x) = 4x$$

$$\Rightarrow \quad f(x) = 2x^2 + C$$

Putting $x = 0$, we get $f(0) = C$

On putting $x = y = 0$ in Eq. (i), we get

$$f(0) = 0 \Rightarrow C = 0$$

$$\therefore \quad f(x) = 2x^2$$

27. (b) $f'(x) = \lim_{h \to 0} \frac{f(x + h) - f(x)}{h} = \lim_{h \to 0} \frac{f(x) \cdot f(h) - f(x)}{h}$

$$= f(x) \lim_{h \to 0} \frac{f(h) - 1}{h}$$

$$= f(x) \lim_{h \to 0} \frac{1 + hg(h) + h^2 g(h)\,\phi(h) - 1}{h}$$

$$= f(x) \lim_{h \to 0} \frac{g(h) + hg(h)\,\phi(h)}{1}$$

$$= f(x) \cdot g(0)$$

$$= a \cdot f(x)$$

28. (c) We have, $f'(x) = \lim_{h \to 0} \frac{f(x + h) - f(x)}{h}$

$$f'(x) = \lim_{h \to 0} \frac{f(x)\, f(h) - f(x)}{h} \quad [\because f(x + y) = f(x) \cdot f(y)]$$

$$= \lim_{h \to 0} \frac{f(x)\,[f(h) - 1]}{h}$$

$$f'(x) = f(x) \cdot \lim_{h \to 0} \frac{f(h) - 1}{h} \quad \ldots\text{(i)}$$

Now, $\quad f(x + y) = f(x) \cdot f(y)$

$\Rightarrow \quad f(x + 0) = f(x) \cdot f(0)$

$\Rightarrow \quad f(x) = f(x) \cdot f(0)$

$\Rightarrow \quad f(x)(1 - f(0)) = 0$

$\Rightarrow \quad f(x) = 0 \quad [\because f(0) \ne 1] \ldots$(ii)

From Eqs. (i) and (ii), we get

$$f'(x) = 0$$

29. (b) $f'(x) = \lim_{h \to 0} \frac{f(x + h) - f(x)}{h}$

$$= \lim_{h \to 0} \frac{f(x) + \lambda xh + 3x^2h^2 - f(x)}{h}$$

$$= \lim_{h \to 0} \lambda x + 3x^2 h$$

$$\therefore \quad f'(x) = \lambda x$$

Now, we have to find λ.

Let $x = 3$ and $y = 2$ in given relation, then

$$f(5) = f(3) + \lambda 6 + 3 \cdot 9 \cdot 4$$

$$52 = 4 + 6\lambda + 108$$

$$\Rightarrow \quad 6\lambda = -60$$

$$\Rightarrow \quad \lambda = -10$$

$$\therefore \quad f'(x) = -10x$$

30. (d) We have, $f\left(\frac{x}{y}\right) = \frac{f(x)}{f(y)}$

On differentiting w.r.t. x, treating y constant, we get

$$f'\left(\frac{x}{y}\right) \cdot \frac{1}{y} = \frac{f'(x)}{f(y)} \quad \ldots\text{(i)}$$

Again, differentinting w.r.t. y, treating x constant, we get

$$f'\left(\frac{x}{y}\right)\left(-\frac{x}{y^2}\right) = f(x) \cdot \left(-\frac{1}{[f(y)]^2}\right) f'(y) \quad \ldots\text{(ii)}$$

On dividing Eq. (i) by Eq. (ii), we get

$$-\frac{y}{x} = -\frac{f(y)\cdot f'(x)}{f(x)\cdot f'(y)} \quad \text{...(iii)}$$

$$\Rightarrow \quad \frac{yf'(y)}{f(y)} = \frac{xf'(x)}{f(x)} = k$$

$$\frac{f'(x)}{f(x)} = \frac{k}{x}$$

$$\because \quad f'(x) = \frac{kf(x)}{x} \quad \text{...(iv)}$$

Now, putting $x = y = 1$ in the given relation, we get $f(1) = 1$

Putting $x = 1$ in Eq. (iv), we get

$$f'(1) = \frac{kf(1)}{1}$$

$$2 = k$$

$$\because \quad f'(x) = \frac{2f(x)}{x}$$

31. (c) We have, $fog(x) = x$

On differentiating w.r.t. x, we get

$$f'og(x)\cdot g'(x) = 1$$

Put $x = a$, we get,

$$f'og(a)\cdot g'(a) = 1$$

$$\Rightarrow \quad f'(b)\cdot 2 = 1$$

$$\therefore \quad f'(b) = \frac{1}{2}$$

32. (b) We have, f and g are inverse functions.

$$\therefore \quad fog(x) = x$$

On differentiating w.r.t. x, we get

$$f'[g(x)]\cdot g'(x) = 1$$

$$\therefore \quad g'(x) = \frac{1}{f'(g(x))} \quad \left[\because f'(x) = \frac{1}{1+x^n}\right]$$

$$= \frac{1}{\dfrac{1}{1+[g(x)]^n}} = 1 + [g(x)]^n$$

$$\therefore \quad g'(x) = 1 + \{g(x)\}^n$$

33. (b) We have, $f(x+y) = 2f(x)\cdot f(y)$

On differentiating w.r.t. x, treating y constant, we get

$$f'(x+y) = 2f'(x)\cdot f(y) \quad \text{...(i)}$$

Again, differentiating w.r.t. y treating x constant, we get

$$f'(x+y) = 2f(x)\cdot f'(y) \quad \text{...(ii)}$$

On dividing Eq. (i) by Eq. (ii), we get

$$1 = \frac{f'(x)\cdot f(y)}{f(x)\, f'(y)}$$

$$\Rightarrow \quad \frac{f'(x)}{f'(x)} = \frac{f'(y)}{f(y)} = k$$

$$f'(x) = kf(x) \quad \text{...(iii)}$$

Put $x = 0$ in Eq. (iii), we get

$$f'(0) = kf(0) = \frac{k}{2} = 3$$

$$\Rightarrow \quad k = 6$$

$$\because \quad f'(x) = 6f(x)$$

$$\because \quad f'(4) = 6f(4) = 6 \times 2 = 12 \quad [\text{given, } f(4) = 2]$$

34. (a) We have, $f\left(\frac{x+y}{2}\right) = \frac{f(x)+f(y)}{2}$ ...(i)

On differentiating Eq. (i) w.r.t. x, treating y constant, we get

$$f'\left(\frac{x+y}{2}\right)\cdot\frac{1}{2} = \frac{1}{2}f'(x) \quad \text{...(ii)}$$

Again, differentiating Eq. (i) w.r.t. y treating x constant, we get

$$f'\left(\frac{x+y}{2}\right)\cdot\frac{1}{2} = \frac{1}{2}f'(y) \quad \text{...(iii)}$$

From Eqs. (ii) and (iii), we get

$$1 = \frac{f'(x)}{f'(y)}$$

$$\Rightarrow \quad f'(x) = f'(y) = k$$

$$\Rightarrow \quad f'(x) = k, \text{ which is constant.}$$

and $f'(0) = -1$

$$\therefore \quad f'(2) = -1$$

35. (c) We have, $f(x) = p[x] + qe^{-|x|} + r|x|^2$

$$\Rightarrow \quad f(x) = \begin{cases} -p + qe^{x} + rx^2; & x < 0 \\ 0 + qe^{-x} + rx^2; & x > 0 \end{cases}$$

Given $f(x)$ is differentiable at $x = 0$.

Hence, $f(x)$ must be continuous at $x = 0$.

At $x = 0$, LHL $= -p + q$ and RHL $= q$

$$\because \quad -p + q = q \Rightarrow p = 0$$

Now, $f'(x) = \begin{cases} qe^{x} + 2rx; & x < 0 \\ -qe^{-x} + 2rx; & x \geq 0 \end{cases}$

$$\Rightarrow \quad \text{LHD} = q \text{ and RHD} = -q$$

$$q = -q \Rightarrow q = 0$$

$$p = 0, q = 0 \text{ and } r \in R$$

36. (a) $f'(x) = \lim_{h \to 0} \frac{f(x+h) - f(x)}{h}$

$$= \lim_{h \to 0} \frac{f(x)\cdot f(h) - f(x)}{h}$$

$$= f(x)\cdot \lim_{h \to 0}\frac{f(h) - 1}{h} = f(x)\cdot \lim_{h \to 0}\frac{1 + hg(h)\log_e 2 - 1}{h}$$

$$= f(x)\cdot \lim_{h \to 0} g(h)\cdot \log_e 2$$

$$= f(x)\cdot \log_e 2\cdot 1$$

$$= \log_e 2^{f(x)}$$

37. (c) We have, $f_1(x) = x$ and $f_2(x) = \begin{cases} \sin\frac{1}{x}; & x \neq 0 \\ x; & x = 0 \end{cases}$

$$f(x) = \begin{cases} x\sin\frac{1}{x}; & x \neq 0 \\ 0; & x = 0 \end{cases}$$

$$\lim_{x \to 0} x\sin\frac{1}{x} = 0\cdot\sin(\infty) = 0\,(-1 \text{ to } 1) = 0$$

$\therefore f(x)$ is continuous, $\forall x \in R$.

Statement I is correct.

$f_1(x) = x$ is continuous everywhere, but $f_2(x) = \sin\frac{1}{x}$ is discontinuous at $x = 0$

Hence, Statement II is incorrect.

38. (b) We have, $f(x) = x - x^2$ and $g(x) = \{x\}$

Then, $f[g(x)] = g(x) - [g(x)]^2 = \{x\} - (\{x\})^2$

We check the continuity at $x = n;\ n \in Z$

At $x = n$,

$$\text{LHL} = \lim_{x \to n^-} f(x) = \lim_{h \to 0} f(n-h)$$

$$= \lim_{h \to 0} \{n-h\} - (\{n-h\})^2$$

$$= \lim_{h \to 0} 1 - h - (1-h)^2 = 0$$

$$\text{RHL} = \lim_{x \to n^+} f(x) = \lim_{h \to 0} f(n+h)$$

$$= \lim_{h \to 0} \{n+h\}^2 - \{n+h\}^2$$

$$= \lim_{h \to 0} h - h^2 = 0$$

$\because$ LHL = RHL

$\therefore$ Statement I is correct.

$f(0) = f(1) = 0$, $g(x) = \{x\}$ is a periodic function with period 1.

$\therefore$ Statement II is also correct.

39. (a) We have,

$$f(x) = |\cos|x|| + \cos^{-1}(\text{Sgn}\, x) + |\log_e x|$$

Since, $|\cos|x||$ is not differentiable at $x = \frac{\pi}{2}, \frac{3\pi}{2}$

$$\cos^{-1}(\text{Sgn}\, x) = \cos^{-1} 1 \text{ in } (0, 2\pi).$$

Hence, differentiable, $\forall x \in (0, 2\pi)$ and $|\log_e x|$ is not differentiable at $x = 1$.

$\because f(x)$ is not differentiable at 3 points in $(0, 2\pi)$.

Statement I is correct.

Statement II is also correct and correct explanation of Statement I.

40. (c) We have, $f(x) = |x| \sin x = \begin{cases} x \sin x; & x \geq 0 \\ -x \sin x; & x < 0 \end{cases}$

$$Lf'(0) = \lim_{x \to 0} \frac{x \sin x - 0}{x} = \lim_{x \to 0} \sin x = 0$$

$$Rf(0) = \lim_{x \to 0} \frac{-x \sin x - 0}{x} = \lim_{x \to 0} -\sin x = 0$$

$\therefore f(x)$ is differentiable at $x = 0$, but $|x|$ is not differentiable at $x = 0$ and $\sin x$ is differentiable at $x = 0$,

but $|x| \sin x$ is differentiable at $x = 0$

Hence. Statement I is correct but Statement II is incorrect.

Revisal Problems (JEE Advanced)

1. (c) Consider the function $h(x) = \max\{x, x^2\}$ at $x = 0$ and $x = 1$,

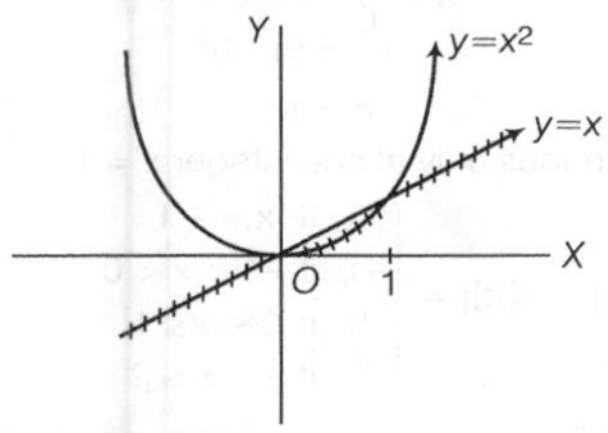

not differentiable at $x = 0, 1$.

Again, consider $h(x) = \max\{x^2, x^2\}$

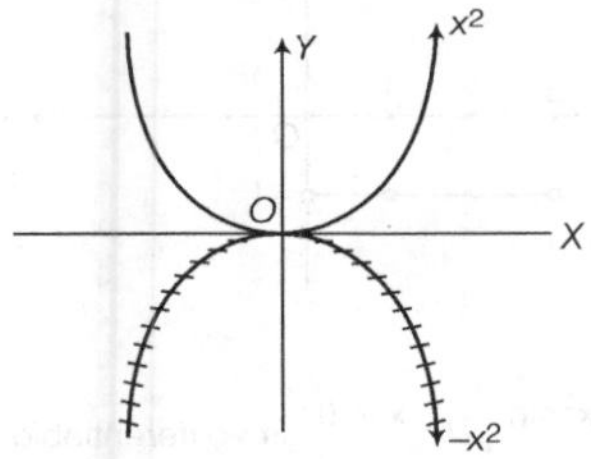

Clearly, differentiable at $x = 0$.

At $x = x_0$, may or may not be differentiable.

But when $f(x_0) \neq g(x_0)$, then always differentiable at $x = x_0$.

2. (a) Let $x = 2/3$, which is rational.

$$\Rightarrow \quad h(2/3) = 1/3$$

$$\lim_{t \to 0} h\left(\frac{2}{3} + t\right) = 0 \Rightarrow \text{ Discontinuous at } x \in Q$$

Let $x = \sqrt{2} \notin Q \Rightarrow h(\sqrt{2}) = 0$ and $\lim_{t \to 0} h(\sqrt{2} + t) = 0$

$\therefore$ Continuous for all irrational.

3. (d) $g(n + h) = f[\{n + h\}] = f(h) = \lim_{h \to 0} \frac{e^h - \cos 2h - h}{h^2}$

$$= \lim_{h \to 0} \frac{(e^h - 1) + (1 - \cos 2h) - h}{h^2}$$

$$= \lim_{h \to 0} \left(\frac{e^h - h - 1}{h^2}\right) + \left(\frac{1 - \cos 2h}{h^2}\right)$$

$$= 1/2 + 2 = 5/2$$

$$g(n - h) = f[1 - \{n - h\}] = f(1 - \{-h\})$$

$$f(h) = \lim_{h \to 0} \frac{e^h - \cos 2h - h}{h^2} = 5/2$$

$$g(n) = 5/2$$

$\therefore g(x)$ is continuous for all $x \in I$ and $g(x)$ is continuous for all $x \in R$.

4. (b) $h(x) = \begin{cases} \dfrac{2\cos x - \sin 2x}{(\pi - 2x)^2}, & x < \pi/2 \\ \dfrac{e^{-\cos x} - 1}{8x - 4\pi}, & x > \pi/2 \end{cases}$

LHL at $x = \pi/2$,

$$\lim_{h \to 0} \frac{2\sin h - \sin 2h}{4h^2} = \lim_{h \to 0} \frac{2\sin h(1 - \cos h)}{4h^2} = 0$$

RHL at $x = \pi/2$,

$$\lim_{h \to 0} \frac{e^{\sin h} - 1}{[(\pi/2) + h] - 4\pi} = \lim_{h \to 0} \frac{e^{\sin h} - 1}{8h} \cdot \frac{\sinh}{\sinh} = \frac{1}{8}$$

$\Rightarrow h(x)$ is discontinuous at $x = \pi/2$.

The irremovable discontinuity at $x = \pi/2$

$$f(\pi^+/2) = 0$$

and $\quad g(\pi^-/2) = 1/8$

$\Rightarrow \quad f(\pi^+/2) \neq g(\pi^-/2)$

5. (c) $f(1^+) = f(1^-) = f(1) = 2$

$f(0) = 1, \quad f(2) = 2$

$f(2^-) = 1, f(2) = 2$

$\therefore f$ is not continuous at $x = 2$.

6. (a) In the immediate neighbourhood of $x = \pi/2$, $\sin x > \sin^3 x$

$\Rightarrow |\sin x - \sin^3 x| = \sin x - \sin^3 x$

For $x \neq \pi/2$,

$$f(x) = \left[\frac{2(\sin x - \sin^3 x) + \sin x - \sin^3 x}{2(\sin x - \sin^3 x) - \sin x + \sin^3 x}\right] = 3$$

Hence, f is continuous and differentiable at $x = \pi/2$.

7. (c) We have, $\quad g(x) = x - [x] = \{x\}$

f is continuous with $f(0) = f(1)$

$$h(x) = f[g(x)] = f(\{x\})$$

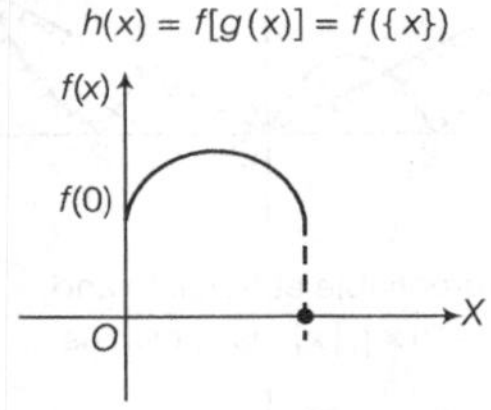

Let the graph of f is as shown in the figure satisfying

$$f(0) = f(1)$$

Now, $\quad h(0) = f(\{0\}) = f(0) = f(1)$

$h(0.2) = f(\{0.2\}) = f(0.2)$

$h = (1.5) = f(\{1.5\}) = (0.5)$ etc.

Hence, the graph of $h(x)$ will be periodic graph as shown.

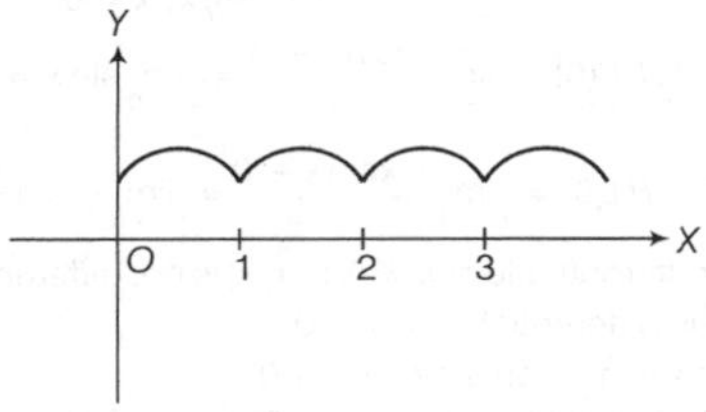

$\therefore$ h is continuous on R.

8. (b) $$f'(x) = \lim_{h\to 0}\frac{f(x+h)-f(x)}{h}$$
$$= \lim_{h\to 0}\frac{f(h)+|x|h+xh^2}{h}$$

where $x = h$ and $y = x$

$\therefore$ $$f'(x) = \lim_{h\to 0}\left[\frac{f(h)-f(0)}{h} + |x| + xh\right] \quad [\because f(0)=0]$$
$$f'(x) = f'(0) + |x| = |x|$$

9. (d) Statements I and II are incorrect. The function $f(x) = 1/x$, $0 < x < 1$, is a counter example.
Statement III is correct. Apply the intermediate value theorem to f on the closed interval $[a, b]$.

10. (b) Graph for $y = |x^2 - 2|x||$, is shown as

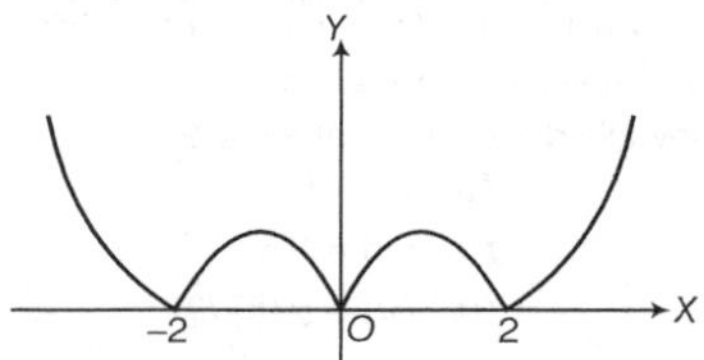

$\therefore$ $|x^2 - 2|x||$ and $|x|$ is shown as

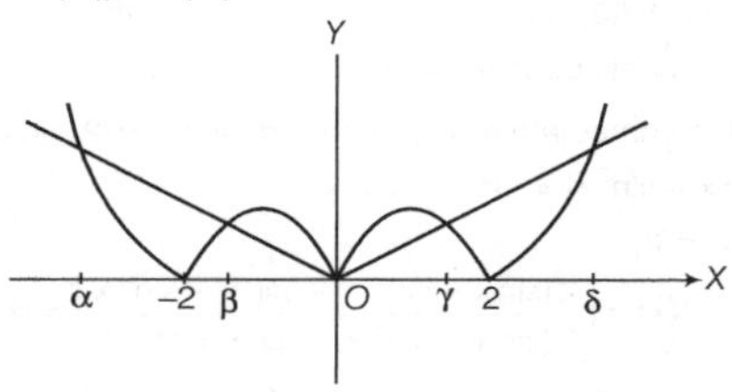

$\therefore$ $f(x) = \max\{|x^2-2|x|\,1, |x|\}$ is shown as

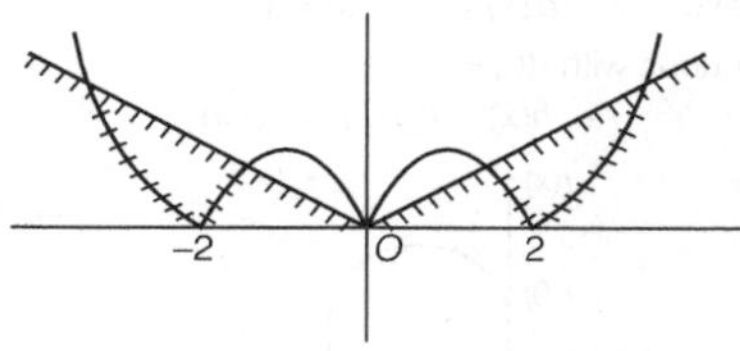

$\Rightarrow f(x)$ is not differentiable at 5 points and
$g(x) = \min\{|x^2-2|x||, |x|\}$ is shown as

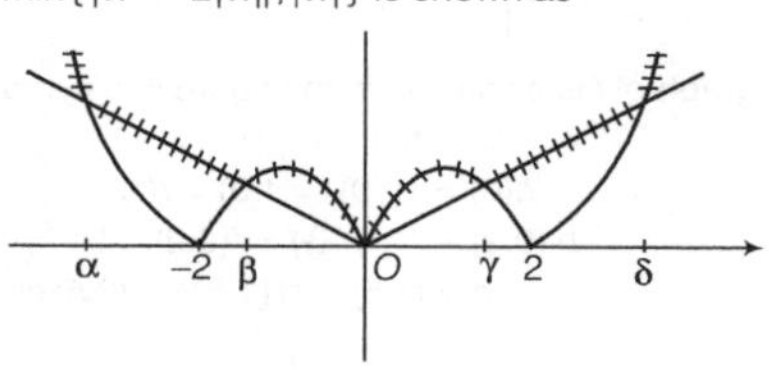

$\Rightarrow$ $g(x)$ is not differentiable at 7 points.

11. (a) $$f(-1) = b(1-1)+1 = 1$$
and $$\lim_{h\to 0} f(-1+h) = 1$$
$$\lim_{h\to 0} f(-1-h) = \sin[(-1+h+a)\pi]$$
$$= -\sin\pi a$$

For continuity, $\sin\pi a = -1 = \sin(2n\pi + 3\pi/2)$

$\Rightarrow$ $\pi a = 2n\pi + 3\pi/2$

$\Rightarrow$ $a = 2n + 3/2$

Hence, $a = 2n + 3/2$, $n \in I$ and $b \in R$.

12. (a,c) $f(x) = \begin{cases} x^3, & \text{if } x \le 1 \\ x^2, & \text{if } x > 1 \end{cases}$

$\Rightarrow f$ is continuous for all x and differentiable for all $x \in (1, \infty)$.
Also, $g(x)$ be continuous at $x \in I$

$$g(n) = n^2;\ g(n^+) = n^2$$
$$g(n^-) = (n-1)^2 + 1$$

$\therefore$ $n^2 = (n-1)^2$

$\Rightarrow$ $n = 1$

$g(x)$ is continuous only at one integer $x = 1$.

13. (a,b,c,d) $[|x|] - |[x]| = \begin{cases} 0, & \text{if } x = -1 \\ -1, & \text{if } -1 < x < 0 \\ 0, & \text{if } 0 \le x \le 1 \\ 0, & \text{if } 1 < x \le 2 \end{cases}$

$\therefore$ Range is $\{0, -1\}$.

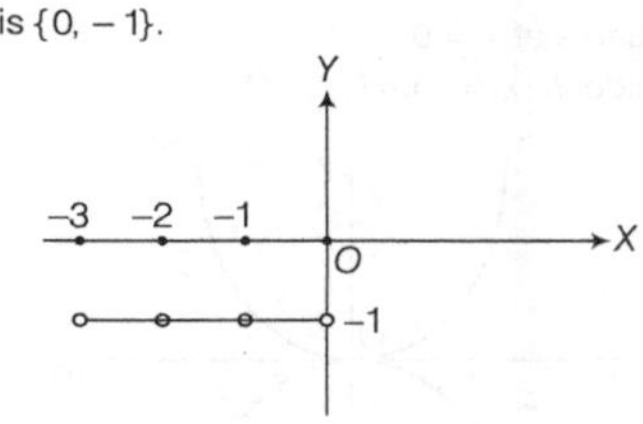

14. (b,c,d)

(a) $f(x) = \begin{cases} x^2\sin\frac{1}{x^2}, & x \ne 0 \\ 0, & x = 0 \end{cases}$ is differentiable but $f'(x)$ is not bounded in $[0, 1]$.

(b) True, e.g. Let $f(x) = \begin{cases} x, & 0 < x < 1 \\ 1, & x = 0 \\ 0, & x = 1 \end{cases}$ bijective but not continuous.

(c) $f(x) = x^2 - \cos\pi x + 4$

Now, $f(-1) = 1 - (-1) + 4 = 6$

and $f(2) = 4 - 1 + 4 = 7$

At f is continuous on $[-1, 2]$, so $f(c) = 2\pi$, for some $c \in (-1, 2)$

(d) $$(f^{-1})'(4) = \frac{1}{f'(0)} = \left(\frac{1}{1+e^x}\right)_{x=0} = \frac{1}{2}$$

15. (a,d) By intermediate value property,
$$\frac{f(0)+f(2)}{2} = f(c),\ 0 < c < 2.$$

By mean value theorem,
$$f(1) - f(0) = f'(c_1),\ 0 < c_1 < 1$$
$$f(2) - f(1) = f'(c_2),\ 1 < c_2 < 2$$

By subtracting,
$$f(0) + f(2) - 2f(1) = f'(c_2) - f'(c_1)$$
$$= (c_2 - c_1)f''(c),\ c_1 < c < c_2$$

$\Rightarrow$ $f(0) + f(2) - 2f(1) < 0$

$\Rightarrow$ $f(0) + f(2) < 2f(1)$

16. (b,c,d) $f'(0^+) = \lim_{h \to 0} \dfrac{h^p \cdot \sin\frac{1}{h} + h(\tan h)^q}{h}$

$= \lim_{h \to 0} h^{p-1} \cdot \sin\frac{1}{h} + (\tan h)^q$

For this limit to exist $(p - 1) > 0$ and $q \in N$.

$\therefore \quad p \geq 2$ and $q \in N$

Again, $\quad f'(0^-) = \lim_{h \to 0} \dfrac{-h^p \cdot \sin\frac{1}{h} - h(\tan h)^q}{-h}$

$= h^{p-1} \cdot \sin\frac{1}{h} + (\tan h)^q$

which is same.

$\therefore \quad p \geq 2$ and $q \in N$

17. (b)(i) $f'(0) = \lim_{h \to 0} \dfrac{\cos h - 0}{h}$ does not exist.

Obviously, $f(0) = f(0^-) = f(0^+) = 1$

(ii) $g(x) = 0$ for all x, hence continuous and derivable.

(iii) As $0 \leq \{f(x)\} < 1$, hence $f(x) = \sqrt{\{x\}^2} = \{x\}$ which is discontinuous, hence non-derivable all $x \in I$.

(iv) $\lim_{x \to 1} x^{1/\log x} = \lim_{x \to 1} x \log_x e = e = f(1)$

$\therefore k(x)$ is constant for all $x > 0$, hence continuous and differentiable at $x = 1$.

Hence, (i) → (p,s), (ii) → (p,q), (iii) → (r,s), (iv) → (p,q)

Explanations for Q. Nos.(18-20)

Since, $f(x)$ is symmetric about $x = 1$ and it is twice differentiable. So, $f'(x)$ must have one root at $x = 1$.

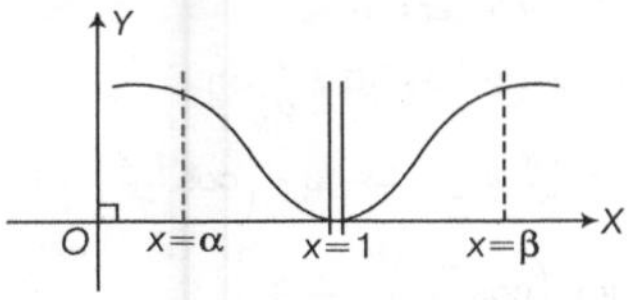

$\therefore \quad f'(x) = a(x-1)(x-\alpha)(x-\beta)$

$f'(x) = a(x-1)[x^2 - (\alpha+\beta)x + \alpha\beta]$

Here, $\quad \dfrac{\alpha+\beta}{2} = 1$. So, $\alpha + \beta = 2$

$f'(x) = a(x-1)(x^2 - 2x + \alpha\beta)$

$= a(x^3 - 2x^2 + \alpha\beta x - x^2 + 2x - \alpha\beta)$

$= a(x^3 - 3x^2 + (\alpha\beta + 2)x - \alpha\beta)$

$f''(x) = a(3x^2 - 6x + \alpha\beta + 2)$

$f''(2) = a(12 - 12 + \alpha\beta + 2) = 0$

$\therefore \quad \alpha\beta = -2$

$\alpha - \dfrac{2}{\alpha} = 2 \Rightarrow \alpha^2 - 2\alpha - 2 = 0$

$\therefore \quad \alpha = 1 - \sqrt{3}, \beta = 1 + \sqrt{3}$

So, sum $= 1 + \alpha + \beta = 3$

$f'(x) = a(x-1)(x^2 - 2x - 2)$

$= a(x-1)[(x-1)^2 - 3]$

$f(x) = a\left[\dfrac{(x-1)^4}{4} - \dfrac{3}{2}(x-1)^2\right] + C$

$\left[\begin{array}{l} \because f(1) = 0, \text{ so } C = 0 \\ f(2) = 1, \text{ so } a = -4/5 \end{array}\right]$

$f(2) = a[1/4 - 3/2] = 1$, so $a = -4/5$

$f(x) = -4/5\left[\dfrac{(x-1)^4}{4} - \dfrac{3}{2}(x-1)^2\right]$

$f(3) = 8/5$ and $f(1+\sqrt{3}) = 9/5$

18. (d) **19.** (c) **20.** (d)

Explanations for Q. Nos.(21-23)

The graph of $f(x)$ and $g(x)$ intersect at two points $x = \pm 1/2$, $g(x)$ is continuous, $\forall x \in R$ and non-differentiable at $x = -2, -1, 0, 1, 2$ i.e. five points.

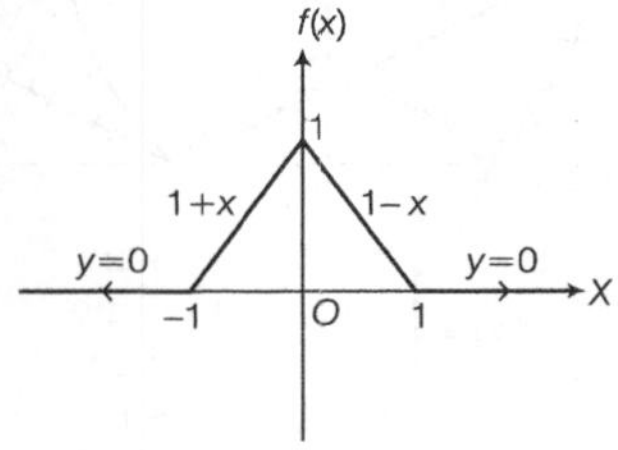

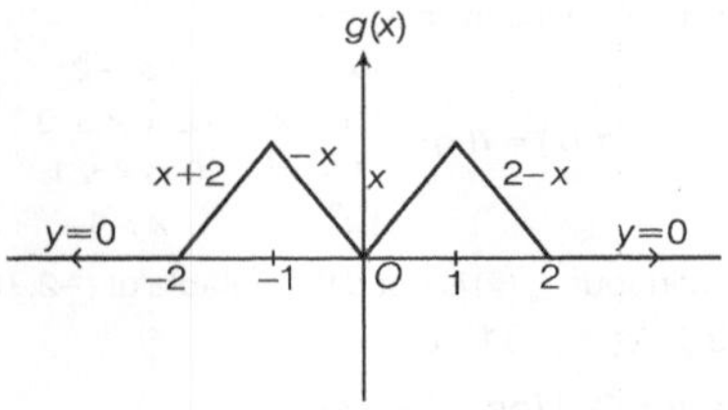

21. (b)

22. (a)

23. (c)

24. (b) Replacing y by $1/x$

$f(x) \cdot f(1/x) = f(x) + f(1/x)$,

Since $f(1) = 2$, we get

$f(x) = 1 + x^2$

25. (a) $f(x) = x^2 + 1$

$\Rightarrow \quad f(x) \geq 1$

$0 < \dfrac{1}{f(x)} \leq 1$

$\Rightarrow \quad \left[\dfrac{1}{f(x)}\right] = \begin{cases} 1, & x = 0 \\ 0, & \text{otherwise} \end{cases}$

$\therefore g(x)$ has only one point of discontinuity.

26. (d) $h(x) = \min\left\{\dfrac{2}{1+x^2}, x^2, |1 - |x||\right\}$, as all functions are even. It is sufficient to look for $x \geq 0$. The required number will be double those of $x \in [0, \infty)$.

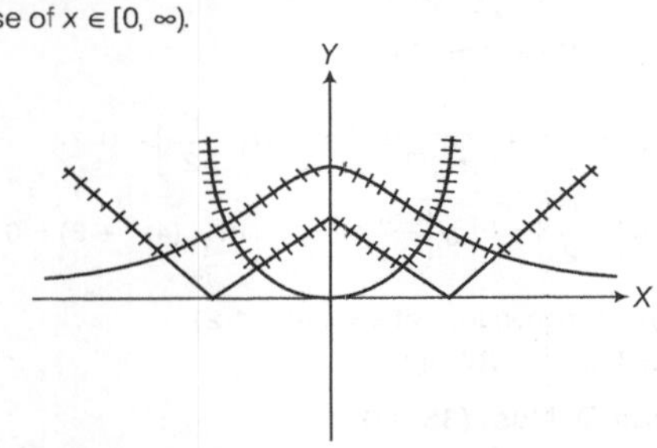

$\therefore$ 6 points of non-differentiability.

27. (c) $f(x) = x^2 - 2|x|$

$f(x) = \begin{cases} x^2 - 2x, & x \geq 0 \\ x^2 + 2x, & x < 0 \end{cases}$

$f'(0)$ does not exist, $f'(x)$ vanishes at $x = 1/2$ and $x = -1/2$.

28. (c) Not differentiable at $x = -2, 0, 2$.

Explanations for Q. Nos. (29-31)

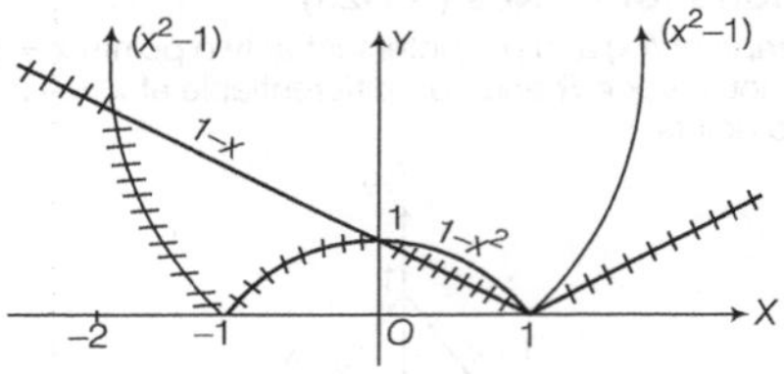

$$f(x)=\begin{cases}x^2-1, & x\le -2\\ 1-x, & -2<x\le 0\\ 1-x^2, & 0<x\le 1\\ x^2-1, & x>1\end{cases}$$

So, $f(x)$ is continuous everywhere.

$$g'(x)=f(x)=\begin{cases}x^2-1, & x\le -2\\ 1-x, & -2<x\le 0\\ 1-x^2, & 0<x\le 1\\ x^2-1, & x>1\end{cases}$$

Thus, continuous, $g(x)$ is not differentiable at $\{-2, 0, 1\}$.

29. (a) **30.** (c) **31.** (b)

Explanations for Q. Nos. (32-34)

$$f(x)=\begin{cases}[x], & -2\le x\le -1/2\\ 2x^2-1, & -1/2<x\le 2\end{cases}=\begin{cases}-2, & -2\le x<-1\\ -1, & -1\le x\le -1/2\\ 2x^2-1, & -1/2<x\le 2\end{cases}$$

$$|f(x)|=\begin{cases}2, & -2\le x<-1\\ 1, & -1\le x\le -1/2\\ |2x^2-1|, & -1/2<x\le 2\end{cases}$$

$$|f(x)|=\begin{cases}2, & -2\le x<-1\\ 1, & -1\le x\le -1/2\\ 1-2x^2, & -1/2<x\le 1/\sqrt{2}\\ 2x^2-1, & 1/\sqrt{2}<x\le 2\end{cases}$$

$$|f(x)|=\begin{cases}-2, & -2\le |x|<-1\\ -1, & -1\le |x|\le -1/2\\ 2|x|^2-1, & -1/2<|x|\le 2\end{cases}=2x^2-1;\ -2\le x\le 2$$

$$\therefore\ g(x)=f(|x|)+|f(x)|=\begin{cases}2x^2+1, & -2\le x<-1\\ 2x^2, & -1\le x\le -1/2\\ 0, & -1/2<x\le 1/\sqrt{2}\\ 4x^2-2, & 1/\sqrt{2}<x\le 2\end{cases}$$

$$\Rightarrow\ g(-1^-)=\lim_{x\to -1}(2x^2+1)=3$$

$$\Rightarrow\ g(-1^+)=\lim_{x\to -1}(2x^2)=2$$

$$g\left(-\frac{1^-}{2}\right)=\lim_{x\to -1/2}2x^2=\frac{1}{2},\ g\left(-\frac{1^+}{2}\right)=0$$

$$g\left(-\frac{1^-}{2}\right)=0,\ g\left(-\frac{1^+}{\sqrt{2}}\right)=\lim_{x\to -\frac{1}{\sqrt{2}}}(4x^2-2)=0$$

$\therefore\ g(x)$ is discontinuous at $x=\{-1, -1/2\}$.

32. (a) **33.** (c) **34.** (b)

Explanations Q. Nos. (35-37)

Graph for $f(x)$ is shown as

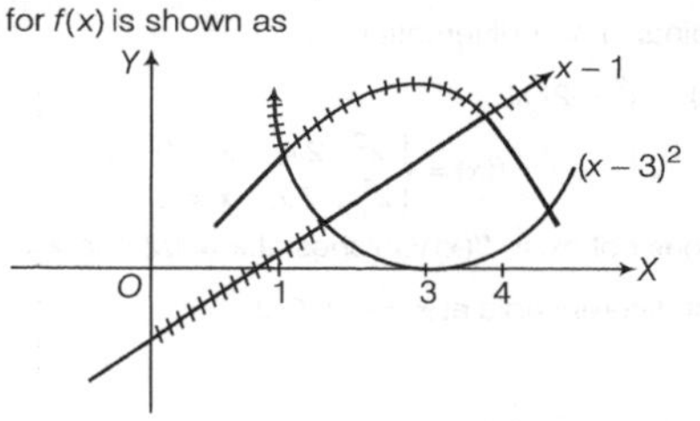

$$\Rightarrow\quad f'(2^-)=-2$$

$$\Rightarrow\quad f'(2^+)=1$$

$$\Rightarrow\quad f'(2^+)-f'(2^-)=1-(-2)=3$$

$f(x)$ is maximum, when

$$x-1=3-\frac{(x-3)^2}{2}$$

$$\Rightarrow\quad 2x+(x-3)^2=8$$

$$\Rightarrow\quad x^2-4x+1=0$$

$$\Rightarrow\quad x=2\pm\sqrt{3}\qquad [\text{neglecting } 2-\sqrt{3}]$$

$$\therefore\quad x=2+\sqrt{3}$$

Now, rate of change of x w.r.t. $f(x)$ at $x = 3$.

$$\Rightarrow\quad f'(x)=1 \text{ at } x=3.$$

$$\therefore\quad \frac{dx}{df(x)}=1$$

35. (c) **36.** (b) **37.** (a)

38. (4) $\because\ [x]+[x+1/4]+[x+2/4]+[x+3/4]=[4x]$

$\therefore\ f(x)=[4x]$, which becomes discontinuous at

$x = 1/4, 2/4, 3/4, 1 \in [0, 1]$

39. (5) $g(x)$ must assume only one integer value

i.e. $g(x)=0,\ \forall\ x\in R$

where $\dfrac{2}{c}<\dfrac{f(x)}{c}<\dfrac{\sqrt{21}}{c}$

$$\Rightarrow\quad \frac{\sqrt{21}}{c}<1\ \Rightarrow\ c>\sqrt{21}$$

$\therefore$ Least positive integer is 5.

40. (2) When, $0<x<2\ \Rightarrow\ 0<\dfrac{x}{2}<1$

$$\therefore\quad 0<\frac{\pi x}{2}<\frac{\pi}{2}\ \Rightarrow\ 0<\left(\cos\frac{\pi x}{2}\right)<1$$

$$\Rightarrow\quad \lim_{n\to\infty}\left(\cos\frac{\pi x}{2}\right)^{2n}\to 0$$

and $f(2)=1$

$\therefore\ f(x)$ is discontinuous at $x = 2$.

41. (1) Here, $f'(x)=3x^2-2x+1>0, \forall x\in R$

$\Rightarrow\ \max f(t)=f(x)$, when $0\le t\le x$

$$\therefore\quad g(x)=\begin{cases}x^3-x^2+x+1, & 0\le x\le 1\\ 3-x, & 1<x\le 2\end{cases}$$

$\Rightarrow g(x)$ is continuous but not differentiable at $x = 1$.

42. (4)

$$f(x)=x,\ \forall\ x\in R \qquad \dots(\text{i})$$

$$f(x)=-x,\ \forall x\in R \qquad \dots(\text{ii})$$

$$f(x)=\begin{cases}x, & x\ge 0\\ -x, & x<0\end{cases} \qquad \dots(\text{iii})$$

$$f(x)=\begin{cases}-x, & x\ge 0\\ x, & x<0\end{cases} \qquad \dots(\text{iv})$$

$\therefore$ Number of functions = 4

43. (6) Given, $f(x)=([2x]+\{2x\})([2x]-\{2x\})$

$$=2x(2x-2\{2x\})=4x^2-4x\{2x\}$$

Hence, 6 points of discontinuity are there as the function is continuous at $x = 0$.

44. (0) Replacing x by $-x$.

$$f(2x^2-1)=-2x^3f(-x)$$

$$\therefore\quad 2x^3f(x)=-2x^3f(-x)$$

$$\Rightarrow\quad f(-x)=-f(x)$$

$$\therefore\quad f^{2016}(0)=0$$

JEE Main & AIEEE Archive

1. (a) $g(x) = \begin{cases} k\sqrt{x+1}, & 0 \le x \le 3 \\ mx+12, & 3 < x \le 5 \end{cases}$

$$\lim_{x \to 3^-} g(x) = \lim_{x \to 3^+} g(x) = g(3)$$

$$\Rightarrow \quad 2k = 3m + 2 = 2k \qquad \ldots(i)$$

$$\therefore \quad g'(x) = \begin{cases} \dfrac{k}{2\sqrt{x+1}}, & 0 \le x \le 3 \\ m, & 3 < x \le 5 \end{cases}$$

LHD at $x = 3 = \lim_{x \to 3^-} g'(x) = \dfrac{k}{4}$

RHDat $x = 3 = \lim_{x \to 3^-} g'(x) = m$

LHD = RHD

$$\frac{k}{4} = m \qquad \ldots(ii)$$

From Eqs. (i) and (ii),

$$m = \frac{2}{5}, k = \frac{8}{5}$$

$$k + m = 2$$

2. (d) Here, $f(0) = 2 = g(1)$

$g(0) = 0$

and $f(1) = 6$

$\because f$ and g are differentiable in (1, 0).

Let $h(x) = f(x) - 2g(x)$

$h(0) = f(0) - 2g(0)$

$h(0) = 2 - 0$

$h(0) = 2$

Now, $h(1) = f(1) - 2g(1) = 6 - 2(2)$

$h(1) = 2, h(0) = h(1) = 2$

Hence, using Rolle's theorem,

There exists $c \in]0,1[$, such that

$h'(c) = 0$

$\Rightarrow \quad f'(c) - 2g'(c) = 0$, for some $c \in]0,1[$

$\therefore \quad f'(c) = 2g'(c)$

3. (a) **Given** A function $f : R \to R$ defined by

$f(x) = [x] \cos \pi \left(x - \frac{1}{2}\right)$, where [·] denotes the greatest integer function.

To discuss The continuity of function f.

Now, $\cos x$ is continuous, $\forall x \in R$.

$\Rightarrow \cos \pi \left(x - \frac{1}{2}\right)$ is also continuous, $\forall x \in R$.

Hence, the continuity of f depends upon the continuity of $[x]$.
Now, $[x]$ is discontinuous, $\forall x \in I$.
So, we should check the continuity of f at $x = n, \forall n \in I$.

LHL at $x = n$ is given by

$$f(n^-) = \lim_{x \to n^-} f(x)$$

$$= \lim_{x \to n^-} [x] \cos \pi \left(x - \frac{1}{2}\right)$$

$$= (n-1) \cos \frac{(2n-1)\pi}{2}$$

$$= 0$$

RHL at $x = n$ is given by

$$f(n^+) = \lim_{x \to n^+} f(x)$$

$$= \lim_{x \to n^+} [x] \cos \pi \left(x - \frac{1}{2}\right)$$

$$= (n) \cos \frac{(2n-1)\pi}{2} = 0$$

Also, value of the function at $x = n$ is

$$f(n) = [n] \cos \pi \left(n - \frac{1}{2}\right)$$

$$= (n) \cos \frac{(2n-1)\pi}{2} = 0$$

$$\therefore \quad f(n^+) = f(n^-) = f(n)$$

Hence, f is continuous at $x = n, \forall n \in I$.

4. (b) **Given** A function f such that

$$f(x) = |x-2| + |x-5|.$$

To discuss Continuity and differentiability of f in interval (2, 5).

We know that,

$$|x-2| = \begin{cases} x-2, & x \ge 2 \\ 2-x, & x < 2 \end{cases}$$

and $$|x-5| = \begin{cases} x-5, & x \ge 5 \\ 5-x, & x < 5 \end{cases}$$

$$\Rightarrow \quad |x-2| = \begin{cases} 2-x, & x < 2 \\ x-2, & 2 \le x \le 5 \\ x-2, & x > 5 \end{cases}$$

and $$|x-5| = \begin{cases} 5-x, & x < 2 \\ 5-x, & 2 \le x \le 5 \\ x-5, & x > 5 \end{cases}$$

$$\Rightarrow \quad f(x) = |x-2| + |x-5|$$

$$= \begin{cases} (2-x)+(5-x), & x < 2 \\ (x-2)+(5-x), & 2 \le x \le 5 \\ (x-2)+(x-5), & x > 5 \end{cases}$$

$$= \begin{cases} 7-2x, & x < 2 \\ 3, & 2 \le x \le 5 \\ 2x-7, & x > 5 \end{cases}$$

Now, we can draw the graph of f very easily.

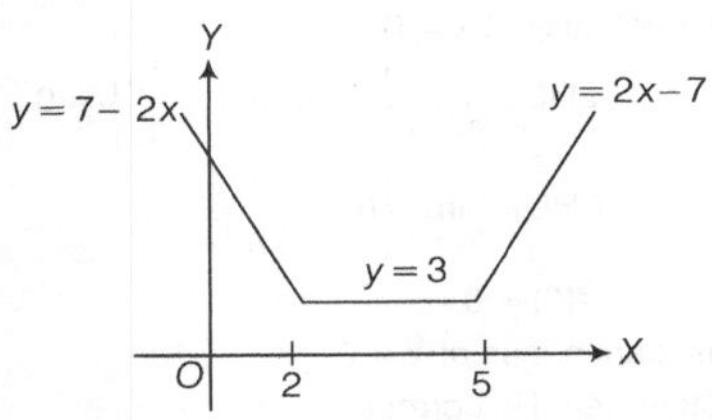

From the above graph, we can analyse all the required things.

Statement I $f'(4) = 0$

It is obviously clear that f is constant around $x = 4$, hence $f'(4) = 0$.

Hence, Statement I is correct.

Statement II

It can be clearly seen that

(i) f is continuous, $\forall x \in [2, 5]$.

(ii) f is differential, $\forall x \in (2, 5)$.

(iii) $f(2) = f(5) = 3$

Hence, Statement II is also correct but obviously not a correct explanation of Statement I.

5. (b) Here, $f(x)=\begin{cases}\dfrac{\sin(p+1)x+\sin x}{x}, & x<0\\ q, & x=0\\ \dfrac{\sqrt{x+x^2}-\sqrt{x}}{x^{3/2}}, & x>0\end{cases}$

Since, $f(x)$ is continuous for $x \in R$.

So, $f(x)$ is continuous at $x = 0$.

RHL at $x = 0$,

$$\lim_{h\to 0}\frac{\sqrt{h+h^2}-\sqrt{h}}{h^{3/2}}$$

$$=\lim_{h\to 0}\frac{\sqrt{h}\,\{\sqrt{h+1}-1\}}{h\sqrt{h}}$$

$$=\lim_{h\to 0}\left(\frac{\sqrt{h+1}-1}{h}\times\frac{\sqrt{h+1}+1}{\sqrt{h+1}+1}\right)$$

$$=\lim_{h\to 0}\frac{(h+1)-1}{h\{\sqrt{h+1}+1\}}$$

$$=\lim_{h\to 0}\frac{1}{\sqrt{h+1}+1}=\frac{1}{2} \quad \ldots\text{(i)}$$

LHL at $x = 0$,

$$\lim_{h\to 0}\frac{\sin(p+1)(-h)+\sin(-h)}{-h}$$

$$=\lim_{h\to 0}\frac{\sin(p+1)h}{h}+\frac{\sin h}{h}$$

$$=(p+1)+1=(p+2) \quad \ldots\text{(ii)}$$

$$f(0)=q \quad \ldots\text{(iii)}$$

From Eqs. (i), (ii) and (iii),

$$\frac{1}{2}=q=p+2$$

$\therefore$ $p=-\dfrac{3}{2}$ and $q=\dfrac{1}{2}$

6. (c) Here, $f(x)=\begin{cases}x\cdot\sin\left(\dfrac{1}{x}\right), & x\neq 0\\ 0, & x=0\end{cases}$

To check continuity at $x = 0$,

$$\text{LHL}=\lim_{h\to 0}\left\{(-h)\sin\left(-\frac{1}{h}\right)\right\}=0$$

$$\text{RHL}=\lim_{h\to 0}\left\{h\sin\left(\frac{1}{h}\right)\right\}=0$$

$$f(0)=0$$

So, $f(x)$ is continuous at $x = 0$.

Hence, Statement I is correct.

$$f_2(x)=\begin{cases}\sin\left(\dfrac{1}{x}\right), & x\neq 0\\ 0, & x=0\end{cases}$$

Here, $\lim_{x\to 0}f_2(x)=\lim_{x\to 0}\sin\left(\dfrac{1}{x}\right)$

which does not exist.

So, $f_2(x)$ is not continuous at $x = 0$.

Hence, Statement II is incorrect.

7. (b) We have, $f:(-1,1)\to R$

$$f(0)=-1,\quad f'(0)=1$$

$$g(x)=[f(2f(x)+2)]^2$$

$$\Rightarrow\quad g'(x)=2[f(2f(x)+2)]\times f'(2f(x)+2)\times 2f'(x)$$

$$\therefore\quad g'(0)=2[f\{2f(0)+2\}]\times f'\{2f(0)+2\}\times 2f'(0)$$

$$=2\,[f(0)]\times f'(0)\times 2f'(0)$$

$$=2\times(-1)\times 1\times 2\times 1=-4$$

8. (c) $f(x)=x|x|$ and $g(x)=\sin x$

$$gof(x)=\sin(x|x|)=\begin{cases}-\sin x^2, & x<0\\ \sin x^2, & x\geq 0\end{cases}$$

$$\therefore\quad (gof)'(x)=\begin{cases}-2x\cos x^2, & x<0\\ 2x\cos x^2, & x\geq 0\end{cases}$$

Clearly, $L(gof)'(0)=0=R(gof)'(0)$

So, gof is differentiable at $x = 0$ and also its derivative is continuous at $x = 0$.

Now, $(gof)''(x)=\begin{cases}-2\cos x^2+4x^2\sin x^2, & x<0\\ 2\cos x^2-4x^2\sin x^2, & x\geq 0\end{cases}$

$\therefore$ $L(gof)''(0)=-2$ and $R(gof)''(0)=2$

$\therefore$ $L(gof)''(0)\neq R(gof)''(0)$

Hence, $gof(x)$ is not twice differentiable at $x = 0$.

Therefore, Statement I is correct, Statement II is incorrect.

9. (d) $f'(1^-)=\lim_{h\to 0}\dfrac{f(1-h)-f(1)}{-h}$

$$=\lim_{h\to 0}\frac{(1-h-1)\cdot\sin\left(\frac{1}{1-h-1}\right)-0}{-h}$$

$$=\lim_{h\to 0}\sin\left(-\frac{1}{h}\right)$$

$$=-\lim_{h\to 0}\sin\frac{1}{h}$$

and $f'(1^+)=\lim_{h\to 0}\dfrac{f(1+h)-f(1)}{h}$

$$=\lim_{h\to 0}\frac{(1+h-1)\sin\left(\frac{1}{1+h-1}\right)-0}{h}$$

$$=\lim_{h\to 0}\sin\frac{1}{h}$$

$\therefore$ $f'(1^-)\neq f'(1^+)$

Hence, f is not differentiable at $x = 1$.

Again,

$$f'(0)=\lim_{h\to 0}\frac{(0+h-1)\sin\left(\frac{1}{0+h-1}\right)-\sin 1}{-h}$$

$$=\lim_{h\to 0}\frac{\left\{(h-1)\cos\left(\frac{1}{h-1}\right)\times\left(\frac{-1}{(h-1)^2}\right)\right\}+\sin\left(\frac{1}{h-1}\right)}{-1}$$

[using L' Hospital's rule]

$=\cos 1-\sin 1$ and

$$f'(0^+)=\lim_{h\to 0}\frac{(0+h-1)\sin\left(\frac{1}{0+h-1}\right)-\sin 1}{h}$$

$$=\lim_{h\to 0}\frac{(h-1)\cos\left(\frac{1}{h-1}\right)\left(\frac{-1}{(h-1)^2}\right)+\sin\left(\frac{1}{h-1}\right)}{1}$$

[using L'Hospital's rule]

$=\cos 1-\sin 1$

$\Rightarrow$ $f'(0^-)=f'(0^+)$

Hence, f is differentiable at $x = 0$.

10. (d) Now, $\lim_{x \to 0}\left(\frac{1}{x} - \frac{2}{e^{2x}-1}\right)$

$$= \lim_{x \to 0} \frac{e^{2x} - 1 - 2x}{x(e^{2x} - 1)}$$

$$= \lim_{x \to 0} \frac{2e^{2x} - 2}{(e^{2x} - 1) + 2xe^{2x}} \quad \text{[using L'Hospital's rule]}$$

$$= \lim_{x \to 0} \frac{4e^{2x}}{4e^{2x} + 4xe^{2x}} = 1 \quad \text{[using L'Hospital's rule]}$$

So, $f(x)$ is continuous at $x = 0$, then

$$\lim_{x \to 0} f(x) = f(0)$$

$$\Rightarrow \quad f(0) = 1$$

11. (b) Since, $f(x) = \frac{x}{1+|x|}$

Let $f(x) = \frac{g(x)}{h(x)} = \frac{x}{1+|x|}$

It is clear that $g(x) = x$ and $h(x) = 1 + |x|$ are differentiable on $(-\infty, \infty)$ and $(-\infty, 0) \cup (0, \infty)$, respectively.

Thus, $f(x)$ is differentiable on $(-\infty, 0) \cup (0, \infty)$.

Now, we have to check the differentiability at $x = 0$.

$$\therefore \lim_{x \to 0} \frac{f(x) - f(0)}{x - 0} = \lim_{x \to 0} \frac{\frac{x}{1+|x|} - 0}{x}$$

$$= \lim_{x \to 0} \frac{1}{1+|x|} = 1$$

Hence, $f(x)$ is differentiable on $(-\infty, \infty)$.

12. (b) $f'(1) = \lim_{h \to 0} \frac{f(1+h) - f(1)}{h}$

$$= \lim_{h \to 0} \frac{f(1+h)}{h} - \lim_{h \to 0} \frac{f(1)}{h}$$

Since, $\lim_{h \to 0} \frac{f(1+h)}{h} = 5$, so $\lim_{h \to 0} \frac{f(1)}{h}$ must be finite as $f'(1)$ exists and $\lim_{h \to 0} \frac{f(1)}{h}$ can be finite only, if $f(1) = 0$ and $\lim_{h \to 0} \frac{f(1)}{h} = 0$.

$$\therefore \quad f'(1) = \lim_{h \to 0} \frac{f(1+h)}{h} = 5$$

13. (d) Given that, $f(1) = -2$ and $f'(x) \ge 2$

$$\Rightarrow \quad \frac{dy}{dx} \ge 2 \Rightarrow dy \ge 2dx$$

$$\Rightarrow \quad \int_{f(1)}^{f(6)} dy \ge 2\int_1^6 dx$$

$$\Rightarrow \quad [y]_{f(1)}^{f(6)} \ge 2[x]_1^6$$

$$\Rightarrow \quad f(6) - f(1) \ge 10$$

$$\Rightarrow \quad f(6) \ge 10 + f(1)$$

$$\Rightarrow \quad f(6) \ge 8 \quad [\because f(1) = -2]$$

Alternate Method

$$\because \quad \frac{f(6) - f(1)}{6 - 1} \ge 2$$

$$\Rightarrow \quad f(6) - f(1) \ge 10$$

$$\Rightarrow \quad f(6) + 2 \ge 10 \Rightarrow f(6) \ge 8$$

14. (c) $\because \quad |f(x) - f(y)| \le (x - y)^2$

$$\therefore \lim_{x \to y} \frac{|f(x) - f(y)|}{|x - y|} \le \lim_{x \to y} |x - y|$$

$$\Rightarrow \quad |f'(y)| \le 0$$

$$\Rightarrow \quad f'(y) = 0$$

$$\Rightarrow \quad f(y) = \text{Constant}$$

$$\Rightarrow \quad f(y) = 0 \quad [\because f(0) = 0, \text{given}]$$

$$\therefore \quad f(1) = 0$$

15. (c) $\because \quad f(x) = \frac{1 - \tan x}{4x - \pi}$

$$\therefore \lim_{x \to \pi/4} f(x) = \lim_{x \to \pi/4} \left(\frac{1 - \tan x}{4x - \pi}\right)$$

$$= \lim_{x \to \pi/4} \left(\frac{-\sec^2 x}{4}\right)$$

[using L'Hospital's rule]

$$= \frac{-\sec^2(\pi/4)}{4} = -\frac{2}{4}$$

$$\Rightarrow \lim_{x \to \pi/4} f(x) = -\frac{1}{2}$$

Also, $f(x)$ is continuous in $[0, \pi/2]$, so $f(x)$ will be continuous at $\frac{\pi}{4}$.

$$\therefore \quad f\left(\frac{\pi}{4}\right) = \lim_{x \to \pi/4} f(x) = -\frac{1}{2}$$

16. (a) $\lim_{x \to a} \frac{f(a)g(x) - f(a) - g(a)f(x) + g(a)}{g(x) - f(x)} = 4$

Applying L'Hospital's rule, we get

$$\lim_{x \to a} \frac{f(a)g'(x) - g(a)f'(x)}{g'(x) - f'(x)} = 4$$

$$\Rightarrow \quad \lim_{x \to a} \frac{kg'(x) - kf'(x)}{g'(x) - f'(x)} = 4$$

$$\therefore \quad k = 4$$

17. (b) Continuity at $x = 0$,

$$\text{LHL} = \lim_{x \to 0^-} f(x)$$

$$= \lim_{h \to 0} (0 - h)e^{-\left(\frac{1}{|-h|} + \frac{1}{(-h)}\right)}$$

$$= \lim_{h \to 0} (-h)e^{-\left(\frac{1}{h} - \frac{1}{h}\right)} = \lim_{h \to 0} (-h) = 0$$

$$\text{RHL} = \lim_{x \to 0^+} f(x) = \lim_{h \to 0} (0 + h)e^{-\left(\frac{1}{|h|} + \frac{1}{h}\right)}$$

$$= \lim_{h \to 0} he^{-\left(\frac{1}{h} + \frac{1}{h}\right)} = \lim_{h \to 0} \frac{h}{e^{2/h}} = 0$$

$$\therefore \quad \lim_{x \to 0^-} f(x) = \lim_{x \to 0^+} f(x) = f(0)$$

Therefore, $f(x)$ is continuous for all x.

Differentiability at $x = 0$,

$$Lf'(0) = \lim_{h \to 0} \frac{(-h)e^{-\left(\frac{1}{h} - \frac{1}{h}\right)} - 0}{(-h) - 0} = \lim_{h \to 0} e^0 = 1$$

$$Rf'(0) = \lim_{h \to 0} \frac{he^{-\left(\frac{1}{h} + \frac{1}{h}\right)} - 0}{h - 0}$$

$$= \lim_{h \to 0} \frac{1}{e^{2/h}} = 0$$

$$\Rightarrow \quad Rf'(0) \ne Lf'(0)$$

Therefore, $f(x)$ is not differentiable at $x = 0$.

JEE Advanced & IIT JEE Archive

1. (7) $\displaystyle \lim_{x\to 1}\frac{\int_{-1}^{x} f(t)\,dt}{\int_{-1}^{x} t\,|f(t)|\,dt} = \frac{f(x)}{xf\{f(x)\}} = \frac{1}{14}$

$$\Rightarrow \quad \frac{\frac{1}{2}}{f\left(\frac{1}{2}\right)} = \frac{1}{14} \Rightarrow f\left(\frac{1}{2}\right) = 7$$

2. (a,d) $g(0) = 0, g'(0) = 0, g'(1) \neq 0$

$$f(x) = \begin{cases} g(x), & x > 0 \\ -g(x), & x < 0 \\ 0, & x = 0 \end{cases}$$

(a) RHD at $x = 0$ $f'(0^+) = \lim_{h\to 0}\frac{f(h) - f(0)}{h}$

$$= \lim_{h\to 0}\frac{g(h) - g(0)}{h} = g'(0) = 0$$

LHD at $x = 0$, $f'(0^-) = \lim_{h\to 0}\frac{f(-h) - f(0)}{-h}$

$$= \lim_{h\to 0}\frac{-g(-h) + g(0)}{-h}$$

$$= g'(0) = 0$$

$\therefore$ Differentiable at $x = 0$

(b) $h(x) = \begin{cases} e^x, & x > 0 \\ e^{-x}, & x < 0 \\ 1, & x = 0 \end{cases}$

$$h'(0^+) = \lim_{t\to 0}\frac{h(t) - h(0)}{t} = \lim_{h\to 0}\frac{e^t - 1}{t} = 1$$

$$h'(0^-) = \lim_{t\to 0}\frac{h(-t) - h(0)}{-t} = \lim_{h\to 0}\frac{e^t - 1}{-t} = -1$$

Not differentiable at $x = 0$.

(c) $foh = f\{h(u)\} = g\{h(u)\}$ as $h(u) > 0$

$$\text{RHD} = \lim_{t\to 0}\frac{g\{h(t)\} - g\{h(0)\}}{t}$$

$$= \lim_{t\to 0}\frac{g(e^h) - g(1)}{t} = g'(1) = k$$

$$\text{LHD} = \lim_{t\to 0}\frac{g\{h(-t)\} - g\{h(0)\}}{-t}$$

$$= \lim_{t\to 0}\frac{g(e^h) - g(1)}{-1} = -g'(1) = -k$$

Not differentiable at $x = 0$.

(d) $hof = h\{f(u)\}$

$$\text{RHD} = \lim_{t\to 0}\frac{h\{g(t)\} - h\{f(0)\}}{t}$$

$$= \lim_{t\to 0}\frac{h\{g(t)\} - h(0)}{t} = \lim_{t\to 0}\frac{h\{g(t)\} - h(0)}{t}$$

As $g'(0) = 0$ $\lim_{h\to 0}\frac{g(h) - g(0)}{h} = 0$

Differentiable at $x = 0$.

3. (3) **Plan**

(i) In these type of questions, we draw the graph of the function.

(ii) The points at which the curve taken a sharp turn, are the points of non-differentiability.

Curve of $f(x)$ and $g(x)$ are

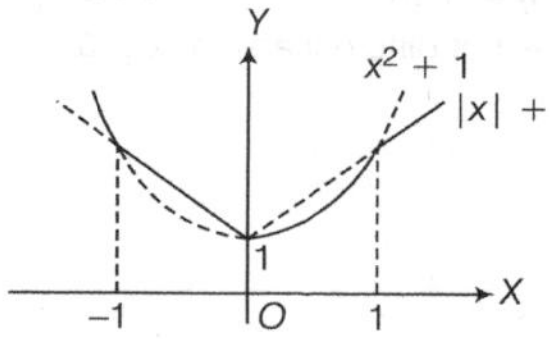

$h(x)$ is not differentiable at $x = \pm 1$ and 0.

As, $h(x)$ take sharp turns at $x = \pm 1$ and 0.

Hence, number of points of non-differentiability of $h(x)$ is 3.

4. (a,c) **Plan** A function $f(x)$ is continuous at $x = a$, if $\lim_{x\to a^-} f(x) = \lim_{x\to a^+} f(x) = f(a)$.

Also, a function $f(x)$ is differentiable at $x = a$, if

$$\lim_{x\to a^-}\frac{f(x) - f(a)}{x - a} = \lim_{x\to a^+}\frac{f(x) - f(a)}{x - a}$$

i.e. $\quad f'(a^-) = f'(a^+)$

Given that, $f:[a, b] \to [1, \infty)$

an $\quad g(x) = \begin{cases} 0, & x < a \\ \int_a^x f(t)\,dt, & a \le x \le b \\ \int_a^b f(t)\,dt, & x > b \end{cases}$

Now, $\quad g(a^-) = 0 = g(a^+) = g(a)$

$$\left[\text{as } g(a^+) = \lim_{x\to a^+}\int_a^x f(t)\,dt = 0 \text{ and } g(a) = \int_a^a f(t)\,dt = 0\right]$$

$g(b^-) = g(b^+) = g(b) = \int_a^b f(t)\,dt$

$\Rightarrow g$ is continuous, $\forall x \in R$.

Now, $\quad g'(x) = \begin{cases} 0, & x < a \\ f(x), & a < x < b \\ 0, & x > b \end{cases}$

$$g'(a^-) = 0$$

but $\quad g'(a^+) = f(a) \ge 1 \quad [\because \text{range of } f(x) \text{ is } [1, \infty), \forall\, x \in (a, b)]$

$\Rightarrow g$ is non-differentiable at $x = a$

and $\quad g'(b^+) = 0$ but $g'(b^-) = f(b) \ge 1$

$\Rightarrow g$ is not differentiable at $x = b$.

5. (b) **Concept Involved** To check differentiability at a point, we use RHD and LHD at a point and if RHD = LHD, then $f(x)$ is differentiable at the point.

Description of Situation

As, $\quad R\{f'(x)\} = \lim_{h\to 0}\frac{f(x+h) - f(x)}{h}$

and $\quad L\{f'(x)\} = \lim_{h\to 0}\frac{f(x-h) - f(x)}{-h}$

Here, students generally get confused in defining modulus.

To check differentiable at $x = 0$,

$$R\{f'(0)\} = \lim_{h\to 0}\frac{f(0 + h) - f(0)}{h}$$

$$= \lim_{h\to 0}\frac{h^2\left|\cos\frac{\pi}{h}\right| - 0}{h} = \lim_{h\to 0} h\cdot\left|\cos\frac{\pi}{h}\right| = 0$$

$$L\{f'(0)\} = \lim_{h\to 0}\frac{f(0 - h) - f(0)}{-h}$$

$$= \lim_{h\to 0}\frac{h^2\left|\cos\left(-\frac{\pi}{h}\right)\right| - 0}{-h} = 0$$

So, $f(x)$ is differentiable at $x = 0$.

To check differentiability at $x = 2$,

$$R\{f'(2)\} = \lim_{h\to 0}\frac{f(2 + h) - f(2)}{h}$$

$$= \lim_{h\to 0}\frac{(2 + h)^2\left|\cos\left(\frac{\pi}{2 + h}\right)\right| - 0}{h}$$

$$= \lim_{h\to 0} \frac{(2+h)^2 \cdot \cos\left(\frac{\pi}{2+h}\right)}{h}$$

$$= \lim_{h\to 0} \frac{(2+h)^2 \cdot \sin\left(\frac{\pi}{2} - \frac{\pi}{2+h}\right)}{h}$$

$$= \lim_{h\to 0} \frac{(2+h)^2 \cdot \sin\left(\frac{\pi h}{2(2+h)}\right)}{h \cdot \frac{\pi}{2(2+h)}} \cdot \frac{\pi}{2(2+h)}$$

$\Rightarrow \quad R\{f'(2)\} = \pi$

$$L\{f'(2)\} = \lim_{h\to 0} \frac{f(2-h) - f(2)}{-h}$$

$$= \lim_{h\to 0} \frac{(2-h)^2 \cdot \left|\cos\frac{\pi}{2-h}\right| - 2^2 \cdot \left|\cos\frac{\pi}{2}\right|}{-h}$$

$$= \lim_{h\to 0} \frac{(2-h)^2 - \left(-\cos\frac{\pi}{2-h}\right) - 0}{-h}$$

$$= \lim_{h\to 0} \frac{-(2-h)^2 \cdot \sin\left(\frac{\pi}{2} - \frac{\pi}{2-h}\right)}{h}$$

$$= \lim_{h\to 0} \frac{(2-h)^2 \cdot \sin\left(-\frac{\pi h}{2(2-h)}\right)}{h \times \frac{-\pi}{2(2-h)}} \times \frac{-\pi}{2(2-h)}$$

$\Rightarrow \quad L\{f'(2)\} = -\pi$

Thus, $f(x)$ is differentiable at $x=0$ but not at $x=2$.

6. (8/3) Given, $f(1) = \frac{1}{3}$ and $6\int_1^x f(t)\,dt = 3x\,f(x) - x^3$ for all, $x \geq 1$, using Newton-Leibnitz formula.

Differentiating both sides, we get

$$6f(x)\cdot 1 - 0 = 3f(x) + 3xf'(x) - 3x^2$$

$\Rightarrow \quad 3xf'(x) - 3f(x) = 3x^2$

$\Rightarrow \quad f'(x) - \frac{1}{x}f(x) = x$

$\Rightarrow \quad \frac{xf'(x) - f(x)}{x^2} = 1$

$\Rightarrow \quad \frac{d}{dx}\left\{\frac{f(x)}{x}\right\} = 1$

Integrating both sides, we get

$$\frac{f(x)}{x} = x + C \qquad \left[\because f(1) = \frac{1}{3}\right]$$

$\Rightarrow \quad \frac{1}{3} = 1 + C \Rightarrow C = -\frac{2}{3}$

$$f(x) = x^2 - \frac{2}{3}x \Rightarrow f(2) = 4 - \frac{4}{3} = \frac{8}{3}$$

Note *Here, $f(1) = 2$ does not satisfy given function.*

$\therefore \quad f(1) = \frac{1}{3}$

For that $f(x) = x^2 - \frac{2}{3}x$ and $f(2) = 4 - \frac{4}{3} = \frac{8}{3}$

7. (b,c) $f(x+y) = f(x) + f(y)$, as $f(x)$ is differentiable at $x = 0$.

$\Rightarrow \quad f'(0) = k \qquad \ldots$(i)

Now, $\quad f'(x) = \lim_{h\to 0} \frac{f(x+h) - f(x)}{h}$

$$= \lim_{h\to 0} \frac{f(x) + f(h) - f(x)}{h}$$

$$= \lim_{h\to 0} \frac{f(h)}{h} \qquad \left[\frac{0}{0}\text{ form}\right]$$

Given, $f(x+y) = f(x) + f(y), \forall\ x, y$

$\therefore \quad f(0) = f(0) + f(0)$

when $x = y = 0 \Rightarrow f(0) = 0)$

Using L'Hospital's rule

$$= \lim_{h\to 0} \frac{f'(h)}{1} = f'(0) = k \qquad \ldots\text{(ii)}$$

$\Rightarrow \quad f'(x) = k$

Integrating both sides, we get

$$f(x) = kx + C, \text{ as } f(0) = 0$$

$\Rightarrow \quad C = 0$

$\therefore \quad f(x) = kx$

$\therefore f(x)$ is continuous for all $x \in R$ and $f'(x) = k$, i.e. constant for all $x \in R$.

8. (a,b,c,d) $f(x) = \begin{cases} -x - \pi/2, & x \leq -\pi/2 \\ -\cos x, & -\pi/2 < x \leq 0 \\ x - 1, & 0 < x \leq 1 \\ \log x, & x > 1 \end{cases}$

Continuity at $x = -\frac{\pi}{2}$,

$$f\left(-\frac{\pi}{2}\right) = -\left(-\frac{\pi}{2}\right) - \frac{\pi}{2} = 0$$

$$\text{RHL} = \lim_{h\to 0} -\cos\left(-\frac{\pi}{2} + h\right) = 0$$

$\therefore f(x)$ continuous at $x = -\frac{\pi}{2}$.

Continuity at $x = 0$,

$$f(0) = -1$$

$$\text{RHL} = \lim_{h\to 0}(0 + h) - 1 = -1$$

$\therefore f(x)$ is continuous at $x = 0$.

Continuity at $x = 1$,

$$f(1) = 0$$

$$\text{RHL} = \lim_{h\to 0} \log(1+h) = 0.$$

$\therefore f(x)$ is continuous at $x = 1$.

Here, $\quad f'(x) = \begin{cases} -1, & x \leq -\pi/2 \\ \sin x, & -\pi/2 < x \leq 0 \\ 1, & 0 < x \leq 1 \\ \frac{1}{x}, & x > 1 \end{cases}$

Differentiability at $x = 0$, LHD = 0, RHD = 1

$\therefore$ It is not differentiable at $x = 0$

Differentiability at $x = 1$, LHD = 1, RHD = 1

$\therefore$ It is differentiable at $x = 1$.

Also, for $x = -\frac{3}{2} \Rightarrow f(x) = -x - \frac{\pi}{2}$

$\therefore$ It is differentiable at $x = -\frac{3}{2}$

9. (b) We have, $\lim_{x\to 0} \frac{g(x)\cos x - g(0)}{\sin x}$; $\qquad \left[\frac{0}{0}\text{ form}\right]$

$$= \lim_{x\to 0} \frac{g'(x)\cos x - g(x)\sin x}{\cos x} = 0$$

Since, $f(x) = g(x)\sin x$

$$f'(x) = g'(x)\sin x + g(x)\cos x$$

and $\quad f''(x) = g''(x)\sin x + 2g'(x)\cos x - g(x)\sin x$

$\Rightarrow \quad f''(0) = 0$

Thus, $\lim_{x\to 0}[g(x)\cos x - g(0)\text{cosec } x] = 0 = f''(0)$

$\Rightarrow$ Statement I is true.

Statement II $f'(x) = g'(x)\sin x + g(x)\cos x$

$\Rightarrow \quad f'(0) = g(0)$

Statement II is not a correct explanation of Statement I.

10. (a)

(i) $x|x|$ is continuous, differentiable and strictly increasing in $(-1, 1)$.

(ii) $\sqrt{|x|}$ is continuous in $(-1, 1)$ and not differentiable at $x = 0$.

(iii) $x + [x]$ is strictly increasing in $(-1, 1)$ and discontinuous at $x = 0$
$\Rightarrow$ not differentiable at $x = 0$.

(iv) $|x-1| + |x+1| = 2$ in $(-1, 1)$
$\Rightarrow$ The function is continuous and differentiable in $(-1, 1)$.

Statement II is also true.

Hence, (i) $\to$ (p,q,r), (ii) $\to$ (p,s), (iii) $\to$ (r,s), (iv) $\to$ (p,q)

11. (b) Since, $f''(x) = -f(x)$

$\Rightarrow \quad \dfrac{d}{dx}\{f'(x)\} = -f(x)$

$\Rightarrow \quad g'(x) = -f(x) \qquad [\because g(x) = f'(x), \text{ given}] \quad \ldots \text{(i)}$

Also, $\quad F(x) = \left[f\left(\dfrac{x}{2}\right)\right]^2 + \left[g\left(\dfrac{x}{2}\right)\right]^2$

$\Rightarrow \quad F'(x) = 2\left[f\left(\dfrac{x}{2}\right)\right]\cdot f'\left(\dfrac{x}{2}\right)\cdot\dfrac{1}{2}$

$\qquad + 2\left[g\left(\dfrac{x}{2}\right)\right]\cdot g'\left(\dfrac{x}{2}\right)\cdot\dfrac{1}{2} = 0$ [from Eq. (i)]

$\therefore \; F(x)$ is constant.

$\Rightarrow \quad F(10) = F(5) = 5$

12. (a) **Plan** $\displaystyle\int \frac{dx}{\sqrt{a^2 - x^2}} = \sin^{-1}\left(\frac{x}{a}\right) + C$

As $g(a)$ is defined in the question, first use the numerical value of 'a' given in question and then proved.

Given, $\quad g(a) = \displaystyle\lim_{h \to 0^+}\int_h^{1-h} t^{-a}(1-t)^{a-1}\,dt$

$\therefore \quad g\left(\dfrac{1}{2}\right) = \displaystyle\lim_{h \to 0^+}\int_h^{1-h} t^{-1/2}(1-t)^{-1/2}\,dt$

$= \displaystyle\int_0^1 \frac{dt}{\sqrt{t - t^2}} = \int_0^1 \frac{dt}{\sqrt{\frac{1}{4} - \left(t - \frac{1}{2}\right)^2}}$

$= \sin^{-1}\left[\left(\dfrac{t - 1/2}{1/2}\right)\right]_0^1$

$= \sin^{-1}1 - \sin^{-1}(-1) = \pi$

13. (d) **Plan** $\displaystyle\int_0^a f(x)\,dx = \int_0^a f(a-x)\,dx$

As $g(a)$ is given, use the numerical value of 'a' given in the question and then proved.

Given that, $g(a) = \displaystyle\int_0^1 \frac{dt}{t^a(1-t)^{1-a}}$

Clearly, $\quad g(a) = g(1-a)$

$\left[\text{using} \displaystyle\int_0^a f(x)\,dx = \int_0^a f(a-x)\,dx\right]$

Now, differentiating w.r.t. 'a', we get

$$g'(a) = g'(1-a)(-1)$$

For $a = \dfrac{-1}{2}$, we have

$$-g'\left(\frac{1}{2}\right) = g'\left(\frac{1}{2}\right)$$

So, $\quad g'\left(\dfrac{1}{2}\right) = 0$

14. (a,d) Here, $\quad f(x) = \min\{1, x^2, x^3\}$ which could be graphically shown as

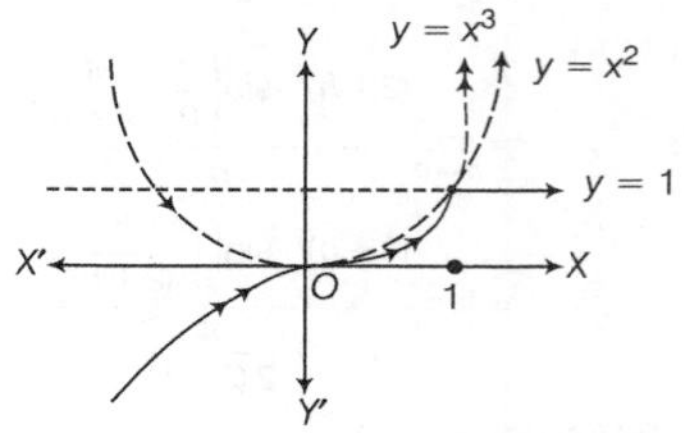

$\Rightarrow f(x)$ is continuous for $x \in R$ and not differentiable at $x = 1$ due to sharp edge.

15. (c) Let $g(x) = f(x) - x^2$

$\Rightarrow g(x)$ has atleast 3 real roots which are $x = 1, 2, 3$

[by mean value theorem]

$\Rightarrow \quad g'(x)$ has atleast 2 real roots in $x \in (1, 3)$.

$\Rightarrow \quad g''(x)$ has atleast 1 real roots in $x \in (1, 3)$.

$\Rightarrow \quad f''(x) - 2\cdot 1 = 0$, for atleast 1 real root in $x \in (1, 3)$.

$\Rightarrow \quad f''(x) = 2$, for atleast one root in $x \in (1, 3)$.

16. (b) Given,

$$f(1) = f\left(\frac{1}{2}\right) = f\left(\frac{1}{3}\right) = \ldots = \lim_{n \to \infty} f\left(\frac{1}{n}\right) = 0$$

as $\quad f\left(\dfrac{1}{n}\right) = 0$; $n \in$ integer and $n \geq 1$.

$\Rightarrow \quad \displaystyle\lim_{n \to \infty} f\left(\frac{1}{n}\right) = 0$

$\Rightarrow \quad f(0) = 0$

Since, there are infinitely many points in neighbourhood of $x = 0$.

$\therefore \quad f(x) = 0$

$\Rightarrow \quad f'(x) = 0$

$\Rightarrow \quad f'(0) = 0$

Hence, $\quad f(0) = f'(0) = 0$

17. (a) Using graphical transformation.

As, we know the function is not differentiable at sharp edges and in figure (ii)

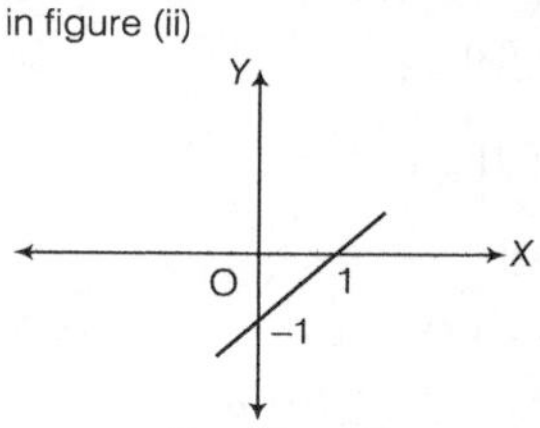

(i) $y = x - 1$

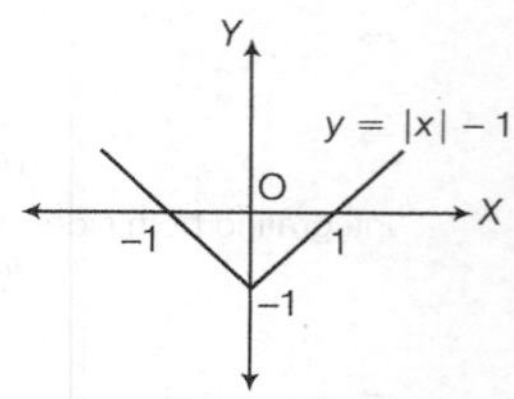

(ii) $y = |x| - 1$

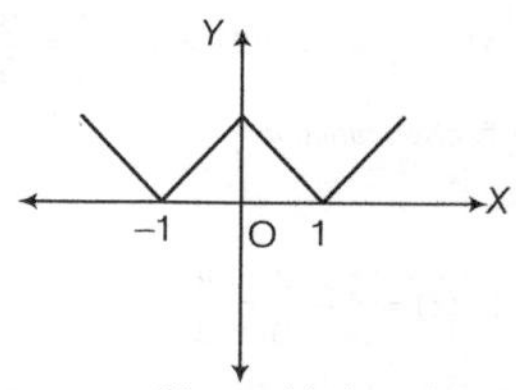

(iii) $y = ||x| - 1|$

In function, $y = ||x| - 1|$ we have 3 sharp edges at $x = -1, 0, 1$.

Hence, $f(x)$ is not differentiable at $\{0, \pm 1\}$.

4. Applications of Derivatives

DPP-1 Derivative as Rate Measure

1. Let A be the area of the rectangle and x be its breadth.
According to the given information,

$$\frac{dA}{dt} = 48 \text{ cm}^2/\text{s}$$

$\therefore$ Breadth $= x$, then length $= x^2$

$$\because \quad \text{Area, } A = \text{Length} \times \text{Breadth} = x^2 \times x = x^3$$

On differentiating both sides w.r.t. 't', we get

$$\frac{dA}{dt} = 3x^2 \frac{dx}{dt}$$

$$\Rightarrow \quad 48 = 3x^2 \frac{dx}{dt}$$

$$\Rightarrow \quad \left(\frac{dx}{dt}\right) = \frac{48}{3x^2}$$

Now,
$$\frac{d}{dt}(x^2) = 2x\frac{dx}{dt}$$

$$\therefore \quad \left[\frac{d}{dx}x^2\right]_{x=4.5} = 2 \times 4.5 \times \frac{48}{3 \times (4.5)^2} \quad \left[\because \frac{dx}{dt} = \frac{48}{3x^2}\right]$$

$$= 7.11 \text{ cm/s}$$

2. Let S be the surface area of balloon. Then, $S = 4\pi r^2$, where r is the radius of the balloon.
According to the given information,

$$\frac{dr}{dt} = 10 \text{ m/s}$$

Now,
$$\frac{dS}{dt} = 4\pi(2r)\frac{dr}{dt}$$

$$= 8\pi r \cdot (10) \quad \left[\because \frac{dr}{dt} = 10\right]$$

$$= 80\pi r$$

$$\therefore \quad \left(\frac{dS}{dt}\right)_{r=15} = 80 \times 15\pi = 1200\pi \text{ cm}^2/\text{s}$$

3. Let x be the length of each edge of the cube, S be its surface area and V be its volume at any time t, then

$$S = 6x^2 \quad \text{and} \quad V = x^3$$

It is given that, $\frac{dV}{dt} = k$ (constant)

Now,
$$V = x^3$$

$$\Rightarrow \quad \frac{dV}{dt} = 3x^2\frac{dx}{dt}$$

$$\Rightarrow \quad k = 3x^2\frac{dx}{dt} \Rightarrow \frac{dx}{dt} = \frac{k}{3x^2}$$

and
$$S = 6x^2$$

$$\therefore \quad \frac{dS}{dt} = 12x\frac{dx}{dt}$$

$$\Rightarrow \quad \frac{dS}{dt} = 12x\left(\frac{k}{3x^2}\right)$$

$$\Rightarrow \quad \frac{dS}{dt} = \frac{4k}{x}$$

$$\therefore \quad \frac{dS}{dt} \propto \frac{1}{x}$$

Hence, the rate of increase in surface area varies inversely as the length of edge of the cube.

4. It is given that the plane is ascending vertically at the constant rate of 100 km/h.

$$\therefore \quad \frac{dh}{dt} = 100 \text{ km/h} \quad \ldots\text{(i)}$$

Height of the plane after 3 min $= 100 \times \frac{3}{60} = 5$ km

[using, $h = v \cdot t$]

Now,
$$A = 2\pi r^2\left(\frac{h}{h+r}\right)$$

$$\therefore \quad \frac{dA}{dt} = 2\pi r^2 \frac{d}{dt}\left(\frac{h}{r+h}\right)$$

$$= 2\pi r^2 \left\{\frac{(r+h)\frac{dh}{dt} - h\frac{d}{dt}(r+h)}{(r+h)^2}\right\}$$

$$= 2\pi r^2 \left\{\frac{(r+h)\frac{dh}{dt} - h\frac{dh}{dt}}{(r+h)^2}\right\} = \frac{2\pi r^3}{(r+h)^2}\frac{dh}{dt}$$

$$= \frac{2\pi r^3}{(r+h)^2} \times 100 \quad \left[\because \frac{dh}{dt} = 100 \text{ km/h}\right]$$

$$= \frac{200\pi r^3}{(r+h)^2}$$

We want to find $\frac{dA}{dt}$, when $t = 3$ min.

At $t = 3$, we have $h = 5$ km

$$\therefore \quad \left(\frac{dA}{dt}\right)_{t=3} = \frac{200\pi r^3}{(r+5)^2}$$

5. Let AB be the position of the ladder at any time t such that $OA = x$ and $OB = y$.

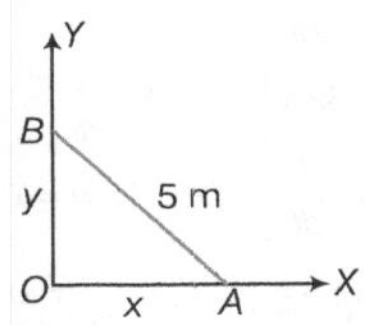

Then,
$$OA^2 + OB^2 = AB^2$$

$$\Rightarrow \quad x^2 + y^2 = 5^2 \quad \ldots\text{(i)}$$

It is given that the bottom of the ladder is pulled along the ground away from the wall at the rate of 2 m/s.

$$\therefore \quad \frac{dx}{dt} = 2 \text{ m/s}$$

Now,
$$x^2 + y^2 = 5^2$$

$$\Rightarrow \quad 2x\frac{dx}{dt} + 2y\frac{dy}{dt} = 0$$

$$\Rightarrow \quad 2x(2) + 2y\frac{dy}{dt} = 0$$

$$\Rightarrow \quad \frac{dy}{dt} = \frac{-2x}{y} \quad \ldots\text{(ii)}$$

On putting $x = 4$ in Eq. (i), we get $y = 3$

On putting $x = 4$ and $y = 3$ in Eq. (ii), we get

$$\frac{dy}{dt} = \left(-\frac{8}{3}\right) \text{m/s}$$

6. Let r be the radius, h be the height and V be the volume of the sand cone at any time t.

Then, $$V = \frac{1}{3}\pi r^2 h$$

$\Rightarrow$ $$V = \frac{1}{3}\pi(36h^2)h = 12\pi h^3 \quad [\because r = 6h]$$

$\Rightarrow$ $$\frac{dV}{dt} = 36\pi h^2 \frac{dh}{dt} \quad \ldots\text{(i)}$$

$\Rightarrow$ $$\frac{dh}{dt} = \frac{1}{3\pi h^2} \quad \left[\because \frac{dV}{dt} = 12\right]$$

$\therefore$ $$\left(\frac{dh}{dt}\right)_{h=4} = \frac{1}{3\pi(4)^2} = \frac{1}{48\pi}$$

Thus, the height of the sand cone is increasing at the rate of $\frac{1}{48\pi}$ cm/s.

7. Let horizontal distance moved by kite is x and length of string y.

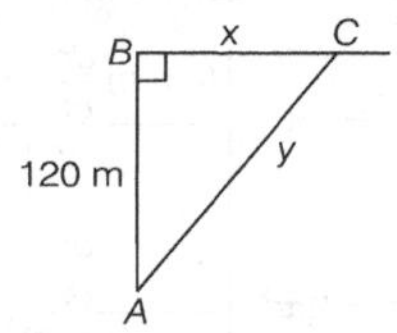

From the above figure, we have

$$y^2 = x^2 + (120)^2 \quad \ldots\text{(i)}$$

$\Rightarrow$ $$2y\frac{dy}{dt} = 2x\frac{dx}{dt} \Rightarrow \frac{dy}{dt} = \frac{x}{y}\frac{dx}{dt}$$

$\Rightarrow$ $$\frac{dy}{dt} = 52 \cdot \frac{x}{y} \quad \left[\because \frac{dx}{dt} = 52\right]$$

On putting $y = 130$ in Eq. (i), we get

$$x = 50$$

$\therefore$ $$\frac{dy}{dt} = \frac{52 \times 50}{130} = 20 \text{ m/s}$$

8. Given equation of ellipse is

$$16x^2 + 9y^2 = 400 \quad \ldots\text{(i)}$$

It is given that, $$\frac{dy}{dt} = \frac{-dx}{dt}$$

From Eq. (i), $$32x\frac{dx}{dt} + 18y\frac{dy}{dt} = 0$$

$\Rightarrow$ $$\frac{dx}{dt}(32x - 18y) = 0$$

$\therefore$ $$\frac{dx}{dt} \neq 0$$

$\therefore$ $$32x - 18y = 0 \Rightarrow x = \frac{18}{32}y$$

$\Rightarrow$ $$\frac{x}{y} = \frac{9}{16} \Rightarrow x = 9k,\ y = 16k$$

On putting these values of x and y in Eq. (i), we get

$$16 \times 81k^2 + 9 \times 256k^2 = 400$$

$\Rightarrow$ $$1296k^2 + 2304k^2 = 400$$

$\Rightarrow$ $$3600k^2 = 400$$

$\Rightarrow$ $$k^2 = \frac{400}{3600} = \frac{1}{9}$$

$\Rightarrow$ $$k = \pm\frac{1}{3}$$

When $k = \frac{1}{3}$, then $x = 3$ and $y = \frac{16}{3}$

when $k = -\frac{1}{3}$, then $x = -3$ and $y = \frac{-16}{3}$

Hence, the required points are $\left(3, \frac{16}{3}\right)$ and $\left(-3, \frac{-16}{3}\right)$.

9. (b) Let $AB = 13$ ft is ladder and $AC = x$, $BC = y$.

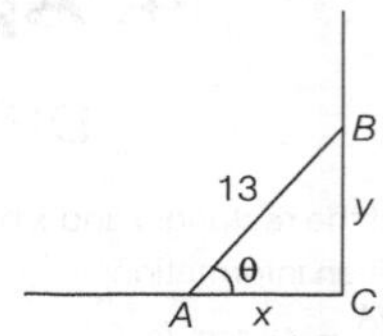

In right angled ΔACB, $x^2 + y^2 = (13)^2 \quad \ldots\text{(i)}$

$\Rightarrow$ $$\tan\theta = \frac{y}{x} \quad \ldots\text{(ii)}$$

It is given that, $$\frac{dx}{dt} = 5 \text{ ft/ s} \quad \ldots\text{(iii)}$$

On differentiating Eq. (i) w.r.t. t, we get

$$2x\frac{dx}{dt} + 2y\frac{dy}{dt} = 0$$

$\Rightarrow$ $$\frac{dy}{dt} = \frac{-x}{y}\frac{dx}{dt} \quad \ldots\text{(iv)}$$

On differentiating Eq. (ii) w.r.t. t, we get

$$\sec^2\theta\frac{d\theta}{dt} = \frac{x\frac{dy}{dt} - y\frac{dx}{dt}}{x^2}$$

$$= \frac{-x \times \frac{x}{y}\frac{dx}{dt} - y\frac{dx}{dt}}{x^2} \quad \text{[using Eq. (iv)]}$$

$\Rightarrow$ $$\sec^2\theta\frac{d\theta}{dt} = \frac{\left(-\frac{x^2}{y} - y\right)\frac{dx}{dt}}{x^2}$$

$\Rightarrow$ $$\frac{d\theta}{dt} = \frac{\left(-\frac{x^2}{y} - y\right)\frac{dx}{dt}}{x^2\sec^2\theta} \quad \ldots\text{(v)}$$

When $x = 12$, then $y = \sqrt{(13)^2 - (12)^2} = 5$

Now, $$\left(\frac{d\theta}{dt}\right)_{x=12,\ y=5} = \frac{\left(\frac{-144}{5} - 5\right)5}{(12)^2\left(\frac{13}{12}\right)^2} \quad \left[\because \sec\theta = \frac{13}{12}\right]$$

$$= \frac{\left(\frac{-144-25}{5}\right) \times 5}{(13)^2} = \frac{-169}{(13)^2} = -1 \text{ rad/s}$$

10. (b) Let α be the semi-vertical angle of the cone $C'AB$ whose height CO is 4 m and radius $OB = 2$ m, then

$$\tan\alpha = \frac{1}{2}$$

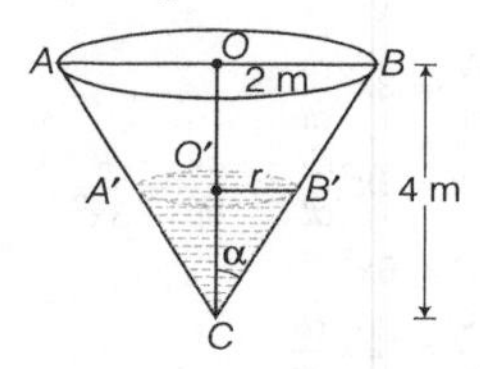

Let V be the volume of water in the cone i.e. the volume of the cone $CA'B'$.

After time t min, h be the height of the water, then

$$V = \frac{1}{3}\pi(O'B')^2(CO')$$

$\Rightarrow$ $$V = \frac{1}{3}\pi h^3\tan^2\alpha \quad \left[\because \tan\alpha = \frac{O'B'}{CO'} = \frac{O'B'}{h} \Rightarrow O'B' = h\tan\alpha\right]$$

$\Rightarrow$ $$V = \frac{\pi}{12}h^3$$

Now, $\dfrac{dV}{dt} = \dfrac{\pi}{12} 3h^2 \dfrac{dh}{dt} = \dfrac{\pi}{4} h^2 \dfrac{dh}{dt}$

$\Rightarrow \quad 77 \times 10^3 = \dfrac{\pi h^2}{4} \cdot \dfrac{dh}{dt}$ $\quad \left[\begin{array}{l} \because 1\,\text{L} = 10^3\,\text{cm}^3 \\ \therefore 77\,\text{L} = 77 \times 10^3 \text{cm}^3 \\ \text{i.e. } \dfrac{dV}{dt} = 77\,\text{L} = 77 \times 10^3\,\text{cm}^3 \end{array}\right]$

$\Rightarrow \quad \dfrac{dh}{dt} = \dfrac{77 \times 4 \times 10^3}{\pi h^2}$

$\therefore \quad \left(\dfrac{dh}{dt}\right)_h = \dfrac{77 \times 4 \times 10^3}{\pi \times (70)^2} = \dfrac{77 \times 4 \times 7 \times 10^3}{22 \times 70 \times 70} = 20\,\text{cm/min}$

11. (c) Given equation of the curve is

$$y^3 = 27x \quad \text{...(i)}$$

On differentiating Eq. (i) w.r.t. y, we get

$$3y^2 = 27\frac{dx}{dy} \Rightarrow \frac{dx}{dy} = \frac{y^2}{9}$$

If abscissa changes at a slower rate than the ordinate, then

$$\left|\frac{dx}{dy}\right| < 1 \quad \Rightarrow \quad \left|\frac{y^2}{9}\right| < 1$$

$\Rightarrow \quad |y^2| < 9$

$\Rightarrow \quad -3 < y < 3$

$\therefore \quad y \in (-3, 3)$ and $x \in (-1, 1)$

12. (a) Given equation of the curve is

$$y = x^{3/2}$$

$\Rightarrow \quad \dfrac{dy}{dt} = \dfrac{3}{2} x^{1/2} \dfrac{dx}{dt} \quad \text{...(i)}$

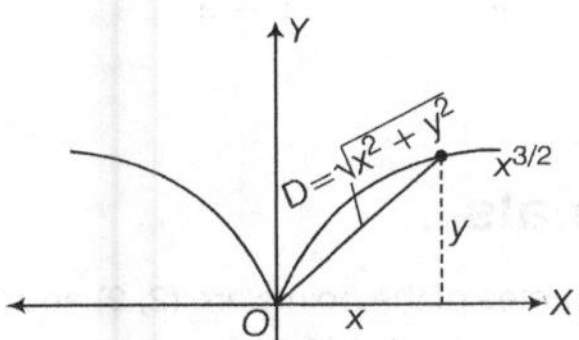

Let D be the distance of particle form origin i.e. $D = \sqrt{x^2 + y^2}$.

$\therefore \quad \dfrac{dD}{dt} = \dfrac{1}{2\sqrt{x^2 + y^2}}\left(2x\dfrac{dx}{dt} + 2y\dfrac{dy}{dt}\right)$

$\Rightarrow \quad \dfrac{dD}{dt} = \dfrac{1}{2\sqrt{x^2 + y^2}}\left(2x\dfrac{dx}{dt} + 2y\dfrac{3}{2}x^{1/2}\dfrac{dx}{dt}\right)$

$\Rightarrow \quad 11 = \dfrac{1}{2\sqrt{x^2 + y^2}}(2x + 3y^{1/2})\dfrac{dx}{dt} \quad \left[\because \dfrac{dD}{dt} = 11\,\text{units/s}\right]$

Now, $\quad \dfrac{dx}{dt} = \dfrac{22\sqrt{x^2 + y^2}}{(2x + 3yx^{1/2})}$

$\therefore \quad \left(\dfrac{dx}{dt}\right)_{x=3} = \dfrac{22\sqrt{9 + 27}}{[2 \times 3 + 3 \times (3)^2]} \quad \left[\begin{array}{l}\text{when } x = 3, \\ \text{then } y = (3)^{3/2}\end{array}\right]$

$= \dfrac{22 \times 6}{33} = \dfrac{132}{33} = 4$

13. (c) Given, x and y are the sides of squares. Then, the area of the squares are x^2 and y^2.

We have to obtain, $\dfrac{d(y^2)}{d(x^2)} = \dfrac{2y\dfrac{dy}{dx}}{2x} = \dfrac{y}{x} \times \dfrac{dy}{dx} \quad \text{...(i)}$

Given curve is $y = x - x^2$

$\Rightarrow \quad \dfrac{dy}{dx} = 1 - 2x \quad \text{...(ii)}$

Thus, $\quad \dfrac{d(y^2)}{d(x^2)} = \dfrac{y}{x}(1 - 2x) \quad$ [from Eqs. (i) and (ii)]

$\Rightarrow \quad \dfrac{d(y^2)}{d(x^2)} = \dfrac{(x - x^2)(1 - 2x)}{x}$

$\Rightarrow \quad \dfrac{d(y^2)}{d(x^2)} = 2x^2 - 3x + 1$

$\therefore \quad \left[\dfrac{d(y^2)}{d(x^2)}\right]_{x=2} = 2 \times 2^2 - 3 \times 2 + 1 = 3$

14. (b)

(i) Given, $r = 5$ cm, $\delta r = 0.06$

$\because \quad A = \pi r^2$

$\therefore \quad \delta A = 2\pi r\,\delta r$

$= 2\pi(5)(0.06) = 0.6\pi$

(ii) Given, $V = x^3$, $\delta V = 3x^2 \delta x$

$\therefore \quad \dfrac{\delta V}{V} \times 100 = 3\dfrac{\delta x}{x} \times 100 = 3 \times 1 = 3 \quad \left[\because \dfrac{\delta x}{x} \times 100 = 1\right]$

(iii) Let $y = \dfrac{x^2}{2} - 2x + 5$

Given that, $\quad \dfrac{dy}{dt} = 2\dfrac{dx}{dt} \Rightarrow (x - 2)\dfrac{dx}{dt} = 2\dfrac{dx}{dt}$

$\therefore \quad x = 4$

(iv) $\because \quad A = \dfrac{\sqrt{3}}{4}x^2$

$\therefore \quad \dfrac{dA}{dt} = \dfrac{\sqrt{3}}{2}\left(x\dfrac{dx}{dt}\right) = \dfrac{\sqrt{3}}{2} \times 15 \times 0.1$

$= \dfrac{15\sqrt{3}}{20} = \dfrac{3\sqrt{3}}{4}$

Hence, (i) $\to$ q; (ii) $\to$ r; (iii) $\to$ p; (iv) $\to$ s

Explanations for Q. Nos. (15 and 16)

Let V be the volume and r be the radius of the balloon at any time, then

$$V = \frac{4}{3}\pi r^3 \Rightarrow \frac{dV}{dt} = \frac{4}{3} 3\pi r^2 \frac{dr}{dt}$$

$\Rightarrow \quad \dfrac{dV}{dt} = 4\pi r^2 \dfrac{dr}{dt}$

$\Rightarrow \quad 40 = 4\pi r^2 \dfrac{dr}{dt} \quad \left[\because \dfrac{dV}{dt} = 40\,\text{cm}^3/\text{min}\right]$

$\Rightarrow \quad 10 = \pi r^2 \dfrac{dr}{dt}$

$\Rightarrow \quad \dfrac{dr}{dt} = \dfrac{10}{\pi r^2} \quad \text{...(i)}$

Again, let S be the surface area of the balloon, when its radius is r_1, then

$$S = 4\pi r^2$$

$\Rightarrow \quad \dfrac{dS}{dt} = 8\pi r \dfrac{dr}{dt} \quad \text{...(ii)}$

From Eqs. (i) and (ii), we get

$$\frac{dS}{dt} = \frac{80}{r}$$

When $r = 8$, then rate of increase of $S = \dfrac{80}{8} = 10\,\text{cm}^2/\text{min}$

$\therefore$ Increase of S in 1/2 min $= 10 \times \dfrac{1}{2} = 5\,\text{cm}^2/\text{min}$

If r_1 is the radius of the balloon after 1/2 min, then

$$4\pi r_1^2 = 4\pi(8)^2 + 5$$

$\Rightarrow \quad r_1^2 - 8^2 = \dfrac{5}{4\pi} = 0.397$ (approx.)

Now, $\quad r_1^2 = 64.397$

$\Rightarrow \quad r_1 = 8.025$ (approx.)

$\therefore$ Required increase in the radius $= r_1 - 8$

$= 8.025 - 8 = 0.025$ cm

15. (b) **16.** (a)

17. (b) Given, $\frac{dV}{dt} = \pi \text{m}^3/\text{s}$

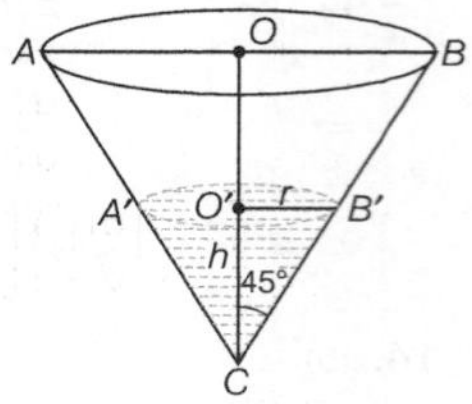

Semi-vertical angle, $\alpha = 45°$

Let $O'B' = r$ and $O'C = h$

In $\Delta O'B'C$, $\tan 45° = \frac{O'B'}{O'C}$

$$1 = \frac{r}{h}$$

$\Rightarrow$ $r = h$

$\Rightarrow$ $V = \frac{1}{3}\pi r^2 h$

$\Rightarrow$ $V = \frac{1}{3}\pi h^3$ $[\because r = h]$

$\Rightarrow$ $\frac{dV}{dt} = \frac{1}{3}\pi \times 3h^2 \frac{dh}{dt}$

$\Rightarrow$ $\frac{dV}{dt} = \pi h^2 \frac{dh}{dt}$

$\Rightarrow$ $\frac{dh}{dt} = \frac{1}{\pi h^2} \times \frac{dV}{dt} = \frac{1}{\pi h^2} \times \pi = \frac{1}{h^2}$ m/s

$\therefore$ $\left(\frac{dh}{dt}\right)_{\text{at } h=2} = \frac{1}{(2)^2} = \frac{1}{4} = 0.25$ m/s

18. (a) Let A be the top surface area of water.

Then, $A = \pi r^2 = \pi h^2$ $[\because r = h]$

$\therefore$ $\frac{dA}{dt} = 2\pi \frac{dh}{dt}$

$\Rightarrow$ $\left(\frac{dA}{dt}\right)_{\text{at } h=1} = 2\pi \times \left(\frac{dh}{dt}\right)_{\text{at } h=1}$

$$= 2\pi \times 1 = 2\pi$$

19. (2) Let V be the volume of sphere.

then, $V = \frac{4}{3}\pi r^3$

$\Rightarrow$ $\frac{dV}{dt} = \frac{4}{3}\pi 3r^2 \frac{dr}{dt}$ ...(i)

It is given that, $\frac{dV}{dt} = \frac{dr}{dt}$ ...(ii)

From Eqs. (i) and (ii), we get

$$r^2 = \frac{1}{4\pi} \Rightarrow r = \frac{1}{2\sqrt{\pi}}$$

But it is given that $r = \frac{1}{k\sqrt{\pi}}$

$\therefore$ $k = 2$

20. (5) Let $PQ = 4$ m be the height of the pole and $AB = 1.6$ m be the height of the man. Let the end of shadow be R and it is at a distance of l from A when the man is at distance x from PQ at some instant.

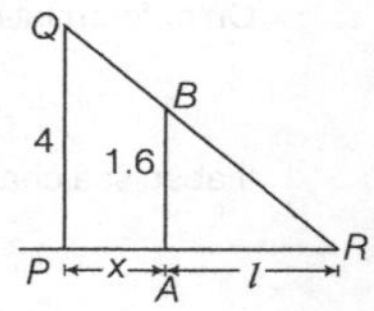

We have, $\frac{PQ}{AB} = \frac{PR}{AR}$

$[\because \Delta PQR$ and ΔABR are similar$]$

$\Rightarrow$ $\frac{4}{1.6} = \frac{x + l}{l} \Rightarrow 2x = 3l$

$\Rightarrow$ $2\frac{dx}{dt} = 3\frac{dl}{dt}$

$\Rightarrow$ $\frac{dl}{dt} = \frac{2}{3} \times 30 \text{ m/min} = 20 \text{ m/min}$

But $\frac{dl}{dt} = k \Rightarrow \frac{k}{4} = \frac{20}{4} = 5$

DPP-2 Tangents and Normals

1. Given equation of curve is

$$3x^2 - y^2 = 8 \quad \text{...(i)}$$

Let the coordinate of the point of contact be (x_1, y_1).

$\therefore$ $(x_1\ y_1)$ lies on the curve (i), then

$$3x_1^2 - y_1^2 = 8 \quad \text{...(ii)}$$

On differentiating Eq. (i) w.r.t. x, we get

$$6x - 2y\frac{dy}{dx} = 0$$

$\Rightarrow$ $\frac{dy}{dx} = \frac{6x}{2y} = \frac{3x}{y}$

$\Rightarrow$ $\left(\frac{dy}{dx}\right)_{(x_1, y_1)} = \frac{3x_1}{y_1}$

Since, normal to the curve is parallel to the line $x + 3y = 4$

i.e. $-\frac{1}{\left(\frac{dy}{dx}\right)_{(x_1, y_1)}} = \text{Slope of line } x + 3y = 4$

$\Rightarrow$ $-\frac{1}{\left(\frac{dy}{dx}\right)_{(x_1, y_1)}} = -\frac{1}{3}$

$\Rightarrow$ $\left(\frac{dy}{dx}\right)_{(x_1, y_1)} = 3 \Rightarrow \frac{3x_1}{y_1} = 3 \Rightarrow x_1 = y_1$ ...(iii)

From Eqs. (ii) and (iii), we have

$$3x_1^2 - x_1^2 = 8$$

$\Rightarrow$ $2x_1^2 = 8 \Rightarrow x_1^2 = 4$

$\Rightarrow$ $x_1 = \pm 2$

When $x_1 = 2$, then $y_1 = 2$

When $x_1 = -2$, then $y_1 = -2$

Thus, coordinates of the points are (2, 2) and (−2, 2).

The equation of normal at (2, 2) is

$$y - 2 = \frac{-1}{3}(x - 2)$$

$\Rightarrow$ $y - 2 = \frac{-1}{3x} + \frac{2}{3}$

$\Rightarrow$ $x + 3y - 8 = 0$

and equation of the normal at (−2, −2) is

$$y + 2 = -\frac{1}{3}(x + 2)$$

$\Rightarrow$ $3y + 6 = -x - 2$

$\Rightarrow$ $x + 3y + 8 = 0$

2. The equation of given curve is

$$y = be^{-x/a} \quad \text{...(i)}$$

Since, it crosses Y-axis at the point, where $x = 0$.

Putting $x = 0$ in Eq. (i), we get

$$y = be^0 = b$$

So, the point of contact is $(0, b)$.

On differentiating Eq. (i) w.r.t. x, we get

$$\left(\frac{dy}{dx}\right) = be^{-x/a}\frac{d}{dx}\left(\frac{-x}{a}\right) = \frac{-b}{a}e^{-x/a}$$

$\therefore$ $\left(\frac{dy}{dx}\right)_{(0, b)} = \frac{-be^0}{a} = \frac{-b}{a}$

The equation of the tangent at $(0, b)$ is

$$y - b = \frac{-b}{a}(x - 0)$$

$\Rightarrow$ $y - b = \frac{-b}{a}x$

$\Rightarrow$ $ay - ab = -bx$

$$\Rightarrow \quad ay + bx - ab = 0$$

$$\Rightarrow \quad \frac{x}{a} + \frac{y}{b} = 1$$

Hence, $\frac{x}{a} + \frac{y}{b} = 1$ touches the curve $y = -be^{-x/a}$ at the point, where it crosses the X-axis.

3. Let the line $x\cos\alpha + y\sin\alpha = p$ touches the curve

$$\frac{x^2}{a^2} + \frac{y^2}{b^2} = 1 \text{ at } (x_1, y_1).$$

$$\therefore \quad \frac{x_1^2}{a^2} + \frac{y_1^2}{b^2} = 1 \quad \ldots\text{(i)}$$

and $\quad x_1\cos\alpha + y_1\sin\alpha = p \quad \ldots$(ii)

On differentiating $\frac{x^2}{a^2} + \frac{y^2}{b^2} = 1$ w.r.t. x, we get

$$\frac{2x}{a^2} + \frac{2y}{b^2}\frac{dy}{dx} = 0$$

$$\Rightarrow \quad \frac{dy}{dx} = \frac{-2x/a^2}{2y/b^2} \quad \Rightarrow \quad \frac{dy}{dx} = \frac{-b^2}{a^2}\frac{x}{y}$$

$$\Rightarrow \quad \left(\frac{dy}{dx}\right)_{(x_1, y_1)} = \frac{-b^2}{a^2}\left(\frac{x_1}{y_1}\right)$$

Now, slope of tangent to the curve = Slope of the line

$$\frac{-b^2}{a^2}\frac{x_1}{y_1} = \frac{-\cos\alpha}{\sin\alpha} \quad \Rightarrow \quad \frac{x_1}{y_1} = \frac{a^2\cos\alpha}{b^2\sin\alpha}$$

$$\Rightarrow \quad x_1 = \frac{a^2\cos\alpha}{b^2\sin\alpha}\cdot y_1 \quad \ldots\text{(iii)}$$

Form Eqs. (ii) and (iii), we have

$$\frac{a^2\cos^2\alpha}{b^2\sin\alpha}y_1 + y_1\sin\alpha = p$$

$$\Rightarrow \quad y_1\left(\frac{a^2\cos^2\alpha}{b^2\sin\alpha} + \sin\alpha\right) = p$$

$$\Rightarrow \quad y_1(a^2\cos^2\alpha + b^2\sin^2\alpha) = p\cdot b^2\sin\alpha$$

$$\Rightarrow \quad y_1 = \frac{pb^2\sin\alpha}{a^2\cos^2\alpha + b^2\sin^2\alpha} \quad \ldots\text{(iv)}$$

and $\quad x_1 = \frac{pa^2\cos\alpha}{a^2\cos^2\alpha + b^2\sin^2\alpha}$

On substituting these values of x_1, y_1 in Eq. (i), we get

$$\frac{1}{a^2}\left[\frac{p^2a^4\cos^2\alpha}{(a^2\cos^2\alpha + b^2\sin^2\alpha)^2}\right] + \frac{1}{b^2}\left[\frac{p^2b^4\sin^2\alpha}{(a^2\cos^2\alpha + b^2\sin^2\alpha)^2}\right] = 1$$

$$\Rightarrow \quad p^2a^2\cos^2\alpha + p^2b^2\sin^2\alpha = (a^2\cos^2\alpha + b^2\sin^2\alpha)^2$$

$$\Rightarrow \quad p^2(a^2\cos^2\alpha + b^2\sin^2\alpha) = (a^2\cos^2\alpha + b^2\sin^2\alpha)^2$$

$$\therefore \quad p^2 = (a^2\cos^2\alpha + b^2\sin^2\alpha)$$

4. The equation of curve is

$$x^m\cdot y^n = a^{m+n} \quad \ldots\text{(i)}$$

and line $\quad x\cos\alpha + y\sin\alpha = p \quad \ldots$(ii)

Let line touches the curve at (x_1, a_1).

$$\therefore \quad x_1^m\cdot y_1^n = a^{m+n} \quad \ldots\text{(iii)}$$

and $\quad x_1\cos\alpha + y_1\sin\alpha = p \quad \ldots$(iv)

Now, differentiating Eq. (i) w.r.t. x, we get

$$mx^{m-1}y^n + x^m ny^{n-1}\frac{dy}{dx} = 0$$

$$\Rightarrow \quad \left(\frac{dy}{dx}\right)_{(x_1, y_1)} = \frac{-mx_1^{m-1}y_1^n}{ny_1^{n-1}x_1^m}$$

Since, line touches the curve.

$$\therefore \quad \frac{-m}{n}\frac{x_1^{m-1}y_1^n}{y_1^{n-1}x_1^m} = -\frac{\cos\alpha}{\sin\alpha}$$

$$\Rightarrow \quad \frac{-m}{n}x_1^{-1}y_1 = \frac{-\cos\alpha}{\sin\alpha}$$

$$\Rightarrow \quad \frac{y_1}{x_1} = \frac{n\cos\alpha}{m\sin\alpha} \quad \ldots\text{(v)}$$

From Eqs. (iv) and (v), we have

$$x_1 = \frac{pm}{(m+n)\cos\alpha}$$

and $\quad y_1 = \frac{pn}{(m+n)\sin\alpha}$

On substituting these values of x_1, y_1 in Eq. (iii), we get

$$\frac{p^n n^n}{\sin^n\alpha(m+n)^n} \times \frac{p^m m^m}{\cos^m\alpha\,(m+n)^m} = a^{m+n}$$

$$\Rightarrow \quad \frac{p^{m+n}n^n\cdot m^m}{(m+n)^{m+n}\sin^n\alpha\,\cos^m\alpha} = a^{m+n}$$

$$\therefore \quad p^{m+n}\cdot m^m\cdot n^n = (m+n)^{m+n}\cos^m\alpha\cdot\sin^n\alpha\cdot a^{m+n}$$

5. The given curves are

$$x = y^2 \quad \ldots\text{(i)}$$

and $\quad xy = k \quad \ldots$(ii)

On solving Eqs. (i) and (ii), we get

$$x = k^{2/3},\ y = k^{1/3}$$

So, the two curves intersect at the point $P(k^{2/3}, k^{1/3})$.

On differentiating Eq. (i) w.r.t. x, we get

$$1 = 2y\frac{dy}{dx}$$

$$\Rightarrow \quad \frac{dy}{dx} = \frac{1}{2y}$$

$$\Rightarrow \quad m_1 = \left(\frac{dy}{dx}\right)_{(k^{2/3},\,k^{1/3})} = \frac{1}{2^{k^{1//3}}}$$

On differentiating Eq. (ii) w.r.t. x, we get

$$x\frac{dy}{dx} + y = 0 \Rightarrow \frac{dy}{dx} = \frac{-y}{x}$$

$$\Rightarrow \quad m_2 = \left(\frac{dy}{dx}\right)_{(k^{2/3},\,k^{1/3})} = -k^{1/3/k^{2/3}} = -\frac{1}{k^{1/3}}$$

For the curves (i) and (ii) to cut at right angled at $(k^{2/3}, k^{1/3})$, we must have

$$m_1\cdot m_2 = -1$$

$$\Rightarrow \quad \frac{1}{2k^{1/3}}\cdot\left(-\frac{1}{k^{1/3}}\right) = -1$$

$$\Rightarrow \quad 2k^{2/3} = 1$$

$$\Rightarrow \quad (2k^{2/3})^3 = 1^3$$

$$\therefore \quad 8k^2 = 1$$

6. Tangent at (h, k) to $y = \sin x$ is

$\frac{y-k}{x-h} = \cos h$, passes through the point (0, 0).

$$\Rightarrow \quad \frac{-k}{-h} = \cos h$$

$$\text{or} \quad \cos h = \frac{k}{h} \quad \ldots\text{(i)}$$

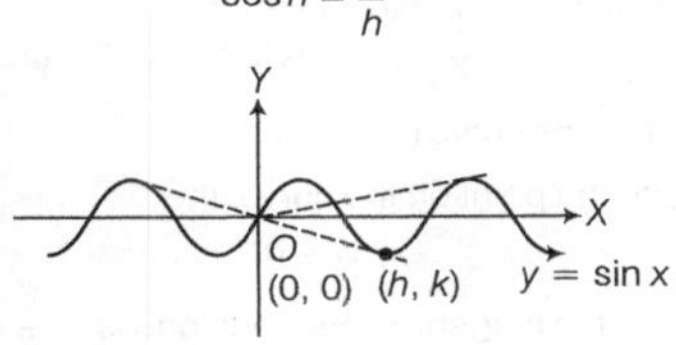

Also, (h, k) lies on $y = \sin x$.

$$\Rightarrow \quad k = \sin h \quad \ldots\text{(ii)}$$

On squaring and adding Eqs. (i) and (ii), we get

$$\Rightarrow \quad \frac{k^2}{h^2} + k^2 = \sin^2 h + \cos^2 h$$

$$\Rightarrow \quad \frac{y^2}{x^2} + y^2 = 1 \Rightarrow x^2y^2 = (x^2 - y^2)$$

7. (b) We have, $x = a\cos^3 t$, $y = a\sin^3 t$

$$\Rightarrow \quad \frac{dx}{dt} = -3a\cos^2 t \sin t, \frac{dy}{dt} = 3a\sin^2 t + \cos t$$

$$\therefore \quad \frac{dy}{dx} = \frac{3a\sin^2 t + \cos t}{-3a\cos^2 t \sin t}$$

$$\frac{dy}{dx} = -\tan t$$

So, the equation of tangent at t is

$$y - a\sin^3 t = -\tan t\,(x - a\cos^3 t)$$

$$\Rightarrow \quad \cos t\,(y - a\sin^3 t) = -\sin t\,(x - a\cos^3 t)$$

$$\Rightarrow \quad y\cos t - a\sin^3 t\cos t = -x\sin t + a\sin t\cos^3 t$$

$$\Rightarrow \quad x\sin t + y\cos t = a\sin t\cos^3 t + a\sin^3 t + \cos t$$

$$\Rightarrow \quad x\sec t + y\operatorname{cosec} t = a$$

8. (d) Given, $y = x + \sin x\cos x$

Now, $$\frac{dy}{dx} = 1 + \cos^2 x - \sin^2 x$$

$$\therefore \quad \left(\frac{dy}{dx}\right)_{x=\frac{\pi}{2}} = 0$$

When $x = \frac{\pi}{2}$, then $y = \frac{\pi}{2}$

$\therefore$ Equation of the normal at $\left(\frac{\pi}{2}, \frac{\pi}{2}\right)$ is

$$y - \frac{\pi}{2} = \frac{-1}{0}\left(x - \frac{\pi}{2}\right)$$

$$\Rightarrow \quad x = \frac{\pi}{2} \Rightarrow 2x = \pi$$

9. (c) Given, $x + y = x^y$ ...(i)

Since, the curve cuts X-axis, where $y = 0$.

$$\therefore \quad x = x^0 \Rightarrow x = 1$$

So the point of contact is (1, 0).

On differentiating Eq. (i) w.r.t. x, we get

$$1 + \frac{dy}{dx} = x^y\left(\frac{y}{x} + \log x \cdot \frac{dy}{dx}\right)$$

$$\Rightarrow \quad 1 + \frac{dy}{dx} - x^y\frac{dy}{dx}\cdot\log x = x^y \cdot \frac{y}{x}$$

$$\Rightarrow \quad \frac{dy}{dx}(1 - x^y \log x) = x^y \frac{y}{x} = -1$$

$$\Rightarrow \quad \frac{dy}{dx} = \frac{x^y\left(\frac{y}{x}\right) - 1}{(1 - x^y\log x)}$$

$$\therefore \quad \left(\frac{dy}{dx}\right)_{(1,\,0)} = \frac{-1}{1} = -1$$

So, the equation of normal at (1, 0) is

$$y - 0 = 1\,(x - 1) \Rightarrow x - y - 1 = 0$$

10. (c) Equation of the curve is $x^2 y = c^3$ ...(i)

Let (x_1, y_1) be the point on the curve, the

$$x_1^2 y_1 = c^3 \quad \text{...(ii)}$$

$\therefore$ Equation of the tangent in intercept form is $\frac{x}{a} + \frac{y}{b} = 1$ ...(iii)

Equation of the tangent at (x_1, y_1) is

$$\frac{x_1}{a} + \frac{y_1}{a} = 1 \quad \text{...(iv)}$$

On differentiating Eq. (i) w.r.t. x, we get

$$2xy + x^2\frac{dy}{dx} = 0$$

$$\Rightarrow \quad \frac{dy}{dx} = \frac{-2xy}{x^2} = \frac{-2y}{x}$$

$$\therefore \quad \left(\frac{dy}{dx}\right)_{(x_1,\,y_1)} = \frac{-2y_1}{x}$$

$$\Rightarrow \quad \frac{-2y_1}{x_1} = \frac{-b}{a} \Rightarrow 2ay_1 = bx_1 \quad \text{...(v)}$$

From Eqs. (iv) and (v), we have

$$x_1 = \frac{2a}{3},\; y_1 = \frac{b}{3}$$

On substituting these values in Eq. (ii), we get

$$\left(\frac{2a}{3}\right)^2\left(\frac{b}{3}\right) = c^3 \Rightarrow a^2 b = \frac{27}{4}c^3$$

11. (b) Given, $\frac{x^4}{2} = x + y$ ...(i)

Let (x_1, y_1) be the point on the curve (i), then

$$\frac{x_1^4}{2} = x_1 + y_1 \quad \text{...(ii)}$$

Also, point (x_1, y_1) lies on the line $3x + 4y = c$.

$$\therefore \quad 3x_1 + 4y_1 = c \quad \text{...(iii)}$$

From Eq. (i), we have

$$\frac{dy}{dx} = 2x^3 - 1$$

$$\Rightarrow \quad \left(\frac{dy}{dx}\right)_{(x_1,\,y_1)} = 2x_1^3 - 1$$

Now, slope of tangent at (x_1, y_3) = Slope of the line

$$\Rightarrow \quad 2x_1^3 - 1 = \frac{-3}{4}$$

$$\Rightarrow \quad 2x_1^3 = \frac{1}{4}$$

$$\Rightarrow \quad x_1^3 = \frac{1}{8} \Rightarrow x_1 = \frac{1}{2}$$

$$\therefore \quad y_1 = \frac{1}{4}\left(c - \frac{3}{2}\right)$$

From Eq. (ii), we have

$$\frac{\left(\frac{1}{2}\right)^4}{2} = \frac{1}{2} + \frac{1}{4}\left(-\frac{3}{2} + c\right)$$

$$\frac{1}{32} = \frac{1}{2} - \frac{3}{8} + \frac{c}{4} \Rightarrow \frac{1}{32} = \frac{1}{8} + \frac{c}{4}$$

$$\Rightarrow \quad \frac{c}{4} = \frac{1}{32} - \frac{1}{8} \Rightarrow \frac{c}{4} = \frac{-3}{32}$$

$$\therefore \quad c = \frac{-3}{8}$$

Hence, only one value of c is possible.

12. (b) Given, $f(x) = x^3 + ax + b, a \neq b$ ...(i)

From Eq. (i), we have

$$f'(x) = 3x^2 + a$$

$$f'(a) = 3a^2 + a$$

$$f'(b) = 3b^2 + a$$

According to the question,

$$f'(a) = f'(b)$$

$$3a^2 + a = 3b^2 + a$$

$$\Rightarrow \quad 3a^2 = 3b^2 \Rightarrow a = \pm b$$

$$\Rightarrow \quad a = -b \quad [\because a \neq b]$$

Now, $$f(1) = 1 + a + b = 1 - b + b \quad [\because a = -b]$$

$$\therefore \quad f(1) = 1$$

13. (b) Given, $3xy^2 - 2x^2y = 1$ ...(i)

$$\Rightarrow \quad 3x2y\frac{dy}{dx} + 3y^2 - 4xy - 2x^2\frac{dy}{dx} = 0$$

$$\Rightarrow \quad (6xy - 2x^2)\frac{dx}{dy} + 3y^2 - 4xy = 0$$

$$\Rightarrow \quad \frac{dy}{dx} = \frac{4xy - 3y^2}{6xy - 2x^2}$$

$$\therefore \quad \left(\frac{dy}{dx}\right)_{(1,\,1)} = \frac{4-3}{6-2} = \frac{1}{4}$$

Equation of the tangent is

$$y - 1 = \frac{1}{4}(x - 1)$$

$$\Rightarrow \quad 4y - 4 = x - 1$$

$$\Rightarrow \quad x - 4y + 3 = 0 \quad \text{...(ii)}$$

From Eqs. (i) and (ii), we have

$$3x\left(\frac{x+3}{4}\right)^2 - 2x^2\left(\frac{x+3}{4}\right) = 1$$

$$\Rightarrow \quad 3x\frac{(x+3)^2}{16} - 2x^2\frac{(x+3)}{4} = 1$$

$$\Rightarrow \quad (x+3)\left[\frac{3x(x+3)}{16} - \frac{x^2}{2}\right] = 1$$

$$\Rightarrow \quad (x+3)\left[\frac{3x^2 + 9x - 8x^2}{16}\right] = 1$$

$$\Rightarrow \quad (x+3)(9x - 5x^2) = 16$$

$$\Rightarrow \quad 9x^2 - 5x^3 + 27x - 15x^2 = 16$$

$$\Rightarrow \quad -6x^2 - 5x^3 + 27x - 16 = 0$$

$$\Rightarrow \quad 5x^3 + 6x^2 - 27x + 16 = 0$$

$$\Rightarrow \quad (x-1)(5x^2 + 11x - 16) = 0$$

$$\Rightarrow \quad (x-1)(5x^2 + 11x - 16) = 0$$

$$\Rightarrow \quad (x-1)(x-1)(5x+16) = 0$$

$$\Rightarrow \quad x = 1, \frac{-16}{5}$$

When $x = \frac{-16}{5}$, then $y = -\frac{1}{20}$

$\therefore$ Other point on the curve where tangent meet again is $\left(\frac{-16}{5}, \frac{-1}{20}\right)$.

14. (c) Equation of the curve is

$$y - e^{xy} + x = 0$$

$$\Rightarrow \quad \frac{dy}{dx} - e^{xy}\left(y + x\frac{dy}{dx}\right) + 1 = 0$$

$$\Rightarrow \quad \frac{dy}{dx}(1 - xe^{xy}) = y\cdot e^{xy} - 1$$

$$\Rightarrow \quad \frac{dx}{dy} = \frac{1 - xe^{xy}}{y\cdot e^{xy} - 1}$$

Clearly, $\frac{dx}{dy} = 0$ at (1, 0)

So, the required point is (1, 0).

15. (c) We have, $\frac{dy}{dx} = 0$ at (0, 1) and (−1, 0)

$$\therefore \quad c = 0 \text{ and } -4a + 3b - c = 0$$

$$\Rightarrow \quad a = 3b/4 \text{ and } c = 0 \quad \text{...(i)}$$

Also, the curve passes through (0, 1) and (−1, 0).

$$\therefore \quad d = 1 \text{ and } 0 = a - b - c + d$$

$$\Rightarrow \quad a - b - c + 1 = 0 \quad \text{...(ii)}$$

From Eqs. (i) and (ii), we get

$$a = 3, b = 4, c = 0, d = 1$$

$$\therefore \quad y = 3x^4 + 4x^3 + 1$$

$$\Rightarrow \quad \frac{dy}{dx} = 12x^3 + kx^{12}$$

Now, $\frac{dy}{dx} < 0$

$$\Rightarrow \quad 12x^3 + 12x^2 < 0$$

$$\Rightarrow \quad x + 1 < 0$$

$$\Rightarrow \quad x < -1$$

16. (b) Here, slope of the tangent is

$$\frac{0 + \lambda}{\lambda/2 - 0} = 2 \quad \text{...(i)}$$

and $y = x^3 - 3x^2 - 7x + 6$

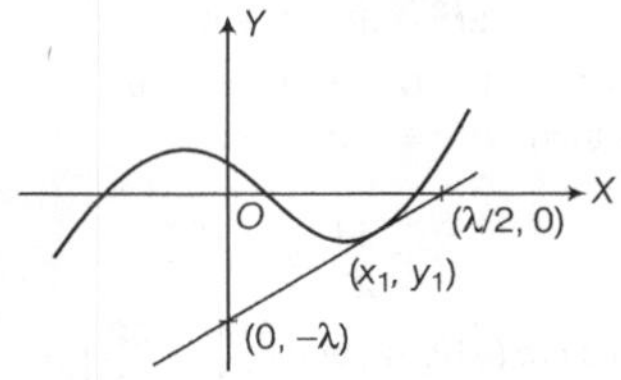

$$\Rightarrow \quad \left(\frac{dy}{dx}\right)_{(x_1,\, y_1)} = 3x_1^2 - 6x_1 - 7 \quad \text{...(ii)}$$

From Eqs. (i) and (ii), we get

$$3x_1^2 - 6x_1 - 7 = 2$$

$$\Rightarrow \quad 3x_1^2 - 6x_1 - 9 = 0$$

$$\Rightarrow \quad x_1^2 - 2x_1 - 3 = 0$$

$$\Rightarrow \quad (x_1 - 3)(x_1 + 1) = 0$$

$$\Rightarrow \quad x_1 = 3 \quad [\text{neglecting } x_1 = -1]$$

Also, $y_1 = x_1^3 - 3x_1^2 - 7x_1 + 6 = -15$

$\therefore$ So, the required point is (3, − 15).

17. (b) Given, $f(x) = ax^3 + bx^2 + cx + d$

$$\therefore \quad f'(x) = 3ax^2 + 2bx + c$$

Since, X-axis is tangent to the curve $f(x)$ at $x = 2$.

$$\therefore \quad f'(2) = 12a + 4b + c = 0 \quad \text{...(i)}$$

Also, $x = -1$ is a zero of $f(x)$.

$$\therefore \quad f(-1) = a(-1)^3 + b(-1)^2 + c(-1) + d = 0$$

$$= -a + b - c + d = 0$$

$$= a - b + c - d = 0 \quad \text{...(ii)}$$

At $x = 0$, $f(0) = -2$

$$\Rightarrow \quad d = -2 \quad \text{...(iii)}$$

From Eqs. (ii) and (iii), we have

$$a - b + c = -2 \quad \text{...(iv)}$$

Now, $x = 2$ is a zero of $f(x)$.

$$\therefore \quad 8a + 4b + 2c + d = 0$$

$$8a + 4b + 2c = 2$$

$$4a + 2b + c = 1 \quad \text{...(v)}$$

From Eqs. (i) and (v), we have

$$a = -1/2, b = 3/2, c = 0, d = -2$$

$$\therefore \quad a + b + c + d = -\frac{1}{2} + \frac{3}{2} + 0 - 2 = 1 - 2 = -1$$

18. (b) Given, $x = t^3 - 4t^2 - 3t$

and $y = 2t^2 + 3t - 5$

$$\Rightarrow \quad \frac{dx}{dt} = 3t^2 - 8t - 3$$

and $\frac{dy}{dt} = 4t + 3$

Now, $\frac{dy}{dx} = \frac{dy/dt}{dx/dt} = \frac{4t + 3}{3t^2 - 8t - 3}$

If the tangent is horizontal, then

$$\frac{4t+3}{3t^2-8t-3}=0$$

$\Rightarrow$ $4t+3=0 \Rightarrow t=-3/4$

$\therefore$ So, the point is $\left(\frac{-27}{64}, \frac{-49}{8}\right)$.

$\therefore$ $H=1$

If the tangent is vertical, then $\frac{dx}{dy}=0$

i.e. $\frac{3t^2-8t-3}{4t+3}=0$

$\Rightarrow$ $3t^2-8t-3=0$

$\Rightarrow$ $(t-3)(3t+1)=0 \Rightarrow t=3, -1/3$

When $t=3$, then $x=-18, y=22$

$t=-1/3$

$\Rightarrow$ $x=\frac{14}{27}, y=\frac{-52}{9}$

So, the points are $(-18, 22)$ and $\left(\frac{14}{27}, -\frac{52}{9}\right)$.

$\therefore$ $V=2$

19. (c) Given, $y=x^n$ $(n \in N)$

On differentiating. w.r.t. x, we get

$$\frac{dy}{dx}=nx^{n-1}$$

$\Rightarrow$ $\left(\frac{dy}{dx}\right)_{(a,\, a^n)}=n\cdot a^{n-1}$

Equation of the normal at (a, a^n) is

$$y-a^n=\frac{-1}{na^{n-1}}(n-a) \quad \ldots(i)$$

Since, Eq. (i) intersect Y-axis at $(0, b)$.

$\therefore$ $b-a^n=\frac{a}{na^{n-1}}=\frac{1}{n}a^{2-n}$

On taking limit $a \to 0$ both sides, we get

$$\lim_{a\to 0} b-\lim_{a\to 0} a^n=\frac{1}{n}\lim_{a\to 0} a^{2-n}$$

$\Rightarrow$ $\frac{1}{2}=\frac{1}{n} \Rightarrow n=2$ $\left[\because \lim_{a\to 0} b=\frac{1}{2}\right]$

20. (a) Equation of the line passes through the point $\left(\frac{1}{2}, 2\right)$ is

$$y-2=m\left(x-\frac{1}{2}\right) \quad \ldots(i)$$

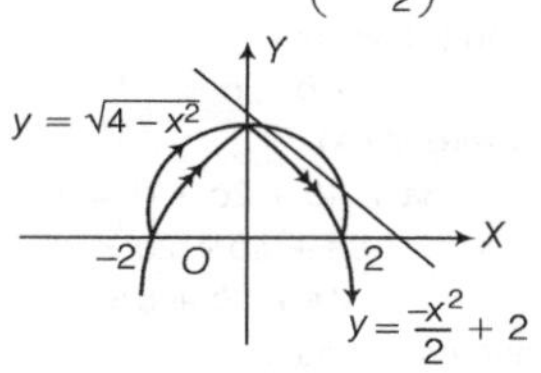

On solving with $y=\frac{-x^2}{2}+2$, we get

$$2+m\left(x-\frac{1}{2}\right)=\frac{-x^2}{2}+2$$

$\Rightarrow$ $\frac{x^2}{2}+mx-\frac{m}{2}=0$

$\therefore$ $D=0 \Rightarrow m^2-4\left(\frac{1}{2}\right)\cdot\left(\frac{-m}{2}\right)=0$

$\Rightarrow m=0, -1$

With $m=0$, tangent is $y=2$ rejected.

With $m=1$, tangent is $y=-x+\frac{5}{2}$ or $2x+2y=5$.

21. (b) Let $P=(x_1, x_1^{3/2})$ and $Q=(x_2, x_2^{3/2})$

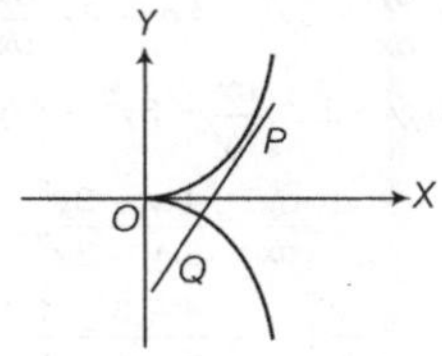

Here, $y^2=x^3$

$\Rightarrow$ $2y\frac{dy}{dx}=3x^2$

$\Rightarrow$ $\frac{dy}{dx}=\frac{3x_1^2}{2y_1}=\frac{3}{2}\frac{x_1^2}{x_1^{3/2}}=\frac{3}{2}x_1^{1/2}$ ...(i)

Slope of $PQ=\frac{x_2^{3/2}-x_1^{3/2}}{x_2-x_1}$ ...(ii)

From Eqs. (i) and (ii), $\frac{x_2^{3/2}-x_1^{3/2}}{x_2-x_1}=\frac{3}{2}x_1^{1/2}$

$\Rightarrow$ $2\left(\sqrt{\frac{x_2}{x_1}}\right)^3-3\left(\sqrt{\frac{x_2}{x_1}}\right)^2+1=0$

On solving $\sqrt{\frac{x_2}{x_1}}=1, -\frac{1}{2}$

Also, $\frac{\tan\alpha}{\tan\beta}=\sqrt{\frac{x_1}{x_2}}=-2$ or 1

22. (a) Given that, $x=a(1+\cos\theta)$, $y=a\sin\theta$

On differentiating w.r.t. θ, we get

$$\frac{dx}{d\theta}=a(-\sin\theta) \quad \text{and} \quad \frac{dy}{d\theta}=a\cos\theta$$

$\Rightarrow$ $\frac{dy}{dx}=\frac{-\cos\theta}{\sin\theta}$

$\therefore$ Slope of normal $=\frac{-1}{-\frac{\cos\theta}{\sin\theta}}$

Equation of normal at the given point is

$$y-a\sin\theta=\frac{\sin\theta}{\cos\theta}[x-a(1+\cos\theta)]$$

Clearly, normal passes through the point $(a, 0)$.

23. (d) We have, $y=x+\frac{4}{x^2}$

On differentiating w.r.t. x, we get

$$\frac{dy}{dx}=1-\frac{8}{x^3}$$

Since, the tangent is parallel to X-axis, therefore

$$\frac{dy}{dx}=0$$

$\Rightarrow$ $x^3=8$

$\therefore$ $x=2$ and $y=3$

24. (a) We have, $y=\int_0^x |t|\,at$, $x \in R$ ...(i)

$\therefore$ $\frac{dy}{dx}=|t|, x \in R$

Let (x_1, y_1) be a point on the curve $y=\int_0^x |t|dt$, where tangent is parallel to the line $y=2x$, then

$$\left(\frac{dy}{dx}\right)_{(x_1,\, y_1)}=2$$

$\Rightarrow$ $|x_1|=2 \Rightarrow x_1=\pm 2$

Since, (x_1, y_1) lies on Eq. (i).

$\therefore$ $y_1=\int_0^{x_1}|t|dt$

When $x_1 = 2$, then

$$y_1 = \int_0^2 |t|\, dt = \int_0^2 t\, dt = \left[\frac{t^2}{2}\right]_0^2 = 2$$

When $x_1 = -2$, then

$$y_1 = \int_0^{-2} -t\, dt = \left[\frac{-t^2}{2}\right]_0^{-2} = -2$$

So, the points on the curve are (2, 2) and (−2, −2).
Equations of the tangent at these points are

$$y - 2 = 2(x - 2) \text{ and } y + 2 = 2(x + 2)$$

$$\Rightarrow \quad y = 2x - 2 \text{ and } y = 2x + 2$$

Hence, the x-intercept of these tangents are ± 1.

25. (d) We have,

$$y = f(x)$$

$$\Rightarrow \quad \frac{dy}{dx} = f'(x)$$

$$\Rightarrow \quad \left(\frac{dy}{dx}\right)_{(3,\, 4)} = f'(3)$$

$$\Rightarrow \quad -\frac{1}{\left(\frac{dy}{dx}\right)_{(3,\, 4)}} = -\frac{1}{f'(3)}$$

It is given that, slope of normal $= \tan\frac{3\pi}{4}$

$$\therefore \quad \tan\frac{3\pi}{4} = -\frac{1}{f'(3)}$$

$$\Rightarrow \quad f'(3) = 1$$

26. (d) We have,

$$y^3 + 3x^2 = 12y \quad \ldots\text{(i)}$$

$$\Rightarrow \quad 3y^2\frac{dy}{dx} + 6x = 12\frac{dy}{dx}$$

$$\Rightarrow \quad 3(y^2 - 4)\frac{dy}{dx} = -6x$$

$$\Rightarrow \quad \frac{dy}{dx} = \frac{-2x}{y^2 - 4}$$

At point(s), where the tangent(s) is (are) vertical, $\frac{dy}{dx}$ is not defined

i.e. $\quad y^2 - 4 = 0$

$$\Rightarrow \quad y = \pm 2$$

From Eq. (i), we have

$$y = 2 \Rightarrow x = \pm\frac{4}{\sqrt{3}}$$

and $\quad y = -2$

$\Rightarrow x^2 = \frac{-16}{3}$, which is not possible.

Hence, the required points are $\left(\pm\frac{4}{\sqrt{3}}, 2\right)$.

27. (a) The equation of the curve is

$$y = x^2 - 5x + 6$$

$$\therefore \quad \frac{dy}{dx} = 2x - 5$$

Let m_1 and m_2 be the slopes of tangents at (2, 0) and (3, 0) to the given curve.

Then, $\quad m_1 = \left(\frac{dy}{dx}\right)_{(2,\, 0)} = 2 \times 2 - 5 = -1$

and $\quad m_2 = \left(\frac{dy}{dx}\right)_{(3,\, 0)} = 2 \times 3 - 5 = 1$

Clearly, $\quad m_1 \cdot m_2 = (-1)(1) = -1$

So the required angle is $\frac{\pi}{2}$.

28. (a) Equation of tangent to the curve $y = e^x$ at (c, e^c) is

$$y - e^c = e^c(x - c) \quad \ldots\text{(i)}$$

Equation of the line joining $(c - 1, e^{c-1})$ and $(c + 1, e^{c+1})$ is

$$y - e^{c-1} = \frac{e^c(e - e^{-1})}{2}(x - c + 1) \quad \ldots\text{(ii)}$$

On subtracting Eq. (i) from Eq. (ii), we get

$$e^c - e^{c-1} = \frac{e^c(e - e^{-1})}{2}(x - c + 1) - e^c(x - c)$$

$$\Rightarrow \quad e^c - e^{c-1} = (x - c)e^c\left(\frac{e - e^{-1}}{2} - 1\right) + e^c\left(\frac{e - e^{-1}}{2}\right)$$

$$\Rightarrow \quad x - c = \frac{(e - 1)^2}{2 - (e - 1)^2} < 0$$

$$\Rightarrow \quad x < c$$

Hence, Eqs. (i) and (ii) intersect at a point on the left of c.

Alternate Method

Clearly, point $P(c, e^c)$ lies in between the points $Q(c - 1, e^{c-1})$ and $R(c + 1, e^{c+1})$ on the curve $y = e^x$ as shown in the figure given below.

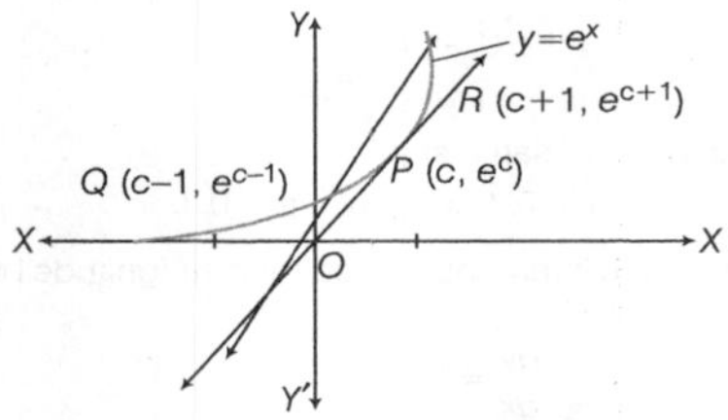

Also, $y = e^x$ is strictly increasing, so the tangent at P intersects line joining Q and R on the left of point P.

29. (c) We have, subnormal, $y = \frac{dy}{dx}$

and $\quad$ subtangent $= \frac{y}{\frac{dy}{dx}}$

$$\Rightarrow \quad \sqrt{\frac{\text{Subnormal}}{\text{Subtangent}}} = \sqrt{\frac{y\frac{dy}{dx}}{y/\frac{dy}{dx}}} = \frac{dy}{dx} = \text{Slope of the tangents}$$

30. (b) Given, $y^2 = 8ax\ (a > 0)$

$$\Rightarrow \quad 2y\frac{dy}{dx} = 8a \Rightarrow \frac{dy}{dx} = \frac{8a}{2y} = \frac{4a}{y}$$

$$\therefore \quad \text{Length of subnormal} = y \cdot \frac{dy}{dx} = y \cdot \frac{4a}{y} = 4a$$

31. (a,b,c,d)

(a) We have, $y^2 = 4ax \quad \Rightarrow \quad m_1 = y' = \frac{2a}{y}$

and $\quad y = e^{-x/2a} \quad \Rightarrow \quad m_2 = y' - \frac{1}{2a}e^{-x/2a} = -\frac{1}{2a}y$

$$\therefore \quad m_1 \cdot m_2 = -1$$

Hence, orthogonal.

(b) We have, $y = 4ax \Rightarrow y' = \frac{4a}{2y} = \frac{2a}{y}(m_1)$ [not defined at (0, 0)]

and $x^2 = 4ay_1 \quad \Rightarrow \quad y' = \frac{2x}{4a} = \frac{x}{2a} = 0$ at (0, 0)

∴ The two curves are orthogonal at (0, 0).

(c) We have, $\quad xy = a^2 \quad \Rightarrow \quad m_1 = y' = \frac{-a^2}{x^2}$

and $\quad x^2 - y^2 = b^2 \quad \Rightarrow \quad m_2 = y' = \frac{2x}{2y} = \frac{x}{y}$

$$\therefore \quad m_1 \cdot m_2 = \frac{-a^2}{xy} = \frac{-a^2}{a^2} = -1 \quad [\because xy = a^2]$$

Hence, orthogonal.

(d) We have, $y = ax \Rightarrow y' = a(m_1)$

and $x^2 + y^2 = c^2$

$$\Rightarrow m_2 = y' = \frac{-x_1}{y_1}$$

$$\therefore m_1 \cdot m_2 = \frac{-ax_1}{y_1} = \frac{-x_1}{y_1} = -1$$

Hence, orthogonal.

32. (a,d) Given, $x = kt$, $y = \frac{k}{t}, k > 0$

$$\Rightarrow \frac{dx}{dt} = k, \frac{dy}{dt} = \frac{-k}{t^2}$$

and $$\frac{dy}{dt} = \frac{-k/t^2}{k} = \frac{-1}{t^2}$$

$\therefore$ Slope of tangent = Slope of line $\left(\frac{x}{a} + \frac{y}{b} = 1\right)$

$$\Rightarrow -\frac{1}{t^2} = \frac{-1/a}{1/b}$$

$$\Rightarrow \frac{1}{t^2} = b/a$$

$$\Rightarrow t^2 = a/b$$

$$\Rightarrow t = \pm\sqrt{a/b}$$

So, a and b are of same sign

i.e. $a > 0, b > 0$ or $a < 0, b < 0$

33. (a,b) Since, the intercepts are equal in magnitude but opposite in sign.

$$\therefore \frac{dy}{dx} = 1$$

Now, $$\frac{dy}{dx} = x^2 - 5x + 7 = 1$$

$$\Rightarrow x^2 - 5x + 6 = 0$$

$$\Rightarrow x = 2 \text{ or } 3$$

When $x = 2$, then $y = 8/3$

When $x = 3$, then $y = 7/2$

So, the points are $(2, 8/3)$ and $(3, 7/2)$.

34. (b,c) Given, $xy = 1$

$$\Rightarrow y = \frac{1}{x} \Rightarrow \frac{dy}{dx} = -\frac{1}{x^2}$$

Then, slope of normal = x^2 (which is always positive) and it is given $ax + by + c = 0$ is normal whose slope = $\frac{-a}{b}$

$$\Rightarrow \frac{-a}{b} > 0 \text{ or } \frac{a}{b} < 0$$

Hence, a and b are of opposite sign.

35. (b,c) Given, $y = ke^{kx}$ ...(i)

$$\Rightarrow \frac{dy}{dx} = k^2e^{kx}$$

Since, curve (i) intersect Y-axis, then $x = 0$

$$\therefore y = k$$

So, the point of intersection is $(0, k)$.

Now, the slope of tangent to the curve at $(0, k)$ is

$$m_1 = \left(\frac{dy}{dx}\right)_{(0, k)} = k^2$$

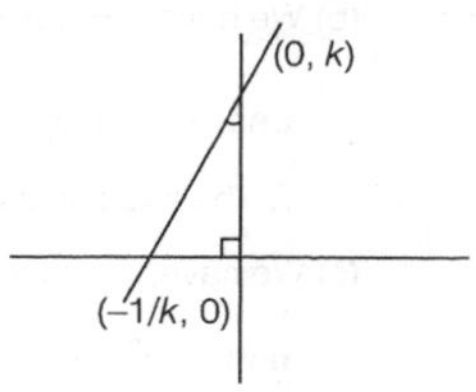

Equation of the tangent is

$$y - k = k^2(x - 0)$$

$$\Rightarrow y - k = k^2x$$

$$\Rightarrow k^2x - y + k = 0 \quad \text{...(ii)}$$

$\therefore$ Angle between the line $k^2x - y + k = 0$ and Y-axis is

$$\tan\theta = \frac{1/k}{k}$$

$$\Rightarrow \tan\theta = \frac{1}{k^2} \Rightarrow \cot\theta = k^2$$

$$\Rightarrow \theta = \cot^{-1}(k^2)$$

$$\therefore \sin\theta = \frac{1/k}{\sqrt{\frac{k^4+1}{k^2}}} = \frac{1}{\sqrt{k^4+1}}$$

$$\Rightarrow \theta = \sin^{-1}\left(\frac{1}{\sqrt{k^4+1}}\right)$$

36. (a,b) Given, $\sqrt{xy} = a + x$

$$\Rightarrow \frac{1}{2\sqrt{xy}}(y + xy') = 1$$

Since, tangent cuts-off equal intercept from the axes.

$$y' = -1$$

$$\Rightarrow y - x = 2\sqrt{xy} = 2(a + x)$$

$$\Rightarrow y = 2a + 3x \Rightarrow x(2a + 3x) = (a + x)^2$$

$$\Rightarrow 2ax + 3x^2 = a^2 + x^2 + 2ax$$

$$\Rightarrow 2x^2 = a^2$$

$$\therefore x = \pm a/\sqrt{2}$$

37. (a,b,d) Given, $y\cot x = y^3\tan x$ ...(i)

$$\Rightarrow \frac{y}{\tan x} = y^3\tan x$$

$$\Rightarrow y = y^3\tan^2 x$$

$$\Rightarrow \frac{dy}{dx} = 3y^2\frac{dy}{dx}\tan^2 x + y^3 2\tan x\sec^2 x$$

$$\Rightarrow \frac{dy}{dx}(1 - 3y^2\tan^2 x) = 2y^3\tan x\sec^2 x$$

$$\frac{dy}{dx} = \frac{2y^3\tan x\sec^2 x}{1 - 3y^2\tan^2 x} \quad \text{...(ii)}$$

When $x = \frac{\pi}{4}$, then $y = 0, \pm 1$

$\therefore$ Points on the curve where abscissa in $\pi/4$ are

$$\left(\frac{\pi}{4}, 0\right)\left(\frac{\pi}{4}, 1\right)\left(\frac{\pi}{4}, -1\right)$$

Now, slope of the tangent at $(\pi/4, 0)$ is

$$\left(\frac{dy}{dx}\right)_{(\pi/4,\ 0)} = 0$$

Equation of the tangent, is $y - 0 = 0$

$$\Rightarrow y = 0$$

Slope of the tangent at $\left(\frac{\pi}{4}, 1\right)$ is

$$\left(\frac{dy}{dx}\right)_{\left(\frac{\pi}{4}, 1\right)} = \frac{4}{-2} = -2$$

Equation of the tangent is

$$y - 1 = -2\left(x - \frac{\pi}{4}\right)$$

$$\Rightarrow y - 1 = -2x + \frac{\pi}{2}$$

$$\Rightarrow 2x + y - 1 - \frac{\pi}{2} = 0$$

$$\Rightarrow 4x + 2y = \pi + 2$$

Slope of the tangent at $\left(\frac{\pi}{4}, -1\right)$ is

$$\left(\frac{dy}{dx}\right)_{\left(\frac{\pi}{4}, -1\right)} = \frac{-4}{-2} = 2$$

Equation of the tangent is

$$y + 1 = 2\left(x - \frac{\pi}{4}\right)$$

$$\Rightarrow \quad y + 1 = 2x - \pi/2$$

$$\Rightarrow \quad 2y + 2 = 4x - \pi$$

$$\therefore \quad 4x - 2y - \pi - 2 = 0$$

38. (b,d) Given, $x = a(\cos\theta + \theta\sin\theta)$, $y = a(\sin\theta - \theta\cos\theta)$

$$\therefore \quad \frac{dx}{d\theta} = a(-\sin\theta + \sin\theta + \theta\cos\theta) = a\theta\cos\theta \quad \ldots\text{(i)}$$

and $$\frac{dy}{d\theta} = a(\cos\theta - \cos\theta + \theta\sin\theta) = a\theta\sin\theta \quad \ldots\text{(ii)}$$

Now, $$\frac{dy}{dx} = \tan\theta$$

$$\therefore \quad \text{Slope of normal} = -\cot\theta = \tan\left(\frac{\pi}{2} + \theta\right)$$

It makes angle $\left(\frac{\pi}{2} + \theta\right)$ with the X-axis.

$\therefore$ Equation of the normal is

$$y - a(\sin\theta - \theta\cos\theta) = -\frac{\cos\theta}{\sin\theta}[x - a(\cos\theta + \theta\sin\theta)]$$

$$\Rightarrow y\sin\theta - a\sin^2\theta + a\theta\sin\theta\cos\theta$$

$$= -x\cos\theta + a\cos^2\theta + a\theta\sin\theta\cos\theta$$

$$\therefore \quad x\cos\theta + y\sin\theta = a$$

$\therefore$ Option (a) is not correct because it does not pass through (0, 0).

Now, its distance from origin $= \left|\dfrac{a}{\sqrt{\cos^2\theta + \sin^2\theta}}\right| = a$, which is a constant.

Explanations for Q. Nos. (39-41)

Let $\quad f(x) = ax^2 - bx + c.$

$$f(0) = 2 \Rightarrow c = 2$$

$$f'(x) = 2xa - b$$

$$f''(x) = 2a$$

$$f'(2) = b,\ f''(3) = c,\ f(1) = a.$$

$$\therefore \quad 4a - b = b,\ 2a = c,\ a - b + c = a$$

$$\Rightarrow \quad a = 1, c = 2, b = 2.$$

$$\therefore \quad f(x) = x^2 - 2x + 2$$

$$\Rightarrow \quad f'(1) = 2a - b = 2 - 2 = 0$$

At $x = 3$, $\quad f(3) = 9 - 6 + 2 = 5$

$\therefore$ Equation of the tangent at (3, 5) is

$$\frac{y-5}{x-3} = 4 \Rightarrow y - 5 = 4x - 12 \Rightarrow y = 4x - 7$$

Intersection point of $y = x^2 - 2x + 2$ and $y = 2e^{2x}$ is

$$(x-1)^2 + 1 = 2e^{2x}$$

$$\Rightarrow \quad x = 0$$

$$\therefore \quad \left(\frac{dy}{dx}\right)_{C_1} = (2x-2)_{x=0} = -2 \text{ and } \left(\frac{dy}{dx}\right)_{C_2} = (4e^{2x})_{x=0} = 4$$

$$\Rightarrow \quad \tan\theta = \left|\frac{4+2}{1-8}\right| = \frac{6}{7}$$

$$\therefore \quad \theta = \tan^{-1}\left(\frac{6}{7}\right)$$

39. (a) **40.** (c) **41.** (d)

42. (b) For $k = 0$, line $y = x$ meets $y = 0$ i.e. X-axis only at one point.

For $k < 0$, $y = ke^x$ meets $y = x$ only once as shown in the figure.

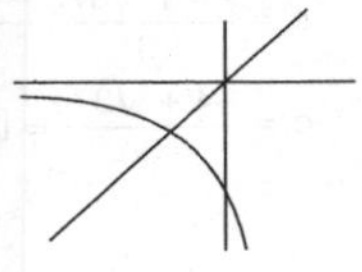

43. (a) Let $f(x) = ke^x - x$

Now, for $f(x) = 0$ to have one root means the line $y = x$ must be tangential to the curve $y = ke^x$.

Let it be so at (x_1, y_1), then

$$\left(\frac{dy}{dx}\right)_{x_1} = ke^{x_1} = 1$$

or $$e^{x_1} = \frac{1}{k}$$

Also, $\quad y_1 = ke^x$ and $y_1 = x_1$

$$\therefore \quad x_1 = 1 \text{ or } 1 = ke \Rightarrow k = \frac{1}{e}$$

44. (a) For $y = x$ to be tangent to the curve $y = ke^x, k = \dfrac{1}{e}$.

For $y = ke^x$ to meet $y = x$ at two points we should have

$$k < \frac{1}{e} \text{ or } k \in \left(0, \frac{1}{e}\right) \text{ as } k > 0.$$

45. (4) Given, $(3 - a)x + ay + (a^2 - 1) = 0$ is normal to $xy = 1$.

$\therefore$ Slope of straight line = Slope of normal

$$\Rightarrow \quad -\frac{(3-a)}{a} = -\left(\frac{dx}{dy}\right)$$

$$\Rightarrow \quad \frac{3-a}{a} = -x^2$$

$$\therefore \quad \frac{3-a}{a} < 0$$

− + − (sign scheme with points 0 and 3)

$$\Rightarrow \quad a < 0 \text{ or } a > 3$$

$\therefore$ Least positive integer value of $a = 4$.

46. (9) Since, $x + 4y = 14$ is normal to the curve $y^2 = \alpha x^3 - \beta$ at (2, 3).

$$\therefore \text{ Slope of } (x + 4y = 14) = \left(\frac{dy}{dx}\right)_{(2,\,3)}$$

$$\Rightarrow \quad -\frac{1}{4} = \left[-\frac{1}{\left(3\alpha\dfrac{x^2}{2y}\right)}\right]_{(2,\,3)}$$

$$\Rightarrow \quad -\frac{1}{4} = -\frac{1}{2\alpha} \Rightarrow \alpha = 2$$

From Eq. (i), we have

$$(3)^2 = 2(2)^3 - \beta$$

$$\Rightarrow \quad 9 = 16 - \beta$$

$$\Rightarrow \quad \beta = 7$$

$$\therefore \quad \alpha + \beta = 2 + 7 = 9$$

47. (2) Here, $1 \le |\sin x| + |\cos x| \le \sqrt{2}$

$$\therefore \quad [|\sin x| + |\cos x|] = 1$$

$$x^2 + 1 = 5 \Rightarrow x = \pm 2$$

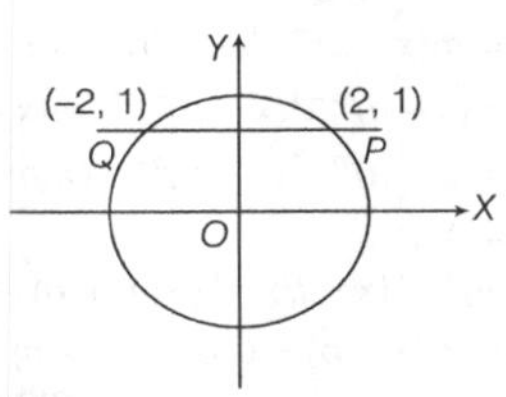

$\therefore \quad P(2, 1)$ and $Q(-2, 1)$.

Slope of tangent of the curve at P is 2 and slope of tangent of the curve at Q is −2.

$\therefore$ Angle of intersection is

$$\tan^{-1}(2) = \tan^{-1}(k)$$

$$\therefore \quad k = 2$$

48. (1) Given, $y = \log_e x$ ...(i)

$\Rightarrow \quad \frac{dy}{dx} = \frac{1}{x} \Rightarrow \left(\frac{dy}{dx}\right)_{(1,\,0)} = 1$

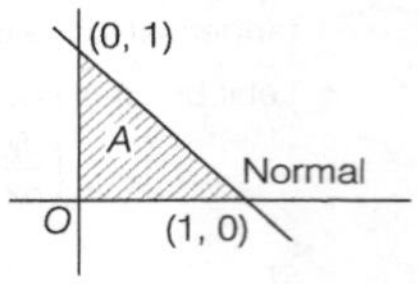

Equation of the normal is

$$y - 0 = -1(x - 1)$$

$\Rightarrow \quad y = -x + 1$

$\Rightarrow \quad x + y - 1 = 0$ ...(ii)

$\therefore$ Required area, $A = \frac{1}{2} \times |x| = \frac{1}{2}$ sq unit

$\Rightarrow \quad 2A = 1$ sq unit

49. (4) Given curves are $\frac{x^2}{36} + \frac{y^2}{4} = 1$ ...(i)

and $x^2 + y^2 = 12$ ...(ii)

Points of intersection of Eqs. (i) and (ii) are $(3, \sqrt{3})$ and $(-3, -\sqrt{3})$.

On differentiating Eq. (i) w.r.t. x, we get

$$\frac{dy}{dx} = \frac{-x}{9y} \Rightarrow \left(\frac{dy}{dx}\right)_{(3,\,\sqrt{3})} = -\frac{1}{3\sqrt{3}}\ (m_1)$$

On differentiating Eq. (ii) w.r.t. x, we get

$$2x + 2y\frac{dy}{dx} = 0 \Rightarrow \frac{dy}{dx} = \frac{-x}{y}$$

$\Rightarrow \quad \left(\frac{dy}{dx}\right)_{(3,\,\sqrt{3})} = -\sqrt{3}\ (m_2)$

$\therefore \quad \tan\alpha = \left|\frac{-\frac{1}{3\sqrt{3}} + \sqrt{3}}{1 + \frac{1}{3}}\right| = \left|\frac{\frac{-1+9}{3\sqrt{3}}}{4/3}\right| = \frac{4}{2\sqrt{3}}$

$\Rightarrow \quad \alpha = \tan^{-1}\left(\frac{4}{2\sqrt{3}}\right) = \tan^{-1}\left(\frac{k}{2\sqrt{3}}\right) \Rightarrow k = 4$

50. (2) Given, $y = -p^2x^2 + 5px - 4$ ...(i)

and $y = \frac{1}{1 - x}$ ...(ii)

$\because$ Chord touches the curve (ii) at $x = 2$, which provide $y = -1$.

Let (x_1, y_1) and (x_2, y_2) be the ends of chord touching the point be middle point $\left(\frac{x_1 + x_2}{2}, \frac{y_1 + y_2}{2}\right)$.

$\therefore \quad \frac{x_1 + x_2}{2} = 2$

$\Rightarrow \quad x_1 + x_2 = 4$

and $y_1 + y_2 = -2$

$\because (x_1, y_1)$ and (x_2, y_2) satisfy the curve.

$\therefore \quad y_1 = -p^2x_1^2 + 5px_1 - 4$ ...(iii)

and $y_2 = -p^2x_2^2 + 5px_2 - 4$ ...(iv)

On subtracting Eq. (iv) from Eq. (iii), we get

$$y_1 - y_2 = -p^2(x_1^2 - x_2^2) + 5p(x_1 - x_2)$$

$\Rightarrow \quad \frac{y_1 - y_2}{x_1 - x_2} = -p^2(x_1 + x_2) + 5p$

$$= -4p^2 + 5p$$

Again, $\left(\frac{dy}{dx}\right)_{x=2} = \left[\frac{1}{(1-x)^2}\right]_{x=2} = 1$

$$= -4p^2 + 5p$$

$\Rightarrow \quad 4p^2 - 5p + 1 = 0$

$\Rightarrow \quad p = 1, \frac{1}{4}$

$\therefore$ So, the number of values of p are 2.

DPP-3 **Mean Value Theorem**

1. We have, $f(x) = (x - a)^m (x - b)^n$, where $m, n \in N$

On expanding $(x - a)^m$ and $(x - b)^n$ by binomial theorem, then taking the product we find that $f(x)$ is a polynomial degree $(m + n)$. Since, a polynomial function is everywhere differentiable and continuous also.

Therefore,

(i) $f(x)$ is continuous on $[a, b]$.

(ii) $f(x)$ is differentiable on (a, b).

Also, $f(a) = f(b)$

Thus, all the three conditions of Rolle's theorem is satisfied.

Now, we have to show that there exists $c \in (a, b)$ such that $f'(x) = 0$.

We have, $f(x) = (x - a)^m (x - b)^n$

$\Rightarrow \quad f'(x) = m(x - a)^{m-1}(x - b)^n + (x - b)^m n(x - b)^{n-1}$

$\Rightarrow \quad f'(x) = (x - a)^{m-1}(x - b)^{n-1}\{m(x - b) + n(x - a)\}$

$\Rightarrow \quad f'(x) = (x - a)^{m-1}(x - b)^{n-1}\{x(m + n) - (mb + na)\}$

$\therefore \quad f'(x) = 0$

$\Rightarrow \quad (x - a)^{m-1}(x - b)^{n-1}\{x(m + n) - (mb + na)\} = 0$

$\Rightarrow \quad (x - a) = 0$ or $(x - b) = 0$ or $x(m + n) - (mb + na) = 0$

$\Rightarrow \quad x = a$ or $x = b$ or $x = \frac{mb + na}{m + n}$

Since, $x = \frac{mb + na}{m + n}$ divides (a, b) into the ratio $m : n$.

Therefore, $\frac{mb + na}{m + n} \in (a, b)$

Thus, $c = \frac{mb + na}{m + n} \in (a, b)$ such that $f'(c) = 0$.

Hence, Rolle's theorem is verified.

2. Given, $f(x) = x^3 + 4x^2 - 7x - 10$

Clearly, $f(x)$ being a polynomial function, is continuous on $[-1, 2]$ and differentiable on $(-1, 2)$.

Also, $f(-1) = (-1)^3 + 4(-1)^2 - 7(-1) - 10$

$$= -1 + 4 + 7 - 10 = 0$$

$\Rightarrow \quad f(2) = (2)^3 + 4(2)^2 - 7(2) - 10$

$$= 8 + 16 - 14 - 10$$

$$= 0$$

$\Rightarrow \quad f(-1) = f(2)$

Thus, $f(x)$ satisfies all the condition of Rolle's theorem.

Now, $f(x) = x^3 + 4x^2 - 7x - 10$

$$f'(x) = 3x^2 + 8x - 7$$

$\therefore \quad f'(c) = 3c^2 + 8c - 7 = 0$

$\Rightarrow \quad c = \frac{-8 \pm \sqrt{64 + 84}}{6}$

$\Rightarrow \quad c = \frac{-8 \pm \sqrt{148}}{6} = \frac{-4 \pm \sqrt{37}}{3}$

$\Rightarrow \quad c = \frac{-4 + \sqrt{37}}{3}, \frac{-4 - \sqrt{37}}{3}$

$\Rightarrow \quad c = \frac{-4 + \sqrt{37}}{3} \in [-1, 2]$

3. We have, $f(x) = x^3 - 2x^2 - x + 3$

We know that a polynomial function is everywhere differentiable and continuous.

So, $f(x)$ being polynomial is continuous in $[0, 1]$ and differentiable in $(0, 1)$.

Thus, $f(x)$ satisfies both the conditions of Lagrange's mean value theorem on $[0, 1]$.

So, there must exist atleast one real number $c \in (0, 1)$ such that

$$f'(c) = \frac{f(1) - f(0)}{1 - 0}$$

Now, $$f(x) = x^3 - 2x^2 - x + 3$$
$$f'(x) = 3x^2 - 4x - 1$$
$$f'(c) = 3c^2 - 4c + 1$$

and $$f(0) = 3, f(1) = 1$$

$\therefore$ $$3c^2 - 4c - 1 = \frac{1-3}{1}$$

$\Rightarrow$ $$3c^2 - 4c - 1 = -2$$

$\Rightarrow$ $$3c^2 - 4c + 1 = 0$$

$\Rightarrow$ $$(3c - 1)(c - 1) = 0$$

$\Rightarrow$ $$c = 1 \text{ or } 1/3$$

$\Rightarrow$ $$c = 1/3 \in (0, 1)$$

4. Given, $f(x) = a_0 x^n + a_1 x^{n-1} + a_2 x^{n-2} + \dots + a_{n-1} x = 0$

$$f'(x) = n a_0 x^{n-1} + (n-1) a_1 x^{n-2} + \dots + a_{n-1} = 0$$

$\because$ $f(0) = 0$, so $f(x) = 0$ has two real roots 0 and α.

$\therefore$ $f'(x) = 0$ has a real root α_1 lying in between 0 and α.

So, $$0 < \alpha_1 < \alpha$$

5. As $f(x)$ and $g(x)$ are continuous and differentiable in $[0, 2]$, then there exists atleast one c such that

$$\frac{f'(c)}{g'(c)} = \frac{f(2) - f(0)}{g(2) - g(0)} = \frac{8-5}{1-0} = 3$$

$\Rightarrow$ $$f'(c) = 3g'(c)$$

6. It is given that f, ϕ and ψ are continuous in $[a, b]$ and derivable in (a, b).

Case I If $f(a) \neq f(b)$, $\phi(a) \neq \phi(b)$, $\psi(a) \neq \psi(b)$, then there exists $c \in (a, b)$ such that

$\therefore$ $$f'(c) = \frac{f(b) - f(a)}{b - a} \Rightarrow (b - a) f'(c) = f(b) - f(a) \quad \dots\text{(i)}$$

[by LMVT]

$$\phi'(c) = \frac{\phi(b) - \phi(a)}{b - a} \Rightarrow \phi'(c)(b - a) = \phi(b) - \phi(a) \quad \dots\text{(ii)}$$

[by LMVT]

and $$\psi'(c) = \frac{\psi(b) - \psi(a)}{b - a} \Rightarrow (b - a)\psi'(c) = \psi(b) - \psi(a) \quad \dots\text{(iii)}$$

[by LMVT]

Now, $$\begin{vmatrix} f(a) & f(b) & f'(c) \\ \phi(a) & \phi(b) & \phi'(c) \\ \psi(a) & \psi(b) & \psi'(c) \end{vmatrix}$$

Applying $C_2 \to C_1 - C$,

$$= \begin{vmatrix} f(a) & f(b) - f(a) & f'(c) \\ \phi(a) & \phi(b) - \phi(a) & \phi'(c) \\ \psi(a) & \psi(b) - \psi(a) & \psi'(c) \end{vmatrix} = \begin{vmatrix} f(a) & (b-a)f'(c) & f'(c) \\ \phi(a) & (b-a)\phi'(c) & \phi'(c) \\ \psi(a) & (b-a)\psi'(c) & \psi'(c) \end{vmatrix}$$

[using Eqs. (i), (ii) and (iii)]

$$= (b - a)\begin{vmatrix} f(a) & f'(c) & f'(c) \\ \phi(a) & \phi'(c) & \phi'(c) \\ \psi(a) & \psi'(c) & \psi'(c) \end{vmatrix}$$

$= (b - a) \times 0$ [$\because c_2$ and c_3 are identical]

$= 0$

Case II If $f(a) = f(b)$, $\phi(a) = \phi(b)$ and $\phi(a) = \phi(b)$, then there exists $c \in (a, b)$ such that

$$f'(c) = 0, \phi'(c) = 0 \text{ and } \psi'(c) = 0$$

[by Rolle's theorem]

$\therefore$ $$\begin{vmatrix} f(a) & f(b) & f'(c) \\ \phi(a) & \phi(b) & \phi'(c) \\ \psi(a) & \psi(b) & \psi(c) \end{vmatrix} = \begin{vmatrix} f(a) & f(b) & 0 \\ \phi(a) & \phi(b) & 0 \\ \psi(a) & \psi(b) & 0 \end{vmatrix} = 0$$

7. Given, $y = \dfrac{2 - x^2}{x^4}$, $x \in [-1, 1]$

$\therefore$ $f(-1) = 1$, $f(1) = 1$

$f(-1) = f(1)$

The given function is continuous and differentiable throughout the interval except at $x = 0$.

Then, there exists some $c \in [-1, 1]$ such that

$$f'(c) = 0$$

Now, $$\frac{dy}{dx} = \frac{x^4(-2x) - (2 - x^2)4x^3}{x^8}$$
$$= \frac{-2x^5 - 8x^3 - 4x^5}{x^8} = \frac{-6x^5 - 8x^3}{x^8} = \frac{-6x^2 - 8}{x^5}$$

$\Rightarrow$ $$f'(c) = \frac{-6c^2 - 8}{c^5} = 0$$

$\Rightarrow$ $$-(6c^2 + 8) = 0 \Rightarrow c^2 = \frac{-8}{6} = \frac{-4}{3}$$

$\Rightarrow$ $$c = \pm \frac{2}{\sqrt{3}} i$$

Thus, there is no real value of c for which $f'(c) = 0$.

Hence, the derivative of this function does not vanish at any point of the given interval.

8. Consider the function f given by

$$f(x) = \log_e x,\ x \in [b, a],\ 0 < b < a$$

Clearly, it is continuous on $[b, a]$ and differentiable on (b, a). So, by Lagrange's mean value theorem, there exists $c \in (b, a)$ such that

$$f'(c) = \frac{f(a) - f(b)}{a - b}$$

$\Rightarrow$ $$\frac{1}{c} = \frac{\log a - \log b}{a - b} \qquad \left[\because f(x) = \log x \Rightarrow f'(x) = 1/x\right]$$

Now, $$c \in (b, a)$$
$$b < c < a$$

$\Rightarrow$ $$\frac{1}{a} < \frac{1}{c} < \frac{1}{b} \qquad [\because 0 < b < a]$$

$\Rightarrow$ $$\frac{1}{a} < \frac{\log a - \log b}{a - b} < \frac{1}{b}$$

$\Rightarrow$ $$\frac{a - b}{a} < \log a - \log b < \frac{a - b}{b}$$

$\therefore$ $$\frac{a - b}{a} < \log \frac{a}{b} < \frac{a - b}{b} \qquad [\because a - b > 0]$$

9. (i) Given that $f(x)$ is differentiable function on $[0, 4]$.

$\therefore$ It will be continuous on $[0, 4]$.

By Lagrange's mean value theorem, we get

$$\frac{f(4) - f(0)}{4 - 0} = f'(a) \text{ for } a \in (0, 4) \quad \dots\text{(i)}$$

Again, since f is continuous on $[0, 4]$ by intermediate mean value theorem, we get

$$\frac{f(4) + f(0)}{2} = f(b) \quad \text{for } b \in (0, 4) \quad \dots\text{(ii)}$$

On multiplying Eqs. (i) and (ii), we get

$$\frac{[f(4)]^2 - [f(0)]^2}{8} = f'(a) \cdot f(b);\ a, b \in (0, 4)$$

or $$[f(4)]^2 - f[(0)]^2 = 8f'(a) f(b)$$

(ii) To prove, $\int_0^4 f(t)\,dt = 2\,[\alpha f(\alpha)^2 + \beta f(\beta^2)], \forall\ 0 < \alpha, \beta < 2$

Let $$I = \int_0^4 f(t)\,dt$$

Put $t = u^2 \Rightarrow dt = 2u\,du$

$$\therefore \quad I = \int_0^2 f(u^2)\,2u\,du \qquad \ldots(iii)$$

Consider $$F(x) = \int_0^x f(u)^2\,2u\,du$$

then, clearly $F(x)$ is differentiable and hence continuous on [0, 2].

By Lagrange's mean value theorem, we get some $u \in (0, 2)$ such that

$$F'(u) = \frac{F(2) - F(0)}{2 - 0}$$

$$\Rightarrow \quad f(u^2)\cdot 2u = \frac{\int_0^2 f(4^2)\,2u\,du}{2} \qquad \ldots(iv)$$

Again, by intermediate mean value theorem, there exists atleast one α, β such that $0 < \alpha < u < \beta < 2$.

$$\Rightarrow \quad F'(u) = \frac{F'(\alpha) + F'(\beta)}{2}$$

$$\left[\begin{array}{l}\text{as } f \text{ is continuous on } (0, 2)\\ \Rightarrow F \text{ is continuous on } (0, 2)\end{array}\right]$$

$$\Rightarrow \quad f(u^2)\,2u = \frac{f(\alpha^2)\,2\alpha + f(\beta^2)\,2\beta}{2}$$

$$\Rightarrow \quad f(u^2)\,2u = \alpha f(\alpha^2) + \beta + (\beta^2) \qquad \ldots(v)$$

From Eqs. (iv) and (v), we get

$$\int_0^2 f(u^2)\,2u\,du = 2\,[\alpha f(\alpha^2) + \beta f(\beta^2)], \text{ where } 0 < \alpha, \beta < 2$$

$$\Rightarrow \quad \int_0^4 f(t)\,dt = 2\,[\alpha f(\alpha^2) + \beta f(\beta^2)],\ 0 < \alpha, \beta < 2$$

10. (d) Let us check the validity of Rolle's theorem for the given function one by one.

(a) $f(x) = \begin{cases} \dfrac{\sin x}{x}, & x \neq 0 \\ 1, & x = 0 \end{cases}; x \in [-1, 1]$

$$\lim_{x \to 0} f(x) = \lim_{x \to 0} \frac{\sin x}{x} = 1$$

Also, $f(0) = 1$

$\lim_{x \to 0} f(x) = f(0) \Rightarrow f(x)$ is continuous in $[-1, 1]$.

$$\therefore \quad Lf'(0) = \lim_{h \to 0} \frac{\frac{\sin(0 - h)}{0 - h} - h}{-h}$$

$$= \lim_{h \to 0} \frac{\frac{-\sin h}{-h} - 1}{-h} \qquad \left[\frac{0}{0} \text{ form}\right]$$

$$= \lim_{h \to 0} \frac{h\cos h - \sin h}{-h^2} \qquad \left[\frac{0}{0} \text{ form}\right]$$

[by L' Hospital's rule]

$$= \lim_{h \to 0} \frac{\cos h - h\sin h - \cos h}{-2h}$$

[by L' Hospital's rule]

$= 0$

and $$Rf'(0) = \lim_{h \to 0} \frac{\frac{\sin(0 + h)}{0 + h} - 1}{h}$$

$$= \lim_{h \to 0} \frac{\frac{\sin h}{h} - 1}{h} \qquad \left[\frac{0}{0} \text{ form}\right]$$

$$= \lim_{h \to 0} \frac{h\cos h - \sin h}{h^2}$$

$$= \lim_{h \to 0} \frac{\cos h - h\sin h - \cos h}{2h} = 0$$

$\because \quad Lf'(0) = Rf'(0)$

$\therefore$ $f(x)$ is differentiable on $(-1, 1)$.

Now, $$f(-1) = \frac{\sin(-1)}{-1} = \sin 1$$

$$f(1) = \frac{\sin(1)}{1} = \sin 1$$

$$f(-1) = f(1)$$

Thus, all the condition of Rolle's theorem are satisfied. Hence, Rolle's theorem is valid for $f(x)$.

(b) $g(x) = \begin{cases} \dfrac{1 - \cos x}{x}, & x \neq 0 \\ 0, & x = 0 \end{cases}; x \in [-2\pi, 2\pi]$

$$\lim_{x \to 0} g(x) = \lim_{x \to 0} \frac{1 - \cos x}{x} = 0$$

Also, $g(0) = 0$

$\therefore \quad \lim_{x \to 0} g(x) = g(0)$

$\Rightarrow$ $g(x)$ is continuous in $[-2\pi, 2\pi]$.

Now, $$Lg'(0) = \lim_{h \to 0} \frac{\frac{1 - \cos(0 - h)}{0 - h} - 0}{-h}$$

$$= \lim_{h \to 0} \frac{\frac{1 - \cos h}{-h} - 0}{-h}$$

$$= \lim_{h \to 0} \frac{1 - \cos h}{h^2} \qquad \left[\frac{0}{0} \text{ form}\right]$$

$$= \lim_{h \to 0} \frac{\sin h}{2h} \qquad \text{[by L' Hospital's rule]}$$

$$= \frac{1}{2}$$

and $$Rg'(0) = \lim_{h \to 0} \frac{\frac{1 - \cos(0 + h)}{0 + h} - 0}{h}$$

$$= \lim_{h \to 0} \frac{1 - \cos h}{h^2} \qquad \left[\frac{0}{0} \text{ form}\right]$$

$$= \lim_{h \to 0} \frac{\sin h}{2h} \qquad \text{[by L' Hospital's rule]}$$

$$= \frac{1}{2}$$

$\because \quad Lg'(0) = Rg'(0)$

$\therefore$ $g(x)$ is differentiable in $(-2\pi, 2\pi)$.

Also, $$g(-2\pi) = \frac{1 - \cos(-2\pi)}{-2\pi} = 0$$

$$g(2\pi) = \frac{1 - \cos 2\pi}{-2\pi} = 0$$

$$g(-2\pi) = g(2\pi)$$

Thus, all the conditions of Rolle's theorem are satisfied. Hence, Rolle's theorem is valid for $g(x)$.

(c) $h(x) = \begin{cases} \dfrac{1 - \cos x}{x^2}, & x \neq 0 \\ 1/2, & x = 0 \end{cases}; x \in [-2\pi, 2\pi]$

For continuity at $x = 0$,

$$\lim_{x \to 0} h(x) = \lim_{x \to 0} \frac{1 - \cos x}{x^2} \qquad \left[\frac{0}{0} \text{ form}\right]$$

$$= \lim_{x \to 0} \frac{\sin x}{2x} \qquad \text{[by L' Hospital's rule]}$$

$$= \frac{1}{2}$$

Also, $$h(0) = \frac{1}{2}$$

$\because \quad \lim_{x \to 0} h(x) = h(0) = \frac{1}{2}$

$\therefore$ $h(x)$ is continuous at $x = 0$.

For differentiability at $x = 0$,

$$\text{Now, } Lh'(0) = \lim_{h \to 0} \frac{\frac{1-\cos(0-h)}{(0-h)^2} - \frac{1}{2}}{-h}$$

$$= \lim_{h \to 0} \frac{\frac{1-\cos h}{h^2} - \frac{1}{2}}{-h} \qquad \left[\frac{0}{0} \text{ form}\right]$$

$$= \lim_{h \to 0} \frac{2 - h\sin h - 2\cos h}{h^3}$$

[by L' Hospital's rule] $\left[\frac{0}{0} \text{ form}\right]$

$$= \lim_{h \to 0} \frac{-\sin h - h\cos h - 2\sin h}{3h^2} \qquad \left[\frac{0}{0} \text{ form}\right]$$

$$= \lim_{h \to 0} \frac{-\cos h + \cos h + h\sin h + 2\cos h}{6h}$$

$$= \lim_{h \to 0} \frac{h\sin h}{6h} = 0$$

$$\text{and } Rh'(0) = \lim_{h \to 0} \frac{\frac{1-\cos h}{h^2} - \frac{1}{2}}{h} \qquad \left[\frac{0}{0} \text{ form}\right]$$

$$= \lim_{h \to 0} \frac{-2 + h\sin h + 2\cos h}{h^3} \qquad \left[\frac{0}{0} \text{ form}\right]$$

[by L' Hospital's rule]

$$= \lim_{h \to 0} \frac{\sin h + h\cos h - 2\sin h}{3h^2}$$

[by L' Hospital's rule]

$$= \lim_{h \to 0} \frac{h\cos h - \sin h}{3h^2}$$

$$= \lim_{h \to 0} \frac{-h\sin h + \cos h - \cos h}{6h}$$

$$= \lim_{h \to 0} \frac{-h\sin h}{6h} = 0$$

$\because \quad Lh'(0) = Rh'(0)$

$\therefore$ $hf(x)$ is differentiable at $x = 0$.

Then, $\quad h(-2\pi) = \dfrac{1-\cos(-2\pi)}{(-2\pi)^2} = 0$

and $\quad h(2\pi) = \dfrac{1-\cos 2\pi}{(2\pi)^2} = 0$

$\therefore \quad h(-2\pi) = h(2\pi)$

Thus, all the condition of Rolle's theorem are satisfied.

Hence, Rolle's theorem are valid for $h(x)$.

(d) $k(x) = \begin{cases} x\sin\left(\frac{1}{x}\right), & x \neq 0 \\ 0, & x = 0 \end{cases}; \; x \in \left[-\frac{1}{\pi}, \frac{1}{2\pi}\right]$

For continuity at $x = 0$,

$$\lim_{x \to 0} k(x) = \lim_{x \to 0} x\sin\left(\frac{1}{x}\right)$$

$= 0 \times$ (A finite number between 1 and –1)

$= 0$

Also, $\quad k(0) = 0$

$\because \quad \lim_{x \to 0} k(x) = k(0)$

$\therefore \quad k(x)$ is continuous for $x \in \left[-\frac{1}{\pi}, \frac{1}{2\pi}\right]$.

For differentiability at $x = 0$,

$$Lk'(0) = \lim_{h \to 0} \frac{(0-h)\sin\left(\frac{1}{0-h}\right) - 0}{-h}$$

$$= \lim_{h \to 0} \frac{-h\sin\left(\frac{1}{h}\right)}{h}$$

$= \lim_{h \to 0} \sin\left(\frac{1}{h}\right)$ = A finite value between –1 and 1

$$\text{and} \quad Rk'(0) = \lim_{h \to 0} \frac{(0+h)\sin\left(\frac{1}{0+h}\right) - 0}{h}$$

$$= \lim_{h \to 0} \frac{h\sin\left(\frac{1}{h}\right)}{h}$$

$$= \lim_{h \to 0} \sin\left(\frac{1}{h}\right)$$

= a finite number between –1 and 1

$\because \; Lk'(0) \neq Rf'(0)$

$\therefore$ $k(x)$ is not differentiable.

Hence, Rolle's theorem is not valid for $k(x)$.

11. (d) $f(x) = \begin{cases} \dfrac{x^3 - 2x^2 - 5x + 6}{x-1}, & x \neq 1 \\ -6, & x = 1 \end{cases}$

To check continuity of $f(x)$ at $x = 1$,

$$\text{LHL} = \lim_{x \to 1^-} f(x) = \lim_{h \to 0} f(1-h)$$

$$= \lim_{h \to 0} \frac{(1-h)^3 - 2(1-h)^2 - 5(1-h) + 6}{1-h-1}$$

$$= \lim_{h \to 0} \frac{(1-h)[1 + h^2 - 2h - 2 + 2h - 5] + 6}{-h}$$

$$= \lim_{h \to 0} \frac{(1-h)[h^2 - 6] + 6}{-h}$$

$$= \lim_{h \to 0} \frac{h^2 - 6 - h^3 + 6h + 6}{-h} = \lim_{h \to 0} \frac{2h - 3h^2 + 6}{-1}$$

$= -6$ [by L' Hospital's rule]

$$\text{RHL} = \lim_{x \to 1^+} f(x) = \lim_{h \to 0} f(1+h)$$

$$= \lim_{h \to 0} \frac{(1+h)^3 - 2(1+h)^2 - 5(1+h) + 6}{1+h-1}$$

$$= \lim_{h \to 0} \frac{3(1+h)^2 - 4(1+h) - 5}{1} \quad \text{[by L' Hospital's rule]}$$

$= -6$

Also, $\quad f(1) = -6$

$\because \quad \text{LHL} = \text{RHL} = f(1) = -6$

$\therefore$ $f(x)$ is continuous at $x = 1$.

To check differentiability of $f(x)$ at $x = 1$,

$$Lf'(1) = \lim_{h \to 0} \frac{(1-h)^3 - 2(1-h)^2 - 5(1-h) + 6}{-1}$$

[by L' Hospital's rule]

$$= \lim_{h \to 0} \frac{3(1-h^2)(-1) - 2 \times 2(1-h)(-1) - 5(1)}{-1}$$

$$= \lim_{h \to 0} \frac{3(1-h)^2 - 4(1-h) - 5}{1}$$

$= -6$

$$Rf'(1) = \lim_{h \to 0} \frac{(1+h)^3 - 2(1+h)^2 - 5(1+h) + 6}{h}$$

$$= \lim_{h \to 0} \frac{3(1+h)^2 - 4(1+h) - 5}{1} \quad \text{[by L' Hospital's rule]}$$

$= -6$

$\because \quad Lf'(1) = Rf'(1)$

$\Rightarrow$ $f(x)$ is differentiable at $x = 1$.

Also, $\quad f(-2) = -8 - 8 + 10 + 6 = 0$

$f(3) = 27 - 18 - 15 + 6 = 0$

$f(-2) = f(3)$

Thus, $f(x)$ satisfies all the conditions of Rolle's theorem.

There exists $c \in [-2, 3]$ such that

$$f'(c) = 0$$

$\Rightarrow \quad (c-1)(2c^2 - 3c + 1) = 0$

$\Rightarrow \quad c = 1 \text{ or } 2c^2 - 3c + 1 = 0$

$\Rightarrow \quad (c-1)(2c-1) = 0$

$\therefore \quad c = 1 \text{ or } 1/2$

12. (a) We have, $f(x) = 2x^2 + 3x + 5$

Since, $f(x)$ is satisfies all the conditions of LMVT at $x = 2$.

$\therefore \quad f'(2) = \dfrac{f(a) - f(1)}{a-1}$

$\Rightarrow \quad 11 = \dfrac{2a^2 + 3a + 5 - 10}{a-1}$

$\Rightarrow \quad 11a - 11 = 2a^2 + 3a + 5 - 10$

$\Rightarrow \quad 2a^2 - 8a + 6 = 0$

$\Rightarrow \quad a^2 - 4a + 3 = 0$

$\Rightarrow \quad (a-3)(a-1) = 0$

$\Rightarrow \quad a = 1 \text{ or } 3$

$\Rightarrow \quad a = 3$

13. (d) Given, $f(x) = 8x^2 - 7x + 5$

$\therefore \quad f'(c) = 16c - 7 = \dfrac{f(6) - f(-6)}{12}$

$= \dfrac{(8 \times 36 - 7 \times 6 + 5) - (8 \times 36 + 7 \times 6 + 5)}{12} = -7$

$\Rightarrow \quad c = 0$

14. (b) It is given that f is continuous and differentiable for all real x.

$\therefore \quad \dfrac{f(4) - f(2)}{4-2} = f'(c) \Rightarrow \dfrac{f(4) - f(2)}{2} \geq 6$

$\Rightarrow \quad \dfrac{f(4) + 4}{2} \geq 6 \Rightarrow f(4) + 4 \geq 12$

$\Rightarrow \quad f(4) \geq 8$

15. (b) We have, $f(x) = x^3 + 7x - 1, x \in [0, 1]$

$\therefore \quad f(0) = -1$

$f(1) = 7$

$f(0) \neq f(1)$

By LMVT, we have

$$\frac{f(1) - f(0)}{1 - 0} = 3c^2 + 7$$

$\Rightarrow \quad 3c^2 + 7 = 8 \Rightarrow 3c^2 = 1$

$\Rightarrow \quad c^2 = \dfrac{1}{3} \Rightarrow c = \pm \dfrac{1}{\sqrt{3}}$

$\therefore \quad c = \dfrac{1}{\sqrt{3}} \in (0, 1)$

16. (c) Given, $f(x) = |1 - x|, 1 \leq x \leq 2$

$\Rightarrow \quad f(x) = -(1 - x), x \in [1, 2]$

$f(1) = 0$

$f(2) = 1$

$f(1) \neq f(2)$

By LMVT, we have

$$\frac{f(2) - f(1)}{2 - 1} = f'(c), \forall c \in (1, 2) \Rightarrow \frac{1-0}{1} = f'(c)$$

$\Rightarrow \quad f'(c) = 1, \quad \forall c \in (1, 2)$

and $\quad g(x) = -(1 - x) + b\sin\left(\dfrac{\pi}{2}x\right) = (x-1) + b\sin\left(\dfrac{\pi}{2}x\right)$

$\Rightarrow \quad g(1) = b \Rightarrow g(2) = 1$

If Rolle's theorem applicable to g, then $b = 1$.

17. (d) For Rolle's theorem in $[a, b]$,

$f(a) = f(b)$, in $[0, 1] \Rightarrow f(0) = f(1) = 0$

$\because$ The function has to be continuous in $(0, 1)$.

$\therefore \quad f(0) = \lim_{x \to 0^+} f(x) = 0$

$\Rightarrow \quad \lim_{x \to 0} x^{\alpha} \log x = 0$

$\Rightarrow \quad \lim_{x \to 0} \dfrac{\log x}{x^{-\alpha}} = 0$

On applying L' Hospital's rule, we get

$$\lim_{x \to 0} \frac{1/x}{-\alpha x^{-\alpha - 1}} = 0$$

$\Rightarrow \quad \lim_{x \to 0} \dfrac{x^{\alpha}}{-\alpha} = 0$

$\therefore \quad \alpha > 0$

18. (c) Given that, $P(x) = 51x^{101} - 2323x^{100} - 45x + 1035$

Using Rolle's theorem, we consider anti-derivative of $P(x)$

i.e. consider $F(x) = \dfrac{x^{102}}{2} - \dfrac{2323x^{101}}{101} - \dfrac{45x^2}{2} + 1035x + c$

Then, being a polynomial function $F(x)$ is continuous and differentibale.

Now, $F(45^{1/100}) = \dfrac{(45)^{\frac{102}{100}}}{2} - \dfrac{2323(45)^{\frac{101}{100}}}{101} - \dfrac{45(45)^{\frac{2}{100}}}{2} + 1035(45)^{\frac{1}{100}} + c$

$= \dfrac{45}{2}(45)^{\frac{2}{100}} - 23 \times 45(45)^{\frac{1}{100}} - \dfrac{45(45)^{\frac{2}{100}}}{2} + 1035(45)^{\frac{1}{100}} + c$

$= c$

and $F(46) = \dfrac{(46)^{102}}{2} - \dfrac{2323(46)^{101}}{101} - \dfrac{45(46)^2}{2} + 1035(46) + c$

$= 23(46)^{101} - 23(46)^{101} - 23 \times 45 \times 46 + 1035 \times 46 = c$

$\therefore \quad F(45^{\frac{1}{100}}) \; F(46) = c$

$\therefore$ Rolle's theorem is applicable.

Hence, there must exist atleast one root of $F'(x) = 0$.

i.e. $P(x) = 0$ in the interval $(45^{1/100}, 46)$.

19. (b,c) We have, $f(x) = 8x^3 - 6x^2 - 2x + 1$

$f(0) = 1$

$f(1) = 8 - 6 - 2 + 1 = 1$

$f(0) = f(1)$,

By Rolle's theorem, we have

$f'(c) = 0, \forall c \in (0, 1)$

$24c^2 - 12c - 2 = 0$

$\Rightarrow \quad 12c^2 - 6c - 1 = 0$

$\Rightarrow \quad c = \dfrac{6 \pm \sqrt{36 + 48}}{24} = \dfrac{6 \pm \sqrt{84}}{24}$

$= \dfrac{2(3 \pm \sqrt{21})}{24}$

$= \dfrac{3 \pm \sqrt{21}}{12}$

$c = \dfrac{3 + \sqrt{21}}{12} \in (0, 1)$

and $\quad c = \dfrac{3 - \sqrt{21}}{12} \in (0, 1)$

Hence, $f'(c)$ vanishes for some $c \in (0, 1)$.

Since, $f'(c) = 0$ this means $f(x) = 0$ has atteast one root $(0, 1)$.

20. (b,d) $f(0) = f(1) = f(2) = 0$

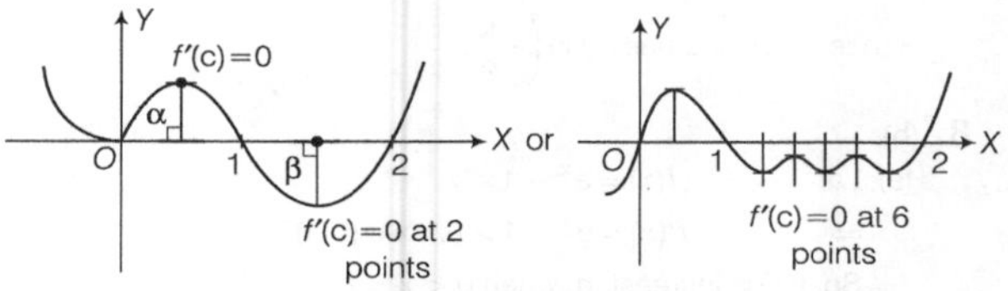

As, $f(x)$ is continuous and differentiable between $x = 0$ and $x = 2$.

$\therefore f'(c) = 0$ for two points $x = \alpha, \beta$.

$\Rightarrow f'(c) = 0$ for atleast two $c \in (0, 2)$.

21. (a) Let $f(x) = e^{10x}(x-1)(x-2)$

$$f(1) = 0 = f(2)$$

Thus, $f(x)$ satisfies all the condition of Rolle's theorem.

$\therefore \quad f'(c) = 0, \forall c \in (1, 2)$

$\Rightarrow \quad e^{10c}[10c^2 - 28c + 17] = 0$

$\Rightarrow \quad 10c^2 - 28c + 17 = 0 \quad [\because e^{10c} \neq 0]$

$$\Rightarrow \quad c = \frac{28 \pm \sqrt{784 - 680}}{20}$$

$$= \frac{28 \pm \sqrt{104}}{20} = \frac{20 \pm 10.19}{20}$$

$$= 1.91 \text{ or } 0.8905$$

$\Rightarrow$ The quadratic equation $10x^2 - 28x + 17 = 0$ has atleast are root in (1, 2).

$\therefore$ Statement I and Statement II are correct and Statement II is the correct explanation of Statement I.

22. (b) We have, $f(x) = 2 + \cos x$

$$f(t) = 2 + \cos t$$

$$f(t + \pi) = 2 + \cos(t + \pi) = 2 - \cos t$$

$f(t) \neq f(t + \pi)$ then there exist $c \in (t, t + \pi)$ such that

$$f'(c) = \frac{2 - \cos t - 2 - \cos t}{\pi}$$

$$-\sin c = \frac{-2\cos t}{\pi}$$

$$\sin c = \frac{\cos t}{\pi/2} = 0$$

$$\Rightarrow \quad c = 0, \pi; t = \frac{\pi}{2}$$

Clearly, Statement II is correct because $\cos x$ is periodic with period 2π.

Hence, Statement I is and, Statement II are correct but Statement II is not the correct explanation of Statement I.

23. (c)

(i) $f'(x) = \log x - \dfrac{3}{x} + 1$

$\Rightarrow \quad f(x) = (x - 3)\log x + c$

$\therefore \quad f(1) = f(3)$

(ii) $f'(x) = 4ax^3 + 3bx^2 + 2cx + d$

$\Rightarrow \quad f(x) = ax^4 + bx^3 + cx^2 + dx + e$

$\because \quad f(0) = f(3)$

$\therefore \; 27a + 9b + 3c + d = 0$

(iii) $\dfrac{f(b) - f(a)}{b - a} = f'(\sqrt{3}) = \dfrac{2}{3}$

$\Rightarrow \quad \dfrac{ab - 1}{ab} = \dfrac{2}{3} \Rightarrow ab = 3$

(iv) $\dfrac{f(b) - f(a)}{b - a} = f'(1/2)$

$\Rightarrow \quad a + b = 1$

Hence, (i) $\rightarrow$ (q, r), (ii) $\rightarrow$ (r), (iii) $\rightarrow$ (q), (iv) $\rightarrow$ (p)

24. (4) Using LMVT for f in [1, 2],

$$\forall c \in (1, 2), \frac{f(2) - f(1)}{2 - 1} = f'(c) \leq 2$$

$$f(2) - f(1) \leq 2$$

$\Rightarrow \quad f(2) \leq 4 \quad \ldots$(i)

Again, using LMVT in [2, 4],

$$\forall d \in (2, 4), \frac{f(4) - f(2)}{4 - 2} = f'(d) \leq 2$$

$\therefore \quad f(4) - f(2) \leq 4$

$$8 - f(2) \leq 4$$

$f(2) \geq 4 \quad \ldots$(ii)

From Eqs. (i) and (ii), we get

$$f(2) = 4$$

25. (5) Given, $f''(x) - g''(x) = 0$,

On integrating both sides, we get

$\Rightarrow \quad f'(x) - g'(c) = c,$

At $x = 1$, $\quad f'(1) - g'(1) = c$

$\Rightarrow \quad c = -2$

$\therefore \quad f'(x) - g'(x) = -2$

Again integrating both sides, we get

$$f(x) - g(x) = -2x + c_1$$

At $x = 2$, $\quad f(2) - g(2) = -4 + c$

$\therefore \quad c_1 = -2$

or $\quad f(x) - g(x) = -2x - 2$

$$\therefore \quad \left| f\left(\frac{3}{2}\right) - g\left(\frac{3}{2}\right) \right| = |-3 - 2| = 5$$

DPP-4 Monotonic Functions

1. (a) We have, $f(x) = x^2(x-2)^2$

$\Rightarrow \quad f'(x) = 2x(x-2)^2 + x^2 \, 2(x-2)$

$$= 2x[(x-2)^2 + x^2 - 2x]$$

$$= 2x(x^2 + 4 - 4x + x^2 - 2x)$$

$$= 2x(2x^2 - 6x + 4) = 4x^3 - 12x^2 + 8x$$

For $f(x)$ to be increasing, we must have

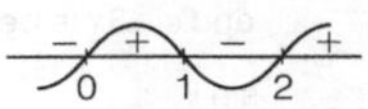

$$f'(x) > 0$$

$$4x^3 - 12x^2 + 8x > 0$$

$$4x(x-2)(x-1) > 0$$

$\therefore \quad x \in (0, 1) \cup (2, \infty)$

2. (a) We have, $f(x) = \tan x - x, \forall x \in R - \left\{(2n+1)\dfrac{\pi}{2}\right\}$

$\Rightarrow \quad f'(x) = \sec^2 x - 1$

$\Rightarrow \quad f'(x) = \tan^2 x \quad [\because \sec^2 x = 1 + \tan^2 x]$

$f(x) = \tan^2 x > 0$ for all x in the domain of f.

$\therefore f(x)$ is always increases.

3. (a) We have, $f(x) = x^3 + 6x^2 + (9 + 2k)x + 1$

It is given that, $f(x)$ is increasing.

$\therefore \quad f'(x) \geq 0 \Rightarrow 3x^2 + 12x + (9 + 2k) \geq 0$

If $D = (12)^2 - 4 \times 3 \times (9 + 2k) \leq 0 \quad \left[\begin{array}{l}\because ax^2 + bx + c \geq 0, \\ \text{if } a > 0 \text{ and } D \leq 0\end{array}\right]$

$\Rightarrow \quad 144 - 108 - 24k \le 0$

$\Rightarrow \quad 36 - 24k \le 0$

$\therefore \quad k \ge 3/2$

4. (d) We have, $f(x) = \sin x - \cos x - ax + b$

$\Rightarrow \quad f'(x) = \cos x + \sin x - a$

It is given that, $f(x)$ decreases for all real values of x.

$\Rightarrow \quad f'(x) \le 0 \Rightarrow \cos x + \sin x - a \le 0$

$\Rightarrow \quad \cos x + \sin x \le a$

$\Rightarrow \quad \sqrt{2}\left(\frac{1}{\sqrt{2}}\cos x + \frac{1}{\sqrt{2}}\sin x\right) \le a$

$\Rightarrow \quad \sqrt{2}\left(\sin\frac{\pi}{4}\cos x + \cos\frac{\pi}{4}\sin x\right) \le a$

$\Rightarrow \quad \sqrt{2}\sin\left(x + \frac{\pi}{4}\right) \le a$

$\therefore \quad a \ge \sqrt{2} \quad \left[\because \text{maximum of } \sin\left(x + \frac{\pi}{4}\right) \text{ is } 1\right]$

5. (c) Given, $f(x) = \int \left(2 - \frac{1}{1 + x^2} - \frac{1}{\sqrt{1 + x^2}}\right)dx$

$\Rightarrow \quad f'(x) = 2 - \frac{1}{1 + x^2} - \frac{1}{\sqrt{1 + x^2}}$

$f'(x) = \frac{2(1 + x^2) - 1 - \sqrt{1 + x^2}}{(1 + x^2)}$

Clearly, $1 + x^2 > 0, \forall\, x$.

For the sign of numerator,

Let $\phi(x) = 2(1 + x^2) - 1 - \sqrt{1 + x^2}$

$\phi(x) = 2 + 2x^2 - 1 - \sqrt{1 + x^2} = 2x^2 - \sqrt{1 + x^2} + 1$

$\phi(x) = 2x^2 + 1 - \sqrt{1 + x^2}$

Now, $\quad 2x^2 > x^2, \forall\, x$

$2x^2 + 1 > x^2 + 1, \forall x$

$\sqrt{2x^2 + 1} > \sqrt{x^2 + 1}, \forall x$

and $\quad 2x^2 + 1 > \sqrt{2x^2 + 1}, \forall x$

$\Rightarrow \quad 2x^2 + 1 > \sqrt{x^2 + 1}, \forall x$

$\Rightarrow \quad 2x^2 + 1 - \sqrt{x^2 + 1} > 0, \forall x$

$\Rightarrow \quad \phi(x) > 0, \forall\, x$

Thus, $f'(x) > 0, \forall\, x$,

i.e. $\quad x \in (-\infty, \infty)$

Hence, $f(x)$ is an increasing function.

6. (b) Given, $\quad f(x) = 4x - \tan 2x$

$\Rightarrow \quad f'(x) = 4 - 2\sec^2 2x = 2(1 - \tan^2 2x)$

For the continuous domain $\left(\frac{-\pi}{4}, \frac{\pi}{4}\right)$,

$f'(x) \ge 0 \text{ in } \left[\frac{-\pi}{8}, \frac{\pi}{8}\right]$

and $\quad f'(x) \le 0 \text{ in } \left(\frac{-\pi}{4}, \frac{-\pi}{8}\right] \cup \left[\frac{\pi}{8}, \frac{\pi}{4}\right)$

So, the required largest continuous interval is $\left[\frac{-\pi}{8}, \frac{\pi}{8}\right]$.

$\therefore$ Longest length $= \frac{\pi}{8} - \left(-\frac{\pi}{8}\right) = \frac{\pi}{8} + \frac{\pi}{8} = \frac{\pi}{4}$

7. (b) We have, $f(x) = \tan^{-1}(\sin x + \cos x)$

$\Rightarrow \quad f'(x) = \frac{1}{1 + (\sin x + \cos x)^2} \times (\cos x - \sin x)$

$\Rightarrow \quad f'(x) = \frac{\cos x}{1 + (\sin x + \cos x)^2} \times (1 - \tan x)$

Clearly, $\quad f'(x) > 0, \forall\, x \in \left(-\frac{\pi}{2}, \frac{\pi}{4}\right)$

Hence, $f(x)$ is increasing in $\left(-\frac{\pi}{2}, \frac{\pi}{4}\right)$.

8. (b)

(a) Let $\quad f(x) = e^x - 1 - x$

$\Rightarrow \quad f'(x) = e^x - 1 > 0, \forall x \in (0, 1)$

So, $f(x)$ is increasing, when $0 < x < 1$

$\Rightarrow \quad f(x) > f(0) \quad \text{or} \quad e^x - 1 - x > 0$

$\Rightarrow \quad e^x > 1 + x$

(b) Let $g(x) = \log_e(1 + x) - x$

$\Rightarrow g'(x) = \frac{1}{1 + x} - 1 = \frac{-x}{1 + x} < 0, \forall x \in (0, 1)$

So, $g(x)$ is decreasing, when $0 < x < 1$

$\Rightarrow \quad g(0) > g(x) \Rightarrow \log_e(1 + x) < x$

(c) Let $h(x) = \sin x - x$

$\Rightarrow h'(x) = \cos x - 1 < 0, \forall x \in (0, 1)$

So, $h(x)$ is decreasing, when $0 < x < 1$

$\Rightarrow \quad h(x) < h(0)$

$\therefore \quad \sin x < x$

(d) Let $g(x) = \log_e x - x$

$\Rightarrow \quad g'(x) = \frac{1}{x} - 1$

$\therefore \quad g'(x) > 0, \forall x \in (0, 1)$

or $\quad g(x) < g(1)$

$\Rightarrow \quad \log_e x - x < -1 \Rightarrow x - 1 > \log_e x$

$\Rightarrow \quad x > \log_e x$

9. (c) We have, $f(x) = \int e^x(x - 1)(x - 2)\,dx$

$\Rightarrow \quad f'(x) = e^x(x - 1)(x - 2)$

For $f(x)$ to be decreasing, we must have

$f'(x) < 0$

$\Rightarrow \quad e^x(x - 1)(x - 2) < 0$

$\Rightarrow \quad (x - 1)(x - 2) < 0$

$\therefore \quad x \in (1, 2)$

10. (a) We have, $f(x) = xe^{x(1 - x)}$

$\Rightarrow \quad f'(x) = e^{x(1 - x)} + x(1 - 2x)e^{x(1 - x)}$

$\Rightarrow \quad f'(x) = (1 + x - 2x^2)e^{x(1 - x)}$

$\Rightarrow \quad f'(x) = -(x - 1)(2x + 1)e^{x(1 - x)}$

Since, $e^{x(1 - x)} > 0$, for all x. Therefore, sign of $f'(x)$ for different values of x are as shown below

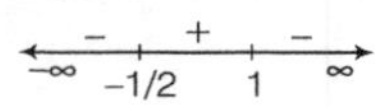

Clearly, $f(x)$ is increasing on $[-1/2, 1]$ and decreasing on $\left(-\infty, -\frac{1}{2}\right] \cup [1, \infty)$.

11. (a) We have, $f(x) = 3\sin x - 4\sin^3 x$

$f(x) = \sin 3x$

We know that, $\sin x$ is increasing on the interval

$\left(2n\pi - \frac{\pi}{2}, 2n\pi + \frac{\pi}{2}\right), n \in I$

and $\sin 3x$ is periodic with period $\frac{2\pi}{3}$, i.e. one third of the period of $\sin x$.

$\therefore$ Length of longest interval

$= \frac{1}{3}\left\{\left(2n\pi + \frac{\pi}{2}\right) - \left(2n\pi - \frac{\pi}{2}\right)\right\} = \frac{\pi}{3}$

12. (c) Here, $f(x) = \dfrac{x}{\sin x}$

$$\Rightarrow \quad f'(x) = \frac{\sin x \cdot 1 - x \cdot \cos x}{\sin^2 x} \quad \ldots \text{(i)}$$

where, $\sin^2 x$ is always positive, when $0 < x \le 1$.

But to check numerator, we again let

$$h(x) = \sin x - x\cos x$$

$$\Rightarrow \quad h'(x) = \cos x - 1 \cdot \cos x + x\sin x$$

$$= x\sin x, \text{ which is positive for } 0 < x \le 1$$

$\therefore \quad h'(x) > 0 \Rightarrow h(x)$ is increasing, when $0 < x \le 1$

$\Rightarrow \quad h(0) < h(x) \Rightarrow 0 < \sin x - x\cos x$

In Eq. (i), $\quad \sin x - x\cos x > 0$

$\Rightarrow \quad f'(x) > 0$, where $0 < x \le 1$

Hence, $f(x)$ is increasing, when $0 < x \le 1$.

Again, $$g(x) = \frac{x}{\tan x} \quad \text{[given]}$$

$$g'(x) = \frac{\tan x - x\sec^2 x}{\tan^2 x} \quad \ldots \text{(ii)}$$

where, $\tan^2 x > 0$

For the sign of $\tan x - x\sec^2 x$, we let $\phi(x) = \tan x - \sec^2 x$

$$\phi'(x) = \sec^2 x - \sec^2 x - x(2\sec x)(\sec x \tan x)$$

$$\phi'(x) = -2x\sec^2 x \tan x$$

As $\quad \phi'(x) < 0, \forall \, 0 < x \le 1$

$\therefore \quad \phi(x)$ is decreasing, when $0 < x \le 1$.

$\Rightarrow \quad \phi(0) > \phi(x)$ or $0 < \tan x - x\sec^2 x$

In Eq. (ii), $\quad \tan x - x\sec^2 x < 0$

$$g'(x) < 0, \text{ when } 0 < x \le 1$$

$\therefore g(x)$ is decreasing, when $0 < x \le 1$.

13. (d) Given, $$f(x) > x \quad \ldots \text{(i)}$$

$$\Rightarrow \quad f[f(x)] > f(x) \quad \ldots \text{(ii)}$$

From Eqs. (i) and (ii), we get

$$f[f(x)] > x$$

$$\Rightarrow \quad f[f(x)] - x > 0$$

$\therefore$ No real root for $f[f(x)] = x$.

14. (b) Given, $x = \dfrac{1}{1+t^2}, y = \dfrac{1}{t(1+t^2)}$

$$\Rightarrow \quad \frac{dx}{dt} = \frac{-2t}{(1+t^2)^2}, \frac{dy}{dt} = \frac{-1+3t^2}{t^2(1+t^2)^2}$$

$$\Rightarrow \quad \frac{dy}{dx} = \frac{1+3t^2}{2t^3}$$

$$\frac{dy}{dx} > 0, \text{ if } t > 0$$

$$\Rightarrow \quad x = \frac{1}{1+t^2} \in (0, 1)$$

Hence, $f(x)$ is increasing in (0, 1).

15. (b) Given, $f(x) = \dfrac{\log(\pi + x)}{\log(e + x)}$

$$\Rightarrow f'(x) = \frac{\log(e+x) \times \dfrac{1}{\pi + x} - \log(\pi + x) \times \dfrac{1}{e + x}}{[\log(e + x)]^2}$$

$$= \frac{(e + x)\log(e + x) - (\pi + x)\log(\pi + x)}{(e + x)(\pi + x)[\log(e + x)]^2}$$

$$= \frac{e\log(e + x) + x\log(e + x) - \pi\log(\pi + x) - x\log(\pi + x)}{(e + x)(\pi + x)[\log(e + x)]^2}$$

$$= \frac{x\log\left(\dfrac{e + x}{\pi + x}\right) + [e\log(e + x) - \pi\log(\pi + x)]}{(e + x)(\pi + x)[\log(e + x)]^2}$$

Now, $\quad \pi + x > e + x \Rightarrow \log\left(\dfrac{e + x}{\pi + x}\right) < 0$

$$\Rightarrow \quad f'(x) < 0$$

and also $e\log(e + x) < \pi\log(\pi + x) \Rightarrow f'(x) < 0$

Thus, $f(x)$ is decreasing on $(0, \infty)$.

16. (a) Given, $3x^2 - 2x^3 = \log_2(x^2 + 1) - \log_2 x$

$$\Rightarrow \quad 3x^2 - 2x^3 = \log_2\left(\frac{x^2 + 1}{x}\right)$$

$$\Rightarrow \quad 2^{3x^2 - 2x^3} = \frac{x^2 + 1}{x}$$

$$\Rightarrow \quad 2^{3x^2 - 2x^3} = x + \frac{1}{x}$$

$$\Rightarrow \quad 2^{3x^2 - 2x^3} = x + \frac{1}{x} \ge 2$$

$$\Rightarrow \quad 3x^2 - 2x^3 = 1$$

$$\Rightarrow \quad 2x^3 - 3x^2 + 1 = 0$$

$$\Rightarrow \quad (x - 1)(2x^2 - x - 1) = 0$$

$$\Rightarrow \quad x - 1 = 0 \text{ or } 2x^2 - x - 1 = 0$$

$$\Rightarrow \quad x = 1 \text{ or } x = \frac{+1 \pm \sqrt{1 + 8}}{4}$$

$$\Rightarrow \quad x = 1 \text{ or } x = \frac{1 \pm 3}{4}$$

$$\Rightarrow \quad x = 1 \text{ or } x = 1, \frac{-1}{2}$$

But $x = \dfrac{-1}{2}$ (not possible as $\log x$ does not exist)

Hence, the number of solution is 1.

17. (d) $h(x) = \dfrac{\log(f(x) \cdot g(x))}{\log(a)} = \log a^{\{a^{|x|}\text{sgn}\, x\} + [a^{|x|}\text{sgn}\, x]}$

$$= \frac{\log a^{a^{|x|}\text{sgn}\, x}}{\log a} = a^{|x|}\text{Sgn}\, x \cdot \frac{\log a}{\log a}$$

$$= a^{|x|}\text{Sgn}$$

$$= \begin{cases} a^x, & x > 0 \\ 0, & x = 0 \\ -a^{-x}, & x < 0 \end{cases}$$

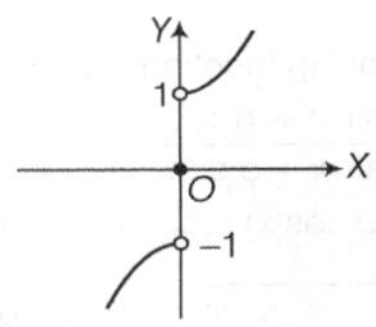

$\therefore h(x)$ is odd and increasing for $a > 1$.

18. (b) Given, $f(x) = \left(\dfrac{\sqrt{p + 4}}{1 - p} - 1\right)x^5 - 3x + \log 5$

$$\Rightarrow \quad f'(x) = 5\left(\frac{\sqrt{p + 4}}{1 - p} - 1\right)x^4 - 3$$

Since, $f(x)$ is decreases for all real x.

$$\therefore \quad f'(x) \le 0$$

$$5\left(\frac{\sqrt{p + 4}}{1 - p} - 1\right)x^4 - 3 \le 0$$

$$\Rightarrow \quad \frac{\sqrt{p + 4}}{1 - p} - 1 \le 0$$

$$\Rightarrow \quad \frac{\sqrt{p + 4} - 1 + p}{1 - p} \le 0$$

$\left[\because \text{given expression is defined for } p \ne 1 \text{ and } p + 4 \ge 0, p \ge -4\right]$

$\Rightarrow \quad \sqrt{p+4}-(1-p) \le 0 \quad$ and $\quad 1-p>0$

or $\quad \sqrt{p+4}-(1-p) \ge 0 \quad$ and $\quad 1-p<0$

$\Rightarrow \quad p+4 \le (1-p)^2 \quad$ and $\quad 1>p$

or $\quad p+4 \ge (1-p)^2 \quad$ and $\quad p>1$

$\Rightarrow \quad p+4 \le 1+p^2-2p \quad$ and $\quad 1>p$

or $\quad p+4 \ge 1+p^2-2p \quad$ and $\quad p>1$

$\Rightarrow \quad p^2-3p-3 \ge 0 \quad$ and $\quad 1>p$

or $\quad p^2-3p-3 \le 0 \quad$ and $\quad p>1$

$\Rightarrow \quad p = \dfrac{3 \pm \sqrt{21}}{2} \quad$ and $\quad 1>p$

or $\quad p = \dfrac{3 \pm \sqrt{21}}{2} \quad$ and $\quad p>1$

$\Rightarrow \quad p = \dfrac{3 - \sqrt{21}}{2} \quad$ and $\quad 1>p$

or $\quad P = \dfrac{3 + \sqrt{21}}{2} \quad$ and $\quad p>1$

Also, $\quad p \ge -4$

$\Rightarrow \quad p \in \left[-4, \dfrac{3-\sqrt{21}}{2}\right] \cup (1, \infty)$

19. (a) Given, $f(x) = x^3 + bx^2 + cx + d,\ 0 < b^2 < c$

$\therefore \quad f'(x) = 3x^2 + 2bx + c$

Discriminant $= 4b^2 - 12c = 4(b^2 - 3c) < 0 \quad [\because 0 < b^2 < c]$

$\therefore \quad f'(x) > 0, \forall x \in R$

$\Rightarrow f(x)$ is strictly increasing, $\forall x \in R$.

20. (c) Given, $g(u) = 2\tan^{-1}(e^u) - \dfrac{\pi}{2}$ for $u \in (-\infty, \infty)$

$$g(-u) = 2\tan^{-1}(e^{-u}) - \frac{\pi}{2} = 2\cot^{-1}(e^u) - \frac{\pi}{2}$$

$$= 2\left[\frac{\pi}{2} - \tan^{-1}(e^u)\right] - \frac{\pi}{2} = \frac{\pi}{2} - 2\tan^{-1}(e^u)$$

$$= -g(u)$$

$\because \quad g(-u) = -g(u)$

So, $g(u)$ is an odd function.

and $g'(u) = \dfrac{2e^u}{1+e^{2u}} > 0 \ \forall u \in R$

$\therefore g$ is strictly increasing function in $(-\infty, \infty)$

21. (a) Given, $f(x) = \dfrac{a\sin x + b\cos x}{c\sin x + d\cos x}$

$$f'(x) = \frac{(c\sin x + d\cos x)(a\cos x - b\sin x) - (a\sin x + b\cos x) \times (c\cos x - d\sin x)}{(c\sin x + d\cos x)^2}$$

$$= \frac{\left[\begin{array}{l} ac\sin x\cos x - bc\sin^2 x + ad\cos^2 x - bd\sin x\cos x \\ -ac\sin x\cos x + ad\sin^2 x - bc\cos^2 x + bd\sin x\cos x \end{array}\right]}{(c\sin x + d\cos x)^2}$$

$$= \frac{(ad - bc)\cos^2 x + (ad - bc)\sin^2 x}{(c\sin x + d\cos x)^2}$$

$$f'(x) = \frac{(ad - bc)(\cos^2 x + \sin^2 x)}{(c\sin x + d\cos x)^2}$$

$$f'(x) = \frac{ad - bc}{(c\sin x + d\cos x)^2}$$

It is given that, $f(x)$ is monotonically increasing.

$\therefore \quad f'(x) \ge 0$

$\Rightarrow \quad \dfrac{ad - bc}{(c\sin x + d\cos x)^2} \ge 0$

$\Rightarrow \quad ad - bc \ge 0$

$\Rightarrow \quad ad \ge bc$

22. (b) Given, $f(x) = x^3 + ax^2 + bx + 5\sin^2 x$ is increasing on R.

$\Rightarrow \quad f'(x) > 0, \forall x \in R$

$\Rightarrow \quad 3x^2 + 2ax + b + 5\sin 2x > 0, \forall x \in R$

$\Rightarrow \quad 3x^2 + 2ax + (b - 5) > 0, \forall x \in R$

$[\because \sin 2x \ge -1]$

Now, $\quad (2a)^2 - 4 \times 3 \times (b - 5) < 0$

$\left[\begin{array}{l}\because \text{if } f(x) = ax^2 + bx + c > 0 \\ \text{and } a > 0 \Rightarrow D < 0\end{array}\right]$

$\Rightarrow \quad 4a^2 - 12(b - 5) < 0$

$\therefore \quad a^2 - 3b + 15 < 0$

23. (a,c) Given, $h(x) = f(x) - [f(x)]^2 + [f(x)]^3$

$\Rightarrow \quad h'(x) = f'(x)[1 - 2f(x) + 3\{f(x)\}^2]$

$$= 3f'(x)\left[\{f(x)\}^2 - \frac{2}{3}f(x) + \frac{1}{3}\right]$$

$$= 3f'(x)\left[\left\{f(x) - \frac{1}{3}\right\}^2 + \frac{2}{9}\right]$$

Note that, $h'(x) < 0$, whenever $f'(x) < 0$ and $h'(x) > 0$, whenever $f'(x) > 0$.

Thus, $h(x)$ increases (or decreases), whenever $f(x)$ increases (or decreases).

24. (a,b,c,d) Given that, $f(x) = \begin{cases} 3x^2 + 12x - 1, & -1 \le x \le 2 \\ 37 - x, & 2 < x \le 3 \end{cases}$, then

In $(-1, 2]$, $f'(x) = 6x + 12$

$f'(x) = 0 \Rightarrow x = -2$

$\Rightarrow \quad f(x)$ decreases in $(-\infty, -2)$ and increases on $(-2, \infty)$.

Also, $\quad f(2^-) = 3(2)^2 + 12(2) - 1 = 35$

$f(2^+) = 37 - 2 = 35$

Hence, f is continuous.

$$f'(x) = \begin{cases} 6x + 12, & -1 < x < 2 \\ -1, & 2 < x < 3 \end{cases}$$

$\Rightarrow \quad f'(2^-) = 24$ and $f'(2^+) = -1$

Hence, $f(x)$ is not differentiable at $x = 2$.

Also, $\quad f(2^+) < f(2)$ and $f(2^-) < f(2)$

Hence, $x = 2$ is the point of maxima.

25. (a,d) Let, $\quad \phi(x) = f(x) \cdot g(x)$

$$\phi'(x) = \underset{(+)}{f(x)}\underset{(+)}{g'(x)} + \underset{(-)}{f'(x)}\,\underset{(-)}{g(x)}$$

$\Rightarrow \quad \phi'(x) > 0$

$\because \phi(x) = f(x)\, g(x)$ is strictly increasing on I.

Again, let $\quad h(x) = f[g(x)]$

$\Rightarrow \quad h'(x) = f'[g(x)] \cdot g'(x)$

$= (-\text{ve}) \cdot (+\text{ve})$

$= -\text{ve}$

$\therefore h(x)$ is strictly decreasing.

26. (a,b,c,d) Given, $f(x) = f(1 - x)$

On differentiating w.r.t. x, we get

$f'(x) = -f'(1 - x)$

Put $x = \dfrac{1}{2}$

$\Rightarrow \quad 2f'\left(\dfrac{1}{2}\right) = 0 \Rightarrow f'\left(\dfrac{1}{2}\right) = 0$

Since, $\quad f'\left(\dfrac{1}{2}\right) = 0$ and $f'\left(\dfrac{1}{4}\right) = 0$

$\Rightarrow \quad f'(x) = 0$ at two points in $[0, 1]$.

Now, $$\int_{-1/2}^{1/2} f\left(x+\frac{1}{2}\right)\sin x\,dx = 0$$

Since, $f\left(x+\frac{1}{2}\right)\sin x$ is an odd function which is clear from the following explanation.

Let $$g(x) = f\left(x+\frac{1}{2}\right)\sin x$$

$$g(-x) = f\left(\frac{1}{2}-x\right)\sin(-x)$$

$$= -\sin x\, f\left[1-\left(\frac{1}{2}-x\right)\right]$$

$$= -\sin x\, f\left(\frac{1}{2}+x\right) = -g(x)$$

Moreover, $\int_{1/2}^{1} f(1-t)\,e^{\sin(\pi t)}\,dt$

$$= \int_0^{1/2} f(x)\,e^{\sin \pi u}du, \text{ where } 1-t = u$$

27. (b,c,d) We have, $$f(x) = x\cos\frac{1}{x},\ x \ge 1$$

$$f'(x) = \cos\frac{1}{x} + \frac{1}{x}\sin\frac{1}{x}$$

$$f''(x) = -\frac{1}{x^3}\cos\frac{1}{x}$$

$\Rightarrow$ $\lim_{x\to\infty} f'(x) = 1$ and $f''(x) < 0, \forall\ x \ge 1$

$\Rightarrow f'(x)$ is strictly decreasing in the interval $[1, \infty)$.

Let $g(x) = f(x+2) - f(x)$,

then $g'(x) = f'(x+2) - f'(x) < 0$ [$\because f'(x)$ is strictly decreasing]

$\Rightarrow g(x)$ is strictly decreasing on $(1, \infty)$.

Now, $\lim_{x\to\infty} g(x) = \lim_{x\to\infty} f(x+2) - f(x)$

$$= \lim_{x\to\infty} (x+2)\cos\frac{1}{x+2} - x\cos\frac{1}{x}$$

$$= \lim_{x\to\infty} x\left(\cos\frac{1}{x+2} - \cos\frac{1}{x}\right) + 2\cos\frac{1}{x+2}$$

$$= \lim_{x\to\infty} 2x\sin\frac{x+1}{x^2+2x}\sin\frac{1}{x^2+2x} + 2\cos\frac{1}{x+2}$$

$$= 2\lim_{x\to\infty} \frac{\sin\left(\frac{x+1}{x^2+2x}\right)}{\frac{x+1}{x^2+2x}} \times \frac{\sin\left(\frac{1}{x^2+2x}\right)}{\frac{1}{x^2+2x}} \times \frac{x(x+1)}{(x^2+2x)^2} + 2\cos\frac{1}{x+2}$$

$$= 2\times 1\times 1\times 0 + 2 = 2$$

As $g(x)$ is decreasing on $[1, \infty)$ and $\lim_{x\to\infty} g(x) = 2$

$\therefore$ $g(x) > 2, \forall\ x \in [1, \infty)$

$\Rightarrow$ $f(x+2) - f(x) > 2, \forall\ x \in [1, 0)$

28. (b,c) Given, $f(x) = \log_e x + \int_0^x \sqrt{1+\sin x}\,dt$

$\Rightarrow$ $f'(x) = \frac{1}{x} + \sqrt{1+\sin x},\ x > 0$

But $f(x)$ is not differentiable in $(0, \infty)$, as $\sin x$ may be -1 and then

$$f''(x) = -\frac{1}{x^2} + \frac{\cos x}{2\sqrt{1+\sin x}} \text{ will not exist}$$

$\Rightarrow f'(x)$ is continuous for all $x \in (0, \infty)$

but $f'(x)$ is not differentiable on $(0, \infty)$.

$\therefore$ Option (b) is true.

Also, $f'(x) \le 3$, if $x > 1$ and $f(x) > 3$, if $x > e^3$

Let $\alpha = e^3$

$\Rightarrow$ Option (c) is true.

Option (d) is not possible as $f(x) \to \infty$, when $x \to \infty$.

29. (b,c,d) Here, $f(x) = \int_0^x e^t (t-2)(t-3)\,dt$

$\Rightarrow$ $f'(x) = e^x (x-2)(x-3)$ [by Newton-Leibnitz's rule]

+   −   +
2   3

$\therefore$ Maximum at $x = 2$,

minimum at $x = 3$ and decreasing on $(2, 3)$.

Also, $f'(x) = 0$ has two roots, i.e. $x = 2, 3$

$\Rightarrow$ $f'(2) = f'(3) = 0$

Then, by Rolle's theorem

$f''(c) = 0$ must have atleast one root $\in (2, 3)$.

30. (b,c) Let $f(x) = x\sin\pi x$

$$f'(x) = \pi x\cos\pi x + \sin\pi x = 0 \Rightarrow \pi x = -\tan\pi x$$

Let $h(x) = \tan\pi x,\ g(x) = -\pi x$

which could be ploted as

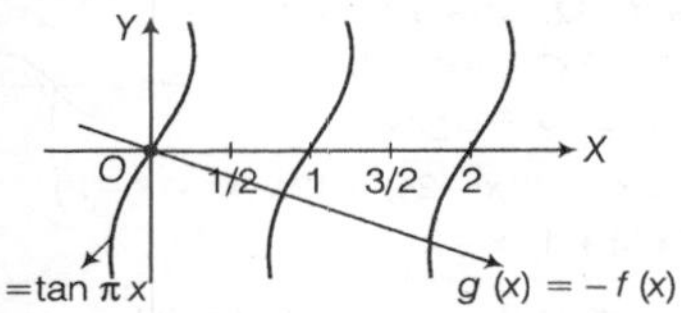

Clearly, $f(x)$ and $g(x)$ intersect, when $\frac{1}{2} < x < 1$

or $$\frac{3}{2} < x < 2$$

or $$\frac{5}{2} < x < 3$$

$\therefore$ A unique point in $\left(n+\frac{1}{2}, n+1\right)$ or $(n, n+1)$.

31. (c) Given, $f(x) = x^3 + x^2 + 3x + \sin x$

$\Rightarrow$ $f'(x) = 3x^2 + 2x + 3 + \cos x$

$\because$ $3x^2 + 2x + 3 > 0, \forall\ x$ and $-1 \le \cos x \le 1$

If $\cos x = -1$

$f'(x) = 3x^2 + 2x + 2 > 0, \forall\ x \in R$ and if $\cos x = 1$

$f'(x) = 3x^2 + 2x + 4 > 0, \forall\ x \in R$

$\therefore f(x)$ is an increasing function.

Hence, f is one-one.

Clearly, Statement I is correct.

32. (a) Let $f(x) = x^{1/x}$

$$f'(x) = x^{1/x}\left[\frac{-1}{x^2}\times\log x + \frac{1}{x}\times\frac{1}{x}\right]$$

$$f'(x) = x^{1/x}\left[\frac{-\log x}{x^2} + \frac{1}{x^2}\right]$$

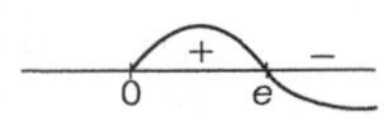

$$f'(x) = x^{1/x}\left[\frac{1-\log x}{x^2}\right]$$

Clearly, $f'(x) > 0$ for $0 < x < e$ and $f'(x) < 0$ for $x > e$

$\therefore$ Hence $f(x) = x^{1/x}$ is increasing for $0 < x < e$ and decreasing for $x > e$.

Using this concept, Statement I is correct.

33. (d) $f(x) = \tan^{-1}(\log_e x),\ x > 0$

$$f'(x) = \frac{1}{1+(\log x)^2}\cdot\frac{1}{x} > 0, \forall\ x \in (0, \infty)$$

$\therefore$ Increasing $\Rightarrow$ injective.

As, $x > 0 \Rightarrow -\infty < \log x < \infty$

$\therefore$ $$-\frac{\pi}{2} < \tan^{-1}(\log x) < \frac{\pi}{2}$$

Range of $f(x)$ = Codomain $\Rightarrow$ Surjective

34. (c) Since, range of $f(x) \in \left(-\frac{\pi}{2}, \frac{\pi}{2}\right)$ and increasing.

$\therefore \quad y = \tan^{-1}(\log_e x)$

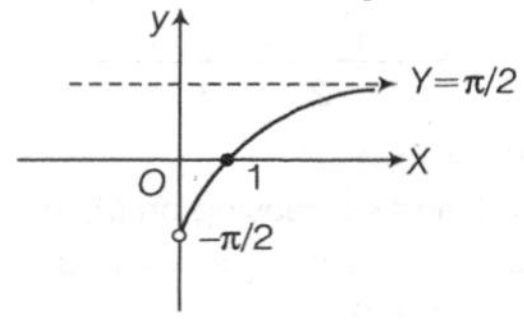

35. (c) From the graph, $g(x)$ is discontinuous at $x = x_1, x_2, x_3$.

$\Rightarrow \quad \tan^{-1}(\log x_1) = -1, \tan^{-1}(\log x_2) = 0, \tan^{-1}(\log x_3) = 1$

$\Rightarrow \quad x_1 = \frac{1}{e^{\tan 1}}, x_2 = 1, x_3 = e^{\tan 1}$

$\therefore \quad x_1 + x_2 + x_3 = \frac{1}{e^{\tan 1}} + 1 + e^{\tan 1} > 3$

Explanations for Q. Nos. (36-38)

Given, $f(x) = 3x^4 - 4x^3 - 12x^2 + 5$

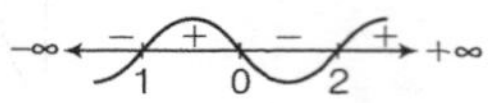

$f'(x) = 12x^3 - 12x^2 - 24x$

$= x(12x^2 - 12x - 24) = 12x(x^2 - x - 2)$

$= 12x(x + 1)(x - 2)$

In $(-\infty, -1)$	decreasing
In $(-1, 0)$	increasing
In $(0, 2)$	decreasing
In $(2, \infty)$	increasing

36. (a) Triplet $(a_1, a_2, a_3) \equiv (-1, 0, 2)$

37. (d) On the basis of given Information graph of $f(x)$, is

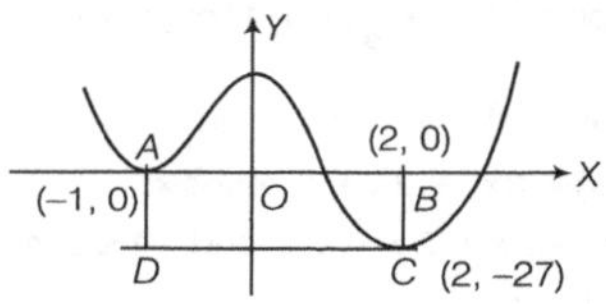

$\therefore$ Area of rectangle $ABCD = 3 \times 27 = 81$ sq units

38. (d) Clearly from the graph, 2 real coincident and 2 irrational roots.

39. (c) Here,

$$f(x) + 2x = (1 - x)^2 \cdot \sin^2 x + x^2 + 2x \quad \ldots \text{(i)}$$

where, $P : f(x) + 2x = 2(1 + x)^2 \quad \ldots$(ii)

$\therefore \quad 2(1 + x^2) = (1 - x)^2 \sin^2 x + x^2 + 2x$

$\Rightarrow \quad (1 - x)^2 \sin^2 x = x^2 - 2x + 2$

$\Rightarrow \quad (1 - x)^2 \sin^2 x = (1 - x)^2 + 1$

$\Rightarrow \quad (1 - x)^2 \cos^2 x = -1$

which is never possible.

$\therefore$ P is false.

Again, let $\quad h(x) = 2f(x) + 1 - 2x(1 + x)$

where $\quad h(0) = 2f(0) + 1 - 0 = 1$

$\quad h(1) = 2f(1) + 1 - 4 = -3$

as $h(0)\,h(1) < 0 \Rightarrow h(x)$ must have a solution.

$\therefore$ Q is true.

40. (b) Here, $\quad f(x) = (1 - x)^2 \cdot \sin^2 x + x^2 \geq 0, \forall x$

and $\quad g(x) = \int_1^x \left[\frac{2(t - 1)}{t + 1} - \log t\right] f(t)\, dt$

$$\Rightarrow \quad g'(x) = \left\{\frac{2(x - 1)}{x + 1} - \log x\right\} \cdot \underbrace{f(x)}_{+\text{ve}} \quad \ldots \text{(i)}$$

For $g'(x)$ to be increasing or decreasing.

Let $\quad \phi(x) = \frac{2(x - 1)}{x + 1} - \log x$

$\phi'(x) = \frac{4}{(x + 1)^2} - \frac{1}{x} = \frac{-(x - 1)^2}{x(x + 1)^2}$

$\phi'(x) < 0$, for $x > 1$

$\Rightarrow \quad \phi(x) < \phi(1)$

$\Rightarrow \quad \phi(x) < 0 \quad \ldots$(ii)

From Eqs. (i) and (ii), we get

$g'(x) < 0$ for $x \in (1, \infty)$

$\therefore \quad g(x)$ is decreasing for $x \in (1, \infty)$.

DPP-5 Maxima and Minima

1. (i) Given $f(x) = 2x^3 - 21x^2 + 36x - 20$

$f'(x) = 6x^2 - 42x + 36$

For maxima or minima,

$f'(x) = 0 \quad \Rightarrow 6x^2 - 42x + 36 = 0$

$\Rightarrow \quad (x - 1)(x - 6) = 0$

$\Rightarrow \quad x = 1, 6$

Now, $\quad f''(x) = 12x - 42$

$f''(x)$ at $x = 1 = -30 < 0$

Local maxima at $x = 1$

and $\quad f'(x)$ at $(x = 6) = 72 - 42 = 30 > 0$

Local minimum at $x = 6$.

(ii) Given, $f(x) = -(x - 1)^3 (x + 1)^2$

$f'(x) = -[3(x - 1)^2 (x + 1)^2 + (x - 1)^3\, 2(x + 1)]$

$f'(x) = -[3(x^2 - 1)^2 + 2(x^2 - 1)(x - 1)^2]$

$= -(x^2 - 1)[3(x^2 - 1) + 2(x - 1)^2]$

$= (x^2 - 1)(5x^2 - 4x - 1)$

For maxima or minima,

$f'(x) = 0$

$\Rightarrow \quad -(x^2 - 1)[3(x^2 - 1) + 2(x - 1)^2] = 0$

$\Rightarrow \quad x = \pm 1 \text{ or } 3x^2 - 3 + 2x^2 + 2 - 4x = 0$

$\Rightarrow \quad x = \pm 1 \text{ or } 5x^2 - 4x - 1 = 0$

$\Rightarrow \quad x = \pm 1 \text{ or } (x - 1)(5x + 1) = 0$

$\Rightarrow \quad x = \pm 1 \text{ or } x = 1, -1/5$

$\therefore$ Critical points are $-1, -1/5, 1$.

Now, $\quad f''(x) = -(2x)(5x^2 - 4x - 1) - (x^2 - 1)(10x - 4)$

$= -[10x^3 - 8x^2 - 2x + 10x^3 - 4x^2 - 10x + 4]$

$= -[20x^3 - 12x^2 - 12x + 4]$

$f''(-1) = -[-20 - 12 + 12 + 4] = 1670$

Local minimum at $x = -1$.

$f''(1) = -[-20 - 12 - 12 + 4] = 0$

Neither maxima nor minima at $x = 1$.

$f''(-1/5) = -[20(-1/5)^3 - 12(-1/5)^2 - 12(-1/5) + 4]$

$= -\left[-\frac{20}{125} - \frac{12}{25} + \frac{12}{5} + 4\right]$

$= -\left[\frac{-20 - 60 + 275 + 500}{125}\right] = -\left[\frac{695}{125}\right] = -\frac{139}{25} < 0$

$\therefore$ $f(x)$ has local maxima at $x = -1/5$.

(iii) Given, $f(x) = x \cdot \log_e x$

$$f'(x) = \left(\log_e x + x \times \frac{1}{x}\right)$$

$$f'(x) = (\log_e x + 1)$$

For maxima or minima,

$$f'(x) = 0$$

$$\log_e x + 1 = 0$$

$$\Rightarrow \quad \log_e x = -1 \Rightarrow x = \frac{1}{e}$$

Now, $f''(x) = \frac{1}{x}$

$$f''(1/e) = e > 0$$

$\therefore$ $f(x)$ has minima at $x = \frac{1}{e}$ and there is no local maxima.

(iv) Given, $y = \dfrac{3x^2 + 4x + 4}{x^2 + x + 1}$

$$\Rightarrow \quad \frac{dy}{dx} = \frac{(x^2 + x + 1)(6x + 4) - (3x^2 + 4x + 4)(2x + 1)}{(x^2 + x + 1)^2}$$

$$\frac{dy}{dx} = \frac{-x^2 - 2x}{(x^2 + x + 1)^2}$$

$$\frac{dy}{dx} = \frac{-(x^2 + 2x)}{(x^2 + x + 1)^2}$$

For maxima or minima, $\frac{dy}{dx} = 0$

$$\Rightarrow \quad \frac{-(x^2 + 2x)}{(x^2 + x + 1)} = 0$$

$$\Rightarrow \quad x^2 + 2x = 0 \quad \Rightarrow x(x + 2) = 0$$

$$\Rightarrow \quad x = 0, x = -2$$

Now, $f''(x)$

$$= \left[\frac{(x^2 + x + 1)^2 (2x + 2) - (x^2 + 2x) 2(x^2 + x + 1)(2x + 1)}{(x^2 + x + 1)^4}\right]$$

$$= -\left[\frac{(x^2 + x + 1)(2x + 2)(x^2 + x + 1) - 2(2x + 1)(x^2 + 2x)}{(x^2 + x + 1)^4}\right]$$

$$= -\left[\frac{-2(x^3 + 3x^2 + x - 1)}{(x^2 + x + 1)^3}\right]$$

$$\Rightarrow \quad f''(x) = \frac{2(x^3 + 3x^2 + x - 1)}{(x^2 + x + 1)^3}$$

$$\therefore \quad f''(0) = \frac{-2}{1} = -2 < 0$$

$f(x)$ has local maxima at $x = 0$.

Now, $f''(-2) = \dfrac{2[(-2)^3 + 3(-2)^2 + (-2) + 1)]}{[(-2)^2 - 2 + 1]^3}$

$$= \frac{2(-8 + 12 - 2 + 1)}{(4 - 1)^3} = \frac{6}{27} = \frac{2}{9} > 0$$

$\therefore$ $f(x)$ has local minima at $x = -2$.

2. (i) $f(x) = 4x - \dfrac{x^2}{2}$; $x \in \left[-2, \dfrac{9}{2}\right]$

$$f'(x) = 4 - x$$

For maxima or minima,

$$f'(x) = 0$$

$$4 - x = 0$$

$$\Rightarrow \quad x = 4$$

Now, $f(-2) = -8 - 2 = -10$

$$f(4) = 16 - 8 = 8$$

$$f\left(\frac{9}{2}\right) = 18 - \frac{81}{8} = \frac{63}{8} = 7.875$$

$\therefore$ Maximum value of $f(x) = 8$ and minimum value of $f(x) = -10$

(ii) $f(x) = 3x^4 - 8x^3 + 12x^2 - 48x + 25$; $x \in [0, 3]$

$$\Rightarrow \quad f'(x) = 12x^3 - 24x^2 + 24x - 48$$

For maxima or minima,

$$f'(x) = 0$$

$$\Rightarrow \quad 12x^3 - 24x^2 + 24x - 48 = 0$$

$$\Rightarrow \quad x^3 - 2x^2 + 2x - 4 = 0$$

$$\Rightarrow \quad (x - 2)(x^2 + 2) = 0$$

$$\Rightarrow \quad x = 2, \neq \sqrt{2}i$$

$\therefore$ $x = 2$ in the only real critical point.

Now, $f(0) = 25$

$$f(2) = 3 \times (2)^4 - 8(2)^3 + 12(2)^2 - 48 \times 2 + 25$$

$$= 48 - 64 + 48 - 96 + 25$$

$$= -39$$

$$f(3) = 3 \times (3)^4 - 8(3)^3 + 12(3)^2 - 48 \times 3 + 25$$

$$= 243 - 216 + 108 - 144 + 25$$

$$= 16$$

$\therefore$ Maximum of $f(x) = 25$ and minimum of $f(x) = -39$.

(iii) $f(x) = \sin x + \dfrac{1}{2}\cos 2x$; $x \in \left[0, \dfrac{\pi}{2}\right]$

$$\Rightarrow \quad f'(x) = \cos x + \frac{1}{2} \times 2(-\sin 2x)$$

$$f'(x) = \cos x - \sin 2x$$

For maxima or minima,

$$f'(x) = 0$$

$$\Rightarrow \quad \cos x - \sin 2x = 0$$

$$\Rightarrow \quad \cos x(1 - 2\sin x) = 0$$

$$\Rightarrow \quad \cos x = 0 \quad \text{or} \quad 1 - 2\sin x = 0$$

$$\Rightarrow \quad x = (2n + 1)\frac{\pi}{2} \quad \text{or} \quad \sin x = \frac{1}{2}$$

$$\Rightarrow \quad x = \frac{\pi}{2} \quad \text{or} \quad \frac{\pi}{6}$$

Now, $f(0) = \frac{1}{2}$

$$f\left(\frac{\pi}{6}\right) = \frac{1}{2} + \frac{1}{4} = \frac{3}{4}$$

$$f\left(\frac{\pi}{2}\right) = \frac{1}{2}$$

$\therefore$ Maximum of $f(x) = \frac{3}{4}$, at $x = \frac{\pi}{6}$

and minimum of $f(x) = \frac{1}{2}$, at $x = 0, \frac{\pi}{2}$

3. Let ABC be a right angled triangle, right angle at B.

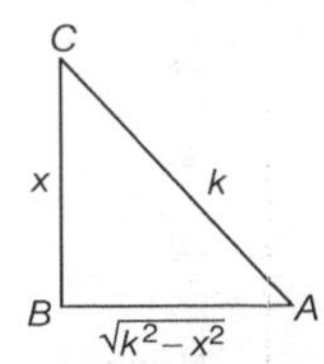

Let $AC = k$, $BC = x$, then

$$AB = \sqrt{k^2 - x^2} \quad \ldots(i)$$

Perimeter $(P) = AB + BC + AC$

$$= \sqrt{k^2 - x^2} + x + k$$

$$\Rightarrow \quad \frac{dP}{dx} = \frac{1}{2\sqrt{k^2 - x^2}}(-2x) + 1 \quad [\because k \text{ is constant}]$$

$$\Rightarrow \quad \frac{dP}{dx} = \frac{-x}{\sqrt{k^2 - x^2}} + 1$$

For maxima or minima, we have

$$\frac{-x}{\sqrt{k^2 - x^2}} + 1 = 0$$

$$\Rightarrow \quad \frac{-x}{\sqrt{k^2 - x^2}} = -1$$

$$\Rightarrow \quad \sqrt{k^2 - x^2} = x \Rightarrow k^2 - x^2 = x^2$$

$$\Rightarrow \quad 2x^2 = k^2 \Rightarrow x^2 = \frac{k^2}{2}$$

$$\Rightarrow \quad x = \pm \frac{k}{\sqrt{2}}$$

Now,
$$\frac{d^2P}{dx^2} = \frac{-\sqrt{k^2 - x^2} - (-x)\dfrac{-2x}{2\sqrt{k^2 - x^2}}}{k^2 - x^2}$$

$$= \frac{-\sqrt{k^2 - x^2} - \dfrac{x^2}{\sqrt{k^2 - x^2}}}{k^2 - x^2} = \frac{-(k^2 - x^2) - x^2}{(k^2 - x^2)^{3/2}}$$

$$\Rightarrow \quad \frac{d^2P}{dx^2} = \frac{-k^2}{(k^2 - x^2)^{3/2}}$$

$$\left(\frac{d^2P}{dx^2}\right)_{\text{at } x = \frac{k}{\sqrt{2}}} = \frac{-k^2}{\left(k^2 - \dfrac{k^2}{2}\right)^{3/2}} = \frac{-k^2}{\left(\dfrac{k^2}{2}\right)^{3/2}} = \frac{-(2)^{3/2}}{k} < 0$$

Thus, P is maximum, when $x = \frac{k}{\sqrt{2}}$.

$$\therefore \text{ Base} = AB = \sqrt{k^2 - x^2} = \sqrt{k^2 - \frac{k^2}{2}} = \frac{k}{\sqrt{2}}$$

$$\Rightarrow \quad AB = BC = \frac{k}{\sqrt{2}}$$

Hence, P is maximum when triangle is isosceles.

4. Let x m be the length of a side of the square and y m be the radius of the circle. Then, we have,

$$4x + 2\pi y = 28 \Rightarrow 2x + \pi y = 14 \quad \text{...(i)}$$

Let ABC be the combined area of the square and the circle, then

$$A = x^2 + \pi y^2 \quad \text{...(ii)}$$

$$\Rightarrow \quad A = x^2 + \pi\left(\frac{14 - 2x}{\pi}\right)^2 \quad \text{[from Eq. (i)]}$$

$$\Rightarrow \quad A = x^2 + \frac{1}{\pi}(14 - 2x)^2$$

$$\Rightarrow \quad \frac{dA}{dx} = 2x + \frac{1}{\pi}(14 - 2x)(-2)$$

$$\Rightarrow \quad \frac{dA}{dx} = 2x - \frac{4}{\pi}(14 - 2x)$$

For maximum or minimum,

$$\frac{dA}{dx} = 0$$

$$\Rightarrow \quad 2x - \frac{4}{\pi}(14 - 2x) = 0$$

$$\Rightarrow \quad 2x - \frac{56}{\pi} + \frac{8x}{\pi} = 0$$

$$\Rightarrow \quad \frac{2\pi x + 8x}{\pi} = 56$$

$$\Rightarrow \quad x = \frac{56\pi}{2\pi + 8} = \frac{28\pi}{\pi + 4}$$

Now,
$$\frac{d^2A}{dx^2} = 2 - \frac{4}{\pi}(-2) = 2 + \frac{8}{\pi} > 0$$

Then, A is maximum, when $x = \frac{28}{\pi + 4}$

On putting $x = \frac{28}{\pi + 4}$ in Eq. (i), we get

$$y = \frac{14}{\pi + 4}$$

So, length of two pieces of wire are

$$4x = 4 \times \frac{28}{\pi + 4} = \frac{112}{\pi + 4} \text{ m}$$

and
$$2\pi y = 2\pi \times \frac{14}{\pi + 4} = \frac{28\pi}{\pi + 4} \text{ m}$$

5. Let α be the semi-vertical angle of a cone of given slant height l. Then,

$$CO = l\cos\alpha, \; OA = l\sin\alpha$$

Let V be the volume of the cone, then

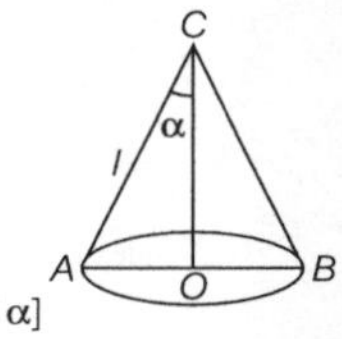

$$V = \frac{1}{3}\pi(OA)^2\,(CO)$$

$$\Rightarrow \quad V = \frac{1}{3}\pi(l\sin\alpha)^2\,(l\cos\alpha)$$

$$\Rightarrow \quad V = \frac{1}{3}\pi l^3 \sin^2\alpha\cos\alpha$$

$$\Rightarrow \quad \frac{dV}{d\alpha} = \frac{\pi}{3} l^3\,[-\sin^3\alpha + 2\sin\alpha\cos^2\alpha]$$

$$\Rightarrow \quad \frac{dV}{d\alpha} = \frac{\pi l^3}{3}\sin\alpha[-\sin^2\alpha + 2\cos^2] \quad \text{...(i)}$$

For maximum or minimum of V, we must have

$$\frac{dV}{d\alpha} = 0$$

$$\Rightarrow \quad \frac{\pi l^3}{3}\sin\alpha\,[-\sin^2\alpha + 2\cos^2\alpha] = 0$$

$$\Rightarrow \quad 2\cos^2\alpha = \sin^2\alpha$$

$$\Rightarrow \quad \tan^2\alpha = 2 \quad \Rightarrow \quad \tan\alpha = \sqrt{2}$$

Now,
$$\tan\alpha = \sqrt{2} \quad \Rightarrow \quad \cos\alpha = \frac{1}{\sqrt{3}}$$

On differentiating Eq. (i) w.r.t. α, we get

$$\frac{d^2V}{d\alpha^2} = \frac{1}{3}\pi l^3\cos^3\alpha\,(2 - 7\tan^2\alpha)$$

$$\Rightarrow \quad \left(\frac{d^2V}{d\alpha^2}\right)_{\tan\alpha = \sqrt{2}} = \frac{1}{3}\pi l^3\left(\frac{1}{\sqrt{3}}\right)^3 (2 - 7 \times 2) = \frac{-4\pi l^3}{3\sqrt{3}} < 0$$

Then, V is maximum, when $\tan\alpha = \sqrt{2}$ or $\alpha = \tan^{-1}\sqrt{2}$, i.e. when the semi-vertical angle of cone is $\tan^{-1}\sqrt{2}$.

6. Given, capacity

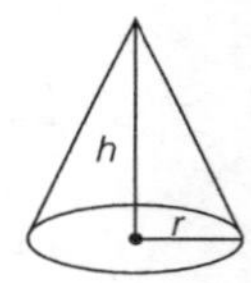

$$\Rightarrow \quad V = \frac{1}{3}\pi r^2 h \quad \text{...(i)}$$

To minimise the canvas required, i.e. CSA.

$$C = \pi r l$$

$$C^2 = \pi^2 r^2 l^2 = \pi^2 r^2 (h^2 + r^2)$$

$$= \pi^2\left[\frac{3V}{\pi h}\right]\left[h^2 + \frac{3V}{\pi h}\right], \quad \text{[from Eq. (i)]}$$

$$\therefore \quad f(h) = 3V\left[\pi h + \frac{3V}{h^2}\right] \quad \text{...(ii)}$$

$$f'(h) = 3V\left[\pi - \frac{6V}{h^3}\right] \quad \text{...(iii)}$$

$$f''(h) = 3V\left[\frac{+18V}{h^4}\right] \quad \text{...(iv)}$$

Put $f'(h) = 0 \Rightarrow h = \left(\frac{6V}{\pi}\right)^{1/3}$, at which $f''(h) > 0$

$\Rightarrow$ CSA is minimum when

$$h^3 = \frac{6V}{\pi}$$

$$\Rightarrow \quad h^3 = \frac{6}{\pi}\left(\frac{1}{3}\pi r^2 h\right)$$

$$\Rightarrow \quad h^2 = 2r^2 \quad \left[\because V = \frac{1}{3}\pi r^2 h\right]$$

$$\therefore \quad h = \sqrt{2}\,r$$

7. Let r be radius, l be the slant height and h be the height of the cone of given surface area S. Then,

$$S = \pi r^2 + \pi r l$$

$$\Rightarrow \quad l = \frac{S - \pi r^2}{\pi r} \quad \text{...(i)}$$

Let V be the volume of the cone, then

$$V = \frac{1}{3}\pi r^2 h$$

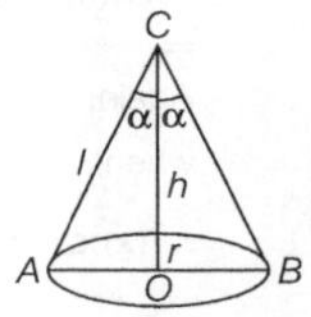

$$\Rightarrow \quad V^2 = \frac{1}{9}\pi^2 r^4 h^2$$

$$= \frac{1}{9}\pi^2 r^4 (l^2 - r^2)$$

$$V^2 = \frac{\pi^2}{9} r^4 \left[\left(\frac{S - \pi r^2}{\pi r}\right)^2 - r^2\right] \quad \text{[from Eq. (i)]}$$

$$V^2 = \frac{\pi^2 r^4}{9}\left[\frac{(S - \pi r^2) - \pi^2 r^4}{\pi^2 r^2}\right]$$

$$\Rightarrow \quad V^2 = \frac{1}{9}S(Sr^2 - 2\pi r^4) = f(r) \quad \text{[say]}$$

$$\Rightarrow \quad V^2 = \frac{1}{9}S(2Sr - 8\pi r^3) \quad \ldots\text{(ii)}$$

For maxima or minima, we must have

$$f'(r) = 0$$

$$2Sr - 8\pi r^3 = 0$$

$$\Rightarrow \quad S = 4\pi r^2 \quad \ldots\text{(iii)}$$

On differentiating Eq. (ii) w.r.t. r, we get

$$f''(r) = \frac{S}{9}(2S - 24\pi r^2)$$

$$= \frac{S}{9}\left[2S - 2\pi\frac{S}{4\pi}\right] \quad \text{[from Eq. (iii)]}$$

$$\Rightarrow \quad f''(r) = -\frac{4S^2}{9} < 0$$

So, $f(r)$ is maximum, when $S = 4\pi r^2$

Hence, V is maximum, when $S = 4\pi r^2$

Now, $\quad S = 4\pi r^2$

$$\Rightarrow \quad \pi r l + \pi r^2 = 4\pi r^2 \Rightarrow l = 3r$$

$$\therefore \quad \sin\alpha = \frac{r}{l} = \frac{r}{3r} = \frac{1}{3}$$

$$\Rightarrow \quad \alpha = \sin^{-1}(1/3)$$

Hence, V is maximum when $\alpha = \sin^{-1}\left(\frac{1}{3}\right)$.

8. Let $ABCD$ be a rectangle and let the semi-circle be described on side AB as diameter.

Let $AB = 2x$ and $AD = 2y$.

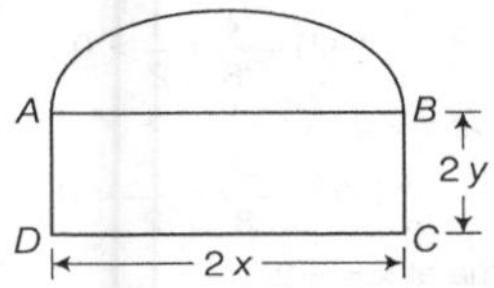

Let p be the perimeter and A be the area of the figure, then

$$p = 2x + 4y + \pi x \quad \ldots\text{(i)}$$

and

$$A = (2x)(2y) + \frac{\pi x^2}{2} \quad \ldots\text{(ii)}$$

$$= 4xy + \frac{\pi x^2}{2}$$

$$= x(p - 2x - \pi x) + \frac{\pi x^2}{2} \quad \text{[from Eq. (i)]}$$

$$= px - 2x^2 - \pi x^2 + \frac{\pi x^2}{2}$$

$$\Rightarrow \quad A = px - 2x^2 - \frac{\pi x^2}{2}$$

$$\Rightarrow \quad \frac{dA}{dx} = p - 4x - \pi x \quad \text{and} \quad \frac{d^2A}{dy^2} = -4 - \pi$$

For maximum or minimum,

$$\frac{dA}{dx} = 0$$

So, $\quad p - 4x - \pi x = 0$

$$\Rightarrow \quad x = \frac{p}{\pi + 4}$$

Clearly, $\quad \dfrac{d^2A}{dx^2} = -4 - \pi < 0, \forall$ values of x.

Now, $\quad A$ is maximum, when $x = \dfrac{p}{\pi + 4}$

$\therefore \quad$ Radius of semi-circle $= x = \dfrac{p}{\pi + 4}$

9. Let x m and y m be the length of the sides of rectangle $ABCD$ and let there be a semi-circle on side CD of length x.

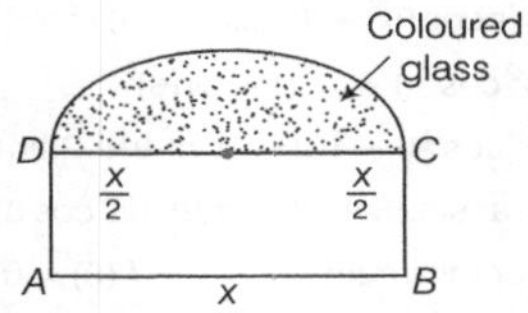

Therefore, perimeter of the window (including the base of arch)

$$= \text{Perimeter of rectangle} + \text{Perimeter of semi-circle}$$

$$= 2x + 2y + \frac{1}{2}\left(2\pi\frac{x}{2}\right)$$

$$= 2x + 2y + \frac{\pi x}{2} = k \quad \text{[constant]}$$

$$\therefore \quad y = \frac{1}{2}\left(k - 2x - \frac{\pi x}{2}\right) \quad \ldots\text{(i)}$$

Let c be the light per square metre transmitted by coloured glass, so that the light transmitted by clear glass will be $3c$ per square metre.

Hence, the total light transmitted by the window is given by

$$A = (\text{Area of coloured glass})\,c + (\text{Area of clear glass})\,3c$$

$$= \frac{1}{2}\pi(x/2)^2 c + xy(3c)$$

$$= \frac{1}{8}\pi c x^2 + 3cx\,\frac{1}{2}\left(k - 2x - \frac{\pi x}{2}\right) \quad \text{[from Eq. (i)]}$$

$$= \frac{1}{8}c(-5\pi x^2 - 24x^2 + 12kx)$$

$$\Rightarrow \quad \frac{dA}{dx} = \frac{1}{8}c(-10\pi x - 48x + 12k)$$

and $\quad \dfrac{d^2A}{dx^2} = -\dfrac{1}{4}(5\pi + 24)c < 0$

For maximum or minimum of A,

$$\frac{dA}{dx} = 0$$

$$\Rightarrow \quad x = \frac{6k}{5\pi + 24}$$

From Eq. (i), $\quad y = \dfrac{(\pi + 6)k}{5\pi + 24}$

Since, $\dfrac{d^2A}{dx^2}$ in negative, therefore A is maximum.

Hence, $\quad$ ratio $= \dfrac{x}{y} = \dfrac{6}{\pi + 6} \quad$ or $\quad \dfrac{y}{x} = \dfrac{\pi + 6}{6}$

10. Let (r, θ) be the polar coordinates of any P on the curve, where r is the distance of the point from the origin.

$$\Rightarrow \quad ar^2\cos^2\theta + 2hr^2\sin\theta\cos\theta + ar^2\sin^2\theta = c$$

$$\Rightarrow \quad r^2(a\cos^2\theta + a\sin^2\theta + 2h\sin\theta\cos\theta) = c$$

$$\Rightarrow \quad r^2 = \frac{c}{a + 2h\sin\theta\cos\theta}$$

r^2 is minimum, when $a + h\sin 2\theta$ is maximum.

$$\Rightarrow \quad r^2 = \frac{c}{a+h} \quad \text{and} \quad \theta = 45^\circ$$

$$\Rightarrow \quad r = \pm\sqrt{\frac{c}{a+h}}$$

$\therefore$ Points are $(r\cos\theta, r\sin\theta) \pm \left(\sqrt{\frac{c}{2(a+h)}}, \sqrt{\frac{c}{2(a+h)}}\right)$

11. Given curve is $\quad 4x^2 + a^2y^2 = 4a^2$

$$\Rightarrow \quad \frac{4x^2}{4a^2} + \frac{a^2y^2}{4a^2} = 1$$

$$\Rightarrow \quad \frac{x^2}{a^2} + \frac{y^2}{4} = 1 \quad \ldots\text{(i)}$$

Let P be $(a\cos\theta, 2\sin\theta)$ on the curve (i).

$\therefore$ Distance of point P from the point $(0, -2)$ is

$$D = \sqrt{(a\cos\theta)^2 + \{2(\sin\theta + 1)\}^2}$$

$$D^2 = a^2\cos^2\theta + 4^2(1 + \sin\theta)^2$$

$$D^2 = a^2\cos^2\theta + 16(1 + \sin^2\theta + 2\sin\theta) = f(\theta) \quad \text{[say]}$$

$$\Rightarrow \quad f'(\theta) = -a^2\sin 2\theta + 16(\sin 2\theta + 2\cos\theta)$$

For maximum or minimum, $\quad f'(\theta) = 0$

$$\Rightarrow \quad -a^2\sin 2\theta + 16\sin 2\theta + 32\cos\theta = 0$$

$$\Rightarrow \quad (16 - a^2)\sin 2\theta + 32\cos\theta = 0$$

$$\Rightarrow \quad \cos\theta\,[2(16 - a^2)\sin\theta + 32] = 0$$

$$\Rightarrow \quad \cos\theta = 0 \quad \text{or} \quad 2(16 - a^2)\sin\theta + 32 = 0$$

$$\Rightarrow \quad \theta = \frac{\pi}{2} \quad \text{or} \quad \sin\theta = -\frac{-32}{2(16 - a^2)}$$

$$\Rightarrow \quad \theta = \frac{\pi}{2} \quad \text{or} \quad \sin\theta = \frac{-16}{(16 - a^2)}$$

$$\Rightarrow \quad \theta = \frac{\pi}{2} \quad \text{or} \quad \sin\theta = \frac{16}{(a^2 - 16)}$$

$$\Rightarrow \quad \theta = \frac{\pi}{2} \quad \text{or} \quad \sin\theta \neq \frac{16}{a^2 - 16} \quad [\because 4 < a^2 < 8]$$

$$\Rightarrow \quad \theta = \frac{\pi}{2}$$

Now, $\quad f''(\theta) = -2a^2\cos 2\theta + 16(\cos 2\theta - 2\sin\theta)$

$$f''\left(\frac{\pi}{2}\right) = 2a^2 + 16(-3)$$

$$= 2a^2 - 48 < 0 \quad [\because 4 < a^2 < 8]$$

$\therefore$ Point is $\left(a\cos\frac{\pi}{2}, 2\sin\frac{\pi}{2}\right)$, i.e. $(0, 2)$.

12. Let S be the square of unit area and $ABCD$ be the quadrilateral of sides a, b, c and d.

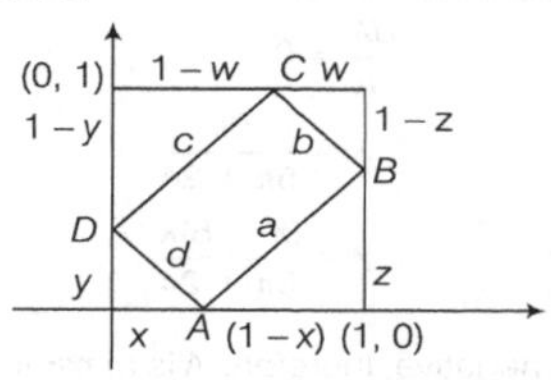

Here, $\quad a^2 = (1 - x^2) + z^2,\ b^2 = w^2 + (1 - z)^2$

$$c^2 = (1 - w^2) + (1 - y^2),\ d^2 = x^2 + y^2$$

Adding all the above equations, we have

$a^2 + b^2 + c^2 + d^2$

$$= \{x^2 + (1 - x)^2\} + \{y^2 + (1 - y)^2\} + \{z^2 + (1 - z)^2\} + \{w^2 + (1 - w)^2\}, \text{ where } 0 < x, y, z, w \le 1$$

Let us consider a function

$$f(x) = x^2 + (1 - x)^2,\ 0 < x \le 1$$

Then, $\quad f'(x) = 2x - 2(1 - x)$

Let $f'(x) = 0$, for maximum and minimum

$$\Rightarrow \quad 4x - 2 = 0 \Rightarrow x = 1/2$$

Again, $\quad f''(x) = 4 > 0$

when $\quad x = \frac{1}{2}$

$\therefore f(x)$ is minimum at $x = \frac{1}{2}$ and maximum at $x = 1$.

$$\Rightarrow \quad 2 \le a^2 + b^2 + c^2 + d^2 \le 4$$

13. (d) Since, $f(x) = 2x^3 - 9ax^2 + 12a^2x + 1$

$$\Rightarrow \quad f'(x) = 6x^2 - 18ax + 12a^2$$

For maxima or minima, $\quad f'(x) = 0$

$$\Rightarrow \quad 6(x^2 - 3ax + 2a^2) = 0$$

$$\Rightarrow \quad x^2 - 3ax + 2a^2 = 0$$

$$\Rightarrow \quad x^2 - 2ax - ax + 2a^2 = 0$$

$$\Rightarrow \quad x(x - 2a) - a(x - 2a) = 0$$

$$\Rightarrow \quad (x - a)(x - 2a) = 0$$

$$\Rightarrow \quad x = a,\ x = 2a$$

Now, $\quad f''(x) = 12x - 18a$

at $x = a$,

$$f''(x) = 12a - 18a = -6a$$

$\therefore f(x)$ will be maximum at $x = a$,

i.e. $\quad p = a$

Again at $\quad x = 2a$

$$f''(x) = 24a - 18a = 6a$$

$\therefore f(x)$ will be minimum at $x = 2a$,

i.e. $\quad q = 2a$

Given, $\quad p^2 = q$

$$\Rightarrow \quad a^2 = 2a$$

$$\therefore \quad a = 2$$

14. (d) Given, $f(x) = \frac{x}{2} + \frac{2}{x} \Rightarrow f'(x) = \frac{1}{2} - \frac{2}{x^2}$

For maximum or minimum, $f'(x) = 0$

$$\Rightarrow \quad \frac{1}{2} - \frac{2}{x^2} = 0$$

$$\Rightarrow \quad \frac{2}{x^2} = \frac{1}{2} \Rightarrow x^2 = 4$$

$$\Rightarrow \quad x = \pm 2$$

Now, $\quad f''(x) = \frac{4}{x^3}$

$$f''(2) = \frac{4}{8} = \frac{1}{2} > 0$$

$f(x)$ has minima at $x = 2$

and $\quad f''(-2) = \frac{-4}{8} = \frac{-1}{2} < 0$

$\therefore f(x)$ has maxima at $x = -2$.

15. (b) Let ABC be a triangular park in which $AB = AC = x$ and $BC = y$

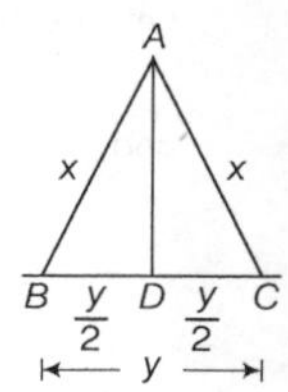

Now, $\quad AD = \sqrt{x^2 - \frac{y^2}{4}}$

$$= \frac{1}{2}\sqrt{4x^2 - y^2}$$

Area of ΔABC $(A) = \frac{1}{2} \times BC \times AD$

$$A = \frac{1}{2} \times y \times \frac{1}{2}\sqrt{4x^2 - y^2}$$

$$A = \frac{1}{4}y\sqrt{4x^2 - y^2}$$

$$\frac{dA}{dy} = \frac{1}{4}\sqrt{4x^2 - y^2} + \frac{y}{4}\frac{1}{2\sqrt{4x^2 - y^2}} \times (-2y)$$

$$= \frac{\sqrt{4x^2 - y^2}}{4} - \frac{y^2}{4\sqrt{4x^2 - y^2}}$$

$$= \frac{4x^2 - y^2 - y^2}{4\sqrt{4x^2 - y^2}} = \frac{4x^2 - 2y^2}{4\sqrt{4x^2 - y^2}}$$

For maximum and minimum,

$$\frac{dA}{dy} = 0$$

$$\Rightarrow \quad 4x^2 - 2y^2 = 0$$

$$\Rightarrow \quad y^2 = 2x^2$$

$$\Rightarrow \quad y = \sqrt{2}x$$

Now,

$$\frac{d^2A}{dy^2} = \frac{4\sqrt{4x^2 - y^2}(-4y) - (4x^2 - 2y^2)\frac{4}{2\sqrt{4x^2 - y^2}}(-2y)}{16(4x^2 - y^2)}$$

$$= \frac{-16y(4x^2 - y^2) + 4y(4x^2 - 2y^2)}{16(4x^2 - y^2)^{3/2}}$$

$$= \frac{-12y(4x^2 - y^2)}{16(4x^2 - y^2)^{3/2}} = \frac{-3y(4x^2 - y^2)}{4(4x^2 - y^2)^{3/2}}$$

$$= \frac{-3y}{4(4x^2 - y^2)^{1/2}}$$

Then, $$\left(\frac{d^2A}{dy^2}\right)_{\text{at } y = \sqrt{2}x} = \frac{-3\sqrt{2}x}{4(x^2 - 2x^2)^{1/2}}$$

$$= \frac{-3\sqrt{2}x}{4\sqrt{2}x} = -3/4 < 0$$

$\therefore$ Area is maximum, when $y = \sqrt{2}x$.

and maximum area $= \frac{1}{4}\sqrt{2}x\,\sqrt{2}x = \frac{1}{2}x^2$

16. (d) We have,

$$P(x) = x^4 + ax^3 + bx^2 + cx + d$$

$$\Rightarrow \quad P'(x) = 4x^3 + 3ax^2 + 2bx + c$$

It is given that, $x = 0$ is a root of $P'(x) = 0$.

$$\therefore \quad P'(0) = 0 \Rightarrow c = 0$$

On putting $c = 0$, we get

$$P'(x) = x(4x^2 + 3ax + 2b)$$

Since, $x = 0$ is the only real root of $P'(x) = 0$.

$\therefore \quad 4x^2 + 3ax + 2b = 0$ has no real root.

$$\Rightarrow \quad 9a^2 - 32b < 0$$

It is given that, $\quad P(-1) < P(1)$

$$\Rightarrow \quad 1 - a + b + c < 1 + a + b + c + d$$

$$\Rightarrow \quad a > 0$$

But $\quad 9a^2 - 32b < 0$

$$\therefore \quad b > 0$$

Now, $P'(x) = x(4x^2 + 3ax + 2b) > 0, \forall x \in (0, 1)$

$\therefore \quad P(x)$ is increasing in (0, 1].

$\Rightarrow P(1)$ is the maximum value of $P(x)$.

Also, $\quad P'(x) = x(4x^2 + 3ax + 2b) < 0, \forall x \in [-1, 0)$

$[\because 4x^2 + 3ax + 2b > 0, \forall x]$

$\Rightarrow P(x)$ is decreasing in (–1, 0).

$\Rightarrow P(-1)$ is not the minimum value of P.

17. (d) If $f(x)$ has a local minimum at $x = -1$, then

$$\lim_{x \to -1^+} f(x) \ge f(-1)$$

$$\Rightarrow \quad \lim_{x \to -1^+} (2x + 3) \ge f(-1)$$

$$\Rightarrow \quad -2 + 3 \ge k + 2$$

$$\Rightarrow \quad k \ge -1$$

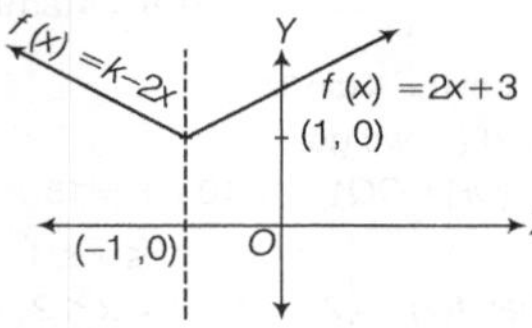

18. (b) We have, $f(x) = \int_0^x \sqrt{t}\sin t\,dt \Rightarrow f'(x) = \sqrt{x}\sin x$

[by Leibnitz's rule]

At points of local maximum or minimum, we have

$$f'(x) = 0 \Rightarrow \sqrt{x}\sin x = 0$$

$$\Rightarrow \quad x = \pi, 2\pi \qquad \left[\because x \in \left(0, \frac{5\pi}{2}\right)\right]$$

Changes in signs of $f'(x)$ in the neighbourhood of π and 2π as shown in figure given below.

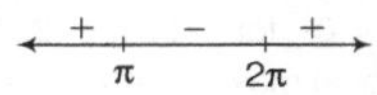

Clearly, $f'(x)$ changes its sign from positive to negative in the neighbourhood of $x = \pi$ and negative to positive in the neighbourhood of $x = 2\pi$.

Thus, $f(x)$ has a local maximum at $x = \pi$ and a local minimum at $x = 2\pi$.

19. (d) Let $f(x) = 2x^3 + 3x + k$

Since, $f(x)$ has two distinct real roots $\in (0, 1)$

Then, $f'(x)$ must be zero for some $x \in (0, 1)$.

Here, $f'(x) = 6x^2 + 3x = 3x(2x + 1) = 0$

$$\Rightarrow \quad x = 0, -\frac{1}{2} \notin (0, 1)$$

$\therefore$ No value of k i.e. k does not exist.

20. (a) At $x = 0$, $f(x)$ is not differentiable. However, $f(x)$ has a local maximum at $x = 0$.

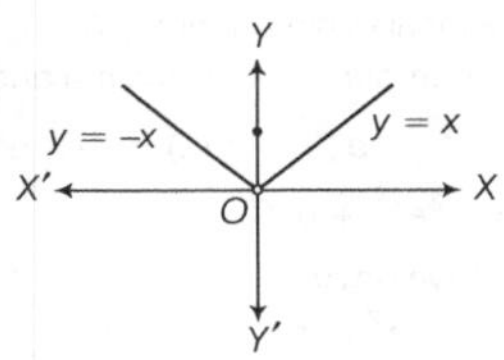

21. (d) Given, $f(x) = (1 + b^2)x^2 + 2bx + 1$

The graph of $f(x)$ is upward parabola and coefficient of x^2 is $1 + b^2 > 0$.

$\Rightarrow$ The range of $f(x)$ is $\left(\frac{-D}{4a}, \infty\right)$, where D is discriminant of $f(x)$.

$$\Rightarrow \quad m(b) = \frac{-4b^2 - 4(1 + b^2)}{4(1 + b^2)}$$

$$\therefore \quad m(b) = \frac{1}{1 + b^2} \in (0, 1]$$

22. (d)

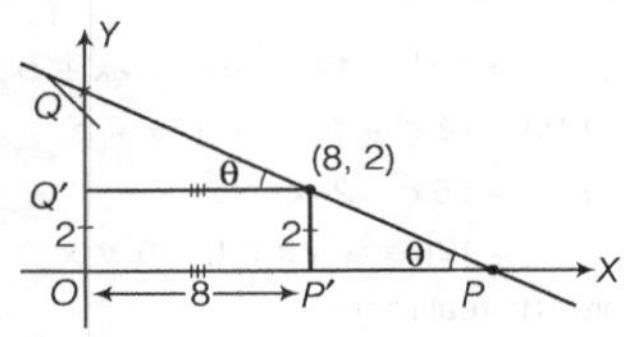

Here, $\quad OP = OP' + PP' = 8 + 2\cot\theta$

$$OQ = OQ' + QQ' = 2 + 8\tan\theta$$

$$\therefore \quad OP + OQ = 10 + 2(\cot\theta + 4\tan\theta) \quad \ldots(i)$$

As, AM ≥ GM

$$\frac{\cot\theta + 4\tan\theta}{2} \geq \sqrt{\cot\theta \times 4\tan\theta}$$

$\Rightarrow \quad \cot\theta + 4\tan\theta \geq 4 \quad \ldots(ii)$

From Eqs. (i) and (ii), we get

$$(OP + OQ)_{min} = 10 + 8 = 18$$

23. (a) It is given that, $f(x) = \begin{cases} e^x, & 0 \leq x \leq 1 \\ 2 - e^x, & 1 < x \leq 2 \\ x - e, & 2 < x \leq 3 \end{cases}$

and $g(x) = \int_0^x f(t)dt$, $x \in [0, 3]$

$\therefore \quad g'(x) = f(x) = \begin{cases} 2 - e^{x-1}, & 0 < x \leq 2 \\ x - e, & 2 < x \leq 3 \end{cases}$

So, $\quad g'(x) = 0$

$\Rightarrow \quad x = 1 + \log_e 2 \quad \text{and} \quad x = e$

Also, $\quad g'(x) > 0 \quad \text{for} \quad x \in (0, 1 + \log_e 2)$

and $\quad g'(x) < 0 \quad \text{for} \quad (1 + \log_e 2, 2)$

So, $g(x)$ attains a local maxima at $x = 1 + \log_e 2$

Similarly, $g'(x) < 0$ for $2 < x < e$ and $g'(x) > 0$ for $e < x < 3$.

$\Rightarrow g(x)$ attains local minimum at $x = e$.

24. (c) Given that, $f(x) = \begin{cases} (2 + x)^3, & -3 < x \leq -1 \\ x^{2/3}, & -1 < x < 2 \end{cases}$

$\Rightarrow \quad f'(x) = \begin{cases} 3(2 + x)^2, & -3 < x < -1 \\ \frac{2}{3} x^{-1/3}, & -1 < x < 2 \end{cases}$

Clearly, $f'(x)$ changes sign from positive to negative as x passes through $x = -1$ from left to right.

So, $f(x)$ attains a local maximum at $x = -1$.

We observe that, $f'(x) > 0$ for all $x \in (-3, -1)$

and $\quad f'(x) < 0$ for $x \in (-1, 0)$.

Also, $\quad f'(x) > 0$ for $x \in (0, 2)$

But $\quad f'(0)$ does not exist.

So, $f(x)$ attains a local minimum at $x = 0$.

Hence, the total number of local maxima and local minima is 2.

25. (d) Given, $f(x) = e^{x^2} + e^{-x^2}$, $\quad g(x) = xe^{x^2} + e^{-x^2}$

and $\quad h(x) = x^2 e^{x^2} + e^{-x^2}$

For any $x \in [0, 1]$, we have

$$x^2 \leq x \leq 1$$

$\Rightarrow \quad x^2 e^{x^2} \leq xe^{x^2} \leq e^{x^2}$

$\Rightarrow \quad e^{-x^2} + x^2 e^{x^2} \leq e^{-x^2} + xe^{x^2} \leq e^{-x^2} + e^{x^2}$

$\Rightarrow \quad h(x) \leq g(x) \leq f(x)$

Now, $\quad f'(x) = 2x(e^{x^2} - e^{-x^2}) > 0, \forall x \in (0, 1]$

$\Rightarrow f(x)$ is increasing on $(0, 1]$.

$\Rightarrow f(1)$ is maximum value of $f(x)$ on $[0, 1]$.

$\Rightarrow \quad 9 + e + e^{-1}$

Also, $\quad f(1) = g(1) = h(1) = e + e^{-1}$

$\therefore \quad a = b = c = e + e^{-1}$

26. (b) We have, $f(x) = 3x^4 - 4x^3 + 6x^2 + ax + b$

$\Rightarrow \quad f'(x) = 12x^3 - 12x^2 + 12x + a$

$\Rightarrow \quad f'(x) = 36x^2 - 24x + 12$

$\quad = 12(3x^2 - 2x + 1) > 0, \forall x.$

$\therefore f(x)$ has only one real root.

Since, $f'(x)$ changes in sign only once.

Therefore, only one extremum possible.

27. (b) Given, $y = \frac{\log x}{x^2}$

The area of rectangle will be maximum at the point, where y is maximum.

$$\therefore \quad \frac{dy}{dx} = \frac{x^2 \times \frac{1}{x} - \log x(2x)}{x^4}$$

For maximum or minimum,

$$\frac{x(1 - 2\log x)}{x^4} = 0 \quad \Rightarrow \quad 1 - 2\log x = 0$$

$\Rightarrow \quad \log x = \frac{1}{2}$

$\Rightarrow \quad x = e^{1/2}$

Now, $\quad \frac{d^2y}{dx^2} = \frac{x^3(-2/x) - (1 - 2\log x)\,3x^2}{x^6}$

$\quad = \frac{x^2[-2 - 3(1 - 2 - 2\log x)]}{x^6}$

$\quad = \frac{-2 - 3 + 6\log x}{x^4} = \frac{-5 + 6\log x}{x^4}$

Then, $\left(\frac{d^2y}{dx}\right)_{x = e^{1/2}} = \frac{-5 + 6\log e^{1/2}}{e^2} = \frac{-5 + 3}{e^2} = -\frac{2}{e^2} < 0$

$\therefore$ Area of rectangle will be maximum at the vertex, when $x = e^{\frac{1}{2}}$ and $y = \frac{1}{2e}$.

Hence, area $= e^{1/2} \times \frac{1}{2e} = \frac{1}{2\sqrt{e}}$ sq unit

28. (a) We have, $f(x) = \frac{ax^3}{3} + (a + 2)x^2 + (a - 1)x + 2$

$\Rightarrow \quad f''(x) = 2ax + 2(a + 2) = 0$

$\Rightarrow \quad x = -\frac{(a + 2)}{a}$, which is a point of inflection.

We must have $-\frac{(a + 2)}{a} < 0$

$\Rightarrow \quad (-\infty, -2) \cup (0, \infty)$

29. (a) Here, $y = e^{-|x|}$, $x > 0$

$$\left[\frac{dy}{dx}\right]_{(x_1, y_1)} = (-e^{-x}) = -e^{-x_1} \quad \ldots(i)$$

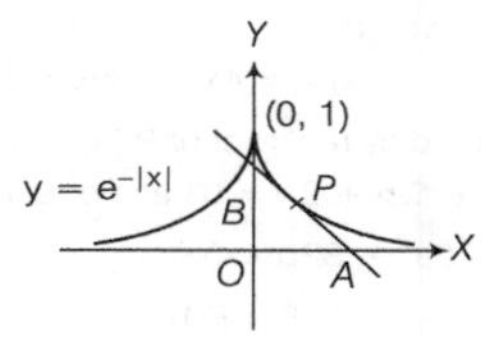

$\therefore$ Equation of tangent at (x_1, e^{-x_1}) is

$$\frac{y - e^{-x_1}}{x - x_1} = -e^{-x_1}$$

$\therefore \quad A(1 + x_1, 0)$ and $B(0, (1 + x_1)e^{-x_1})$

$\Rightarrow$ Area of $\Delta OAB = \frac{1}{2}(1 + x_1)^2 e^{-x_1}$

For maximum area of ΔOAB,

$$f(x_1) = \frac{1}{2}(1 + x_1)^2 \cdot e^{-x_1}$$

$$f'(x_1) = \frac{1}{2}[2(1 + x_1) \cdot e^{-x_1} - (1 + x_1)^2 \cdot e^{x_1}]$$

$$= \frac{1}{2} e^{x_1} [(1 + x_1) \cdot (2 - 1 - x_1)]$$

$$= \frac{e^{x_1}}{2}(x_1 + 1)(1 - x_1)$$

– + –
–1 1

For area of ΔOAB to be maximum $x = 1$
i.e. maximum area $= e^{-1}$

or coordinate of point P is $\left(1, \frac{1}{e}\right)$.

Similarly, when $x < 0 \Rightarrow y = e^x$

The coordinate of point P is $\left(-1, \frac{1}{e}\right)$.

30. (d) Since, $a = \left[\frac{4}{\sin x} + \frac{1}{1 - \sin x}\right]$, a is least

$$\Rightarrow \quad \frac{da}{dx} = \left[-\frac{4}{\sin^2 x} + \frac{1}{(1 - \sin x)^2}\right] \cos x = 0$$

We have to find the value of x in the interval $\left(0, \frac{\pi}{2}\right)$.

$\Rightarrow \cos x \neq 0$ and other factor when equals to zero.

Given, $\quad \sin x = 2/3$

$$\text{Now,} \quad \frac{d^2a}{dx^2} = \left[-\frac{4}{\sin^2 x} + \frac{1}{(1 - \sin x)^2}\right](-\sin x) + \left[\frac{8}{\sin^3 x} + \frac{2}{(1 - \sin x)^3}\right]\cos^2 x$$

Put $\sin x = \frac{2}{3}$ and $\cos^2 x = 1 - \frac{4}{9} = \frac{5}{9}$

$$\therefore \quad \frac{d^2a}{dx^2} = 0 + \left[\frac{8}{8/27} + 2 \times 27\right]\frac{5}{9} = 81 \times \frac{5}{9} = 45 > 0$$

$\Rightarrow$ a is minimum and its value is

$$\frac{4}{2/3} + \frac{1}{1 - 2/3} = 6 + 3 = 9$$

31. (a,c) Here, $l = 15x - 2a$, $b = 8x - 2a$ and $h = a$

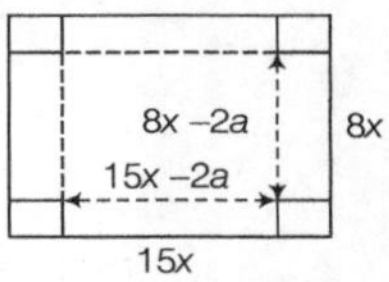

$\therefore$ Volume $= (8x - 2a)(15x - 2a)$

$V = 2a \cdot (4x - a)(15x - 2a)$ ...(i)

$$\frac{dV}{du} = 6a^2 - 46ax + 60x^2$$

$$\frac{d^2V}{dx^2} = 12a - 46x$$

Here, $\left(\frac{dV}{da}\right) = 0 \Rightarrow 6x^2 - 23x + 15 = 0$

At $a = 5$, $\quad x = 3, 5/6$

$$\frac{d^2V}{da^2} = 2(30 - 23)x$$

At $x = 3$, $\quad \frac{d^2V}{da^2} = 2(30 - 69) < 0$

$\therefore$ Maximum at $x = 3$, also at $x = 5/6$

$$\Rightarrow \quad \frac{d^2V}{da^2} = 0$$

$\therefore$ At $x = 5/6$, V is minimum.

Thus, sides are $8x = 24$ and $15x = 45$.

32. (a,b) Here, $f(x) = 2|x| + |x + 2| - ||x + 2| - 2|x||$

$$= \begin{cases} -2x - (x + 2) + (x - 2), & \text{when } x \leq -2 \\ -2x + x + 2 + 3x + 2, & \text{when } -2 < x > -2/3 \\ -4x, & \text{when } -2/3 < x \leq 0 \\ 4x, & \text{when } 0 < x \leq 2 \\ 2x + 4, & \text{when } x > 2 \end{cases}$$

$$= \begin{cases} -2x - 4, & x \leq -2 \\ 2x + 4, & -2 < x \leq -2/3 \\ -4x, & -2/3 < x \leq 0 \\ 4x, & 0 < x \leq 2 \\ 2x + 4, & x > 2 \end{cases}$$

Graph for $y = f(x)$ is shown below

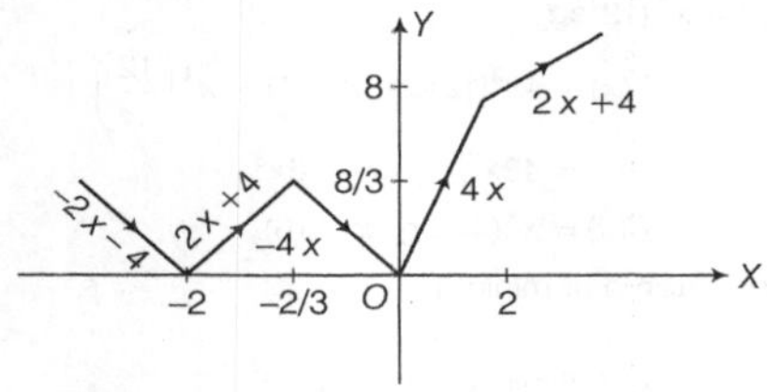

33. (a,b,c,d) Given, $f(x) = \int_0^x \sqrt{1 - t^4}\, dt$

$$\Rightarrow \quad f'(x) = \sqrt{1 - x^4} > 0 \text{ in } (-1, 1)$$

$\Rightarrow f$ is increasing.

$$\text{Now,} \quad f(x) + f(-x) = \int_0^x \sqrt{1 - t^4}\, dt + \int_0^{-x} \sqrt{1 - t^4} dt$$

$$= \int_0^x \sqrt{1 - t^4}\, dt + \left[-\int_0^y \sqrt{1 - y^4}\, dy\right] t = -y$$

$$= 0$$

$\Rightarrow$ $f(x)$ is odd.

Again, $f''(x) = \frac{-4x^3}{2\sqrt{1 - x^4}}$ which is vanished at $x = 0$ and changes sign.

$\Rightarrow (0, 0)$ is inflection, since f is well defined in $[-,1\ 1]$.

34. (a,b,c) Given, $f(x) = \frac{\sin(x + a)}{\sin(x + b)}$

$$f(x) = \frac{\sin(x + b) \times \cos(x + a) - \sin(x + a)\cos(x + b)}{\sin^2(x + b)}$$

$$= \frac{\sin(b - a)}{\sin^2(x + b)}$$

If $\sin(b - a) = a$, then $f'(x) = 0 \Rightarrow f(x)$ will be constant.

i.e. $b - a = n\pi$ or $b - a = (2n + 1)\pi$ or $(b - a) = 2n\pi$,

then $f(x)$ has no minima.

35. (b,c) Since, $f(x)$ has local maxima at $x = -1$ and $f'(x)$ has local minima at $x = 0$.

$$\therefore \quad f''(x) = \lambda x$$

On integrating, we get

$$f'(x) = \frac{\lambda x^2}{2} + c \qquad [\because f'(-1) = 0]$$

$$\Rightarrow \quad \frac{\lambda}{2} + c = 0 \Rightarrow \lambda = -2c \qquad \text{...(i)}$$

Again, on integrating both sides, we get

$$f(x) = \frac{\lambda x^3}{6} + cx + d$$

$$f(2) = \lambda(8/6) + 2c + d = 18 \qquad \text{...(ii)}$$

$$\text{and} \quad f(1) = \frac{\lambda}{6} + c + d = -1 \qquad \text{...(iii)}$$

From Eqs. (i), (ii) and (iii), we get

$$f(x) = \frac{1}{4}(19x^3 - 57x + 34)$$

$$\Rightarrow \quad f'(x) = \frac{1}{4}(57x^2 - 57) = \frac{57}{4}(x - 1)(x + 1)$$

For maxima or minima, put $f'(x) = 0 \Rightarrow x = 1, -1$

$$\text{Now,} \quad f''(x) = \frac{1}{4}(114x)$$

At $x = 1$, $\quad f''(x) > 0$, minima

At $x = -1$, $\quad f''(x) < 0$, maxima

$\therefore f(x)$ is increasing for $[1, 2\sqrt{5}]$.

$\Rightarrow$ $\quad f(x)$ has local maxima at $x = -1$

and $\quad f(x)$ has local minima at $x = 1$.

Also, $\quad f(0) = 34/4$

36. (b)

(i) $f(x) = x^4(12\log_e x - 7)$

$$f'(x) = 4x^3(12\log_e x - 7) + x^4\left(\frac{12}{x}\right)$$
$$= 48x^3\log_e x - 16x^3$$
$$f'(x) = x^3(48\log_e x - 16)$$

For maxima or minima,

$$f'(x) = 0$$
$$x^3(48\log_e x - 16) = 0$$
$$\Rightarrow \quad x = 0,\ 48\log_e x - 16 = 0$$
$$\Rightarrow \quad x = 0,\ \log_e x = \frac{1}{3}$$
$$\therefore \quad x = 0,\ x = e^{1/3}$$
$$\Rightarrow \quad f''(x) = 3x^2(48\log_e x - 16) + x^3\left(\frac{48}{x}\right)$$
$$= x^2(144\log_e x - 48 + 48)$$
$$= 144x^2\log_e x$$

Here, $f''(x)$ changes sign at $x = 1$

$\therefore a = 1$ is point of inflection.

Now, $f''(0) =$ Not defined

$$f''(e^{1/3}) = \frac{144}{3}e^{2/3} > 0$$

$\therefore x = e^{1/3}$ is point of minima.

(ii) $12t = 12 \times \frac{1}{3} = 4$

(iii) If graph is concave downward, then

$$f''(x) < 0$$
$$\Rightarrow \quad 144x^2\log_e x < 0$$
$$\Rightarrow \quad \log_e x < 0$$
$$\Rightarrow \quad 0 < x < 1$$

$\therefore$ Graph of the function is concave downward in the interval (0, 1).

Hence, $d + 3e = 0 + 3 \times 1 = 3$

(iv) Graph is concave upward, if $f''(x) > 0$

$$\Rightarrow \quad 144x^2\log_e x > 0$$
$$\Rightarrow \quad \log_e x > 0$$
$$\Rightarrow \quad x > 1$$
$$\Rightarrow \quad x \in (1, \infty)$$

So, least value of p is 1.

Hence, (i) $\rightarrow$ (s), (ii) $\rightarrow$ (r), (iii) $\rightarrow$ (p), (iv) $\rightarrow$ (q)

Explanations for Q. Nos. (37-39)

$$\lim_{x \to 0} \frac{1}{x} \log \begin{vmatrix} \frac{f(x)}{x} & 1 & 0 \\ 0 & \frac{1}{x} & 1 \\ 1 & 0 & \frac{1}{x} \end{vmatrix} = 2$$

$$\Rightarrow \quad \lim_{x \to 0} \frac{\log\left[\frac{f(x)}{x^3} + 1\right]}{x} = 2 \qquad \text{...(i)}$$

For limit to exist, $\lim_{x \to 0} \frac{f(x)}{x^3} = 0$

$$\Rightarrow \quad f(x) = a_0x^6 + a_1x^5 + a_2x^4$$

Also, $f'(0) = f'(2) = f'(1) = 0$

$$\Rightarrow \quad f'(x) = 6a_0x^5 + 5a_1x^4 + 4a_2x^3$$
$$= x^3(4a_2 + 5a_1x + 6a_0x^2)$$
$$f'(2) = 0 \Rightarrow 24a_0 + 10a_1 + 4a_2 = 0 \qquad \text{...(ii)}$$
$$f'(1) = 0 \Rightarrow 6a_0 + 5a_1 + 4a_2 = 0 \qquad \text{...(iii)}$$

From Eq. (i), we get

$$\log\left\{\lim_{x \to 0}\left(\frac{f(x)}{x^3} + 1\right)^{1/x}\right\} = 2 \quad \Rightarrow \log\left\{e^{\lim_{x \to 0}\frac{f(x)}{x^4}}\right\} = 2$$

$$\Rightarrow \quad \lim_{x \to 0} \frac{a_0x^6 + a_1x^5 + a_2x^4}{x^4} = 2$$

$$\Rightarrow \quad a_2 = 2 \qquad \text{...(iv)}$$

From Eqs. (ii), (iii) and (iv), we get

$$\Rightarrow \quad a_1 = -\frac{12}{5},\ a_0 = \frac{2}{3} \qquad \text{...(iv)}$$

$$\therefore \quad f(x) = \frac{2}{3}x^6 - \frac{12}{5}x^5 + 2x^4$$
$$f'(x) = 4x^5 - 12x^4 + 8x^3$$
$$= 4x^3 \cdot (x - 1)(x - 2)$$

– + – + (sign scheme at 0, 1, 2)

Graph for $f(x)$ is

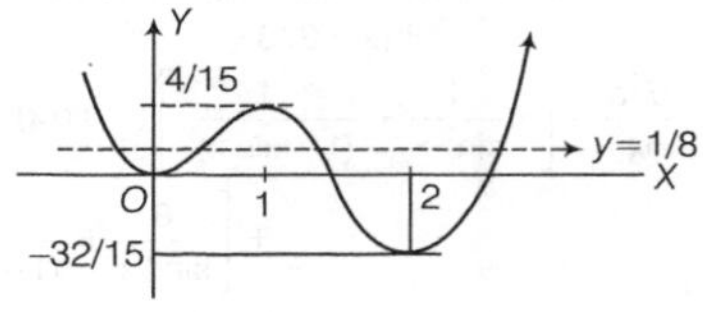

37. (d) **38.** (a) **39.** (b)

40. (a) $f(x) = \frac{x^2 - ax + 1}{x^2 + ax + 1},\ 0 < a < 2$

$$f(x) = \frac{(x^2 + ax + 1) - 2ax}{x^2 + ax + 1} = 1 - \frac{2ax}{x^2 + ax + 1}$$

$$\Rightarrow \quad f'(x) = -\left[\frac{(x^2 + ax + 1)2a - 2ax(2x + a)}{(x^2 + ax + 1)^2}\right]$$

$$= -\left[\frac{-2ax^2 + 2a}{(x^2 + ax + 1)^2}\right] = 2a\left[\frac{x^2 - 1}{(x^2 + ax + 1)^2}\right] \qquad \text{...(i)}$$

$$f''(x) = 2a\left[\frac{(x^2 + ax + 1)^2(2x) - 2(x^2 - 1)(x^2 + ax + 1)(2x + a)}{(x^2 + ax + 1)^4}\right]$$

$$= 2a\left[\frac{2x(x^2 + ax + 1) - 2(x^2 - 1)(2x + a)}{(x^2 + ax + 1)^3}\right] \qquad \text{...(ii)}$$

Now, $f''(1) = \frac{4a(a + 2)}{(a + 2)^3} = \frac{4a}{(a + 2)^2}$

and $f''(-1) = \frac{4a(a - 2)}{(2 - a)^3} = \frac{-4a}{(a - 2)^2}$

$$\therefore \quad (2 + a)^2 f''(1) + (2 - a)^2 f''(-1) = 4a - 4a = 0$$

41. (a) When $x \in (-1, 1)$, $x^2 < 1 \Rightarrow x^2 - 1 < 0$

$\therefore$ $f'(x) < 0$, $f(x)$ is decreasing.

Also at $x = 1$, $f''(1) = \frac{4a}{(a + 2)^2} > 0$ $[\because 0 < a < 2]$

$\therefore$ $f(x)$ has local minimum at $x = 1$.

42. (b) $g'(x) = \frac{f'(e^x)}{1 + (e^x)^2} \cdot e^x = 2a\left[\frac{e^{2x} - 1}{(e^{2x} + ae^x + 1)^2}\right]\left(\frac{e^x}{e^{2x} + 1}\right)$

$\Rightarrow g'(x) = 0$, if $e^{2x} - 1 = 0$, i.e. $x = 0$

If $x < 0, e^{2x} < 1 \Rightarrow g'(x) < 0$

43. (7) $f(x) = 2x^3 - 15x^2 + 36x - 48$

$\Rightarrow f'(x) = 6x^2 - 30x + 36 \Rightarrow f'(x) = 6(x - 2)(x - 3)$

So, $f(x)$ is increasing in $(-\infty, 2) \cup (3, \infty)$.

Also, $A = \{4 \le x \le 5\}$

$\therefore$ $f_{max} = f(5) = 7$

44. (0) Given, $\lim_{x \to 0} \left[\frac{1 + p(x)}{x^2}\right] = 2$

$\therefore \quad \lim_{x \to 0} \frac{p(x)}{x^2} = 1$

Consider $p(x) = ax^4 + bx^3 + x^2 \Rightarrow p'(x) = 4ax^3 + 3bx^2 + 2x$

Now, $\quad p'(1) = 4a + 3b + 2 = 0$

$\Rightarrow \quad 4a + 3b = -2 \quad \ldots(i)$

and $\quad p'(2) = 32a + 12b + 4 = 0$

$\Rightarrow \quad 32a + p2b = -4$

$\Rightarrow \quad 8a + 3b = -1 \quad \ldots(ii)$

On solving Eqs. (i) and (ii), we get

$a = 1/4, b = -1$

$\therefore \quad p(x) = \frac{1}{4}x^4 - x^3 + x^2$

$\Rightarrow \quad p(2) = 4 - 8 + 4 = 0$

45. (1) $f(x) = \ln\{g(x)\}$

$\therefore \quad g(x) = e^{f(x)}$

$\Rightarrow \quad g'(x) = e^{f(x)} \cdot f'(x)$

$\Rightarrow \quad g'(x) = 0 \Rightarrow f'(x) = 0$ as $e^{f(x)} \neq 0$

$\Rightarrow 2010(x - 2009)(x - 2010)^2 (x - 2011)^3 (x - 2012) y = 0$

So, there is only one solution of local maxima.

46. (5) We have, $f(x) = |x| + |x^2 - 1| = \begin{cases} -x + x^2 - 1, & x \leq -1 \\ -x - x^2 + 1, & -1 < x < 0 \\ x - x^2 + 1, & 0 \leq x < 1 \\ x + x^2 - 1, & x \geq 1 \end{cases}$

$\therefore \quad f'(x) = \begin{cases} 2x - 1, & x < -1 \\ -2x - 1, & -1 < x < 0 \\ -2x + 1, & 0 < x < 1 \\ 2x + 1, & x > 1 \end{cases}$

Clearly, $f(x)$ is not differentiable at $x = -1, 0, 1$. The changes in sign of $f'(x)$ for different values of x are shown in figure given below

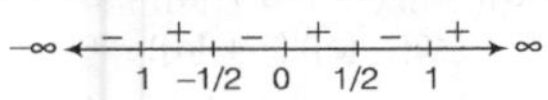

So, $f'(x)$ changes is sign at 5 points. Hence, total number of points of local maxima or local minima of $f(x)$ is 5.

47. (9) Since, $x = 1$ and $x = 3$ are extreme points of $P(x)$.

$\therefore \quad x = 1$ and $x = 3$ are roots of $P'(x) = 0$

Now, $\quad P'(x) = k(x - 1)(x - 3) = k(x^2 - 4x + 3)$

$\Rightarrow \quad P(x) = k\left(\frac{x^2}{3} - 2x^2 + 3x\right) + c$

Now, $P(1) = 6$ and $P(3) = 2$

$\Rightarrow \quad 6 = k\left(\frac{1}{3} - 2 + 3\right) + c$ and $2 = k(9 - 18 + 9) + c$

$\Rightarrow \quad 6 + \frac{4k}{3} + c$ and $c = 2 \Rightarrow c = 2$ and $k = 3$

$\therefore \quad P'(x) = 3(x^2 - 4x + 3)$

Hence, $\quad P'(0) = 9$

48. (5) Here, $x^2 + y^2 = r^2$ and tangents from $P(6, 8)$ are shown as

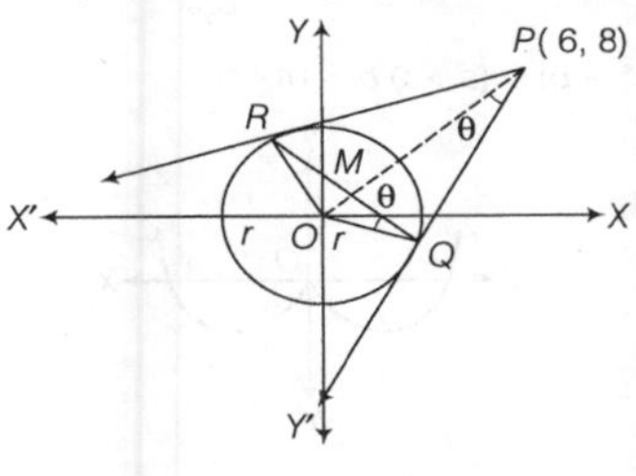

From the figure, in ΔOMQ, we have

$\cos\theta = \frac{MQ}{OQ}$ and $\sin\theta = \frac{OM}{OQ}$

$\therefore \quad MQ = r\cos\theta$ and $OM = r\sin\theta$

$QR = 2r\cos\theta$

$\Rightarrow \quad PM = OP - OM = 10 - r\sin\theta$

Area of $\Delta PQR = \frac{1}{2}(2r\cos\theta)(10 - r\sin\theta)$

$\therefore \quad f(\theta) = r\cos\theta(10 - r\sin\theta)$

$\left[\text{using } \frac{OQ}{OP} = \sin\theta \Rightarrow r = 10\sin\theta\right]$

$f(\theta) = 100\sin\theta\cos 3\theta$

$f'(\theta) = 100(\cos^4\theta - 3\cos^2\theta\sin^2\theta)$

$f'(\theta) = 100(-10\cos^3\theta\sin\theta + 6\sin^3\theta\cos\theta)$

Put $f'(\theta) = 0$, then

$\tan^2\theta = \frac{1}{3}$ or $\theta = \frac{\pi}{6}$

$f''(\pi/6) = 100\left(\frac{-15\sqrt{3}}{8} + \frac{\sqrt{3}}{8}\right) < 0$

$\therefore$ Area is maximum when $\theta = \frac{\pi}{6}$ and hence, $r = 10\sin\frac{\pi}{6} = 5.$

49. (6) We have, $f(x) = x^4 + bx^2 + 8x + 1$

$f'(x) = 4x^3 + 2bx + 8$

$f''(x) = 12x^2 + 2b$

$\therefore$ Tangent is horizontal, i.e. parallel to X-axis.

Now, $\quad f'(x) = 0$

$4x^3 + 2bx + 8 = 0 \quad \ldots(i)$

For point of inflection,

$f''(x) = 0$

$\Rightarrow \quad 12x^2 + 2b = 0$

$\Rightarrow \quad x^2 = -\frac{b}{6} \quad \ldots(ii)$

[this is only possible when $b < 0$]

From Eqs. (i) and (ii), we have

$x = 1$ and $b = -6$

$\therefore \quad |b| = 6$

50. (9) We have, $f(x) = ax + \cos 2x + \sin x + \cos x$

$\Rightarrow \quad f'(x) = a - 2\sin 2x + \cos x - \sin x$

As $f'(x) \geq 0$

$\Rightarrow \quad a \geq 2\sin 2x + \sin x - \cos x$

Let $t = \sin x - \cos x = \sqrt{2}\sin\left(x - \frac{\pi}{4}\right)$

$\Rightarrow \quad -\sqrt{2} \leq t \leq \sqrt{2}$

So, the inequality can be written as

$a \geq -2t^2 + t + 2$

Let $g(t) = -2t^2 + t + 2 = -2\left(t - \frac{1}{4}\right)^2 + \frac{17}{8}$

The range of $g(t)$ for $-\sqrt{2} \leq t \leq \sqrt{2}$ is

$g(-\sqrt{2}) \leq g(t) \leq g\left(\frac{1}{4}\right)$

$\Rightarrow \quad -2 - \sqrt{2} \leq g(t) \leq \frac{17}{8}$

So, the range of a can be found.

$\Rightarrow \quad a \geq \max_{|t| \leq \sqrt{2}}$

$\Rightarrow \quad a \geq \frac{17}{8}$ or $a \in \left[\frac{17}{8}, \infty\right) = \left[\frac{m}{n}, \infty\right)$

$\therefore \quad m - n = 17 - 8 = 9$

Revision Problems (JEE Main)

1. (d) Here, $(f'(x))^2 = f(x) \cdot f''(x)$

$\Rightarrow \quad (y')^2 = y \cdot y''$

$\Rightarrow \quad \int \frac{y'}{y} dx = \int \frac{y''}{y'} dx \quad \Rightarrow \quad \log y = \log y' + C_1$

as $\quad f(0) = 1, f'(0) = 1 \quad \Rightarrow \quad C_1 = 0$

$\therefore \quad y = y'$

$\Rightarrow \quad \int \frac{y'}{y} dx = \int dx \quad \Rightarrow \quad \log y = x + C_2$

as $\quad f(0) = 1 \quad \Rightarrow \quad C_2 = 0$

$\therefore \quad \log y = x \quad \Rightarrow \quad y = e^x$

$\Rightarrow \quad y'' > 0, \forall \; x \in R$

2. (c) For the intersection of the given curves

$$|x^2 - 1| = |x^2 - 3|$$

$\Rightarrow \quad (x^2 - 1)^2 = (x^2 - 3)^2$

$\Rightarrow \quad (x^2 - 1)^2 - (x^2 - 3)^2 = 0$

$\Rightarrow \quad [(x^2 - 1) - (x^2 - 3)]\,[(x^2 - 1) + (x^2 - 3)] = 0$

$\Rightarrow \quad 2\,[2x^2 - 4] = 0$

$\Rightarrow \quad 2x^2 = 4$

$\Rightarrow \quad x = \pm\sqrt{2}$

Neglecting $\quad x = -\sqrt{2}$ as $x > 0$

We have point of intersection as $x = \sqrt{2}$

Here, $y = |x^2 - 1| = (x^2 - 1)$ in the neighbourhood of $x = \sqrt{2}$

and $\quad y = -(x^2 - 3)$ in the neighbourhood of $x = \sqrt{2}$

$\Rightarrow \quad \left(\frac{dy}{dx}\right)_{c_1} = 2x = 2\sqrt{2}$

and $\quad \left(\frac{dy}{dx}\right)_{c_2} = -2x = -2\sqrt{2}$

Hence, if θ is angle between them

$\Rightarrow \quad \tan\theta = \left|\frac{2\sqrt{2} - (-2\sqrt{2})}{1 + 2\sqrt{2}(-2\sqrt{2})}\right| = \left|\frac{4\sqrt{2}}{-7}\right| = \left(\frac{4\sqrt{2}}{7}\right)$

3. (c) Given, $x = f'(t)\sin t + f''(t)\cos t$

$y = f'(t)\cos t - f''(t)\sin t$

$\Rightarrow \quad \frac{dx}{dt} = f''(t)\sin t + \cos t\; f'(t) + f'''(t)\cos t - f''(t)\sin t$

$= \cos t\;[f'(t) + f'''(t)]$

$\frac{dy}{dt} = f''(t)\cos t - f'(t)\sin t - f'''(t)\sin t - f''(t)\cos t$

$= -\sin t\;[f'(t) + f'''(t)]$

Now $\frac{dS}{dt} = \sqrt{\left(\frac{dx}{dt}\right)^2 + \left(\frac{dy}{dt}\right)^2} = \sqrt{[f'(t) + f'''(t)]^2\,(\sin^2 t + \cos^2 t)}$

$V = \frac{dS}{dt} = f'(t) + f'''(t)$

4. (a) Since, f is differentiable.

$\Rightarrow$ f is also continuous.

Thus, by Lagrange's mean value theorem, $a \in (0, 4)$ such that

$$f'(a) = \frac{f(4) - f(0)}{4 - 0} = \frac{f(4) - f(0)}{4} \quad \ldots(\text{i})$$

Also, by Intermediate mean value theorem, there exists $b \in (0, 4)$ such that

$$f(b) = \frac{f(4) + f(0)}{2} \quad \ldots(\text{ii})$$

From Eqs. (i) and (ii), we get

$$f'(a) \cdot f(b) = \frac{f(4) - f(0)}{4} \times \frac{f(4) + f(0)}{2}$$

$\Rightarrow \quad \{f(4)\}^2 - \{f(0)\}^2 = 8f'(a)\,f(b)$

5. (d) We have, $f(x) = 8ax - a\sin 6x - 7x - \sin 5x$

$\Rightarrow \quad f'(x) = 8a - 6a\cos 6x - 7 - 5\cos 5x$

$= (8a - 7) - 6a\cos 6x - 5\cos 5x$

$\because$ $f(x)$ is increasing.

$\therefore \quad f'(x) \geq 0$

$\Rightarrow \quad (8a - 7) - 6a\cos 6x - 5\cos 5x \geq 0$

$\Rightarrow \quad 8a - 7 \geq 6a\cos 6x + 5\cos 5x$

$\Rightarrow \quad 8a - 7 \geq 6a + 5 \quad [\because -1 \leq \cos x \leq 1]$

$\Rightarrow \quad 2a \geq 12 \quad \Rightarrow \quad a \geq 6$

$\Rightarrow \quad a \in [6, \infty)$

6. (b) We have, $f(x) = \{x\}$

As we know, for discontinuous functions, maximum and minimum at $x = a$ is attained when

$$f(a) \geq f(a + h) \quad \text{and} \quad f(a) \geq f(a - h)$$

$\Rightarrow$ $f(x)$ is maximum at $x = a$

and $\quad f(a) \leq f(a + h) \quad$ and $\quad f(a) \leq f(a - h)$

$\Rightarrow$ $f(x)$ is minimum at $x = a$

$f(x) = \{x\}$ is discontinuous at $x = 5$, where $f(5) = 0$

$f(5 + h) > 0 \quad$ and $\quad f(5 - h) > 0$

So, $\quad f(5) < f(5 + h) \quad$ and $\quad f(5) < f(5 - h)$

$\Rightarrow$ $f(x)$ is minimum at $x = 5$

$\therefore \quad f(x)$ for $x = 5$ attains local minima.

7. (d) Let $f(x) = x^3 - 3x + [a]$

$$f'(x) = 3x^2 - 3$$

Let $f'(x) = 0 \quad \Rightarrow \quad 3x^2 - 3 = 0$

$\Rightarrow \quad x = \pm 1$

For three distinct real roots

$$f(1)\,f'(-1) < 0$$

$\Rightarrow \quad (1 - 3 + [a])\,(-1 + 3 + [a]) < 0$

$\Rightarrow \quad (-2 + [a])\,(2 + [a]) < 0 \quad \Rightarrow \quad [a]^2 - (2)^2 < 0$

$\Rightarrow \quad [a]^2 < 4 \quad \Rightarrow \quad [a] < \pm 2$

$\Rightarrow \quad -2 < [a] < 2 \quad \Rightarrow \quad a \in [-1, 2)$

8. (a)

(i) $y = ax^2 - bx \; (a > 0, b > 0)$

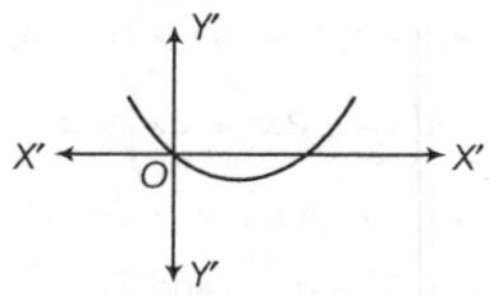

(ii) $y = ax^2 - bx (a > 0, b < 0)$

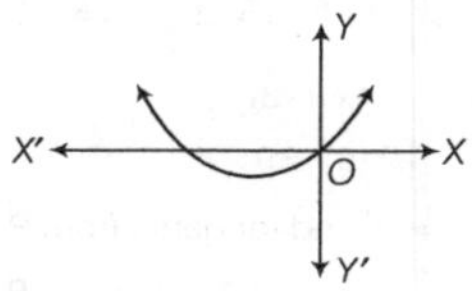

(iii) $y = ax^2 - b|x| \; (a > 0, b > 0)$

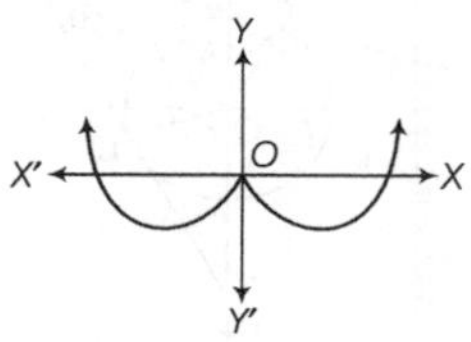

(iv) $y = ax^2 - b|x|\ (a > 0, b < 0)$

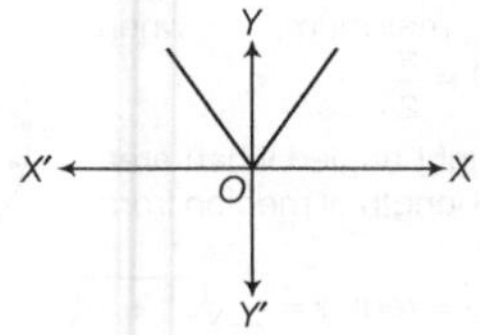

9. (b) We have,

$$f(x) = 2x^3 - 3(a+1)x^2 + 6ax - 12$$

$\Rightarrow \quad f'(x) = 6x^2 - 6(a+1)x + 6a$

$\Rightarrow \quad f''(x) = 12x - 6(a+1)$

Since, $f(x)$ has maxima at $x = x_1$.

$\therefore \quad f''(x_1) = 12x_1 - 6(a+1) < 0$

$\Rightarrow \quad x_1 < \dfrac{6(a+1)}{12} = \dfrac{a+1}{2}$

and $f(x)$ has minima at $x = x_2$.

$f''(x_2) = 12x_2 - 6(a+1) > 0$

$\Rightarrow \quad x_2 > \dfrac{a+1}{2}$

$\Rightarrow \quad 2x_1 > \dfrac{a+1}{2} \quad [\because 2x_1 = x_2]$

$\Rightarrow \quad 2\left(\dfrac{a+1}{2}\right) > \dfrac{a+1}{2}$

$\Rightarrow \quad a = \dfrac{1}{2}$

10. (d) Since, $f(x)$ has local maxima at $x = 1$.

$\Rightarrow \quad f(1) > f(1^-)$

$\Rightarrow \quad -6 > \tan^{-1}\alpha - 5$

$\Rightarrow \quad \tan^{-1}\alpha < -1$

$\Rightarrow \quad \alpha < -\tan 1 < -1$

$\therefore$ Only the possible option is (d).

11. (b) Time taken by the truck $= \dfrac{300}{x}$ h

$\therefore$ Fuel consumed $= \left(2 + \dfrac{x^2}{600}\right)\cdot\dfrac{300}{x}$

$\therefore$ Expenses on travelling

$\Rightarrow \quad E = 200 \times \dfrac{300}{x} + \left(2 + \dfrac{x^2}{600}\right)\cdot\dfrac{3000}{x}$

$\therefore \quad \dfrac{dE}{dx} = -\dfrac{66000}{x^2} + 5 < 0, \forall\ x \in [30, 60]$

$\therefore$ Most economical speed is 60 km/h.

12. (b) $y = 2e^x \sin\left(\dfrac{\pi}{4} - \dfrac{x}{2}\right)\cos\left(\dfrac{\pi}{4} - \dfrac{x}{2}\right)$, where $0 \le x \le 2\pi$

$y = e^x \sin 2\left(\dfrac{\pi}{4} - \dfrac{x}{2}\right)$

$y = e^x \sin\left(\dfrac{\pi}{2} - x\right)$

$y = e^x \cos x$

$y' = e^x \cos x - e^x \sin x$

$= e^x(\cos x - \sin x)$ = slope of tangent

$\Rightarrow \quad y'' = e^x(\cos x - \sin x) + e^x(-\sin x - \cos x)$

$= e^x[\cos x - \sin x - \sin x - \cos x]$

$y'' = e^x[-2\sin x]$

For maxima or minima of y',

$y'' = 0 \Rightarrow -2e^x \sin x = 0$

$\Rightarrow \quad \sin x = 0 \Rightarrow x = \pi$

13. (c) Let each side of regular hexagon is x cm and lateral edge is 1 cm.

Let $OA = h$ cm be height of regular hexagon.

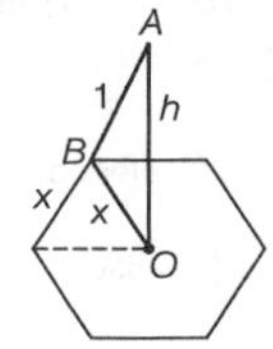

In ΔAOB, $\quad OA^2 + OB^2 = AB^2$

$\Rightarrow \quad h^2 + x^2 = 1^2$

$\Rightarrow \quad h = \sqrt{1 - x^2}$

Volume of pyramid,

$$V = \frac{1}{3} \times \text{Area of base} \times \text{Base of height}$$

$$= \frac{1}{3} \times 6 \times \frac{\sqrt{3}}{4}x^2 \times \sqrt{1-x^2} = \frac{\sqrt{3}}{2}x^2\sqrt{1-x^2}$$

Now, $\dfrac{dV}{dx} = \dfrac{\sqrt{3}}{2}\left[2x\sqrt{1-x^2} + x^2\dfrac{-2x}{2\sqrt{1-x^2}}\right]$

$= \dfrac{\sqrt{3}}{2}\left[2x\sqrt{1-x^2} - \dfrac{x^3}{\sqrt{1-x^2}}\right]$

$= \dfrac{\sqrt{3}}{2}\left[\dfrac{2x(1-x^2) - x^3}{\sqrt{1-x^2}}\right] = \dfrac{\sqrt{3}}{2}\left[\dfrac{2x - 3x^3}{\sqrt{1-x^2}}\right]$

$\Rightarrow \quad \dfrac{d^2V}{dx^2} = \dfrac{\sqrt{3}}{2}\left[\dfrac{\sqrt{1-x^2}(2 - 9x^2) - (2x - 3x^3)\dfrac{-2x}{2\sqrt{1-x^2}}}{(1-x^2)}\right]$

$\Rightarrow \quad \dfrac{d^2V}{dx^2} = \dfrac{\sqrt{3}}{2}\left[\dfrac{(1-x^2)(2-9x^2) + (2x^2 - 3x^4)}{(1-x^2)^{3/2}}\right]$

For maxima or minima, $\dfrac{dV}{dx} = 0 \Rightarrow \dfrac{2x - 3x^3}{\sqrt{1-x^2}} = 0$

$\Rightarrow \quad 2x - 3x^3 = 0 \Rightarrow x(2 - 3x^2) = 0$

$\Rightarrow \quad x = 0$ or $x = \pm\sqrt{2/3}$

$$\left(\frac{d^2V}{dx^2}\right)_{x=\sqrt{2/3}} = \frac{\sqrt{3}}{2}\left[\frac{\left(1-\frac{2}{3}\right)\left(2 - 9\times\frac{2}{3}\right) + \left\{2\left(\frac{2}{3}\right) - 3\left(\frac{2}{3}\right)^2\right\}}{\left(1-\frac{2}{3}\right)^{3/2}}\right]$$

< 0

$\therefore$ Volume is maximum, when $x = \sqrt{\dfrac{2}{3}}$

$\therefore \quad h = \sqrt{1-x^2} = \sqrt{1 - \dfrac{2}{3}} = \sqrt{\dfrac{1}{3}} = \dfrac{1}{\sqrt{3}}$

14. (b) Given, $f(x) = \begin{cases} \dfrac{4-x}{2-\sqrt{x}}, & \text{for } 0 < x < 4 \\ 4, & \text{for } x = 4 \\ 16 - 3x, & \text{for } 4 < x < 6 \end{cases}$

For continuity at $x = 4$, LHL $= \lim\limits_{h\to 0} f(4-h)$

$= \lim\limits_{h\to 0}\dfrac{4-(4-h)}{2-\sqrt{4-h}} = \lim\limits_{h\to 0}\dfrac{h}{2-\sqrt{4-h}} \quad \left[\dfrac{0}{0}\text{ form}\right]$

$= \lim\limits_{h\to 0}\dfrac{1}{-\dfrac{1}{2\sqrt{4-h}}(-1)} = \lim\limits_{h\to 0} 2\sqrt{4-h} = 4$

RHL $= \lim\limits_{h\to 0} f(4+h) = \lim\limits_{h\to 0}\dfrac{4-(4+h)}{2-\sqrt{4+h}}$

$= \lim\limits_{h\to 0}\dfrac{-h}{2-\sqrt{4+h}} = \lim\limits_{h\to 0}\dfrac{1}{\dfrac{1}{2\sqrt{4+h}}} = \lim\limits_{h\to 0} 2\sqrt{4+h} = 4$

Also, $\quad f(x) = 4$

$\because \quad$ LHL = RHL = $f(x)$

$\therefore$ $f(x)$ is continuous at $x = 4$.

15. (d) $f(x)$ vanish at point, where

$$\sin\frac{\pi}{x} = 0, \text{ i.e. } \frac{\pi}{x} = k\pi, k = 1, 2, 3, \ldots$$

Hence, $x = \frac{1}{k}$

Also, $f'(x) = \sin\frac{\pi}{x} - \frac{\pi}{x}\cos\frac{\pi}{x}$, if $x \neq 0$, $f'(x) = 0$

$\Rightarrow$ $\tan\frac{\pi}{x} = \frac{\pi}{x}$

which is possible for infinite points as $x \in (0, 1)$.

16. (a) We have, $x^2 e^{|x|} = 1$

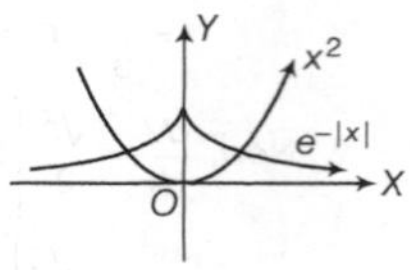

$\Rightarrow$ $e^{|x|} = \frac{1}{x^2}$

$\Rightarrow$ $e^{-|x|} = x^2$

Hence, the number of solutions are 2.

17. (b) We have, $f''(x) = 6(x - 1)$

On integrating, we have

$$f'(x) = 3(x - 1)^2 + c \quad \ldots(i)$$

At (2, 1), $y = 3x - 5$ is tangent to $y = f(x)$

Thus, $f'(2) = 3$

From Eq. (i), we have

$$3 = 3(2 - 1)^2 + c$$

$\Rightarrow$ $c = 0$

$\therefore$ $f'(x) = 3(x - 1)^2$

Again integrating, we have

$$f(x) = (x - 1)^3 + c_1$$

Since, the curve passes through (2, 1).

$\therefore$ $1 = (2 - 1)^3 + c_1 \Rightarrow c_1 = 0$

$\therefore$ $f(x) = (x - 1)^3$

18. (c) Given, $g(x) = [f'(x)]^2 + f''(x) f(x) = \frac{d}{dx}[f(x) f'(x)]$

Let $h(x) = f(x) f'(x)$

Since, $f(a) = 0, f(b) = 2, f(c) = -1, f(d) = 2, f(e) = 0$

$f(x) = 0$ has four roots namely a, α, β, e, where $b < \alpha < c$ and $c < \beta < d$ and $f'(x) = 0$ at three points k_1, k_2, k_3, where $a < k_1 < \alpha$, $\alpha < k_2 < \beta$, $\beta < k_3 < c$ [since between any two roots of a polynomial function $f(x) = 0$, there lies atleast one root of $f'(x) = 0$]

Therefore, there are atleast 7 roots of $f(x) f'(x) = 0$

Therefore, there are atleast 6 roots of $\frac{d}{dx}[f(x) f'(x)] = 0$

i.e. $g(x) = 0$

19. (a) We have, $f(x) = \begin{cases} \sin\frac{\pi x}{2}, & 0 \le x < 1 \\ 3 - 2x, & x \ge 1 \end{cases}$

$$\text{LHL} = \lim_{x \to 1^-} f(x) = \lim_{h \to 0} f(1 - h)$$

$$= \lim_{h \to 0} \sin\frac{\pi(1 - h)}{2} = 1$$

$$\text{RHL} = \lim_{x \to 1^+} f(x) = \lim_{h \to 0} f(1 + h)$$

$$= \lim_{h \to 0} 3 - 2(1 - h)$$

$$= 1$$

Also, $f(1) = 3 - 2 \times 1 = 1$

$\therefore$ $f(x)$ is continuous at $x = 1$.

In the left neighbourhood of $x = 1$, we have

$$f'(x) = \frac{\pi}{2}\cos\frac{\pi}{2}x > 0$$

In the right neighbourhood of $x = 1$, we have

$$f'(x) = -2 < 0$$

Hence, at $x = 1$, $f(x)$ has local maxima.

20. (a) Area of $\Delta ABC = \frac{1}{2} ab \sin\theta$

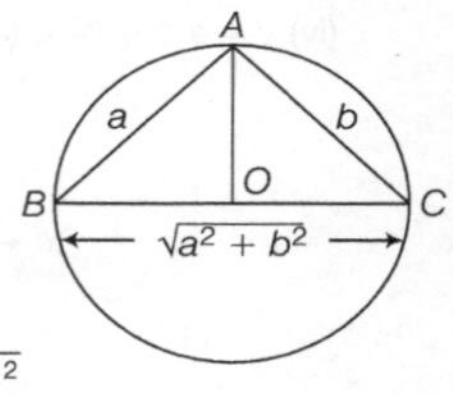

which is maximum, when $\sin\theta = 1 \Rightarrow \theta = \frac{\pi}{2}$

Thus, ΔABC is right angled when area is maximum and length of median from A is

$$AO = \text{radius} = \frac{1}{2}\sqrt{a^2 + b^2}$$

21. (a) Let the equation of line be $\frac{x}{a} + \frac{y}{b} = 1$

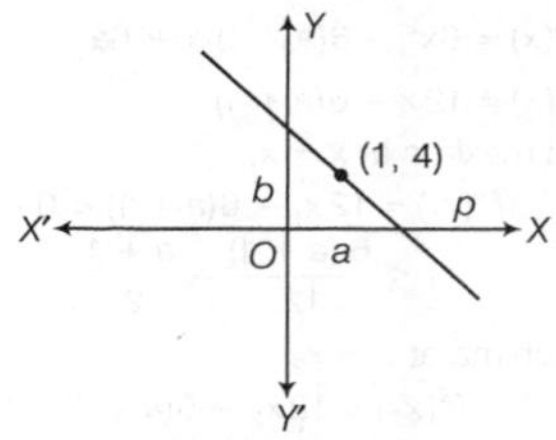

Since, it passes through (1, 4).

$\therefore$ $\frac{1}{a} + \frac{4}{b} = 1$

$\Rightarrow$ $\frac{4}{b} = 1 - \frac{1}{a} \Rightarrow \frac{4}{b} = \frac{a - 1}{a}$

$\Rightarrow$ $\frac{b}{4} = \frac{a}{a - 1} \Rightarrow b = \frac{4a}{a - 1}$

Sum of intercept on positive axes

$$S = a + b$$

$$S = a + \frac{4a}{a - 1} = \frac{a^2 - a + 4a}{(a - 1)} = \frac{a^2 + 3a}{(a - 1)}$$

$$\frac{dS}{da} = \frac{(a - 1)(2a + 3) - (a^2 + 3a)}{(a - 1)^2} = \frac{a^2 - 2a - 3}{(a - 1)^2}$$

For maxima or minima, $\frac{dS}{da} = 0$

$\Rightarrow$ $a^2 - 2a - 3 = 0 \Rightarrow (a - 3)(a + 1) = 0$

$$a = 3, -1$$

$\Rightarrow$ $$\frac{d^2S}{da^2} = \frac{(a - 1)^2(2a - 2) - (a^2 - 2a - 3) \times 2(a - 1)}{(a - 1)^4}$$

$$= \frac{(a - 1)[(a - 1)(2a - 2) - 2(a^2 - 2a - 3)]}{(a - 1)^4}$$

$$= \frac{2a^2 - 4a + 2 - 2a^2 + 4a + 6}{(a - 1)^3}$$

$$= \frac{8}{(a - 1)^3}$$

at $a = 3$

$$\frac{d^2S}{da^2} = \frac{8}{(3 - 1)} = 1 > 0$$

$\therefore$ S is minimum, when $a = 3$

$\Rightarrow$ $b = 6$

$\therefore$ Equation of line $= \frac{x}{3} + \frac{y}{6} = 1$

$\Rightarrow$ $2x + y = 6$

22. (b) Let the width of the brick be a.

$\therefore$ Length $= 3a$

Let h be the height of the brick.

$\therefore$ Volume $= l \times b \times h$

$$1 = 3a \times a \times h \Rightarrow h = \frac{1}{3a^2}$$

Now, surface area = $2(lb + bh + hl)$

$$S = 2\left(3a^2 + \frac{1}{3a} + \frac{1}{a}\right)$$

$$\frac{dS}{da} = 2\left[6a - \frac{1}{3a^2} - \frac{1}{a^2}\right]$$

For maxima or minima,

$$\frac{dS}{da} = 0$$

$$\Rightarrow \quad 6a - \frac{1}{3a^2} - \frac{1}{a^2} = 0 \Rightarrow a^3 = \frac{2}{9}$$

$$\Rightarrow \quad \frac{d^2S}{da^2} = 2\left[6 + \frac{2}{3a^3} + \frac{2}{a^3}\right]$$

$$\therefore \quad \left(\frac{d^2S}{da^2}\right)_{a = \left(\frac{2}{9}\right)^{1/3}} = 2\left[6 + \frac{2 \times 9}{3 \times 2} + 2 \times \frac{9}{2}\right]$$

$$= 2\,[6 + 3 + 9] = 36 > 0$$

So, surface area is minimum, when $a = \left(\frac{2}{9}\right)^{1/3}$, i.e. $a^3 = \frac{2}{9}$

23. (d) Given, $g(x) = \log[h(x)], \forall x \in J$

$$\Rightarrow \quad g'(x) = \frac{1}{h(x)} h'(x), \quad \forall x \in J$$

$$\Rightarrow \quad g''(x) = \frac{h(x)h''(x) - [h'(x)]^2}{[h(x)]^2}$$

Clearly, $\quad [h(x)]^2 > 0$

Since, $\quad [h'(x)]^2 > h(x)\,h''(x)$

$$\Rightarrow \quad h(x)\,h''(x) - [h'(x)]^2 < 0 \Rightarrow g''(x) < 0$$

$\Rightarrow g(x)$ is concave down on J.

24. (d) Let $h(x) = f(x) + g(x), \forall x \in [-1, 3]$

Now, $\quad h'(x) = f'(x) + g'(x), \forall x \in [-1, 3]$

$\Rightarrow \quad h''(x) = f''(x) + g''(x), \forall x \in [-1, 3]$

$\Rightarrow \quad h''(x) > 0 \quad [\because f''(x) > 0, g''(x) > 0]$

$\Rightarrow h(x)$ is concave upward, i.e. $f(x) + g(x)$ is concave upward.

25. (a) Compare the greatest value of the function appearing on the LHS of the equation with the least value appearing on RHS $\Rightarrow x = 1$

Note that RHS minimum value at $x = 1$ but LHS has maximum value at $x = 1 \Rightarrow x = 1$ can be the only solution.

26. (c) We have, $P(x) = a_0 + a_1x^2 + a_2x^4 + \cdots + a_nx^{2n}$

$$P'(x) = 2a_1x + 4a_2x^3 + \cdots + 2na_nx^{2n-1}$$

For maximum or minimum, $P''(x) = 0$

$\Rightarrow \quad x(2a_1 + 4a_2x^2 + \cdots + 2na_nx^{2n-2}) = 0$

$\Rightarrow \quad x = 0 \quad [\because$ each $a_i > 0$ and powers of x are even]

Now, $\quad P''(x) = 2a_1 + 12a_2x^2 + \cdots + 2n(2n-1)\,a_nx^{2n-2}$

$\therefore \quad [P''(x)]_{x=0} = 2a_1 > 0$

i.e. $P(x)$ has a minimum at $x = 0$ only.

27. (d) Since, $V = \frac{4}{3}\pi r^3$

$$\frac{dV}{dt} = 4\pi r^2 \frac{dr}{dt} \Rightarrow -72\pi = 4\pi r^2 \frac{dr}{dt}$$

$$\Rightarrow \quad \frac{dr}{dt} = \frac{-18}{r^2}$$

$$\Rightarrow \quad \int r^2 dr = -18 \int dt$$

$$\Rightarrow \quad \frac{r^3}{3} = -18t + c \text{ at } t = 0, r = 15\text{ m}$$

$$\therefore \quad c = 1125 \Rightarrow r^3 = -54t + 3375$$

At $t = 49, r = 9$ m

$$\therefore \quad \left(\frac{dr}{dt}\right) = -\frac{-18}{9^2} = \frac{2}{9}$$

28. (c) If $f(x)$ has a local minimum at $x = -1$, then

$$\lim_{x \to -1^+} f(x) \geq f(1)$$

$$\Rightarrow \quad 1 \geq b + 2$$

$$\Rightarrow \quad b \leq -1$$

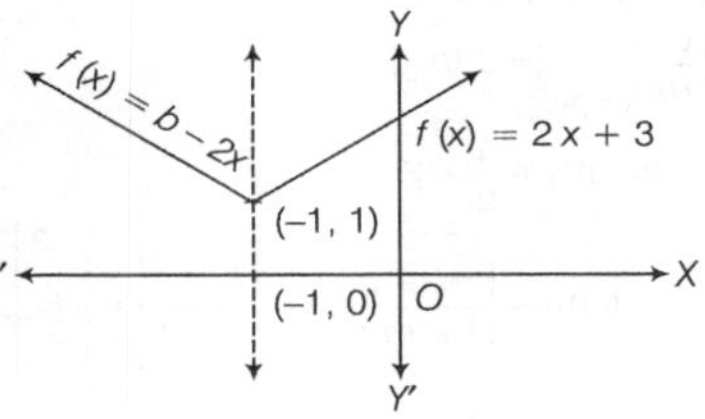

29. (b) $f(x) = \begin{cases} 4x - (a + b + c + d), & x \geq d \\ 2x - (a + b + c - d), & c \leq x < d \\ c + d - a - b, & b \leq x < c \\ b + c + d - a - 2x, & a \leq x < b \\ a + b + c + d - 4x, & x < a \end{cases}$

which can be shown as below

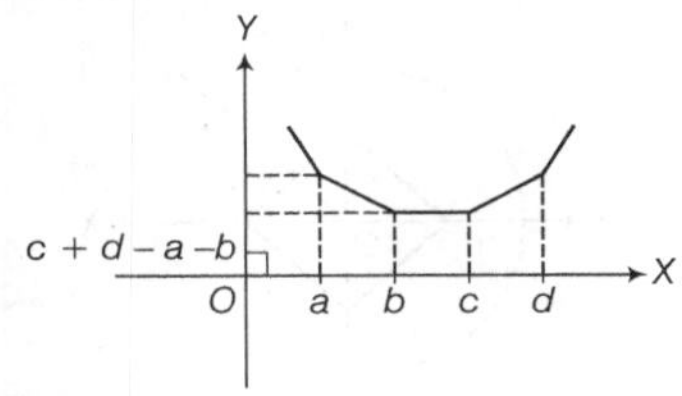

$\therefore$ Least value of y

$= |x - a| + |x - b| + |x - c| + |x - d|$ is $(c + d - a - b)$.

30. (c) $f(x) = \int_{-1}^{x} (t^2 + 2t)(t^2 - 1)\,dt$

$f'(x) = (x^2 + 2x)(x^2 - 1)$ [by Leibnitz's rule]

$= x(x + 2)(x^2 - 1)$

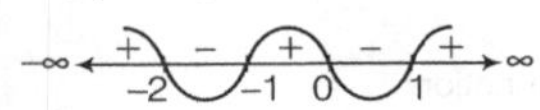

Thus, $\quad f'(x) > 0$ for $(-\infty, -2) \cup (-1, 0) \cup (1, \infty)$

31. (a) Let the slope of tangent be denoted by $\tan\psi$.

Length of tangent = $y\,\text{cosec}\,\psi$

Length of normal = $y\sec\psi$

$$\therefore \quad \frac{\text{Length of tangent}}{\text{Length of normal}} = \cot\psi \propto \frac{1}{y}$$

Statement I is correct.

Length of normal = $y\sec\psi = |y\sqrt{1 + m^2}|$

Length of tangent = $y\,\text{cosec}\,\psi = \left|\frac{y\sqrt{1 + m^2}}{m}\right|$

$\therefore$ Statement II is correct explanation of Statement I.

32. (d) We have, $\quad y^2 = 16x \quad \ldots$(i)

and $\quad x^2 = 16y \quad \ldots$(ii)

From Eq. (i), we have $2y\frac{dy}{dx} = 16$

$$\frac{dy}{dx} = \frac{8}{y} \quad \ldots\text{(iii)}$$

From Eq. (ii), we have

$$\frac{dy}{dx} = \frac{1}{16}(2x) = \frac{x}{8} \quad \ldots\text{(iv)}$$

Clearly, the given curves intersect at (0, 0) and (16, 16).

$\therefore$ From Eq. (iii), we have

$$\left(\frac{dy}{dx}\right)_{(16,\,16)} = \frac{1}{2}(m_1) \quad \text{[say]}$$

From Eq. (iv), we have

$$\left(\frac{dy}{dx}\right)_{(16,\,16)} = 2\,(m_2) \quad \text{[say]}$$

$\therefore \quad m_1 \cdot m_2 = \frac{1}{2} \times 2 = 1$

$$\Rightarrow \quad \tan\theta = \left|\frac{m_1 - m_2}{1 + m_1 m_2}\right| = \left|\frac{\frac{1}{2} - 2}{1 + 1}\right| = \left|\frac{\frac{-3}{2}}{2}\right| = \frac{3}{4}$$

$\therefore$ Statement I is incorrect and Statement II is correct.

33. (d) Common normal is $y = x$

Solving $x + y = 2 \Rightarrow (1, 1)$

and $x^2 + y^2 = 16$

$\Rightarrow (2\sqrt{2}, 2\sqrt{2})$

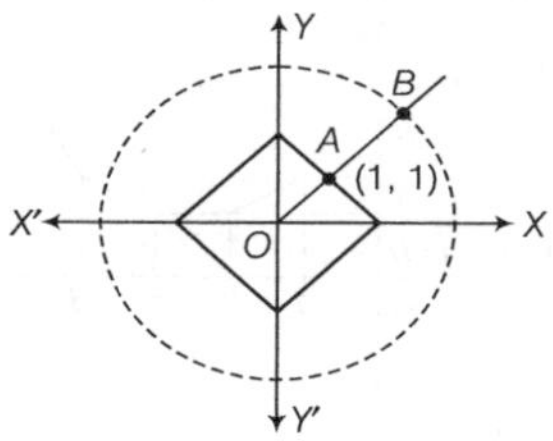

The distance between AB is $4 - \sqrt{2}$.

But as curves are not smooth, check at slope point.

The coordinates in Ist quadrant are (2, 0) and (4, 0) and have distance = 2

$\therefore 4 - \sqrt{2}$ is not shortest.

34. (a) Statement II is obviously true.

Statement I,

Consider the function,

$$f(x) = e^x, P(x_1, e^{x_1}) \text{ and } Q(x_2, e^{x_2})$$

are two points on the curve $y = f(x)$ and a point R divides the line joining P and Q internally in the ratio 1 : 2, then coordinates of R are

$$\left(\frac{2x_1 + x_2}{3}, \frac{2e^{x_1} + e^{x_2}}{3}\right)$$

$$\therefore \quad \frac{2e^{x_1} + e^{x_2}}{3} > e^{\frac{2x_1 + x_2}{3}}$$

$\therefore$ Statement I is correct and Statement II is correct explanation of Statement I.

35. (b) Let $g(x) = f(x) - x^2$

We have, $g(1) = 0, g(2) = 0, g(3) = 0$

$[\because f(1) = 1, f(2) = 4, f(3) = 9]$

By Rolle's theorem on $g(x)$,

$g'(x) = 0$ for at least $x \in (1, 2)$

Let $g'(c_1) = 0$, where $c_1 \in (1, 2)$

Similarly, $g(x) = 0$ for at least one $x \in (2, 3)$

Let $g'(c_2) = 0$, where $c_2 \in (2, 3)$

By Rolle's theorem, atleast one $x \in (c_1, c_2)$

such that $g''(x) = 0$

$\Rightarrow f''(x) = 2$ for some $x \in (1, 3)$

Statement I is correct.

Statement II

$g(x) = x^2$

$\Rightarrow g'(x) = 2x \Rightarrow g''(x) = 2, \quad \forall x \in R$

Statement II is also correct but not correct explanation of Statement I.

36. (d) Let $g(x)$ be the inverse function of $f(x)$.

Then, $f[g(x)] = x$

$\therefore f'[g(x)]\, g'(x) = 1$

i.e. $g'(x) = \dfrac{1}{f'[(g(x)]}$

$$\therefore \quad g''(x) = -\frac{1}{f'[g(x)]^2} f''[g(x)]\, g'(x)$$

In Statement I, $f''[g(x)] > 0$

and $g'(x) < 0 \Rightarrow g''(x) < 0$

$\Rightarrow$ Concavity $f^{-1}(x)$ is upward.

$\therefore$ Statement I is incorrect.

In Statement II,

$f''[g(x)] > 0$

and $g'(x) < 0 \Rightarrow g''(x) < 0$

$\Rightarrow$ Concavity of $f^{-1}(x)$ is upward.

$\therefore$ Statement II is correct.

37. (d) $f(x) = 5 - 4(x - 2)^{2/3}$ attains greatest value at $x = 2$.

Statement II is obviously correct.

38. (c) Statement I is correct.

Statement II is incorrect, as both $f(x) = x$ and $g(x) = x^3$ are increasing in $(-1, 0)$ but $h(x) = x \cdot x^3$ in decreasing.

39. (a) Let $f(x) = 0$ has two roots say $x = r_1$ and $x = r_2$, where $r_1 r_2 \in [a, b]$

$\Rightarrow f(r_1) = f(r_2)$

Hence, $\exists$ some $c \in (r_1, r_2)$, where $f'(c) = 0$

But $f'(x) = x^6 - x^5 + x^4 - x^3 + x^2 - x + 1$ for $x \geq 1$

$f'(x) = (x^6 - x^5) + (x^4 - x^3) + (x^2 - x) + 1 > 0$ for $x \leq 1$

$f'(x) = (1 - x) + (x^2 - x^3) + (x^4 - x^5) + x^6 > 0$

Hence, $f'(x) > 0$ for all x.

$\therefore$ Rolle's theorem fails.

$\Rightarrow f(x) = 0$ cannot have two or more roots.

40. (d) **Statement I**

$$f(x) = \log_{(e + x)}(\pi + x) \Rightarrow f(x) = \frac{\log_e(\pi + x)}{\log_e(e + x)}$$

$$\Rightarrow \quad f''(x) = \frac{\log(e + x) \times \frac{1}{(\pi + x)} - \log(\pi + x) \times \frac{1}{e + x}}{[\log(e + x)]^2}$$

$$= \frac{(e + x)\log(e + x) - (\pi + x)\log(\pi + x)}{(e + x)(\pi + x)[\log(e + x)]^2}$$

$(e + x)(\pi + x) > 0$ and $[\log(e + x)]^2 > 0$

But $(e + x)\log(e + x) \ngtr (\pi + x)\log(\pi + x)$

$\therefore f'(x) \ngtr 0$

$\therefore$ Statement I is incorrect and Statement II is correct.

Revisal Problems (JEE Advanced)

1. (b) We have, $f(x) = x(\log x - 2)$

$\Rightarrow \quad f'(x) = (\log x - 2) + x \times \frac{1}{x}$

$\Rightarrow \quad f'(x) = \log x - 2 + 1$

$\Rightarrow \quad f'(x) = \log x - 1$

For maxima or minima,

$f'(x) = 0$

$\Rightarrow \quad \log x - 1 = 0$

$\Rightarrow \quad x = e$

At $x = 1$, $f(1) = -2$

At $x = e$, $f(e) = -e$

At $x = e^2$, $f(e^2) = 0$

Maximum of $f(x)$ is 0 and minimum is $-e$.

$\therefore$ Difference $= 0 - (-e) = e$

2. (b) The graph of $y = a^x$ and $y = x$ is shown below

$a > 1$

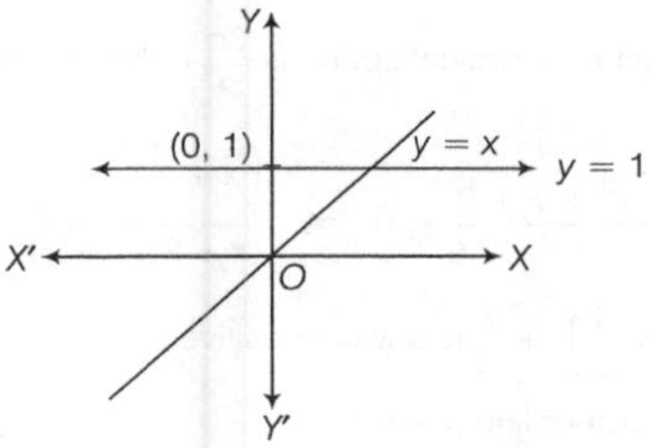

$0 < a < 1$

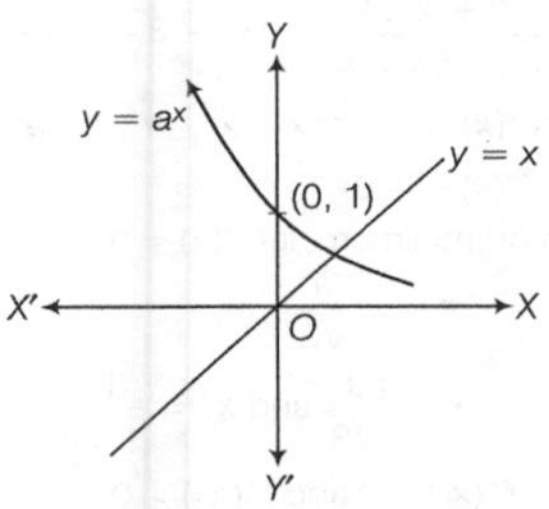

$\Rightarrow \quad a \in (0, 1]$

From the above figure, $a = 1$

3. (a) $L = 4 - x + 2\sqrt{9 + x^2}$, where $0 \le x \le 4$

$$\frac{dL}{dx} = \frac{2x}{\sqrt{9 + x^2}} - 1 = 0$$

$\Rightarrow \quad 4x^2 = 9 + x^2$

$\Rightarrow \quad x = \sqrt{3}$

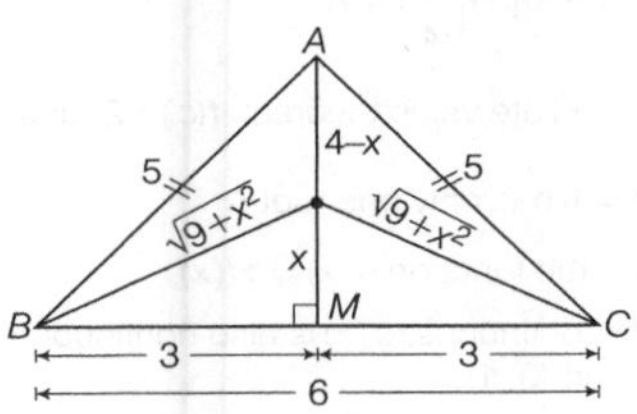

Now, $L(0) = L(4) = 10$

$L(\sqrt{3}) = 4 - \sqrt{3} + 2 \cdot \sqrt{12}$

$= 4 - \sqrt{3} + 4\sqrt{3} = 4 + 3\sqrt{3}$

$\therefore$ Minimum length of wire $= 4 + 3\sqrt{3}$.

4. (d) We have, $g'(x) = \frac{2}{x + g(x)} > 0, \forall x \in [1, 6]$.

$\Rightarrow g(x)$ is increasing function on $[1, 6]$.

$$\therefore \quad \int_1^6 g'(x)\,dx \le \int_1^6 \frac{2}{x}\,dx \Rightarrow [g(x)]_1^6 \le 2[\log x]_1^6$$

$\Rightarrow \quad g(6) - g(1) \le 2 \log 6$

$\therefore \quad g(6) \le 2 \log 6 \qquad [\because g(1) = 0]$

5. (b) $\tan\theta = \frac{x}{r}$ or $x = r\tan\theta$

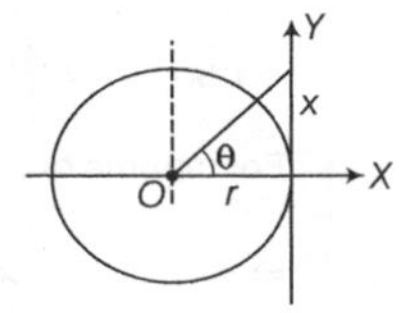

or $\frac{dx}{dt} = r\sec^2\theta\left(\frac{d\theta}{dr}\right)$

$= r\omega\sec^2\theta = v\sec^2\theta$

$[\because v = r\omega$, where ω is angular velocity$]$

where $\theta = \frac{2\pi}{8}$

$\therefore \quad \frac{dx}{dt} = v\sec^2\left(\frac{\pi}{4}\right) = 2v = 40$ km/h

6. (c) Let each side of regular hexagon be x cm and lateral edge be 1 cm.

Let $OA = h$ cm be height of regular hexagon.

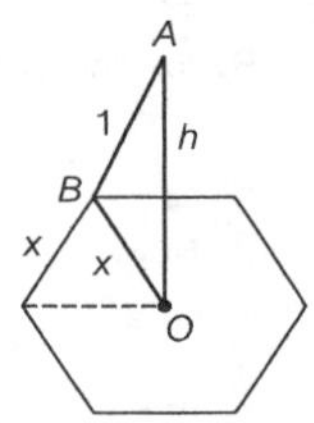

$\therefore$ In ΔAOB, $OA^2 + OB^2 = AB^2$

$\Rightarrow \quad h^2 + x^2 = 1^2$

$\Rightarrow \quad h = \sqrt{1 - x^2}$

Volume of pyramid

$= \frac{1}{3} \times$ Area of base $\times$ Height

$= \frac{1}{3} \times 6 \times \frac{\sqrt{3}}{4}x^2 \times \sqrt{1 - x^2}$

$V = \frac{\sqrt{3}}{2}x^2\sqrt{1 - x^2}$

Now, $$\frac{dV}{dx} = \frac{\sqrt{3}}{2}\left[2x\sqrt{1 - x^2} + x^2\frac{(-2x)}{2\sqrt{1 - x^2}}\right]$$

$$= \frac{\sqrt{3}}{2}\left[2x\sqrt{1 - x^2} - \frac{x^3}{\sqrt{1 - x^2}}\right]$$

$$= \frac{\sqrt{3}}{2}\left[\frac{2x(1 - x^2) - x^3}{\sqrt{1 - x^2}}\right] = \frac{\sqrt{3}}{2}\left[\frac{2x - 3x^3}{\sqrt{1 - x^2}}\right]$$

$$\Rightarrow \quad \frac{d^2V}{dx^2} = \frac{\sqrt{3}}{2}\left[\frac{\sqrt{1 - x^2}\,(2 - 9x^2) - (2x - 3x^3)\frac{(-2x)}{2\sqrt{1 - x^2}}}{(1 - x^2)}\right]$$

$$\therefore \quad \frac{d^2V}{dx^2} = \frac{\sqrt{3}}{2}\left[\frac{(1 - x^2)(2 - 9x^2) + (2x^2 - 3x^4)}{(1 - x^2)^{3/2}}\right]$$

For maxima or minima, $\frac{dV}{dx} = 0$

$\Rightarrow \quad \frac{2x - 3x^3}{\sqrt{1 - x^2}} = 0 \Rightarrow 2x - 3x^3 = 0$

$\Rightarrow \quad x(2 - 3x^2) = 0 \Rightarrow x = 0$ or $x = \pm\sqrt{2/3}$

$$\Rightarrow \quad \left(\frac{d^2V}{dx^2}\right)_{x = \sqrt{\frac{2}{3}}} = \frac{\sqrt{3}}{2}\left[\frac{\left(1 - \frac{2}{3}\right)\left(2 - 9 \times \frac{2}{3}\right) + \left[2\left(\frac{2}{3}\right) - 3\left(\frac{2}{3}\right)^2\right]}{\left(1 - \frac{2}{3}\right)^{3/2}}\right]$$

< 0

$\therefore$ Volume is maximum, when $x = \sqrt{2/3}$.

$\therefore \quad h = \sqrt{1 - x^2} = \sqrt{1 - \frac{2}{3}} = \sqrt{\frac{1}{3}} = \frac{1}{\sqrt{3}}$

7. (c) Obviously, f is increasing and g is decreasing in R.

Hence, $f[g(\alpha^2 - 2\alpha)] > f[g(3\alpha - 4)]$

$\Rightarrow$ $g(\alpha^2 - 2\alpha) > g(3\alpha - 4)$ [$\because f$ is increasing]

$\Rightarrow$ $\alpha^2 - 2\alpha < 3\alpha - 4$ [$\because g$ is decreasing]

$\Rightarrow$ $\alpha^2 - 5\alpha + 4 < 0$

$\Rightarrow$ $(\alpha - 1)(\alpha - 4) < 0$

$\therefore$ $\alpha \in (1, 4)$

8. (c) $f(x) = \dfrac{t + 3x - x^2}{x - 4}$

$$f'(x) = \frac{(x-4)(3-2x) - (t + 3x - x^2)}{(x-4)^2}$$

For maxima or minima,

$$f'(x) = 0$$

$\Rightarrow$ $-2x^2 + 11x - 12 - t - 3x + x^2 = 0$

$\Rightarrow$ $-x^2 + 8x - (12 + t) = 0$

For one M and m $D > 0$

$$64 - 4(12 + t) > 0$$

$\Rightarrow$ $16 - 12 - t > 0 \Rightarrow t < 4$

9. (c) Since, $F(x)$ is the anti-derivative of $f(x)$.

$\therefore$ $\int f(x)\,dx = F(x)$

$\Rightarrow$ $F'(x) = f(x)$ and $F''(x) = f'(x)$

Now, $F'(x) = 0 \Rightarrow f(x) = 0$

i.e. at $x = \dfrac{\pi}{2}, \pi, \dfrac{3\pi}{2}$

At $x = \dfrac{\pi}{2}$, $F'(x)$ changes sign from positive to negative.

Hence, $y = F(x)$ has maxima at $x = \dfrac{\pi}{2}$ at $x = \pi$, $F'(x)$ does not change sign.

$\Rightarrow$ Point of inflection at $x = \pi$.

At $x = \dfrac{3\pi}{2}$

$F(x)$ changes sign from negative to positive.

$\Rightarrow$ Minima at $\dfrac{3\pi}{2}$

10. (b) We have,

$$f(x) = \frac{2}{3}\sqrt{x^3} - \frac{x}{2} + \int_1^x \left(\frac{1}{2} + \frac{1}{2}\cos 2t - \sqrt{t}\right) dt$$

$$f'(x) = \frac{2}{3} \times \frac{1}{2}(x^3)^{-1/2} 3x^2 - \frac{1}{2} + \left(\frac{1}{2} + \frac{1}{2}\cos 2x - \sqrt{x}\right)$$

$$= (x^3)^{-1/2} \cdot x^2 - \frac{1}{2} + \left[\frac{1}{2}(1 + \cos 2x) - \sqrt{x}\right]$$

$$= x^{1/2} - \frac{1}{2} + \frac{1}{2}(1 + \cos 2x) - \sqrt{x}$$

$$= \frac{1}{2}\cos 2x$$

Put $f'(x) = 0$, then

$$\frac{1}{2}\cos 2x = 0$$

$\Rightarrow$ $\cos 2x = 0$

$\Rightarrow$ $2x = (2n + 1)\dfrac{\pi}{2}, n \in I$

$\Rightarrow$ $x = (2n + 1)\dfrac{\pi}{4}, n \in I$

But $x > 0$ [as $\sqrt{x}$ and $\sqrt{x^3}$ defined for $x > 0$]

$\therefore$ $x = \dfrac{\pi}{4}, \dfrac{3\pi}{4}, \dfrac{5\pi}{4}, \dfrac{7\pi}{4}$

So, there are four critical points.

11. (b) Let the speed of steamer be v m/h, then velocity of the steamer relative to the current $= (v - c)$ m/h.

If s miles is the distance covered, then the time taken to cover this distance is $t = \dfrac{s}{v - c}$ h.

Since, the petrol burnt $= kv^3$ per hour, where k is constant.

The total amount of petrol burnt for a distance of s miles

$$z = kv^3 \frac{s}{v - c}$$

$\therefore$ $$\frac{dz}{dv} = \frac{2ksv^2\left(v - \frac{3c}{2}\right)}{(v - c)^2}$$

For maximum or minimum of z, $\dfrac{dz}{dv} = 0$ or $v = \dfrac{3c}{2}$ of v is little less or little greater than $\dfrac{3c}{2}$ the sign of $\dfrac{dz}{dv}$ changes from negative to positive .

Hence, z is minimum, when $v = \dfrac{3c}{2}$ m/h.

Since, minima is the only extreme value, z is least at $v = \dfrac{3c}{2}$,

i.e. the most economical speed is $\dfrac{3c}{2}$ m/h = 1.5 cm/h

12. (d) Here, $\dfrac{x^2 + x + 2}{x^2 + 5x + 6} < 0 \Rightarrow \dfrac{\left(x + \frac{1}{2}\right)^2 + \frac{7}{4}}{(x + 2)(x + 3)} < 0$

where $\left(x + \dfrac{1}{2}\right)^2 + \dfrac{7}{4}$ is always positive.

$\therefore$ Using number line rule for $(x + 2)(x + 3)$ as shown figure, we get

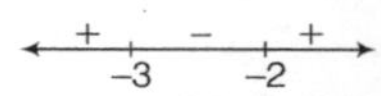

$$\frac{x^2 + x + 2}{x^2 + 5x + 6} < 0 \Rightarrow -3 < x < -2 \quad \text{...(i)}$$

Now, consider $f(x) = 1 + a^2x - x^3$, $f'(x) = a^2 - 3x^2$

$$f''(x) = -6x$$

For maximum or minimum, let $f'(x) = 0$

$\Rightarrow$ $x = \pm \dfrac{a}{\sqrt{3}}$

Let $x_1 = \dfrac{|a|}{\sqrt{3}}$ and $x_2 = -\dfrac{|a|}{\sqrt{3}}$

$\therefore$ $f''(x_1) < 0$ and $f''(x_2) > 0$

$\therefore$ $f(x)$ is maximum at $x = x_1$ and $f(x)$ is minimum at $x = x_2$,

i.e. $-3 < x_2 < -2 \Rightarrow -3 < \dfrac{-|a|}{\sqrt{3}} < -2$

$\Rightarrow$ $3\sqrt{3} > |a| > 2\sqrt{3}$

$\therefore$ $a \in (-3\sqrt{3}, -2\sqrt{3}) \cup (2\sqrt{3}, 3\sqrt{3})$

13. (b) Let $f(x) = 3\tan x + x^3 - 2 \Rightarrow f'(x) = 3\sec^2 x + 3x^2 > 0$

So, $f(x)$ is increases.

Also, $f(0) = -2$ and $f\left(\dfrac{\pi}{4}\right) > 0$

So, by Intermediate value theorem, $f(c) = 2$ for some c in $\left(0, \dfrac{\pi}{4}\right)$.

Hence, $f(x) = 0$ has only one root.

14. (d) Consider, the function $g(x) = xf(x)$

Since, $f(x)$ is continuous, $g(x)$ is also continuous in [0, 1] and differentiable in (0, 1).

As, $f(1) = 0$

$\therefore$ $g(0) = 0 = g(1)$

Hence, Rolle's theorem is applicable for $g(x)$. Therefore, there exists atleast one $c \in (0, 1)$ such that $g'(c) = 0$

$\Rightarrow$ $xf'(x) + f(x) = 0 \Rightarrow cf'(c) + f(c) = 0$

15. (c) Let x tree be added, then

$$p(x) = (x + 50)(800 - 10x)$$

Now, $p'(x) = 0$

$\Rightarrow$ $50(800 - 10x) + (x + 50)(-10) = 0$

$\therefore$ $x = 15$

16. (b) Slope of the given line $3x + 2y + 1 = 0$ is $-3/2$.

Let us locate the point on the curve at which the tangent is parallel to the given line.

On differentiating the curve both sides w.r.t. x, we get

$$6x - 8y\frac{dy}{dx} = 0 \Rightarrow \left(\frac{dy}{dx}\right)_{(x_0, y_0)} = \frac{3x_0}{4y_0} = -\frac{3}{2}$$

[$\because$ tangent is parallel to $3x + 2y = 1$]

Also, the point (x_0, y_0) ies on $3x^2 - 4y^2 = 72$

$$3x_0^2 - 4y_0^2 = 72 \Rightarrow \frac{3x_0^2}{y_0^2} - 4 = \frac{72}{y_0^2}$$

$\Rightarrow$ $3(4) - 4 = \dfrac{72}{y_0^2}$ $\left[\text{as } \dfrac{x_0}{y_0} = -2\right]$

$\Rightarrow$ $y_0^2 = 9 \Rightarrow y_0 = \pm 3$

So, the required points are $(-6, 3)$ and $(6, -3)$.

Distance of $(-6, 3)$ from the given line $= \dfrac{|-18 + 6 + 1|}{\sqrt{13}} = \dfrac{11}{\sqrt{13}}$

and distance of $(6, 3)$ from the given line.

Thus, $(-6, 3)$ is the required point $= \dfrac{|18 - 6 + 1|}{\sqrt{13}} = \sqrt{13}$

$$x_0 + y_0 = -6 + 3 = -3$$

17. (b) We have, $f(x) = x^2 \sin\left(\frac{1}{x}\right) + x^3 \cos\left(\frac{1}{2x}\right)$

Here, $f'(x) = 2x \cdot \sin\left(\frac{1}{x}\right) + x^2 \cdot \cos\left(\frac{1}{x}\right)\cdot\left(-\frac{1}{x^2}\right) + 3x^2 \cdot \cos\left(\frac{1}{2x}\right)$

$+ x^3 \cdot \left[-\sin\left(\frac{1}{2x}\right)\right]\cdot\left(-\frac{1}{2x^2}\right)$

$\Rightarrow$ $f'(x) = 2x \sin\left(\frac{1}{x}\right) - \cos\left(\frac{1}{x}\right) + 3x^2 \cdot \cos\left(\frac{1}{2x}\right) + \frac{x}{2} \cdot \sin\left(\frac{1}{2x}\right)$

$f'\left(\frac{1}{2\pi}\right)$ and $f'\left(\frac{1}{\pi}\right)$ changes sign.

$\Rightarrow f'(x) = 0$ atleast once, also $f(x)$ is continuous and differentiable in $\left[\frac{1}{3\pi}, \frac{1}{\pi}\right]$.

Also, $f\left(\frac{1}{3\pi}\right) = 0 = f\left(\frac{1}{\pi}\right)$.

[only in this interval this will be true]

So, $f(x)$ satisfies Rolle's theorem.

Hence, there exists some $c \in \left[\frac{1}{3\pi}, \frac{1}{\pi}\right]$ such that $f'(c) = 0$.

18. (b) Here, $g(x) = f(\tan^2 x - 2\tan x + 4), 0 < x < \frac{\pi}{2}$

$\Rightarrow$ $g'(x) = f'(\tan^2 x - 2\tan x + 4)(2\tan x \sec^2 x - 2\sec^2 x)$

$= f'(\tan^2 x - 2\tan x + 4)\, 2\sec^2 x(\tan x - 1)$

For $g(x)$ to be increasing $g'(x) > 0$

$\Rightarrow$ $f'(\tan^2 x - 2\tan x + 4)\, 2\sec^2 x(\tan x - 1) > 0$

$\Rightarrow$ $f'[(\tan x - 1)^2 + 3] \cdot 2\sec^2 x(\tan x - 1) > 0$ ...(i)

[as $f''(x) > 0 \Rightarrow f'(x)$ is increasing $f'[(\tan x - 1)^2 + 3] > f'(3) = 0$]

For all $x \in \left(0, \frac{\pi}{4}\right) \cup \left(\frac{\pi}{4}, \frac{\pi}{2}\right)$

Thus, equation hold for $\tan x - 1 > 0$

$\Rightarrow$ $\tan x > \phi, \forall x \in \left(\frac{\pi}{4}, \frac{\pi}{2}\right)$

19. (a) $\because$ $f'(x) = |x| - \{x\}$

$\therefore$ $f(x)$ is decreasing.

$\therefore$ $f'(x) < 0$

$|x| - \{x\} < 0$

$|x| < \{x\}$

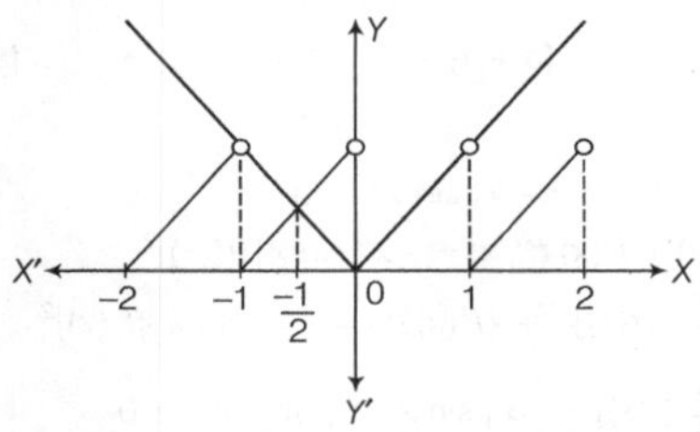

It is clear from the figure, $x \in (-1/2, 0)$.

20. (c) We know that, if $f'(x) > 0$ and $f''(x) > 0$, then graphically it can be expressed as let $x_1 < x_2$

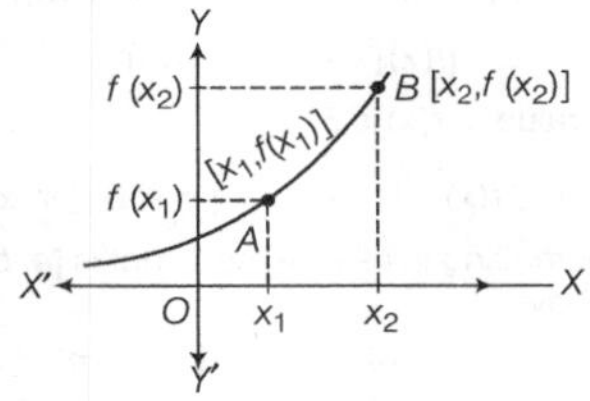

and $x_1 < \dfrac{x_1 + x_2}{2} < x_2$

and $\dfrac{f(x_1) + f(x_2)}{2}$ is the mid-point of the chord joining A and B.

Thus, it can be expressed from the figure as

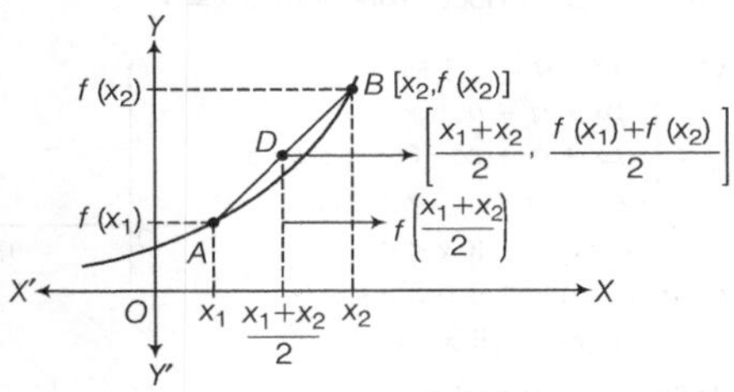

$\therefore$ $f\left(\dfrac{x_1 + x_2}{2}\right) < \dfrac{f(x_1) + f(x_2)}{2}$

21. (c) Given, $f'(\sin x) < 0, f''(\sin x) > 0, \forall x \in \left(0, \frac{\pi}{2}\right)$

$g(x) = f(\sin x) + f(\cos x)$

$\Rightarrow$ $g'(x) = f'(\sin x) \cdot \cos x + f'(\cos x)(-\sin x)$

$\Rightarrow$ $g''(x) = -f'(\sin x)\sin x + \cos^2 x\, f''(\sin x)$

$+ f''(\cos x)\sin^2 x - f'(\cos x)\cos x > 0, \forall x \in \left(0, \frac{\pi}{2}\right)$

$\left[\begin{array}{l}\text{as it is given, } f'(\sin x) = f'\left[\cos\left(\frac{\pi}{2} - x\right)\right] < 0 \\ \text{and } f''(\sin x) = f''\left[\cos\left(\frac{\pi}{2} - x\right)\right] > 0\end{array}\right]$

$\Rightarrow$ $g'(x)$ is increasing in $\left(0, \frac{\pi}{2}\right)$ and $g'\left(\frac{\pi}{4}\right) = 0$

$\Rightarrow$ $g'(x) > 0, \forall x \in \left(\frac{\pi}{4}, \frac{\pi}{2}\right)$

and $g'(x) < 0, \forall x \in \left(0, \frac{\pi}{4}\right)$

22. (a) $f'(x) = \begin{cases} 1 & , x \geq 1 \\ -3x^2, & x < 1 \end{cases}$

$f(x)$ is increasing in $[1, \infty)$ and $f(x)$ is decreasing in $(-\infty, 1)$.

$\Rightarrow f(x)$ has minimum at $x = 1$.

$\therefore \quad f(1^-) \geq f(1)$

$\Rightarrow \quad [a + 1] - 1 + 1 \geq 0 \quad \Rightarrow \quad [a] \geq -1$

$\Rightarrow \quad a \geq -1$

23. (c) $f(x) + f''(x) = -x|\sin x| \cdot f'(x)$

$f'(x) \cdot f(x) + f'(x) f''(x) = -x|\sin x| \cdot [f'(x)]^2$

$\Rightarrow \frac{1}{2} \cdot \frac{d}{dx}[\{f(x)\}^2 + \{f'(x)\}^2] = -x|\sin x| \cdot [f'(x)]^2$

$\Rightarrow \frac{1}{2} \cdot \frac{d}{dx}[f(x)] = -x|\sin x| \cdot [f'(x)]^2$, as $x \geq 0$

$\Rightarrow F'(x) < 0 \Rightarrow F(x)$ is decreasing function.

As, $x \geq 0 \Rightarrow F(x) \leq F(0)$

$\Rightarrow \quad [f(x)]^2 + [f'(x)]^2 \leq [f(0)]^2 + [f'(0)]^2$

$\Rightarrow \quad [f(x)]^2 \leq 25 - [f'(x)]^2$

$\therefore$ Maximum value of $f(x)$ is 5.

24. (d) Let $a < b$ and $f(x) = |x - a| + |x - b|, \forall x \in R$

So, $f(x)$ is decreasing in $(-\infty, a]$ constant is $[a, b]$ and increasing in $[b, \infty)$, we have

$f(0) = f(1) = f(-1) \Rightarrow \{-1, 0, 1\} \in [a, b]$

$\therefore \quad |a - b| = 2$

25. (c) As, $f(1) = 0$

$f(1^+) > 0$

$f(1^-) < 0$

Hence, there are no local extremum at $x = 1$.

26. (c) $f(x) = |px - q| + r|x|$

$= \begin{cases} -px + q - rx, & x \leq 0 \\ -px + q + rx, & 0 < x \leq q/p \\ px - q + rx, & x > q/p \end{cases}$

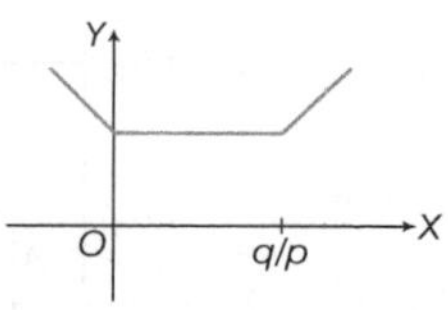

For $r = p$, $\begin{cases} f'(x) < 0, \text{ if } x \leq 0 \\ f'(x) = 0, \text{ if } 0 < x \leq q/p \\ f'(x) > 0, \text{ if } x > q/p \end{cases}$

$\therefore$ Infinite points of minimum.

If $r > p$ or $r < p$, then only one point of minimum.

$\therefore$ When $r \neq p \Rightarrow$ one point of minimum.

27. (a) $f(x) + f'''(x) = -x\,g(x) f'(x)$

Let $\quad h(x) = f^2(x) + [f'(x)]^2$

$\Rightarrow \quad h'(x) = 2f(x)f'(x) + 2f'(x)f'''(x)$

$= 2f'(x)[-x]\,g(x)f'(x) = -2x\,[f'(x)]^2 g(x)$

$\therefore x = 0$ is a point of maxima for $h(x)$.

28. (a,c,d) Here, $f(x) = (x^2 - 1)^n (x^2 + x + 1)$

has local extremum at $x = 1$

$f(1) = 0$

and $\quad f(1) < f(2 - h)$ and $f(1) < f(2 + h), \forall h > 0$

$f(2 - h) > 0$ and $f(2 + h) > 0$

$\Rightarrow \quad [(2 - h)^2 - 1]^2 [(2 - h)^2 + (2 - h) + 1] > 0$

and $\quad [(2 + h)^2 - 1]^n [(2 + h)^2 + (2 + h) + 1] > 0$

$\Rightarrow \quad (3 - h)^n (1 - h)^n [h^2 - 5h + 4] > 0$

and $\quad (h + 3)^n (h + 1)^n [h^2 + 5h + 6] > 0$

$\Rightarrow \quad (-h)^n > 0$

$\Rightarrow n$ is an even number.

29. (a,b,d) $f(x) = \begin{cases} x + 2, & x < -1 \\ x^2, & -1 \leq x < 1 \\ (x - 2)^2, & x \geq 1 \end{cases}$

At $x = -1$, LHL $= \lim_{h \to 0} f(-1 - h) = \lim_{h \to 0} (-1 - h + 2) = 1$

At $x = -1$, RHL $= \lim_{h \to 0} f(-1 + h) = \lim_{h \to 0} (-1 + h)^2 = 1$

Also, $\quad f(-1) = (-1)^2 = 1$

$\therefore f(x)$ is continuous at $x = -1$.

At $x = 1$, LHL $= \lim_{h \to 0} f(1 - h) = (1 - h)^2 = 1$

At $x = 1$, RHL $= \lim_{h \to 0} f(1 + h) = \lim_{h \to 0} (1 + h)^2 = 1$

Also, $\quad f(1) = (1 - 2)^2 = 1$

$\therefore f(x)$ is continuous at $x = 1$.

$\therefore f(x)$ is continuous for all $x \in R$.

$f'(x) = \begin{cases} 1, & x < -1 \\ 2x, & -1 \leq x < 1 \\ 2(x - 2), & x \geq 1 \end{cases}$

Clearly, $f'(x)$ changes sign at $x = -1, 0, 1, 2$.

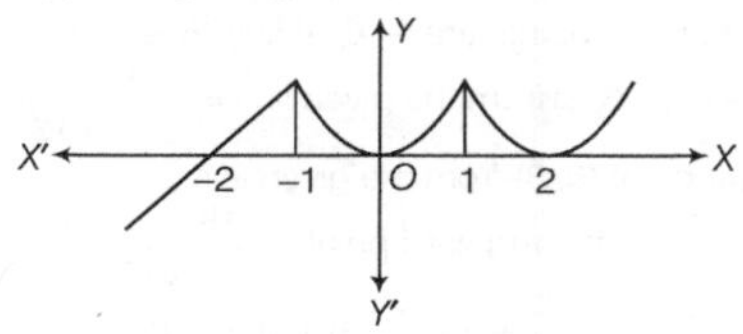

From the figure, it is clear that

$f(x)$ is not differentiable at $x = 0, -1, 1, 2$.

$\therefore f(x)$ has two local maxima and two local minima.

30. (a,c,d)

(a) Let $\quad f(x) = x - \tan^{-1} x$

$\Rightarrow \quad f'(x) = 1 - \frac{1}{1 + x^2}$

$\Rightarrow \quad f'(x) = \frac{x^2}{1 + x^2} \geq 0, \forall x \in (0, 1)$

Then, $f(x)$ is increasing function.

(as we know $x_1 \leq x_2 \Rightarrow f(x_1) \leq$ terms for increasing function)

$\therefore \quad x \geq 0, \forall x \in (0, 1)$

$\Rightarrow \quad f(x) \geq f(0), \forall x \in (0, 1)$

$\Rightarrow \quad x - \tan^{-1} x \geq 0 - \tan^{-1}(0), \forall x \in (0, 1)$

$\Rightarrow \quad x \geq \tan^{-1} x, \forall x \in (0, 1)$

(b) Let $f(x) = \cos x - 1 + \frac{x^2}{2}$

$\Rightarrow f'(x) = -\sin x + x > 0, \forall x \in (0, 1)$

$f(x)$ is increasing in $(0, 1)$.

$\therefore \quad f(x) > f(0)$

$\cos x - 1 + \frac{x^2}{2} > 0$

$\Rightarrow \quad \cos x > 1 - \frac{x^2}{2}$

(c) Let $f(x) = 1 + x \log(x + \sqrt{1 + x^2}) - \sqrt{1 + x^2}$

$\Rightarrow f'(x) = \log(x + \sqrt{x^2 + 1}) + \frac{x}{x + \sqrt{x^2 + 1}} \times \left[1 + \frac{x}{\sqrt{1 + x^2}}\right] - \frac{x}{\sqrt{1 + x^2}}$

$= \log(x + \sqrt{x^2 + 1})$

As $x + \sqrt{x^2 + 1} \geq 1$ for $x \geq 1$

$\therefore \quad \log (x + \sqrt{x^2 + 1}) \geq 0$

$\therefore \quad f'(x) \geq 0, \forall\ x \in (0, 1)$

Thus, $f(x)$ is increasing function.

Now, for $x \geq 0 \Rightarrow f(x) \geq f(0)$

$\Rightarrow \quad 1 + x \log (x + \sqrt{x^2 + 1}) - \sqrt{1 + x^2} \geq 0$

$\Rightarrow \quad 1 + x \log (x + \sqrt{x^2 + 1}) \geq \sqrt{1 + x^2}$

(d) Let $f(x) = \log (1 + x) - x^2 + \dfrac{x^2}{2}$

$\Rightarrow f'(x) = \dfrac{1}{1 + x} - 2x + x = \dfrac{1}{1 + x} - x > 0, \forall\ x \in (0, 1)$

$f(x)$ is an increasing function.

Now, $\quad x \geq 0$

$f(x) \geq f(0)$

$\Rightarrow \log(1 + x) - x^2 + \dfrac{x^2}{2} \geq 0 \Rightarrow \log(1 + x) \geq x^2 - \dfrac{x^2}{2}$

31. (a,b,c) If $f'(x) = 0$ has n real roots.

$\Rightarrow f(x) = 0$ has atmost $(n + 1)$ roots.

If $f'(x) = 0$ has 2 real roots, then.

(a) $f(x) = 0$ has 1 real root.

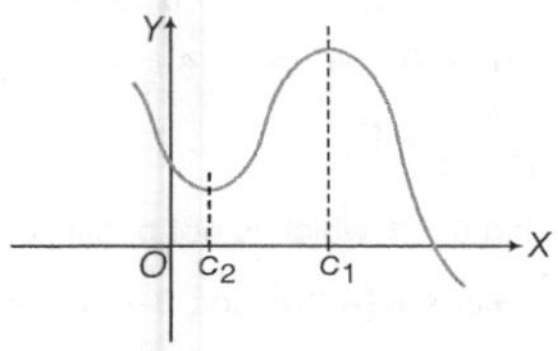

(b) $f(x) = 0$ has 2 real roots.

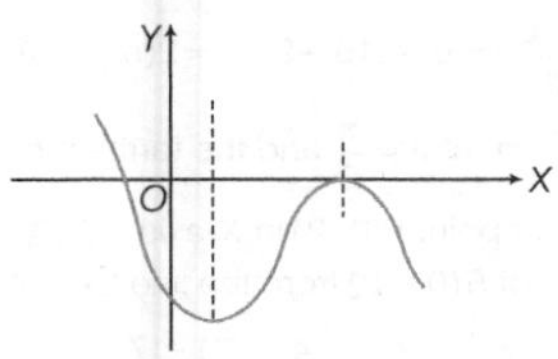

(c) $f(x) = 0$ has 3 real roots.

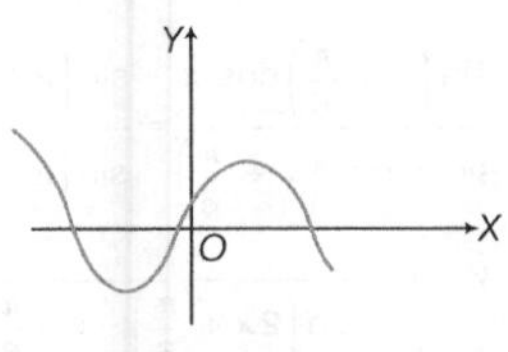

32. (a,c) Clearly, $\lim_{x \to a} [f(x)]$ is an integer and LHL and RHL should be same for existence of $\lim_{x \to a} f(x)$. Let $\lim_{x \to a} [f(x)] = n\ (n \in I)$

Clearly, LHL and RHL both should be just greater than n as $f(x)$ is continuous at $x = a$.

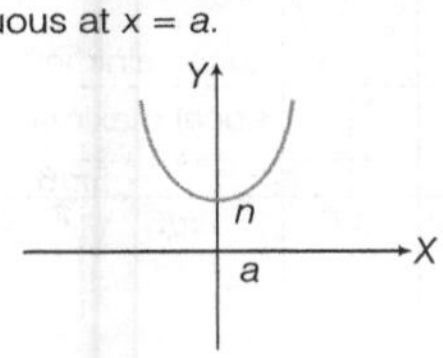

$\therefore$ $f(x)$ has local minimum at $x = a$.

33. (a,b,c)

(a) $f(x) = \begin{cases} 1, & x = 1 \\ 0, & 0 \leq x < 1 \\ x, & -1 \leq x < 0 \end{cases} \Rightarrow$ not differentiable at $x = 0$ in $(-1, 1)$

(b) $f(0) = 0$ and $\lim_{x \to 0} \dfrac{\tan x}{x} = 1 \Rightarrow$ not continuous at $x = 0$

(c) $f(x) = \begin{cases} 1, & x \notin \text{integer} \\ 0, & x \in \text{integer} \end{cases} \Rightarrow$ not continuous at $x = 0$

(d) $f(x) = \begin{cases} x - \sin x, & 0 \leq x \leq 1 \\ -x + \sin x, & -1 \leq x < 0 \end{cases} \Rightarrow$ continuous and differentiable at $x = 0$.

34. (a,b) Given, $f(x) = 1 + x \log(x + \sqrt{x^2 + 1}) - \sqrt{1 + x^2}$

$h(x) = f(x) - f^2(x) + f^3(x)$

$\Rightarrow \quad h'(x) = f'(x) - 2f(x)\,f'(x) + 3f^2(x)f'(x)$

$= f'(x)[1 - 2f(x) + 3f^2(x)]$

We know that, $1 + x\log(x + \sqrt{x^2 + 1}) - \sqrt{1 + x^2} > 0$

$\Rightarrow \quad f(x) > 0$

Now, $\quad 1 - 2f(x) + 3f^2(x) > 0, \forall\ x \in (0, \infty)$

and $\quad 1 - 2\,f(x) + 3f^2(x) < 0, \forall\ x \in (-\infty, 0)$

Hence, $h(x)$ is increasing in $(0, \infty)$ and decreasing in $(-\infty, 0)$.

35. (c,d) Given, $f(x) = a(x - x_1)(x - x_2)$

$f(x) = a(x + x_2)(x - x_2)$

$f(x) = a(x^2 - x_2^2) \quad [\because x_1 + x_2 = 0]$

$\Rightarrow \quad f'(x) = a(2x - 2x_2)$

$f'(x) = 2a(x - x_2)$

$f''(x) = 2a > 0$

$\Rightarrow f(x)$ has an extremum.

Now, $\quad f'(x) = 2a(x + x_1) \quad [\because x_1 + x_2 = 0]$

From this expression, we cannot say that

$f'(x) > 0$ or $f'(x) < 0, \forall\ x \in R$

So, $\quad f(x)$ is non-monotonic on R.

Explanations for Q. Nos. (36-38)

Here, $y = \dfrac{x^2}{x^2 - 1}$; not defined at $x = 1, -1$.

$\Rightarrow \quad \dfrac{dy}{dx} = -\dfrac{2x}{(x^2 - 1)^2}$

$\Rightarrow \quad \dfrac{dy}{dx} = 0 \Rightarrow x = 0 \quad$ [point of maxima]

As, $x \to 1^+, y \to \infty, x \to 1^-, y \to -\infty$

Similarly, $x \to -1^+, y \to -\infty, x \to -1^-, y \to \infty$

Then, the graph of $y = \dfrac{x^2}{x^2 - 1}$ is shown as

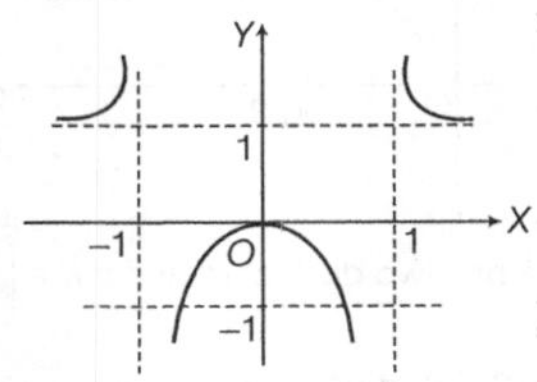

36. (b)

37. (d)

38. (a)

Explanations for Q. Nos. (39-41)

We have, $f(x) = x^2e^{-|x|} = \begin{cases} x^2e^{-x}, & x \geq 0 \\ x^2e^{x}, & x < 0 \end{cases}$

$\Rightarrow \quad f'(x) = \begin{cases} x \cdot e^{-x} \cdot (2 - x), & x \geq 0 \\ x \cdot e^{x} \cdot (x + 2), & x < 0 \end{cases}$

$f(x)$ is increasing in $(-\infty, -2) \cup (0, 2)$ and $f(x)$ is decreasing in $(-2, 0) \cup (2, \infty)$.

Now, $\lim\limits_{x \to +\infty} f(x) = 0$ and $\lim\limits_{x \to \pm 2} f(x) = \dfrac{4}{e^2}$, $f(0) = 0$

$\therefore$ Graph of $f(x)$ will be as shown in the figure given below

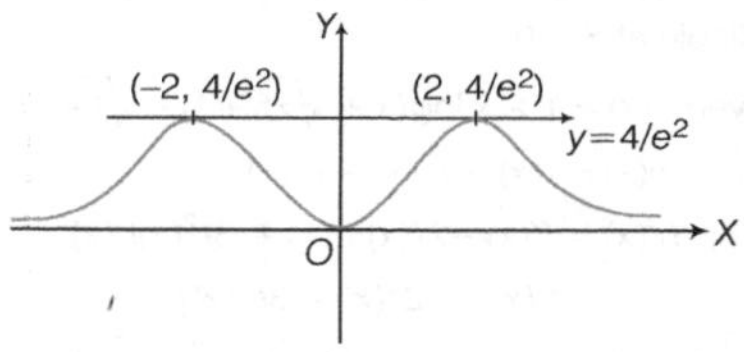

$y = kx^2$ will intersect $y = e^{|x|}$,

then, $kx^2 = e^{|x|} \Rightarrow x^2e^{-|x|} = \dfrac{1}{k}$

So, $y = x^2e^{-|x|}$ will be cut by line $y = \dfrac{1}{k}$

At exactly two points, if $\dfrac{1}{k} = \dfrac{4}{e^2}$

$\Rightarrow \quad k = \dfrac{e^2}{4}$

$\therefore$ Area $= 2\int_0^2 x^2e^{-x}dx$

$= 2\left\{[-x^2e^{-x}]_0^2 + \int_0^2 2xe^{-x}dx\right\}$

$= 2\left\{-\dfrac{4}{e^2} + 2[-xe^{-x}]_0^2 - 2[e^{-x}]_0^2\right\} = 2\left(2 - \dfrac{10}{e^2}\right)$

From the above figure

$$\text{Range} = \left[0, \frac{4}{e^2}\right]$$

39. (c) **40.** (a) **41.** (b)

Explanations for Q. Nos. (42-44)

We have, $f(x) = x \cdot 2^{-x}$

$\therefore \quad f'(x) = 2^{-x}(1 - x\log 2)$

and $f''(x) = 2^{-x}\log 2\,(x\log 2 - 2)$.

Clearly, $f(x)$ is increasing in $\left(-\infty, \dfrac{1}{\log 2}\right)$ and decreasing in $\left(\dfrac{1}{\log 2}, \infty\right)$.

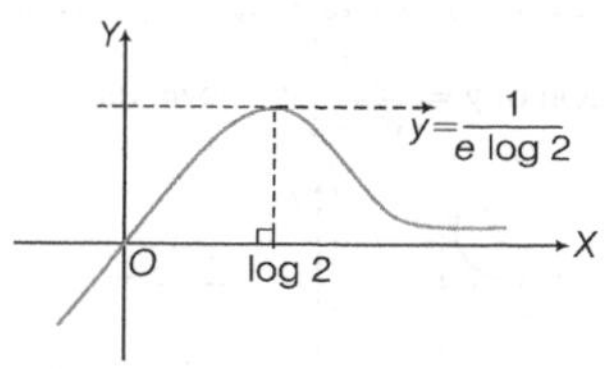

Clearly, $f(x) = k$ has two distinct roots for $k \in \left(0, \dfrac{1}{e\log 2}\right)$.

Given, $f(x) = x \cdot 2^{-x}$ and $g(x) = \max\{f(t) : x \leq t \leq x + 1\}$

As, $f(x)$ is increasing in $\left(-\infty, \dfrac{1}{\log 2}\right)$, hence the maximum value of $g(x)$ occurs at $t = x + 1$.

$\therefore \quad g(x) = f(x + 1) = (x + 1) \cdot 2^{-(x+1)}$

42. (d) **43.** (b) **44.** (d)

45. (3) The equation of the given curve can be expressed as shown in the figure given below

$$\frac{x^2}{\alpha^2} + \frac{y^2}{4} = 1, \text{ where } 4 < \alpha^2 < 8$$

which is equation of the ellipse.

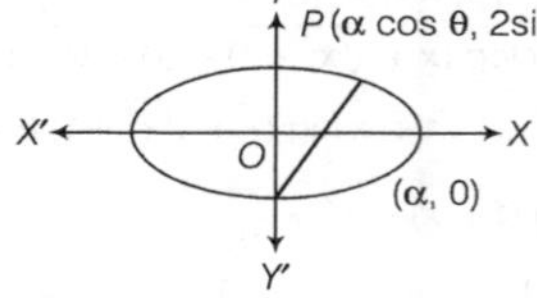

Let us consider a point $P(\alpha\cos\theta, 2\sin\theta)$ on the ellipse.

Let the distance of $P(\alpha\cos\theta, 2\sin\theta)$ from $(0, -2)$ is L, then

$$L^2 = (\alpha\cos\theta - 0)^2 + (2\sin\theta + 2)^2$$

$\therefore \quad \dfrac{dL^2}{d\theta} = \cos\theta\,[-2\alpha^2\sin\theta + 8\sin\theta + 8]$

Now, $\dfrac{dL^2}{d\theta} = 0$

$\Rightarrow \quad \cos\theta\,[-2\alpha^2\sin\theta + 8\sin\theta + 8] = 0$

Either $\cos\theta = 0$ or $(8 - 2\alpha^2)\sin\theta + 8 = 0$

$\Rightarrow \quad \theta = \dfrac{\pi}{2}$ or $\sin\theta = \dfrac{4}{\alpha^2 - 4}$

Since, $\alpha^2 < 8 \Rightarrow a^2 - 4 < 4$

$\Rightarrow \quad \dfrac{4}{\alpha^2 - 4} > 1$

$\therefore \quad \sin\theta > 1$, which is not possible.

Further, $\dfrac{d^2L^2}{d\theta^2} = \cos\theta\,[-2\alpha^2\cos\theta + 8\cos\theta]$

$+ (-\sin\theta)\,[-2\alpha^2\sin\theta + 8\sin\theta + 8]$

At $\theta = \dfrac{\pi}{2}$, $\dfrac{d^2L^2}{d\theta^2} = 0 - (16 - 2\alpha^2) = 2(\alpha^2 - 8) < 0$ [as $\alpha^2 < 8$]

So, L is maximum at $\theta = \dfrac{\pi}{2}$ and the farthest point is $(0, 2)$.

The reflection of point $P(0, 2)$ in X-axis is $R(0, -2)$.

Now, distance of $R(0, -2)$ from the line $3x - 4y + 7 = 0$,

$$D = \left|\frac{3 \times 0 - 4(-2) + 7}{\sqrt{(3)^2 + (-4)^2}}\right| = \left|\frac{15}{5}\right| = 3$$

46. (3) Here, $y = \dfrac{2\sin\left(x + \dfrac{\pi}{6}\right)\cos x}{2\sin x \cdot \cos\left(x + \dfrac{\pi}{6}\right)} = \dfrac{\sin\left(2x + \dfrac{\pi}{6}\right) + \sin\dfrac{\pi}{6}}{\sin\left(2x + \dfrac{\pi}{6}\right) - \sin\dfrac{\pi}{6}}$

$\therefore \quad y = 1 + \dfrac{1}{\sin\left(2x + \dfrac{\pi}{6}\right) - \sin\dfrac{\pi}{6}}$

y is minimum, if $2x + \dfrac{\pi}{6} = \dfrac{\pi}{2}$.

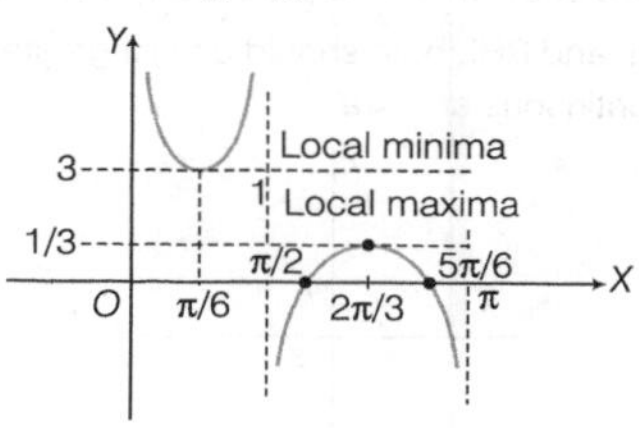

$\therefore \quad x = \dfrac{\pi}{6}$

$\Rightarrow \quad y_{\min} = 1 + 2 = 3$

47. (2) Minimum distance is the distance along the common normal to both the curves i.e. $y = x$ must be parallel to the tangent as both the curves are inverse of each other.

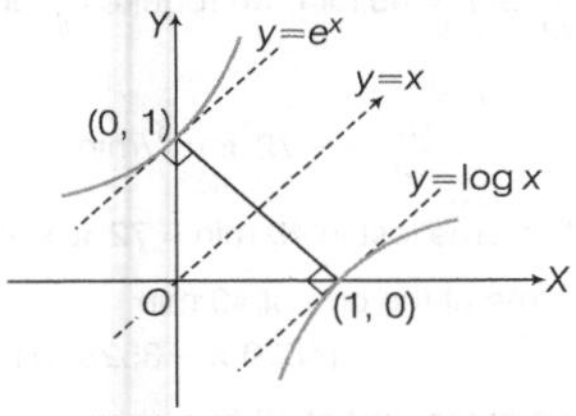

$$\left(\frac{dy}{dx}\right)_{x_1} = e^{x_1} = 1 \Rightarrow x_1 = 0 \text{ and } y_1 = 1$$

$\therefore \quad AB = \sqrt{2} = \sqrt{k}$

$\Rightarrow \quad k = 2$

48. (5) Let the corner A of leaf $ABCD$ be folded over to A which is the inner edge BC of the page.

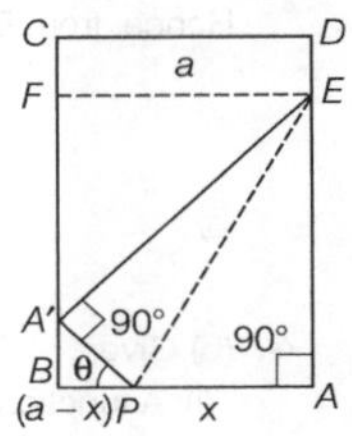

Let $AP = x$, then $\quad AB = a$

$\therefore \quad BP = a - x$

If $\angle A'PB = \theta$ B_{a-x}, then

$\angle EA'F = \theta$

Since, EF is parallel to AB, then $EF = a$

In $\Delta A'BP$, $\cos\theta = \dfrac{BP}{PA'} \Rightarrow \dfrac{a-x}{x}$

In $\Delta A'FE$, $A'E = EF \operatorname{cosec}\theta = \dfrac{a}{\sqrt{1-\cos^2\theta}}$

$$= \frac{a}{\sqrt{1-\left(\dfrac{a-x}{x}\right)^2}} = \frac{ax}{\sqrt{x^2-(a-x)^2}} = \frac{ax}{\sqrt{2ax-a^2}} = AE$$

Now, ΔAPE is folded to $A'PE$ = Area of folded part

$= \text{Area of } \Delta PAE = \dfrac{1}{2} AP \cdot AE$

$= \dfrac{1}{2} x \dfrac{ax}{\sqrt{2ax-a^2}} = A$ [say]

$$\therefore \quad A^2 = \frac{a^2x^4}{4(2ax-a^2)} = \frac{a^2/4}{\left(\dfrac{2a}{x^3}-\dfrac{a^2}{x^4}\right)} = \frac{a^2/4}{y}$$

where, $y = \dfrac{2a}{x^3} - \dfrac{a^2}{x^4}$; $0 < x < a$

Obviously, A^2 ($1 \in A$) is minimum, when y is maximum.

Then, $\quad y = \dfrac{2a}{x^3} - \dfrac{a^2}{x^4} \Rightarrow \dfrac{dy}{dx} = -\dfrac{6a}{x^4} + \dfrac{4a^2}{x^5}$

and $\quad \dfrac{d^2y}{dx^2} = \dfrac{24a}{x^5} - \dfrac{20a^2}{x^6}$

For maxima or minima of y,

$$\frac{dy}{dx} = -\frac{6a}{x^4} + \frac{4a^2}{x^5} = 0$$

$\Rightarrow \quad x = 2a/3$

When $x = \dfrac{2a}{3}$, then $\dfrac{d^2y}{dx^2} = \dfrac{4a}{x^5}\left(6 - \dfrac{5a}{x}\right)$

$= 4a(3/2a)^5\left(6 - 5a\dfrac{3}{2a}\right)$

$= -4a\,(3/2a)^5 \cdot \dfrac{3}{2} < 0$

$\Rightarrow y$ is maximum i.e. A is minimum when $x = \dfrac{2a}{3}$, which is the only critical point (least),

So, the folded area is least, when $\dfrac{2}{3}$ of the width of the page in folded over.

$\Rightarrow \quad \dfrac{p}{q} = \dfrac{2}{3}$

$\therefore \quad p + q = 5$

49. (2) $f(x) = \dfrac{1}{x^2-4}$ is shown as below

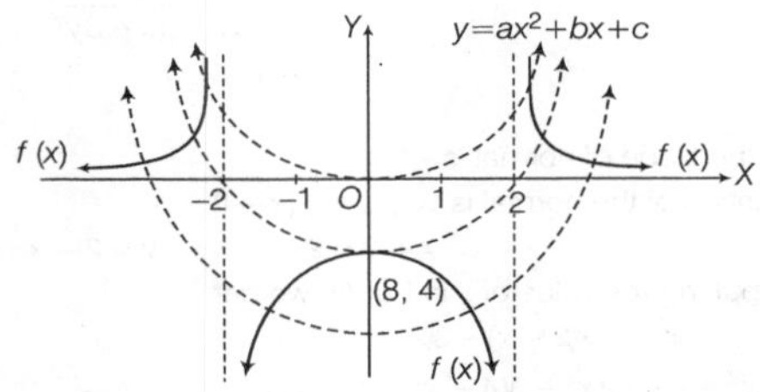

From the above figure, the minimum number of point of intersection is 2.

50. (6) We have, $\quad f(x) = \sqrt{16-(x-4)^2} - \sqrt{1-(x-7)^2}$

Now, consider $\quad y = \sqrt{16-(x-4)^2}$

$\Rightarrow \quad (x-4)^2 + y^2 = 16,\ y > 0$

is a semi-circle with centre (4, 0) and radius 4.

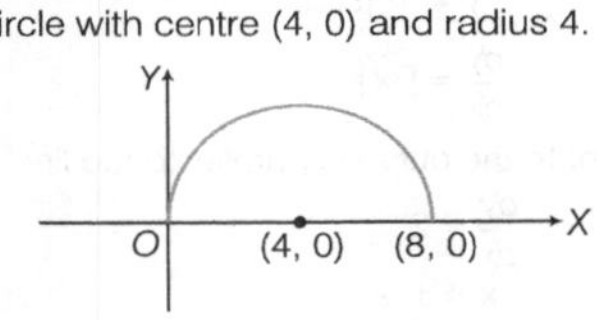

Similarly, $\quad y = \sqrt{1-(x-7)^2}$

$\Rightarrow \quad (x-7)^2 + y^2 = 1,\ y > 0$

is a semi-circle with centre (7, 0) and radius 1.

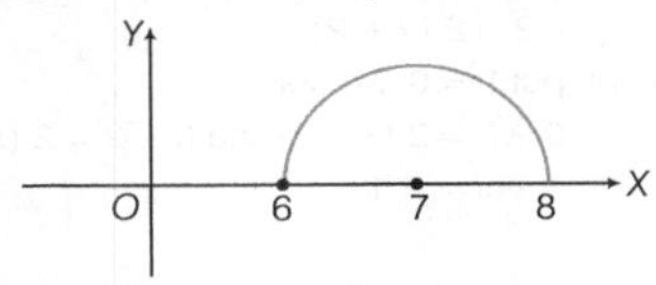

On combining the above two figures, we have

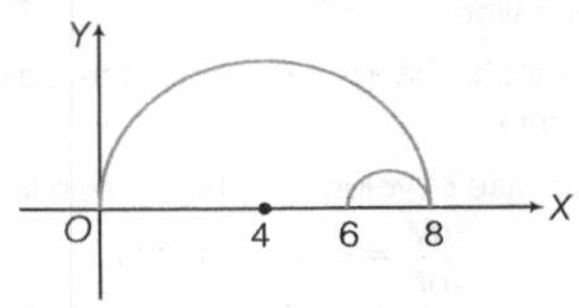

$[f(x)]_{\max}$ = Maximum vertical distance between the two curves which occurs when $x = 6$.

$\therefore \quad [f(x)]_{\max} = \sqrt{16-(6-4)^2} - 0$

$= \sqrt{12} = \sqrt{k}$

$\therefore \quad k = 12 = 2^2 \times 3^1$

So, the number of divisors is 6.

JEE Main & AIEEE Archive

1. (d) Given, $x^2 + 2xy - 3y^2 = 0$ ...(i)

On differentiating. Eq (i) w.r.t. x, we get

$$2x + 2\left(x\frac{dy}{dx} + y\right) - 6y\frac{dy}{dx} = 0$$

$$\Rightarrow \quad 2x + 2x\frac{dy}{dx} + 2y - 6y\frac{dy}{dx} = 0$$

$$\Rightarrow \quad (2x - 6y)\frac{dy}{dx} + (2x + 2y) = 0$$

$$\Rightarrow \quad \frac{dy}{dx} = \frac{-(x+y)}{(x-3y)}$$

$$\therefore \quad \left(\frac{dy}{dx}\right)_{(1,1)} = 1$$

So, the slope of normal is -1.

Equation of the normal is $y - 1 = -(x-1)$

$$x + y = 2 \quad \Rightarrow \quad y = 2 - x$$

On putting the value of y in Eq. (i), we get

$\Rightarrow \quad x^2 + 2x(2-x) - 3(2-x)^2 = 0$

$\Rightarrow x^2 + 4x - 2x^2 - 3(4 + x^2 - 4x) = 0$

$\Rightarrow x^2 + 4x - 2x^2 - 12 - 3x^2 + 12x = 0$

$\Rightarrow \quad -4x^2 + 16x - 12 = 0$

$\Rightarrow \quad x^2 - 4x + 3 = 0$

$\Rightarrow \quad (x-1)(x-3) = 0 \Rightarrow x = 1, 3$

So, $x = 1, y = 1$ or $x = 3, y = -1$

2. (a) Given, $\quad y = \int_0^x |t|\, dt$

$\therefore \quad \frac{dy}{dx} = |x|$

Since, tangent to the curve is parallel to the line $y = 2x$.

$\Rightarrow \quad \frac{dy}{dx} = 2$

$\therefore \quad x = \pm 2$

Now, points, $\quad y = \int_0^{\pm 2} |t|\, dt = \pm 2$

Equation of tangents are

$$y - 2 = 2(x-2)$$

and $\quad y + 2 = 2(x+2)$

For x-intercept, put $y = 0$, we get

$$0 - 2 = 2(x-2) \text{ and } 0 + 2 = 2(x+2)$$

$\therefore \quad x = \pm 1$

3. (c) **Given**

(i) Volume ($V = 4500\,\pi\ m^3/\text{min}$) of the helium gas filled in a spherical balloon.

(ii) Due to a leak, the gas escapes the balloon at the rate of $72\,\pi\ m^3/\text{min}$.

$\therefore$ Rate of decrease of volume of the balloon is

$$\frac{dV}{dt} = -72\,\pi\ m^3/\text{min}$$

To find The rate of decrease of the radius of the balloon 49 min after the leakage started.

i.e. $\quad \frac{dr}{dt}$ at $t = 49$ min

[assuming that the leakage started at time $t = 0$]

Now, the balloon is in spherical shape, hence the volume of the balloon is $V = \frac{4}{3}\pi r^3$.

On differentiating both sides w.r.t. t, we get

$$\frac{dV}{dt} = \frac{4}{3}\pi\left(3r^2 \times \frac{dr}{dt}\right)$$

$$\Rightarrow \quad \frac{dr}{dt} = \frac{dV/dt}{4\pi r^2} \quad \text{...(i)}$$

Now, to find $\frac{dr}{dt}$ at $t = 49$ min, we require $\frac{dV}{dt}$ and the radius (r) at that stage,

$$\frac{dV}{dt} = -72\,\pi\ m^3/\text{min}$$

$\therefore$ Amount of volume lost in 49 min $= 72\,\pi \times 49\ m^3$

Now, final volume at the end of 49 min

$$= (4500\,\pi - 3528\,\pi)\ m^3 = 972\,\pi\ m^3$$

If r is the radius at the end of 49 min, then

$$\frac{4}{3}\pi r^3 = 972\pi$$

$$\Rightarrow \quad r^3 = 729 \Rightarrow r = 9$$

$\therefore$ Radius of the balloon at the end of 49 min = 9 m

Hence, from Eq. (i), we get

$$\frac{dr}{dt} = \frac{dV/dt}{4\pi r^2}$$

$$\Rightarrow \quad \left(\frac{dr}{dt}\right)_{t=49} = \frac{(dV/dt)_{t=49}}{4\pi(r^2)_{t=49}} = \frac{72\pi}{4\pi(9^2)} = \frac{2}{9}\ \text{m/min}$$

4. (b) Given,

(i) A function f, such that

$f(x) = \log|x| + bx^2 + ax, x \neq 0$

(ii) The function f has extrema at $x = -1$ and $x = 2$, i.e. $f'(-1) = f'(2) = 0$ and $f''(-1) \neq 0 \neq f''(2)$.

Now, given function f is

$$f(x) = \log|x| + bx^2 + ax$$

$$\Rightarrow \quad f'(x) = \frac{1}{x} + 2bx + a$$

$$\Rightarrow \quad f''(x) = \frac{-1}{x^2} + 2b$$

Since, f has extrema at $x = -1$ and $x = 2$.

Hence, $\quad f'(-1) = 0 = f'(2)$

$\quad f'(-1) = 0$

$\Rightarrow \quad a - 2b = 1$ ...(i)

and $\quad f'(2) = 0$

$\Rightarrow \quad a + 4b = \frac{-1}{2}$ ...(ii)

On solving Eqs. (i) and (ii), we get

$$a = \frac{1}{2} \text{ and } b = \frac{-1}{4}$$

$$\Rightarrow \quad f''(x) = \frac{-1}{x^2} + \frac{-1}{2} = -\left(\frac{x^2+2}{2x^2}\right)$$

$\Rightarrow \quad f''(-1) < 0$ and $f''(2) < 0$

Therefore, f has local maxima at both $x = -1$ and $x = 2$.

Hence, Statement I is correct.

Also, while solving for Statement I, we found the values of a and b, which justify that Statement II is also correct.

However, Statement II does not explain Statement I in any way.

5. (c) Here, $f(x) = \int_0^x \sqrt{t}\sin t\, dt$, where $x \in \left(0, \frac{5\pi}{2}\right)$

$\therefore \quad f'(x) = \{\sqrt{x}\sin x - 0\}$ ...(i)

[using Newton-Leibnitz's formula]

Now, $\quad f'(x) = \sqrt{x}\sin x = 0$

$\Rightarrow \quad \sin x = 0$

$\therefore \quad x = \pi, 2\pi$

Now, $f''(x) = \sqrt{x}\cos x + \dfrac{1}{2\sqrt{x}}\sin x$

and $f''(\pi) = -\sqrt{\pi} < 0$

So, $f(x)$ has local maximum at $x = \pi$.

and $f''(2\pi) = \sqrt{\pi} > 0$

So, $f(x)$ has local minimum at $x = 2\pi$.

6. (b) $f(x) = \begin{cases} \dfrac{\tan x}{x}, & x \neq 0 \\ 1, & x = 0 \end{cases}$

As $\dfrac{\tan x}{x} > 1, \forall\ x \neq 0$

$\therefore$ $f(0 + h) > f(0)$

and $f(0 - h) > f(0)$

At $x = 0$, $f(x)$ attains minima.

$$\therefore\quad f'(0) = \lim_{h \to 0} \frac{f(h) - f(0)}{h} = \lim_{h \to 0} \frac{\frac{\tan h}{h} - 1}{h}$$

$$= \lim_{h \to 0} \frac{\tan h - h}{h^2}$$

$$= \lim_{h \to 0} \frac{\sec^2 h - 1}{2h} \quad \text{[using L' Hospital's rule]}$$

$$= \lim_{h \to 0} \frac{\tan^2 h}{2h^2} \cdot h \quad [\because \tan^2\theta = \sec^2\theta - 1]$$

$$= \frac{1}{2} \cdot 0 = 0 \quad \left[\because \lim_{\theta \to 0} \frac{\tan\theta}{\theta} = 1\right]$$

So, Statement II is correct.

Hence, both statements are correct but Statement II is not the correct explanation of Statement I.

7. (d) We have, $y = x + \dfrac{4}{x^2}$

On differentiating w.r.t. x, we get

$$\frac{dy}{dx} = 1 - \frac{8}{x^3}$$

Since, the tangent is parallel to X-axis, therefore

$$\frac{dy}{dx} = 0 \Rightarrow x^3 = 8$$

$\Rightarrow$ $x = 2$ and $y = 3$

8. (d)

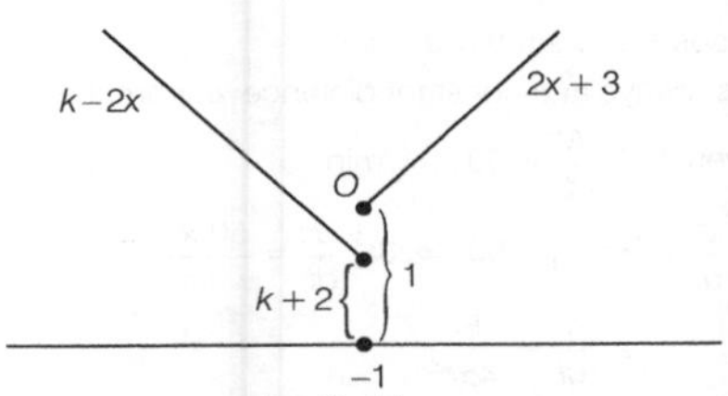

$\because$ $k + 2 \leq 1$

$\therefore$ $k \leq -1$

9. (b) Given, $P(x) = x^4 + ax^3 + bx^2 + cx + d$

$\Rightarrow$ $P'(x) = 4x^3 + 3ax^2 + 2bx + c$

Since, $x = 0$ is a solution for $P'(x) = 0$, then

$$c = 0$$

$\therefore$ $P(x) = x^4 + ax^3 + bx^2 + d$ ...(i)

Also, we have $P(-1) < P(1)$

$\Rightarrow$ $1 - a + b + d < 1 + a + b + d$

$\Rightarrow$ $a > 0$

Since, $P'(x) = 0$, only when $x = 0$ and $P(x)$ is differentiable in $(-1, 1)$, we should have the maximum and minimum at the points $x = -1, 0$ and 1.

Also, we have $P(-1) < P(1)$

$\therefore$ Maximum of $P(x) = \text{Max}\{P(0), P(1)\}$

and minimum of $P(x) = \text{Min}\{P(-1), P(0)\}$

In the interval $[0, 1]$,

$$P'(x) = 4x^3 + 3ax^2 + 2bx$$

$$= x(4x^2 + 3ax + 2b)$$

Since, $P'(x)$ has only one root $x = 0$, then $4x^2 + 3ax + 2b = 0$ has no real roots.

$\therefore$ $(3a)^2 - 32b < 0 \Rightarrow \dfrac{3a^2}{32} < b$

$\therefore$ $b > 0$

Thus, we have $a > 0$ and $b > 0$.

$\therefore$ $P'(x) = 4x^3 + 3ax^2 + 2bx > 0, \forall\ x \in (0, 1)$

Hence, $P(x)$ is increasing in $[0, 1]$.

$\therefore$ Maximum of $P(x) = P(1)$

Similarly, $P(x)$ is decreasing in $[-1, 0]$.

Therefore, minimum $P(x)$ does not occur at $x = -1$.

10. (c) Let $f(x) = x^7 + 14x^5 + 16x^3 + 30x - 560$

$\therefore$ $f'(x) = 7x^6 + 70x^4 + 48x^2 + 30 > 0, \forall\ x \in R$

So, $f(x)$ is increasing.

Hence, $f(x) = 0$ has only one solution.

11. (b) Let $f(x) = x^3 - px + q$

Then, $f'(x) = 3x^2 - p$

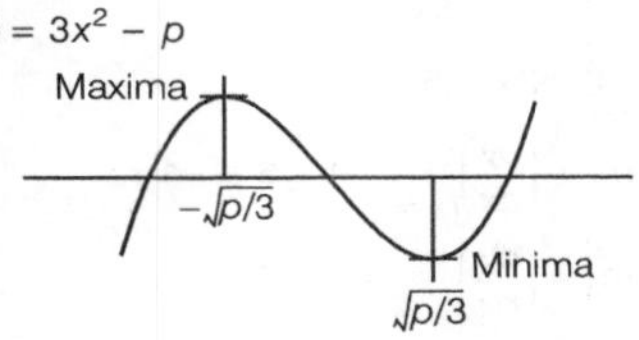

Put $f'(x) = 0$, then $x = \sqrt{\dfrac{p}{3}}, -\sqrt{\dfrac{p}{3}}$

Now, $f''(x) = 6x$

At $x = \sqrt{\dfrac{p}{3}}$, $f''(x) = 6\sqrt{\dfrac{p}{3}} > 0$ [minima]

and at $x = -\sqrt{\dfrac{p}{3}}$, $f''(x) < 0$ [maxima]

12. (a) Using Mean value theorem,

$$f'(c) = \frac{f(3) - f(1)}{3 - 1} \quad \left[\because f'(c) = \frac{f(b) - f(a)}{b - a}\right]$$

$$\Rightarrow \quad \frac{1}{c} = \frac{\log_e 3 - \log_e 1}{2}$$

$$\therefore \quad c = \frac{2}{\log_e 3} = 2\log_3 e$$

13. (d) Let the equation of normal be

$$Y - y = -\frac{dx}{dy}(X - x)$$

It meets the X-axis at G. Therefore, coordinates of G are $\left(x + y\dfrac{dy}{dx}, 0\right)$.

According to given condition,

$$x + y\frac{dy}{dx} = 2x$$

$$\Rightarrow \quad y\frac{dy}{dx} = x \Rightarrow y\,dy = x\,dx$$

On integrating both side, we get

$$\frac{y^2}{2} = \frac{x^2}{2} + C \Rightarrow x^2 - y^2 = -2C$$

which shows a hyperbola.

14. (c) $\because f(x) = \min\{x+1, |x|+1\}$

$f(x) = x + 1, \forall x \in R$

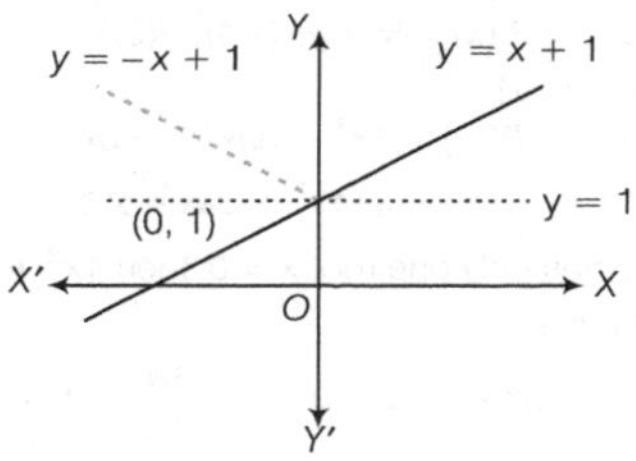

It is clear from the figure that, $f(x)$ is differentiable everywhere.

15. (b) Since, $f(x) = \tan^{-1}(\sin x + \cos x)$

On differentiating w.r.t. x, we get

$$f'(x) = \frac{1}{1+(\sin x + \cos x)^2}(\cos x - \sin x)$$

$$= \frac{\sqrt{2}\left\{\cos x \cdot \cos\frac{\pi}{4} - \sin x \cdot \sin\frac{\pi}{4}\right\}}{1+(\sin x + \cos x)^2} = \frac{\sqrt{2}\cos\left(x+\frac{\pi}{4}\right)}{1+(\sin x+\cos x)^2}$$

For $f(x)$ to be increasing,

$$-\frac{\pi}{2} < x + \frac{\pi}{4} < \frac{\pi}{2} \Rightarrow \frac{-3\pi}{4} < x < \frac{\pi}{4}$$

Hence, option (b) lies in the above interval.

16. (a) $\because \quad y = x^2 - 5x + 6$

$\therefore \quad \frac{dy}{dx} = 2x - 5$

Now, $\quad m_1 = \left(\frac{dy}{dx}\right)_{(2,\,0)} = 4 - 5 = -1$

and $\quad m_2 = \left(\frac{dy}{dx}\right)_{(3,\,0)} = 6 - 5 = 1$

Now, $\quad m_1 m_2 = -1 \times 1 = -1$

Hence, angle between the tangents is $\frac{\pi}{2}$.

17. (d) $\because \quad f(x) = \frac{x}{2} + \frac{2}{x}$

$\therefore \quad f'(x) = \frac{1}{2} - \frac{2}{x^2}$

For maxima or minima, put $f'(x) = 0$

$\therefore \quad \frac{1}{2} - \frac{2}{x^2} = 0 \Rightarrow x^2 = 4$

$\Rightarrow \quad x = \pm 2$

Now, $\quad f''(x) = \frac{4}{x^3}$

$\Rightarrow \quad f''(2) = \frac{4}{8} = \frac{1}{2} > 0$ [minima]

and $\quad f''(-2) = -\frac{4}{8} = -\frac{1}{2} < 0$ [maxima]

Hence, $f(x)$ is minimum at $x = 2$.

18. (a) Let $f(x) = \frac{3x^2 + 9x + 17}{3x^2 + 9x + 7} = 1 + \frac{10}{3\left(x^2 + 3x + \frac{7}{3}\right)}$ [by division algorithm]

$$= 1 + \frac{10}{3\left[\left(x+\frac{3}{2}\right)^2 + \frac{1}{12}\right]}$$

Hence, $f(x)$ will be maximum at $x = -\frac{3}{2}$.

So, the maximum value of $f(x) = 1 + \frac{10}{3\left(\frac{1}{12}\right)} = 1 + 40 = 41$

19. (b) Let $\quad f(x) = x^3 + 6x^2 + 6$

On differentiating w.r.t. x, we get

$$f'(x) = 3x^2 + 12x = 3x(x+4)$$

For $f(x)$ to be increasing, $f'(x) > 0$

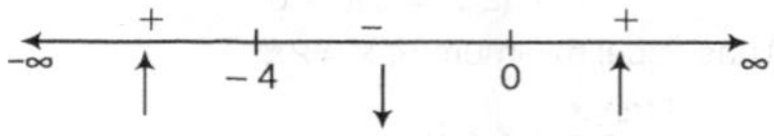

$\Rightarrow \quad x \in (-\infty, -4) \cup (0, \infty)$

Let $\quad f(x) = 3x^2 - 2x + 1$

$\therefore \quad f'(x) = 6x - 2$

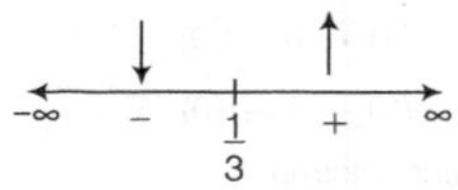

$\Rightarrow \quad f'(x) > 0, \ \forall \ x \in \left(\frac{1}{3}, \infty\right)$

Since, this is wrong.

20. (a) Given that, $x = a(\cos\theta + \theta\sin\theta)$

and $\quad y = a(\sin\theta - \theta\cos\theta)$

On differentiating w.r.t. θ respectively, we get

$$\frac{dx}{d\theta} = a(-\sin\theta + \sin\theta + \theta\cos\theta)$$

$\Rightarrow \quad \frac{dx}{d\theta} = a\theta\cos\theta$ ...(i)

and $\quad \frac{dy}{d\theta} = a(\cos\theta - \cos\theta + \theta\sin\theta)$

$\Rightarrow \quad \frac{dy}{d\theta} = a\theta\sin\theta$ ...(ii)

On dividing Eq. (ii) by Eq. (i), we get

$$\frac{dy}{dx} = \tan\theta$$

Since, slope of normal $= -\frac{dx}{dy} = -\cot\theta$

So, the equation of normal is

$$y - a\sin\theta + a\theta\cos\theta = -\frac{\cos\theta}{\sin\theta}(x - a\cos\theta - a\theta\sin\theta)$$

$\Rightarrow y\sin\theta - a\sin^2\theta + a\theta\cos\theta\sin\theta$

$= -x\cos\theta + a\cos^2\theta + a\theta\sin\theta\cos\theta$

$\Rightarrow \quad x\cos\theta + y\sin\theta = a$

So, it is always at a constant distance 'a' from the origin.

21. (c) Given that, $\frac{dV}{dt} = 50\ \text{cm}^3/\text{min}$

$\therefore \quad \frac{d}{dt}\left(\frac{4}{3}\pi r^3\right) = 50 \Rightarrow 3r^2\frac{dr}{dt} = \frac{50 \times 3}{4\pi}$

$\Rightarrow \quad \frac{dr}{dt} = \frac{50}{4\pi r^2}$

$\therefore \quad \left(\frac{dr}{dt}\right)_{r=15} = \frac{50}{4\pi \times 225} = \frac{1}{18\pi}$ cm/min

22. (b) Let lizard catch the insect C and distance covered by insect be S.

Then, time taken by insect, $t = \frac{S}{20}$ ...(i)

and distance covered by lizard $= 21 + S$

$\Rightarrow \quad 21 + S = \frac{1}{2}(2)\cdot t^2$ ...(ii)

$\left[\because S = ut + \frac{1}{2}at^2;\ \text{here}\ u = 0, a = 2\ \text{cm/s}^2\ \text{and}\ S = 20t\right]$

$\Rightarrow \quad 21 + 20t = t^2$ [from Eq. (i)]

$\Rightarrow \quad t^2 - 20t - 21 = 0$

$\Rightarrow \quad t^2 - 21t + t - 21 = 0$

$\Rightarrow \quad t(t-21)+1(t-21)=0$

$\Rightarrow \quad (t+1)(t-21)=0$

$\Rightarrow \quad t=-1, 21$

$\therefore \quad t=21\,s \quad$ [neglecting $t=-1$]

23. (d) Given that,

$$u=\sqrt{a^2\cos^2\theta+b^2\sin^2\theta}+\sqrt{a^2\sin^2\theta+b^2\cos^2\theta}$$

$$\therefore \quad u^2=a^2\cos^2\theta+b^2\sin^2\theta+a^2\sin^2\theta$$

$$+b^2\cos^2\theta+2\sqrt{(a^2\cos^2\theta+b^2\sin^2\theta)}$$

$$\times\sqrt{(a^2\sin^2\theta+b^2\cos^2\theta)}$$

$$\Rightarrow u^2=a^2+b^2+2\sqrt{x(a^2+b^2-x)}$$

[where, $x=a^2\cos^2\theta+b^2\sin^2\theta$]

$$\Rightarrow \quad u^2=(a^2+b^2)+2\sqrt{(a^2+b^2)x-x^2}$$

On differentiating w.r.t. θ, we get

$$\frac{du^2}{d\theta}=\frac{2}{2\sqrt{(a^2+b^2)x-x^2}}(a^2+b^2-2x)\times\frac{dx}{d\theta}$$

and $\dfrac{dx}{d\theta}=(b^2-a^2)\sin 2\theta \quad [\because x=a^2\cos^2\theta+b^2\sin^2\theta]$

$$\Rightarrow \quad \frac{du^2}{d\theta}=\frac{(a^2+b^2-2x)}{\sqrt{(a^2+b^2)x-x^2}}\times(b^2-a^2)\sin 2\theta$$

For maxima and minima, put $\dfrac{du^2}{d\theta}=0$

$\therefore \quad a^2+b^2=2(a^2\cos^2\theta+b^2\sin^2\theta)$

and $\quad \sin 2\theta=0 \Rightarrow \cos 2\theta\,(b^2-a^2)=0$

and $\quad \sin 2\theta=0 \Rightarrow \cos 2\theta=0$

and $\quad \theta=0 \Rightarrow 2\theta=\dfrac{\pi}{2}$

and $\quad \theta=0 \Rightarrow \theta=\dfrac{\pi}{4}$

and $\quad \theta=0$

So, u^2 will be minimum at $\theta=0$ and will be maximum at $\theta=\dfrac{\pi}{4}$.

$\therefore \quad u^2_{min}=(a+b)^2$

and $\quad u^2_{max}=2(a^2+b^2)$

Hence, $\quad u^2_{max}-u^2_{min}=2(a^2+b^2)-(a+b)^2$

$\qquad =(a-b)^2$

24. (d) Equation of parabola is $y^2=18x$.

On differentiating w.r.t. t, we get

$$2y\frac{dy}{dt}=18\frac{dx}{dt}$$

$\Rightarrow \quad 2\cdot 2y=18 \quad \left[\because \dfrac{dy}{dt}=2\dfrac{dx}{dt}\right]$

$\Rightarrow \quad y=\dfrac{9}{2}$

From equation of the parabola,

$$\left(\frac{9}{2}\right)^2=18x \Rightarrow \frac{81}{4}=18x$$

$\Rightarrow \quad x=\dfrac{9}{8}$

Hence, the required point is $\left(\dfrac{9}{8},\dfrac{9}{2}\right)$.

25. (b) Since, $\quad f''(x)=6(x-1)$

On integrating both sides, we get

$$f'(x)=3(x-1)^2+C \quad \text{...(i)}$$

Also, at the point (2, 1), the tangent to graph is

$$y=3x-5$$

$\because$ Slope of tangent $=3$

$\Rightarrow \quad f'(2)=3$

$\therefore \quad f'(2)=3(2-1)^2+C=3 \quad$ [from Eq. (i)]

$\Rightarrow \quad 3+C=3 \Rightarrow C=0$

From Eq. (i), $\quad f'(x)=3(x-1)^2$

On integrating both sides, we get

$$f(x)=(x-1)^3+K \quad \text{...(ii)}$$

Since, graph passes through (2, 1).

$\therefore \quad 1=(2-1)^2+K$

$\Rightarrow \quad K=0$

Hence, equation of function is $f(x)=(x-1)^3$.

26. (a) Given that, $\quad x=a(1+\cos\theta)$, and $y=a\sin\theta$

On differentiating w.r.t. θ, we get

$$\frac{dx}{d\theta}=a(-\sin\theta) \text{ and } \frac{dy}{d\theta}=a\cos\theta$$

$$\therefore \quad \frac{dy}{dx}=\frac{-\cos\theta}{\sin\theta}$$

$\therefore$ Slope of normal $=\dfrac{-1}{(-\cos\theta/\sin\theta)}$

Equation of normal at the given point is

$$y-a\sin\theta=\frac{\sin\theta}{\cos\theta}[x-a(1+\cos\theta)]$$

It is clear that in the given options, normal passes through the point $(a, 0)$.

27. (b) Let $f(x)=x+\dfrac{1}{x} \Rightarrow f'(x)=1-\dfrac{1}{x^2}$

For maxima and minima, put $f'(x)=0$

$\Rightarrow \quad 1-\dfrac{1}{x^2}=0 \quad \Rightarrow \quad x=\pm 1$

Now, $\quad f''(x)=\dfrac{2}{x^3}$

At $x=1$, $\quad f''(x)=+\text{ve} \quad$ [minima]

and at $x=-1$, $\quad f''(x)=-\text{ve} \quad$ [maxima]

Thus, $f(x)$ attains minimum value at $x=1$.

28. (c) $\because \quad f(x)=2x^3-9ax^2+12a^2x+1$

$\therefore \quad f'(x)=6x^2-18ax+12a^2$

For maxima or minima, put $f'(x)=0$

$\therefore \quad 6(x^2-3ax+2a^2)=0$

$\Rightarrow \quad x^2-3ax+2a^2=0$

$\Rightarrow \quad x^2-2ax-ax+2a^2=0$

$\Rightarrow \quad x(x-2a)-a(x-2a)=0$

$\Rightarrow \quad (x-a)(x-2a)=0$

$\Rightarrow \quad x=a$, and $x=2a$

Now, $\quad f''(x)=12x-18a$

At $x=a$, $\quad f''(x)=12a-18a=-6a$

So, $f(x)$ will be maximum at $x=a$.

i.e. $\quad p=a$

Again, at $x=2a$, $\quad f''(x)=24a-18a=6a$

So, $f(x)$ will be minimum at $x=2a$.

i.e. $\quad q=2a$

Given, $\quad p^2=q \quad \Rightarrow \quad a^2=2a$

$\therefore \quad a=2$

29. (c) Since, $\quad f(x)=\cot^{-1}x+x$

On differentiating w.r.t. x, we get

$$f'(x)=-\frac{1}{1+x^2}+1=\frac{x^2}{1+x^2}\geq 0$$

Hence, $f(x)$ is increasing function for all $x\in(-\infty,\infty)$.

30. (b) Given that, $f(x) = (x+1)^{1/3} - (x-1)^{1/3}$

On differentiating w.r.t. x, we get

$$f'(x) = \frac{1}{3}\left[\frac{1}{(x+1)^{2/3}} - \frac{1}{(x-1)^{2/3}}\right]$$

$$= \frac{(x-1)^{2/3} - (x+1)^{2/3}}{3(x^2-1)^{2/3}}$$

Clearly, $f'(x)$ does not exist at $x = \pm 1$.

Now, put $f'(x) = 0$, then

$$(x-1)^{2/3} = (x+1)^{2/3}$$

$$\Rightarrow \quad x = 0$$

At $x = 0$, $\quad f(x) = (0+1)^{1/3} - (0-1)^{1/3} = 2$

Hence, the greatest value of $f(x)$ is 2.

31. (a) The equations of two curves are

$$x^3 - 3xy^2 + 2 = 0 \quad \ldots \text{(i)}$$

and $$3x^2y - y^3 - 2 = 0 \quad \ldots \text{(ii)}$$

On differentiating Eqs. (i) and (ii) w.r.t. x, we get

$$\left(\frac{dy}{dx}\right)_{C_1} = \frac{x^2 - y^2}{2xy}$$

and $$\left(\frac{dy}{dx}\right)_{C_2} = \frac{-2xy}{x^2 - y^2}$$

Now, $$\left(\frac{dy}{dx}\right)_{C_1} \times \left(\frac{dy}{dx}\right)_{C_2} = \left(\frac{x^2-y^2}{2xy}\right)\left(\frac{-2xy}{x^2-y^2}\right) = -1$$

Hence, the two curves cut at right angle.

JEE Advanced & IIT JEE Archive

1. (4) $\because$ Volume, $\quad V = \pi (r-2)^2 h$

Volume of the material used,

$$V_m = 4h\left(\frac{r + r - 2}{2}\right)\pi + 2\pi r^2$$

$$= 4\pi h(r-1) + 2\pi r^2$$

$$= \frac{4(r-1)v}{(r-2)^2} + 2\pi r^2$$

Now, $$\frac{dV_m}{dr} = 4V\left[\frac{(r-2)^2 - (r-1)\,2\,(r-2)}{(r-2)^4}\right] + 4\pi r = 0$$

Put, $r = 12$ (given)

$$\therefore \quad 4V\left[\frac{100-220}{10000}\right] + 48\pi = 0$$

$$\Rightarrow \quad \frac{-48V}{1000} + 48\pi = 0$$

So, $$\frac{V}{250\pi} = 4$$

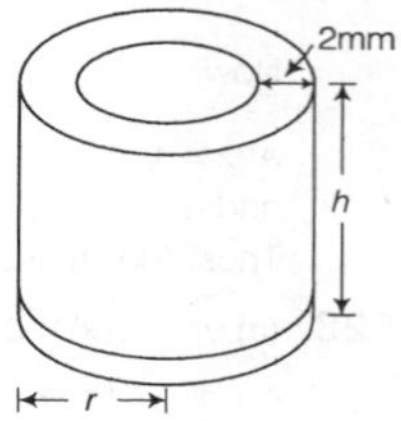

2. (a,b,d) $\because x^2 - y^2 = 1$

$$\Rightarrow \quad 2x - 2yy' = 0$$

$$\Rightarrow \quad y' = \frac{x}{y} \quad \ldots \text{(i)}$$

$$\therefore \quad \frac{x}{y'} \frac{y}{x_1 - x_2} = -1$$

$$\Rightarrow \quad x_2 = 2x_1 \quad \ldots \text{(ii)}$$

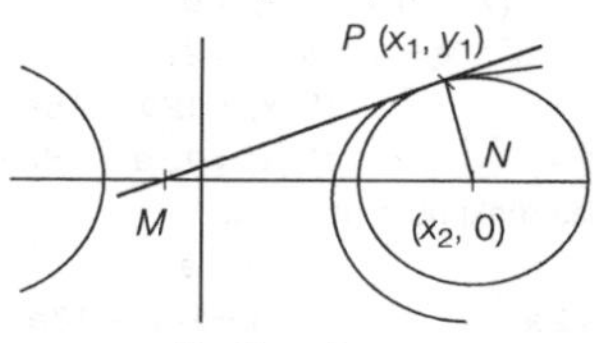

Equation of the PM is $\dfrac{y - y_1}{x - x_1} = \dfrac{x_1}{y_1}$

Put $y = 0$, the $\quad x = \dfrac{x_1^2 - y_1^2}{x_1} = \dfrac{1}{x}$

$\therefore M \equiv \left(\dfrac{1}{x_1}, 0\right)$, $\quad N \equiv (2x_1, 0)$, $P = (x_1, y_1)$

Now, $\quad l = x_1 + \dfrac{1}{3x_1} \quad \Rightarrow \quad \dfrac{dl}{dx_1} = 1 - \dfrac{1}{3x_1^2}$

$\Rightarrow \quad m = \dfrac{y_1}{3} \quad \Rightarrow \quad \dfrac{dm}{dy_1} = \dfrac{1}{3}$

Also, $$m = \frac{1}{3}y_1 = \frac{1}{3}\sqrt{x_1^2 - 1}$$

$$\therefore \quad \frac{dm}{dx_1} = \frac{x_1}{3\sqrt{x_1^2 - 1}}$$

3. (b,c) Let $h(x) = f(x) - 3g(x)$

$$h(-1) = 3$$
$$h(0) = 3$$
$$h(2) = 3$$
$$h'(x) = f'(x) - 3g'(x)$$

$\Rightarrow f'(x) - 3g'(x) = 0$ has exactly one solution is $(-1, 0)$

and $f'(x) - 3g'(x) = 0$ has exactly one solution is $(0, 2)$.

4. (a,c,d) **Plan**

1. If $I(x) = \int_{\phi(x)}^{\psi(x)} f(t)\,dt$, then
   $\dfrac{d}{dx}[I(x)] = f\{\psi(x)\}\left\{\dfrac{d}{dx}\psi(x)\right\} - f\{\phi(x)\}\left\{\dfrac{d}{dx}\phi(x)\right\}$
2. If $f'(x) > 0$, $\forall\ x \in [a, b]$, then $f(x)$ is monotonically increasing on $[a, b]$.
3. $\int_a^b f(x)\,dx = -\int_b^a f(x)\,dx$
4. If $f(-x) = -f(x), \forall\ x \in R$, then $f(x)$ is an odd function of x on R.

Given, $$f(x) = \int_{1/x}^{x} \frac{e^{-\left(t + \frac{1}{t}\right)}}{t}\,dt$$

$$f'(x) = 1 \cdot \frac{e^{-\left(x + \frac{1}{x}\right)}}{x} - \left(\frac{-1}{x^2}\right)\frac{e^{-\left(\frac{1}{x} + x\right)}}{1/x}$$

$$= \frac{e^{-\left(x + \frac{1}{x}\right)}}{x} + \frac{e^{-\left(x + \frac{1}{x}\right)}}{x} = \frac{2e^{-\left(x + \frac{1}{x}\right)}}{x}$$

As, $\quad f'(x) > 0, \forall x \in (0, \infty)$

$\therefore$ $f(x)$ is monotonically increasing on $(0, \infty)$.

Now, $$f(x) + f\left(\frac{1}{x}\right) = \int_{1/x}^{x} \frac{e^{-\left(t + \frac{1}{t}\right)}}{t}\,dt + \int_{x}^{1/x} \frac{e^{-\left(t + \frac{1}{t}\right)}}{t}\,dt$$

$$= 0, \forall x \in (0, \infty)$$

Now, let $$g(x) = f(2^x) = \int_{2^{-x}}^{2^x} \frac{e^{-\left(t + \frac{1}{t}\right)}}{t}\,dt$$

$$g(-x) = f(2^{-x}) = \int_{2^x}^{2^{-x}} \frac{e^{-\left(t + \frac{1}{t}\right)}}{t}\,dt = -g(x)$$

$\therefore$ $f(2^x)$ is an odd function.

5. (8) **Plan** Slope of tangent at the point (x_1, y_1) is $\left(\frac{dy}{dx}\right)_{(x_1, y_1)}$.

Given curve $\quad (y - x^5)^2 = x(1 + x^2)^2$

$$\Rightarrow \quad 2(y - x^5)\left(\frac{dy}{dx} - 5x^4\right) = (1 + x^2)^2 + 2x(1 + x^2)\cdot 2x$$

Put $x = 1, y = 3$

$$\therefore \quad \frac{dy}{dx} = 8$$

6. (a,c) **Concept Involved**

The problem is based on the concept to maximise volume of cuboid.

i.e. to form a function of volume, say $f(x)$ find $f'(x)$ and $f''(x)$.

Put $f'(x) = 0$ and check $f''(x)$ to be positive or negative for minimum and maximum, respectively.

Here, $\quad l = 15x - 2a, b = 8x - 2a$

$h = a$

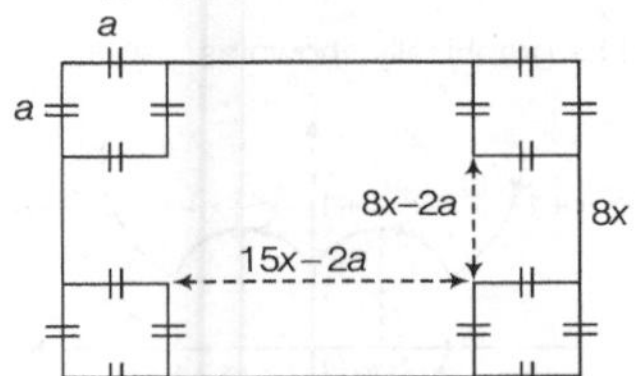

$$\therefore \quad \text{Volume} = (8x - 2a)(15x - 2a)a$$

$$V = 2a\cdot(4x - a)(15x - 2a) \quad \ldots\text{(i)}$$

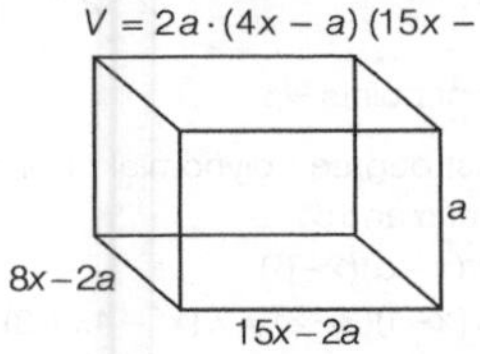

$$\frac{dV}{da} = 6a^2 - 46ax + 60x^2$$

$$\frac{d^2V}{da^2} = 12a - 46x$$

Here, $\quad \left(\frac{dV}{da}\right) = 0$

$$\Rightarrow \quad 6x^2 - 23x + 15 = 0$$

At $a = 5 \Rightarrow x = 3, \frac{5}{6}$

$$\left(\frac{d^2V}{da^2}\right) = 2(30 - 23x)$$

At $x = 3, \left(\frac{d^2V}{da^2}\right) = 2(30 - 69) < 0$

$\therefore$ Maximum when $x = 3$, also at $x = \frac{5}{6}$

$$\Rightarrow \quad \left(\frac{d^2V}{da^2}\right) > 0$$

At $x = 5/6$, volume is minimum.

Thus, sides are $8x$ i.e. 24 and $15x$ i.e. 45.

7. (a,b) **Concept Involved**

We know that, $\quad |x| = \begin{cases} x, & x \ge 0 \\ -x, & x < 0 \end{cases}$

$$\Rightarrow \quad |x - a| = \begin{cases} x - a, & x \ge a \\ -(x - a), & x < a \end{cases}$$

and for non-differentiable continuous function, the maximum or minimum. Can be checked with graph as

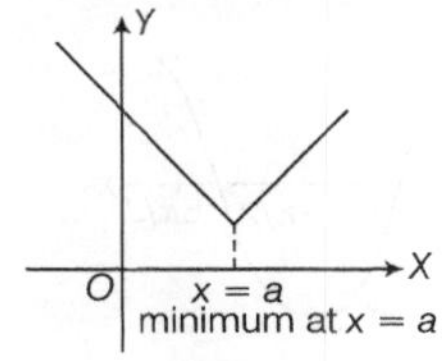

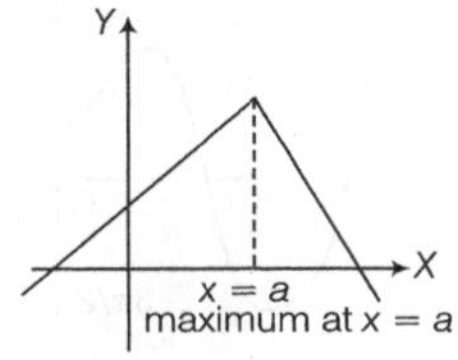

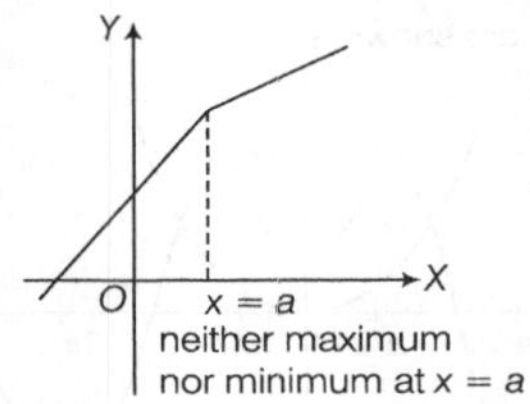

Here, $f(x) = 2|x| + |x + 2| - ||x + 2| - 2|x||$

$$= \begin{cases} -2x - (x + 2) + (x - 2), & \text{when } x \le -2 \\ -2x + x + 2 + 3x + 2, & \text{when } -2 < x \le -2/3 \\ -4x, & \text{when } -2/3 < x \le 0 \\ 4x, & \text{when } 0 < x \le 2 \\ 2x + 4, & \text{when } x > 2 \end{cases}$$

$$= \begin{cases} -2x - 4, & x \le -2 \\ 2x + 4, & -2 < x \le -2/3 \\ -4x, & -2/3 < x \le 0 \\ 4x, & 0 < x \le 2 \\ 2x + 4, & x > 2 \end{cases}$$

Graph for $y = f(x)$ is shown as

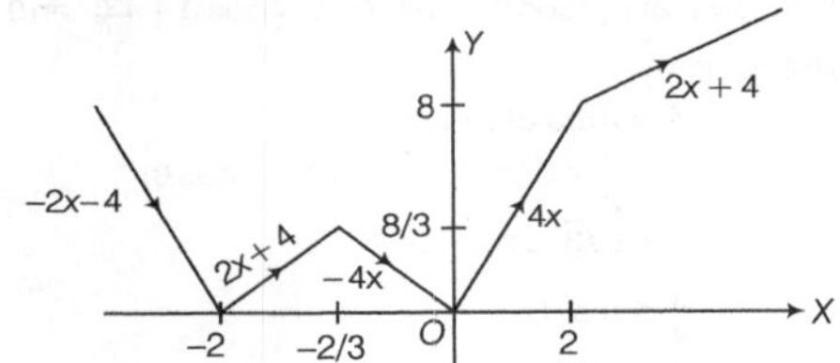

8. (c) **Concept Involved**

The given equation contains algebraic and trigonometric functions called transcendal equation. To solve transcendal equations, we should always plot the graph for LHS and RHS.

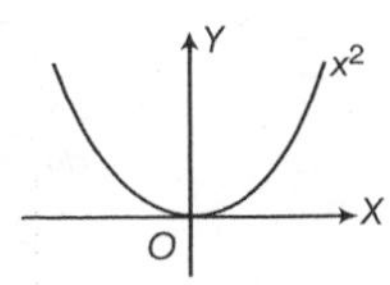

Here, $\quad x^2 = x\sin x + \cos x$

Let $\quad f(x) = x^2$

and $\quad g(x) = x\sin x + \cos x$

We know the graph for $f(x) = x^2$

To plot, $\quad g(x) = x\sin x + \cos x$

$$g'(x) = x\cos x + \sin x - \sin x$$

$$g'(x) = x\cos x \quad \ldots\text{(i)}$$

$$g''(x) = -x\sin x + \cos x \quad \ldots\text{(ii)}$$

Put $g'(x) = 0 \Rightarrow x\cos x = 0$

$$\therefore \quad x = 0, \frac{\pi}{2}, \frac{3\pi}{2}, \frac{5\pi}{2}, \frac{7\pi}{2}, \ldots$$

At $x = 0, \frac{3\pi}{2}, \frac{7\pi}{2}, \ldots; \quad f''(x) > 0 \quad$ [minimum]

At $x = \frac{\pi}{2}, \frac{5\pi}{2}, \frac{9\pi}{2}, \ldots$; $f''(x) < 0$ [maximum]

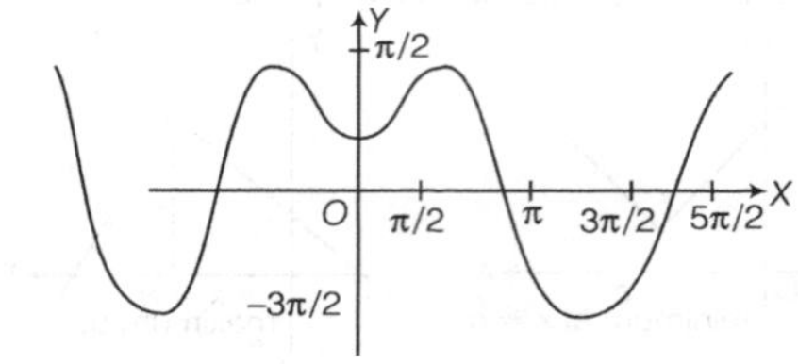

$\therefore$ $f(x)$ and $g(x)$ are shown as

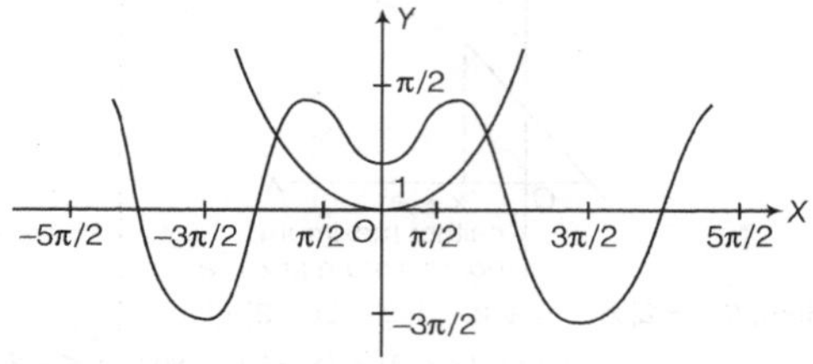

Hence, the number of solutions are 2.

9. (9) As to maximise or minimise area of triangle, we should find the area in terms of parametric coordinate and we apply second derivative test.

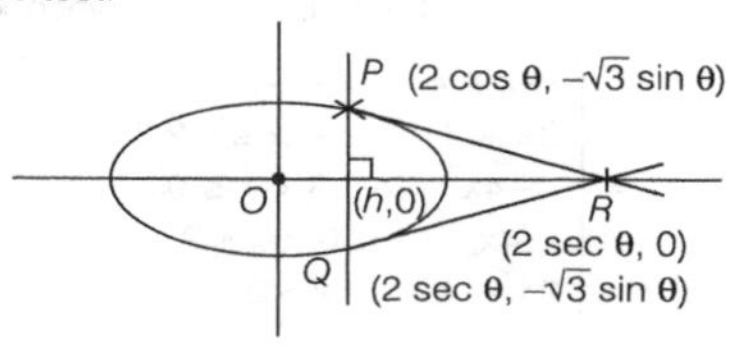

Here, tangent at $P(2\cos\theta, \sqrt{3}\sin\theta)$ is $\frac{x}{2}\cos\theta + \frac{y}{\sqrt{3}}\sin\theta = 1$

$\therefore$ $R(2\sec\theta, 0)$

$$\Rightarrow \quad \Delta = \text{Area of } \Delta PQR$$

$$= \frac{1}{2}(2\sqrt{3}\sin\theta)(2\sec\theta - 2\cos\theta)$$

$$= 2\sqrt{3}\cdot\sin^3\theta/\cos\theta \quad \ldots\text{(i)}$$

Since, $\frac{1}{2} \le h \le 1,$

$\therefore$ $\frac{1}{2} \le 2\cos\theta \le 1$

$\Rightarrow$ $\frac{1}{4} \le \cos\theta \le \frac{1}{2}$ ...(ii)

$$\therefore \quad \frac{d\Delta}{d\theta} = \frac{2\sqrt{3}\{\cos\theta\cdot 3\sin^2\theta\cos\theta - \sin^3\theta\,(-\sin\theta)\}}{\cos^2\theta}$$

$$= \frac{2\sqrt{3}\cdot\sin^2\theta}{\cos^2\theta}[3\cos^2\theta + \sin^2\theta]$$

$$= \frac{2\sqrt{3}\sin^2\theta}{\cos^2\theta}\cdot[2\cos^2\theta + 1]$$

$$= 2\sqrt{3}\tan^2\theta\,(2\cos^2\theta + 1) > 0$$

when, $\frac{1}{4} \le \cos\theta \le \frac{1}{2}$

$\therefore$ When $\cos\theta = \frac{1}{4}$,

$$\Delta_1 = \Delta_{max} \text{ occurs at } \cos\theta = \frac{1}{4} = \left(\frac{2\sqrt{3}\cdot\sin^3\theta}{\cos\theta}\right) = \frac{45\sqrt{5}}{8}$$

when $\cos\theta = \frac{1}{2}$,

$$\Delta_2 = \Delta_{min} \text{ occurs at } \cos\theta = \frac{1}{2} = \left(\frac{2\sqrt{3}\sin^3\theta}{\cos\theta}\right) = \frac{9}{2}$$

$$\therefore \quad \frac{8}{\sqrt{5}}\Delta_1 - 8\Delta_2 = 45 - 36 = 9$$

10. (5)

(i) Local maximum and local minimum are those points at which $f'(x) = 0$, when defined for all real numbers.

(ii) Local maximum and local minimum for piecewise function are also been checked at sharp edges.

Description of Situation $y = |x| = \begin{cases} x, & x \ge 0 \\ -x, & x < 0 \end{cases}$

Also, $y = |x^2 - 1| = \begin{cases} (x^2-1), & x \le -1 \text{ or } x \ge 1 \\ (1-x^2), & -1 \le x \le 1 \end{cases}$

$$y = |x| + |x^2 - 1| = \begin{cases} -x + 1 - x^2, & x \le -1 \\ -x + 1 - x^2, & -1 \le x \le 0 \\ x + 1 - x^2, & 0 \le x \le 1 \\ x + x^2 - 1, & x \ge 1 \end{cases}$$

$$= \begin{cases} -x^2 - x + 1, & x \le -1 \\ -x^2 - x + 1, & -1 \le x \le 0 \\ -x^2 + x + 1, & 0 \le x \le 1 \\ x^2 + x - 1, & x \ge 1 \end{cases}$$

which could be graphically shown as

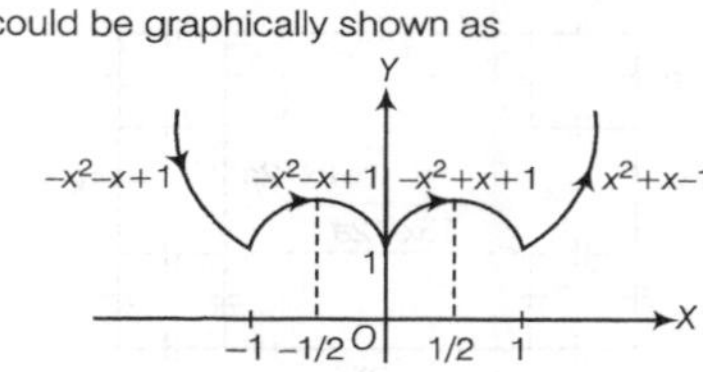

Thus, $f(x)$ attains maximum at $x = \frac{1}{2}, \frac{-1}{2}$ and $f(x)$ attains minimum at $x = -1, 0, 1$.

$\therefore$ Total number of points = 5

11. (9) If $f(x)$ be least degree polynomial having local maximum and local minimum at α and β.

Then, $f'(x) = \lambda(x-\alpha)(x-\beta)$

Here, $p'(x) = \lambda(x-1)(x-3) = \lambda(x^2 - 4x + 3)$

Integrating both sides between 1 to 3, we get

$$\int_1^3 p'(x)dx = \int_1^3 \lambda(x^2 - 4x + 3)dx$$

$$\Rightarrow \quad [p(x)]_1^3 = \lambda\left(\frac{x^3}{3} - 2x^2 + 3x\right)_1^3$$

$$\Rightarrow \quad p(3) - p(1) = \lambda\left[(9 - 18 + 9) - \left(\frac{1}{3} - 2 + 3\right)\right]$$

$$\Rightarrow \quad 2 - 6 = \lambda\left\{\frac{-4}{3}\right\} \Rightarrow \lambda = 3$$

$$\therefore \quad p'(x) = 3(x-1)(x-3)$$

$$\therefore \quad p'(0) = 9$$

12. (a,b,c,d) Use of Newton's- Leibnitz's formula,

$$\frac{d}{dx}\left\{\int_{f(x)}^{g(x)} \phi(t)\,dt\right\} = \phi(g(x))\cdot g'(x) - \phi(f(x))\cdot f'(x)$$

Here, $f(x) = \int_0^x e^{t^2}(t-2)(t-3)\,dt$

$\Rightarrow$ $f'(x) = e^{x^2}(x-2)(x-3)$

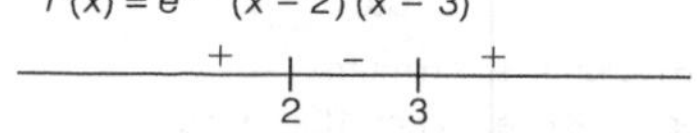

$\therefore$ Maximum at $x = 2$

and minimum at $x = 3$

decreasing on (2, 3)

Also, $f'(x) = 0$ has two roots $x = 2$ and $x = 3$

i.e. $f'(2) = f'(3) = 0$

By Rolle's theorem,

$f''(c) = 0$ must have atleast one root $\in (2, 3)$.

13. (2) $f(x) = x^4 - 4x^3 + 12x^2 + x - 1$

$f'(x) = 4x^3 - 12x^2 + 24x + 1$

$f''(x) = 12x^2 - 24x + 24 = 12(x^2 - 2x + 2)$

$= 12\{(x-1)^2 + 1\} > 0$ for all x

$\Rightarrow f'(x)$ is increasing.

Since, $f'(x)$ is cubic and increasing.

$\Rightarrow f'(x)$ has only one real root and two imaginary roots.

$\therefore$ $f(x)$ cannot have all distinct roots.

$\Rightarrow$ Atmost 2 real roots.

Now, $f(-1) = 15, f(0) = -1, f(1) = 9$

$\therefore$ $f(x)$ must have one root in $(-1, 0)$ and other in $(0, 1)$.

$\Rightarrow$ 2 real roots.

14. (2) Let $f(\theta) = \dfrac{1}{\sin^2\theta + 3\sin\theta\cos\theta + 5\cos^2\theta}$

Again, let $g(\theta) = \sin^2\theta + 3\sin\theta\cos\theta + 5\cos^2\theta$

$$= \frac{1-\cos 2\theta}{2} + 5\left(\frac{1+\cos 2\theta}{2}\right) + \frac{3}{2}\sin 2\theta$$

$$= 3 + 2\cos 2\theta + \frac{3}{2}\sin 2\theta$$

$\therefore$ $g(\theta)_{\min} = 3 - \sqrt{4 + \frac{9}{4}} = 3 - \frac{5}{2} = \frac{1}{2}$

$\therefore$ $f(\theta) = \dfrac{1}{g(\theta)_{\min}} = 2$

15. (9) The equation of the tangent at (x, y) to the given curve $y = f(x)$ is $Y - y = \dfrac{dy}{dx}(X - x)$.

y-intercept $= y - x\dfrac{dy}{dx}$

According to the question,

$$x^3 = y - x\frac{dy}{dx} \Rightarrow \frac{dy}{dx} - \frac{y}{x} = -x^2$$

which is linear in x.

$$\text{IF} = e^{\int \frac{-1}{x}dx} = \frac{1}{x}$$

$\therefore$ Required solution is

$$y\cdot\frac{1}{x} = \int -x^2\cdot\frac{1}{x}dx \Rightarrow \frac{y}{x} = \frac{-x^2}{2} + C \Rightarrow y = \frac{-x^3}{2} + Cx$$

At $x = 1, y = 1$, $\quad 1 = \dfrac{-1}{2} + C \Rightarrow C = \dfrac{3}{2}$

Now, $\quad f(-3) = \dfrac{27}{2} + \dfrac{3}{2}(-3) = \dfrac{27-9}{2} = 9$

16. (1) Let $g(x) = e^{f(x)}, \forall\ x \in R$

$\Rightarrow g'(x) = e^{f(x)}\cdot f'(x)$

$\Rightarrow f'(x)$ changes its sign from positive to negative in the neighbourhood of $x = 2009$

$\Rightarrow f(x)$ has local maxima at $x = 2009$

So, the number of local maximum is one.

17. (b,c) Here, $f'(x) = 1/x + \sqrt{1+\sin x}$, $x > 0$ but $f(x)$ is not differentiable in $(0, \infty)$ as $\sin x$ may be -1 and then $f''(x) = -\dfrac{1}{x^2} + \dfrac{\cos x}{2\sqrt{1+\sin x}}$ will not exist.

$\Rightarrow f'(x)$ is continuous for all $x \in (0, \infty)$ but $f'(x)$ is not differentiable on $(0, \infty)$.

$\therefore$ Option (b) is true.

Also, $f'(x) \le 3$, if $x > 1$ and $f(x) > 3$, if $x > e^3$

$\therefore$ Let $\alpha = e^3$

$\Rightarrow$ Option (c) is true.

Option (d) is not possible as $f(x) \to \infty$ when $x \to \infty$.

18. (d) Given function, $f(x) = e^{x^2} + e^{-x^2}, g(x) = xe^{x^2} + e^{-x^2}$ and $h(x) = x^2e^{x^2} + e^{-x^2}$ are strictly increasing on $[0, 1]$.

Hence, at $x = 1$, the given function attains absolute maximum all equal to $e + 1/e$. $\Rightarrow$ $a = b = c$

19. (b) We have,

$$e^{-x}f(x) = 2 + \int_0^x \sqrt{t^4+1}\,dt \quad x \in (-1, 1)$$

On differentiating w.r.t. x, we get

$$e^{-x}[f'(x) - f(x)] = \sqrt{x^4+1}$$

$\Rightarrow$ $f'(x) = f(x) + \sqrt{x^4+1}\,e^x$

$\because$ f^{-1} is the inverse of f.

$\therefore$ $f^{-1}[f(x)] = x$

$\Rightarrow$ $f^{-1'}[f(x)]f'(x) = 1$

$\Rightarrow$ $f^{-1'}(f(x)) = \dfrac{1}{f'(x)}$

$\Rightarrow$ $f^{-1'}(f(x)) = \dfrac{1}{f(x) + \sqrt{x^4+1}e^x}$

At $x = 0$, $f(x) = 2$

$\Rightarrow$ $f^{-1'}(2) = \dfrac{1}{2+1} = \dfrac{1}{3}$

20. (7) Given, $A = \{x \mid x^2 + 20 \le 9x\} = \{x \mid x \in [4, 5]\}$

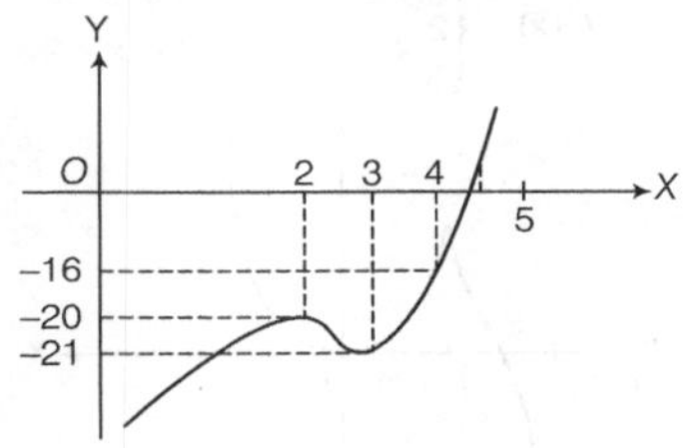

Now, $\quad f'(x) = 6(x^2 - 5x + 6)$

Put $f'(x) = 0$, then $x = 2, 3$

$f(2) = -20,$

$f(3) = -21,$

$f(4) = -16,$

$f(5) = 7$

From graph, maximum of $f(x)$ on set A is $f(5) = 7$.

21. (b,c,d) Given, $f(x) = x\cos\dfrac{1}{x}$, $x \ge 1$

$\Rightarrow$ $f'(x) = \dfrac{1}{x}\sin\dfrac{1}{x} + \cos\dfrac{1}{x}$

$\Rightarrow$ $f''(x) = -\dfrac{1}{x^3}\cos\left(\dfrac{1}{x}\right)$

Now, $\displaystyle\lim_{x\to\infty} f'(x) = 0 + 1 = 1$

$\therefore$ $x \in [1, \infty)$

$\Rightarrow$ $\dfrac{1}{x} \in (0, 1]$

$\Rightarrow$ $f''(x) < 0$

As $\quad f'(1) = \sin 1 + \cos 1 > 1$

$f'(x)$ is strictly decreasing and $\displaystyle\lim_{x\to\infty} f'(x) = 1$

So, graph of $f'(x)$ is shown as below

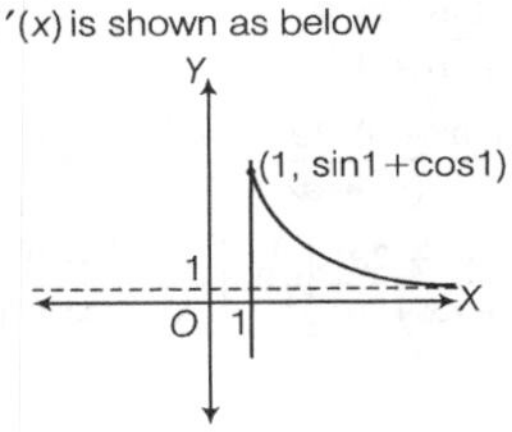

Now, in $[x, x+2]$, $x \in [1, \infty)$, $f(x)$ is continuous and differentiable, so by LMVT,

$$f'(x) = \frac{f(x+2) - f(x)}{2}$$

As $\quad f'(x) > 1, \forall\, x \in [1, \infty)$

$$\Rightarrow \quad \frac{f(x+2)-f(x)}{2} > 1$$

$$\Rightarrow \quad f(x+2) - f(x) > 2, \forall\, x \in [1, \infty)$$

22. (c) Given, $\quad g(u) = 2\tan^{-1}(e^u) - \frac{\pi}{2}$ for $u \in (-\infty, \infty)$

$$g(-u) = 2\tan^{-1}(e^{-u}) - \frac{\pi}{2}$$

$$= 2[\cot^{-1}(e^u)] - \frac{\pi}{2}$$

$$= 2\left[\frac{\pi}{2} - \tan^{-1}(e^u)\right] - \frac{\pi}{2}$$

$$= \pi/2 - 2\tan^{-1}(e^u)$$

$$= -g(u)$$

$\therefore \quad g(-u) = -g(u) \Rightarrow g(u)$ is an odd function.

23. (c) Given that, $f(x) = \begin{cases} (2+x)^3, & -3 < x \le -1 \\ x^{2/3}, & -1 < x < 2 \end{cases}$

$$\Rightarrow \quad f'(x) = \begin{cases} 3(x+2)^2, & -3 < x \le -1 \\ \frac{2}{3}x^{-1/3}, & -1 < x < 2 \end{cases}$$

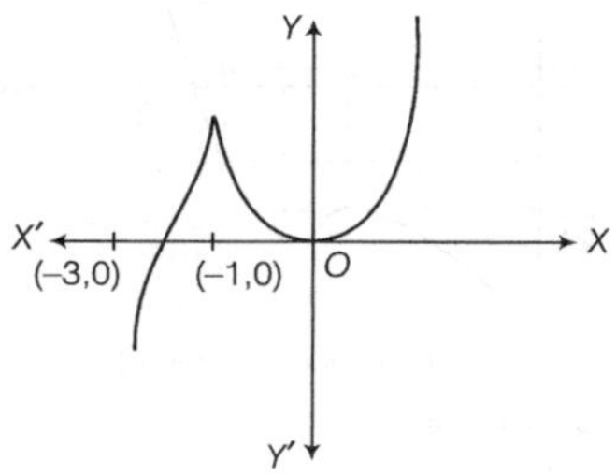

Clearly, $f'(x)$ changes its sign at $x = -1$ from +ve to –ve and so $f(x)$ has local maxima at $x = -1$.

Also, $f'(0)$ does not exist but $f'(0^-) < 0$ and $f'(0^+) < 0$. It can only be inferred that $f(x)$ has a possibility of a minima at $x = 0$. Hence, the given function has one local maxima at $x = -1$ and one local minima at $x = 0$.

24. (a) $\quad \frac{d}{dx}(x + \sin x) = 1 + \cos x = 2\cos^2\frac{x}{2} > 0 \quad$ for $\quad -\frac{\pi}{2} < x < \frac{\pi}{2}$.

Therefore, $x + \sin x$ is increasing in the given interval.

Again, $\frac{d}{dx}(\sec x) = \sec x \tan x$ which is > 0 for $0 < x < \pi/2$

and $\qquad < 0$ for $\frac{-\pi}{2} < x < 0$

Therefore, $\sec x$ is neither increasing nor decreasing in the given interval.

Hence, (i) → (p), (ii) → (r)

25. (a) $f(x) = \frac{(x^2 + ax + 1) - 2ax}{x^2 + ax + 1}$

$$= 1 - \frac{2ax}{x^2 + ax + 1}$$

$$f'(x) = -\left[\frac{(x^2 + ax + 1)\cdot 2a - 2ax(2x + a)}{(x^2 + ax + 1)^2}\right]$$

$$= -\left[\frac{-2ax^2 + 2a}{(x^2 + ax + 1)^2}\right] = 2a\left[\frac{(x^2 - 1)}{(x^2 + ax + 1)^2}\right] \qquad \text{...(i)}$$

$$f''(x) = 2a\left[\frac{(x^2 + ax + 1)^2(2x) - 2(x^2 - 1)(x^2 + ax + 1)(2x + a)}{(x^2 + ax + 1)^4}\right]$$

$$= 2a\left[\frac{2x(x^2 + ax + 1) - 2(x^2 - 1)(2x + a)}{(x^2 + ax + 1)^3}\right] \qquad \text{...(ii)}$$

Now, $\quad f''(1) = \frac{4a(a+2)}{(a+2)^3} = \frac{4a}{(a+2)^2}$

and $\quad f(-1) = \frac{4a(a-2)}{(2-a)^3} = \frac{-4a}{(a-2)^2}$

$\therefore \quad (2 + a)^2 f''(1) + (2 - a)^2 f''(-1) = 4a - 4a = 0$

26. (a) When $x \in (-1, 1)$, $\quad x^2 < 1 \Rightarrow x^2 - 1 < 0$

$\therefore \qquad f'(x) < 0$

$\Rightarrow f(x)$ is decreasing

Also, at $\quad x = 1, f''(1) = \frac{4a}{(a+2)^2} > 0 \qquad [\because 0 < a < 2]$

$f(x)$ has local minimum at $x = 1$

27. (b) $g'(x) = \frac{f'(e^x)}{1 + (e^x)^2}\cdot e^x = 2a\left[\frac{e^{2x} - 1}{(e^{2x} + ae^x + 1)^2}\right]\left(\frac{e^x}{1 + e^{2x}}\right)$

$g'(x) = 0$, if $e^{2x} - 1 = 0$, i.e. $x = 0$

If $\quad x < 0, e^{2x} < 1$

$\Rightarrow g'(x) < 0$.

28. (a) Slope of the line joining the points $(c - 1, e^{c-1})$ and $(c + 1, e^{c+1})$ is equal to $\frac{e^{c+1} - e^{c-1}}{2} > e^c$

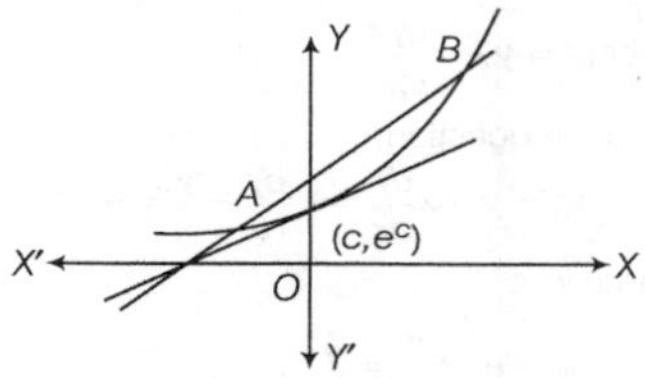

$\Rightarrow$ Tangent to the curve $y = e^x$ will intersect the given line to the left of the line $x = c$.

Alternate Method

The equation of the tangent to the curve $y = e^x$ at (c, e^c) is

$$y - e^c = e^c(x - c) \qquad \text{...(i)}$$

Equation of the line joining the given points is

$$y - e^{c-1} = \frac{e^c(e - e^{-1})}{2}[x - (c - 1)] \qquad \text{...(ii)}$$

Eliminating y from Eqs. (i) and (ii), we get

$$[x - (c - 1)][2 - (e - e^{-1})] = 2e^{-1}$$

$$\Rightarrow \quad x - c = \frac{e + e^{-1} - 2}{2 - (e - e^{-1})} < 0 \Rightarrow x < c$$

29. (b,c) Since, $f(x)$ has local maxima at $x = -1$ and $f'(x)$ has local minima at $x = 0$.

$$\therefore \quad f''(x) = \lambda x$$

On integrating both sides, we get

$$f'(x) = \lambda\frac{x^2}{2} + C \qquad [\because f'(-1) = 0]$$

$$\Rightarrow \quad \frac{\lambda}{2} + C = 0$$

$$\Rightarrow \quad \lambda = -2C \qquad \text{...(i)}$$

Again, integrating both sides, we get

$$f(x) = \lambda \frac{x^3}{6} + Cx + D$$

$\Rightarrow$ $f(2) = \lambda \left(\frac{8}{6}\right) + 2C + D = 18$ ...(ii)

and $f(1) = \frac{\lambda}{6} + C + D = -1$ ...(iii)

From Eqs. (i), (ii) and (iii), we get

$$f(x) = \frac{1}{4}(19x^3 - 57x + 34)$$

$\therefore$ $f'(x) = \frac{1}{4}(57x^2 - 57)$

$$= \frac{57}{4}(x-1)(x+1)$$

For maxima or minima, put $f'(x) = 0$

$\Rightarrow$ $x = 1, -1$

Now, $f''(x) = \frac{1}{4}(114x)$

At $x = 1$, $f''(x) > 0$, minima

At $x = -1$, $f''(x) < 0$, maxima

$\therefore$ $f(x)$ is increasing for $[1, 2\sqrt{5}]$.

$\therefore$ $f(x)$ has local maximum at $x = -1$ and $f(x)$ has local minimum at $x = 1$.

Also, $f(0) = 34/4$

30. (a,b) Given,

$$f(x) = \begin{cases} e^x, & 0 \le x \le 1 \\ 2 - e^{x-1}, & 1 < x \le 2 \\ x - e, & 2 < x \le 3 \end{cases}$$

and $g(x) = \int_0^x f(t)\,dt$

$\Rightarrow$ $g'(x) = f(x)$

Put $g'(x) = 0$

$\Rightarrow$ $x = 1 + \log_e 2$

and $x = e$.

Also, $g''(x) = \begin{cases} e^x, & 0 \le x \le 1 \\ -e^{x-1}, & 1 < x \le 2 \\ 1, & 2 < x \le 3 \end{cases}$

At $x = 1 + \log_e 2$,

$g''(1 + \log_e 2) = -e^{\log_e 2} < 0$, $g(x)$ has a local maxima.

Also, at $x = e$,

$g''(e) = 1 > 0$, $g(x)$ has a local minima.

$\because$ $f(x)$ is discontinuous at $x = 1$, then we get local maxima at $x = 1$ and local minima at $x = 2$.

31. (c) Let $f(x) = bx^2 + ax + c$

$\because$ $f(0) = 0 \Rightarrow c = 0$

and $f(1) = 1 \Rightarrow a + b = 1$

$\therefore$ $f(x) = ax + (1-a)x^2$

Also, $f'(x) > 0$, for $x \in (0, 1)$

$\Rightarrow$ $a + 2(1-a)x > 0$

$\Rightarrow$ $a(1-2x) + 2x > 0$

$\Rightarrow$ $a > \frac{2x}{2x-1}$

$\Rightarrow$ $0 < a < 2$, since $x \in (0, 1)$

$\therefore$ $f(x) = ax + (1-a)x^2$; $0 < a < 2$

32. (d) The tangent at (1, 7) to the parabola $x^2 = y - 6$ is

$$x(1) = \frac{1}{2}(y + 7) - 6$$

[replacing $x^2 \to x x_1$ and $2y \to y + y_1$]

$\Rightarrow$ $2x = y + 7 - 12$

$\Rightarrow$ $y = 2x + 5$ ...(i)

which is also tangent to the circle

$$x^2 + y^2 + 16x + 12y + c = 0$$

i.e. $x^2 + (2x+5)^2 + 16x + 12(2x+5) + c = 0$ must have equal roots i.e. $\alpha = \beta$

$\Rightarrow$ $5x^2 + 60x + 85 + c = 0$

$\Rightarrow$ $\alpha + \beta = -\frac{60}{5}$

$\Rightarrow$ $\alpha = -6$

$\therefore$ $x = -6$

and $y = 2x + 5 = -7$

$\therefore$ Point of contact is $(-6, -7)$.

33. (a) Here, $y^2 = 16x$, $0 \le y \le 6$

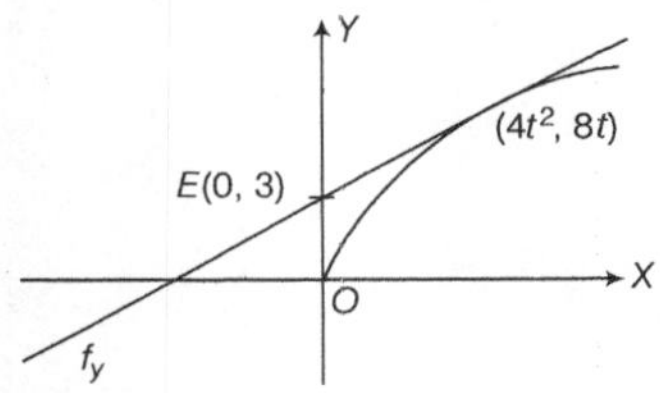

Tangent at F, $yt = x + at^2$

At $x = 0$, $y = at = 4t$

Also, $(4t^2, 8t)$ satisfy $y = mx + c$

$\Rightarrow$ $8t = 4mt^2 + 3$

$\Rightarrow$ $4mt^2 - 8t + 3 = 0$

$\therefore$ Area of $\Delta = \frac{1}{2}\begin{vmatrix} 0 & 3 & 1 \\ 0 & 4t & 1 \\ 4t^2 & 8t & 1 \end{vmatrix} = \frac{1}{2} \cdot 4t^2(3 - 4t)$

$$A = 2[3t^2 - 4t^3]$$

$\therefore$ $\frac{dA}{dt} = 2[6t - 12t^2]$

$$= -12t(2t - 1)$$

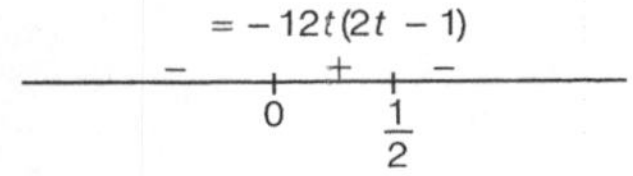

$\therefore$ Maximum at $t = \frac{1}{2}$ and $4mt^2 - 8t + 3 = 0$

$\Rightarrow$ $m - 4 + 3 = 0$

$\Rightarrow$ $m = 1$

$\therefore$ $G(0, 4t) \Rightarrow G(0, 2)$

$\Rightarrow$ $y_1 = 2$

$\Rightarrow$ $(x_0, y_0) = (4t^2, 8t) = (1, 4)$

$\Rightarrow$ $y_0 = 4$

$\therefore$ Area $= 2\left(\frac{3}{4} - \frac{1}{2}\right) = \frac{1}{2}$

Hence, (i) $\to$ (s), (ii) $\to$ (p), (iii) $\to$ (q), (iv) $\to$ (r)

Last 3 Years' Questions
JEE Main & Advanced
(2016-2018)

JEE Main

2016

1. Let $p = \lim_{x \to 0^+} (1 + \tan^2 \sqrt{x})^{1/2x}$, then $\log p$ is equal to **[Limits]**

(a) 2 (b) 1 (c) $\frac{1}{2}$ (d) $\frac{1}{4}$

2. For $x \in R$, $f(x) = |\log 2 - \sin x|$ and $g(x) = f(f(x))$, then **[Continuity and Differentiability]**

(a) g is not differentiable at $x = 0$
(b) $g'(0) = \cos(\log 2)$
(c) $g'(0) = -\cos(\log 2)$
(d) g is differentiable at $x = 0$ and $g'(0) = -\sin(\log 2)$

3. A wire of length 2 units is cut into two parts which are bent respectively to form a square of side $= x$ units and a circle of radius $= r$ units. If the sum of the areas of the square and the circle so formed is minimum, then **[Applications of Derivatives]**

(a) $2x = (\pi + 4)r$ (b) $(4 - \pi)x = \pi r$
(c) $x = 2r$ (d) $2x = r$

4. $\lim_{n \to \infty} \left[\frac{(n+1)(n+2)\dots 3n}{n^{2n}}\right]^{1/n}$ is equal to **[Limits]**

(a) $\frac{18}{e^4}$ (b) $\frac{27}{e^2}$
(c) $\frac{9}{e^2}$ (d) $3\log 3 - 2$

5. Let P be the point on the parabola, $y^2 = 8x$, which is at a minimum distance from the centre C of the circle, $x^2 + (y+6)^2 = 1$. Then, the equation of the circle, passing through C and having its centre at P is **[Applications of Derivatives]**

(a) $x^2 + y^2 - 4x + 8y + 12 = 0$ (b) $x^2 + y^2 - x + 4y - 12 = 0$
(c) $x^2 + y^2 - \frac{x}{4} + 2y - 24 = 0$ (d) $x^2 + y^2 - 4x + 9y + 18 = 0$

2017

6. If 20 m of wire is available for fencing off a flower-bed in the form of a circular sector, then the maximum area (in sq m) of the flower-bed is **[Applications of Derivatives]**

(a) 12.5 (b) 10 (c) 25 (d) 30

7. For $x \in \left(0, \frac{1}{4}\right)$, if the derivative of $\tan^{-1}\left(\frac{6x\sqrt{x}}{1-9x^3}\right)$ is $\sqrt{x} \cdot g(x)$, then $g(x)$ equals **[Applications of Derivatives]**

(a) $\frac{9}{1+9x^3}$ (b) $\frac{3x\sqrt{x}}{1-9x^3}$
(c) $\frac{3x}{1-9x^3}$ (d) $\frac{3}{1+9x^3}$

8. $\lim_{x \to \pi/2} \frac{\cot x - \cos x}{(\pi - 2x)^3}$ equals

[Limits]

(a) $\frac{1}{24}$
(b) $\frac{1}{16}$
(c) $\frac{1}{8}$
(d) $\frac{1}{4}$

2018

9. For each $t \in \mathbf{R}$, let $[t]$ be the greatest integer less than or equal to t. Then,

$$\lim_{x \to 0^+} x\left(\left[\frac{1}{x}\right] + \left[\frac{2}{x}\right] + \ldots + \left[\frac{15}{x}\right]\right)$$

[Limits]

(a) is equal to 0
(b) is equal to 15
(c) is equal to 120
(d) does not exist (in $\mathbf{R}$)

10. Let $S = (t \in \mathbf{R} : f(x) = |x - \pi|(e^{|x|} - 1)\sin|x|$ is not differentiable at $t\}$. Then, the set S is equal to **[Continuity and Differentiability]**

(a) ϕ (an empty set)
(b) $\{0\}$
(c) $\{\pi\}$
(d) $\{0, \pi\}$

11. Let $f(x) = x^2 + \frac{1}{x^2}$ and $g(x) = x - \frac{1}{x}, x \in \mathbf{R} - \{-1, 0, 1\}$. If $h(x) = \frac{f(x)}{g(x)}$, then the local minimum value of $h(x)$ is **[Applications of Derivatives]**

(a) 3
(b) -3
(c) $-2\sqrt{2}$
(d) $2\sqrt{2}$

JEE Advanced

2016

1. The least value of $\alpha \in R$ for which $4\alpha x^2 + \frac{1}{x} \geq 1$, for all $x > 0$, is

[Applications of Derivatives, Type 1]

(a) $\frac{1}{64}$
(b) $\frac{1}{32}$
(c) $\frac{1}{27}$
(d) $\frac{1}{25}$

2. Let $f : R \to R, g : R \to R$ and $h : R \to R$ be differentiable functions such that $f(x) = x^3 + 3x + 2, g(f(x)) = x$ and $h(g(g(x))) = x$ for all $x \in R$. Then,

[Methods of Differentiation, Type 2]

(a) $g'(2) = \frac{1}{15}$
(b) $h'(1) = 666$
(c) $h(0) = 16$
(d) $h(g(3)) = 36$

3. Let $f : (0, \infty) \to R$ be a differentiable function such that $f'(x) = 2 - \frac{f(x)}{x}$ for all $x \in (0, \infty)$ and $f(1) \neq 1$. Then **[Continuity and Differentiability, Type 2]**

(a) $\lim_{x \to 0+} f'\left(\frac{1}{x}\right) = 1$
(b) $\lim_{x \to 0+} x\, f\left(\frac{1}{x}\right) = 2$
(c) $\lim_{x \to 0+} x^2 f'(x) = 0$
(d) $|f(x)| \leq 2$ for all $x \in (0, 2)$

4. Let $\alpha, \beta \in R$ be such that $\lim_{x \to 0} \frac{x^2 \sin(\beta x)}{\alpha x - \sin x} = 1$. Then, $6(\alpha + \beta)$ equals

[Limits, Type 3]

5. Let $a, b \in R$ and $f : R \to R$ be defined by $f(x) = a\cos(|x^3 - x|) + b|x|\sin(|x^3 + x|)$. Then, f is **[Continuity and Differentiability, Type 2]**

(a) differentiable at $x = 0$, if $a = 0$ and $b = 1$
(b) differentiable at $x = 1$, if $a = 1$ and $b = 0$
(c) not differentiable at $x = 0$, if $a = 1$ and $b = 0$
(d) not differentiable at $x = 1$, if $a = 1$ and $b = 1$

Note ***Type-1*** *Only one correct option,* ***Type-2*** *More then one correct option,* ***Type-3*** *Single digit Answer,* ***Type-4*** *Numerical value based*

6. Let $f(x)=\lim_{n\to\infty}\left[\dfrac{n^n(x+n)\left(x+\frac{n}{2}\right)\ldots\left(x+\frac{n}{n}\right)}{n!(x^2+n^2)\left(x^2+\frac{n^2}{4}\right)\ldots\left(x^2+\frac{n^2}{n^2}\right)}\right]^{x/n}$,

for all $x = 0$. Then **[Limits, Type 2]**

(a) $f\left(\frac{1}{2}\right)\geq f(1)$
(b) $f\left(\frac{1}{3}\right)\leq f\left(\frac{2}{3}\right)$
(c) $f'(2)\leq 0$
(d) $\dfrac{f'(3)}{f(3)}\geq\dfrac{f'(2)}{f(2)}$

7. Let $f: R\to(0,\infty)$ and $g: R\to R$ be twice differentiable functions such that f'' and g'' are continuous functions on R.

Suppose $f'(2)=g(2)=0$, $f''(2)\neq 0$ and $g'(2)\neq 0$. If $\lim_{x\to 2}\dfrac{f(x)g(x)}{f'(x)g'(x)}=1$, then

[Applications of Derivatives, Type 2]

(a) f has a local minimum at $x = 2$
(b) f has a local maximum at $x = 2$
(c) $f''(2) > f(2)$
(d) $f(x) - f''(x) = 0$, for atleast one $x\in R$

8. Let $f:\left[-\frac{1}{2},2\right]\to R$ and $g:\left[-\frac{1}{2},2\right]\to R$ be functions defined by $f(x)=[x^2-3]$ and $g(x)=|x|\,f(x)+|4x-7|\,f(x)$, where $[y]$ denotes the greatest integer less than or equal to y for $y\in R$. Then, **[Continuity and Differentiability, Type 2]**

(a) f is discontinuous exactly at three points in $\left[-\frac{1}{2},2\right]$
(b) f is discontinuous exactly at four points in $\left[-\frac{1}{2},2\right]$
(c) g is not differentiable exactly at four points in $\left(-\frac{1}{2},2\right)$
(d) g is not differentiable exactly at five points in $\left(-\frac{1}{2},2\right)$

2017

9. Let $[x]$ be the greatest integer less than or equals to x. Then, at which of the following point(s) the function $f(x)=x\cos(\pi(x+[x]))$ is discontinuous ?

[Continuity and Differentiability, Type 2]

(a) $x=-1$ (b) $x=1$ (c) $x=0$ (d) $x=2$

Directions (Q.Nos. 10-12) by appropriately matching the information given in the three columns of the following table.

Let $f(x)=x+\log_e x - x\log_e x,\ x\in(0,\infty)$

Column 1 contains information about zeros of $f(x)$, $f'(x)$ and $f''(x)$.
Column 2 contains information about the limiting behaviour of $f(x)$, $f'(x)$ and $f''(x)$ at infinity.
Column 3 contains information about increasing/decreasing nature of $f(x)$ and $f'(x)$.

	Column-1		Column-2		Column-3
(I)	$f(x)=0$ for some $x\in(1,e^2)$	(i)	$\lim_{x\to\infty}f(x)=0$	(P)	f is increasing in $(0, 1)$
(II)	$f'(x)=0$ for some $x\in(1,e)$	(ii)	$\lim_{x\to\infty}f(x)=-\infty$	(Q)	f is decreasing in (e, e^2)
(III)	$f'(x)=0$ for some $x\in(0,1)$	(iii)	$\lim_{x\to\infty}f'(x)=-\infty$	(R)	f' is increasing in $(0, 1)$
(IV)	$f''(x)=0$ for some $x\in(1,e)$	(iv)	$\lim_{x\to\infty}f''(x)=0$	(S)	f' is decreasing in (e, e^2)

[Applications of Derivatives]

10. Which of the following options is the only INCORRECT combination?

(a) (I) (iii) (P) (b) (II) (iv) (Q) (c) (II) (iii) (P) (d) (III) (i) (R)

11. Which of the following options is the only CORRECT combination?

(a) (I) (ii) (R) (b) (III) (iv) (P) (c) (II) (iii) (S) (d) (IV) (i) (S)

12. Which of the following options is the only CORRECT combination?

(a) (III) (iii) (R) (b) (IV) (iv) (S) (c) (II) (ii) (Q) (d) (I) (i) (P)

13. If $f: R \to R$ is a twice differentiable function such that $f''(x) > 0$ for all $x \in R$, and $f\left(\frac{1}{2}\right) = \frac{1}{2}$, $f(1) = 1$, then **[Continuity and Differentiability, Type 1]**

(a) $f'(1) \le 0$ (b) $f'(1) > 1$ (c) $0 < f'(1) \le \frac{1}{2}$ (d) $\frac{1}{2} < f'(1) \le 1$

14 Let $f(x) = \dfrac{1 - x(1 + |1 - x|)}{|1 - x|} \cos\left(\dfrac{1}{1 - x}\right)$

for $x \ne 1$. Then **[Limits, Type 2]**

(a) $\lim_{x \to 1^+} f(x) = 0$ (b) $\lim_{x \to 1^-} f(x)$ does not exist

(c) $\lim_{x \to 1^-} f(x) = 0$ (d) $\lim_{x \to 1^+} f(x)$ does not exist

15. If $f(x) = \begin{vmatrix} \cos(2x) & \cos(2x) & \sin(2x) \\ -\cos x & \cos x & -\sin x \\ \sin x & \sin x & \cos x \end{vmatrix}$, then **[Methods of Differentiation, Type 2]**

(a) $f(x)$ attains its minimum at $x = 0$ (b) $f(x)$ attains its maximum at $x = 0$

(c) $f'(x) = 0$ at more than three points in $(-\pi, \pi)$ (d) $f'(x) = 0$ at exactly three points in $(-\pi, \pi)$

2018

16. For every twice differentiable function $f: R \to [-2, 2]$ with $(f(0))^2 + (f'(0))^2 = 85$, which of the following statement(s) is (are) TRUE ? **[Continuity and Differentiability, Type 2]**

(a) There exist $r, s \in R$, where $r < s$, such that f is one-one on the open interval (r, s)

(b) There exists $x_0 \in (-4, 0)$ such that $|f'(x_0)| \le 1$

(c) $\lim_{x \to \infty} f(x) = 1$

(d) There exists $\alpha \in (-4, 4)$ such that $f(\alpha) + f''(\alpha) = 0$ and $f'(\alpha) \ne 0$

17. Let $f: R \to R$ and $g: R \to R$ be two non-constant differentiable functions. If $f'(x) = (e^{(f(x) - g(x))}) g'(x)$ for all $x \in R$ and $f(1) = g(2) = 1$, then which of the following statement(s) is (are) TRUE? **[Continuity and Differentiability, Type 2]**

(a) $f(2) < 1 - \log_e 2$ (b) $f(2) > 1 - \log_e 2$

(c) $g(1) > 1 - \log_e 2$ (d) $g(1) < 1 - \log_e 2$

18. For each positive integer n, let $y_n = \frac{1}{n}((n+1)(n+2)\dots(n+n))^{1/n}$.

For $x \in R$, let $[x]$ be the greatest integer less than or equal to x. If $\lim_{n \to \infty} y_n = L$, then the value of $[L]$ is .... **[Limits, Type 4]**

19. Let $f: (0, \pi) \to R$ be a twice differentiable function such that $\lim_{t \to x} \dfrac{f(x)\sin t - f(t)\sin x}{t - x} = \sin^2 x$ for all $x \in (0, \pi)$.

If $f\left(\frac{\pi}{6}\right) = -\frac{\pi}{12}$, then which of the following statement(s) is (are) TRUE? **[Limits, Type 2]**

(a) $f\left(\frac{\pi}{4}\right) = \frac{\pi}{4\sqrt{2}}$

(b) $f(x) < \frac{x^4}{6} - x^2$ for all $x \in (0, \pi)$

(c) There exists $\alpha \in (0, \pi)$ such that $f'(\alpha) = 0$

(d) $f''\left(\frac{\pi}{2}\right) + f\left(\frac{\pi}{2}\right) = 0$

20. Let $f:R\to R$ be a differentiable function with $f(0)=0$. If $y=f(x)$ satisfies the differential equation $\frac{dy}{dx}=(2+5y)(5y-2)$, then the value of $\lim_{x\to-\infty} f(x)$ is .... **[Limits, Type 4]**

21. Let $f:R\to R$ be a differentiable function with $f(0)=1$ and satisfying the equation $f(x+y)=f(x)f'(y)+f'(x)f(y)$ for all $x, y\in R$.
Then, the value of $\log_e(f(4))$ is .... **[Continuity and Differentiability, Type 4]**

22. Let $f_1 : R\to R$, $f_2 : \left(-\frac{\pi}{2},\frac{\pi}{2}\right)\to R$, $f_3 : (-1, e^{\pi/2}-2)\to R$ and $f_4 : R\to R$ be functions defined by **[Continuity and Differentiability]**

(i) $f_1(x)=\sin(\sqrt{1-e^{-x^2}})$,

(ii) $f_2(x)=\begin{cases}\dfrac{|\sin x|}{\tan^{-1}x} & \text{if } x\neq 0\\ 1 & \text{if } x=0\end{cases}$, where the inverse trigonometric function $\tan^{-1}x$ assumes values in $\left(-\frac{\pi}{2},\frac{\pi}{2}\right)$,

(iii) $f_3(x)=[\sin(\log_e(x+2))]$, where for $t\in R$, $[t]$ denotes the greatest integer less than or equal to t,

(iv) $f_4(x)=\begin{cases}x^2\sin\left(\dfrac{1}{x}\right) & \text{if } x\neq 0\\ 0 & \text{if } x=0\end{cases}$

	List-I		List-II
P.	The function f_1 is	1.	NOT continuous at $x=0$
Q.	The function f_2 is	2.	continuous at $x=0$ and NOT differentiable at $x=0$
R.	The function f_3 is	3.	differentiable at $x=0$ and its derivative is NOT continuous at $x=0$
S.	The function f_4 is	4.	differentiable at $x=0$ and its derivative is continuous at $x=0$

The correct option is

(a) P $\to$ 2; Q $\to$ 3; R $\to$ 1; S $\to$ 4
(b) P $\to$ 4; Q $\to$ 1; R $\to$ 2; S $\to$ 3
(c) P $\to$ 4; Q $\to$ 2; R $\to$ 1; S $\to$ 3
(d) P $\to$ 2; Q $\to$ 1; R $\to$ 4; S $\to$ 3

Answer *with* Explanations

JEE Main

1. *(c)* Given, $p = \lim_{x \to 0^+} (1 + \tan^2 \sqrt{x})^{\frac{1}{2x}}$ [1^∞ form]

$$= e^{\lim_{x \to 0^+} \frac{\tan^2 \sqrt{x}}{2x}}$$

$$= e^{\frac{1}{2} \lim_{x \to 0^+} \left(\frac{\tan \sqrt{x}}{\sqrt{x}}\right)^2} = e^{\frac{1}{2}}$$

$\therefore \quad \log p = \log e^{\frac{1}{2}} = \frac{1}{2}$

2. *(b)* We have, $f(x) = | \log 2 - \sin x |$

and $\quad g(x) = f(f(x)), x \in R$

Note that, for $x \to 0$, $\log 2 > \sin x$

$\therefore \quad f(x) = \log 2 - \sin x$

$\Rightarrow \quad g(x) = \log 2 - \sin (f(x))$

$\quad = \log 2 - \sin (\log 2 - \sin x)$

Clearly, $g(x)$ is differentiable at $x = 0$ as $\sin x$ is differentiable.

Now, $g'(x) = - \cos (\log 2 - \sin x) (- \cos x)$

$\quad = \cos x \cdot \cos (\log 2 - \sin x)$

$\Rightarrow \quad g'(0) = 1 \cdot \cos (\log 2)$

3. *(c)* According to given information, we have

Perimeter of square + Perimeter of circle = 2 units

$\Rightarrow \quad 4x + 2\pi r = 2$

$\Rightarrow \quad r = \frac{1 - 2x}{\pi}$ ...(i)

Now, let A be the sum of the areas of the square and the circle. Then,

$$A = x^2 + \pi r^2 = x^2 + \pi \frac{(1 - 2x)^2}{\pi^2}$$

$\Rightarrow \quad A(x) = x^2 + \frac{(1 - 2x)^2}{\pi}$

Now, for minimum value of $A(x)$, $\frac{dA}{dx} = 0$

$\Rightarrow \quad 2x + \frac{2(1 - 2x)}{\pi} \cdot (-2) = 0$

$\Rightarrow \quad x = \frac{2 - 4x}{\pi}$

$\Rightarrow \quad \pi x + 4x = 2$

$\Rightarrow \quad x = \frac{2}{\pi + 4}$ ...(ii)

Now, from Eq. (i), we get

$$r = \frac{1 - 2 \cdot \frac{2}{\pi + 4}}{\pi}$$

$$= \frac{\pi + 4 - 4}{\pi(\pi + 4)} = \frac{1}{\pi + 4} \quad \text{...(iii)}$$

From Eqs. (ii) and (iii),

we get $\quad x = 2r$

4. *(b)* Let $l = \lim_{n \to \infty} \left[\frac{(n + 1) \cdot (n + 2) \dots (3n)}{n^{2n}}\right]^{\frac{1}{n}}$

$$= \lim_{n \to \infty} \left[\frac{(n + 1) \cdot (n + 2) \dots (n + 2n)}{n^{2n}}\right]^{\frac{1}{n}}$$

$$= \lim_{n \to \infty} \left[\left(\frac{n + 1}{n}\right)\left(\frac{n + 2}{n}\right) \dots \left(\frac{n + 2n}{n}\right)\right]^{\frac{1}{n}}$$

On taking log both sides, we get

$$\log l = \lim_{n \to \infty} \frac{1}{n} \left[\log \left\{\left(1 + \frac{1}{n}\right)\left(1 + \frac{2}{n}\right) \dots \left(1 + \frac{2n}{n}\right)\right\}\right]$$

$\Rightarrow \quad \log l = \lim_{n \to \infty} \frac{1}{n} \left[\log\left(1 + \frac{1}{n}\right) + \log\left(1 + \frac{2}{n}\right) + \dots + \log\left(1 + \frac{2n}{n}\right)\right]$

$\Rightarrow \quad \log l = \lim_{n \to \infty} \frac{1}{n} \sum_{r = 1}^{2n} \log\left(1 + \frac{r}{n}\right)$

$\Rightarrow \quad \log l = \int_0^2 \log (1 + x)\, dx$

$\Rightarrow \quad \log l = \left[\log(1 + x) \cdot x - \int \frac{1}{1 + x} \cdot x\, dx\right]_0^2$

$\Rightarrow \quad \log l = [\log (1 + x) \cdot x]_0^2 - \int_0^2 \frac{x + 1 - 1}{1 + x}\, dx$

$\Rightarrow \quad \log l = 2 \cdot \log 3 - \int_0^2 \left(1 - \frac{1}{1 + x}\right) dx$

$\Rightarrow \quad \log l = 2 \cdot \log 3 - \left[x - \log |1 + x|\right]_0^2$

$\Rightarrow \quad \log l = 2 \cdot \log 3 - [2 - \log 3]$

$\Rightarrow \quad \log l = 3 \cdot \log 3 - 2$

$\Rightarrow \quad \log l = \log 27 - 2$

$\therefore \quad l = e^{\log 27 - 2} = 27 \cdot e^{-2}$

$\quad = \frac{27}{e^2}$

5. *(a)* Centre of circle $x^2 + (y + 6)^2 = 1$ is $C(0, -6)$.

Let the coordinates of point P be $(2t^2, 4t)$.

Now, let $D = CP$

$\quad = \sqrt{(2t^2)^2 + (4t + 6)^2}$

$\Rightarrow \quad D = \sqrt{4t^4 + 16t^2 + 36 + 48t}$

Squaring on both sides

$\Rightarrow \quad D^2(t) = 4t^4 + 16t^2 + 48t + 36$

Let $\quad F(t) = 4t^4 + 16t^2 + 48t + 36$

For minimum, $\quad F'(t) = 0$

$\Rightarrow \quad 16t^3 + 32t + 48 = 0$

$\Rightarrow \quad t^3 + 2t + 3 = 0$

$\Rightarrow (t+1)(t^2 - t + 3) = 0$

$\Rightarrow \quad t = -1$

Thus, coordinate of point P are $(2, -4)$.

Now ,

$$CP = \sqrt{2^2 + (-4+6)^2}$$
$$= \sqrt{4+4}$$
$$= 2\sqrt{2}$$

Hence, the required equation of circle is

$$(x-2)^2 + (y+4)^2 = (2\sqrt{2})^2$$

$\Rightarrow x^2 + 4 - 4x + y^2 + 16 + 8y = 8$

$\Rightarrow \quad x^2 + y^2 - 4x + 8y + 12 = 0$

6. (c) Total length $= 2r + r\theta = 20$

$$\Rightarrow \quad \theta = \frac{20 - 2r}{r}$$

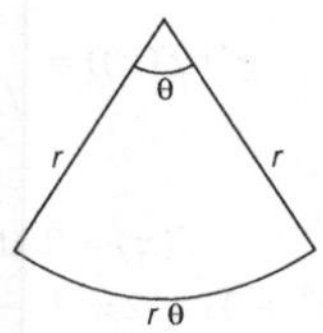

Now, area of flower-bed,

$$A = \frac{1}{2}r^2\theta \Rightarrow A = \frac{1}{2}r^2\left(\frac{20-2r}{r}\right)$$

$\Rightarrow \quad A = 10r - r^2$

$\therefore \quad \frac{dA}{dr} = 10 - 2r$

For maxima or minima, put $\frac{dA}{dr} = 0.$

$\Rightarrow \quad 10 - 2r = 0 \Rightarrow r = 5$

$$\therefore \quad A_{max} = \frac{1}{2}(5)^2\left[\frac{20 - 2(5)}{5}\right]$$
$$= \frac{1}{2} \times 25 \times 2 = 25 \text{ sq m}$$

7. (a) Let $y = \tan^{-1}\left(\frac{6x\sqrt{x}}{1 - 9x^3}\right)$

$$= \tan^{-1}\left[\frac{2 \cdot (3x^{3/2})}{1 - (3x^{3/2})^2}\right]$$

$$= 2\tan^{-1}(3x^{3/2}) \quad \left[\because 2\tan^{-1}x = \tan^{-1}\frac{2x}{1-x^2}\right]$$

$$\therefore \quad \frac{dy}{dx} = 2 \cdot \frac{1}{1 + (3x^{3/2})^2} \cdot 3 \times \frac{3}{2}(x)^{1/2}$$

$$= \frac{9}{1 + 9x^3} \cdot \sqrt{x}$$

$$\therefore \quad g(x) = \frac{9}{1 + 9x^3}$$

8. (b) $\lim_{x \to \pi/2} \frac{\cot x - \cos x}{(\pi - 2x)^3} = \lim_{x \to \pi/2} \frac{1}{8} \cdot \frac{\cos x(1 - \sin x)}{\sin x\left(\frac{\pi}{2} - x\right)^3}$

$$= \lim_{h \to 0} \frac{1}{8} \cdot \frac{\cos\left(\frac{\pi}{2} - h\right)\left[1 - \sin\left(\frac{\pi}{2} - h\right)\right]}{\sin\left(\frac{\pi}{2} - h\right)\left(\frac{\pi}{2} - \frac{\pi}{2} + h\right)^3}$$

$$= \frac{1}{8}\lim_{h \to 0} \frac{\sin h\,(1 - \cos h)}{\cos h \cdot h^3}$$

$$= \frac{1}{8}\lim_{h \to 0} \frac{\sin h\left(2\sin^2\frac{h}{2}\right)}{\cos h \cdot h^3}$$

$$= \frac{1}{4}\lim_{h \to 0} \frac{\sin h \cdot \sin^2\left(\frac{h}{2}\right)}{h^3 \cos h}$$

$$= \frac{1}{4}\lim_{h \to 0}\left(\frac{\sin h}{h}\right)\left(\frac{\sin\frac{h}{2}}{\frac{h}{2}}\right)^2 \cdot \frac{1}{\cos h} \cdot \frac{1}{4}$$

$$= \frac{1}{4} \times \frac{1}{4} = \frac{1}{16}$$

9. (c) **Key idea** *Use property of greatest integer function* $[x] = x - \{x\}$.

We have, $\lim_{x \to 0^+} x\left(\left[\frac{1}{x}\right] + \left[\frac{2}{x}\right] + \ldots + \left[\frac{15}{x}\right]\right)$

We know, $[x] = x - \{x\}$

$$\therefore \quad \left[\frac{1}{x}\right] = \frac{1}{x} - \left\{\frac{1}{x}\right\}$$

Similarly, $\left[\frac{n}{x}\right] = \frac{n}{x} - \left\{\frac{n}{x}\right\}$

$\therefore$ Given limit

$$= \lim_{x \to 0^+} x\left(\frac{1}{x} - \left\{\frac{1}{x}\right\} + \frac{2}{x} - \left\{\frac{2}{x}\right\} + \ldots \frac{15}{x} - \left\{\frac{15}{x}\right\}\right)$$

$$= \lim_{x \to 0^+} (1 + 2 + 3 + \ldots + 15) - x\left(\left\{\frac{1}{x}\right\} + \left\{\frac{2}{x}\right\} + \ldots + \left\{\frac{15}{x}\right\}\right)$$

$$= 120 - 0 = 120$$

$$\left[\begin{array}{l}\because 0 \le \left\{\frac{n}{x}\right\} < 1, \text{therefore} \\ 0 \le x\left\{\frac{n}{x}\right\} < x \Rightarrow \lim_{x \to 0^+} x\left\{\frac{n}{x}\right\} = 0\end{array}\right]$$

10. (a) We have,

$$f(x) = |x - \pi|(e^{|x|} - 1)\sin|x|$$

$$f(x) = \begin{cases} (x - \pi)(e^{-x} - 1)\sin x, & x < 0 \\ -(x - \pi)(e^{x} - 1)\sin x, & 0 \le x < \pi \\ (x - \pi)(e^{x} - 1)\sin x, & x \ge \pi \end{cases}$$

We check the differentiability at $x = 0$ and π.

We have,

$$f'(x) = \begin{cases} (x-\pi)(e^{-x}-1)\cos x + (e^{-x}-1)\sin x \\ \quad + (x-\pi)\sin x e^{-x}(-1), x < 0 \\ -[(x-\pi)(e^{x}-1)\cos x + (e^{x}-1)\sin x \\ \quad + (x-\pi)\sin x e^{x}], 0 < x < \pi \\ (x-\pi)(e^{x}-1)\cos x + (e^{x}-1)\sin x \\ \quad + (x-\pi)\sin x e^{x}, x > \pi \end{cases}$$

Clearly, $\lim_{x\to 0^-} f'(x) = 0 = \lim_{x\to 0^+} f'(x)$

and $\lim_{x\to \pi^-} f'(x) = 0 = \lim_{x\to \pi^+} f'(x)$

$\therefore$ f is differentiable at $x = 0$ and $x = \pi$

Hence, f is differentiable for all x.

11. *(d)* We have,

$$f(x) = x^2 + \frac{1}{x^2} \text{ and } g(x) = x - \frac{1}{x} \Rightarrow h(x) = \frac{f(x)}{g(x)}$$

$$\therefore h(x) = \frac{x^2 + \frac{1}{x^2}}{x - \frac{1}{x}} = \frac{\left(x - \frac{1}{x}\right)^2 + 2}{x - \frac{1}{x}}$$

$$\Rightarrow \quad h(x) = \left(x - \frac{1}{x}\right) + \frac{2}{x - \frac{1}{x}}$$

$$x - \frac{1}{x} > 0, \left(x - \frac{1}{x}\right) + \frac{2}{x - \frac{1}{x}} \in [2\sqrt{2}, \infty)$$

$$x - \frac{1}{x} < 0, \left(x - \frac{1}{x}\right) + \frac{2}{x - \frac{1}{x}} \in (-\infty, 2\sqrt{2}]$$

$\therefore$ Local minimum value is $2\sqrt{2}$.

JEE Advanced

1. *(c)* Here, to find the least value of $\alpha \in R$, for which $4\alpha x^2 + \frac{1}{x} \geq 1$, for all $x > 0$.

i.e. to find the minimum value of α when $y = 4\alpha x^2 + \frac{1}{x}$; $x > 0$ attains minimum value of α.

$$\therefore \quad \frac{dy}{dx} = 8\alpha x - \frac{1}{x^2} \quad \ldots\text{(i)}$$

$$\text{Now,} \quad \frac{d^2y}{dx^2} = 8\alpha + \frac{2}{x^3} \quad \ldots\text{(ii)}$$

when $\frac{dy}{dx} = 0$,

then $8x^3\alpha = 1$

$\frac{d^2y}{dx^2} = 8\alpha + 16\alpha = 24\alpha$, Thus, y attains minimum when

$$x = \left(\frac{1}{8\alpha}\right)^{1/3}; \alpha > 0.$$

$\therefore$ y attains minimum when $x = \left(\frac{1}{8\alpha}\right)^{1/3}$.

$$\text{i.e. } 4\alpha\left(\frac{1}{8\alpha}\right)^{2/3} + (8\alpha)^{1/3} \geq 1$$

$$\Rightarrow \quad \alpha^{1/3} + 2\alpha^{1/3} \geq 1$$

$$\Rightarrow \quad 3\alpha^{1/3} \geq 1$$

$$\Rightarrow \quad \alpha \geq \frac{1}{27}$$

Hence, the least value of α is $\frac{1}{27}$.

2. *(b, c)* As, $g(f(x)) = x$

Thus, $g(x)$ is inverse of $f(x)$.

$$\Rightarrow \quad g(f(x)) = x$$

$$\Rightarrow \quad g'(f(x)) \cdot f'(x) = 1$$

$$\therefore \quad g'(f(x)) = \frac{1}{f'(x)} \quad \ldots\text{(i)}$$

[where, $f'(x) = 3x^2 + 3$]

When $f(x) = 2$, then

$$x^3 + 3x + 2 = 2 \Rightarrow x = 0$$

i.e. when $x = 0$, then $f(x) = 2$

$$\therefore \quad g'(f(x)) = \frac{1}{3x^2 + 3} \text{ at } (0, 2)$$

$$\Rightarrow \quad g'(2) = \frac{1}{3}$$

$\therefore$ Option (a) is incorrect.

Now, $h(g(g(x))) = x$

$$\Rightarrow \quad h(g(g(f(x)))) = f(x)$$

$$\Rightarrow \quad h(g(x)) = f(x) \quad \ldots\text{(ii)}$$

As $g(f(x)) = x$

$$\therefore \quad h(g(3)) = f(3) = 3^3 + 3(3) + 2 = 38$$

$\therefore$ Option (d) is incorrect.

From Eq. (ii),

$$h(g(x)) = f(x)$$

$$\Rightarrow \quad h(g(f(x))) = f(f(x))$$

$$\Rightarrow \quad h(x) = f(f(x)) \quad \ldots\text{(iii)}$$

[using $g(f(x)) = x$]

$$\Rightarrow \quad h'(x) = f'(f(x)) \cdot f'(x) \quad \ldots\text{(iv)}$$

Putting $x = 1$, we get

$$h'(1) = f'(f(1)) \cdot f'(1)$$
$$= (3 \times 36 + 3) \times (6) = 111 \times 6 = 666$$

$\therefore$ Option (b) is correct.

Putting $x = 0$ in Eq. (iii), we get

$$h(0) = f(f(0)) = f(2)$$
$$= 8 + 6 + 2 = 16$$

$\therefore$ Option (c) is correct.

3. *(a)* Here, $f'(x) = 2 - \frac{f(x)}{x}$

or $\frac{dy}{dx} + \frac{y}{x} = 2$ [i.e. linear differential equation in y]

Integrating Factor, IF

$$= e^{\int \frac{1}{x} dx} = e^{\log x} = x$$

$\therefore$ Required solution is

$$y \cdot (\text{IF}) = \int Q(\text{IF}) dx + C$$

$$\Rightarrow \quad y(x) = \int 2(x)\, dx + C$$

$$\Rightarrow \quad yx = x^2 + C$$

$$\therefore \quad y = x + \frac{C}{x} \quad [\because C \neq 0, \text{ as } f(1) \neq 1]$$

(a) $\lim_{x \to 0^+} f'\left(\frac{1}{x}\right) = \lim_{x \to 0^+} (1 - Cx^2) = 1$

$\therefore$ Option (a) is correct.

(b) $\lim_{x \to 0^+} x\, f\left(\frac{1}{x}\right) = \lim_{x \to 0^+} (1 + Cx^2) = 1$

$\therefore$ Option (b) is incorrect.

(c) $\lim_{x \to 0^+} x^2 f'(x)$

$$= \lim_{x \to 0^+} (x^2 - C) = -C \neq 0$$

$\therefore$ Option (c) is incorrect.

(d) $f(x) = x + \frac{C}{x}, C \neq 0$

For $C > 0$, $\lim_{x \to 0^+} f(x) = \infty$

$\therefore$ Function is not bounded in (0, 2).

$\therefore$ Option (d) is incorrect.

4. *(7)* Here, $\lim_{x \to 0} \frac{x^2 \sin(\beta x)}{\alpha x - \sin x} = 1$

$$\Rightarrow \lim_{x \to 0} \frac{x^2\left(\beta x - \frac{(\beta x)^3}{3!} + \frac{(\beta x)^5}{5!} - \ldots\right)}{\alpha x - \left(x - \frac{x^3}{3!} + \frac{x^5}{5!} - \ldots\right)} = 1$$

$$\Rightarrow \lim_{x \to 0} \frac{x^3\left(\beta - \frac{\beta^3 x^2}{3!} + \frac{\beta^5 x^4}{5!} - \ldots\right)}{(\alpha - 1)x + \frac{x^3}{3!} + \frac{x^5}{5!} - \ldots} = 1$$

Limit exists only,

when $\alpha - 1 = 0$

$$\Rightarrow \quad \alpha = 1 \quad \ldots(\text{i})$$

$$\therefore \lim_{x \to 0} \frac{x^3\left(\beta - \frac{\beta^3 x^2}{3!} + \frac{\beta^5 x^4}{5!} - \ldots\right)}{x^3\left(\frac{1}{3!} - \frac{x^2}{5!} - \ldots\right)} = 1$$

$$\Rightarrow \quad 6\beta = 1 \quad \ldots(\text{ii})$$

From Eqs. (i) and (ii),

we get

$$6(\alpha + \beta) = 6\alpha + 6\beta$$
$$= 6 + 1 = 7$$

5. *(a, b)* Here,

$$f(x) = a\cos(|x^3 - x|) + b|x|\sin(|x^3 + x|)$$

If $x^3 - x \geq 0$

$\Rightarrow \cos|x^3 - x| = \cos(x^3 - x)$

$x^3 - x \leq 0$

$\Rightarrow \cos|x^3 - x| = \cos(x^3 - x)$

$\therefore \cos(|x^3 - x|) = \cos(x^3 - x), \forall x \in R$ ...(i)

Again, if $x^3 + x \geq 0$

$\Rightarrow |x|\sin(|x^3 + x|) = x\sin(x^3 + x)$

$x^3 + x \leq 0$

$\Rightarrow |x|\sin(|x^3 + x|) = -x\sin\{-(x^3 + x)\}$

$\therefore |x|\sin(|x^3 + x|) = x\sin(x^3 + x), \forall x \in R$ ...(ii)

$\Rightarrow f(x) = a\cos(|x^3 - x|) + b|x|\sin(|x^3 + x|)$

$\therefore f(x) = a\cos(x^3 - x) + bx\sin(x^3 + x)$ ...(iii)

which is clearly sum and composition of differential functions.

Hence, $f(x)$ is always continuous and differentiable.

6. *(b, c)* Here, $f(x)$

$$= \lim_{n \to \infty} \left[\frac{n^n (x + n)\left(x + \frac{n}{2}\right) \ldots \left(x + \frac{n}{n}\right)}{n!(x^2 + n^2)\left(x^2 + \frac{n^2}{4}\right) \ldots \left(x^2 + \frac{n^2}{n^2}\right)}\right]^{\frac{x}{n}} \quad x > 0$$

Taking log on both sides, we get $\log_e \{f(x)\}$

$$= \lim_{n \to \infty} \log\left[\frac{n^n(x + n)\left(x + \frac{n}{2}\right) \ldots \left(x + \frac{n}{n}\right)}{n!(x^2 + n^2)\left(x^2 + \frac{n^2}{4}\right) \ldots \left(x^2 + \frac{n^2}{n^2}\right)}\right]^{\frac{x}{n}}$$

$$= \lim_{n \to \infty} \frac{x}{n} \cdot \log\left[\frac{\prod_{r=1}^{n}\left(x + \frac{1}{r/n}\right)}{\prod_{r=1}^{n}\left(x^2 + \frac{1}{(r/n)^2}\right)\prod_{r=1}^{n}(r/n)}\right]$$

$$= x \lim_{n \to \infty} \frac{1}{n} \sum_{r=1}^{n} \log\left[\frac{x + \frac{n}{r}}{\left(x^2 + \frac{n^2}{r^2}\right)\frac{r}{n}}\right]$$

$$= x \lim_{n \to \infty} \frac{1}{n} \sum_{r=1}^{n} \log\left(\frac{\frac{r}{n} \cdot x + 1}{\frac{r^2}{n^2} \cdot x^2 + 1}\right)$$

Converting summation into definite integration, we get
$\log_e\{f(x)\}$

$$= x\int_0^1 \log\left(\frac{xt+1}{x^2t^2+1}\right)dt$$

Put $\quad tx = z \Rightarrow xdt = dz$

$$\therefore \quad \log_e\{f(x)\} = x\int_0^x \log\left(\frac{1+z}{1+z^2}\right)\frac{dz}{x}$$

$$\Rightarrow \quad \log_e\{f(x)\} = \int_0^x \log\left(\frac{1+z}{1+z^2}\right)dz$$

Using Newton-Leibnitz formula, we get

$$\frac{1}{f(x)}\cdot f'(x) = \log\left(\frac{1+x}{1+x^2}\right) \quad \ldots\text{(i)}$$

Here, at $x = 1$,

$$\frac{f'(1)}{f(1)} = \log\ (1) = 0$$

$$\therefore \quad f'(1) = 0$$

Now, sign scheme of $f'(x)$ is shown below

+ ——— $x=1$ ——— −

$\therefore$ At $x = 1$, function attains maximum.
Since, $f(x)$ increases on (0, 1).

$$\therefore \quad f(1) > f(1/2)$$

$\therefore$ Option (a) is incorrect.

$$f(1/3) < f(2/3)$$

$\therefore$ Option (b) is correct.
Also, $f'(x) < 0$, when $x > 1$

$$\Rightarrow \quad f'(2) < 0$$

$\therefore$ Option (c) is correct.

$$\text{Also,} \quad \frac{f'(x)}{f(x)} = \log\left(\frac{1+x}{1+x^2}\right)$$

$$\therefore \quad \frac{f'(3)}{f(3)} - \frac{f'(2)}{f(2)} = \log\left(\frac{4}{10}\right) - \log\left(\frac{3}{5}\right)$$

$$= \log\ (2/3) < 0$$

$$\Rightarrow \quad \frac{f'(3)}{f(3)} < \frac{f'(2)}{f(2)}$$

$\therefore$ Option (d) is incorrect.

7. **(*a*, *d*)** Here, $\lim\limits_{x\to 2} \dfrac{f(x)\cdot g(x)}{f'(x)\cdot g'(x)} = 1$

$$\Rightarrow \lim_{x\to 2} \frac{f(x)g'(x) + f'(x)g(x)}{f''(x)g'(x) + f'(x)g''(x)} = 1$$

[using L' Hospital's rule]

$$\Rightarrow \quad \frac{f(2)g'(2) + f'(2)g(2)}{f''(2)g'(2) + f'(2)g''(2)} = 1$$

$$\Rightarrow \quad \frac{f(2)g'(2)}{f''(2)g'(2)} = 1 \quad [\because f'(2) = g(2) = 0]$$

$$\Rightarrow \quad f(2) = f''(2) \quad \ldots\text{(i)}$$

$\therefore$ $f(x) - f''(x) = 0$, for atleast one $x \in R$.
$\Rightarrow$ Option (d) is correct.
Also, $f: R \to (0, \infty)$

$$\Rightarrow \quad f(2) > 0$$

$$\therefore \quad f''(2) = f(2) > 0 \quad \text{[from Eq. (i)]}$$

Since, $\quad f'(2) = 0$ and $f''(2) > 0$

$\therefore$ $f(x)$ attains local minimum at $x = 2$.
$\Rightarrow$ Option (a) is correct.

8. **(*b*, *c*)** Here, $f(x) = [x^2 - 3] = [x^2] - 3$

$$= \begin{cases} -3, & -1/2 \le x < 1 \\ -2, & 1 \le x < \sqrt{2} \\ -1, & \sqrt{2} \le x < \sqrt{3} \\ 0, & \sqrt{3} \le x < 2 \\ 1, & x = 2 \end{cases}$$

and $\quad g(x) = |x|f(x) + |4x - 7|f(x)$

$$= (|x| + |4x - 7|)f(x)$$

$$= (|x| + |4x - 7|)[x^2 - 3]$$

$$= \begin{cases} (-x - 4x - 7)(-3), & -1/2 \le x < 0 \\ (x - 4x + 7)(-3), & 0 \le x < 1 \\ (x - 4x + 7)(-2), & 1 \le x < \sqrt{2} \\ (x - 4x + 7)(-1), & \sqrt{2} \le x < \sqrt{3} \\ (x - 4x + 7)(0), & \sqrt{3} \le x < 7/4 \\ (x + 4x - 7)(0), & 7/4 \le x < 2 \\ (x + 4x - 7)(1), & x = 2 \end{cases}$$

$$\therefore \quad g(x) = \begin{cases} 15x + 21, & -1/2 \le x < 0 \\ 9x - 21, & 0 \le x < 1 \\ 6x - 14, & 1 \le x < \sqrt{2} \\ 3x - 7, & \sqrt{2} \le x < \sqrt{3} \\ 0, & \sqrt{3} \le x < 2 \\ 5x - 7, & x = 2 \end{cases}$$

Now, the graphs of $f(x)$ and $g(x)$ are shown below.

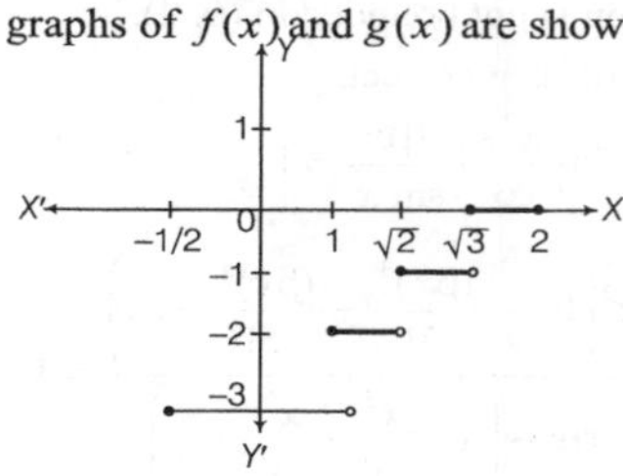

Graph for $f(x)$

Clearly, $f(x)$ is discontinuous at 4 points.
$\therefore$ Option (b) is correct.

Graph for $g(x)$

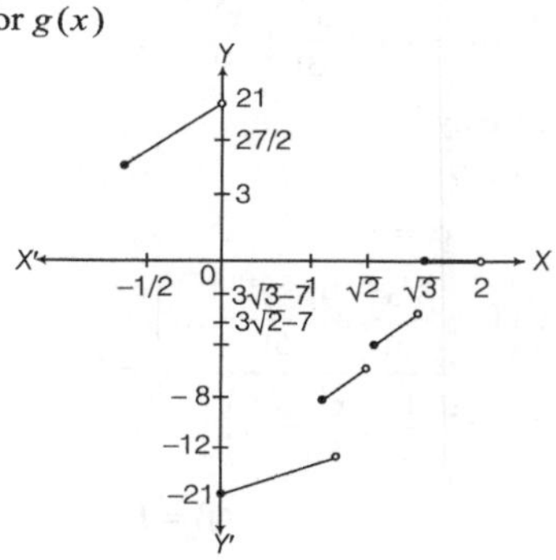

Clearly, $g(x)$ is not differentiable at 4 points, when

$$x \in (-1/2, 2).$$

$\therefore$ Option (c) is correct.

9. *(a,b,d)* $f(x) = x\cos(\pi(x + [x]))$

At $x = 0$

$$\lim_{x\to 0} f(x) = \lim_{x\to 0} x\cos(\pi(x + [x]) = 0$$

and $f(x) = 0$

$\therefore$ It is continuous at $x = 0$ and clearly discontinuous at other integer points.

Solutions. (Q.Nos. 10-12)

$$f(x) = x + \ln x - x\ln x$$
$$f(1) = 1 > 0$$
$$f(e^2) = e^2 + 2 - 2e^2 = 2 - e^2 < 0$$

$\Rightarrow$ $f(x) = 0$ for some $x \in (1, e^2)$

$\therefore$ I is correct

$$f'(x) = 1 + \frac{1}{x} - \ln x - 1 = \frac{1}{x} - \ln x$$

$f'(x) > 0$ for $(0, 1)$

$f'(x) < 0$ for (e, ∞)

$\therefore$ P and Q are correct, II is correct, III is incorrect.

$$f''(x) = \frac{-1}{x^2} - \frac{1}{x}$$

$f''(x) < 0$ for $(0, \infty)$

$\therefore$ S, is correct, R is incorrect.

IV is incorrect.

$$\lim_{x\to\infty} f(x) = -\infty$$
$$\lim_{x\to\infty} f'(x) = -\infty$$
$$\lim_{x\to\infty} f''(x) = 0$$

$\therefore$ ii, iii, iv are correct.

10. *(d)* **11.** *(c)* **12.** *(c)*

13. *(b)* $f'(x)$ is increasing

For some x in $\left(\frac{1}{2}, 1\right)$

$f'(x) = 1$ [LMVT]

$\therefore$ $f'(1) > 1$

14. *(c,d)* $f(x) = \frac{1 - x(1 + |1 - x|)}{|1 - x|}\cos\left(\frac{1}{1 - x}\right)$

Now, $\lim_{x\to 1^-} f(x)$

$$= \lim_{x\to 1^-} \frac{1 - x(1 + 1 - x)}{1 - x}\cos\left(\frac{1}{1 - x}\right)$$

$$= \lim_{x\to 1^-} (1 - x)\cos\left(\frac{1}{1 - x}\right) = 0$$

and $\lim_{x\to 1^+} f(x) = \lim_{x\to 1^+}$

$$\frac{1 - x(1 - 1 + x)}{x - 1}\cos\left(\frac{1}{1 - x}\right)$$

$= \lim_{x\to 1^+} -(x + 1)\cdot\cos\left(\frac{1}{x + 1}\right)$, which does not exist.

15. *(b,c)* $f(x) = \begin{vmatrix} \cos 2x & \cos 2x & \sin 2x \\ -\cos x & \cos x & -\sin x \\ \sin x & \sin x & \cos x \end{vmatrix}$

$\cos 2x(\cos^2 x + \sin^2 x) - \cos 2x$

$(-\cos^2 x + \sin^2 x) + \sin 2x(-\sin 2x) = \cos 2x + \cos 4x$

$$f'(x) = -2\sin 2x - 4\sin 4x = -2\sin 2x(1 + 4\cos 2x)$$

At $x = 0$

$f'(x) = 0$ and $f(x) = 2$

Also, $f'(x) = 0$ $\sin 2x = 0$ or $\cos 2x = \frac{-1}{4}$

$\Rightarrow$ $x = \frac{n\pi}{2}$ or $\cos 2x = -\frac{1}{4}$

16. *(a, b, d)* We have,

$$(f(0))^2 + (f'(0))^2 = 85$$

and $f: R \to [-2, 2]$

(a) Since, f is twice differentiable function, so f is continuous function.

$\therefore$ This is true for every continuous function.

Hence, we can always find $x \in (r,s)$, where $f(x)$ is one-one.

$\therefore$ This statement is true.

(b) By L.M.V.T

$$f'(c) = \frac{f(b) - f(a)}{b - a}$$

$$\Rightarrow \quad |f'(c)| = \left|\frac{f(b) - f(a)}{b - a}\right|$$

$$\Rightarrow \quad |f'(x_0)| = \left|\frac{f(0) - f(-4)}{0 + 4}\right|$$

$$= \left|\frac{f(0) - f(-4)}{4}\right|$$

Range of f is $[-2, 2]$

$\therefore$ $-4 \le f(0) - f(-4) \le 4$

$$\Rightarrow \quad 0 \le \left|\frac{f(0) - f(-4)}{4}\right| \le 1$$

Hence, $|f'(x_0)| = 1$.

Hence, statement is true.

(c) As no function is given, then we assume $f(x) = 2\sin\left(\frac{\sqrt{85}x}{2}\right)$

$\therefore$ $f'(x) = \sqrt{85}\cos\left(\frac{\sqrt{85}\,x}{2}\right)$

Now, $(f(0))^2 + (f'(0))^2 = (2\sin 0)^2 + (\sqrt{85}\cos 0)^2$

$$(f(0))^2 + (f'(0))^2 = 85$$

and $\lim_{x\to\infty} f(x)$ does not exists.

Hence, statement is false.

(d) From option b, $|f'(x_0)| \le 1$

$$x_0 \in (-4, 0)$$

$\therefore$ $(f'(x_0))^2 \le 1$

Hence, $g(x_0) = (f(x_0))^2 + (f'(x_0))^2 \le 4 + 1$ $[\because f(x_0) \in [-2, 2]]$

$\Rightarrow \quad g(x_0) \le 5$

Now, let $p \in (-4, 0)$ for which $g(p) = 5$

Similarly, let q be smallest positive number $q \in (0, 4)$ such that $g(q) = 5$

Hence, by Rolle's theorem is (p, q)

$g'(c) = 0$ for $\alpha \in (-4, 4)$ and since $g(x)$ is greater than 5 as we move form $x = p$ to $x = q$

and $\quad f(x))^2 \le 4$

$\Rightarrow \quad (f'(x))^2 \ge 1$ in (p, q)

Thus, $\quad g'(c) = 0$

$\Rightarrow \quad f'f + f'f'' = 0$

So, $\quad f(\alpha) + f''(\alpha) = 0$ and $f'(\alpha) \ne 0$

Hence, statement is true.

17. *(b, c)* We have, $f'(x) = e^{(f(x) - g(x))} g'(x) \forall x \in R$

$$\Rightarrow \quad f'(x) = \frac{e^{f(x)}}{e^{g(x)}} g'(x)$$

$$\Rightarrow \quad \frac{f'(x)}{e^{f(x)}} = \frac{g'(x)}{e^{g(x)}}$$

$$\Rightarrow \quad e^{-f(x)} f'(x) = e^{-g(x)} g'(x)$$

On integrating both side, we get

$$e^{-f(x)} = e^{-g(x)} + C$$

At $x = 1$

$$e^{-f(1)} = e^{-g(1)} + C$$

$$e^{-1} = e^{-g(1)} + C \quad [\because f(1) = 1] \ldots(i)$$

At $x = 2$

$$e^{-f(2)} = e^{-g(2)} + C$$

$$\Rightarrow \quad e^{-f(2)} = e^{-1} + C \quad [\because g(2) = 1] \ldots(ii)$$

From Eqs. (i) and (ii)

$$e^{-f(2)} = 2e^{-1} - e^{-g(1)} \quad \ldots(iii)$$

$$\Rightarrow \quad e^{-f(2)} > 2e^{-1}$$

We know that, e^{-x} is decreasing

$$\therefore \quad -f(2) < \log_e 2 - 1$$

$$f(2) > 1 - \log_e 2$$

$$\Rightarrow \quad e^{-g(1)} + e^{-f(2)} = 2e^{-1} \quad \text{[from Eq. (iii)]}$$

$$\Rightarrow \quad e^{-g(1)} < 2e^{-1}$$

$$-g(1) < \log_e 2 - 1$$

$$\Rightarrow \quad g(1) > -\log_e 2$$

18. *(1)* We have,

$$y_n = \frac{1}{n}[(n+1)(n+2)\ldots(n+n)]^{1/n}$$

and $\lim_{n \to \infty} y_n = L$

$$\Rightarrow \quad L = \lim_{n \to \infty} \frac{1}{n}[(n+1)(n+2)(n+3)\ldots(n+n)]^{1/n}$$

$$\Rightarrow \quad L = \lim_{n \to \infty}\left[\left(1+\frac{1}{n}\right)\left(1+\frac{2}{n}\right)\left(1+\frac{3}{n}\right)\ldots\left(1+\frac{n}{n}\right)\right]^{\frac{1}{n}}$$

$$\Rightarrow \quad \log L = \lim_{n \to \infty} \frac{1}{n}\left[\log\left(1+\frac{1}{n}\right) + \log\left(1+\frac{2}{n}\right) \ldots \log\left(1+\frac{n}{n}\right)\right]$$

$$\Rightarrow \quad \log L = \lim_{n \to \infty} \frac{1}{n}\sum_{r=1}^{n} \log\left(1+\frac{r}{n}\right)$$

$$\Rightarrow \quad \log L = \int_0^1 \underset{\text{II}}{1} \times \underset{\text{I}}{\log(1+x)}\, dx$$

$$\Rightarrow \quad \log L = (x \cdot \log(1+x))_0^1 - \int_0^1\left[\frac{d}{dx}(\log(1+x)\int dx\right] dx$$

[by using integration by parts]

$$\Rightarrow \log L = [x \log(1+x)]_0^1 - \int_0^1 \frac{x}{1+x}\, dx$$

$$\Rightarrow \log L = \log 2 - \int_0^1\left(\frac{x+1}{x+1} - \frac{1}{x+1}\right) dx$$

$$\Rightarrow \log L = \log 2 - [x]_0^1 + [\log(x+1)]_0^1$$

$$\Rightarrow \log L = \log 2 - 1 + \log 2 - 0$$

$$\Rightarrow \log L = \log 4 - \log e = \log \frac{4}{e}$$

$$\Rightarrow \quad L = \frac{4}{e}$$

$$\Rightarrow \quad [L] = \left[\frac{4}{e}\right] = 1$$

19. *(b, c, d)* Given,

$$\lim_{t \to x} \frac{f(x)\sin t - f(t)\sin x}{t - x} = \sin^2 x$$

Using L' Hospital rules

$$\lim_{t \to x} \frac{f(x)\cos t - f'(t)\sin x}{1} = \sin^2 x$$

$$\Rightarrow \quad f(x)\cos x - f'(x)\sin x = \sin^2 x$$

$$\Rightarrow \quad f'(x)\sin x - f(x)\cos x = -\sin^2 x$$

$$\Rightarrow \quad \frac{f'(x)\sin x - f(x)\cos x}{\sin^2 x} = -1$$

$$\Rightarrow \quad d\left(\frac{f(x)}{\sin x}\right) = -1$$

On integrating, we get

$$\frac{f(x)}{\sin x} = -x + C$$

$$\Rightarrow \quad f(x) = -x\sin x + C\sin x$$

It is given that $x = \frac{\pi}{6}, f\left(\frac{\pi}{6}\right) = -\frac{\pi}{12}$

$$\therefore \quad f\left(\frac{\pi}{6}\right) = -\frac{\pi}{6}\sin\frac{\pi}{6} + C\sin\frac{\pi}{6}$$

$$= -\frac{\pi}{12} = -\frac{\pi}{12} + \frac{1}{2}C$$

$$\Rightarrow \quad C = 0$$

$\therefore \; f(x) = -x\sin x$

(a) $f(x) = -x\sin x$

$$f\left(\frac{\pi}{4}\right) = -\frac{\pi}{4}\sin\frac{\pi}{4} = -\frac{\pi}{4\sqrt{2}} \quad \text{false}$$

(b) $f(x) = -x \sin x$

$\sin x > x - \dfrac{x^3}{6}, \forall\, x \in (0, \pi)$

$\Rightarrow \quad -x \sin x < -x^2 + \dfrac{x^4}{6}$

$\Rightarrow \quad f(x) < \dfrac{x^4}{6} - x^2, \forall\, x \in (0, \pi)$

It is true

(c) $f(x) = -x \sin x$

$f'(x) = -\sin x - x\cos x$

$f'(x) = 0$

$\Rightarrow \; -\sin x - x\cos x = 0$

$\tan x = -x$

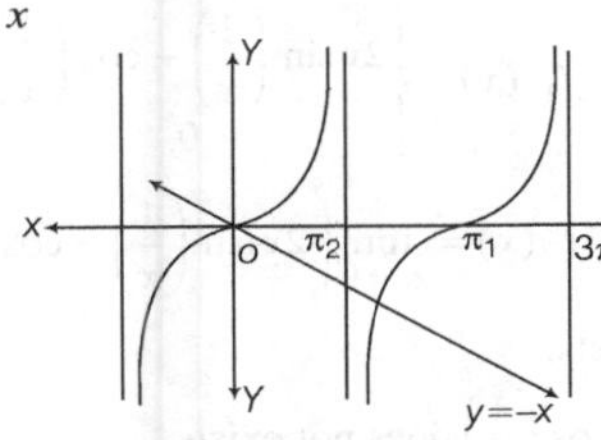

$\Rightarrow$ Their exists $\alpha \in (0, \pi)$ for which $f'(\alpha) = 0$

It is true

(d) $f(x) = -x \sin x$

$f'(x) = -\sin x - x \cos x$

$f''(x) = -2\cos x + x \sin x$

$f''\left(\dfrac{\pi}{2}\right) = \dfrac{\pi}{2},\; f\left(\dfrac{\pi}{2}\right) = -\dfrac{\pi}{2}$

$\therefore \quad f''\left(\dfrac{\pi}{2}\right) + f\left(\dfrac{\pi}{2}\right) = 0$

It is true.

20. *(0.4)* We have,

$$\frac{dy}{dx} = (2 + 5y)(5y - 2)$$

$$\Rightarrow \quad \frac{dy}{25y^2 - 4} = dx$$

$$\Rightarrow \quad \frac{1}{25}\left(\frac{dy}{y^2 - \frac{4}{25}}\right) = dx$$

On integrating both sides, we get

$$\frac{1}{25}\int \frac{dy}{y^2 - \left(\frac{2}{5}\right)^2} = \int dx$$

$$\Rightarrow \quad \frac{1}{25} \times \frac{1}{2 \times 2/5} \log\left|\frac{y - 2/5}{y + 2/5}\right| = x + C$$

$$\Rightarrow \quad \log\left|\frac{5y - 2}{5y + 2}\right| = 20(x + C)$$

$$\Rightarrow \quad \left|\frac{5y - 2}{5y + 2}\right| = Ae^{20x} \qquad [\because e^{20C} = A]$$

when $x = 0 \Rightarrow y = 0$, then $A = 1$

$$\therefore \quad \left|\frac{5y - 2}{5y + 2}\right| = e^{20x}$$

$$\lim_{x \to -\infty}\left|\frac{5f(x) - 2}{5f(x) + 2}\right| = \lim_{x \to -\infty} e^{20x}$$

$$\Rightarrow \quad \lim_{n \to -\infty}\left|\frac{5f(x) - 2}{5f(x) + 2}\right| = 0$$

$$\Rightarrow \quad \lim_{n \to -\infty} 5f(x) - 2 = 0 \quad \Rightarrow \quad \lim_{n \to -\infty} f(x) = \frac{2}{5} = 0.4$$

21. *(2)* Given,

$f(x + y) = f(x)\, f'(y) + f'(x) f(y), \forall x, y \in R$

and $f(0) = 1$

Put $x = y = 0$, we get

$$f(0) = f(0)\, f'(0) + f'(0)\, f(0)$$

$$\Rightarrow \quad 1 = 2f'(0) \Rightarrow f'(0) = \frac{1}{2}$$

Put $x = x$ and $y = 0$, we get

$$f(x) = f(x)\, f'(0) + f'(x)\, f(0)$$

$$\Rightarrow \quad f(x) = \frac{1}{2} f(x) + f'(x)$$

$$\Rightarrow \quad f'(x) = \frac{1}{2} f(x) \quad \Rightarrow \quad \frac{f'(x)}{f(x)} = \frac{1}{2}$$

On integrating, we get

$$\log f(x) = \frac{1}{2}x + C$$

$$\Rightarrow \quad f(x) = Ae^{\frac{1}{2}x}, \text{ where } e^C = A$$

If $f(0) = 1$, then $A = 1$

Hence, $f(x) = e^{\frac{1}{2}x}$

$$\Rightarrow \quad \log_e f(x) = \frac{1}{2}x$$

$$\Rightarrow \quad \log_e f(4) = \frac{1}{2} \times 4 = 2$$

22. *(d)*

(i) Given, $f_1 : R \to R$ and $f_1(x) = \sin\left(\sqrt{1 - e^{-x^2}}\right)$

$\therefore \quad f_1(x)$ is continuous at $x = 0$

Now, $f_1'(x) = \cos\sqrt{1 - e^{-x^2}} \cdot \dfrac{1}{2\sqrt{1 - e^{-x^2}}}(2xe^{-x^2})$

At $x = 0$

$f_1'(x)$ does not exists.

$\therefore \quad f_1(x)$ is not differential at $x = 0$

Hence, option (2) for P.

(ii) Given, $f_2(x) = \begin{cases} \dfrac{|\sin x|}{\tan^{-1} x}, & \text{if } x \neq 0 \\ 1, & \text{if } x = 0 \end{cases}$

$$\Rightarrow \quad f_2(x) = \begin{cases} \dfrac{-\sin x}{\tan^{-1} x} & x < 0 \\ \dfrac{\sin x}{\tan^{-1} x} & x > 0 \\ 1 & x = 0 \end{cases}$$

Clearly, $f_2(x)$ is not continuous at $x = 0$.

$\therefore$ Option (1)for Q.

(iii) Given, $f_3(x) = [\sin(\log_e(x+2))]$, where [ ] is G.I.F.

and $f_3 : (-1, e^{\pi/2} - 2) \to R$

It is given

$$-1 < x < e^{\pi/2} - 2$$

$\Rightarrow$ $-1 + 2 < x + 2 < e^{\pi/2} - 2 + 2$

$\Rightarrow$ $1 < x + 2 < e^{\pi/2}$

$\Rightarrow$ $\log_e 1 < \log_e (x+2) < \log_e e^{\pi/2}$

$\Rightarrow$ $0 < \log_e (x+2) < \frac{\pi}{2}$

$\Rightarrow$ $\sin 0 < \sin \log_e(x+2) < \sin \frac{\pi}{2}$

$\Rightarrow$ $0 < \sin \log_e (x+2) < 1$

$\therefore$ $[\sin \log_e (x+2)] = 0$

$\therefore$ $f_3(x) = 0, f'_3(x) = f_3''(x) = 0$

It is differentiable and continuous at $x = 0$.

$\therefore$ Option (4) for R

(iv) Given, $f_4(x) = \begin{cases} x^2 \sin\left(\frac{1}{x}\right), & \text{if } x \neq 0 \\ 0, & \text{if } x = 0 \end{cases}$

Now, $\lim\limits_{x\to 0} f_4(x) = \lim\limits_{x \to 0} x^2 \sin\left(\frac{1}{x}\right) = 0$

$$f_4'(x) = 2x\sin\left(\frac{1}{x}\right) - \cos\left(\frac{1}{x}\right)$$

For $x = 0$, $f_4'(x) = \lim\limits_{h\to 0} \frac{f(0+h) - f(0)}{h}$

$\Rightarrow$ $f_4'(x) = \lim\limits_{h \to 0} \frac{h^2 \sin\left(\frac{1}{h}\right) - 0}{h}$

$\Rightarrow$ $f_4'(x) = \lim\limits_{h\to 0} h \sin\left(\frac{1}{h}\right) = 0$

Thus, $f_4'(x) = \begin{cases} 2x \sin\left(\frac{1}{x}\right) - \cos\left(\frac{1}{x}\right), & x \neq 0 \\ 0, & x = 0 \end{cases}$

Again, $\lim\limits_{x\to 0} f'(x) = \lim\limits_{x \to 0} \left(2x \sin\left(\frac{1}{x}\right) - \cos\left(\frac{1}{x}\right)\right)$

does not exists.

Since, $\lim\limits_{x\to 0} \cos\left(\frac{1}{x}\right)$ does not exists.

Hence, $f'(x)$ is not continuous at $x = 0$.

$\therefore$ Option (3) for S.